EDUCATIONAL PSYCHOLOGY

Effective Teaching, Effective Learning

EDUCATIONAL PSYCHOLOGY

Effective Teaching, Effective Learning

John F. Travers
Boston College

Stephen N. Elliott
University of Wisconsin-Madison

Thomas R. Kratochwill
University of Wisconsin-Madison

WCB Brown & Benchmark
PUBLISHERS

Madison,Wisconsin•Indianapolis, Indiana
Melbourne,Australia•Oxford, England

Book Team

Editor *Michael Lange*
Developmental Editor *Sheralee Connors*
Production Editor *Michelle M. Campbell*
Designer *K. Wayne Harms*
Art Editor/Processor *Joseph P. O'Connell*
Photo Editor *Judi L. David*
Permissions Editor *Vicki Krug*
Visuals/Design Consultant *Marilyn A. Phelps*
Marketing Manager *Steven Yetter*
Advertising Manager *Jodi Rymer*

WCB Brown & Benchmark

A Division of Wm. C. Brown Communications, Inc.

Vice President and General Manager *Thomas E. Doran*
Editor in Chief *Edgar J. Laube*
Executive Editor *Ed Bartell*
Executive Editor *Stan Stoga*
National Sales Manager *Eric Ziegler*
Director of CourseResource *Kathy Law Laube*
Director of CourseSystems *Chris Rogers*
Director of Marketing *Sue Simon*
Director of Production *Vickie Putman Caughron*
Manager of Visuals and Design *Faye M. Schilling*

Design Manager *Jac Tilton*
Art Manager *Janice Roerig*
Publishing Services Manager *Karen J. Slaght*
Permissions/Records Manager *Connie Allendorf*

Wm. C. Brown Communications, Inc.

Chairman Emeritus *Wm. C. Brown*
Chairman and Chief Executive Officer *Mark C. Falb*
President and Chief Operating Officer *G. Franklin Lewis*
Corporate Vice President, President of WCB Manufacturing *Roger Meyer*

Cover © Superstock (5 photos) and © Wm. C. Brown Communications/Bob Coyle
Photographer (background images).

Cover design by Sailer & Cook Creative Services.

Copyedited by Barbara Bonnet.

The credit section for this book begins on page 551 and is considered an extension of the
copyright page.

Printed in the United States of America by Wm. C. Brown Communications, Inc.,
2460 Kerper Boulevard, Dubuque, Iowa 52001

10 9 8 7 6 5 4 3 2 1

To my wife, Barbara,
whose love, support, and encouragement
have been a source of inspiration
through the years.

John Travers

•

To Bob and Jean, who taught me;
to Anita, who teaches me;
and to Dustin Rhodes and Andrew Taylor,
who I aspire to teach and to learn from,
with love.

Stephen N. Elliott

•

To my family, Carol, Tyler, and Rudy,
and especially in loving memory of
the late Donna Ehrler Ryan, my sister-in-law,
who wanted me to complete this book.

Thomas R. Kratochwill

Brief Contents

Contents

Introduction

The Development of Students

4 Psychosocial and Moral Development 92

5 Social Relationships: Teachers-Students-Parents-Peers 118

SECTION 3

Learning Theories and Practices

6 Behavioral Psychology and Learning 154

7 Cognitive Psychology and Learning 190

8 Thinking and the Teaching of Critical Thinking Skills 222

9 Problem-Solving Skills and Strategies 252

10 Motivation of Students and Teachers 282

SECTION 4

The Design and Management of Classroom Instruction

11 Instructional Objectives and Essential Learning Outcomes 318

12 Effective Teaching Strategies and the Design of Instruction 350

maybe

SECTION 5

Assessing Educational Outcomes

16 Standardized Tests in the Classroom 498

Preface

Teaching and learning are complex and exciting processes that bring people together in a way that changes their lives. Educational psychologists have been at the center of this teaching-learning interaction for nearly a century. Their theoretical and applied work has provided educators significant guidance toward the goals of effective teaching and learning.

Individuals entering the education profession are often both excited and anxious, and they may have many questions and many ideas about teaching and learning. For example, what shall I teach? How shall I teach it? Will my students like me? What if I have a discipline problem right away? Even experienced teachers approach that first class meeting in September with similar, though perhaps less intense, feelings.

We are aware, however, that a dynamic field such as educational psychology must incorporate not only vital facts but also offer teachers data and teaching suggestions for the changes that any society inevitably experiences. Since more children of widely different backgrounds are entering our classrooms, schools and teachers must be prepared to recognize and respect the values, beliefs, and behaviors of these students. Thus, we have interwoven throughout the text, in both the core of the chapters and the boxed material, frequent *multicultural* discussions accompanied by distinct examples of how to apply the content to classroom work.

Educational psychology textbooks provide insights into the teaching-learning process and student behavior, as well as research data, theory analysis, and illustrations, all dealing with actual classroom application of psychological principles. Consequently, those taking an educational psychology course and reading an educational psychology textbook should enter a classroom with greater confidence in their ability to teach well.

To accomplish this goal, we have presented the basic principles of effective teaching and effective learning in a book that has a balanced theoretical orientation. Becoming a successful teacher depends to a considerable extent upon acquiring an understanding of students, how they learn, and the most effective means of teaching. Since teaching is reaching, that is, reaching students, we—the authors of *Educational Psychology: Effective Teaching, Effective Learning*—have attempted to present the latest and most pertinent data available, to apply those theories that best explain a particular classroom situation, and to constantly illustrate in classroom examples how these theories and data "work." In this way, we provide readers with a practical and useful book that will provide knowledge, support, and guidance, not only for course work but also during teaching.

Organization of the Text

Writing an educational textbook that is both practical and useful demands that certain decisions must be made: What is to be presented and how is it to be organized? Answering these questions forced us to select and organize the most pertinent and critical data around the core concepts of educational psychology. These core concepts, which are the heart of educational psychology, and the chapters that include them are as follows. (These topics appear in chapter 1, Table 1.1, where they will be more fully explained.)

Core Concepts and Chapter Coverage

Introduction	1. Educational Psychology: Teaching and Learning
	2. Research and Educational Psychology
The Development of Students	3. Cognitive and Language Development
	4. Psychosocial and Moral Development
	5. Social Relationships: Teachers-Students-Parents-Peers
Learning Theories and Practices	6. Behavioral Psychology and Learning
	7. Cognitive Psychology and Learning
	8. Thinking and the Teaching of Critical Thinking Skills
	9. Problem-Solving Skills and Strategies
	10. Motivation of Students and Teachers

Note the emphasis on students, learning, and teaching. We believe that this organization helps the reader to focus on the *learner* and development, the *learner* and learning, the *learner* and teaching, and the assessment of the *learner* by teachers. Thus the book stresses the interactions between students or learners and teachers.

Content of the Text

Any text's content must present not only the basic principles of the discipline but must also reflect changes in the field. In an attempt to address both of these concerns, we have presented in five sections what we think are the most important elements of educational psychology. *Section one* is an overview of the field and demonstrates the important link between educational psychology and teaching. We have also included a strong research component to help readers evaluate the studies that appear throughout the book and judge the value of the suggestions that have been made about improving America's schools.

Section two is devoted to a careful analysis of how students develop, from their early years that can be so important to those later years that prepare for higher education or an occupation. Teachers are often told to present material that is "biologically and psychologically appropriate." We have attempted to help readers follow this guideline by introducing cognitive, linguistic, moral, and psychosocial data relating to various age levels. We then use these developmental perspectives to examine important school relationships, for example, those between students and teachers, students and students, and teachers and parents.

Section three takes the reader into the world of learning, both theory and practice. Here we examine the details of behavioral and cognitive theories of learning and their implications for the classroom. A major portion of this section is devoted to methods of teaching students how to improve their thinking skills, which helps them improve their academic performance and also helps them to transfer classroom learning to their daily lives. As a follow-up to the thinking skills work, we developed a problem-solving model (DUPE) that provides students a useable method to attack problems they meet in and out of the classroom. Needless to say, none of this will occur without motivated students, and we conclude this section by discussing and illustrating the most pertinent motivational information available.

Section four concentrates on teaching and classroom management. In a sense, *Educational Psychology: Effective Teaching, Effective Learning*, represents a hierarchy: knowing how students develop helps teachers to select appropriate materials and learning techniques. Teachers can then encourage their students to become more effective thinkers and problem solvers and base their teaching strategies and methods of classroom management upon this knowledge.

The section opens with a discussion of instructional objectives since clearly formulated, precise objectives lead to meaningful teaching. Once teachers have a firm idea of what they want to accomplish and what they think their students should achieve, they can then devise suitable teaching strategies. Teaching strategies are effective to the extent that both teachers and their students know what is expected (for class work and for personal behavior), which leads us to an analysis of the most productive means of managing a classroom. Successful classroom management is most likely to occur when teachers are aware of the individual differences of their students, from slow to gifted, from withdrawn to outgoing.

Finally, *Section five* addresses the issue of assessment, both teacher-made and standardized assessment. Given the controversy surrounding testing in our classrooms and society, we have included both traditional and innovative methods of assessment, presenting as wide a range of opinion and fact as is possible. Since assessment is a critical part of good teaching and learning, readers should know the best techniques available for the optimal assessment of their students.

Pedagogical Features of the Text

Helping readers to master a text's contents in as uncomplicated and meaningful a manner as possible has been the most important pedagogical goal of our work. To accomplish this task, we have built a number of helpful features into each chapter.

- *A chapter table of contents.* The major topics of each chapter are presented initially so that readers may quickly find the subject they need. This tactic also aids retention and is an efficient method for reviewing content.

• *Boxes.* Rather than present boxed material randomly, we have designed four types of boxes that expand on the text under discussion but do so in a manner calculated to aid student retention. The four types of boxes are as follows:

1. Focus on Schools
2. Focus on Classrooms
3. Focus on Teachers
4. Focus on Students

These four categories are a progression from the general to the specific and help readers make a firm connection to the topic under discussion in the boxes.

• *Teacher-student interactions boxes.* A fifth category of boxed material *Teacher-Student Interactions* is found at the end of each chapter and after discussion of major topics. These boxes suggest techniques for applying the text's content to classroom situations. Important statements from the chapter are repeated, and specific examples are given of how that content could be used at various grade levels. We believe this feature will help readers understand how the chapter's theoretical and factual material can be translated into classroom usage.

• *Conclusion.* At the end of each chapter the reader will find a brief concluding statement that summarizes the main theme(s) of the chapter. This statement provides the reader with a quick check of the content covered and the purpose of the chapter.

• *Chapter highlights.* Following the brief concluding section is a more detailed number of summary statements that are grouped according to the major topics of the chapter. This enables readers to review the chapter quickly and thoroughly by turning to the chapter's table of contents and then checking against the chapter highlights to determine how successful they were in recalling the pertinent material of the chapter and how it could be used in the classroom.

• *Key terms.* Readers will find at the end of each chapter a list of those terms that are essential to understanding the chapter's ideas and suggestions. These terms are highlighted when used and explained in the context of the chapter. Readers are urged to spend time to master the meaning of each of these terms and relate them to the context in which they appear.

• *Suggested readings.* At the end of each chapter, readers will find an annotated list of four or five books or journal articles that we think are particularly well-suited to supplement the contents of the chapter.

These references are not necessarily textbooks; they may not deal specifically with either education or psychology. We believe, however, that they shed an illuminating light upon the chapter's material.

• *Supplementary materials.* We have worked with the publisher and a group of very talented individuals to put together a quality set of supplementary materials to assist instructors and students who use this text.

• *Instructor's course planner.* The key to this teaching package was created by Lynne Blesz Vestal. This flexible planner provides a variety of useful tools to enhance your teaching efforts, reduce your workload, and increase your enjoyment of teaching. For each chapter of the text, the Planner provides an outline, overview, learning objectives, and key terms. These items are also contained in the Student Study Guide. The Planner also contains lecture suggestions, classroom activities, discussion questions, integrative essay questions, a film list, and a transparency guide. The Instructor's Course Planner is conveniently housed within an attractive 11 x 13 x 9 carrying case. This case is designed to accommodate the complete ancillary package by containing each chapter's material within a separate hanging file, allowing you to keep all your class materials organized at your fingertips.

• *The Test Item File* was also constructed by Lynne Blesz Vestal. This comprehensive test bank includes over 1,000 multiple choice and true/false questions that are keyed to the text and learning objectives. Each item is designated as factual, conceptual, or applied.

• *The Student Study Guide* was created by Lynne Blesz Vestal. For each chapter of the text, the student is provided with an outline, an overview, learning objectives, key terms, a guided review, study questions (with answers provided for self-testing), and an integration and application question. The study guide begins with a section on "Developing Good Study Habits" to help students study more effectively and efficiently.

• *The Educational Psychology Transparency Set* is also available to adopters of this text. The set consists of 40 acetate transparencies or slides of key tables and graphics from the text. The images have been carefully chosen to provide comprehensive coverage of the major topics in *Educational Psychology* and to aid the instructor in explaining intricate and complex concepts presented in the text.

- *Brown & Benchmark TestPak 3.0* is an integrated computer program designed to print test masters; to permit on-line computerized testing; to help students review text material through an interactive self-testing, self-scoring quiz program; and to provide instructors with a gradebook program for classroom management. Test questions can be found in the Test Item File, or you may create your own. You may choose to use Testbank A for exam questions and Testbank B in conjunction with the quiz program. Printing the exam yourself requires access to a personal computer—an IBM® that uses 5.25-inch or 3.5-inch diskettes, an Apple IIe or IIc®, or a Macintosh®. TestPak requires two disk drives and will work with any printer. Diskettes are available through your local Brown & Benchmark sales representative or by phoning Brown & Benchmark Educational Services at 800–338–5371. The package you receive will contain complete instructions for making up an exam.

- *Brown & Benchmark customized reader* allows instructors to select over 80 different journal or magazine articles from a menu provided by a Brown & Benchmark sales representative. These readings can be custom printed and bound into an attractive 8.5 x 11 book, giving instructors an opportunity to tailor-make their own student reader.

- *Our custom publishing service* will also allow you to have your own notes, handouts or other classroom materials printed and bound for your course use very inexpensively. See your Brown & Benchmark representative for details.

- *The Brown & Benchmark Customized Transparency Program* provides you with acetate transparencies of your choice of illustrations from *Educational Psychology*. The program is available to adopters of our text based upon the number of textbooks ordered. Consult your Brown & Benchmark representative for ordering policies.

- *Videotapes.* A large selection of videotapes is also available to adopters based upon the number of textbooks ordered directly from Wm. C. Brown Communications by your bookstore.

Finally, we believe the most important feature of the text is its useability. We have attempted to write a book that readers can turn to, even while they are teaching, as a source of ideas, support, and reassurance.

Acknowledgments

We would particularly like to express our thanks to our editor, Michael Lange, for his insights and support during the writing of this book. His expertise and encouragement have been dual pillars of strength that were constantly present. We would also like to thank Sheralee Connors, our development editor, for her management skills and ability to smooth troubled waters. Michelle Campbell gracefully saw the book through its production schedule, while at the same time Judi David was obtaining delightful and pertinent photos and Vicki Krug was carefully obtaining needed permissions.

Several of our colleagues contributed to our work. We would like to thank the following individuals for their helpful suggestions.

Deborah S. Brown, Friends University

Robert J. Crowley, Sangamon State University

Daniel Fasko, Jr., Morehead State University

Craig L. Frisby, University of Florida

Susan P. Lajoie, McGill University

B. L. McInnis, University of Lowell

Mary Ann McLaughlin, Clarion University of Pennsylvania

Sharon L. McNeely, Northeastern Illinois University

Judith M. Sgarzi, Western New England College

Susan M. Sheridan, University of Utah

1

Introduction

Educational Psychology: Teaching and Learning

As you think about entering the classroom as a teacher, perhaps for the first time, or at the opening of another school year, you probably feel some trepidation. Think, however, of times past, times when conditions were far different from what they are now. Recall the classroom in which Charles Dickens' *Nicholas Nickleby* found himself as an assistant to Mr. Squeers. Nicholas described the boys as follows:

> With every kindly sympathy and affection blasted in its birth, with every young and happy feeling flogged and starved down, with every vengeful passion that can fester in swollen hearts eating its evil way to their core in silence, what an incipient Hell was building here.

Mr. Squeers had his own way of maintaining discipline. "Let any boy speak a word without leave," said Mr. Squeers mildly, "and I'll take the skin off his back." As you can imagine, this had the desired effect.

Or can you recall from your reading of many years ago, an incident in Mark Twain's *Tom Sawyer* when Tom, again late for school, was called to the front of the room by the master.

"Come up here. Now, sir, why were you late again, as usual?"

Noting that the only vacant place in the classroom was next to the desirable Becky Thatcher and wanting to be punished by sitting next to her, Tom uttered the dreadful words, "I stopped to talk with Huckleberry Finn."

The master, shocked, ordered Tom to take off his jacket and he whipped him with a switch until his arm was tired.

"Now, sir, go and sit with the *girls*. And let this be a warning to you." Tom, delighted though sore, had won again.

For most teachers and students the educational environment has changed from this dismal picture of past days. In some schools of the United States teachers and students find themselves in cheerful, roomy buildings. Classrooms are bright and stocked with materials. Students in these schools are no longer threatened by switches and beatings. Rather they interact with teachers in a positive atmosphere for learning. In these schools, teachers are not seen as dictators in their classrooms but as professionals whose skills are dedicated to the fulfillment of their students' potential.

In other parts of the country, however, schools and classrooms are old and rundown, and there is no money for materials and repair. Some schools can even be dangerous environments for teachers and students as a result of crime in the school itself or on the school grounds. Drugs may be sold openly.

You can see, then, that the culture of our contemporary society affects the education of our youth. Teachers also must be prepared to work competently and harmoniously with the growing number of multicultural students entering our classrooms. Minority children have unique experiences that influence their educational lives. This range of educational settings serves to make teaching in the nineties both complex and challenging.

What do we mean by **teaching**? There are many different definitions of teaching, but each seems to share several common critical attributes, such as the following (Anderson & Burns, 1989, pp. 7–8).

- **Teaching can be considered a process** since teaching involves action. You perform when you teach.
- **Teaching can be regarded as an interpersonal activity** since a teacher interacts with one or more students. The interaction can be bidirectional (teachers influence students and students influence teachers). This activity is also known as reciprocal interactions.
- **Teaching is intentional.** When you teach, you do so with a purpose or purposes.

Considering these attributes, Anderson and Burns (1989) provide the following useful definition of teaching: "Teaching is an interpersonal, interactive activity, typically involving verbal communication, which is undertaken for the purpose of helping one or more students learn or change the ways in which they can or will behave" (p. 8).

The acquisition of teaching skills is a complex process but one that can be mastered. Any course or book on educational psychology should have as its major emphasis the ways and means of providing students and

School environments vary greatly and influence learning and attitudes about the importance of learning.

readers with insights into the teaching-learning process. To accomplish that aim means that you acquire both knowledge and understanding of your students, what teaching is, how learning occurs, how classrooms are run, and, in general, what schools are all about. This text will help you to apply the principles of educational psychology to learning environments extending from those of young children to those of adulthood.

It is an exciting time to teach; our nation wants good teachers in the classroom. In a recent statement, Lamar Alexander, U.S. Secretary of Education presented the *America 2000* Education Strategy, which includes the national goals adopted by President Bush and the governors in 1990. The America 2000 strategy is defined as follows:

An action plan to move America toward the six national goals through a populist crusade, by assuring accountability in today's schools, unleashing America's genius to jump-start a new generation of American schools, transforming a "Nation at Risk" into a "Nation of Students," and nurturing the family and community values essential to personal responsibility, strong schools, and sound education for all children (p. 25).

The proposal is a nine year plan to move toward the following educational goals.

1. All children in America will start school ready to learn.
2. The high school graduation rate will increase to at least 90 percent.
3. American students will leave grades four, eight, and twelve having demonstrated competency in challenging subject matter including English, mathematics, science, history, and geography; and every school in America will ensure that all students learn to use their minds well, so that they may be prepared for responsible citizenship, further learning, and productive employment in our modern economy.
4. U.S. students will be first in the world in science and mathematics achievement.
5. Every adult American will be literate and will possess the knowledge and skills necessary to compete economically and exercise the rights and responsibilities of citizenship.
6. Every school in America will be free of drugs and violence and will offer a disciplined environment conducive to learning (p. 9).

In this first chapter, we'll begin to address these issues by exploring the link between educational psychology *and* teaching. We'll next examine what it means to teach. Good teaching, however, just doesn't happen; you must be part artist and part scientist, which we'll explore as our next topic. Next we'll look at the schools in which you'll do your teaching; what are today's schools like? Finally, you'll be asked to think about educational psychology itself—what it is and how it relates to teacher effectiveness.

When you finish your reading of this chapter, you should be able to:

- define educational psychology
- identify the major issues facing teachers today
- describe qualities that contribute to excellent teaching
- assess your expectations for teaching
- compare teaching viewed as an art and as a science
- evaluate the relationship between effective teachers and effective schools.

So You Want to Teach

We have recently seen a spate of *joy* books—*The Joy of Cooking, The Joy of Running, The Joy of Shopping.* Most experienced teachers would also endorse a *Joy of Teaching* book. Will you have your down days? Of course; you cannot escape that in any profession. But you probably have been attracted to teaching by one, or a combination, of several reasons—you enjoy working with young people; you like a particular subject; or you enjoy being in an environment where people want to learn. Before examining how educational psychology can help your teaching and your students' learning, let's look at what it means to teach.

What It Means to Teach

Concern with our schools and a desire to improve student achievement reflect a national interest in education. Prestigious and widely-publicized national reports such as *A Nation At Risk, A Nation Prepared,* and *Tomorrow's Teachers* have specifically addressed the role of teachers. Among their recommendations are the following:

- Persons preparing to teach should be required to meet high educational standards, to demonstrate an aptitude for teaching, and to demonstrate competence in an academic discipline.
- Reaffirm that the teaching profession is the best hope for establishing new standards of excellence as the hallmark of American education.
- Salaries for teachers should be increased and made professionally competitive. Any advances should be tied to an effective evaluation system.
- Career ladders for teachers must be identified.
- Nonschool personnel such as experts in science and mathematics from business and government should be hired.
- Incentives should be used to attract outstanding graduates into teaching.
- Master teachers should be used in designing teacher preparation programs and in supervising novice teachers.
- Schools should be restructured to provide a professional environment for teachers.

That these suggestions need thoughtful consideration is reflected in Brophy's comment (1988) that although most competent adults could survive in a classroom, most could not teach effectively. Teaching, a sophisticated and demanding task, requires high levels of energy, motivation, and subject matter knowledge for effective instruction.

What Are Your Expectations?

You can't see them, but classrooms are filled with expectations: yours, your students', parents', administrators'. Here we'll concentrate on *your* expectations: What awaits you when you walk into that school?

Your main concern probably centers on students—what type of student behavior can I anticipate, and how much should I expect from students academically? There are, however, a range of school responsibilities that face you as a teacher, not all of which are directly related to your teaching (Kim & Kellough, 1991).

For example, some responsibilities are related to managing the physical aspects of teaching, such as keeping attendance, preparing schedules, and ordering equipment (including textbooks). Other responsibilities relate to student supervision, such as supervising halls, lunchrooms, advising clubs, and producing programs such as plays and school exercises. Still other responsibilities will involve you in community activities, such as participating in parent-teacher organization meetings and representing the school at community functions. Some responsibilities will involve your professional advancement, such as joining professional associations and engaging in graduate work. Instructional responsibilities include the daily preparation of lessons, evaluation of students, and the individual advisement of students. Thus your responsibilities will cluster around four categories (Montagu, Huntsberger, & Hoffman, 1989).

• **The Institutional Function.** You will spend time in nonacademic and personal activities (perhaps collecting lunch money or turning in attendance reports) that you must manage efficiently to avoid any undue loss of instructional time.

• **The Managerial Function.** For students to learn, they must have clear objectives, know exactly what is expected of them, and develop positive relationships in the classroom. Establish your classroom rules early, create as few as possible, and make sure that everyone understands them. We'll discuss this function in greater detail in chapter 13.

• **The Academic Function.** You want your students to learn as much as their potential allows. They'll achieve to the extent that your instructional objectives, teaching strategies, and your students' learning abilities and motivational level come together harmoniously.

• **The Professional Development Function.** Standards that regulate entrance into the teaching profession are becoming steadily higher, a change that implies a rising level of minimal professional competence. Graduate work, in-service meetings, and workshops all serve a professional development function.

Teaching and Educational Issues

You will also find yourself involved in and making decisions about many sensitive issues. These issues are likely to involve students who possess a wide range of abilities; teaching techniques and classroom management; evaluation and grading of students; communication with parents; and the use of research to guide teaching and interacting with students. Let's examine several specific issues that we'll address in greater detail in later chapters.

Language

A major change in the teaching of reading and writing is a concept known as **whole language.** Rather than teach phonics isolated from meaning, students learn to read by obtaining the meaning of words from context, with phonics introduced as needed. For example, if, while reading a story, one of your students has difficulty with the word *dish,* you would stop and sound it out. Students don't use basal readers; they read appropriate level literature about themes that interest them and then write about these ideas. Teachers who have begun to use this new technique believe that it motivates their students better than the older methods. Not everyone agrees with this approach, however, and we'll discuss this hotly contested issue in greater detail in chapter 3.

Mathematics

International comparisons of students on mathematics achievement tests have repeatedly found Americans doing poorly. As a result, the country will soon experience another wave of publicity about a revision of the mathematics curriculum. You may have heard about the "new math" of the 1960s, followed a few years later by the "back-to-basics" movement. One of the reasons that the new math was not an unqualified success was that public school teachers had little to say about it. It was simply imposed on them.

Today's emphasis is less on skills for their own sake and more on thinking about and understanding the meaning of numbers. For example, the mathematician J. Paulos (1988) quotes a couple as saying they're not going to Europe because of all the terrorists. In 1985, 17 of the 28 million Americans who traveled abroad that year were killed by terrorists. That same year, 45,000 people were killed on American highways: that statistic means one chance in 5,300 of being killed in a car crash. Understanding the numbers involved helps you to evaluate which situation contains the greatest potential danger.

The National Council of Teachers of Mathematics recommends that students use calculators at all times and urges teachers to emphasize problem solving skills (see chapter 8) and the practical side of mathematics. The goal is to make mathematics seem less threatening and more useful.

Science

Estimates are that fewer than 10 percent of high school graduates have the scientific skills necessary to perform satisfactorily in college-level courses. Attempting to combat this trend, many science educators turn today to a more "hands-on" approach to their teaching. Instead of having their students memorize lengthy formulas, they have them do experiments starting in the early grades. For example, instead of reading about the principle of buoyancy, students in the lower grades make lumps of clay into various shapes, put them into plastic bags, and discover which shapes float and which sink.

You may argue that there's nothing new in this technique; good teachers have been doing it for years. There are differences, however. Where this approach has been successful, teachers have acted as facilitators, not directors. Teachers need not teach a specific amount of material; in a sense, teaching less can result in teaching more. That is, by teaching generalizable problem solving strategies along with the concepts of basic subject matter, and by emphasizing that learners should know themselves, teachers can prepare students for a lifetime of learning.

Retention in Grade

Consider this possible future scenario. You are meeting with the parents of one of your students and they ask you if their child should be retained in third grade. What would you say to them? Making students repeat a year's work has come under heavy attack recently, with opponents claiming that it usually doesn't work. After reviewing studies comparing the education of students who were retained with students of comparable achievement and maturity who were promoted, Holmes (1990) concluded that retained students were no better off than those who went on to the next grade. Retention, either because of immaturity or lack of achievement, is a common practice in our schools, a practice which raises many questions (Medway & Rose, 1986).

- Does grade retention produce academic achievement superior to that found in comparable students who are promoted?
- Do students who have been retained drop out of school more frequently than comparable students who were promoted?
- Does a policy of retention discriminate against particular groups of students?
- What evidence does a school use in its decision to retain?
- Does eliminating grade retention mean a return to a policy of social promotion?
- What are the legal ramifications of grade retention?

Although evidence is accumulating that retention has not been a uniformly successful policy, the issue today is widely debated.

THE FAR SIDE
BY GARY LARSON

"Well, I've got your final grades ready, although I'm afraid not everyone here will be moving up."

The practice of retention is being seriously questioned today. There is little research to support it and several major reviews that condemn it.

Homework

Homework, that in-and-out of favor subject, is once again enjoying renewed acceptance. (Homework usually refers to school-assigned academic work that is to be completed outside school, usually in the home.) At the turn of the twentieth century, homework was considered vital, its popularity declined in the 1940s, reemerged in the 1950s (after Sputnik), fell into disfavor in the 1960s because it was seen as a form of useless pressure, and now, with reports of the poor achievement of American students, is once more viewed as essential. Research shows that for high school students two or more hours increases achievement, that junior high school students benefit from one to two hours of homework, and that there seems to be a slight relationship between homework for elementary school students and improved achievement (Cooper, 1989). Homework at the elementary school level, however, brings home and school closer together and encourages students to realize that they can learn on their own. Homework should not be a burden for students and their parents but should be asssigned to meet demonstrated needs.

The point of introducing these selected but representative issues at this stage of your work is to make you aware of how educational psychology can help you reach decisions. For example, reading about language and development should help you answer questions about whole language programs (see chapter 3). The details of problem solving that you'll read about in chapter 8 should help you in judging science and math methods.

Understanding possible alternatives to retention in grade helps in weighing the pros and cons of this controversial topic. You can better assess the value of homework by using your knowledge of development and learning. To use your knowledge of educational psychology most effectively, however, you must act as both artist and scientist.

Teaching as an Art and Science

Although teachers have always needed professional skills to be successful in the classroom, perhaps few periods in history have dictated a greater need for teachers who are competent, thoughtful, and imaginative. A combination of factors, ranging from changing social conditions to a continuing knowledge explosion, demands teachers who possess abilities that go beyond the sheer mechanics of teaching.

Teaching as an Art

You must know your subject, which implies that you grasp not only the material that you currently are presenting in class, but also the core of the subject, and what researchers are discovering at the frontiers of the discipline. In an age devoted to empirical research, the expansion of knowledge necessitates constant independent study to prevent personal obsolescence.

Teachers will avoid such work unless they like their subject and enjoy interacting with students. To devote hours of study beyond the demands of duty requires a commitment to a discipline and the company of the young, both of which can be provocative masters. You have already made a commitment, which reflects a love of study and pleasure in working with youth. These categories actually mirror two basic themes that are at the heart of this book: the teacher as a person and the teacher as a professional.

A Modern Art of Teaching

In a modern version of *The Art of Teaching* (the name of a graceful overview of teaching originally written by Gilbert Highet in 1950), Flinders (1989), after observing public school teachers, notes that the concept of

Teaching is an art in the sense that the teacher must be part actor, part nurturer, part cheerleader, part psychologist, and part coach. The art of teaching involves compassion, commitment, and caring for students as individuals.

professionalism in education fails to capture the "artistry of teaching." Observing the way that teachers use body language to communicate a message, or their use of silence to motivate, Flinders believes that such skills reveal the grace, subtlety, and drama of everyday teaching.

Analyzing these behaviors, Flinders suggests several categories that capture the art of teaching:

1. **Communication. Communication** goes beyond speaking or writing. It includes body language, the use of space (stepping toward a student, for example), voice intonation, and eye contact. All of these nonverbal cues are coordinated to convey a message of caring about students.

2. **Perception.** When teachers adapt their methods to the "mood" of the class, they are reading cues that describe the emotional context of the group. How many times have you heard teachers talk about the vibes they pick up from a class? **Perception,** then, reflects a sensitivity to students and a capacity (and willingness) to adapt, and characterizes good teaching.

3. **Cooperation.** Any classroom functions more smoothly when teachers and students get along well with each other. Working *with* students is much more effective than talking *to* them. Among the strategies that Flinders recommends to encourage cooperation are these:
   a. using humor to promote solidarity between you and your class,
   b. allowing students to choose activities,
   c. providing opportunities for student recognition, and creating pockets of time for one-to-one contact.

4. **Appreciation.** Although appreciation is not something teachers "do," it is an important part of job satisfaction. **Appreciation,** then, is a product of artistry—knowing you have done a good job.

Flinders (1989) in no sense diminishes the professionalism of teaching: the knowledge that teachers possess, their ability to apply various teaching strategies, and their skill at achieving different kinds of student learning. Rather he urges a recognition of those principles that Highet expressed so well many years ago.

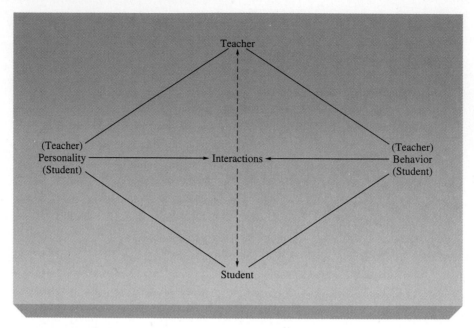

Figure 1.1 Student-teacher interactions.

Remember: as an individual personality with your own needs, characteristics, strengths, and weaknesses, you will adopt certain techniques and styles in the classroom that you decide are best suited for you. How your students respond to your classroom style determines how successful the interactions in your classroom will be. Figure 1.1 illustrates the process.

Figure 1.1 emphasizes that the behavior of both teacher and student produces a series of reciprocal interactions that will eventually culminate in a relationship. The quality of the relationship, positive or negative, goes far in determining your success as a teacher. This important topic will be explored in detail in chapter 5. (Also, a section of each chapter in this book will illustrate teacher-student interactions as they relate to the chapter's topic.)

One of the objectives of this text is to present a range of ideas, theories, and research that will enable you to apply the best and most recent data about teaching and learning that reflect your needs and characteristics. To make these decisions, you must be familiar with data concerning teacher characteristics, student characteristics, teaching, and learning. As we shall see, such knowledge defines the field of educational psychology and the remaining chapters of this book are designed to facilitate effective teaching and learning.

Teaching as a Science

Considering teaching as strictly an art, however, is too limiting. Given the knowledge that we have acquired about the nature of instruction and about the methods of inquiry into any discipline, we should explore the notion that teaching can also be considered a science.

Most teachers, knowingly or not, adopt—and adapt—the scientific method in their work. Teachers may adopt the role of experimenter as they try new instructional methods and classroom procedures (even something as simple as changing the seating arrangement). Any scientific analysis will include the following four steps:

1. **Identifying the problem**—for teachers this means deciding exactly what you want your students to learn;
2. **Formulating a logical series of steps to reach a goal**—for teachers this means deciding not only what but how they will present a topic; that is, teachers are acting as decision makers;
3. **Gathering the data**—for teachers this means deciding just what student behavior is to be measured and what is the best means of measurement;
4. **Interpreting the data**—for teachers, this means deciding if the students' performance (the results of the teacher's strategy and testing) achieved the desired goal.

Teachers, by following the "scientific method" in their instruction and by their involvement at various levels of scientific inquiry, act as scientists: they identify objectives, devise strategies, evaluate their data, and communicate their results.

In a thoughtful attempt to bridge the gap between teaching as an art and teaching as a science, Gage (1977,

1985) urged that we distinguish between a science of teaching and a scientific basis for the art of teaching. He noted that the idea of a science of teaching is probably erroneous because we cannot predict that good teaching inevitably follows from adherence to rigorous laws that yield high predictability and control. (As we shall see later in our work, some psychologists who have applied their work to teaching and learning might disagree with Gage's conclusion, especially B. F. Skinner.)

Gage (1985) argued, however, that it is possible to develop a scientific base for teaching. For example, in teaching as in any science, the laws and trends relating any two variables are subject to modification by the influence of a third variable. He then gives the example of the relationship between teacher criticism and student achievement. It may be negative for students with lower academic orientation and positive for students with higher academic orientation. Thus, a third variable—the pupil's degree of academic orientation—influences the relationship between teacher criticism and student achievement.

To say that teaching has a scientific basis means that educational researchers have accumulated, carefully and painstakingly, a body of knowledge concerning regular, nonchance relationships about teaching and learning. This type of research is difficult and time-consuming, yet "in the long run, the improvement of teaching—what is tantamount to the improvement of our children's lives—will come in large part from the continued search for a scientific basis for the art of teaching" (Gage, 1977, p. 41). So we conclude as we began—teaching is both art and science, a needed combination for changing classrooms.

Research and Teaching

In a thoughtful analysis of the value of educational research, Berliner (1987) believes that in the last few years educators have come closer than ever before to identifying a scientific basis for the art of teaching. While embracing the belief of teaching as an art, Berliner states that such artistry should be research based. He goes on to argue that educational research is as reliable and valid as research in the "hard sciences."

For example, one technique for examining the quality of research in any discipline is to determine if the research results relating to a particular topic are consistent over time. Inspecting a series of experiments in particle physics, Berliner found that in 6 of 13 reviews, significant statistical differences appeared. He then checked 13 psychological reviews and found that 6 of the 13 showed significant statistical differences—similar to the results discovered in the physics review. In other words, research in the social sciences is no better or worse than that in the hard sciences.

Berliner then indicated how educational research helps to improve teaching and learning. For example:

- students (particularly young students) need high rates of success to learn academic matter. This technique is especially true for lower-class students and when the curriculum is hierarchically organized.
- structuring (providing clear directions, objectives, reviews, and advance organizers) improves classroom achievement.
- the most effective teachers provide academic feedback, both positive and negative. (Note: A negative teacher response is a positive predictor of achievement as long as it is task-related.)
- differing expectations for students produce differing results and are a matter of continuing concern (that is, those students of whom you expect more, achieve better).
- cooperative learning methods have helped raise student achievement and have also helped to improve the self-esteem of students. (For a more detailed discussion of cooperative learning, see chapter 9.)

These are only a few of the findings that Berliner discussed but the conclusion is clear: educational research is both good and practical.

With these ideas behind us, we turn now to the relationship of educational psychology to both teaching and learning. Speculating about the definition of educational psychology, Harre and Lamb (1983) stated that it is too simple to say that educational psychology is the psychology of learning and teaching in school. Rather it is concerned with the development and education of children from birth to adulthood; thus it helps to answer many of the questions that you may have about teaching.

For nearly a century there has been no common agreement on a definition of educational psychology. The definition that receives the most acceptance is that educational psychology involves the application of psychology to the study of development, learning, motivation, instruction, and any related issues that occur in educational settings. After a review of the historical literature in educational psychology, Glover and Ronning (1987, p. 14) suggested that educational psychology includes topics that span human development, individual differences, measurement, learning, motivation, and humanistic views of education and is both data- and theory-driven.

Questions That Teachers Ask

How can educational psychology help you to recognize your own needs and also help you to become a true professional? You probably have a list of questions about teaching that you would like answered, such as:

It would be as absurd for one to undertake to educate the young with no knowledge of. . .psychology, as for one to attempt to produce a sonata while ignorant of the phenomena of sound.

Louisa Parsons Hopkins, Educational Psychology, 1986.

- **When are students ready for certain experiences?** Are there developmental data that provide clues to the ideal time and circumstances for teaching different subjects? (Reading instruction is a good illustration.)
- **Are there different teaching techniques that are better suited for some students than for others?** For example, do some students learn better when they are required to discover (with guidance) things for themselves; are there others who do better with more direct instruction?
- **Does a knowledge of learning theory help in the classroom?** For example, does understanding the fundamentals of memory enable teachers to help students retain their learning and transfer it to other subjects?
- **Does knowing the details of test construction really matter?** For example, if we understand the theory behind test making, does it help us to be more certain about the extent and quality of a student's learning?

- **What does the latest research say about classroom discipline?** Here is a question that students and beginning teachers usually ask first. Students need a happy blend of firmness and freedom, but how do we arrive at this happy medium?

These are practical questions that have direct classroom application and as we attempt to answer them, they'll guide your reading throughout the text. When you complete your reading, if you are a beginning teacher, you should face the first day with more confidence. If you are an experienced teacher, you should have new ideas to test, new techniques to try.

Our Multicultural Classrooms

You are probably also concerned that you will be teaching students from different cultures. America today is welcoming great waves of immigrants; thus many immigrant and minority children will be in our classrooms. Priding ourselves on our cultural tolerance, we believe that cultural diversity brings a special strength and vitality

Focus on Teachers

Generalizations About Teachers and Teaching

Anderson and Burns (1989) presented several generalizations that they drew from more than 50 years of research on teachers, teaching, and instruction. The authors noted that the generalizations are fairly conservative and should stimulate discussion and innovation among researchers and practitioners. These generalizations appear in Box Table 1.1. As you read these items, remember that these topics will appear in subsequent chapters. Decide if you agree or disagree with the points, and when you have completed your reading of this book, return to these points and determine if your agreements and disagreements remain the same.

Box Table 1.1

Generalizations About Teachers, Teaching, and Instruction

Category	Generalization
Teachers	Teachers assume a very central, directive and active role in the classroom. Differences in individual teaching behaviors are not reliably associated with differences in student achievement. Teacher characteristics do not impact directly on student achievement. Teachers progress through a fairly predictable set of qualitatively distinct stages as they move from novice to expert status.
Teaching	If teaching behaviors are to be reliably associated with student achievement, then patterns, groupings, or clusters of these behaviors must be identified. Furthermore, experimental or quasi-experimental studies may be necessary to produce the variation in these behavioral clusters that is needed to properly examine the relationships between teacher behavior and student achievement. Considering teaching from a functional, rather than behavioral, point of view is more likely to result in a greater understanding of teaching in general and effective teaching in particular.
Instruction	The subject matter being taught impacts on some, if not all, of the other components of instruction. Although the academic demands on students tend to be fairly minimal, the greater the emphasis on these demands and the students' need to meet them, the greater their achievement in the basic skills. Although lecture, recitation, and seatwork predominate in classrooms, there is little if any evidence that changes in format would result in higher levels of student achievement. Though most teaching and learning takes place in whole-class settings, there is increasing evidence that grouping within the classroom is beneficial for student learning. Instructional time, content coverage, and pacing are associated with higher levels of student achievement.

Note. From *Research in classrooms: The study of teachers, teaching, and instruction* (pp. 343-353) by L. W. Anderson and R. B. Burns, 1989, New York: Pergamon. Reproduced by permission.

(Hirsch, 1987). As we greet these newcomers, however, a basic question remains, one that has always troubled us as a nation: How much do we encourage assimilation into one national culture and still preserve the rich cultural heritage of various groups? Yet, with regard to immigration, one guiding principle remains intact: Our nation broadens its horizons by encountering cultures other than its own (Hirsch, 1987).

As we begin our discussions of **multicultural classrooms** (discussions that will appear in each chapter), we should be aware of the meaning of the terms used. *Culture* refers to those values, beliefs, and behaviors characteristic

There are growing numbers of minority children in our classrooms. Children will increasingly have the opportunity to interact with peers of great cultural diversity.

of a large group of people—for example, those of Hispanic origin. *Ethnic,* however, usually applies to national or linguistic backgrounds and can be included within the larger culture—Mexican Americans. *Race,* on the other hand, does not refer to nationality, culture, or language but is identified by blood-type, such as African. Anthropologists have identified nine major groups: African, American Indian, Asian, Australian, European, Indian, Melanesian, Micronesian, and Polynesian (Tiedt & Tiedt, 1990).

Schools across the country are now welcoming a growing number of multicultural students. Enjoying your work with young people is a necessity for good teaching. For many prospective—and veteran—teachers, this means knowing and understanding an increasing number of multicultural students. Our concern with minority students has ebbed and flowed through the years but the success of the Civil Rights movement and a growing awareness of the effects of poverty have produced a renewed interest in multicultural matters.

Figure 1.2 illustrates the surge in legal immigration for the years 1981–1990.

This is the *third* great immigration we have seen in this country. The first occurred in the mid-1800s with the arrival of immigrants from England, Ireland, Germany, and Scandinavia. The second movement took place between 1900 and 1920 and was dominated by immigrants from Southern Europe—Italy, Hungary, Poland—and many from Russia. In 1907, alone, 1.3 million immigrants entered the United States (Kellogg, 1988). The third major migration began in the late 1960s and continues. The origin of these new immigrants is as follows (Kellogg, 1988): Asia—34 percent, Latin America—34 percent, Europe—16 percent, and Other—16 percent. In 1985, 80 percent of all immigrants came from Mexico and Asia.

Among the most important characteristics of this new group with direct implications for the schools are the following: a) *they are young* and will be in our educational system for many years; b) *they have remarkable language diversity,* which points to the need for definite policy decisions in the schools; and c) *many of the children have not yet mastered their own language.*

As an example of what these figures mean, consider the various birth rates. Although Americans now average 1.7 children per lifetime, black Americans average 2.4 children per lifetime, Cambodians average 7.4, Laotians average 4.6, Vietnamese average 3.4, and Mexican-Americans average 2.9. Thus, the population in our schools will shift to reflect these figures.

Kellogg (1988) reports that the class of 2001 (which started kindergarten in September, 1988) mirrors the changing face of America. For example, minority enrollment ranges from 70 percent to 96 percent in the nation's fifteen largest school systems. What can we conclude from this brief summary? Our public schools will be serving an ever-growing number of immigrant students. In Lowell, Massachusetts, for example, the number of Southeast-Asian students jumped from 98 in 1980 to 2,000 today. The same phenomenon is happening across the country.

Of the four major minority groups—African-American, Asian-American, Hispanic-American, and Native

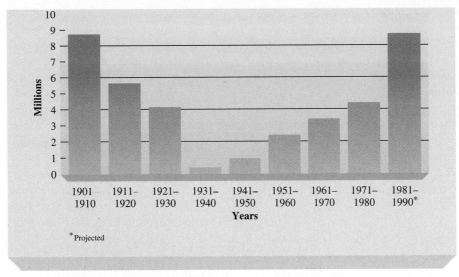

Figure 1.2 Legal immigrants to the United States by decade.

Source: Data from *Current Population Survey 1983*, U.S. Bureau of the Census.

Focus on Students

African–American Students in the Classroom

Noting that 50 percent of urban students are African-American, Lomotey (1990) asks what is happening to these students in our public schools? Too frequently they are labelled as dropouts, at risk students, or children of the underclass, usually by those from outside the African-American community. In his thoughtful overview of the current educational scene, Lomotey identifies academic success as an elusive goal for the large majority of African-American students at all school levels. For example, the 50 percent of urban students who are African-American have a dropout rate of 50 percent.

In attempting to combat this unacceptable condition, educators have come to realize that teachers must move beyond merely understanding the child, long a hallowed objective. Today's understanding must encompass a student's cultural world, those personal experiences that a student brings into the classroom (Boateng, 1990). Otherwise the following persistent pattern that characterizes the educational paths of many African-American students will continue:

- They are more likely to be placed in special education classes.
- They are more likely to be placed in vocational programs in high school.

- They are less likely to be placed in gifted and talented programs.
- They are less likely to be placed in academic tracks in high school.
- They are less likely to receive adequate math, science, and social studies instruction in high school.
- They are less likely to have adequate access to school computers (Lomotey, 1990).

Since there is widespread agreement today that no intellectual differences exist among the various racial groups and that African-American students have shown that they can do well in school, educators would do well to examine the school environments that have successfully engaged these students (see chapter 12).

Classroom instruction should reflect the cultural diversity that is a source of such great strength in our society, and today's teachers need familiarity with the communication, human relationship, learning, and motivation patterns that African-American students (and other minority groups—see **One State's Experience** in the following pages) bring to the classroom. Concepts such as racism and assimilation should appear across the curriculum with various cultural groups used to illustrate these ideas (Boateng, 1990).

Americans—the greatest amount of research has been done with African-Americans. Attention to this group remains high as a result of the declining developmental and educational status of a significant number of African-American children (McLoyd, 1990). Researchers study-

ing any of the minority groups, however, should be alert to the dangers of the "race-comparative" design; that is, how minority children differ from Anglo-American children and then interpreting these differences as deficits. This strategy has been particularly true of studies of

African-American children, which ignores the developmental path of these youngsters, their individual differences, and how some children deviate from the norms of development within the group (McLoyd, 1990).

Students with varied backgrounds, languages, and cultures pose a challenge to all of us as teachers. As McBay (1990) noted, the primary mandate for teachers, administrators, and curricula is to meet the individual needs of multicultural students. Thus each chapter in this book will have a section devoted to multicultural education as it relates to that chapter's topic. For now, the best words of advice are: work diligently to understand **all** the students in your classroom.

One State's Experience

It is often said that "as California goes, so goes the nation." Although this may not be quite accurate because of California's unique location, nevertheless, many of the issues that California is now addressing will soon be faced by other localities around the country. Consequently, the way that California's educators have faced the problems associated with increased immigration may provide insights for the nation as a whole.

One in six California students is foreign-born; *one in four* public school students comes from a non-English speaking home. Thus, educators must address the need for new teaching techniques and new programs that are appropriate for a multiethnic, multiracial, and multilingual student population. Most of these new immigrants come from the Pacific Rim countries of Asia, Mexico, and Central America (Olsen, 1988).

For example, the Asian-American population grew by 70 percent in the years 1980–1988, a rate seven times as fast as that of the general population. From 3.8 million in 1980, the Asian-American population grew to 6.5 million in 1988. One-third of these settled in California (Takaki, 1989).

This influx has been accompanied by the usual problems: schools caught unaware, uncertainty about needed changes, resistance to change, hostility to the new. One project—*California Tomorrow*—has arranged interviews with immigrant children, their parents, teachers, administrators, policy makers, and community advocates in an attempt to identify unmet needs. Since these students have a dropout rate from 50–70 percent, the problem is real, immediate, and growing.

Only about one in four of the foreign-born students begin their American education in the elementary grades, a fact which means that many of the older children lack the necessary basics. Here are several techniques that the schools have used to adapt to these new needs (Olsen, 1988):

- Some schools have turned to new assessment techniques, such as centralized centers that test basic academic skills in the child's native language, offer health screening, and evaluate English proficiency.
- An orientation for parents and those students entering American schools for the first time.
- Slide shows and orientation booklets in the student's native language.
- American students assigned as helpers to immigrant students.
- To reduce misunderstandings and any feelings of hostility, some schools (especially at the secondary level) use videotapes of both immigrant and American born students speaking of an immigrant's difficulties in a new land.

These are merely a few of the innovations that schools and teachers have devised to meet the new challenge.

> We need schools that deal fully with issues of diversity; schools that look frankly at matters of prejudice and equity; schools that support, celebrate, and integrate the cultures, languages, and backgrounds of their students; schools that incorporate the curriculum and the teaching strategies appropriate to the vast range of learning styles and cultures that are found in our multiethnic, multiracial society (Olsen, 1988, p. 218).

Effective Schools

Consistent findings testify to the conclusion that differences among schools are related to different levels of student performance, even beyond those that would be expected from the individual differences of students. During the past 20–25 years, educational research has quite clearly identified those characteristics that mark an **effective school.** Schools whose students achieve well and where morale is high possess the following attributes:

- **Good instructional leadership,** which means that principals, teachers, students, and parents agree on goals, methods, and content.
- **A respected principal** who is known for clear and consistent decisions.
- **An orderly environment** in which positive discipline encourages academic achievement and personal fulfillment.
- **Instructional practices** that blend both the teaching of basics and techniques designed to encourage discovery.

Focus on Schools

The National Assessment of Educational Progress

We are in a time when accountability is the watchword of reform, and testing has become the means for holding schools accountable (Koretz, 1989). These concerns have led to considerable interest in the workings of the **National Assessment of Educational Progress (NAEP)**, a federally-funded testing program now ending its second decade of activity. The NAEP collects data on American students in various subjects, using students 9, 13, and 17 years of age and students in grades 4, 8, and 11.

In reviewing the forces that shaped the NAEP, Messick, Beaton, and Lord (1983) identify four major influences.

1. **The changed federal role** since the 1960s has seen the federal government more active in education, a situation that raised tensions between federal agencies and state officials. NAEP was originally intended to collect representative data while reassuring state administrators that federal control was not imminent. Today these fears, though not totally eliminated, have receded, and states seem more open to the use of comparative data on educational achievement.
2. **The states' improved capacities** to aid local communities have given them more confidence to seek and use such data.
3. **Educational credibility has slipped** in the eyes of the public, and with this reaction has come a call for standards, as seen in the growing number of states using minimum competency tests. NAEP can help to facilitate this trend by providing comparative data.
4. **Fiscal pressure in the states** has resulted in fewer funds available for education. NAEP can help by furnishing data about the effectiveness of school practices, thus aiding state planning by addressing state-specific needs.

NAEP should be able to provide information that helps to answer such questions as:

- Are today's students learning the skills necessary for productive functioning in the 1990s?
- Are students in urban, suburban, and rural schools being adequately prepared?
- What are the competencies of students in math, science, and reading?
- What are the career goals of high school students?
- How do student/teacher ratios relate to achievement?
- Do students with preschool and/or kindergarten experiences perform better than those without these programs?

This list gives you an idea of what NAEP hopes to accomplish.

Others are not as positive about the role of NAEP. For example, Koretz (1989) believes that this new direction of NAEP (as a measure of accountability) will dilute its effectiveness as an indicator of achievement. By raising expectations, Koretz fears that teachers will resort to "teaching to the test," forgetting that it is just another test, subject to the strengths and weaknesses of all tests. (We'll discuss these issues in chapters 15 and 16.)

Finally, Koretz believes that NAEP will not tell us much about the comparative quality of schools because differences among the scores of students in the various states may reflect influences other than the quality of the schools. Nevertheless, given today's public impression of the schools, NAEP will undoubtedly assume a more significant national role. We'll use NAEP data in coming chapters, which will help you to judge its value as a national tool.

- **Collegiality among teachers** in which there is a "working together" to aid student achievement and adjustment.
- **Teachers with realistic but high expectations** for all of their students.
- **A frequent monitoring** of student progress (Good & Weinstein, 1986).

What do we know about the circumstances in which you find—or will find—yourself?

A Place Called School

In his 1984 and 1990 studies, John Goodlad has commented on the results of a sweeping survey of American schools. Intended to further understanding of our schools

and the problems that face them, Goodlad presented a timely picture of what is happening in our schools.

Table 1.1 illustrates many student activities you will initiate depending on the class level.

Four aspects of classroom life struck the investigators as persistent and important.

1. Regardless of organization, **the total group** is the vehicle for teaching and learning. Much of what occurs in a classroom depends on the orderly relationship among all its members. It is within this total organization that individual students work and achieve.
2. **Teachers are the strategic figures in this group.** They determine the activities, their sequence, and the tone of the classroom. As Goodlad (1984,

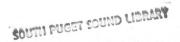

Table 1.1

Snapshot Data: Rank Order of Activities by Probability of Students Having Been Observed Participating in Each at Any Particular Moment

Early Elementary Activity	%	Upper Elementary Activity	%
Written work	28.3	Written work	30.4
Listening to Explanations/Lectures	18.2	Listening to Explanations/Lectures	20.1
Preparation for Assignments	12.7	Preparation for Assignments	11.5
Practice/Performance—Physical	7.3	Discussion	7.7
Use of AV Equipment	6.8	Reading	5.5
Reading	6.0	Practice/Performance—Physical	5.3
Student Non-task Behavior—No Assignment	5.7	Use of AV Equipment	4.9
Discussion	5.3	Student Non-task Behavior—No Assignment	4.8
Practice/Performance—Verbal	5.2	Practice/Performance—Verbal	4.4
Taking Tests	2.2	Taking Tests	3.3
Watching Demonstrations	1.5	Watching Demonstrations	1.0
Being Disciplined	0.5	Simulation/Role Play	0.4
Simulation/Role Play	0.2	Being Disciplined	0.3

Junior High Activity	%	Senior High Activity	%
Listening to Explanations/Lectures	21.9	Listening to Explanations/Lectures	25.3
Written work	20.7	Practice/Performance—Physical	17.5
Preparation for Assignments	15.9	Written work	15.1
Practice/Performance—Physical	14.7	Preparation for Assignments	12.8
Taking Tests	5.5	Student Non-task Behavior—No Assignment	6.9
Discussion	4.2	Taking Tests	5.8
Practice/Performance—Verbal	4.2	Discussion	5.1
Use of AV Equipment	4.1	Practice/Performance—Verbal	4.5
Student Non-task Behavior—No Assignment	3.6	Use of AV Equipment	2.8
Reading	2.8	Reading	1.9
Watching Demonstrations	1.5	Watching Demonstrations	1.6
Simulation/Role Play	0.2	Simulation/Role Play	0.1
Being Disciplined	0.2	Being Disciplined	0.1

From John Goodlad, *A Place Called School*. Copyright © 1984 McGraw-Hill, Inc., New York, NY. Reprinted by permission of McGraw-Hill, Inc.

p. 123) stated, the teacher is virtually autonomous with respect to classroom decisions.

3. **The classroom group** behaves in a manner calculated to maintain the teacher's strategic role. Even when the class is divided into smaller groups they tend to do those things previously determined by the teacher.

4. **The emotional tone of the classroom** tends to be level. Goodlad described students as "passively content"; that is, they felt generally positive about

peers and teachers and usually liked subjects and activities. These findings are almost identical with those reported by Philip Jackson twenty years ago—1968—and are a positive sign that the vast majority of students are prepared to like schools and teachers.

What Do Teachers Say?

Earlier in this chapter the topic of teacher needs and characteristics was mentioned as a subject of concern in this text. When questioned as to why they decided to

Table 1.2

Percentage of Teachers Who Felt Not Adequately Prepared (NAP) in Subject(s) They Are Currently Teaching

Subject	Senior High Schools		Junior High/Middle Schools		Elementary Schools	
	N teaching	NAP, %	N teaching	NAP, %	N teaching	NAP, %
English	159	5.9	126	3.2	234	4.7
Math	101	4.0	93	4.3	201	2.0
Soc. st.	111	0.0	66	4.5	175	4.6
Science	91	6.6	55	7.3	150	23.3
Arts	88	1.1	59	0.0	148	29.1
For. lang.	36	5.6	11	0.0	8	12.5
Ind. arts	39	0.0	17	0.0	3	0.0
Bus. ed.	48	2.1	10	0.0	1	0.0
Home ec.	29	0.0	15	0.0	3	33.3
P.E.	72	1.4	39	2.6	59	18.6
Spec. ed.	24	12.5	32	6.2	22	4.5
Gen. ed.	23	8.7	20	5.0	103	1.0
Total*	814		543		1107	
Overall % NAP		3.57		3.50		10.48

*At the elementary level, where one teacher teaches several subjects, this N represents the number of responses. This occurred also at the two secondary levels but much less frequently.
From John Goodlad, *A Place Called School.* Copyright © 1984 McGraw-Hill, Inc., New York, NY. Reprinted by permission of McGraw-Hill, Inc.

teach, the majority of teachers (57 percent in Goodlad's survey) stated that their decision had to do with the nature of teaching itself:

- the desire to teach in general or to teach a particular subject (22 percent);
- the idea of teaching as a desirable profession (18 percent);
- a desire to serve others (17 percent).

Fifteen percent of the elementary and 11 percent of the secondary teachers stated that liking children was their primary reason.

The teachers who entered the profession because of its inherent value, a desire to teach a specific subject, or liking for children felt that their expectations had been fulfilled. They also stated that they would choose a teaching career if starting again. Those who were influenced by compensation felt least fulfilled and 74 percent of all the teachers questioned stated that their career expectations had been fulfilled.

Finally, the teachers in the survey perceived themselves to be competent, autonomous, and influential

regarding classroom decisions. In other words, most teachers think they are well-prepared to teach. It is interesting to identify those subjects in which they regard themselves as weak. Table 1.2 presents a summary of their responses.

Note that at the secondary level science seemed to be more of a concern than others—with the exception of special education where greater support at this level seems to be needed. Elementary teachers felt inadequately prepared in art, physical education, home economics, science, and foreign languages. Here we have an agenda for improving the academic preparation of teachers, and for helping the schools to become more effective.

Effective Schools—Effective Teachers

Schools are effective to the extent that they are staffed by effective teachers. As you continue your reading you will find several chapters directed to an analysis of teaching and classroom management. Here, however, it would help to mention briefly what research has discovered about effective teachers. In this way, you can see

TEACHER ←→ STUDENT
INTERACTIONS

Relating to Students

At various points in each chapter, boxes entitled *Teacher-Student Interactions* will appear. These are specifically designed to help you translate the theory and research you have been reading about into classroom practice. For example, you read about teaching and the schools in this chapter. Let's assume that you are taking a test on educational psychology and you are asked to list the qualities of a good teacher.

1. List 10 of the most desired qualities of the good teacher.

   1.   6.
   2.   7.
   3.   8.
   4.   9.
   5.   10.

Can you group these in any way? Are some personal characteristics? Are others professional? Which would help you to relate more positively to your students?

2. Among the personal qualities most valued are caring (understanding, patient), sense of humor (relaxed but effective) and fair. The most valued instructional qualities are interesting (varies style), knowledgeable, well-organized, and enthusiastic.

3. Reinforcing what was stressed in this chapter concerning teacher-student relations, remember:
   • a teacher's ability to relate to students is positively related to student achievement;
   • a teacher's ability to relate to students is positively related to enhanced student self-concept;
   • a teacher's ability to relate to students is positively related to student achievement.

more clearly the link between personal and professional characteristics and a smoothly functioning classroom that contributes to students' achievement.

The following features will help us to identify what we know about effective teachers (Cruickshank, 1986):

• **Classroom organization.** Findings support the conclusion that good **classroom organization** refers to those teachers who play a major role in the classroom but involve students in planning and organizing. (See chapter 13.) Having a structured curriculum and setting high goals that are communicated to students also were featured.

• **Didactic teaching. Didactic teaching** refers to a teacher's persistence in seeking goals, following a daily schedule, selecting appropriate content and teaching methods, and involving students. Research (to be discussed in chapter 2) indicates that good teachers also insist on student responsibility.

• **Classroom management. Classroom management** refers to those teachers who set and maintain clear rules and consistently apply them using positive reinforcement.

• **Teacher characteristics. Teacher characteristics** include the more personal features of the teacher. The need to be well-organized, efficient, task-oriented, knowledgeable, fluent, and alert to student differences seem to represent a common thread throughout the studies. These are coupled with such other characteristics as clarity, enthusiasm, self-confidence, friendliness, warmth, encouraging, and supportive.

The blend of teacher, student, and school characteristics needed to produce optimal learning is one that we'll refer to constantly throughout this book. Figure 1.3 illustrates teacher, student, and school variables that have a powerful influence on learning.

Much more will be said throughout this book about the variables that affect learning and teaching. Up to this point we have emphasized the importance and need of excellent teaching to encourage student learning. We now turn our attention to the specific role of educational psychology in helping to improve teaching and learning.

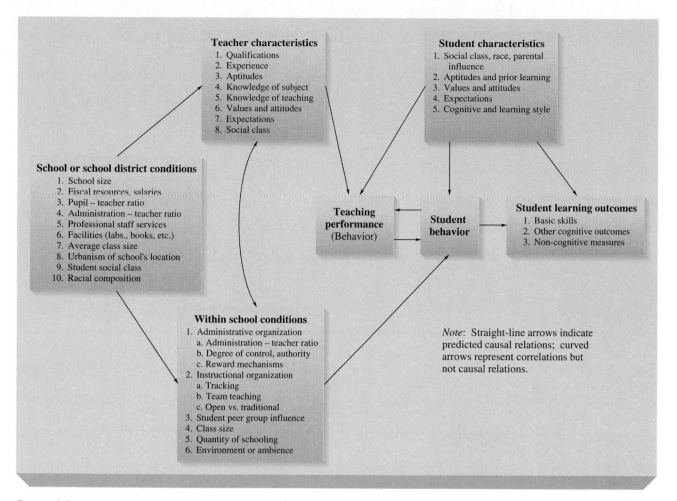

Teacher characteristics
1. Qualifications
2. Experience
3. Aptitudes
4. Knowledge of subject
5. Knowledge of teaching
6. Values and attitudes
7. Expectations
8. Social class

Student characteristics
1. Social class, race, parental influence
2. Aptitudes and prior learning
3. Values and attitudes
4. Expectations
5. Cognitive and learning style

School or school district conditions
1. School size
2. Fiscal resources, salaries
3. Pupil – teacher ratio
4. Administration – teacher ratio
5. Professional staff services
6. Facilities (labs., books, etc.)
7. Average class size
8. Urbanism of school's location
9. Student social class
10. Racial composition

Teaching performance (Behavior)

Student behavior

Student learning outcomes
1. Basic skills
2. Other cognitive outcomes
3. Non-cognitive measures

Within school conditions
1. Administrative organization
   a. Administration – teacher ratio
   b. Degree of control, authority
   c. Reward mechanisms
2. Instructional organization
   a. Tracking
   b. Team teaching
   c. Open vs. traditional
3. Student peer group influence
4. Class size
5. Quantity of schooling
6. Environment or ambience

Note: Straight-line arrows indicate predicted causal relations; curved arrows represent correlations but not causal relations.

Figure 1.3 Structural model of school and teacher variables influencing student learning outcomes.

Educational Psychology: The Core Concepts

Thus far we have stressed the notion of teachers as persons and professionals leading their students to higher levels of excellence. We also believe that educational psychology can play a key role in this process. To help you understand this critical function consider the core concepts of educational psychology and their relationship to the classroom.

Educational Psychology and the Classroom

First is the need to understand what it means to teach. We hope that as a result of reading chapter 1, you have a better grasp of "life in the classroom." You must, however, have a basis to make decisions about your teaching and your students' learning. To help you with these decisions, chapter 2 presents a careful analysis of the research techniques that support the studies mentioned in this book. If you understand these methods, you can feel confident

Focus on Teachers

A Testimonial to Teachers

In a testimonial to the effect that good teachers had on them (Lynn, 1985), several outstanding public figures made statements that summarized the characteristics of good teachers.

1. **Christa McAuliffe**, teacher and astronaut, was the first teacher chosen to travel in space. Dedicated to her profession, she constantly acknowledged the influence of teachers in her life.
2. **Elizabeth Dole** (former U.S. Secretary of Labor, current director of American Red Cross) recalled that her concept of service was inspired by teachers who took the concept of leadership seriously.
3. **Sally Ride** (first woman astronaut) was motivated to continue her interest in science by an outstanding high school chemistry teacher.

4. **Steve Jobs** (founder of Apple Computers) remembers his fourth grade teacher's saying that somewhere in a classroom, sitting at a desk just like yours, is someone who is going to change the world.
5. **Hugh Downs** (TV newscaster) notes that he remembers those teachers who didn't patronize or talk down. He believes that we must have people telling young people that they can do it—"that's what I built on."
6. **Michael Jordan** (basketball superstar) repeatedly has stated that his teachers, especially his fourth-grade teacher, had an enormous impact on his life.

Such comments can only encourage and motivate teachers, for they contain a simple but powerful message: teachers make a difference.

that by adopting (and perhaps adapting) the suggestions offered here, you are following the most recent and carefully researched teaching techniques now available.

Second is the belief that if you are to teach effectively, you must have as much knowledge about your students as possible: their needs, characteristics, and differences. Consequently, chapter 3 is devoted to tracing the cognitive and language development of children, while chapter 4 focuses on their psychosocial and moral development. If you become a regular classroom teacher, you will come into contact with one or more students who are exceptional. There is not one type of exceptional student, but rather many different types, including the gifted and talented, those experiencing sensory handicaps, communication disorders, physical and health impairments, behavior disorders, learning disabilities, and mental retardation. Chapter 14 provides valuable information about the typical characteristics of those students who are exceptional.

Third is the commitment to understanding the learning process, which guides all else since students are in school to learn. Chapters 6 and 7 focus on behavioral and cognitive explanations of learning and provide numerous examples of how these theoretical explanations of learning can be translated into classroom practice. Chapters 8 and 9 have been written to help you turn students into better problem solvers by presenting many techniques and "tips" that have proven helpful. Motivation, the subject of

chapter 10, is so essential that we can safely state that without it, learning will not occur.

Fourth is the function of instruction, beginning with the objectives that teachers wish to attain. Chapters 11, 12, and 13 concentrate on those instructional strategies that research has shown to be effective. Learning, however, does not occur in a vacuum. You must understand as fully as possible the circumstances in which learning is to occur. Consequently, chapter 13 presents in some detail successful strategies for managing a classroom, focusing on those techniques shown by both theory and research to be effective. For example, psychologists and educators now realize that many of the problems that teachers experience in the classroom can be prevented, thus reducing the need for teachers to use specific control techniques.

Fifth are those techniques that you will use to determine how successful your students are in attaining the objectives. Today, perhaps more than ever, assessing students' knowledge and skills is a central issue in schools. From a teacher's perspective, two of the most relevant purposes for assessment are: (a) to identify students who are in need of educational or psychological assistance, and (b) to provide information to teachers that will help them develop instructional programs to facilitate students' functioning. Assessment involves the use of many tools and techniques, which will be examined in detail in chapters 15 and 16. Table 1.3 summarizes the

Table 1.3

Core Concepts and Chapter Coverage	

Core Concepts	Chapters
Introduction to Teaching	1. Educational Psychology: Teaching and Learning
	2. Research and Educational Psychology
The Development of Students	3. Cognitive and Language Development
	4. Psychosocial and Moral Development
	5. Social Relationships: Teachers-Students-Parents-Peers
Learning Theories and Practices	6. Behavioral Psychology and Learning
	7. Cognitive Psychology and Learning
	8. Problem Solving Skills and Strategies
	9. Teaching Thinking Skills
	10. Motivation of Students and Teachers
The Design and Management of Classroom Instruction	11. Instructional Objectives and Essential Learning Outcomes
	12. Effective Teaching Strategies
	13. Classroom Management: Organization and Control
	14. Individual Differences and Diversity in the Classroom
Assessing Educational Outcomes	15. Classroom Tests and the Assessment of Students
	16. Standardized Tests in the Classroom

relationship between the core concepts of educational psychology and the chapters of this text.

Throughout this text you will constantly find suggestions for maintaining good relationships with your students. Understanding student characteristics, using techniques for enhancing motivation, and applying recommendations for improving the learning atmosphere all contribute to establishing warm interactions with your students. The circle is now complete: the characteristics of effective teaching are reflected in the core concepts of educational psychology, which constitute the structure of this book.

Conclusion

In this chapter, we urged you to think about two things: yourself as a teacher and how educational psychology can help you to attain your goals, both as a person and as a professional. As knowledge about teachers and learning grows, so does our ability to help our students achieve as well as they can. This chapter, with its overview of what it means to teach, is intended to help you acquire a perspective on teaching and illustrate how educational psychology can help.

Educational psychology, as a basic discipline for teachers, offers support and guidance. By understanding its theories, research, and methodological suggestions, you can gain insights into yourself as a person and as a professional, thus helping you to become a better learner and a more effective teacher.

Within the core concepts of educational psychology that you read about, you will find two recurring themes in this book: the importance of understanding our multicultural students and the necessity of positive teacher-student relationships. As you can tell from reading the introduction to our multicultural work, Amcrica's classrooms are changing, and, as they do, teachers must adapt to these changes. Also, nothing is more important to your success as a teacher than your relations with your students. You want them to be as positive as possible, both for your own satisfaction and your students' achievement.

Chapter Highlights

So You Want to Teach

- Teachers have their own, unique expectations as they enter the classroom.
- Teachers are intimately involved with the changes shaping America's schools today.
- Teaching, as an art and a science, is today recognized as one of the most exciting and important professions you could enter.
- Today's changing classrooms reflect the population's multicultural mix.
- Educational psychology today is concerned with the development and education of individuals from birth to adulthood.

The Schools Themselves

- Concern with education is apparent in a series of important, far-reaching national reports.
- Definite characteristics mark the effective school.
- National assessments of educational progress have charted important changes in the forces that shape education.

Educational Psychology: The Core Concepts

- Educational psychology, as a discipline, is intended to clarify and improve the interaction between teaching and learning.
- In pursuing this mission, educational psychologists have developed a body of empirical research and theoretical insight that contributes to effective teaching and learning.

Key Terms

Academic function
America 2000
Classroom management
Classroom organization
Communication
Cooperation
Didactic teaching
Effective schools
Homework
Institutional function
Instruction
Managerial function
Multicultural classrooms
Perception
Professional development function
Teacher characteristics
Teaching
Whole language

Suggested Readings

Gage, N. L. (1977). *The scientific basis of the art of teaching.* New York: Teachers College Press. An excellent and insightful examination of the relationship between teaching as an art and teaching as a science. Readable and provocative, Gage presents his rationale for the scientific basis of teaching.

Goodlad, J. (1984). *A place called school.* New York: McGraw-Hill. Examining the effectiveness of American schooling, Goodlad and his colleagues studied the "commonplaces" of schooling: teaching practices, content, materials, physical plant, activities, and leadership among other variables. In so doing, he focused on the perspectives of students, teachers, administrators, and parents. This is a thoughtful, insightful look at the realities of American education.

Research and Educational Psychology

Paul Anderson, one of the third grade elementary teachers at Northside Elementary School, had made up his mind that he would talk to his fellow teachers about the new Assertive Discipline program that the school was adopting for all the elementary classrooms in the district. In fact, the school board had adopted the program, and principals had already ordered material for dissemination. Soon letters would be sent out to parents informing them of the school policy and components of the program.

When Paul arrived at the faculty lounge, he met Mary Sisco. Paul opened the conversation. "Mary, do you know about the new discipline program?" Mary noted that she had heard some of the teachers talking about the program after the faculty meeting last week, which Paul had missed. Paul, further curious about the program asked, "Did the principal say anything about research to support the program? Is it effective with students and does it really help?" Mary noted that little was said about research on the program, but that it is used in many schools across the country. Many teachers at Northside said that given the rise in discipline problems recently, they would like to see the program in their school.

Paul was still concerned about adopting only this program because he recently had enrolled in a classroom management class at the local university. The program introduced at Northside School was not one of those the professor identified as having considerable research support. Paul was skeptical about this program's chances of ultimately improving student academic skills. He wanted the school to consider another program that involved preventing classroom management problems. Mary, who was always trying to get Paul to do more than talk about school issues, said, "Perhaps you could get involved with folks at the University and do some research on the effectiveness of the program. I bet that Mrs. Allen (the principal) would support the project."

Paul Anderson was raising some important questions that you will often face when you enter the teaching profession. The question here is one of research support for a particular program implemented at Northside School and in other schools around the country. Paul was recognizing the important role that research can play in making critical decisions on behalf of students, teachers, and parents. In this chapter we will explore the role that various forms of scientific research can play in educational psychology.

Here we see an example of the need to obtain solid data before making any decisions that could affect the well-being of students, teachers, and parents. It is not, however, enough to collect isolated scraps of information that may or may not be useful. What is needed are carefully designed studies that will provide pertinent and reliable information that will guide decision-making.

Consequently, in this chapter you will discover the vital relationship between research and effective schooling. You will also explore the various methods used to obtain data and the specific purposes for which each method is intended. Finally, you will be asked to think about an issue that is becoming increasingly critical for those of us who work with other individuals—the ethical and legal aspects of research.

When you finish reading this chapter, you should be able to:

- identify the sources of knowledge that lead to educational decisions.
- distinguish the various types of research methods.
- describe the techniques used by educational researchers.
- demonstrate competence in writing a research report.
- classify the various types of research methods according to the purposes for which they are intended.

Research and Effective Schooling

Teachers are always concerned about the effectiveness of their methods, and they like to try different techniques. Teachers who are alert to the latest research and the methods that are appropriate for them to use become increasingly more skillful in their classroom instruction. This chapter is designed to acquaint you with ways in which educational research is conducted and the ways in which it contributes to our understanding of schools, teaching, and learning. *Research answers questions.* Most research is designed to answer questions about causation, relationships, or effectiveness. Examples of such questions relevant to many educators include: What effect do teachers' oral questions have on students' attention and comprehension of material? What is the relationship between amount of time on homework and classroom test performance? Which social skills program, Program A or Program B, is most effective with

"Okay— who asked it about the chicken and the egg?"

H. Schwadron in *Phi Delta Kappan.*

Table 2.1

Common Sources of Knowledge About People and the Environment

Source	Example
Authority	The earth is flat.
Tradition	Children should begin school at age six years.
Expert opinion	Detention of student is unlikely to improve academic functioning.
Personal experiences	Mothers should breast feed.
Documentation	More children attend school today than in 1900.
Scientific research	Some forms of mental retardation are genetic in origin.

regard to increasing students' cooperation skills? *Research guides practice, and in turn practice informs research.*

Sources of Knowledge

Much of the systematic knowledge we have about human behavior has resulted from the application of scientific methods to the study of certain events. A major goal of scientific study is to explain, predict, and/or control these events. Yet, the application of scientific procedures is a relatively recent happening in history. It is also true that although such study has contributed greatly to the understanding of ourselves and others, knowledge is obtained from many sources (see Table 2.1).

Authority

Individuals in a position of status or authority have provided people or societies with the so-called "truth." One prominent example was the belief that the earth was flat. Scholars and mapmakers proclaimed this "fact" with absolute confidence. As you can see, depending on this type of knowledge can lead to trouble if the so-called authority is incorrect. The information conveyed to others will be in error. Of course, authority may not be incorrect in all cases.

Tradition

Knowledge is also obtained from tradition. Did you begin your formal education around the age of six years? If you did, you were one of millions of children who started school at six (either kindergarten or first grade) because traditionally, this was the appropriate age to begin formal schooling. Moreover, there has been a tradition of American schools closing for the summer for agricultural necessities. Such a rationale is no longer necessary, but tradition has prevailed. Knowledge based

on tradition can also be inaccurate. Formal educational experiences begin much earlier than age six. In fact, many children in the United States begin some type of formal education by age two or three. Consequently, there is considerable debate over tradition as a source of knowledge.

Expert Opinion

Another influential source of knowledge comes from the opinion of experts. Certain individuals may take positions that dramatically influence people's beliefs. Many readers of this book may have been reared according to the practices suggested by Dr. Benjamin Spock in his book *Baby and Child Care (1957)*. There have been many other popular books (e.g., *How to Parent* by Fitzhugh Dodson, 1970; *How to Raise Independent and Professionally Successful Daughters* by Rita and Kenneth Dunn, 1977; *How Children Fail* by John Holt, 1964) that influenced the thinking and behavior of parents and teachers. If you are considering having a baby, your thinking on the birth process may be influenced by the popular Lamaze method. Thus, many practices now in vogue are the ideas of various experts and have had a tremendous impact on child rearing and social practices.

Personal Experience

We gain a considerable amount of knowledge from personal experience, although not all of it is accurate. In many instances we may change our beliefs through knowledge from different sources. You might adopt a classroom management program because your personal experiences with the techniques suggest that it will likely be effective with your students. However, the approach may have little or no research support. One limitation of personal experiences is that certain evidence may be omitted or that individuals may be too subjective in their beliefs.

Personal experience. Should you change your answers on multiple-choice tests? Student common sense would say no. You have probably heard the folk wisdom, "Don't change your answers on exams, because you'll be more likely to change a right answer to a wrong answer than a wrong answer to a right answer." You might be surprised that scientific research has consistently found that students are slightly more likely to change a wrong answer to a right answer than a right answer to a wrong answer (Skinner, 1983).

Focus on Classrooms

Rival Hypotheses

Modeling Clay

Jean Piaget is a well-known Swiss psychologist whose ideas have transformed the field of developmental psychology over the past few decades. Many students associate him with conservation tasks, such as how a child learns that 200cc of water is the same in a tall skinny glass as in a short fat glass, despite the difference in the water level. A similar task involving a clay ball and a clay cylinder (each with the same volume of clay) was one of a number of conservation tasks used in a study comparing modeling and nonmodeling instructions given to six-year-olds.

In this study, a random sample of twenty-eight Chicano children were drawn from the first grade of a school located in a *barrio* area of Tucson, Arizona. The children were all from Spanish-speaking homes and were in their first few months of school (median age was 6.3 years). The children were randomly assigned to one of two groups; each group included seven boys and seven girls. Some children (those in the modeling group) were allowed to watch the experimenter transform an object from one shape to another while listening to another child (the model) answer the experimenter's questions about the transformation. Those in the nonmodeling instructions group were not shown the transformation process but were instead presented with "be fore" and "after" objects. This group was told that the objects

were equivalent. Analysis of variance showed significant differences between the two groups, with the modeling group showing superiority on the conservation tasks. Furthermore, according to the authors, the nonmodeling instructions produced no reliable changes.

What do you think? Do you agree that the modeling approach is clearly superior? Before continuing your reading, write your reasons for either agreeing or disagreeing with the authors' conclusions.

Rival Hypothesis

Although we are generally sympathetic towards social learning theory and its methods (including modeling), we have difficulty accepting this study as evidence in its favor. Though the authors are to be commended for the design (true random selection and assignment) and analysis (appropriate use of the analysis of variance,) we wonder about the effectiveness of English instructions being given to children for whom Spanish is a first language. We would have recommended that the entire experiment be conducted in Spanish to eliminate the plausible rival hypothesis that the nonmodeling instructional group received its instructions in a foreign language.

Documentation

Another knowledge source comes through the documentation of events in which a record is kept of various events or phenomena. Today, there is rather extensive documentation of data that is easily accessible through the use of computer technology. For example, we can document that a number of children in a large city have received inoculations against a certain disease. As a form of information and knowledge, documentation is a relatively new source. In many cases we must speculate on certain events in history because important documentation is incomplete or fragmented. Documentation is a good source of knowledge but has its limitations. People can be biased in providing certain information. Nevertheless, documentation is a step in the right direction in obtaining scientific data as a source of knowledge.

Scientific Research

The final source for gaining information is the use of scientific research. "Scientific research is the systematic, controlled, empirical, and critical investigation of hypo-

thetical propositions about the presumed relations among natural phenomena" (Kerlinger, 1973, p. 11). This definition implies that scientific investigation is an orderly endeavor so that the researcher can have confidence in the outcomes. Thus, scientific research typically is carried out under controlled conditions. Educational researchers are empirical in that they make available both the procedures and findings to outside evaluation or criticism.

With this information available (procedures, findings, and conclusions), other reviewers of a study may propose rival hypotheses or different interpretations of the data from those drawn by the original researchers (Huck and Sandler, 1979). In this chapter, we'll present two studies as summarized by Huck and Sandler (1979) along with rival hypotheses. After you read the summary of the study, suggest an alternative and then read what the authors had to say about the research. (You will find these in boxes entitled *Rival Hypotheses*.)

Although the scientific form of investigation generally is regarded as an important method of generating knowledge, there is considerable disagreement about what are the best methods. Scientific methods of investigation have evolved over a considerable period of time. In the next section we review some of the historical features of scientific research.

Influences on Research Methods

The contemporary study of students and schools has evolved from philosophical and theoretical positions. Philosophers have written about students and have dealt with issues that have influenced study by educational psychologists. For example, some early philosophers thought of children as essentially "evil"; others suggested that children were born with the capacity for being good; still others viewed children as having the predisposition to both good and evil. These ideas have provided somewhat different ways of studying students and aspects of their learning.

Philosophical viewpoints toward research emphasize the relationship between children's early experiences and future adult life. In *The Republic,* Plato recommended that children's inherent aptitudes be discovered so that unique talents could be cultivated. These were thought to be fulfilled ultimately through the development of the mind (rational thought).

Jean Jacques Rousseau, a French philosopher, took the position that children are born with an innate moral sense. Rousseau's "inherently good" position was presented in his book *Emile* (1792), in which ideal methods of child-rearing were presented. He believed the educational system should encourage self-expression in children rather than exercise the rigid control that was common in his day. His positions are similar to more contemporary progressive educational practices that emphasize intrinsic motivation and matching activities to learner interest.

Near the end of the seventeenth century John Locke, a British philosopher, suggested in his book *Essay Concerning Human Understanding* (1691) that the child's mind was essentially blank at birth (tabula rasa), and thus, highly impressionable. He believed children learned through perception and through associating ideas in the mind. He was the first major philosopher since Plato who viewed the human organism as a neutral rather than predisposing being.

Theoretical viewpoints, representing the predominant modes of theorizing in educational psychology (e.g., behavioral, cognitive), take different approaches to the study of students. Research strategies can be conceptualized on two dimensions—namely, the *subject* (species) to be studied and the *methodology* to be used

(Endler, Boulter, & Osser, 1976). On the subject dimension, the researcher must decide whether to study a human being directly or simpler organisms such as rats, monkeys, dogs, or other infrahuman organisms. In some cases, the researcher is restricted to a human subject as in verbal learning or interview methods. Researchers must also decide what methodology or form of investigation to use. Typically, the researcher chooses between naturalistic observation or an experimental mode; there are times when both strategies are used in the same study. Both strategies are discussed in detail later in the chapter.

The particular model or theoretical orientation held by the researcher will influence the particular method of scientific study. The behaviorist is usually interested in providing a careful analysis of observable influences on behavior. The cognitive researcher focuses on the conceptual processes within the mind, with their research methods tailored to fit this focus.

The Emergence of Research on Children

Long before people developed systematic experimental procedures to study children, an interest in documenting child behavior was evolving. Some of these procedures, such as baby biographies and individual case studies, represented a dominant form of investigating aspects of a child's development. Although both of these techniques are still used in educational psychology, they generally have been replaced by more credible strategies based on principles of scientific research.

Baby Biographies

Maintaining records of one's children is a relatively common practice. It is likely this practice has existed since various forms of written communications were developed. However, it was not until the end of the eighteenth century that some individuals began to share formally and publicly their observations on children. For example, Johann Pestalozzi, a Swiss educator, published observations on the development of his 3 1/2-year-old son in 1774, in which he reflected the innate goodness of the child. In 1787 Dieterich Tiedeman published his observations of an infant during the first 2 1/2 years of life, in which aspects of sensory motor, language, and intellectual growth were reported.

Systematic observation of children continued into the nineteenth century. Two important publications were instrumental in promoting a long series of observational studies of children. In 1877 Charles Darwin published *A Biographical Sketch of an Infant,* an account of his infant son. Likewise, in 1882, William Preyer published a book of his son's first four years of life. The involvement of

THE FAR SIDE

By GARY LARSON

"No doubt about it, Ellington—we've mathematically expressed
the purpose of the universe. Gad, how I love the thrill
of scientific discovery!"

these professionals facilitated the proliferation of the baby biography as a method of child study. These biographies also focused attention on important aspects of child development and created interest in child study in general.

Despite these positive contributions of the baby biography in child study, the method is not held in high regard in the scientific community. There are several reasons for this. First, the biography represents a subjective description of events and cannot be independently

Focus on Students

The Case Study

The following case study is a direct and brief account of the efforts of a public school speech therapist who, by working with a classroom teacher, a school principal, and the parents, was able to help a boy, LeRoy, overcome his fear of speaking in public situations.

LeRoy, who had never spoken in school, was referred to the speech therapist during the second semester of first grade. The boy showed good comprehension, did all his silent work, was careful with minute details, and was very good in art; but he had never read aloud nor taken part in rhythmic work and singing. LeRoy's intelligence was average, and his score on the Detroit First Grade Reading Test was 92, well above average.

His parents said that LeRoy talked with his family and played well alone. He would never play with other children or go to their homes. His speech with the family was normal. The only reason his mother could give for his behavior was that he was bashful. But the speech therapist felt this remark had been made so often that LeRoy had been encouraged to develop his anti-social tendencies rather than to overcome his natural shyness.

The speech therapist was called in because, by school rules, LeRoy could not advance to second grade until he could read aloud. The first session showed almost no progress, although, of course, the speech therapist did not wish to rush the child. He obviously could hear well and take directions; vocabulary and memory were no problem to him, as his comprehension and seat work showed. At the second session, the therapist began to gain his confidence, and when asked, LeRoy timorously showed both his tongue and his teeth.

During the third session, he uttered his first word in school. Knowing his interest in coloring, the therapist had brought some attractive colored pictures of animals and children. His interest in these was used as the first step in breaking through his withdrawal and silence. To see the pictures, LeRoy repeated "come" and then other first-grade reading words.

At the next meeting, he read a book for the therapist. He read well, and was, of course, praised generously. Later he agreed to "surprise the principal" by reading aloud for her, and also for his teacher, although he would stop if anyone else came into the room.

He remained completely withdrawn from peers, although he would read for a few adults. At an outdoor picnic the following September, he held his ice cream cone in his hand while it melted, and he did not move until he was told to throw his soggy cone away—which he did. He watched the other children having fun but showed no indication that he was enjoying himself.

As LeRoy's second grade year progressed, the therapist encouraged him to read for, and later play with, two neighbor boys who were in his schoolroom. After she suggested that he visit one of them to watch television, LeRoy did so. He had never before gone to another child's house to play. His conversation then was in one-word sentences, but he had no speech defects.

One day the therapist suggested that LeRoy's two friends each bring another boy to be surprised at how well LeRoy read. He assented. His classroom teacher, who was very cooperative, was asked to send first the boys, then the girls, one at a time, at about two-minute intervals. The children came, one by one, and the group moved to a larger room, but LeRoy continued to read for them. They all moved back to the classroom, where everyone could have a seat. And there LeRoy walked to the front of the room, sat in the teacher's chair, and read to the children of his class.

The next day he stayed home; the shock must have been too much for him. The speech therapist went to his home, and he returned eagerly to school with her. When he arrived, his classmates had chosen colored paper to make Easter baskets. He was asked what color he wanted, and he answered "green." The following day LeRoy's teacher noted that he had read aloud in class and that the children had chosen him for games, although he would not participate in the poems or rhythmic actions.

Three weeks later, just before his second grade ended, his teacher reported that he was participating more and that "he beams," whereas before he had shown no facial expression. His withdrawal and silence were rapidly breaking down, and his behavior appeared to be that of a normal, happy child.

Dr. John R. Bergan, interview script.

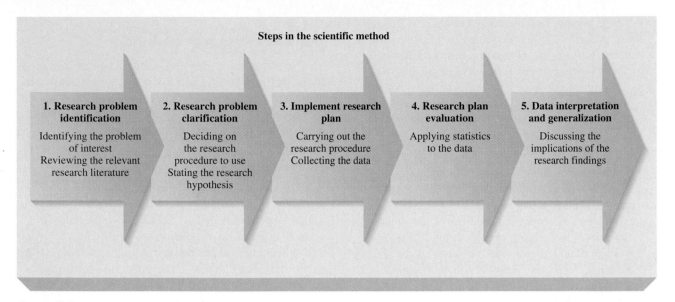

Steps in the scientific method

1. **Research problem identification**	2. **Research problem clarification**	3. **Implement research plan**	4. **Research plan evaluation**	5. **Data interpretation and generalization**
Identifying the problem of interest	Deciding on the research procedure to use	Carrying out the research procedure	Applying statistics to the data	Discussing the implications of the research findings
Reviewing the relevant research literature	Stating the research hypothesis	Collecting the data		

Figure 2.1
The scientific method.

evaluated and replicated by others. Second, typical observations made by individuals are unsystematic and may be taken at irregular intervals. Third, the descriptions of behavior may represent the bias of the individual who holds certain conceptions of human development. Fourth, it is difficult to generalize data from biographies as a result of the aforementioned problems.

Case Studies

Case studies have played an important role in research investigation during the history of psychology and education and are still used in psychology and psychiatry. As a form of research methodology, case studies evolved as individuals from various theoretical orientations became involved in treating people with personality and behavior problems. Though case studies commonly are used in reporting therapeutic interventions with children and adults, they also have been used widely in psychology and education. Novel and innovative therapeutic techniques were shared in professional journals through "case study" methods (Kazdin, 1991), which remained a primary form of methodology of clinical investigations through the first half of this century. The case study reported in the Focus on Students illustrates its usefulness in a contemporary school setting.

Case study investigation has been useful in advancing knowledge, particularly in psychotherapy. Barlow and Hersen (1984) noted that case studies can (a) foster clinical innovation, (b) cast doubt on certain theoretical positions, (c) permit study of uncommon problems, (d) develop new technical skills, (e) support theoretical views, (f) promote refinement in various techniques, and

(g) provide data that can be used to design more highly controlled research. For example, Dukes (1965) reviewed over 200 case studies over a 25-year period from many areas of psychology, noting that in many instances the reports provided evidence of findings that changed the course of future study.

Despite positive features, case studies, such as baby biographies, have many problems and generally are not regarded as reliable research procedures. Case studies typically are characterized by subjective impression, bias, and inadequate description of the procedures used to treat a person, and they are difficult to replicate. Replication is a key concern. For example, it would be virtually impossible to replicate the procedures used by the speech therapist with LeRoy. Thus, case study methods are increasingly being replaced by single case time-series research strategies that are designed to make replication possible. These strategies are described later in the chapter.

Scientific Influences

Researchers embarking on the systematic study of education have many techniques to use in this endeavor. Contemporary research in educational psychology is guided by scientific methods. We use the term "methods" because there is no one scientific method. Scientific research generally is guided by the following five steps used to study a particular topic or problem (see Figure 2.1). We'll examine these steps in the context of an applied educational problem that was investigated by researchers in a preschool setting (Twardosz, Cataldo, & Risley, 1974).

Step 1: Research problem identification. A first step in conducting scientific research involves the identification of a problem or question. There is great interest in knowing how the physical environment influences the behavior and learning of children (Dunn, 1987). One aspect of the problem identified in the study by Twardosz et al. (1974) was determining how an open day-care environment influenced the sleep of infants and toddlers.

Step 2: Research problem clarification. The specific aspects of the problem must be analyzed and the nature, scope, and specifics of the situation identified. The researchers must address the problem of how to examine the variables that might influence sleep. Any ideas? If you choose the conditions of noise and light versus quiet and dark, you are on the right track.

Step 3: Implement research plan. In this step the researchers stated the problem and tested the plan and program implemented to answer the question. They measured the percent of sleeping and crying repeatedly over 47 days under the conditions of noise and light (door left open and light could enter the room) and quiet and dark (door was closed and light was shut out).

Step 4: Research plan evaluation. This step involves making decisions based upon the data collected from the study. The data may or may not support the hunches (hypotheses) of the researchers. Any guesses as to how it turned out? The researchers found *no* differences between the conditions of noise and light—*and*—quiet and dark (i.e., none of the children's sleep was adversely affected by noise and light).

Step 5: Data interpretation and generalization. The final step involves interpretation and generalization of the researcher's findings into a larger body of knowledge related to the problem under study. Results may be integrated into existing knowledge or suggest topics for future research. How would you explain these findings? Perhaps the conditions of noise and light were not strong enough to make a difference. Would you generalize the results of the study by telling people that noise and light have no effect on a child's sleep patterns? You may be "going beyond the data" to suggest this, but as you will see in later chapters, research data in educational psychology are sometimes misrepresented.

Major Research Methods

To a greater or lesser degree the above steps are involved in the major types of research conducted in schools and about schooling. These approaches to research include (a) historical, (b) descriptive, (c) correlational, (d) comparative, and (e) experimental research.

Historical Research

As the name implies, **historical research** involves studying, understanding, and explaining past events. A major purpose of historical research is to formulate conclusions about causes, effects, or trends of past events that either help explain current events or anticipate future events. Typically, individuals conducting historical research do not gather data by administering tests or observing behavior. Rather, they use data that are already available. For example, if educational researchers wanted to examine the factors that influence academic achievement of children in orphanages, they would conduct a search of the literature of follow-up studies of achievement of children in this type of institution.

Descriptive Research

In **descriptive research** the investigator examines and reports things the way they are. In this type of study the researcher collects data to test a hypothesis or answer questions concerning the status of some issue or problem. Instruments such as surveys, questionnaires, interviews, or observational codes may be developed for this type of investigation. The year-round school is an educational alternative being examined by many public school systems. If you were interested in studying the attitudes of students, parents, and teachers about a year-round school, you might develop a questionnaire and send it to a select sample of children, their parents, and teachers. This would be an example of descriptive research.

Correlational Research

In **correlational research,** the researcher attempts to determine if a relation exists between two or more variables. Variables can refer to a range of human characteristics such as height, weight, sex, intelligence, and so forth. For example, a researcher may be interested in examining the relation between intelligence and creativity. But, the finding that there is a relation between intelligence and creativity does not mean that intelligence "causes" creativity. Finding a high correlation only indicates that most people with high intelligence have higher creative behavior, and that most people with lower intelligence have lower evidence of creativity. Thus, the finding that two variables are highly related (correlated) does not mean that one caused the other; a third variable may cause or strongly influence the variables. Thus, it may be that some degree of intelligence is necessary, but not the only requirement to promote creativity.

The degree of relation between two or more variables generally is expressed as a correlation coefficient (labeled "r"), that is represented by a number between .00 (no relation) and 1.00 (perfect relation). Of course, two variables can be negatively related, a situation that occurs when a high score on one variable is accompanied by a low score on the other variable. The more two variables approach 1.00 the better the researcher is able to make a prediction. Most correlations are less than 1.00; thus prediction is far from perfect. Nevertheless, predictions based on known relations are useful in understanding the nature of child behavior.

Comparative Research

In **comparative research** the investigator searches for direct relations among variables that are compared with each other. Typically, comparative research involves the comparison of groups that are different before the study begins. For example, if researchers are interested in examining the effect of socioeconomic status (SES) on drug usage in adolescents, they might form several different groups on the basis of SES (i.e., the non-manipulated independent variable). Much research in educational psychology is conducted in this fashion, but the scientific community does not regard this type of research as reliable and credible as studies in which variables are manipulated directly. Since there is no manipulation or control over extraneous events, the relations established in comparative research must remain tentative. Thus, in the above example, we would have to consider that variables other than SES accounted for different patterns of drug usage. Although comparative research is not as predictable as experimental research, it has the following advantage: Many variables cannot be manipulated or controlled by the educational researcher; thus this form of research provides a useful option.

Experimental Research

Experimental research involves the active manipulation of an independent variable to observe changes in the dependent variable. In experimental research the **independent variable** frequently is called the experimental or treatment condition. Treatment conditions may be compared with each other or to a control condition—a condition in which no treatment is administered, although the group is the same as the treatment group in all other respects. The most important feature of experimental research is that researchers are able to manipulate variables and control sources of influence that could affect the results. Thus, researchers attempt to make the groups as equal as possible on all variables except the independent variable.

An example of experimental research occurs when an investigator forms two groups by assigning subjects randomly to these conditions. By random assignment we mean any individual going into the two groups has an equal chance of ending up in either group. Thus, no bias is introduced into the experiment by having more of one type of subject in some groups, such as age, sex, and so forth. For example, let's assume that you're the researcher and you want to discover the effectiveness of a new method of teaching reading. You have decided that you are interested in discovering the effects of a new type of reading instruction for fifth graders. Thus, you have selected the independent variable. One of the criteria for a true experiment has been met. You next randomly assign the fifth grade students to one of two groups: the first group receives the new reading instruction while the second group continues with the traditional method. You have met *both* of the criteria for experimental research: *control of the independent variable and random assignment of subjects.* By meeting these two criteria, the researcher, if the study is carefully done, can point to a cause and effect relationship. That is, the researcher can state that the new type of reading instruction did cause an improvement in pupils' reading scores if the average scores for the students in the group that received the new method were higher than those of the students in the group that received the traditional reading method.

The variable (reading method) that you manipulated or directly controlled is, as we have seen, the independent variable. The experimental subjects must respond to some task (a reading test) that you selected to determine the effect of the independent variable. The way in which the subjects respond (test performance) is the **dependent variable.** The design is as follows:

$$Eb— X—Ea$$

$$Cb—X—Ca$$

In this illustration, E is the experimental group, C is the control group, X is the independent variable, b is before, and a is after the experiment. If the study has been carefully controlled, any differences on the reading test should be the result of X, the new method of teaching reading.

Table 2.2

Classification and Description of Major Research Methods

Historical Research

Involves studying, understanding, and explaining past events.

Example: Factors leading to the development and growth of the use of teaching machines.

Descriptive Research

Involves collecting data to test hypotheses or answer questions related to the current status of a problem.

Example: How do new parents share responsibilities in child rearing? New parents would be observed for a period of time and results could be reported as percentages (e.g., Feeding: Mother 60%, Father 40%, Diaper changing: Mother 95%, Father 5%, etc.).

Correlational Research

Involves the process of determining whether, and to what extent, a relation exists between two or more variables.

Example: The relation between intelligence and achievement. Scores on an intelligence test would be obtained from each individual in a certain group. The two sets of scores would be correlated, and the resulting correlation coefficient would indicate the degree of relation between intelligence and achievement.

Comparative Research

Involves establishing a direct relation between variables that are compared, but that are not manipulated by the researcher.

Example: The effect of preschool attendance on achievement at the end of first grade. The independent variable (or presumed cause) is preschool attendance; the dependent variable (or effect) is measured achievement at the end of first grade. Groups of first-graders would be identified—some that had attended preschool and some that had not—and the achievement would be compared.

Experimental Research

Involves a study in which a researcher actually manipulates at least one independent variable to observe the effect on one or more dependent variables.

Example: The effect of positive reinforcement on the number of math problems completed by second-grade children. The independent variable is the reinforcement (praise statements by teachers); the dependent variable is the number of problems completed. Two groups would be exposed to essentially the same experiences except for the reinforcement. After some time, their output on math problems would be compared.

Which type of research is best? Many educational researchers believe that experimental research is the most useful form of scientific investigation. Since experimental research allows control of many factors that potentially bias results, it is preferred in the scientific world. However, determining which method of research is best depends on numerous factors such as the problem under investigation, subjects to be studied, instruments used to collect data, and previous work in the field. The purpose of the research helps determine if correlational, comparative, or well-controlled experimental studies are to be conducted. For example, when one is interested in reviewing historical events that led to some current school practice, historical research is the most appropriate.

Thus, many factors must be examined to decide which research method is best under what circumstances; no single research method is always the best. These five types of research are summarized in Table 2.2.

Techniques Used by Researchers

Researchers in the field of educational psychology use many different approaches to gather data. In the following sections, we review some of the more common techniques and procedures used in research. These techniques include surveys, interviews, and observations, and the procedures to be highlighted are cross-sectional and longitudinal methods. Time-series and cross-cultural research are also discussed.

Surveys

In survey research the investigator asks a group of individuals questions about a particular issue. **Survey** research often is used to study teachers, particularly their attitudes, beliefs, opinions, and behavior. Surveys actually are conducted through a variety of methods such as interviews,

Table 2.3

Advantages and Disadvantages of Survey Data Collection Methods

	Direct Administration	Telephone	Mail	Interview
Comparative cost	Lowest	About the same	About the same	High
Facilities needed?	Yes	No	No	Yes
Require training of questioner?	Yes	Yes	No	Yes
Response rate	Very high	Good	Poorest	Very high
Group administration possible?	Yes	No	No	Yes
Allow for random sampling?	Possibly	Yes	Yes	Yes
Require literate sample?	Yes	No	Yes	No
Permit follow-up questions?	No	Yes	No	Yes
Encourage response to sensitive topics?	Somewhat	Somewhat	Best	Weak
Standardization of responses	Easy	Somewhat	Easy	Hardest

questionnaires (called direct administration), the telephone, and mail (Fraenkel & Wallen, 1990). Regardless of the method, the heart of good survey research is the development of a meaningful survey tool—one that clearly communicates questions or concerns in an unbiased fashion, can be completed in a time efficient manner, and scored or interpreted reliably. Each of these methods has various advantages and disadvantages as can be observed in Table 2.3.

As an illustration of the proper use of the survey method, let's begin by agreeing that few topics have caused as much controversy in American public schools as the use of corporal punishment. You might wonder how often corporal punishment is used in schools. Who administers the punishment? Is it used equally across the grades? These are but a few of the questions that Rose (1984) was able to address in a school discipline survey that was mailed to 324 principals in 18 randomly selected states representing the nine U.S. Census districts. Table 2.4 displays several items from the actual questionnaire and the frequency of responses to each item. Rose found that 74.1 percent of the principals responding to the survey used corporal punishment with their students! Corporal punishment was used more with male students than with female students. If you look closely at the table, you can also observe other interesting trends in the study. Do you think the results would be different today? We will discuss the issue of punishment in chapters 6 and 13,

where you will read about alternative classroom management procedures.

Survey research, like that described in the Rose study, has the advantage of wide scope in that a great deal of information can be obtained from a large population (e.g., principals in the U.S.). Generally, survey research provides a good representation of sources of information. Survey research also has disadvantages. First, survey methods may not allow very detailed information on the issue being researched. Second, survey research can also be expensive and time-consuming. Third, another concern is that one may introduce into the study sampling error that can bias the results. Perhaps all states should have been sampled in the Rose (1984) study. Fourth, survey research is subject to faking responses and bias in responding to questions. Even with these limitations, the survey method can provide useful information in research.

Interviews

Although **interviews** are used often in survey research, they are used in many other forms of research as well. Have you ever been interviewed by someone who was conducting a study on some problem or issue? If so, you were exposed to another common method of obtaining information for research purposes. The interview procedure involves a face-to-face situation in which an interviewer asks another individual questions designed

Table 2.4

Frequencies and Percentages of Responses to Questionnaire Items in the Rose Survey

Item	Frequency	Percentage
Demographic		
1. Approximate size of community in which your school is located:		
A. Rural, unincorporated	14	6.0
B. Incorporated, under 1,000	12	5.2
C. 1,000-5,000	36	15.5
D. 5,000-10,000	31	13.4
E. 10,000-50,000	50	21.6
F. 50,000-100,000	25	10.7
G. 100,000-500,000	46	19.8
H. 500,000 or more	18	7.8
2. Number of students in your school:		
A. 0-300	46	19.8
B. 301-600	84	36.2
C. 601-900	58	25.0
D. 901-1,200	20	8.6
E. 1,200 or more	24	10.3
Discipline		
7. Is corporal punishment used in your school?		
A. Yes	172	74.1
B. No	60	25.9
If Question 7 is yes, please complete the remainder of the questionnaire.		
8. Who administers corporal punishment?		
A. Referring teacher	6	3.7
B. Principal	34	21.0
C. Other teacher	0	—
D. Other administrative personnel (e.g., assistant principal)	16	9.9
E. Combination	106	65.4

to obtain answers relevant to the research problem. Of course, interview procedures are used for purposes other than research, such as those interviews usually conducted to fill job openings.

In research, interviews are typically categorized as *structured and unstructured* or *standardized and unstandardized.* In a standardized interview, the interviewer asks questions in which the sequence and wording are fixed. Thus, the interviewer has little freedom to depart from a prepared script. In contrast, unstandardized interviews are more flexible and open in that the interviewer determines what will be asked. Thus, the unstandardized, nonstructured interview is an open format whereas the standardized, structured interview is a closed format.

Interview strategies allow the researcher to obtain a great deal of information, particularly when the situation is open. The interview can also be made flexible to meet the need of situation, problem, and person. This flexibility is an advantage with children since questions can be reworded so that a child can understand the question. Interviews are often used as adjunct methods to probe individuals after an experiment or to follow-up on a written survey response. On the negative side, interviewee responses can be faked, are subject to interpretation, and can take a lot of time.

Item	Frequency	Percentage
For the following three items, circle the number of students in each category who received corporal punishment in the last month.		
14. Male:		
A. 0-5	69	44.8
B. 6-10	35	22.7
C. 11-15	28	18.2
D. 16-20	8	5.2
E. 21-25	2	1.3
F. 26 or more	12	7.8
Do you feel that corporal punishment is effective in:		
18. Maintaining the general level of discipline in your school?		
A. Yes	130	83.3
B. No	26	16.7
19. Reducing specific behavior problems for specific students?		
A. Yes	141	88.1
B. No	19	11.9
20. Maintaining teacher morale?		
A. Yes	111	73.0
B. No	41	27.0
21. Demonstrating your support of your teachers?		
A. Yes	141	73.1
B. No	42	26.9
22. List the offense that most often leads to corporal punishment (categorized subsequent to responses).		
Fighting	72	51.4
Disruptive in class	30	21.4
Disrespect for authority	19	13.5
Disobedience	9	6.4
Truancy	6	4.3
Miscellaneous	4	2.8

From T. L. Rose, Current Uses of Corporal Punishment in American Public Schools in *Journal of Educational Psychology, 76,427-441*, 1984. Copyright © 1984 by the American Psychological Association.

Observation

One of the most common ways we obtain information is through **observation.** Systematic observation has also evolved as a basic scientific tool for gathering data in research on teaching (Evertson & Green, 1986). As noted earlier in the chapter, many early researchers made observations of their own child. A special branch of psychology called *ecological psychology* was developed out of naturalistic observational techniques used by Barker (1968, 1978). In this form of observation, teams of observers view children throughout a typical day's activities. The observers may literally follow the child for the entire day, recording virtually every event.

The observational form of research has opened many new possibilities in the field of educational psychology. It has also been useful for studying children and adolescents in their natural environment. Observational research is expensive and time-consuming, both in training observers and in conducting the observations in the natural environment.

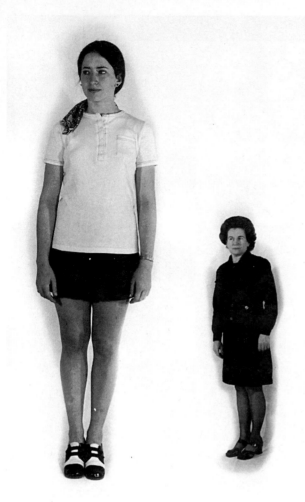

Figure 2.2
Actual photographs from the Kratochwill and Goldman (1973) study depicting an adolescent and an adult in two sizes. Children under the age of 7 generally indicated that the adolescent on the left was older because she was taller.

Cross-Sectional and Longitudinal Research

Two broad, contrasting approaches used to study students in schools exist: cross-sectional and longitudinal. A main feature of the **cross-sectional** approach is the selection of different groups of children at a variety of age levels for study. Typically, a researcher separates the children into different age levels and studies the problem of interest. Here is an example: Have you ever wondered when children are able to judge age accurately? Kratochwill and Goldman (1973) noted that previous research found that it was not until approximately age nine that children are able to judge age accurately. Kratochwill and Goldman believed that results in previous studies were influenced by the ambiguity of the drawings

used (cartoon characters), and their study was designed to investigate children's judgments of age when more realistic stimuli (photographs) were used.

The primary focus of the study was on evaluating a cross-section of children (ages 3, 4, 5, 6, 7, 8, and 9 years) on developmental changes in judgments by relating people's age with their physical size. The photographs consisted of males and females at four age levels—infant, child, adolescent, and middle-aged adult. Each figure was reproduced in two sizes. Using a paired-comparison procedure, experimenters presented a cross-section of children from ages three through nine years (there were 16 children at each age level) with either the male or female photographs. (See female photographs in Figure 2.2 for one example of the paired-comparison). The authors found that the accuracy of children's judgments increased in a generally orderly fashion, improving from 47 percent at age three to 59 percent at age six and to 100 percent at age nine. In comparison to a previous study (Looft, 1971) that used cartoon-like drawings, Kratochwill and Goldman's use of photographs improved the children's accuracy in age judgments. In contrast with previous research (Looft, 1971), the errors children made were primarily the result of basing age judgments on size.

A major advantage of cross-sectional research is that data can be collected across a wide age range in a relatively short time period. Kratochwill and Goldman (1973) evaluated age judgments within a few days. They did not have to measure three-year-olds at one-year intervals for six years to examine the same problem. The advantage is even more apparent when the comparisons involve longer age periods. The major disadvantage of cross-sectional research is that it yields no information about the history of age-related changes. Thus, knowing how children in cross-sectional research would have responded at earlier ages is impossible.

A second form of educational research is called **longitudinal** because the subjects are assessed repeatedly over a longer period of time. Technically, one could study the same individuals from birth to death, but this strategy would likely involve more than one team of researchers. An example of the longitudinal method of research is the Fels study begun in 1929 at the Fels Research Institute in Ohio. Initially 89 subjects (44 males and 45 females) were enrolled to participate in the study. In the study, children were repeatedly weighed, measured, and assessed to identify various developmental changes. For example, at least twice a year, from the children's birth to age 6, a trained interviewer visited the parents' home for a half-day. Thereafter, for the next six years researchers interviewed mothers annually to assess their attitudes toward their children. Most children

Table 2.5

Cross–Sectional and Longitudinal Development Research Strategies Compared

Characteristics	Design Type	
	Cross-sectional	Longitudinal
Research procedure	Measurement of several groups on different development dimensions (e.g., age) simultaneously over a short time period.	Repeated measurement of the same group over long periods of time
Time investment	Short time to conduct (e.g., days, weeks, months)	Long time to conduct (e.g., years, decades)
Expense	Typically inexpensive	Typically expensive
Resources	Relatively few researchers needed	Typically many researchers or research teams, depending on the time period
Major advantage	Relatively large amounts of data can be gathered on a large age span within a short period of time	Researchers can study individual developmental changes within groups
Major disadvantage	Analysis of individual change is obscured	Requires considerable time and resources; subjects may leave study

between the ages of 2 to 2 1/2 also attended the Institute's Nursery for two three-week sessions, and researchers observed peer interaction at the Fels Day Camp in children ages 6 to 10. Such measures as achievement, aggression, conformity, dependency, imitation, language, sex-role, and sociability were rated repeatedly. This study was later followed up by Kagan and Moss (1962) who brought back 71 of the original 89 Fels subjects who were then between 20 and 29 years old. Thus, longitudinal studies can extend for a long time, even beyond that originally intended by the initial research team.

A major advantage of the longitudinal research approach compared to cross-sectional research is that the researcher can study the *same* subjects at each stage or age interval so that he/she can record the patterns of an individual's behavior. In this regard, a researcher can assess the influence of early events on later behavior. There are also some disadvantages. The longitudinal approach is very expensive and time-consuming. Subjects may also leave the study as a result of such factors as moving, illness, death, and loss of motivation to participate. When the sample of subjects changes dramatically, the researcher cannot be sure that subjects who left the study are similar to those that remain. This problem could cause a bias in the results. Some of the major features of cross-sectional and longitudinal methods of educational research are summarized in Table 2.5.

Cross-Cultural Research

Many of the studies cited in this text present research that took place within the context of American culture. Yet, as many educational researchers recognize, **cross-cultural research** should be conducted to determine which factors are related to a particular culture. For example, people from a traditional American culture differ considerably from people from Eastern cultures in the way they behave, think, and approach problems. Consider our earlier example of children's judgment of age. From research conducted in the United States, research-ers have found that children living in American culture become aware sometime during the first two to three years of life that there is a correlation between the physical size of people and their age. Looft, Raymond, and Raymond (1972) attempted to determine the characteristics of age judgments by children in a non-American culture—Sarawak, of the Federation of Malaysia. Children in the study made age judgments on cartoon drawings of four different male drawings (infant, child, adolescent, and adult). The procedures were much the same as those described earlier in the Kratochwill and Goldman (1973) study.

Looft and his associates found that older children in the sample were more accurate in determining the older of the two persons on each stimulus card than the younger children were. The children's explanations for their judgments revealed the importance of fatness and strength in their decisions. Fifty-five percent of the Sarawak children used the word "stronger" in their explanations for their judgments; this was never offered by American children in comparable research (Kratochwill & Goldman, 1973; Looft, 1971). Also 64 percent of the children mentioned the degree of fatness or thinness in their responses, whereas in the American research descriptions almost always pertained to height.

To account for these differences, Looft et al. (1972) noted that the cultural differences relate to the status and occurrence of obesity in Sarawak. A fat person is regarded as one who has accumulated considerable wealth—enough to allow him/her to eat well and not work hard. In contrast to American culture, most people associate fatness with older individuals since they would presumably live longer. Thus, a child would commonly judge the infant drawing that has a protruding belly to be older than the adolescent figure and to explain that the infant was "bigger and fatter."

Time-Series Research

A research approach that is similar to the longitudinal methods discussed above is called time-series or single-case design. Like the repeated measurement feature of the longitudinal design, **time-series research** emphasizes the repeated analysis of a group or individual subject over a definite time period. However, in the time-series research strategy, the repeated measurement is taken at more frequent intervals (e.g., hours, days, weeks) over a relatively short period of time (several weeks or months). At some point in the data series, an intervention is introduced and the researcher evaluates the effect. Time-series designs can involve any number of subjects—for example, ranging from 1 to 1,000,000.

Time-series designs are used most commonly in psychological research in behavioral or operant psychology (see chapter 6). However, the designs are not limited to this orientation and are currently used in psychology, sociology, medicine, and education (Kratochwill, 1978; Kratochwill & Levin, 1992). The major advantage of time-series research is that formal measurement takes place, some credible design is used to evaluate treatments, and reliable data are gathered.

Many time-series designs are used in applied settings where the researcher wishes to demonstrate that some treatment was effective with an identified problem. Narayan, Heward, and Gardner (1990) demonstrated the use of single case times-series methodology in their investigation of a strategy to increase active student responding in the classroom. Based on educational research that has shown a positive relationship between active student responding and academic achievement, the authors were looking for a time and cost efficient way to increase student responding. Traditionally, a teacher would call upon one student at a time to respond. As an alternative the authors devised a response card that can be held up simultaneously by every student in the class to respond to a question by the teacher.

To evaluate their strategy, Narayan and associates selected a regular fourth-grade classroom in an urban public elementary school. There were 20 students in the class and 6 were identified to participate. The authors measured four dependent variables in the study: (a) teacher presentation rate, (b) number of student responses, (c) accuracy of student responses, and (d) daily quiz scores. The study consisted of two independent variables, hand raising and write-on response cards that were alternated in a replication type design. During the baseline, the teacher called upon one student who raised his/her hand in response to a teacher question. In the response-card condition, each student in the class was presented with a white laminated board on which to write one- or two-word answers in response to teacher questions.

The results of the study for each of the six selected students is presented in Figure 2.3. As you can observe from the graphs, the rate of active student response during instruction was higher with the use of response cards than with the hand raising. Also, most of the students scored better on daily quizzes following the sessions in which the response cards were used than they did on quizzes that followed the hand-raising. What do you think that the students had to say about the procedure? Interestingly, 19 of 20 students in the class preferred the response cards over hand raising.

Primary, Secondary, and Meta-Analysis

Have you ever wondered how educational researchers draw conclusions from a body of research evidence? The process of drawing conclusions is not as straightforward as you might think. After the researcher completes the data-gathering phase of the investigation, the data are analyzed in some manner. Typically, some form of statistical test is applied to the data. The first or original analysis of the data that takes place is called *primary analysis.* This primary analysis is usually done by the individual who designed and conducted the research. Following the analysis and discussion of the results, the researcher may share the findings with the scientific community. Once the results are published, they may influence future research, practice, or even public policy.

Not all published research is accepted at face value. Sometimes other researchers wish to re-examine the original data analysis. This procedure is called *secondary*

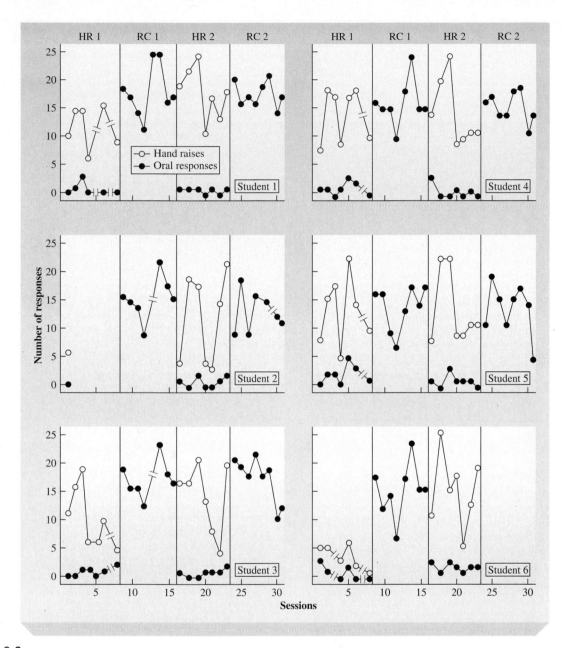

Figure 2.3

Number of responses and hand raises by students 1−6 during hand-raising (HR) and response-card (RC) conditions. Breaks in data paths indicate student absences.

From J.S> Narayan, et al., "Using Response Cards to Increase Student Participation in an Elementary Classroom" in the *Journal of Applied Behavior Analysis*, 23:483-490, 1990. Copyright © 1990 *Journal of Applied Behavior Analysis*, Lawrence, KS. Reprinted by permission of the publishers and authors.

analysis (Cook, 1974). Secondary analysis refers to the re-analysis of data to clarify the original research questions with better statistical procedures or to answer new questions with old data. For example, a researcher may want to examine some early research data on the effect of class size on student achievement. Perhaps the re-analysis will pose some new issues or even different conclusions from those reached by the original researcher's

data analysis. Secondary analysis depends greatly on the availability of the original data. Such data are not always easy to come by. Sometimes they are lost, or coded so that it is difficult to understand the original analysis scheme.

Another form of analysis is called **meta-analysis**— the analysis of analyses (Glass, McGaw, & Smith, 1981). Meta-analysis refers to the statistical analysis of a large

Focus on Classrooms

Rival Hypotheses

Head Start

In the early and middle 1960s there was a great emphasis in this country on early education. Two prime examples are the Sesame Street television show and the Head Start preschool program. Both of these efforts, of course, were developed during this period to prepare disadvantaged children for entrance into elementary school.

In the opinion of many, Sesame Street has been more successful in helping middle- and upper-middle-class children than it has been in helping disadvantaged children. Since it benefited the constituents of most congressional representatives, such criticism was not taken as seriously as that made of Head Start—a program that restricted its benefits to those below a certain level of income. By the late 1960s, as Congress was attempting to cut spending on social programs by dismantling Lyndon Johnson's "Great Society," Head Start became a prime target. The chief ammunition was a national evaluation carried out jointly by Westinghouse and Ohio University, in which the results of a number of separate studies were reported and the conclusion drawn that Head Start had not been overly successful in reaching its goals.

In general, studies of Head Start's effectiveness compared the IQs and educational achievements of children in the program to those of a control group made up of children not in Head Start. In the absence of any researcher's ability to assign children at random to poverty, the control groups tended to be constructed by matching. Based on IQ, children in other preschools were initially matched with Head Start children. Then, pretest-posttest designs were normally used to compare gains made by the two groups. Needless to say, the finding of no significant difference led to great controversy over continued federal spending for Head Start.

> If you had been asked to vote on Head Start, how much weight would you have given this report? Would you have agreed with the authors' conclusions? Before continuing your reading, write your reasons for either agreeing or disagreeing.

Head Start

We know how much weight Donald Campbell and Albert Erlebacher (two psychologists at Northwestern University) would give to the Westinghouse/Ohio University report—very little. They made their position quite clear in a paper criticizing both the methodology and the statistical procedures used in studies of Head Start programs. Since the statistical discussion is quite technical, we will concentrate only on the methodology.

Campbell and Erlebacher's chief criticism was of the effect of matching on the results. Since it would be more difficult to find matches for the most disadvantaged children, it is likely that the studies ended up matching those at the upper end of distribution in the Head Start classroom with those at the lower end of the control classroom. Thus, both samples being compared were extreme relative to their respective populations. Any time the samples are chosen as a consequence of being extreme, we can expect to find the statistical artifact of regression toward the mean. That is to say, the mean of a group chosen because it is extreme will tend to be less extreme (closer to the population mean) when measured a second time.

The amount of regression is a function of the correlation between the two measures, with lower correlations resulting in greater regression. This is a consequence of the chance component of the scores at the first measurement, in that high scorers were "lucky" the first time measured and will be less so the second time. Similarly, low scorers were "unlucky" the first time and will also be less so on second measurement. Thus, in the absence of any differential treatment of the two groups, we would expect the lower-class group mean to decrease and the middle-class group mean to increase as a function of the less-than-perfect correlation from error of measurement. If we now add a constant to each child's score (both maturation and testing would have this effect) in order that all changes will be in the positive direction, the results will show greater gains for the middle-class control group than for the Head Start group—in other words, exactly the findings reported in the Westinghouse/Ohio University evaluation.

The irony of these findings is heightened when we consider the effects of matching on posttest scores. Campbell and Erlebacher used this procedure on data from a computer simulation and concluded that of children scoring the same at time two, the Head Start children have gained .495 points while the Control children have lost .152. This will make sense when you realize that the pretest mean of the Head Start group will have been lower initially, while that of the control group will have been higher. Thus, in the absence of adding the constant, the control group would appear to have lost ground from the pretest to the posttest.

Although there were criticisms of Campbell and Erlebacher's criticism, we chose to side with them. We assume that you will do the same.

H. Schwadron in *Phi Delta Kappan.*

collection of analysis results from individual studies for the purpose of integrating the findings. Meta-analysis is a relatively recent procedure, first coming into prominence during the mid-1970s. It was designed to replace narrative review of research studies—something that most of us have done as students when writing a term paper. Some authors have recommended that traditional narrative review be combined with meta-analysis (e.g., Slavin, 1991), a strategy called "best-evidence synthesis."

Applications of meta-analysis have been quite controversial. For example, Smith and Glass (1977) coded and integrated statistically the results of nearly 400 controlled evaluations of psychotherapy and counseling. Their findings provided convincing evidence of the effectiveness of psychotherapy. Specifically, the individual receiving therapy was better off than 75 percent of untreated individuals. In another study, Smith and Glass (1980) conducted a meta-analysis of research on class size and its relationship to attitudes. They found that advantages of reduced class size are greater in class size ranges from 1 to 15, than at higher ranges (i.e., only small differences occur between class sizes ranging from 20 to 60). Some researchers have been especially critical

of meta-analysis because in making general statements about a particular research topic, it does not discriminate between good and poor studies. The future, however, will likely see more of the meta-analysis research strategy used in educational psychology (Asher, 1990; Walberg, 1986).

Conclusion

This chapter introduced you to the field of research in educational psychology. We noted that some philosophical and theoretical viewpoints have greatly influenced the types of research that are conducted.

Baby biographies and case studies were a common way of gathering information about students when research methods were developing. Neither procedure is considered very scientific today, and most educational researchers reject both.

Contemporary research methods that involve carefully conceived, scientifically based procedures include: historical, descriptive, correlational, comparative, and experimental research. Each is a valid procedure for gaining data on human behavior. The purpose of the re-

Understanding the Research Article

As you continue your reading and work in Educational Psychology, your instructor will undoubtedly ask you to review pertinent articles that shed light on the topic you're studying. Many of these articles will present the results of an experiment that reflects the scientific method.

The typical research article contains four sections: the *Introduction*, the *Method* section, the *Results* section, and *Discussion* (Moore, 1983). We'll review each of these sections using a well-designed study—*The Effects of Early Education on Children's Competence in Elementary School*, published in *Evaluation Review* (Bronson, Pierson, & Tivnan, 1984)—to illustrate each of the four parts.

1. The Introduction

The introductory section will state the purpose of the article (usually as an attempt to solve a problem) and predict the outcome of the study (usually in the form of hypotheses). The introduction section will also contain a review of the literature. In the introductory section of the Bronson et al. article, the researchers state that their intent is to coordinate the effects of early education programs on the performance of students in elementary school. They concisely review the pertinent research and suggest a means of evaluating competence.

2. The Method Section

The method section informs the reader about the subjects in the experiment (Who were they? How many? How were they chosen?), a description of any tests that were used, and a summary of the steps taken to carry out the study. In the Bronson et al. study, the subjects were 169 second-grade children who had been in an early education program and 169 other children who had not been in the pre-school program. The outcome measure was a classroom observation instrument. The authors then explained in considerable detail how they observed the pupils.

3. The Results Section

Here the information gathered on the subjects is presented, together with the statistics that help us to interpret the data. In the article we are using, the authors present their data in several clear tables and present differences between the two groups, using appropriate statistics.

4. Discussion

Finally, the authors of any research article will discuss the importance of what they found (or didn't find) and relate their findings to theory and previous research. In the Bronson et al. article, the authors report that the students who had experienced any early education program showed significantly greater competence in the second grade. The authors conclude by noting the value of these programs in reducing classroom behavior problems and improving students' competence.

Don't be intimidated by research articles. Look for the important features described here and determine how the results could improve classroom practice.

search generally determines what type of study should be conducted. For example, correlational studies attempt to discover the relationship between two or more variables. Remember that a correlation tells us nothing about the cause and effect of the variables measured. We may find that on a particular test all the students who wore red shirts or blouses scored quite highly. Is there a relationship between the red clothing and the scores? Obviously the answer is yes. Did the red clothing cause the high scores? Obviously the answer is no. The value of correlational studies is in the useful information they provide about the strength of a relationship between two variables. Such information may be valuable in itself or may lead to future experimental research to determine possible cause and effect connections.

One of the major concerns of researchers is a lack of control, particularly with regard to the random assignment of subjects. This concern leads us to a considera-

tion of the quasi-experimental method. Let's return to our example of reading methods. We wanted to determine if teaching reading by the phonics method or the whole word method is superior and we chose two classrooms in which the methods were already in use. In other words, we did not assign some students to the classroom using the phonics method and other students to the classroom using the whole word technique. We did not have absolute experimental control. Consequently, these conditions meet the criteria of a quasi-experimental design.

The technique perhaps most favored by researchers, however, is the experiment. In experiments, the researcher has control over the independent variable. Cross-sectional research has the advantage of investigating human behavior across several age ranges simultaneously. We might ask junior high, high school, and college students their   attitudes toward employment procedures in their future. In contrast, longitudinal research has the advantage of investigating human behavior across time. Thus, we may ask junior high students their attitudes toward future employment and continue to measure their attitudes as they become high school and college students.

Methods for reviewing a body of research literature were presented in the chapter. Three techniques have been used including the traditional narrative review, meta-analysis, and best-evidence synthesis. Narrative review involves a survey of the original studies and some commentary on the overall results. The meta-analysis technique involves locating the studies, developing a common metric across studies to determine the effect size, and a statistical analysis to determine if the results are significant. Best-evidence synthesis is a combination of narrative review and meta-analysis.

Finally, as an Appendix to this chapter, you will find some ethical considerations that researchers take into account when conducting research. Most educational researchers adhere to the principles proposed by the American Psychological Association in their research activities.

Chapter Highlights

Research and Effective Schooling

- One of the most important sources of knowledge about human behavior is scientific research.
- Research answers questions about the effectiveness of educational practices.

Influences on Research Methods

- Scientific research is systematic, controlled, empirical, and involves a critical study of some issue or problem.
- Scientific research has been subjected to many and varied influences.
- Scientific research typically follows a series of steps that consists of identifying, clarifying, implementing, evaluating, and interpreting procedures.

Major Research Methods

- Research into educational problems may be historical, descriptive, correlational, comparative, or experimental.
- Historical research involves studying, understanding, and explaining past events.
- Descriptive research involves collecting data to test hypotheses or answer questions related to the current status of the problem.
- Correlational research involves the process of determining whether, and to what degree, a relation exists between two or more variables.
- Comparative research involves establishing a direct relation between variables that the researcher compares, but that she/he does not directly manipulate.
- Experimental research involves a study in which the researcher actually manipulates at least one independent variable to observe the effect on one or more dependent variables.

Techniques Used by Researchers

- The more common research techniques used today are surveys, interviews, observations, and cross-sectional, and longitudinal studies.
- Research can be conducted with large groups of subjects or with a single student subject.
- Cross-cultural research helps to explain differences in how individuals behave, think, and attempt to solve problems.
- Meta-analysis, the analysis of the results of a large number of individual studies, is increasingly popular today.
- No one research method is always best; the research question and issues investigated often determine the method that the researcher will use.

Key Terms

Case studies
Comparative research
Correlational research
Cross-cultural research
Cross-sectional research
Dependent variable
Descriptive research
Experimental research
Historical research
Independent variable
Interviews
Longitudinal research
Meta-analysis
Observation
Surveys
Time-series research

Suggested Readings

Agnew, N. M., & Pyke, S. W. (1987). *The science game* (4th ed.). Englewood Cliffs, NJ: Prentice-Hall. An entertaining presentation of the scientific activities of researchers.

Best, J. W., & Kahn, J. V. (1989). *Research in education* (6th ed.). Englewood Cliffs, NJ: Prentice-Hall. This text illustrates clearly and carefully the methods of educational research and data analysis.

Cook, T. D., & Campbell, D. T. (1979). *Quasi-experimental design and analysis issues for field settings*. Chicago: Rand McNally. This book presents some quasi-experimental designs and design features that can be used in many social research settings. The designs presented probe causal hypotheses about a wide variety of substantive issues in both basic and applied research.

Glass, G. V., McGraw, B., & Smith, M. L. (1981). *Meta-analysis in social research*. Beverly Hills, CA: Sage Publications. This book presents a basic introduction and overview of the use of meta-analysis in psychological and developmental research. Numerous examples are provided within the context of conducting a meta-analysis.

Kazdin, A. E. (1991). *Research design in clinical psychology*. New York: Pergamon Press. This volume presents an up-to-date, comprehensive overview of various research designs and methodological issues in applied and clinical research.

Appendix A

Ethical and Legal Considerations in Research in Education

Research with human subjects carries with it special responsibilities for the educational researcher. A major goal of research is to generate knowledge that will be useful in advancing the human condition. Bersoff (1978) raised several issues in research with human participants:

1. In what way does research invade the private lives of those we study?
2. In the light of potential invasion, how must we accommodate our procedures so that we meet both ethical demands and legal requirements?
3. In particular, what are the kinds of information that we should give our potential subjects so that they may make an informed choice as to their participation?
4. How do we obtain the consent of those who may have a limited capacity to consent—children, the mentally retarded, the severely disturbed—and those whose very situation may preclude free choice—the institutionalized and the imprisoned—while respecting the dignity, humanness, and right to self-determination of these potential research subjects?
5. When may the risks of injury be so great that the researcher should feel obliged to forego the research, even though there may be some potential benefits to either participants or society as a whole? (Bersoff, 1978, pp. 364–365).

Increasingly, ethical and legal guidelines have been advanced for individuals conducting research with children and adults. The American Psychological Association (APA) undertook one such effort in its formulation of a code of "Ethical Standards for Research with Human Subjects" (APA, 1982). The guidelines provide researchers with direction when undertaking scientific investigation.

APA Ethical Standards for Research with Human Participants

The decision to undertake research rests upon a considered judgment by the individual psychologist upon how best to contribute to psychological science and human welfare. Having made the decision to conduct research, the researcher considers alternative directions in which research energies and resources might be invested. On the basis of this consideration, the researcher carries out the investigation with respect and concern for the dignity and welfare of the people who participate and with cog-

nizance of federal and state regulations and professional standards governing the conduct of research with human participants.

A. In planning a study, the investigator has the responsibility to make a careful evaluation of its ethical acceptability. To the extent that the weighing of scientific and human values suggests a compromise of any principle, the investigator incurs a correspondingly serious obligation to seek ethical advice and to observe stringent safeguards to protect the rights of human participants.

B. Considering whether a participant in a planned study will be a "subject at risk" or a "subject at minimal risk," according to recognized standards, is a primary ethical concern to the investigator.

C. The investigator always retains the responsibility for ensuring ethical practice in research. The investigator is also responsible for the ethical treatment of research participants by collaborators, assistants, students, and employees, all of whom, however, incur similar obligations.

D. Except in minimal-risk research, the investigator establishes a clear and fair agreement with research participants, prior to their participation, that clarifies the obligations and responsibilities of each. The investigator has the obligation to honor all promises and commitments included in that agreement. The investigator informs the participants of all aspects of the research that might reasonably be expected to influence willingness to participate and explains all other aspects of the research about which the participants inquire. Failure to make full disclosure prior to obtaining informed consent requires additional safeguards to protect the welfare and dignity of the research participants. Research with children or with participants who have impairments that would limit understanding and/or communication requires special safeguarding procedures.

E. Methodological requirements of a study may make the use of concealment or deception necessary. Before conducting such a study, the investigator has a special responsibility to (1) determine whether the use of such techniques is justified by the study's prospective scientific, educational, or applied value; (2) determine whether alternative procedures are available that do not use concealment or deception; and (3) ensure that the participants are provided with sufficient explanation as soon as possible.

F. The investigator respects the individual's freedom to decline to participate in or to withdraw from the research at any time. The obligation to protect this freedom requires careful thought and consideration when the investigator is in a position of authority or influence over the participant. Such positions of authority include, but are not limited to, situations in which research participation is required as part of employment or in which the participant is a student, client, or employee of the investigator.

G. The investigator protects the participant from physical and mental discomfort, harm, and danger that may arise from research procedures. If risks of such consequences exist, the investigator informs the participant of that fact. Research procedures likely to cause serious or lasting harm to a participant are not used unless the failure to use these procedures might expose the participant to risk of greater harm or unless the research has great potential benefit, and each participant has provided fully informed and voluntary consent. The participant should be informed of procedures for contacting the investigator within a reasonable time period following participation should stress, potential harm, or related questions or concerns arise.

H. After the data are collected, the investigator provides the participant with information about the nature of the study and attempts to remove any misconceptions that may have arisen. Where scientific or humane values justify delaying or withholding this information, the investigator incurs a special responsibility to monitor the research and to ensure that there are no damaging consequences for the participant.

I. Where research procedures result in undesirable consequences for the individual participant, the investigator has the responsibility to detect and remove or correct these consequences, including long-term effects.

J. Information obtained about a research participant during the course of an investigation is confidential unless otherwise agreed upon in advance. When the possibility exists that others may obtain access to such information, this possibility, together with the plans for protecting confidentiality, is explained to the participant as part of the procedure for obtaining informed consent.

Code of Ethics of the Education Profession*
Preamble

The educator, believing in the worth and dignity of each human being, recognizes the supreme importance of the pursuit of truth, devotion to excellence, and the nurture of democratic principles. Essential to these goals is the protection of freedom to learn and to teach and the guarantee of equal educational opportunity for all. The educator accepts the responsibility to adhere to the highest ethical standards.

The educator recognizes the magnitude of the responsibility inherent in the teaching process. The desire for the respect and confidence of one's colleagues, of students, of parents, and of the members of the community provides the incentive to attain and maintain the highest possible degree of ethical conduct. The *Code of Ethics of the Education Profession* 1975 indicates the aspiration of all educators and provides standards by which to judge conduct.

The remedies specified by the NEA and/or its affiliates for the violation of any provision of this *Code* shall be exclusive and no such provision shall be enforceable in any form other than one specifically designated by the NEA or its affiliates.

Principle I
Commitment to the Student

The educator strives to help each student realize his or her potential as a worthy and effective member of society. The educator therefore works to stimulate the spirit of inquiry, the acquisition of knowledge and understanding, and the thoughtful formulation of worthy goals.

In fulfillment of the obligation to the student, the educator—

1. Shall not unreasonably restrain the student from independent action in the pursuit of learning.
2. Shall not unreasonably deny the student access to varying points of view.
3. Shall not deliberately suppress or distort subject matter relevant to the student's progress.
4. Shall make reasonable effort to protect the student from conditions harmful to learning or to health and safety.

5. Shall not intentionally expose the student to embarrassment or disparagement.
6. Shall not on the basis of race, color, creed, sex, national origin, marital status, political or religious beliefs, family, social, or cultural background, or sexual orientation, unfairly—
   a. Exclude any student from participation in any program.
   b. Deny benefits to any student.
   c. Grant any advantage to any student.
7. Shall not use professional relationships with students for private advantage.
8. Shall not disclose information about students obtained in the course of professional service, unless disclosure serves a compelling professional purpose or is required by law.

Principle II

Commitment to the Profession

The education profession is vested by the public with a trust and responsibility requiring the highest ideals of professional service.

In the belief that the quality of the services of the education profession directly influences the nation and its citizens, the educator shall exert every effort to raise professional standards, to promote a climate that encourages the exercise of professional judgment, to achieve conditions which attract persons worthy of the trust to careers in education, and to assist in preventing the practice of the profession by unqualified persons.

In fulfillment of the obligation to the profession, the educator—

1. Shall not in an application for a professional position deliberately make a false statement or fail to disclose a material fact related to competency and qualifications.
2. Shall not misrepresent his/her professional qualifications.
3. Shall not assist any entry into the profession of a person known to be unqualified in respect to character, education, or other relevant attribute.
4. Shall not knowingly make a false statement concerning the qualifications of a candidate for a professional position.
5. Shall not assist a noneducator in the unauthorized practice of teaching.
6. Shall not disclose information about colleagues obtained in the course of professional service unless disclosure serves a compelling professional purpose or is required by law.
7. Shall not knowingly make false or malicious statements about a colleague.
8. Shall not accept any gratuity, gift, or favor that might impair or appear to influence professional decisions or action.

SECTION

2

The Development
of Students

3

Cognitive and Language Development

It was the week after school opened and five-year-old Kenny Wilson and his eleven-year-old sister Alice had just transferred to the Brackett School District. Mrs. Allan, the principal, took both students to their new classrooms and introduced them to their teachers.

"Good morning, Kenny. I'm delighted that you're going to be in this classroom," said Mrs. Groves, the first grade teacher. "Some of the boys and girls in this room live near you. By the way, do you like your new house?"

Kenny, at first nervous, began to respond to Mrs. Groves' warm manner. "Oh, yes. I have my own bedroom. It has big windows."

Mrs. Groves laughed. "Can you see the moon from your window?" she asked.

"You bet. It follows me around the room," said Kenny.

At the same time, Alice was talking with Mr. Gallo, the sixth grade teacher. "Welcome to the Brackett sixth grade, Alice. I think you'll enjoy being here," said Mr. Gallo. "Can you give me an idea of the kind of work you were doing?"

"Well, the social studies teacher was helping us with research skills," said Alice. "We were doing a project on Egypt and we had to pick one specific topic like housing. Then we outlined it and made a report to the class."

"That sounds as if you were doing good work, Alice. You'll like it here; we're doing a lot of the same things."

oth teachers were listening to and observing their pupils as they spoke, searching for clues that would help them work with these new students in their classrooms. And the clues were there, as you can tell from both conversations. Though each student spoke well, there are significant differences in both the thinking and speech of the two students. For example, Kenny's statement that the moon follows him around furnishes clues to his level of cognitive development. Alice's skillful explanation of her use of research methods also revealed a level of cognitive development one would expect of a typical sixth grader.

To interpret Kenny's and Alice's behavior, however, you should be aware of the normal path of development that your students follow. Understanding development will also help you to adapt your instruction to meet their needs. In this chapter, then, you will explore cognitive development, especially the work of Jean Piaget. Since cognition and language are so tightly intertwined, our discussion will then turn to the language development of your students.

When you finish reading this chapter, you should be able to:

- apply your knowledge of cognitive development to the classroom through the appropriate selection of materials and the perceptive use of instructional methods.
- use your classroom as a means of providing needed opportunities for the cognitive and linguistic achievement of your students.

- use language data for the purpose of improving your students' entire range of language behavior—reading, writing, speaking, listening, spelling.

The Meaning of Development

When you think about development, your first inclination is probably to think of physical development; that is, you think of an increase in size. But for a psychologist, development also means an increasing ability to understand abstract ideas (cognitive development), and to get along with others (social development).

As Figure 3.1 illustrates, physical, cognitive, and social development do not occur at the same rate. Your students may be all the same chronological age, but their growth ages will vary. Some will be tall for their age, and some will be short; others may be mentally delayed or accelerated.

If you are aware of the processes of development, you can reassure a self-conscious adolescent whose growth in height is slightly delayed but whose weight is normal. You can look for opportunities to reinforce the social skills of a student whose mental growth has outpaced her social growth. Or you may realize that several members of your eighth grade civics class are floundering because they haven't fully acquired the ability to think abstractly, so you provide additional "hands-on" assignments for the class. Familiarity with developmental theory and

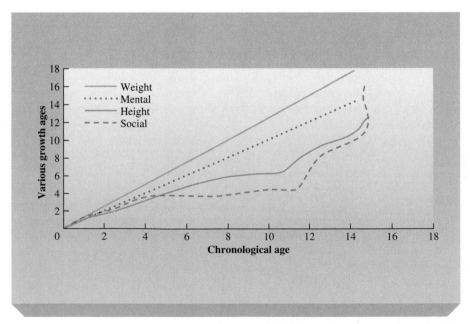

Figure 3.1
The complexity of development.

(a)

(b)

(c)

(d)

The young child's development of fine motor coordination reflected in the ability to hold a pencil. (a) The toddler grabs the whole crayon and is able to make only crude markings with it. (b, c) During early childhood, children use fewer arm and shoulder movements and more finger movements. (d) By the end of early childhood, children have learned to use their fingers and wrist to manipulate the tip rather than the whole pencil (Goodman, 1979, p. 96).

characteristics will enable you to determine appropriate techniques and content to match individual differences.

Although the various facets of development—physical, cognitive, social—do not proceed at the same pace, they do share common trends (Salkind, 1981).

- *Development proceeds from the general to the specific.* For example, an infant's undifferentiated crying soon focuses on a specific cause, such as hunger or discomfort.
- *Development shows an increase in complexity.* For example, the way that children solve problems shows increasing sophistication.

- *A child's behavior gradually becomes more integrated.* Thinking and feeling complement each other.
- *Egocentrism slowly diminishes.* Children gradually realize that the world does not center on them.
- *Children become more independent and self-sufficient.* Their dependence on parents to satisfy their needs typically recedes.

Today we have accumulated considerable data about the development of our students, and the cognitive and language theorists we are about to study offer us a means of integrating a wealth of information and applying it to the classroom. As you read their ideas, use these questions to guide your thinking and to form classroom applications.

- In what way does the age group you are teaching (or plan to teach) see the world differently from you?
- How can you recognize signs of developmental growth in students and use these signs to determine their readiness to acquire new skills?
- Do these theorists provide any insights into the relationship between the abilities of your students and their classroom performance?

An example of a theorist who has thought deeply about cognitive development and whose ideas about the role of culture in development have direct classroom application is Lev Vygotsky. Born in Russia in 1896, Vygotsky was educated at Moscow University and quickly turned his attention to educational psychology, developmental psychology, and psychopathology. He was particularly concerned with applying psychological data to the practical problems facing the Russian schools. Although his career was abruptly terminated by his death from tuberculosis in 1934, his work has attracted considerable recent attention because of the central role that he allotted social processes in cognitive development.

Vygotsky and Mental Development

For Vygotsky (1962, 1978), the clues to understanding mental development lie in children's social processes; that is, cognitive growth depends on children's interactions with those around them. The adults around children interact with them in a way that emphasizes those things that a culture values. For example, a child points to an object; those around the child respond in a way that not only conveys information about the object but also indicates how the child should behave. To understand mental development, we need to concentrate **not** on the products of development but on the social processes that establish these higher mental forms.

It is here that Vygotsky introduces his belief in qualitative shifts in development. Biological explanations can account for only so much of development, and then social forces become a powerful factor in development. Consequently, no single explanation can account for development; rather we must search for multiple influences that help to explain the nature of developmental change (Wertsch, 1985).

He also makes a distinction between "elementary" and "higher" mental processes. For example, children use a practical intelligence during their preverbal days by using their bodies and the objects around them. They will pull themselves up by a chair or table to obtain an attrac-

tive object. As soon as speech appears, their actions are transformed. They can ask for that same object and, as they do, they initiate verbal relationships with those around them.

Speech helps them in their efforts at mastery, producing new, verbal relationships with the environment. Control of these developing higher mental functions gradually shifts from the environment to the individual. Children then use inner speech for themselves (for example, to solve problems) and for others to enhance interpersonal relations (Vygotsky, 1978, p. 25). An interesting question here is: can learning facilitate the shift?

The Zone of Proximal Development

Commenting on the relationship between learning and development, Vygotsky (1978) noted that learning, in some way, must be matched with a student's developmental level, which is too frequently identified by an intelligence test score. Vygotsky believed, however, that we cannot be content with the results of intelligence testing, which provide only a student's present developmental level. For example, after administering a Stanford-Binet Intelligence test, we find that a student's IQ on this test is 110, which would be that student's current level of mental development. We then assume that the student can work only at this level. Vygotsky argue, however, that with a little help, students might be able to do work that they could not do on their own.

We know that students who have the same IQ are quite different in other respects. Motivation, interest, health, and a host of other conditions produce different achievement levels. For example, our student with an IQ of 110 may be able to deal effectively with materials of various levels of difficulty. That is, when working alone, this student may be able to do addition problems but can solve subtraction problems only with the teacher's help.

To explain this phenomenon, Vygotsky introduced his notion of the **zone of proximal development.** He defines the zone of proximal development as the distance between a child's actual developmental level as determined by independent problem solving and the higher level of potential development as determined by problem solving under adult guidance or in collaboration with more capable peers (Vygotsky, 1978). It is the difference between what pupils can do independently and what they can do with help.

As Vygotsky noted (1978), instruction is good only when it proceeds ahead of development. That is, teaching awakens those functions that are maturing and that are in the zone of proximal development. Although teaching and learning are not development, they can act to stimulate developmental processes.

Lessons to Be Learned from Cross-Cultural Psychology

Vygotsky stressed the role that culture plays in development. Cross-cultural research enables us to use cultural variation as a means of determining the developmental differences that can be attributed to culture (Rogoff & Morelli, 1989). For example, how do gender differences emerge in different cultures? How does compulsory schooling, as opposed to age, affect the advancement of intellectual skills? What part of the environment most appeals to students of different cultures?

Cross-cultural studies help us to test the universality of developmental theories that have mainly evolved from the study of Western children. For example, do Piaget's stages of cognitive development (which we are about to study) apply to children from different cultures? Does the attachment literature accurately reflect mother-infant relations in various cultures?

We are more aware today that each of our students grows up in a particular culture that contributes to that student's knowledge and affects how the student will react to schooling. In one sense, all education is multicultural since both teachers and students represent many cultures (Tiedt & Tiedt, 1990). Viewed in this manner, multicultural education is an integrated part of the curriculum and not an isolated few pages in a textbook.

Vygotsky's ideas concerning how culture affects development help us to realize that we cannot understand development without considering the social processes acting on children. Vygotsky traces mental development to the interactions between changing social conditions and a biological organism. His fundamental claim is that human mental processes can be understood only by considering how and where they occur (Wertsch, 1985). Thus, understanding human development requires knowledge of that culture in which development occurs.

As we have seen, Vygotsky (1978) believed that cognitive development occurs in those circumstances in which an adult guides a pupil's thinking (Rogoff, 1990). These skilled adults (parents, teachers) aid cognitive development by using cultural tools (for example, language, mathematics). Institutions such as the school and inventions such as the computer provide critical help in a student's cognitive development. Thus, for Vygotsky, children depend on the social basis of mind to develop cognitively (Rogoff, 1990).

Vygotsky's ideas of mental development stand in contrast to those of Jean Piaget. Although both appeal to a cognitive interpretation of mental development, Vygotsky, as we have seen, turned to social processes to explain a child's cognitive development. Piaget, on the other hand, believed that children construct their own ideas of how

What African–American Children Consider Important

Although students attend to both the physical and social aspects of their environments, they seem to prefer one more than the other, and their preference depends on the guidelines of their culture. The urban environment and the social milieu in which African-Americans develop seem to predispose them toward the social elements of their environment, which then affects their school performance. Understanding the influence of this orientation on the achievement of these students requires an examination of the mechanisms by which students organize their lives. Three categories seem to be significant.

- the physical environment that a family uses to shape a child's interactions with symbols and objects;
- the interpersonal relations that provide feedback to students for their expectations and performances;
- the emotional and motivational climates that influence a student's personality and behavior (Shade, 1987).

Within these categories, visual forms and family interaction patterns are particularly relevant. For example, research suggests that the visual forms within African-American homes were usually those of people (Martin Luther King, Jr., Jesse Jackson, John and Robert Kennedy). Middle-class white homes had more abstract paintings, pictures of flowers, and landscape scenes.

Interpersonal relationships within the family play a large role in the socialization of African-American children with the ultimate goal of helping children to function independently within and without the family (Clark, 1983). Parents attempt to prepare their children for interactions with both peers and teachers and how to act in social situations. Thus, parents are trying to provide a set of guidelines for behaving in novel situations (Shade, 1987).

With regard to the impact on personality and behavior, these socialization practices point to the importance of people to African-American students. Damico's (1985) study is a good example. She asked both white and black adolescents to take those pictures that they think best describe their school. Most of the pictures taken by the African-American students were of people. Other studies indicate that teachers of African-American students concentrate on classroom management and reinforce these students for personable behavior, while rewarding white children for their academic performance (Shade, 1987).

In teaching African-American students, then, remember the importance they place on social interactions, and try to structure the classroom environment in a way that encourages the social dimensions of learning.

the world around them "works"; they function as "little scientists." Their ideas about the world and its objects change as they pass through four identifiable stages. Teachers following Vygotsky's ideas would turn to his Zone of Proximal Development, while teachers using Piaget's ideas would encourage more independent work.

Cognitive Development

Probably no one has influenced our thinking about cognitive development more than Jean Piaget. Born in Neuchatel, Switzerland in 1896, Piaget was trained as a biologist, and his biological training made a major impact upon his thinking about cognitive development. Piaget insisted upon calling himself a "genetic epistemologist," a term that reflected his interest in how the manner in which individuals acquire knowledge changes as they develop. He became fascinated by the processes that led children to make incorrect answers in reasoning tests and turned his attention to the analysis of children's developing intelligence. Until his death in 1980, Piaget remained active in his research into cognitive development, and many believe that he was responsible for the resurgence of interest in cognitive studies.

You will find his ideas challenging, but you will reap a rich reward for your efforts. The insights that you will gain from understanding his theory will afford you a unique method for comprehending the cognitive processes underlying children's behavior. This brief summary will introduce you to his system, present the basic ideas, trace the four stages of cognitive development, and offer suggestions for the classroom.

In a perceptive statement about the science and psychology of education, Piaget (1971) raised three fundamental questions:

1. What is the aim of teaching: To accumulate knowledge? To teach students to learn? To produce innovative students?
2. What materials and subjects are vital? Which are irrelevant? Which should be avoided for the attainment of specific objectives?
3. How does mental development guide selection of those methods best suited for achieving desired goals?

Piaget constantly urged teachers to use his theory. Decide what you want your students to achieve; determine the ideal content for them to attain these goals; never forget that your teaching methods and the subject matter that you use must match your students' cognitive level.

Jean Piaget (1896-1980), one of the most influential developmental psychologists who has significantly influenced educational theories and practices.

Central to Piaget's thinking is the assumption that mental abilities, like physical abilities, go through a process of maturation. Before toddlers are ready to walk, they must have gained the ability to stand. In the same way, a child must develop the capacity for symbolic representation before being ready to read—the child must first comprehend that things have names and that those names can be represented by a pattern of lines and curves on a piece of paper.

Piaget's analysis of cognitive development can help you match curriculum to the abilities of your students. Say, for example, you are working with an eleven- or twelve-year-old student who seems to be having trouble with comprehension (perhaps both verbal and mathematical). Referring to Piaget's ideas suggests that you should provide more concrete examples and more tangible materials because most preteens are not yet ready to do much abstract thinking.

Key Concepts in Piaget's Theory

After many years of observing children of all ages, Piaget deduced that cognitive development has four stages, each of which builds on the previous one. Cognitive functioning begins as responses to concrete phenomena—babies know only what they can touch, taste, or see. Our ability to use symbols and to think abstractly increases with each subsequent stage until we are able to manipulate abstract concepts and consider hypothetical alternatives.

Cognitive Structures

Just as the physical structure of the eye enables us to see and the physical structure of the ear enables us to hear, the psychological **structures** of the mind, or cognitive structures, enable us to think and know. Cognitive development is the result of changes in our cognitive structures. For example, although the one-year-old child cannot comprehend written words (an infant's structures cannot accept them), the same child at seven years easily incorporates words. The child's cognitive structures have changed; intellectual growth has occurred.

Functional Invariants

Piaget believed that we inherit a method of intellectual functioning that enables us to respond to our environment by forming cognitive structures. He suggests that two psychological mechanisms, **adaptation** and **organization,** are responsible for the development of our cognitive structures. Because we use these two mechanisms constantly throughout our lives, Piaget named them **functional invariants.**

Adaptation

We adjust to the environment in two ways: through assimilation and accommodation. Piaget believed that adaptation consists of **assimilation** and **accommodation.** When we assimilate something we incorporate it; we take it in. Think of eating. We take food into the structure of our mouths and change it to fit the shape of our mouths, throats, and digestive tract. We take objects, concepts, and events into our minds similarly: we incorporate them into our mental structures, changing them to fit the structures as we changed the food to fit our physical structures.

For example, you are now studying Piaget's views on cognitive development. These ideas are unique and will require effort to understand them. You are attempting to comprehend them by using the cognitive structures you now possess. You are assimilating Piaget's ideas; you are mentally taking them in and shaping them to fit your cognitive structures. But we also change as a result of assimilation. The food we eat produces biochemical changes; the stimuli we incorporate into our minds produce mental changes. We change what we incorporate; we are also changed by it. For example, not only are you taking in Piaget's ideas, but they are also changing your views on intelligence and cognitive development. Your cognitive structures are changed, and if you understand his concepts, you will never look at your students in quite the same way again. The change in your cognitive structures will produce corresponding behavioral changes; this is the process of **accommodation.**

The adaptive process is the heart of Piaget's explanation of learning. Students begin by trying to "fit" new material into existing cognitive structures, to assimilate the material, a process called **equilibration.** Students (and all of us) try to strike a balance between assimilation and accommodation. That is, students will make mistakes but by continued interaction with the environment, they correct their mistakes and change their cognitive structures (they have accommodated).

Organization

Once a structure is formed it is connected with other structures, and this organization enables us to engage in ever more complex thinking. Organization and adaptation are inseparable. As Piaget states (1952), they are two complementary processes of a single mechanism. Every intellectual act is related to other similar acts.

Physical structures can again provide an analogy for the abstract concept of organization. To read this text you are balancing it, turning the pages, and moving your eyes. All of these physical structures are organized so that you can read. Likewise, for you to understand the material, your appropriate cognitive structures are organized so that they assimilate and accommodate.

If some stimulus is radically different (for example, something written in another language), you may be unable to assimilate it because you do not have the necessary cognitive structures; the material remains meaningless. You must not permit your students just to memorize and then merely repeat it on demand with little, if any, comprehension. Such "learning" will persist only for a brief moment, and students will not relate it to other topics; it will not expand or enrich their knowledge. Although Piaget was primarily interested in the development of thinking, his work has great value for teachers: providing insight into comprehension, transfer, and problem solving ability.

Content

Content is Piaget's term for behavior—talking, acting. Content can provide you with a mirror of your students' cognitive structures. If you observe your students carefully, you begin to discover why they behave as they do. You can use content to identify the level of their functioning and to match appropriate materials and methods to that level. For example, if a student is frowning when you give directions, you can probably conclude that the student didn't understand you.

Schemes

Schemes are organized patterns of thought and action (you may also see the term "schema" but since we are more accustomed to "scheme," it will be used throughout this discussion). They are the cognitive structures *and* behavior that help us to adapt to our environment. They may be best thought of as the inner representation of our activities and experiences. A scheme is named by its activity: the *grasping* schema, the *sucking* schema.

It is not merely the activity, but the activity plus the underlying cognitive structure(s) that constitutes the scheme. For example, by reaching out and touching something, say a blanket, a child begins to learn about the material—its heaviness, its size; the child is forming a cognitive structure about the blanket. When the child combines knowledge about the blanket with the act of reaching for it, Piaget called this behavior a scheme—in this case, the grasping scheme.

How do these concepts "work" in Piaget's theory? If you think of his theory in this way, it may help. Stimuli come from the environment and are filtered through the functional invariants. Adaptation and organization use the stimuli to form new structures or change existing structures. (For example, you may have had your own idea of what intelligence is, but now you change your structures relating to intelligence because of your new knowledge about Piaget.) Your content or behavior now changes because of the changes in your cognitive structures.

One of Piaget's classic experiments can graphically illustrate how content reveals cognitive structures. To replicate this experiment, you'll need a five-year-old child (in Piaget's preoperational stage), a seven-year-old child (in Piaget's concrete operational stage), six black tokens, and six orange tokens. Make a row of the black tokens. If you give the five-year-old child the orange tokens with instructions to match them with the black tokens, the child can easily do it. When the tokens are in a one-to-one position, a five-year-old can tell us that both rows have the same number.

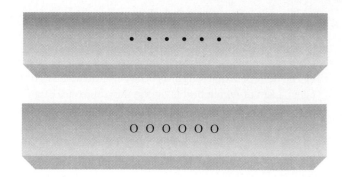

But if we spread the six black tokens to make a longer row, the five-year old will tell us that the row has more tokens!

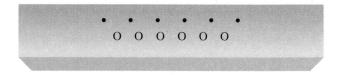

Even when Piaget put the tokens on tracks and let the child move and match them, the child still believed the longer row had more tokens.

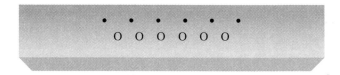

Present the seven-year-old with the same problem. The child will think it is a trick—both rows obviously still have the same number.

This experiment is similar to the one conducted by Kratochwill and Goldman (1973) reported in chapter 2 as an example of developmental research. You will remember that the children in the study were presented with photographs of people of varying sizes. Until the age of seven years the children judged age on the basis of height, judging the taller person as older. When people in the photographs were of different ages but made to look the same size in the photograph, children under the age of 7 judged them as the same age. These findings were consistent even when a young child was paired with an old adult.

These and related experiments hold an important lesson for teachers: cognitive structures change with age. Consequently, teachers should present subject matter in a form that matches the cognitive structures of students. For example, a kindergarten teacher often has to show her students how to hold the paper, grasp the pencil, and print on the line. By the time these students are in the

Table 3.1

The Four Periods of Intellectual Development

The Cognitive Periods and Approximate Ages

1. The sensorimotor period (birth to 18 - 24 months).
2. The preoperational period (2 to 7 years).
3. The concrete operational period (7 to 11 years).
4. The formal operational period (over 11 years).

Note: This is a "stage invariant" theory, which means that the order of the stages does not vary; everyone passes through these stages in this sequence. It is not an "age invariant" theory, which means that a child's age may vary at any one of the periods. For example, although most children reach the concrete operational period at seven years, others may not reach it until eight or nine years.

third grade, they immediately know how to adjust the paper, hold the pencil, and print on the line.

Piaget's Four Stages of Cognitive Development

For Piaget, cognitive development means passage through four stages or periods: **sensorimotor, preoperational, concrete operational, and formal operational** (Table 3.1). The age at which children reach the four stages varies, but the sequence of the stages never varies. In other words, Piaget's theory is stage invariant, age variant. Every child must pass though the sensorimotor stage before the preoperational, the preoperational before the concrete operational, and the concrete operational before the formal operational.

The Sensorimotor Period

The **sensorimotor** period extends from birth to about two years. The cognitive development of infants and toddlers comes mainly through their use of their bodies and their senses as they explore the environment—hence the label sensorimotor.

Infants "know" in the sense of recognizing or anticipating familiar, recurring objects and happenings, and they "think" in the sense of behaving towards these objects and events with mouth, hand, eye, and other sensory-motor instruments in predictable, organized, and often adaptive ways (Flavell, 1985). A good example of this behavior is apparent in the way a baby follows a mother with its eyes and how often it will smile at a mother's face, expecting pleasant consequences.

Features of the Sensorimotor Period

Recent research has shown that children are active processors of information from birth. They are not mere passive recipients of stimuli; they see and hear at birth and immediately commence the task of regulating their environment. Although their main efforts are devoted to homeostatic control (establishing rhythmic respiratory and cardiac rates, clearing air passages), they occasionally, for brief moments, demonstrate intense attention to the environment. These moments signal their search for stimulation; they indicate an ability to process information.

- *Egocentrism.* The child's universe is initially egocentric, entirely centered on self. Piaget uses egocentric in a cognitive sense; that is, egocentric adults know there are other viewpoints but disregard them; egocentric children are simply unaware of any other viewpoint. Very young children lack social orientation: they speak at rather than to each other, and two children in conversation will be discussing utterly unrelated topics. Through cognitive development, however, they will learn that others exist, that there is a world beyond themselves.
- *Object permanence.* An object or person removed from an infant's field of vision ceases to exist. If the toy an infant is playing with is put behind a chair and thus out of sight, the child simply stops searching for it. This explains the pleasure infants manifest when someone plays peek-a-boo with them. The face no longer exists when it is hidden, since the child has not yet acquired object permanence.
- *Concepts of space and time.* Gradually, as children begin to crawl and walk, they realize that there is distance between the objects that they are using to steady themselves. For example, how many times have you seen infants pull themselves up by a chair, drop to the floor, crawl some distance, and then pull themselves up by a table. By moving from object to object, they learn about space and the time it takes to move from object to object.
- *Causality.* As children use their growing sensorimotor intelligence, they begin to find order in the universe. They begin to distinguish their own actions as a cause, and they begin to discover events that have their cause elsewhere, either in other objects or in various relationships between objects (Piaget & Inhelder, 1969). For example, infants will push a toy, perhaps a truck, and watch it roll. They gradually come to realize that their actions caused the truck to roll.

Infants pass through *six subdivisions of the sensorimotor period* (Table 3.2). As they do, they progress from

(a)

(b)

(c)

(d)

For Piaget, development is a continuous creation of more complex forms. Piaget described development as occurring in four stages: (a) sensorimotor, (b) preoperational, (c) concrete operational, and (d) formal operational.

reliance on reflex actions (such as sucking and grasping) to a basic understanding of the world around them and the beginnings of the ability to represent the world through language. The infant will achieve a practical and comparatively coherent organization of elementary motor and perceptual acts. Although an infant's cognitive structures are too primitive to permit any symbolic manipulation of objects, the sensorimotor schemes developed during this period are the basis of the logical, abstract schemes of the adult. Even at the end of this period, they don't understand why you can't see what they're looking at when you're on the other side of the room.

Educational Implications

Piaget's analysis of infant cognitive development is important not only for daycare staff and others who care for infants, but it also has implications for the classroom. What happens during the first two years of life provides the foundation for more formal work. Children's cognitive achievements during the sensorimotor period enable them eventually to go on to the use of symbols (such as those used in language and mathematics).

If you work with infants in a daycare setting, remember Piaget's (1969) suggestions for furthering cognitive development.

- *Provide multiple objects* of various sizes, shapes, and colors for them to use. Think about the label sensorimotor for a moment. What meanings do you attach to it? One undoubtedly includes the active use of the senses or body; through bodily use (reaching, touching, creeping), infants learn about the environment. Consequently, parents and daycare centers should furnish toys and objects that are circular, square, soft, hard, stationary, or mobile. (These needn't be expensive: blocks of wood, rubber balls, and pieces of fruit are perfectly satisfactory.) By manipulating these simple objects, children form the cognitive groundwork of their lives.
- *If infants are to develop cognitively as fully as their potential permits, they must actively engage environmental objects.* They must touch them, push them, pull them, squeeze them, drop them, throw them—and any other action we can conceive— because infants learn through sensory and motor activity. The ball they push and see roll, the square block that falls and makes different sounds when it falls on the wooden floor or a rug, or the different sounds that come from kicking the rungs of the crib

---

Table 3.2

Outstanding characteristics of the Sensorimotor Period

The Six Subdivisions of This Period

STAGE 1	During the first month the child exercises the native reflexes, for example, the sucking reflex. Here is the origin of mental development, for states of awareness accompany the reflex mechanisms.
STAGE 2	Piaget refers to Stage 2 (from 1 to 4 months) as the stage of primary circular reactions. Infants repeat some act involving the body, for example, finger sucking. (*Primary* means first, *circular reaction* means repeating the act.)
STAGE 3	From 4 to 8 months *secondary circular reactions* appear; that is, the children repeat acts involving objects outside themselves. For example, infants continue to shake or kick the crib.
STAGE 4	From 8 to 12 months, the child "coordinates secondary schemata." Recall the meaning of schema—behavior plus mental structure. During Stage 4, infants combine several related schemata to achieve some objective. For example, they will remove an obstacle that blocks some desired object.
STAGE 5	From 12 to 18 months, *tertiary circular reactions* appear. Now children repeat acts, but not only for repetition's sake; now they search for novelty. For example, children of this age continually drop things. Piaget interprets such behavior as expressing their uncertainty about what will happen to the object when they release it.
STAGE 6	At about 18 months or 2 years, a primitive type of representation appears. For example, one of Piaget's daughters wished to open a door but had grass in her hands. She put the grass on the floor and then moved it back from the door's movement so that it would not blow away.

From J. Flavell, *Cognitive Development*. Copyright © 1985 Prentice-Hall, Inc., Englewood Cliffs, NJ. Allyn & Bacon, Inc., Needham Heights, MA.

TEACHER ←→ STUDENT
INTERACTIONS

The Sensorimotor Period

1. Piaget believed that infants learn about other human beings from the way they are treated from birth.
   - A parent's or daycare provider's face is the most exciting plaything an infant experiences. It changes, makes noises, and responds to the baby. Use pictures of faces in magazines, photographs, or even circles with features drawn on them to help infants respond positively to those around them.
   - Talk to infants, not at them. We have learned that infants find adult speech, properly used, one of the most stimulating parts of their environment.
2. We now know that children are active processors of information from birth.
   - Since newborns can see to a distance of only about 10 inches, place objects such as mobiles and rattles within that range.
   - Have them look at colorful objects with high contrast (red, black and white, navy and white).
   - Infants will move their hands toward an object as their eyes go back and forth between the object and their hands. Hang a soft animal or a cloth ball within their range to attract their attention and stimulate movement.
3. Infants use their bodily actions to discover cause and effect relationships.
   - Use toys that are fun to touch for their texture but that also make noises when squeezed or shaken.
   - Towards the end of the first year, use real toys or plastic cups of varying sizes, wooden spoons, or measuring spoons so infants can learn how things work. For example, encourage them to stack the cups and discover the difference in sound when they bang the wooden or metal spoons.

as compared to the solid front and back—these actions all further cognitive development.

The Preoperational Period

When Piaget refers to **operations** (as in the term **preoperational**), he means actions that we perform mentally in order to gain knowledge (Ginsburg & Opper, 1988). To know an object is to act on it. You mentally compare it, change it, and then return it to its original state. Piaget (in Ripple & Rockcastle, 1964) stated that *knowledge is not just a mental image of an object or event.* It is not enough to look at it, to picture it. You must modify the object; that is, you do something to it.

You compare it with other similar objects, noting similarities and differences; you place it in a particular order;

you measure it; you take it apart and then put it back together. Piaget believed that mental objects are reversible; that is, you can think in opposite directions: you add, but you can also subtract; you join things mentally, but you can also separate them. For example, if 2 is added to 2, the result is 4; but if 2 is taken away from 4, the original 2 returns.

Preoperational, then, refers to a child who has begun to use symbols but is not yet capable of mentally manipulating them. Children who cannot take something apart and put it together again, who cannot return to the beginning of a thought sequence (that is, who cannot comprehend how to reverse the action of 2 + 2), who cannot believe that water poured from a short, fat glass into a taller, thinner one retains the same volume—these children are at a level of thinking that precedes operational thought.

By approximately two years of age, when children are making the transition from the sensorimotor period, they use language constantly and give discernible signs of their growing symbolic ability. Between approximately two and seven years of age, children pass through the preoperational period.

Features of Preoperational Thought

The Ability to Represent. For Piaget, the great accomplishment of the preoperational period is a growing ability to *represent,* which is the manner in which we record or express information. For example, the word *car* is a representation since it represents a certain idea. Pointing an index finger at a playmate and saying "Stick 'em up" is also an example of representation. Although symbolic activity steadily develops during the preoperational period, several important limitations still exist.

Centering, or concentrating on only part of an object or activity. Children ignore the relationship among the various parts. Recall Piaget's experiment with the tokens. When the tokens were spread out, preoperational children could not relate space to number.

Egocentrism, a central characteristic of the preoperational as well as the sensorimotor period. For preoperational children things can be only as they want them; other opinions are meaningless. Kenny Wilson in the chapter opener is a good example of this type of thinking. The moon was following *him* around; everything focused on him.

Irreversibility, or the inability to reverse one's thinking. Preschoolers cannot return to the original premise. They may have learned 2 + 2 = 4, but they cannot yet grasp that 4 − 2 = 2.

Between the ages of two and seven, children are starting to recognize that there's a world out there that exists independently of them. Recognizing the abilities of young children and their cognitive limitations that we have just discussed, we can identify the following features of preoperational thought: realism, animism, artificialism, and transductive reasoning.

Realism, slowly distinguishing, and accepting, a real world, thus identifying both an external and internal world. Piaget believes that youngsters initially confuse internal and external; they confuse thought and matter. The confusion disappears at about seven years of age. For example, a young child who is jealous of a new born sibling gradually realizes that parents "can't take it back."

Animism, considering as alive and conscious a large number of objects that adults consider inert. For example, a child who sees a necklace wound up and then released explains that it is moving because it "wants to unwind." Children overcome this cognitive limitation as they recognize their own personalities. They then refuse to accept personality in things. Piaget believes that comparison with the thoughts of others—social intercourse—slowly conquers animism as it does egocentrism. Piaget identifies four stages of animism:

a. almost everything is alive and conscious;
b. only those things that move are alive;
c. only those things that manifest spontaneous movements are alive;
d. consciousness is limited to the animal world.

Artificialism, assumption that everything is the product of human creation. For example, when asked how the moon began, some of Piaget's subjects replied, "because we began to be alive." As egocentrism decreases, youngsters become more objective, and they steadily assimilate objective reality to their cognitive structures. They proceed from a purely human or divine explanation to an explanation that is half natural, half artificial: the moon comes from the clouds, but the clouds come from people's houses. Finally, at about nine years of age they realize that human activity has nothing to do with the origin of the moon. (Realism and artificialism are examples of both the abilities and limitations of preoperational thought that we previously mentioned. The decline of artificialism is paralleled by the growth of realism.)

Transductive Reasoning, reasoning that is neither deductive nor inductive; rather it is from particular to particular—and is quite characteristic of preschool children. The following are examples of transductive reasoning:

The sun won't fall down because it's hot.

The sun stops there because it's yellow.

TEACHER ◀▶ STUDENT INTERACTIONS

The Preoperational Child

1. Children learn through active explorations and interactions with adults, other children, and materials.
   - Teachers of kindergartners can help them to make short story books such as "What 's on My Street?" Use vocabulary words that they have already learned and have them illustrate their stories. Then have the children take their stories home and read them aloud to their parents.
   - Toward the end of the preoperational period, when teaching a unit like the solar system to second graders, have the children play the role of the planets, the satellites, and the sun. Cut large circles in poster board, label them, and attach a string so that the students can hang them around their necks, indicating what they are. The students can then act out their roles.
2. Piaget believed that the great accomplishment of the preoperational period is a growing ability to represent.
   - Encourage students to put things in the order in which they see them to help with their reading.
   - Put a series of circles and lines on the board. Give students a few minutes to study the sequence; then erase it. Have them write the circles and lines in the same sequence on their papers.
   - Have one child dress to go outdoors and have that child put on boots, a hat, a coat, and mittens. Then tell a second child to dress in exactly the same way as the first child did. Have the rest of the group do the same thing.
   - Provide opportunities for students to tell jokes. They like to do this, and it promotes socialization, improves memory, and aids pragmatic skills.
3. Be aware of the egocentrism of preoperational pupils.
   - Have students play games such as *Simon Says* in which they learn that they can't always be the winner.
   - Rotate special, and usually desired, duties such as *Teacher's Helper* so that students learn that they must take turns.

Educational Implications

Certain activities typical of preoperational children reflect their use of internal representation (Piaget & Inhelder, 1969):

1. *Deferred imitation.* Preoperational children can imitate some object or activity that they have previously witnessed; for example, they walk like an animal that they saw at the zoo earlier in the day.

Conservation During the concrete operational stage, the child exhibits conservation. The child comes to realize that changing the form of something does not change its amount. In a classic demonstration used by Piaget, a child is shown two containers holding equal amounts of liquid. When the fluid in one container is poured into a tall, narrow container, the preoperational child will believe that container contains more fluid than the short, wide container. In contrast, the concrete operational child realizes that both containers hold the same amount of fluid.

2. *Symbolic play.* Children enjoy pretending that they are asleep, or that they are someone or something else.
3. *Drawing.* Children of this age project their mental representations into their drawings. Highly symbolic, their art work reflects the level of their thinking and what they are thinking. Encourage children to talk about their art.
4. *Mental images.* Preoperational children can represent objects and events, but they cannot change or anticipate change in their thinking. Recall Piaget's experiment with the five-year-old who thought there were more tokens in a row when they were spaced farther apart.
5. *Language.* For preoperational children, language becomes a vehicle for thought. Let them have ample opportunities to talk with you and with each other.

The Concrete Operational Period

Children at the concrete operational stage demonstrate striking differences in their thinking compared to children at the preoperational stage. Between seven and eleven or twelve years, children overcome the limitations of preoperational thinking and accomplish true mental operations. Now students can reverse their thinking and group objects into classes.

The transition from preoperations to concrete operations is a transition from subjective centering to a cognitive, social, and moral decentering (Piaget & Inhelder, 1969). There are still limitations at the concrete operations stage, however. Children can perform mental operations only on concrete (tangible) objects or events and not on verbal statements. For example, if they are shown blocks A, B, and C, concrete operational children can tell you that A is larger than B, that B is larger than C; and that, therefore, A is largest of all. But if you tell them that

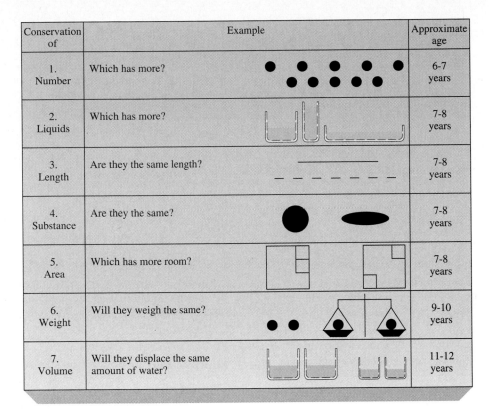

Conservation of	Example		Approximate age
1. Number	Which has more?		6-7 years
2. Liquids	Which has more?		7-8 years
3. Length	Are they the same length?		7-8 years
4. Substance	Are they the same?		7-8 years
5. Area	Which has more room?		7-8 years
6. Weight	Will they weigh the same?		9-10 years
7. Volume	Will they displace the same amount of water?		11-12 years

Figure 3.2
Different kinds of conservation appear at different ages.

Liz is taller than Ellen, who is taller than Jane, they cannot tell you who is tallest of all (especially in the early years of the period). These results explain why Piaget designated the period "concrete operations."

Features of Concrete Operational Thought

Several notable accomplishments mark the period:

1. **Conservation,** or the realization that the essence of something remains constant although surface features may change. In Piaget's famous water jar problem, children observe two identical jars filled to the same height. While they watch, the contents of one container are poured into a taller and thinner jar so that the liquid reaches a higher level. By the age of seven most children will state that the contents are still equal; they **conserved** the idea of equal amounts of water by decentering; that is, by focusing on more than one aspect of the problem. They can now reverse their thinking; they can mentally pour the water back into the original container.

    Different types of conservation appear at different times during the concrete operational period as Figure 3.2 shows.

Piaget (1973) believed that youngsters use three arguments to conserve:

a. *The argument of identity.* The concrete operational child says that since no water has been removed or added to either jar, it is still the "same thing." By eight years of age, children are amused by the problem, not realizing that a year earlier they probably would have given a different answer.
b. *The argument of reversibility.* Concrete operational children state that you just have to pour the water back and it is the "same thing."
c. *The argument of compensation.* Concrete operational children will say that the water is higher in the taller beaker, but that it is narrower. That is, these youngsters compensate for the height increase by noting the circumference decrease and realize that it is the "same thing."

2. **Seriation,** or the ability to arrange objects by increasing or decreasing size. As we noted above, concrete operational children can arrange concrete objects, such as blocks. If, however, the operation is in pure language, such as the word problem mentioned above comparing the heights of three

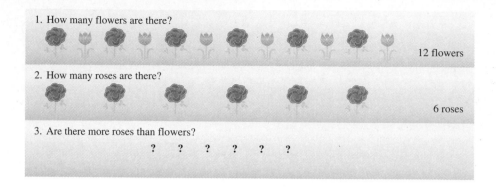

Figure 3.3
Classification.

girls, it becomes more complicated, and the concrete operational child cannot solve it.

3. **Classification,** or the ability to group objects with some similarities within a larger category. If a preoperational child is shown a picture of six roses and six tulips, the child will be able to answer correctly questions about the number of tulips and the number of roses, but when asked "Are there more roses than flowers?" the child will answer "Roses." The concrete operational child, however, is able to classify both roses and tulips as flowers. See Figure 3.3.

In a classic experiment illustrating mastery of classification, Piaget showed children at both the preoperational and the concrete operational levels 20 wooden beads, 16 of which were brown and four of which were white. When he asked, "Are there more brown beads than wooden beads?" the preoperational children typically answered "Brown" while the older children answered correctly.

4. **Number concept,** which is not the same as the ability to count. As Piaget's experiment with the two rows of tokens showed, even though the preoperational child can count, one isn't always one. When the five tokens in one row were spread out, the child was convinced that it contained more than five tokens. Only after children acquire the concepts of seriation and classification will they be able to understand the "oneness of one"—that one boy, one girl, one apple, and one orange are all one of something.

These thought systems of the concrete operational child gradually come into a well-organized equilibrium, which Piaget refers to as **cognitive operations.** When children reach this phase of cognitive development, they are on the threshold of adult thought, or formal operations.

Middle childhood students have experienced an intellectual revolution. Their thinking has become logical and more abstract, their attention improves, and memory becomes more efficient as they develop new strategies.

Educational Implications

Piaget's concrete operational level signals readiness for increasingly abstract tasks that youngsters face in elementary school. The ability to read and translate symbols reaches across the curriculum into almost all subjects. Reading ability largely determines academic success or failure.

Are youngsters capable of meeting the problems they face? Yes and no. They can assimilate and accommodate the material they encounter but at their level. Elementary school youngsters up to the age of 10 or 11 are capable of representational thought but only with the concrete, the tangible. Consequently, we cannot expect them to comprehend fully any abstract subtleties.

The Formal Operational Period

According to Piaget, the **formal operational** period, during which the beginnings of logical, abstract thinking appears, commences at about 11 or 12 years. During this period, youngsters demonstrate an ability to reason realistically about the future and consider possibilities that they actually doubt. Teenagers look for relations; they separate the real from the possible; they test their mental solutions to problems; they feel comfortable with verbal statements (Manaster, 1989). In short, the period's great achievement is a release from the restrictions of the tangible and the concrete (Ginsburg & Opper, 1988).

Piaget and Inhelder (1969) sum up the difference between concrete operations and formal operations with an example from their research: when younger children

The Concrete Operational Child

1. Since concrete operational students can conserve, reverse their thinking and classify, begin to have them compare, contrast, and classify, using materials that offer hands-on learning.
   - Have them construct objects or replicas of events they have studied and relate them to their reading. Ask them to write about their experiences, and then discuss the topic with them and their classmates. In short, constantly blend the concrete with the abstract to develop a readiness for increasingly abstract material.
   - Have your students design floats made from shoeboxes about the states (or countries) they are studying. Print the state's motto on the side of the float. On separate pieces of paper, have each student illustrate the specific state, including the state's emblem. Have them prepare an outline of the state's outstanding features.
2. Provide opportunities for students to develop classification skills.
   - Have students play a classification game by pairing common household objects like a knife and a fork, a towel and a bar of soap, a toothbrush and toothpaste, a brush and comb. Include some pairs that are obvious and some less so. Have one pair for each child. Spread all objects on a table. Let each student have a turn at choosing two items that belong together. Have them explain why they grouped the objects as they did.
   - Celebrate with a "food fest" in social studies. Assign two students to explore research materials about a particular country, perhaps the country from which their family originated. Locate recipes and types of food. Enlist the parents' help to cook the food. Make decorations, costumes, and provide music for your celebration.
   - Have students break down all the activities they engage in during the week. Now work with them to develop categories—such as Home, School, Play— and have them put their activities in the appropriate categories.
3. Concrete operational students are able to reverse their thinking.
   - Use origami techniques (Japanese paperfolding) to have students design shapes (such as birds and flowers). Then ask them how they would get back to the original shape of the paper.
   - Look at an island on a map. Tell students that they can fly there, but that their plane becomes disabled. How would they return?

were asked to assume that coal is white, they replied that coal has to be black, whereas adolescents accepted the unreal assumption and reasoned from it.

Another of Piaget's experiments demonstrated the difference in reasoning strategies between concrete operations and formal operations. Upper elementary school children and adolescents were presented with five jars containing colorless liquids and asked to find the combination of liquids that would produce a yellow color. The concrete operational children combined two jars and then tried them all together. The adolescents systematically tried various combinations of all jars and quickly discovered that jars A, C, and E would produce yellow (jar B contained bleach and jar A contained water).

Students at the formal operational stage usually can function effectively at the level of hypotheses, utilizing propositions that are independent of immediate concrete observations. Piaget and Inhelder (1969) believe that the adolescent's emerging abilities signal the establishment of a new group of structures. Until this period, logical thinking depended on concrete material, not on the manipulation of hypotheses, which is now the case. Remember, though, that some students at this level may still be concrete operational or only into the initial stages of formal operations. Many adolescents have just consolidated their concrete operational thinking and continue to use it consistently. Unless they find themselves in situations that demand formal operational thinking (science, math), they will continue to be concrete operational thinkers. For example, estimates are that only about 1 in 3 young adolescents think at the formal operational level (Santrock, 1992). With these students you must continue to blend concrete and abstract materials.

Another interesting feature of adolescent thought is what Elkind (1981) refers to as **adolescent egocentric thinking.** He states that adolescents assume that everyone else thinks as they do and shares their concerns. This is a result of the changes occurring in their bodies and their sensitivity to others, which leads to intense concentration on themselves. "But why is everyone looking at me?" They thus create an **imaginative audience.**

Features of Formal Operational Thought

There are several essential features of formal operational thinking:

1. *The adolescent's ability to separate the real from the possible,* which distinguishes the concrete operational from the formal operational child. The adolescent tries to discern all possible relations in any situation or problem and then, by mental experimentation and logical analysis, attempts to

discover which are true. Flavell (1963) notes that there is nothing trivial in the adolescent's accomplishment; it is a basic and essential reorganization of thought processes that permits the adolescent to exist in the world of the possible.

2. *The adolescent's thinking is propositional,* which means that the adolescent uses not only concrete data but also statements or propositions that contain the concrete data. Dealing with abstract concepts no longer frustrates them. For example, a history teacher can ask a class, "What were the real reasons for our struggle with the Japanese in World War II?" and expect that the students will be able to respond.

3. *The adolescent attacks a problem* by gathering as much information as possible and then making all the possible combinations of the variables that he/she can. Adolescents proceed as follows. *First,* they organize data by concrete operational techniques (classification, seriation). *Second,* they use the results of concrete operational techniques to form statements or propositions. *Third,* they combine as many of these propositions as possible (These are hypotheses, and Piaget often refers to this process as hypothetico-deductive thinking.) *Fourth,* they then test to determine which combinations are true.

Educational Implications

When we turn to the classroom, we can see the practical applications of Piaget's work. Teachers can aid their students' cognitive development by analyzing their content (what they do), which enables instructors to infer the type of underlying cognitive structure and then utilize methods and materials that will help their students to assimilate and accommodate. If you recall Piaget's statement that children construct their own world, then students must manipulate material as much as possible.

Although most adolescents are comfortable with these materials and activities, teachers should be careful not to exaggerate their abilities. Provide as many concrete examples as you think are necessary before attempting to have them formulate general principles.

Try to discover how students sequence materials and activities so that you can match their developmental levels. The activities should challenge a student's thinking but should not be so difficult as to frustrate and cause failure. Students should concentrate upon the activities, and not the teacher, thus permitting the teacher more time to observe and to guide.

TEACHER ◄──► STUDENT
I N T E R A C T I O N S

The Formal Operational Period

1. Formal operational students can engage in propositional thinking.
   - Teachers can now use verbal materials in their instruction. After presenting the basic facts about the end of the Cold War have the students adopt pro and con positions about the actual causes.
   - Set up debating teams; have students act as the political or military leaders of the times.
2. Adolescents gather as much information as possible about a problem.
   - Ask your students to list what they think are the major environmental problems of advanced technology: nuclear waste disposal, nuclear weapons, air and water pollution, energy shortages, depletion of natural resources.
   - Now ask students how many of these problems affect all nations. How does the fact that nations share these problems illustrate our interdependence?
3. Formal operational students can generate many possible solutions to problems.
   - Ask your students how THEY could actively participate in solving some of the problems discussed above.
   - Discuss with your students how things would be different today if the following imaginary event had occurred:
     a) In 1492, Christopher Columbus sailed west into an area known as the Bermuda Triangle and mysteriously disappeared.
     b) Martin Luther King was not assassinated in 1968.
     c) George Washington proclaimed himself as King of America instead of the first president.

Criticisms of Piaget

Although Piaget has left a monumental legacy, his ideas have not been unchallenged. Piaget was a believer in the stage theory of development. That is, development is seen as a sequence of distinct stages, each of which entails important changes in the way a child thinks, feels, and behaves (Scarr et al., 1986).

Rest (1983) argues that the acquisition of cognitive structures is gradual rather than abrupt and is not a matter of all-or-nothing; for example, a child is not completely in the preoperational or concrete operational stage. A child's level of cognitive development seems to depend more on the nature of the task than on a rigid classification system.

In a wide-ranging review of hundreds of studies that have tested Piaget's ideas, Gelman and Baillargeon (1983) also question the idea of broad stages of development, although they support the notion of cognitive structures that assimilate and accommodate the environment. The idea of stages with no overlap seems to lack empirical evidence to support it.

In a typical Piagetian experiment, a doll was placed at different positions around a model of three mountains, and children were asked how the mountains look at each position. Children under six reported their own view and not the doll's. Yet when Gelman and Baillargeon (1983) showed cards with a different picture on each side to three-year-old children, the children correctly reported what they saw and what the tester would see.

Can preschoolers be trained to accomplish a concrete operational task? In a classic experiment, Gelman (1969) worked with five-year-olds who had failed to conserve number, length, and liquid amount. She trained the children to focus on the relevant relations (teaching them to attend to rows of sticks of equal length, for example). Following this training, when the children were asked to select rows of equal length sticks, they chose correctly. They were later able to transfer this ability to other Piagetian conservation tasks.

Although this study shows that preschoolers are probably more cognitively competent than their failure on concrete operational tasks suggests, we may well question whether these five-year-olds might have been on the verge of concrete operations and if the training Gelman offered "pushed" them into concrete operational thought. Summarizing Gelman's work, we can say: structures, yes; stages, no.

Scarr, Weinberg, and Levine (1986) offer a modification: structures, yes; approximate stages, yes. There probably are cognitive stages but especially in the beginning or the middle of the stage, children may not consistently demonstrate all the stage's characteristics. For example, they may understand conservation of liquid but not conservation of number. Even if stages may not be as dramatically different and clearly defined as in Piaget's model, cognitive structures do change and "the idea of stages is useful in identifying these major mental reorganizations" (Scarr et al., 1986, p. 355).

Piaget Across Cultures

Piaget's work has been criticized because it was done with middle-class Swiss children. Consequently, we may ask if Piaget's ideas cross cultures. On this point, there are mixed reviews.

Children from different cultures show different rates for acquiring different concepts. Eskimo children, for example, develop spatial concepts more rapidly than Ivory Coast African children. But African farm children acquire conservation of quantity, weight, and volume more quickly than children from other societies. We know that children acquire concepts that their society values more quickly than they acquire concepts that are of little value to their society.

Most cross-cultural research has attempted to discover if children develop and use cognitive structures and the sequence of developmental stages that Piaget outlined (Bullinger & Chatillon, 1983). Results indicate that almost all children demonstrate behavior that confirms the sensorimotor and preoperational stages. Many adolescents and adults of non-Western cultures, however, do not demonstrate concrete and/or formal operational behavior (Fischer & Silvern, 1985). But the tests of cognitive functioning may be at fault because they were designed for Western European children. While almost all adults in Geneva, Paris, London, and New York display concrete operational thinking on conservation tasks, many adults in Third World capitals do not (Stigler, et al., 1990). Tests that use culturally familiar tasks yield findings of concrete and formal operational behavior.

In their thoughtful commentary on the relationship between culture and thought, Cole and Scribner (1974) conclude that there are no cultural differences in basic component cognitive processes. No cultural group lacks a basic process such as abstraction. What appears to differ is the involvement of a given process in performance.

For example, studies conducted with 3- and 4-year-olds in Britain and Iran about knowledge of their neighborhoods showed no differences in accuracy but differences in style of reporting. Iranian children were more pictorial. Studies comparing sentence integration strategies used by 2- and 5-year-old American and Italian children showed that although Americans relied on word order, the Italian youngsters used semantic cues (Segal, 1986). A review of the major Piagetian studies of cognitive development in several African nations provides evidence of the impact of cultural factors upon the testing situation (Malone, 1984). For example, African children who have gone to school show more advanced cognitive development on Piagetian tests than do children who have not attended school because schools:

- emphasize the search for general rules,
- rely heavily on verbal instructions,

- teach specific skills intended to obtain specific information, and
- teach literacy (Rogoff, 1981).

We must know more about how tasks are interpreted in light of cultural variables before we can reach definite conclusions about the universality of Piaget's ideas.

For the Classroom

Piaget (1971) insisted that the essential functions of intelligence consist of understanding and inventing. Our students build cognitive structures by structuring reality. Preschool children, for example, may have had some experience with numbers (perhaps from a TV show such as *Sesame Street*). Parents and teachers have shown them two apples, two spoons, two shoes. By "operating" on twos (actually touching, moving, comparing the sets of two), they form the cognitive structure of twoness. It is, however, a limited structure. The preoperational child gradually learns that putting 2 twos together produces 4. Getting back to 2, however, poses an obstacle since subtraction requires **reversibility,** which the child is not yet cognitively mature enough to accomplish.

A secondary school student, however, not only knows needed facts but can use them. If you ask high school pupils, once they have developed the cognitive structures necessary for understanding the Civil War, to describe what might have happened to the Union Army without Ulysses S. Grant, they have little difficulty in reversing. That is, they can "remove" Grant and invent new outcomes for the various battles. Their cognitive development permits them not only to understand abstract facts but, using these facts, also to invent and to suggest hypothetical variations. Thus, your students will gain knowledge *not* from copying reality but from *acting* on it.

Knowledge of Piaget's theory helps you to assess the level of a student's cognitive development. By observing your students closely you can link behavior to cognitive level and utilize appropriate subject matter. For example, curriculum planners can profit from Piaget's findings by attempting to answer two questions. Are there ideal times for the teaching of certain subjects? Is there an ideal sequence for a subject that matches Piaget's sequence of cognitive development?

Piaget's work provides data for the formulation of optimal learning conditions. For example, during the first two periods (sensorimotor and preoperational) youngsters should constantly interact physically with their environment. During the concrete operational period students should be able to use as many tangible objects as possible.

Finally, adolescents should encounter verbal problems, master learning strategies, and test their solutions. Remember:

- Piaget always insisted that his was an interactionist system; students must "operate" on curricular materials. For example, adolescents with reading problems must have materials that are appealing and actively involve them in skill development and comprehension.
- Carefully consider how much direction and guidance each of your pupils needs. A youngster who has a language problem requires prompt assistance to prevent a persistent speech deficit. But a student who has the necessary formula to solve a math problem should be permitted to make a few mistakes and to discover the correct solution rather than being told.
- Be careful concerning the materials that you use. If you encourage interactive learning, what you have your students "operate on" must be appropriate for them physically (can they physically manipulate the materials?) and cognitively (can they understand what they are supposed to do?).
- Use instructional strategies appropriate to your students' ethnic and racial backgrounds (Ornstein & Levine, 1982). For example, studies of Hispanic students have shown that they tend to be **field-sensitive;** that is, they are influenced by personal relationships and praise or disapproval from authority figures. Pueblo Indian children from the American Southwest show higher achievement when instruction utilizes their "primary learning" patterns (those that occur outside the classroom). These students respond well when instruction incorporates the concerns and needs of the community. For example, measuring the amount of rainfall (in inches) per year and relating it to crop production can be used in math classes.

Cognitive Development and AIDS Prevention

Piaget's ideas on cognitive development have also been used to formulate programs in related fields, such as health and AIDS prevention. For example, Walsh and Bibace (1990, 1991) have proposed a developmentally-based program that attempts to educate, not merely inform, students about the reality of AIDS. Knowledge about AIDS is growing, but information is not education and does not induce behavioral change.

One method of reaching school children has been suggested by Walsh and Bibace (1990, 1991). Arguing that the schools will inevitably be drawn into the struggle to contain the spread of AIDS, these researchers urge that

HIV/AIDS programs be included at every school level. To be most effective, such programs should be developmentally-based since children understand themselves and their world according to their level of cognitive development. Even with this caution, program designers should remember that not all students of the same age are at the same level of cognitive development.

One technique for designing an AIDS education program is to base its content and methodology on the processes children use to develop their ideas of illness. Three types of explanation have been identified by Walsh and Bibace (1990).

1. *Explanations based on association.* Here children describe an illness according to specific, external situations with which they have linked the sickness. It is a highly personal explanation in which they pay little attention to the cause of an illness. "You know; it's poison ivy, that itchy stuff. It comes by magic."

2. *Explanations based on sequence.* Here children's explanations include both internal and external symptoms, and they tend to identify something concrete, often "bad" that caused the illness. They realize that this bad something can appear in a variety of situations; thus they now have the ability to generalize their conclusions. Their explanations also include a mechanism or sequence of events to explain the cause: "You know, Billy touched those bushes and then he got that itchy rash;" "Of course Maddy got sick; she got wet in the rain and stayed outside in wet clothes to play. The cold got on her and went inside her nose and throat, and now she's sneezing all over the place."

3. *Explanations based on interactions.* Children describe illness as a bodily malfunction whose ultimate outcome depends on the interplay of a variety of factors: time, body condition, medical care, and environmental conditions. "When you touch a poison ivy plant, it leaves an oil trace on your body or clothes. The oil gets into your skin and causes a rash to appear; it makes little blisters that break; and then the itch hits you. Remember: Leaves of three; leave them be."

Children seem to follow a similar pattern in understanding AIDS. For example, Walsh and Bibace (1990) state that young children (about four or five years old) remain quite egocentric, with a tendency to focus on external events and don't show much concern for cause and effect. They define AIDS by something with which they are familiar. It's a "bad" sickness and anyone who is seriously ill can have AIDS. Those working with children at this level should be concerned with the fears that they

have about the illness. Reassurance and correcting any erroneous views are probably the best technique to use.

Children who are older and at a concrete level of cognitive development (about seven to eleven years) can differentiate more accurately and interpret AIDS according to specific bodily symptoms. They initially interpret cause in concrete terms: "A bug caused it;" "Using someone else's straw." Later at this level, they begin to describe the cause of AIDS in a more sequential manner: "A bug gets inside your blood, infects you, makes you sick, and then you die." Those working with children at this level should appeal to their ability to make distinctions: for example, doing drugs with dirty needles can transmit the virus.

Older children (11 years+) are capable of more complex thinking and can understand the possibility that many interacting elements may be at work in disease. For example, they realize that AIDS may be caused by sex and/or dirty needles, but that those behaviors may not always cause AIDS (Walsh & Bibace, 1990). Individuals working with children at this level can appeal to their more abstract thinking ability to explain modes of transmission. Table 3.3 summarizes the basics of a developmentally-based AIDS/HIV educational program.

Such a program goes a long way to answering a pertinent question raised by Quackenbush and Villarreal (1988): What do you need to know to talk about AIDS? As these authors note, to be comfortable in discussing this sensitive topic with students you need familiarity with the following:

- Child development. You should be prepared to give appropriate answers to their questions about health, personal relationships, and sexuality. Appropriate in this sense means the type of discussion or program based on the ideas suggested by Walsh and Bibace (1990).
- Basic AIDS information. To answer students' questions accurately, you need to be knowledgeable about the transmission, prevention, and path of AIDS. In other words, before you shape your answers to a child's cognitive level, you need to have mastered the fundamental information so that you don't either overinform or misinform.
- The types of questions that students of different ages and stages will ask. For example, "What is AIDS?" "How do people get AIDS?" "What does 'sharing needles' mean?" (For an excellent overview of this topic see Quackenbush and Villarreal, 1988, pp. 27–42.)
- Timing. You should know a student(s) well enough to realize when the time is right to introduce the topic and how much time is needed for adequate coverage.

Table 3.3

Developmentally-Based AIDS/HIV Education

	Younger Children (5-7)	Intermediate Children (8-10)	Older Children (11++)
Fear	Vague fears; need reassurance from authority figures about their non-vulnerability	Concrete fears; need strategies for excluding potential causes; need concrete information about noncauses	Healthy fear; need specifics of biological mechanisms underlying causes and preventive behavior
Cause	Unconcerned with cause	Preoccupied with discrete causes; need list of noncauses; not concerned with details of mode of transmission	Understand body systems; detailed biological explanations of various causes and mechanisms of transmission helpful
Prevention	Unconcerned with prevention	Beginning concept of prevention; introduce notion of prevention across many illnesses including AIDS; broad categories of preventive behavior	Understand prevention; need detailed biological explanations of preventive behavior and conditions under which it operates and which affect use

From M. E. Walsh and R. Bibace, "Developmentally-based AIDS/HIV Education" in *Journal of School Health*, 60: 256-261, 1990. Copyright, 1990. American School Health Association, Kent, Ohio 44240. Reprinted by permission.

Alternatives to Piaget

As you can well imagine, other cognitive theorists have offered insights into cognitive development that offer different emphases and different interpretations. Those advocating an information processing perspective believe that cognitive development is better understood by breaking down a child's solution to a problem into small, detailed steps. Kurt Fischer (Fischer & Silvern, 1985), for example, proposed an elaborate theory of cognitive development from infancy to adulthood that encompasses ten stages: three at the sensorimotor level, three at the representational level, and four at the abstract level. Unlike Piaget, however, Fischer believes that development is much more uneven than previously realized.

Another theorist who has elaborated on Piaget's ideas is Robbie Case (1985). Believing that development proceeds by the use of ever improving cognitive strategies, Case relies on a construct called the **M-space,** or mental space. Essentially a memory concept, the M-space holds the number of schemes that a student has available for a specific task. As these schemes are used more and more frequently and with increasing age, they become more automatic and free up more M-space. This increase in memory capacity is the major mechanism for cognitive development. The *total* capacity for memory does not change, but the *available* capacity at any time can increase because of more efficient functioning (Miller, 1989).

Changes in cognitive development occur as children find themselves in problem situations. Relying on what Case calls executive control structures, children identify goals and the strategies needed to reach the goals by using their innate processing abilities. That is, children determine what is needed to solve the problem, activate appropriate mental structures, and then evaluate the results. For example, in solving a word problem, children may decide that they must find the cost of one orange by applying their knowledge of division, then multiply by the number of oranges that the problem calls for. Once students learn to apply their mathematical knowledge automatically, they can go on to more difficult problems.

As you see, Piaget has had a great influence on other cognitive theorists, and his ideas on cognitive development have had wide impact. Piaget has also proposed a theory of language development. Before we examine his and other theories of language development, however, let's first trace the path by which children acquire language.

Language Development

From the first random sounds, to the precise and direct expressions of the first grader, to the sophisticated conversation of the teenager, language offers definite clues to personality, intelligence, education, and occupation. For example, an infant's cries may betray fear or discomfort. (Today's advanced technology offers hope that analysis of crying will lead to the early detection of emotional difficulties.)

By the time children reach the age of six, you can expect them to exhibit language mastery and to use language to control their environment. Instead of leaving the table, walking to the refrigerator, and taking out the milk, they may simply ask someone else to do it for them.

We take language acquisition for granted, but closer inspection of this accomplishment testifies to the enormity of the task. Children seem to be programmed to talk and to use all forms of language to adjust to their environment. The form that the particular language takes—whether English, Arabic, or Chinese—is incidental. From birth, children tune into the language that they hear around them and feed these sounds into their unique ability to master language.

Language Accomplishments

When children acquire a language, they learn a code; they use symbols (letters, words, sentences) to represent the people, objects, and events in their environment. These symbols are arbitrary; for example, American children learn *book,* French youngsters learn *livre,* and Spanish children learn *libro.* Each child will learn the word for *book* at approximately the same time, however. What varies from culture to culture is the symbol used to represent the object, person, or idea.

Children quickly master this code (not just the words but the grammar, such as plurals and past and future tenses). They soon learn that only certain sounds form certain words and that these words form sentences according to a definite and prescribed set of rules. In other words, without actual instruction, children realize that there are elaborate rules that dictate what sounds can be combined and how words can be combined.

For example, adults often ask about what is "normal" in the child's speech development. Experts in speech and language development believe that "normal" is actually a range of performance. Eisenson (1986) summarized some broad implications from questions frequently asked about normal development.

- Children should begin to understand things said to them between the ages of six to nine months (unless some handicap is present).
- Most children who are going to talk will say their first word by fifteen months; some, however, will speak as early as eight or nine months.
- Within a few months after children have begun to develop a naming or labeling vocabulary, they will usually begin using some of the words to make things happen. For example, a child may say "wawa" to request a drink of water.

Children acquire the basics of their language easily and continue to refine it, using language to adapt to and control their environment.

- Once children have achieved a vocabulary of 50–60 words as labels or demands, they usually can combine them into two-word statements. This ability typically occurs by eighteen months.
- Children's comprehension of language exceeds their ability to speak, and this feature of language continues throughout life.

If you listen carefully to young children speak, you will rarely hear a sentence duplicated. The symbols (the sounds and the words) are relatively limited, but the rules facilitate almost unlimited combinations. What is remarkable is how quickly children master these complex rules. Children at an early age demonstrate two innovative accomplishments:

1. They master word order.

   Daddy came home.

Here we see subject, predicate, and object, and tense is also indicated.

2. Once they acquire word order, youngsters begin to vary the elements. That is, they convey identical meanings but shift or change the elements. For example, the following sentences are slightly different, but the meaning remains unchanged.

   The man wound up the clock.

   The man wound the clock up.

When linguists examine a language, they identify four major components:

1. sound, or **phonology**
2. meaning, or **semantics**
3. grammar, or **syntax**
4. use, or **pragmatics**

Every language possesses certain distinctive, fundamental sounds, which are the **phonemes** of that language. These are the smallest language unit. For example, the words thin and shin sound alike, but the initial sounds differ sufficiently so as to distinguish the words, thus qualifying the initial sounds as phonemes.

The smallest unit of language to have meaning is the **morpheme.** Morphemes may be whole words or a part of a word that signifies meaning—er, ed, ing. The word older has two morphemes: old signifying age and er signifying comparison. Morphemes are composed of a series of phonemes (the morpheme "er" consists of two phonemes, while "old" consists of three phonemes).

Morphemes are arranged in the grammar or **syntax** of a language. The task of any syntax is to arrange morphemes in meaningful sentences. Grammatical studies have repeatedly shown that any speaker can say and any listener can understand an infinite number of sentences.

Grammar seems to be designed to convert ideas into word combinations. The relationship between ideas and words is the source of meaning or **semantics.** To integrate language elements, children must be able to represent various kinds of knowledge to combine them, and to evaluate their relevance in context (Shatz, 1983).

Children must also learn how to use their language, a concept which brings us to the development of **pragmatic** skills. Language is a remarkably sophisticated developmental accomplishment, one part of which is the success children have in making their communication clear. A snatch of a bedtime conversation between a father and small daughter demonstrates the complexity of language:

> Father: "——and then Trina (the canine heroine of his impromptu narrative) was chased by another dog. I wonder what happened next."
>
> Girl: "I know—the dog catched her!" (Flavell, 1985, p. 243).

What language skills has that little girl already acquired? *First,* she shows considerable phonological development. But it's more than knowing the sounds of a language. She also shows that her language is both innovative and rule-governed. *Second,* her speech shows evidence of linguistic meaning. She knows how concepts and relationships can be expressed by words and word combinations. For example, she knows that "chase" implies more than "run." Or that the "I" her father uses does not refer to the same "I" that she uses. *Third,* the child has a striking knowledge of grammar. She knows that word order and word formation give clues to word meaning. For example, she realizes it was not Trina that did the chasing. *Fourth,* she understands the pragmatics of language. She knows that her speech must flow with that of others to engage in reasonable conversation.

All children, no matter what their native tongue, manifest similar patterns of language development. The basic sequence of language acquisition is as follows:

- *at about 3 months* children use intonations similar to those of adults;
- *at about 1 year* they begin to use recognizable words;
- *at about 4 years* they have acquired the complicated structure of their native tongue;
- *at about 6 or 7 years* they speak and understand sentences that they have never previously used or heard.

Table 3.4 reviews these developmental changes during the early years.

Table 3.4

The Sequence of Infant Language Development

Language	Age
Crying	From birth
Cooing	2–4 months
Babbling	4–6 months
Single words	12 months
Two words	18 months
Phrases	2 years
Short sentences and questions	2–3 years

Language Development in Infancy

Infants tune into the speech they hear and immediately begin to discriminate distinctive features. They also seem to be sensitive to the context of the language they hear; that is, they identify the *affective* nature of speech. The origins of language appear immediately after birth in infants' gazes and vocal exchanges with those around them. Although these are not specific language behaviors, they are an integral part of the language continuum.

Neonates vocalize by crying and fussing, which are forms of communication. At about the sixth to eighth week, **cooing** (sounds that resemble vowels and consonants) appears. These precursors of language blend with **babbling**, which then merges into the first words, and is then continuous with the appearance of two words, phrases, and sentences. The sequence is as follows:

- *At about four months, children begin to babble, that is, to make sounds that approximate speech.* For example, you may hear an "eee" that makes you think that the infant is saying "see." It seems, however, that babbling does not depend on external reinforcement: deaf as well as hearing children babble, but deaf children continue to babble past the age when hearing children begin to use words. Babbling probably appears initially as a result of biological maturation. Late in the babbling period, children use consistent sound patterns to refer to objects and events. These sound patterns are called **vocables** and seem to indicate that children have discovered that meaning is associated with sound. For example, a child may hear the doorbell and say "ell." The use of vocables may

be a link between babbling and the first intelligible words (DeVilliers & DeVilliers, 1978). These speechlike sounds increase in frequency until about one year, when children begin to use single words. At this stage, babbling is still interspersed among the single words.

- *At about one year, the first words appear.* (The age can vary markedly, however, depending on how the proud parents or other observers define what qualifies as a word.) Often called **holophrastic speech**, these first words are difficult to analyze. They are usually nouns, adjectives, or self-invented words, and they may even represent multiple meanings. "Ball" may mean not only the ball itself but "Throw the ball to me." Children's first words show a phonetic similarity to adult words, and children consistently use these words to refer to the same objects or events.

The single-word period flows into the use of multiple words and is continuous at the other end with the development of grammar. Between the ages of about one year and eighteen months, *children begin to use these single words to convey multiple meanings.* At first, "ball" refers to a round, moving object. Gradually, "ball" acquires the meaning of "give me the ball," "throw the ball," or "watch the ball roll." Ball now means much more than a round object. When toddlers begin to use their words to convey these more complex ideas, they are getting ready to move to the next stage of language development.

- *When the two-word stage appears, at about eighteen months,* youngsters initially struggle to devise some means of indicating tense and number, and they typically experience difficulty with grammatical correctness. At first they use word order to suggest meaning. They do not master inflections (plurals, tense, possessives) until they begin to form three-word sentences. A youngster's efforts to inject grammatical order into language is a good sign of normal language development.

- *At about two years of age children expand their vocabularies rapidly, and simple sentences, or telegraphic speech, appear.* Although young children use primarily nouns and verbs (not adverbs, conjunctions, prepositions), their sentences demonstrate definite syntactic structure. Although the nouns, adjectives, and verbs of children's sentences differ from those of adults, the same organizational principles are present. **Telegraphic speech,** like holographic speech, contains considerably more meaning than the sum of its words. For example, "milk gone" means "my milk is all gone."

Once syntactic structure emerges in two-word sentences, inflection soon appears, usually with three-word sentences. The appearance of inflections seems to follow a pattern: first the plural of nouns, then tense and person of verbs, and then possessives.

- *Vocabulary constantly expands.* As their symbolic activity increases and becomes more abstract, youngsters learn that everything has a name, and their vocabulary expands at an enormous rate (which explains why these months are often called the time of the *language explosion*). Between the ages of one and two, a toddler's vocabulary grows by at least 2,500 percent to as much as 6,000 percent. The growth rate in the subsequent years of early childhood is less spectacular but quite remarkable. Estimates of vocabulary are extremely tentative, however, since youngsters know more words than they articulate. Table 3.5 presents the approximate number of words that appear at various ages.

Speech Irregularities

When should a teacher be concerned about the possible existence of a language problem? Youngsters who consistently miss the milestones should receive a more detailed examination. Professionals who are trained in speech and language problems are identified as speech/language pathologists. These individuals are often available in the schools, and you should contact them if you have any questions. Don't confuse a serious language problem (such as lack of comprehension), with temporary setbacks or with speech irregularities that are a normal part of development.

When speech emerges, certain irregularities appear that are quite normal and to be expected. For example, **overextensions** mark children's beginning words. A child who has learned the name of the family pet—"doggy"—may for a while use that label for cats, horses, donkeys, cows or any other animal with a head, tail, body, and four legs. As children learn about their world, they quickly eliminate overextensions.

Overregularities are a similar fleeting phenomenon. As youngsters begin to use two- and three-word sentences, they struggle to convey more precise meanings by mastering the grammatical rules of their language. For example, many English verbs add *ed* to indicate past tense.

I wanted to play ball.

Some verbs, however, form the past tense by a change in the root.

Daddy came home.

Most children, even after they have mastered the correct form of such verbs as come, see, and run, still add *ed* to

Table 3.5

The Pattern of Vocabulary Development—Estimates

Age (Years)	Number of Words	
	Low	High
1	2-3	4-6
2	50	250
3	400	2000
4	1200	6000
5	1500	8000
6	2500	10,000

the original form. That is, youngsters who know that the past tense of "come" is "came" will still say:

Daddy comed home.

This tendency to overregularize persists only briefly. It is another example of the close link between language and thought. We know that from birth children respond to patterns. Infants look longer at the human face than they will at diagrams because the human face is more complex. Once children have learned a pattern such as adding *ed* to signify past tense, they have considerable difficulty in changing the pattern.

Language Development in Early Childhood

Children will not speak before they are about one year old—this is a biological given and nothing will change it. But once language appears, it is difficult to retard its progress. Usually only some traumatic event such as brain damage or dramatically deprived environmental conditions will hinder development.

As children come to the end of the early childhood period, they will have reached several language milestones (Anselmo, 1987):

- They become skillful in building words, adding suffixes such as er, man, and ist to form nouns—for example, the person who performs experiments is an experimenter.
- They begin to be comfortable with passive sentences—for example, the glass was broken by the wind.
- By the end of early childhood, children can pronounce almost all speech sounds of their native language accurately.

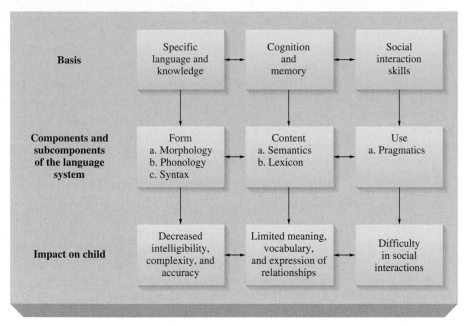

Figure 3.4
The language system: components and subcomponents.

- As we have noted, infancy and early childhood is the time of the "language explosion" and vocabulary has grown rapidly.
- Children of this age are aware of grammatical correctness.

Children proceed from hesitant beginnings to almost complete acquisition of their native language by the time they are about seven years old. Children manifest similar patterns of speech development whether they live in a ghetto or a wealthy suburb. A particular culture has little to do with language emergence, although it has everything to do with the shape that language assumes. Children in France and Spain, for example, may use different words for the same objects, but the appearance of single words, two-word sentences, and other achievements follow the same developmental pattern.

Metalinguistic Awareness

Metacognition refers to children's ability to step back and look at the various cognitive skills that have developed within themselves (Keil, 1979). One of these cognitive skills is language, and probably nothing reveals the close link between cognitive and language development more than a youngster's acquisition of metalinguistic awareness. At about the age of six, youngsters acquire this ability to "look at language and not through it."

The stages in the acquisition of metalinguistic awareness have been summarized as follows by Bullinger and Chatillon (1983):

For four year olds, words exist on the same plane as the things to which they refer. "Train is a long word because a train has a lot of cars."

From five to six years, children identify words with the activity of speaking. "A word is when you talk."

From six to seven years, words are differentiated from what they represent. Youngsters now begin to show an understanding of language.

A good example of this understanding is seen in the developmental progression of listening skills (McDevitt et al., 1990). In a study of first, third, and fifth graders, they found that the older children relied less on behavioral cues and more on comprehension. Children of all ages responded to speakers by combining their judgments of the speaker's competence with the norms of the situation (home, school).

Communication Disorders

As children develop language, there are many possibilities for language and communication disorders to occur in relationship to the form, content, and use of the language system (Kaiser, Hemmeter, & Alpert, 1992). In Figure 3.4, Kaiser and her associates have presented the interrelationships between the components and subcomponents of the language system and the potential impact of various communication disorders on language use.

Three aspects of Figure 3.4 are important in understanding communication disorders. *First,* the form, content, and use of language are related to a student's specific linguistic knowledge, cognitive development, and social interaction skills. For example, a student who has an emotional problem that involves social interaction may develop communication difficulties. *Second,* each subcomponent of the language system has the capacity for causing disruption. That is, specific syntax problems can significantly affect communication performance. For example, some children tend to slur their speech, which can make it difficult for others to understand them. *Third,* each of the language components has an impact on the others. A student who is experiencing difficulties in language form will have trouble relating to other children and adults.

Adequate communication skills are essential for the appropriate development of academic and social competence throughout the school years. Early detection of language problems is essential for a student's success in school. Again, if you suspect that a student is having language or communication problems, it is important to contact a professional who can provide the necessary assessment and treatment services.

The Whole Language Movement

Building on a growing knowledge of language development, educators, long dissatisfied with the teaching of reading and writing, have adopted a new strategy. Called **whole language,** it is a movement that is sweeping the country and refers to a technique by which all language processes (speaking, listening, reading, and writing—including spelling and handwriting) are studied in a more natural context, as a whole and not as a series of facts.

The whole language movement rests on the basic premise that infants learn their language by actually using it, and that this should be the acquisition model for learning reading and writing. This premise leads to several educational guidelines:

- the acquisition of language is tied tightly to meaning;
- written language is language;
- what is true for language is true for written language;
- language usage always occurs in context; and
- the language situation is crucial for the comprehension of meaning (Altwerger, Edelsky, & Flores, 1987).

The proponents of whole language believe that it is consistent with Piaget's theory of human development because the individual child's use of language materials matches that child's level of cognitive development. Proponents also claim that it is consistent with Vygotsky's work because of the important role that context plays in a child's attempts to master reading and writing (McCaslin, 1989). Still others believe that the whole lan-

guage movement is a natural outgrowth of several earlier educational beliefs such as the emphasis on the integrated curriculum and individualized reading (Goodman, 1989).

How The Whole Language Concept "Works"

Shifting from dependence on a basal language series to whole language requires teachers to re-think their assumptions about literature and language learning. For example, many teachers will work with themes: friendship, loyalty, honesty. First, students will read a story that illustrates the theme. This is known as *experiencing the literature.* Next, the teacher may read a related story or poem; students are listening to the literature.

Now the teacher may attempt to *expand* the concepts that the students experienced in their literature and simultaneously work on vocabulary using various techniques. Next, students may read the selection cooperatively (taking turns with their partners or reading aloud about a particular character in the story). They can then discuss the characters in the story.

At this point, they may *respond* to the literature by completing a story form (sentences with missing words, explaining the beginning and ending, telling how the story's problem was solved). The teacher may ask them to evaluate the characters' actions in the story or give their own opinions about the story. Some students may explore language; that is, if they need help with vocabulary or phonics, or with general reading strategies, they are now guided to appropriate activities.

The students here shift from reading to writing. For example, they may write a paragraph explaining a particular part of the story. They use the words they have learned in their reading and now apply them to their writing. They can be taught how to proofread and to revise in this phase.

With their reading and writing experiences completed, and if time permits, they may *extend their reading experiences.* That is, if the theme of their work was friendship, they may do independent research that could include examples of friendship in stories, friendship between leaders of nations, or friendship between people of different cultures.

The ideal time for the introduction of whole language is during the early childhood period. Children of this age are experiencing a rapid natural growth of language and enjoying the newfound power that language confers, which seems to be an ideal time to harness this exuberance and use it to further their learning.

Can Language Learning Be Easy?

By making language learning meaningful and relevant to students in such a way that they actually use it for their own purposes, supporters believe that the teaching of language becomes simpler and more appealing. Meaningful language learning helps students to make sense out of their worlds because while they are learning language, they are also learning *through* language. That is, comprehension of meaning is always the goal of readers, and expression of meaning is always the goal of writers (Goodman, 1986).

One way of motivating students to continually search for meaning is to turn to literature. Literature has proven to be a superb vehicle for developing, enhancing, and enriching lifelong, active literacy (Routman, 1988). The reasons for using literature as the foundation for a reading and writing program are the following:

- Literature encourages meaning. Children beginning to read immediately search for meaning, and stories that make sense are easy for them to discuss and recall.
- Literature has students focus on reading as a whole, something natural rather than an isolated series of parts.
- Literature-based programs encourage a positive self-image because students instantly see themselves as readers.
- Literature encourages language development by exposing students to a variety of correct, creative, and imaginative language that also aids comprehension and vocabulary development.

Bilingualism

You have just entered your first classroom to meet your pupils. Much to your surprise, several students whom you will be teaching during the year do not speak or write English as their primary language. This situation is becoming more and more common in our schools. All evidence points to the conclusion that our country today is more diverse ethnically and linguistically than ever before. For example, while the country's population increased by 11.6 percent between the years 1970–1980, the Asian-American community increased by 233 percent, Native Americans by 71 percent, Hispanics by 61 percent, and African Americans by 17.8 percent. Moreover, estimates are that at least 3.4 million students are limited in English language skills in a school system primarily designed for those who speak English (Lindholm, 1990).

The rights of language-minority students have come increasingly under analysis with specific implications for the schools and professionals who work in them. Some of the rights of these students are as follows (Garcia, 1990):

- There is a legally acceptable procedure for identifying all students who have problems speaking, understanding, reading, or writing English.

A difficult task faced by the more than 6 million children who come from homes in which the primary language is not English is to master both their native tongue, spoken at home, and English, to make their way in the larger society.

- Once these students are identified, there are minimal standards for the educational program that is provided for them. For example, some courts have noted that the teacher must have special training in working with these students and that the students receive adequate time to acquire English skills.
- A school district is advised, but not compelled, to offer instruction in the student's native language as well as English.
- A school system may not deny services to a student because only one or a few students in the district speak the specific language.

Many misconceptions have surrounded the educational progress of those students with an ability to speak two or more languages. For example:

- It is a misconception to assume that introducing a second language hurts the development of the student's primary language.
- It is a misconception to assume that bilingual children will become semilingual (going back and forth between the two languages) or confused in their language development.
- It is a misconception to assume that students will acquire languages easily. Older students learn syntactic and semantic aspects of a new language faster than younger students under appropriate conditions (McLaughlin, 1990).

In the past, a common practice has been to emphasize English and minimize the student's primary language, a practice which has caused McLaughlin (1990) to note:

> Educational programs that do not attempt to maintain the child's first language deprive many

children of economic opportunities they would otherwise have as bilinguals. This is especially true of children who speak world languages used for international communication such as Spanish, Japanese, Chinese, and the like. If these children's first languages are not maintained, one of this country's most valuable resources will be wasted (p. 74).

We can only conclude that you, as the classroom teachers of today and the future, will continue to work with growing ethnic and linguistic diversity. Consequently, learn as much about your students as possible, and search constantly for the most effective means of communicating with them.

Language Development in Middle Childhood

As youngsters mature, their vocabulary (both speaking and comprehension) increases enormously to match their expanding cognitive activity. For example, children of this age recognize sarcastic remarks, probably more from intonation than context (Capelli, et al., 1990). Yet they understand the intent of the statement. It has now become increasingly difficult to continue to match age with language accomplishment. Table 3.6 illustrates general language achievements for the preteen years.

It is an interesting chart because it encompasses almost all aspects of development for these years. Note the steady progression in motor skills—from acquiring the ability to grasp a pencil and print at about age seven to writing lengthy essays just three years later. Increasing visual discrimination is apparent in the accurate description of events and the elimination of letter reversals (for example, b for d). The growth in cognitive ability is seen in the detection of cause and effect and the appeal of science and mystery stories.

For children between 6 and 10 years, the relationship of language development (in the sense of mastering a native tongue) to reading is crucial. From signs on buses and streets as they go to school, to an educational curriculum that is overwhelmingly verbal, children must interpret the written word. In our society the functional illiterate faces a daily battle for survival.

Theories of Language Acquisition

Many of the language achievements that we take for granted are actually amazing accomplishments and defy easy explanation. Imitation, although a powerful linguistic force, does not seem to be the sole explanation for a youngster's intuitive grasp of grammar since a child

Table 3.6

Some Typical Language Accomplishments

Age (years)	Language Accomplishments
6	Vocabulary of about several thousand words Understands use and meaning of complex sentences Uses language as a tool Possesses some reading ability
7	Motor control improves; able to use pencil Can usually print several sentences Begins to tell time Losing tendency to reverse letters (b, d)
8	Motor control improving; movements more graceful Able to write as well as print Understands that words may have more than one meaning (ball) Uses total sentence to determine meaning
9	Can describe objects in detail Little difficulty in telling time Writes well Uses sentence content to determine word meaning
10	Describes situations by cause and effect Can write fairly lengthy essays Likes mystery and science stories Masters dictionary skills Good sense of grammar

hears so many incorrect utterances. Imitation also does not explain the manner by which thoughts are translated into words.

Lenneberg's Biological Explanation

Linguistic achievements that cannot be explained by imitation or some other cause have led some to a biological interpretation of language. What else could be the explanation in the cases of five- or six-year-old children who, in the course of two years of instruction, progressed from no speech whatever to the level of the normal youngster of the same age?

And what else but an innate capacity for language can explain the innovative nature of language? Children do not merely imitate those around them. If you listen care-

Table 3.7

Piaget—Language and Thought

Period (Age in Years)	Outstanding Characteristics	Language Equivalent
Sensorimotor (0-2)	1. Egocentrism 2. Organizes reality by sensory and motor abilities	1. Language absent until final months of period
Preoperational (2-7)	1. Increasing symbolic ability 2. Beginnings of representation	1. Egocentric speech 2. Socialized speech
Concrete operations (7-11)	1. Reversibility 2. Conservation 3. Seriation 4. Classification	1. Beginnings of verbal understanding 2. Understanding related to concrete objects
Formal operations (over 11)	1. Development of logico-mathematical structures 2. Hypothetico-deductive reasoning	1. Language freed from the concrete 2. Verbal ability to express the possible

fully to the young children, you will distinguish unique combinations of words, words that they never heard before. They may have heard the words "man," "doll," and "walk," but never the combination "man walk doll." Such novel utterances testify to the creative aspects of language. The work of Eric Lenneberg (1967) offers insights into the biological bases of the capacity for language.

The Language Spurt

Lenneberg's initial premise is that at a certain time in development, children show an amazing spurt in the ability to name things. There is a rapid increase in vocabulary from between 14 and 30 months. At the end of the third year children have a speaking vocabulary of about 1,000 words and probably understand thousands of other words. This explosion in vocabulary occurs at about the same age for every normal child in the world.

The specific causal elements and the underlying cerebral mechanisms for the language explosion are still unknown. Lenneberg believes that imitation, conditioning, and reinforcement—all external factors—are inadequate explanations for language development, and that anatomical and physiological agents—internal factors—play a major part.

Language and Behavior

Any theorist who endeavors to explain language development must account for a subtle form of behavior. In normal children, for example, there is initially nothing to show that the various steps of language development are about to occur. And rapid vocabulary growth is only one of the amazing features that we have yet to explain. Youngsters, without instruction, are also learning the rules of language so that by the age of four, they have acquired the essentials

of adult speech. The sheer mechanisms of speech production demand a high order of interpretation and an entire complex of special physiological adaptations.

Lenneberg postulates that language development follows a biological schedule, which is activated when a state of "resonance" exists, that is, when children are "excited" in accordance with the environment, the sounds that they have been hearing suddenly assume a new, meaningful pattern.

Language development parallels motor and cognitive ability. Standing, walking, and general muscular coordination approximate the appearance of certain language characteristics. Motor, cognitive, and language schedules seem to follow genetically programmed instructions and manifest steady, sometimes spectacular, development, level off, and slowly decline. Consequently, if children of an appropriate age are placed in any language community, they will immediately and with little difficulty, acquire that language.

Piaget and Language Development

Piaget believed that language emerges, not from a biological timetable such as Lenneberg suggests, but rather from existing cognitive structures and in accordance with the child's needs. Piaget began his basic work on language, *The Language and Thought of the Child* (1926), by asking, What are the needs that a child tends to satisfy when he talks? What is the function of language for a child? Piaget answered this question by linking language to cognitive structures. Thus, language function differs at each of the four cognitive levels (see Table 3.7).

Recording the speech of two six year-old children, Piaget identified two major speech categories of the preoperational child: egocentric speech and socialized speech. Children engage in **egocentric speech** when they do not care to whom they speak, or whether anyone is listening to them (Piaget, 1926, p. 32). There are three types of egocentric speech:

1. *Repetition,* which children use for the sheer pleasure of talking and which is devoid of social character.
2. *Monologue,* in which children talk to themselves as if they were thinking aloud.
3. *Collective monologue,* in which other children are present but not listening to the speaker.

Children engage in **socialized speech** when they exchange views with others, criticize one another, ask questions, give answers, and even command or threaten. Piaget estimates that about 50 percent of the six-year-old's speech is egocentric and that what is socialized is purely factual. He also warns that although most children begin to communicate thought between seven and eight years of age, their understanding of each other is still limited.

Seven or eight years of age sees the slow but steady disappearance of egocentrism, except in verbal thought, in which traces of egocentrism remain until about 11 or 12 years of age. Usage and complexity of language increases dramatically as children pass through the four stages of cognitive development. Piaget insists that the striking growth of verbal ability does not occur as a separate developmental phenomenon but reflects the development of cognitive structures.

Chomsky and Psycholinguistics

Similar to Lenneberg, Noam Chomsky, (1928–) a professor of linguistics at the Massachusetts Institute of Technology, believes that all humans have an innate capacity to acquire language as a result of our biological inheritance. Trained in linguistics, mathematics, and philosophy, Chomsky went farther than Lenneberg in his views: not only do we have a biological predisposition for language, but we also have an innate knowledge of language. He calls it our **Language Acquisition Device (LAD)**. Chomsky (1957) also stated that no one acquires a language by learning billions of sentences of that language. Rather children acquire a grammar that can generate an infinite number of sentences in their native language.

Chomsky's work is usually referred to as **psycholinguistics,** a combination of psychology and linguistics. Linguistics is the study of the rules of any language, while psychology focuses on behavior. Linguists assume that the rules of language are part of our knowledge; psychologists have attempted to discover how these rules are represented in our minds (especially the capacities that children must have to master the rules of their language). The combination of the two approaches has produced the field of psycholinguistics (Gardner, 1982).

Children possess an innate competence for language acquisition, just as they possess an innate capacity for walking. No one has to tell children *how* to walk—they walk and talk without consciously knowing how they did either. Although all normal children possess approximately the same language competence, their performance, or use of language, varies increasingly as they grow older. This variation is largely a result of differences in opportunities to learn how to use language, which includes not only speaking but also listening, writing, and reading. Thus, even though all preschoolers may have roughly the same linguistic abilities, the language abilities of adults vary widely.

The view of language as an unfolding of innate capacities, as seen in the work of Chomsky and others, offers clues as to the teaching of second languages. For example, teachers have long worried that the acquisition of a first language may interfere with the learning of a second. Recent research suggests that the native language does not in any significant way interfere with the development of the second language. The acquisition of both seem to be guided by common language principles that are a part of the human cognitive system. In fact, success in the acquisition of the second language is closely related to the proficiency level of the first language, which indicates that the two languages share a common base (Hakuta, 1986).

Language and the Classroom

As we conclude our analysis of language development, it is possible to see the classroom impact of the various theories we have discussed, especially with regard to current curriculum changes. The whole language concept, which is an approach to teaching reading that focuses on meaning, is a good example. The whole language technique incorporates all aspects of language—listening, speaking, reading, writing, spelling, thinking—by using children's literature and trade books across the curriculum. The meaning that pupils derive from such involvement is, in turn, related to cognitive ability, which reflects Piaget's belief that language development depends on cognitive development.

TEACHER ⬄ STUDENT
INTERACTIONS

1. Language is an integral part of instruction in the content areas, which emphasizes its importance to students.
   - Insure access to a wide range of appropriate books.
   - Schedule class time for independent reading.
   - Encourage class discussion of the books that the students read.
   - Derive activities that focus on a story or author; for example, role play an author to discover how and why that author wrote the story, or turn a story into a classroom play.
2. Understanding the spoken word and using a variety of words in their own speech prepares children for meeting words on the printed page. Use these activities to promote students' language development."
   - Encourage children to make place associations with this game. Tell your students that for the next minute they are to name everything they can think of that they might find in a grocery store, on a farm, or in a sports shop. Encourage students to use specific names for people and objects.
   - Show students pictures of everyday objects, such as a bicycle, toothbrush, an umbrella, and so on. Ask students to describe how the objects are used and for what they are used.
   - Pose problems for children to solve on their own or by acting out the situations with puppets. For example, give students the following scenario: Four friends were going on a picnic, but it has started to rain and they have to stay inside. What can they do now to have fun? Insist that students use complete sentences as they make up their dialogues.

- Test language skills and creativity by having students tell a story in the round. Seat the class in a circle on the floor. Begin a story; then after several minutes, tap the child next to you and say, "Please continue." The child now adds to the story for a few minutes and then taps the child next to him or her. Continue around the circle, asking the last child to make up an ending.
- See how well students listen and understand what they hear by giving children verbal directions for drawing a mystery object on paper. Have a picture of the object ready for students to check against their own drawings.
- Check problem-solving abilities and language skills by giving students a story problem, but omitting vital information needed to solve it. Ask students to pinpoint what else they need to know before they can figure out the answer.
3. As children acquire their language, they must also learn to use it properly.
   - Read aloud to your students as often as possible. Children like to listen and as they do, they are learning about language as communication. It is a technique that also increases their motivation to read.
   - Ask children to retell stories in their own words. This is a procedure that aids sequencing, helps in learning about story structure, and aids comprehension."
   - Use prompts, such as "What comes next?" "What problems did they face?" "How did they overcome them?"

Chomsky's ideas on the relationship of performance to opportunity can be seen in the suitable occasions that the whole language technique offers across the curriculum. Language activities become an integral part of instruction in content areas, thus assuming a more meaningful and functional place in a student's life.

Conclusion

In this chapter we have examined the work of several of the leading developmental theorists. Their conclusions offer considerable insights into developmental processes and should help you to understand your students better. For example:

- by understanding Piaget's work, you can appreciate the characteristics and complexities of the various ages and stages. You have a framework for identifying the kinds of tasks that your students (whatever their age) should be able to grasp;
- by utilizing knowledge of cognitive development, you can encourage the emerging mental abilities of your students;
- by tracing the sequence of language development, and placing your students in that sequence, you can devise means of improving their communication skills.

Chapter Highlights

The Meaning of Development

- Vygotsky's zone of proximal development offers insight into the relationship among learning, development, and social processes.
- Culture plays a key role in development.
- Important cognitive milestones, such as object permanence, are achieved during the sensorimotor period.
- Knowledge of cognitive development aids in instructional decisions.

Piaget and Cognitive Development

- Piaget's basic ideas help teachers to decide on developmentally appropriate materials and instructions.
- Piaget's theory aids us in understanding that "children think differently."
- His stages of cognitive development help us to comprehend what we can expect cognitively from students of different ages.
- Piaget's belief that students must interact with the environment for learning to occur has classroom implications.

Language: Theories and Development

- Several different explanations of language—biological, cognitive, innate—have led to the formulation of specific theories.
- Language acquisition offers definite clues to a student's developmental progress, which can aid teachers in working with students.
- Recognizing the importance of language in a student's life and its critical role in academic success can help you to search for the signs that could impede progress.

Key Terms

Accommodation
Adaptation
Adolescent egocentric thinking
Animism
Artificialism
Assimilation
Babbling
Bilingualism
Centering
Classification
Cognitive operations
Concrete operations
Conservation
Content
Cooing
Egocentric speech
Egocentrism
Equilibration
Field sensitive
Formal operations
Functional invariants
Holophrastic speech
Imaginative audience
Irreversibility
Language Acquisition Device (LAD)
Metacognition
Morpheme
M-space
Number concept
Operations
Organization
Overextension
Overregularity
Phonemes
Phonology

Pragmatics
Preoperational
Psycholinguistics
Realism
Reversibility
Schemes
Semantics
Sensorimotor
Seriation
Socialized speech
Structures
Syntax
Telegraphic speech
Transductive reasoning
Vocables
Whole language
Zone of proximal development

Suggested Readings

Anselmo, S. (1987). *Early childhood development: Prenatal through age eight.* Columbus, Ohio: Merrill. One of the best books you could read about early childhood. Ranging from observation techniques to social and cognitive development, it offers a readable, comprehensive account of these years.

Flavell, J. (1985). *Cognitive development.* Englewood Cliffs, N.J.: Prentice-Hall. If you would like to compare Piagetian theory with information processing, this is the book. Typical Flavell—carefully researched, well-written, thorough.

Ginsburg, H., and Opper, S. (1988). *Piaget's theory of intellectual development.* Englewood Cliffs, N.J.: Prentice-Hall. This slim paperback is one of the best introductions to Piaget's work that you could read. Well-organized and carefully written, it presents the reader with an excellent theoretical and practical overview.

Tittnich, E., Bloom, L., Schomburg, R., & Szekeres, S. (Eds.). (1990). *Facilitating children's language: Handbook for child-related professionals.* New York: The Haworth Press. This book is a useful resource if you are looking for a theoretical background review and practical strategies for facilitating children's language development.

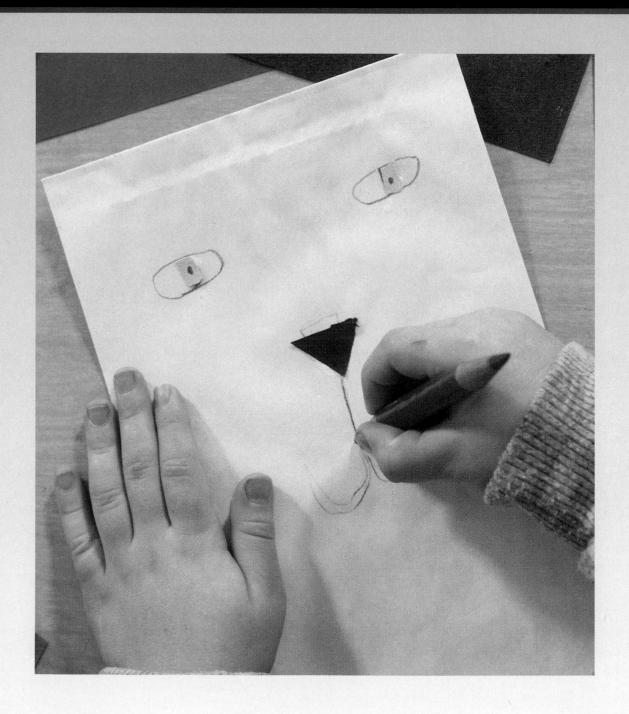

Psychosocial and Moral Development

Bill Brown, who was in the eighth grade at Junior High West, kept staring at the ground in the school's parking lot. Although all the students in the school were milling around, talking and trying to discover the exact location and cause of the fire, Bill stayed by himself. With a troubled expression he watched the firemen quickly extinguish the small blaze. He knew who had set the fire.

Earlier in the day, Jim Weston, another eighth grader, said to him, "It's time we had a little excitement around here. It's been pretty dull lately. Watch what happens in science today."

"What's up, Jim? You're not going to try anything in Johnson's class, are you? (Pete Johnson was the eighth grade science teacher.) "He's a pretty good guy."

"What difference does that make? Let's liven things up."

When the officials from the fire department gave the all clear and the students returned to the building, Bill walked by the science lab and saw the damage caused by the small fire. He liked Mr. Johnson; he had been Bill's Little League coach and had always been fair to him.

Pete Johnson saw him standing at the doorway and said, "This is a tough one, Bill. The fire inspector said it was set. I can't believe anyone would do this. Think of the damage and what could have happened to some of the students. Who could possibly do something like this?"

Bill looked at the teacher. He knew that Jim Weston wasn't really bad; he just didn't think that others really liked him, so he was always looking for attention. "Why, he even told me something would happen, just to make sure somebody would know," thought Bill. "If I tell Mr. Johnson what I know, maybe he could straighten Jim out. But Jim could be in a lot of trouble, maybe even expelled."

Bill stood there, not sure what to do next.

Torn between loyalty to a friend and yet knowing that his friend's actions are wrong, Bill is faced with a dilemma that has strong implications for psychosocial and moral development. If he decides to confide in the teacher whom he likes, what will the rest of his friends think? Peer influence at this age is a powerful motivator of behavior. Yet, as we realize from reading Piaget in chapter 3, a student of this age *knows* when something is wrong. Will Bill reconcile his behavior with what he thinks, and at the same time be trusted by his friends? Or will he compromise what he believes to be right to stay "in" with his friends?

To help you take a position on these questions, this chapter will explore the dimensions of psychosocial development, primarily through the work of Erik Erikson. Erikson has traced this phase of development through eight stages, several of which have important implications for the classroom.

But as you can tell from Bill Brown's dilemma, moral issues are also at stake, so Lawrence Kohlberg's insights into the path of moral development will be presented. Kohlberg's ideas, which have been directly applied to the classroom, should help you to understand the reasoning behind your students' behavior.

When you complete your reading of this chapter, you should be able to:

- interpret students' behaviors according to Erikson's stages of psychosocial development.
- appeal to the strengths of the stage, and help students adjust to the crises that eventually await them.
- use developmental knowledge to encourage and maintain a secure and free classroom atmosphere.
- use developmental knowledge to establish positive relationships with students.
- apply Kohlberg's ideas to your classroom, having a firmer idea of the type of moral thinking students are capable of.
- formulate moral education techniques through Kohlberg's use of moral dilemmas.
- use your ideas of moral development to establish a moral classroom environment.

Psychosocial Development

We are intensely aware today that children are deeply affected by the social agents (family, school, peers, media) that surround them. By linking children's development to the interactions and interrelationships with the critical agents in their environment, Erik Erikson has dramatically called our attention to the significance of social context (Isenberg, 1987). Born in Frankfurt, Germany in

Erik Erikson, whose psychological theory of human development offers insights into the challenges that people face at various stages of their lives.

1902, Erikson as a young man became interested in both education and psychoanalysis. He came to the United States in 1933, settling in Boston, where he was the first child psychoanalyst in the city.

Erikson's views on development and the search for identity are widely popular today. Working with American Indian tribes and treating World War II veterans helped Erikson to realize that many emotional problems were the result of identity confusion. He proposed a series of psychosocial stages of development during which an individual has to establish changing concepts of self and reality. During the "working out" of the psychosocial stages, students must grapple with both positive and negative elements as they strive for self-identity.

Erikson's Eight Stages

Erikson believes that personality emerges from a series of inner and outer conflicts, which, if resolved, result in a greater sense of self. These crises arise at each of eight stages of life identified by Erikson. Each crisis results in a period of increased vulnerability and heightened potential, which can lead to possible maladjustment or to increased psychic strength. During the adolescent years, for example, teenagers are besieged by self-doubt—about their bodies, their abilities, their popularity—yet with patience and proper guidance, they can acquire a positive self-identity.

In his famous *Childhood and Society* (1950), Erikson stated the two basic assumptions underlying his eight stages:

1. Personality develops according to one's ability to interact with the environment;

Table 4.1

Erikson's Eight Stages—Crises, Strengths, Influences

Age (years)	Stage	Psychosocial Crisis	Psychosocial Strength	Environmental Influence
1	Infancy	Trust vs. mistrust	Hope	Maternal
2-3	Early childhood	Autonomy vs. shame, doubt	Willpower	Both parents or adults substitutes
4-5	Preschool, nursery	Initiative vs. guilt	Purpose	Parents, family, friends
6-11	Middle childhood	Industry vs. inferiority	Competence	School
12-18	Adolescence	Identity vs. identity confusion	Fidelity	Peers
18-35	Young adulthood	Intimacy vs. isolation	Love	Partners: spouse/lover friends
35-65	Middle age	Generativity vs. stagnation	Care	Family society
Over 65	Old age	Integrity vs. despair	Wisdom	Mankind

Source: Data from Erik Erikson, *Childhood and Society*, 1950.

2. Society invites this interaction with the environment and encourages and safeguards the successive appearance of the stages. The crises, strengths, and major environmental influences that characterize each stage are outlined in Table 4.1.

As you continue your reading, use these questions to help you assess Erikson's ideas.

- Given your age and ability to recall crucial experiences, do you think that Erikson's stages (including crises, strengths, and influences) are realistic?
- Are the crises, strengths, and influences that Erikson identifies for your stage meaningful for you?

Stage 1 Trust versus Mistrust (first year)

Erikson believes that a healthy personality requires a sense of trust, toward one's self and the world, a sense that develops during the first year. Infants derive security and comfort from a warm relationship with their parents. Cold parental care and rejection causes mistrust and affects all later development (for an exhaustive summary of human studies, see Rutter, 1980).

As infants develop greater control over their body (e.g., more accurate grasping of objects) they learn to trust their bodies as well, thus increasing their psychological sense of security. The world becomes a safe and orderly place as children take their first steps toward personal mastery.

Attachment

Development during the first year of life can have long-term consequences. Research demonstrates that attachment (usually to the mother) appears during the last half of the first year (Ainsworth, 1979; Bowlby, 1969). If **attachment** is not nurtured by the mother or other caregiver, however, children may not develop the trust necessary to establish lasting relationships with others.

Although relationships with parents are a key element in the development of attachment, other developmental factors also contribute. For example, a child's inborn temperamental tendency to be fearful or relaxed in unfamiliar situations affect a child's behavior. In other words, children are psychologically different from birth, a fact that has been ignored in the attachment studies (Kagan, 1989).

Reciprocal Interactions

Infants in Erikson's first period of Trust versus Mistrust have as much influence on surrounding adults as the adults have on them, a phenomenon known as **reciprocal**

Focus on Students

The Strange Situation Technique

Ainsworth (1979) devised the **strange situation** technique to study attachment experimentally. Placing young children in a strange situation enables researchers to classify their reactions following separation from their mothers. (Attachment appears for most youngsters during the last half of the first year.)

Before we continue, imagine the setting. A toddler, alone with its mother in a strange room, suddenly sees the mother leave. A stranger enters; the child is visibly upset; the stranger leaves; the mother returns. What do you think the child's reaction will be?

Ainsworth has identified three major reactions in one-year-old infants.

1. *Type A children* (about 20 percent of American children) rarely cried during separation and avoided their mothers at reunion. The mothers of these babies seemed to dislike or were indifferent to physical contact.
2. *Type B children* (about 67 percent of American children) were secure and used the mother as a base from which to explore. Separation intensified their attachment behavior; they exhibited considerable distress, ceased their explorations, and at reunion sought contact with mothers. The mothers of these children were nurturant yet also encouraged independent and exploratory behaviors.
3. *Type C children* (about 15 percent of American children) manifested anxiety before separation and were intensely distressed by the separation. Yet on reunion they displayed ambivalent behavior toward their mothers; they sought contact but simultaneously seemed to resist it. The mothers of these children have given conflicting signals so that the infants are confused by the relationship.

Examining the nature of these mother-infant interactions, Ainsworth (1979) states that feelings, close bodily contact, and face-to-face interactions seem to be equally as important in the child's expectations of the mother's behavior. The security attained during the early attachment phases seems to have enduring qualities. For example, securely attached infants later have more positive and cooperative relations with family members, are more competent, and have better interactions with their peers. Group A babies later showed more aggressive behavior, and Group C infants were more easily frustrated, less persistent, and less competitive.

interactions (Brazelton & Als, 1979) or **transactions** (Sameroff, 1975). As research has shown, children are born with temperamental differences; thus, they respond in unique ways to their parents' efforts to communicate. Each infant instantly demonstrates a special, individual style that has a decided impact on its parents. For example, some infants from birth are irritable, cry frequently, and are difficult to console; others are calm, easy-going, and console themselves. Partly because of these innate temperamental differences, parents treat each of their children differently; studies of identical twins, whose mothers admit that they respond differently to each child, support this conclusion.

The pattern of interactions between a mother and her newborn infant becomes quite consistent during the first week after birth, and the style of the relationship persists (Osofsky, 1976). The stage is set and reciprocal interactions will continue: the child acts on the parents and changes them; these changes are then reflected in the parents' behavior toward the child. The constantly crying child can provoke impatient responses from its parents; parental impatience only further irritates the child. The nature of these interactions will create a particular level of trust or mistrust, which will usually color all of a child's relationships, including those with teachers.

The parents' **sensitive responsiveness,** or the ability to recognize the nonverbal cues an infant provides, also affects interactions with the child, as well as the child's subsequent relationships. Although sensitive responsiveness seems to be more natural for some adults than others, it also seems to be a skill that one can acquire and improve upon with knowledge and experience. Moreover, this skill is as useful to teachers as it is to parents. The better able you are to recognize the clues that your students provide about what they're thinking and feeling, the more effectively you can manage your classroom. For example, the usually pleasant, responsive student who comes to class and sullenly stares at you is presenting a clear signal that something is wrong.

Educational Implications

Youngsters who have experienced a warm, positive attachment come to school better prepared to deal with school content (because of greater competence) and better able to get along with peers (because of more positive relationships). If parental relations remain warm and supportive, students maintain the confidence to explore, to develop self-esteem, and to achieve.

Teachers can also help students form positive relationships. When teachers, especially during the early years of schooling, establish a warm atmosphere, they help their pupils find a sense of security in another human being—not an easy task, but one that sometimes can be accomplished. This example demonstrates the critical role that teachers can play in the socialization of their pupils.

Stage 2 Autonomy versus Shame, Doubt (2–3 years)

For Erikson, the theme of the second stage is **Autonomy** versus Shame and Doubt, a concept which usually appears during toilet training. During this period, personality is shaped by learning the meaning of self-control. This stage is decisive for establishing a proper balance between loving goodwill and hateful self-insistence, between compulsive self-restraint and meek compliance. Parental reactions are crucial since the objective of this stage is the child's development of self-control with no loss of self-esteem. Loss of self-control because of parental overcontrol results in self-doubt and shame.

At this age children are becoming more and more vocal, and adults must respond to the growing demands of language. (Remember: these are the years that Lenneberg refers to as the time of the "language explosion.") They must also respond appropriately to the child's increasing physical mobility; too many restrictions work against self development, yet adults must also consider the child's safety. A delicate interplay between freedom and restraint is needed. At the end of Erikson's second stage, children should be relatively self-sufficient, but still willing recipients of adult guidance, demonstrating growing autonomy with diminishing feelings of shame and doubt.

Although children need to maintain a sense of trust in a manner calculated to further self-confidence, adults (parents and teachers of day care and nursery schools) must also introduce restraints that will help youngsters develop self control, competence, and maturity. For example, youngsters of this age, when playing in a sandbox, have a tendency to throw sand in the face of other children. They need to learn not to do things even when they are provoked that can hurt other children.

Educational Implications

Ideally, youngsters should achieve considerable self-control as well as control of their bodies by the age of seven years. To accomplish this goal, here are some objectives for adults working with young children:

1. Protect youngsters from injury.
2. Prevent them from harming others.

"Miss Cobb, there's something you should know. We were having a contest to see who could lean out the window the farthest, and Tommy Bishop won."

© Glenn Bernhardt.

3. Provide them with opportunities to exercise and develop their talents.
4. Enable them to acquire sufficient self-mastery to understand both limitations and opportunity.

How you accomplish these objectives will depend on your individual style of interacting with others and the unique personality of the child. From Erikson's perspective, this means never humiliating a child, either physically or verbally, when you must impose restrictions. Firm but tactful restraint implies that youngsters recognize and respect you as an authority figure while retaining their sense of autonomy and initiative.

To help youngsters to attain autonomy without lingering shame or doubt, consider the characteristics of young children and adapt your teaching accordingly. Here are some guidelines that should help:

1. *Young children require consistent and reasonable discipline.* Since children are so attuned to adult authority, any adult behavior that confuses them can have a lasting impact. For example, a pattern of inconsistent discipline whereby an offense (such as deliberately dropping things) is sometimes punished and then at other times is ignored or even condoned with a smile causes confusion and uncertainty. As they grow older, they must abide by rules; these years are the time for them to respect reasonable rules reasonably administered. They won't always obey, of course, and when you must reprimand, do so, and then as soon as possible offer a warm response for acceptable behavior.

Table 4.2

Common Fears in Children

0–6 months	Loss of support, loud noises
7–12 months	Fear of strangers, fear of sudden, unexpected, and looming objects
1 year	Separation from parent, toilet, injury, strangers
2 years	A multitude of fears including loud noises (vacuum cleaners, sirens/alarms, trucks, and thunder), animals (e.g., large dogs), dark room, separation from parent, large objects/machines, change in personal environment
3 years	Masks, dark, animals, separation from parent
4 years	Parent separation, animals, dark, noises (including at night)
5 years	Animals, "bad" people, dark, separation from parent, bodily harm
6 years	Supernatural beings (e.g., ghosts, witches, "Darth Vader"), bodily injuries, thunder and lightning, dark, sleeping or staying alone, separation from parent
7–8 years	Supernatural beings, dark, fears based on media events, staying alone, bodily injury
9–12 years	Tests and examinations in school, school performance, bodily injury, physical appearance, thunder and lightning, death, dark (low percentage)

R. J. Morris and T. R. Kratochwill, *Treating Children's Fears and Phobias.* Copyright © 1983 Pergamon Press, Inc., Elmsford, NY. Allyn & Bacon, Inc. Needham Heights, MA.

2. *Young children need ample opportunities to do things for themselves* such as arranging furniture, obtaining materials, helping around a room. Any activities that you can devise will help them to gain mastery over themselves and their surroundings, thus contributing to autonomy. Children of this age usually want to help their parents when they see their mothers or fathers working around the house. For example, a father who lets his son or daughter water the flowers with a hose is contributing to his child's sense of autonomy.

3. *Young children need good models.* At this age, children love to imitate, so you will have many pertinent opportunities. For example, assume that you are working with children of this age, and the group wants to play a board game. You took it home, however, to study the rules and forgot to bring it back. By immediately admitting your mistake, you teach the children about honesty and accepting responsibility for your behavior.

4. *Young children should be protected from unwarranted fears.* Because young children have a limited cognitive capacity plus an aptitude for fantasy, they may become subject to unreasonable anxieties and fears (Morris & Kratochwill, 1983).

Table 4.2 lists some common fears that children experience.

Although children experience many normal fears, unreasonable punishment or, conversely, excessive permissiveness can cause them to become unduly fearful of a parent or teacher, and that fear may transfer to other adults. Your best reaction to a child's unwarranted fear is to listen, to explain, and to set a positive example. For example, how often have you heard an older child—especially a brother or sister—tell a youngster how terrible Mrs. Smith is and what she'll "do to them" next year. If unchecked, a child can acquire an unreasonable fear that may spread to all teachers and the school itself.

5. *Young children need boundaries,* not to restrict them, but to give them the security and comfort of an ordered world. For example, many young children are quite cautious about cars as a result of the warnings of their parents. They have learned that they just can't dash out into the street; they might get hurt. With this learning comes a gradual realization that the reasonable restrictions of the adults around them come from love and are designed for their safety, which is another step in the development of trust and autonomy.

Stage 3 Initiative versus Guilt (4–5 years)

Children in Erikson's third stage show greater freedom of movement, perfection of language, and expansion of imagination. A sense of **initiative** emerges that will serve as a basis for realistic ambitions and purposes. As Erikson notes, the indispensable contribution of this stage to later development is to free the child's initiative and sense of purpose for adult tasks that promise fulfillment of human capacities.

Erikson notes that preschoolers realize who they are, have a lively imagination, are mobile, and have a good grasp of language. Their world challenges them to master new tasks, such as learning to read, adapting to school, and dressing themselves. Their growing symbolic ability, which was discussed in the section on Piaget's preoperational stage, enables them to meet the challenges that Erikson identifies for these years. Parents who encourage children to do things (to play, to help in the home) encourage a sense of initiative. Scoffing at children's ideas and efforts produces a sense of guilt.

The Importance of Play

Children play constantly during these years. Einon (1985) describes what happened when her three-year-old daughter poured water into the bathtub. By pouring the water, the little girl was learning the bodily movements necessary to hold a container and to pour accurately, making adjustments as the water container became lighter. She also learned that containers are heavier when full. Einon concludes that the three-year-old, although playing, was also conducting early scientific experiments. This is an excellent example of how play can further cognitive development.

As you can see from this example, children play for various reasons, chief of which are the following:

- *Play aids cognitive development.* Through play, children learn the objects in their world, what these objects do (balls roll and bounce), what they consist of (toy cars have wheels), and how they work. To use Piaget's term, children "operate" on objects through play and also learn behavioral skills that will be of future use.
- *Play helps social development.* The involvement of others demands a give-and-take that teaches young children the basics of forming relationships. As cognitive skills require the sequential mastery of fundamentals, so social skills demand the same building process. Why are some five- and six-year-olds more popular with their classmates than others? Watching closely, you can discover the reasons:

decreasing egocentrism, recognition of the right of others, and a willingness to share. These social skills do not simply appear; they are learned, and much of the learning comes through play.

- *Play provides an emotional release.* There is not the right-or-wrong, life-and-death feelings that accompany interactions with adults. Children can be creative without worrying about failure. They can also work out emotional tensions through play. In short, play is a powerful developmental instrument: it stimulates learning by encouraging the freedom to explore and to discover what works and what doesn't, it provides an imaginary escape world, and it helps to build interpersonal relations (Caplan & Caplan, 1983).

The Development of Play

Does play change over time? Are there age-related features of play that we can identify? It is difficult, if not impossible, to link a specific age with a specific kind of play. But it is possible to link the characteristics of a particular level (early childhood, middle childhood) with kinds of play.

Pretend play seems most characteristic of the type of play during early childhood. Preoperational children show an increasing ability to represent. They are better able to engage in abstract thinking, to let one thing represent another. They can pretend.

Pretend play becomes more social with age and seems to entail a three-stage sequence (Rubin, Fein, & Vandenberg, 1983).

1. Pretend play becomes increasingly dramatic until the early elementary school years.
2. Pretend play becomes more social with age.
3. Pretend play gradually declines during middle childhood and games with rules replace it.

Pretend play begins with simple actions such as pretending to be eating or asleep. But as symbolic ability, the nature of pretending changes. Very young children will use toy telephones to talk. Youngsters who are a little older will pick up a banana and pretend to talk on the telephone. Pretend play steadily becomes more elaborate. Youngsters will serve tea to a group of dolls or feed soldiers; they also begin to enact the role of others, all of which supports Erikson's belief in the importance of initiative in development.

During these preschool days, children display awareness of the emotional states of others. By 3 1/2 to 4 years, most children will respond positively to those in need (Denham et al., 1990). Children who don't react in this way seem to be disliked. Thus, youngsters assess the

The role of play in the early childhood years is especially important because of its influence on physical, cognitive, social, and emotional development.

individual differences of their peers and make judgments based on these observations.

Another interesting development during this stage is the *emerging role of conscience.* Children now have the ability to cope with the environment, but they are also encountering yes and no reactions from their parents. Consequently they experience guilt feelings when they know they have done something of which parents or teachers disapprove. If children face too many restrictions, they can acquire emotional problems early in life.

These characteristics of preoperational children have led to a concern for *developmentally appropriate curricula.* The National Association for the Education of Young Children, in a series of papers (Calvert, 1986), has urged greater attention to "learning through active exploration and interaction with adults, other children, and materials." Teachers of these children, as active observers, prepare the environment in a developmentally appropriate way.

That is, they make sure that the children have the necessary muscular development and coordination needed to feel, handle, and manipulate the toys or objects they are using. Children at the beginning of this period, for example, need to use large crayons when drawing. Consequently, the best advice for dealing with preoperational children is to meet them on their level but challenge them.

Educational Implications

Youngsters who acquire a sense of initiative will bring to the classroom a healthy desire to face challenges. These are the pupils who will try to read the sentence, who will attempt the new activity, who are undaunted by facing the computer.

Young children have much to learn about the world, and a well-structured environment—appropriate objects in a wide variety of colors, plants, animals—helps them to label and order their world, thus extending cognitive, language, and psychosocial development. Schooling at this level must capitalize on a child's spontaneous learning, thus aiding the development of competence and security, two of the great objectives of this period.

Stage 4 Industry versus Inferiority (6–11 years)

Children now possess a sense of being able to do things well; they want to win recognition by producing things, which is the meaning of **industry.** Youngsters in elementary school are coming into their own: they sense their growing competence, both physical and mental, and if challenges match ability, they feel fulfilled. Horizons widen as children encounter a wide variety of people, tasks, and events.

During these years the school becomes a proving ground. Can they establish a positive relationship with teachers? Can they do well in subjects? Are they able to form friendships? Some degree of success contributes to both personal adjustment and social acceptance. Conversely, children who despair of their skills and their status with their peers can easily acquire a sense of inadequacy.

TEACHER ⟷ STUDENT
INTERACTIONS

Erikson's Early Stages

1. A healthy personality requires a sense of trust, towards oneself and the world.
   - If you find yourself working with infants in a daycare setting, provide as much physical contact with the infants as possible. For infants, physical contact helps to establish a sense of security and trust.
   - Once separation anxiety appears, be careful of how you leave infants. Although you can't be with each child every minute, you can contribute to children's psychological comfort and trust in those around them by doing such simple things as putting a familiar toy with a child before you leave.
   - From about one to two years, think of yourself as a learning consultant. For example, play games that help them acquire a better understanding of the world; take their questions seriously and answer them carefully.
2. For healthy development, children must acquire not only control over their bodies but also self-control.
   - Help students who tend to lose their tempers easily to change. Talk to them and remind them of any times when they maintained control—"Do you remember last week when Jimmy pushed you; you didn't scream; you acted very grown-up. You told him to stop or you would tell me."
   - Stress to your students that everybody gets mad and wants to strike out. The difference is, however, that they don't. Use examples of children in the class who do not yell or scream every time something goes wrong.

   - Encourage self-control in students by asking "How would you feel if somebody picked on you?" Help them to understand someone else's feelings: other students don't feel very good when someone constantly tells them they're wrong.
   - Explain to children who "go off the wall" too frequently that they might have to back away from arguments. Nobody likes a "sore loser." Encourage self-esteem in the classroom by occasionally allowing these children to be your helper. In this way, they can still feel good about themselves even when they lose an argument.
3. With developing control, children begin to manipulate their environment, thus acquiring feelings of competence. More is said about teaching self-control to students in chapter 5.
   - Encourage children who have difficulty controlling their emotions to engage in a physical activity, such as bike riding, throwing a ball, or running, in which they have physical control.
   - Help children to eliminate jealousy. If others get a better grade, remind them of their past accomplishments. You might even put them on a special card as a reminder.
   - Help children to avoid keeping annoying things to themselves to the point that they become preoccupied with them. Encourage them to talk to others about those things that bother them.

Erikson's ideas of industry and inferiority are particularly relevant for multicultural students. Entering a classroom in which language and customs may seem strange, these students may feel overwhelmed by self-doubt. If you encourage them to bring elements of their culture into the classroom, you help to enhance their self-esteem by accepting their identity as a member of a particular group. Your behavior thus sets an example for your students and motivates multicultural students to participate more fully in classroom activities. You can then use their strengths as a competent member of their culture as a bridge to successful classroom work in this new environment (Tiedt & Tiedt, 1990).

The Tasks of Middle Childhood

Twelve "developmental missions" guide elementary school children in their quest for growth, fulfillment, and self-identity (M. Levine et al., 1980). These 12 missions constitute the basic concerns of this age group.

1. *To sustain self-esteem.* The lives of school children present diversified opportunities either to enhance or reduce feelings of self-esteem. Feedback from peers and adults, school achievement, and social successes are all strong reinforcing agents that influence self-esteem. Youngsters' evaluation of self-esteem will vary throughout the period, but at its conclusion they should emerge with a good, positive self-concept. Am I all I can be?
2. *To find social acceptance.* For some youngsters, leaving the protective shield of the family and finding acceptance in a peer group is easy, for others difficult, and for both, enormously important. Do my peers accept me?
3. *To reconcile individuality with conformity.* Children are unique beings with individual preferences and abilities, which may or may not be valued by the group. Modifying, not sacrificing their strengths in search of social acceptance remains a major mission

for the middle childhood youngster. Is this right for me?

4. *To select appropriate role models.* In their search for identity children often use peers, older children, and adults as models, which may be positive or negative depending on the model. Is he/she really what I would like to be?

5. *To examine values.* The values of home may not be the values of the group or the school, and a changing cognitive perspective may force youngsters to weigh cherished home beliefs against new, interesting, and persuasive ideas. Should I or shouldn't I?

6. *To grow within the family.* Although dependence on the family lessens with new friends and new ideas, children still want harmonious relations with parents and siblings, to be considered successful by them. Am I comfortable with my family?

7. *To explore autonomy and its limits.* With competence comes a desire to test boundaries. In a sense, youngsters are testing not only adult restrictions but themselves; "Will I be able to make it without adult help?"

8. *To acquire knowledge and skill.* Although skills are attained physically and socially, school remains the great testing ground. How do I measure up against my peers?

9. *To live within one's body.* Children of this age now are aware of their growing physical competence, and the task is to acquire the use of these abilities most effectively. What can and should I do?

10. *To deal with fears.* Along with competence come new tests, new trials that may be cognitive, psychosocial, and/or physical. How do I learn not to be overwhelmed by novel and unexpected challenges?

11. *To deal with appetites and drives.* Maturity brings desires; how do I learn the self-control necessary for success, happiness, and adjustment?

12. *To refine self-awareness.* The school years can be harshly objective in revealing to children where their strengths and weaknesses lie. As children reach 12 years of age, the manner in which the previous eleven missions have been fulfilled force them to face reality. Am I willing to accept who I am?

Sports and Competition

The search for accomplishing the twelve developmental missions reflects the individual differences of youngsters. Desiring social acceptance, elementary school children strike out in many directions in their endeavors to achieve status. Many paths attract them: school paper, dancing, band, and, increasingly, sports. These years see many youngsters, both boys and girls, coordinating their physical abilities and showing definite signs of athletic skill. Little League baseball, youth hockey, Pop Warner football, and soccer all become showcases for their athletic talent.

If parents, coaches, and youngsters maintain their perspective, sports can be a healthy vehicle to carry children to a desirable sense of industry. Adults who transmit a "win at any cost" attitude do little, however, to help a 10-year-old maintain perspective. Parents, realizing that they have a skilled athlete in the family, and facing formidable college tuition costs, may push their child too hard and too fast. (Because of the recent availability of federal monies linked to sex discrimination legislation, girls are beginning to feel the same pressures that boys have long experienced.)

Sports are an excellent outlet for youngsters—but in their place. What happens to educational values if a youngster's life becomes totally immersed in sports at a time when the content of classes is becoming increasingly abstract? The stories of athletes who drop out of college in their senior year and of high school graduates who cannot read but are accepted into major universities are a grim reminder that we are faced with a national problem, one that we continue to ignore at our educational peril.

Competition in sports is keen, as it is also in the classroom and raises certain issues.

- *Competition is a fact of life*—in the home, in school, in work. Races should be run and scores should be kept.

- *Excessive motivation produces negative results* (for more on motivation, see chapter 8). Recall the athlete who, under enormous pressure from some unthinking coach, hides a potentially crippling injury "to help the team to win."

- *Excessive emphasis upon grades and honors* turns a student's focus away from the intrinsic value of learning to the transient value of material objects.

- *Intense competition* turns youngsters against each other, and, if prolonged, leads to undesirable concentration upon self—I must win—regardless. Under these conditions, too often the end justifies the means, and unhealthy behavioral patterns become routine.

- *Competition is probably inevitable in the classroom.* But teachers must work to instill self-competition. Competition with self is closely related to many other motivational topics: setting reasonable goals, a moderate level of self-competition, a realistic level of need achievement. Teachers who strive for intrinsically motivated students by encouraging realistic self-competition not only foster learning, but they also provide a means for coping with life.

TEACHER ⟷ STUDENT
INTERACTIONS

Erikson's Elementary School Years

1. Elementary school children need to acquire a sense of accomplishment.
   - Congratulate your students aloud for their successes; help students in your class not only to feel proud individually but also to feel proud of each other.
   - Arrange a table in your room "All About Me." This could be a week-long display of items that are special to that particular child (collections, sports mementos, photos, baby toys, etc.), things that he or she brings from home. On Friday, the spotlight child shares what he or she has brought.
   - Ask children to write a compliment about another child on a white piece of paper with a white crayon. The "invisible ink" papers are then delivered to the designated person. The recipient paints his or her paper with watered-down tempera paint. As the student paints, a message appears (as well as a smile on the student's face as he or she sees the message).
   - Take a picture of each child on the first day of school. Mount the pictures on a bulletin board. Keep the display up all year. Outside the hall or in the classroom, reserve a bulletin board for a brag board. When a child wins an award, writes an outstanding paper, etc., put his or her snapshot on the board. Put the photos in a scrapbook at the end of the year.
   - Ask your students to define their interest and hobbies to determine an area in which they are an expert. Then ask them to find out where and to whom they could go for more information on that topic, and what subjects they would like to know more about. After the students choose a subject, they are assigned to research their topic and then present their findings in a five-minute oral report. Make sure to leave time for a question and answer period. The whole class learns from the resident "experts."

2. During these years, children acquire knowledge about the world beyond their families.
   - Ask your children to participate in a "worldly project to track down the origins of foreign products. Students check their clothing labels to find manufacturing locations. Locate these places on a world map and encourage children to speculate about how the items arrived in your area. Next, ask pupils to look through their kitchen cupboards at home. Are any food products from out of the country? Mark these spots on your map, too. And finally, investigate the origins of toys, appliances, even cars. Help students develop a growing awareness of how they are "connected" to the rest of the world.
   - Ask children how they got their names. You may discover that they are named after a grandparent from another country, or simply because of the way they looked when they were born.
   - Ask parents to cook ethnic dishes to share with the class while they talk about the country. Children may bring in items common to their heritage and wear native costumes to school when studying different cultures.
   - Have children study folktales from other countries. Discuss common themes and point out differences.
   - Explore local history. Visit historical houses; discuss how children lived in those days compared to today.
   - Develop ways your pupils can keep in touch with the community: field trips to manufacturing plants, museums, hospitals, community centers, nursing homes, etc.
   - Celebrate Grandparents and Senior Citizens Day, when older residents are invited to spend a day at school. Build a unit around these visits—perhaps called "Living History"—and search for ways to record and publish the information (perhaps in a local paper).
   - Adopt a downtown building and have students learn as much as they can about it and its present and former inhabitants. With scissors, rulers, and paints in hand, create a replica of Main Street. Have the project supervised by local shopkeepers.

3. In the elementary school years, children learn from almost everything that they do.
   - Have your students share a cooking experience to promote social interaction and language skills. When they feel successful in completing (and eating) a cooking project, their self-image is enhanced.
   - After a tour or a field trip, use dramatics to encourage your children to reenact what they observed.
   - Encourage creative thinking during your students' free time by setting up centers where students may write and "publish" their own books, make puppets and write short skits, design posters, or create their own "inventions."
   - Plan a celebration like a fiesta or a fair to study other times or countries. Relate your language arts activities to the celebration (food, art, handicrafts, songs).
   - Explore science through nature walks. Invite the children to bring in their insect collections from home. Review the life cycle of the monarch butterfly. Make a hands-on bulletin board or activity where students demonstrate the scientific words they have learned. Write a class journal about the experiences of their walk. Have the children make clay models or drawings of what they saw on their walk. Design a mural with your class about what they observed.

Educational Implications

Erikson aptly described the elementary school years as "I am what I learn." For youngsters at this stage, learning occurs from almost everything they do. They learn through play, from their peers, in sports, and other activities, and, of course, in school.

Elementary school youngsters understandably are eager to use the abilities that they developed during their first six or seven years. This eagerness means they will inevitably encounter failure as well as success, especially in their school work. The balance between these two outcomes will decisively affect a child's self-esteem. Your task is to channel the child's energy and talent in positive directions.

Teachers can do much to help students gain a sense of mastery over the environment by matching content with ability (or level of cognitive development, as emphasized by Piaget) so that they can achieve at their level. Knowing what your students can do from their behavior (recall Piaget's use of *content*), from tests, and from their classroom work, you can direct them to tasks that are challenging but within their range of ability. Children can gain a feeling of competence, a sense of being capable, if their performance attains tangible goals.

Moreover, achievement and acceptance go hand-in-hand in this socially significant stage. Youngsters of this age who do well in the spelling bees, who become team leaders in subject matter areas, and who read well usually are popular. Thus, your efforts to match content with cognitive level—*for all pupils*—have intellectual, emotional, and social consequences.

Stage 5 Identity versus Identity Confusion (12–18 years)

Erikson's fifth stage witnesses the end of childhood and the beginning of adulthood. Youngsters become concerned with what others think of them, and peer opinion plays a large part in how they think of themselves. If uncertainty at this time results in *identity confusion,* a bewildered youth may withdraw, run away, or turn to drugs. Youngsters faced with the question "Who am I?" may be unable to answer. The challenges are new; the tasks are difficult; the alternatives are bewildering. Needless to say, adults must have patience and understanding.

Minority children may be particularly susceptible to these concerns. To help them cope with their search for identity, Spencer and Markstrom-Adams (1990) recommend that everything possible should be done to keep these youths in school, attempt to make them more health conscious, identify potential social support sys-

"Your teacher tells me you've become the class clown."

Cartoon © Mike Shapiro.

tems, develop a sense of group pride, and, finally, sensitize teachers to the needs of these students.

Erikson believes that the young in our society are searching for something, someone to be true to. They yearn for stability in an age of change, and their search may lead to extremes. But the search is a time for testing both self and the world.

The Search for Identity

Adolescence is the period Erikson is most often associated with, mainly because of his speculations about the adolescent **identity crisis**. Faced with a combination of physical, sexual, and cognitive changes joined with heightened adult expectation and peer pressure, adolescents understandably feel insecure about themselves—who they are and where they're going. By the end of adolescence, those who have resolved their personal crises have achieved a sense of identity. They know who they are. Those who remain locked in doubt and insecurity experience what Erikson calls **identity confusion.** His views on identity have generated considerable speculation, theorizing, and research.

For example, Marcia (1966, 1980), in a series of studies, notes that adolescents seem to respond to the need to make choices about their identity (particularly regarding career, religion, or politics) in one of four ways:

1. **Identity diffusion,** or inability to commit themselves to choices—the lack of a sense of direction.
2. **Identity foreclosure,** or making a commitment only because someone else has prescribed a particular choice; being "outer-directed."
3. **Identity moratorium,** or desiring to make a choice at some time in the future but being unable to do so.
4. **Identity achievement,** or committing oneself to choices about identity and maintaining that commitment under all conditions.

Self-Esteem Enhancement

In this chapter we have noted that development of self-esteem in children and adolescents is important to their mental health and overall performance in school. Recently, concern about the gender gap in self-esteem has caused educators and psychologists to examine the causes of a drop in self-confidence in girls in the adolescent years. One of the major reasons contributing to this decline is the reaction of adult family members and teachers. Girls may discover that some adults believe that males can do things that females can't. Boys simply feel that they are fairly good at a lot of things (Friberg, 1991).

Self-esteem is an evaluation of the information contained in the self-concept; it emanates from what the child is as a person (Pope, McHale, & Craighead, 1988). Pope and her associates have developed a program for self-esteem enhancement that can be of great benefit to school children and adolescents. The authors note that it is useful to examine children's self-esteem in five areas:

1. *Social,* which involves children's feelings about themselves as friends to others;
2. *Academic,* which deals with children's evaluations of themselves as students;
3. *Family,* which includes children's feelings about membership in their families;
4. *Body Image,* which involves children's perceptions of their physical appearance and capabilities and is based on their satisfaction with the way that they look and perform; and
5. *Global Self-Esteem,* which entails a general evaluation of the self.

These authors have also developed a program to enhance self-esteem in children and adolescents. The program, based on social learning theory, has several features that teachers and other professionals can use in schools. The program focuses on the following eight components:

1. *Social problem solving.* In this part of the program, students are taught to adopt a social problem solving perspective.
2. *Self-statements.* Students are taught to change self-statements that are negative and to use more positive statements about themselves.
3. *Attributional style.* This component entails teaching a special type of self-statement to explain positive and negative events.
4. *Self-control.* Students are taught cognitive strategies to help them change their behavior.
5. *Standard setting.* Students are taught to evaluate their performance by the link between cognitions and behavior.
6. *Social understanding and skills.* Students are taught to use their previously learned skills to evaluate their own thoughts and feelings as well as the thoughts and feelings of others.
7. *Communication skills.* Students are taught to communicate effectively with others.
8. *Body image.* Students are taught to accept their physical selves.

Educational psychologists have been increasingly concerned about the connection between emotional well-being and success in school. You should be alert to those students who appear to have low self-esteem. Fortunately, there are programs (such as the one just described) in which students can participate to facilitate their self-esteem and improve their academic functioning.

Educational Implications

For teachers working with adolescents, integrating the physical, sexual, and cognitive changes of adolescence and focusing adolescents on particular and clearly defined goals becomes the crucial task, one whose successful attainment leads to healthy feelings of identity.

Teachers can help their students acquire psychosocial maturity by:

- treating them as *almost adult*; that is, providing them with independence, freedom, and respect. For example, give them the chance to discuss, argue, and present their own views but always within the framework of classroom control;
- challenging them with realistic goals that coordinate classroom activities with college and career choices. For example, have them research ways in which the math or science that they are studying in class relates to job skills;
- using materials that challenge, not defeat, and that are both biologically and psychologically appropriate. For example, if you have a student who has difficulty reading at the secondary level, try to find reading material that is interesting but not too difficult; that is, high interest, low vocabulary; these students would resist using a reader from an obviously lower level; and
- constantly recalling the issue of identity versus identity diffusion. For example, help your students to discover their strengths and weaknesses through their classroom work. Suggest they read stories in which the characters work out a personal problem and in so doing find out about themselves.

TEACHER ◄──► STUDENT
INTERACTIONS

Erikson's Adolescent Years

1. During the adolescent years, teenagers engage in excruciating self-scrutiny.
   - Consider giving your teenage students "free time." Have an interesting classroom full of learning aids, interest areas (books, microscopes, educational games, etc.) easily accessible to students. Let students use the items at their discretion. After establishing a few rules for "free time" (ordinary rules of conduct are to be followed: only a certain number are allowed in any one area at a time; when the teacher says that time is up, each person must clean up the area in which he or she is working), walk around, talking, explaining when asked, but mainly listening. You demonstrate your trust in them; they in turn reveal the academic areas in which they are weak. They may also reveal personal problems as well as topics that interest them.
   - Each student writes a journal entry and submits it to you. Students can write about anything they wish. Many will write about personal problems. You write back, answering their questions and commenting on the information used in the entries after each is submitted.
   - Develop communication strategies such as rap sessions and pep talks. Get your students to ask: Is this really worth getting upset about? Present hypothetical situations that relate to their experiences and have the students judge whether the matter is worth their consideration. If a student feels that it is, ask why. Are there other solutions to the situation?
   - Encourage your students to give themselves a pat on the back when they handle personal situations competently.
2. Rapidly occurring developmental changes—physical, sexual, cognitive, and social—can lead to an identity crisis.
   - Have on hand popular teenage guides that they may borrow about sex and drugs, AIDS, and other current social problems; or suggest they find them at the library.
   - Develop your own sensitive responsiveness towards their emotional needs.
   - Encourage your students to join extracurricular activities you think may interest them.
   - Coordinate with the guidance and career counselors programs that will help students plan for their future.
   - Keep in touch with parents by telephone or by personally inviting them to school programs.
3. Teachers, through classroom work, can help students to acquire a needed sense of identity.
   - Develop academic units that will highlight their expertise. You may have a student in your class who has traveled to a country you are studying. If so, in a social studies class, for example, encourage the student who has been there to share experiences with the class.
   - Stress the skill of communication. By being able to express how they feel in groups and with individuals and by learning how to listen, teenagers will realize that they are not the only confused human beings, and they will learn numerous ways to deal with their fears.
   - Encourage teenagers to be assertive. If they are in a highly stressful situation, by asking questions and expressing their needs, they can identify and relieve their stress.
   - Teach them problem solving strategies. Show them how to break a problem down into a series of steps so that it no longer seems mountainous. Problem solving also involves thinking about alternative ways to deal with a situation so that it is not necessary to respond in the same way every single time something happens.
   - Be sympathetic to the student who is not doing well, who is showing signs of buckling under accumulated pressures or is withdrawing from situations. Teenagers often need a confidant in such cases.

Stage 6 Intimacy versus Isolation (18–35 years)

Erikson believes that a sense of **intimacy** goes beyond being sexual and involves the capacity to develop a true and mutual psychosocial intimacy with friends, the ability to care for others without fearing a loss of self-identity. Young people of this age continue to develop their identity by close relationships with others. If the young adult fails to acquire a sense of intimacy with others, a sense of isolation may appear. They avoid relationships and there is a refusal to commit to others.

Stage 7 Generativity versus Stagnation (35–65 years)

During middle age, individuals think about the future of both society and their own children. Care for others is an outstanding characteristic of this period, which implies an obligation to guide the next generation by passing on

Learning is enriched when individuals from more than one generation share knowledge and experiences.

desirable social values. If a sense of **generativity** (similar to productivity and creativity) is lacking, individuals may stagnate, suffering from morbid self-concern. Basic to a sense of generativity is care, which means that individuals assume responsibility for the well-being of the next generation.

Stage 8 Integrity versus Despair (over 65 years)

As Erikson (1950) stated, those individuals who have taken care of things and people and have adapted to the triumphs and disappointments of life are the people who reap the harvest of the first seven stages. The person who can view his or her life with satisfaction and accept its ups and downs has achieved a sense of **integrity,** which implies that one looks back and sees meaning in life. No despair over age, failure, and missed opportunities clouds this outlook. Basic to a sense of integrity is wisdom, a detached yet active concern with life and its meaning.

For the Classroom

In a thoughtful commentary on the role of schools, Erikson states that children require systematic instruction. He believes that good teachers, those who are trusted and respected by the community, know how to alternate play with work, games with study. They also know how to work well with those students to whom school is just not important right now, something to endure rather than enjoy.

Effective teachers know how to pace their instruction to maximize learning. (This topic is discussed in greater detail in chapter 12.) If we link the importance of pacing to Erikson's comments, we can see that optimal scheduling and time on task demands a good knowledge of students: attention span, interests, and motivation.

Regardless of the level at which you teach, students are on the move. Elementary school students may move from room to room: special projects, assignments, special classes (reading, music, art, science, and physical education, among others). At the secondary level students move from class to class and have study periods, lunch periods, and free periods.

Teachers quickly become aware of the classroom implications of these activities and build their techniques around them. For example, pupils coming into the classroom from recess need a few minutes to settle down. Adolescents returning from a lunch period usually are not ready to immerse themselves instantly in a subject; they must be led into it: questions, announcements, or anything that sets the tone for instruction.

Remember that student attitudes toward school itself will affect your pacing. In the early grades, students tend to be swept up in the academic life of the school. It is the reason they are there. At the secondary level, however, school adds a new dimension; learning must compete with friendships, peer pressure, and rivalries. Good teachers accept these facts of school life and build them into their planning.

Finally, Erikson states that educators must avoid two extremes that have exercised a fascination in the history of education. *First,* early school life should not be a grim reflection of the tensions of adulthood; otherwise students become slaves to formal, and ultimately sterile, regulations. For example, many parents today are determined to turn their children into "Superstudents," regardless of ability or inclination. Under these conditions students will learn what is absolutely necessary but at the risk of a rigid self-restraint that will make miserable their own lives and those of others. *Second,* educators must not fall prey to the seduction of learning as all play, and only when students "feel like it."

Erikson's message is clear: Make every effort possible to understand your students, and the teacher-learner interaction can be both productive and enjoyable for you and your students.

Moral Development

What do you mean by the term "moral"? The very use of the word can cause heated debate. Consequently, educators approach the topic cautiously (if at all), but in a time of terrorism, assassinations, nuclear arms, war, and a burgeoning drug culture, moral education deserves consideration.

What is the school's role in moral education? Some believe that moral issues do not belong in the classroom; others state that moral education goes on in every classroom every day. Students learn about and discuss revolution in history, honesty in leaders, and other moral issues.

Given these realities, many schools have felt the necessity to address the role of moral development through education. Even if your school has not initiated a formal program, you will find it useful to be aware of the theory and research that attempt to describe the moral development of your students (Stigler et al., 1990). Teachers face an unavoidable fact: they make moral decisions every day on such real issues as stealing, cheating, and lying.

Jean Piaget was one of the first psychologists to consider the moral development of children. He formulated his ideas on moral development from observations of children playing a game of marbles. Watching the children, talking to them, and applying his cognitive theory to their actions, he identified the following stages of moral development—how children actually conform to rules.

- Stage 1. Children simply played with the marbles, making no attempt to conform to rules. Piaget (1965) referred to this as the *stage of motor rules.*
- Stage 2. Between about three and six years, children seem to imitate the rule behavior of adults, but they still play by themselves and for themselves. Piaget calls this the *egocentric stage.*
- Stage 3. During the seventh and eighth years, children attempt to play by rules, even though they understand the rules only vaguely. This is the *stage of incipient cooperation.*
- Stage 4. Finally, between the ages of 11 and 12, children play strictly by the rules. Piaget calls this the *stage of codification of rules.*

After youngsters reach Stage 4, they realize that rules emerge from the shared agreement of those who play the game and, therefore, rules can be changed by mutual agreement. They gradually understand that intent becomes an important part of right and wrong, and their decreasing egocentrism permits them to see how others view their behavior. Peers help here because in the mutual give-and-take of peer relations, they are not forced to

accept an adult view. This activity is referred to as the *morality of cooperation.*

Kohlberg's Theory of Moral Development

Fascinated with the study of a child's moral development during his doctoral work at the University of Chicago, Lawrence Kohlberg (1927-1987) attempted to apply Piaget's cognitive rationale to moral development. His doctoral dissertation forced a rethinking of the traditional ideas on moral development. After teaching at the University of Chicago for six years, Kohlberg accepted an invitation to join the Harvard faculty where he continued his longitudinal studies of moral development until his death.

Kohlberg believed that moral stages emerge from a child's active thought about moral issues and decisions (Colby et al., 1983; Kohlberg, 1975). Kohlberg's view of moral development extends from about four years of age through adulthood and traces moral development through three levels that encompass six stages. (Be sure to distinguish stages from levels as you read this section; if you are confused, check Table 4.3.) Passage through the six stages occurs by successive transformations of a child's cognitive structures. The six stages are grouped into three levels: *Preconventional* (4 to 10 years), *Conventional* (10 to 13 years), and *Postconventional* (13 years and over).

Kohlberg believed that moral judgment requires us to weigh the claims of others against self-interest. Thus, youngsters must overcome their egocentrism before they can legitimately make moral judgments. Children who still believe that the world centers on them can't recognize the legitimate claims of others. Also, the level of moral development (what one knows) may differ from the content of moral judgment (what one does). That is, people may know what is right but do things they know are wrong.

Kohlberg's six stages of moral development are illustrated in Table 4.3.

Level 1 Preconventional Morality

Moral development begins during infancy because children are rewarded for what their parents believe is right and punished for wrongdoing. With cognitive growth, moral reasoning appears and control, as we have seen, gradually begins its shift from external sources to more internal self-control.

For youngsters at Kohlberg's **Preconventional Level** *(approximately ages 4 to 10),* punishment and obedience

Table 4.3

Kohlberg's Stages of Moral Development

Level I. Preconventional (about 4 to 10 years).
During these years children respond mainly to cultural control to avoid punishment and attain satisfaction. There are two stages:

Stage 1. Punishment and obedience. Children obey rules and orders to avoid punishment; there is no concern about moral rectitude.

Stage 2. Naive instrumental behaviorism. Children obey rules but only for pure self-interest; they are vaguely aware of fairness to others but only for their own satisfaction. Kohlberg introduces the notion of reciprocity here: "You scratch my back, I'll scratch yours."

Level II. Conventional (about 10 to 13 years).
During these years children desire approval, both from individuals and society. They not only conform, but actively support society's standards. There are two stages:

Stage 3. Children seek the approval of others, the "good boy-good girl" mentality. They begin to judge behavior by intention: "She meant to do well."

Stage 4. Law-and-order mentality. Children are concerned with authority and maintaining the social order. Correct behavior is "doing one's duty."

Level III. Postconventional (13 years and over).
If true morality (an internal moral code) is to develop, it appears during these years. The individual does not appeal to other people for moral decisions; they are made by an "enlightened conscience." There are two stages:

Stage 5. An individual makes moral decisions legalistically or contractually; that is, the best values are those supported by law because they have been accepted by the whole society. If there is conflict between human need and the law, individuals should work to change the law.

Stage 6. An informed conscience defines what is right. People act, not from fear, approval, or law, but from their own internalized standards of right or wrong.

From L. Kohlberg, "Moral Stages and Moralization: The Cognitive Developmental Approach" in *Moral Development and Behavior: Theory, Research, and Social Issues*, edited by Thomas Lickona. Copyright © 1976 Holt Rinehart and Winston, Inc., New York, NY. Reprinted by permission of Thomas Lickona.

still determine what is right or wrong. As their abstract abilities increase, however, youngsters begin to understand that if I do A, I'll be punished, while B will bring something pleasant. Not concerned with moral correctness, they basically try to avoid unpleasant consequences.

Lickona (1983), using Kohlberg's theory but giving it a more practical orientation, devised the following scheme for analyzing moral development at the preconventional level.

- *Two to three years of age.* Love, attachment, and independence mark these years and are the basis for moral reasoning. When the first signs of moral reasoning become apparent, Lickona noted that adults should adopt two techniques to aid development:
- stay within the confines of children's moral stage, helping them to use and consolidate the cognitive and moral tools they possess. For example, a parent may want to teach a child that it's wrong to throw things on the floor, and say to the child, "Jackie, you wouldn't want to break that pretty glass, would you?"
- occasionally challenge their level of moral reasoning and force them to think in a new dimension, to prod them to a higher level. For example, using the previous example, a parent could say, "Jackie, what

would happen if you threw the pretty glass on the floor?"

- *About four years of age.* These youngsters begin to show concern for what's fair, but they are still highly egocentric; fairness is what *they* designate. On a playground, for example, you often see a youngster leave a swing, but when another child starts to use it, the first youngster runs back, saying it's not fair for anyone else to use it "because it's mine." They may revert to lies to get what they want and often become expert manipulators of adults. They are also compassionate and can be challenged to think at a higher moral level. Youngsters at this age are often attached to baby brothers and sisters and become quite protective of them.
- *About five to six years of age.* As children become less egocentric and self-assertive, they may become easier to handle and more obedient. These years probably reflect most strongly the belief that what is right is what adults say. Lickona suggests that you urge children to higher-order moral reasoning while simultaneously appealing to your authority. For example, "Jackie, I wouldn't take Zack's toy. Why not?"

TEACHER ⬌ STUDENT INTERACTIONS

Moral Development—The Early Years

1. Moral development occurs because of a child's active thought about moral issues and decisions and interactions with others.
   - Pose a situation for your class in which each class member pretends to be the teacher. The teacher in the story is upset because he knows that someone in his class is breaking bottles on the playground, but no one will admit it. The teacher must decide if he should punish the whole class or ask class members if they knew who did it. Have each of the students write down what he or she would do if he/she were the teacher. After students have done this, use their answers for class discussions.
   - Ask your students what they would do in this situation. You have just seen your best friend cheat on an important test that will decide who receives the class prize. Should you tell the teacher? Should you pretend you didn't see it? What will you say to your friend later? If you were the teacher and discovered it, what would you do? Why?
   - You probably will want to structure situations in which boys and girls work together. Ask your class what they would do if, while working in teams of two boys or two girls, one of the girls was sick and couldn't come to school. Should a team of two boys work with the girl who was in school? Do you think the girl would want to work with the boys? Shouldn't boys and girls work together?
2. Moral judgments necessitate weighing the claims of others against self-interest.
   - Frequently, two of your students constantly will be at each other. The tension between them may even flow into your classroom. Have a discussion with them in which you act as moderator. Try to get each of them to see the other's point of view, and work out a plan that when one irritates the other, they won't start to fight immediately.

- You will inevitably be faced with a situation in which your students can think only of themselves. It may be as simple as a time conflict between two fourth grades over the use of a VCR. Take this, or similar opportunities, and talk with your class about the rights of others. "We used the VCR this time last week; I know you really want to see this film, but it's not our turn. That wouldn't be fair."
- One way of getting your students to think about the needs and wishes of others is to form groups that must solve individual problems. As students work together, they are forced to take the viewpoints of others into consideration.
- Elementary school children love to use the telephone. This is an excellent way to introduce a language lesson—perhaps on pragmatics—and as you do you can emphasize that other family members may also like to use (or need to use) the phone.
3. Challenging children to think of moral issues at a higher level can advance moral reasoning.
   - Use classic stories such as Huckleberry Finn in which the relationship between Huck and Jim changed as Huck moved beyond mere self-interest to a concern for Jim.
   - Engage a student in role-playing in which the character acts on moral principles higher than those of the student. Have the student identify those qualities that he most admires in the character's personality.
   - Opportunities to discuss ways of improving race relations are an integral part of most social studies curricula. Involve your students in a discussion of busing as a means of insuring racial equality in the schools. Why do some people oppose having their children bused? Why are others in favor of it? Why do people become part of a mob?

- *About six to nine or ten years of age.* Youngsters at this stage show signs of increasing self-awareness. Their sense of interpersonal relationships enlarges to include the notion of two-sidedness. "I'll obey the rules, but there should be something in it for me." Home conditions determine when Stage Two appears. A home atmosphere of mutual respect and fairness encourages the appearance of this stage as early as six years.

Educational Implications

Because young children are highly dependent on adults for their ideas of right and wrong, they are particularly susceptible to being taught, both directly and by example, basic moral principles such as honesty, trustworthiness, and cooperativeness.

- Reinforce examples of desired behavior: praise a child in front of the other children for returning money found in the room.
- Prod young children toward higher order thinking. Encourage them to talk things over with you, giving you the chance to specify what is right or wrong but also explaining why. "Why shouldn't you take your brother's money from the table?" "Yes, you probably would be punished, but you wouldn't want anyone to steal from you, would you?"

• Teach directly; set an example; use stories, movies, school plays, and where possible, urge your students to think about *WHY*.

For teachers and parents meeting youngsters at Stage Two, Lickona suggests tolerance of a youngster's changed concept of the adult-child relationship; that is, children's awareness that *they* have their own ideas. Also, adults can possibly use a youngster's changed concept: if I do something that pleases you, isn't it right that you should do something to please me?

Elementary school children obey because they either expect something in return or want to avoid punishment. Urge them, when you can, to move beyond this level of moral reasoning by helping them to be more sensitive to the feelings of others. When they hurt a brother, sister, or friend, talk about it with them and help them to understand what happened. Appeal to your expectations for them, rather than have them concentrate on rewards and punishment.

Level 2 Conventional Morality

Moral development during the middle childhood years continues to develop from the merger of two influences, authority and mutuality (Kohlberg, 1975). Children at the **conventional level** of moral development are still susceptible to authority, but cognitive and psychosocial changes are beginning to produce differences in outlook. For example, youngsters realize that the opinions and feelings of others matter—what "I" do might hurt someone else.

By the end of the period, children clearly include intention in their thinking. For the typical 6-year-old, stealing is bad because "I might get punished"; for the 11- or 12-year-old, stealing may be bad because "it takes away from someone else." During the elementary school years, children move from judging acts solely by their enormity or **degree** of punishment to judging intention and motivation.

The two sources of influence for elementary school children—namely adults and peers—can cause a frustrating dilemma when the actions of either come into conflict with what the child's changing cognitive capacity determines is wrong. Again we are reminded that a youngster's understanding of moral right or wrong is no guarantee of appropriate moral action.

A new level of moral reasoning—being a good person to please others—appears in the middle to late elementary school years and lasts into the teens (Kohlberg, 1975). This turn to adult authority is marked, and parents mainly shape a youngster's developing conscience. Towards the end of the period peers also become influential.

Educational Implications

We can draw certain conclusions about moral development from the cognitive and psychosocial characteristics of elementary school children.

• They can reason about their actions.
• Their level of moral reasoning may not be an accurate indication of their moral behavior.
• They are influenced strongly by both adults and peers.

These conclusions may seem to point in different directions for a teacher's efforts to improve moral reasoning—for example, discussions of moral dilemmas (see box on page 113) to assess children's level of moral reasoning and to enable them to test the limits of that reasoning.

If you were working with an eight-year-old child, you might pose the following dilemma: you need money for a ticket to a skating party, and you find a wallet with $10.00 in it, but it also contains the owner's name and address. Question the child about returning the wallet: you found it, so would keeping the money be stealing? Why should you return it? What if you don't get a reward? If the child says, "I might get into trouble," you have identified a Stage I child.

By varying your questions, you will discover the range of the child's moral reasoning. Knowing the upper limits gives you a yardstick for measuring that child's behavior and helps you to motivate the child to act at the appropriate level.

Level 3 Postconventional Morality

As youths move into the teenage period, they seem to be equally divided between Kohlberg's Stage 2 and Stage 3; that is, they retain elements of both preconventional and conventional moral reasoning (Colby et al., 1983). By the end of adolescence, most are solidly entrenched in Stage 3, the conventional level. It is not until early adulthood that a few people begin to reason in postconventional ways (Santrock, 1992). Teenagers want to do the "right thing," but their dependence on others clouds their reasoning. Adults, primarily teachers and parents, may advise behavior that is the opposite of what their peers advise, leading to conflict. For example, adolescents whose friends are saying "Well, the clubs are open to two o'clock so it must be OK" may have trouble with parents who are saying "One o'clock and no later." It is in these situations that treating adolescents as "almost adults," that is, reasoning with them, can prove valuable advice.

Although "other-directedness" characterizes adolescents' judgments, their thinking represents a more abstract and sophisticated mode of thought. Cognitive subtleties appear in Stage 3 thinking: no longer bound solely by personal concerns, adolescents consider the reactions of others.

Educational Implications

The developmental changes of the teenage years explain many of the conflicts that seem to buffet Stage 3 youth. Frequently, in critical self-examination, they dislike what they see; they become desperate to be popular and retreat into "everybody's doing it" excuses. Working with teenagers requires some special strategies.

1. *Maintain as positive a personal relationship as possible.* Reason with them by trying to explain your thinking; talk things over with them as often as seems feasible; don't dictate to them.
2. *Work with teens to form a good self-image.* Stress their strengths and absolutely refuse to compare them to others.
3. *Teach moral values by example.* In spite of apparent unconcern, teenagers are impressed by displays of fairness and honesty. Provide a classroom atmosphere in which honesty prevails, and you will have taken a major step toward enlisting class cooperation. Conversations with high school teachers reinforce this point. Secondary school teachers believe that today's students have few "heroes" but do look up to and admire fair, honest teachers.
4. *Balance independence and control.* Your task will be to have students accept your control. Fairness in dealing with your students, when accompanied by appropriate opportunities for independent action, help to establish a harmonious, healthy classroom climate. Remember: you are dealing with "almost adults" (Lickona, 1983).

Criticisms of Kohlberg's Theory

The subjects of a 20-year longitudinal study of moral development by Kohlberg and his colleagues were 58 boys who were 10, 13, and 16 when they were initially tested (Colby, Kohlberg, Gibbs, & Lieberman, 1983). They were tested six times (the original testing plus five followups) at three- to four-year intervals. All subjects progressed through Kohlberg's stages in the suggested sequence; no one skipped a stage. The subjects' moral judgments were closely related to their age, socioeconomic status, IQ, and education.

For his school age subjects, the age breakdown was as follows:

- most 10-year-olds were between stages 1 and 2;
- most of the 13- to 14-year-olds were somewhere between stages 2 and 3 (a few were at either 2 or 3);
- most of the 16-year-olds were at stage 3.

As a result of these and similar studies, considerable support has arisen for Kohlberg's assumption that children proceed through stages of moral development in an invariant sequence. But several commentators remain concerned by the small number of subjects who reach the upper moral stages and by Kohlberg's use of an all-male group.

Most notably, Gilligan (1977, 1982) has questioned the validity of Kohlberg's theory for women. Gilligan believes the qualities the theory associates with the mature adult (autonomous thinking, clear decision making, and responsible action) are qualities that have been traditionally associated with "masculinity" rather than "femininity." The characteristics that define the "good woman" (gentleness, tact, concern for the feelings of others, display of feelings) all contribute to a different concept of morality.

Noting that women's moral decisions are based on an *ethics of caring* rather than on a *morality of justice,* Gilligan argues for a different sequence for the moral development of women (Brabeck, 1983). For boys and men, separation from mothers is essential for the development of masculinity, whereas for girls femininity is defined by *attachment to mothers.* Thus, male gender identity is threatened by attachment, whereas female gender identity is threatened by separation. Consequently, women define themselves through a context of human relationships and judge themselves by their ability to care (Gilligan, 1982, p. 17). As a result of her studies, Gilligan formulated a developmental sequence with three levels, based on the ethic of care as seen in Table 4.4.

Gilligan does not argue for the superiority of either the male or female sequence but urges that we recognize the difference between the two. As she notes, by recognizing two different modes, we can accept a more complex account of human experience that sees the importance of separation and attachment in the lives of men and women and discover how these events appear in different modes of language and thought.

For the Classroom

Schools are in the moral education business, either directly or indirectly. Whatever they do to influence how students think, feel, and act regarding matters of right and wrong becomes a matter of moral education. Some districts have well-planned moral education programs. In others, the curriculum in morality is unwritten. It is reflected, for example, in the attitudes of teachers toward minority and handicapped students and in the attitudes of the community toward academics and athletics (Benninga, 1988, p. 415).

Teachers of adolescents cannot avoid moral issues in the classroom. They will face ethical and value questions

Table 4.4

Gilligan's Theory of Moral Development for Women

Level I: Orientation to Individual Survival
Here decisions center on the self and concerns are pragmatic.

First Transition: From Selfishness to Responsibility
As attachment to others appears; self-interest is redefined in light of "what one should do."

Level II: Goodness as Self-Sacrifice
A sense of responsibility for others appears (the traditional view of women as care-takers). Goodness is equated with self-sacrifice and concern for others.

Second Transition: From Goodness to Truth
Women begin to include concern for self with their concern for others. Is it possible to be responsible to one's self as well as to others? The answer requires knowledge, hence the shift from goodness to truth. Recognizing one's needs is not being selfish but rather being honest and fair.

Level III: The Morality of Nonviolence
Resolution of the conflict between concern for self and concern for others results in a guiding principle of nonviolence. Harmony and compassion govern all moral action involving self and others. Level III defines both femininity and adulthood.

The Moral Dilemma

Kohlberg devised a modified clinical technique—the **moral dilemma**, a conflict causing subjects to justify the morality of their choices—to discover the structures of moral reasoning and the stages of moral development. Here is an example of the moral dilemmas that Kohlberg (1969) presented.

A woman needs a miracle drug to save her life. The druggist is selling the remedy at an outrageous price, which the woman's husband cannot meet. He collects about half the money and asks the druggist to sell it to him more cheaply or allow him to pay the rest later. The druggist refuses. What should the husband do: steal the drug or permit his wife to die rather than break the law?.

Note: You project your own views in your answer.

Asking what kind of person we want emerging from our attempts at moral education, the *ASCD Panel on Moral Education* (1988) concluded that the moral person values morality and then acts on these values. The panel stated that a morally mature person possesses six major characteristics that come from universal moral and democratic principles:

• Respect for human dignity,
• Concern for the welfare of others,
• Integration of individual interests with social responsibilities,
• Demonstrations of that integrity,
• Reflection about moral choices, and
• Active preference for peaceful resolution of conflicts.

Using Moral Dilemmas

Many teachers are now using moral dilemmas in their classrooms. These are thought-provoking dialogues that probe the moral basis of people's thinking. They are real or imaginary conflicts involving competing claims, for which there is no clear, morally correct solution.

Since most students have had little experience in resolving moral dilemmas, teachers should initially be active during the discussion and only later introduce more complex issues that require resolution at the stage above the student's present moral level. Certain strategies will help you make classroom discussions of moral dilemmas most effective:

• Asking *why* to help students identify the dilemma and discover their level of moral reasoning; for example, why is yours a good solution?

in almost every class. Classroom work designed to facilitate moral development can be divided roughly into two types: *informal and formal.*

The *informal* treatment of moral issues occurs in those communities where no commitment has been made to introduce moral education into the curriculum. In those situations, teachers, by the manner in which they interact with their students, by the type of classroom atmosphere they create, and by their handling of sensitive curriculum issues (such as race relations, religion, and aggression) become moral educators.

In a more *formal* setting, specific class time is designated for moral instruction as part of the curriculum. This moral instruction usually entails the discussion of moral dilemmas. Instructors, without dominating the discussion, ask students to explain the basis of their discussions, always gently urging them to a higher state of reasoning and encouraging them to listen to each other, question each other, respond to each other. These formal programs seem to be effective in raising a student's level of moral reasoning.

- *Complicating* the circumstances to add a new dimension to the problem. For example, imagine an official in the East German government with family in the West. When the separation between East and West occurs, he is torn between trying to retain power in the East or moving to the West and rejoining his family. A teacher could begin by discussing loyalty and gradually introduce complications, such as civil conflict, family ties, regional or national commitment, and then ask, "What would you have done?"
- *Presenting examples,* based on incidents at school, such as the student who surreptitiously set off an alarm that disrupted the entire school. The teacher threatens to punish the whole class unless the offender confesses. His friend knows who did it. When the offender doesn't admit his guilt, what should his friend do: let the innocent class be punished or tell on his friend?
- Alternating *real and hypothetical* dilemmas, so that students are encouraged to live by their beliefs. For example, it can be difficult for a student to befriend another student when classmates are mocking him/her because of a different language or customs. But if students have encountered similar situations in literature and in moral dilemma discussions, they are more likely to stand by their principles.

Effective discussions of moral dilemmas also require a conducive atmosphere, which can be encouraged by the teacher's attention to the following four points:

1. You must create an atmosphere of trust and fairness in which students are willing to reveal their feelings and ideas about the moral dilemma with which the group is wrestling. In the lower grades, teachers can avoid becoming the authority when resolution of the issue remains elusive; in the upper grades, teachers must work to bring older students to the point where they will share their beliefs with others.
2. Such an atmosphere results from respecting your students and valuing their opinions. Teachers who are decent and fair in their relations with their students and who respect their students can do much to create a positive atmosphere for moral instruction.
3. An atmosphere conducive to moral instruction does not appear overnight. Students need time to evaluate you, to judge how you react to them as persons. They also need time to decide how you will handle sensitive discussions and to feel secure that they will not be ridiculed or humiliated by their peers or by a teacher.
4. You must be sensitive to what your students are experiencing. Watch for those students who find the

discussion painful, for whatever reason. Make every effort to provide a forum—within the group or in private conversation—for them to express their feelings, which must be on their terms.

The Teacher's Role

Meaningful discussion of moral issues requires careful preparation. For example, a teacher, described by Lickona (1985), was determined to foster such desirable moral qualities in her students as justice, truth, and fairness. She initiated discussions involving these qualities (using the moral dilemma technique) and encouraged her students to search for them and talk about them in their group meetings. When she observed their behavior in typical class situations, she discovered—nothing!

Analyzing her own behavior she realized that her behavior reflected her values and that her students searched for what they thought *she* wanted. She felt that she conveyed the impression that only she had the wisdom to answer the question; thus discussion within the group was limited. After this honest self-evaluation, she reduced the size of discussion groups to six, frequently adopted a devil's advocate position on issues, and encouraged interaction among the children.

She also began to use classroom dilemmas that had moral dimensions and were personally meaningful to the children—why two boys were fighting or why one class kept a movie projector to the exclusion of others. These in-school dilemmas gradually led to a discussion of issues that occur outside the classroom. With a talented teacher, the moral and academic curriculum can be two sides of the same coin. For example, it is almost impossible to read the story of Anne Frank without commenting on the courage of the family that hid her, or during a civics class pointing out the responsibility to vote, or the injustice and unfairness of treating people as unequal because of color or religion.

Talented teachers who are committed to moral education can play a major role in the process. Moral education also can be more effective if teachers follow a few guidelines (Harmin, 1988):

- Speak up for morality. When something is wrong, teachers should speak up forcibly—to explain, for example, that picking on a smaller child is wrong.
- State personal opinions when they feel strongly about an issue—for example, no politician, whether mayor or president, is above the law. When expressing opinions, be sure that you allow others to be heard.
- Take the time to explain rules or positions of right and wrong, not just to announce them. In chapter 13, we'll discuss the need for classroom rules to be clearly understood so that they can work for the good of all.

Focus on Schools

Schools and Character Development

Because there's no way to know what another person is really thinking, we can identify good character only by watching and listening to our students (Wynne, 1988). Therefore, it makes sense for schools to encourage and reward the good conduct of their students. For example, the *For Character* program developed in the Chicago area publicly acknowledges the good conduct and academic efforts of its students, including the following character-building activities:

- tutoring peers or students in other grades,
- serving as a crossing guard,
- acting as a student aide,
- acting as a class monitor,
- engaging in school activities,
- raising funds for the school or community, and
- joining school or community projects.

The program also provides opportunities for motivating students: public recognition through awards and ribbons presented at school assemblies and through mention over the school's public address system and in school bulletins. Such recognition is given to individual pupils, groups of students, and entire classes. The relationship between academic learning and character development is mutually supportive because educators get back what they put into their work (Wynne, 1988, p. 426).

With teachers and students working together to attain moral objectives, students should begin to develop the following characteristics:

1. A sense of self-respect that emerges from positive behavior toward others
2. Skill in social perspective-taking that asks how others think and feel
3. Moral reasoning about the right things to do
4. Moral values such as kindness, courtesy, trustworthiness, and responsibility
5. The social skills and habits of cooperation
6. An openness to the suggestions of adults

Moral Development and Forgiveness

Robert Enright and his associates (in press) have developed a cognitive model of **forgiveness** as a specific application of mercy. His work focuses on the individual who forgives, not on the one seeking forgiveness. The work is an extension of the Kohlbergian justice presenta-

tion, but there are clear differences. Enright et al. present the issues as follows:

> When we ask the fairest solution to a problem, forgiveness never enters the picture. As an example, suppose Billy runs to Mom, telling her that Jill unfairly took all the marbles. Although Mom could ignore it, she probably would engage in some form of justice reasoning. Whether she uses distributive justice, punitive justice, care reasoning, or another form, she is reasoning with a justice strategy of some kind. The parent would not think of forgiving the child in this context. On the other hand, Mom may ask Billy to forgive Jill. If so, and this is the crux of the justice-forgiveness distinction, she is abandoning her quest for the *fair* solution. Instead, she is seeking the compassionate solution, or the one beneficial to Billy's emotional health, or even the one most beneficial to Billy and Jill's relationship (p. 136).

The forgiveness option is distinguished from the justice strategy. Enright notes that in the Heinz dilemma (discussed previously in the chapter), he would focus on a different aspect than Kohlberg by asking individuals what Heinz should do if the druggist conceals the drug. The options may be to use a justice strategy to decide whether to seek retribution on his own, use the courts to sue, or to forgive. Enright has drawn some useful distinctions between the Kohlbergian justice sequence and the stages of forgiveness (see Table 4.5). Teaching students to forgive is an important skill, one that requires both an understanding of how they reason and an awareness of their problems.

Conclusion

In this chapter, we have examined the psychosocial and moral aspects of development, with particular attention paid to the work of Erik Erikson and Lawrence Kohlberg. Your reading about the work of these theorists and the possibility of applying their ideas to the classroom should help you in your teaching. For example, what does Erikson say about a teenager who is caught in the search for identity? Does moral development theory and research help in analyzing students' objectionable behavior when you realize that they know better?

School is a rich social experience for students and teachers, providing numerous opportunities for activities that aid moral development. Try to model appropriate social problem solving and have your students share their responses with their peers.

Table 4.5

Stages of Justice and Forgiveness Development

	Stages of Justice	Stages of Forgiveness
Stage 1	Punishment and Obedience Orientation. I believe that justice should be decided by the authority, by the one who can punish.	Revengeful Forgiveness. I can forgive someone who wrongs me only if I can punish him or her to a similar degree to my own pain.
Stage 2	Relativist Justice. I have a sense of reciprocity that defines justice for me. If you help me, I must help you.	Restitutional or Compensational Forgiveness. If I get back what was taken away from me, then I can forgive. Or, if I feel guilty about withholding forgiveness, then I can forgive to relieve my guilt.
Stage 3	Good/Boy/Girl Justice. Here, I reason that the group consensus should decide what is right and wrong. I go along so that others will like me.	Expectational Forgiveness. I can forgive if others put pressure on me to forgive. It is easier to forgive when other people expect it.
Stage 4	Law and Order Justice. Societal laws are my guides to justice. I uphold laws in order to have an orderly society.	Lawful Expectational Forgiveness. I forgive when my religion demands it. Notice that this is not Stage 2 in which I forgive to relieve my own guilt about withholding forgiveness.
Stage 5	Social Contract Orientation. I am still interested in that which maintains the social fabric but I also realize that unjust laws exist. Therefore, I see it as just, as fair, to work within the system to change.	Forgiveness as Social Harmony. I forgive when it restores harmony or good relations in society. Forgiveness decreases friction and outright conflict in society. Note that forgiveness is a way to control society; it is a way of maintaining peaceful relations.
Stage 6	Universal Ethical Principle Orientation. My sense of justice is based on maintaining the individual rights of all persons. Conscience rather than laws or norms determines what I will accept when there are competing claims.	Forgiveness As Love. I forgive unconditionally because it promotes a true sense of love. Because I must truly care for each person, a hurtful act on his or her part does not alter that sense of love. This kind of relationship keeps open the possibility of reconciliation and closes the door on revenge. Note that forgiveness is no longer dependent on a social context, as in Stage 5. The forgiver does not control the other by forgiving; he or she releases the other.

From R. D. Enright and the Human Development Study Group (in press), "The Moral Development of Forgiveness" in W. Kurtines and J. Gewirtz, editors, *Handbook of Moral Development*, Volume 1, pages 123-152. Copyright © Lawrence Erlbaum Associates, Hillsdale, NJ.

Chapter Highlights

Erikson and Psychosocial Development

- Erikson's eight stages of psychosocial development provide a structure for analyzing the crises and strengths of students' lives.
- Understanding the meaning of these stages in your students' lives can only help to enhance and enrich the teacher-learner interactions.
- Psychosocially, youngsters need those around them to whom they can attach, thus acquiring a sense of security about their surroundings.
- The emergence of self-control is a critical feature of psychosocial growth as children develop their ideas of right and wrong.

- In today's classrooms, students will interact with youngsters from many cultures, which should broaden their sensitivity to and understanding of others.

Kohlberg and Moral Development

- Children begin to understand the moral consequences of their actions as they are rewarded or punished for their behavior.
- To explain this phenomenon, Kohlberg has formulated a cognitive interpretation of moral development that incorporates Piagetian thinking.
- Using the technique of moral dilemmas and analyzing an individual's reasoning, Kohlberg has traced progress through stages of moral development.

TEACHER ⬌ STUDENT
INTERACTIONS

Moral Development—The Later Years

1. Moral development during the elementary school years can be traced to the merger of two influences: authority and a student's growing cognitive capacity.
   - Discuss issues of right and wrong on which there would be agreement: lying, stealing, cheating, and the like. Now ask the class to suggest ways of dealing with these problems if they should occur in the classroom.
   - When students' moral ideas are challenged, they find it painful. Students, for example, can be scornful of "those foreigners. Why worry about their rights—after all, isn't this our country?" Classmates may point out that they have the same rights as everyone else, and discussion can be heated. Encourage students to express their feeling of doubt and confusion as they are prodded to a higher level of moral thinking.
   - Raise such direct questions as "Why is it wrong to cheat?" Try to get your students to realize that cheating is a lie (it's not what you know), people will find out and won't trust you any more, and it's not fair to all your classmates who don't cheat.
   - As Lickona noted, try to teach students to think first and act later. Do this in three steps:
     1. Do I have any options?
     2. What will happen if I do any of these (the options)?
     3. What's the best decision for myself (that is, what do I think is right?) and for others?

2. Understanding what is right or wrong is no guarantee of appropriate moral action.
   - Arrange discussion groups that will address such topics as "What kind of person am I? What kind of person would I like to become?"
   - Organize students into groups to research and to talk to younger students about the effects of using drugs and alcohol.
   - Discuss how movies and television sometimes depict figures that break the law as exciting and charismatic. What effect will that have on younger students? What happens when popular actors and actresses are in such shows?

3. Students are impressed by the moral behavior of their teachers.
   - Show your students that you respect them, by listening to their opinions and acting on them when you can.
   - Be consistent in your own behavior; don't just talk about fairness and justice to all but demonstrate these traits when you interact with all of your students, regardless of race, color, and beliefs.
   - Treat all of your students in the same manner; what's wrong for one is wrong for all.
   - Ask your students to write an essay about desirable moral qualities for teachers. You will usually discover much about yourself and what students think of your behavior.

- Kohlberg's ideas have been challenged, especially by Carol Gilligan, who proposes a different path for a woman's moral development.
- Educators believe that the concepts of moral development can be translated into classroom practice.

Reciprocal interactions
Pretend play
Self-esteem
Sensitive responsiveness
Strange situation
Transactions

Key Terms

Attachment
Autonomy
Conventional level
Forgiveness
Generativity
Identity achievement
Identity confusion
Identity crisis
Identity diffusion
Identity foreclosure
Identity moratorium
Industry (versus inferiority)
Initiative (versus guilt)
Integrity (versus despair)
Intimacy (versus isolation)
Moral dilemma
Preconventional level

Suggested Readings

Bowlby, J. (1969). *Attachment*. New York: Basic. Here is the major work that provided impetus to the study of attachment behavior. Written in an engaging manner, Bowlby traces the background of his work and the gradual insights that led him to recognize the significance of a child's first attachments.

Dacey, J., & Kenny, M. (in press). *Adolescents today*. Dubuque, Iowa: Wm. C. Brown. A readable account of the adolescent years with strong emphasis on Erikson, this book is particularly relevant for an understanding of today's teenagers.

Lickona, T. (1985). *Raising good children*. New York: Bantam. An enjoyable and practical introduction to the world of a child's moral development. Working from Kohlberg's basic framework, Lickona nicely integrates theory and practice with case studies.

Social Relationships: Teachers-Students-Parents-Peers

Ruth Groves stirred her coffee slowly as she talked with Ann Kline and Mary Powers in the faculty room. "I went to an open lecture at the university last night," she said, "and it was pretty good. They had a guest lecturer commenting on changes in education for the nineties and he really emphasized the need to analyze the relationships in our school."

Mary Powers laughed. "Does he think we have relatives on the payroll?"

Ruth joined in the laughter and then said, "No, his point was that we should look carefully at teacher-student, student-student, and teacher-parent relationships."

Just then Ron Gallo walked in and said, "We have PTO meetings; we see parents when a problem develops. What else can we do?"

"Well, replied Ruth, "He pointed out that with everything around us changing so rapidly, students have even more challenges and need help from many different sources."

"What's new about that?" snorted Ron.

Ann Kline spoke up for the first time. "The thing is, Ron, there's a lot of expertise among our parents, and perhaps we should call on them more."

"Not only with the parents, Ann," said Mary Powers. "Some of our own students are terrific at different things. We have sixth graders, for example, who are super with computers."

Ruth enthusiastically interrupted. "That's great. It's not only a matter of sharing knowledge, but it encourages the idea of working together."

Phyllis Allan entered, and jokingly said, "What revolution are you people planning?"

"Nothing as exciting as that, I'm afraid, Phyllis," said Ruth. "We were just talking about ways of getting us all—students, teachers, parents, and administrators—to work together even more closely."

R uth Groves' comments are particularly pertinent when we consider the changes in our society and around the world. As the number of multicultural students in our schools increases, greater opportunities arise for understanding other cultures by interacting positively with these students.

This opportunity for interaction leads us into the world of relationships. "For most of us, relationships with other people are the most important part of our lives" (Hinde, 1979, p. 3). This statement by Robert Hinde, a well-known English scientist, probably reflects what most of us think about our dealings with others. Further reflection, however, leads to the observation that relationships between adults and children (especially teachers/parents and children), and among peers, constitute a major force in learning and development.

In this chapter, you'll examine the nature of relationships to determine their meaning and development. You'll then trace how teacher-student, student-student, and teacher-parent relationships all affect a student's achievement.

When you complete your reading of this chapter, you should be able to:

- define the role that relationships play in learning and development.
- analyze a specific relationship by its constituent interactions.
- differentiate categories of interactions in the classroom.
- evaluate relationships between teachers and students as either positive, neutral, or negative.
- identify significant relationships among students.
- detect how specific peer relationships are influencing a student's behavior.

(a)

(b)

(c)

(d)

Schooling and the process of learning cultivates a variety of interpersonal relationships: (a) teacher-student relationships, (b) parent-student relationships, (c) parent-teacher relationships, and (d) student-peer relationships.

Table 5.1

Sources of Students' Relationships

Parent-Adult	Sibling-Relatives	School	Peers	Others
Mother-father	Brothers	Principal	Male	Day-care personnel
Mother-stepfather	Sisters	Teacher(s)	Female	Friends (family)
Father-stepmother	Stepbrothers	Classmates	Group	Neighbors
Father	Stepsisters	(older, younger)		Religious personnel
Mother	Extended relatives			Medical personnel
Mother-other	(cousins, etc.)			Psychologist
Father-other				Specialists (coaches,
Relatives (aunt, uncle,				counselors, music,
grandparents)				art teachers, etc.)
Foster parent				
Adoptive parent				
Institutional personnel				

• suggest ways of improving teacher-parent relationships.

First, let's turn our attention to the nature of relationships and decide if we agree with Hinde's rather dramatic statement.

The Importance of Relationships

The discussion among the teachers at the chapter's opening points to a conclusion that is becoming daily more evident: a school is a community of relationships. At the heart of students' social and psychological needs lies the urge for harmonious relations with others. The manner in which a student forms relationships, with whom, and the nature of the relationships help to determine the atmosphere in which learning occurs. Examined in this manner, the cumulative effect of relationships weighs heavily on educational outcomes. A poor teacher-student relationship can have decidedly negative effects on learning.

New findings about the origin and nature of relationships provide opportunities for improving learning and development. These data, translated into meaningful, practical suggestions, can offer teachers rich insights into their students' behavior and help both teachers and students in their adjustments to each other. For example, students whose parents are divorcing may have strained relationships with one or both parents, and the strain may be affecting classroom behavior and performance.

Life inside the classroom is not the only significant element in determining what type of teacher-student relationship evolves. A changing social environment means that teacher-student relationships differ from those of a generation or even a decade ago. Teachers must adapt to students whose experiences with peers, television, cable TV, VCRs, subtle and overt sexuality, and drugs (among other challenges) are a frequent occurrence. Working mothers and single parents introduce new variables into knowledge of students and their relationships.

To help you understand the key role that relationships play in schooling, this chapter will first explore the nature of relationships, then focus on such specific relationships as student-student, teacher-student, and teacher-parent.

The Nature of Relationships

During the past decade there has been sharpened interest in the role that interpersonal relationships play in human development (Brazelton, 1984; Damon, 1983; Hartup, 1983; Osofsky & Connors, 1979). Since 1977, researchers have displayed an increasing fascination with the kinds of interactions that influence children, especially the interactions between mother-child (Ainsworth, 1979; Bakeman & Brown, 1980) and teacher-student (Clark & Peterson, 1986; Hartup, 1983).

To give you some idea of the many complex relationships in which a student may engage, examine Table 5.1. Here you see the possible partners in their relationships, many of whom a student will contact in any one day.

The Meaning of Relationships

A relationship implies a pattern of intermittent interactions between two people involving interchanges over an extended period of time (Hinde, 1979, 1987). The **interactions** are mutual; each person's behavior in a dyadic relationship (two people) acknowledges the behavior of the other person. Teachers react to students according to the way that they behave. If one student withdraws after a reprimand and another talks back, you act differently toward each.

The term **relationship** also suggests continuity among interactions; you may have a relationship with a school friend whom you have not seen for years. You know that when your students enter your room in September, your interactions with them will last until June—or even longer if a positive, friendly relationship develops.

Since relationships emerge from the sequence of interactions, more is involved than the overt behavior of both participants. Perceptual, cognitive, and affective elements are particularly pertinent to the nature of any relationship. It is not only what one says or does that is significant but also how the partner perceives that behavior.

You will react differently to different students because of how you perceive them and how you feel about their behavior. Finally, you constantly will make judgments, based on personal emotions and cognitions, about a partner's thoughts and feelings: teachers about students, students about teachers.

These ideas are highly significant for understanding the developing relationship between teachers and students. Note the emphasis on perceptual, cognitive, and affective features. When we link these to a student's competence, it becomes clear that students react to far more than our behavior; the quality of the interactions instantly begins to establish the nature of the relationship.

Characteristics of Relationships

Eight categories of dimensions are useful for analyzing relationships (Hinde, 1987). These categories are the content of interactions, the quality of interactions, the diversity of interactions, the frequency and patterning of interactions, reciprocity vs complementarity, intimacy, interpersonal perception, and commitment. Read these carefully and try to understand them so that you can apply them when and where appropriate. When you examine your interactions with students, parents, colleagues, and administrators, analyze your relationships by using these categories.

The Content of Interactions

The **content of interactions** refers to what participants do together and distinguishes the kind of relationship. For example, teacher-student specifies a definite range of

---

Focus on Teachers

Checking Your Relationships with Students

If we pause for a moment and consider the implications of the type of interactions you have with your students, you can better understand how a particular relationship has developed. Recall the previous discussion about instructional techniques and the kinds of functions you perform—all involving interactions with students.

For example, you explain either to a group or to individuals. You provide correction and feedback. You answer questions. We could create a lengthy list of activities, but, in all of these, you are interacting with students. Do you ever step back and analyze the interactions you engage in with your students? You would find it profitable; you may improve relationships and improve achievement.

Occasionally during the year, once your rules are in place and your class knows what is expected, why not try something like this. Ask your students to complete a check list—about you—involving topics such as the following. Put a check on the line where you think your teacher (name) belongs. (Make it as easy as possible for them.)

	High	Low
1. Fair		
2. Plays favorites		
3. Firm		
4. Easy		
5. Helpful		
6. Ignores students		
7. Friendly		
8. Aloof		
9. Concerned		
10. Disinterested		

Obviously you can include many other and different items, but you can see how you get an appraisal of your relationships with your students. Whatever technique you decide on, it's a good idea to evaluate yourself; if a negative profile emerges, you have a chance to assess what is wrong and take corrective measures.

---

interactions, what teachers and students do in a classroom. It is not how the interactions are conducted but the behaviors that characterize the relationship. You talk to your students; you direct them; you ask them questions; you encourage discussion.

Every type of interaction that we can think of need not be present for us to designate a relationship as teacher-student. For example, should we distinguish the teacher-student relationship of the regular classroom teacher from that of a student with a substitute teacher? Although certain interactions may be lacking in the substitute teacher-student relationships, the basic interactions are present that enable us to identify "teacher-student."

The Diversity of Interactions

Do individuals engage in only one type of interaction or many? Different relationships usually entail many types of interactions. Teachers not only teach, but they also act as role models, counsel, and even play with students. The more ways in which you interact with your students, the more you will understand them.

Diversity of interactions has special significance for understanding relationships. Teachers who restrict their interactions to lecturing, for example, limit the possibility of exploring the deeper dimension of a particular subject and encouraging a student's social development by other types of interactions.

The Qualities of Interactions

The **quality of an interaction** depends not only on what the participants are doing but also on how they are doing it (Hinde, 1979). For example, a teacher may discipline harshly or firmly, thus suggesting a relationship that the content of the interactions alone cannot define. The responses of each of the participants appear to be central to the notion of quality. If you use the checklist mentioned on p. 122, you should get some sense of the quality of your interactions with your students.

The Relative Frequency and Patterning of Interactions

The consequences of interactions may depend not just on their frequency but on frequency in relation to other types of interactions. **Frequency and patterning of interactions** refer not only to the number of interactions but also to interactions of different types.

Before we can describe a teacher-student relationship as warm, we must assess many kinds of interactions. How does a teacher behave during instruction or react to inattention? Some interactions are the opposite of each other but are still classified in the same category. Teacher effectiveness, for example, involves both helping and disciplining when required.

Reciprocity versus Complementarity

Reciprocity refers to those interactions in which the participants do the same thing either simultaneously or in turn, such as children's play: one runs after the other and then the roles are reversed. **Complementarity** refers to those interactions in which the behavior of both participants is quite different yet blends together harmoniously—for example, the interactions between teachers and their students.

In the teacher-student relationship, as in all close personal relationships, both participants are satisfying their needs. Teachers like young people and usually enjoy working with their subject matter; students require considerable learning to adapt to a complex society. Here we see the complementary nature of the interaction. Teachers ask questions; students answer. Students ask questions; teachers answer. These are examples of reciprocity.

Intimacy

Intimacy means the extent to which participants in a relationship are prepared to reveal aspects of themselves to each other. In this way, each member acquires knowledge of the other as a total person. Yet intimacy is never complete; there is always the tendency to withhold something. In the classroom, for example, both teachers and students engage in so many interactions that they should understand each other's behavior in different situations.

Interpersonal Perception

Interpersonal perception refers to how each partner in a relationship sees the other. Each of us has a sense of self that our perceptions of what others think of us has strongly shaped. The nature of the relationships that we all experience from birth has, to a considerable extent, made us what we are.

If reactions of others powerfully influence a student's sense of self, then the impact of family, school, and friends indeed is critical. As we mentioned previously, it is not just a student's or teacher's behavior that is important. How the partner in the relationship perceives the behavior is crucial.

Commitment

Commitment defines those situations where one or both parties either accept their relationship as continuing indefinitely or direct their behavior toward insuring its continuance or bettering the relationship. Commitment requires time, or acceptance of the bad with the good, and provides a sharing that affords mutual support.

Once a relationship is established, the participants behave in a manner calculated to maintain the relationship until circumstances dictate otherwise. For students, however, the chance of placement in a particular classroom establishes relationships over which they have no control.

Table 5.2

Dimensions of a Relationship

Category	Meaning
Content	What the partners do together helps to label the relationship (teacher-student)
Diversity	The type and extent of interactions
Quality	How the interactions are conducted—are they pleasant or nasty?
Relative frequency and patterning of interactions	Does the relation among the interactions suggest a pattern: friendly, hostile?
Reciprocity versus complementarity	Do the interactions "fit"? Are they smooth and agreeable, not erratic? Do they contribute to a comfortable relationship?
Intimacy	The extent to which the partners know each other determines the kind of interactions possible.
Interpersonal perceptions	How each partner sees the other affects the self-concept of both.
Commitment	Degree to which both partners accept the relationship—for a relationship to be successful each partner must have faith in the other's commitment.

Table 5.2 summarizes Hinde's eight categories. With Hinde's dimensions as a guide for assessing relationships, we can now turn our attention to the powerful role of reciprocal interactions in developing relationships.

The Reality of Reciprocal Interactions

Among the socializing agents in your students' lives are parents, siblings, peers, and television. The major socializing agent within the school, however, is the student's teacher. As a major force in the social development of your students, teachers (and the school in general) face a constant challenge: how can teachers structure their students' relationships to preserve individuality but simultaneously help them to conform to society's expectations? Teachers play a key role here because, for their students, they represent society's values. Thus the teacher-student relationship can help students to be themselves and also to be productive members of society.

At the heart of any discussion about relationships, especially those that occur in the classroom, are **reciprocal interactions.** Picture yourself interacting with a student:

you both are constantly changing, and these changes then affect the interactions that make up the relationship between the two of you. What you learn about students and what they learn about their teacher continually changes, even if slightly, the nature of the relationship.

Examining the interpersonal relationships in this manner dramatizes the necessity to look beyond "the relationship" between teacher-student or mother-child. The interactions of the specific relationship differ; they differ from relationship to relationship. The interactions between teacher and student differ distinctly from those between mother and child, and they differ within any one relationship. At times teachers must be firm; at other times, they must be warm.

The purpose of the interactions, then, varies for each individual, reflecting the past experiences of each. For example, think of the relationship between a teacher and a student. Within the structure of the classroom, the teacher-student relationship emerges, in which the purpose of the instructor is to provide for educational needs (sometimes physical and psychological), while the student's intent focuses almost exclusively on learning.

Students' Perceptions of the Teacher-Student Relationship

Although the primary emphasis in this chapter is on the teacher, researchers are beginning to gather important data on what students think of classroom processes. Teachers bring their own expectations to their relationships with students. (We'll say more about this later in the chapter.) Students react, positively or negatively, to these teacher behaviors. For example, Wittrock (1986) reported that students' perceptions of their teachers have a strong impact on achievement and that this effect begins as early as first grade. Not only does this perception affect achievement, but students also use teacher interactions as one source of knowledge about their self-concepts and ability. This should come as no surprise since we know that seven-year-old students begin to develop deeper and more abstract perceptions of adults.

As students perceive and think about the interactions occurring in the classroom between themselves and the teacher and between the teacher and others, they begin to discriminate any differential treatment. They notice that boys seem to receive different treatment from girls, low achievers from high achievers, and they may even note differences based on social class distinctions.

These facts of classroom life become an integral part of the teacher-student relationship that begins tentatively; slowly firms; and, finally, sets both the emotional and cognitive tone of academic life. The final, established relationship emerges from the kind of interactions that have taken place between the teacher and student. In this chapter we'll trace the origins of these interactions and what influences the kinds of interactions that appear.

But for now remember that what happens in the classroom—the relationship between you and your students, and among students—will influence the success of your teaching and the extent to which your students learn.

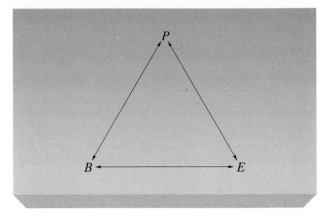

Figure 5.1

Schematic representation of Bandura's reciprocal determinism model of human behavior.

The interactions that constitute this relationship—talking, showing, correcting, and listening are mainly complementary, and though they are obviously different, they just as obviously "fit." Consequently, "fit" refers to the match between a student's and teacher's behavior. If the fit is appropriate, then the relationship, with its interactions, will be a positive and powerful force toward learning and development.

Although our main concern is with teacher-student relationships, your students will form relationships with a remarkable variety of individuals: parents, siblings, peers, teachers, counselors, and many others. Some are much more significant than others, but all leave their mark.

The success of school relationships, both with teachers and peers, often influences the form that social development takes. But to analyze these significant interactions adequately requires that we learn more about the nature, givens, and origins of relationships. Once we have accomplished this, it is then possible to study more carefully student-student, teacher-student, and teacher-parent relationships.

We know now that students are temperamentally distinct from the moment of birth. Think for a moment about the different reactions of children to punishment for misbehavior: some sulk, some become surly, some become aggressive, and some become withdrawn and passive. Do you react to each of these behaviors in an identical manner? Of course not. Your reactions change because of the different behaviors toward you. The sequence is as follows:

- I do something to you—you change
- As a result of the changes in you, I change
- As a result of my change, you change
- As a result of your change, I change

Bandura's (1978) **reciprocal determinism** model, deduced from social learning theory, nicely captures these ongoing interactions between a student and a teacher. Bandura conceptualizes human behavior as a continuous reciprocal interaction among an individual's thoughts, behaviors, and environmental factors. He uses the term determinism to "signify the production of effects by events, rather than in the doctrinal sense that actions are completely determined by a prior sequence of causes independent of the individual" (1978, p. 345). Schematically (see Figure 5.1), Bandura represents reciprocal determinism as a triadic or three-way interaction among behavior (B), cognitions and other internal events that affect perceptions and actions (P), and external environment (E). External events can be the actions/reactions of other people, such as a peer, a teacher, or a parent, or external events can involve inanimate objects or conditions.

Students are not passive recipients of information from teachers. They choose to attend or not; they assimilate the content according to the structures of their existing knowledge; and they retain or not. Even the apparently passive student is continually judging the teacher and class content, deciding whether or not "to go along with it." It is a sobering thought.

Particularly important in interacting with students is the notion of **sensitive responsiveness.** Although we have a way to go before we have adequate concepts or adequate measures of what sensitive responsiveness means, we are beginning to realize its significance in our relations with others. For example, you may know that individual students respond to certain parts of your instruction. Why are they sensitive to some and not others? Why are you sensitive to certain student behaviors and not others? The answers seem to involve not only the discrimination between different cues provided by students, but in addition the giving of appropriate responses.

Thus the stage is set and the cycle commences: students act on adults and change the adults; adult behavior directed at the student then reflects these changes. The tone of the interactions between students and teachers assumes a definite structure that will characterize the relationship for the time they spend together, introducing the issue of the individuals involved in the relationship.

The Person in the Relationship

In any dyadic relationship, such as teacher-student, both individuals bring to the relationship physical and biological characteristics that range from appearance to genetic endowment. Since some of these characteristics, especially physical appearance and temperament, are what we notice about another person, we should attempt to understand their functions in emerging relationships.

Physical Appearance

For good or ill, physical appearance affects the manner in which others react to us. Attractiveness is as important for students as it is for adults. Langlois and Downs (1979) studied the effect of physical attractiveness on peer relations and discovered a definite developmental pattern. Reasoning that we all—teachers and students alike—evaluate the behavior of others as a function of attractiveness, the authors speculated that physical attractiveness is highly significant in the development and expression of relationships.

The issue that Langlois and Downs addressed was whether there were behavioral differences between at-tractive and unattractive children. They studied 64 children who were judged attractive or unattractive by 20 adult females who were shown full-face black-and-white photographs of the youngsters. Clothing cues were eliminated, and children with eye glasses or facial deformities were excluded. Half of the subjects were three years old, while the remainder were five years old. The dyads were two attractive children, two unattractive children, and mixed pairs. The authors found that the most aggressive behavior appeared between the five-year-old dyads where one child was unattractive. The activity level between the attractive-unattractive children was significantly higher than that between attractive children. Thus, unattractive children seem to be more aggressive and active, a pattern that appears with age.

Two conclusions are possible from this study: unattractive children (in the eyes of adult raters) actually behave differently, an idea which is highly unlikely. Or these behavioral differences may be the result of negative expectancies. Since the people around these youngsters may anticipate difficulty (solely on the basis of appearance), the children quickly learn the appropriate behavior. Conclusion: Don't let a student's appearance affect the relationship with you.

Temperament

A personal characteristic that appears equally as influential as physical appearance is that of **temperament.** As Carey (1981) stated, children's temperaments contribute significantly to their interactions with their environments, interactions that then immediately begin to structure emerging relationships. Carey defines temperament as an individual's behavioral style in interacting with the environment. Temperament used in this sense describes how a student behaves, rather than what is done or why it is done.

Thomas and Chess (1980) identified nine temperament variables that they believe qualify as stylistic: emotional intensity, activity level, response threshold, biological rhythmicity, adaptability to altered social circumstances, approach/withdrawal tendency in new social situations, distractibility, persistence, and mood. These researchers argue that collectively these nine variables result in differing behavioral styles that characterize emotional functioning of individuals.

Social Skills

Developing the skills for successful relationships with one's peers, parents, and teachers is one of the most important accomplishments of childhood. This interpersonal social process, although not fully understood, begins soon after birth and is influenced by organismic variables such as one's own physical abilities, language,

Focus on Classrooms

"Goodness of Fit" in the Classroom

Research clearly indicates that temperament is largely constitutional, observable during the first days of life, stabilizes at three or four months, remains remarkably consistent, and continually interacts with the environment (see Buss & Plomin, 1985; Carey 1981; Thomas & Chess, 1980). As Goldsmith (1983) noted, we ignore the action of genetic factors in temperament at our own risk. Twin studies, adoption studies, and family studies all testify to the notion of an inborn temperamental disposition. (For a more detailed analysis of this growing belief, see Matheney, 1980 and Torgerson, 1981.)

The recent research concerning the roots of temperament suggests that students have an inborn personality that the environment in which they find themselves modifies. For example, one student's disposition may be basically impulsive; another's may be essentially withdrawn. Remember that you also possess a definite personality that enables you to be more compatible with some students than with others.

The idea of different personalities working together introduces the concept of **goodness of fit**, which describes the consonance between the properties of the classroom (including you) with its expectations and demands, and your students' characteristics, behaviors, and types of behaving. Goodness of fit is a practical and pertinent notion in any analysis of relationships, especially that of teacher and student. If you view a relationship as a series of interactions over time, you become aware of those behaviors and attitudes—both yours and your students'—that could lead to personality conflicts.

You may be having difficulty with a student who seems to take forever to master something, yet the student is bright and willing, but seems to be growing sullen. You may be quick and active, a difference that creates a situation that could lead to a personality conflict. If you now think of the temperamental differences that are brought to any relationship, you may better understand that your student is simply demonstrating a behavioral style that, although not yours, suits the student's temperament. You can then temper your impatience, give more time whenever possible, and provide a goodness of fit to your relationships.

and communication skills, and environmental variables such as family members' and peers' involvement and interactions.

Behaviors such as sharing, helping, initiating relationships, requesting help from others, giving compliments, and saying "please" and "thank you" are socially desirable behaviors that most everyone would agree are examples of social skills. In general, social skills may be defined as socially acceptable, learned behaviors that enable a person to interact with others in ways that elicit positive responses and assist in avoiding negative responses (Gresham & Elliott, 1984).

The normal course of the development of social skills in young children generally has been studied in one of two ways: a) those investigations whose purpose is the description of increasing sociability with increasing age; and b) studies that identify the cognitive, linguistic, and behavioral components of successful sociability. The classic observational investigation of preschool children's free play by Parten (1932) established the early assumption that, developmentally, there is a progression from solitary (2 to 2 1/2 years) to parallel (2 1/2 to 3 years) to cooperative (4 1/2 years) play. Solitary play literally means playing alone or at least away from others. Parallel play is illustrated when children play alongside each other, but do not (or infrequently) interact and are probably engaged in different activities. Cooperative play involves frequent interactions between children around a common activity. More recent research, however, has cast doubt on that sequence of development. For example, Smith (1978) found that parallel play was characteristic of the youngest children, but that the older children (three- and four-year-olds) alternated between solitary and interactive play. Smith's findings reflect a current re-evaluation of the developmental status of solitary and parallel play and the continued interest in the social development of young children.

Having reported the general agreement that social interaction does indeed increase with age, and that interactive behaviors occur earlier developmentally than first imagined, other empirical work has directed our attention to the behavioral components of successful interaction. Findings from these studies are especially relevant to efforts to remediate social skill deficits in children having difficulty interacting effectively (cf. Eisenberg & Harris, 1989).

Social Initiation

Leiter (1977) found requests to play that were accompanied by whining, crying, begging, or coercion were more likely to be denied, while friendly, smiling initiations with suggestions for an activity were more likely to be accepted. This is not to say, however, that children who are ingratiating have success at social initiation. Rather, a judicious balance between assertiveness and accommodation to others' interests constitutes a successful strategy (Lamb & Baumrind, 1978). Similarly, Hazen, Black, and Fleming-Johnson (1984) found that popular children who were successful at entering others' play situations were able to alter their entry communications to fit the demands of ongoing play situations, reflecting not

Learning how and when to enter groups in a socially appropriate way is an important social skill.

only the knowledge of a wide array of social initiation strategies, but also the adaptability to use them appropriately. In all, it is apparent that successful social initiation is characterized by specific nonverbal and verbal communication behaviors that clearly transmit the entering child's desire, as well as his/her awareness of the contextual accommodations that must be made.

Social Interactions

Other skills enhance the maintenance of social interaction. Asher (1990) described the characteristics of these maintenance skills frequently used by children. These range from complex perspective-taking abilities, such as adjusting the effectiveness of one's communications to other children's needs, to more straightforward reinforcement strategies, such as offering other children praise and approval, as well as going along with another child's plan or wishes. Related to these maintenance skills is the manner in which children who exhibit successful interaction styles manage interpersonal conflict. In their study of preschool children's friendships, Hartup, Laursen, Stewart, and Eastenson (1988) found that

conflicts among friends did not differ from those among nonfriends in situational inducement, frequency, or duration. What did make them distinct was the effort to maintain the interaction in spite of the disagreement.

The previous brief review illustrates some important aspects of normative social development of young children. As children develop, Gresham and Elliott (1990) documented the development and daily use of social skills in five basic domains: cooperation, assertion, responsibility, empathy, and self-control. Gresham and Elliott used the acronym of CARES to facilitate memory of these five domains of behavior, which can be characterized as follows:

1. **Cooperation**—behaviors such as helping others, sharing materials with a peer and complying with rules.
2. **Assertion**—initiating behaviors such as asking others for information and behaviors that are responses to others' actions, such as responding to peer pressure.
3. **Responsibility**—behaviors that demonstrate the ability to communicate with adults and concern about one's property.
4. **Empathy**—behaviors that show concern for a peer's or significant adult's feelings.
5. **Self-control**—behaviors that emerge in conflict situations, such as responding appropriately to teasing or to corrective feedback from an adult.

Children ages three through eighteen were found to exhibit behaviors in these five basic social skills domains; of course, as you would expect, the meaningful use and frequency of occurrence of such behaviors generally increases with age. Significant deficits in these basic social skill domains were evident in many handicapped students (Gresham, Elliott, & Black, 1987; Stinnett, Oehler-Stinnett, Stout, 1989) and correspondent to poorer academic achievement (Frentz, Gresham & Elliott, 1991; Gresham & Elliott, 1990).

Several researchers have concluded that most schools have a "hidden" curriculum for social skills (Cartledge & Milburn, 1986). That is, teachers clearly value prosocial behaviors such as those representative of the basic social skill domains we reviewed, yet most teachers do not explicitly or directly teach students these behaviors. In an interesting investigation of teachers' social validity ratings of social skills, Gresham and Elliott (1988) learned that teachers who taught mainstreamed handicapped and non-handicapped students (grades 1–8) were in relatively high agreement about the social skills they valued most in their classrooms. The most highly-rated or most important social skills in the eyes of teachers involved academic-related behaviors. For example, following the teacher's verbal directions, requesting assistance from the teacher, and attending to class speakers were all rated highly by teachers. Other important social skills, according to the teachers, were controlling one's temper, sharing materials with others, and responding appropriately to teasing by a peer.

Of the student characteristics we have discussed (i.e., physical appearance, temperament, and social skills) that influence interpersonal relationships, social skills are the most malleable. In fact, numerous social skills curricula have been published and are frequently being used in schools to explicitly teach students basic social problem-solving techniques and social skills (Elliott & Gresham, 1991). An instructional skill unit from the *Social Skills Intervention Guide* (Elliott & Gresham, 1991) is illustrated in the Teacher-Student Interaction box on pages 130–131. Note that in the box a five-step instructional model (Tell-Show-Do-Follow Through/ Practice-Generalization) is used to teach the social skill and is directed by a teacher or trained group leader.

Having reviewed some of the important building blocks of social relationships, we may now ask: How can knowledge of relationships help at school and in the classroom? We will first examine peer or student-student relationships, then turn to teacher-student relationships.

Peer Relationships

As children grow they expand their contacts beyond those with parents and siblings and quickly establish a network of peer relationships whose influence rivals the family only. The number of relationships expands dramatically as a youngster enters school, for example. **Peer** means equal and, used developmentally, equal typically refers to age (that is, children within twelve months of each other). Children, however, need not be equal in any other characteristic; they may be quite different with regard to intelligence, physical skills, social skills, and almost any attribute that we wish to mention, differences that quite accurately describe the classroom environment. The assumption of equal age in peer relations may be a myth since most children interact with others who are more than twelve months older. Often chronological

age differs, but students may be at the same level cognitively, socially, and/or emotionally (Hartup, 1983).

The interactions appear to fall into a definite pattern. For example, certain social actions such as nurturance are more frequent with older children. Some actions occur more frequently with age-mates (e.g., aggression), while other actions are more frequently directed toward older children (e.g., dependency). Finally, a majority of the social actions of children are with same sex peers.

The Developmental Sequence

Is there a developmental progression to the relationships that children form? Given the rapid changes in all aspects of development, variety in both peers and interactions seems inevitable. The general sequence of development is as follows.

Infancy

Infant relationships may well become one of the most important research topics of the future because of changing societal conditions. As of now, the best that we can do is to make rather general statements concerning the social interactions of infancy.

- Most infants have contacts with other infants.
- Infants lack social skills.
- Infants exhibit interest in other infants.
- During the 6–12 month period, developmental changes appear in the interactions between infants (specifically, interactions are more frequent and complex).

With growing numbers of infants appearing in daycare centers as early as three months of age, we can only speculate about changes that could occur in the social development of these youngsters. Certainly, developmental restraints are present that will restrict the extent of interactions in spite of the circumstances: limitations of speech, physical mobility, perceptual skills, and cognitive competence.

More contacts with others, however, facilitate a sharpening of social skills. Other language modes such as reaching and touching increase. Greater following tendencies, at first with eyes and later, during the 6–12 month period, with creeping and crawling. Their attention also becomes more focused. If these changes turn out to be consistent for all daycare children, we may conclude that the potential exists for changes in social interactions.

TEACHER ⬌ STUDENT
INTERACTIONS

Teaching Students Social Skills

Teaching children social skills involves many of the same methods used to teach academic concepts. Effective teachers of both academic and social skills model correct behavior, elicit an imitative response, provide corrective feedback, and arrange for opportunities to practice the new skills.

Elliot and Gresham (1991), the authors of the *Social Skills Rating System*, recently published the *Social Skills Intervention Guide* to facilitate a link between assessment results and interventions for children who have social skills deficits. The following skill training unit on "Responding to Teasing from Peers" illustrates a basic instructional sequence that teachers can use successfully to teach students appropriate social skills.

Domain: Self-control

Subdomain: Anger control

Skill: Responds to teasing from peers appropriately

Definition of skill: Student responds to teasing from peers by ignoring, changing the subject, making a joke, or complimenting the other person

Learning objective: Student will appropriately respond to teasing or name-calling from peers

Tell Phase

1. Introduce skill by asking questions such as:
   - Have you ever been teased by your peers? How does this make you feel?
   - Why do you think people sometimes like to tease others? (makes them feel better, like to see other people squirm, etc.)
   - What have you done when you were teased by others?
   - What happened? How did you feel afterwards?
   - What are some ways you could respond to being teased? (get angry; get feelings hurt; ignore it; change the subject; make a joke; compliment other person)
2. Read definition of skill to be taught and discuss it to ensure understanding by students (key terms are noted below).
   - Key terms: teasing, name-calling, being butt of jokes, complimenting, changing the subject
3. Rationale for importance of skill:
   - Sometimes you can get people to stop teasing you by ignoring them. They don't get a charge out of teasing if you don't get upset by it.
   - Many times you can stop being teased by just changing the subject.
   - Often, if you compliment the other person who is teasing you, he/she will stop.
   - Sometimes making a joke about yourself takes the fun out of teasing.
4. Steps in performing the skill:
   a. Decide if you are being teased.
   b. Try to understand why you are being teased.
   c. Choose a strategy (ignoring, making a joke, complimenting, changing the subject).
   d. Implement strategy.
   e. Evaluate how you did and how other person reacted.

Show Phase

1. Group leader models the skill:
   a. Positive modeling: Use steps identified in 4 above.
   b. Negative modeling: Model inappropriate ways of performing skill such as teasing back, showing your feelings are hurt, yelling or screaming, pushing or shoving other person.
2. Group leader models skill again but this time emphasizes and comments on each step as it is performed.

Figure 5.2 summarizes this sequence beginning with the origins of interactions, identifying major developmental changes that are known to occur, and ending with recognition of emerging relationships across the lifespan.

Once the need for relationships has been established, it remains relatively constant throughout our lives, even extending into the classroom. Relationships among students in your class are either continued from other years or quickly formed among new classmates. From a teacher's perspective, of course, relationships with stu-

dents become vital, since harmonious interactions with students contribute to a successful—both personally and professionally—classroom environment.

Relationships in the classroom follow a sequential hierarchy similar to the following:

- All of us have a need for relationships.
- With age changes, different partners fulfill this need.
- Peer relationships extend into the classroom and can affect learning.
- Inborn temperamental dispositions affect the quality of interactions.

3. Group leader role plays skill with other students. Read the following vignette and role play:
   - Julie is climbing on the monkey bars during recess. A couple of kids behind her yell at her to get off. They say "Hurry up and get off, Fatso. You're no good at climbing." They continue to call her "Fatso."
4. Group leader leads a discussion of alternative ways the person could have performed the skill. Decide if students need another role play. If so, choose one of the following vignettes and role play:
   - (optional)
     Anthony is playing on the playground with his class. Several students from another class taunt and tease Anthony by saying: "You're in the stupid kid class; you're retarded."
   - (optional)
     Donna is in a wheel chair. Some girls yell at her when she goes down the hall, "Where did you get those wheels, crippo?"
   - (optional)
     Bill has struck out for the third time during the softball game. His teammates say, "You're a bad player, four eyes. You can't even see the ball."

Do Phase

1. Ask students to define skill verbally. At least half the group provides definitions. Refine and clarify definitions as needed.
2. Ask students to provide a rationale for performing skill. Ask group members who do not provide a definition to provide rationales.
3. Ask students to list critical steps in performing skill. List steps in proper sequence on chalkboard or flip chart.
4. Ask students to model the behavior. Use vignettes not used in Show Phase for role plays.
5. Student-directed role plays. Have students generate new or novel situations in which skill could be performed.
   a. Non-participating students provide feedback on role-plays.
   b. Group leader provides informative feedback of individual student performances.

Follow Through and Practice Phase

1. Periodically review and practice steps in performing the skill. Watch for instances of teasing and appropriate as well as inappropriate use of skill.
2. Have students generate a list of things that kids get teased about and discuss how they could respond.
3. Make a list of "good-natured" teasing incidents and discuss how this form of teasing is not something to get upset about or feel bad about.
4. Have students monitor the times they are teased for one week. Be sure they record who, what, when, where, and how they responded.

Generalization Phase

1. Teach self-instructional strategy for responding to teasing and name-calling. Have students write down steps for skill performance on note cards. Have them memorize steps, verbalize steps aloud, whisper them, and finally use covert speech to repeat steps for dealing with teasing.
2. Role play different situations in which children are teased. Use situations generated in the Follow Through Phase (#2) for role plays.
3. Role play situations in which children are teased by familiar and unfamiliar peers.
4. Discuss and role play alternative ways that students could appropriately respond to teasing. Use ways generated under #4 of the Show Phase for this activity.

Social Skills Intervention Guide by Stephen N. Elliott and Frank M. Gresham © 1991 American Guidance Service, Inc., 4201 Woodland Road, Circle Pines, MN 55014-1796. All rights reserved.

- Recognizing temperamental characteristics can help teachers to achieve a "goodness of fit" in relationships with students.

Remember: If your relationships with students are positive, you will usually have a pleasant, productive year. Occasionally you will be at cross purpose with a student whose misbehavior defies your efforts to reach him/her. If this is an unusual case, then don't feel guilty; it probably has little to do with you and reflects factors outside the classroom and your control.

Early Childhood

Most studies of peer relationships during the early childhood period (two–six years) have been conducted at daycare centers and nursery schools. Again we note the age progression in developing relationships: social contacts occur more frequently among five-year-olds than three-year-olds. Aggressive interactions are quite common in the period, although aggression decreases in proportion to friendly interactions (especially true among middle class boys).

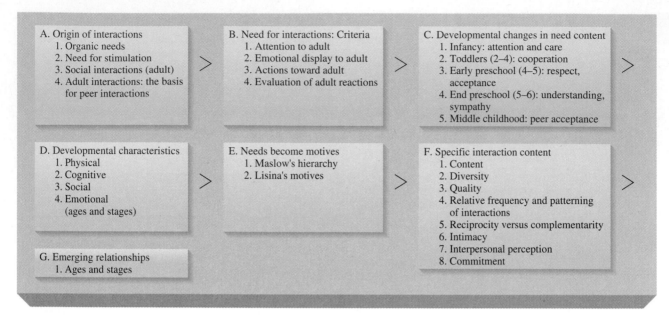

Figure 5.2
The origin and development of relationships.

Particularly interesting are the changes in quarreling during these years. Similar to their other social exchanges, older youngsters (four, five, six years) engage in fewer but longer quarrels with members of their own sex (Hartup, 1983). Boys quarrel more frequently among themselves than girls, usually over objects. We previously mentioned the gradual change from physical to verbal aggression toward the end of the period.

Recall those characteristics of the early childhood youngsters that we discussed in chapters 3 and 4, especially language and play, which further the development of relationships. Although solitary activity persists, older children of this period are more obviously bidding for the attention of their peers.

Middle Childhood

With school entrance a child's world alters dramatically. Peer relationships become more intense; a child must get along with peers, which entails new ways of thinking about others. Teachers become a force to be reckoned with. No longer may a child ignore the wishes and ideas of other children. Evaluation of, if not acceptance of, others can no longer be avoided, and again we witness the influence of developmental changes on social interactions. Verbal aggression advances while overt physical aggression declines (more so for girls than boys); moodiness becomes more common.

These changes match the developmental path of students. Cognitive development, for example, enables a

student to understand more clearly the dynamics of various relationships, especially such dimensions as perception and commitment. Students' developing cognitive abilities enable them to make definite decisions about the behavior of their peers (Dodge et al., 1990). Concrete operational children have acquired flexibility in their thinking and manifest a basic form of perspective-taking. They become more astute at detecting meaning in facial expressions and vocal intonations. As their communication ability increases, they begin to incorporate multiple sources of information, a skill that helps them to assess any relationship.

Adolescence

As noted in chapter 4, adolescence becomes a time of testing for most teenagers. They still want to remain close to parents, but the tugs of separation and independence are sharp and can be difficult to handle harmoniously. While these strains occur in the home, the attraction of peer relationships grows intense and assumes a sensitivity and sense of belongingness that challenges adults—teachers and parents—to remain "sensitively responsive."

How many times have you heard teenagers say, "I can't talk to my parents." If the relationships within the home are poor, adolescents turn to others who appear sympathetic to their views. As a teacher, work hard to develop sensitive responsiveness to the clues that students offer.

Table 5.3

Selman's Levels of Perspective-Taking

Level	Friends	Peers	Adult-Child
0—Undifferentiated and egocentric (3-6 years)	Friendship depends on physical closeness	Something physical holds group together (play ball)	Adult seen as boss; are physical needs met?
I—Differentiated and subjective, separates physical from psychological (5-9 years)	Someone does what child wants	Forms unilateral relations, no complementary roles	Adults seen as caretakers and helpers
II—Develops reciprocal concept of people—can look at self objectively, realizes that others can do what they do (I know that you know) (7-12 years)	Interactions become desirable in themselves	Realizes that relationships can exist	Adults seen as counselors; both can help each other
III—More complex concept of people—can have mixed feelings about same person (10-15 years)	Recognizes relationship, mutual sharing	Sees group as social whole	Adults are tolerated but begins to sense mutual satisfaction in relationship
IV—Symbolic concept of people, realizes complexity of relationships (12 years)	Different relationships satisfy different needs	Begins to understand how group works	Recognizes a changing system of interactions

Understanding the Changes

Acceptance of the role that peer relations play in development has mounted, and attention has centered on a child's interpretation of these relationships. Why do your students react as they do? As in all considerations of developmental change, we see the interactions of young people in a particular setting such as the classroom. Thus, to shed light on developing peer relationships (as in all relationships) the environment, the nature of relationships, and their developmental progression all require scrutiny. Are there any explanations for the different ways that students look at relationships as they develop?

Selman and Interpersonal Understanding

Focusing on children themselves, Selman (1980) attempted to clarify emerging interpersonal relationships. He formulated a theory of **social perspective-taking** levels that incorporates a social-cognitive developmental framework. Selman (1980, p. 24) stated that it is impossi-

ble to separate children's views of how to relate to each other from their personal theories concerning the psychological characteristics of individuals. Thus, children construct their own version of what it means to be a "self" or "other."

As a result of investigations of children's interactions with others and guided by the theoretical speculations of such theorists as Piaget, Flavell, Mead, and Kohlberg, Selman proposed four levels of social-perspective taking. Table 5.3 presents a summary of thinking at each level and how it affects a student's perception of friends. Note how continued cognitive development leads to growing sophistication in interpreting the dynamics of the relationship and in satisfying ever more complex needs.

If we apply these concepts to schooling and conceive of the classroom as a network of interpersonal relationships structured to facilitate the attainment of educational goals, we can agree with Johnson (1981) when he noted that peer experiences are no superficial luxury. Rather maximum achievement demands constructive student-student relationships.

Peer Relationships and Social Status in the Classroom

Whom do you like the best? Whom do you like to work with the most? Whom do you like the least? These are typical questions used to discover relationships among students in a classroom and can be used to summarize any given student's status among his or her peers. Such an approach to characterizing students' social status is called sociometry or **sociometrics.** Sociometrics have a long history in applied research on children's friendships and social status. Two basic approaches to sociometrics have been prevalent in the research literature: peer nominations and peer ratings. In general, nominations are considered to measure popularity, whereas ratings are indicative of acceptance.

A sociometric nomination procedure developed by Coie, Dodge, and Coppotelli (1982) has become one of the methods researchers and school psychologists alike use most frequently. The Coie system is both simple and sophisticated—it uses simple questions to generate a rather sophisticated five-category classification system of social status. Specifically, all the students in a given classroom are asked to select the three classmates whom they like most (LM) and the three they like least (LL). The confidential nominations, both LM and LL, for each student are used to compute social preference (SP = LM - LL) and social impact (SI = LM + LL) scores. Social preference and social impact scores are then used to identify students in one of five social status groups: popular, average, controversial, neglected, and rejected. (Technically, the SP and SI scores must be transformed using a simple statistical Z-score transformation.)

Box Figure 5.1, using the dimensions social preference and social impact, illustrates the relative relationships among these five social status groups. From this figure, one concludes that *popular* students are preferred by many of their peers and have a moderate to high impact on them; *controversial* students are liked most by some, but liked least by about an equal number of peers (regardless of their preference, they do make a high impact on others); *neglected* students are not really noticed by their peers (few, if any, nominated them as like most or like least, and they seem to have little or no impact on others); finally, *rejected* students are actively disliked by many and seem to have a moderate to high impact on other students. Coie (1982) and others have found that those students in the rejected group are at-risk for poor interpersonal relationships and later maladjustment.

Many children are concerned about who likes them and have fears about not being liked.

PEANUTS reprinted by permission of UFS, Inc.

Educators are using the sociometric techniques, such as the one we have described above, more frequently to gain an understanding of the social relationships within classrooms and to screen for children who may be at-risk for interpersonal difficulties. Admittedly, however, some educators have expressed concern about the use of negative nominations (i.e, naming someone whom you do not like), assuming that they might result in increasing negative interactions among students. Several alternative methods have been designed to overcome this concern. One is the use of teacher nominations. Ollendick and his colleagues have demonstrated that teachers can reliably identify aggressive, withdrawn, and popular children when provided objective criteria of these categories (Ollendick, Oswald, & Francis, 1989).

Regardless of the specific methods you use, consider routinely monitoring the social status of students in your classrooms once they have had a couple of weeks to get to know each other. For more details on the use of sociometric techniques in your classroom, consult the work of McConnell and Odom (1986).

Johnson (1981) identified several reasons for this conclusion:

• peer relationships influence educational aspirations and achievement, especially with regard to motivation and a supportive environment;

• peer relationships also contribute to the socialization of students—the acquisition of attitudes, values, and information;

• peer relationships can predict future psychological health, especially as a sign of the ability to maintain cooperative relationships;

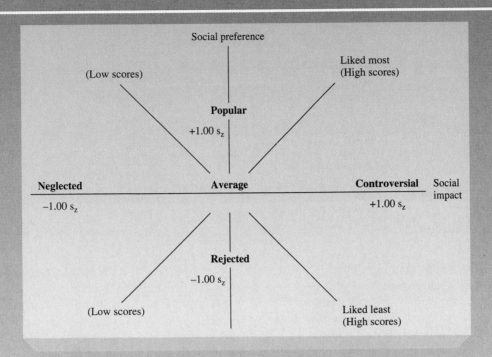

Box Figure 5.1

Relationships among positive and negative social choice measures, the dimensions of social preference and social impact, and five types of social status.

From J. D. Coie, et al., "Dimensions and Types of Social Status: A Cross-Age Perspective" in *Developmental Psychology*, 18(4), 557-570, American Psychological Association. Reprinted by permission.

• peer relationships contribute to the development of sex-role identity, control of impulsive behavior, and the growth of necessary social competencies.

As Johnson noted, simply putting students together will not produce positive relationships. You must be sure that students positively interact with each other in a supporting context. Johnson insists that you must control the major factors affecting the interactions, especially the way you structure goals (cooperative and not always competitive) and the way in which you manage conflict. The inevitable conclusion: You need to work at

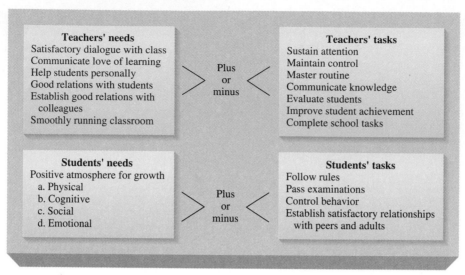

Figure 5.3
Reconciliation of needs and tasks.

establishing positive student-student relationships as well as teacher-student relationships.

With this work on the nature of relationships and the influences of peers as background, let us now turn to the specifics of teacher and student relationships.

Teacher-Student Relationships

Our basic concern is with a teacher's response to the press of classroom responsibilities: establishing effective routines, instruction, managing groups, keeping records, evaluating students, and communicating with parents and other school staff. Given this array of classroom pressures, teachers must learn to respond quickly and decisively.

Why, then, should teachers be overly concerned with relationships in the classroom when they are so busy? Many teachers react as Ron Gallo did in the chapter opening: Who has the time? What's new about attending to relationships? One answer is that the latest research indicates just what a positive force the various relationships that occur within the school can be.

The Classroom Context

As we have just noted, individual characteristics alone cannot explain the dynamics that exist between teachers and students. The school itself, as an institution, offers certain norms, regulations and opportunities that affect an individual's reactions to them—both teacher and student. The school, also, must respond to the particular pressures of the community. Thus the relationships that emerge take shape within a total educational culture.

Nevertheless, our basic concern here is with the classroom and a teacher's response to the press of activities, especially the press of instruction, managing groups, keeping records, evaluating students and establishing effective routines. How do positive teacher-student relationships develop within this context?

When teachers respond to students, they enter into a relationship where they must resolve the issue of warmth and distance that arises in teacher-student relationships. As Feiman-Nemser and Floden (1986) noted, teachers have the dual responsibility of maintaining control and attention in their groups while simultaneously encouraging an openness to learning. The first task demands distance while the second requires warmth and involvement. Teachers must be aware of the tasks they are responsible for without losing sight of students' needs. Figure 5.3 illustrates some of the needs and tasks of both teachers and students.

If after reviewing the figure, you feel that you have several minuses, then you can assess what you must do to restore balance. That is, your needs are being met while you simultaneously satisfy those obligations that accompany teaching. You can see how the many variables must intermingle smoothly if need satisfaction is to occur. Even if you are satisfied with the flow of events in your classroom, remember that conditions change and that you must be prepared to change with them to maintain balance.

Teacher Roles

A teacher's role can be divided into two categories: those that relate to the adults in the school system—employee, subordinate, adviser, and colleague—and those that

Focus on Classrooms

The Power of Role

Here we should consider several ramifications of the term "role." **Role** usually refers to behavior, or certain expectancies about behavior, associated with a particular position in society. You have certain expectations about how a mother should act, how a doctor should perform duties, or how a mechanic should work on your car. You also have certain ideas about a teacher's duties and how students should behave.

If you think of the school as the institution, teachers and students have roles, and you can more easily visualize how the expectations for both roles reflect the school's place in a particular community. Your interpretation of the proper behaviors for both roles should meet the school's and your students' expectations; students' behavior should, in turn, fall within the school's and teacher's accepted bounds. Otherwise, the possibility of role conflict arises.

Never underestimate the power of role as an influence on behavior. In the famous prison study by Haney et al. (1973), 24 male college students were randomly selected from a pool of volunteers to act as either prisoners or guards in a mock prison constructed in the basement of Stanford University's psychology building. The subjects were told, as prisoners, that they should expect surveillance and harassment, such as having their rights curtailed, but that no physical abuse would be allowed. The "guards" were told to maintain order for effective functioning of the "prison." Following their arrest and booking, the subjects were imprisoned.

In less than two days, trouble erupted. Prisoners barricaded themselves, screamed, and cursed at the guards, while the guards in turn increased their harassment and intimidation of the prisoners. Within several days, some prisoners became so emotionally upset that they had to be released, and the experiment was halted.

Here we see a clear example of how the expectations associated with role affect behavior. If your expectations of how students should behave are at odds with your students, then the potential for role conflict exists. If a student does not live up to expectations, or has different views about acceptable behavior, or cannot understand how the teacher interprets a role, conflict can arise. Thus, role conflict emerges if there are significant digressions from role expectations.

Remember the implications of the prison study: We react strongly to role expectations, tend to behave accordingly, and become upset when others fail to meet our expectations. If you have trouble with a student, or students, take the time to examine your role expectations for students—your role expectations may be either too high or too low.

relate to the students—instructor, disciplinarian, parent substitute, confidante, and motivator. When we examine these categories in light of Goodlad's survey of American schooling (1984), we conclude that teachers feel most influential with regard to curriculum, instruction, student behavior, and communicating with parents. They feel less influential regarding fiscal management and the selection and evaluation of colleagues. They also have a sense of powerlessness on matters directly affecting them; that is, they feel more secure about policies concerning students than they do about issues concerning their own destiny.

Thus, teachers still see themselves as the central figure in the classroom: establishing a classroom atmosphere and directing activities. This role is also apparent in their manner of instruction: the authority figure in control.

Bruner (1960) examined the classroom functions of the instructor, and identified three sources of teacher behavior. *First, the teacher is a communicator of knowledge,* which implies mastery of the knowledge to be communicated and mastery of effective methods of communication. Both could result from more careful recruiting of teachers and better preparation in teacher-training institutions. *A second role of the teacher is that of a model,* an individual who is both competent and exciting, and who will inspire in students a love of learning. *Finally, the teacher is a symbol,* the immediate representative of "education."

In a sense, teachers represent all adult society and can be particularly significant figures in shaping a youth's attitudes, interests, opinions, and values, let alone intellectual achievement. As we noted earlier, teachers will be successful to the extent that they introduce knowledge, discipline, and motivation into their relationships with students.

There are less complicated roles: friend of youth, member of a profession, member of a community, and the teacher as an individual—different roles, different skills, different behavior, same person. One may well question whether the task is even possible. Yet all teachers exhibit strength in some of these roles, and in them you should attain your maximum impact.

What Influences a Teacher's Role Performance?

What skills does a teacher need, and what are some characteristics that may influence role function? Certain roles are exercised outside the classroom: faculty member, community liaison officer, and learner. Other tasks require skills that place the teacher in an administrative

Table 5.4

Description of Teacher Roles

Instructor*	Classroom Manager	Communicator	Decision Maker
Conducts effective lessons based on: a. gaining attention b. clear objectives c. review d. presenting effective stimuli e. guiding learning f. involving students g. providing feedback h. aiming for retention i. aiming for transfer j. planning for evaluation	Establishes classroom rules Formulates routine Plans for orderly transition Maintains class control Plans assignments, materials, and lessons Keeps orderly records Completes school tasks	Clear dialogue with students Successful relations with colleagues Positive interactions with administrators Keeps parents informed and accepts their support	Concerning student achievement Concerning student behavior Concerning curriculum Concerning school policy Concerning parental input

*From R. Gagne, *Essentials of Learning for Instruction.* Copyright © 1988 Prentice-Hall Inc., Enlglewood Cliffs, NJ. Allyn & Bacon, Inc., Needham Heights, MA.

role: disciplinarian, keeper of records, learning-aids officer, and program director. Instructional roles include motivator, resource person (involves telling, explaining, and demonstrating) and evaluator and adapter (adjusting material to individual differences). In other words, a teacher must be a first-class facilitator.

Several influences suggest success or failure in the performance of each. For example, a teacher's social class strongly governs classroom interactions. Researchers repeatedly have demonstrated differences in the relationship between middle class teachers and lower class students, and middle class teachers and middle or upper class children. Teachers in a preparatory school may relate quite differently to their students than teachers do to students in an inner city school. Student ability, the organizational climate of the school (autocratic versus democratic), student and teacher expectations, and the teacher-student interaction all affect a teacher's perception of role.

Among the personality characteristics that affect a teacher's selection of roles and skillful performance in them are needs. A secure, confident teacher, for example, is open to questions and discussion about issues while someone less secure may interpret questions and disagreements as a personal challenge.

Teacher roles have long fascinated psychologists and educators and understandably so, since success in the various roles ultimately determines teaching success. Table 5.4 summarizes these roles of instructor, classroom manager, communicator, and decision maker.

Teachers' Thought Processes

The subtle and complex process that we have been describing—how situational variables interact with personality variables and role perspective—move to a deeper dimension when we introduce the notion of teachers' thought. Recently attracting substantial research interest, teachers' thought processes can determine, either positively or negatively, how they will interact with individual students, especially when linked with classroom context and role perspective. (See Figure 5.3)

Our particular concern here rests on the belief that what teachers think will affect their behavior while teaching. For example, Clark and Peterson (1986) videotaped twelve experienced teachers each teaching a 2 1/2-hour social studies lesson to three groups of seventh and eighth grade students. Segments of the tape were then shown to the teachers, and the teachers were asked the following questions:

- What were you doing in the segment and why?
- Were you thinking of any alternative strategies?
- What were you noticing about your students?
- How are the students responding?
- Did any students' responses cause you to act differently from what you had planned?
- What were your particular objectives in this segment?
- Was there anything in this segment that affected what you did?

From this and similar studies, Clark and Peterson (1986) concluded that a small portion of teachers' reports

Focus on a Leading Researcher

Penelope L. Peterson, professor, Department of Educational Psychology and Teacher Education, Michigan State University.

Source: Klausmeier, H., and Wisconsin Associates (1990). *The Wisconsin Center for Education Research: Twenty Five Years of Knowledge Generation and Educational Improvement.* Madison, WI: Wisconsin Center for Education Research.

Penelope L. Peterson received her Ph.D. from Stanford University in 1976. She is Professor of Educational Psychology and Teacher Education at Michigan State University. Currently, she is Co-director of the Institute for Research on Teaching and the Center for the Learning and Teaching of Elementary Subjects at Michigan State University. In addition, she is a senior researcher in the Center for Policy Research in Education (CPRE) funded by OERI. In her CPRE work, Peterson is examining the relationship between new roles for teachers and classroom practice in restructured schools. She is also co-directing with David Cohen an OERI–and NSF-funded study of the effects on classroom practice of the state-level reform of elementary school mathematics in California.

about their thought processes during instruction dealt with instructional objectives (14 percent). Another small portion was devoted to subject matter (5–14 percent), while a larger percentage of time was given to thinking about instruction itself—for example, "They could use some positive reinforcement" (20–30 percent). Finally, teachers reported that the largest amount of "thinking" time focused on the learner—for example, "Nobody seems to be listening;" "I thought Timmy would get that" (40–60 percent).

In an informative analysis of these data, Clark and Peterson (1986) discovered that a large proportion of teachers' statements about learners could be included in the following four categories:

1. Perceptions—teachers responded to a sensory experience—a pupil might frown, indicating a lack of understanding.

2. Interpretations—teachers attached meaning to perception—"Marcia seems to be having trouble with this problem."
3. Anticipations—predictions made about what would happen during the lesson—"I'll bet they'll have trouble with this."
4. Reflections—thoughts about related events but other than what had been done—"Alex did a much better job in math this morning."

When the percentages in each of these learner categories were analyzed over a wide range of studies, a remarkable consistency appeared—*about 50 percent of teachers' thought about learners falls into these four categories.* We can summarize, then, by stating that the greatest amounts of teachers' interactive thoughts (thoughts during actual teaching) were concerned with learners.

Teacher Attributions

Any discussion of teachers' thought processes would be incomplete without including attribution theory (see chapter 10). Among the most important beliefs that teachers have about students are those that involve teachers' perceptions of the causes of students' behavior, that is, teachers' attributions for these causes. Attribution theory, as you will read in chapter 10, uses the categories of *ability, effort, task difficulty, and luck* to explain one's successes or failures. In addition, teachers often tend to attribute students' successes and failures to themselves (taking responsibility for students' behavior) or to the students (effort, ability, and thus placing responsibility upon the student).

Teachers' ego-involvement may also be part of the attribution process. In other words, since I am so active in my students' learning, I take responsibility for any student's successes but place the blame for failure on my students. Researchers have also found (Peterson & Barger, 1984) that teachers use students' past performances in making attributions about present performance. Thus, high ability students are "expected" to be successful.

Attribution seems also to be linked to the feedback that teachers provide students. For example, perceived effort was highly valued and a major determinant of reward and punishment. Among the findings of studies of the relationship between teachers' attributions and teachers' behavior are the following:

- *Low student effort* results in considerable negative feedback.
- *Perceived responsibility for success* does not predict teacher praise.
- *Failure caused by external events* received least teacher criticism.

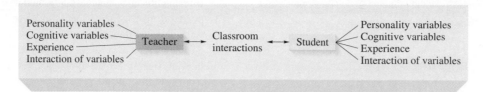

Figure 5.4
Classroom interactions.

• *Failure caused by internal events* (attention, effort) received greater teacher criticism.
• *Teachers' attributions* significantly predicted teachers' use of criticism.

Teachers' attributions influence the pattern of feedback, the number and kind of teacher-student interactions, the types of goals that teachers set for particular students, and role perception. For example, to what do I attribute my students' academic achievement?

Arguing that attributions involve one's personal values, Ames (1983) suggested that teachers proceed through a chain of beliefs to explain the cause-effect relationship between instruction and student outcome. Each link in the chain leads to a possible positive outcome:

• teaching is important
• teachers intentionally act to produce positive outcomes
• achieving success, even with the inherent restrictions imposed by the school, is possible.

Believing that teaching is a valuable activity that demands considerable personal competence leads one to a definite role perception from which flows a consistent and predictable pattern of behavior.

Finally, we have seen that each partner in the relationship—the teacher and the individual students—must determine the limits of the relationships. How much warmth? How much closeness? You must establish the terms of the relationship and adhere to the norms of behavior decided upon. Inconsistency in your behavior, reflecting your roles, leads inevitably to trouble because students can never be sure what their interactions with you should be.

The opinions, prejudices, interests, and skills of everyone in the classroom will affect the performance of each student to a greater or lesser degree. Although you bear the main responsibility for determining the form of interactions, there are limitations inherent in any classroom. For example, some students resist communication; others do not. The grade level strongly shapes the type of interaction, as does the nature of the class (shop, art) and the class size.

The classroom is a "behavior setting" composed of students with characteristics, teachers with characteristics, the characteristics of the group, and behaviors of teachers and students. Accordingly, teachers design classroom objectives to facilitate interactions so that students acquire cognitive, affective, and psycho-motor skills more efficiently.

Perhaps the most neglected part of this entire discussion of interactions is the effect that students have on teachers. Regardless of the personality of the teacher, students' reactions definitely influence a teacher's behavior. Student reactions inevitably color your performance. Aggressive, hostile, and unruly students will elicit far different teacher activities than an alert, interested group. Recall the meaning of reciprocal interactions, and you can better understand the dynamic changes that inevitably occur between teacher and student. Figure 5.4 illustrates the dynamics of classroom interactions between teachers and students.

Note the cooperative, yet complicated, series of interdependent pressures at work. The cooperative phenomenon makes understanding interactions difficult because once others become part of the interactions, results become unpredictable. That is, it is not just the teacher and a student; other influences are at work: the behavior of other students, peer influence, personal feelings.

Conditions also change: a silent, passive group will alter a teacher's behavior, both with regard to nature and effectiveness. Teachers may prefer a more responsive group with whom they can engage in a dialogue. So the teachers' methods must change from group 1 to group 2, and then effectiveness may change as well.

Educational history gives many examples of the positive interactions of great teachers. William James and his friendliness, Cattell and his extroversion, Judd and his pugnacity, Terman and Dewey with their need of quiet cooperation—all represent instructors at peak efficiency, but we can only wonder if environmental conditions for these outstanding personalities had been different, would their performances also have been different?

Table 5.5

Students' Opinion of the Teacher–Student Relationship

Directions: Check the appropriate box.

Statement	Agree	Uncertain	Disagree
Students in this class like the teacher.			
The teacher is fair to everybody.			
Students work hard in this class.			
At least in this class you know what you're supposed to do.			
It's easy to talk over a problem with this teacher.			
Some students seem to be unhappy here.			
It's hard to be in a room where the teacher plays favorites.			
It's hard when you don't know what you're supposed to do in class.			
Students are afraid to ask this teacher any questions.			

Classroom Interactions

Do the interactions that take place between teacher and student constitute a relationship? If you recall the definition presented earlier in the chapter, all the essentials seem to be present.

A relationship implies a pattern of intermittent interactions over an extended period of time.

Certainly this describes what occurs in the classroom during the school year.

Although teachers have been the focus of our discussion, you must also take into account students' perception of the relationship. Table 5.5 presents an example of student opinion that you could use as a check of your students' reactions to classroom interactions. It should provide you with valuable feedback.

Students and Interactions

Do any clues exist as to why interactions can vary so widely from student to student? One possibility lies in the developmental stage of your students. Schools are quite different social contexts at preschool, elementary, and secondary levels. They are organized differently, students perceive them differently, and different kinds of social behavior are expected at different levels (Minuchin & Shapiro, 1983).

If we now turn to the way that teachers interact with different types of students, we may acquire additional insights into classroom relationships. Again, we must begin with the notion of **reciprocal interactions**; no longer can we believe that active teachers do something to passive students. As we now know, changes in one member of the relationship produce changes in the other.

You change as the result of changes in your students. What also seems clear is that teachers give more attention and different attention to some students than to others. The findings about teachers' differential treatment of their students fall into several categories.

- *Personal characteristics.* For some reason, which may be quite private, teachers manifest liking, indifference, or outright rejection toward certain students. Teachers show affection and care for those students who are achieving and conforming, and who make legitimate demands. They tend to be indifferent toward withdrawn, silent children and initiate much less contact with them than with the first group. Students with behavior problems invite rejection. Remember: these are generalizations and do not apply to all teachers, but appear with sufficient frequency to identify a pattern.
- *Teachers' expectation.* Given the reality of teacher expectations, differential treatment of students can come as no surprise but as something to be aware of and to be avoided. If you expect low achievers not to know and not to participate, you must force yourself to initiate contact with them as much as with others. Note how attribution has affected our thinking about expectations: We attribute behavior to low ability and expect minimum performance; we attribute excellent performance to high ability and attribute failure to a lack of effort.
- *Social class and background.* This subject has been so well-documented, both through research and in the popular press, that it needs little discussion here. Since mostly white, middle-class teachers staff the schools, differential treatment of minority low socioeconomic status (SES) or problem students has often been reported. As sensitivity to this issue has grown, teachers themselves, as well as teacher-training institutions, have become more alert to the problem and have taken steps to check its spread. Menuchin and Shapiro (1983) stated that any type of discrimination because of race, ethnicity, SES, or gender has negative effects that are not confined to the immediate individuals involved. The classroom is a public place, and everyone in it, witnessing such treatment, develops interpretations of how certain individuals should be treated.
- *Gender differences.* Another well-documented finding is that many teachers treat boys differently from girls (Berk, 1992). The elementary school has frequently been characterized as a feminine domain, more conducive to the needs and interests of girls than boys. But several interesting issues arise upon examining the data more carefully. Although girls, in general, do better than boys in the elementary grades, girls lose this achievement edge in secondary school, especially in such subjects as science and mathematics. Why? One reason may be an extension into the classroom of stereotypic attitudes toward gender: Boys are reinforced for intellectual pursuits, girls for nurturing activities. Teachers more frequently attribute failure in boys to lack of motivation, while they more frequently see girls as lacking ability. Table 5.6 summarizes the differential responses of teachers that researchers and experienced teachers report commonly occur in classrooms.

The subtle consequences of the interaction of these variables cannot be exaggerated. Students absorb teacher assessments and add them to their own assessments that may or may not be accurate. Students then perform to the standard that they have set for themselves.

Teacher-Student Relationships: A Summary

Regardless of a student's actual ability, teachers form certain expectations for their students based on a number of variables, as we have repeatedly seen. They then, subtly or otherwise, communicate these feelings to the individual student who quickly grasps the message and reacts to it accordingly. Students begin to see themselves as bright or slow, someone of whom much is expected or little is expected.

Here once again, you can observe the telling impact of reciprocal interactions. You behave toward a student in a certain way; the student reacts to your behavior; you, in turn, react. The norms are set and the student performs in a manner consistent with the interactions that shape the relationship between the two of you.

We have concentrated upon the classroom context, role perspective, and thought processes as the basis of our analysis of teacher-student relationships. Teacher and students each bring givens with them, and the interaction of distinct personalities sets the initial tone of the relationship. The experiences of each with previous teachers and classrooms demand consideration as each participant has his or her own idea of his or her role. The

Table 5.6

Differential Responses of Teachers

Category	Teacher Responses
Pupil characteristics	
Achieving	Positive attachment
Conforming	
Withdrawn	Indifferent
Problems	Rejection
Teachers' expectations	
High achievers	More interactions, greater opportunities, more praise
Low achievers	Expected not to know, little participation, fewer opportunities
Social class	
High	May overrate, expectations higher, more interactions
Low	Tend to reject, lower expectations, disbelief in high IQ
Gender	More interactions, more criticism, react more harshly to misbehavior, may have higher expectations
Male	
Female	More accepting, reinforce "feminine" behavior, milder discipline, may have lower expectations

thought processes of each encompass the pertinent cognitive variables—what are their thoughts while in the classroom?

Put them all together, and the resultant complex mixture of interactions identifies the relationship. If you think about your role and how you visualize your instruction, you should become more sensitive to the reasons for your reactions to specific students. As you do, try to assess your interactions with particular students: good, positive, too negative, too infrequent? If you decide a change in a particular relationship is necessary, focus on the interactions and attempt to determine why you (and this student) are acting as you do. Are you reacting to a stereotype? Have you formed prior expectations?

Hinde's statement that relationships are the most important part of our lives applies as forcefully to the classroom as to any setting, and we may add that the quality of your relationships with your students will determine the success of your instruction, your management, and your students' learning.

Relationships in the Classroom

Learn about your students and try to understand their needs.

1. Teacher-student relationships are crucial for learning and development.
   - Work hard at recognizing your students as persons; they must not be merely a face-in-the-crowd. React to them personally when they return from an illness or if something has gone wrong at home. Recognize publicly their achievements; if they have accomplished something significant—in or out of class—let them talk about it to the rest of the class.
   - Although we will stress the need for rules and routine in later chapters, once you come to know your students well, there will be times when you will want to react individually to a child. For example, if you sense that a good student is upset and likely to explode, send this student on an errand or talk to the child individually about some unrelated matter.
   - If you have a student with whom you find it difficult to relate (as we all do occasionally), list the eight categories of interactions mentioned earlier in the chapter and honestly characterize each one. Examine your evaluation of each category and think of ways that you could change the interactions.
   - Don't take any student for granted. Your daily interactions will change because of the many influences acting on students, both in and out of class. Get to know your students, be sensitive to any clues, and act appropriately.
2. A teacher's interactions with a student determines the value of the relationship.
   - A teacher characteristic that students cherish and that affects a teacher-student relationship is fairness. Check your behavior often in this regard. Keep these questions in mind: Am I fair to all of my students? Do I treat them all in the same way?
   - Remember to use humor in your interactions with your students. Don't attempt to be a stand-up comic, but realize that students appreciate it when you react humorously to some light-hearted incident in class or if you can joke about an innocent mistake in class.
   - Remember to treat your students with dignity and respect. If you treat them courteously, the majority of students will respond in kind. In any survey of desirable teacher characteristics, students always say something like, "(S)He always acted nice towards us; you feel good as a person." Dignity, respect, and courtesy are powerful forces on a positive relationship.
   - Remember: Students take their cues from you and in their interactions, they are assessing your tone of voice, facial expressions, and behavior. As you are sensitive to them, they also are sensitive to you; if you are usually patient but on this occasion you seem to be abrupt, the interactions change, and student behavior is affected, perhaps for the day, if you are unaware of what happened.
3. Strive for a "goodness-of-fit" in your relationships with your students.
   - Be clear in your own mind about how you feel a teacher should act, that is, your role. Try not to be blinded by the "teacher-as-authority" role. You certainly are the authority figure, but you also want your students to see you as a real person. Acting with dignity, using humor, and perhaps using a few personal experiences can be quite helpful. Be yourself.
   - To help you and your students define your roles in the classroom, put a VENN diagram (overlapping circles) on the board. Entitle one large section *Teacher*, the other large sections *Student*, and where they overlap, *Both*. Now with your students, fill in the appropriate roles for each area.
   - When the "goodness-of-fit" is lacking and you find it difficult to relate to a student, don't deny it. Face up to it and watch your own behavior. Don't overlook any misbehavior but, when you can, force yourself to take the extra step—furnish as much positive reinforcement as you can. Usually this helps and reciprocal interactions take over—as you change, the student changes.

Teacher-Parent Relationships

Teacher-parent relationships introduce a different perspective. No matter how different the perspective, however, the principles governing relationships apply here equally as well. As the interactions change, however, so also does the relationship, and for some parents the interactions with teachers are so infrequent and perfunctory that no relationship whatsoever exists. This situation is unfortunate since interested parents can be an integral part of a student's learning experience. Though most discussions of teacher-parent relationships focus on formal functions—PTA activities, Parents' Nights—there is another, highly significant role that parents play—that of the parent-volunteer.

Ruth Groves' views in the chapter opening suggest the changing concept of the parental role—not merely custodial but as a source of expertise to be capitalized upon. Parents who have the time and desire can help teachers in many ways. They can serve in the school library, act as expert sources of information, and join field trips as supervisors. These are but a few of the services that parents can offer and, as they do, they add another positive element to the home-school relationship, increase their child's motivation, and encourage achievement.

A Changing Relationship

As family conditions have changed, as parents have become more educated, and as they have become more aware of their rights as parents of school children, teacher-parent relationships have changed accordingly. An increasing number of single parents has led to a corresponding increase in working mothers who have expressed concern about the unsupervised time that their children have. Such concerns have led many parents to question the length of the school day and to urge school boards to require schools to provide after school activities or to lengthen the school day. Teachers have usually resisted both efforts on the grounds that students cannot sustain attention, motivation, and learning capacity for such a lengthy time. They also argue that constant peer activities become self-defeating socially and emotionally.

Parents have grown more sophisticated and critical concerning school practices, subjects taught, and methods of instruction. These parents are active in school affairs and wish to become involved in a partnership with teachers in their child's education. For example, the consideration given to special education students can be directly attributed to the role of parents.

Finally, legislation passed in the 1970s provided parents with the impetus and right to play a more influential role in school life. The Family Educational Rights and Privacy Act of 1974 (the Buckley Amendment) contained four major provisions.

1. Parents of students under the age of 18 years and eligible students have the right to review and inspect the student's educational records.
2. Parents and eligible students have the right to challenge the contents of records that they believe to be inaccurate.
3. Educational institutions cannot disclose information in a student's records without the written consent of the parent or eligible student.
4. Educational institutions must notify parents and eligible students of their rights.

The second major piece of legislation dealing with parents' rights was P.L. 94-142, passed in 1975 and now referred to as the Individuals with Disabilities Act. This legislation focuses on educational services for handicapped children and specifies involvement of parents on the assessment and decision-making process prior to any educational changes for a student. This legislation was recently amended (PL99-457) to extend more services to at-risk or handicapped preschool children and to increase services to the children's parents.

The combination of these three events—family conditions, parental education, and supportive legislation—have all contributed to a more alert and active parental role, one that has in many cases altered the teacher-parent relationship.

Positive Outcomes of Teacher-Parent Relationships

Militancy and legislation, however, are poor substitutes for productive relationships, and the interactions of teachers with parents proves no exception. Ample evidence exists detailing how fruitful harmonious relationships can be. During the 1960s and the 1970s, the so-called War on Poverty spawned numerous intervention programs that demanded a close link between home and school. Basic to this union of home and school was the belief that parents were a key element in a child's school success.

To support this belief, Lazar and Darlington (1982) studied the long-term effects of twelve Head Start programs and reported significant effects on school competence, families, and attitudes about self and school. Among the techniques used by the various programs were constant communication with parents, training of mothers in the use of educational activities in the home, and periodic home visits. Data from these studies indicated:

- children who attended these programs were less likely to be retained in grade and more likely to meet their schools' requirements.
- these children attained higher IQ scores than their controls.
- these children demonstrated higher self-concepts and were proud of their school accomplishment.
- mothers of program graduates were more satisfied with their child's school performance than were control mothers; they also had higher occupational aspirations for their children than did control mothers.

These results were obtained several years after the children had left the program and suggest the benefits of positive parental involvement in school affairs.

Parental Participation

The Parental Education Follow Through Program (PEFTP) devised by Gordon (1977) stressed parental involvement in its program. Gordon's basic premise stated that if intervention were to be successful, it should start early and involve the parents. A key feature was to use community women as paraprofessionals trained to function as home educators. They assisted in the classrooms in the mornings and visited homes in the afternoon.

The key relationships, then, incorporate children, parents, and teachers, with teachers and parents sharing the instructional focus. The major aspects of the program included:

- comprehensive services (medical, social, psychological); weekly home visits by the paraprofessionals stressing home learning and parental teaching behavior; and parental participation: volunteer, employee, advisor (Rubin et al., 1983).

A paraprofessional visiting the home of a kindergarten parent, for example, might use large and small different colored balloons, asking a child to sort them by size and color. With regard to the teaching behaviors, parents were encouraged to explain what they were going to do, give youngsters time to become familiar with the materials, ask questions requiring multiple-word answers, encourage the learner to ask questions, give learners time to answer, and use feedback judiciously.

Gordon reported strong and consistent effects for those youngsters who remained in the program for two to three years. Long-term effects were equally as impressive: only 10 percent of these students dropped out of school before high school graduation, compared to 31 percent for control groups. Thus cognitive and achievement growth satisfied everyone—students, parents, teachers.

Role of Parents: Teachers' Views

How do teachers view this partnership? Although little evidence exists to answer this question definitively, an extensive survey conducted by Becker and Epstein (1982) offers interesting insights into teachers' reactions. Contacting almost 3,700 public elementary school teachers in the state of Maryland, the authors concluded that their survey results showed a positive orientation to parent involvement but divergent ideas as to the ideal method of furthering this objective.

Teacher-parent contacts are almost universal: 95 percent of the teachers in the survey talked with parents, sent notices home, and met with parents on openhouse nights. A high percentage of teachers asked parents to check and sign students' homework, but even in these standard practices, teachers' interactions differed. For example Becker and Epstein report that about 65 percent of their teachers discussed how parents can help their children, while the other 35 percent do likewise but only as the need arises. Only a small number of teachers venture beyond these activities. Seven percent of teachers in the survey had workshops or group meetings with parents aside from school-sponsored events. Principals showed the same patterns as teachers: supporting traditional practices, but also advocating the use of parent volunteers in the classroom.

How to improve the process remains an enigma to most teachers. Much of this uncertainty comes from insecurity on both parts. Here are some suggestions to help you ease any tension you may feel in meeting with parents.

- *Don't become too technical in discussions with parents.* Be sure you use terms they can understand.
- *Don't be the "expert."* Discuss a student as positively as possible, but be completely honest. Remember: Don't surprise parents. If a student is doing poorly and may face academic problems later, tell the parent.
- *Stick to the topic.* You're not there to discuss any other student or teachers. Concentrate on what you know.
- *Be careful about offering personal advice.* You're not a certified counselor, and becoming involved in family matters can too easily cause problems and jeopardize relationships.
- *Be professional.* You're a teacher with knowledge about educational matters; use this knowledge courteously and in a manner designed to help the student and to lead to a continued positive interaction with parents.

How to Involve Parents

Here are several techniques that teachers stated they use to involve parents in home learning activities (Becker & Epstein, 1982).

1. Techniques involving reading books was one of the most frequently mentioned activities involving parents. Almost two-thirds of the teachers frequently ask parents to read to their elementary school children, particularly those in the early grades. Teachers also stated that they requested parents to take their children to the library; they likewise reported loaning books and materials to parents.
2. Learning through discussion was often mentioned by the respondents. Believing that their students can learn from conversations and discussion, teachers asked parents to discuss a particular television program with their children and to talk over school activities and homework assignments.
3. Informal learning activities at home, such as acting as a role model were also encouraged by teachers. Reading to children, questioning them, and reviewing homework were all favorably mentioned.
4. *Teacher-parent contracts* are formal agreements between teachers and parents in which the parents assume responsibility for certain activities. These most frequently take two forms: parents are urged to apply sanctions for school-related behavior (loss of privileges for problem behavior, access to rewards for desired behavior) and those where parents agree to supervise or assist with homework or other projects. About 60 percent of the teachers surveyed believed these practices were worthwhile. Kelley (1990) recently has written an entire book on the use of School-Home Notes (i.e., contracts) to facilitate children's classroom success. This practical book has many examples of actual contracts and behavior management plans.
5. Helping parents to teach, encompassing such activities as direct instructional aid for parents for home use, classroom observation, and parental responses to teachers' questionnaires about their child's school progress, was less frequently used by teachers. When they did adopt this technique, teachers most frequently selected classroom observation by parents.

Summarizing their work, Epstein and Becker (1982) noted that teachers have honest differences of opinion about parental involvement, differences that reflect three rather different perspectives.

1. Parents care but cannot do much to improve their child's learning.
2. Parents care but should not help with school learning.
3. Parents care and can be of great help if they are shown how to help.

The Role of Parents: A Warning

In a thoughtful essay about recent emphasis on parental involvement in the schools' work, Heath and McLaughlin (1987) urge caution concerning "excessive expectations" about such activities. Tracing the history of educational panaceas, the authors note that the renewed stress on science after Sputnik, the War on Poverty, the focus on illiteracy, the return to basics, the "blame the teacher" movement all moved to center stage briefly, undoubtedly led to real, if short-lived improvements, and then faded. Still the feeling persists that all is not right with our schools: illiteracy proves hard to overcome, reading scores decline, public school graduates seem ill-prepared to confront a technological society.

In the early 1980s, reports such as *A Nation at Risk* warned that blaming teachers was an oversimplified solution. Only the interplay of several forces—school, family, community, and workplace—could satisfy the needs of today's schools. Thus attention shifted to the parent as the "problem" of today's education.

Economic and emotional stress in the modern family have often resulted in poor parenting, which then carries over to children, causing inadequacies in coping skills. Conclusion: Make parents partners in the school enterprise. Educators are urged to view parents as extensions of the schools. Parents can reinforce school values, support home-based school activities (homework) and monitor student behavior. The goal, of course, is to improve the chances of greater academic achievement and successful futures. These latter themes have been echoed in recently published issues of *Educational Leadership* (1989, October) and the *Elementary School Journal* (1991, January).

Parents as Saviors

Heath and McLaughton's summary of parental involvement, then, accurately reflects present concerns. But they fear that these efforts will be doomed to failure for two reasons. *First,* parents as solution focuses too narrowly on academic achievement. Other outcomes such as emotional stability, physical and mental health, and cognitive abilities (thinking skills) are equally as important objectives and cannot be served by our schools. *Second,* viewing parents as saviors rests on an outdated concept of family. As we have seen, family structure has been altered dramatically. Today's family cannot offer the support demanded in the latest proposals.

In many cases, the problem runs far more deeply than supervising homework activities; youngsters come to school with no breakfast or inadequate clothing. Cultural differences, resulting in vastly different expectations for children, affect both the school performance of these youngsters and the relationship of their parents with the school. The authors use the example of a minority group such as the Vietnamese who came to this country under church sponsorship and received considerable local support. Their children (and the families themselves) have fared well in school and career. On the other hand, many Mexican migrants have had to rely solely on family networks and have fared less well.

Another example of assuming too much from parental relationships is found in the work of Stevenson et al. (1990). Studying math and reading achievement scores of almost 3,000 first, third, and fifth graders in 20 Chicago schools, these investigators found that black and Hispanic students had lower scores. Yet the mothers of almost all of the students tried to help because they thought schooling was important for their children. They had a firm belief in their children's abilities, were strong advocates of homework, and urged a longer school day.

Although the expectations that Hispanic mothers had for their children's futures were lower than those of the mothers of the black and white children, differences among the groups were not significant. Yet far more minority children are dropping out of school. If student abilities are similar across groups, and parental support is evident, then the search for causes of failure and dropouts must turn elsewhere. Consequently, today's students must have at their disposal a range of resources that stretch far from home and school. Think for a moment about the conditions we have sketched: radically altered family conditions, shrinking role of the schools, and technological advancement. No single solution seems adequate.

One possibility that the authors suggest resides in the community: open up the resources of volunteer agencies and community institutions to provide students access to adults with a wide range of talents and perspectives that cannot be found in any one family. Students then would have the opportunity to learn and to work, and to develop social competence in their individual performances and as group members. *Single-policy solutions no longer remain feasible.* Concern with the functions of educating demands a role for children as "actors in a larger social system," using the family as a base but moving beyond their limited resources and engaging appropriate environmental networks. The school then becomes one of a series of institutions serving students, acting as a broker rather than the sole deliverer of services.

Heath and McLaughlin presented an insightful essay that addresses a major concern facing our schools today. They have attempted to sketch a broad outline that places students at the center of a network of educational and cultural opportunities intended to aid learning, motivation, and adjustment.

Several of our larger school systems have attempted some variation of these ideas, and all have reported success (higher test scores, better school attendance). This scheme has deep roots in educational history. One of the chief reasons for its limited success has been the lack of sustained attempts by all concerned parties to maintain cooperative efforts at a sufficiently high level to insure continued student enthusiasm and realistic opportunities. As these efforts lose momentum, forces would then shift once again to single issues: parents, teachers, curriculum. So although these cooperative efforts suggested by Heath and McLaughlin are to be lauded, we must also continue our striving to improve teacher education and parental involvement.

Parental Involvement: Conclusions

What can we conclude from this analysis of teacher-parent relationships? The most obvious deduction we can make is that the topic lacks the evidence that points to policy. We simply are not sure, for example, how much (if at all) parental involvement improves school learning. From work reported by surveys such as Epstein and Becker's (1982) we can conclude:

- supervising school work at home may be the most educationally significant activity for parents;
- some parents will work with their children at home with or without teachers' suggestions;
- the attitudes, training, and experience of teachers affect their commitment to, and type of, parental involvement;
- acting as a manager of parental involvement changes the teacher's role;
- different types of activities need different parental roles.

Again, these conclusions represent generalizations based on observation. Research is urgently needed to provide data leading to implementation.

Recognizing the lack of definitive data, Lombana (1983) proposed a program development model that could be used as a first step in securing needed information. Start with the relative number of parents who might need or want involvement with the school. Identify parents' greatest needs, which seem to center on general participation in school activities.

Now you can begin to differentiate the various elements around which program development can commence. Usually schools begin with general parental participation: sharing information, volunteer activities, advisory council. Once this structure is in place, schools can refine the process and analyze in greater detail the strengths and weaknesses of the community's parents, thus leading to a more accurate, productive utilization of parental talent.

TEACHER ⬌ STUDENT
INTERACTIONS

Peer and Parent Relationships

1. Peer relationships extend into the classroom and can affect learning.
   - In the elementary school, to help students understand each other (especially at the beginning of the school year) have each child paste his/her picture on a piece of construction paper with a few sentences expressing likes and dislikes. Mount them around the classroom and arrange time for students to discuss their "autobiographies." When you are finished with this part of the assignment, collect them into a class yearbook and have students add to their comments during the year.
   - At the secondary level (especially if you have a homeroom), decide on certain times of the year to highlight various ethnic groups. February could be African-American month, April Asian-American month. Assign students to research famous persons, outstanding music, art, and books. Try to obtain guest lecturers to elaborate on the themes that the class is studying. In this way, you help to break down stereotypes and bring students to a better understanding of each other.
   - Consider establishing a peer or cross-age tutoring program. Explain the purpose of the program to the class, select and prepare the tutors, and carefully monitor the progress of the various groups. Don't always pick the same students as tutors; try to find some strengths in a low achiever that could usefully be passed on to the group. Be clear to the tutors in not only what you want them to do but also how to do it: discuss, demonstrate, etc.
2. Positive and productive teacher–parent relationships help to improve students' achievement and maintain a harmonious classroom atmosphere.
   - Aside from formal open houses, encourage parents to contact you during the first month of school. You may do this by sending home (or mailing) letters that explain your willingness to meet with parents as soon as possible.
   - Be as flexible as you can concerning scheduling since some parents can come only early in the morning or later in the afternoon.
   - Be positive about a student, but let parents know what you expect and ask them what they expect from you.
   - Try to discover what their expectations are for their child and work with them to help them formulate realistic goals.
   - Have examples of the student's work so you can discuss—and verify—their child's strengths and weaknesses.
   - As the year progresses, accumulate a folder of representative work for each student so you can trace improvements, slumps, or subjects that need remedial work.
   - When you conclude a meeting with a parent(s), try to end with a positive outlook and urge parents to keep in close contact with you.
3. If your interactions with your students are friendly and positive, the resulting classroom atmosphere can only encourage learning. When you have the opportunity, determine how you're doing with your students by completing the following checklist.

Put a check in column
   1 if you are satisfied with your interactions with your class.
   2 if you think there is room for improvement.
   3 if you're uncertain whether the interactions are positive or negative.
   4 if you think the interactions are more negative than positive.
   5 if you think the interactions are mainly hostile.

(You can also use this technique to determine the nature of your relationship with an individual student.)

	1	2	3	4	5
Content					
Diversity					
Quality					
Frequency-patterning					
Reciprocal-complementary					
Intimacy					
Interpersonal perception					
Commitment					

If you are objective and completely honest with yourself, you can discover any problems in classroom interactions and focus on that particular category to improve the relationship.

When parents are actually participating, an assessment can be conducted to determine the specific needs of the parents. Focus should be on the readiness of the involved individuals, their preferences for types of involvement, and the skills they may require or can offer to the program.

Here are some categories that will help you to think about ways of designing a program involving teachers and parents.

- *Program design* refers to program objectives, instructional techniques, and program strategies. For example, one program objective could be to improve communications with parents. Strategies could include a newsletter to be sent home, regularly scheduled monthly conferences, parental observations in the classroom, and weekly progress reports.

- *Program implementation* indicates activities, statements of progress, and constant monitoring of the activities. Review of activities should suggest changes while the program is in action: Are the strategies actually producing progress toward the stated objectives? Do parents believe that communication with the school is improving?
- *Evaluation* refers to a formal assessment of the program, rather than the in-process monitoring just mentioned, and should lead to decisions about the program's effectiveness. Were the objectives achieved? If not, what should be done?

These measures can lead to more useful teacher-parent relationships and, perhaps equally as important, lead to strategies for obtaining much needed data. Some type of teacher involvement with parents has always been, and will continue to be, present. From treating parents as distant individuals who must be met on open house nights to more recent views of "parents as saviors," teacher-parent relationships have been a constant. We are now witnessing the initial stages of still another phase: parents as one of a cluster of potential school partners. Perhaps the best way to conclude is to urge establishing warm and harmonious relationships with parents, engaging them as you think they can help fulfill your students'

needs. Then continue the search for the hard evidence that we require to utilize as fully as possible the fruits of productive teacher-parent intentions.

Conclusion

We finish this chapter as we began: Relationships with other people are the most important part of our lives. As we have seen, Hinde's statement is as true for the classroom as elsewhere. Remember that you must be sensitive and responsive to students so that the reciprocal interactions between you and your students are positive.

Classroom context, role perspective, and thought processes interact in both teacher and student, to shape reciprocal interactions. Both teachers and students interpret the behavior of the other, a process that can be influenced by the temperament and appearance of both.

As the interactions between teacher and students continue to build throughout the school year, the relationship is also affected by the reactions of parents and by the interactions among peers. The interactions between teachers and students and among peers exert their influence and help to determine the nature of the reciprocal interactions in the classroom.

A means of monitoring or evaluating your relationships is to use Hinde's eight categories and then work to improve those interactions that could be adversely affecting the classroom atmosphere. Finally, the evolving roles of parents and their relationships with teachers were examined. Home-school collaboration is a popular theme today and serves to challenge teachers to use parents in constructive ways.

Chapter Highlights

The Importance of Relationships

- Relationships with other people may be the most important part of our lives, and a poor teacher-student relationship negatively affects learning.
- Reciprocal interactions, which are at the core of any relationship, help to explain the changes that occur as individuals interact. As you respond to a student, that student changes; you then change in reaction to the student's change. This constant change in the interactions that make up a relationship defines reciprocal interactions.
- Your relationships with your students consist of a pattern of intermittent interactions that affect your judgments about them. These judgments then become part of your behavior toward a particular student.

- By analyzing the characteristics of a relationship, it becomes possible to specify just where the strengths and weaknesses exist in a particular relationship. For example, once you are familiar with the eight categories of a relationship discussed in this chapter, you may decide that the quality of your interactions with a student is more consistently negative than with other students.
- To the extent that you are successful in establishing a "goodness of fit" atmosphere in your classroom, the greater will be your satisfaction and pleasure in working with your students.

Teacher-Student Relationships

- The notion of reciprocal interactions will help you to understand that your relationships with your students rarely remain static. Even with those students whom you have decided are the "best" or the "most difficult," a changing pattern of interactions is inevitable.

- Your vision of your role and the role of your students must be consistent with the school's and community's expectations. Role has a powerful influence on behavior, and if your expectations for your students agree with their role assessment, you will have a smoothly running classroom.
- Recent research on teachers' thought processes has emphasized that what teachers think affects their behavior while teaching. Particularly important is a teacher's attributions for the causes of their students' behavior.
- As you examine the interactions that constitute your relationship with any student, be aware of those characteristics of the student that may influence you, as well as your own expectations for that student.

Peer Relationships

- Peer relationships follow a developmental pattern that reflects those age characteristics that students bring to your classroom.
- Peer relationships extend into the classroom, influencing both students' interactions with teachers and affecting the extent of their own achievement.

Teacher-Parent Relationships

- Teacher-parent relationships range from perfunctory contacts to situations where parents are actively involved in the school's life. As conditions in society change, parents are becoming more engaged in the school's functioning, from aiding in the selection of a superintendent to serving on curriculum committees.
- Most teachers and researchers recognize that parental interest can be a positive force in a school's life but remain uncertain as to the best method of capitalizing on this interest.

Key Terms

Assertion
Commitment
Content of interactions
Cooperation
Diversity of interactions

Reciprocal determinism
Sensitive responsiveness
Empathy
Goodness of fit
Interactions
Interpersonal perception
Intimacy
Peer
Quality of an interaction
Reciprocal interactions
Reciprocity versus complementarity
Relationship
Relative frequency and patterning of interactions
Responsibility
Role
Self-control
Social perspective-taking
Sociometrics
Temperament

Suggested Readings

Buss, A. H., and Plomin, R. (1985). *Temperament: Early developing personality traits.* Hillsdale, N.J.: Erlbaum. These authors present a detailed examination of the notion that temperament is an inborn characteristic, with all that it implies for student personalities.

Damon, W. (1983). *Social and personality development.* New York: Norton. In this work, Damon begins with the socialization-individuation concept and uses it for the basis of his analysis of personal development—an excellent piece of work.

Hinde, R. (1979). *Towards understanding relationships.* New York: Academic. Here is the "bible" of interpersonal relationships. Hinde has developed eight categories that can be used to analyze relationships and can be particularly helpful in examining classroom relationships (student-student, teacher-student, teacher-parent).

Lombana, J. (1983). *Home-school partnership: Guidelines and strategies for educators.* New York: Grune and Stratton. A practical guide to various techniques for insuring harmonious relationships with parents and also specific suggestions for conducting home-school activities.

Learning Theories and Practices

Behavioral Psychology and Learning

Alice West, the ninth grade social studies teacher at the Junior High, had caught one of her students, Pam Jones, smoking in the restroom that morning. She told Pam to meet her in her homeroom after school. Alice, who cared about her students, knew she had to take some action and thought for the rest of the day about what she should do.

When Pam came to her room later that day, Alice told her to sit down and then said to her, "You're lucky in one way, Pam. There was no one else who saw you smoking."

Pam looked puzzled and said, "I don't understand, Ms. West."

"If someone else saw you, I'd have to make an example of you," replied Alice. "Why do you think that we have rules about smoking on school property? Did you ever think about the possibility of a fire and what could result from that? Didn't you listen to the fire marshall when he spoke to the group? He wasn't just trying to scare you."

"I know, Ms. West. But it's more of a habit now than anything else."

"OK, Pam. Let's try this. You know how you like to be part of the tutoring teams that visit the elementary schools; if you don't do this again, I'll put you on the team."

"I won't, Ms. West. I hadn't really thought of what could happen. Besides, I really like working with the kids."

In her concern for the safety of her students, Alice West turned to the use of a behavioral technique. By attempting to use reinforcement skillfully, teachers are bringing into the classroom those theories that have strong implications for behavior change.

In this chapter, as in this example, the focus is on behavior. Behaviorism, as the name suggests, applies to those who believe that any analysis of learning should focus on the observable behavior of our students. Traditionally, behaviorists believe that studies of ideas, percepts or concepts, such as cognitive theorists propose, are fruitless; we must work with behavior. (Certain behaviorists such as Bandura, who are frequently called **neobehaviorists,** attempt to include cognitive processes such as motivation and intention.)

To help you understand the differences among the outstanding behaviorists, we'll first examine Pavlov's **classical conditioning** and Thorndike's **connectionism.** Next we'll analyze Skinner's **operant conditioning** and point out key differences between Pavlov and Skinner. Bandura's **neobehaviorism** deserves our attention because of its importance for learning and development. Finally, we'll turn to behaviorism's impact on the classroom, concentrating on management techniques. These theorists have continuing and direct relevance for classroom teachers.

After you read this chapter, you should be able to:

- distinguish between classical and operant conditioning.
- recognize how students may acquire fears by classical conditioning.
- explain how a theory such as Thorndike's Connectionism had such widespread classroom application.
- identify the major elements of operant conditioning.
- understand how the principles of reinforcement and punishment can be used in the classroom.
- apply the principles of social cognitive theory— imitation, modeling—to your instructional techniques.

Classical Conditioning

Much of the affective behavior that your students demonstrate in class can be explained by the work of the Russian physiologist, Ivan Pavlov. For example, many of your students' fears, anxieties, or joys can be traced to conditions within the classroom, frequently without the awareness of teachers.

Pavlov's Work

Many years after his death, Pavlov's best known writings, *Conditioned Reflexes* (1927) and *Lectures on Conditioned Reflexes* (1928) remain highly influential. His studies of digestion in animals led to the discovery of an important psychological discovery—the **conditioned re-**

Ivan Pavlov (1849–1936). Pavlov is shown in his laboratory flanked by his assistants and one of his dogs.

flex. For example, the anticipation of food caused the flow of saliva in his experimental dogs.

Saliva flowed at the dog's sight of the food dish or of the attendant, perhaps even at a sound the attendant usually made during feeding. We can understand how food can cause the flow of saliva, but sights and sounds (the attendant, a bell) don't usually cause saliva to flow. Somehow Pavlov's dogs "learned" that these sights and sounds signalled the appearance of food, as in Figure 6.1.

Pavlov called the signal (sights, sounds) that produced saliva the **conditioned stimulus.** He next turned his attention to the planned establishment of these conditioned reflexes. You may be familiar with the model he used.

A hungry dog was harnessed with a ticking metronome present (the conditioned stimulus). After a controlled interval, food (the unconditioned stimulus) was placed in the dog's mouth. After several repetitions, saliva began to flow during the interval when the metronome was ticking, before any food appeared. Thus Pavlov had established a conditioned reflex, with the metronome acting as the conditioned stimulus. The sequence in **classical conditioning** is as follows:

1. US (unconditioned stimulus) produces UR (unconditioned response)

    food——saliva

2. CS (conditioned stimulus) produces no response

    metronome alone——no response

3. CS + US (conditioned + unconditioned stimulus) produces UR (unconditioned response)

    metronome plus food——saliva

4. CS (conditioned stimulus) produces CR (conditioned response)

    metronome alone——saliva

Thus the conditioned stimulus (sight of the attendant, sound of the metronome) has come to acquire some of the response-producing potential of the unconditioned stimulus (the food). Note that the neutral or conditioned stimulus has been conditioned to the unconditioned stimulus.

Pavlov believed that if he could establish conditioned reflexes through this technique, extinction or elimination of reflexes must also be possible. The dog was placed in the usual situation with the metronome ticking and saliva flowing, but the dog was given no food. After several pairings of the ticking metronome and lack of food, saliva no longer flowed when the metronome ticked. Extinction of the conditioned response had occurred.

Features of Classical Conditioning

Before discussing the classroom implications of Pavlov's work, we should review several principles of classical conditioning that Pavlov discovered (Kalish, 1981). These include stimulus generalization, discrimination, and extinction.

- **Stimulus generalization** refers to the process by which the conditioned response transferred to other stimuli that were similar to the original conditioned stimulus. For example, once having learned that the color "red" means stop, we tend to stop or hesitate at red lights, signs, or flashing red bulbs. Stimulus

Figure 6.1

Pavlov's research apparatus. In studying the digestive process, Ivan Pavlov would present a dog with meat powder and collect saliva through a tube inserted into one of the dog's salivary glands. The amount of salivation was recorded by having a stylus write on a rotating drum. Pavlov found that dogs would salivate to stimuli associated with the presentation of food, such as the mere sight of the laboratory assistant who brought the food.

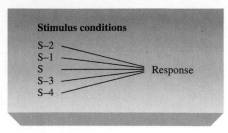

Figure 6.2
Stimulus generalization. The response—stopping—is made to S_1, red traffic light, S_2, red light over door, S_3, red stop sign.

generalization is a process that lies at the heart of transfer of learning in the classroom.

We want our students to be able to use the material they learn in class in a variety of circumstances. Teenagers who have learned to avoid drug usage in schools through the use of written and visual materials, will, we hope, avoid them when and if they are actually offered to them on the street. In Figure 6.2, think of the various stimuli as different types of the red condition meaning *stop*.

Remember, though, the less closely the stimulus resembles the conditioned stimulus, the weaker the response will be. Reading about a drug transaction is far different from being approached by someone—maybe even a friend—attempting to sell drugs.

Generalization appears to explain the transfer of a response to a situation other than that in which the original learning occurred. A first grade youngster terrified by a stern teacher may transfer that fear or anxiety to anything about schools: teachers, books, the school building itself. These circumstances meet all of Pavlov's criteria for conditioning. Two facts about generalization are worth noting.

- Once conditioning to any stimulus occurs, its effectiveness is not restricted to that stimulus.
- As a stimulus becomes less similar to that originally used, its ability to produce a response lessens accordingly (Hulse, Egeth, & Deese, 1980).
- **Discrimination** refers to the process by which we learn not to respond to similar stimuli in an identical manner. You would be well advised not to yell at a uniformed police officer as you would a uniformed opposing football player. We make these distinctions by a process known as discrimination, which is just the opposite of generalization. Whereas generalization means responding in the same way to two different stimuli, discrimination implies responding differently to two stimuli.

For example, if in the morning your car absolutely refuses to start—nothing happens—you can be quite sure that the problem is electrical. It might be the battery; it might be the starter. If, however, you hear a clicking sound, the chances are good that the starter is faulty. Because of prior experiences, you have discriminated the starter as the problem. We respond differently to stimuli because of our previous experiences—which established that certain of our responses were successful in the presence of certain stimuli.

We again can draw important classroom implications. Youngsters learning to read may have serious difficulties if they cannot discriminate circles from curved lines, or horizontal from vertical lines. They then could not, or at least not consistently, discriminate v from u or b from d, which could lead to reading problems. Similar discrimination challenges exist for young learners when confronted with numbers such as 21 and 12 or 25 and 52. Learning to make discriminations of form and, later in life, of substance is a critical component of successful learning.

- **Extinction** refers to the process by which conditioned responses are lost. Through his experiments, Pavlov found that by presenting the sound of the metronome alone (that is, with no food) he could eliminate the conditioned response. The student whose older brother or sister warned her of that "terrible Mrs. Smith" she would have as her teacher next year could easily cause the younger student to associate anxiety with Mrs. Smith. After several nervous weeks at the beginning of school, however, she finds Mrs. Smith a pleasant person and gradually extinguishes her anxiety.

Other behaviorists, however, are more interested in the consequences of the responses that students make and in deliberately shaping behavior, which leads us to the work of E. L. Thorndike.

Thorndike's Connectionism

Edward Lee Thorndike (1874–1949) believed that all learning is explained by connections (or bonds) that are formed between stimuli and responses. These connections occur mainly through trial and error, which Thorndike later designated as learning by selecting and connecting. Thorndike formulated laws of learning, which were not inflexible laws but rules that learning seemed to obey. His three major laws of learning (Readiness, Exercise, and Effect) have had direct application to education.

TEACHER ⬅➡ STUDENT
INTERACTIONS

Using Classical Conditioning in the Classroom

1. Generalization is the process by which a conditioned response transfers to other stimuli that are similar to the original conditioned stimulus.
    *   If you suspect that a student is nervous in your class, try to discover what circumstances triggered the anxiety; that is, try to identify the stimuli acting at the time. For example, what could cause anxiety in students?
    *   Assume that you have found that your anxious students are relaxed elsewhere in school. Observe them carefully and identify the situations where they are most anxious (in the classroom? or on the playground? or walking to school?).
    *   Continue to narrow your search to discover the stimuli that actually produce the anxiety. It may be a larger classmate who bullies your student on the way to and from school. With supervised activity on the playground and in the classroom, everything seems fine. Or you may discover that anxiety appears in your relationship with this student. Have **you** done something or could it be anxiety over grades? You may find that your student's nervousness results from fear of adults or parental pressure over grades.
    *   If grades are the cause, then the fear or anxiety is the unconditioned response. Take definite steps to introduce non-fear provoking stimuli with those stimuli that cause the anxiety. You could have the student practice with tests (with reassurance that "they won't count"). Try to obtain parental cooperation—ask parents to downplay any "life and death" feelings about their youngster's grades; help in preparing for exams by reassuring the child. Finally, without showing favoritism, help this student to succeed. (Note in all of these examples that the intent is identical—change the circumstances.)
2. If you want students to transfer the material you are presenting, then you must provide ample opportunity for them to discover the relationship that the subject has to other situations.
    *   Since you want your students to learn more about numbers than merely memorizing them, give practical examples, preferably using community sources with which the children are familiar. "When you came by Mr. Smith's store this morning, did you notice the four rows and four columns of oranges? How many were there altogether?"
    *   In teaching subjects such as the American Revolution or the French Revolution, point out to students how people can live under tyranny for only so long before they rebel. Remind them of recent events in which many of the Communist countries overturned their governments.
3. Discrimination is the process by which we learn not to respond to similar stimuli in an identical manner.
    *   Stress to your students how important it is to distinguish things that seem alike but mean something different. One ring of the school bell may mean recess; continuous ringing means a fire drill or alarm.
    *   Provide continued practice for your students so that they become accustomed to searching for differences. This is true at all grade levels. In the early grades, students must learn to look for the difference that makes one number 6 and not 9. At the secondary level, the search for differences becomes more subtle: in *Tom Sawyer*, both boys run away but for different reasons. Encourage your students to discover the differences and discuss them.
4. Extinction is the process by which conditioned responses are lost.
    *   Students in California, for example, may be anxious about earthquakes. Help them to make their concern realistic by explaining to them how the school was constructed to protect them from earthquakes, by showing films of boys and girls leaving a school quietly and in good order, by practicing leaving the building while you talk to them in a reassuring manner. The same procedures can be used for other situations such as fires or tornadoes.
    *   During written work the class clown may continue to act up, even after you have reprimanded him. In many cases, teachers turn away after a scene, and other students, by gesture or whisper, may urge him on. If you continue to monitor the situation, they will be unable to offer encouragement, and the behavior should cease.

The importance of classical conditioning for teachers is that awareness of its principles enables you to be more alert to the role that stimuli can play in a student's behavior.

The Law of Readiness

When organisms, both human and animal, are ready to form connections, to do so is satisfying and not to do so is annoying. Thorndike believed that readiness is an important condition of learning because satisfaction or frustration depends on an individual's state of readiness. He stated (1913, p. 133) that readiness is like an army sending scouts ahead of a train whose arrival at one station sends signals ahead to open or close switches. Schools can't force students to learn if they aren't biologically and psychologically prepared.

Edward Thorndike (1874–1949).

"Archives of the History of American Psychology, The University of Akron."

The Law of Exercise

Any connection is strengthened in proportion to the number of times it occurs and in proportion to the average vigor and duration of the connection. Conversely, when a connection is not made between a stimulus and response for some time, the connection's strength decreases. Continued experimentation and criticism forced Thorndike after 1930 to revise the original law of exercise. He realized that practice alone was insufficient for improvement. There must also be a strengthening of the bond by reinforcement; that is, the law of effect must also operate. When students practice, they should be aware of the consequences of what they are doing. Otherwise, practice becomes ineffective and even harmful if error creeps in.

The Law of Effect

Probably the most important of Thorndike's laws, the Law of Effect, states that responses accompanied by satisfaction are more firmly connected with the situation; responses accompanied by discomfort have their connections weakened. The greater the satisfaction or discomfort, the greater is the strengthening or weakening of the bond. In 1932, Thorndike revised the law to stress that reward has a much greater strengthening effect than punishment has a weakening effect. Pupils tend to learn more effectively (and easily) and to retain that learning longer, if it has pleasant consequences.

For many years, Thorndike had a powerful influence on educational practice because of his insistence on a scientific basis for education. For example, his explanation of the transfer of learning is still meaningful. Called **identical elements,** the theory states that learning can be

applied to new situations only when the learner sees similar features—the identical elements—in both situations.

Hergenhahn (1988) states that Thorndike believed good teaching begins with knowing what you want to teach—the stimuli. You must also identify the responses you want to connect to the stimuli and the timing of appropriate satisfiers. As Thorndike would say:

- Consider the pupil's environment.
- Consider the response you want to connect with it.
- Form the connection (with satisfaction).

Thorndike's remarkable energy and drive led to an astounding number of publications and provided education with the scientific emphasis it so desired. His work with the Law of Effect was an early statement of the importance of positive reinforcement, a concept B. F. Skinner greatly expanded.

Operant Conditioning

B. F. Skinner (1904–1990) received his doctorate from Harvard and after teaching for several years at the Universities of Minnesota and Indiana, he returned to Harvard. It was there that he continued to refine the differences between classical and operant conditioning and applied his ideas to a wide range of human endeavors.

Skinner, convinced of the importance of reinforcement, developed an explanation of learning that stressed the consequences of behavior—what happens after we do something is all-important. Alice West, the teacher in the vignette in the chapter opening, decided that she would react to her students' behavior by reinforcing the desired behavior. Reinforcement has proven to be a powerful tool in the shaping and control of behavior, both in and out of the classroom.

Skinner's Views

B. F. Skinner has been in the forefront of psychological and educational endeavors for the past several decades. Innovative, practical, tellingly prophetic, and witty, Skinner's work has had a lasting impact. In several major publications, *The Behavior of Organisms* (1938), *Science and Human Behavior,* (1953), *Verbal Behavior* (1957), *The Technology of Teaching* (1968), *Beyond Freedom and Dignity* (1971), *About Behaviorism* (1974), and in a steady flow of articles, Skinner has reported his experiments and developed and clarified his theory. He has never avoided the challenge of applying his findings to practical affairs. Education, religion,

B. F. Skinner (1904–1990).

psychotherapy, and other subjects have all felt the force of Skinner's thought.

Although Skinner initially made his impact during the 1930s when the classical conditioning of Pavlov was popular and influential, he demonstrated that the environment had a much greater influence on learning and behavior than Pavlov realized. Skinner, in his explanation of **operant conditioning,** argued that the environment (parents, teachers, peers) reacts to our behavior and either reinforces or eliminates that behavior. The environment holds the key to understanding behavior (Bales, 1990).

For Skinner, behavior is a causal chain of three links: (a) an operation performed upon the organism from without—a student comes to school without breakfast; (b) some inner condition—the student gets hungry; and (c) a kind of behavior—listless behavior in the classroom.

Lacking information about inner conditions, we cannot indulge in speculation. For example, a student is listless and disinterested during class. Skinner scoffed at those who say the student is unmotivated. What does this mean? How can you explain it behaviorally? The problem is that the teacher or counselor searching for causes has stopped at the second link: some inner condition. The answer lies in the first link: something done to the student, such as lack of breakfast, physical difficulty, or trouble with parents.

Until his death in 1990, Skinner emphasized the importance of consequences on behavior and cautioned us about the limitation of a cognitive-oriented psychology.

> So far as I'm concerned, cognitive science is the creationism of psychology. It is an effort to reinstate that inner initiating-originating-creative self or mind which, in a scientific analysis, simply does not exist. I think it is time for psychology as a profession and as a science in such fields as psychotherapy, education, developmental psychology and all the rest, to realize that the science which will be most helpful is not cognitive science searching for the inner mind or self, but selection by consequences represented by behavior analysis.
>
> Looking back on my life—sixty-two years as a psychologist—I would say that what I have tried to do, that what I have been doing, is to make that point clearer; to show how selection by consequences in the individual can be demonstrated in the laboratory with animals and with human subjects and to show the implications of that for the world at large—in not only the profession of psychology, but in consideration of what is going to happen in the world unless some very vital changes are made. Any evidence that I've been successful in that is what I should like to be remembered by (Skinner, 1990).

Skinner and Reinforcement

Throughout our analysis of Skinner's system we will constantly encounter the term **reinforcement,** which Skinner uses as a key element to explain how and why learning has occurred. Reinforcement is typically used as follows:

- *A* **reinforcer** *is a stimulus event,* which, if it occurs in the proper temporal relation with a response, tends to maintain or increase the strength of a response, a stimulus-response connection, or a stimulus-stimulus connection (Hulse, Egeth, & Deese, 1980, p. 23). Praise, for example, may be a powerful reinforcer. If you praise a student's correct responses immediately, the student knows that you are reinforcing a specific behavior.
- *The principle of reinforcement* refers to an increase in the frequency of a response when certain consequences immediately follow it. The

consequence that follows behavior must be contingent upon the behavior. A contingent event that increases the frequency of behavior is referred to as a reinforcer (Kazdin, 1989, p. 105). Once you praise a student's correct response, you increase the probability that the student will remember the response and use it in future, similar situations.

- *Be sure to distinguish reward from reinforcement.* Nonpsychologists use the term "reward"; parents may buy a child an ice cream cone for "being good"; a basketball coach may take his squad to a pizza parlor for a "good game." This is a broad interpretation since no specific behavior is identified. Psychologists, however, view the process quite differently. They believe that reinforcement becomes effective when applied to *specific* behaviors: a student receives a teacher's praise for the solution to a problem or the correct answer to a question.

The Skinnerian model attempts to link reinforcement to response as follows:

?—response—reinforcement

The question mark represents the range of environmental stimuli, the unknown antecedents acting on the organism at any time. If we focus on the observable (the response) and reinforce it, control of behavior passes to the environment (teachers, parents). (Note that Pavlov concentrated on conditioned stimuli, which is why his theory is called Type S conditioning. Skinner focused on responses, and thus his theory is called Type R conditioning.)

The Nature of Reinforcement

In his analysis, Skinner (1953) concentrated on behavior that affects the surrounding world because the consequences of that behavior feed back into the organism, thus increasing the tendency to reproduce that behavior under similar circumstances. Once Skinner reached that conclusion, he had at his disposal a powerful tool for analyzing behavior.

Using Reinforcement

Imagine that once again you are a ten-year-old with a sweet tooth. Your father has constantly prodded you all summer to mow the lawn: do it today; do it before I get home, or else. But your mother, with a shrewd understanding of human behavior, discovers that the local variety store carries a new brand of ice cream bars that you like—but they're rather expensive. She promises you a package each week after mowing the lawn. By the end of the summer you are cutting the grass on a regular basis with no threats, coercion, or scoldings.

This simple illustration contains all of the elements that made fervent believers of many of Skinner's readers. It also demonstrates why Skinner was dissatisfied with the Pavlovian model as a technique for explaining all of our behavior. Skinner was determined that he would work only with the observable in order to build a scientific structure of learning and behavior.

In our example, no one can identify the stimulus that caused you to mow the lawn during August. The only tangibles that we have to work with are your behavior and the reinforcers. (Remember: Your father told you and you avoided the task.) Skinner began his analysis with pigeons and rats in exactly the same manner and quickly recognized that the consequences of behavior—the reinforcers—were powerful controlling forces. Perhaps we could summarize his thinking by saying, *control the reinforcers, control the behavior.* We saw an example of this technique in the chapter opening. By controlling the reinforcement (tutoring elementary school students), Alice West was attempting to encourage her student to obey the school's rule on smoking.

Thus far we have been discussing positive reinforcers, or events that are presented after a response has been performed and that increase the behavior or activity they follow. There is also *negative reinforcement* that refers to events (aversive stimuli) *removed* after a response has been performed and that also increase the behavior or activity they follow (Kazdin, 1989). That is, both positive and negative reinforcement functionally increase behavior. Negative reinforcement should not be confused with punishment, which, as we shall see later in the chapter, decreases behavior.

Skinner (1953) noted that some event is a negative reinforcer only when its removal increases performance of the response. You can probably think of many things that are aversive in the environment. Consider, for example, adolescents who have loud music playing in their room. This situation is an aversive event for the parents who deplore the sound and would rather listen to country and western. To eliminate the adolescents' music, the parents shout and threaten to stop phone privileges unless the music is turned off. If the threat stops the playing of the music, the behavior of not playing loud music has been negatively reinforced.

You can understand how negative reinforcement operates in many situations, but it is necessary for some aversive event to be present for the principle to operate. Since you want to avoid establishing aversive events in the classroom, this procedure should be used infrequently in educational programs. Nevertheless, it is important to understand the concept and its potential strong impact on behavior.

The Keller Plan

Utilizing many of the behavioral principles we have just discussed, Keller (1968) devised a technique for individualized instruction. Using a **Personalized System of Instruction (PSI)**, students proceed at their own pace through a series of self-contained curricular segments. Each student responds to written stimulation and is reinforced for a correct response. Several steps are involved.

- Decide on the material to be covered.
- Divide the material into self-contained segments.
- Determine the most efficient means of evaluation.
- Permit students to move from step to step at their own pace.

In a **PSI** classroom, you see students working independently at their desks and a teacher moving from student to student. Upon passing a mastery test, the student moves onto the math unit (Stallings & Stipek, 1986).

Hergenhahn (1988), summarizing the results of PSI, concludes that students seem to achieve at a superior level if the principles of learning in the system are carefully followed. Criticisms of PSI focus on the lack of reciprocal interactions between teachers and students and whether all curricular material can be so easily segmented.

Types of Reinforcers

As he continued to study behavior from this viewpoint, Skinner examined reinforcers more carefully and categorized them according to their power.

1. **Primary reinforcers** are those that affect behavior without the necessity of learning: food, water, sex. In this sense, they are natural reinforcers.

2. **Secondary reinforcers** are those that acquire reinforcing power because they have been associated with primary reinforcers. For example, if one of Skinner's pigeons pecked a disc, a green light would go on, followed a second later by a piece of corn. The green light remains on and, after repeated trials, gradually acquires reinforcing potential of its own.

3. **Generalized reinforcers,** a form of secondary reinforcers, are those that acquire reinforcing power because they have accompanied several primary reinforcers. Money illustrates this category because it leads to food, liquids, and other positive things; it then becomes a generalized reinforcer for a multitude of behaviors. Table 6.1 illustrates the various types of reinforcers.

Table 6.1

Categories of Reinforcers

Category	Types	Usage
Primary	1. Biological (natural) a. food, liquids, sensory	Usually with young, or special students. Example: candy, ice cream, soft music

Secondary	1. Social
	   a. facial expression
	   b. proximity
	   c. words
	   d. privileges
		Frowning, smiling
		Changing seats
		Praise
		Appointment to leadership role

	2. Activity a. pleasant or "high frequency" behavior	Playing a game following completion of class assignment

	3. Generalized
	   a. tokens
	   b. points
	   c. anything that can be used to obtain pleasure
		Compiling 25 points enables student to select pleasant activity such as free reading, playing a game, building models

For many years, the two Freds (Fred S. Keller and B. Fred Skinner) educated and entertained those attending the annual behavior analysis convention. This entertaining exchange was entitled "Old Friends" and occurred at the Midwestern Association for Behavior Analysis convention in Chicago, 1976.

Photo by G. K. Hare.

Schedules of Reinforcement

Skinner identified two kinds of intermittent reinforcement: interval and ratio. **Interval reinforcement** refers to a schedule whereby reinforcement occurs at definite established time intervals; for example, you may decide to praise a talking out student only if that student remains quiet for five minutes. Following the praise, no additional reinforcement is given until another five minutes passes.

A **ratio schedule** means that reinforcement occurs after a certain number of responses. For example, you may insist that one of your students completes four math problems before a game activity. If the ratio is slowly altered, an amazing number of responses may result from a very low number of reinforcements. Skinner also developed variable schedules for both interval and ratio reinforcement, whereby reinforcement appears at any time or after any response (Ferster & Skinner, 1957).

The importance of reinforcement and the identification of classes of reinforcers led Skinner to consider what happens to behavior that escapes (for whatever reason) constant reinforcement. You don't reinforce your students for every desired response they exhibit. They receive periodic grades; workers receive weekly or monthly checks; but both students and workers continue to behave appropriately.

The answer lies in the effectiveness of **intermittent reinforcement,** especially the notion of schedules of reinforcement. Studies of four classes of schedules have produced consistent findings.

1. **Fixed ratio,** in which reinforcement depends on a definite number of responses. If you require your students to complete thirty workbook examples before they can do something else, perhaps more exciting, you have put them on a fixed ratio schedule.
2. **Variable ratio,** in which the number of responses needed for reinforcement will vary from one reinforcement to the next. Required responses may vary, and subjects never know which response will be reinforced. For example, some teachers don't want to see only the completed project. They ask to see it during various stages of progress and mark what has been done.
3. **Fixed interval,** in which a response results in reinforcement after a definite time. The sequence is as follows: reinforcement—twenty seconds—reinforcement; reinforcement—twenty seconds—reinforcement. Note that responses made during the twenty-second interval are not reinforced. Teachers occasionally fall into a pattern in which they have a class work and then perhaps every ten or fifteen minutes into the class, ask for responses. Students know this and start to work just before the teacher is due to call on them.
4. **Variable interval,** in which reinforcement again depends on time and a response, but the time between reinforcements varies on this schedule. In the above example, rather than waiting for the ten or fifteen minutes to go by, teachers ask for responses at different times—immediately, later, in the middle of the class.

What can we conclude from Skinner's analysis of reinforcement schedules?

First, continuous reinforcement produces a high level of response only as long as reinforcement persists. The lesson for teachers: don't constantly reinforce your students; they come to expect it. (You like students, or you wouldn't be teaching, and probably tend to use praise excessively; be careful.)

Second, intermittent reinforcement, although producing slower acquisition of responses, results in greater resistance to extinction (loss of response).

Third, ratio schedules can be used to generate a high level of responding, but fatigue may hinder performance. Fixed ratios are common in education; we reinforce our students for papers, projects, and examinations. However, after students respond and receive reinforcement, behavior drops off sharply and learning efficiency suffers (Skinner, 1953).

Focus on Classrooms

Identifying Rewards for Students

Teachers sometimes are unaware of the types of things students find rewarding. Many things students will work for are either free or inexpensive. For example, free time in the classroom or extra recess are things that are free and available in every school and are motivating to students. Administer the following questionnaire to the target student to find out the things he/she finds rewarding.

Name   Grade   Date

1. Name three things you most like to do at school.
   a.
   b.
   c.

2. If you had fifteen minutes of free time at school to do what you wanted, what would you do?

3. Name three special jobs you would like to do at school.
   a.
   b.
   c.

4. If you could choose to work with someone in your class, who would it be?

5. Name three things that you most like to do at home.
   a.
   b.
   c.

Activities are a potent reinforcer for children's behavior. They can often be established as part of the normal routine in home and school settings.

Fourth, interval schedules produce the most stable behavior. Skinner (1968, p. 159) summarized the meaning of these schedules for education as follows:

> The student will be less dependent on immediate and consistent reinforcement if he is brought under the control of intermittent reinforcement. If the proportion of responses reinforced (on a fixed or variable ratio schedule) is steadily reduced, a stage may be reached at which behavior is maintained indefinitely by an astonishingly small number of reinforcements.

Table 6.2 illustrates the various reinforcement schedules.

Skinner and Punishment

Thus far we have stressed the key role of reinforcement (both positive and negative) in controlling behavior in

Skinner's theory. Now we turn our attention to the two types of reinforcers that Skinner has identified: **positive reinforcers** (those stimuli whose presentation strengthens behavior) and **negative reinforcers** (those stimuli whose withdrawal strengthens behavior).

What happens when a teacher or parent withdraws a positive reinforcer (a child cannot go to the movies) or introduces something unpleasant (slapping, scolding)? Skinner believed that these two conditions establish the parameters of punishment.

Kazdin (1989, p. 144) defines punishment more formally as follows:

> Punishment is the presentation of an aversive event or the removal of a positive event following a response that decreases the frequency of that response.

Table 6.2

Schedules of Reinforcement

Type	Meaning	Outcome
Fixed ratio (FR)	Reinforcement depends on a definite number of responses—for example, every tenth response	Activity slows after reinforcement and then picks up
Variable ratio (VR)	Number of responses needed for reinforcement varies—ten responses, reinforcement; five responses, reinforcement	Produces greatest activity of all schedules
Fixed interval (FI)	Reinforcement depends on a fixed time—for example, every thirty seconds	Activity increases as deadline nears (students must finish paper by a certain date)
Variable interval (VI)	Time between reinforcements varies	Produces steady activity

Examining Skinner's description and Kazdin's definition, note that they mention two aspects of punishment.

1. *Something aversive (unpleasant) appears after a response.* This is called an **aversive stimulus.** For example, a mother may slap a child who yells at her; teachers may reprimand students who are talking in class. In each case, something unpleasant follows behavior.
2. *Something positive (pleasant) disappears after a response.* A child who slaps another youngster while playing may be sent indoors. A teenage son may violate his curfew and loses use of the car the next weekend. In both instances something unpleasant followed undesirable behavior.

Note: Punishment always is intended to decrease a certain type of behavior.

Categories of Punishment

In behavioral programs punishment refers to presentation or removal of some event that results in a reduction in the frequency of a behavior. There are three general categories of punishment: the presentation of aversive events, withdrawal of positive consequences, and consequences based on effort or activity (Kazdin, 1989).

The most commonly recognized form of punishment involves presenting something aversive following performance or the response of an individual. If the event presented reduces the frequency of the behavior, it would be functionally defined as punishment. Remember, certain aversive events (such as shouting) may actually increase some behavior, and, therefore, shouting would be defined as a reinforcer. Verbal statements such as reprimands commonly function as punishment but may lose their effectiveness over extended applications. Other aversive events such as physical intervention (corporal punishment) have been identified as having functional punishing effects but should not be used except in extraordinary circumstances, and even then their use remains quite controversial.

Withdrawal of positive consequences can also serve to reduce the frequency of some behavior and may serve as punishment. The two major forms of withdrawal of positive consequences are **time-out** from reinforcement and **response cost.** Time-out from reinforcement has a long history of use in educational settings. You may have heard of or seen instances in which students were involved in "time-out" by being placed in a chair in the hall or sent to the principal's office. Many of these procedures did not qualify as punishment and may have actually led to greater misbehavior.

Focus on Teachers

Don't Rely on Punishment

In a perceptive analysis, Skinner questioned the reasons for teaching failure and settled upon the excessive reliance upon punishment (Skinner's expression for this: **aversive stimuli**). Although corporal punishment, legal in some states, is used infrequently today, other forms of punishment, perhaps even more damaging psychologically, such as ridicule and sarcasm, have grown more common. With these forms of aversive control, we can force students to read books, listen to lectures, and take tests; but if these activities are disliked, they are usually accompanied by unwanted by-products. In fact, some behaviorists argue that behavior problems can be solved with non-aversive strategies under virtually all conditions (LaVigna & Donnellan, 1986).

Students are ingenious in their methods of avoiding and escaping from aversive stimuli: they come late; they become truants; they develop school phobia; they feign illness; they simply "turn off" on the teacher and anything educational. They may even become abusive and destructive, turning to vandalism.

Note: There is a difference between escape and avoidance behavior.

1. **Escape behavior** occurs when a response eliminates an aversive event. Keeping a student from joining classmates in a pleasant activity until a task is completed illustrates the escape technique: when the appropriate responses are made, the aversive stimulus or punishment (in this case, isolation) is removed.

2. **Avoidance behavior** allows a student to prevent or postpone contact with something aversive. Feigning illness in the morning to stay home so as to avoid a teacher's punishment is a good example of avoidance behavior.

Attractive settings, multisensory materials, and insultingly easy material provide few, if any, answers. Students will not learn unless positive reinforcement prevails. Students remember what happened in school and transfer that learning to new situations because of the consequences of their behavior in the classroom. If we present material mechanically and don't offer students the opportunity to respond in order that we may reinforce those responses, school becomes meaningless for students.

Teaching will become more pleasant, teachers more successful, and teacher-student relationships more positive when teachers abandon aversive techniques in favor of designing personally satisfying schedules of reinforcement for students (Skinner, 1968).

Time-out from positive reinforcement refers to the removal of all positive reinforcers for some time period. Time-out is often not effective because not all sources of reinforcement are removed. For example, a student sent to the hallway for a time-out period may actually receive considerable attention from peers who happen to be walking by. Brief time-out has been found to be effective but has some disadvantages in educational settings. First, there is a tendency for teachers and others to use time-out as a sole method of discipline. During these periods the child is often excluded from learning activities. There is also the danger that teachers might revert to longer and longer time-out periods with no real benefit to the student.

Response cost involves a loss of a positive reinforcer and, unlike time-out, does not involve a period during which positive events are unavailable. Response cost most often involves a fine or penalty of some sort. For example, students given access to some reinforcer for a specified period of time may have that time taken away for inappropriate behavior. Like time-out, response cost should be used with positive procedures. Indeed, response cost depends on positive events being present to work effectively.

A relatively new class of punishment techniques is based on *effort following some response*. For example, requiring a person to do something that involves effort or work may reduce the response and therefore, serve as punishment. **Overcorrection** is a procedure that is included in this category. It involves a penalty for some inappropriate behavior with two procedures. First, restitution is involved since the person corrects the effects of some negative action. A student who breaks another student's pencil would be required to replace it. Second, positive practice is included and consists of repeatedly practicing an appropriate behavior. A student may be required to demonstrate the correct use of a pencil as in writing. Of course, not all behaviors that one is trying to reduce would be handled with both components of overcorrection.

How Punishment Works

Studying the psychological mechanisms underlying punishment, researchers have identified several key elements that influence its effectiveness (Kazdin, 1989).

1. *Schedule of punishment.* Generally, punishment is more effective when it is delivered every time rather than intermittently. However, when you discontinue punishment, recovery of a response originally punished is greater under conditions of continuous punishment than with intermittent applications. A teacher who reprimands a student for some rule

infraction would be advised to use the reprimand each time the problem behavior occurs. Nevertheless, once a behavior has been suppressed, the punishment procedure need be used only intermittently to keep it from reappearing.

2. *Intensity of punishment.* It was once believed that increasing the intensity of punishment increases its effectiveness. However, this is not the case. If punishment is to be considered, you should use mild forms.

3. *Source of reinforcement.* Punishment is usually enhanced when other sources of reinforcement that maintain the behavior are removed. It is important to recognize that behavior (both positive and negative) is maintained by various reinforcement contingencies. Therefore, punishment will be more effective when a certain behavior is not reinforced at the same time punishment contingencies are involved. For example, when a teacher tries to use punishment in the classroom, it is often common for a student's peers to reinforce the child's inappropriate behavior through laughing or clapping. Thus, punishment would be expected to be less effective when peers reinforce the child.

4. *Timing of reinforcement.* Most student behavior consists of a series of actions that make up a response class or group of behaviors. Punishment is usually more effective when it is delivered early in a sequence of behaviors that form a response group. Consider the student who throws spit wads in the classroom. The act of throwing spit wads is actually made up of a series of actions that lead to the final act of throwing. The child usually takes out a piece of paper, rolls it into a ball, puts the magic solution on the ball, and proceeds to toss it across the room. Punishment early in the sequence leading to the act of throwing will be more effective in breaking up the chain of problematic behaviors.

5. *Delay of punishment.* The longer the interval between behavior and punishment, the less effective the punishment. The consequences of behavior, pleasant or painful, are most effective when they immediately follow that behavior. The explanation for the effectiveness (or not) of punishment lies in the interval between behavior and punishment: if lengthy, the unwanted behavior may be reinforced by something or someone else in the environment. By the time you get around to disciplining a student, he or she may have received the attention of peers, who may laugh and encourage additional misbehavior or give the "thumbs-up" signal or some other form of support.

Also, punishment becomes more effective (in a positive sense) if students know exactly why you're punishing them. Punishing an entire class for something a few may have done can only produce bad feelings and tension. Make sure students understand the what and why of punishment and be consistent: if you punish something once, you must punish the behavior each time it appears—regardless of the offender. Otherwise students are confused and continue to exhibit the behavior.

6. *Variation of punishment.* Kazdin (1989) notes that although punishment usually consists of a contingency applied after some behavior, varying the punishment that follows a behavior can actually enhance the effects. It is possible that some type of adaptation to the repeated effects of the same punishment occurs (e.g., always reprimanding the child will be less effective over repeated applications). Kazdin, however, is careful to point out that variation does not imply combination. Combining several aversive events would be objectionable on ethical and practical grounds.

7. *Reinforcement of alternative behaviors.* Kazdin makes two important points that you must consider in any use of punishment techniques. First, aversive events of relatively weak intensity can effectively suppress behavior if reinforcement is also provided for an alternative positive response. Second, punishment usually trains a person in what not to do rather than in what to do. Thus, it is important that you follow up with positive reinforcement when punishment is used because it will increase the effectiveness of punishment as a procedure, focus your attention on teaching positive behaviors to replace the negative ones you are trying to reduce, and reduce the negative side effects of using aversive strategies.

At this point you should consider two generalizations about punishment: (a) regardless of what you may personally think of punishment as a means of controlling behavior, properly used, punishment is highly effective; (b) there is also little doubt that the side effects of punishment, most of which are undesirable, accompany punishment that is routinely, even thoughtlessly, applied.

Suggestions for Using Punishment

Remember these suggestions for using punishment:

- It is confined to the *immediate situation* and may have no effect in the future. A good example is gum chewing. Look at your classmates during your next class. Some will almost surely be chewing gum. Ask

"First, she tells us how much fun reading is. Then, she assigns me three extra chapters as punishment when I snicker."

Try to avoid using school work as a means of punishment. Think of alternatives—preferably reinforcement of an alternative desired behavior.

Robert Hageman, Courtesy of *Phi Delta Kappan.*

if any one of them has ever been punished for chewing gum in school. Invariably some will recall that during elementary school they either had to stay after class, do extra work, or wear the gum on their nose. Yet here they are chewing noisily.

- There may be a *future effect* if the punished behavior later produces conditioned stimuli that evoke unpleasant emotional responses. For example, when a youngster begins to chew gum in school, the memory of previous punishment arouses feelings of guilt and anxiety that will inhibit gum chewing. One immediate difficulty is that previously punished behavior may become acceptable under different circumstances. For example, a boy or girl from a devoutly religious family may have had premarital sex followed by feelings of remorse, guilt, and acute anxiety—all forms of self-punishment. It is possible that these feelings become so intense that they affect sexual life after marriage.
- Any stimulus accompanying the aversive stimulus may be *conditioned* to that behavior. A student who has a nagging, sarcastic teacher in the first or second grade may react with fear to any classroom setting.

Should teachers resort to punishment? The practical answer is yes. Problems arise in a classroom where a teacher must act quickly and decisively or lose control of an entire class. But teachers should use punishment sparingly, carefully, and as a last resort. One reason is that we simply do not understand

punishment's effects. If you must use it, here are some suggestions.

- *Be sure that you later have the student do something that you can reinforce positively.* Do not have your use of punishment produce a hostile, defiant student who sees teachers as nothing more than punishing agents.
- *Punish individuals, not classes.* Nothing is as ludicrous as having an entire class remain late, or do some exercise, because one or two individuals caused trouble.
- *Avoid using school subjects as punishment.* There is no better way to teach students to dislike math or spelling than having them solve hundreds of extra problems or copy endless lists of words.
- *Avoid sending youngsters to others for punishment.* You only inform students that you cannot control them. Also the students will develop antagonistic or fearful feelings toward the principal or whoever dispenses punishment.
- *If at all possible, ignore aggravating behavior.* Skinner called this extinction. Some youngsters like to be punished; they enjoy the attention, which they find reinforcing. By not supplying the attention or reinforcement, teachers can encourage the disappearance of the behavior. If a student's behavior is so disruptive that it affects an entire class, then naturally it cannot be ignored. You must act. Remember, you evaluate punishment through its consequences. Something that you think is punishment may not decrease a behavior.

No one can tell you the best way for you to control a class. You must discover what works best for you. You will encounter problems; everyone does. Refuse to panic and try various techniques until you discover your most effective method. Always remember that positive reinforcement is much more satisfying than punishment for you and your students. Problems are minimal in a pleasant, exciting atmosphere that encourages activity and cooperation.

For the Classroom

Skinner was a constant and critical observer of current educational practices. Using the teaching of arithmetic as an example, Skinner noted that students must learn special verbal responses—words, figures, signs—that refer to arithmetic functioning. Consequently, teachers must help their students to bring this behavior under stimulus control.

Students must learn to count, add, subtract, multiply, and divide before they can solve problems. Teaching

Focus on Classrooms

Skinner and the Reluctant Mathematician

You may agree or disagree with Skinner's system, but his identification of the reluctant mathematician is at once perceptive and telling. We are all familiar with those who freeze at the sight of numbers (are you one?). Skinner, of course, argued that such behavior can be directly traced to the lack of adequate and correct contingencies of reinforcement.

If you are comfortable with figures, you should have no difficulty with these simple problems. If, however, you are one of the frozen, your reactions should be interesting.

1. Examine the following columns of figures for about thirty seconds. Don't try to add them. Just scan each column and estimate the four that have the highest totals.

```
A B C D E F G H I
3 9 5 7 1 8 3 2 3
8 0 3 7 2 5 9 8 4
3 8 8 5 3 2 1 4 3
6 2 2 2 4 3 6 5 1
8 7 5 4 5 6 5 7 9
5 1 2 6 6 1 5 6 3
2 1 2 6 6 1 5 7 9
7 4 9 3 8 8 7 9 6
```

2. Fill in the blanks to make this a correct multiplication problem.

$$
\begin{array}{r}
\text{-}7 \\
\times 8\text{-} \\
\hline
\underline{} \\
\underline{} \\
2\_8
\end{array}
$$

These are relatively simple problems that some of you will solve easily, while others will experience difficulty. Can you explain why this is so, linking your answer to Skinner's operant conditioning?

Answers:
1. H = 48, A = 42, G = 41, D = 40
2. 27, 84

Skinner believed that schools should search for positive reinforcers that they now have at their disposal, such as paper, paints, puzzles, and activities that students enjoy. The next step would be to make them contingent upon desired behavior. One way of combining both of these features would be the use of **teaching machines,** which divide materials to be learned into small units and reinforce successful behaviors. These devices are mechanical (which students usually like) and they provide positive reinforcement (which everybody likes). They also eliminate aversive stimuli.

There are several advantages in the use of teaching machines.

- Reinforcement for the right answer is immediate; just using these machines can be reinforcing.
- Machines make possible the presentation of carefully controlled material in which one problem can depend on the answer to the preceding problem, eventually leading to the development of complex behaviors.
- If the material lacks sufficient inherent reinforcing characteristics, other reinforcers (such as those just mentioned) can be made contingent upon completion of the program (Skinner, 1986).

Tracing the history of teaching machines, Skinner (1986) noted that teaching machines are a great asset for motivation, attention, and appreciation. For example, motivation is enhanced because good programs "maximize the effects of success" by having students take small steps and helping them to do so successfully (Skinner, 1986, p. 108). Attention increases because students (like all of us) attend to those things that reinforce us. Appreciation of art, music, or a discipline is enhanced by a carefully arranged series of reinforcements.

Having students proceed, successfully, at their own rate means that some students will master many fields quickly, while those who move more slowly will, nevertheless, survive as successful students. Education can become more efficient if it utilizes the existing technology of teaching machines and moves away from those ideas that have proven fruitless for the past several decades. Today's more sophisticated teaching machines include desk top models with earphones and voice feedback and microcomputers designed for programmed instruction.

Finally, Skinner's work has definite implications for teachers:

- *Reinforcement remains such a powerful tool in controlling behavior* that teachers should constantly be aware of their consequences.
- *The well-known* **Premack principle** has valuable classroom implications. David Premack (1965) has stated that all organisms engage in some activities more than others. After noting a student's preferred

these procedures entails the proper use of positive reinforcement, which should be immediate and frequent (particularly in the first stages of instruction). For example, Skinner has estimated that during the first four school years teachers can arrange only a few thousand behavior-reinforcement contingencies but that efficient mathematical behavior requires at least *25,000 contingencies* during these years (Skinner, 1968).

Using Operant Conditioning in the Classroom

1. Operant conditioning is concerned with the consequences of behavior.
   - A good general principle for teaching is that when students respond, react to their behavior as quickly as possible, immediately if you can. Your reaction may be either positive or negative, but you can be sure that if you allow enough time to elapse between a student's response and your reaction, what you say or do will have lost much of its impact.
   - Don't assume that you know why students do or don't do something. Skinner would say that you are guessing. Work with what your students say or do and reinforce (or punish) that behavior in an attempt to shape their behavior in the desired direction.
   - Be sure that you know exactly what you want your students to do; otherwise you reinforce behavior that may or may not lead to desirable objectives. Must a student have the correct answer to receive positive reinforcement; would a partial answer suffice; or would a positive attitude toward the task be enough to warrant reinforcement? These are important questions that you must think about to become skillful in applying reinforcement.

2. Control the reinforcers, control the behavior.
   - Once you get to know your students, you'll be able to identify those reinforcers that they particularly like. In the chapter's opening vignette, the secondary school student liked working with the younger students. Allowing her to do so illustrates the application of a powerful reinforcer. The opposite also holds true: knowing your students well enables you to take away something pleasurable (working with younger students) or to introduce something unpleasant (extra work after school). In either case, your control of the reinforcers permits you to shape students' behavior.
   - Be sure students understand why they are being reinforced. Teachers who stand in front of a class and say "That's very good" to the entire class are reinforcing unknown behaviors, some of which may be objectionable.
   - When you apply reinforcers, remember Skinner's advice: apply them to specific behaviors. "That's good"

   is too vague. "Good, Billy. You got the right answer this time." By merely saying "That's good," you can't be sure of what you're reinforcing. Billy may have stopped trying to get the answer when you spoke to him.
   - If you must use punishment, be careful of how you use it and be sure that it is appropriate for the particular behavior. A secondary school teacher recently related how he had been pushing a good student ("Do you call that good work?" When are you going to turn in something that you're proud of?"). The student, a good worker and usually pleasant and good-natured, turned one day and shouted at the teacher. Though there will unquestionably be times when you must punish, try not to misjudge the situation the way that this teacher did. Know your students, know what they are capable of, and know what they can tolerate.

3. Be aware of the nature and timing of your reinforcements.
   - Teachers are often criticized for giving too much positive reinforcement. Decide how frequently you must reinforce a student, since the frequency will vary from student to student. Discover what individual students consider as important reinforcers; some will respond well to teacher praise, while others will need more tangible reinforcers, such as being appointed teacher's helper, leading traffic patrols, or being designated class messenger for the week.
   - Students who have a problem with their self-esteem or lack confidence in a particular subject may need frequent reinforcement. Provide as much as you think is necessary and then gradually reduce it. Initially, you may reinforce their general behavior in your class (let them select the posters for the month), then restrict it to the subject matter (reinforce partially correct answers), and, finally, limit reinforcement to the necessary minimum (tests, projects).
   - Teachers who reinforce too frequently find that students work only for the reinforcement and that reinforcement becomes meaningless after awhile. If you find this happening, initiate class discussions in which you try to lead students to the realization that learning itself is satisfying and important.

---

activities, you can then use them as positive reinforcers. For example, noting that several boys who avoid anything mathematical enjoy playing ball, a shrewd teacher could promise them free time after completing their math work.

- *Aversive stimulation (punishment) may cause more problems than it solves.* Use punishment sparingly and carefully, although there may be occasions when

nothing else works. If you must punish, try to get the offending student to do something that you can positively reinforce—and do it as soon as possible.

- *Be alert to the timing of your reinforcement.* Though it may be impossible to reinforce all desirable behaviors, when you decide that a certain behavior is critical, reinforce it immediately. Do not let time elapse.

• *Determine precisely what you want your students to learn*, and then arrange the material so that they make as few mistakes as possible.

A study of disruptive behavior in secondary school classes illustrates these ideas (McNamara, Evans, and Hill, 1986). The classes were in remedial math; one consisted of 17 pupils, twelve to thirteen years old; the other had 15 pupils aged thirteen to fourteen. Both groups were noisy and disruptive at the start of class; they pushed their tables together and talked loudly, making it impossible to begin the lesson.

The teacher, a 23-year-old woman, had one year of experience teaching in the school and felt that she related well to the students individually but lacked group control. Several procedures were suggested as the intervention technique.

    a. The tables were set in rows with two students at each table. (Here the teacher was attempting to structure the classroom environment to aid in her use of behavior techniques.)

    b. Rules of the classroom were displayed on a large chart placed at the front of the classroom. The rules were also printed on sheets of paper and distributed to the class. The rules were: arrive on time, work quietly, bring necessary materials, no shouting, don't bother others. (This procedure identified acceptable behavior.)

    c. The teacher was asked to make evaluative statements about conduct at the end of the lesson. (Here assessment measures were introduced.)

    d. If the evaluation was positive, the class could spend the final ten minutes of the lesson doing puzzles. (Recall the Premack principle.)

    e. Self-assessment consisted of the students' checking the rules that they had followed (on the sheets that had been distributed). (Here the teacher was striving for student self-control.)

The results showed a substantial improvement in student on-task behavior and a notable increase in positive teacher behavior. (We shall return to Skinner's ideas on behavior modification in greater detail in chapter 13.)

Social Cognitive Learning

Albert Bandura (1925–) received his doctorate in 1952 from the University of Iowa, where he was influenced by the learning research tradition. Applying these principles to human behavior, Bandura initiated a sweeping pro-

Older siblings in the family have a strong modeling influence on younger family members.

gram of theory and research that led to the development of social cognitive learning. Considerable evidence exists that learning occurs through observing others, even when the observer does not reproduce the model's responses during acquisition and therefore receives no reinforcement (Bandura et al., 1963). For Bandura, **social cognitive learning** means that the information we process from observing other people, things, and events influences the way we act.

Children in all cultures learn and develop by observing more experienced people engaged in culturally important activities. In this way, teachers and parents help students to adapt to new situations, aid them in their problem-solving attempts, and guide them to accept responsibility for their behavior (Rogoff, 1990).

Observational learning has particular classroom relevance since children do not do just what adults tell them to do but rather what they see adults do. If Bandura's assumptions are correct, teachers can be a potent force in shaping the behavior of their students with the teaching behavior they demonstrate in class. The importance of models is seen in Bandura's interpretation of what happens as a result of observing others.

• The observer may acquire new responses.
• Observation of models may strengthen or weaken existing responses.
• Observation of a model may cause the reappearance of responses that were apparently forgotten.

If students witness undesirable behavior that is either rewarded or goes unpunished, undesirable student behavior may result; the reverse is also true. Classroom implications are apparent: positive, consistent teacher behavior contributes to a healthy classroom atmosphere. To understand the power of modeling, study the accompanying pictures carefully. Note the children's aggressive behavior after observing the model.

In a classic study, Bandura, Ross, and Ross (1963) studied the effects of live models, filmed human aggression, and filmed cartoon aggression on preschool children's aggressive behavior. The filmed human aggression portrayed adult models displaying aggression toward an inflated doll; the filmed cartoon aggression portrayed a cartoon character displaying the same behavior as the humans; the live models displayed the identical aggression as the others. Later all the children exhibited significantly more aggression than youngsters in a control group. Also, filmed models were as effective as live models in transmitting aggression. Research suggests that prestigious, powerful, competent models are more readily imitated than models who lack these qualities (Bandura et al., 1963).

An Explanation of Modeling

Modeling behavior may be described as one person observing another's behavior and acquiring that behavior in representational form without simultaneously performing the responses (Bandura, 1977, 1986). Four important processes seem to be involved in observational learning.

1. *Attention.* Mere exposure to a model does not insure acquisition of behavior. An observer must attend to and recognize the distinctive features of the model's response. The modeling conditions also must incorporate the features previously mentioned, such as attractiveness in the model and reinforcement of the model's behavior. Students who recognize these characteristics in their teachers will attend to the important features of their instructors' presentation. That our students are attracted to the compelling features of desirable models can be seen in their imitation of the clothing, hair styles, and mannerisms of today's rock stars, athletes, actors, and actresses.
2. *Retention.* To reproduce the desired behavior implies that a student symbolically retains the observed behavior. Bandura believes that "symbolic coding" helps to explain lengthy retention of observed behavior. For example, a student codes, classifies, and reorganizes the model's responses into personally meaningful units, thus aiding retention. What does this mean? As your students observe you, they must also form some type of image or mental

schemata that corresponds to what you are actually doing. (Note: they cannot form this mental picture unless they attend.) Your task is to urge them, either covertly or overtly (or both) to form this image while you are demonstrating.

3. *Motor reproduction processes.* Bandura believes that symbolic coding produces internal models of the environment that guide the observer's future behavior. The cognitive guidance of behavior is crucial for Bandura because it explains how modeled activities are acquired without performance. But cognitive activity is not autonomous—stimulus and reinforcement control its nature and occurrence. Again, what does this mean? After observation and after urging your students to form an image of the task's solution, have them demonstrate the solution as soon as possible. Can they do it? You can then reinforce correct behavior and alter any incorrect responses. Don't be satisfied with "show and tell"; have them reproduce the necessary behavior so that all of learning's mechanisms are utilized: stimulus—cognition—response—reinforcement.
4. *Motivational processes.* Although an observer acquires and retains the ability to perform modeled behavior, there will be no overt performance unless conditions are favorable. For example, if reinforcement previously accompanied similar behavior, the individual tends to repeat it. But vicarious reinforcement (observing a model reinforced) and self-reinforcement (satisfaction with one's own behavior) are powerful human reinforcers.

Bandura introduces a subtle distinction here that helps to distinguish social learning theory from Skinner's operant conditioning. Reinforcement acts on our students' motivation to behave and not on the behavior itself. In this way, Bandura believes that the resulting learning is stronger and longer lasting than that produced by reinforcing behavior alone.

Self-efficacy

As we have seen, social cognitive learning results from the interactions among behavior, environmental variables, cognitive processing, and personal factors (Schunk, 1989). These factors, especially the environment (in the form of modeling or the feedback we get from others), influence our feelings of competency on a particular task or skill. Such feelings of competency, called **self-efficacy,** develop from information conveyed by four sources (Bandura, 1981, 1986).

Photographs of children reproducing the aggressive behavior of the female model they had observed on film.
From Bandura, Ross, & Ross, 1963a.

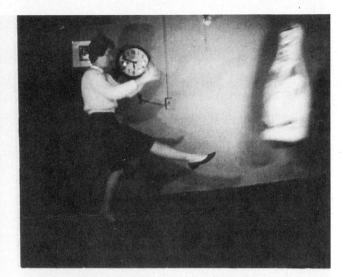

1. *Performance accomplishments.* We acquire personal and effective information from what we do; we learn from first-hand experience how successful we are in mastering our environment.
2. *Vicarious experience.* Watching "similar others" perform, we persuade ourselves that we can probably do it also. The reverse is also true.
3. *Verbal persuasion.* Persuasion can lead our students into believing that they can overcome their difficulties and improve their performance.
4. *Emotional arousal.* Stressful situations constitute a source of personal information. If we project an image of ourselves as inept and fearful in certain situations, then we enhance the possibility of just that behavior. But if an admired model demonstrates "coolness under fire," that behavior reduces our tendency toward debilitating emotional behavior.

Receiving data from these sources enables us to judge the extent of our self-efficacy; that is, success raises our sense of self-efficacy, while failure diminishes it. You can see how your feedback to your students can have a powerful effect on their feelings of competency. As a respected model, your evaluations carry significant weight. When you say, "Of course you can do it, Heather," you are providing strong verbal persuasion. You should then follow through on this encouragement by insuring that the student's performance accomplishment meets your (and your student's) expectations.

Your instructional techniques are also important. Research has consistently shown that when students are taught how to go about a task—that is, when they are given strategy training—their performance improves (Paris, Cross, and Lipson, 1984). This in turn influences their self-efficacy since a belief that you know what you are doing improves your control over a situation.

Using models can also be effective in improving self-efficacy. Working with elementary school children who were experiencing difficulty in mathematics, Schunk, Hanson, and Cox (1987) had the students observe videotapes of students under different learning conditions.

• Some of the students observed a teacher helping students solve problems.
• Others observed peer models who solved the problems easily and then made positive statements reflecting self-efficacy.
• Still others observed coping models in which the students had difficulty and made mistakes but also uttered coping statements ("I'll have to work hard on this"). They were then shown to become more skillful.

Self-efficacy develops from performance accomplishments, vicarious experience, verbal persuasion, and emotional arousal.

Observing the coping models seemed to produce the most beneficial results.

Thus far we have indicated that social cognitive learning offers pertinent suggestions for understanding our students' behavior, particularly by making us aware of the modeling power of our behavior and the importance of self-efficacy to our students' learning. How can we apply these principles to the classroom?

Multicultural Models

Our discussion of modeling provides an excellent opportunity to stress the benefits of presenting models from various cultures. Different cultures have different values, beliefs, and motives that appear in the behavior of members of that culture. Consequently, if you are able to introduce into your classroom outstanding representatives of a particular culture, you can then reinforce the characteristics, abilities, and behaviors that members of that culture hold in esteem.

The visit of Nelson Mandela to the United States is a good example. His trials and ultimate triumph have been a source of inspiration to black youth. You not only engender pride in black students but you remind the other students of the respect and honor that these models command. By inviting such individuals into your classroom or initiating study projects about outstanding figures, you also have the chance to promote intercultural understanding. Individuals honored by their culture because of furthering interpersonal relations teach your students an important lesson.

With regard to inviting models, consider these questions that can help your selection.

- Do they have status? They should possess those features that lead to status: they are knowledgeable, educated, admired.
- Are they competent? They must be or they would not have achieved status.
- Are they respected? Though we may quibble over the definition of "respect," outstanding individuals eventually must behave in a manner that elicits the respect of others.

Children from different cultures, like the rest of us, try to make sense of their world by developing an explanatory model. By reinforcing the values and attitudes that express the best in their culture, you help to instill pride in these students and contribute to greater intercultural understanding.

For the Classroom

Bandura's ideas have particular relevance for the classroom, especially as they furnish information about the characteristics of desirable models and the personal features of students, notably their self-efficacy. Certain characteristics of models seem to relate positively to observational learning: those who have high status, competence, and power are more effective in prompting others to behave similarly than are models of lower standing (Bandura, 1977, p. 88).

The behavior of those who have achieved status and distinction undoubtedly has produced successful consequences, thus suggesting a high functional value for observers. The model's behavior, then, also furnishes information about the probable consequences of similar behavior by the observer. Thus, model characteristics not only attract observers because they have achieved status, even adulation as in the example of rock stars, but their behavior also resulted in tangible rewards: money, power.

As for students, Bandura (1981) has expressed concern about the development of self-knowledge, particularly the notion of **self-efficacy,** which he states "is concerned with judgments about how well one can organize and execute courses of action required to deal with prospective situations that contain many ambiguous, unpredictable, and often stressful, elements" (1981, p. 201).

Estimates of self-efficacy affect choices of activities and situations: we avoid situations that we fear will exceed our abilities but confidently perform those activities that we think we can handle. It also affects the quality of our behavior and our persistence on difficult tasks. For an example of how observational learning improves task persistence, consider Craske's research.

In a study of 37 male (mean age = 11.4) and 28 female pupils (mean age = 10.11), Craske (1985) used a social learning theory strategy to increase the persistence of the subjects who had been identified as *learned helplessness* children (children who feel helpless when faced with almost any kind of challenge). Subjects were taught to attribute failure to a lack of effort rather than a lack of ability. The subjects observed an eight-minute film in which a model answered a set of eighteen puzzles and was reinforced for each correct response. The model was also told that the correct answer resulted from "trying hard."

The results in the study indicated females were helped significantly while the males improved but not to the same extent. These results are particularly interesting as they relate to self-efficacy. The girls saw themselves as needing help, but the boys' judgments of themselves as competent individuals caused them to downplay any support.

The schools offer an excellent opportunity for the development of self-efficacy; consequently, educational practices should reflect this reality (Bandura, 1981). That is, materials and methods should be evaluated not only for academic skills and knowledge but also for what they can accomplish in enhancing students' perceptions of themselves.

Finally, to translate social learning theory into meaningful classroom practice, remember:

1. Just what is it you wish to present to your students? (the specific behaviors to be modeled);
2. Is it worth their doing? (the kinds of reinforcements available for the correct response);
3. How are you going to tell them, show them, and urge them to visualize the desired behaviors?
4. Does the lesson possess qualities that will improve your students' self-efficacy?

Social Cognitive Learning in the Classroom

1. Learning occurs from observing others even when the observer doesn't practice the observed behavior.
   - Film a video while groups of your students make social studies presentations (using maps, transparencies, models, etc.). As they watch the video, let them criticize the quality of their presentation, their methods, how they gained (or did not gain) the interest of the class, and how they would improve their presentation.
   - Show a filmstrip or a video of a favorite story. Set up groups in the class to critique the filmstrip and compare it to the story. Is it true to the book? Are the characters depicted the way you imagined they would be? What did they learn from observing the way that the characters acted?
   - Discuss the subject of "heroes" with your students. Who are they? What makes them heroes? Are they all particularly courageous? Did they take risks and overcome obstacles to achieve outstanding goals? Did they contribute something of lasting value to society? Do you believe that a person has to give up his or her life to become a hero? Under what circumstance? What is the difference between an idol and a hero? Do popular culture heroes fit the criteria of a hero? Your class may want to make a Hall of Fame and nominate their heroes for membership.
2. Several important processes are involved in observational learning.
   - Reinforcement occurs when children reenact what they have observed after a tour or a field trip. (For example, in the early elementary classes, after a trip to a dentist, use a high stool for a dental chair and large white shirts buttoned down the front as dentists' smocks and let the children act out what they have seen and heard.)
   - After reading a story aloud to a middle school group, select students to be the main characters, and after a brief "rehearsal" let them reproduce a scene for the class; *then* discuss with them the main idea, the characterization, the plot.
   - Draw high school students' attention to the sequencing of steps during a chemical experiment. Once they have seen it performed and understand the procedure, they perform the experiment themselves. Those who perform it well may help their classmates who are having difficulty. In this way, all of the students should better be able to retain and use the material.
3. For teachers who use observational learning there are several significant sources of information available that are also excellent motivational tools.
   - Cooperative learning provides students with the opportunity to show each other how to work together to complete a project.
   - Peer tutoring is another method to encourage one child to imitate another's skill in performing a special task.
   Older children help younger children to learn when they demonstrate their knowledge to them. They may present puppet shows for them, help them with their reading, play games with them in the school yard, assist them in using the computer, or be a "buddy" to a child with special needs.

Behaviorism and Teaching

Our objective thus far in this chapter has been to explain the theory and research that comprises behaviorism while offering general applications. With this as a basis we can now turn to specific illustrations of how the theory "works" in the classroom. Our discussion will include techniques for increasing, decreasing, and maintaining behavior. Also, since the use of behavioral principles has not been without criticism, we shall conclude this section by considering certain ethical issues.

Techniques to Increase Behavior

If you recall our earlier discussion of reinforcement, we emphasized that only those events that strengthen or increase behavior could be called reinforcement. Positive reinforcement is any event following behavior that increased the future rate and probability of responding. Negative reinforcement involves an increase in the probability of some behavior following the removal of an aversive event after the behavior is performed.

As we have seen, consequence must be contingent upon the appropriate behavior. The sequence in positive reinforcement is as follows:

1. You have made it quite clear to a student that the math seatwork must be finished before he/she plays with a puzzle or game.
2. Your student completes an assignment.
3. The student commences play with game.
4. There is increased probability that this student will complete seatwork in the future.

Figure 6.3 illustrates the process.

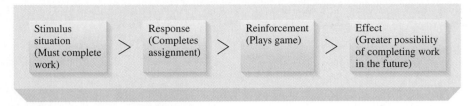

Figure 6.3
Contingency of reinforcement.

Effective Reinforcers

It is not always easy to identify positive reinforcers since what one student reacts well to may antagonize another. Attention is a good example. Adolescents particularly can show considerable variation in their reactions to teacher attention. For a few, it is something they wish to escape from or avoid, depending upon their reinforcement history. Occasionally when reinforcement does not seem to produce the desired result, it is not that reinforcement principles are faulty but rather that inappropriate reinforcers have been chosen.

If you wish to use positive reinforcers (and we all do, deliberately or otherwise), then be aware of the manner in which you apply them.

One way of selecting appropriate reinforcers is to consult to the motivation chapter and base your choices on those reinforcers that are natural for whatever age group you teach. You may want to use the following list as a guide in selecting reinforcers.

- Consider age, interests, and needs of your students. Pieces of candy are not too motivating for adolescents.
- Know precisely the behavior you wish to strengthen and make your reinforcer sufficiently desirable.
- List potential reinforcers that you think would be desirable. The reinforcer menu could be valuable here.
- Don't forget the demonstrated effectiveness of the Premack Principle.
- Vary your reinforcers.
- Keep a record of the effectiveness of various reinforcers on individual students.

Secondary Reinforcers

Earlier in this chapter (see p. 163) we discussed the difference between primary and secondary reinforcers. (Primary reinforcers are those that have biological importance; secondary reinforcers are those that acquire their power through association with primary and/or secondary reinforcers.) Most teachers will use **secondary reinforcers** frequently. These can be grouped into three major categories (Alberto & Troutman, 1986).

1. **Social reinforcers**, which typically include attention, can be verbal or nonverbal. For example, the expression on your face can carry an unmistakable message to a student. Usually, however, social reinforcers are verbal, either accompanying some other form of reinforcement ("John, you can act as class monitor because of the way you behaved in gym") or as words of praise that signal your pleasure about a specific behavior. Consequently, social reinforcers may include expression, contact, proximity, privileges, and words.

2. **Activity reinforcers,** which the "Premack Principle" previously mentioned, are high frequency behaviors. As reinforcers they are used following low frequency behaviors (see p. 180). For example, working on a ship model as a class project may appeal to a student and can be used to reinforce the behavior of turning in an assignment when due. Again, however, be sure you know what your individual students like.

3. **Generalized reinforcers** are those associated with a variety of other reinforcers (see p. 163). Smiling at a student, for example, has a history of being associated with a variety of pleasant experiences. Generalized reinforcers may also be a thing—moncy or a token—that may be exchanged for something of value.

Suggestions for Use

Positive reinforcement is a powerful principle and can be applied to great advantage in the classroom. All of us who teach, from the preschool to the doctoral level, whether we are behaviorists or not, use positive reinforcement. We must avoid, however, making students too dependent on the reinforcement we provide, particularly if we have initiated structured programs for students. *We want them to work for those reinforcers that are natural to them.*

Reducing dependence on such reinforcers as points or tokens, or any other artificial reinforcer, is called **thinning,** which means that reinforcement is provided less frequently. Greater amounts of appropriate behavior must occur before reinforcement occurs. You should realize the following benefits from thinning:

- more constant rate of responding with appropriate behavior (your students consistently follow classroom rules);
- a lessened anticipation of reinforcement (your students learn not to rely on outside reinforcement);
- control shifts to typical classroom procedures such as occasional praise (your students gradually acquire a sense of satisfaction from their own classroom successes);
- appropriate behavior is maintained over longer periods of time.

To conclude this section, we can summarize several aspects of positive reinforcement that you will find helpful. Remember: the correct use of positive reinforcement demands that you present the reinforcing stimulus (praise, candy, tokens, points) as soon as the appropriate behavior appears.

Techniques to Decrease Behavior

The use of positive procedures should be your goal as often as possible. Sometimes when the goal is to reduce or eliminate misbehavior, teachers consider using punishment (aversive procedures). A word of warning: don't fall into the trap of relying on punishment. It's easy; it frequently works for a short period of time (although not so easily with secondary school students); it gives you a feeling of having established control, which is fine unless you rely exclusively on punishment as a means of maintaining order. It also can destroy your rapport with students if excessively used; it produces a ripple effect that touches all students and affects your own teaching; it may have side effects of which you may be unaware.

Alternatives to Punishment

In recent years, there has been considerable discussion about the use of aversive techniques (see Repp & Singh, 1990 for a review of various perspectives). The use of punishment may even be associated with some myths such as the following (Donnellan & LaVigna, 1990):

- Punishment is necessary. Positive reinforcement can be used as an alternative.
- Punishment is more effective than other control techniques. Evidence to support this statement is not clear.
- Punishment is easier. The ease with which punishment is applied may lead to its too frequent use when other procedures are available.

Analyzing punishment and its alternatives, Alberto and Troutman (1986) offer a sequential hierarchy with

There are many alternatives to punishment.

four levels as a means of reducing inappropriate behavior. This hierarchy begins at Level I with the least restrictive and least aversive methods and gradually progresses to Level IV methods that are more restrictive and aversive. The best professional practice dictates beginning with Level I and moving to a higher level only when a student's behavior does not improve in a reasonable time period.

1. Level I strategies. These procedures are designated as the preferred option because by using them, teachers use positive techniques. They are based on the idea of differential reinforcement; that is, they rely on reinforcement to decrease or completely eliminate some behavior. For example, differential reinforcement of low rates of behavior is a technique designed to prevent that same behavior from becoming disruptive: you want students to contribute to but not dominate group discussion. For example, you may wish to eliminate a student's talking out behavior. Using differential reinforcement of low rates of behavior, you would select a period of time, perhaps ten minutes, and when the student remains silent, you offer praise and time to work on a model plane. You can gradually stretch the time for remaining silent.

   Differential reinforcement of incompatible behavior means that you reinforce some totally incompatible behavior. For example, you may decide to reinforce silent reading; a student cannot read silently while talking out.

2. Level II strategies. The strategies of this category are intended to reduce misbehavior by withholding reinforcement. As Alberto and Troutman (1986) note, teachers use extinction to reduce behavior that is being maintained by their attention. (Again, note the need to know what reinforces students.)

Extinction is best used in conjunction with the positive reinforcement of appropriate behavior.

Don't be discouraged if the effects of extinction are not immediate, because students will be demonstrating a phenomenon called resistance to extinction. You may even encounter an increased rate of misbehavior before the effects of extinction become noticeable. Even after the misbehavior disappears, it may occasionally surface once again, a phenomenon called spontaneous recovery. (Once this happens, however, ignoring it causes it to disappear rapidly.)

You must be careful that other students don't pick up the misbehavior when they see you ignoring it in one of their classmates. You are the only judge of that, but if you are successful at identifying the source of the misbehavior (perhaps peer attention), you can usually manipulate other reinforcers to bring about a combination of extinction and positive reinforcement.

3. Level III strategies. Note that Level III strategies involve the use of punishment techniques, from less to more severe. In the first of the suggested strategies, response cost (see p.167), you attempt to reduce behavior by removal of a reinforcer (Alberto & Troutman, 1986, p. 246). Once the targeted misbehavior occurs, specific reinforcers are withdrawn.

For example, telephone companies, at different times in different localities, have addressed the problem of excessive requests for information about telephone numbers. They typically provided this service free-of-charge, certainly a positive reinforcer for the caller. When companies begin to charge for this service, the number of requests drops dramatically. Withdrawal of reinforcement (free service) acts as punishment.

You can adopt similar practices in your classroom. A technique proven to be effective combines a token reinforcement system with response cost. Students can not only earn tokens toward something desirable, but they can also lose tokens by misbehavior. A talking out student acquires tokens by periods of silence but also loses a token by inappropriate talking.

Consider these suggestions for productive use of the response cost technique (Alberto & Troutman, 1986).

• Be sure that you actually withdraw the reinforcers when needed. It is probably best to avoid using anything physical (if you move to take away candy with younger students, they may put as much as possible in their mouths and eat it). Taking tokens away from a six foot, four inch football player would be considerably more difficult. Try positive reinforcement initially.

• Know what reinforces individual students.
• Be sure that students understand clearly what constitutes misbehavior and its cost.
• Don't trap yourself; be certain that you can indeed withdraw a reinforcer.
• Combine response cost with positive reinforcement for behavior.

The second of the Level III strategies entails the use of **time-out** procedures (see p. 166), which means that students are denied reinforcement for a specific period. Again you must be sure that you know exactly what reinforces your individual students.

There are two basic time-out procedures:

a. Nonseclusionary time-out: the student remains in the classroom but is barred from normal reinforcement. "Put your head on your desk for the next five minutes" prevents the student from receiving reinforcement from either the teacher or classmates. Any type of procedure that prevents reinforcement while keeping the student in the classroom belongs in this category;

b. Seclusionary time-out: here the student is removed from an activity or the actual classroom. You may resort to this technique by seating a student alone in a remote corner of the room for some specified period. Putting a student in a separate room is usually reserved for special situations and must be used with sensitivity and caution.

4. *Level IV strategies*. This level involves the use of aversive stimuli and is what is most frequently regarded as punishment. Since we have discussed the pros and cons of punishment in considerable detail earlier in this chapter, we can conclude by stressing that regardless of the procedure used to reduce or eliminate behavior, remember to combine these techniques with positive reinforcement.

Techniques to Maintain Behavior

Once a student's behavior has changed, you want that student to maintain the desirable behavior over time and without programmed reinforcement. You also want students to demonstrate appropriate behavior in other classes. For example, while you may have successfully reduced talking out behavior in your history class, this student should also reduce talking out in English. In other words, teachers strive for generalization.

Strategies for Facilitating Generalization

When you teach students in your classroom, you hope that what they learn will transfer to other settings and be remembered over time. Behavioral researchers have developed a technology that teachers can use in classrooms to help students generalize their knowledge and behavior. Building on some of the classic work of Stokes and Baer (1977), White and his associates (1988) presented a review and update of the strategies for facilitating generalization that will be of special value to teachers. They describe the following twelve strategies:

1. *Teach and hope.* In this traditional strategy the teacher provides regular instruction and hopes that the child's behavior will generalize. For example, the teacher introduces some new vocabulary words in class, emphasizing their meaning. Some children may remember, but more likely some do not. You hope that most will remember. Teach and hope is actually the absence of any special techniques to facilitate generalization and is common in most classrooms.

2. *Teach in the natural setting.* Teaching is conducted directly in at least one setting in which the skill or knowledge will actually be used. Generalization is then assessed in other nonteaching settings. For example, the teacher might ask parents to teach the new words at home after they are taught in the classroom. Actually, effective teachers use this tactic quite often.

3. *Teach sequential.* This strategy is an extension of # 2 since teaching is conducted in one setting and generalization is assessed in other settings. If necessary, teaching is conducted sequentially in more and more settings until generalization to all the desired settings is observed. For example, a teacher interested in teaching social skills might schedule teaching of the skill in settings such as school, home, and playground.

4. *Introduce students to natural maintaining contingencies.* In this strategy, the teacher ensures that the student experiences the natural consequences of a skill learned by (a) teaching a functional skill that is likely to be reinforced outside of the instructional setting; (b) teaching to a level of proficiency that makes the skill truly useful; (c) making sure that the learner actually experiences the natural consequences; and (d) teaching the learner to seek reinforcement outside of the instruction. As an example, you may consider using academic content that will be useful to the student outside the classroom: teaching words that students would likely use when interacting with peers and adults.

5. *Use indiscriminable contingencies.* Sometimes natural consequences cannot be expected to facilitate and maintain generalization. In such cases it may be necessary to use artificial consequences. It is best that the learner cannot determine precisely when

those consequences will be available. Teaching social skills to preschoolers, a teacher might praise the children after progressively greater delays rather than after each skill is demonstrated, as would be the strategy during initial teaching.

6. *Train to generalize.* With this strategy, students are reinforced only for performing some generalized instance of the skill. Performing a previously reinforced version of the skill is no longer reinforced. For example, students could be taught the names of various shapes. Reinforcement is then provided when students name shapes that were not previously taught in the classroom.

7. *Program common stimuli.* The teacher can select a salient, but not necessarily task-related, stimulus from the situation to which generalization is desired and include that stimulus in the teaching program. Students might be taught a skill in the presence of their peers. These skills would then be expected to be available in other settings when the peers are present (that is, when the stimuli are present).

8. *Use sufficient exemplars.* This strategy entails the sequential addition of stimuli to the teaching program until generalization to all related stimuli occurs. Different skills may require a different number of examples to ensure generalization, and you should make this determination based on a student's performance.

9. *Use multiple exemplars.* Using this technique means that you will teach, at the same time, several examples of the stimulus class to which generalization is desired. The teacher who uses multiple examples of a concept or skill will increase the chances that a student will use the skill in a nonteaching setting.

10. *Conduct general case programming.* To use this strategy, the teacher must conduct a careful analysis of both the skill and the environment to which generalization is desired. Thereafter, stimuli in the presence of which the skill should be used, stimuli in the presence of which the skill should not be used, and stimuli that should not affect skill use, but could inappropriately do so, are selected for teaching. For example, in teaching high school students to use a stick shift in driver education class, it would be useful to analyze the range of stick shift options found in most cars and trucks and teach this universe of options. One could then anticipate that good generalization to most cars in the community would occur.

11. *Teach loosely.* By teaching loosely we do not mean that you should become an incompetent teacher. What we mean is that you should teach in a variety

of ways so as to avoid a ritualized, highly structured, invariate program that inhibits generalization. Teaching that involves a variety of settings, materials, and reinforcers will help facilitate generalization.

12. *Mediate generalization.* This tactic involves teaching a strategy or other procedure so that the student can remember when to generalize, or at least reduce the differences between the teaching and generalization settings. Students can be taught to self-monitor their own behavior across settings.

Each of the twelve strategies to facilitate generalization will be helpful to you in teaching your students. It is important to remember that you can use the strategies in combination to increase the chances that your students will transfer their knowledge and skills. Remember: according to behavioral educators, teaching is not enough. You must do more than teach and hope: use those strategies that facilitate generalization.

Techniques of Self-Control

Since you cannot monitor a student constantly, a major objective in working with students is to have them accept responsibility for their own behavior, that is, to exercise self-control. Kazdin (1980, p. 249) offers a good definition of self-control.

> As a general definition, self-control usually refers to those behaviors a person deliberately undertakes to achieve self-selected outcomes.

In aiding your students to acquire this ability, be sure that they know precisely what behavior produced reinforcement. Encourage them to talk about why they were or were not reinforced, thus aiding them to understand their behavior. Remember: it is the students' self-control; therefore they must be active in the process.

Once you have made them aware of the inappropriateness of their behavior and they are willing to cooperate, have them note, with your help at first, the frequency of their misbehaviors—a kind of self-recording device.

Next involve them in the management of reinforcement: what reinforcers should be used, when should they be given, what constitutes misbehavior, how much should each instance of misbehavior cost them. In this way responsibility slowly shifts from you to the student.

Teaching Students Self-Control

Some children learn to regulate their own behavior during their early years within the family. Many children, however, can benefit from learning some strategies to help them control their own behavior in social and learn-

ing settings. In recent years, psychologists have developed programs that teachers and other professionals can use to help children in their psychosocial development (Esveldt-Dawson & Kazdin, 1982; Workman, 1982). There are three components of self-control that you can use to teach your students self-control: (a) self-assessment or self-analysis; (b) self-monitoring; and (c) self-reinforcement.

Self-assessment requires that students examine their own behavior or thinking and determine whether they have performed some behavior or thought process. For example, a teacher might ask one of her students if she has been completing her math assignments. It is important that children have some idea or standard that they can use in self-assessment, which often comes from the performance of significant adults and peers. Remember, all students do not routinely set self-standards and, therefore, it is helpful to teach these skills.

Self-monitoring is a procedure in which students record their performance or keep a record of what they are doing. Interestingly, the very act of recording some action has been shown to change performance. For example, if you try to encourage kind or positive statements from students when they interact with peers, self-monitoring of this social interaction is likely to increase. Researchers have shown that self-monitoring can increase academic performance but may not be sufficient in itself to sustain any improvement (Piersel & Kratochwill, 1979).

Self-reinforcement refers to students' giving themselves a reward following successful completion of the activity being monitored. Self-reinforcement can be a very potent strategy for increasing the occurrence of a student's performance. Students can be taught to praise themselves or arrange some pleasant activity as a self-reward, which then acts to sustain performance.

Workman (1982) has identified several advantages of using self-control strategies:

- Self-control strategies allow students to manage their own behavior in the absence of the teacher or other adults.
- Self-control strategies can help students develop responsibility for their own behavior.
- Self-control can help improve the chances that a student's behavior will transfer to other settings and with other individuals.

Although some students appear to regulate their behavior quite well without formal attempts to teach this skill, others may need additional assistance to regulate their behavior. Teaching self-control strategies to these students can increase both their sense of self-efficacy and their sense of responsibility.

Focus on Classrooms

Recording Student Behavior

Before you begin to use any form of behavior change, you must know precisely what you want to change, the best way to change it, and if you actually brought about the change. To accomplish these objectives you should know exactly how often the misbehavior occurs and under what circumstance. This is not as arduous as it sounds, particularly if you follow fairly simple, but proven procedures. (For detailed discussion of observation, collection, and interpretation of data see Alberto & Troutman 1986; Sulzer-Azaroff & Reese, 1982; Fromberg & Driscoll, 1985; Gelfand & Hartmann, 1986.) These and similar techniques that we have mentioned help not only teaching and learning but also help to improve your relationships with your students.

You have identified the behavior you want to change and are now ready to determine just how bad things are; you must collect data. There are several ways that you can do this; (Sulzer-Azaroff, 1991):

1. *Permanent product recording*—measurement of tangible outcomes of behavior (grades, number of tasks completed, number of problems solved);
2. *Event recording*—how often the behavior occurs during a specified period (number of questions asked, number of episodes of talking out);
3. *Duration*—how long the behavior persists (does a student talk out during the entire period or only at the beginning or end?);
4. *Latency recording*—how soon after a stimulus (the start of a class) the misbehavior commences;
5. *Interval recording*—if a thirty-minute class is divided into ten-minute intervals, determine when the behavior occurs;
6. *Time sampling*—at specified periods you can check to see if the behavior is occurring—perhaps every ten minutes. This is a relatively simple procedure—easy to use, not too intrusive, and not too demanding of your time.

Let's assume you have targeted the behavior and made your observations. You now must put it in some manageable form that is readily understandable, something you can look at and judge if your efforts have been successful. Graphing

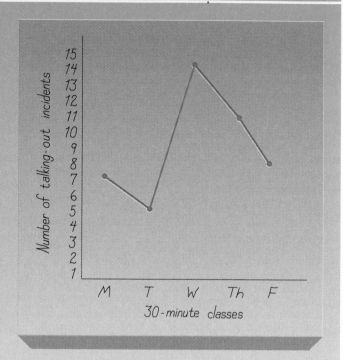

data can be useful to you, students, parents, counselors, and administrators.

You have recorded the number of times a student has talked out during a thirty-minute class and now wish to plot your graph. Remember that your basic graph has two axes: the horizontal (abscissa or x-axis) and the vertical (ordinate or y-axis). Behavior is plotted on the ordinate; time on the abscissa.

Using your record sheets, place a dot at the proper intersection of the two axes. Now connect the dots and you have a graphic illustration of this student's inappropriate behavior. Continue this practice after you begin your program, and you will have telling evidence of the success or failure of your efforts.

Collecting data in this fashion need not be confined to misbehavior. You can use the same technique to assess the effectiveness of a remedial math program for a student who is having trouble. Students, as well as teachers, like to see their progress.

Ethical Considerations

Since one of the objectives of schooling is to effect change, those techniques that rely on more overt methods, such as behavior control, are often subject to harsh criticism. Such criticism seems to stem from two sources:

1. a misunderstanding of the procedures
2. incorrect application.

The principles of behavior control discussed in this chapter have arisen from careful human experimentation (Alberto & Troutman, 1986). They *do not* include such procedures as hypnosis, brain surgery, drugs, or electric shock. Opponents of behavioral procedures argue that any technique of control is inhumane, since they deprive students and patients of their freedom.

Proponents, on the other hand, disagree, stating that by understanding and controlling their behavior, individuals have a greater choice of options. The student who has frittered away school time—for whatever reason—and consistently failed is not free to choose a college. Perhaps the main issue is *what* techniques to use to bring about change (Kazdin, 1989).

The *misuse* of behavioral techniques has probably generated the most heated controversy since extreme applications of aversive stimuli have been documented: "water treatment" in which a patient is buffeted by water projectiles; harsh buzzer sounds applied to the ears; slapping; prolonged isolation. Though these have been discovered in use mainly in special situations (institutionalized children), they have raised questions about the continued use of behavioral principles. (For a more detailed discussion of ethical and legal aspects, see Kazdin, 1989; Sulzer-Azaroff & Riese, 1982.)

Although classroom teachers rarely resort to extreme measures, a good suggestion is to follow guidelines suggested by Alberto and Troutman (1986). Since all teachers are concerned with ethical issues because of their desire to do what is best for students, we must be sensitive to community feelings, what the law says, and our own responsibilities.

You can best accomplish your objectives if you are competent in your application of behavioral principles; select attainable, appropriate goals; and finally, are accountable for your techniques. What this means is that there must be clearly stated and accepted goals, a statement of procedures, and an honest rendering of results.

Behaviorism and the Future

Behaviorism, which has remained remarkably stable in its basic orientation, has recently shown signs of change. Behaviorists, faced with the challenge of a renewed, dynamic cognitive psychology, have reacted by adopting several strategies. They have attempted to

• strengthen and refine their methodology;
• accept the warnings of the ethologists concerning constraints on learning; and
• incorporate, on behavioral terms, cognitive concepts within their framework.

Behaviorists have made significant contributions to education. For example, behavioral studies have demonstrated that almost all students, regardless of preparedness, disabilities, or deprivation, can learn. Behaviorism has also helped to remove blocks to student learning (Sulzer-Azaroff, 1991).

Applying Behavior Analysis to Schooling

In this chapter, we have noted that many of the behavioral procedures urged by Skinner have been successfully applied to educational problems. As Skinner has stated (1984), the survival of humankind depends on how well we educate. Education has not widely adopted many of his suggestions, however. Critics of behavioral techniques (such as Brophy, 1983) have noted that behavioral procedures are often ignored because they are applied to circumscribed or isolated problems in the schools.

To increase the use of behavioral procedures in the schools, Greer and his associates at Columbia University Teachers College have developed a model called the Comprehensive Application of Behavior Analysis to Schooling (CABAS) (Greer, in press; Selinske, Greer, & Lodhi, 1991). The model is designed to apply behavior analysis to the school roles of students, teachers, and supervisors. It also includes such behavioral components as direct instruction, personalized system of instruction, programmed instruction, and an organizational behavior management component for supervision and administration. Following is a description of each of the components:

• *Application to students.* This section consists of collecting data for all instructional trials. Scripted curricula specifying the antecedent stimuli, responses, and consequences for all instruction are used. The following is an example of a one-trial teaching sequence for handicapped children:

> The student was presented with a three-dimensional object (e.g., a cube); the student felt the object and the teacher asked "what shape?" The student had a five-second period (for example) to produce the correct signed or vocal response. An incorrect response resulted in a correction procedure (i.e., "This is a cube."). A correct response resulted in praise and the presentation of an edible reinforcer, a token, or a brief activity period with a toy. The teacher recorded a minus for the lack of a response or an incorrect response or a plus for a correct response, and then proceeded to the next trial (Greer, in press, pp. 109–110).

- *Application to teachers.* This section involved instructing the teachers to use the skills and terminology of behavior analysis with on-the-job-training and out-of-class instruction through a personalized system of instruction. The teachers applied the behavioral principles with the students.
- *Application to supervisors.* Supervisors were involved in the training of the teachers. Specifically, they designed the teacher modules and tutored the teachers to the point of mastery. The supervisors also maintained a log of their activities, and they themselves had to meet criteria for job performance.

Greer and his associates (Selinske et al., 1991) evaluated the CABAS program in a small school that served blind students with multiple handicaps. The program produced educationally significant increases in trials taught and correct trials; also it identified student objectives. Teachers also evaluated the program positively. Support for the program has been modest, however, because of its limited application in a small school that serves handicapped students. Though a better test would be in a regular public school, the program does indicate that a combination of behavioral principles has merit in teaching academic skills.

Skinner's Suggestions

As you might expect, Skinner (1984) pronounced on the state of American education and found it wanting, mainly because it neglects behaviorist principles. Skinner believed that the resurgence of humanistic and cognitive psychology has proven a major obstacle to any progress in our schools (progress, by the way, that he believes began with his work on programmed instruction).

To solve our educational dilemma, Skinner (1984) recommended a return to the principles and objectives of behaviorism.

1. *Be clear about what is to be taught,* which implies that you should concentrate on what is to be learned. For example, we don't teach "spelling"; we teach students how to spell words.
2. *Teach first things first.* You should avoid any attempt to reach the final product too quickly, since any subject and its subdivisions contain a series of steps that students must master before reaching the final stage.
3. *Teach to individual differences.* Here is one of Skinner's favorite themes: students can progress only at their own rates. To respond to this truism, Skinner long advocated teaching machines, programmed instruction, and computers.
4. *Program subject matter.* Unlike typical texts, individual programs induce students to do or say the things that they are to do or say. Skinner called this "priming" the behavior, and the prompts that are built into the program must be gradually eliminated until the behavior appears without help. At that point, the reinforcing consequences of being right become highly effective in sustaining behavior.

Referring to concerns about education, Skinner stated:

> There is a better way: give students and teachers better reasons for learning and teaching. That is where the behavioral sciences can make a contribution. They can develop instructional practices so effective and so attractive in other ways that no one—student, teacher, and administrator—will need to be coerced into using them (Skinner, 1984, p. 952).

Among the accomplishments behaviorists claim are the following:

1. Although behaviorism has proven its worth in the successful education of disabled youngsters, its range of achievements also incorporate the other end of the spectrum since its carefully controlled techniques have likewise been shown to help students to learn at *advanced levels.*

2. Though behaviorism is usually thought to be effective in teaching simple topics, evidence exists that *complex behaviors* are equally as teachable. Complex procedures such as shaping, differential reinforcement, and fading have all become tools of educators.

3. Behaviorism has made clear to educators that the key to teaching complex skills is to distinguish, clearly and precisely, the *critical features* of the task—exactly what behavior is to change under what conditions. Closely allied to the careful identification of objectives is the use of effective and natural reinforcers. (See the work of the Veroffs (1980) in the motivation chapter for a more detailed discussion of natural reinforcers.)

4. Behaviorism has attacked the problem of individual differences in the classroom in a different manner. If any of your students fail to achieve objectives, it may well be that *they lack the basic prerequisite skills.* Your task, then, is to divide the learning task into its component parts, including those subskills that lead to complexity. You cannot expect students to solve division problems until they can add, subtract, and multiply.

If behaviorism is to continue to progress, certain barriers must be overcome.

- Many educators simply lack information about the value of behavioral strategies.
- Even those who appreciate the benefits of behavioral techniques may lack the skills to implement them.
- Current societal contingencies impede the implementation of behavioral techniques.

By working to overcome these challenges, most behaviorists feel confident about the future of their theory, both its viability and application.

Conclusion

Behaviorism, with its emphasis on observable behavior, has remained a popular explanation of learning. But behaviorism may take one of several interpretations, which can influence what you do in the classroom. The four most popular forms of behaviorism and the individuals most clearly associated with them are:

Pavlov's Classical Conditioning

Thorndike's Connectionism

Skinner's Operant Conditioning

Bandura's Observational Learning

Classical conditioning, which emphasizes the presentation of stimuli, is a highly effective technique in producing emotional learning. We have seen how this affects a student's feelings about school. Operant conditioning, which emphasizes reinforcement, has been responsible for many instructional techniques: reinforcement schedules, more efficient use of positive and negative reinforcers, teaching machines. Observational learning, which emphasizes modeling, has been shown to be a powerful instrument of learning. Dramatic studies of how children's behavior changes as a result of watching a model testify to its potential for learning in the classroom.

Each of these explanations has practical implications for the classroom. If we concentrate on observable behavior, then by formulating instructional suggestions from these theories, we can devise strategies that increase, decrease, and maintain behavior. These theories can also be used to help students learn how to control their own behavior.

As with any powerful means of controlling behavior, abuse may set in and lead to extremes and undesirable measures. Consequently, suggestions for the ethical use of behavioral techniques have been widely adopted.

Chapter Highlights

Classical Conditioning

- Pavlov's work has educational implications, especially with regard to generalization, discrimination, and extinction of behavior.
- Conditioning principles should make teachers aware of a need to use classroom stimuli sensitively.

Thorndike's Connectionism

- Thorndike was a powerful force in American psychology and his ideas remain influential even today, especially the Law of Effect.
- Thorndike's Law of Effect remained popular for years (influencing Skinner), and his views of exercise and transfer are still applicable.

Operant Conditioning

- Skinner's interpretation of conditioning has become the most accepted and widely used form of behaviorism today. Its impact is felt in education, psychology, and business.
- His views of punishment have clarified its meaning and use.
- Skinner's ideas on reinforcement have led to broad acceptance of programmed instruction and computers as effective teaching tools.

Social Cognitive (observational) Learning

- Bandura's stress on the impact of modeling has shown the potency and far-reaching effects of this type of learning.
- Observational learning attempts to include the influence of cognitive processes within a behavioral framework.
- The principles of observational learning emphasize the need for multicultural models that meet the needs of a variety of students.

Behaviorism and Teaching

- The principles of behaviorism are widely used in today's classrooms.
- Techniques for shaping behavior can be effectively used in the classroom, if thoroughly understood and carefully applied.

Behaviorism and the Future

- The future success of behaviorism demands clear adherence to its basic principles, while introducing compatible changes from related disciplines.

Key Terms

Activity reinforcers
Aversive stimuli
Avoidance behavior
Classical conditioning
Conditioned reflex
Conditioned stimulus
Connectionism
Discrimination
Escape behavior
Extinction
Fixed interval
Fixed ratio
Generalized reinforcers
Identical elements
Intermittent reinforcers
Interval reinforcement
Negative reinforcers
Neobehaviorists
Nonseclusionary time-out
Operant conditioning
Overcorrection
Personalized System of Instruction (PSI)
Positive reinforcers
Premack principle
Primary reinforcers
Ratio schedule
Reinforcer
Response cost
Seclusionary time-out
Secondary reinforcers
Self-assessment
Self-efficacy
Self-monitoring
Self-reinforcement
Social cognitive learning
Social reinforcers
Stimulus generalization
Teaching machine
Thinning
Time-out
Variable interval
Variable ratio

Suggested Readings

Alberto, P. & Troutman, A. (1986). *Applied behavior analysis.* Columbus, Ohio: Merrill. One of the best accounts of applied behavioral principles. Soundly rooted in behaviorism, the authors present a variety of practices that can be extremely helpful in the classroom.

Bandura, A. (1986). *Social foundations of thought and action.* Englewood Cliffs, N.J.: Prentice-Hall. The most recent statement of social learning by the leader in the field. It would be well worth your time and effort to explore Bandura's ideas.

Kazdin, A. (1989). *Behavior modification in applied settings (4th ed.). Pacific Groves, CA: Brooks/Cole.* Outstanding overview of behavioral principles in action. Available in paperback, it offers the reader a summary of the ethical and legal issues that have sprung up around the use of behavior modification.

Skinner, B. F. (1953). *Science and human behavior.* New York: Macmillan. If you want to understand Skinner's operant conditioning, this is the book. Don't be put off by the date; it contains the basic ideas that are as fresh today as when written. By the way, Skinner was an excellent writer.

Skinner, B. F. (1990). *Skinner's keynote address: Lifetime scientific contributions remarks.* Washington, DC: American Psychological Association. This videotape presents Skinner's last keynote address and public appearance at the American Psychological Association in 1990. This already classic tape provides most informative viewing.

Cognitive Psychology and Learning

Barbara Cotter, an English teacher at Junior High West, was concerned about her Modern Literature course. She too frequently felt that she was fighting a losing battle in trying to get her students interested in many of the ideas that were central to the stories she was teaching. Such concepts as loyalty and persistence, among others, seemed to escape her students. She wondered if she should look at her problem psychologically; perhaps something was at work that she hadn't identified. She decided to discuss it with her class.

At the beginning of class the next day, she mentioned her concern. "Look, I want to be very honest with you. I know you think you're working hard, and I appreciate your cooperation. But something seems to be missing."

Jake, a good student but also a bit of a class clown, asked, "Why, did someone take something, Miss Cotter?"

The teacher decided to go along with the good humor. "No, that would be the least of my problems, Jake. What's missing is some spark, some clue that you really like reading these stories. After all, reading is something that will stay with you all your life."

Andrea, a serious student, raised her hand and said, "I know what you mean. I think I'm going to enjoy one of these stories and then something seems to happen. Everything goes dead."

With that, other students began to raise their hands.

The teacher pointed to a student and said, "OK, Alex. What do you think?"

The student hesitated a bit and said, "Well, gosh, Miss Cotter, it could be the way that we're going about this."

With this, the teacher knew that a start had been made. "What do you mean, Alex?"

"Well, you keep telling us how important these stories are—and I'm sure you're right. But maybe we should find out for ourselves."

Andrea chimed in rather excitedly. "That's right. Instead of you or the guide telling us what's important, I'd like to make a list of my own ideas, what categories are most important to me."

Sandra joined in from the other side of the room. "Yes, and then when each of us does this, perhaps we could put together a list of the traits of the leading characters—what's good and what's bad—and try to relate them to the story's theme."

"Right," said Alex. "That makes sense. You know, it would mean more to us and help us to remember the story better. Now that I think of it, why don't we try to develop some memory aids that will help us all?"

The conversation between this teacher and her students reflects many of the features of this chapter. If you can have your students develop their own concepts and relate them to other parts of the subject you're teaching, your work will be much easier and probably more efficient.

Before teachers can hope to improve thinking skills, however, they themselves must be knowledgeable about their students' cognitive competence and capacity to engage in abstract thought. In this chapter, which explores the relationship between cognitive psychology and learning, you will note the clear implications for the classroom.

The pace of change in cognitive work during the past two decades has been rapid, and as the field has sharpened its focus on information processing, its contribution to teaching and learning has grown noticeably. (In chapter 8 we shall discuss in greater detail the classroom applications of cognitive theory, such as mnemonics, problem solving strategies, and other related topics.)

We'll examine the major themes of cognitive psychology in this chapter and attempt to indicate pertinent classroom application such as the origins of a cognitive science—from where it was to where it is. Also, you'll read about the significance of mental representations in cognitive studies. Current interpretations of perception, recent studies and speculation concerning classification, the changing status of memory work, and the logic—or illogic—of our reasoning processes will also be presented.

When you finish your reading, you should be able to:

- understand the key role that representation plays in learning.
- help students to construct categories to aid their learning.
- distinguish between recognition and recall of material.
- recognize those distractions that affect student memory.

- accept that the manner in which you frame or structure your material will influence your students' thinking and decision-making.

Before we commence our work, however, try the simple exercise that appears in the Focus box on page 193.

The Meaning of Cognitive Psychology

What does cognitive psychology mean? Cognitive scientists are in general agreement that their work encompasses the study of memory, attention, perception, language,

Central to cognitive psychology is the concept of mental representations. External events are coded and become retrievable in internal form.

Focus on Students

How Much Do You Remember?

In the early 1930s, the British psychologist, F. C. Bartlett, became convinced that studies of memory actually ignored clues that explained much of remembering and forgetting. Read the following passage (a legend found in a Pacific Northwest Indian group). Later in the chapter, when you again meet Bartlett's work, write the legend as you recall it.

"The War of the Ghosts"

One night two young men from Egulac went down to the river to hunt seals, and while they were there it became foggy and calm. Then they heard war cries, and they thought: "Maybe this is a war party." They escaped to the shore, and hid behind a log. Now canoes came up, and they heard the noise of paddles, and saw one canoe coming up to them. There were five men in the canoe, and they said:

"What do you think? We wish to take you along. We are going up the river to make war on the people."

One of the young men said: "I have no arrows."

"Arrows are in the canoe," they said.

"I will not go along. I might be killed. My relatives do not know where I have gone. But you," he said, turning to the other, "may go with them."

So one of the young men went, but the other returned home.

And the warriors went on up the river to a town on the other side of Kalama. The people came down to the water, and they began to fight, and many were killed. But presently the young man heard one of the warriors say: "Quick, let us go home: that Indian has been hit." Now he thought: "Oh, they are ghosts." He did not feel sick, but they said he had been shot.

So the canoes went back to Egulac, and the young man went ashore to his house, and made a fire. And he told everybody and said: "Behold I accompanied the ghosts, and we went to fight. Many of our fellows were killed, and many of those who attacked us were killed. They said I was hit, and I did not feel sick."

He told it all, and then he became quiet. When the sun rose he fell down. Something black came out of his mouth. His face became contorted. The people jumped up and cried.

He was dead.

reasoning, problem solving and creativity. That is, cognitive psychology is the study of the structures and components for processing information (Phye & Andre, 1986). Central to cognitive psychology is a belief in **mental representations**; in other words, external events can be coded so that they become retrievable in an internal form (Glass, Santa & Holyoak, 1987). As you can see, this is a departure from early behaviorism, which we discussed in chapter 6. Table 7.1 illustrates these differences.

Stored in memory, these mental representations have become a legitimate focus of speculation and research. Cognitive psychologists firmly, even fiercely, believe that the stimulus situation does not directly determine our behavior and the behavior of our students. For example, the way that your students think about you, your classroom, and the school influences their learning. Interposed between stimulus and response is cognitive activity. Thus our thought processes are not an accumulation of stimulus-response connections; cognition intervenes and distinctly colors our reactions.

Today, cognitive psychology enjoys great appeal and, as we noted in the chapter opening, has become a potent force in the classroom. One source of cognitive appeal is its perspective on human beings. Your students organize information processes into goals and subgoals in a fraction of a second and achieve remarkable results: they remember, they decide, they solve problems, they learn (Siegler, 1983). If you can aid your students in organizing and processing information, you will help them to become more competent and to improve their learning both in and out of the classroom (Glaser, 1991).

Cognitive conceptions of learning have reached into the classroom with far-reaching effects. For example, today we are much more aware of the importance of students' **prior knowledge** on present learning and the significance of memory strategies for student learning, among many other cognitive insights (Shuell, 1986).

But we also face cognitive limitations: our students, like ourselves, can simultaneously manipulate only a certain number of symbols at a definite speed (Kinsbourne, 1986). Consequently, they invent strategies to help them overcome these obstacles: they organize material to help them remember; they rehearse data over and over; they devise schemes to help them solve problems. (These techniques are analyzed in some depth in chapter 8.)

The Emergence of Cognitive Psychology

The history of any science is rooted in many fields, and cognitive psychology follows that familiar format. Today's cognitive psychology flows from the conceptual

Table 7.1

Comparison of Behavioral and Traditional Cognitive Theories of Learning and Cognition

Behavioral Learning Theory	Traditional Cognitive Theory
1. Learner is seen as passive and reactive to environment.	1. Learner is seen as active and mastering the environment.
2. Learning occurs because of associations among stimuli or between stimuli and responses.	2. Learning occurs because the learner actively tries to understand the environment.
3. Knowledge consists of whatever pattern of associations have been learned.	3. Knowledge consists of an organized set of mental structures and procedures.
4. Learning is the acquisition of new associations.	4. Learning consists of changes in mental structure brought about by mental reasoning.
5. Prior knowledge influences new learning primarily through indirect processes such as positive or negative transfer because of similarity of stimuli between situations.	5. New learning is based on using prior knowledge to understand new situations, and changing prior knowledge structures to deal with new situations.
6. Discussion of the activities of the mind is not permitted.	6. Discussion of activities of the mind is the central issue in psychology.
7. Strong experimental research tradition. Theories can only be verified through experiment.	7. Weak experimental research tradition. Observational research, thought experiments, and logical analysis can be used.
8. Education consists of arranging stimuli so that desired associations are made.	8. Education consists of allowing/encouraging active mental exploration of complex environments.

From Gary Phye and Thomas Andre, Classroom Cognitive Learning. Copyright © 1986 Academic Press, Orlando, FL.

framework of Gestalt psychology, especially its emphasis on perception, an emphasis that strongly shaped the thinking of such modern cognitivists as Jerome Bruner.

The Influence of the Gestaltists

The early Gestaltists—Max Wertheimer, Wolfgang Köhler, and Kurt Koffka—were firmly convinced that behaviorism could not account for the full range of human behavior. Consequently, they launched a determined and effective attack against early behaviorism.

Wertheimer, the founder of the movement, discovered that if two lights were turned off and on at a definite rate, one received the impression that a single light was moving back and forth. This finding, which Wertheimer called the phi phenomenon, could not be effectively explained by a stimulus and response model; humans, when processing these stimuli, add something to the incoming sensory data to form their perception of movement. See page 195 for an illustration of the experimental setup for testing the phi phenomenon.

From their academic base in Germany, the Gestaltists earned rapid acceptance from their European colleagues, but it was not until Wertheimer, Koffka, and Köhler were forced to flee Nazi Germany that Gestalt psychology was recognized as a viable psychological force in America. Given the preeminence of behaviorism in American psychology, the Gestaltists were attempting no small feat in their direct challenge to behaviorism.

With their views of perception and perceptual learning finding acceptance in many quarters, the Gestaltists widened their efforts to bring a cognitive interpretation to human development, intelligence, and especially problem solving. One of the lasting legacies of Gestalt theory has been the principles of perceptual organization, which we'll discuss in the perception section of this chapter. (The Gestaltists' work still has current significance; for example, see Michael Wertheimer's proposal (1985) for a gestaltist perspective on computer simulation of cognitive processes.)

Focus on Students

Monitoring Cognitive Strategies

As an example of the manner in which cognitive theory has influenced current thinking about learning, consider the following example. Ghatala, Levin, Pressley, and Ledico (1985) devised an experiment in which second grade children were trained to monitor their cognitive strategies and then tested on an associative learning task. The procedure was as follows:

1. 126 second grade children (mean age 7.6 years) were divided into three groups.
2. The children in the strategy-monitoring group were taught that some strategies are better than others for improving performance (using a cookie cutter to draw a circle rather than attempting it free-hand; arranging letters in as meaningful manner as possible to improve memory). The children were verbally reinforced and reminded to monitor their performance.
3. Youngsters in a "strategy-affect" group were told that some ways of playing games were "more fun" than others. They then used the circle-drawing technique and were asked which way they had more fun and why.
4. The control group played an equivalent amount of time with the experimenter, using the same tasks as the experimental group, but received no instruction nor reinforcement.
5. All groups were told they were going to play another game that involved remembering pairs of words. The children were then given three paired associate list of words. In the first condition (memorizing the list of words), the children were simply told to remember them as best they could.
6. On the second list, half the children were told to make up a story to help them remember. The other half of the group were instructed to count the letters in each pair of words, a strategy known to decrease performance.
7. All the children were tested on the third list.
8. One week and eight weeks later, the children were retested.

The results clearly indicated that those youngsters who had received the original "strategy-monitoring" training showed long-term recall, while all of the children who received the affective strategy on the second list demonstrated short-term recall. The authors believe that these results testify to the value of including strategy-monitoring techniques in an instructional design.

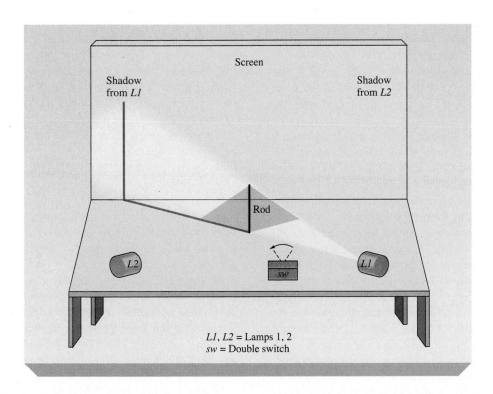

The phi phenomenon.

Bartlett and the Schema

Unhappy with existing methods to study memory, Bartlett (1932) presented exotic stories to his subjects and then asked them to recall the stories at different times. You were asked to read "The War of the Ghosts" at the beginning of the chapter. *Stop now and rewrite that story as you recall it, without again looking at it.*

Now check your story against the original. How different is it? Did you add to or subtract from the original? Is it essentially the same story? When asked to recall the story, most subjects impose an order and organization on it that are missing from the original. With increasing time, subjects made the story even more meaningful, more logical. Thus **schema** (**schemata**) of events are mental frameworks that modify incoming data so that they "fit" the person's experiences and perceptions (Phye & Andre, 1986).

When presenting new material, teachers quickly learn to expect a familiar refrain. One of the students will undoubtedly say, "That's like Mrs. Anderson said last year." The student is trying to fit something new into an existing cognitive framework—the schema.

Introducing the Schema

In 1967, Pompi and Lachman conducted an experiment in which subjects read stories that lacked words ordinarily associated with the theme of the story. For example, one story concerned a surgical operation, but words such as doctor, nurse, scalpel, and operation were lacking.

After reading the story, subjects were then given a list of words that included doctor, nurse, scalpel, and operation and asked if these words had appeared in the story. Subjects invariably stated that these words had appeared in the story.

The investigators believed that people grasp a story theme, compare it with the test words, and then match on the basis of familiarity. The stimulus for the subjects' responses must have been mental; that is, they used their knowledge of medicine and surgery in their replies, even though no such specific cues appeared in the story.

To explain this tendency toward logic and the familiar, cognitive psychologists turned to the schema, a term that refers to some form of abstract cognitive structure. These schemas are the basis of memory and result from our previous experiences, which we organize in an individual manner. The organization of information is at the heart of the concept of schema. Organization of one's knowledge is a central ingredient of learning. Consequently, organization is important at three levels: (a) organization that already exists in one's long-term memory; (b) organization that can be perceived or generated within the material to be learned; (c) organization

that links the first two levels, thus allowing new material to be integrated with one's existing knowledge (Baddely, 1990).

For example, after listening to, or reading, "The War of the Ghosts," you would use your own schemata (plural of schema) to interpret and recall the story's theme. You may have some familiarity with canoes; you may have had previous encounters with ghost stories or Indian adventure stories. If these matched corresponding parts of the story, you may recall these themes quite accurately.

If, however, your schemata vary widely from the story's themes, you probably add to "The War of the Ghosts" from your own schemata, introduce a more acceptable (to you) story theme, and distort the theme even further on additional recalls. Thus memory is not a passive re-telling of past events; rather activity, spirit, and even creativity characterize our recall.

The Schema Today

Schema has remained a viable concept in cognitive psychology (Phye & Andre, 1986). Think of a schema as a unit of organized knowledge about events, situations, or objects, one which guides informational input and retrieval (Leahey & Harris, 1985). A schema may be quite specific, such as the technique needed to add a column of numbers, or quite general, such as an interpretation of intelligence. In other words, the materials that your students must learn will not in themselves explain exactly what is learned. The material contains potential information; that is, it possesses cues and directions that should guide students to use their own knowledge, thus obtaining the fullest possible information that they can. (See section on Ausubel and meaningful learning.)

The rationale for accepting the notion of schema has been a growing realization that we do not approach any topic totally devoid of knowledge; we have both prior knowledge and present expectations. We possess schemata that shape how we encode incoming material, and indeed, even affect how we "feel" about such material.

As an example of how the latest theories and results from research into cognitive psychology are finding their way into the classroom, consider the following experiment. Rahman and Bisanz (1986) were interested in how students used a schema of story to aid recall and to discover how a schema affected strong reconstruction. Working on the assumption that inadequate knowledge of a story's structure could cause difficulty for poor readers, the authors were directly reflecting the most recent thinking about schema theory.

Rahman and Bisanz (1986) attempted to answer four questions.

Focus on Students

Would You Make a Good Eyewitness?

The notion of schema has important consequences for many facets of our lives. As one example, consider the testimony of eyewitnesses in a court of law. The amount of reconstruction—or even creativity—in an eyewitness' account of a crime cuts to the heart of our system of justice. Repeated studies have shown that even immediately after the event has occurred, inaccuracies consistently appear in testimony. (In a recent publication of the American Psychological Association [Doris, 1991], the suggestibility of children's recollections and its implications for eyewitness testimony was discussed.)

Attorneys typically ask a set of standard questions of an eyewitness:

- Under what circumstances did the eyewitness view the defendant at the time of the crime?
- Does present testimony match any prior description (for example, immediately after a crime or accident)?
- Was the identification of the person (defendant) accurate?

Stressful conditions do not lend themselves to reliable testimony, and the courts have become increasing skeptical about such accounts. Since three-quarters of all trials involve police testimony, the significance of distortion of recall cannot be ignored.

Skilled questioning can shape even the testimony of truthful witnesses. Loftus and Palmer (1974) showed students a film of a collision between two cars. They then asked their subjects one of two questions:

1. About how fast were the cars going when they hit each other?
2. About how fast were the cars going when they smashed into each other?

Students have higher estimates of speed when answering the second question, and when asked the same question one week later, erroneously reported broken glass at the scene.

The relevance of schema and the danger of distortion of recall also have direct classroom relevance. If you have some knowledge of a topic, such as the nature of intelligence (a schema for intelligence), you use that schema in attempting to understand Piaget's views. (You may have already reacted in this way to the development chapter.) In answering examination questions did you fuse, that is, distort, your knowledge? In these and similar conditions, cognitive psychologists have provided considerable insight into how cognitive processes affect memory (Baddeley, 1988).

1. Do both good and poor readers typically utilize a story schema?
2. Can both groups ignore the standard sequence of the story and retrieve information from a jumbled format?
3. Can both groups use a story schema when cued to do so?
4. Do poor readers improve when the task is repeated?

They studied 48 good readers (mean age 11.5 years) and 48 poor readers (mean age 11.8 years) from sixth grade. The students heard a story in either standard or scrambled form. They were then told to recall and reconstruct the order of the story as they heard it or as it should be. The same procedure was repeated in a second phase with one change: before hearing the story, the subjects were told about the story's format and ways to rearrange it if the story's sequence was askew.

The authors were able to draw several conclusions concerning schema use.

- Both poor and good readers could recall and reconstruct a story presented in standard form. (Poor readers' stories were not well-developed.)
- Good readers consistently used a strong schema when cued to do so on any task (both standard and scrambled) while poor readers could only demonstrate a story schema with a standard format.
- In the second phase of the experiment poor readers improved only on the standard format.

The authors concluded that comprehension research is vital in studies of poor readers and, in so doing, emphasize the growing importance of cognitive research for the classroom. Their findings point to the need to provide poor readers with a clear structure of what they are reading. If their comprehension is to improve, then techniques such as outlining, sequencing, and finding main features must be incorporated into their programs. The student's learning style will largely determine which techniques to use with individual students (see chapter 8). We want to find the best way that students represent material.

Meaningful Learning

In his analysis of learning, David Ausubel (1968, 1977, Ausubel et al., 1978) made two basic distinctions: one between *reception and discovery learning* and the other between *rote and meaningful learning*. He believed that the first distinction is significant because most of your students' learning, both in and out of school, is presented to them, that is, reception learning. Reception learning, however, need not be rote; it can be quite meaningful for students.

Reception learning and discovery learning pose two different tasks for students. In reception learning, the potentially meaningful material becomes meaningful as students internalize it. With discovery learning, however, students must discover what is to be learned and then rearrange it to integrate the material with existing cognitive structures.

Ausubel has long been an outspoken advocate of **meaningful learning,** which he defines as the acquisition of new meanings. Note: there are two important ideas contained in his definition. Meaningful learning implies that the material to be learned is potentially meaningful (is it appropriate for the student?). *The acquisition of new meanings* refers to the process by which students turn potentially meaningful material into actual meaningfulness.

Ausubel noted that meaningful learning occurs when the material to be learned is related to what students already know. If, for example, Barbara Cotter, the English teacher we meet at the chapter's opening, is teaching Hemingway's *For Whom the Bell Tolls* in her Modern Literature course, she could help her students' attempts to transfer potentially meaningful material (belief in a cause, loyalty to others) into actual meaning by relating the story's themes to their own schemata, such as their willingness to help one of their friends or joining a student club dedicated to fighting the use of drugs. She would then have utilized the important ideas in Ausubel's definition of new meanings.

Advance Organizers

One of Ausubel's most important ideas for teachers is that of **advance organizers**, which he described as a form of expository teaching, that is, explaining what is to come (Williams, 1986). Ausubel (1960, 1980) defined an advance organizer as an abstract, general overview of new information to be learned that occurs in advance of the actual reading. In teaching *For Whom the Bell Tolls,* for example, Barbara Cotter, the teacher we met at the beginning of the chapter, could summarize the major features of the novel before her students read the book. She could then lead a discussion of important concepts such as loyalty and steadfastness in terms that her students understand.

This introductory material is intended to help students ready their cognitive structures for incorporating potentially meaningful material. Advance organizers are presented before introducing the new material and at a slightly higher level of abstraction because meaningful material is better learned and retained if it can be subsumed under already existing relevant ideas. Your students already have their own ideas about loyalty to friends.

To help your students acquire meaning, Ausubel suggests that you identify relevant **anchoring ideas** that your students already possess (in their cognitive structures). That is, attempt to relate new, potentially meaningful material to some topic with which students are familiar. You read earlier in this book (chapter 3) about Piaget initiating this process when he described *assimilation and accommodation.* He constantly referred to the biological processes: we use the structure of the mouth to eat; therefore it is logical to assume that we use cognitive structures to think.

Advance organizers are effective when they utilize the anchoring ideas already present in the students' cognitive structures, thus helping to reduce the students' dependence on rote memorization. Ausubel summarized the principal function of advance organizers as bridging the gap between what your students already know (their ideas of loyalty to their friends, for example) and what they need to know before they can successfully learn new material (the abstract notion of loyalty inherent in the novel). In this way, learners receive an overview of the material before they actually encounter it and are provided with organizing elements that are the core of the new material.

Ausubel's ideas, however, must be used with caution. Advance organizers have not always produced more efficient learning, although the results of recent research indicate that advance organizers have a consistent, moderate, and positive effect on learning (Corkill, Glover, Bruning, & Krug, 1989). Such learning variables as a student's cognitive structures and general state of developmental readiness must be taken into consideration. In other words, potentially meaningful material must be biologically and psychologically appropriate. Introducing a preschooler's story by referring to concepts such as loyalty without giving appropriate examples frustrates the entire process of meaningful learning. By talking about the relationship between a child and dog, the teacher can introduce the concept at the proper psychological level and then gradually help the students apply a label to it. (For additional applications of Ausubel's theory, see Smith, 1984.)

How can you help students effectively use their schemata in the acquisition of meaningful learning, yet avoid distortion? First, you must discover just what knowledge they possess about a topic, since this will guide their organization of the new material. Second, try to link the new work to specific themes in their knowledge. If you are teaching twentieth century American history, for example, you might ask your students to link as many of the characteristics of George Bush to other modern presidents as they can. Finally, be certain that your students have mastered the pertinent facts before you expect them to generalize; otherwise you may inadvertently encourage distortion. Students must be familiar with the American Presidents before they can compare them to George Bush.

Although Ausubel emphasized meaningful reception learning, another famous cognitive psychologist, Jerome Bruner, concentrated his efforts on **discovery learning.** Bruner's work has also been in the forefront of those forces that have been influential in the development and acceptance of cognitive psychology. Let's now turn our attention to Bruner's work.

The Contribution of Jerome Bruner

The ideas that flourished during the early years of cognitive "science" could not be ignored and had a decided influence on the creative minds of such young psychologists as George Miller and Jerome Bruner. These two cognitivists continued in the tradition we have been tracing and founded the *Center for Cognitive Studies* at Harvard in 1960.

We have previously mentioned the high regard in which Miller's colleagues held him. The impact of Miller's article, "The Magical Number Seven, Plus or Minus Two," was enormous. Bruner believes that if there were a retrospective Nobel Prize in Psychology for the mid-1950s, George Miller would win it on the basis of that one article. It is about the limitations on human information capacity. The magic number was the number of alternatives that a human being could keep in mind in immediate memory—7 ± 2 (1983, p. 97).

A Study of Thinking

Jerome Bruner (1915–) received his PhD. from Harvard in 1941 and immediately became involved in the American war effort, especially in psychological warfare. He was a Professor of Psychology at Harvard from 1945 until 1972, where from 1960 to 1972 he was also Director of Cognitive Studies. He was at England's Cambridge University from 1972 until 1979. Presently he is at the New School for Social Research in New York.

Bruner, with colleagues Jacqueline Goodnow and George Austin, published in 1956 an ingenious and important account of categorization called *A Study of Thinking*. In it they analyzed categorizing and believe it explains why humans are not overwhelmed by environmental complexity. The authors state that three types of concepts exist: conjunctive, disjunctive, and relational.

1. **Conjunctive concepts** rely upon the joint presence of several attributes. These attributes are abstracted from many individual experiences with the object, thing, or event. So there are categories such as boy, car, book, and orange.

2. **Disjunctive concepts** are composed of concepts, any one of whose attributes may be used in classification. That is, one or another of the attributes enable an object to be placed in a particular category. A good example of the disjunctive category is the strike in baseball. A strike may be either a ball thrown by the pitcher that is over the plate and between a batter's shoulders and knees, or a ball at which the batter swings and misses, or a ball that the batter hits foul (outside the playing limits of the diamond). Any one of these attributes enables the observer to classify it as a strike.

3. **Relational concepts** are formed by the relationship that exists among defining attributes. The authors illustrate this category by using income brackets. There are many income levels or classes, all of which exist because of the relationship among income, eligible expenses, and number of dependents. The combination of these properties determines an individual's income class. These are relational categories.

Bruner, Goodnow, and Austin concluded that categorizing implies more than merely recognizing instances. Rules are learned and then applied to new situations. Students learn that a sentence—subject, object, predicate—is the basic unit in writing, in history as well as English. The various categories (conjunctive, disjunctive, relational) are really rules for grouping attributes to define the positive instances of any concept.

With these ideas, Bruner, Goodnow, and Austin effectively showed that their subjects actively participate in the classification process. As you can imagine, the great value of Bruner's work in the 1950s and 1960s lay in the energy it supplied to the renewed cognitive movement. Gardner (1985) notes that subjects were treated as active, constructive problem solvers rather than as simple reactors to whatever stimuli were presented to them. Actively constructing solutions to problems implies that students turn to their cultural environment for clues to aid them in their quest.

Cognition Across Cultures

In their classic analysis, *Culture and Thought* (1974), Cole and Scribner provided interesting observations into the cognitive differences in various cultures. Noting that perceptual variations are common among different peoples, Cole and Scribner state that our modes of responding to stimuli are not "experience-free." Rather our reactions depend on our past histories of dealing with similar stimuli.

Stating that what children "see" in geometric patterns may be related to what actions they are asked to perform

TEACHER ←→ STUDENT
INTERACTIONS

Classroom Implications of Cognitive Psychology

1. Mental representations are at the heart of cognitive psychology. Thus the use of active learning methods increases the depth of information processing and the likelihood that it will be memorable. Some suggestions to improve memory and comprehension of important material follow.
   - Have your students listen to tapes of great speeches, such as Martin Luther King's *I Have A Dream* so that they gain insight into the Civil Rights Movement.
   - Have elementary school students perform historical skits about important events such as the discovery of America or the coming of the Pilgrims so that they can better understand their place in American history and remember their significance for longer intervals.
   - Conduct a classroom or school-wide election to simulate state and federal elections. Help students transfer these external events into mental representations by using such memory techniques as rehearsal and urging them to compare different elections.
2. Children can be taught to monitor their own cognitive strategies.
   - Encourage upper elementary and middle school students to check their report-writing skills by having them use reference materials such as the dictionary to correct their spelling, the thesaurus to rewrite information in their own words, and the almanac to give them up-to-date facts and statistics.
   - Develop kindergarten and elementary school children's ability to monitor their own sequencing and classification skills by using such techniques as a cooking class. Emphasize that they should concentrate on the needed steps as they themselves cook. Stress the importance of paying close attention to detail and using the correct utensils.
   - Ask your high school students who are learning to write journal articles to make certain their articles answer the questions *who, what, where,* and *how.* Ask them to edit their articles before submitting them to make sure they have answered all the questions.
3. Schema, or mental frameworks, can help students not only to learn more effectively but also to recall

information over longer periods of time.
   - Develop units of study such as the value of water by first relating the topic to your students' prior knowledge. For children of the northwest and northeast, you may offer the example of snow melt, then ice backup.
   - When you develop a unit such as holidays, remember that children of various cultures celebrate holidays differently but that all students have a schema for holidays to which you can relate your activities. With young children, challenge their knowledge of familiar words by using "interrupted reading." Before you read a story or a book, explain to them that when you stop, they have to think of a word the author would use. For example, "The graceful animal that came to the watering hole for a drink had only one horn. He must be a ——."
4. Meaningful learning and discovery learning pose two different tasks for students.
   - (For meaningful learning) Before you explain a scientific fact to lower elementary school students (e.g. how a caterpillar turns into a butterfly), first discuss the importance of steps that happen in a specific order. As an advance organizer you may illustrate a sequence with pictures of a butterfly's life cycle: egg, caterpillar, chrysalis, butterfly.
   - (For discovery learning). Explain to your children that they are going to find out how a caterpillar turns into a butterfly by watching the caterpillar itself as it eats the leaf, then turns into a chrysalis, and finally a caterpillar which will be released in the playground.
   - (For meaningful learning). Introduce the concept of career planning by discussing a recent career article in a journal or magazine. Using charts and diagrams, demonstrate how many students their age would like to study medicine, law, or education. As an advance organizer, the class may like to discuss friends or relatives who are engaged in these careers.
   - (For discovery learning). Divide your students into small groups to take a poll of their classmates to discover what careers they are interested in pursuing. Tabulate the results and make a report to the class.

(recognize the pattern, copy it, or reconstruct it), Cole and Scribner believed that different actions require different perceptual information. Consequently, children master their perceptual worlds as they master new activities. An example of this can be seen in the authors' work in Liberia. They asked some subjects to sort cards and others to describe the cards. The two groups showed different preferences for stimuli, depending on whether they were asked actually to sort (preference: form) or verbally describe (preference: color).

With regard to such conceptual processes as classifying, we see similar differences. The characteristic used for classifying reflects the nature of the task: how familiar, what is the source of the task (for example, animal or plant), and in what form they were presented.

Classifying processes seem to change with experience. For example, when people moved from an isolated village to a city or town or were exposed to a Western-type education, class membership seemed more important for grouping items. Schooling also contributes in a similar manner to the way in which people describe and explain their own mental operations.

Culture influences how people think, relate, and learn. Consequently, we can too frequently misperceive and misunderstand our students' behavior when we interpret it solely from our own cultural perspective. Cognitive activities occur in cultural situations (such as the classroom) that involve interpretations and values by both teachers and students.

Students who come from different racial, ethnic, or socioeconomic backgrounds than their teacher and the school administrators may have values, goals, and interests that are highly acceptable to their families and communities but not to the school community. Consequently, educators may not be able to accept behavior that the students and their parents find completely appropriate (Grossman, 1990, p. 339).

A good example of this difference can be found in the school's expectations and assumptions. Most schools and teachers expect that their students will function cognitively in a verbal and analytic manner (Tharp, 1989). Students who conform to these expectations, such as Japanese-American and Chinese-American students, are more likely to succeed than students who do not. Their patterns of cognitive functioning "fit" school expectations. Native Americans, on the other hand, perform better on performance and spatial tasks than on verbal ones. Consequently, their achievement suffers in traditional settings.

To offset these disadvantages, the concept of "contextualized instruction" has been introduced, which means that a student's personal experiences in a particular culture are used to introduce new material (Tharp, 1989). Materials that reflect the student's cultural community are utilized to provide a basis for developing school skills. These various levels of contextualization—personal, community, and cultural—seem to result in improved academic performance.

For example, Navajos reject the idea of "tough" at one extreme and "nice" at the other. Educators who are unaware of these beliefs can be ineffective in their methods of reinforcement and punishment. The Navajos resist open displays of affection but respect their children's individuality and independence. Thus efforts to control behavior by punishment or obvious rewards violate cultural values and are doomed to failure. Consequently, when teachers embed cultural values in classroom practices, they see greater student participation and higher levels of achievement (Tharp, 1989).

These ideas reflect the tendency to view mental life as consisting of two quite different methods of functioning: the logical, abstract manner of scientific thinking and *narrative* thinking, a much more personal kind of thinking that concentrates on people and the causes of their behavior (Bruner, 1986). Thus, stories of their particular culture greatly influence children, and they make up stories about their own lives; that is, they interpret their lives as stories or narratives (Howard, 1991).

If you have multicultural students in your classroom, take the time to discover the outstanding features of their culture, how they respond to various stimuli, and any notable cultural variations in behavior. You will find that the resulting positive relationships with these students will be well worth your effort.

The Importance of Information Processing

As we begin to examine specific aspects of cognition, the significance of information processing for both teachers and students becomes more apparent. Think of information processing as encompassing such topics as attention, perception, thinking, memory, and problem solving strategies. These are the subjects that were addressed in the chapter's opening.

Remember, though, that *representation* lies at the very heart of information processing. Its importance for teachers becomes apparent from observing students' behavior. How many times have you said to yourself, "I wonder what he's thinking?" or asked yourself, "Now, how could she have arrived at that answer?"

Cognitive psychologists are attempting to discover techniques that will allow us to analyze our students' thinking, which, if successful, has positive and far-reaching implications for both understanding learning and improving instruction. It seems reasonable to assume that our students have ideas or use symbols, but translating these simple statements into testable situations demands that researchers explore the domain of representation: symbols, schemas, images, ideas, and their interactions.

The Meaning of Representation

The manner in which information is recorded or expressed is a **representation** of that information (Glass, Holyoak, & Santa, 1987). The simple word "car" is a representation since it represents a certain idea; the idea conveyed can also be represented in different ways: auto, automobile, or motor car. In each example, however, the information represented remains the same; this common

Cognitive psychologists are attempting to discover techniques that will allow us to analyze our students' thinking, which, if successful, has positive and far-reaching implications for both understanding learning and improving instruction.

Are You a Visual or an Auditory Learner?

In a simple, and what has become a classic, experiment in cognitive psychology, Conrad (1964) had college students memorize lists of six written letters (such as T A V R B K). The students read the letters silently; the letters were removed; the subjects were asked to repeat the letters in order. Conrad was fascinated by the mistakes the students made, in particular, the letter substitutions they made. If the students recalled the letters visually (that is, using the same code in which the letters were originally presented), you would expect them to use a substitute letter that looked like the original letter—C for O. Most students, however, substituted letters that sounded like the original—V for C. Conrad concluded the students had recoded the letters, substituting a speech code for a visual code. (Incidentally, this is an excellent example of information processing.)

The results of Conrad's research are particularly interesting for us because they raise questions about classroom practice.

1. Will all students recode visual letters into a speech code?
2. Would individual differences explain students' preferences for particular sensory modes? That is, will some students learn better by acoustical means than by verbal?
3. Is it possible to identify the mode that a student prefers?

Although the answers to these questions remain elusive, some clues are being furnished. For example, Conrad found that with deaf subjects who cannot speak, letter substitutions were visual rather than auditory; they tended to substitute C for O and not V for C. Consequently, we can conclude that the chances are high that not all students will use the same code to represent information in memory. This and similar studies emphasize that teachers must be constantly alert to the clarity of their presentations, both visual and auditory.

represented information is called the *content* of the representation; the different ways that the information can be expressed is called the *representational code*.

How We Represent Information

If you recall the meaning of representation presented earlier in this section—the manner in which we record or express information—then knowing how our students represent the material they encounter in the classroom raises important issues both for curriculum and instruction (Phillips, 1983). We appear to use two types of codes for representing information: **mental imagery** and **verbal processing** (Foster, 1986).

Mental Imagery

Stop for a moment and think about the last time you went to the beach. Were there waves? Was the beach crowded? What color was the water? Answering these questions takes you into the world of mental imagery, a world that

has long intrigued philosophers and psychologists. You undoubtedly formed a "picture in your mind" to answer each of the questions. Your mental image represented or resembled the waves, the people at the beach, the color of the water. If you think about your answers, you will sooner or later question the accuracy of your image—just how precise was it? Was the water exactly that blue-green color you recalled? Though almost all of us use mental imagery, today's psychologists are more concerned with the reliability of our reports.

For example, Paivio (1974) asked his subjects to imagine two clocks whose times were 12:05 and 9:15. On which clock do the hands form the larger angle? Think about it for a moment. How did you answer the question? Didn't you form an image of each clock similar to the following?

Paivio's subjects reported that they had formed pictures of the clocks; they also needed more time if the angles were similar: 12:05, 1:10.

Another example of mental images can be found in the work of Stephen Kosslyn (1980), who attempted to have readers get an intuitive feeling for the topic by trying to answer the following questions: What shape are a German Shepherd's ears? Is a tennis ball larger than a pear? Does a bee have a dark head? Is a Christmas tree darker green than a frozen pea? Most people report that they mentally picture the named objects in the course of trying to answer these questions.

Images and Pictures

Any discussion of imagery must reckon with the widespread conviction that a visual image is a picture in our memory, much as a snapshot is stored in a photo album (Kosslyn, 1980). Yet an image is not like a picture stored in memory, waiting to be retrieved. Imagine a tiger. How many stripes does it have? You may have difficulty with this notion; it is difficult to "pull" a tiger picture from memory and count its stripes. Images are abstract, while pictures are linked to the visual properties of actual objects.

Our general knowledge can distort our images (Anderson, 1985). For example, subjects were told that two circles connected by a straight line was either a dumbbell or eyeglasses.

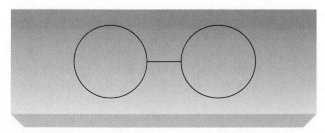

When asked to draw the object from memory, subjects who had been given the label eyeglasses often bent the connecting line.

Those who were given the label dumbbell strengthened or doubled the connecting line.

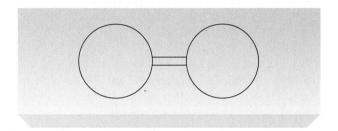

Anderson interprets these results to indicate that the subjects' general knowledge distorted their memories of the physical properties of the objects. Reproducing an actual picture would not result in such distortions.

Thus, though image may be difficult to define, we can specify several properties of images (Anderson, 1985).

- Images represent continuously varying information.
- Images possess the capability of responding to certain mental operations (for example, we can "rotate" them: imagine a cat's face, now its tail).
- Images are not linked to a "picture" of the object, but are part of our representational system.
- Images often change because of the knowledge that we possess (recall the dumbbell experiment).

Verbal Processing

Unlike mental imagery, verbal processing does not resemble in any way what it represents. Language is a good example: in no way does "car" resemble an actual automobile. The distinction between mental imagery and verbal processing has classroom significance when you consider that although most of us use both codes, we typically prefer one over the other.

If you can determine which code your individual students prefer, then you should use instructional methods that match a preferred code whenever possible. For example, several methods to be described in the next chapter are designed to help students with their memory.

Some of these methods such as rehearsal appeal to verbal processes, while others such as method of loci appeal to mental imagery.

For the Classroom

One way of improving your relationships is to help students decrease their feelings of frustration when faced with a challenging situation. As an example of how mental representations affect classroom performance, even at higher levels, consider an experiment described by de-Jong and Ferguson-Hessler (1986). Using evidence indicating that possession of knowledge does not necessarily lead to effective problem solving, the authors wished to investigate the problem schemata that their students used. (By problem schemata, they mean those sets of elements of knowledge that are linked together within the knowledge base of the problem.)

Experts utilize more adequate and complete problem schemata; that is, they attack problems according to underlying principles while novices fixate on the surface characteristics of a problem. Problem solvers tend to use the correct data and appropriate procedures.

Studying 47 first year university physics students, the authors presented them with 12 problems that involved 65 elements. (The subject matter was electricity and magnetism.) The 65 elements were then printed on cards, and the students were asked to sort them into coherent piles: the cards in any one pile were more closely connected to each other than to cards in other piles.

The authors found that the good problem solvers organized their knowledge in a much more *problem-type centered fashion* than did the poor problem solvers; they used problem schemata. Interestingly, a high correlation was discovered between course examination scores and problem-centered scores.

Utilization of problem schemata thus appears to be an extremely efficient way both to solve problems and to do well on examinations. To encourage this ability in students, the authors urged teachers to help their students to organize memory by the characteristics of the problem situation, the necessary data, and the correct procedural knowledge.

Consequently, try to have students feel comfortable with the basic types of problems in a given subject, make sure they master the fundamental data, and insure that they are familiar with the necessary steps to solve a problem (for example, changing signs when an amount is moved from one side of an equation to another). If you work at this technique, you will help your students to form more positive attitudes toward a subject and reduce the chances of unhappiness and discipline problems (Foster, 1986).

The Role of Perception

If you stop your reading for a moment and look around, you may see some things that you recognize immediately, such as your computer or a dictionary. You may also notice something that is totally different or new—perhaps the internal mechanism of your computer if you are seeing it for the first time (Shuell, 1986). Our ability to recognize the familiar and to realize what we do not know is **perception.** Perceiving something means that:

- you can recall past experiences with this person, object, or event;
- you experience meaning;
- you have certain expectations about the object or event.

Consequently, perception seems to entail more than just the ability to react to something; considerable processing is necessary to integrate multiple sources of information into a single representation.

Explanation of the Perceptual Process

We do not respond to our environment on a one-to-one basis. For example, examine the following figure.

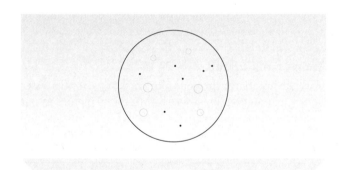

What do you see? Undoubtedly your reply would be something like, "I see a circle with dots and smaller circles inside it." You would not say, "I see one dot, and another dot, and another dot, and a small circle, and another small circle, and a line around all of them." You grouped the stimuli and expressed your answer in some related manner. You utilized your past experience by combining it with this present experience.

When someone asks you what time it is, do you carefully observe all of the minute markings on your watch? No, your past experience enables you to ignore the irrelevant and concentrate on the section where the hands and numbers are.

You organized the relevant stimuli, ignored the irrelevant, and moved them into the background, thus creating

Figure 7.1
Gradual differentiation of a face.

a figure-ground relationship. The more prominent qualities of the stimulus pattern emerge more clearly (figure) while the less prominent qualities recede (ground). In the example of telling time, the hands resting on the minute markings of five o'clock are the figure, while the remainder of the face of the watch represents the ground.

Perception is giving meaning to the discrete, meaningless stimuli that initially aroused awareness. The meaning that you give any stimulus depends upon the manner in which you pattern it. For example, a young boy hears a sound. From his past experiences he realizes that it is a whistle. As he continues to relate this stimulus to his experience, perceptual meaning becomes richer. He notes the time element; the whistle always blows at seven o'clock, morning and evening. Passing through town one evening at seven o'clock, he hears the whistle from the fire station. He has located its source. Now when he hears it, he identifies it as the seven o'clock whistle coming from the firehouse.

How you structure stimuli determines the quality of the percept and, ultimately, the concept. Teachers should use materials that form a meaningful pattern for youngsters. The strong reaction against history as the memorization of dates, and against geography as the memorization of places, is a negative example of perceptual meaning. Presented as a mass of sheer facts, students are unable to form patterns and establish meaningful relations among such stimuli or to link them with their own past experiences. The result is a distorted concept of all aspects of history and geography and a distressing tendency to avoid these subjects later in life.

Only then can they hope to encourage students to see the value of a particular subject and help them to make the topic more meaningful. This in itself is no easy chore; it requires a thorough knowledge of individual students. But the effort is richly rewarded when students acquire awareness and begin to discern meaning in their classroom.

For the Classroom

We have emphasized that perception is a crucial element in learning. The sensory experiences that students en-counter are not just mechanically registered and then filed away. Incoming data merge with past, similar experiences and combine with present physiological and psychological states to produce a particular perception (Speth & Brown, 1988). Perception, then, depends on both learning and maturation.

Patterns of Stimuli

Almost from birth, students react to patterns of stimuli as they perceive them at the moment. Learning, maturation, emotions, needs, and values are all intertwined in perception. In one classic study, (Bruner & Goodman, 1947) several ten-year-old children from poor homes and a like number from rich homes were asked to estimate the size of coins. The experimenters first showed the youngsters coins ranging in value from a penny to a half dollar and then asked them to duplicate the coin sizes by adjusting a knob that projected circles on a screen. The circle on the screen could be made larger or smaller. Interestingly, the poor children greatly overestimated the size of the coins since the value they placed had affected their perceptions. The rich youngsters only slightly overestimated the size.

How do students proceed from a gross reaction to a discriminated response? In Figure 7.1 a gradually more detailed pattern of a face is given. Older subjects often identify it as a face as early as the second figure, while students of even third or fourth grade age are unable to identify it until the last line is drawn. Why? What delays the recognition? The older students, because of their experiences, added the necessary details themselves. (The ability to perform these closure tasks is a good predictor of reading readiness.)

Fantz' work (1961, 1963) also indicated that newborn infants not only see but also have preference for certain patterns. He studied 18 infants under 5 days of age by placing them in the bottom of a test chamber. At the top of the chamber was an illuminated slot into which cards could be placed, and a peephole next to the slot enabled the investigator to observe the infant's eyes. When the image was established in the eye, the length of time that the infant focused on a particular color, pattern, or form was recorded. The infant was given a range of choices: a schematic face, a patch of newsprint, a bull's eye, and a red, a white, and a yellow circle. The subjects looked longest at facial patterns, then at the newsprint, and then the bull's eye. None looked longest at the circles.

What can we conclude from these results? We cannot conclude that there is any instinctive reaction to the human face. But the environment seems to suggest that there are definite properties in the visual world of the infant, since visual attention focuses earlier on patterns than on color differences. If this is so, and all evidence supports this conclusion, then perceptual training should commence much earlier in life, since children show an early readiness for perception.

For classroom purposes, it is especially significant that developmental changes occur in the attainment of perceptual acuity. Consider some perceptual phenomena that illustrate these developmental changes by answering the four questions next to the illustrations below.

In examining these illustrations, you probably answered as follows:

- Three figures of XO (You grouped them.)
- You probably identified B as the larger. (Objective measurement reveals that they are identical; the surrounding elements affect your perception of the middle circle.)
- You probably saw an O in the first illustration and an X in the second. (The difference between the central figure and its surrounding elements is so striking that you focused on the central figure.)
- Your first reaction was probably line b. (Measurement shows that they are the same length.)

Helping Students with Their Perceptual Acuity

As adults, our experience enables us, with little difficulty, to overcome our initial responses. Younger students are more easily confused (they may, for example, confuse b with d), but they gradually develop less susceptibility to complex stimulus patterns. The task then becomes one of aiding them to acquire perceptual acuity as early as possible, since this is a capacity they possess almost from birth (Foster, 1986). For example, many of the skills that a child must master in school, such as reading, require accurate discriminations and competence in detecting the unchanging nature of stimulus patterns in spite of possible surface changes. Such added knowledge of the perceptual process would aid both the construction of suitable curriculum materials and the nature of instruction.

Teachers can capitalize on their students' tendency to group; that is, students want to organize and structure, and you can help them by recalling certain principles.

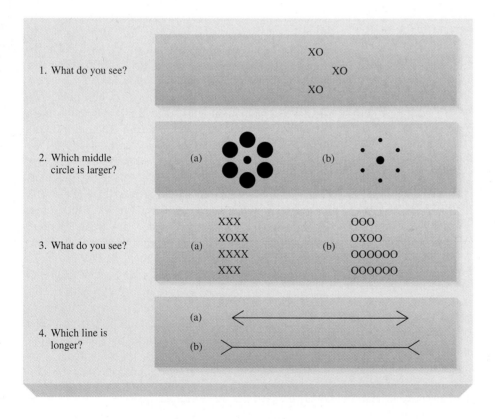

1. What do you see?

2. Which middle circle is larger? (a) (b)

3. What do you see? (a) XXX / XOXX / XXXX / XXX (b) OOO / OXOO / OOOOOO / OOOOOO

4. Which line is longer? (a) (b)

Focus on Students

Structure and Memory

As we have mentioned, your students learn better when material is somewhat familiar or can be organized into structures. Try this experiment yourself. It is similar to what your students encounter. Memorize this list of words.

A	B	C
grass	paper	the
furnace	rod	morning
snow	white	sky
orange	read	is
picture	girder	beautiful
lamp	print	when
cellar	strong	the
oxygen	cover	sun
hockey	bar	is
cement	scrap	rising

As you attempt to recall them, certain patterns emerge. You probably had difficulty with the words in column A—they were meaningless. Column B was easier—not only

did the words possess meaning, but they clustered around two key words: book and steel. Column C was probably the easiest—the words were logically organized into a meaningful structure. You thus have a dual task. You must either relate new material to what your students already know, or you must make new material as meaningful as possible.

You can help your students by following the organization principles suggested by the Gestaltists. For example, what do you see in the diagram shown above?

Most readers say that it is a square, but it is a square of circles; individual identity is absorbed by the larger unit. Four of these "circles" now become "corners."

---

1. What do you see in the following figure?

You saw two groups of circles, not ten isolated figures.

2. Objects that are similar form natural groups. What do you see in the following figure?

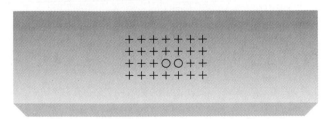

You saw a group of crosses and two circles because we group similar things.

These basic perceptual principles aid meaning because students can then organize material. So you should attempt:

- to use the familiar to introduce the novel.
- to relate new material to some structure that the students already possess.
- to stress any meaningful relations within the material.

You cannot overemphasize the importance of meaning and structure to your students. We often experience difficulty in thinking and problem solving because "facts" are buried by their surroundings—they are "camouflaged." Can you find the digit 4 in the following diagram?

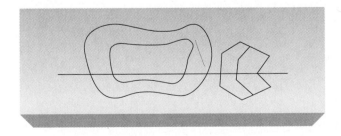

If you have trouble, turn to the next page.

It is buried within unfamiliar shapes, and you probably had trouble finding it. Students have exactly the same trouble discovering and finding meaning within unfamiliar subjects. Your students' past experiences should be used to form cognitive schemata in their efforts to master new materials, solve problems, and look at subjects more creatively.

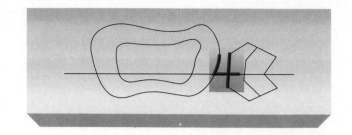

TEACHER ⟷ STUDENT INTERACTIONS

Information Processing in the Classroom

1. The manner in which information is recorded or expressed is a representation of that information.
   - Show your students pictures or actual objects used in various occupations: paint brush, easel, stethoscope, baker's hat, spatula, wrench, etc. Have them guess how each object is used and what the user's career is.
   - Tell the story of the blind men and the elephant and discuss how important perception is in the story and why the men's perception was distorted.
   - For older children, describe a hypothetical automobile accident. Ask the children to accept roles as witnesses. Ask what each witness could have seen. Point out how each person may have seen something that another did not.
   - Select a short mystery (by an author like Donald Sobel) to read to your class. Before you begin, however, ask the children to listen carefully for clues. Towards the conclusion, ask them how they think the mystery should be solved and then compare their projected solutions to the author's.

2. Students use two techniques for representing information: mental imagery and verbal processing.
   - Mental Imagery: In kindergarten and lower grades, show students pictures of every day objects such as broom, comb, ball, etc. and ask your students to describe how these objects are used and what they are used for.
     Train your students to "use their third eye" as each one takes a turn to continue the story that you begin.
   - Use a game like "Blind Man's Bluff" to teach the alphabet to young children. Have one child blindfolded. Select another child to take a large oak tag letter off the wall. The blindfolded child traces around the letter with her hands, trying to determine which one it is.
   - In math, to determine what a problem wants you to find, ask your students to picture what facts are present and which are missing. It is easier to decide what steps they must take to find the missing facts

when they know what is present. Sometimes it helps to draw a picture of the problem. Use concrete models such as a diagram, coins, or plastic chips labeled for value to help students think a problem through using these visualization techniques.

Verbal processing:
   - For older students organize a debate, e.g. whether there should be a dress code, a change in academic requirements to graduate, etc.
   - Arrange a forum; invite guests knowledgeable in their field to discuss with students current topics, e.g. should driving lessons be part of the school curriculum; should students be forced to pay a fee for sports; do you agree that there should be a ban on smoking in public places?
   - For younger students play games such as "I went to the market and brought home" where each student, using each letter of the alphabet, says one thing that the following child must repeat.

3. Perception is giving meaning to the stimuli that come from the environment.
   - Develop a keener perception in your students by having them research the various cultures that are represented in their class. Ask them to find out their traditional dress, their food, family attitudes, etc. Children who may have "immaturely" ridiculed or called others names should have a deeper appreciation of their classmates after completing such a project.
   - In kindergarten, select a child to be a "buddy" to another who is having difficulty. By watching the more competent child, the other child will learn more quickly how to fold her paper, hang up her jacket, put her toys away, etc.
   - In upper classes, organize children into several small cooperative learning groups to help one another develop perceptual awareness.

How Students Categorize

Students interact successfully with their environment according to their ability to organize information. Placing objects into categories and then inventing a name for the category is one of the fundamental organizing activities in which all students engage. Book, pupil, teacher, car, doll, and water are examples of your tendency to categorize. With this skill, you avoid the necessity of responding separately to each and every object in your environment. When you hear the word "book," you need not seek an actual book to ascertain its characteristics. If you have a concept of book, you have placed it in a category with other similar objects that are made of bound sheets and have pages with words and illustrations. Upon hearing "book" you recall the concept that possesses the common properties of that category.

Forming Categories

Bruner, Goodnow, and Austin (1956) summarized the importance of categorizing information, and their insights, although dated, have stood the test of time and are worthy of repeating today.

1. *Categorizing reduces the complexity of the environment.* Abstraction enables students to group objects, and then students gradually respond to classes of objects rather than respond to each and every thing they encounter.
2. *Categorizing permits us to identify the objects of the world.* We identify objects by placing them in a class, and when similar objects are met, we can say, "Ah, there is another one of those little redheaded Venusians."
3. *Categorizing allows humans to reduce their need of constant learning.* Each time we experience an object, we are not forced to form a new category; we merely categorize with no additional learning. This object has attributes X, Y, Z; therefore, it belongs to the category entitled "car."
4. *Categorizing provides direction for instrumental activity.* When we see a road sign that reads *Danger Ahead,* we alter our driving to the anticipated conditions. We become more alert, proceed more cautiously, and drive more slowly.
5. *Categorizing encourages the ordering and relating of classes.* Since we react to systems and patterns, once we place an object in a category we vastly increase the possibilities of establishing relationships for that particular object. For example, once students decide on the characteristics of the "good" president, they can then match any president to this category.

Recent Research

This classic view of how we organize information (how we form categories or concepts) has come under considerable revision so that a more novel interpretation has been widely accepted. The impetus for the assault began with research into how we name colors.

If you think about it, there is no clear rationale for the color names that we have designated since color is actually a continuum. We arbitrarily divide color as we see fit. A question that intrigued cognitive psychologists was: Does the manner in which we label things structure the way that we classify them? Brown and Lenneberg (1954), using English-speaking subjects, showed them 24 colors and asked them to label the colors. Those readily named were called *codable.* Another group of subjects was shown a small set of colors and then a large set and asked to specify what they had seen before. Subjects readily recognized those colors that the researchers had identified as codable.

The matter rested there until 1973 when Eleanor Rosch, studying a Stone Age tribe in New Guinea that had only two color terms (one for bright, one for dark), discovered that although her subjects had difficulty identifying by name the intermediate colors, they showed the same recognition characteristic as English-speaking subjects. Thus differences in naming between the two cultures did not reflect differences in memory storage: cognitive processing determined the color categories they formed.

Upon her return to America and with continued experimentation, Rosch (Mervis & Rosch, 1981) concluded that her work with color categories extended throughout the classification process to how we form categories. The classic theory of classification described at the beginning of this section holds that a category consists of certain definite criteria. If an object possesses these criteria, it belongs to that category; if it lacks the defining criteria, it must be a member of another category.

But all categories do not seem to possess a neat, defining set of criteria. Gardner (1985, p. 345) noted that some categories are better identified by the actions that they signify. For example, a "drinking vessel" is defined by its potential for being held and poured from. These and similar difficulties caused Rosch to propose an explanation that cuts across many natural categories. The explanatory concept she proposed is called a **prototype,** which does not contain clearly defined critical attributes but a common standard form—the prototype (Glass, Holyoak, & Santa, 1987, p. 343–345). For example, though chickens and robins are technically birds, most people would state that the robin is a more typical example of a bird; it is more natural—it is a prototype.

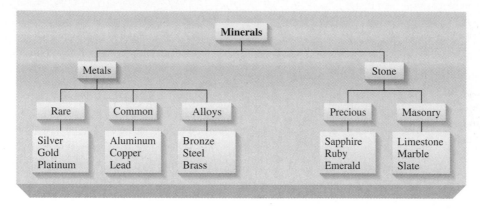

Figure 7.2
A conceptual hierarchy for the concept of minerals.

For the Classroom

What does this change in thinking about classification mean for teachers? It probably reinforces what teachers have been doing intuitively for years. When teaching an idea—a concept—good teachers never had their students memorize long lists of attributes that best described it. Rather, they consistently gave examples; they compared the concept to other categories that were not the same. Macintosh and Delicious apples are both apples; an orange is not an apple. Good teachers have generally appealed to information in a child's natural world and did not depend solely on artificial criteria.

Try to structure classroom experiences to provide as many rich and meaningful impressions as possible. The following principles should help:

1. *Remember that concepts are only as valuable as the meaning they convey.* Be careful that you do not accept the symbol alone as evidence that students have attained a concept. You should continually probe to guarantee that meaning is associated with the symbol. For example, you probably can define concept, but can you describe it, give examples, and explain the various types (Wilson, 1987)?

2. *Provide varied experiences for the learner.* Students should encounter the concept under different conditions. Where possible they should see and feel and talk about it, connecting the object with as many senses as possible. Learners should occasionally encounter examples of what a concept is not. That is, some negative examples are effective if mixed with many positive, clear instances.

3. *Utilize assorted methods of presenting the concept.* Different techniques of presentation are most efficient. You cannot be satisfied with one method, whether it is telling, discovery, or reading. A combination of methods is definitely indicated.

4. *Encourage self-activity in the search for common elements.* This principle is almost a subdivision of item three. All learning increases with a student's activity, which is also true for concept formation. Students should spend substantial time in searching for the necessary properties of the concept. The time spent should be proportionate to the other methods you employ for the acquisition of any concept. That is, you must decide, at least initially, how much time should be given to search, and how much to telling. The concept's abstractness will unquestionably influence the teacher. For example, teaching a student the concept of ball entails considerable self-activity. Learning about deoxyribonucleic acid demands substantial direction, especially in the initial phases of concept acquisition.

5. *Encourage students to apply the concept.* Once students have partially attained the concept, they should begin to use it. They should read it and explain it; they should furnish it as a missing word; they should use it to solve problems. Above all, if they are to use it outside the classroom, teachers should supply experiences that are not routinely educational. Students must realize that they can use it at home, work, or play, which is exactly what is meant by concepts aiding in the economical adjustment to the environment.

6. *Relate the concept or category to your students' prior knowledge in a systematic manner.* Encourage students to think about how they organize their knowledge about a particular set of concepts or categories. For example, if they are studying about metals such as silver and gold, have them relate this content to existing information they may have about minerals.

Depending on the student's prior knowledge and schema about metals, they may find the hierarchical organization (like that illustrated in Figure 7.2) similar to their own organized schema. If not, such a graphic organizer should facilitate further inquiries and learning. In some cases where hierarchical organization of information is not known or readily apparent, encourage students to create their own subjective representation of information (Baddeley, 1990).

Concepts are vital to thinking, reasoning, and perceiving relationships. The quality of a student's concepts is the best measure of probable success in learning because meaning is basic to learning. Also, concepts determine what we know, believe, and do. Concepts, then, are vital to all phases of life. They order the environment, add depth to perceptual relationships, clarify thinking, and, particularly, facilitate the entire learning process. Meaningful concepts are also a great aid to memory.

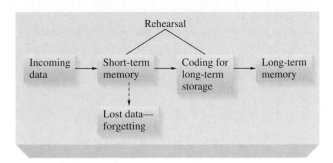

Figure 7.3
An early multi-store model.

Memory at Work

Acquiring concepts is in itself, however, not enough; we want our students to remember what they acquire. As the reborn cognitive movement carried into the late 1960s and 1970s, the study of memory attracted considerable attention. An analysis of memory that cognitive psychologists widely accepted was the distinction made between episodic and semantic memory (Tulving, 1972).

- **Episodic memory** is your recall of personal experiences within a specific context or period of time. Think of it as autobiographical; episodic memory provides you with a personal history. For example:
    (a) John and I watched the Red Sox play the Yankees last Friday night.
    (b) I saw Rex Harrison play Henry Higgins in *My Fair Lady* when it first opened in New York.

- **Semantic memory** is the memory necessary for the use of language, a kind of dictionary without reference to our personal experiences and which represents our general knowledge. It is the organized knowledge that a person possesses about words and other verbal symbols. For example:
    (a) I know that Albany is the capital of New York.
    (b) I know that "friend" is an acceptable English word.

Note that we can verify the accuracy of semantic memory. Written testimony (geography books, state and federal listings) attest to the truthfulness of the statement that Albany is the capital of New York. No such tests exist for episodic memory.

In a particularly influential model of episodic memory, Atkinson and Shiffrin (1968) proposed a three-store system: the sensory register, the short-term store, and the long-term store. These three stores are structurally distinct because they hold information differently, for varying times, and for different purposes. The authors also stated that the three stores lose information differently. Figure 7.3 illustrates a multi-store model.

The sensory register holds input in almost the same form as the sensory image; that is, cognitive processes do not begin to alter it until after data pass through the sensory register. Information is lost from the register in less than a second, either through spontaneous decay or through the entry of new data. The sensory register momentarily preserves information so that it can be selectively transmitted into the memory system. The selective characteristic of the sensory register prevents us from being overwhelmed by the sensory input. For example, what attracts the attention of some students does not work with others.

The short-term store is seen as our working memory, which entails conscious processes. Input to the short-term store comes from both the sensory register and the long-term store, which feed data to the short-term store for conscious manipulation. Information can be held indefinitely here if attention remains constant; otherwise decay commences and data are lost in 15 to 30 seconds. The critical nature of the short-term store lies in its conscious content; neither the sensory register nor the long-term store entails consciousness. The longer that information remains in the short-term store, the greater the chance that it will be transmitted to the long-term store (George Miller's reference to the magical number seven as our storage capacity applied to short-term memory).

Long-term store holds both conscious and unconscious data. For example, you can recall how the clams tasted at a beach cookout when you were a child. You probably still talk about the smell of the kitchen when an apple pie was baking. Although information may be stored indefinitely, data still may be lost (interference, perhaps even sheer decay). The significance of long-term memory lies in its survival and adaptation value; we require an enormous amount of information to survive in a modern society.

Consequently, the more meaningful that you can make material for your students, the better that you relate it to their experiences, and the more successful you are in motivating them, the greater will be their level of understanding since they processed it at a deeper level.

New Directions in Memory Studies

Although multistore models of memory have a neatness and elegance that many find appealing, the interests of most cognitive scientists are shifting away from this view (Baddeley, 1990). Consequently, several cognitivists advocate a **levels of processing** analysis (Craik & Lockhart, 1972), which focuses on the depth of processing. Information is not transformed by moving through a series of stores. Data are processed by various operations called perceptual-conceptual analysis.

The perceptual-conceptual analysis reflects an individual's attention. If you deem incoming material worthy of long-term recall, you will analyze it differently from material you judge as relatively unimportant. Whether the stimulus is processed at a shallow level or at a deeper level depends on the nature of the stimulus, the time available for processing, and the subject's own motivation, goals, and knowledge base. Thus, the operations performed during input determine the fate of the incoming information.

Consequently, the initial processing of a word will determine the length of time students remember it. For example, if you are interested only in the color of a word's printed letters, you will not remember that word as you would if you had examined the word for its meaning (Sherry & Schachter, 1987).

Memory remains a major research interest for today's cognitive psychologists (Baddeley, 1990). A question now frequently asked is: Should memory be studied naturally, that is, by using everyday experiences (Conway, 1991), or by using strict laboratory techniques?

In an attempt to illustrate the value of both these techniques, Ceci and Bronfenbrenner (1991) used a thirty-minute cake-baking experiment in which the children were observed while they waited for the cupcakes to bake. There were three conditions: some children did the baking in the laboratory, others in their homes, and others in a kitchen in a university building. The authors report that the children in the lab checked the clock 30 percent more frequently than those in their own homes but with no greater degree of punctuality. As a result, the authors urge that memory researchers adopt both techniques in the study of memory.

Yet certain basic questions remain to be answered: Why do we forget? Do all individuals experience the same type of problems with memory? Are there specific

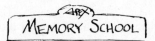

"You simply associate each number with a word, such as 'lipoprotein' and 3,467,009."

© 1991 by Sidney Harris—Science Magazine.

types of memory problems or are they related? How exactly do we memorize? How can we become skillful at remembering (Neisser, 1982)?

As a result of decades of research, speculation, and common sense reasoning, certain generalizations are possible. Among them are the following:

- similarity of material can cause interference;
- meaningful material aids recall;
- time on task helps students to remember;
- rehearsal (going over something repeatedly) is an important memory strategy.
- mnemonic strategies can help students remember.

Before proceeding further, we should pause and make some basic distinctions that will help to clarify a complex topic.

Recognition, Recall, and Forgetting

We have previously commented on the shifting focus in memory research, from reliance on multistore models to a concern with levels of processing and have noted Tulving's identification of episodic and semantic memory. You should also distinguish between **storage** and **retrieval.** Storage implies "putting information into" memory, which occurs as a result of attending, encoding, and the use of memory strategies. Retrieval, on the other hand, implies recognizing, recalling, and reconstructing what we previously "put in."

For example, your students may have memorized the names of the major battles of the Civil War on Monday, but on Wednesday some of the class can't recall them. You then furnish a cue. "Henry, how would you describe the tip of your pencil?" "It's sharp, Miss Smith. Oh, I get it. Sharpesville is the name." This student knew the name but couldn't retrieve it without help. Two other topics that have special relevance for the classroom are recognition and recall.

If you think for a moment, you will quickly realize the importance of these concepts for the classroom. In your teaching you constantly appeal to your students' basic knowledge; you are asking them to recognize something familiar in a new work that you are teaching. In testing, you want them to recognize familiar cues in the questions. Academic success or failure is closely tied to both recognition and recall.

Recognition

Recognition means that we compare a present, incoming representation with a representation already stored in memory. Is the number of your apartment 29? Here we see a recognition task; note: you were not asked to recall the number of your apartment.

There are three major elements involved in recognition: similarity, prior experience, expectation and context. Similarity seems obvious since we probably will not recognize something we have not encountered before or something familiar in a radically altered form—for example, a friend at a costume party. As obvious as it sounds, the notion of similarity can lead to difficulty in the classroom. If you use multiple choice questions, the alternate answers you select, if too similar, can hinder recognition. Prior experience refers to the frequency and recency of your encounters with the object, event, or person. Repetition exercises a strong impact upon recognition. Expectation and context means that we expect to meet certain things or people in certain circumstances. For example, youngsters in the early grades are almost always surprised to meet a teacher in the supermarket. They do not expect to see them in these circumstances. The expectations that arise from context, of course, are not limited to elementary school youngsters. A continuing frustration for teachers relates to some student's inability, almost refusal, to recognize and apply mathematical principles in anything but a math class. Different context; different expectations.

Recall

What are the names of the Great Lakes? Who won the 1986 World Series? Who was the President of the United States before Lyndon Johnson? These questions force you to **recall** information, which goes beyond recognition because you are not given a "copy" of the representation. Any retrieval cue is minimal; consequently, students must generate their own cues in their search for the necessary information. For a search to be effective,

the information sought must have been stored in a reasonably organized manner; otherwise the target information remains elusive and recall usually falters. Again we note the importance of schema—or organizational property—for understanding cognitive processes.

Since the strategies to aid recall are so central to memory, learning, and problem solving, chapter 8 is devoted to their analysis.

Forgetting

Forgetting, unfortunately, is a normal process and here does not refer to an abnormal loss of memory occasioned by aging, shock, or brain injury. Under normal daily conditions, what causes your students to forget previously acquired material? Theorists have proposed several explanations (Sherry & Schachter, 1987).

• *Forgetting as disuse or fading.* Once it is learned, students will forget an item unless they use it. This explanation of forgetting has been referred to as the trace decay hypothesis (Ebbinghaus, 1885). Deterioration of the information develops and learning slowly fades. Though still a popular belief, today psychologists question it. For example, if subjects memorize a list of words to errorless recall, and then wait for various times before testing, the loss is illustrated in Figure 7.4.

   The exact details of the curve may vary depending upon the nature of the material, the degree of overlearning, and other material studied between the time of learning and the time of recall. But note two items with important implications for teaching:

   • the rapid decline after initial learning;
   • the stability of retained materials with increasing time.

   Other possible interpretations of the forgetting curve exist. Certain skills, such as riding a bicycle, swimming, or ice skating, show remarkable endurance. Even some verbal material is not quickly forgotten. You probably recall several lines from an elementary school play or show, while forgetting something you learned last semester, which decay over time does not explain; other variables, such as motivation, also must influence retention. Still time exacts its toll, and you should consider this in your teaching by conducting periodic, meaningful reviews.

• *Motivated forgetting,* or repressed forgetting. Unquestionably you have had experiences that you try to forget because of the unpleasantness, fear, or anxiety associated with them. If experiences are sufficiently severe, amnesia—either partial or total loss of memory—results. The extent of repression as a cause of normal forgetting remains unestablished because of the lack of experimental control that can be introduced.

• *Forgetting because of interference.* Psychologists agree that most forgetting happens because new

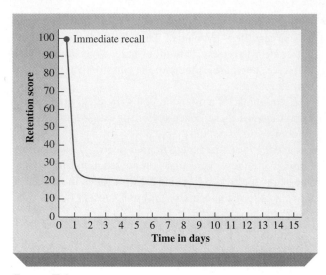

Figure 7.4
The curve of retention.

learning interferes with past learning. The proactive retroactive process illustrates this theory.

• *Forgetting because of extinction and reorganization.* Because of disuse and a lack of reinforcement, students forget a response. When forced to recall it, they apply newly acquired experiences and undoubtedly reshape the original response so that it may or may not suit the original stimulus. We have seen an example of this in "The War of the Ghosts."

Given the present understanding of the forgetting and retention phenomenon, what are some specific measures you can adopt to aid your students' storage and retrieval?

1. *Repeatedly urge students to remember.* This does not mean obvious exhortation but refers to student self-activity, whereby material acquires both meaning and personal significance: it is organized and stored. For example, overlearning aids memory because it more sharply distinguishes the item to be stored and facilitates coding, which lowers the possibility of negative transfer and increases the possibility of positive transfer.

2. *Comprehension, not mere mastery of facts, should be the aim of your instruction.* This understanding depends upon the kind of material and how you present it. As words are remembered better than nonsense syllables, so solutions of problems are better remembered than isolated facts. Try to guide students to perceive and use relationships within the material and between the topic and the learner's background. (Note: Throughout this work on verbal learning, three essentials have been stressed: *meaning, organization, and structure.*)

Given that much of what students must remember will be based on material they read, you should be aware of several strategies for increasing comprehension of written material. These include the following (Pressley & Harris, 1990):

- *summarization,* which means creating a representation of the central idea;
- *imagery,* which means constructing an internal visual representation of text content;
- *story grammar,* which means identifying the setting, problem, goal, action, and outcome in a story;
- *prior knowledge activation,* which means that students relate what they already know to the content of the text;
- *self-questioning,* which means devising questions that help to integrate the content being read;
- *question-answer,* which means teaching students to analyze questions carefully as a way of helping them to respond.

3. *Provide distributed rather than mass practice and insure that overlearning occurs.* It is better to teach ten foreign language words a day for five days than to force memorization of all fifty words in a single period. Periodic review of lecture notes surpasses cramming.

4. *Conduct periodic review.* Review soon after learning and at short intervals, gradually widening the time between reviews. Review need not be dogmatic, formal sessions. Quizzes, assignments, and use of material are effective review techniques. Periodic reviews are especially significant when you recall the retention curve, which dramatically illustrated the initial loss of learning. Meaningful reviews are an excellent tool to overcome this loss.

5. *Reduce interference.* Recalling the proactive-retroactive inhibition paradigm, teachers, and especially administrators, should try to schedule subjects that reinforce and not interfere with each other. After a history period involving names, dates, and places, you would probably not want to move into a discussion of Henry V in an English class.

For teachers, the customary method of recall is to ask students to retrieve information in its original form. If you present cues (questions) different from the form in which the information was originally stored, students experience much greater difficulty. Consequently, teachers should use questions carefully, so that they may aid a student to acquire a method of problem solving or to think creatively. To demand recall in the original form is to promote *convergent* thinking (certainly but not always a needed and desired technique) at the expense of *divergent* or creative thinking. Try to encourage both types of thinking, convergent at the beginning of a topic when mastery of facts is required and divergent once facts have been acquired and problem solving and creativity can be encouraged.

For the Classroom

If students rapidly learn a large amount of nonmeaningful material, they will forget it just as quickly. The rate of loss slows when most of the material is forgotten. But occasionally a surprising phenomenon seems to occur: after a rest period, there may be an actual gain in retention.

For example, after thirty minutes of studying twenty spelling words, students may be able to spell fifteen of them correctly. Yet the next morning they may spell seventeen correctly. This **reminiscence** is hard to explain. Is it true learning, or is it the product of faulty experimentation? There are two possible causes of reminiscence.

1. Fatigue developed during the original learning and affected retention, which then improved after rest.
2. The experiment was faulty because the initial test of retention was actually another learning experience that aided performance in the next test of retention.

Another important feature relates to the position of items to be memorized. Students learn the beginning and end of any memory task much more easily than the middle elements. Undoubtedly this is a function of interference; isolated items are learned more readily and retained longer. What can you do to help students with that difficult middle section? One technique is to furnish some organization or structure to which they can relate it. For example, ask them to select two or three words in the section that have particular meaning for them and have them use these words as clues, or have them imagine a picture related to the section, or use some words to form pictures.

This procedure helps to reduce interference, which may produce the phenomenon seen in Table 7.2.

Procedure A is the control; there is no interference; procedure B is retroactive inhibition; that is, new material (Task 2) interferes with previously learned material (Task 1). Procedure C is proactive inhibition; that is, previously learned material interferes with the recall of new material. For example, studying the same period in English and history could lead to either proactive or retroactive interference unless students have formulated a clear structure of the topic in both subjects.

Help to eliminate inhibition by ensuring that the material to be learned is meaningful and organized. Learning meaningful material to mastery lessens your students' susceptibility to interference. If students comprehend

Table 7.2
The Problem of Interference

Tasks		Retention
A. Task 1		Test Task 1
B. Task 1	Task 2	Test Task 1
C. Task 1	Task 2	Test Task 2

the meaning inherent in any content, they learn it more rapidly and retain it longer. The meaningfulness in material depends upon either some pattern that the learner recognizes (1, 7, 13, 19, 25, 3l) or the familiarity of the material (previously learned details).

You have probably determined by now that students differ in their abilities to remember. Psychologists have become interested in the reasons for these differences and have attempted to discover whether students can learn to improve their performance. These efforts have led to the phenomenon of **metacognition,** the ability to examine one's own cognitive processes (see chapter 3).

Metacognition

Although interest in metacognition is relatively recent, its content has always been with us—for example, our thoughts about a decision we made or "how we are doing on a project" all entail metacognitive processes. When we discussed Piaget's stage of formal operations (see chapter 2), we were exploring metacognitive thinking about hypotheses and possibilities.

Metacognitive skills seem to be involved in many classroom cognitive activities: comprehension, evaluation, reading, writing, and problem solving, among others. Discussing metacognition, Flavell (1985) analyzes it by two domains: metacognitive knowledge and metacognitive experiences.

Metacognitive Knowledge

Metacognitive knowledge refers to our knowledge and beliefs about cognitive matters gained from experience and which we have stored in our long-term memory (Flavell, 1985, p. 105). We acquire metacognitive knowledge about people, tasks, and strategies.

- An example of metacognitive knowledge of people is an important concept for the classroom. You may

have come to believe that a particular person just doesn't like you; a student may decide that you have little confidence in his ability.

- With regard to tasks, we know that the nature of a task forces us to think about how we'll manage. If it's difficult, perhaps we'll need more time, or perhaps we should prepare an outline.
- As for strategies, we should make a distinction between cognitive strategies (achieving a goal) and metacognitive strategies (monitoring your progress toward that goal). Over time, we have all learned much about strategies (which are best suited for success on a particular task?). For example, you have a strategy for recalling what you have read in this chapter. These strategies (to be discussed in detail in chapter 8) may be simple (repeatedly going over the material) or complex (imagining that you place certain topics in different parts of your house).

Since learning strategies can be taught, you can help your students appreciate their value by having them concentrate on just what they do when they must learn. Here is an example of the importance of learning strategies (Derry, 1989). Imagine that you are a student who has arrived at school and discovered that your first period teacher is giving a test on chapter 5. You studied chapter 4. You have fifteen minutes before the class. How would you most wisely use the time? (Derry actually assigned a reading, allowed fifteen minutes, and then tested her students.)

At the end of the quiz she asked them to describe in detail what they did when they studied. Not many did well on the quiz. One who did stated that she initially read the chapter summary and then skimmed the chapter, concentrating on the chapter headings, looking for organization. With the remaining time, she read the topic sentences in as many paragraphs as possible. Another student who did poorly said he felt panic and started to read through the chapter as fast as he could but didn't get too far.

Here is a striking example of the differences between successful and unsuccessful learning strategies. You can see that the plan you use for attaining a goal is your learning strategy. By teaching your students how to attack a problem, you can do much to improve their achievement.

Metacognitive Experiences

Metacognitive experiences are either cognitive or affective experiences that relate to cognitive activities. For example, while you are reading this chapter, you may feel a little uncertain or doubtful about one of the topics, or you may be quite concerned that you didn't understand it. As

Flavell (1985) notes, metacognitive experiences are most likely to occur when careful, conscious monitoring of your cognitive efforts are required. The uncertainty, or confidence, that you may feel about a topic is tied to relevant metacognitive knowledge.

You can see, then, how valuable these metacognitive experiences can be. If you are puzzled by one of these topics, then your sense of uncertainty will cause you to read the section again, perhaps discuss it with other students, or bring up questions in class.

By making students aware that they can "think about their thinking," you will also help them to improve those cognitive behaviors that result in better classroom performance. This ability becomes apparent when students—and all of us—make decisions.

Decision-Making and Reasoning

Do you consider yourself logical? How good are you at making decisions? Do you pride yourself in your accurate thinking? Although we all want to think that we are models of logical thinking, facts seem to tell us otherwise. How would you respond to the situations in the Focus on Teachers box?

We have long believed that, as humans, we think, reason, and solve problems on the basis of rational processes. Decision-making has long been described as a process in which individuals examine alternatives according to their probability, utility, and value (Krouse, 1986).

Representativeness

Tversky and Kahneman appeal to the principle of representativeness to explain these apparent variations in our thinking by which they mean our tendency to compare things, people, or events to see how well they resemble each other. Gardner (1985) uses the following example to illustrate the principle of representativeness.

Consider the case of Linda: 31-years-old, single, very bright, and outspoken. As a student, she majored in philosophy and participated in anti-nuclear demonstrations and was active in campus issues involving discrimination and social justice. Given the following statements, which do you think is more probable?

1. Linda is a psychiatric social worker.
2. Linda is a bank teller.
3. Linda is a bank teller and active in the feminist movement.

Which did you select? Many readers probably selected the third alternate, but if you pause for a moment, you may have second thoughts. Was Linda trained as a psy-

Focus on Teachers

What Would You Do?

How would you answer these questions?

1. Imagine that you were lucky enough to obtain two tickets to the great Broadway musical *42nd St.* for $70.00. As you walk down the street to the theatre, you discover that you have lost the tickets. You can't remember the seat numbers. Would you go to the ticket window and buy another pair of tickets for $70.00?
2. Imagine that you are on the way to the theatre to buy tickets for the Broadway play, *42nd St.* They will cost you $70.00. As you approach the ticket window, you discover that you have lost $70. Would you still pay $70.00 for the tickets?

These questions, originally posed by Tversky and Kahneman (1981), usually elicit some interesting answers. How did you answer them? Among their subjects, 46 percent answered yes to question 1, while 88 percent answered yes to question 2. Note: Many more people said they would buy new tickets if they had lost the money than if they had lost the tickets. Yet the two situations are actually identical—in each instance you would have lost $70.00.

How can we explain the difference in the responses? Tversky and Kahneman believe that the way a problem is "framed" helps to explain our response. As they state (1981, p. 453):

> The frame that a decision-maker adopts is controlled partly by the formulation of the problem and partly by the norms, habits, and personal characteristics of the decision-maker.

This latest research holds much promise for learning, instruction, and curriculum construction because the manner in which material is packaged (books, kits) and presented (instructional techniques) goes far in determining the responses of your students.

chiatric social worker? Nothing was mentioned except her work in philosophy. It certainly makes more sense to assume that Linda is a bank teller rather than a bank teller and an active feminist since the probability is higher that a person will have one characteristic than two. Yet, as Gardner indicates, 80 percent of subjects (even those knowledgeable about statistics) select item three.

Why? Representativeness is at work here. We assume because a person has certain characteristics that others will also be present. Consequently, knowing that Linda has certain specific characteristics (activist at school, outspoken), we then add other characteristics that are representative of "this kind" of person.

TEACHER ◄──► STUDENT
I N T E R A C T I O N S

Cognition in the Classroom

1. Students will be successful—both in and out of class—to the extent that they acquire the ability to place objects in categories.
   - For older students:
     Suggest a research project about possible careers to be divided into categories, such as those that require a college education and those that demand a high school diploma, those that require clerical skills and those that don't, those that traditionally recruit males and those that attract females.
   - For younger students:
     Encourage recycling among your students. Have them collect trash for the school day in a paper bag and then divide it into biodegradable, degradable, and nondegradable materials.
   - Plan an outdoor treasure hunt. Give each student a list of items to find. When the class returns, divide all the items into their proper categories.

2. Helping students improve their memory will aid their successful achievement throughout life.
   - Suggest that your students be "picture helpers"; train them to use mental pictures to keep track of a numbered series of items.
   - Show them that using key words derived from the fact to be remembered can help their long-term memory. A

good key word is one that sounds or looks like the word to be memorized, is familiar to the students, and is concrete in the sense that a picture can be drawn to represent the word.
   - Demonstrate how they may draw pictures illustrating their key words and show them to the class while describing them. Then encourage the students to think back to their pictures when they are trying to remember the words they have to memorize.

3. The manner in which a teacher presents material helps to shape the responses that students make.
   - Ask yourselves these questions when you're presenting material:
     1. Am I a cheerful, enthusiastic speaker, or a boring, predictable droner?
     2. Is the length of my lessons appropriate to my students' attention span?
     3. Do I avoid abstractions and try to be as concrete as possible?
     4. When I realize students don't understand, do I rephrase my comments or just repeat them?
     5. Do I speak at a rate appropriate to my students' ability level?

For the Classroom

If the manner in which you present a problem influences both how your students process this information and their responses to it, then the classroom implications are far-reaching (Tennure, 1986). An initial question that requires answering relates to the developmental characteristics of our students. It is one thing to state that our students use representations, either through verbal processes and/or mental imagery, or that certain organizational principles govern their perceptions. It is quite another thing to state that the nature of our students' responses are influenced by the manner in which we **frame** material.

Students' Decision Making

Addressing this question, Krouse (1986) studied 90 students, 30 each from grades one, three, and six (48 boys, 42 girls). Employing the *Concept Assessment Kit (Conservation)* and a variety of Tversky-Kahneman tasks, Krouse sought to determine if any relationship existed between children's decision-making behavior (as determined by Tversky-Kahneman tasks) and certain variables: educational level, level of cognitive development, sex of child.

Though no sex differences appeared and level of cognitive development was not significant, Krouse found that educational level made a difference. Third and sixth graders demonstrated the same variations in decision-making as adults, a particularly interesting finding in the light of cognitive theory. Recalling our discussion of attention, perception, representation, classification, and memory, we could conclude, not surprisingly, that our students' processing capacities are fairly restricted during the early years. To what do young children attend? Are they capable of discriminating loss of money from loss of object, or is it just something "I lost"?

Younger students (preschoolers to the early elementary grades (1, 2) could not judge their mental capabilities as accurately as the older students, an ability that gradually and consistently improves during the elementary school years. Whatever the reason, a developmental shift seems to occur around the third grade, a finding that reinforces the concern you should have for carefully framing material during instruction.

Conclusion

With cognitive psychology's long and rich tradition, its emergence as a popular explanation of human behavior should come as no surprise. Some of the leading figures in the history of psychology have made major contributions to our knowledge of cognition. The study of memory, in particular, has been enriched by their work.

Research techniques that have become increasingly sophisticated have led to a greater comprehension of the meaning of representation, leading to a recognition that individuals may depend on different modes to represent. Cognitive research into perceiving and categorizing have also made us aware of various means of improving our students' skills. Recent investigations into our decision-making strategies promise even more exciting insights into the cognitive processes we use, both in and out of the classroom.

From our perspective, the educational implications to be derived from cognitive psychology are enormous. Not only do we benefit from a greater understanding of human behavior, but we also gain additional practical suggestions for improving our students' learning.

Chapter Highlights

The Meaning of Cognitive Psychology

- The concept of representation is basic to an understanding of cognitive psychology.
- We attend, perceive, and reason, and these cognitive activities affect our behavior.

The Emergence of Cognitive Psychology

- Cognitive psychology has a long and rich tradition, with its roots in many disciplines.
- Among modern cognitive psychologists, Jerome Bruner has been particularly influential.
- Bruner's studies on perception and thought have been landmarks in modern cognitive psychology.
- Studies of memory have long fascinated cognitive psychologists because of its critical role in thought and decision-making.

The Importance of Information Processing

- Representation, which is at the heart of information processing, is the manner in which information is recorded or expressed.

- No matter how data are represented, the information remains the same; this is called the content of representation.
- The different ways that information can be expressed are called the representational code; these codes may be either mental or verbal.

The Role of Perception

- Perceiving is an active process demanding our involvement with the objects, events, and people in our environment.
- The active process of perception helps us to give information from our environment.
- Helping students structure, or organize, their environment aids their perceptual processes, thus furthering learning.

How Our Students Categorize

- The better that students categorize (form classes and put information in these categories) the more efficient learners they become.

Key Terms

Advance organizers
Anchoring ideas
Conjunctive concepts
Discovery learning
Disjunctive concepts
Episodic memory
Forgetting
Frame
Levels of processing
Long-term store
Meaningful learning
Mental images
Mental representation
Metacognition
Metacognitive experience
Metacognitive knowledge
Perception
Prior knowledge
Recall
Recognition
Relational concepts
Reminiscence
Representation
Retrieval
Schema (schemata)
Semantic memory
Sensory register
Short-term store
Storage

Suggested Readings

Bruner, J. (1983). *In search of mind.* New York: Harper and Row. The autobiography of one of the leading cognitive psychologists of our time. Following his life in this charming paperback is also an excursion through the history of cognitive psychology.

Gardner, H. (1986). *The mind's new science.* New York: Basic. One of the best single summaries of the field of cognitive psychology, past, present, and projected. Available in paperback, it is a good example of Gardner's ability to translate complex ideas into simple language with no loss of meaning.

Glover, J. A., Ronning, R. R., & Bruning, R. H. (1990). *Cognitive psychology for teachers.* New York: Macmillan. This book is designed to provide teachers a solid foundation in cognitive psychology and includes both a discussion of introductory issues and a cognitive approach to subject-matter instruction.

Miller, G. (1956). The magical number seven, plus or minus two. *Psychological Review, 63,* 81-97. Make every effort to read this fascinating article that is a milestone in the history of cognitive psychology. Your library should have this issue.

Thinking and the Teaching of Critical Thinking Skills

W alter Grimes, the superintendent of schools, had the assistant superintendents and principals gathered in his office for a meeting as a follow-up to the memo he had circulated concerning a thinking skills program. There was unanimous support in the group for the idea. Everyone realized that given the rapid changes that students faced in their daily lives, they needed help to prepare for unique challenges.

The superintendent had asked the assistants to prepare a report that would be discussed at this meeting. His only charge to them was to make sure that it was a "solid program." In this, he was reflecting a concern that with the growing popularity of incorporating thinking skills in the classroom, some superficial programs would appear.

The assistant superintendents made their presentations. Jack Cunningham spoke of the need to have any thinking skills work rooted in a sound scientific, philosophical, and educational base. Harry Walker addressed the issue of relating any program to intellectual skills. Helen Turnbul talked about the various taxonomies of thinking skills currently available and the possibility of adapting them for individual usage. Finally, Alice Cury outlined the important points of several outstanding programs.

It was a lengthy meeting, but the principals recognized the significance of the topic and began to ask specific questions.
Will there be a formal program?
How can we insure teacher cooperation?
Have any of these programs been used elsewhere?
How much time would be allotted?
Were there materials available for distribution?

They all agreed, however, that a thinking skills program could be a significant way of helping their students adapt to change.

A dministrators, teachers, and parents are not shocked to be told that we are living in an age of enormous and rapid change. In the meeting between Walter Grimes and his assistants, several issues arose that will guide our work in this chapter

As our society moves from an industrial base to one committed to an information technology, the skills that our students need to adapt to these new directions likewise change. Unless teachers equip themselves with the ability to teach innovative skills, their students will be woefully unprepared to meet new demands. If the reports discussed in chapter 1 are accurate, and repeated evidence testifies to their accuracy, our concerns about these new skills become more pressing.

After a general discussion of thinking skills, the topics that will occupy our attention for the remainder of the chapter are the following:

1. What is the role of the brain in relation to thinking skills?
2. Does intelligence have a special meaning for thinking skills?
3. Are there interpretations of thinking skills that meet the above criteria?
4. What kind of programs have been devised to further the acquisition of thinking skills?
5. Are there specific suggestions that will help in teaching this subject?

When you complete your reading of this chapter, you should be able to:

- identify those strategies that help students acquire fundamental facts and skills;
- apply those strategies that help students develop reasoning skills, concepts, and problem solving processes;
- suggest strategies that help students search for insights in their learning;
- guide students in the use of those strategies that help them to learn about relationships and how to work together, with humor, enthusiasm, and a tolerance for ambiguity.

Think for a moment about the high school dropout rate: Estimates are that 25 percent of the 14–18-year-old population no longer attend school. These ex-students now lack the skills needed to advance in today's markets; the numbers of students unprepared to cope with changing conditions must be reduced by a concerted effort to have our school population equipped with those skills that will enable them to adapt to change.

"I don't get it! They make us learn reading, writing, and arithmetic to prepare us for a world of videotapes, computer terminals, and calculators!"

H. Schwadron in Phi Delta Kappan.

Thinking Skills

Thinking skills (or simply critical thinking) have infused educators with an enthusiasm for both their ultimate value and present utility. Since an information technology is marked by a swift proliferation of knowledge, mastery of available content will not suffice once our students leave school and attempt to become productive citizens. Rather, they need skills and strategies that will enable them to adapt to constant change. That is, critical thinkers are self-correcting; they discover their own weaknesses and act to remove obstacles and faults (Lipman, 1987).

As stated in the influential report *Educating Americans for the 21st Century,* schools must return to basics, but not merely the basics of the past: communication skills and problem solving skills are the "thinking" tools needed in a technological society. An examination of thinking skills and methods of teaching students to think critically will occupy us for the remainder of the chapter.

Critical Thinking: A Definition

Two definitions of **critical thinking** will be offered here as a reference for our work. The first is offered by Robert Ennis and is rooted in philosophy.

Critical thinking is reasonable reflective thinking that is focused on deciding what to believe or do (Ennis, 1987, p. 10). Ennis believes that five key qualities are inherent in this definition: *practical, reflective, reasonable, belief, and action.* Thus critical thinking becomes an activity, both practical and reflective, that has reasonable belief or action as its goal. When we come to investigate the skills that emerge from this definition, we'll discover that Ennis' definition includes dispositions as well as abilities.

The second definition is proposed by Robert Sternberg and reflects Sternberg's psychological concerns about thinking and intelligence.

> Critical thinking comprises the mental processes, strategies, and representations people use to solve problems, make decisions, and learn new concepts (Sternberg, 1985, p. 46).

As Sternberg notes, his definition emerges from a psychological analysis of critical thinking, especially as it is related to intelligence. Tracing Sternberg's view of intelligence will help us to discover those skills that seem most closely associated with critical thinking.

As we have seen thus far, critical thinking entails the judicious use of a set of skills that will be at the heart of our discussion. Another topic that applies to both the principal's dilemma and your thinking about claims is the role of knowledge. The more knowledge that students possess about any topic, the better their thinking.

As an example of the key role of knowledge consider a classic study devised by deGroot (1965), who was fascinated by the clearly superior play of expert chess masters compared to less accomplished players. Initially deGroot believed that the experts could think of more possible moves and could think further ahead, thus exploiting the weaknesses of opponents. He had both masters and those less accomplished attempt to plan the next move in an actual game while they thought aloud. What do you think happened?

Circle the letter of the correct answer.

a.	The masters thought further ahead.	T	F
b.	The masters planned more moves.	T	F
c.	Both of the above are true.	T	F
d.	None of the above is true.	T	F

If you circled d, you were correct. Contrary to deGroot's expectations, the masters used neither of these strategies; rather their initial choice of moves seemed far superior to the others. Their experience provided the knowledge that let them devise a superior first move.

Finally, before we commence our actual work, recall that in the chapter opening we saw a superintendent of schools discussing thinking skills with his associates. Their worry about "solid" programs is timely. The topic of thinking skills is "hot" today, and a real danger exists that this serious and urgently needed topic could become a fad and quickly be relegated to obscurity. One way of avoiding this fate is to accept—in whole or part depend-

Focus on Teachers

Reacting to a Claim

Many of the situations we encounter in our daily lives involve claims. Claims are statements that are either true or false (Moore & Parker, 1986). Moore and Parker believe that our ability to accept, reject, or suspend judgment about a claim defines critical thinking. A claim serves one of three purposes: to convey information, to affect our attitudes, or to influence our behavior. These are so intertwined that occasionally it is impossible to distinguish them.

Now let's assume that you are a sixth-grade teacher, and several computers were sent to your building as part of the new computer curriculum. Accompanying the shipment was a memo from the superintendent regarding security. Two days later the computers are stolen, and the computer program is inescapably delayed.

One of your angry colleagues asks the principal's secretary if the principal read the memo. The reply:

> He didn't have a chance to read the entire report; after all, it was six double-spaced pages.

Obviously the secretary is attempting to defend the principal by making a claim. What was the claim? Do you accept it? Why? Why not? Certainly the excuse seems weak; either the principal was negligent, a slow reader, or too busy to respond to an important issue. You must decide if the reasons behind the claim are credible and, if not, if there are any unstated reasons that would cause you to accept the claim.

ing on how you evaluate their claims—*only those theories that have a solid philosophical and/or scientific basis.* The interpretations of thinking skills presented in this chapter are solidly rooted in a philosophical or psychological basis.

The Brain and Thinking

We begin by asking a fundamental question: Can there be learning, developing, and thinking without a biological substrate? Although no one would argue against this premise, considerable controversy arises when we speculate about the relationship between brain and mind, that is, thinking.

For an overview of basic brain anatomy examine Figure 8.1, keeping in mind the relationship of brain location to function. Note the basic brain areas identified by lobe; function has also been assigned to the various areas.

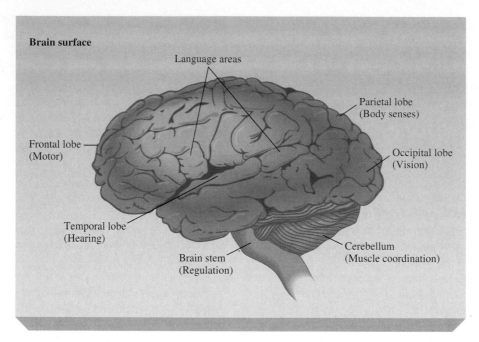

Figure 8.1
Brain and function.

Brain and Mind: The Relationship

Until recently, extreme positions have been the rule when it comes to discussing the brain-mind relationship. Philosophical advocates have virtually ignored the existence of brain, and more currently physiologists and biologists have insisted that mind is nothing more than a system of connecting neurons. Rose (1987) raised the question: How are data transformed from a series of electrical signals passing along particular nerves to central brain regions where they interact with one another, thus producing certain kinds of responses? One attempt to answer this question was proposed by Alexander Luria.

Luria's Work

The Russian neuropsychologist Alexander Luria (1980) proposed a less extreme but still neurological view. Intellectual activity begins with analyzing the conditions of the task and then identifying its most important elements. For example, Luria (1973) traces the thinking process through several stages.

- Thinking begins only when a person is motivated to solve a problem for which there is no ready solution. When students recognize problems and realize that they have the tools to solve them, their motivation remains high.
- The second stage is not an attempt to solve the problem immediately. Rather, it entails the restraint of impulsive responses. Any possible solutions must be carefully investigated. We have commented previously on the need to identify the problem's basic elements.
- Next is the selection of what seems to be the most satisfactory alternative and the creation of a general plan. Students must be taught to pause, use the critical elements they have identified, and take the time to plan for a solution.
- Finally, the methods and operations of the proposed solution must be put into action. Does it work? Have I reached a satisfactory solution?

Neuropsychological deficits differentiate specific aspects of the brain-mind relationship. Noting that lesions in different cerebral locations cause different types of intellectual disturbances, Luria describes the impact of frontal zone lesions on the ability to formulate plans and notes that such patients manifest an inability to form a preliminary basic plan of action. Any system of connections that arises will be random, having lost its goal-directed and selective character.

This testimony to the relationship between brain and mind establishes a firm rationale for the need to include information about brain functioning in our analysis of thinking skills. We'll now examine those brain characteristics (plasticity, pattern matching, lateralization, and learning) that appear particularly suited to expand our views of thinking.

Plasticity

Human beings show amazing resiliency, which is the meaning of **plasticity**; recovery from insult has been a well-documented fact of biological and psychological research. Yet the limits of plasticity are not infinite, and thus we are faced with a dilemma: Under what conditions will children and adults recover from damage? As you can well imagine, the research and literature that have addressed this problem are enormous.

Plasticity, as used here, implies flexibility or resiliency. In the current psychological climate, plasticity is contrasted with continuity. What stand you take on the meaning of these terms has important implications that extend well beyond the home and the classroom. Consider, for example, those that believe in continuity: Whatever happens to a child leaves an indelible mark; the damage will be continuous for that child's life. Why, then, should you support government programs, costing millions of dollars, for the relief of early disadvantage if there can be no relief? Adherents of plasticity take exactly the opposite viewpoint: Since human beings demonstrate tremendous recuperative powers, refusal to undertake such efforts border on the criminal. The child-rearing, educational, economic, and political consequences of either of these positions spread throughout the entire fabric of our society.

Pattern Matching

In chapter 7, when we examined cognitive explanations of learning, constant reference was made to the **pattern match** between our cognitive capacities and the external world. Here we address the role of the brain in the process since pattern detection seems to be an inherent function of the brain. In fact, some authors (Caine & Caine, 1990) believe that the brain resists having meaningless patterns imposed on it.

Hubel (1979), discussing how the brain organizes information (by patterns), noted that, at the input end, the brain is primarily preoccupied with extracting from the outside world information that is biologically interesting. At the output end, nerve impulses stimulate behavioral responses. What happens between input and output remains vague, and, as Hubel stated, understanding the neural mechanisms that explain perception (pattern matching) remains a major goal.

Hart (1983), commenting on the brain's tendency to match patterns, stated that the brain detects, constructs, and elaborates patterns as a basic, built-in, natural function. He believes that there is no concept, no fact in education, more important than the brain's pattern matching function because it is at the heart of all learning.

Hart (1983, p. 67) summarized his thinking about the brain's pattern matching ability as follows:

- The brain is naturally a pattern matcher, even in infants.
- Pattern matching utilizes both specific elements and relationships and is aided by the effective use of clues.
- Negative clues play an important role since they instantly alert the brain that "something is wrong."
- The brain uses clues in a probabilistic manner; that is, we use a minimum number of clues to reach a correct decision or solution.
- Pattern matching depends on the experiences you bring to any situation; the more clues we recognize, the quicker the match.
- Patterns are continually changing to meet the demands of new experiences.

Since our brain seems predisposed to search for patterns, you can help your students to improve their classroom performance by using what we know of pattern matching. For example, one technique is to have them develop chronological pattern guides. After students have read a story (or page or paragraph), give them a mixed series of statements and ask them to arrange these statements in the order in which they appeared in the story. Students react well to such exercises because they are predisposed to identify patterns. For example, daydreaming is a form of patterning, as is critical thinking. Teaching that attempts to present information in a way that helps their brains to extract patterns—such as an integrated curriculum, thematic teaching, and the current interest in whole language—helps students to make sense of what they are learning (Caine & Caine, 1990).

Lateralization

Which hand do you use for writing? If you were to kick a football, would you use the leg on the same side of your body as the hand you use for writing? Pick up a pencil or ruler and assume it is a telescope. Which eye do you use? Are you using the same side of the body that you used for writing and kicking? Your answers to these questions should give you some idea of the meaning of **cerebral lateralization.**

We tend to think of the brain as a single unit, but actually it consists of two halves: the cerebral hemispheres. The two halves are connected by a bundle of nerve fibers (the corpus callosum), and the left hemisphere controls the right side of the body while the right hemisphere controls the left side of the body. Although the hemispheres seem to be almost identical, your answers to the above few questions provide clues about important differences between the two.

Figure 8.2
Lateralization of handedness.

These differences, called **functional asymmetry,** offer insight to your brain's organization. If you are right-handed, for example, your left cerebral hemisphere is lateralized for handedness and also for control of your speech. You are "left lateralized." There is general agreement today that although there may be some rationale for the distinction between left and right hemispheric dominance, both hemispheres are involved in all activities (Caine & Caine, 1990). Figure 8.2 illustrates the relationship between one's left and right hemispheres and handedness.

Much of our knowledge of cerebral lateralization has resulted from brain damaged patients. Patients with left hemisphere damage, for example, typically encounter speech difficulties; damage to the right hemisphere frequently causes perceptual and attentional disorders. The right hemisphere has often been relegated to a "minor" position because as humans we rely so heavily on language that the left hemisphere came to be thought of as the dominant or "major" hemisphere. Today, however, much importance has been placed on the right hemisphere's control of visual and spatial activities.

As interesting as these data are, our concern must focus mainly on developmental and educational implications. Data clearly suggest functional asymmetry between the hemispheres at all ages and between both sexes. Rourke, Bakker, Fisk, and Strang (1983) reported an age-related shift in scanning letters from LFA (left field advantage) to RFA (right field advantage). The shift occurred from approximately 6 to 7 years to 11 to 12 years. They give the example of presenting both a seven-year-old and a fourteen-year-old with a simple sentence. Rourke and his colleagues believe that these children probably generate different strategies to process the sentence. They also doubt that this processing occurs in the same brain structures. The authors speculate that the younger child is likely to respond to the visual configuration of the sentence, thus signalling visual-spatial predominance (right hemisphere). The older reader, however, probably responds, almost automatically, with a perceptual analysis, thus indicating greater syntactical and semantic awareness (left hemisphere).

Lateralization in the Classroom

Can we draw implications from the lateralization literature with regard to education? Answering this question requires two significant considerations.

1. *Are there sex differences that are definitely related to lateralization?* Without reviewing the enormous literature addressed to this question, we can safely state that sex differences exist in certain abilities such as verbal and spatial skills. Females generally seem superior in anything relating to language, while males excel in spatial tasks. But these differences tell us nothing about why they exist. They may result from either biological or cultural factors, or both. The differences are too tenuous and too subject to a variety of interpretations (Caine & Caine, 1990).

    Our interest, however, focuses on one question: Should these demonstrated differences dictate different instructional practices for both sexes? Though these research results should be taken into consideration, they should not be the basis for curriculum construction or different instructional techniques. For one thing, males and females are much more alike in brain functioning than they are different; some women have greater spatial ability than men, and some men have greater language skills than women. Second, we are a nation that cultivates individual differences and should foster unique talents.

2. *To what extent, then, should education recognize these differences?* Since the results of lateralization studies have become known, criticism has been directed at the schools for "teaching to the left hemisphere." Reading, writing, and mathematics all favor logical, sequential processing—left hemisphere functions. Should we teach to the right hemisphere?

Although the temptation to teach for right hemispheric involvement is great, research to date remains vague as to how much involvement of either hemisphere is present in the activities of the other—how much one interferes with the other. Perhaps we can best conclude that acceptance of current findings means that we should accept the reality of greater or lesser hemispheric activity in any particular activity but also be aware that human activity, especially learning, entails the commitment of both hemispheres. Once again, the best advice you can follow to maintain positive relationships with your students is to teach to their individual needs.

One way of integrating current knowledge of lateralization into the curriculum is to become aware of your reliance on verbal directions (Grady, 1984). Most teachers depend heavily on linear tasks, such as having students respond to specific questions or following directions. Try also to present material graphically, in visual form, and encourage students to express their understanding of a topic in a creative manner.

Learning

Regardless of hemispheric lateralization and our efforts to capitalize on current findings, we can safely state that classroom learning finds its biological base in the cerebral cortex. For the successful functioning of such complex mental processes as perception, cognition, and decision-making, perfectly tuned and smoothly operating synapses are essential.

What seems to distinguish the human brain is the variety of specialized activities it is capable of learning (Geschwind, 1979). The difficulty still facing investigators lies in the unexplored gap between the psychological reality of learning and knowledge about the structure, biochemistry, and physiology of the brain. One possible approach to bridging this gap would be to determine if brain cells undergo change because of learning.

Hyden (1985) discovered, through animal research, that during and after learning both brain cells and their synapses show an increase in protein production. Hyden believed that a "wave of protein synthesis" pervades the brain at learning; that is, system changes occur in brain cell protein during learning. He then hypothesized that when learning begins, inner and outer stimuli cause electrical changes in the nervous system that induce the production of specific proteins in the brain. Calcium production also increases.

What also should interest us are the developmental changes that occur in brain structures—size, number of connections, and changes in such brain support systems as the glial cells. The growth of intellectual capacity in our students undoubtedly matches the brain's anatomical and biochemical changes. Although this match still lacks biological proof, the brain's role in learning seems well-established and testifies to the need for comprehensive theory of thinking to acknowledge a brain basis.

For example, all teachers know that some students prefer to learn with noise surrounding them, or while they move around, talk to others, or just fidget. They don't act in this manner to irritate a teacher. They are, however, responding to signals from their central nervous systems (Garger, 1990). Frequently a student's approach to learning (for example, wanting to listen to music while studying) is a neurophysiological response.

Thinking Skills and Multicultural Students

You may occasionally be thwarted by what appears to be unrelated answers by multicultural students, but remember one guiding principle: Their perception of the problem may be quite different from yours (Rogoff, 1990). For example, Greenfield (1966) conducted a series of studies among the Wolof of Senegal in which she investigated their attainment of Piagetian conservation abilities. Greenfield *found that the manner of questioning influenced children's answers.* When children were asked about the amount of water in two identical beakers, Greenfield noticed that if the question was asked directly—Why do you think this glass has more than the other?—she seldom received an answer. When she asked the question in a less personal manner—Why is this true?—the children answered easily and correctly.

Greenfield also discovered that *the children's reasoning for non-conservation answers was related to the person who poured the water* and not to the logic of the problem. When the experimenter poured the liquid into a new container, 25 percent of the youngsters said the new container had more because the adult poured it. When the children themselves poured the liquid, 70 percent of the six- and seven-year-olds gave conservation answers. Thus when children poured the water, their conservation answers didn't depend upon a cultural tendency to attribute power to an adult.

TEACHER ⟷ STUDENT
INTERACTIONS

The Brain and Thinking Skills

1. Thinking ability is closely linked to its biological basis.
   • Given different rates of maturation, students will differ in their ability to process subject matter content. Be on the lookout for those students who have trouble with abstract topics and adjust your teaching methods accordingly. Don't hesitate to provide considerable visual material and "hands-on" experiences.
   • The brain continually searches for patterns, and students who are disorganized in their study habits are at a disadvantage. Help these students by having them write simple linear outlines, which should start them thinking about patterns. Since learning styles differ, try other techniques such as using arrows, graphs, webs, and a series of dots to show how ideas are connected; use color to illustrate similar meanings of words and passages.
   • Encourage students to react to patterns by the types of visual displays you have in the classroom. Use charts, pictures, and art work to emphasize the importance of searching for patterns.
   • Balance your teaching methods and use teaching materials in a variety of ways that appeal to both visual and verbal processing.

2. Efforts to improve student performance or introduce remedial work should reflect the resiliency of your students.
   • Research results have shown that a supportive environment can help to ease the impact of a particular deficit. As much as you can, adapt your classroom to your students' needs. Give students who do better in an informal setting assignments that permit them, with your guidance, to work at their own pace with few directions and deadlines. The point here is to address their unique learning preferences and subject weaknesses by as individualized an approach as you can devise.
   • Some students seem to prefer more structure in their work. Use small, carefully organized, sequential steps. Check their comprehension at each step.
   • In your efforts to help students work to their potential, use many different teaching techniques—text, reading,

filmstrips, tapes, discussion, writing assignments, games, art, and music to appeal to them visually, verbally, and motorically.
   • As part of a warm, supportive environment, provide as much positive reinforcement as possible to enhance their self-esteem. Try to reinforce positively in front of the group when you can—**but** be sure your behavior is realistic, that you offer deserved reinforcement.

3. Teachers can utilize differences in their students' learning styles to make classroom work as meaningful as possible for individual students.
   • Present a problem to your group: Mr. Lewis' variety store is losing business to a new supermarket two blocks away. What should he do to remain in business? Have students play the role of Mr. Lewis and observe their strategies for solving the problem, which will help you to identify specific learning styles.
   • Now, using their answers, develop charts, diagrams, and any pertinent visual and outline their strategies. As you do, point out the strengths and weaknesses of each: This part is good; this part won't work—why? What will this accomplish? In this way you can make them aware of what they do best and how they can use this strength in all of their work.
   • For those students who seem to learn better visually, help them by using color. For example, give them colored cards in which each card represents a part of speech (noun, verb, etc.). Now have them analyze stories by the color of the cards. You have helped them to become familiar with parts of speech and with the way that words "work."
   • Have students select a topic related to current work in class and ask them to demonstrate how they would teach it. What is the best way to teach it—verbally, visually, formally, or informally? Why? How will they pace it? Will they allow questions? What is the purpose of their presentation? How will they have their classmates follow up on their lesson? When they are finished, ask them what they learned about themselves and the topic.

Research has consistently upheld this finding: No matter how diverse the cultural group, evidence testifies to the existence of commonly held cognitive abilities (Miller-Jones, 1989). What previously obscured this fact was a failure to recognize the importance of the experimental method, as we have just seen in Greenfield's work. Once a cognitive task was presented in a culturally

appropriate way, similar cognitive skills (memory, classification) appeared.

When we translate these and similar findings to our classrooms, we find the same cultural tendencies at work. Problems with language, trouble with standardized tests, and difficulties with a novel environment all translate into behavior that can too easily be interpreted as deficient. Yet when teachers view these students as assets, and are able to communicate with them, their thinking skills are on a par with other students.

What is needed? We need schools that accept diversity, encourage and integrate the cultures, languages, and backgrounds of their students, and incorporate the curriculum and the teaching strategies appropriate to the vast range of learning styles and cultures that are found in our multiethnic, multiracial society (Olsen, 1988, p. 218).

Intelligence and Thinking

Having established the connection between thinking and its biological base, the brain, we now turn our attention to the relationship between intelligence and thinking. We have all taken cognitive abilities tests and speculated about their results in comparison to our own assessment of our potential. You probably think exactly the same way about your students: Are they working to potential? How can I help them to improve their performance?

But if we are to help students improve their performance on IQ tests, achieve better grades, and prepare for life's problems, we would be wise not to be trapped by traditional views of intelligence. If, by directly teaching thinking skills, we hope to aid our students, we must turn to a broader, more qualitative view of intelligence.

Intelligence Tests: Some Unresolved Issues

Enthusiasm for psychometric interpretations of intelligence dimmed when IQ tests failed to resolve several critical issues and apparently produced conflicting outcomes concerning the relationship between intelligence (or aptitude) and learning performance. For example, advocates of intelligence testing claimed that *these instruments measured an individual's capacity or innate potential for learning,* a remarkable accomplishment since the claim implied that significant variables such as education or socioeconomic status did not affect IQ test scores. Results, however, consistently have shown that more education and higher social class are the inevitable partners of rising intelligence test scores.

A second issue plaguing the intelligence testing movement concerns the *nature versus nurture (heredity vs. environment) controversy.* To what extent do test scores indicate genetic influences and to what extent environmental forces? The history of psychology is marked by this controversy with opinion at one time leaning heavily toward the hereditarian view and at another to the environmental view. An intensely emotional ques-

tion, it has been accompanied by a distressing tendency to confuse individual differences in ability with group differences: genetic superiority or inferiority then become confused with race or color. If the measurement of pure capacity eludes detection by IQ tests, then the heredity-environment controversy becomes meaningless.

The third issue relates directly to learning: *There is apparently a low correlation between aptitude scores and learning.* During the first few decades of this century, intelligence was widely equated with learning ability. After the early enthusiasm for mental tests wore off about 1930, the concept of a general ability has been under recurrent challenge. Noting that it has become fashionable to criticize the use of general ability or intelligence tests—criticism so intense that it has occasionally caused the elimination of these tests in some public schools—Cronbach and Snow believe that they have found "nearly ubiquitous evidence that general measures predict amount learned or rate of learning or both" (1977, p. 496).

With this in mind, let's turn to three current interpretations of intelligence that have particular relevance for the teaching of thinking skills. These include Sternberg's Triarchic Model, Gardner's Multiple Intelligences, and Perkins' Thinking Frames.

Sternberg's Triarchic Model of Intelligence

Any explanation of intelligence must be able to do three things (Sternberg, 1986, 1987, 1988): (a) It should be able to relate intelligence to an individual's internal world and explain what happens when a person thinks intelligently; (b) Any theory of intelligence must accept the relation between the external world and that person's intelligence and explain how intelligence functions in the "real world" and (c) Any intellectual theory must relate intelligence to the individual's experiences.

Sternberg believes that intellectual skills and thinking skills are inseparable, although there is more to intelligence than thinking. With this as background, Sternberg developed a **triarchic theory of intelligence** consisting of three elements designed to explain each of his three ideas of what intelligence "should do." He has labeled these three elements: *componential, experiential, and contextual.* Let's examine each of these components in some detail.

1. *Componential.* Sternberg identifies three types of information-processing components that constitute the initial segment of our intelligence: metacomponents, performance components, and knowledge-acquisition components.

Robert Sternberg, a cognitive psychologist and leading theorist concerning human intelligence and problem solving.

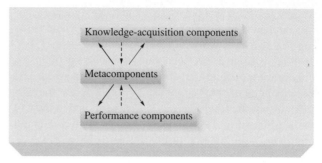

Figure 8.3
The integration of intellectual components.

a. **Metacomponents** are the executive components of intelligence used to plan, monitor, and evaluate our problem solving strategies. Sternberg (1986) suggests ways of improving our strategies and provides sample problems to solve. These topics are discussed in more detail in chapter 9 and refer to a student's ability to identify the nature of a problem, selecting the steps necessary to solve it, devise a plan, and evaluate a solution.

b. **Performance components** help us execute the instructions of the metacomponents; they are the implementation segment of intelligence. Among the most important of these are inferring relations, applying these relations to new stimuli, and comparing attributes of stimuli. Students must learn when to use the various components and to use them in as wide a variety of situations as possible. Inference is particularly important. You hear a friend is in the hospital and infer that she is ill or injured. Could she have taken a job there? Students should learn that they need as much information as possible before making any inferences. (Again, note how impulsivity works against a student's achievement.)

c. **Knowledge-acquisition components** refer primarily to our ability to acquire and use language, thus enabling us to seize on contextual cues in solving problems. The key here is to help students determine which facts are pertinent. Sternberg (1988) identified three crucial processes: (a) *selective encoding,* in which you detect relevant facts that are not immediately obvious. In the discovery of penicillin, for example, Fleming noticed that although mold had ruined his experiment, it had also killed the bacteria; (b) *selective combination,* in which you see a way of combining unrelated facts; and (c) *selective comparison* in which you combine old and new information. For example, a teacher who conducts his class according to cognitive principles encounters a student who is not doing well with these methods. He recalls his educational psychology course of a few years ago and that the instructor, in discussing behaviorism, mentioned that some students need a carefully planned reinforcement schedule.

Sternberg notes that these three components are highly interactive: planning, acting, providing feedback, and generally acting in tandem. Figure 8.3 illustrates the integration of these three components.

2. *Experiential.* The second aspect of intelligence that Sternberg identified is experiential, which is that point in our experiences where intelligence becomes most critically involved. Our experiences increase our ability to deal with novel tasks and to make information processing more automatic. In other words, there are times in which our intelligence must deal with novelty, with new conceptual systems, when our traditional mode of intellectual functioning is inadequate. For example, reading about an electric motor doesn't mean you can repair it. You must experience the novelty of actually taking it apart and putting it together again. These situations demand creative responses. There are other times and situations, however, when to pause

and analyze each element retards intellectual functioning. Reading is a good example; to ponder each letter would be devastating. Needed are those automatic processes that enable us to solve complex problems.

3. *Contextual.* The third aspect of intelligence in Sternberg's model specifies the functions to which components are applied in coping with the external world (Sternberg, 1987, p. 198). In other words, the major thrust of contextual intelligence is adaptation. Adaptation as used here has three connotations: (a) *adaptation to existing environments* so that we may fit better into our environment; (b) *shaping existing environments,* which implies changing the present environment to more suitably meet your needs; and (c) *selecting new environments,* which involves evaluation of present environments and selection of a new, more favorable environment.

If you apply these descriptions to yourself and others whom you know, you probably can identify which aspect of intelligence is predominant. For example, those who excel in analytic thinking usually do quite well on traditional IQ tests. Their componential aspect seems to eclipse the others. We can draw similar conclusions about those who exhibit high creativity, or those who always seem to know "the right thing to do." Recognizing these individual differences inflicts no damage on Sternberg's insistence on the integrated nature of the triarchic model; rather it recognizes our unique abilities as real and inevitable.

Sternberg devised a program for teaching to improve intellectual skills (see especially Sternberg (1986). The program consists of five parts. *The initial section* provides background information and discusses the triarchic theory of intelligence. *The second phase* provides training materials pertinent to those intellectual skills related to the individual's internal world (the metacomponents, performance components, and knowledge-acquisition components). Sternberg offers an example of how these components act together. Consider the following problem.

Washington: 1 as Lincoln: 5 12 16 20

Metacomponents identify the nature of the problem and determine the steps necessary to solve it. (If Washington was the first president, Lincoln was the?) Performance components then activate these steps, although the knowledge acquisition components had been previously acquired; that is, we had earlier learned how to use these steps (add, multiply, subtract, divide, or, in our example, the order of the presidents). *The third part* of the program furnishes instruction and practice on varied problems. *The fourth segment* contains examples and exercises of

Howard Gardner, a psychologist who has offered an appealing theory of multiple intelligences.

intelligence applied to our everyday lives. Sternberg's intent here is to stress the function of intellectual skills in daily living and not merely in the classroom. *The fifth segment* discusses motivational and emotional blocks. Among the blocks identified are lack of perseverance, inability to complete tasks, too little or too much self-confidence, and lack of impulse control.

Though it is too early to judge the impact of Sternberg's model, the triarchic theory offers promising insights into qualitative intelligence as long as Sternberg resists the temptation to become too mechanistic as he moves into the testing side of the model and refuses to allow its three segments to become too rigid.

Gardner and Multiple Intelligences

Our second link between intelligence and thinking skills is Howard Gardner's theory of **multiple intelligences** (1983, 1985, 1991). Gardner's speculations are particularly fascinating since any model of thinking skills contains several basics that reflect intellectual ability. But what is especially intriguing is that the same individual who can form penetrating mathematical insights may be quite baffled by the most obvious musical clues. Gardner's ideas, though still theoretical, attempt to address this issue.

Identifying Intelligences

Gardner begins by noting that his theory of multiple intelligences accepts a cultural input into intelligence as well as its biological basis. Next Gardner explains his eight criteria for identifying any intelligence.

1 *Potential isolation by brain damage.* If brain damage can destroy a particular ability, it seems likely that this ability is not dependent on any other ability.

2. *Existence of exceptional populations.* Those individuals who exhibit outstanding but uneven abilities testify to a particular ability. For example, one child may be mathematically precocious, with other abilities not at the same level. The idiot savant is another example, those individuals who may exhibit a single prodigious ability and who may otherwise be mentally retarded.

3. *Core operations.* These include basic information-processing operations that are highly unique to a particular ability. The gifted athlete for example, evaluates multiple stimuli, judges their value, and instantly communicates information to the body.

4. *A distinctive developmental history.* Any intelligence must possess discernible developmental stages through which individuals pass, some remaining at low levels of expertise while others pass on to high levels of performance.

5. *An evolutionary history.* Antecedents of the intelligence should be able to be identified in other species. These may appear as discrete elements in other species and be integrated only in humans.

6. *Experimental evidence.* Precise methodology must be available to study the details of the particular intelligence. In this way, the autonomy of the intelligence may be probed; do the facts support the theory?

7. *Support from psychometric findings.* Standardized tests (similar to the IQ test) offer clues as to the existence of any intelligence when test items correlate with some tasks and not others.

8. *Susceptibility to encoding in a symbol system.* There must be some means of capturing the information content in an intelligence.

The Seven Intelligences

Using the above criteria, Gardner goes on to identify seven intelligences that are relatively autonomous. He believes that human cognitive competence is better described as a set of abilities, talents, or mental skills, which we call "intelligence." Everyone possesses each of these skills to some extent, but we differ in the degree of skill and how we combine them. Here are Gardner's seven types of intelligence.

1. *Linguistic intelligence.* The first of Gardner's intelligences to meet these criteria is language. For example we can trace the effects of damage to the language areas of the brain; we can identify the core operations of any language: phonology, syntax, semantics, and pragmatics; its developmental history has been well-documented and supported by empirical investigations. Gardner considers language a preeminent instance of human intelligence.

2. *Musical intelligence.* One has only to consider the talent and career of a Yehudi Menuhin to realize that there is something special about music. At three years of age, Menuhin became fascinated by music and by age ten he had been performing on the international stage. The early appearance of musical ability suggests some kind of biological preparedness. The right hemisphere of the brain seems particularly important for music, and musical notation clearly indicates a basic symbol system. Though musical skill usually is not considered "intelligence" in most theories, in satisfying the criteria posed by Gardner, it demands inclusion.

3. *Logical-mathematical intelligence.* Theoreticians of intelligence have so commonly accepted scientific thinking that we may safely assume that L-M intelligence completely satisfies Gardner's criteria.

4. *Spatial intelligence.* Brain research has linked spatial ability to the right side of the brain. For example, the national system of maps requires the use of symbols based on spatial abilities, which demands the involvement of spatial intelligence to interpret the data.

5. *Bodily-kinesthetic intelligence.* The left hemisphere's control of the body's right side and vice-versa is so well-known that it requires no additional comment here. The developmental schedule of bodily movements has been carefully recorded. Thus Gardner has identified the control of bodily motions and the ability to handle objects skillfully as core operations. Although the concept of "body as intelligence" may at first surprise you, Gardner notes that such feelings do not characterize other societies that cherish harmony between mind and body.

6. *Interpersonal intelligence and*

7. *Intrapersonal intelligence.* Gardner refers to these two categories as the "personal" intelligences. Interpersonal intelligence builds on a core capacity to recognize what is distinctive in others.

Table 8.1

Gardner's Intelligences

Type of Intelligence	Meaning
Linguistic	Communication; a pre-eminent example of human intelligence
Musical	Linked to brain location and a basic symbol system
Logical-mathematical	What we usually identify as "intelligence"
Spatial	Linked to brain location and utilizes symbol systems
Bodily-kinesthetic	Smooth development of bodily movements aids adjustment and adaptation
Interpersonal Intrapersonal	Linked to frontal lobe of brain; recognize what is distinctive in others

Intrapersonal intelligence utilizes a core capacity to understand one's own feelings, to discriminate among them, and to express feelings through a symbolic code. Autistic children are good examples of a deficit in this latter form of intelligence—often competent in a certain skill, they may be nearly incapable of ever referring to themselves. Table 8.1 summarizes Gardner's types of intelligences.

Unlike Sternberg, who has recently turned his attention to the testing implications that his theory suggests, Gardner has focused on the educational ramifications of multiple intelligence. Beginning with the need for mastery in a technological society, Gardner traces educational needs through these early years to the need for adolescents to be assisted in their choice of careers.

Accepting the multiple intelligence model raises questions about career choice since "intelligence" may interact in any given occupation. Although physicians obviously must bring their logical-mathematical intelligence to a high skill level, they also must master interpersonal skills in treating patients and bodily-kinesthetic skills in surgery.

To acquire a needed minimum in all intelligences and extraordinary proficiency in one or two, we must remember that instructional needs will vary throughout development. The detailed instruction needed to acquire notational systems during the early years becomes inappropriate at the upper levels. Sole reliance upon a notational system

Focus on Teachers

Ranking the Intelligences

Take a moment to read through Gardner's types of intelligences again. Now rank them by the importance you place on each.

____ Linguistic intelligence
____ Musical intelligence
____ Logical-mathematical intelligence
____ Spatial intelligence
____ Bodily-kinesthetic intelligence
____ Interpersonal intelligence
____ Intrapersonal intelligence

What do you think? Are some more relevant for teachers than others?

Check your classmates' lists. How similar are they to yours?

Are there differences between the elementary and secondary majors in the class? Had you expected this?

Are there differences within each group (elementary/secondary)?

If differences exist within groups, are they by subject?

Do your answers to these questions tell you anything about you as a teacher?

for instruction during the early years is also inappropriate since an enriched sensory environment is also suitable. Finally, Gardner believes that excessive emphasis on linguistic and logical-mathematical intelligences is short-sighted given the role that spatial, interpersonal, and bodily skills play in many career choices. Consequently, Gardner (1987) recommends that educators become "assessment specialists" and search for strengths in students indicating high levels of spatial and personal intelligences, for example.

Perkins and Thinking Frames

Perkins (1986, 1987), believing that schools must address thinking skills, states that any perspective on the teaching of thinking must confront the problem of intelligence. If for no other reason, we must decide whether those we teach are already functioning at their intellectual ceilings. Can we improve intelligence by teaching our students to think better?

Perkins urges us to avoid too narrow a view of intelligence lest we become trapped by a concept of intelligence such as that measured by IQ tests. He believes that the key question is: What psychological factors contribute to a broader, more qualitative model of intelligence? Answering his own question, he states that modern psychologists have adopted one of three concepts of intelligence:

1. **a power theory of intelligence,** which is solely dependent on the neurological efficiency of the brain, a genetic interpretation
2. **a tactical theory of intelligence,** which holds that those who think better do so because they know more tactics about how to use their minds
3. **a content theory of intelligence,** which reflects a view of intelligence as a rich knowledge base. Mastery of factual material is at the heart of thinking and problem solving.

Perkins believes that no one of these views contains all the answers about intelligence that we have been searching for; a combination of all three seems more promising. Therefore, he conceptualizes intelligence as:

Intelligence = Power + Tactics + Content

Perkins next turns his attention to ways that teaching thinking skills can improve intelligence. Noting that the schools can do little about the power side of intelligence, and perhaps have done too much in the teaching of content, Perkins focuses upon the tactics as our best hope. Stating that tactical intelligence refers to a bag of tricks, he proposes the term thinking frames to describe the "tricks that make up tactical intelligence."

David Perkins, whose studies of thinking have helped us to understand the relationship among teaching and intelligence.
Source: Harvard University

Thinking frames are representations intended to guide the process of thought by supporting, organizing, and activating that process (Perkins, 1986, p. 7). A simpler definition would be a guide to organizing and supporting thought processes (Perkins, 1987, p. 47). How can students acquire these frames? Perkins hypothesizes that we learn thinking frames through a three-stage process involving acquisition, internalization, and transfer.

- *Acquisition,* by which students encounter and transfer the basics of a frame by direct instruction, or invention. The teacher's task is to help them to form a representation of the topic.
- *Internalization,* or making the process automatic. Internalization comes about through practice on simple examples until it becomes fluent and spontaneous. Memory gradually becomes an important support, only to recede as the process becomes automatic. Meaningful practice and memory aids (see chapter 9) lead to automatic processing.
- *Transfer,* or using the frame in a wide variety of contexts. Since transfer or generalization does not occur spontaneously, we must teach for it.

TEACHER ⬌ STUDENT
INTERACTIONS

Intelligence and Thinking Skills

1. The triarchic theory of intelligence consists of componential, experiential, and contextual elements.
   - You can help students improve their thinking skills by combining their preferred learning styles with their inclination to pattern matching. Ask individual students to give you directions to their houses from the school. Some students will tell you, others will write out directions, and still others will draw you a map. Make them aware of these differences and encourage them to capitalize on their strengths.
   - Give students a list of words in which each word is somehow related to another. You are encouraging them to infer relationships. For example:

     heel
     train
     liar
     track
     feel
     rail
     ⎯⎯

     heel—feel
     train—track
     liar—rail (liar backwards)

   - Encourage your students to focus only on relevant information. Try analogies such as the following:

     Beds have sheets.

     Building is to dome as bed is to: pillow canopy hotel room

     The first statement (beds have sheets) is not relevant to the problem.

   - Frame your questions in a way that encourages your students to think creatively and hypothetically and that leads them to make judgments.

2. The theory of multiple intelligences has attracted considerable attention.
   - Help students to become comfortable with language by giving examples of how the arrangement of words can change meaning. Why are these sentences the same? Why are they different?

     The cow was hit by the helicopter.

     The helicopter hit the cow.

   - Appeal to the use of as many intelligences as possible. Assign your students to groups and ask them to draw the shape of an island. Have them put in rivers, lakes, valleys, crops, mineral deposits, and any other data you think are important. Now ask them to put in cities, transportation facilities, occupations, etc. You can use similar activities at the various grade levels by using more abstract and sophisticated analyses but, in each case, you are asking students to use their spatial, logical-mathematical, language, and personal intelligences.
   - Use varied activities that require your students to apply their different intelligences. For example:

     Play charades to reinforce the learning of people, places, and events in social studies classes.

     Start a collection of twentieth century heroes: why this person? List specific achievements, background, and relevance to the topic you're studying; defend your selection to the class.

     Select a different period of American history and have groups explain what it would have been like for a family to live in those times.

     Do the same thing for different cultures.

3. Teaching thinking skills is a means of improving tactical intelligence.
   - Don't be satisfied with questions and assignments that are restricted to data collection. Pose themes or problems that require students to make judgments, hypothesize, and react creatively.
   - Ask your students to predict what the community they're living in will be like in twenty years. Have them hypothesize, collect data, and then justify their predictions.
   - Pick a sport with which your students are familiar—for example, baseball. Divide them into teams and have each member of each team write a question about the subject(s) they're studying. You then assign a value to each question: single, double, triple, home run. Each team member takes a turn as the pitcher and "throws" a question at the opposition. You can act as scorekeeper. The students are working together, collecting data for their questions, writing the questions, and reviewing material for their answers.

Teaching About Frames

If your "thinking frames about thinking frames" are in order, you should be ready to ask how Perkins' view of intelligence and thinking can help your teaching. Anticipating this question, Perkins believes that you must consider a startling variety of thinking frames. Some are general or specific, some emphasize process versus product, and some urge structure over style.

A comprehensive program designed to cultivate thinking skills should encompass each of these types. Consequently, to evaluate your efforts to teach thinking skills, consider the following suggestions:

1. Be sure they are varied and include the three stages just mentioned.
2. Use frames that offer leverage, that specify what to do, when to do it, and how to do it with regard to definite tasks.
3. Frames that students master should help them to master other frames.
4. You should be able to teach the frame directly.
5. Examples of how to use the frame should lead to automatic performance by students.
6. Teach, teach, teach for transfer.

As Perkins notes, what happens in a classroom helps to shape minds, either by art or accident. We surely need more art and fewer accidents.

Thinking Skills: An Analysis

Now that we have established a neurological and an intellectual base for thinking skills programs and instructional suggestions, we can discuss several taxonomies of thinking skills that have been proposed. We'll consider three of the most widely accepted taxonomies.

For our purposes, three taxonomies with sound rationales and precise objectives as well as practical utility are: Benjamin Bloom's *Taxonomy of Educational Objectives—Cognitive Domain*; Robert Ennis' *Taxonomy of Critical Thinking Dispositions and Abilities,* and Arthur Costa's *Model of Critical Thinking Skills.* Each of these systems offers a solid basis for the skills it proposes: Bloom's in educational objectives, Ennis' in philosophy, and Costa's in curriculum goals.

The Bloom Taxonomy

In 1956, Benjamin Bloom and his colleagues published an enduring classification of educational goals entitled *Taxonomy of Educational Objectives, Handbook 1: Cognitive Domain.* Bloom had several goals in mind. *First,*

he believed that the taxonomy would help in curriculum construction. *Second,* it would identify certain behaviors in any plan (recall, define, compare). *Third,* it would help in the preparation of both learning experiences and evaluation devices. *Fourth,* it could serve as a tool to analyze educational processes. (See chapters 10 and 15 for additional applications of Bloom's work.)

Bloom's taxonomy, embedded in the history of educational evaluation and precise in its objectives and terminology, has enjoyed widespread acceptance and today forms the core of many thinking skills programs. The main purpose of the taxonomy is to provide a classification of the goals of our educational system (Bloom Ed., 1956, p. 1). The taxonomy consists of three major sections: the cognitive, the affective, and the psychomotor domains. Our concern here is with the cognitive taxonomy, which is divided into the six major classes listed below:

1.00 Knowledge—recall of specific facts

2.00 Comprehension—understanding what is communicated

3.00 Application—generalization and use of abstract information in concrete situations

4.00 Analysis—breakdown of a problem into subparts and detection of relationships among the parts

5.00 Synthesis—putting together parts to form a whole

6.00 Evaluation—using criteria to make judgments

Each category is further subdivided into other, more specific objectives. Bloom and his associates state that these six classes represent the hierarchical order of the different classes of objectives. The objectives of each class usually depend on the preceding classes (Bloom Ed., 1956, p. 18). Educators have found the upper levels of the taxonomy (analysis, synthesis, and evaluation) particularly helpful in constructing a taxonomy of thinking skills.

Bloom justifies the simple to complex sequence of the categories by noting that a simple behavior may become integrated with other, equally as simple behaviors, to form a more complex behavior. Addition, subtraction, and multiplication are needed to master long division. As you can see, the educational implications of the taxonomy can be quite explicit.

Educational objectives follow from the various taxonomic categories and are interpreted to specify exactly how the educative process is to change students; what precisely do I want my students to learn? The use of a taxonomy of thinking skills provides a useful organization of

Focus on Classrooms

The Taxonomy in Casablanca

As an example of how the six categories of Bloom's cognitive domain can be used as thinking skills, consider the following example:

1. *Knowledge*, as used in the taxonomy, entails the recall of specific facts. Although remembering is the key process, relating is also involved since organizing and reorganizing material is necessary to solve a problem with the specific facts you have at your disposal. For example:
   - Who played the role of Rick in *Casablanca*?
   - Who played Ilsa Lund?
   - What was the title of the famous theme song?

2. *Comprehension* represents the lowest level of understanding. You understand what is being communicated and can make use of the material. Write a brief essay in which you describe the circumstances of the story. What role did the city of Paris play in the story?

3. *Application* refers to the use of abstract thinking in particular and concrete situations; they are generalizations that can be used. In what way did Rick's sense of honesty shape the outcome of the story?

4. *Analysis* refers to the breakdown of a problem into manageable parts while simultaneously detecting relationships among the parts and discerning the manner in which they are related. An example would be deductive reasoning.

Does it seem logical to you that Captain Renault would join with Rick to fight the Nazis? How can you explain Rick's refusal to allow Ilsa Lund to remain with him in Casablanca?

5. *Synthesis* is the putting together of parts and elements to form a whole or pattern not previously evident. Generally, synthesis involves a recombination of parts of previous experience with new material to form a new whole. If Rick and Ilsa had remained together in Casablanca, what would have happened to them? If Rick had not shot and killed the Nazi officer, would circumstances have changed in Casablanca?

6. *Evaluation* refers to making value judgments, using previously determined criteria, about ideas, solutions, etc. Was Rick wrong in shooting to kill? Should all of the leading characters have been allowed to escape?

Bloom and his colleagues discovered that most schools were primarily concerned with knowledge and comprehension skills, especially recall and recognition. Most teacher-made and standardized tests focus on the three lower levels of thinking, ignoring analysis, synthesis, and evaluation, which are precisely the skills needed in adult adaptation. If you think of your own status, you will realize that most of the problems you encounter demand much more than recall. Do I want a long-lasting relationship with this particular person? Which school offers the best preparation for my needs? Which of these two positions offers the best opportunities now and the most promising future?

---

knowledge about thinking and facilitates answering questions such as:

- What do we know about students—their developmental paths, needs, and interests?
- What is in the nature of the subject matter that can help to shape objectives?
- What does the psychology of learning tell us about the appropriate placement of objectives in the learning sequence? Do the ways that students learn suggest a series of steps that must be mastered?

Many educators have felt that the elegant simplicity of Bloom's logic and the detailed presentation of the various categories of the taxonomy have not been fully utilized. With today's interest in teaching thinking skills, many concerned teachers and administrators have turned to Bloom's categories of analysis, synthesis, and evalua-

tion as the best means available for organizing the teaching of higher order thinking skills. You might try something like this. Find a theme in literature, science, or social studies that students can read and enjoy. Then ask questions that will test and develop their thinking skills.

Using Questions to Improve Thinking Skills

Even before Socrates, questioning was one of teaching's most common and most effective techniques. Some teachers ask hundreds of questions, especially when teaching science, geography, history, or literature. Using questions is a specific example of how teachers can help students to improve their thinking skills. In 1966, Norris Sanders analyzed classroom questions and identified seven levels.

1. *Memory*—recall or recognize previously learned ideas
2. *Translation*—restate an idea in a different manner
3. *Interpretation*—compare ideas or use an idea to solve a problem when told to do so
4. *Application*—use an idea to solve a problem when not told to do so but when the problem requires
5. *Analysis*—solve a problem following logical steps
6. *Synthesis*—create something with data you are given
7. *Evaluation*—make a value judgment.

Now identify the level of the following questions based on this situation.

Wanted: Thinking Students

Are you tired of being frustrated during examinations?

Do you refuse to settle for second best?

Do you want to succeed?

Do you know how to analyze a problem?

Do you even know how to begin to attack a problem?

If your answers to these questions indicate that you are unhappy with your present level of thinking skills, meet me in Room 211 at 3:00 p.m.

Indicate the level of the following questions by filling in the blank.

1. Imagine that you see this notice taped to the classroom bulletin board. How would you reply?
_____

2. Who wrote this notice? _____

3. Do you think this is an appealing notice? _____

4. How would you rewrite it to make it more attractive? _____

5. What type of student do you think would respond to this notice? _____

6. What type of problem do you see in using the questions in the notice? _____

7. When the interested students report to Room 211, what will they be told?_____

Here are the levels. Argue about them if you will. (6, 1, 7, 2, 3, 5, 4) By using this and similar techniques, you can help your students to achieve higher levels of thinking and improve their methods of attacking problems.

Questions, however, take different forms and place different demands on students. Some questions require only factual recall and do not provoke analysis. For example, of more than 61,000 questions found in the teacher guides, student workbooks, and tests for nine history textbooks, more than 95 percent were devoted to factual recall. This is not to say that questions meant to

"I don't know why you're so surprised by his poor grades. Every day you asked him what he did at school, and every day he answered, 'Nothing.'"

© Art Bouthiller

elicit facts are unimportant. Students need basic information to engage in higher level thinking processes and discussions. Such questions also promote class participation and provide a high success rate in answering questions correctly.

The difference between factual and thought-provoking questions is the difference between asking: "Where did Lincoln deliver the Gettysburg Address?" and asking, "Why was Lincoln's Gettysburg Address an important speech?" Each kind of question has its place, but the second question requires the student to analyze the speech according to the issues of the Civil War.

Although both kinds of questions are important, students achieve more when teachers ask thought-provoking questions and insist on thoughtful answers. Students' answers may also improve if teachers wait longer for a response, giving students more time to think. Table 8.2 provides several examples of questions that require varying levels of thinking.

Improving Teachers' Questions

Worried about their students' inability to draw inferences, two elementary school administrators, Falkoff and Moss (1984) turned to the improvement of teacher questions. Beginning with a series of workshops, they introduced their teachers to several theorists, beginning with Bloom. Next, they matched types of questions with the categories from the taxonomy.

Table 8.2

Using Bloom's Taxonomy of Thinking Skills to Guide the Development of Questions for Students

Level of Thinking	Example of Questions
Knowledge	Who did _____ ?
	When was _____ completed?
	Identify the _____ in the list.
	What does 2 + 6 equal?
Comprehension	Provide a good title for the story you read.
	In your own words, what was the main theme of the story?
Application	Use the word correctly in a sentence.
	Design a model that illustrates your understanding of the concept.
Analysis	Categorize all of the elements of the problem.
	What is the function of _____ ?
	How is A related to B?
Synthesis	Identify the common pattern resulting from all of the pictures.
	Summarize the various points that were made by stating a rule.
	Integrate the various pieces of information to create a profile of the person.
Evaluate	Judge the best method for testing the hypothesis.
	Rank order the projects, using stated criteria, from best to worst.
	Decide which problems were solved correctly.

Question	Taxonomy
1. Factual	Knowledge, comprehension
2. Interpretative	Application/analysis
3. Creative	Synthesis
4. Evaluative	Evaluation

Students then had to be taught to respond appropriately to the various types of questions. Working with both students and teachers, they found that interpretative questions served as the best vehicle to achieve higher order thinking. They also discovered that if students were to answer such questions, they must be taught to make inferences.

Therefore, they initiated a three-stage sequence to help their students.

- *Inferences from sensory cues* involved such techniques as standing in front of students with tight lips and folded arms. Ask students how you are feeling but then ask them "why"?
- *Inferences from visual cues* require attention to details. For example, what can you tell about a culture from some artifacts, perhaps an old coin?
- *Inferences about relationships* force students to conceptualize attributes and then search for common themes. Students were also required to discuss their rationale for making a relationship. They were then encouraged to compare and contrast.

These strategies are an excellent example of Bloom's ideas built into the teaching of thinking skills. Let's now examine a second approach to teaching critical thinking skills.

Ennis' Taxonomy

Presenting a model of thinking skills clearly based in logic, Ennis (1987, p. 11), stated that "reflectively and reasonably deciding what to believe or do can be broken down into a set of critical thinking dispositions, three basic areas of critical thinking ability, and an area of strategical and tactical ability in employing critical thinking." The thinking dispositions constitute a way of thinking rather than specific skills. As Ennis noted, if sensitivity to others is lacking, critical thinking may be useless, a belief that is closely akin to Sternberg's personal intelligences.

Addressing the abilities of his model, Ennis has divided them into four major groups: clarity, basis, inference, and interacting with others.

Clarity means "being clear about what is going on." Included in this category are the elementary abilities of focusing on a question, analyzing arguments, asking questions, and the more advanced abilities of defining terms and identifying assumptions; Why? What is the main point? Give an example. What is not an example?

Basis means identifying a reasonable basis for a judgment; Ennis believes we search for support for our inferences. Three abilities are included here: *judging, credibility* (note the earlier discussion of claims), and *observing.* For example, you might ask students if they believe the authors' account of what happened in the Soviet Union at the time of Eastern European independence. Why? Can you think of any reasons why the authors might be biased in their interpretation of the facts? Did their conclusions agree with those of other authorities?

Inference means a logical and reasonable foundation for inferring. Three abilities are included: *deducing, inducing,* and *making value judgments.* Ennis raises a point here that we stress in the next chapter on problem solving strategies: *background information* is essential for critical thinking. A student who lacks fundamental knowledge rarely makes good inferences.

Interacting with others involves discussion, debate, and in general, the exchange of ideas with others, a crucial element in critical thinking.

Up to now Ennis has concentrated on acquiring information as the basis for reasonable judgments and beliefs. But the process must conclude with action based on acquired knowledge and reasonable inference. Finally, Ennis (1987) concludes that the significant features of his model of critical thinking are:

- focusing on belief and action
- making action decisions
- criteria for evaluation
- dispositions and abilities
- organization for curriculum construction

Costa and Thinking Skills

Costa's (1985) rationale for his discussion of thinking skills is as simple as it is far-reaching: thinking is hard work, but with proper instruction human thought processes can be more broadly applied, more spontaneously generated, more precisely focused, more intricately complex, more metaphorically abstract, and more insightfully divergent. With this statement, Costa takes a firm stand in favor of *direct instruction* thinking skills.

Teaching about thinking can be divided into three components: *brain functioning, metacognition,* and *epistemic cognition.* Knowing how our brains work, being conscious of our own thinking, and learning how knowledge is produced by studying the lives of great composers, scientists, or writers all contribute to our teaching for, of, and about thinking.

Following this introductory work, Costa turns his attention to a model of human intellectual functioning since he believes that an information processing model should be the basis for any definition of thinking, instructional strategies, and teaching behaviors. The main features of any such model are as follows:

- Processing through the senses implies that students are alert to problems, consider as many variables as possible, identify pertinent data, and devise a system for collecting vital information.
- Students derive meaning from data by defining a problem, determining the goal, searching for relationships, and formulating a strategy.
- Students apply and evaluate a decision by communicating it to others after checking it against possible alternative solutions.
- Students become aware of their own behaviors as they attempt to reach decisions.

Costa's next step is to suggest a four-level hierarchy of thinking skills that should be helpful in teaching, curriculum construction, and developing instructional materials. The four levels are as follows:

Level I: The Discrete Level of Thinking

This level of thinking involves individual skills prerequisite to more complex thinking. For example, what demands are made on students' vocabulary? Can students comprehend the material?

Level II: Strategies of Thinking

This second level of thinking skills involves the combination of individual, discrete skills to formulate strategies. Do students understand the ideas presented and can they combine them in a way that leads to problem solving?

Level III: Creative Thinking

This level of thinking skills requires the use of strategies to create new thought patterns and innovative solutions. For example, can students apply what they have learned about America's original break with England to the current changes in Eastern Europe?

Level IV: The Cognitive Spirit

Although we can generate numerous lists of skills, that alone is insufficient. Thus this level of thinking requires students' willingness, disposition, inclination, and commitment to think.

What can teachers do to foster thinking skills? Costa believes that certain teacher behaviors can be quite effective in their impact on thinking skills. Four categories of behavior seem particularly relevant—questioning, structuring, responding, and modeling—all of which should occur within a discussion format.

Questioning. Costa (1985, p. 126) states that students derive their cues for expected behavior almost totally from teacher questions and statements. If we assume a relationship between the level of thinking in a teacher's statements and questions and the level of student thinking, then questions containing higher order thinking will require students to use higher order thinking skills to answer them.

If you return to Costa's ideas of intellectual functioning, you realize that questions can activate each part of the model. For example, to aid input, questions that require your students to name, describe, define, and observe are effective tools. To help students process data, questions that require your students to search for relationships, to synthesize, analyze, compare, and contrast are appropriate. Questions that force students to apply data in a novel manner should have them evaluate, judge, imagine, and predict.

Structuring. Costa uses structuring in the traditional manner to mean how teachers control the classroom environment. We have long known that teaching success is tightly linked to a well-structured classroom. Note: Well-structured and controlled does not imply rigid and unbending rules and discipline; rather the term applies to a situation in which both teacher and students know what the structure is (firm, tight, relaxed, friendly) and in which the structure remains consistent.

Structuring your classroom to improve your students' thinking skills demands clear objectives that they can understand. Costa believes such structure emerges from three instructional goals: (a) instructional clarity, (b) structuring time and energy, and (c) carefully organizing your interactions with your students.

Responding. In attempting to create a climate conducive to developing student thinking skills, Costa focuses on the nature of teacher responses. Teacher responses, which are extremely influential in shaping student behavior, fall into two major categories: closed responses or open responses. *Closed responses* include criticism and praise. Critical responses (in the sense of a "put down") add little to the attainment of thinking skills. Praise must be used judiciously; otherwise it is relatively ineffective. If used carefully with students experiencing difficulty and if matched with clear standards of achievement for all students, praise seems to be positive. Referring once again to the motivation chapter, we can safely say that intrinsic motivation should be our constant goal. *Open responses* include silence, accepting, clarifying, and facilitating. We can summarize this category by stating that you should give students time to answer your question, be nonjudgmental, clearly indicate when you do not understand an answer, and provide feedback.

Modeling. Avoid any inconsistencies between what you say and what you do. Students are remarkably perceptive and will quickly discern any discrepancies. If you want students to improve their thinking skills, you must show them that you place a high value on these behaviors. If you truly appreciate innovative solutions, careful inferences, and well-planned predictions, demonstrate your enthusiasm by your own behavior. Look for challenges and welcome obstacles.

What you say and do greatly influences students; show how much you value thinking skills. Try to do it in a way that reflects the thoughtful analysis of the strengths of good programs that guided the discussion between Superintendent Grimes and his colleagues that we saw in the chapter's opening.

Selected Programs

With these taxonomies of thinking skills as background, we can now turn our attention to how "thinking skills" have been translated into programs. We shall again discuss only well-documented, carefully researched programs. Four programs will be discussed here: Sternberg and Gardner's Practical Intelligence for School, Feuerstein's Instrumental Enrichment, Lipman's Philosophy for Children, and deBono's CoRT Thinking Program. Other worthwhile programs will be briefly summarized.

Practical Intelligence for School

Students must learn to use their **practical intelligence** effectively in school because that's where so much of their lives takes place. Yet, according to Sternberg and his colleagues, many teachers neither make explicit their

Intellectual domains (Multiple Intelligences)	Componential ——————→ Contextual ——————→ Experiential		
	Examples of mental processes:	*Practical application:*	*Transfer to new situations:*
Linguistic	Selecting the steps needed to solve a problem.	How to organize your thoughts in order to write a book report.	Writing a history report. Writing a letter. Giving directions to someone.
Logical-mathematical	Ordering the components of problem solving.	How to complete a math worksheet accurately.	Figuring out the steps for balancing a budget.
Musical	Selecting revelant information.	How to pick out the melody from the harmony.	Recognizing the main theme in a musical work.
Spatial	Selecting a mental representation for information.	How to make pictures in your mind to help you remember what you read.	Using a schematic to assemble a piece of electronic equipment. Reading a map.
Bodily-kinesthetic	Allocating your resources.	How to pace yourself throughout a long-distance run.	Adjusting your physical exertion during a basketball game or ballet performance.
Interpersonal	Solution monitoring.	How to understand your teacher's comments on your history report.	Restating what someone is telling you to be sure you understand him or her.
Intrapersonal	Identifying a problem.	Figuring out that something bothers you in school.	Figuring out that you are getting annoyed by your brother's teasing.

Figure 8.4
Intellectual operations.

expectations nor share the tacit knowledge that is necessary for success both inside and outside of school (Sternberg, Okagaki, & Jackson, 1990). Since 1987, Sternberg and his team of researchers have worked with Gardner's research team cooperatively to develop a theory-based curriculum called Practical Intelligence for School (PIFS).

The PIFS program is an outgrowth of the combination of Sternberg's Triarchic Model of Intelligence and Gardner's Multiple Intelligences Model. Figure 8.4 illustrates how these models of intelligence, which we discussed earlier in this chapter, are combined in the PIFS program. Note that Gardner's theory expresses the domains in which intelligence manifests itself (linguistic, logical-mathematical, musical, etc.), whereas Sternberg's componential subtheory identifies the mental processes involved in these domains. His contextual subtheory defines the practical ways in which the processes are applied, and the experiential subtheory deals with the transfer of skills to new situations.

The total PIFS curriculum is comprised of two parts: (a) the Yale portion designed to teach skills used across content areas, and (b) the Harvard portion designed to teach specific skills within a subject. The organization of the PIFS curriculum is based on three kinds of tacit knowledge: managing oneself, managing tasks, and working with others. Figure 8.5 illustrates the three types of tacit knowledge along with seven subdivisions and forty-eight specific skills.

The forty-eight practical intelligence skills are systematically taught. First, instruction focuses on the man-

aging yourself skills. Once these are mastered, instruction turns to the managing tasks skills. Finally, the cooperating with others are taught. Teachers are provided a guide that emphasizes learning in a social context. Thus, students work together in a large group (class) initially to discuss a skill and then move to small groups to apply that skill. At the end of each session, students evaluate their use of the new knowledge and material. Later teachers provide integrative activities that encourage students to apply their new learning in their lives.

According to Sternberg and his associates, teaching practical intelligence for schools is not easy. For those teachers who were evaluated in their project, successfully teaching the PIFS curriculum required a fundamental reorientation of attitudes and teaching style. "In particular, teachers need to come to value a kind of knowledge that they usually do not teach, despite expecting students to somehow learn it (Sternberg, Okagaki, & Jackson, 1990, p. 38). They argue that teaching practical intelligence skills like those in the PIFS curriculum can foster success in all students.

Instrumental Enrichment

Originally proposed by Reuven Feuerstein (1980), **instrumental enrichment** rests on the assumption that we can modify our cognitive structures. Feuerstein believes that the root problem of poor learners lies in the reduced level of modifiability that such students exhibit. Cognitive growth occurs as a result of both **incidental**

I. Managing yourself

   A. Overview of managing yourself

      1. Introductory Lesson
      2. Kinds of Intelligence: Definitions and Principles
      3. Kinds of Intelligence: Multiple Intelligences
      4. Kinds of Intelligence: Academic or Practical Intelligence
      5. Understanding Test Scores
      6. Exploring What You May Do
      7. Accepting Responsibility
      8. Collecting Your Thoughts and Setting Goals

   B. Learning styles

      9. What's Your Learning Style?
    10. Taking In New Information
    11. Showing What You Learned
    12. Knowing How You Work Best
    13. Recognizing the Whole and the Parts

   C. Improving your own learning

    14. Memory
    15. Using What You Already Know
    16. Making Pictures in Your Mind
    17. Using Your Eyes—A Good Way to Learn
    18. Recognizing the Point of View
    19. Looking for the Best Way to Learn
    20. Listening for Meaning
    21. Learning by Doing

II. Managing tasks

   A. Overview of solving problems

    22. Is There a Problem?
    23. What Strategies Are You Using?
    24. A Process to Help You Solve Problems
    25. Planning a Way to Prevent Problems
    26. Breaking Habits
    27. Help with Our Problems

   B. Specific school problems

    28. Taking Notes
    29. Getting Organized
    30. Understanding Questions
    31. Following Directions
    32. Underlining—Finding the Main Idea
    33. Noticing the Way Things Are Written
    34. Choosing Between Mapping and Outlining
    35. Taking Tests
    36. Seeing Likenesses and Differences in Subjects
    37. Getting It Done on Time

III. Cooperating with others

   A. Communication

    38. Class Discussions
    39. What to Say
    40. Tuning Your Conversation
    41. Putting Yourself in Another's Place
    42. Solving Problems in Communication

   B. Fitting into school

    43. Making Choices—Adapting, Shaping, Selecting
    44. Understanding Social Networks
    45. Seeing the Network: Different Roles
    46. Seeing the Network: Figuring Out the Rules
    47. Seeing the Relationship Between Now and Later
    48. What Does School Mean to You?

Figure 8.5

Practical intelligence for school curriculum.

© Art Bouthillier.

learning (exposure to a changing environment) and **mediated learning** (the training given to learners by experienced adults). Of the two, mediated learning is by far the most important. By scheduling, sequencing, and grouping stimuli, adults order and regulate the learner's environment, thus forming the **Mediated Learning Experience** (**MLE**). The program is intended to improve the cognitive performance of low-achieving adolescents by enhancing their modifiability as a result of exposure to new experiences.

Specifically, the IE program consists of a series of paper and pencil exercises that take about 200 to 300 hours to complete over two to three years. Feuerstein calls these exercises "instruments" rather than lessons because they are intended to be content-free. The various tasks are clustered into 20 instruments, 15 of which comprise the total program. Each instrument focuses on one or more cognitive functions, while simultaneously promoting others. The program takes about three to five hours per week and is presented by a specially trained teacher who is a regular staff member.

Among the instruments used are the following:

- *Organization of dots,* a technique that is divorced from any school subject and one that forces students to break a task into parts and search for relationships among the reorganized parts. The cognitive processes needed in this task will also transfer to other thinking skills.
- *Orientation in space I* is designed to promote the formation of specific strategies that will help students acquire frames of reference for spatial relations, gradually culminating in a personal frame of reference. Students learn that perception of an object, event, or person depends on their personal vantage point and that relationships can shift depending on a person's position.
- *Temporal relations* furnishes systems whereby students can first understand time as a fixed, measurable interval, then slowly introduces the relative quality of present, past, and future with its irreversible flair. This instrument encourages students to search for proper starting points and consider all relevant information, thus reducing impulsivity.

• *Transitive relations* is a more advanced instrument that concentrates on drawing inferences from relations that can be described as larger than, equal to, or smaller than.

These are but a few of the twenty instruments Feuerstein and his colleagues devised, but they indicate the type of learning experience provided, one that is essentially content-free and based upon the mediated learning experience.

The rationale, instruments, and theoretical concepts are sharply focused on one goal: Improvement of students' thinking skills. It is a complicated system, one in which teachers need careful training.

Thus the main goal of Instrumental Enrichment (IE) is to develop thinking and problem solving abilities in students so that they become autonomous learners. It is assumed that intelligence is dynamic and that cognitive development demands direct and mediated intervention to build the mental processes for learning. This program is intended for upper elementary, middle, and secondary levels.

Philosophy for Children

Matthew Lipman (1987) stated that the goal of the Philosophy for Children program is to promote excellent thinking, creative as well as critical, imaginative as well as logical, inventive as well as analytical. But, as he notes, to encourage children to think well, we must first teach them to think. To capture their imagination, while simultaneously prodding their thinking skills, Lipman decided to turn to the "magic of fiction."

By showing youngsters, in fictional form, other children inquiring about truth, friendship, and freedom, for example, Lipman believed he could motivate students to think about their thinking. Six programs have been developed thus far, each consisting of a novel (about 100 pages) and a 400-page instructor's manual with exercises and discussions keyed to the novel's concepts and skills. Two of the programs, *Pixie,* and *Kio and Gus,* are designed for the first four grades. *Harry Stottlemeier's Discovery* is intended for grades 5 and 6 (here children are introduced to logic), while the remaining three novels, *Lisa, Suki,* and *Mark,* apply the reasoning skills previously learned to specific school content.

As the novels unfold, the characters in them use many of the same thinking skills that we would like students to use. Lipman's goal, of course, is to have students reenact the thinking processes that the characters use, not only in their own thoughts but also in class discussion.

In the *Philosophy for Children* program, the sharpening of thinking skills does not take place exclusively in classroom discussions, but the exercise and strengthen-

Stimulating inquiry in students is one of the most important roles of a teacher. Opportunities to discover and to respond are critical components of effective teaching.

ing of such skills is most evident in the classroom. Some children like to read and some like to write, but almost all love to talk. The problem is to transform this energy into cognitive skill, much as the transmission system of an automobile transforms the raw power of the engine into the disciplined and directed movement of the wheels.

Mere talking must be converted into conversation, discussion, and dialogue, which means learning to listen to others, as well as to respond effectively. It means learning to follow the various lines of reasoning taking place as the discussion proceeds: sizing up the assumptions that underlie each utterance, drawing inferences, testing for consistency and comprehensiveness, and learning to think independently by freely choosing one's own premises.

At any given moment in a conversation, each participant engages in countless mental acts, some in harmony with others, some quite independent of others, some convergent, others divergent. But the dialogue must be disciplined. This is accomplished by having the participants utilize the rules of logic as criteria for distinguishing between good and poor thinking (Lipman, 1983, p. 86).

Applying this scheme to the novels expressly written for the course, we discover Lipman's objectives for teaching thinking skills at each level. In the *Pixie* and *Kio and Gus* novels, Lipman emphasizes reasoning about nature, especially animals and the environment. *Pixie* stresses language and reasoning skills, especially analogical thinking. *Harry Stottlemeier's Discovery* explores the principles of reasoning. The *Lisa* program (specifically designed for grades 7 and 8) applies the intellectual tools previously acquired to ethical reasoning. *Suki* highlights the integration of thinking and writing.

Finally, in *Mark,* Lipman introduces reflective thinking in the social sciences. For example, consider this statement in *Mark*: "When we have a bunch of criteria, is it possible we still need another criterion to be able to decide which of the first bunch we should pick?"

Lipman summarizes the program as follows: The elementary section of the programs furnishes situations that require students to use their reasoning and inquiry skills; the middle portion introduces them to the principles underlying these skills; the secondary part has them apply their cognitive skills to academic and life situations.

The major instructional features of the **Philosophy for Children** curriculum include:

- modeling, with focus on discussion;
- operationalizing concepts or stressing how ideas work;
- using students' experiences;
- encouraging group dialogue;
- responding to students' desire for meaning; and
- teaching thinking skills separately.

Thus the main goal of the Philosophy for Children curriculum is to improve children's reasoning abilities by having them "think about thinking." It assumes children are interested in such issues as truth and fairness and should learn to think for themselves. The curriculum is intended for kindergarten through high school students.

The CoRT Thinking Program

As our final example of thinking skills programs, we turn to de Bono's work on **Cognitive Research Trust (CoRT)**, which has a different objective from either Feuerstein's or Lipman's. Although these two programs concentrated on the means of acquiring thinking skills, de Bono is more concerned with problem solving ability. Linking his theory of thinking skills to a neurological and information-processing base, de Bono (1985a) argues forcefully for the direct teaching of thinking skills to students. The *CoRT program* has several objectives.

- The program should be *simple and practical.* A successful program must be teachable for instructors and understandable for students. Expensive materials and special audiovisual materials are unnecessary.
- The program should *apply to a wide range of ages* since de Bono believes that thinking processes are fundamental.
- The thinking skills taught should be *those required in real life*; for this reason the program emphasizes "projective" thinking: gathering information, inferring from it, and acting on it.
- The program should be *independent of any detailed knowledge base.* Thinking skills needed throughout our lives aren't tied to a specific subject; we need vital thinking skills in all subjects and problem areas.
- Students should be able to *transfer the thinking skills* they acquire to all of life's situations. By the mixture of items in the CoRT program, de Bono believes that students' attention can be directed at necessary thinking processes.

So what is the CoRT method? It is best to illustrate this method with an example from deBono (1985a).

> I was teaching a class of thirty boys, all eleven years of age, in Sydney, Australia. I asked if they would each like to be given $5 a week for coming to school. All thirty thought this was a fine idea. "We could buy sweets or chewing gum.... We could buy comics.... We could get toys without having to ask Mum or Dad."
>
> I then introduced and explained a simple tool called the PMI (which I will describe later). The explanation took about four minutes. In groups of five, the boys applied the PMI tool to the suggestion that they should be given $5 a week for coming to school. For three to four minutes they talked and thought on their own. At no time did I interfere. I never discussed the $5 suggestion, other than to state it. I did not suggest that the youngsters consider this, think of that, and so forth. At the end of their thinking time, the groups reported back to me: The bigger boys would beat us up and take the money.... The school would raise its charges for meals.... Our parents would not buy us presents.... Who would decide how much money different ages received?... There would be less money to pay teachers ... There would be less money for a school minibus.
>
> When they had finished their report, I again asked the boys to express their views on the suggestion of pay for attending school. This time, twenty-nine of the thirty had completely reversed their opinion and thought it a bad idea. We subsequently learned that the one holdout received no pocket money at home. The important point is that my contribution was minimal. I did not interact with the boys. I simply explained the PMI tool, and the boys then used it on their own—as their tool. My "superior" intelligence and broader experiences were not influences. The boys did their own thinking (de Bono, 1985a).

The *PMI* de Bono referred to represents *plus* (the thinker's first attempt to discover the good points in a

"I expect you all to be independent, innovative, critical thinkers who will do exactly as I say."

situation), *minus* (the negative features), and *interesting* (things worth noting). In de Bono's usage, PMI becomes a scoring tool, one that students find easy to remember, easy to pronounce, easy to use.

The CoRT method encompasses the following features as major concepts of the system:

- *The role of perception in thinking.* The intent of the program is to enable students to view things more clearly by providing a "perceptual map" to guide behavior.
- *CoRT attention tools.* The PMI is an example of an attention tool since it forces students to go beyond their initial reactions. Using such a tool provides students with a frame that highlights details and enriches perception.
- *CoRT practice items.* The important point here is de Bono's insistence that thinking skills, not the content, are to be practiced.
- *Strategies for encouraging transfer.* Once students learn to focus attention on their thinking skills, the program has them use these skills in a variety of situations.
- *Identification of skills* in which to offer instruction. Each lesson in the program focuses on a different

thinking skill that was selected because of its applicability to a wide variety of situations.

For students who enter a CoRT program, de Bono's expectation is that they will reach one of four levels of achievement.

- *Level 1.* A general awareness of thinking as a skill, a willingness to explore and think about a topic.
- *Level 2.* A more structured approach to thinking, that considers the consequences of a plan or action and a search for alternatives.
- *Level 3.* Focused and deliberate use of several of the CoRT tools.
- *Level 4.* Fluid and appropriate use of such metacognitive aspects as thinking about thinking.

Thus the main goal of the CoRT program is to teach thinking skills that are useful in and out of school. It assumes lateral thinking is unconventional and nonsequential and may not always be right. Intelligent people aren't necessarily skillful thinkers. Finally, the CoRT program is supposedly useful for students of all ability levels ranging in ages from eight to twenty-two.

TEACHER ◄►STUDENT
INTERACTIONS

Analyzing Thinking Skills

1. Thinking skills programs must be based on a sound rationale and precise objectives.

   • Try to engage students in all categories of Bloom's taxonomy. Rather than ask simple factual questions, such as "Who won the battle of Yorktown?" ask "What do you think would have happened if England had won the Revolutionary War?"

   • After students have prepared their answers, have them share their speculations with the class. Have them draw maps that would reflect this new territory and prepare an outline indicating how the American people would be different today.

   • Help your students to develop the habit of analyzing, to identify the parts in a problem or situation and to see how they relate to the whole. This is common in math and science, but students should grow accustomed to using this technique in all parts of the curriculum. For example, after reading a story or description of some event, ask them to identify the main features (people, events) and how the relationships among them explained the final outcome.

   • Insist that your students not be satisfied with the first thing they do. At the secondary level, you could assign groups specific topics relating to what you're teaching (a novel, the Reconstruction period, the discovery of DNA). Each student in the group is to research a particular aspect of the topic, but before submitting it to the group, the student must evaluate the work according to certain criteria: Did I get all the information I could? Does it "fit" the topic? Is it what I was supposed to do? Then have the total group evaluate each report before they present to the entire class. Allow class time for this work.

   • At the elementary level, you could focus on a school problem: why has there been so much fighting in the schoolyard lately? Write your students' responses on the board and, with the class, discuss the strengths and weaknesses of each. Finally, have the class vote for the two best solutions.

2. Teaching strategies can help to improve students' thinking skills.

   • To help your students improve the clarity of their thinking, emphasize one thing at a time. In a way that they can understand, teach them to look for a logical sequence. Before proposing a solution for the problem of why there are so many fights on the playground, students must determine several things: Where did the trouble occur? Was it always in the same place? Did it happen at about the same time? Who was involved? Were any teachers around? Help them to realize that this strategy applies to their school subjects as well.

   • Tell students that you want them to invent something. Give them simple examples, such as the need for a back-scratching instrument or a device that will pick up pins and needles from the floor. You can structure it in the form of a "back-to-the-future" game. But make your students justify their invention: Is it necessary? What is the problem it will solve? Are materials available to build it? How much will it cost? You are forcing them to examine the basis of their judgments.

   • Have groups of students research the countries of origin of several of their classmates. Create a "cultural corner" where one group at a time puts their reports, magazines, pictures, literature about the country, and any other materials they may have collected. Design holiday cards for the special holidays of that country and then specify class time for oral reports.

   • Make your students aware of current environmental concerns by bringing in news accounts of dangerous incidents, such as oil spills, toxic waste, etc. Form discussion groups whose objectives are to suggest ways of dealing with the various problems. Have them write letters to the local papers expressing their concerns. In this way, you are encouraging them to work together to solve problems.

Conclusion

The teaching of thinking skills is becoming an integral part of the curriculum in many classrooms. What could prevent this change from continuing is the rapid proliferation of programs that have no realistic basis (biological, philosophical, psychological), and which offer little research evidence about their effectiveness, and which have not had follow-up studies conducted on their projected outcomes.

Though few thinking skills programs have yet had the benefit of careful study, some have their roots firmly entrenched in long-established traditions. Our work in this chapter concentrated on such programs. After arguing for recognition of the link between the brain and thinking, we turned our attention to several current theories of intelligence. These theories also help to establish the basis of thinking skills programs on a solid footing since academic success usually reflects these skills.

Which thinking skills analyses offer the most promise for building successful programs? We selected four that seemed to represent the high qualitative and quantitative standards previously discussed. We chose them because they provided a basis for their practical applications and because they showed considerable promise for helping students.

Thus we formulated a chain of reasoning in our work: a rationale that should help you to select the program you decide is best suited for your students' needs. We conclude as we began—properly scrutinized and used, the teaching of thinking skills is here to stay.

Chapter Highlights

Thinking Skills

- Educators today believe that students need more than facts; they need those skills and strategies that enable them to adapt to constant change.
- The concept of thinking skills will become part of the curriculum only if programs have meaningful connections to such disciplines as philosophy, psychology, or biology.
- If thinking skills programs claim biological roots, their designers must demonstrate a discernible link with such brain phenomena as plasticity, pattern matching, and lateralization.
- Multicultural students may possess particular thinking skills that cultural differences mask and which may remain hidden unless teachers are aware of a culture's expectancies.

Intelligence and Thinking

- Given the more restricted view that educators and psychologists now have of intelligence tests, new theories of intelligence have appeared that offer considerable support for the role of thinking skills in the curriculum.
- Sternberg's Triarchic model attempts to explain what intelligence "should do" and by recognizing a range of intelligence from metacognitive to contextual, he provides a qualitative means of devising thinking skills programs for each segment of the model.
- Many psychologists have long sought an explanation of intelligence that accounts for its varied nature. Gardner's proposal of Multiple Intelligences addresses this issue and contains clear implications for teaching and learning.

- Concerned about narrow views of intelligence, Perkins has concentrated upon thinking skills that are designed to supplement his view of tactical intelligence. Perkins introduces the term "thinking frames" to indicate those representations that guide our thought processes.

Thinking Skills: An Analysis

- Several taxonomies of thinking skills are available that meet the criteria of a carefully designed program with a discernible link to disciplinary roots.
- Bloom's Taxonomy of Educational Objectives is intended to specify desirable cognitive objectives in behavioral terms, to suggest means of evaluating the attainment of these goals, and to aid in curriculum construction.
- Ennis' Taxonomy of Critical Thinking Skills, with its philosophical basis, attempts to encourage a way of thinking rather than accumulate specific skills.
- Costa's Thinking Skills program is based upon knowledge of how the brain works, our awareness of our thinking, and acquiring knowledge. He urges that an information processing model should be the basis for teaching, learning, and curriculum construction.

Selected Programs

- The Practical Intelligence for School program is designed to encourage students to use their intelligence effectively in school.
- Feuerstein's Instrumental Enrichment program rests on the assumption that our cognitive structures can be modified. The goal of the program is to help students develop thinking and problem solving abilities so that they may become autonomous learners.

- In the Philosophy for Children program, Lipman used fictional stories in an effort to promote excellent thinking by having students "think about their thinking."
- As a means of facilitating lateral thinking, de Bono's CoRT program identifies learning strategies. The thinking skills that students acquire should be useful in and out of school.

Key Terms

Cerebral lateralization
Content theory of intelligence
Cognitive Research Trust (CoRT)
Critical thinking
Functional asymmetry
Incidental learning
Instrumental enrichment
Knowledge-acquisition components
Mediated learning
Mediated learning experience (MLE)
Metacomponents
Multiple intelligences
Pattern matching
Performance components
Philosophy for Children
Plasticity
Power theory of intelligence
Practical intelligence
Tactical theory of intelligence
Thinking frames
Thinking skills
Triarchic theory of intelligence

Suggested Readings

Costa, A. (Ed.). (1985). *Developing minds.* Alexandria, Va.: ASCD. A collection of essays written by outstanding authors of the leading thinking skills programs. A valuable guide to recent work in this field.

Gardner, H. (1983). *Frames of mind.* New York: Basic. Here Gardner presents his concept of "multiple intelligences," a work that is well-written and quite provocative. You can read this for information and enjoyment.

Rourke, B., Bakker, D., Fisk, J., & Strang, J. (1983). *Child neuropsychology.* New York: Guilford. You could have no better guide to brain development, problems, case studies, and practical application than this excellent text. This text is highly recommended if you wish to explore this field in greater depth.

Sternberg, R. (1988). *The triarchic mind: A new theory of human intelligence.* New York: Viking. Sternberg's views on intelligence in which he develops his thesis that intelligence is composed of three elements. This is not strictly a theoretical presentation, however, since Sternberg furnishes many practical examples of intelligence "in action" and means of assessing the three elements.

Problem-Solving Skills and Strategies

Alice Jenkins, the fifth-grade teacher at Brackett School, was worried about one of her students. Timmy, a bright, alert boy in good health seemed to be at a loss when he was faced with a problem. Unless a question was simple and obvious, he seemed to have difficulty in knowing how to begin.

After talking with him, Alice was convinced that Timmy's confusion was related to the way that he organized his work. She discussed the problem with Mr. Abrams, the school counselor, who suggested that she attempt to teach Timmy some learning strategies that would give him confidence and provide him a basis for attacking problems in all of his subjects. Remembering what she had read about general and specific problem-solving techniques, Alice decided to ask Timmy some specific questions about his work habits.

Keeping him after school for a few minutes, Alice asked, "Timmy, are you still going to Disney World this summer?"

Timmy said, "My mother and father think we're going during the spring vacation."

"That sounds great. When you get there, what will you do first? Do you think you'll run in and see as much as you can at first, or will you think about what you want to do first, second, and so forth."

"I don't know," replied Timmy. "I read some of the folders and there's so much there, I don't know where to begin."

Alice laughed but realized that this was exactly the same behavior Timmy showed when faced with a problem in school. "Look, Timmy," she said, "Let's try to figure out what you should do first and then go from there."

Timmy thought for awhile and then replied, "OK, but I'm not sure how I'll decide."

"Well, let's try to draw up a plan that you can follow. You know, Timmy, if you get in the habit of thinking about what's important and then making a plan to get it, it helps you in everything you do."

"Sometimes it's awfully hard to find out what's important. There's just so much that I get baffled."

After several more questions, Alice knew that Timmy had no idea how to attack problems. She also knew that this was characteristic of some students. The encouraging part of students with this kind of difficulty is that they usually can be helped by mastering several easy-to-learn techniques that will be the focus of this chapter.

How would you react to the following situation?

At the end of 1989 and continuing into 1990, amazing changes occurred in Eastern Europe. Poland, in its quest for freedom, first captured the imagination of the world. The division between East and West Germany crumbled. Hungary and Czechoslovakia opted for free elections. The Baltic states were seething with unrest, and the march toward democracy seemed unstoppable.

Now assume that during these times you are an advisor to the President of the United States and are committed to helping other peoples in their struggle for freedom. Your course of action, however, isn't as clear as you might like. The problem is that your advice to the President must be such that the United States encourages these movements but in a way that does not cause violent repressions. What path do you suggest he should follow?

There is no escaping problem solving. Although dramatic historical events, such as just described in Eastern Europe, capture the world's attention and illustrate the nature of problem solving in vivid fashion, for most of us it is the daily routine of our lives that occupies our problem solving energies. From the moment that we decide what to eat for breakfast, what route to take to work, what television show to watch in the evening, our day's activities reflect a series of problems to which we must react.

Learning is an excellent example of problem solving in action. As you can tell from the conversation of the Brackett teacher and student (discussed in the chapter's opening), educators are concerned with how they can improve the problem solving abilities of their students. They are also worried, however, about students' ability to engage in productive problem-solving behavior outside the classroom. The problem to be solved, the activities involved, and the strategies that we adopt all represent problem-solving behavior.

Thanks to recent research, especially into information processing, we are now more aware of the procedures involved in solving problems. From increased knowledge has come insights into various strategies that can improve our ability to solve problems. For example, different kinds of memory techniques are better suited for different types of content. Not only will such knowledge aid us in solving our problems but we can teach these techniques and strategies to our students.

In a sense, this chapter and chapter 8 (*Thinking and the Teaching of Critical Thinking Skills*) are about **metacognition,** the ability we develop "to think about thinking" that we discussed in chapter 7. We not only know something, but we also begin to think about what we can do with this knowledge. We develop strategies to solve the problems we face.

In this chapter we'll discuss the nature of problem solving, why some of us avoid problems, and the typical kinds of strategies we use when we attempt problem solving. Next we'll examine the details of the **DUPE** model, which presents a formula for determining the dimensions of a problem, understanding its nature, planning for its solution, and finally, evaluating the success of the solution. We have presented several interesting problems throughout the chapter to help you learn about your own problem-solving ability and to help you understand better the techniques that your students must master to become good problem solvers.

When you complete your reading of this chapter, you should be able to:

- help your students identify the nature of a problem;
- improve your students' willingness to undertake problem solving;
- teach your students the basics of a problem-solving model that they can apply both in and out of school;
- identify the weaknesses in your students' problem-solving skills.

First, however, what do we mean by "a problem?"

What Is a Problem?

Have you ever sat baffled while you read an arithmetic word problem? Have you ever been assigned a term paper and were bewildered about where to start? In each of these instances you have a problem; you cannot get where you want to go. There is a void, a gap, that you must cross to solve your problem. When dealing with students' learning or behavior problems, *we like to think of a problem as occurring when there is a significant discrepancy between the actual behavior and the desired behavior.*

Using this definition, some problems concern deficits (actual behavior is problematic and is below the desired standard). Other problems concern excess (actual behavior is problematic and exceeds the desired standard of behavior). As we shall see later when we examine the nature of a problem in more detail, problem solving requires that we understand the meaning of the gap or discrepancy (we try to represent it in some manner) and we then construct ways of bridging the gap.

To illustrate what is meant by representing the gap and then bridging it, try to solve this problem.

Two motorcyclists are 100 miles apart. At exactly the same moment they begin to drive toward each other for a meeting. Just as they leave, a bird flies in front of the first cyclist to the front of the second cyclist. When it reaches the second cyclist it turns around and flies back to the first. The bird continues flying in this manner until the cyclists meet. The cyclists both traveled at the rate of 50 miles per hour, while the bird maintained a constant speed of 75 miles per hour. How many miles will the bird have flown when the cyclists meet?

Students need time to reflect on problems.

Many readers, examining this problem, will immediately begin to calculate distance, miles per hour, and constancy of speed. Actually this is not a mathematical problem; it is a word problem. Carefully look at it again. Both riders will travel for one hour before they meet; the bird flies at 75 miles per hour; therefore, the bird will have flown 75 miles. No formulae or calculations are needed, just a close examination of what is given.

Improving Problem-Solving Skills

You may scoff and state that any problem is easy when you know the answer. True, but there is another lesson here. Regardless of how you react to problems, it is possible to improve your ability to solve them. If such a possibility exists for us, it also holds true for your students. It is an exciting prospect because no matter what a student's intelligence, or socioeconomic level, or whatever other variable we could mention, that same student can enhance learning skills.

Individual differences in problem-solving ability exist; some of us are simply better at solving problems than others. There are many explanations for these differences: Some have had previous experience in similar activities; some, with more enriching educations, bring more knowledge to a problem, and some are motivated to solve problems. These are not the issue. Regardless of advantages, there is probably no such thing as the perfect problem solver. There are, however, individuals who can improve their skills by attending more closely to the na-

ture of the problem that faces them, by better understanding their own thinking processes, and by using mistakes to improve their skills.

Those of you reading this text have already had the benefit of considerable education. To be successful thus far you must be a fairly competent problem solver, even though you may not have thought of it in just this way. As an example of how you can improve your skills, you will do better with the problems that you will encounter in the remainder of this chapter because you will be more cautious and attentive after analyzing the bird and the motorcyclists. Try this.

> There are 3 separate, equally sized boxes, and inside each box there are 2 separate small boxes, and inside each of the small boxes there are 4 even smaller boxes. How many boxes are there altogether?

Your attempt to solve this problem is another excellent example of individual differences in problem solving, especially those differences that relate to problem-solving style. Though many readers will try to solve it "in their heads" (some form of internal representation), others will immediately turn to paper and pencil and draw the various stages (external representation). If we could survey the readers, our guess would be that more solved the second problem than the first. You attended to it more carefully and considered as many alternatives as possible. (The answer is 33: 3 large boxes + 6 small boxes + 24 smaller boxes.)

When you directly teach learning strategies and tactics to your students, it is reasonable to expect that their ability to solve problems, both in and out of the classroom, will improve. Timmy, in the opening vignette, is a good example. With guidance in how to attack problems, Timmy, and other students like him, will have a much better chance of succeeding.

Although efforts to incorporate problem-solving activities and content within the curriculum are increasing, it is still, for the most part, a solitary effort by individual teachers. Rarely are students taught to think; typically the focus is on what to learn, which is unfortunate since most teachers are good problem solvers. However, as noted in the previous chapter, several psychologists and educators are developing for children programs designed to teach critical thinking skills. Unfortunately, many teachers have never been taught to scrutinize thought processes; consequently, they tend to overlook these abilities as valuable tools for their students to master.

Sources of Error

Whimbey and Lochhead (1985) believe that we can improve our analytical skills by becoming aware of the kinds of errors that we frequently make in attempting to solve problems. As these authors note, most errors are not because people lack information about the problem. Even with the necessary facts present, individuals have difficulty with problems because they do not attend well nor fully employ their reasoning processes. As an example of the type of error that ensnares many problem solvers, the authors offer the following example.

> In a different language *liro cas* means red tomato, *dum cas dan* means big red barn, and *xer dan* means big horse. What is the word for barn in this language?
>
> (a) dum (b) liro (c) cas (d) dan (e) xer

Here we have a fairly simple problem, but one that demands we make a systematic comparison of phrases and a careful matching of words. Poor problem solvers often jump at the first clue, with the result that they choose b, c, d, or e. Aside from mechanical mistakes in problem-solving procedures, emotional elements can also be influential.

Among the most common sources of error are the following:

- Failure to observe and use all the relevant facts of a problem. Did you account for each word in the language problem?
- Failure to adopt systematic, step-by-step procedures. The problem solver may skip steps, ignore vital information, and leap to a faulty conclusion. Did you

make a check, or some other mark, against each word?
- Failure to perceive vital relationships in the problem. Did you discover the order of the words?
- Frequent use of sloppy techniques in acquiring information and using one's reasoning processes. Did you guess at the meaning of any of the words?

Retreating from Problems

None of us enjoys having to cope with difficult situations. It is much easier to ignore or avoid problems that demand considerable effort to solve. If motivated individuals feel this way, imagine how much more difficult it must be for those students who constantly experience frustration in school and who are more accustomed to failure than success. These students can react only negatively to any problem that they encounter in the classroom, and as we shall see, they transfer this attitude to other problems they meet. Mathematics is an example of a subject that produces negative reactions even in experienced adult learners. For whatever reason—poor instruction, poor materials, lack of motivation at a critical time—these individuals either avoid or simply refuse to attempt to solve a math problem. As an example of this reaction, try to solve the following problem.

> Group these numbers in such a way that when you total the groups, they add up to the sum of 1,000.
>
> 88888888

Some elementary school youngsters will find the solution almost immediately, but there will be many readers who simply ignore the problem and continue their reading. Others will routinely read the problem while their thoughts are on something totally different. Still others react in an almost reflex manner by saying, "Math—that's not for me."

Your inability to solve a problem may not be solely the result of faulty attention, dislike of math, or even lack of motivation. You may have acquired a general feeling of anxiety about certain types of problems, or all problems. If this is true of successful students, why should less mature students, with a history of failure and lacking problem-solving skills, even try to solve any educational problems? Their experiences, which probably have contributed to feelings of futility, can generate only a negative reaction to anything resembling a problem, both in and out of school.

(In case you are still searching for the answer, try this line of reasoning. How many groups are required to produce a 0 in the units column when you add them? This is the key to solving the problem, since five is the first number that will result in $0 : 5 \times 8 = 40$. Try working with five groups.

(Solution: $888 + 88 + 8 + 8 + 8$.)

Excuses, Excuses, Excuses

There are those who will not attempt to search for a solution. As Lewis and Greene (1982) noted, too many people just give up or decide immediately that they would be unsuccessful. Lewis and Greene attribute these attitudes to several myths about mental abilities, the most prominent of which are the following:

- *I just wasn't born smart.* This myth retains its popularity because it shifts responsibility for failure from the individual to some genetic blueprint (Lewis & Greene, 1982). But current interpretations of intelligence have led us to conclude that it is primarily a collection of experiences, particularly as we measure it. Enrich the experiences; improve the performance. This in no way, of course, ignores the inherited ability that establishes a ceiling for potential. However, since potential is rarely, if ever, approached, there exists ample opportunity to improve performance and enhance self-esteem.
- *I have a terrible memory.* Another misleading belief is that our storage capacity for memory is severely restricted when studies have clearly shown that our ability to retain is much greater than commonly realized. Retrieval is undoubtedly the issue here because under hypnosis or through the use of electric brain probes, the average person's memory has been proven to be amazingly detailed.
- *You can't teach an old dog new tricks.* The third myth refers to the belief that mental ability declines with age. Again, research has demonstrated that aside from physical damage or disease, there is little actual decline in brain functioning. Too often we live up to expectations: if you're old, you're forgetful or would find it difficult to learn anything new.

  Regardless of the reasons for retreating from problems, it is a difficult task to help anyone, adult or student, break away from customary attitudes and beliefs. Creative thinking (searching for alternatives to solve problems) is concerned with breaking away from old ideas. This leads to changes in both attitudes and approach; we look differently at situations. Because this approach is novel, most people feel uncomfortable in trying it. It is much easier to do the same things, even if they have previously led to failure. If, however, you can teach your students to use the strategies discussed in this chapter, the chances are that they will experience greater success, which will then encourage them to try.

Problem-Solving Strategies

What are these strategies that would help your students in their work? They range from general problem-solving techniques to specific and simple tactics. For example, you are probably more cautious about any problem that you now meet in this chapter—you are attending more carefully to detail, a simple suggestion but one that can be enormously helpful. Try this problem, one that appears in almost any analysis of problem solving.

What day follows the day before yesterday if three days from now it will be Monday?

Good problem solvers analyze details with considerable care and usually break a problem into sections. They might proceed as follows:

- If three days from now it will be Monday, today must be Friday.
- If today is Friday, yesterday was Thursday.
- Then the day before yesterday was Wednesday.
- The following day is Thursday.

Although superficially simple, attending to detail is a powerful tool in solving problems. It makes no difference if the strategy is general or specific, *attending must be the initial step,* and it is from this beginning that strategies take shape. A problem-solving strategy is a means of putting things in place carefully and with a great deal of thought, which is just the opposite of hoping something will happen or taking a wild guess (deBono, 1984).

problem-solving strategies are usually divided into two categories: general (also called weak) and strong (also called specific or detailed).

1. **General strategies.** A general strategy, according to deBono (1984), is a set of principles and guidelines that may apply to any situation. He uses the example of an interviewer who always selects people who are rated number two: they achieve almost as well as those who rank first but temperamentally they are less likely to be difficult to work with. Thus, operational structures seem to be the basis of general problem solving and lead to a set of highly general methods that constitute the core of problem-solving behavior.

   Bransford and Stein (1984) likewise offer specific examples of general strategies. Working a problem backwards is a general strategy that eases problem solution. If you have a 9:00 a.m. examination and you can't be late, one technique would be to decide that you want to arrive at 8:45 a.m.; it takes thirty minutes for the trip; you want to allow fifteen minutes for potential traffic slowdowns; therefore, you should leave at 8:00 a.m. Bransford and Stein believed that working backwards is especially helpful whenever the goal is clear and the initial state of the problem is vague.

2. **Strong strategies.** A strong strategy is one designed for a specific purpose, that is, those strategies that seem to be unique to a particular subject. Anyone familiar with the core concept of a subject is better able to initiate steps to solve a problem involving that knowledge. The most powerful approach to problem solving is to become familiar with concepts that others have invented (Bransford & Stein, 1984). These concepts, then, provide the tools for representing and solving problems. For example, researchers who are thoroughly versed in the basic concepts of genetics and molecular biology are also the most suitably equipped to explore the biological frontiers where ultimately the problems of cancer and heart disease will be solved.

The Good Problem Solver

Are there discernible characteristics that identify the good problem solver? Whimbey and Lochhead (1985) believe that an accumulation of research has resulted in the identification of the following categories that identify the "good problem solver."

- *Positive attitude.* Good problem solvers believe that they can solve problems by careful, persistent analysis. Poor problem solvers, on the other hand, believe that you either know the answer or you don't; if you don't, why bother trying? They have not learned that a problem that at first appears confusing can be broken down into parts and gradually analyzed. Poor problem solvers have not learned how to analyze, and thus they have little experience with successful solutions and even less self-confidence.
- *Concern for accuracy.* The good problem solver takes pains to grasp the facts and relationships that the problem presents. Poor problem solvers are rather casual: a quick reading, an immediate reaction, little concern for details. Here is an excellent example of what was previously mentioned about improving performance: simply by teaching students to read more carefully—reread—and to look for the details that are given, they can grasp the problem more accurately, thus improving their problem-solving skills.
- *Breaks the problem into parts.* Good problem solvers consistently try to break a problem into parts, analyze each part, and then integrate the parts in an attempt to

reach a solution. Poor problem solvers fail to see any sequence in a problem; they view it as total confusion. By teaching them to search for parts and then to try to understand the parts, we can ensure that poor problem solvers will increase their chances for success.
- *Avoids guessing.* Poor problem solvers tend to jump at the first answer that comes to mind. They frequently "play a hunch" (with few facts) or simply stop in the hunt for a solution; both of these tendencies reflect a lack of the first three categories of the good problem solver and are major sources of errors for students.
- *Active problem solver.* Good problem solvers just do more things than poor problem solvers as they search for a solution. If the problem is wordy, they may outline; if the problem is complicated, they may draw a diagram; they will continuously ask themselves questions about the problem. Each of these activities improves accuracy and sharpens focus on the problem.

Different Cultures—Different Perspectives

Problem-solving strategies provide unique insights into the cultural differences you will find in your classroom and what they mean for learning. Consider these statements (taken from New Voices, 1988).

- Don't take offense if Southeast Asian or Hispanic children don't look you in the eye—it's a sign of respect.
- Don't pat Southeast Asian children on the head— that's insulting.
- If you cross your fingers (considered good luck by Americans), many Southeast Asians think you have made an obscene gesture.
- Cambodians are insulted by anyone who calls to them by hand gestures.

These are but a few examples of cultural variation that can affect achievement. We also must avoid stereotypes: African-American students will fail; Asian-American students will succeed. Remember that "Asian" also includes Korean, Vietnamese, Filipino, Cambodian, and Chinese and that remarkably few studies have been done on Asian-American students who fail (Slaughter-Defoe et al., 1990).

The differences we have described may affect the way that students from different cultures attack problems. Remember: Students from different cultures may initially differ in what they identify as a problem. What you consider highly significant may appear irrelevant to them (Goodnow in Stigler et al., 1990). For example, Cole and Scribner (1974) described differences in the way that children from different cultures attempt to solve problems. If a metal box is divided into three sections—A,B,C—the subject is taught to push a button in the middle of the door to A to obtain a marble. Next the subject learns to push door C to receive a ball bearing. Then the subject can acquire a piece of candy by putting the marble in section B. Finally, all three doors are opened together, and the subject is told to do whatever is necessary to get the candy. Note that the subjects must combine two learned acts to get the candy: get the marble and then put it in box B. Liberian children had great difficulty with this task, but most American youngsters mastered it quickly. You can see how easy it would be to jump to conclusions about the problem-solving abilities of American and Liberian children.

When the authors changed the task by using materials more familiar to the Liberian youngsters (using keys painted red and black instead of pushing buttons to open the boxes), their success rate jumped to about 80 percent, and with prompting, to about 90 percent. The lesson should be clear: By adjusting the circumstances surrounding a task, we can help students from different cultures to use their abilities and thus improve their achievement.

In teaching multicultural students, try to detect any characteristics in their learning style that could affect their learning (as we have just seen in the above experiment). The following are especially significant differences among students of varied cultures (Grossman, 1990):

- whether your students rely on internal clues (ideas, feelings, values) to learn and solve problems or tend to use information from their environment.

- whether they prefer working alone or with others.

- whether they function better in competitive or cooperative situations.

- whether they prefer to work independently or seek feedback and guidance from others.

- whether they prefer abstract activities (such as math or science) or are interested in more affective subjects, such as history.

- whether they respond to praise or criticism from others or are relatively indifferent to the opinions of others.

Keeping in mind the characteristics of a good problem solver and the nature of tasks, we propose several strategies to help individuals master effective problem-solving techniques.

The DUPE Model

Many models have been proposed to help people solve a wide variety of problems. Often they use a series of steps in the form of an acronym (SAC—Strategic Air Command, NATO—North Atlantic Treaty Organization, HOMES—The names of the Great Lakes: Huron, Ontario, Michigan, Erie, Superior). For our purposes, we shall use an acronym that you can pass on to your students, one which they should be able to remember easily and which they can transfer to any problems. It will also be the model for the remainder of the chapter. The acronym is **DUPE** and its intent is to convey the message: *don't let yourself be deceived*. The meaning of each letter is as follows:

D—Determine just exactly what is the nature of the problem. Too often we are deceived by meaningless elements in the problem situation; it is here that attention to detail is so important.

U—Understand the nature of the problem. It is not enough to realize that a particular problem exists; you must also comprehend the essence of the problem if your plan for solution is to be accurate. For example, teachers frequently state that a student's classroom difficulties are the result of hyperactivity. Thus, the problem is identified but to understand the cause of the hyperactivity—physical, social, psychological—requires additional information.

P—Plan your solution. Now that you know that a problem exists and you understand its nature, you must select strategies that are appropriate for the problem. It is here that memory plays such an important role.

E—Evaluate your plan, which usually entails two phases. First you should examine the plan itself in an attempt to determine its suitability. Then you must decide how successful your solution was.

The model you are about to analyze offers several metacognitive strategies that you can pass on to your students. The first element in the DUPE model, then, is to determine the nature of the problem.

TEACHER ⬅➡ STUDENT
I N T E R A C T I O N S

Helping Students Meet Problems

1. You can help your students improve their problem-solving skills.
   - Begin with simple problems such as asking them to think of a different way of coming to school from their homes. Since your students will be familiar with the neighborhood, the problem is not difficult, but it does challenge them to think of something new.
   - Ask your class to write down all of the streets that they crossed that morning on their way to school. Simple tasks such as this will help them to become alert to details. When you are working with your students on solving problems, constantly urge them to pay attention to the details.
   - While they are listing the streets that they crossed, watch to see how each student does it. Some will sit there for a few minutes and then start writing; they have done it "in their heads." Others will draw a map of their route. It is the difference between internal and external representation. Encourage your students to do what comes naturally for them.
2. Teach your students about the common mistakes that people make in trying to solve problems.
   - To help them avoid becoming too impulsive when they meet a problem, ask questions using material with which they are familiar: Who was the third president before George Bush? Invariably, some pupils will blurt out the first name that comes to their minds, an action which provides you with the opportunity to stop the lesson and emphasize how important it is to think about the problem.
   - Ask your students to take the letters in the word *March* and rearrange them to form a different word. Some of your students will immediately say, "I can't do that." Use this opportunity to teach them to stop, try different

combinations, and keep trying until they get it. You can use this technique at both the elementary and secondary levels by varying the difficulty of the words used. Emphasize that they never should retreat from a problem.
   - Go back to the problem on p. 254 (the motorcyclists driving toward each other and the bird flying back and forth) and emphasize to students how important it is to take time and search for the givens of a problem. Now point out they must take the givens and match them against what is asked for. In the motorcycle problem, some of the givens were unnecessary for the solution.
3. Stress the characteristics of the good problem solver.
   - Begin with a problem that your students will find challenging but well within their competence. For example, casually ask your students how many months of the year have 28 days in them. After the usual responses, some student will probably look at you and say, "They *all* have 28 days." This provides you with an opportunity to point out the need for accuracy; don't jump at the first answer that comes to mind, but look at the problem more carefully.
   - Stress the value of breaking a problem into parts. Start with a simple problem such as this. *A clock takes two seconds to strike two o'clock. How long will it take to strike three o'clock?* The first part of this problem is the two seconds it takes to strike two o'clock; that is, one interval (between the sounds) takes the two seconds. The next part of the problem is the time it takes to strike three o'clock, in which there are two intervals of two seconds. Thus, four seconds are required. Most students love these brainteasers, which enable you to teach the basics of problem solving.

Determining the Nature of a Problem

How do we know that a problem exists? Students are often baffled when confronted by a problem; they have no idea of how to begin since they are unable to identify the nature of the problem. They have a vague sense that they "just can't do something." In the classroom they are usually told about the problem or read about it, and yet even these clues may offer little tangible help because the nature of the problem still eludes them.

They are not alone in their bewilderment. How would you go about solving this problem?

There is a super psychic who can predict the score of any game before it is played. Explain how this is possible.

This problem, taken from Bransford and Stein (1984), poses a challenge to most of us because, as the authors noted, it is difficult to generate a reasonable explanation. If you are having difficulty, it is probably because you have made a faulty assumption about the nature of the problem. You were not asked about the final score; the score of any game before it is played is 0 to 0. We deliberately presented a tricky problem to stress that you must attend to details.

The Elements of a Problem

Psychologists usually divide problems into two classes: **well-defined and ill-defined.** A well-defined problem is one in which the steps to solution are specified clearly in the problem's statement. The major focus in the solution of such problems is on the sequence of steps needed.

> If 3 oranges cost 99 cents how much does each orange cost?
>
> The facts are clearly stated; what is needed are the steps.
>
> 1. Three cost 99 cents
> 2. To find the cost of one, divide 99 by 3
> 3. Answer: 33

An ill-defined problem is one in which the givens are much more vague and the steps to solution more elusive. As Sternberg notes, such problems require one or two insights into their nature, insights that usually are difficult to achieve. Once they are achieved, however, the problem is quickly resolved.

The problems presented earlier in this chapter are examples of this type. If you had difficulty with the eight 8s, you could not solve it until you achieved the insight that there must be five groups. In the problem with the motorcycles and the bird, once you realized that the solution depended on the bird's speed per hour (since the cyclists traveled for one hour), the answer came quickly.

In his classic study of problem solving, Wickelgren (1974) stated that problems provide three types of information: givens, operation, and goals.

- **Givens.** These are the facts that are presented in the problem as we commence work, including representations of objects, things, and events as well as expressions representing assumptions, definitions, and facts. For example, you were given eight 8s to work with. A kind of implicit given is that you may need additional knowledge from other sources. As Wickelgren noted, you should be alert to this type of implicit information, again reinforcing the importance of attention. Carefully attending to the details in the problem helps you to grasp its nature and decide if you need additional information, and if you do, from what source.

Wickelgren's advice is excellent; even recognizing the relevant properties of the givens, with no additional background information needed, we still fail to explore the possible uses of these properties to solve the problem. This failure is especially detrimental in efforts to solve insight problems where the relationships among the properties are often critical for solution. The opposite advice to this, of course, is not to become dazzled by the irrelevant givens that appear in the problem. For example, in the motorcycle and bird problem, to concentrate on how many times the bird would fly back and forth between the cyclists would be merely distracting.

- **Operations.** By operations, Wickelgren means the actions that you can perform on the givens. These are the actions that are permitted within the framework of the problem. How do you solve the following problem?

> The perimeter of a rectangle is 25 feet greater than the sum of its length and width. If the length is 15 feet longer than the width, what are its dimensions?

1. What is required? (The rectangle's dimensions.)
2. What am I asked to do? (Solve for length and width.)
3. What am I given? (The perimeter and the length.)
4. What shall I do? (Use the given data: The perimeter $P = x + (x + 15) + x + (x + 15)$ is 25 feet greater than the sum of length and width.
5. Solve:

$$x + (x + 15) + x + (x + 15) = x + (x + 15) + 25$$
$$4x + 30 = 2x + 15 + 25$$
$$4x + 30 = 2x + 40$$
$$2x = 10$$
$$x = 5$$

The solution to this problem demonstrates all that we have been discussing thus far:

- Attention to detail (What is required?);
- What am I asked to do? (Understand the nature of the problem.);
- What are the givens? (Is additional information needed?);
- What shall I do? (Plan and represent the solution.).

With regard to operations, certain mathematical rules that are essential to the problem's solution determine your actions. You must remove parentheses and change signs when you move an item from one side of the equation to the other. Most of us are quite familiar with these operations, but other actions, which are almost as familiar, can remain tantalizingly elusive. Try to solve this much used balance problem.

> In a collection of 12 cans of soda, 11 cans have exactly the same weight, while one is heavier than the others. How would you determine which is the heavy can if you are provided with a balance scale that will weigh as many cans as

you wish to put on each side of the scale? The problem is that you must discover the heavy can in the least number of weighings.

A quick reaction to this problem is to divide the 12 cans into 2 sets of 6, select the set of 6 that is heavier, and divide this into 2 sets of 3. It is here that your strategy breaks down. How will you assess the final set of 3: 1 against 1, and then a final set of 1 versus 1?

Actually, however, the scale offers three options for solution: heavier, lighter, or equal. Consequently, by dividing the original 12 cans into 3 sets of 4, you can weigh one set of 4 against the other, thus immediately determining which set of 4 contains the heavy can. If the first two sets balance, then the heavy can is in the third set. Now balance 2 against 2, and finally 1 against 1. You have solved the problem in three steps.

By carefully considering the operations required and understanding the most efficient way that they can be employed you can avoid miscalculations that frustrate problem solution.

- **Goals.** When you cannot get where you want to go—you can't immediately solve the problem—you must devise a means of bridging the gap as economically as possible. Accurately representing the information contained in a problem depends on a precise and correct definition of the goal. You should have a clear, precise statement of the goal, rather than some vague formulation, which may do considerable harm when you attempt to solve a problem (Wickelgren, 1974, p. 37).

    The goal must be perfectly clear in your mind since it influences the choice of strategies that you select for solution: What is the goal as stated in the problem or posed by the situation? What do I need to attain the goal? Was I successful? It is here that we see the value of categorizing problems as ill- or well-structured. Although the basic strategies that lead to solution are probably the same for both, there are surface differences that affect the ease and quality of solution. For ill-structured problems that require more background information, your perspective on the problem continues to change as you secure new data. But it is your definition of the goal that shapes all else that follows.

Realizing that a problem exists and having determined its basic dimensions, the second stage of our DUPE model takes us more deeply into the nature of problems.

Understanding the Nature of the Problem

Understanding the nature of a problem implies that we can both define and represent it, which has several sig-

nificant implications. Before you define a problem you must have a sufficient amount of knowledge to recognize the givens. You must also have adequate problem-solving skills that permit you to represent it. Both of these prerequisites suggest the relevance of categorizing problems as ill- or well-defined. Many of life's daily problems are vague; we can label them as ill-defined. If we lack problem-solving strategies, then our task is next to impossible. Here is one of the major reasons why there is growing pressure for schools to teach problem-solving skills, either as a separate course or as a part of a course's content.

As an example of the value of teaching problem-solving strategies consider the following.

> Tom either walks to work and rides his bicycle home or rides his bicycle to work and walks home. The round trip takes one hour. If he were to ride both ways, it would take 30 minutes. If Tom walked both ways, how long would a round trip take?

This problem (based on Wickelgren, 1974, p. 104) illustrates a basic problem solving strategy of dividing the givens into subgoals. Think for a moment: What are the givens? How long would it take to ride one way? (15 minutes) How long is a round trip? (one hour) How long does it take to walk one way? (45 minutes) How long is the round trip if Tom walked both ways? (45 + 45 = 90 minutes)

The Knowledge Base

Compare the givens of the above problem with the example Hayes (1989) uses to stress the importance of prior knowledge (based on Smith & Van Ness, 1959).

> Liquid water at 212° F and 1 atm has an internal energy (on an arbitrary basis) of 180.02 BTU/lb. The specific volume of liquid water at these conditions is 0.01672 ft/lb. What is the enthalpy?

For anyone with a knowledge of thermodynamics this is not a particularly difficult problem. If you lack the necessary prior knowledge, however, you are defeated before you start. If you are missing relevant knowledge, an easy problem may appear difficult, if not impossible. *Remember: Much that passes for cleverness or innate quickness of mind actually depends on specialized knowledge* (Hayes, 1989). This helps to explain current interest in the role of prior knowledge in problem solving.

Recent cognitive research demonstrates that an understanding of cognitive processes demands recognition of the role of knowledge and its internal representation. In their studies of expert chess players, Chase and Simon (1973) discovered that experts differed from novices in playing chess, not by employing different processes but in the knowledge base that they use for their strategies.

What has also become more apparent is that the acquisition of knowledge in itself is not enough; what is also critical is the availability of knowledge when needed. (Retrieval from memory, which we shall discuss in the next section, is an example of getting at and using information that we have previously stored.)

Available knowledge also serves another function, that of assisting the individual in deciding what information provided by the problem is or is not pertinent. Analyzing the givens that we have discussed previously illustrates this function. In the problem of the eight 8s, the number of digits is obviously pertinent; what is not as equally pertinent is the manner in which the 8s must be grouped. In this problem, pertinence must emerge from background knowledge, which demonstrates that both pertinence and availability are key issues in problem solving.

Problem Representation

The first and most basic step in problem solving is to represent the information in either symbolic or diagrammatic form. Symbolic form casts the problem's information in words, letters, or numbers, while diagrammatic form expresses the information by some collection of lines, dots, or angles. The first step, then, in solving a problem is to take the givens and cast them in some form that is more personally meaningful.

Representation may be either internal or external. When we initially begin problem solving, we mentally visualize and arrange the givens, so all representation commences as internal. There can be as many diverse schemes of internal representation as there are people. First, however, let's examine external representation.

External Representation

Following this beginning phase, some of us with almost all problems and all of us with complex problems turn to **external representation** (drawing parts, expressing the givens as symbols). The value and applicability of our external representation is highly dependent on the quality and perceptiveness of the internal representation.

Lewis and Greene (1982, p. 204) offer the following problem as an example of using internal or external (or both) representation.

> As principal of a school with 1,000 students, you have the task of ordering textbooks for each course. Students can elect to study either language or a science, and this semester you learn from the language department that 400 have elected to take Spanish and 300 will take French. One hundred fifty of the language students want to take both. How many science books must you order to be sure that each student not electing language will have one?

Good problem solving requires gathering and organizing facts.

Once again we have a problem that incorporates much of what we have discussed. It is well-structured, but the givens require careful attention. Although some readers will derive the solution in their heads, others will immediately reach for paper and pencil. A quick reading of the problem might lead you to conclude that 300 science books should be ordered. But note that 150 students are taking both French and Spanish.

Representing the givens externally, you could proceed as follows.

Total number of students	1,000
Taking Spanish	400
Taking French	300
Taking both	150

The total number taking French and Spanish is 700, but 150 of these are the same students; thus, 550 students will take language, leaving 450 students needing science books.

Here we have an excellent example of how external representation can help in problem solving. Wickelgren (1974, pp. 186–187) offered several reasons for the use of external representation.

• Writing down a problem's givens focuses your attention on the most important concepts.

Teaching Students to Construct Graphic Representations

Graphic representations are visual illustrations of verbal statements and can be helpful in understanding a problem and in mapping a solution to a problem. Many researchers discuss the uses and effects of graphic representations in problem solving (Bransford, Sherwood, Vye, & Rieser, 1986; Silver, 1987) and in creative thinking (McTighe & Lyman, 1988).

Undoubtedly you are familiar with graphic representations such as flow charts, pie charts, and family trees. Box Figure 9.1*a* and *b* present other graphic representations that are useful in facilitating students' comprehension, summarizations, and synthesis of complex ideas.

Students who used graphic structures like these were better able to select important ideas and recall details, as well as detect missing information and unrelated connections from the material they read (Jones, Pierce, & Hunter, 1988). These researchers also noted that the use of graphic representations seemed to foster nonlinear thinking and provide input into both visual and verbal modes of processing information.

Thus, an effective graphic representation can show at a glance the key parts of a whole and their relations, thereby allowing a holistic understanding that words alone can't convey.

Jones and her colleagues recommend a five-step procedure for teaching students to use graphic representations in their work. The five steps are:

1. Present at least one good example of a graphic outline that matches the type of outline you will teach.
2. Model how to construct either the same graphic outline or the one to be introduced.
3. Provide procedural knowledge about when and why they should use a particular type of graphic structure.
4. Coach students in the use of graphic structures by asking them to explain the structures they choose and then give them feedback about their choices.
5. Give students opportunities to practice outlining with graphic structures and provide them feedback.

"Here's your problem; you had a fold in your plans."

(a)

Graphic representations are visual illustrations of verbal statements. Frames are sets of questions or categories that are fundamental to understanding a given topic. Here are shown nine "generic" graphic forms with their corresponding frames. Also given are examples of topics that could be represented by each graphic form. These graphics show at a glance the key parts of the whole and their relations, helping the learner to comprehend text and solve problems.

Spider map

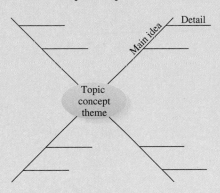

Used to describe a central idea: a thing (a geographic region), process (meiosis), concept (altruism), or proposition with support (experimental drugs should be available to AIDS victims). Key frame questions: What is the central idea? What are its attributes? What are its functions?

Series of events chain

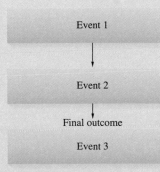

Initiating event

Event 1

Event 2

Final outcome

Event 3

Used to describe the stages of something (the life cycle of a primate); the steps in a linear procedure (how to neutralize an acid); a sequence of events (how feudalism led to the formation of nation states); or the goals, actions, and outcomes of a historical figure or character in a novel (the rise and fall of Napoleon). Key frame questions: What is the object, procedure, or initiating event? What are the stages or steps? How do they lead to one another? What is the final outcome?

Continuum/Scale

Low   High

Used for time lines showing historical events or ages (grade levels in school), degrees of something (weight), shades of meaning (Likert scales), or ratings scales (achievement in school). Key frame questions: What is being scaled? What are the end points?

Compare/Contrast matrix

	Name 1	Name 2
Attribute 1		
Attribute 2		
Attribute 3		

Used to show similarities and differences between two things (people, places, events, ideas, etc.). Key frame questions: What things are being compared? How are they similar? How are they different?

Problem/Solution outline

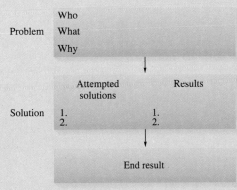

Used to represent a problem, attempted solutions, and results (the national debt). Key frame questions: What was the problem? Who had the problem? Why was it a problem? What attempts were made to solve the problem? Did those attempts succeed?

Box Figure 9.1
Graphic forms with corresponding text frames.

(continued on next page)

Teaching Students to Construct Graphic Representations
Continued

(b)

Network tree

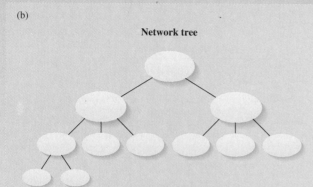

Used to show causal information (causes of poverty), a hierarchy (types of insects), or branching procedures (the circulatory system). Key frame questions: What is the superordinate category? What are the subordinate categories? How are they related? How many levels are there?

Fishbone map

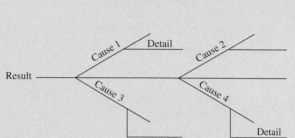

Used to show causal interaction of a complex event (an election, a nuclear explosion) or complex phenomenon (juvenile delinquency, learning disabilities). Key frame questions: What are the factors that cause X? How do they interrelate? Are the factors that cause X the same as those that cause X to persist?

Human interaction outline

Goals		Goals
Person 1		Person 2
Group 1		Group 2

Interaction

Action ⟶ Reaction

Action ⟶ Reaction 1
⟶ Reaction 2

Outcomes		Outcomes
Person 1		Person 2
Group 1		Group 2

Used to show the nature of an interaction between persons or groups (European settlers and American Indians). Key frame questions: Who are the persons or groups? What are their goals? Did they conflict or cooperate? What was the outcome for each person or group?

Cycle

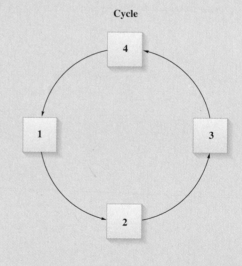

Used to show how a series of events interact to produce a set of results again and again (weather phenomena, cycles of achievement and failure, the life cycle). Key frame questions: What are the critical events in the cycle? How are they related? In what ways are they self-reinforcing?

Box Figure 9.1 (Continued)
Graphic forms with corresponding text frames.

- You begin to see relationships among the givens.
- If the problem is complex, representing the intermediate steps aids memory.
- Some givens, such as tables or graphs, are quite difficult to visualize in detail.

In no way is the emphasis on external representation intended to diminish the vital role of internal representation, which is the basis of all symbolic and diagrammatic forms.

Internal Representation

It is a mistake to conceive of **internal representations** as an external copy of an external situation because internal representation entails the addition and elimination of details from the original and the interpretation of information (Hayes, 1989). As a simple example of Hayes' intent, close your eyes for a moment and picture some location in which you typically relax and enjoy yourself, say a particular beach. You probably added details that are not part of the beach—people, boats, parasols. You undoubtedly omitted some details that usually are present, perhaps seaweed. Finally, you probably experienced pleasant feelings as you thought about the beach—you interpreted the data.

Each of us also forms a different representation of the same circumstances; some of us tend to represent visually, others verbally, while still others may use auditory images. There are no rigid distinctions among these various kinds of representations, although one form is usually dominant; teachers, for example, tend to be quite verbal.

The manner in which we represent a problem determines the ease or difficulty with which we solve it, if at all. A good example of the importance of representation is seen in the classic nine dots problem.

> Without taking your pencil from the paper, connect each of the dots by using four straight lines. Each dot must be touched.

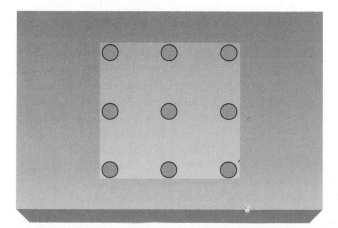

Difficulty arises for those who attempt the following solution.

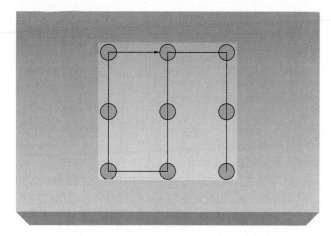

There are variations of this strategy, but they always reach the same conclusion: one dot remains untouched. *You will never solve the nine dots problem until you change your representation,* which you can do if you attend to the givens in the instructions. Nowhere were you told to remain within the confines of a square. (We too often impose limits on ourselves when we face problems.) Once you change your representation, the solution follows easily.

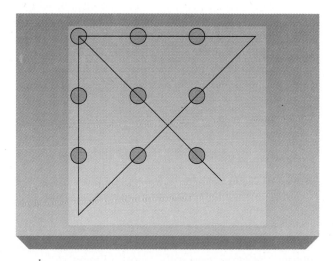

Representation, then, is basic for planning an accurate solution and you should remember, and encourage your students to remember, that if you are having difficulty in solving a problem, consider changing your representation.

Planning the Solution

Once you have a workable representation of the problem, you now must devise a plan for its solution, which involves two critical aspects. It is at this stage that students like Timmy can be helped. If students can't organize the material satisfactorily (that is, in accordance with their learning styles), they will have difficulty in solving problems.

First, there is the need to be familiar with the core concepts required for solution. If the problem demands basic arithmetic facts, then your students must be able to do the addition or division that is required. We have previously seen the necessity for conceptual tools in the problem concerning thermodynamics: for those of us lacking prior knowledge in this field, the problem remains insoluble since we lack the strong strategies.

Second, there is the need to apply certain general strategies that seem appropriate. We have mentioned some of these such as working backwards, which can be helpful if the goal and givens are stated clearly. Means-end analysis is another general strategy that aids solution when the goal is obvious. Assume that your house needs painting and you decide to do it yourself. The goal is clear, but the means to achieve it require additional planning.

If the old paint is peeling, then it first must be scraped and roughed up with a wire brush. You must then decide if these spots need priming. Is there hardware you should remove? What kind of paint is best suited to the weather conditions in your area: latex or oil? How you answer this question dictates the kind of paint brush you should use. Though these steps seem simple, if you omit one—such as scraping—the solution is faulty.

Helping You Plan

Now that you have done the basic preparation for attacking the problem, you can select an array of learning strategies that will help you to formulate a plan for solution. Hayes (1989) suggests seven learning strategies that reflect much of the work that we discussed in the preceding chapter, especially the role of memory.

1. **The Structuring Strategy.** This strategy is intended to have you search for relations in the learning material; it is a method for discovering structures. What is the relationship among the eight 8s that will enable you to solve the problem? Once you uncover these relations, they may reveal categories, hierarchies, or networks that will help you to understand the material. The use of graphic representations, as described in the previous teacher-student interactions box, is an illustration of a structuring strategy.

2. **The Context Strategy.** In the context strategy, you are urged to search for relations within the material to be learned. This differs from the structuring strategy in that the relations may be between the learning material and what we already know. You know that $8 \times 5 = 40$; therefore five groups are needed. If you have learned how to disassemble a one-barrel carburetor, it is much easier to repair a two-barrel carburetor than if you had no experience whatsoever.

3. **Monitoring.** Monitoring requires that you constantly teach yourself to see what you have or have not learned. In problem solving you can constantly question yourself to determine if each detail of your plan is moving you closer to solution. Now that I know I need five groups, how many 8s should be in each group?

4. **Inferencing.** Inference strategy also involves asking yourself questions, but the questions are not merely factual. They are intended to generate inferences about the material to evaluate its importance or implications for problem solution. In the nine dots problem, you may well begin to wonder, "What would happen if I extend the lines outside the square?" Or in the eight 8s problem, "Can I use more than one 8 in each group? How many 8s should be in the first group?"

5. **Instantiation.** Instantiation means to furnish an example. Are there problems similar to the one I am attempting to solve? We may also try to create examples for ourselves or others. If you were trying to explain a foul in baseball, your listeners may find it helpful if you tell them that if the baseball stays outside the white lines before it reaches either first or third bases (first and third), it is a "foul."

6. **Multiple Coding.** Can we represent the information—the givens in our problem—in more than one way: verbally or through mental imagery? As you attempted to solve the problem of the cyclists and the bird, you may have made the givens more meaningful by using them in a story or by forming mental pictures of the cyclists moving toward each other and the bird racing between them.

7. **Attention Management.** What do you do with your time? If you face a problem, do you find yourself daydreaming? Hayes suggests that you allow yourself enough time to study a problem, organize your schedule, and stay with it.

The Role of Memory

As we saw in chapter 7, one of the most powerful strategies in solving problems is the efficient use of memory. All memory strategies, however, are not equally as effective. The appropriateness of the strategy depends on the level of material involved and the conditions under which the information must be remembered. Try this memory problem.

The following list contains 25 words. Take 90 seconds to study the following words. When time runs out, write as many of the words as you can without looking at the list.

book	word
page	mirror
wheel	pear
ball	truck
apple	court
light	wrench
net	tree
orange	tire
branch	minutes
sneaker	minutes
leaf	brake
basket	column
referee	

How did you do? Or more importantly from our perspective, how did you do it? Were these among the strategies you used?

• Rehearse (repeat) each word until you were sure you had memorized it: tire, tire, tire; book, book, book; branch, branch, branch.
• Rehearse several words: ball, apple, referee; ball, apple, referee.
• Organize the words by category. Note that several words related to cars; others could be grouped as fruit; still others could be categorized as relating to books.
• Did you construct a story to relate as many of the words as possible?
• Did you form images of words or groups of words?

You may have tried one or a combination of these strategies, but note that you were not told to memorize them in any particular manner. If you had received specific instructions, each of these strategies would not have been equally as effective. When we are asked to remember a particular telephone number, the tendency is to rehearse it for as long as we need to recall it. But if you had been directed to memorize them in a certain order (the way that they were presented), grouping items by categories would not have been efficient; thinking of a story to link them in the correct order would have been much more efficient (Kail, 1984).

(If you attempted to memorize these 25 words by straight rehearsal—not by grouping or any other technique—then you undoubtedly could recall from 5 to 9 words; the average memory span for familiar words is 5.86.)

Retrieval Aids

A major issue for most of us is what psychologists call **storing** and **retrieving.** Much too frequently we have something in our memory (we have stored it) but we cannot get at it (we cannot retrieve it). We know what the answer is but just can't recall it; it's on the "tip of my tongue."

Think for a moment about the list of words you were asked to memorize. A few of them were probably on the "tip of your tongue." If an instructor were to ask you, "Who is Larry Bird?" you may hesitate. Then the instructor adds, "Boston." It is as if you opened a door: Bird, Boston, Boston Celtics, basketball, most valuable player.

There are several techniques that can help us to trigger our memory. Among the most effective retrieval aids are the following:

• **Cues.** Although you were supplied with the cue (Boston) in the above example (Larry Bird), the most effective cues for your students (and for all of us) are those that we generate ourselves. Regardless of the task that we face, we almost always believe that we learned more than we recall; we simply "cannot get at" the material. Try this memory problem.

Read each of the following sentences once, spending about (no more than) three seconds on each. As soon as you are finished, put the list out of sight and write as many of the sentences as you can recall.

Thomas Jefferson was a Virginian.
The tide was high at 10:45 A.M.
Evergreens are not deciduous.
Our new car is a turbo diesel.
The lawnmower has a rotary construction.
Light travels at the rate of 186 million miles/second.

"We don't learn at school anymore, Mom. We retrieve."

© Mike Streff.

John F. Kennedy was born in Brookline, Massachusetts.

Richard Feynman won the Nobel Prize for physics in 1965.

In the colder climates, lobsters usually shed their shells in July.

The new generation of printers is based on laser principles.

Most readers will recall 6 or 7 of these 10 sentences. Our interest is in what happened to the other 3 or 4. Did you fail to encode them? Did you lose them almost immediately? Use these words as retrieval cues for the sentences you cannot recall.

laser	rotary
Virginian	deciduous
tide	lobsters
Brookline	light
turbo	Nobel

This time you probably remembered most, if not all, the sentences that you initially failed to retrieve. Your students, with instruction and guidance, can easily master this technique and will improve not only their problem-solving skills but also their memory in all subjects. Initially, you can teach them how to utilize this technique by providing them with tangible cues for the material you are presenting. Your ultimate objective is to help them devise their own cues for any subject they encounter.

A particularly effective cue is the use of acronyms and acrostics. As mentioned earlier, an acronym is a word consisting of the letters of a series of words (DUPE). There is a two-fold value to acronyms: (a) the compression of several facts into a smaller number (which reflects Miller's magic number 7 + 2), and (b) the cues it provides for remembering large amounts of data; DUPE acts as a trigger, releasing the facts incorporated under each letter.

A second strategy is to devise a sentence or phrase with words whose first letter is the cue for certain information. Most of us who are non-musicians relied on an acrostic to recall the lines of a G clef.

e very

g ood

b oy

d oes

f ine

Using an acrostic is an effective strategy as long as the material is not too complicated or unique. The strategy should never be more difficult than the task; the goal is to simplify.

- **Imagery.** Some students—as well as readers—tend to visualize objects or events; they function more efficiently in this mode rather than relying on verbal processes that are less dependent on concreteness. You can encourage the use of imagery in all students, and they will find it helpful.

  Urge them to form a picture that links the items that they are to remember. For example, if students must remember that John Adams was the second president of the United States, ask them to picture Adams standing for a portrait and holding a large card with the number 2 on it. For those students who function best in this mode, and even for those who are more verbal, encouraging them to use imagery can aid retention and recall.

- **The Method of Loci.** The above techniques are excellent provided that the retrieval cues are appropriate. Lacking appropriate stimuli, however, you still can devise your personal cues to help you remember and recall unrelated items. The method of loci—using familiar locations—was originally used by the Greeks and Romans to recall items in a fixed sequence. By utilizing a series of familiar visual images and linking each image to the object to be retained, you have formulated your personal retrieval cues.

  Since the rooms in your house are firmly locked in your memory, they are suitable "locations" in which to place the items to be remembered. First, form an image of the object that you must recall and then, second, place it somewhere in one of the rooms. Use each location only once; if you placed the word "educational psychology" on the couch in the living room, do not use that specific location again. Try using the method of loci.

  Here are several words that I would like you to be able to define and use. Map out a path that you would walk in your home, arranging the rooms along the path in the most economical manner possible. Now "picture" each word and place it somewhere on your route.

  assimilation

  concrete operations

  learning

  locus of control

  cognitive

  attribution

  value

  strategy

  iconic

  accommodation

Elaboration

To elaborate is to add information to what you are trying to learn so that the material becomes more personally meaningful. According to Weinstein and others (1988/1989), "**Elaboration** involves using what we already know to help make sense of what we are trying to learn. 'What we already know' includes our prior knowledge, our experiences, our attitudes, our beliefs, and our values" (Weinstein, et al., 1989/1990, pp. 17–18).

Elaboration strategies that improve students' recall of material are effective because they produce an increased depth of processing (more involvement with material). Elaboration also facilitates storage of new information with related information that is well known to the learner (Weinstein & Mayer, 1986). The effective use of elaboration strategies depends on students' relating what they are trying to learn to what they already know. The way learners enact this strategy can involve a number of specific tactics, such as creating analogies, paraphrasing, summarizing in their own words, transforming information into another form such as a chart or diagram, using comparison and contrast methods, or trying to teach what they are learning to someone else.

Teachers can help students develop fluent and flexible elaboration tactics by encouraging them to answer questions about the material they are learning. Questions that have been shown to be helpful include:

- What is the main idea of this story?
- What does this material remind me of?
- How can I put this into my own words?
- What is a good example of this that I am familiar with?
- How does this apply to my life?

Teachers can help students to use elaboration tactics by creating opportunities for students to answer questions like those above and then test their recall of the information they have acquired.

These are the most prominent of several techniques designed to improve retention and recall. They can be extremely helpful to you and your students if you remember two warnings: (a) be sure that the strategy itself is not so complex and cumbersome that it requires more effort to remember than the content; (b) be sure that you and your students adopt techniques that are best suited to you. Your personal style should determine the strategy with which you are most comfortable.

Finally, try to devise your own method of improving retention. When you are faced with the task of mastering material, how do you go about it? What is your general strategy? Now, applying the suggestions just offered, can you refine and improve your strategy?

For example, a student will occasionally describe a strategy of attempting to visualize the page on which the material to be memorized is located. If successful, the words on that particular page seem to come alive in memory. Performance was aided by suggesting the use of cues within this student's preferred general strategy.

You can improve your memory by:

- knowing as much about different techniques as possible;
- discovering those techniques that seem to work particularly well for you;
- practice, practice, practice.

These techniques for improving memory are intended to be used with other strategies discussed in this section so that you have a wide variety of choices to help you select the most effective plan possible, one that is most pertinent for a particular problem. With this accomplished, it is time to move to the evaluation stage of the DUPE model.

Evaluating the Solution

If all has gone well, you have formulated a plan that incorporates careful attention to the givens, either an internal or external representation of the problem (or both), and a plan that you can effectively use. Evaluation now plays an important role in your search for a solution.

Examining Your Plan and Solution

Two aspects of evaluation seem especially pertinent:

1. *The necessity to stop here and evaluate your plan.* Does it include all of the vital givens? Does your representation account for the givens in a way that reflects the essence of the problem? Does your plan use both the vital facts and your representation of the problem so that it is calculated to reach the required solution?
2. *If your answers to these and similar questions are affirmative,* then the first evaluative phase is complete and you should activate your plan. After you have worked through the plan, a second evaluative phase is needed in which you must decide if you have found a solution or if you are totally satisfied with the solution that you have achieved. As Hayes (1989, p. 46) noted, the critical question in evaluation is: Does the answer I propose meet all of the goals and conditions set by

the problem? If you were told to solve for x, the mere fact that you have x on one side of your equation and everything else on the other does not necessarily mean that you are right.

As one means of addressing the issues raised by evaluation, Sternberg and Salter (1982) introduced the concept of "component," which they define as an elementary information process that operates upon internal representations of objects or symbols. One of the derivatives of components is what Sternberg designates **metacomponents,** higher order control processes used in planning, determining alternate courses of action, and monitoring the success of the plan. Metacomponents activate and receive feedback from other components, thus insuring a constant monitoring process. Though metacomponents may be highly speculative, Sternberg's work indicates intense interest in the evaluative phase of problem solving.

What happens if you negatively answer the question just posed: "No, I have not reached the correct solution." You must continue the search process and not let frustration halt your continued search. We are all creative to a certain extent, and knowledge about the creative process may help you through these periods of frustration.

Creativity and Evaluation

Have you ever done something totally novel, at least for you? Have you fit a part into a toaster or iron so that it works? Have you discovered a solution to a math problem, a solution that was not in the back of the book? Creative behavior involves acts that are both novel and of value. Thus creativity can be a critical part of the problem-solving evaluation process. As Perkins noted (1981), there is nothing odd or novel about the idea of inventing behavior to help with thinking, problem solving, or invention. Discussing the notion of generating novel solutions when your efforts are blocked, Perkins described the results of research on heuristics that has emerged from recent analyses of "teaching thinking."

Heuristics

Assume that you are frustrated in your efforts to solve a particular problem. You have used all the suggested techniques: attention to detail, breaking into parts, formed representations, searched for relationships. None of these well-known techniques helps. *Therefore, you must generate new solutions.* One way is by teaching yourself (and your students) to use alternative search strategies, a process called **heuristics.**

Perkins contrasts heuristics with algorithms. An algorithm is a precise series of steps that leads to solution. Solving for the perimeter of a rectangle is a good example; you must place the correct expressions on the proper side of the equation and then solve for x by a series of definite steps.

Using algorithms to solve many (if not most) of your problems is impossible, especially with ill-defined daily problems. Consequently, we tend to use heuristics and engage in searches that are highly selective (that is, highly individualistic) and usually incomplete. Then why use them?

Heuristics are personal guidelines based on your knowledge, your experiences, your learning style, and your choice of strategies. They are effective when they call your attention to overlooked facts, hidden relationships, ties to something you already know. They can be effective even while being incomplete because they initiate a different kind of effort, a different type of search. All the evidence need not be present before we reach a solution. Recall the Gestalt principle of closure and examine the drawing below.

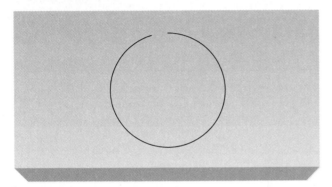

You instantly identified a circle. Heuristics functions in exactly the same way. What do we know about creative individuals that could help us in our work with students?

The Creative Student

Who are the creative students? Remember: Creative is not identical with gifted. Gifted is too restricted an interpretation of creative since it has been amply demonstrated that intelligence test items have a low correlation with creativity (Dacey, 1989a). Among the characteristics of creative people are the following:

- *Cognitive Skills.* Certain cognitive elements are necessary for creative thinking. These include memory and evaluation. Divergent elements, such as originality, flexibility, and sensitivity, are indispensable. Another outstanding characteristic of the creative thinker is the ability to sense problems, a realization that some ambiguity exists.
- *Motivation-Interest.* Creative people are curious; they like to manipulate ideas. They have a high achievement need that is linked with an intellectual persistence. They seek challenges, prefer the complex, and can tolerate uncertainty. They like to look at things in a new way (Dacey, 1989a). An inevitable conclusion is that creative thinkers have an intense commitment to their work.

- *Personality.* Creative persons are independent, inclined to take risks, resourceful, adventurous, and complex. They also possess an excellent sense of humor and see themselves as getting along well with others (Dacey, 1989a).

As a teacher, you are probably most interested in discovering if there have been any links between age and creativity. There seem to be three stages of creative change (Lesner & Hillman, 1983):

1. *From birth to 11 years old,* a time of "creative internal enrichment," during which children develop their own distinct personalities;
2. *From 12 to 60 years old,* a time of "creative external enrichment," during which there occurs a transition to a more outward, socially aware orientation;
3. *From age 60 to death,* a time of "creative self-evaluation," during which individuals assess their life's accomplishments.

Dacey (1989b) has made a more recent attempt to address this issue. Noting that most people, under the right circumstances, can greatly improve their creative ability, Dacey (1989b) argues that there are six peak periods in the growth of creativity, which follow these general age guidelines:

For Males	For Females
1. 0–5 years	0–5 years
2. 11–14 years	10–13 years
3. 18–20 years	18–20 years
4. 29–31 years	29–31 years
5. 40–45 years	40–45 years
6. 60–65 years	60–65 years

These are the periods that seem more intellectually volatile than others, and Dacey argues that substantial increases in creativity are less likely with each succeeding period. For our purposes, note how the first three periods include both the preschool and school years. Of particular importance is the 10- to 14-year-old period. Noting that students of this age are attempting to define their self-concept, Dacey believes that this is an ideal time to foster creativity since these students are open to new ideas as they intensify their search for their identity.

How can you help your students to fulfill their creative potential?

Fostering Creativity

There is nothing trivial about any discussion of creativity because society urgently needs a steady supply of creative minds to insure not only progress but its very survival. Creativity by its very nature requires fertile grounds in which to flourish, one of which, and perhaps the most important, is the classroom. To help you think about your

Table 9.1

Analyzing Your Personal Learning Style

The questions that Lewis and Greene (1982, pp. 149–150) used to assess learning style are as follows. (Answer these carefully and learn something about your personal learning style.)

1. When studying an unfamiliar subject do you:
   a. prefer to gather information from many topic areas?
   b. prefer to stay fairly close to the central topic?
2. Would you prefer to:
   a. know a little about a great many subjects?
   b. become an expert on just one subject?
3. When studying from a textbook do you:
   a. skip ahead and read chapters of special interest out of sequence?
   b. work systematically from one chapter to the next, not moving on until you have understood earlier material?
4. When asking other people for information do you:
   a. tend to ask broad questions that call for general answers?
   b. tend to ask narrow questions that demand specific answers?
5. When browsing in a library or bookstore do you:
   a. look at books on many different subjects?
   b. stay in one section, concentrating on one or two subjects?
6. Are you best at remembering:
   a. general principles?
   b. specific facts?
7. When performing some task do you:
   a. like to have background information not strictly related to the work?
   b. prefer to concentrate on strictly relevant information?
8. Do you think that educators should:
   a. give students exposure to a wide variety of subjects in college?
   b. ensure that students mainly acquire extensive knowledge related to their specialties?
9. When on vacation would you sooner:
   a. spend a short amount of time in several different places?

b. stay in just one place the whole time and really get to know it?
10. When learning something would you rather:
    a. follow general guidelines?
    b. work to a detailed plan of action?
    Now add up your a's and b's; if you scored six or more a's you are holist, or to use the terminology of Lewis and Greene, a **grouper**; if you scored six or more b's, you are a **stringer**. The higher you score in either of the categories, the more closely your learning style approximates the following descriptions.

1. *Groupers.* Groupers have the following characteristics:
   - *Description.* Preferring as wide a grasp of a subject as possible, groupers like to learn general principles and attempt to relate the topic under consideration to as many related subjects as possible. They usually learn better in unstructured situations, tending to resist detailed classes and instructional methods. Groupers may experience difficulty with much of current educational practice that is based on systematic, step-by-step techniques.
   - *Learning strategies.* Lewis and Greene (1982, p. 152) stated that groupers should begin by studying general concepts and the total situation or problem before commencing more detailed analysis. For example, a grouper beginning to study the workings of a particular computer should start by acquiring knowledge about the history of computers, something about the general technology, and perhaps several examples of computer usage in our society. Then you can set the more systematic study of a particular computer within this broad framework of knowledge. This approach to a problem matches the learning style of a grouper. The weakness of this technique is that groupers or holists tend to ignore essential details that could impair problem solution.
   - *Organizing material.* Groupers learn most efficiently and most successfully when they are able to relate the material being studied to a wide range of topics. Lewis and Greene (1982, p. 159) suggested that if four topics

classroom as a stimulating environment for creative behavior, consider the following general suggestions.

- *Try to ensure that the material that you use to encourage creativity in the classroom matches the developmental level of the child.* If you recall Piaget's stages of cognitive development, you know that young children can have difficulty with material that is too abstract, so at these early stages, although you

can encourage them to be innovative, you must also use content suitable for their cognitive abilities.
- *Give children experience in deriving as many and different responses to a problem as possible.* Select a word such as book and ask students to think of as many uses as possible for it. List them on the board and then ask the children for more uses. You are fostering divergent thinking, not just requiring one

are to be learned, groupers should learn the first two separately but rehearse them together. Topics three and four should be learned the same way; then items one and two should be recalled. Finally, rehearse all four items together.

2. *Stringers.* Stringers have the following characteristics: *Description.* Rather than a global preference, stringers opt for a systematic, methodical analysis that leads to mastery of details. They are comfortable with this strategy, and it is only after they have acquired specifics that they will turn to more general concepts. Knowledge is acquired sequentially and gradually, and it must be information that is directly related to the task. Since most academic work is highly structured, stringers usually receive grades that are commensurate with their abilities.

- *Learning strategies.* Stringers should begin by identifying the goal that they want to achieve and then carefully planning the steps that lead to it, insuring a well-structured situation (the problem space). Such planning enables stringers to feel in control, thus eliminating anxiety about how to proceed. For example, in the computer illustration, stringers would be initially concerned about learning the keyboard and any vital commands. They may become frustrated and tense if initially they were forced to consider computer history.

   Although the description of stringers could lead you to conclude that they will be most successful in school because their minds are especially good at grasping specific details and forming associations between groups of facts, they can sometimes overlook equally essential broad concepts (Lewis & Greene, 1982, p. 159).

- *Organizing material.* In studying four topics, study each of the first two separately, then rehearse them. Next, study topic three separately and rehearse all three together. Now do topic four and then rehearse it with the three other items. The best advice to stringers is to build knowledge in a systematic way, beginning with the essentials (Lewis & Greene, 1982).

correct answer. What can you do with a book? Obviously, read it. But you can also use it as a doorstop, a weight, or even as a ruler in an emergency.

Ask them to imagine, to go beyond the data. For example, assume that the class is studying the opening of the American West. They could write essays that incorporate the basic facts but go far beyond. A popular book takes the life of General Custer, presents the facts, and then asks the reader to believe that Custer, critically wounded, survived Big Horn and had to stand trial for his role in the massacre. *The Trial of George Armstrong Custer* is a lesson in creativity. Try something like it.

- *Encourage your students to search for relationships.* Creativity tests often ask you to name one word that can be linked to others. Devise lists that are appropriate for your students and that require similar thinking.
- *One of the most important aspects of creativity is the ability to tolerate ambiguity.* Fear of failure and fear of the unknown usually drive us (especially children) to reach some solution, suitable or not. Directly teach students that it is better to pause, to muse, to think of alternatives, to search for the better way.

In addition to fostering creative behavior, you can encourage students to become more flexible in their approach to problem solving by using techniques that teach them about themselves. Here is one fairly simple method.

Helping Students Learn About Themselves

In the chapter opener we read about Timmy, a student who seemed to need help in identifying and attacking a problem. One of the first tasks in helping your students learn how to solve problems is to make them aware of how they prefer to go about it. What strategies are they comfortable with? You can help them to make decisions about selecting appropriate and useful strategies by first encouraging them to discover things about themselves they probably don't know, especially their learning styles. Lewis and Greene (1982) believe that you can improve your problem-solving ability by reflecting on your personal learning style, which should then help you to organize material (the givens) in a way that is personally meaningful. Their suggestions about "learning how to learn" are particularly relevant for our work here.

Basing their strategies on the work of the British educational psychologist, Gordon Pask, they have devised a set of ten questions, the answers to which reveal much about your personal learning style. Pask (1976), using a "conversational" technique that allows mental activities to be described in behavioral terms, was able to analyze students' learning strategies into the opposite categories of holist and serialist. Having adopted one of these learning styles, students are reluctant to abandon it (even in the face of failure) unless they receive definite instructions for altering their strategy. Holists have many goals and will consider many topics as they attempt to solve problems, while serialists tend to concentrate on one goal and one working topic. (See Table 9.1.)

Focus on Teachers

Social Problem Solving

Solving interpersonal problems is a challenge that confronts all students and adults. Learning how to get along with others, how to communicate successfully to avoid disputes, and how to help in ways that do not hinder others requires many of the same problem-solving skills that we have presented as relevant to solving academic problems. Teaching students to be good social problem solvers has become an important part of social skills, drug prevention, and sexual awareness programs in many schools today. The basis for many of these programs is the work on *Interpersonal Cognitive Problem Solving* or *ICPS* (Spivak & Shure, 1974).

Interpersonal Cognitive Problem Solving (ICPS) was originally designed to teach young children how to think, not what to think. In other words, the goal was to teach children a process for thinking about problems they would encounter, not the solutions to the problems. Teaching solutions would be an endless task for even the best teacher, so the goal of any ICPS program is to teach students to identify alternative solutions to problems and to evaluate each solution on the basis of its potential consequences. Six specific problem-solving skills constitute the major instructional components of ICPS.

- *Alternative solution thinking.* This component stimulates students to search for new solutions by combining old solutions or by inventing truly new solutions.
- *Consequential thinking.* This component stimulates students to look continually for new solutions by combining old solutions or by inventing truly new solutions.
- *Causal thinking.* This component stresses the relationships between events and requires students to have the ability to relate one event to another over time. Causal thinking is a more direct or exacting extension of consequential thinking.
- *Interpersonal sensitivity.* This component concerns one's awareness that an interpersonal problem actually exists. Given that students (and adults) do not always perceive that a problem exists between themselves and others, it is necessary to teach them to listen to and observe others' actions and attitudes.

- *Means-ends thinking.* This component involves planning a step-by-step plan to achieve a given goal. Students initially must identify their goal and then to consider systematically the resources and skills needed to reach their goal. Finally, they must plan for setbacks and not being able to reach a goal immediately.
- *Perspective taking.* This component emphasizes that different people have different motives and viewpoints, and thus may respond differently in any given situation. Perspective taking involves role taking and empathy, and thus is a complex cognitive skill for many students.

Research investigating the application of ICPS has been conducted with mixed results. Most of the major reservations about ICPS concern research methodology (e.g., absence of control groups, bias in evaluations of teachers who have been actively involved in ICPS training, the use of many other training components such as modeling and coaching along with ICPS). It is widely agreed, however, that the thinking and acting skills stressed in the ICPS approach are meaningful and are significantly related to successful interpersonal relationships. Research and the application of ICPS and its problem-solving subcomponents will most certainly continue in schools.

The original ICPS work of Spivack and Shure has influenced many psychologists and educators interested in the development of students' social competence. For example, ICPS is a major component in the popular *Think Aloud* classroom program (Camp & Bosh, 1981) and in *The Prepare Curriculum* (Goldstein, 1988). The problem-solving components of ICPS are also evident in a parenting program entitled *Teach Your Child Decision Making* (Clabby and Elias, 1987). Box Figure 9.2 is from the *Think Aloud* classroom program and illustrates a basic four-step problem-solving sequence: state the problem, think about alternative plans, select a plan and carry it out, and self-evaluate the plan's success. Programs like *Think Aloud* and *The Prepare Curriculum* originally were designed for use with aggressive and impulsive students, but as they have been used more, teachers are finding that all students can benefit from learning how to be good problem solvers.

Teaching Problem-Solving Techniques

Consequently, the strategies that cut across situations and that are not confined to a specific subject are those that will concern us in this section, which introduces the topic of the transfer of learning.

Helping Students to Transfer Their Learning

Once we have taught students basic knowledge, learning strategies, and problem-solving techniques, we want them to use these tools in a variety of situations and not to think of them as applying only to the classroom. Transfer of learning refers to attempts to understand how learning one topic influences later learning.

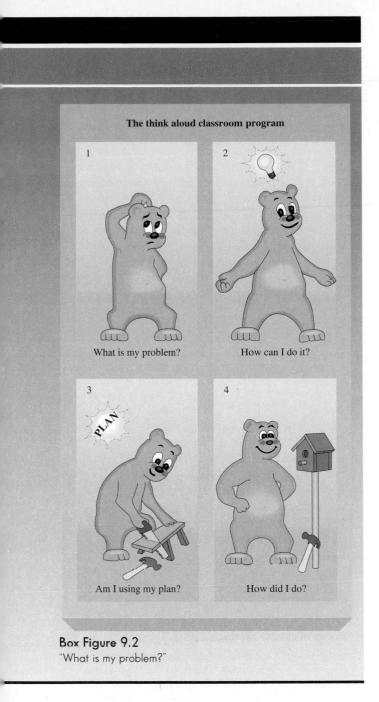

The think aloud classroom program

1 — What is my problem?

2 — How can I do it?

3 — Am I using my plan?

4 — How did I do?

Box Figure 9.2
"What is my problem?"

Transfer may be positive, such as when learning one topic helps you to learn another—knowing how to add and subtract helped you to master long division. It may also be negative, however, such as when learning one topic hinders the learning of another—knowing one word processing program may interfere with the learning of a new, more powerful program.

Influences on Transfer

Certain conditions influence what and how much will be transferred. Among these are the following (Ellis & Hunt, 1989):

- *Task similarity exercises a strong influence on transfer.* Imagine changing the color of the traffic lights that govern our driving. Instead of stopping at a red light, we must now stop at the orange signal. Would this bother us? Not too much because orange is similar to red, and it would be relatively easy to transfer the stopping habit. Learning to make the same response to new but similar stimuli usually produces positive transfer.

  Now let's change the conditions. Instead of stopping at red, we must stop at green and go on red. The pattern is completely reversed. What will happen? Drivers, making new and opposite responses to red and green, will undoubtedly get into more accidents. Here we see an instance of negative transfer—what was previously learned interferes with the new learning. Is it any wonder that students can have difficulty with some English sounds? How will you sound *ou: though, tough, ouch?* Consequently, in your teaching be alert to the impact that similarity can have on transfer.

- *The degree of original learning is an important element in transfer.* More practice on and greater familiarity with the original material produces more positive transfer. If students are thoroughly familiar with multiplication, for example, they have little trouble in a store determining how much 8 apples at 9 cents each will cost.

- *Personal variables such as intelligence, motivation, and past experiences are important, but difficult to control, influences on transfer.* Your personal knowledge of your students will help you to insure transfer since you know something about the extent of their past learning. You can usually relate some aspect of their experiences to new material, thus facilitating transfer. For example, knowing places that your students have visited can make a social studies lesson more meaningful for an entire class.

Implications for the Classroom

For transfer to occur, your students must see something similar in both situations and must have a good grasp of the original material. Courses in driver education should produce students who obtain their driving licenses and have good safety records. If algebra is intended to be used in physics and chemistry classes, then students should demonstrate this transfer in their science classes.

Here are several suggestions that will help your students to be aware of the value of transfer.

- *Teach to overlearning.* The more experience that students have with the material to be transferred, the more successful will be the transfer. A good idea is to give verbal examples of how material can be transferred and then provide circumstances that encourage your students to use the material. In class discussions, assignments, and quizzes, urge your students to search for transfer.

- *Be certain that the material you teach is well-organized.* Meaningful material is more easily transferred. We have previously mentioned how important it is for students to recognize the organization and structure of material. If you can bring them to this realization, they will discover principles and generalizations that they can use in many situations. For example, if students thoroughly grasp the reasons for Lincoln's desire not to punish the Southern states, they will transfer this knowledge to modern times and appreciate why presidents tolerate dissent for the sake of national unity.

- *Use advance organizers if possible.* When you are about to teach abstract material it may be useful to furnish your students with Ausubel's "advance organizers." These general principles will help your students to see that the abstract material they are encountering possesses more structure than if they had met it unprepared. You must know both your students and subject to formulate effective advance organizers because your introductory work reflects what you think is important, and it must match your students' ability level.

- *Emphasize the similarity between classroom work and the transfer situation.* If you are concerned with transfer, you must attempt to make the classroom condition similar to the transfer situation. For example, most algebra tests involve word problems, so as soon as possible have your students work with word problems, perhaps incorporating terms from chemistry and physics. If you teach reading, be sure that the letters and words you teach have the same form that the youngsters will see in their readers. Sometime during your teaching, students should receive practice under conditions similar to the working or transfer environment.

- *Specify what is important in the task.* Identifying the important features of a task helps youngsters to transfer these elements or to guard against potential difficulties. For example, children frequently confuse *b* with *d,* so teachers should stress the distinction and give them considerable experience with words

containing these letters. Again in algebra, students consistently forget to change signs (+ -) when moving terms from one side of the equation to the other. Constantly calling students' attention to the required change of sign, instructors should provide numerous instances that require transposition.

- *Try to understand how students perceive the possibility of transfer.* Instructors teach what they know and have organized. How do students view the process? Is it meaningful to them? Do they see how they can use the material in different circumstances? If you attempt to see your teaching and the subject from your students' viewpoint, you may present it quite differently, capitalize more on their background, and offer more practical possibilities of transfer. This is more easily said than done, but once you try it, you will be more conscious of the need for emphasizing strategies, meaning, organization, and structure.

Using Problem-Solving Strategies

Among the many suggestions for achieving the goal of using problem-solving strategies are the following:

- *problem-solving instruction* should begin with content that students are comfortable with, and only gradually should you introduce slightly different notions (Rummelhart & Norman, 1981). For example, before you ask students what they think caused the changing political climate in Eastern Europe, they should have a basic knowledge of the geography and history of these nations.

- In his discussion of problem-solving methods, Doyle (1983) distinguishes between *direct and indirect instruction*; in direct instruction the tasks are clearly defined with definite steps for mastering each step for solution. Indirect instruction involves less clearly defined tasks, and students use considerable self-discovery in their striving for solution. Instruction is intended to provide opportunities for students to initiate their own generalizations and procedures.

    For those students who need help in solving problems, direct instruction is probably best. You could begin by asking them for reasons why an oppressed people would risk overthrowing their government, after first discussing with them ideas of freedom, self-determination, and the like. Then, as their problem-solving abilities grow, switch to more indirect methods by posing more general questions, such as asking them to consider what neighboring countries would do in this situation.

    Doyle believes direct instruction is most suitable for teaching elementary school students, those with

TEACHER ←→ STUDENT
INTERACTIONS

Using Problem–Solving Strategies in the Classroom

From our discussion thus far we can be encouraged by the knowledge that our students can improve their problem-solving methods. Here are a few pertinent suggestions based on the work reviewed in this chapter that you should find useful.

1. *Analyze the difficulties in individual student's problem-solving behavior.* These difficulties usually result from any or all of five causes:

   a. *Intelligence.* Even if some students have relatively low ability, you can still improve their problem-solving technique, but keep the problem manageable for them; that is, the problem cannot be too abstract. For those of greater ability, problems should become progressively more abstract. Show these students films and filmstrips about England; show them pictures of, and discuss the merits of, some of England's great leaders over the years. In this way, gradually lead them to understand England's emergence as a world leader.

   b. *Motivation.* Often students are so discouraged by previous attempts to solve problems that they either stop immediately or guess. No one has taken the time to help them. If you provide tangible help and manageable problems, they will show immediate improvement. Keep the problems simple at first, such as tracing the factors that led to England's rise. Combine a manageable problem with teaching the problem-solving strategies that we have discussed in this chapter.

   c. *Information.* Either the problem does not provide sufficient data, or students cannot relate information they possess to the problem. You must know your students so that you can satisfactorily match problem with student. In working with your students, be sure that the problem has sufficient "givens" (see p. 261) for them to recognize. A good technique to use here is means-end analysis—do I have the means to solve this problem?

   d. *Experience.* In initially attempting to solve problems, students are usually bewildered. You must actively demonstrate techniques and then let them practice with simple problems. Once you have brought your students to a realization that they have solved a

   problem—England's status, for example—then emphasize the techniques that they used and point out how they can be used in different situations.

   e. *Set.* Teach students to look initially for several possible solutions and to test them mentally to determine which is most feasible. Emphasize that they should not necessarily use the first solution they think of. For example, if the class is mature enough, you could have them try both the nine-dot and the cyclists problems.

2. *Correct students' difficulties.* Teach students to search diligently for clues that organize the problem and to use their existing knowledge, plus the problem's data, to solve it. By urging students to separate the problem into meaningful parts, you not only aid analysis by helping them to simplify it, but you also encourage a more positive attitude about their ability to solve problems. In this way, you have taught them to think, not only of England, *but about ways of solving a problem.*

3. *Teach—directly teach—problem solving techniques.* Do not assume that presenting a problem to students will automatically activate some problem-solving mechanism. Teach the ideas discussed here and stress the use of errors. Help them to use their errors. "No, Betty. It wasn't just their army that helped England. When you look at all that water around them, they must have needed what?"

   Students must learn to expect errors, but not to cease searching for a solution. Why was it an error? At what stage? Do I need more information? Can I use here what I learned elsewhere? These are the questions that can help students to use errors intelligently.

4. *Give your students the opportunity to solve problems.* Success in life is determined by the ability to see, to analyze, and to solve problems. Admittedly it is a time-consuming process, and it would be much easier to tell students the answer. But that offers little support when they meet other, different obstacles. It is the technique that will transfer and assist your students in all situations. Nowhere in your teaching can you better serve your students than by helping them to remove those intellectual blocks that both frustrate and defeat.

---

low ability and those who lack expertise in a particular subject. Indirect instruction is best suited for those students who possess the required knowledge base and general strategies.

• Frederiksen (1984) commented that among the attributes of a *good instructional program* are the

following: instruction in the necessary knowledge base (teach your students what they need to know about England's rise to great power status), instruction in strategies for developing internal representations (picture this string of small islands that became powerful), and finally, link what we know about problem-solving processes to teaching techniques (teach according to the DUPE model), using such techniques as means-end analysis, identifying goals and subgoals, and changing internal representations. These general strategies resist application without considerable domain-specific knowledge.

Conclusion

Since life, both in and out of the classroom, consistently poses problems, helping students to learn different ways of attacking these problems can be of great value. Initially, though, we must be aware that a problem exists. Then, having determined the nature of a problem, you can devise strategies that are appropriate for this problem and your personal learning style. However, you must master certain fundamentals if you are to become a successful problem solver.

For example, the more knowledge you have about a problem, the greater your chances of solving it. Having acquired the necessary knowledge, you can then form a representation of the problem, which can be either internal or external. You can now decide what the best strategies are, best for this problem and for you.

A problem solving model was then introduced to help you—the **DUPE** model.

    D—Determine that a problem exists.

    U—Understand its nature.

    P—Devise a plan for its solution.

    E—Evaluate the plan and solution.

Finally, you were urged to master the problem-solving strategies presented in this chapter, both to help you and so that you can pass them on to your students.

Chapter Highlights

What Is a Problem?

- Problem solving is a constant in our lives, and students every day are faced with problems, both in and out of the classroom.
- Though some students are probably better than others at solving problems, the problem solving ability of all students can be improved.
- Difficulty in solving problems can come from simple mistakes, such as failing to use all of the clues present in the problem.
- Negative attitudes toward classroom problems can transfer to all problems in all aspects of a student's life.
- Problem-solving strategies can be divided into general and specific (also called strong) techniques. General strategies are those that you may use in any situation, while specific strategies are used for a particular topic.
- Students from different cultures may attempt to solve problems in different ways.
- Various models such as DUPE have been proposed to help in solving problems.

Determining the Nature of the Problem

- Determining the nature of a problem is a basic first step.
- Identifying the givens of a problem and then deciding what actions can be performed on them helps to

specify the problem's goal, that is, "bridging the gap" between where you are or where you want to go.

Understanding the Nature of the Problem

- Understanding the nature of a problem means that you have identified the nature of the problem and that you also can represent it.
- Students must possess the basic knowledge that a problem requires for solution, or they have little hope of success.
- Representing a problem means that you can cast its information in either symbolic (internal) or graphic (external) forms.

Planning the Solution

- Once you represent a problem, you can devise a plan for its solution.
- Planning requires that you possess the knowledge needed to solve the problem. If the solution involves the use of algebra, then students must have that information if they hope to succeed.
- The appropriate use of memory is a powerful aid in solving problems.

Evaluating the Solution

- Evaluation of your problem-solving plan can occur at two stages: after you have devised your plan (is it adequate?) and after your proposed solution (did it work?).
- If you are unhappy with your solution, or it simply "doesn't work," you must creatively devise a new plan for a revised solution.

Teaching Problem-Solving Techniques

- If you are well-versed in the various problem-solving strategies, you can teach them to your students as a form of knowledge.
- Perhaps the best advice to remember is: directly teach problem-solving techniques.

Key Terms

Attention management
Context strategy
Cues
DUPE
Elaboration strategy
External representation
General strategies
Givens
Goals
Groupers
Heuristics
Imagery
Inferencing
Instantiation
Internal representation
Metacognition
Metacomponents
Method of Loci
Monitoring
Multiple coding
Operations
Retrieving
Storing
Stringers
Strong strategies
Structuring strategy
Well defined and ill defined

Suggested Readings

Bransford, J., & Stein, B. (1984). *The ideal problem solver*. New York: Freeman. If you could read only one source about problem solving, this would be it. Presenting their own model of problem solving and combining it with tantalizing problems, the authors provide an excellent overview of the field.

Hayes, J. (1989). *The complete problem solver*. Philadelphia: The Franklin Institute Press. A comprehensive analysis of problem-solving behavior that emphasizes the use of representation. An excellent section on the use of memory.

Lewis, D., & Greene, J. (1982). *Thinking Better*. New York: Pauson, Wade. A popular practical guide full of cogent suggestions to encourage and improve thinking.

Motivation of Students and Teachers

arbara Cotter, the junior high English teacher we met earlier, was worried about the motivational level of one of her classes. It just lacked "the spark" that she felt with other classes. Casting about for ideas that could increase the level of motivation in her class, she decided to tell the class about her concern and ask them if they felt the same way.

She mentioned it to her students at the beginning of the next class and received an immediate response. Tom, who planned to become an English major, was quite frank. "You know, Mrs. Cotter, we all like this class, but I'm not sure that the direction it's going meets my needs for college."

At that, Susan, a quiet student who usually said little but who did well on her written work, rather hesitatingly raised her hand and said, "If I'm able to go to college, I'm going to need as much financial support as possible, so I need good marks, but I find it hard to study for this class."

Le Yang, who had entered this school in November, stood up. "I know my English isn't perfect," he said carefully, "but I study a lot and try hard in class. I just don't know why I'm not doing better."

Zack, an outstanding athlete whom the teacher felt could do much better, surprised her by saying, "This is a good class, Mrs. Cotter. You can tell from what's been said that we all like it, but something about it seems to bother us. I just don't know what I'm getting out of it."

Elaine, who was rather dramatic, sighed, and said, "I would love to be a writer. Maybe if we used more examples of today's writers, I would be more excited."

These students, in their own way, were expressing something they felt was lacking in class: unmet needs, lack of achievement, the exact cause of a grade, lack of reinforcement, and the need for models. Satisfying all of these students may seem like a formidable task (and it is); nevertheless, motivated students go a long way to meeting their own demands.

This teacher, as is true for us all, recognizes the critical role that motivation plays in learning and wants to take steps to be certain that motivation is a plus and not a minus in her class. Focusing on motivation can also increase multicultural sensitivity by providing opportunities for students to discover interesting features of other cultures.

Motivation is a subject that intrigues teachers since they realize—both professionally and instinctively—that here is a topic that can mean the difference between success and failure in the classroom. Studying motivation also illustrates how educational psychology reaches into our classrooms and has considerable significance for everyone interested in improving the quality of education. As you can well imagine, motivation is a critical element in a student's learning and a teacher's instruction.

A bright student with a handicap, for example, may be doing poorly in school. To help and support such a student requires data from multiple sources: What is the specific nature of the handicap? What is the student's academic potential? Has learning been affected in earlier grades? What has been the impact on the student's self-concept? Focusing on forces either internal or external to the student would be severely limiting. Using the best information about both internal and external forces from a variety of sources is the most suitable method for aiding and motivating students.

When you complete your reading of this chapter, you should be able to answer a series of questions about motives, students, and the classroom.

- What causes motivation? Here we shall examine the theories that attempt to explain the nature of motivation.
- What affects students' motives? The focus of this section will be those states (anxiety, curiosity, attitudes) that influence student behavior.
- What interests students? There will be a developmental thrust to this section since different things and activities interest students at different times in their lives.

- What are the effects of motivation? Here the intent will be to relate motivational knowledge to a positive classroom atmosphere.
- What are the educational implications of motivation? Here we shall examine the specific relationship of motivation to both teaching and learning.

Motivation: Meaning and Myths

When people (including teachers) ask about motivation, their intent is usually to discover:

- What causes a student to act in a particular way?
- What occurs inside students; what are their inner feelings?
- What do students want; what is their goal?

These questions serve as an excellent guide to studying the topic of motivation, but first what is meant by motivation, a central construct in both educational and psychological research for the past sixty years (Weiner, 1990). With regard to education, motivation has always been tied to learning activities and often inferred from the outcome of learning. Motivation theorists in the 1940s (such as Hull and Spence) focused on hunger and thirst drives or sexual stimulation (Freud). Efforts to apply the results of motivational research to education produced a greater emphasis on the cognitive aspects of motivation. Work by Lewin (1935) on level of aspiration and Atkinson (1964) on achievement motivation were meaningful additions to the education literature.

Today, a cognitive emphasis with a focus on the self-system dominates motivational theory and research. For example, causal attributions, self-efficacy, learned helplessness, test anxiety, locus of control, competitive versus cooperative activities, and intrinsic versus extrinsic rewards are all used to explain human motivation. All of these topics are examined in recent works on *Research on Motivation in Education,* Volumes 1–3 , (C. Ames & R. Ames, 1984, 1985, 1989) and in a recent issue of the *Journal of Educational Psychology* (Schunk, 1990, 82–84).

No single best definition of motivation is recognized. To clarify the roles and responsibilities of school personnel in helping students achieve, however, Brophy's (1986) discussion about motivation to learn provides a meaningful operational definition of motivation. He noted (p. 16), "Students reveal motivation to learn when they try, attend to lessons or assignments, strive to get the initial benefits, understand, and remember what they are supposed to learn."

If you were asked to provide a list of highly motivated individuals, the chances are that your list would include the names of some great athletes. These gifted people did not arrive at their present lofty position by ability alone. Talent plus dedicated determination helped them to achieve their "world-class" accomplishments.

Psychologists are convinced that today's great athletes have not yet reached their physiological limitations and that any restraints on performance are psychological. In their efforts to help athletes to overcome these restraints, sports psychologists have devised techniques that can help not only athletes but also classroom teachers.

For example, runners are urged to imagine the noise of the crowd, the sound of their own breathing, their position at the starting line, the starter's gun, their first steps, the encouragement of their teammates, and the feeling of the track under their spikes. They are likewise directed to see themselves crossing the finish line first and receiving a victory medal.

The intent of the sports psychologists is to produce in the athletes a feeling of their own competence, which is a strong motivating force. That is, not only can they do it, but they want to do it. Similar techniques can be effective in the classroom. It is entirely possible that if you match a task with a student's ability, having that student imagine successful performance will produce more effective behavior, which then will aid motivation for the next task. For example, urge students to picture themselves studying. Then have them visualize understanding the material. Finally, have them see themselves in the classroom, relaxed and ready for a test.

Will students learn even if they are poorly motivated? They will learn something, but will they learn what we want them to learn? Everything that we know about learning indicates that if motivation is faulty, learning will suffer: Attention is limited; behavior is not directed at objectives; discipline may become a problem; learning has gone awry.

Although it is relatively easy to describe motivated individuals, it is difficult to specify just what motivation is. When you are motivated, or when you see your students motivated, you usually can discover what conditions caused the behavior. Something acted on you, or your students, to produce a certain kind of behavior, which was maintained at a certain level of intensity, and which was directed at a definite goal. *Thus motivation arouses, sustains, directs, and integrates your behavior.*

For example, one of your students may have been promised a ticket to a rock concert for passing an algebra course. You wish a good grade in your educational psy-

chology course so that your transcript will be attractive to a future employer. In both examples, a certain type of behavior was aroused and maintained long enough to achieve a specific goal.

What Are the Myths About Motivation?

Wlodkowski (1986) and Grossnickle and Thiel (1988) believe that the concept of motivation is shrouded in myths that can mislead and confuse. Some of these myths focus on students, while others concern teachers. Among the most damaging are the following:

- *When students are not actively involved in their work, they are unmotivated.* Nothing could be more misleading; if students are doing anything, they are motivated. They may not be motivated to learn, but they are motivated to do something, and that something could lead to a serious discipline problem.
- *Failure is a good motivator.* Experience may be a valuable teacher, but chronic failure often begets more of the same unless a better way is substituted. Success, even small successes, is a more potent motivator for most students.
- *Learning is more important than motivation.* Since students must learn to survive, schools must force students to learn regardless of the conditions. Though this belief may produce immediate learning, the ultimate consequences may be negative. Students may not use their learning since it was meaningless, and worse, they simply may be repelled by the thought of any additional learning (Moses, 1991b). That this view is changing is seen in the work of Russell and Morrow (1986), who report that in their studies of secondary school social studies teachers, the teachers were more concerned with motivational techniques than they were with knowledge of subject matter.
- *Teachers motivate students.* Teachers do *not* motivate students. The best that we can do is to make conditions as attractive and stimulating as possible. Your students' perceptions, values, personalities, and judgments ultimately determine motivation (Wlodkowski, 1986). By matching task with ability under meaningful and pleasant conditions (including teacher encouragement), we can encourage students' self-motivation (Thorkildsen, 1988).
- *Threats increase motivation.* By using the threat of low grades, retention, and parental notification, some teachers (especially new teachers) believe that they motivate students. Although stern measures are occasionally necessary and must be used, to build a

classroom atmosphere around threats is counter-productive.

- *Learning automatically improves with increased student motivation.* Positive evidence is lacking to show that motivation always improves learning. Motivation is certainly a condition for learning, but if other vital conditions are lacking, we can only question the extent of the learning. For example, a teacher may have motivated students, but if the lesson is not well-planned, if the teacher cannot control the class, or if a teacher's presentation is vague, then motivated students will probably learn but less than if conditions were more favorable.

Motivation in the Classroom

Try to analyze the motives of your students (or your classmates in this course), much as the teacher in the chapter opening did. Do they want to come to class? Do they love to learn? Or do they hate learning and dread coming to school? Why do they feel as they do? If they enjoy the work, try to discover what they like and link it to the classroom atmosphere. If they are reluctant scholars, try to discover what has gone wrong. Is there anything in the classroom atmosphere that explains what happened?

Attempting to answer these and similar questions, Brophy (1987b) argued that no motivational strategies will succeed if certain preconditions are not met.

- Classroom conditions must be supportive, warm, and encouraging so that students are sufficiently secure to take risks without fear of criticism.
- The challenges that students face are appropriate, which occurs only if teachers know and understand their students.
- Worthwhile, meaningful objectives that are clearly understood by the class can be powerful motivators.
- Motivational strategies should be moderate and monitored; that is, students can't be kept at too high or too low a level of motivation.

Teachers must adjust these preconditions, however, according to the developmental level of their students. For example, children enter school primarily attending to social feedback; their perception of their own competence remains positive. After the first few grades, objective feedback becomes more important and they learn that high academic performance is valued. They now begin to assess their performance more realistically. By the sixth grade they learn that ability is a stable factor in their performance (Stipek, 1984).

The more that you know about your students as individuals, and the more that you know about motivation,

"I'd like to dedicate this day to all my students who complain that nothing interesting ever happens in school."

© Randy Glasbergen.

the more effective your teaching will be and the more your students will learn. To produce this condition in your classroom requires a judicious blending of intrinsic and extrinsic motivation.

Intrinsic motivation means that students themselves want to learn in order to achieve a specific objective. Obviously this is an ideal state that results in considerable learning and a minimum of discipline problems. You can help your students acquire intrinsic motivation by relating your knowledge of their abilities, needs, and interests to meaningful goals. For example, knowing that a student is interested in the medical field and knowing the student's ability enables you to channel that interest in an appropriate direction.

Although this is ideal, intrinsic motivation can be elusive. Consequently, marks, prizes, and other tangible rewards are used. Since rewards and inducements are external to a student, they are characterized as **extrinsic motivation.** Even when using these methods, you should always attempt to have students transfer these temporary external devices to intrinsic motives. Typically, the motivation to learn for any age student is influenced by both intrinsic and extrinsic factors. Subject matter that is not of high interest and/or complicated usually requires the use of more extrinsically-oriented methods.

The Results of Boredom

Your efforts spent in understanding and implementing motivation can save you untold problems since poorly motivated students frequently are discipline problems. This was the concern of the teacher in the chapter opening. Realizing that disinterested students quickly become behavior problems, she wanted to forestall any difficulties and turned to cooperative learning to help her.

A study that has become a classic in the psychological literature, *The Pathology of Boredom* (Heron, 1957), still offers clues for today's teachers and learners. Beginning with the assumption that monotony is an important and enduring human problem, investigators at McGill University studied the effects of a prolonged and boring environment. The subjects in the experiment—male college students—were paid $20 per day to participate. They lay on a comfortable bed 24 hours a day as long as they wanted, only taking time to eat their meals while sitting on their beds. They wore plastic visors to cut down on visual stimulation; cotton gloves prevented them from experiencing touch perception; and the steady hum of an air conditioner and the use of rubber pillows stifled auditory perception.

Before the experiment the subjects stated that they would use time to prepare for examination and to do term papers. Soon after the experiment began, however, the subjects reported that they were unable to think clearly about anything for any length of time and that their thinking had become disoriented. Concentration was impossible and some of them began to hallucinate.

Here is a clear example of what a prolonged monotonous environment can do. A changing sensory environment is necessary for all of us, including students. Watch your students for signs of restlessness. If you detect them, change the pace, introduce something new, move swiftly to involve them actively in the classroom activities. A boring classroom can cause unruly students, discipline problems, and discouraged teachers.

What Causes Motivation?

Since motivated students are obviously the most desirable to teach, it is well worth the time and effort for teachers (and future teachers) to learn as much as possible about motivation. For example, Serna (1989) discovered motivation was needed to have students actually use study skills. Providing a rationale, setting goals, using shaping procedures, and aiming for errorless learning all encouraged students to apply the study skills.

One way of coming to grips with the nature and meaning of motivation is to examine several motivational theories. Although there are numerous theoretical explanations of motivation—biological, learning, cognitive—we shall include only those that have direct classroom application. If you grasp the meaning of the theories, you will be in a much better position to understand motivation, or its lack, in your individual students. A good beginning for acquiring an understanding of students' motivation and objectives is to examine the needs hierarchy of Abraham Maslow.

Maslow and the Needs Hierarchy

Tom, the student who was concerned whether Barbara Cotter's English class was meeting his needs, is an example of the importance of need satisfaction. One of Maslow's (1987) most famous concepts is that of **self-actualization,** which means that we use our abilities to the limit of our potentialities. If we can convince students that they should—and can—fulfill their promise, they are then on the path to self-actualization. *Self-actualization is a growth concept;* students move toward this goal as they satisfy their basic needs. It is movement toward physical and psychological health.

Need Satisfaction

Growth toward self-actualization requires the satisfaction of a hierarchy of needs. There are five basic needs in Maslow's theory: *physiological, safety, love and belonging, esteem, and self-actualization.* Figure 10.1 illustrates the hierarchy of needs, with those needs at the base of the hierarchy assumed to be more basic relative to the needs above them in the hierarchy.

1. *Physiological needs.* Physiological needs, such as hunger and sleep, are dominant and are the basis of motivation. Unless they are satisfied, everything else recedes. For example, students who frequently do not eat breakfast or suffer from poor nutrition generally become lethargic and non-interacting; their learning potential is severely lowered. Note: This is particularly true of adolescents who can be extremely sensitive to their weight.
2. *Safety needs.* These needs represent the importance of security, protection, stability, freedom from fear and anxiety, and the need for structure and limits. Any of your students who are afraid of school, of peers, of a teacher, or of a parent's reaction have their safety needs threatened, and these fears can affect classroom performance.
3. *Love and belongingness needs.* This category refers to our need for family and friends. Healthy, motivated people wish to avoid feelings of loneliness and isolation. Students who feel alone, not part of the group, or who lack any sense of belongingness usually have poor relationships with others, which can then affect classroom learning.
4. *Esteem needs.* These needs encompass the reactions of others to us as individuals and our opinion of ourselves. We want a favorable judgment from others, which should be based on honest achievement. Our own sense of competence combines with the reactions of others to produce our sense of self-esteem. As a teacher be sure to provide

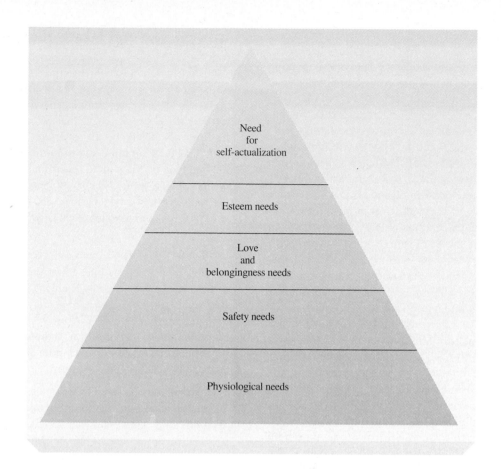

Figure 10.1
Maslow's hierarchy of needs.
Source: Data for diagram based on Hierarchy of Needs from *Motivation and Personality*, Third Edition, by Abraham H. Maslow. Revised by Robert Frager, et al., Harper/Row, Publishers, Inc., 1954, 1987.

Young children are usually highly motivated to demonstrate they "know" the answer to a question.

opportunities for students to satisfy this need: Help students to achieve and receive deserved reinforcement.

5. *Need for self-actualization.* Here Maslow was referring to that tendency, in spite of the satisfaction of lower needs, to feel restless unless we are doing what we think we are capable of doing. Encourage your students to recognize their potential and guide them into activities that will enable them to feel both competent and fulfilled.

For the Classroom

Examining Maslow's hierarchy, you can see how a deficit in any one need category will affect student performance. Hungry students, for example, usually are not scholars; their hunger overwhelms all other concerns. Similarly, fearful students (for whatever reason) may find it difficult to concentrate on their studies. Those students who feel rejected and isolated may refuse to participate fully in your class activities.

Teachers experience similar needs. Ratliff (1988) compared the perceived need differences between teachers and workers in government, retail sales, and industry. He discovered that many teachers had significantly higher physiological, safety, and love and belongingness needs, with lower needs for self-esteem and self-actualization than the other workers.

Students—and all us—need to feel that we are worthy of respect, both from ourselves and others, a respect that is based on actual achievement. Finally, unless students believe that they are doing all that they could be doing, they will be plagued by feelings of restlessness and even discontent. As you can see, Maslow's remarkably perceptive analysis of human needs furnishes us with rich general insights into human behavior.

Bruner and Motivation

In his little classic, *The Process of Education* (1960), Bruner stated that any attempt to improve education inevitably begins with the motives for learning. He asked: What results from emphasis upon examinations, grades, and promotion? Does it intensify motivation? How intense should motivation be? Bruner believed that there is some ideal level of arousal between apathy and wild excitement, since passivity causes boredom while intense activity leaves little time for reflection and generalization.

One possible solution is Bruner's notion of **discovery learning,** which has captured many educators' imagination with its insights into classroom motivation. Arguing that discovery is rearranging or transforming evidence so that one goes beyond the evidence to form new insights, Bruner states that discovery proceeds from the well-prepared mind. Encouraging discovery causes students not only to organize material to determine regularities and relationships but also to avoid the passivity that blinds them to the use of the information learned.

The result is that students learn to manipulate their environment more actively and achieve considerable gratification from personally coping with problems. We know that students like tasks that permit them to respond actively by interacting with teachers or with each other (Brophy, 1987b).

Bruner emphasizes that the goal of discovery learning is to have students use their information in solving problems in many different circumstances. One of Bruner's basic assumptions underlying discovery learning is that individuals behave according to their perceptions of their environment. That is, students see meaning in knowledge, skills, and attitudes when they themselves discover it.

Focus on Classrooms

Conceptual Blockbusting

In a practical demonstration of a cognitive interpretation of motivation, Adams (1986) introduced the notion of conceptual blockbusting. Students frequently lack motivation because they simply are unaware of how to attack a lesson, do a paper, study, or do any independent work. Increasing competence means increasing motivation. People like to do what they do well. Adams' ideas on conceptual blockbusting offer excellent suggestions that could help students begin to attack several perceptual blocks.

- *Difficulty in isolating the problem.* Students just cannot identify the problem, which may be answering a question or completing a written exercise. They use inadequate clues to leap to a solution (usually incorrect), or they use misinformation. One of your first tasks should be to help your students isolate the problem—what precisely needs to be done. Students will learn that their initial effort saves time and poses solutions.

- *Tendency to limit the problem too closely.* Everyone, especially children, tends to be bound by his or her experience. If students solved a particular problem by addition, they are reluctant to try multiplication on the next problem. They impose imaginary boundaries and refuse to cross them. Teach your students to try different methods once they have identified a problem, not just what was previously successful.

- *Seeing what you expect to see.* This is closely related to the second obstacle and can be disastrous for motivation. Recall the discussion of the development of a "mathematical sense," which many lack. Why? The answer probably is that you could not isolate the problem (new symbols, new vocabulary). When you succeeded, you tended to repeat the solution, right or wrong, and as you failed, you came to expect failure.

- *Failure to utilize all sensory inputs.* Students need help and often rely excessively upon a single channel of communication. Concentrating upon words, they may neglect illustrations that help to clarify; they may not use tapes or discussion with others as sources of information. Try to help your students to use as many and different sensory inputs as possible.

One conclusion is clearly apparent from Adams's work—helping students to acquire a technique or to recognize, isolate, and solve problems is also a powerful motivational device.

As we have emphasized repeatedly in preceding chapters, your task is to arrange classroom materials and activities so that students learn with a maximum of personal involvement and a minimum of teacher intervention. Try to make the material you're presenting as personal, concrete, and familiar as possible. Relate the material to their personal experiences, use anecdotes, and show how the material applies to their lives (Brophy, 1987b).

Students will always have mixed motives for learning. They must please parents, impress peers, and acquire mastery. But how can you help your students to appreciate the world of ideas for their own sake? One recommendation is to increase a student's inherent interest by insuring that you present ideas at their level so that they achieve a sense of discovery. If you succeed, you not only teach a subject but also instill attitudes and values about intellectual activity. (See chapter 8 for a detailed discussion of Bruner's suggestions about instructional strategies that encourage discovery learning and motivation.)

It is worth quoting Bruner here:

> If teaching is done well and what we teach is worth learning, there are forces at work in our contemporary society that will provide the external prod that will get children more involved in the process of learning than they have been in the past (1960, p. 73).

Finally, Bruner noted that knowledge of results (feedback, reinforcement) is valuable if it comes when learners compare their results with what they attempt to achieve. Even then, learners use feedback according to their internal state, that is, their interests, attitudes, anxieties, and the like. Information is least useful when learners are highly anxious or focus on only one aspect of a problem too closely. For Bruner, information is most helpful when it is at the learner's level and encourages self-activity and intrinsic motivation.

McClelland and Need Achievement

Students differ in their **need achievement.** Some can be described as driven, while others manifest a magnificent indifference. To give you an idea of how your students feel about motivation, try this simple exercise, which should help you to discover where students believe that the responsibility for motivation lies (Bragstad & Stumpf, 1987). Put these categories on the board.

Teacher   Student   Other (parents, principal)

Now have your students put in each column a percentage figure that represents the amount of responsibility for learning that each of these categories carries. For example:

Teacher	Student	Other
45%	45%	10%

Even from this cursory description, you can tell that achievement motivation relates to competence—judging it and increasing it. As Dweck and Elliott (1983) noted, three competence goals are involved: a "learning" goal to increase competence (acquiring new knowledge or skills, or understanding something new), and two "performance" goals (obtaining favorable judgments of one's competence, and avoiding unfavorable judgments).

Need achievement theory emerged from a motivational model called **expectancy-value** in which motivation is a function of an individual's expectancy of success, the incentive value of success and failure, and the strength of the motive. (The student in the chapter opening who was worried about her grades affecting scholarship possibilities demonstrates a need for achievement.)

Studying Need Achievement

The attempt to identify and measure an individual's level of achievement and then apply the results for practical purposes has been one of the major objectives of David McClelland. *Defining the need to achieve as a spontaneously occurring concern to do things better* (people may be unaware that they possess this need), McClelland (1987) stated that such individuals seek out challenging, moderately difficult tasks, do well at them, want all possible feedback, and become bored with steady success.

To measure the need for achievement (nAch), McClelland gave his subjects achievement-oriented tasks. For example, male college students were told the tests they were taking would reflect their intelligence and reliably discriminate people of high ability. The students thus were motivated to do as well as possible.

When the tests were completed, the subjects' fantasies were studied by having them respond to pictures (depicting work) that were flashed on a screen. The subjects were given five minutes to write a story about the pictures. The themes of their stories were then compared with those of similar subjects who had not been given the test and the accompanying instructions. The stories of the test subjects showed many more references to standards of excellence, to doing well, or wanting to do well.

Is it possible to raise a student's level of achievement? Possible clues can be found in McClelland's work with Indian businessmen. Using basically the same techniques just described, McClelland had the Indian subjects continue to rewrite their responses (under conditions of achievement arousal) until they reflected a high level of need achievement. He had them play business games with attainable goals and use problem solving methods to reach their objectives. He discovered that his subjects eventually started more businesses, invested more capital, and created more jobs than a control group.

Meaning and Motivation

Recent studies of motivation in school settings have been influenced by the need achievement work, but as Maehr (1984) notes, not everyone in a school is concerned with need achievement. Many other needs are also at work: self-esteem, affiliation, reinforcement, which leads Maehr to believe that teachers should view classroom motivation from a broader perspective, one that recognizes the personal investment of all involved.

There are three propositions to this notion. First is the relationship between motivation and behavior, which has often been ignored in the past. For example, teachers don't ask about the motivation of a student to read because they see a need. They are prompted to ask motivational questions because of what they see a student doing, that is, the student's behavior.

Second is the concept of **personal investment,** which refers to an individual's persistence, continuing motivation, variation in activity level, and goals. For example, when teachers see a student consistently working on vocabulary to improve reading and using free time to go to the library table, they realize that these students are investing their personal resources in a particular way (Maehr, 1984).

Finally, the meaning that students perceive in a situation revolves around their sense of self and the options that are open to them to seek a relevant goal. Consequently, choice of behavior, feelings of competency, and meaningful goals all combine in an individual to determine motivation in any situation. Maehr's ideas suggest that we examine achievement motivation by recognizing the personal dimension, for, as he notes in a realistic example, children may do their homework not to achieve but to continue to receive their allowance.

For the Classroom

Do these results have educational implications? Having demonstrated that adult levels of achievement can be raised, McClelland next turned his attention to students. He used tactics similar to the Indian experience: Teaching children how to think, talk, and act like persons with high nAch. After this he asked them what they were planning to do in the future. His study used two procedures.

- First, McClelland's staff taught students the techniques of raising levels of need achievement. The results of this procedure showed that although higher levels of need achievement did not increase grade

scores, there were other positive outcomes. When the subjects were interviewed eight to eighteen months later, they were spending their time in a much more achievement-related way. For example, they reported they believed they were doing better in school or work.

- Second, the teachers themselves were trained to introduce achievement motivation concepts into the classroom. This group demonstrated considerable improvement in academic performance.

What conclusions emerged from these studies that could benefit classroom teachers?

- *Important sex differences appeared.* Girls benefitted more if the training were structured, while boys showed improvement if they were given more freedom within the training.
- *Achievement motivation training seems to be related to subject matter.* Performance under these conditions improved more in math and science classes than in social studies.
- *A forced restructuring of the classroom* similar to the format of the training seminars produced few, if any, results. Having teachers specifically include achievement motivation instruction in their regular work seems more effective.
- *Teachers who were involved in the research* became more alert to the need to involve their students actively, to encourage all students to participate, and, finally, to provide tangible feedback to student responses.
- *Don't be discouraged if your efforts are not successful with all students.* From your reading of the individual differences literature you can now more readily understand that certain students are unconcerned about achievement. But these same students may be intensely interested in task mastery for its own sake. Understanding the various theories will make you much more aware of these different motivations.

Weiner and Attribution Theory

Even with a need to achieve, students will either succeed or fail. As they do, they search for reasons for their success or failure—they attribute their performance to a specific cause: The test was difficult; the teacher dislikes me; I'm good in this subject. Your students' attributions then serve as a guide to their expectations for future success or failure in that subject (Moses, 1991b). Le Yang, the student who couldn't understand why he wasn't doing better, may have attributed his performance to language difficulties. Like most of us, he was searching for a cause to explain his behavior.

We are all similar in this respect. If, when you are with a certain person, you consistently have an enjoyable time, then your expectation is that you will continue to have a good time in the future. Students who consistently do poorly in a subject expect to continue to do poorly. But before you can hope to have success in changing a student's performance, you must know to what that student attributes subpar performance.

Attribution theory rests on three basic assumptions (Petri, 1991). First, people want to know the causes of their own behavior and of others, particularly behavior that is important to them. Second, attribution theory assumes that we do not randomly assign causes to our behavior. There is a logical explanation for the causes to which we attribute our behavior. Third, the causes that we assign to our behavior influence subsequent behavior. If we attribute our failure to a particular person, we may come to dislike that person. The student who believes that "no matter what I do, Mr. Smith won't give me a good grade" will come to dislike Mr. Smith.

Attribution theory also relates well to the need for achievement. Weiner (1980, 1984, 1990) believes that when achievement is aroused, we tend to attribute our performance to one of four elements: ability, effort, task difficulty, or luck. Figure 10.2 presents an expanded version of the attribution concept and the many factors that influence students' attributions.

Ability

These attributions of success and failure have important implications for teaching since students' assumptions about their abilities are usually based upon past experiences. It is precisely here that we find explanations for math phobia, reading problems, or dislike of science. Students have a history of failure, and they often make the devastating assumption that they lack ability. This tendency is particularly true if others do well on the task.

Once students question their abilities, this doubt spreads to other subjects and other tasks. Soon there is a generalized feeling of incompetence that paralyzes initiative and activates an expectation of failure. Schunk (1985), studying the relationship between self-efficacy (that is, personal judgments of performance capabilities on any task) and learning, reported that students enter a classroom with aptitudes and experiences that affect their self-efficacy for initial learning. When successful, students' sense of self-efficacy increases, it in turn, enhances motivation.

Students who consistently question their own abilities pose a serious challenge since their history of failure and feelings of incompetence undercut motivation and learning. Your initial assumption about these students should be that there must be something that they can do well. Consequently, search for tasks that they can perform

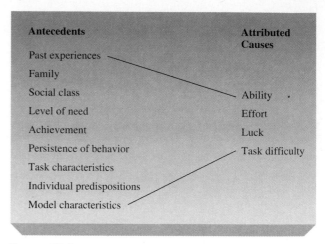

Figure 10.2
Conditions and characteristics that often influence students' attributions about successes or failures.

with competence and publicly reward them for their success. Remember: Avoid the danger of attributing their initial failure to a lack of ability before searching for alternate causes.

Effort

Weiner (1990) also made the interesting discovery that students usually have no idea how hard they try to succeed. Students (and all of us) judge their efforts by how well they did on a particular task. Even in tasks involving pure chance, successful students believed that they tried harder than those who were unsuccessful. An important cycle is thus established: Success increases effort; effort produces more success.

The educational implications are real and significant. If a skill is to be mastered and your teaching is consistent for your entire group, then student performance will vary because of motivation. Here again we note the importance of insuring success as a means of encouraging further effort.

Task Difficulty

Task difficulty usually is judged by the performance of others on the task. If many succeed, the task is perceived as easy, and vice versa. An interesting phenomenon can develop here. If a student consistently succeeds on a task at which others fail, that student will attribute success to ability. But if individual success is matched by the success of others, then the source of the success is seen in the task. Weiner's findings emphasize once again the importance of matching a task with a student's ability, thus enhancing ability and increasing effort.

Luck

Finally, if there is no tangible link between behavior and goal attainment, the tendency is to attribute success to

Focus on Teachers

Positive Reinforcement—Again

Skinner believed that today's education is failing because students for the most part see little or no results of their studying. When apathy is coupled with few demands and lack of reinforcement, schooling suffers.

The antidote? Teachers must improve their control over the classroom, not abandon it. (According to Skinner, the modern teacher is more actor and tour director than educator.) The answer for Skinner lies in the arrangement of **positive reinforcers** so that teachers can compete with the myriad distractions of today's society. Tokens, credit point systems, and programmed instruction all have proven to be effective techniques for affecting behavior.

You should also think about the amount of learning that your students must demonstrate before they are reinforced. If you do not demand sufficient change at each step, you will reinforce often, but your students will progress slowly. If you demand too much, no response may be satisfactory. (Again, note the need to try to match a student's ability with material.) If you successfully reduce the number of reinforcements, students will reach a point at which behavior is maintained indefinitely by an astonishingly small number of reinforcements.

Skinner believed (1968) that the most important consequence of motivation is what students do when they are no longer being taught. The teacher's attention, approval, and affirmation may have no real life counterpart. Unless intrinsic motivation has been established, the desirable behaviors fostered in class may be lost. If, however, students are exposed to carefully designed schedules of positive reinforcement, intrinsic motivation should maintain this behavior. They will continue to read for pleasure, listen to good music, and attend to national affairs—all without the urging of a teacher. Finally, Skinner noted that if we understand the proper use of reinforcers, we should be able to make students eager and diligent and be fairly confident that they will continue to enjoy learning for the rest of their lives.

Charting students' accomplishments provides opportunities for both intrinsic and extrinsic rewards and is useful in providing feedback. Reinforcement and feedback are central components in motivating students.

---

luck. Those students who have little faith in their abilities attribute their success on almost any task to luck, thus shortcircuiting the motivational network just described. Success in this case will not increase effort; lack of effort does nothing to bolster a belief in one's ability, and tasks remain an overwhelming obstacle.

For the Classroom

In applying his interpretation of attribution theory to the classroom, Weiner (1990) stated that there is a relationship among a student's attributions (ability, luck, effort, task difficulty), the stability of the attribution, its resistance to extinction, and expectancy of future goal attainment. Consequently, in achievement-related situations,

students experience both cognitive and emotional reactions such as the following:

"I just failed this exam," accompanied by feelings of frustration and upset, such as the following:

A. "I failed because I didn't try hard enough," followed by feelings of shame and guilt.
B. "I just don't have the right stuff," followed by feelings of low self-esteem, lack of worth, and hopelessness.

It is a complicated mixture, one to which you should be alert. For as you attempt to help students, you must be aware of your own causal attributions. It is quite easy to be deceived by a student's apparent effort and assign higher ability to that student than warranted. Students may also deliberately minimize effort to avoid the suggestion that they lack ability (Covington, Spratt, & Omelich, 1980).

Examining the subtleties of motivation leads to the conclusion that certain motivational aspects involve learning. Some motivation is learned: we learn to want definite objects; we learn to expect certain outcomes; we learn to fear certain things. But the relationship between learning and motivation is bi-directional—new learning depends upon motivation. Motivation is heightened for many students when interesting, new learning opportunities are presented.

As we shall see in the next section, learning theorists view learning quite differently, and their explanations of motivation reflect their beliefs about learning. Among the most prominent of the learning theorists is B. F. Skinner, whose system is usually referred to as operant or instrumental conditioning.

Skinner and Motivation

Skinner stated (1971) that if you ask people why they go to the theater and they reply that they feel like going, you are usually satisfied. It would be more revealing, however, if you knew what happened when they previously attended the theater, what they had read about the play, and what else induced them to go.

According to Skinner, behavior is shaped and maintained by its consequences. Thus, the consequences of previous behavior influence students. There is no major internal or intrinsic motivational component in the process. According to Skinner, motivated behavior results from the consequences of similar previous behavior. If students obtain reinforcement for certain behavior, they tend to repeat it with vigor. If they don't, such as Zack, the athlete we described in the chapter opening, students (like all of us) tend to lose their interest and their performance suffers.

For the Classroom

Students should not study merely to avoid the consequences of not studying, which may be something aversive such as punishment. Under aversive conditions students will engage in truancy, vandalism, disruptive behavior, or apathy. How can teachers improve their control over the classroom and not abandon it? Skinner believes that the answer lies in the appropriate use of *positive reinforcement schedules.*

Students are immediately encouraged upon giving correct responses and are not merely punished for incorrect responses. Such students come to feel free and happy in the classroom and when outside school because they have established behavioral patterns that produce

THE FAR SIDE   By GARY LARSON

© Chronicle Features. 1982   *Larson*

"Say ... Look what THEY'RE doing."

Models can serve as an important stimulus to motivate learners to try new behaviors or tasks.

The Far Side cartoon by Gary Larson is reprinted by permission of Chronicle Features, San Francisco, CA.

success, pleasant relations with others, and a deserved sense of accomplishment. These feelings have developed because a student learning to read has been reinforced when spoken responses to verbal stimuli are correct. You are reinforced during a lecture when the words you hear or see correspond to the responses that you anticipated. (Skinner believed that this is an important component in listening or reading with understanding.) If your students—or you—have been fortunate enough to have received such positive reinforcement, you can understand what Skinner means by self-motivation.

Finally, in analyzing the relationship between positive reinforcers and motivation, Skinner stated that telling students they don't know something is not highly motivating. Rather he suggested that you cover small amounts of material that you can immediately and positively reinforce. Much more about Skinner's views of motivation and human behavior will appear in chapter 13, Classroom Management, because many of the most challenging issues facing teachers pertain to students' motivation.

Bandura and Social Cognitive Learning

The final theorist whom we shall consider is Albert Bandura, who has attempted to combine both cognitive and behavioral elements in his explanation of motivation. Bandura's social learning theory has particular relevance for motivation. Students who come to your classroom are all able, and some willing, to imitate. A more permanent impression is made on students not by telling them what to do, but by setting an example for them. Teachers should be models as much as possible since your behavior can be a powerful motivating force for student behavior.

Observation of a model can produce significant changes in your students' behavior. Among these are the following: (a) an observer may acquire new responses; (b) observing models may strengthen or weaken existing responses; (c) observing models may cue the appearance of apparently forgotten responses. (The accompanying box illustrates the steps in using modeling in the classroom to teach a social skill.)

Obtaining Information About Yourself

If modeling is to be a motivational force, then your students' self-knowledge is crucial. Bandura (1981, 1986) believes that self-knowledge is gained from information conveyed by either personal or socially mediated experiences. There are four major sources of information available to students: performance accomplishments, vicarious experience, verbal persuasion, and emotional arousal.

- **Performance accomplishments.** Bandura states that we acquire personal and effective information from what we do. Students learn from first-hand experiences how successful they are in mastering classroom challenges. Their grades and the reactions of their classmates leave no room for doubt. When we realize the validity of Bandura's statement and combine it with conclusions from attribution theory, the necessity of arranging carefully planned schedules of positive reinforcement is clearly demonstrated. Be sure that your students encounter challenges that they realistically have a chance of mastering.
- **Vicarious experience.** This is Bandura's expression for watching "similar others" perform. If others can perform a task successfully, students usually feel more optimistic when they begin. Unfortunately, the opposite is also true.

  This source of information can be a major motivational device for teachers. If you are aware of the modeling power of your behavior, you can use it to urge students to improve their performance. You will also be more alert to the need to provide reasonable tasks for your class. If students look around and see that everyone is struggling, even the brightest, many students will simply give up.

Focus on Teachers

Guidelines for Using Modeling to Teach Social Skills

1. *Establish the need to learn the skill.* It is important to "sell" the social skill to students. Consider doing the following:
   a. Ask students why the skill might be important to them.
   b. Point out potential consequences of using the skill and not using the skill.
   c. Use examples from books, television, and the like in which characters used the skill.
   d. Identify situations in which the skill could come in handy for students.

2. *Identify skill components.* It is important that the social skill be task-analyzed for students. Students must know what steps and in what order the behaviors must be performed. Consider doing the following:
   a. Present a social skill (e.g., starting a conversation).
   b. Ask students what they would have to do to start a conversation with someone else.
   c. Write **all** of their suggestions on a chalkboard or flip chart.
   d. Discuss the relevance of each suggestion with the group. Decide with the group what behaviors would be important and unimportant and why.
   e. Decide with the group the list of behaviors that would be most important in performing the skill.
   f. Decide with the group the order in which the behaviors should be performed. Identify potential problems that might occur in performing the skill (e.g., the other person ignores you).

3. Present the modeling display.
   a. Decide if you or another child will model the skill.
   b. Be sure to have each of the steps in performing the skill written in view of group members.
   c. Review the steps to be performed before presenting the modeling display.
   d. Instruct students to watch to see if each step is performed in the proper sequence.
   e. Model the skill for the group.
   f. After modeling, discuss with students what they say and have them evaluate the modeling sequence.

4. Rehearse the skill. Have different students rehearse the modeled skill.

5. Provide specific feedback.
   a. Point out the correct things students did in performing the skill.
   b. Offer suggestions for how the performance could be improved. Remodel the skill if necessary and have students rehearse.

Reproduced from Social Skills Intervention Guide (Elliott & Gresham, 1991), American Guidance Service.

Table 10.1

Motivational Theorists and Their Basic Ideas

Name	Theory	Central Element of Theory	Explanation of Motivation
Maslow	Humanistic	Needs Hierarchy	Need Satisfaction
Bruner	Cognitive	Intrinsic Processes	Mixed Motives
McClelland	Achievement	Need to Achieve	Changes in Need Achievement
Weiner	Attribution	Causes of Behavior	Identifying Perceived Causes of Behavior
Skinner	Operant Conditioning	Reinforcement	Schedules of Reinforcement
Bandura	Social Cognitive	Imitation	Modeling

- **Verbal persuasion.** Here Bandura means that students can be led, through persuasion, into believing that they can overcome any difficulties and improve their performance. If you, as the instructor, are respected and admired by students, then your suggestions become a potent influence on your students' behavior.
- **Emotional arousal.** By this expression Bandura means that stressful situations constitute a source of personal information. If students see themselves as inept and fearful in certain situations and with certain subjects, then the possibility of that fearful behavior appearing is enhanced.

For the Classroom

The role of imitation in motivation and learning has direct classroom implications. Students' successful imitation of what they see and hear in the classroom is partially influenced by how you—the model—respond to them. If you recall, you were asked earlier what makes modeling effective. When you answered that question, you should have included references to *attention, retention, and reinforcement.*

Students must *attend* if they are going to imitate; they must *remember* what they have imitated if they are to reproduce it in the future; and their imitating behavior must have been reinforced for them to remember and later use. We can thus conclude that students will imitate when you provide incentives for them to do so and when you attend to what they have done. Elaine, the student who wanted to see some writings of modern authors, is a good example of a student who is looking for a model to imitate.

Note the two-way influence process described here (Bandura, 1986). Your students attend to and imitate you; you then attend to and reinforce them. Imitative per-

formance reflects not only the competencies of students but the reactions of the model (teachers). If you respond equally to performances that are markedly different in quality, your students will not imitate successfully. But if you attend to their behavior and reinforce them appropriately, they will accurately reproduce behavior.

As students grow older and move through the grades, their intellectual abilities increase and they become capable of delayed imitation. They can witness a modeled performance and later perform that task without having practiced it. If you recall Piaget's discussion of cognitive development, the growth of cognitive structures permits students to cope with increasingly more abstract material, retain that material, conserve it, and finally use it.

If you now apply these concepts to Bandura's work, you realize that your students can mentally rehearse what they view. With this increasing cognitive sophistication, they will soon escape the limitations of direct imitation and form new patterns of modeled behavior (Bandura, 1977, p. 33). This is especially true when students become comfortable with verbal symbols.

You can describe a course of action to them; *they will attend, retain, rehearse, and imitate* according to the verbal stimuli that you have presented to them. For example, before assembling equipment necessary for a science project, you can describe it and draw pictures of it, thus helping your students in the actual assembly.

As we conclude Bandura's work, remember: Students who observe enthusiastic, knowledgeable teachers tend to imitate that behavior and become enthusiastic and knowledgeable themselves.

Table 10.1 summarizes the major ideas of the motivational theorists we have reviewed. Which theory is most compatible with your thoughts about motivation and learning?

TEACHER ⬌ STUDENT
I N T E R A C T I O N S

Motivation and Learning

1. Intrinsic motivation is the ideal state for student learning.
   - Provide a comfortable area and adequate time in your classroom for students to lose themselves in a book of *their* choice. The joy of reading, then, will be its own reward.
   - Establish a corner with "hands on" science materials, e.g. shells, rocks, etc. so that students will find pleasure in identifying the various specimens and explaining them to classmates.
   - Have at your students' fingertips the reference books they need to do their own research (or just to browse through when they have free time).

2. Understanding students' needs is a critical factor in facilitating teaching and learning.
   - Be aware of any "hidden" difficulties of your students (e.g. slight hearing loss, minor eye problems, etc) when writing on the board, giving directions, assigning seats, etc.
   - Develop the skill of "sweeping" your classroom regularly to discern how your students react to each other, to new work, to interruptions.
   - Take time to talk individually to each of your students often about outside activities and events that are important to each of them.

3. Explanations of motivation help teachers, not only in understanding the motivational process, but also in their practical classroom work.
   - Knowledge of Bandura's theory will encourage you to be the model your students will imitate. Your enthusiasm for your subject and your encouraging attitude will help them to overcome their fear of attempting new assignments.
   - Knowledge of Skinner's theory, for example, will encourage you to praise and reward their good work. One suggestion to continue throughout the year is a series of attractive bulletin boards that recognize your students' good behavior or improved work; another is the presentation of awards for accomplishments.

Knowledge of your students' attributions will encourage you to assess their abilities, understand their efforts, and acknowledge that sometimes luck does play a part in a person's success. Your ability to admit that you too can make a mistake will encourage your students to apologize for theirs, correct them, and continue to succeed.

What Affects Students' Motivation?

The teacher in the vignette at the chapter's opening reflected a real concern for implementing motivational techniques and demonstrated her understanding of how motives affect students. As we have seen, several theorists have attempted to explain the nature of motivation with varying degrees of success. In their speculations each of the theorists has had to account for those individual motives that influence behavior. Given the importance of motivation to learning, it would be good for you to be aware of several of the most crucial of these motives. Among them would be anxiety, attitude, curiosity, locus of control, learned helplessness, and students' environments.

Anxiety

Were you anxious before your last exam? How do you feel when you must speak in public? Are there certain situations in which you feel particularly anxious, regardless of your preparation? We are all alike in this regard: anxious in some conditions, not in others. Terms to describe this condition are **situational, state, or normal anxiety.** There are other individuals, however, who are constantly in a state of anxiety, which is often called neurotic or **trait anxiety.**

Within the classroom setting, there are numerous sources of anxiety for students: teachers, examinations, peers, social relations, achievement settings, what girls think of boys, what boys think of girls, like or dislike of subjects, and distance from home for younger students. Whatever the cause, whatever the level of anxiety, you can be sure of one thing: Anxiety will affect student performance. Keep in mind, however, anxiety at relatively low to moderate levels can be constructive; anxiety at relatively high levels can be destructive and non-adaptive.

Since our concern is primarily with anxiety's effect on achievement, you should realize that extremely intense motivation that produces high anxiety has a negative effect on performance. Moderate motivation seems to be the desirable state for learning complex tasks. This is the Yerkes-Dodson law, which states that ideal motivation for learning decreases in intensity with increasing task difficulty. Figure 10.3 illustrates this concept. Note how increasing intensity improves performance only to a certain level, and then continued intensity results in a deteriorating performance. Think about some task that you generally do well; now think about your motivation for it. Would you characterize it as high or low? Usually as tasks become more difficult, students have fewer successes and subsequently become less motivated to continue the task.

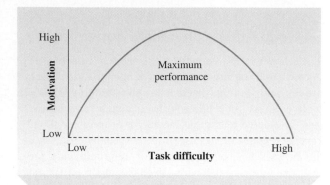

Figure 10.3

The Yerkes-Dodson law explaining the relationship between motivation and task difficulty.

Classroom Conditions

You will encounter exactly the same phenomenon in your classroom, which means that knowledge of anxiety can benefit both you and your students. Anxiety may appear at any time, be confined to one situation, or generalize widely. *Anxiety may be defined as an unpleasant sensation that is usually experienced as feelings of apprehension and general irritability accompanied by restlessness, fatigue, and various somatic symptoms such as headaches and stomach aches* (Chess & Hassibi, 1978, p. 241).

Many classroom implications emerge from this general overview. One is the distinct possibility that anxiety may generalize from one subject or teacher to another. Older students may develop a distaste for school that affects their achievement. Younger students may develop school phobia, a psychological condition producing such physical manifestations as crying and vomiting before school in the morning, thus hoping to avoid school attendance.

The following personality and behavioral characteristics are typical of the anxious student and reflect the opinion of the students themselves, other classmates, teachers, and parents:

- Anxious students develop negative attitudes about themselves and persistently blame only themselves for any failures. They tend to become dependent and are reluctant to display curiosity;
- Peers view anxious classmates negatively and may take advantage of them. Anxious students usually are not popular; they are rarely chosen either by peers or teachers for leading roles in classroom activities;
- Teachers typically perceive anxious students as more poorly adjusted than their classmates and as displaying more negative personality characteristics. For example, these students are seen as less secure and less task-oriented;

- Parents, especially fathers, see their anxious children as less mature, less well-adjusted, and more dependent.

It is clear from this brief summary that anxious students carry a heavy burden, which, as we have seen, can affect their classroom performance, especially in test-taking. Although anxiety affects all aspects of behavior, no topic has been more carefully researched in educational psychology than test anxiety.

Test Anxiety

The construct of **test anxiety** has been used for well over four decades to describe the behavior and emotions of students who find preparing for and taking tests stressful. Sarason's (1980, p. 476) summary of the main characteristics of test anxiety includes the following: (a) the test situation is seen as difficult, challenging, and threatening, (b) students see themselves as ineffective or inadequate in handling the task, (c) students focus on undesirable consequences of personal inadequacy, (d) self-deprecatory preoccupations are strong and interfere with task-relevant cognitive activity, and (e) students expect and anticipate failure and loss of regard by others.

Researchers have documented that test anxiety first appears in children at an early age—perhaps as early as age 7—and persists well into high school (Hembree, 1988). Estimates are that as many as 30 percent of school children suffer from debilitative test anxiety (Hill & Wigfield, 1984). This translates into a figure of eight to nine million children in American schools who may experience debilitating anxiety in academic performance situations. Approximately 20 percent of all test-anxious children will drop out of school because of repeated academic failure (Tobias, 1979).

Research on test anxiety can be divided into two types: laboratory research focusing on characteristics of test anxious students and clinical research focusing on methods for reducing test anxiety and its undesirable effects. In an exhaustive meta-analytic study of 562 research reports on test anxiety, Hembree (1988) concluded the following major points:

- Test anxiety and academic performance are significantly inversely related at grade three and above.
- Test anxiety occurs in students from all sociocultural groups in our society.
- Females exhibit more test anxiety than males, but as a group females are more likely to admit and self-report test anxiety.
- Average students, as measured by standardized tests, experience higher levels of test anxiety compared to both higher and lower ability students.

- High-test anxious students perform better under conditions that include low stress instructions, provisions for memory supports, performance incentives, and minimal classroom distractions.
- Worry components of test anxiety (e.g., negative self-talk and cognitions) appear to be stronger than emotional components (e.g., heartbeat, sweaty palms, and upset stomach).
- Test anxiety is directly related to fears of negative evaluation, dislike of tests, cognitive self-preoccupation, and less effective study skills.
- High test-anxious students hold themselves in lower esteem than do low test-anxious students.
- Finally, high-anxious students spend more time than low-anxious students attending to task-irrelevant behaviors such as negative self-statements, attention towards physical discomfort, and watching others in the classroom, and as a result, their performance suffers.

These research results describe characteristics of students and test conditions that may be manipulated to reduce anxiety and to enhance test taking performances. The research on treating test anxiety, however, more directly provides information on how to reduce test anxiety and is worth reviewing here, given the prevalence of test anxiety in school children.

Nicaise (1991) identified three major treatment philosophies for test anxiety. These can be characterized as (a) behavioral systematic desensitization with relaxation training, (b) skills training, and (c) cognitive-behavioral attention training. Each of these approaches is based on a different view of what the basic source of the problem is with a test anxious student. The desensitization/relaxation approach assumes that relaxation and test anxiety are conflicting responses. Strengthening the adaptive response of relaxing in the presence of a stimulus (i.e., a test) that evokes anxiety will result in the incremental weakening and eventual elimination of the anxiety response to the stimulus. The skills training approach assumes that poor test-taking performance is caused by a lack of knowledge, inadequate study habits, or deficient test-taking skills. The skills training approach involves procedures designed to enhance skills in each of these behaviors. The cognitive-behavioral attention training approach assumes self-talk and self-monitoring treatment procedures can be used to reduce students' preoccupied worrying and increase their attention task-relevant cues.

Nicaise (1991) recently summarized the major reviews of treatments for test anxiety. Her examination indicated that no single treatment is the best for every student. In fact, there are data to support the use of treatments characterizing all three of the major approaches

we have briefly described, with perhaps those treatments combining relaxation, study skill training, and attentional self-talk providing the most effective and long lasting treatment for test anxiety.

A final word of caution is necessary here. Teachers are not therapists. As much as you want to help, and try to help, there are times when a student needs professional help. Know when that time is reached and consult a school psychologist or counselor for assistance.

Attitudes

Psychologists typically define an **attitude** *as a relatively permanent way of feeling, thinking, and behaving toward something or somebody.* These feelings, thoughts, and actions reflect your perceptions of a situation or a person. There is an important implication for teaching in this analysis: The more that you know about somebody or something and the more strongly that you feel, the less likely is your attitude to change.

Pause for a moment and consider what this means for the classroom. If other teachers, especially those you respect, have spoken negatively and with feeling about a student, your attitude toward that student will probably be negative and will be difficult to change. Also, if you have had difficulty with one member of a family, then you must guard against being negative about any brothers or sisters that you may later have.

In both examples, care is needed to prevent rigid attitudes from obstructing learning. What is clear, then, is the necessity to insure as positive an attitude as possible—both students' and teachers'—to facilitate motivation and learning.

Attitude Change

Any instance of attitude change involves persuasion. The student who enters your classroom with a negative attitude toward you, the subject, or both must be persuaded to change that attitude. McConnell (1980) stated that there are four main elements in persuasive communication: the communicator, the message, the audience, and the audience-communicator feedback loop.

The communicator in our example is the teacher. The one feature that seems to mark the effective communicator is credibility. In a classic study, Hovland, Janis, and Kelley (1953) wrote a statement about the importance of atomic submarines and attributed it to two sources, one of high credibility, the other of low credibility. The source of the message strongly affected the subjects' attitudes; subjects given the message from the high credibility source tended to accept the argument, while the other group rejected it.

A month later the investigators retested their subjects. They were amazed to discover that the high credibility group had become less positive, while the low credibility group had become more positive. What had happened was that the subjects began to forget the source of their information and began to concentrate on the information itself.

If we translate the findings from the Hovland study into suggestions for the classroom, it seems that teachers as the sources of information have an immediate and strong effect on students, but if it is to be long lasting, then the information itself should be accurate, pertinent, and interesting.

The message refers to the information that you transmit to your class. Given the accuracy of the material that you are presenting to your class, your next concern should be the manner in which you present it. This is not a matter of the methods that you select. Rather it refers to the emotional accompaniments of the message.

Do you present it with a "do it, or else" attitude, hoping that fear will be a strong motivating force? If you do, consider follow-up studies to the television film, *Scared Straight.* This film showed prison inmates telling young people in graphic detail about prison brutality. Follow-up studies showed that more of those who participated in the study later committed offenses than subjects in a control group.

Yelling and frightening young people for a brief time does not provide them with the skills necessary to cope with their environment. What seems to be much more effective is teaching those skills that promise success and that promote self-esteem.

The audience in our example is a class of students. The individual personalities that compose a class demand careful and continuous scrutiny so that you can shape subject matter in a way that captures their attention and interest. Again, we see the need to match material with ability and interest.

Learn to know your students and translate this knowledge into classroom action. For example, you may identify a student with a negative attitude toward history, determine the cause of the attitude (to what does the student attribute such behavior?), arrange for successful experiences, all the while carefully shaping classroom material to the student's needs.

The audience-communicator feedback loop refers to the response that a class actually makes to a teacher and is a guide to future work. It is deceptively easy to assume that because you have presented something in what you were sure was a stimulating manner that your class grasped it fully. You must take the time to determine if the students can respond cognitively (do they understand what you taught?) and what their affective reaction is (do they enjoy this work?). Seeking and reviewing feedback

about one's performance is a critical component of successful communication and teaching.

For the Classroom

Attitudes are powerful motivational influences that can be either positive or negative. Students' attitudes decisively affect their learning and are our concern in this section. Their attitudes toward school arise from a number of sources: parents, siblings, peers, their own performance, and teachers, among others. Since students' attitudes toward school are a given when they arrive at school, one's chances of successfully changing those attitudes will come from directly working with the student as seen in the following examples.

Students' attitudes toward teachers. Here are several strategies for fostering positive attitudes toward teachers.

- Make every effort to share something with individual students. By giving a student time on a special basis (not forced, but in as natural a way as possible), you convey a sense of caring that even students with negative attitudes appreciate. If teachers combine this with an obvious liking for the subject(s) they teach, students begin to think of teachers as something more than a distant figure in the front of the room.
- There is a cliche' (true, as are most cliches) that warns teachers to accept students but not necessarily their behavior. Acceptance is not always easy; there are some students who are difficult to like. Students with negative attitudes are expecting rejection. When we accept their positive behavior, it frustrates their expectancies and may provide the opportunity for attitude change.

Students' attitudes toward subjects. Rare indeed is the student without a negative attitude toward some subject. This is to be expected; even teachers like some subjects better than others. But an overall negative attitude is damaging to a student and can, if unchecked, affect an entire classroom. Learning suffers and cynicism is rampant, especially with older students. Suggestions to improve attitudes toward subjects include the following:

- Teachers must show enthusiasm about their subjects. You can accomplish this by becoming expert in your field and permitting your students to see how much you like what you are doing. Relate the subject to your students' knowledge—about home, community, activities, sports, or anything that your class is interested in.
- Be careful about what surrounds your teaching of the subject. Although this sounds simple, you should be aware of anything negative that could have an impact on your teaching. For example, avoid using extra

assignments in your subject as punishment. If there has been an unpleasant incident in class, it may be well to turn to written work rather than new instruction. (You could be seen as the villain, and any negative feelings will transfer to the material you are presenting.)

- Demonstrate how meaningful your subject is. For example, many students dislike anything geographical because of past experiences—forced to memorize capitals, products, rivers, and the like. But if geography is linked to such current events as environmental pollution or tense world situations, the subject takes on new meaning.

Students' attitudes toward themselves. Poor self-opinion can have devastating consequences for motivation. Behavior is consistent with self-opinion; thus a realistic objective is to aid in the development of a positive attitude toward self. Here are several suggestions that you may find helpful.

- *Guarantee success.* However you do it, make certain that students with poor self-concepts experience earned success. Honesty is fundamental here since if a student discovers that the achievement was unwarranted, self-esteem and trust in the teacher would diminish sharply.
- *Be prepared to offer nearly constant encouragement.* It is insufficient to structure a learning situation for these students. If their self-esteem is low, they may not have the motivation to commence the task. Initially, you must be with them to recognize any effort and any success. Work closely with them at the beginning of the task and minimize any mistakes. Stress learning from mistakes and reinforce effort.

Curiosity

If students are relatively relaxed and willing to work (as are most students), then you could reasonably expect them to have some interest in their environment. Curiosity can be one of a teacher's best friends because it signals a motivated student, eager to learn. Your task as a teacher, then, is to capitalize on this interest by further stimulating students and maintaining an optimal level of curiosity. But first it is necessary to explain what we mean by curiosity.

What Is Curiosity?

Curious behavior is often described by other terms, such as exploratory, manipulative, or active, but all have a similar meaning. To identify the origin of curiosity is difficult. Explanations have focused on the external (something in the student's environment is attractive) or the

internal (human beings need stimulation; recall the McGill experiments on boredom). Current interpretations include both.

Researchers (Dacey, 1989b) have established that certain correlates of curiosity appear consistently, although not with high significance. For example, there seems to be a low to moderate correlation between intelligence and curiosity. Measures of achievement relate somewhat to curiosity, but the most significant relationship is between curiosity and creativity.

For the Classroom

Curiosity is a natural phenomenon that you should encourage within the limits that you establish for your class. A relaxed atmosphere, freedom to explore, and an acceptance of the unusual all inspire curiosity. The development of curiosity should be encouraged as soon as possible—during the preschool and elementary years. If you recall your earlier developmental reading, the early years are a time for the formation of cognitive structures that furnish a basis for future cognitive activity. Students not only acquire knowledge, but they also learn about learning. They become curious if their environment is stimulating.

Youngsters are naturally curious, and if their curiosity is encouraged, it will probably last a lifetime. Here are some suggestions for engaging curiosity.

- *Enthusiasm for a subject* should be discernible to students. By using questions related to the material, teachers can tease students into exploring this new vista.
- Depending upon a student's level of sophistication, stimulate cognitive *conflicts, cause some apparent confusion* but simultaneously provide clues to the solution. Some of the problems we posed in chapter 8 on problem solving are good examples of stimulating and potentially confusing problems that many curious students like.
- When possible, *allow students to select topics* that they are curious about. Give them the freedom, and the direction, to explore for themselves.
- Model curious, inquiring behavior. Tell students the things you are curious about and model some of the resourceful behavior that curious people use to solve problems.

Locus of Control

Did you do well in your last test in this course? Why? Were you well-prepared? Or does the instructor like you? Or were you just plain lucky? If you think about your answers to these questions, and consider how other

Curiosity is a meaningful concept of motivation. Try to set up learning events that allow for "discoveries" and fuel curiosity.

students might answer them, you can discern possible patterns that identify your **locus of control.**

Internals-Externals

Some students' answers to these questions suggest that anything good that happens to a person is caused by chance; the replies of other students indicate that if anything good happens, it was deserved. For most of us, our responses follow a definite form: If we attribute responsibility to ourselves, we are called **internals.** If we attribute the causes of our behavior to somebody or something outside ourselves, we are called **externals.**

Parents, peers, and a student's total environment subtly interact to produce these feelings of confidence or uncertainty about life's challenges. Using more refined and sophisticated versions of this basic theme, Rotter (1966, 1975) and Phares (1973) analyzed individuals to determine their locus of control. If students believe they have little control over the consequences of their actions, they are said to have an external locus of control; if they believe they can control what happens to them, they are thought to have an internal locus of control.

For example, if students believe that success and rewards come from skill and not luck, they then assume that they have control over their own destinies. On the other hand, if students believe that rewards come from luck and not skill, they assume that they have little control over their own destinies.

The internal-external dimension seems to be a generalized interpretation of the reasons that some behavior is rewarded and other is punished. What is significant about the locus of control concept is that it can be used as a personality characteristic or tendency that has implications for learning. Researchers have shown, for example, a positive relationship between externality and the use of extrinsic forms of motivation in experienced teachers (Trice & Wood-Shuman, 1984). In a recent investigation, Wigfield (1988) found that age and past successes and failures have a significant effect on students' attributions of control. In general, as students become more mature and as they experience more success, their attributions about control become more internal.

Locus of control, however, is susceptible to change under certain conditions, such as experiences that meaningfully

Focus on Students

Internals and Externals in the Classroom

Locus of control provides another opportunity to improve your relationships with your students. By getting to know and understand them, you can assess their self-concepts and build on their strengths and work on their weaknesses. Individuals are neither all internal nor all external, but one of these traits is typically dominant. Since internals are seen as independent, alert, competent, and self-confident, it is difficult to avoid the conclusion that internality is the preferable personality characteristic. Rotter (1975) cautioned against such speculation, however, noting that internals may be too confident and withdrawn, while externals can be quite appealing and socially attractive.

Externality may also help some students to adapt successfully in situations where internality could cause problems. For example, some students with extremely authoritarian parents realistically assume that they have little control over their actions. Students from impoverished environments may also realistically assume that their well-being depends on others. Rotter is not making a value judgment here; he is simply making a practical assessment of how things often are in our society. Nevertheless, examining the characteristics of internality and externality makes it clear why internality is favored.

Internals
alert
competent
resists influence
domineering
achievement-oriented
independent
self-confident
skillful

Externals
less attentive
erratic performers
influenced by status
influenced by group members
believe they are controlled by others
lack confidence in their ability
random reactions

For the Classroom
A review of many studies of locus of control in school settings suggest the following (Dacey, 1989b):

- teachers tend to attribute more negative characteristics to external students than internals, and external students described their teachers more negatively than did internals;
- external students perform better when they receive specific comments about teachers' expectations;
- teachers, regardless of their own locus of control, are more impressed by the initial performance of students than by recent performances.
- internal students are more effective than external students in recognizing and using available information.
- external students do less well in competitive situations than internal students, which seems to be a result of their higher level of anxiety.

Regardless of a student's locus of control, consider these suggestions. First, present them with realistic challenges, which implies that you must know the students so that you can determine what is realistic for them. Second, carefully reward their accomplishments or at least their efforts. Reinforcement must be based on actual accomplishment; otherwise students will quickly identify it as a sham. Also reinforce their effort; be specific in noting that you realize that they took the responsibility. Finally, use any initial successes, and attempt to foster a habit of trying and taking responsibility for one's actions.

Learned Helplessness

For some students the best opportunity for change may be in the classroom, and if this chance is lost, they may experience a condition called **learned helplessness** (Seligman, 1975). What seems to happen is that after repeated failure students become frustrated and simply will not try. The evidence—both animal and human—strongly supports this conclusion. In a series of experiments by Seligman and Maier (1967), harnessed dogs encountered one of three conditions. An *escape* group learned to escape shock while harnessed by pressing a panel with their noses. A *yoked* group received precisely the same shocks as the escape group, but they could do nothing to reduce or escape the shock. A *naive* group received no shock while in the harness. After twenty-four hours all three groups were moved to a shuttle box where they could escape the shock by jumping over a barrier. Both the escape and naive groups quickly learned to escape the shock, but the yoked group showed little, if any, ability to learn how to avoid the shock. It could not have

alter the relationship between act and outcome. If students think that their success resulted from a teacher's manipulation of their work, there will be little change in their locus of control. It is only when they perceive that *their actions* were instrumental in achieving success that real change may occur.

been the shock itself that made the yoked dogs unable to learn the escape response because dogs in the escape group had been equally shocked. It was the lack of control that sealed their fate when they were later in a position where they could control the shock.

The yoked group's response when presented with a situation that they could control—yet did not—is called learned helplessness. It appears a subtle combination of cognitive, motivational, and emotional elements caused the subject to fail to see the necessary relationships. The animals refused even to try to escape and exhibited signs of stress and depression.

Learned helplessness also applies to humans, as seen in the work of Hiroto (1974). Using three groups, Hiroto subjected them to a loud, unpleasant noise. The escape group could stop the noise by pushing a button. The yoked group experienced the same noise with no way of reducing or eliminating it. The third group received no noise. In the follow-up condition all groups could escape the noise by moving one of their hands in a shuttle box from one side to the other. Again, the escape and naive groups did well, but those who had experienced unavoidable noise simply sat and made no move to eliminate the noise.

If for noise we substitute failing grades, sarcasm at home and school, and ridicule, then it becomes possible to trace a possible developmental path of learned helplessness. Students who experience nothing but failure and abuse at home and school have little chance of obtaining positive reinforcement for their behavior. If you discover such students, though it may sound simple, make every effort to combat this habit of "giving up."

Schools and Learned Helplessness

Investigating learned helplessness in fifth graders, Dweck and Repucci (1973) had one teacher give solvable problems and another teacher give unsolvable problems to their students. Later when the teacher who had given the unsolvable problems instead gave students solvable problems (like those given by the other teacher), the researchers observed that many students could not solve the problems, even though they had previously done so with another teacher.

In a follow-up to the Dweck and Repucci study, Diener and Dweck (1978) investigated the differences in students' reactions to failure. They identified two groups of students, "helpless" and "mastery-oriented." When helpless students failed, they tended to ruminate about the cause of their lack of success. In contrast, when the mastery-oriented students had a failure experience, they focused on finding a solution to the problems they failed. Diener and Dweck also reported that the helpless students

underestimated their number of successes and overestimated their number of failures. When the helpless students had successes, they often reported that they didn't expect them to continue.

One of the practical outcomes of Dweck's research on learned helplessness is knowledge about training students to overcome learned helplessness by attributing their failures to a lack of effort rather than ability. Dweck (1975) used an attribution training procedure that taught students to stress lack of motivation and effort as the primary determinants of failure.

In summary, the concept of learned helplessness has provided a meaningful way to understand the behavior of some students who have repeatedly over several years experienced many more failures than successes. It does not appear that simply increasing the number of their successes will significantly influence their outlook on learning. Teaching students to realistically assess their failures and to focus on increasing their effort or motivation are necessary components in overcoming feelings of helplessness.

Three components of learned helplessness have particular pertinence for the classroom: failure to initiate action, failure to learn, and emotional problems.

1. *Failure to initiate action* means that students who have experienced helplessness tend not to initiate responses in new learning. Passivity becomes the predominant behavior.
2. *Failure to learn* means that even when new directions are given to these students, they still learn nothing from them.
3. *Emotional problems* seem to accompany learned helplessness. Frustration, depression, and incompetence are frequent accompaniments.

Self-Efficacy and Its Role in Motivation

Self-efficacy refers to individuals' beliefs in their capabilities to exert control over aspects of their lives. Self-efficacy theory suggests that efficacy beliefs are the product of one's own performances, vicarious experiences, verbal persuasion from others, and emotional arousal (Bandura, 1977, 1986). Students who believe they are not efficacious in coping with environmental demands tend to focus on their inefficiency and exaggerate potential difficulties. Students who have a strong sense of efficacy, however, tend to focus their attention and effort on the demands of tasks and minimize potential difficulties (Bandura, 1986).

Interest in self-efficacy and its role in motivation has grown immensely as evidenced by a special section in the *Journal of Educational Psychology* on motivation and efficacy (Schunk, 1990). Viewing motivation and efficacy as interacting mechanisms has important theoretical and practical implications for educators. As noted by Schunk, "A sense of efficacy for performing well in school may lead students to expend effort and persist at tasks, which promotes learning. As students perceive their learning progress, their initial sense of efficacy is substantiated, which sustains motivation" (Schunk, 1990, p. 33). Researchers have demonstrated that even when students have encountered prior difficulties, the students' belief that they are capable of succeeding can override negative effects of prior performances and produce motivated behaviors (Rosenthal & Zimmerman, 1978; Schunk, 1989a).

In self-efficacy theory, *efficacy expectations* are differentiated from *outcome expectations*. That is, an outcome expectation represents a person's estimate that a given behavior will lead to a certain outcome. In contrast, an efficacy expectation means that individuals believe that they can perform the behavior or behaviors required to produce certain outcomes. Outcome and efficacy expectations are differentiated because students can believe certain behaviors will produce an outcome, but they may not believe that they can execute the behaviors that will produce the outcome. Figure 10.4 provides an illustration of this difference.

Individuals may possess low perceptions of efficacy in one skill domain (e.g., academics) and high perceptions of efficacy in other skill domains (e.g., social, physical). Moreover, self-perceptions of efficacy often vary as a function of setting. For example, it is a well-established finding that many handicapped children have higher self-concepts in self-contained special education classrooms than in regular education classrooms (Kaufman, Agard, & Semmel, 1985).

In the development of a scale to measure student's self-efficacy, Gresham, Evans, and Elliott (1988) found that the self-efficacy ratings of gifted, nonhandicapped, and mainstreamed mildly handicapped students consistently varied. Social, physical, and academic variations were observed both intraindividually and interindividually. As expected, the handicapped students rated themselves as less efficacious in the academic skill domain than the other domains and in comparison to the nonhandicapped and gifted students. The gifted students rated themselves on average highest in the academic domain and lowest in the social domain. In some cases, the gifted students also rated themselves as less efficacious in the social and physical domains than the nonhandicapped students. Thus, students' perceptions of their self-efficacy vary across skill domains and in comparison to fellow students who are known to function at different levels academically, socially, and physically.

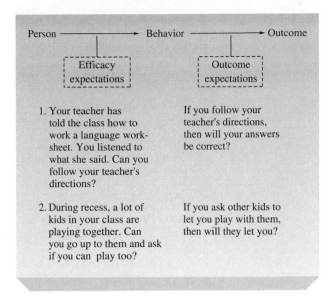

Figure 10.4

Representation of the difference between efficacy expectations and outcome expectations within Bandura's (1977) theory of self-efficacy with example items.

Students and Help-Seeking Behavior

Perceived self-efficacy affects a student's functioning by influencing an individual's choice of activities, effort expenditure, and persistence in the face of difficulties (Bandura, 1986). The ramifications of self-efficacy for a student's classroom learning appear to be tremendous. Researchers interested in the role of self-efficacy in teacher-student interactions have recently reported some important findings about students' help-seeking behaviors (Newman, 1990) and teachers' help-giving behavior (Graham & Barker, 1990). Let's examine several of these studies in detail, given the important role that asking and giving help plays in the classroom.

As Newman (1990) noted, students who ask questions and obtain assistance when it is required alleviate immediate learning difficulties and also acquire knowledge and skills that they can use for self-help later. Despite the obvious importance of help-seeking in the classroom, many students do not ask teachers for help or avail themselves of help when they need it (Good & Weinstein, 1986).

Newman was curious about why children often were reluctant to seek academic assistance from teachers, so he designed a study with 177 third, fifth, and seventh graders. Newman assessed the students' perceived academic competence, intrinsic orientation, and attitudes and intentions regarding help-seeking in math class. The data for these students were used to answer the question: How do student's efforts at academic help-seeking vary according to

(a) characteristics of the students and (b) social-interactional conditions in the classroom? Here are some of the major findings from Newman's (1990) study:

- The influence of motivational factors on the children's intentions to seek help with an academic problem was stronger for the third and fifth graders than for the seventh graders. The stronger the belief that help-seeking is beneficial and the weaker the belief that it has associated costs, the greater the student's expressed likelihood of seeking help.
- For all grades, the greater the student's perceived competence, the less strongly the student felt there was cost associated with seeking help. The implication regarding students with low perceived competence are the same as that regarding low achievers: Those most in need of help may be those most reluctant to seek help.

Newman concluded that his findings were consistent with a vulnerability hypothesis of help-seeking. According to this hypothesis, students with low self-esteem or efficacy have a greater need than students with high self-esteem to avoid situations in which they feel threatened by an admission of failure. Thus, students with low self-efficacy are less likely to seek help. Giving them help remains an important task of teachers.

Giving help to students is not always easy nor without some possible negative side effects for students. According to a recent investigation by Graham and Barker (1990) with children ranging in age from four to twelve, they found that when teachers help students, it can be interpreted as indicating the student lacks ability. Specifically, Graham and Barker found that unsolicited teacher assistance signaled low ability to students. Compared with a nonhelped peer, a student receiving teacher assistance was judged less smart, less proud of success, more grateful, less likely to be successful in the future, and less preferable as a workmate. The cuing function of teachers' assistance was not present in the four- and five-year-olds, so it appears to emerge with the advent of schooling. This study has important implications for help-givers and alerts us to the potential negative side of help for students. In addition it, along with the theoretical work on self-efficacy, emphasizes how instructional practices affect not only students' acquisition of skills but also their motivation and efficacy for learning.

Motivation and Multicultural Students

In this section on what affects a student's motivation, nothing can be more important than the adjustment that a student makes to the environment—new country, new customs, new friends, new classrooms. These new features of life inevitably affect the learning and achievement of many students, with motivation usually a critical element. In this section, we have discussed anxiety, attitude, curiosity, locus of control, learned helplessness, and self-efficacy, any or all of which can affect multicultural students.

One of the major contributions teachers can make to the successful integration and accomplishments of multicultural students is to provide an understanding, supportive environment. The first step is to be certain that all school personnel treat all students with respect and dignity. Be especially alert to the needs of those students whose physical appearance, speech, and behavior may differ from other students, which means that you must be familiar with their cultural backgrounds.

For example, Hawaiian children come from a culture in which collaboration, cooperation, and helping one another are an integral part of their way of life and sibling caretaking is common. Teachers who are aware of these characteristics will design instructional techniques and involve students in small group activities and peer teaching-learning interactions (Tharp, 1989).

This general technique applies to working with all multicultural students. What seems to be most urgent for them? A good guide to helping is Maslow's hierarchy of needs, especially the safety needs. Does this student feel secure in this novel, perhaps frightening environment? What about a student's belongingness needs? Is the student a member of the group or isolated from others because of language or customs? If the answers to these questions are negative, the chances are high that such a student's self-esteem must also be suffering.

As you can well imagine, language is a serious obstacle to acceptance for many students. A practical technique for helping students overcome language barriers is described by First (1988). Called the "English Plus" program, it was developed for the Washington, D.C. schools and involves special strategies to supplement other language programs. For example, although multicultural students may be learning English, the English Plus program uses peers and adults to work with students in their own language. You can see how this and similar strategies can motivate and improve learning by providing both subject matter help and role modeling.

No class is completely homogeneous, and teachers learn to expect differences among their students and search for the best ways to reach their multicultural students. One recommendation is to make sure these students experience immediate success by assigning tasks within their capability and rewarding them for successful performance (Sleeter & Grant, 1988, p. 55).

Among their suggestions are the following:

- individualize instruction as much as possible by sequencing and pacing the programs as correctly as possible for individual children.
- multicultural students have their own strengths; capitalize on these, thus providing positive reinforcement and enhancing a student's self-concept.
- consider using a classwide peer tutoring program or cooperative learning groups.

Although not specifically designed to facilitate the learning and adjustment of minority students, instructional techniques based on cooperative learning principles have been used effectively with a wide range of students. Let's examine this popular instructional intervention next.

Cooperative Learning and Motivation

The dynamics of classrooms are deeply enmeshed in the give-and-take among classroom members—students and students, students and teachers. Though our analysis of relationships appeared in chapter 5, we can comment here on the effect that classroom atmosphere has on motivation and learning, especially the impact of competition and cooperation and the integration of minority students.

We have previously commented on the care with which teachers must handle competition in the classroom (see chapter 6). Can we reach equally as definite conclusions about the results of **cooperative learning,** as the teacher did in the chapter opening? Although this topic has a briefer history, recent research offers several interesting and potentially useful classroom applications.

Defining cooperative learning as a set of instructional methods in which students are encouraged or required to work together on academic tasks, Slavin (1987c) notes that such methods may include having students sit together for discussion, or help each other with assignments, and more complex requirements. He distinguishes cooperative learning from peer tutoring by noting that all students learn the same material, that there is no tutor, and that the initial information comes from the teacher.

Increases in student achievement depend on the conditions of cooperative learning, which has important motivational consequences. Motivation for cooperative learning is associated with the goal structures and potential rewards for group members. Group members can attain their personal goals only if *the group* is successful.

Consequently, two conditions must be met if cooperative learning is to be effective. First, the cooperating groups must have a *group goal* that is meaningful to them (a prize, recognition, free time). Second, the group's success must emerge from the individual learning of *all* group members (Slavin, 1988a). If these two conditions

are met—group effort and individual accountability—then students are motivated to help each other learn.

Cooperative learning involves two aspects of classroom organization: *task structure and reward structure* (Slavin, 1987c). In cooperative learning, the task structures insure that group members work with each other. Reward structures may depend on the performance of the total group (a product they produce), or on the sum of the individual learning performances.

In a series of investigations, Johnson and Johnson (1987) have introduced the concept of goal structures, which refers to the way that students relate to each other as they pursue similar goals (for example, understanding the causes of the American Revolution). Goal structures can be classified as follows:

- *cooperative,* in which students work *together* to achieve a goal;
- *competitive,* in which students work *against* each other while pursuing an instructional goal;
- *individualistic,* in which students' activities are unrelated to each other as they work toward a goal.

For example, during an election, students in a political science or history class may poll different neighborhoods and combine their results to predict a winner (cooperative learning). Some instructors have the disconcerting habit of announcing to a class that "only four people in this class can get an A, and there will be only eight Bs," a classic example of fostering competitive learning. Finally, "I do my work, you do yours; we receive grades based on how well we do individually."

You can see how each of these goal structures establishes a different learning atmosphere and different types of relationships in the classroom. Motivation also varies for each condition. Each of these conditions can serve a definite purpose, but be aware of what you are trying to accomplish in a class and how you are doing it.

For example, there are circumstances best suited for each condition. A course in marketing techniques is obviously designed to teach students how to present their products in a manner superior to a competitor. A large class in a core subject (English, history) usually represents an individualistic goal structure: attend the lectures, take the tests, pass in the assignments, receive the grade. Discussing social action or community involvement offers opportunities for cooperative learning in which students help each other to achieve goals.

In an attempt to develop techniques designed to further cooperative learning, Slavin (1987c) proposes the following:

- Students should work in small, mixed-ability groups of four members: one high achiever, two average achievers, and one low achiever.

Focus on Students

Motivating the At-Risk Student

In a recent article, Alderman (1990) provided a heuristic model of motivation that nicely integrates many of the theoretical and practical points we have emphasized in this and the previous chapter on learning strategies. Alderman has drawn heavily from the teacher expectancy literature and stresses that teachers must show students that they want them to succeed and also that they expect students to achieve the major learning objectives for a class. Referring to her work as *The Link Model*, Alderman emphasizes that students must see a link between what they do and a given learning outcome.

Box Figure 10.1 illustrates Alderman's Link Model and highlights its four main linking components: proximal goals, learning strategies, successful experiences, and attributions for success. Let's briefly explore each of these components.

Link 1: *Proximal Goals.* Goals play an important role in the development of self-motivation by establishing targets by which students can evaluate their own progress. To be effective, goals should be specific rather than general, attainable, and proximal or close at hand rather than long-term (Bandura & Schunk, 1981). Box Figure 10.2 illustrates the steps involved in planning and evaluating one's goals.

Link 2: *Learning Strategies.* Low-achievers often are inefficient learners; that is, they fail to apply a learning strategy that would facilitate their performance. In Link 2, students are asked to identify an effective learning strategy that will help them to accomplish their goals.

Link 3: *Successful Experience.* A learning goal is the key to success in this component. Students measure their success using the proximal goal as the criterion. Teachers play a valuable role by creating

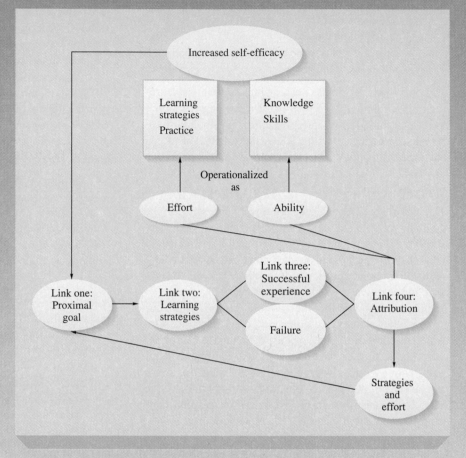

Box Figure 10.1
Motivational links to success.

opportunities for students to work on their goals and fostering effective learning conditions.

Link 4: *Attributions for Success.* Students are encouraged to attribute their success to their personal efforts or abilities. Teachers can help students make appropriate attributions, for example, by asking, "What did you do when you tried?" For difficult tasks, teachers' attributional feedback should begin with a focus on effort and then shift to students' abilities.

The Link Model for fostering motivation goes "full circle." Students who have succeeded and attributed their success to their own effort and ability have concrete performance feedback that will lead them to increased self-efficacy, which in turn will

• Students in each group are responsible for the material taught under regular classroom conditions but also for helping other group members to learn and to achieve a group goal.

One such technique is the *Student Teams-Achievement Division or STAD,* which consists of a definite cycle of activities. The teacher initially presents a lesson under regular classroom conditions. Students then attempt to master the material in their four-member group. For example, if the subject is math, students may work on problems, compare their answers, and attack any difficulties that arise. Students now take individual tests during which they cannot help each other.

The teacher next sums the results of the quizzes to obtain a team score. Since this is cooperative learning, however, the focus is on improvement. Therefore, the teacher compares students' scores on the test with their average scores on previous tests. If a score is ten percent above the average, that student earns three points for the group. An improvement of five to nine points earns two points, four points above to four points below the average earns one point, and anything below five points receives zero points.

Stating that research supports the superiority of this technique over other methods, Slavin (1987b) warns that simply putting students together will not produce learning gains. Students need to work toward a group goal and all members must contribute, not just the smartest. Slavin (1991) stated that the most successful approaches to cooperative learning incorporate two key elements: group goals and individual responsibility.

When these two features are used, achievement effects are consistently positive. For example, 37 of 44 experimental/control studies of at least four weeks' duration found significantly positive results. These positive effects are about the same at all grade levels, in all major subjects, in urban, rural, or suburban schools, and for high, average, or low achievers. Positive effects also have been found on such outcomes as self-esteem, intergroup relations, acceptance of academically handicapped students, and attitudes toward school (Slavin, 1991).

Slavin's concerns reflect persistent criticisms of cooperative learning. Will certain students dominate the groups? Will all students learn as much as possible? Will other students feel less motivated because the teacher is not directly involved? Does personality make a difference (will shy students lose out)?

Regardless of these issues, which have not as yet been fully resolved, cooperative learning seems to be a technique whose time has come. You may want to think of experimenting with it in your classes since, if properly

---

Make your goal as specific as possible:

Planning

1. My specific learning goals for this week (today) are:

2. I will know I have accomplished my goals by:

3. Actions or steps I will take to accomplish these goals:

4. Possible blocks, both personal and outside, that may interfere with my goals:

5. If I need help, I can go to:

6. My confidence in reaching my goal is:

No confidence	Very confident
0	25

Evaluating

7. My satisfaction with my goal attainment is:

Very unsatisfied	Very satisfied
0	25

8. Reasons for attaining or not attaining my goal:

Box Figure 10.2
Proximal goals and progress.

---

lead to increased confidence about goal accomplishments. All students will not consistently experience success; some failures will always occur.

When failure does occur, students' attributions for it are important determinants of their future expectations for success. Students who attribute failure to the use of a weak or inappropriate strategy are more likely to try again. Attributing failure to a lack of effort when students feel they have put forth a strong effort can be a damaging attribution. Working closely with students to assess their performance and helping them to make realistic attributions about their successes and failures is an important task for teachers and parents. The Link Model provides a useful organizer for working with students who are at-risk for motivation problems.

TEACHER ⟷ STUDENT
I N T E R A C T I O N S

Influences on Students' Motivation

1. Classroom conditions greatly affect motivation.
   - The teacher establishes the atmosphere where a student feels safe and able to share interests, reactions, and insights with the teacher and other students. To motivate good reading, for example, the teacher should talk about and bring in books and share interesting stories, jokes from magazines and newspapers, and other sources with the class.
   - The teacher provides interest centers in the classroom. For example, to motivate good reading for reluctant middle school youngsters, the teacher could organize a sports corner.
   - To accompany the sports corner the teacher may involve these students by providing activity cards, suggesting that they categorize the players by teams or batting average, or contribute to a scrapbook, or keep up statistics, charts, etc. about certain players.
2. Curious, enthusiastic students usually have good self-concepts.
   - To develop a good self-concept in less curious and less enthusiastic students, and motivate them to read, for example, older students can write books for primary children and read them to the younger children. They will feel more enthusiastic when they see the enjoyment younger students derive from their picture books and easy readers.
   - Students who are less than enthusiastic about studying math, for example, will become better motivated when

they understand how math works in their daily life. Have them list at least five uses they have for math; make a list of jobs (including schooling and salary) and ask students to choose the jobs on the list they would like to have, and then have them investigate further into the math they would need to know to do the job.
3. Multicultural students may require particular attention to maintain positive motivation.
   - As a classroom teacher, find out about your students' learning histories at the beginning of the year. They may write essays or prepare journals with pictures. Then you can select materials that are compatible with their culture. Sometimes multicultural students are faced with culturally incompatible material and respond only to factual questions, failing to use higher-level skills such as predicting and inferring.
   - Be aware that multicultural children may not complete home assignments for various reasons. You may want to initiate a parent survey to find out if lighting, quiet, and resources are available in their homes. If not, you may decide to seek help from the community to develop a study center or make the school library available for them after school hours.
   - Organize your students of different ethnic and racial groups into cooperative teams where they work together to solve math problems, improve reading comprehension etc.

---

handled, it can enhance motivation, encourage students of all races to work together, and introduce into the classroom an element of tolerance that might otherwise be lacking.

But what does all of this motivational work mean for teaching and learning?

Educational Implications of Motivation

In a perceptive analysis of motivation and teaching, Wlodkowski (1986) noted that in any learning event there are three critical periods during which varying motivational strategies exercise a decisive influence: (a) the beginning, when students commence the learning process; (b) during the learning, when students are involved with the content of the lesson; (c) the ending, when students are completing the process.

The Beginning of Learning

There are two key motivational processes involved at this stage: attitudes and needs.

Attitude. What are students' feelings about themselves, school, teachers, and the subject? The main thrust of the discussion regarding student attitudes relates to you as a communicator. Given the three attitudes—*cognitive, affective, behavioral*—you must identify what exactly is causing a student's negative attitude. Is a student uncomfortable with a subject, either because of its novelty or as a result of unsuccessful previous experiences with it? Has a student missed the fundamentals that are necessary for work in your class? Once you have located the problem, then you can precisely direct your efforts toward its solution.

For example, if some students believe that they simply lack the ability to succeed in a subject, your task will be to assess their level of competence and then construct a base from which they can experience success. If their

Focus on Students

Do Your Students Feel They Belong?

Here are several strategies that will help to increase your students' feelings of belonging.

- Use materials and specific examples that relate directly to the love and belongingness of your students. For example, stories that have a positive theme concerning belongingness are an excellent source; the humorous stories of Beverly Cleary for younger children, or books such as *Room For One More* for adolescents are especially pertinent.
- Create a learning atmosphere that clearly informs students that they are wanted. Such simple techniques as quickly learning the names of your students and taking the time to talk individually with them are extremely effective. Such efforts reflect a social constructivist interpretation of motivation: motivation is inseparable from the instructional process and the classroom atmosphere (Sivan, 1986).
- Be sure that all students are involved in classroom functions; rotate leadership roles, duties, and privileges as frequently as possible.

Esteem needs are two-fold, those arising from a need for self-esteem and esteem from others. With your concern for matching material with a student's ability and encouraging students to take responsibility for their actions, you already have provided a sound basis for achievement and esteem. Now give students an opportunity to display their achievements before their classmates, thus publicly enhancing their reputation.

If you can help students to satisfy their needs in a way that offers both intrinsic and extrinsic satisfaction, you have furnished practical aid in their search for self-actualization.

difficulty seems to be mainly affective—they simply don't like the material—then one technique would be to assign them to a group that enjoys the subject.

The issue of attitudes illustrates clearly the interrelationship of motivational elements. A student may have a rather negative attitude toward your subject but need it for admission to a particular program. If you can seize on this need with stimulating material and positive reinforcement, this student may well complete the work, both liking it and feeling competent with it.

Needs. Are there certain needs working on students during this time of their lives and at this particular moment? If you recall Maslow's hierarchy of needs discussed earlier, you will recall that there are five basic

categories. The first four of these—physiological, safety, love and belongingness, and esteem needs—are essentially *deficiency* needs, while the fifth, self-actualization, is a *growth* need. This combination of needs will appear, in some form, in all of your students.

Remember that students will act to eliminate deficiency needs, and whichever need is most predominant at any moment will be a student's primary concern. You may have prepared an extremely stimulating lesson, but it is lost on the student who skipped breakfast and is ravenous by eleven o'clock. Be guided by the indisputable fact that for most of us, physiological needs demand our immediate consideration.

Safety needs require a different type of response. Most students are secure in their rights since their fundamental safety needs have been met through their homes, which is not to say that they are incapable of feeling anxiety. High anxiety does not correlate with high achievement; consequently, anything that you can do to relieve this condition will help both the student and achievement.

Since there are fears that accompany each developmental stage, classroom work can help to combat them. For example, young children are afraid of the dark, the unknown, animals, and loud noises; from ages nine to eighteen fears relate to school failure and social relations. Probably the best advice to be offered with regard to the safety needs is: Make your classroom as physically and psychologically safe as possible.

During the Learning

The key motivational processes involved during the middle stage of learning are stimulation and affect.

Stimulation. To what are the students attending during the learning experience? Are there elements in the material or in the environment that attract—or distract—their attention?

One of most effective means of insuring that students find a lesson stimulating is to involve their need for achievement. Working on the assumption that personal motives and increased individual effort can be stimulated in the classroom, deCharms (1976) believes that motivation is tightly linked to students' identification of the origin of their actions.

Origins and pawns are terms used to distinguish the two motivational states that are basic to personal causation. Origins are those who feel that they control their own fate; pawns feel that they are at the mercy of everyone and everything. People are not always origins or pawns, but one of these feelings usually predominates. (It is a concept similar to locus of control, but deCharms believes that locus of control emphasizes reinforcement, while the origin-pawn concept stresses the feeling that students determine their own goals and the course of action needed to attain them.)

To enhance the motivation of teachers, the first step is to have them focus on their own motives. In his workshops deCharms asked teachers to write imaginative stories in response to six pictures. This is similar to the technique McClelland used in India and is intended to assess an individual's need for achievement.

The teachers were then asked to write an essay in response to the question "Who am I?" The teachers were encouraged to tell the group something about themselves—goals, values, hobbies, life-style. As the group members became more comfortable with each other, discussion became more open.

While this was going on, each teacher was asked to step outside where each was introduced to the ring toss game. A stake was set up at one end of the room with three-foot distances marked off from it. Each participant was given four rings to toss from any distance desired. The only stipulation was that all rings had to be thrown from the same distance. The objective of the game is to demonstrate the level of an individual's need achievement. Interestingly, those individuals who stood far from the stake and those who stood quite close had lower need achievement than those who selected an intermediate distance. The rationale is that the intermediate group realistically decided that this distance was a challenge for them, a decision that indicated a high need for achievement.

Another technique used was the Blindfold game. Here one teacher was blindfolded and a partner was chosen to be the guide. The guide was responsible for taking the blindfolded member to dinner and back to the meeting room. The purpose of this exercise is to demonstrate individual differences in giving and receiving help and to make the teachers aware of feelings of power and control.

Similar techniques were suggested to the teachers for use with their students. For example, the teachers were urged to have their students write stories with achievement themes but in a different manner than McClelland had used in India. The teachers did not deliberately introduce achievements for the students to use; rather they attempted to elicit the themes from the children. A class could be told that they are to think about a story that they will write on Friday. The discussion during the week will focus on a main character trying to do better. The stories could then be used in a weekly essay contest judged by the students.

The suggestions of deCharms are practical and easy to implement. You can test yourself on the ring toss game (objectively!) and train yourself to write stories with a high need achievement theme. You can also readily adapt to your own classroom his suggestions for working with students.

Affect. What are the emotional consequences of the lesson? How do students feel about it? It seems quite reasonable to assume that motivated students constantly attribute causes to their behavior. If you recall Weiner's work on attributions, there are four major categories for classifying the causes of our behavior: ability, effort, task difficulty, and luck. These attributions for behavior result from a complicated mixture of cognitive and emotional elements that we have previously experienced.

If affect is a constant companion of learning, actually an integral part of the process, then student attributions have practical implications for the classroom. Anytime that students assign a reason for behavior, that assignment carries with it strong emotional overtones.

For example, in one study, Weiner, Russell, and Lerman (1978) had subjects read a brief story about success and failure that also contained the reasons for the success and failure. Here is one of the stories.

> *Francis studied intensely for a test he took. It was very important for Francis to record a high score on this exam. Francis received a very high score on the test. Francis felt that he received this high score because he studied so intensely. How do you think Francis felt upon receiving this score?*

Subjects were asked to respond to the emotional reaction of the person in the story by selecting affective words from a list presented to them. There were ten different stories with ten different reasons for success. Some words appeared in almost all of the attributions for success: pleased and happy. But the reasons for the success influenced the words chosen. For example, if success were attributed to an unstable effort, words like ecstatic and uproarious were chosen.

Eleven other stories were written that attributed failure to luck, ability, and fatigue. When ability was mentioned, subjects chose words such as incompetent and inadequate; when the cause was given as luck, the response was stunned and overwhelmed. Thus it seemed possible to discriminate between the attributions by the affective word chosen.

Weiner's studies have direct implications for teachers: Different emotions are associated with different attributions for success and failure. If students succeed at a task because they think that they were lucky, there will be no feeling of pride at the outcome. Similarly, if failure is attributed to lack of effort and not lack of ability, there may be feelings of shame but no loss of confidence.

Your efforts to identify what students believe caused their behavior can help you to formulate means to combat negative attributions and emotions. Not that you should deceive students; you must aid them in realistically assessing their strengths and weaknesses. But by matching task with ability you can help them to achieve honest successes that they can attribute to ability and effort. It is particularly important since the attributions that they make about their successes and failures influence their expectancies about future successes and failures. The emotions that develop around these expectancies also shape attitudes that students bring into the classroom with them in the future.

When Learning Ends

The key motivational processes involved during the last stage of learning are competence and reinforcement.

Competence. Have students achieved a sense of mastery as a result of this lesson? Does it translate into a sense of confidence, a willingness to undertake something that might previously have intimidated them?

If by competence we mean a feeling of controlling our environment, then competence, as a motive, is a powerful influence in our lives. Bandura's ideas that we have previously discussed have particular relevance for the classroom. Especially pertinent are his views concerning modeling and self-efficacy. Bandura believes that observational learning occurs through four processes:

1. Attention
2. Retention
3. Motor reproduction processes
4. Motivational processes.

Of the four component processes Bandura identifies, two are main explanations for securing attention: *the characteristics of the model*—the teacher—and *the characteristics of the observer*—the students. Although a model who is distinctive captures attention, a word of caution is necessary. Distinctive should not be too unusual; if a teacher's behavior is radically dissimilar, there will be little for students to imitate. Yelling, screaming, and standing on table tops are not ideal types of behavior to be learned.

The selection of model characteristics is a difficult task and cannot be based on preconceived judgments. Experiment with those characteristics that you feel are valuable and with which you are comfortable.

1. *Retention* is aided by describing the behavior to be modeled in terms that your students can readily grasp and by having students actually practice the behavior where feasible (motor reproduction). *Watch*

how I'm adjusting the microscope. Don't move it too quickly. OK, now you try it. Be sure that your students have the capability of acquiring the behavior that you are modeling, and when the desired behavior appears, arrange for immediate reinforcement.

If students see themselves as competent, it not only reduces fear and anxiety for a task but also increases the effort expended; thus **self-efficacy** becomes a powerful motivating force (Bandura, 1977). Although modeling enhances self-efficacy, students are not impressed with the facile performance that denotes a lack of commitment. It is the honest performance suggesting determined effort that students find most compelling. As Bandura notes, modeling is productive because it provides students with specific examples of mastery during the course of their work.

2. *Reinforcement.* Since the theoretical aspects of reinforcement were thoroughly discussed in chapter 6, our focus here will be on specific classroom use. Here are three basic rules to follow.
   a. Reinforce immediately. Provide reinforcement whenever possible while students are still learning.
   b. Reinforce with small amounts rather than large amounts. Whatever you decide to use as a reinforcer—praise, stars, points—use it frequently but in sufficiently small amounts to avoid having it become meaningless for students.
   c. Reinforce small improvements in learning and motivation. A common mistake of teachers is to demand too much before they reinforce, thus discouraging students and interrupting the flow of learning.

Whatever the secondary motives may be, the basic motivation for teaching seems to be a combination of a liking for young people and a fondness for working with meaningful materials. Keep in mind that motivation is a concern throughout the learning process, from beginning to end.

Conclusion

In this chapter we addressed a fascinating aspect of student behavior—in fact, of human behavior—that powerfully affects classroom learning: motivation. You discovered that the various motivational theories all shed light on certain features of motivation, though none seemed to be a thoroughly satisfying explanation in itself. Presently, motivation in the classroom is being influenced by humanistic (Maslow), cognitive (Weiner), cognitive-behavioral

TEACHER ◄──► STUDENT
INTERACTIONS

Motivation and Learning

1. Identifying the natural incentives of the age group you're teaching helps to initiate and sustain motivation.
   - Try establishing interest centers like a "Kids Did It" Corner for elementary and middle school age students. Students can bring in projects they made or display awards or accomplishments. If a student has won a medal at the state fair, for example, she could bring it in and write about her experiences. Such descriptions could be in a special folder for others to read.
   - Using an individual student's interest in a special hobby, ask that child to write a report or make an oral presentation demonstrating the hobby. Encourage other students to seek more information about that hobby (or others) by going to the library and reading books about it.
   - Divide your class into small heterogeneous groups to research a topic of their choice: animals, sports, costumes, underwater adventure, etc. They then choose the method by which they will present their findings to the class: by using the overhead projector, making a filmstrip, a video, a movie, a model, etc.

2. In the initial phase of learning, be sure you identify the attitudes and needs of your students.
   - Examine your students carefully to make sure their negative attitudes and needs are not causing them to fail. They may have phobic reactions to particular subjects (such as math, spelling, computers). Discuss with them how these fears could interfere with their success. If they persist, suggest counseling, remedial work, or even academic therapy.
   - Learn as much as possible about your students' attitudes and needs. You may want to use a temporary divider in your classroom to create a testing area in a classroom corner. Present each task to the student with careful explanations. Then ask the child to do the task independently. Watch her/his responses to various aspects of training and analyze what the child needs to learn.

3. Knowing your students well enables you to determine the appropriate level of stimulation to use in your teaching.
   - In the lower elementary grades, encourage your class to talk about their families; discuss family concepts with them, and point out ways that you as a teacher and the children in your class care for one another at school in some of the ways family members care at home. In ways such as this, the classroom teacher becomes a friend of the very young student.
   - In lower grades, teachers could take a photograph of each child and mount it on a sheet of construction paper. Have each child write (or dictate several sentences) telling you about his/her likes or dislikes and other information. Keep this information in a folder and refer to it from time to time as a means of getting acquainted with your students and offering them the stimulation they need to become motivated students.
   - In middle school, especially, try to look for clues that will help you get to know students who are erratic and difficult to stimulate. Do they like to work alone or in small groups? Do they have rigid thought patterns and need structure to succeed, or do they thrive on change and novelty? Examine your teaching style. Are you highly structured or relaxed? Do you rely heavily on verbal instruction, or do you use lots of visuals? You may find clues that will help you to coordinate your teaching style with the learning style of these students.

(Bandura), and behavioral (Skinner) theories. Each of these theories has led to pragmatic classroom practices that influence learning and behavior. Examples of these practices were highlighted with beginning, middle, and end stages.

We then turned to certain topics that affect motivation and examined them in light of their ultimate impact on learning. This was particularly true of **natural incentive,** those spontaneously occurring motivational elements that appear at certain times in our lives. If identified and capitalized on, they can be a fruitful source of classroom motivation.

Finally, we examined the application of various motivational strategies that seem most effective. These included modeling, attributional knowledge, and reinforcement. A particularly appropriate means of furthering both motivation and learning is the method of cooperative learning. By distinguishing learning as a three-stage process, you can utilize the different teaching techniques, thus helping to arouse, sustain, and direct your students' motivation.

Chapter Highlights

Motivation: Meaning and Myths

- Motivation arouses, sustains, and integrates behavior.
- Several myths have grown up around motivation that can obscure its actual meaning and cause classroom difficulty.
- Recognizing the distinction between intrinsic and extrinsic motivation can help you to devise techniques that improve learning in your classes.

What Causes Motivation?

- Of the various attempts to explain motivation, Maslow's need hierarchy has had a lasting impact as a result of the appeal of its theoretical and practical implications.
- McClelland's explanation of need achievement has direct classroom bearing, especially its identification of the importance of your students' expectations and values.
- Students search for the causes of their behaviors just as teachers do. To explain this phenomenon, Weiner has been a leader in the development of attribution theory. Knowing that students attribute their behaviors to ability, effort, task difficulty, and luck can help you to improve their self-concepts, by realistically examining their abilities in light of the task, thus furthering learning.
- Skinner has long believed that the proper use of schedules of reinforcement (see chapter 4) can improve motivation and, in general, enhance classroom performance.
- According to Bandura, your performance in the classroom can be a powerful model for your students to imitate. Once you recognize desirable behavior in your students, act swiftly to reinforce that behavior.

What Affects Students' Motivation?

- Among the most potent influences on motivation are anxiety, attitude, curiosity, and locus of control.
- Anxiety, either situational or trait, affects classroom performance either positively or negatively. Increasing anxiety lessens performance as task complexity increases.
- A positive attitude toward school and learning increases achievement. Be particularly concerned not only with your students' attitudes toward you and the subjects you are teaching but also with their attitudes about themselves.
- All of your students possess a certain degree of curiosity that, if capitalized upon, can lead to richer and more insightful learning. Structured but relaxed classroom conditions—in the sense of an acceptance of students' ideas—can encourage the creative use of curiosity.
- The locus of control concept can be useful in improving the achievement of your students, especially the "externals." By carefully providing reinforcement for selected behaviors, you not only improve their learning but also help them develop a more positive self-concept.
- Repeated criticism and failure can produce learned helplessness, a form of behavior that causes students to give up, just refusing to try. If you find such students, your first task will be to get them to try, to make an effort so that you can begin to reinforce them.

Educational Implications of Motivation

- Considering various stages of learning—beginning, during, ending—leads to the direct application of motivational theory and research in the classroom, both for you and your students.
- Enjoying young people and finding satisfaction in working with meaningful material may well be the basic motives for teaching.

Key Terms

Anxiety
Attitude
Attribution theory
Cooperative learning
Discovery learning
Emotional arousal
Expectancy-value
Externals
Extrinsic motivation
Internals
Intrinsic motivation
Learned helplessness
Locus of control
Natural incentives
Need achievement theory
Normal anxiety
Operant or instrumental conditioning
Performance accomplishments
Personal investment
Positive reinforcement
Self-actualization
Self-efficacy
Situational anxiety
State anxiety
Test anxiety
Trait anxiety
Verbal persuasion
Vicarious experience

Suggested Redings

deCharms, R. (1976). *Enhancing motivation: Change in the classroom.* New York: Irvington. In this book, deCharms presents a well-written and soundly reasoned analysis of "origins" and "pawns," and excellent suggestions for classroom activities.

First, J. (1988, November). Immigrant students in U. S. public schools: challenges with solutions. *Phi Delta Kappan, 70,* 205–210. In these few pages you get an understanding of the problems multicultural students can face and what you can do to help them.

Houston, J. (1985). *Motivation.* New York: Macmillan. If you still feel a little shaky about your motivational knowledge, this is probably the best single reference to use. Carefully crafted with excellent examples, it will be most helpful.

Veroff, J. and Veroff, J. *Social incentives.* New York: Academic. This important work presents the Veroffs' ideas on natural motivators, which have practical classroom application. If your students want to do something themselves, it presents you with a fine opportunity to capitalize on intrinsic motivation.

SECTION

4

The Design and
Management of Classroom
Instruction

Instructional Objectives and Essential Learning Outcomes

I n his thoughtful collection of essays, *Late Night Thoughts On Listening to Mahler's Ninth Symphony*, Lewis Thomas ponders the role of the social sciences. Noting that the social sciences still have a long way to go, Thomas nevertheless believes that they may be up to the most important business of all, *if they only ask the right questions.*

Thomas' conclusion is particularly true for educators if we substitute "objectives" for "the right questions." Goals and objectives have always concerned those who care about our schools. Thomas Jefferson, for example, believed that the most important goal of the schools was to guard our freedom and happiness, which could be accomplished only by knowledgeable citizens. The more pragmatic Benjamin Franklin stated that it would be good if students could be taught "everything that is useful and everything that is ornamental. But art is long and their time is short." He then went on to describe the need for students to master reading, writing, arithmetic, and especially history.

As we come to the end of the twentieth century, concerns have increased about our urban schools. A recent task force has identified the following six goals that reflect existing needs:

- increase the level of expectations for all students
- make sure that students are ready to begin school
- decrease the dropout rate
- insure better preparation for higher education and successful employment
- recruit a qualified teaching force
- rid the schools of drugs and alcohol

When we turn to the classroom, how will you define your teaching as successful? The only answer to this question can be that your teaching is successful if your students learn. The next question would be: What is it my students are expected to learn? Answer: Students are supposed to attain the purposes of instruction, which *both* teacher and students must clearly understand.

When students don't know what is called for, their performance suffers. A teacher's effectiveness in the classroom also falters since the focus of instruction is dissipated. What precisely do you want your students to accomplish in this lesson, this unit, this course? These concerns take us into the world of **objectives**.

Having analyzed the major features and theories of development and having examined the intricacies of the learning process, we come now to the teaching act itself—what you do in the classroom. Before commencing our work, we should step back and ask ourselves, "Why am I doing this? What do I hope to attain? What should students take from their endeavors?" In other words, our concern in this chapter will be with the objectives of instruction.

First, we must make the distinction between the goals of education, those broad, general aims of schooling that are desirable for all of our citizens and those more narrowly defined objectives of instruction that are particularly suited for individuals and classes.

Second, we'll focus on specific objectives, illustrating the nature of the "good" objective and suggesting several sources that you would find helpful in stating objectives that are pertinent for your purposes.

Third, our concern will shift to the role of educational psychology in helping you formulate valuable objectives. One way of accomplishing this task is to present problems identified by educational psychologists in various subjects. For example, the coding process in reading, the nature of error in mathematics, and the role of knowledge structures in science all can help you to focus your instructional objectives.

Fourth, what are your objectives with regard to computer usage, both for yourself and your students?

When you have finished reading this chapter, you should be able to:

- recall the benefits of formulating pertinent objectives,
- recognize the characteristics of good objectives,
- recognize suitable methods for deriving relevant and important objectives,
- acquire information about the major published sources of objectives,
- acquire information about the challenges to learning that are inherent in the subject you're teaching,
- recall those proposals stressing the purposes of general education, and
- describe the positive use of computers in the classroom.

Deciding on Educational Objectives

Throughout this chapter we'll concentrate on the role of objectives in instruction—why we should take the time to think about them, write them, and attempt to achieve them. Before we do, however, we should concentrate on some practical benefits that come to us all—teachers and students—from our concern with objectives. The point in all of this relates to *you and your students.* It's deceptively easy to become enmeshed in *this* day's work, *this* lesson, and *this* test. There's nothing wrong in such planning; in fact you won't do a good job on any particular day if you don't devote thought to your work for that day.

For example, research has shown that most teachers aren't initially concerned with specific objectives to be attained by their students at the end of a unit. Experienced teachers seem to engage in about eight types of planning: weekly, daily, long range, short range, term, and yearly, lesson planning, unit planning. Note that six of these relate to time (Clark & Peterson, 1986). Teachers usually plan activities to fill available instructional time. They also use teachers' editions of text books and curriculum guides, but it is only later that they measure their work against objectives (D. Brown, 1988).

Although research is scanty about the planning of secondary school teachers, elementary teachers' planning seems to focus on daily plans within the context of weekly, unit, term, and yearly plans. The organizational context (materials, tests, curriculum guides) greatly influences teachers.

Studying the planning of twelve middle school teachers (grades 7 and 8) by interviews and by analyzing their plans, D. Brown (1988) found that that planning involved "nested" decision making (general to specific, yearly to daily). One of the most interesting findings was the teachers' tendencies to rely on experience—their own notes, handouts, and work sheets, audiovisuals, and tests. In other words, the teachers turned to what they had successfully used in the past, an interesting finding that requires more research in an attempt to discover what guides teachers in their initial planning.

The basis of their planning included the following:

- what topics to cover tomorrow
- what materials to prepare for tomorrow

"I'm usually three days ahead of a regular class, one day ahead of the fast learners and two days behind a classful of them."

Learning suffers when objectives are missing or poorly stated.

© 1992 by Sidney Harris.

- how to conduct lessons
- what topics to review from yesterday
- how to sequence activities
- what kinds of discussions to have with students
- what to use for written activities
- what homework to assign
- when to schedule tests
- how to test

As a result of this study, D. Brown (1988) concluded that teachers act as curriculum implementors and not curriculum planners. Also, if teachers depend heavily on their unit notebooks, then we must determine the reasons that teachers include what they do in these planning books. Finally, it seems clear that teachers' initial planning is limited and gradually broadens to include long-term objectives.

Our task, then, is to encourage teachers to encompass their daily concerns within the scope of specific objectives. By focusing on what you and your students are doing now in relation to what they'll be doing in the future, together with what they are learning and why they're learning this material, you take your work to another level. You will have linked practical and theoretical considerations in a way that makes learning more meaningful and useful. A path has been charted that should help your students to learn more meaningfully now and aid them in using and applying such learning to their future work. How does today's lesson on *Hamlet* relate to the goals of the unit? Is there any potential transfer to history or current events?

To do so, however, requires clear and accurate statements of just what you intend to do. In their excellent analysis of objectives, Bloom, Madaus, and Hastings (1981) noted that statements of educational objectives describe, in a relatively specific manner, what a student should be able to produce or do, or what characteristics students should possess after the learning.

Focus on Schools

High Achieving African-American Schools

Sizemore (1990) graphically traced, in her description of a primarily African-American school in the Pittsburgh, Pennsylvania system, what goes into the making of a high-achieving school. In 1979 there were five high-achieving out of twenty-one African-American (70 percent or more African-American students) elementary schools in Pittsburgh. High achievement was determined by reading and math scores. This forced the board of education to search for an explanation to explain these different outcomes.

When Sizemore first compared the differences between low- and high-achieving schools, she found that in the high-achieving schools, parents were treated as equal members in a partnership and were welcomed in the school; principals were more authoritarian; they were more independent of the central office (which enabled them to respond more quickly to community needs); they assumed responsibility for student discipline, and that there was a consensus among teachers, parents; and principals that high achievement should be the priority.

In the low-achieving school, there was no such consensus. The principal felt restrained by the central office, she did not stand with teachers in discipline problems, and she tended to retain unsatisfactory teachers rather than undertake the sometimes difficult task of "persuading" them to leave. Student achievement was lower, absenteeism higher, morale lower, and the principal spent less time interacting with students than the principals of the high-achieving schools.

When Sizemore returned five years later, a new, systemwide school improvement had been put into practice, a new principal was in place, and excellence had become the major objective. The new principal, who was mildly authoritarian, had convinced staff and community that high achievement was the top priority. This had not been done without a struggle: weak teachers were persuaded to leave; revolts against the principal failed because of the support of the majority of the staff and community; questionable programs were eliminated, thus providing more time-on-task for students; and the principal devoted considerable time to student interactions, helped teachers with their discipline problems, and did not hesitate to refer for suspension those students who had committed serious breaches of discipline. Once this policy of student responsibility for their actions was recognized, the number of serious problems decreased dramatically.

As a result of these changes, Sizemore (1990) identified the following features that characterized those schools with high-achieving African-American students:

- a moderately authoritarian principal
- a principal who does not fear to be different in order to help students achieve to the best of their ability
- agreement between school and community concerning high achievement as the top priority objective
- an educational environment contributing to high expectations for student achievement
- clearly stated rules and regulations intended to help students realize their goals
- the willingness of teachers and principals to fight for those policies and programs that lead to high achievement

---

In our analysis, we'll move from discussing the general lofty goals that society assigns to our schools to specific objectives in specific subjects.

The Paideia Proposal

In a more recent examination of educational goals Mortimer Adler (1982) stated that though the quantity of education is similar for all (the availability of twelve years of basic public schooling), the quality of these twelve years is far from similar. Yet if we truly believe in school equality, the need for equal quality schooling for all becomes a major objective.

In the *Paideia Proposal,* Adler advocated a one-track system of public schooling that has three main objectives:

1. self-improvement
2. enlightened citizenship
3. a productive career

To achieve these goals, public schooling must be general and liberal, not specialized and vocational. These are not contradictory statements since preparation for an occupation is inextricably intertwined with understanding the demands of a technological society.

The course of study to be followed for twelve years should be required for all, with only one exception: the choice of a second language. Electives are to be eliminated during these years since they are intended to prepare for specialization.

Some subjects (language, mathematics, natural science) are indispensable to basic schooling; lacking mastery of any one of these produces a flawed education. Here are those skills that are fundamental to learning—*using* language (spelling, writing), competence with computers and other instruments. Note that language and mathematics are in both categories but, first, knowledge is required; then come the "how to do" skills. Finally, Adler believes that we must engage students in the active use of their minds in searching, exploring, and solving problems related to their reading and activities.

Integration of these three ideas occurs as students acquire basic knowledge, use that knowledge in education, but then go on to apply knowledge for varied purposes. Although the model is not rigid and is subject to adaptation, the three categories must be present and specialized activities eliminated (Adler, 1982).

What Place Schooling?

In 1984, John Goodlad's widely discussed text, *A Place Called School,* was published, and in it he asked a simple but unsettling question: "Can we have effective schools?" The implication, of course, is that current popular opinion is skeptical, if not downright hostile, toward public education. But as Goodlad noted, such negative reactions appear to be directed at "education" in general. Most of the parents surveyed stated that although schools across the country are doing a poor job, *my* child's school is doing just fine. This is an interesting distinction and one that leads to an analysis of our expectations, our goals, for our public schools.

Tracing educational literature for more than three hundred years, Goodlad and his colleagues concluded that four broad areas of school goals have emerged:

1. academic, which includes all intellectual skills and domains of knowledge;
2. vocational, which is intended to enhance self-responsibility;
3. social and civic, which are intended to prepare for socialization into a complex society; and
4. personal, which emphasizes the development of individual responsibility, talent, and free expression.

Given the variety of tasks that we expect our schools to accomplish (see chapter 1), articulation of clear and nationally accepted goals is no easy assignment, even with widespread recognition of broad, desirable educational concerns—for example, the school should do a good job in academic matters. Goodlad (1984) believes that two prerequisites must be met if today's schools are to succeed: a) society's charge to the schools must be understood by those the school serves as well as professional educators; and b) a new coalition, similar to the forces that gave rise to our present system, must emerge.

Lack of a clear mandate has resulted in a lack of clear goals. In an effort to suggest national guidelines, Goodlad has proposed a set of goals derived from a review of aims that have appeared throughout the history of American schooling and from analyzing state guides to education. Several highlights of his exhaustive list follow. These appear in Table 11.1.

Table 11.1

Goals for Schooling in the United States

A. Academic goals

1. Mastery of basic skills and fundamental processes.
   1.1 Learn to read, write, and handle basic mathematical operations.
   1.2 Learn to acquire ideas through reading and listening.
2. Intellectual development
   2.1 Develop the ability to think rationally, including problem solving skills, application of principles of logic, and skill in using different modes of inquiry.
   2.2 Develop the ability to use and evaluate knowledge.

B. Vocational goals

3. Career education-vocational education
   3.1 Learn how to select an appropriate occupation.
   3.2 Learn to use knowledge of career options for decision-making.

C. Social, civic, and cultural goals

4. Interpersonal understandings
   4.1 Develop knowledge of different value systems and their effect on individuals and society.
   4.2 Develop effective communication skills.
5. Citizenship participation
   5.2 Develop knowledge of the basic workings of government.
   5.7 Develop those economic and consumer skills necessary to enhance one's quality of life.

D. Personal goals

8. Emotional and physical well-being
   8.4 Learn to use leisure time effectively.
   8.6 Develop the ability to engage in constructive self-criticism.
9. Creativity and aesthetic expression
   9.1 Develop the ability to solve problems in original ways.
   9.5 Develop the ability to evaluate various forms of aesthetic expression.

These general goals suggested by Goodlad, though more detailed and extensive than those posed by Adler, nevertheless mirror the same concerns. Such general targets point the way for schools without dictating the specific needs of individual communities and students. Our next task, then, is to discover the means by which you can implement them in your classroom. Before we do, however, we must define the various terms in any discussion of "objectives" (see Table 11.2).

As you complete this initial section of the chapter, think back on your own schooling for a moment. Perhaps both you and your classmates, in answering the following questions, can share your educational experiences in class.

1. Do you think that you were adequately prepared (in both your elementary and secondary education) for your present work?
2. Do you have an understanding of the basic disciplines—math, science, language—or do you feel inadequate when class discussions shift to topics in which your grasp of fundamentals should be the basis for your contribution?
3. Did your schooling meet the three objectives Adler mentions in the *Paideia Proposal* (self-improvement, enlightened citizenship, productive career)?

Regardless of how you answered these questions, your replies point to the reality of identifying and attempting to attain clearly defined general objectives. Now let's turn our attention to **instructional objectives.**

The Role of Objectives in Instruction

It is the end of August, and you know that on the Wednesday after Labor Day you will be facing your class(es) for the first time. Whether you are teaching subtraction in an elementary school or teaching Biology 1 in a secondary school, you are faced with the same question: What exactly do I want these students to learn?

You quickly realize, however, that what you decide is not enough. What kinds of behaviors will you accept in your students as evidence that they have learned? Having determined what you want to accomplish and what your students should know, you can now turn your attention to the techniques and materials you will use (Lovell-Troy, 1989). Finally, since you cannot guess that your students have learned, you must devise some means of evaluating their performance.

In short, you must have clearly defined *instructional objectives* that form an integrated whole to guide your teaching: *plan, teach, test.*

Why Bother with Objectives?

To write good objectives is a time-consuming, thoughtful task. Why should you bother? For a very good reason: many students simply don't know what teachers expect.

Table 11.2

Definition of Terms

Term	Meaning
Goal	Those broad, general aims (such as Goodlad's list) that identify educational priorities for a society
Objectives	Those instructional outcomes that encompass the range of student learning (uses the computer as a word processor)
Learning outcomes	An instructional outcome stated as specific student behavior (can insert and delete material by using the correct computer commands)

By writing clearly stated objectives, teachers keep their instruction focused, and students quickly learn what is expected of them. For example, Muth and others (1988) found that when instructional objectives were closely tied to content, their students recalled more information. When you think about what you want to do and force yourself to articulate those ideas, you become a better teacher. It is as simple as that. But you are not the only beneficiary. Your students will learn more and enjoy it more, and the resulting feedback will cause you more pleasure in your teaching.

Description, Goals, or Objectives

Although we have moved from a consideration of educational goals such as Goodlad's "mastery of basic skills and fundamental processes" to a more restricted, attainable level of instructional objectives, we can make further distinctions.

Educational psychology is a course designed to familiarize students with the basic processes of development, learning, and instruction.

Stop for a moment and think about this statement. Is it an educational goal? Why? Why not? Is it an instructional objective? Why? Obviously it is neither. It is a course description that could appear in any university catalog in the country.

Students should develop respect for different ethnic groups, people of different colors, and individuals of different religious beliefs.

Focus on Teachers

Teachers, Students, and Objectives

In his little classic, *Preparing Instructional Objectives*, Robert Mager (1975) noted that without clearly defined goals, evaluating a lesson, course, or program efficiently is impossible. How can you evaluate your teaching and your students' performance unless you measure outcome against stated objectives?

Bloom, Madaus, and Hastings (1981) identified a variety of benefits derived from formulating and selecting pertinent objectives.

- Writing clear, specific behavioral statements of objectives requires you to think about the changes you want to accomplish.
- The process helps you discover any non-essentials that might obscure your main objectives.
- Clearly stated objectives help you to group students more efficiently.
- Stating objectives helps you in selecting proper methods and materials.
- Once you recognize exactly what you want to achieve, your evaluative techniques become more precise and meaningful.
- Stated objectives can facilitate communication among teachers since, in a sense, you are talking "the same language." Such commonality facilitates the exchange of ideas among teachers as they attempt to improve courses or programs.
- When both you and your students clearly understand what is to be attained, communication improves and learning increases.
- Precisely stated objectives also improve communication between teachers and parents. When parents know just what is expected of their children, they better understand a child's strength and weakness, and knowing what is expected helps them to join with teachers in combatting weaknesses.

Focusing on objectives in this manner improves the quality of the entire learning environment. Students clearly recognize what is expected of them, and they understand the basis of your marks and grades. You can see, then, how precisely defined objectives help to establish and maintain positive teacher-student relationships.

How would you categorize this statement—description, goal, or objective? You probably realized immediately that here is one of those broad educational goals we previously discussed.

> As you read this text in educational psychology, you should use those learning strategies discussed in chapter 7.

How do you classify this statement? Is it a general educational goal? No. Is it a course description? No. What we see here is a statement regarding the processes you should be using; it says nothing about product.

> When you complete this text, you should be familiar with those topics that comprise educational psychology.

Is this an objective? Yes. What kind of objective? Here is an example of what Gronlund (1985) calls a "general instructional objective," which is stated as a broad learning outcome.

> When you complete this text, you should be able to list and explain Skinner's two dimensions of punishment.

At this point we have become much more specific about an expected learning outcome and indicated exactly what behaviors are anticipated. You can see how precisely stated objectives will define and improve evaluation.

Goals and Multicultural Students

Before we complete this section on goals and objectives, we should review the recommendations recently made by the National Coalition of Advocates for Students, since these are a good example of goal statements. As they note (New Voices, 1988), most young immigrants coming to the United States bring with them a passion for freedom, education, and for gaining economic and personal security. Unless our schools are ready to capitalize on these motivations, most students will be unable to attain their goals. To help these students, the NCAS suggests the following goals:

- Be sure that everyone (parents, other students, and school personnel) understand that immigrant children have a legal right to a free, public education.
- Be sure that appropriate assessment and placement are available for immigrant students.
- Be sure that classmates respect the student's native language and culture.
- Be sure that English-speaking programs are in place to ensure that immigrant students can become competent in the use of English.
- Be sure that your classroom is free of harassment and conflict.
- Promote the success of immigrant students by offering as much support as possible.
- Work hard to develop the necessary skills to teach successfully foreign-born students and help to prevent any potential conflicts in the classroom.
- Be sure that there are sufficient resources for immigrant students.

- Encourage the parents of immigrant children to participate fully in the education of their children.

Noting that youthful immigrants tend to be a group without a constituency, the NCAS report urges that community agencies work together to support the welfare of potentially vulnerable students.

In this way, you can help these students to develop and maintain a strong sense of their personal and cultural self-esteem by aiding them to recognize those influences that have shaped their thinking and behavior (Tiedt & Tiedt, 1990). Emphasize that any differences in the way that they dress or act reflect their traditions and heritage, which can enrich—or has enriched—American culture.

Outcomes as Objectives

The objectives you have just read represent different kinds of outcomes. For our purposes, **general and specific instructional objectives** are most pertinent since they can structure your teaching methods and evaluative techniques. Such objectives also help to guide your students' study habits. As you have seen, these two types of objectives (general and specific) vary in their specificity. The classic work of Tyler (1950) offers good examples of the more general category, and Gagne's analysis of tasks (1988) offers excellent insights into the preparation of specific outcomes.

The Tyler Rationale

Since its publication, the Tyler Rationale has enjoyed great popularity, and deservedly so, because it has enabled educators to improve curriculum and instruction by stating objectives that are exact and uniquely suited to a particular system.

The Tyler Rationale is designed to provide the answers to four questions:

1. What are the educational objectives that the school should seek to attain?
2. What type of learning experiences are conducive to the achievement of these goals?
3. How may these learning experiences best be organized?
4. What is the most desirable method of determining if these objectives were attained?

The answers to these questions are relevant for any or all school systems. Tyler recommends that the four questions be answered by:

1. *Obtaining data about the learner.* This information should review characteristics of all learners, and then information about the youth of the city or town where the school is located. For example, after

fourth-, fifth-, and sixth-grade students of a particular community take a standardized reading test, school officials discover that these students are substantially below national norms. Such reliable information about students will influence any statement of objectives.
2. *Obtaining data about society in general,* and the community in particular. For example, if the national juvenile delinquency rate were significantly lower than the rate in our hypothetical community; it may indicate the need for expanded afterschool activities and job opportunities for adolescents.
3. *Obtaining data on academic subjects from acknowledged specialists.* The use of subject-matter experts, particularly at the university level, to aid in curriculum evaluation has become common, a desirable tendency in an age when knowledge is accumulating at a rapid rate. Specialists who are aware of developments at the frontiers of their subject, as well as its core, can vastly enrich the typical curriculum.

The above process will result in many objectives, some of which will not be pertinent to the needs of the school system. All objectives are now screened by the philosophy of education and psychology of learning that determine the school's policy. This screening process is vital before a school adopts any objectives.

Assume that the data obtained show that more local youngsters are involved in automobile accidents involving drinking than the national average. There would appear to be a need for discussion of this topic in class. But this particular school is dedicated to more traditional and classical aims. Consequently, its philosophy of education would challenge this objective.

The objectives that survive the first obstacle now are passed through the school's psychology-of-learning screen. Records may show that the juvenile crime rate has increased alarmingly in crimes against person and property. Consequently, a statement concerning minimum standards of behavior seems to be needed. Again, the school system may be committed to a psychology of learning that rejects ethical questions in the classroom. It assumes automatic transfer from the great works of literature to today's problems. The psychology screen would then eliminate this objective.

These examples illustrate the operation of the Tyler Rationale, particularly in the formation of objectives. Once objectives are stated in exact, practical language, attention can be directed to the means of their attainment. How should the courses within the curriculum be developed and taught? What learning experiences are most suitable?

Table 11.3

Focus on Practice: Kindergarten ELOs

A common trend among school districts is to establish expected learner outcomes (ELOs) for each primary grade. Part of the basic competency movement in education, ELOs are used to communicate a school district's learning expectations to parents, teachers, and students. Well-written ELOs list curriculum-referenced cognitive and behavior objectives that can be empirically assessed.

Many school districts use their ELOs in making decisions about school entry and grade retentions. Ideally, preschool screening tests should be highly congruent with a school's kindergarten ELOs. Thus, when selecting preschool screening measures, you can assess their content validity by systematically comparing them to the ELOs developed by the schools the children will attend.

A representative set of kindergarten ELOs for reading, writing, and mathematics follows:

Kindergarten ELOs—Reading*

1. Identify common objects or pictures in the environment.
2. Identify these positions: above-below, behind-in front, top-bottom, and left-right.
3. Distinguish likenesses and differences.
4. Identify lowercase manuscript letters.
5. Identify uppercase manuscript letters.
6. Identify rhyming pictures.
7. Match upper- and lowercase manuscript letters.
8. Sequence pictures.
9. Select pictures that show story endings.
10. Recognize words that begin with the same sound.

Kindergarten ELOs—Writing

1. Identify these positions: above-below, behind-in front, top-bottom, and left-right.
2. Distinguish likeness and differences.
3. Identify lowercase manuscript letters.
4. Identify uppercase manuscript letters.
5. Match upper- and lowercase manuscript letters.
6. Sequence pictures.

Kindergarten ELOs—Mathematics

1. Identify elements of a set.
2. Identify the smaller or larger object.
3. Identify these simple closed figures: circle, triangle, and square.
4. Compare the number of elements in two sets and indicate which is greater.
5. Classify objects or pictures according to color and shape.
6. Count concrete objects.
7. Count to ten by ones.
8. Identify one-half of a concrete object.
9. Identify these coins: penny, nickel, dime, and quarter.
10. Identify sets with an equal number of elements.
11. Identify the cardinal number of a set of not more than ten elements.
12. Identify the primary colors.

Finally, when schools have formulated objectives, determined organization of the curriculum, and selected learning experiences, how can the school best determine if educational objectives actually were acquired? Here the vital role of measurement in the learning process is seen. If there is no accurate assessment of behavioral change, the value of the educational effort remains vague and uncertain.

The work of Tyler and others has stimulated many school districts to establish **expected learner outcomes,** or **ELOs,** for each primary grade. ELOs are used to communicate a school district's learning expectations to students, teachers, and parents. Many school districts use their ELOs to make decisions about school entry and grade retention. Table 11.3 illustrates a representative set of kindergarten ELOs for reading, writing, and mathematics.

Gagne and Task Analysis

A much more specific type of analysis is found in the work of Robert Gagne (1988). His work is provocative and stimulating, especially sections relating **task analysis** to efficient learning. Classifying tasks by elements that produce substantial learning could be critical for teachers at all levels. Consequently, many psychologists have concentrated upon "the task" as a more fertile source of learning principles.

For example, in a unit on American history, after students have studied about the American presidents, a teacher may say, "Today we're going to see how some former presidents led the country in times of peril. We'll use Washington, Lincoln, and Franklin Roosevelt."

Task analysis would require this teacher to decide first how these lessons relate to the unit's objectives. Next, the teacher would have to be sure that the students

An Example of Task Analysis

Usually, the task analysis approach requires that an algorithm of instruction be specified in constructing the task components. The work of Salvia and Hughes (1990) provides an example of this requirement when they illustrate the teaching of division to elementary school students. As noted in the picture below, there are three methods for teaching simple division. The first strategy is called the *goes into* method and involves the sequence 3 goes into 21 exactly 7 times. The second method sometimes used in special classes involves a subtraction algorithm and is sometimes called *cumulative subtraction:* subtract 3 from 21, 3 from 18, etc. count the tallies, and the answer is 7. The third algorithm for teaching division is the *button to button* method. The students are usually taught to use hand calculators to solve the problem sequence by learning the appropriate order of pushing buttons on the devices.

Different algorithms for teaching division.

have the skills to carry out the assignment. Do they have the necessary reading skills? Do they know how to do independent research? Have they been taught outlining skills? Can they write a research paper?

Next, the teacher would have to decide on materials and methods. Different stimuli will be used (pictures, stories, movies), both direct teaching and group activities. Finally, the teacher must decide what kinds of student behavior to accept as evidence of learning.

To make learning more responsive to environmental stimuli, *Gagne advocates analysis of the task into its component parts.* These task elements may react to a varying pattern of stimuli that demand differing teaching techniques. If teachers can establish that content is capable of numerous and different methods of presentation, and the effectiveness of each, the implications for teaching for individual differences are significant.

If there is some *hierarchical* order to the component task, students should understand the logical sequence and the necessity to integrate all components for achievement of the completed task. Teaching the separate elements requires constant reference to the whole task to furnish direction and meaning to the learning. In a geography class, for example, a student must know the fundamental facts about a country, but the teacher should relate these to an ultimate objective: determining the causes of a country's foreign policy and attempting to predict future action.

Task analysis requires even closer examination of educational objectives, the behavior needed to attain these objectives, and the terminology required to state clearly and unequivocally the relationship between student performance and school goals. Specifically, there must be a decision as to *definite, intelligible, attainable goals.*

Exactly what is it that we wish our students to achieve (for example, knowledge of the actions of presidents in troubled times)? What tasks must students undertake to gain these goals (for example, reading, writing, outlining, research)? What stimuli must we provide to insure the necessary knowledge and skill to complete these tasks (for example, books, films, group discussion)? Using present information about varied curricula,

Table 11.4

Identifying Learning Outcomes: A Contrast

	Tyler's Rationale	Gagne's Task Analysis
Data Needed	1. Information about learner 2. Information about society 3. Information about subject matter	1. Information about learning tasks 2. Information about component parts 3. Information about possible hierarchy
Means of Obtaining Data	1. Identify educational objectives 2. Identify pertinent learning experiences 3. Organize learning experiences 4. Identify accurate learning measures	1. Identify dimensions of task 2. Identify component parts 3. Identify steps needed to master each part 4. Identify necessary prerequisites for each step 5. Identify conditions of learning
Application of Data	1. Articulate school's (system's) philosophy of education 2. Organize learning experiences into curriculum 3. Assess degree of attainment	1. Design instructional sequence 2. Facilitate individualized instruction 3. Identify significant learning outcomes

techniques of grouping, assessment of capacity, and the like, students could progress by a graded series of discernible stages.

The process is as follows:

- Any human task may be analyzed into a set of component tasks that are distinct from each other in the experimental operations needed to produce them (reading is distinct from outlining).
- These task components are mediators of the final task performance (good readers will probably have a better final product).
- The basic steps in training design are (a) identify the component tasks of a final performance, (b) insure that each component task is mastered, and (c) arrange the total learning situation in a sequence to provide optimal transfer from one component to another.

Table 11.4 summarizes Gagne's and Tyler's views.

What Are Good Objectives?

Once you have determined the type of objectives needed, you must express them in such a way that everyone clearly understands them; they are meaningful in the sense that they are worth the time and effort to achieve; they are expressed in behavioral terms that can guide your teaching and enable you to assess whether students have or have not obtained these outcomes.

Gronlund (1985) offers the following excellent guidelines:

- Do your objectives include all important outcomes? You should be cautious that your teaching and testing do not focus on one type of objective, a trap that can lure us all. Typically we focus on cognitive outcomes (especially knowledge of facts), that are most familiar to us. Don't forget those affective outcomes that can be important to the total learning environment, as well as any essential psychomotor skills.
- Are your objectives consistent with the general goals of the school? As Gronlund noted, one of the difficulties in answering this question relates to the usual lack of clearly stated school goals. In most cases you are on your own and must determine if the community's and school's aims for their children are in harmony with yours.
- Are your objectives in harmony with sound principles of learning? Be sure that your desired learning outcomes match your students' developmental level, are attainable, and can help your students in other situations as well as in your class.

• Are the objectives realistic when you consider your students' abilities and the time and facilities available? This question reflects our earlier concern with the worthwhileness of the objectives you formulate. Realistic objectives apply to multicultural as well as typical students. Your knowledge and understanding of multicultural students will give you confidence in helping them fulfill their needs, which then become part of your objectives.

With these guidelines in mind, we can now turn our attention to those specific instructional objectives that will guide your teaching. These instructional objectives are an intent communicated by a statement describing a proposed change in the learner—a statement of what the learner is to be able to do upon completion of the learning experience (Kim & Kellough, 1991). Thus, an instructional objective requires a demonstrable behavioral change in the learner. Consequently, we can tell that learning has occurred only when we observe a change in behavior.

Note the essential ingredients of this description:

• student-centered
• learning outcomes
• observable behavior

In other words, your objective states what the student is expected to accomplish, the products of that learning (not the activities), and clearly defined student levels of performance.

Evaluating Objectives

Your reading thus far should help you to be aware of the characteristics of good objectives. How would you evaluate these objectives according to the criteria just discussed?

1. To appreciate the insights offered by educational psychology.
2. To present to you, the reader, several examples of clearly stated objectives.
3. To study the application section of the summary at the end of the chapter and refer to the appropriate parts of the chapter.
4. To write ten instructional objectives that reflect the content of educational psychology described in this book.

Let's look at each of these.

1. The first objective is so vague as to be meaningless. What do you mean by appreciate? What insights?

2. Here we have an objective for the teacher and not for students.
3. This objective tells students what to do (a learning activity) and does not refer to a learning outcome. Be careful of these; although student-centered, they lack any reference to performance.
4. This meets the criteria of the good objective: student-centered, a learning outcome, and observable.

Before we turn our attention to the actual writing of objectives, consider Robert Mager's (1975) reminder that desirable objectives have three characteristics.

1. What is *the behavior* that should result? Here you are concerned with identifying the specific behavior that signals that the learner has achieved the objective. Remember that your statement of the desired behavior also should specify an acceptable level. For example, if you give students ten problems, you might decide that seven correct solutions is an acceptable performance level. This description is sometimes called *performance-based* or *outcome-based* instruction (Kim & Kellough, 1991).
2. What are the *conditions* under which the specific behavior should occur? For example, calculating with paper and pencil differs from calculating by a computer. Mager strongly urges that you describe enough conditions for the objective to write appropriate test items.
3. What are the *criteria* that inform you that students have achieved an objective at the proper level? In other words, how well must a student perform to be judged successful? Is it the number of items correct? Is it time? Whatever the criteria, be sure that students understand the minimal acceptable level of performance.

Writing Acceptable Objectives

Keeping in mind the essential criteria of good objectives, you can now begin to formulate your own objectives. *First,* decide on the content that you wish your students to learn. What are the major concepts that must be included? Are they appropriate for your course, the curriculum, and your students? *Second,* what are the general goals for this course? What are the goals for the individual sections or units of the course? Answering these questions leads you to consider the general instructional objectives mentioned earlier and the manner in which

Table 11.5

Desired Characteristics of Objectives

Characteristics	Meaning
Specified content	Content should be precisely stated in behavioral terms.
Specified outcome	Students' behavior, as a result of learning, should be stated as observable outcomes.
Specified level of performance	Expected student behavior should not only be specified, but the exact degree of attainment should be clear to both teacher and students.
Specified outcome in clear, exact terms	Use verbs, such as name, identify, classify, order, avoid, and understand.

you sequence the objectives (Nesbit & Hunka, 1987). *Third,* break down these general goals into specific, observable outcomes. Recall the general goal that referred to the "topics of educational psychology." If we move to a more specific, observable level, our objective might read:

> Given that "learning" is an essential topic in educational psychology, students should be able to identify five cognitive theorists and the concepts that are central to their theories.

Fourth, be sure your objectives are clear and appropriate.

Table 11.5 summarizes the characteristics of appropriately stated instructional objectives as suggested by Bloom, Madaus, and Hastings (1981) and Gronlund (1985).

If we now translate these ideas into action, our first step should be cautionary: use precise terminology. As Gronlund noted (1985, p. 45) the action verbs you use should satisfy two criteria.

- They should clearly convey your instructional intent.

- They should precisely state the behavior and level of performance expected of students (use verbs such as identify, name).

Writing objectives can become more focused if you follow the suggestions offered by Armstrong and Savage (1983). Their ABCD format includes four elements:

> A—the audience for which the objectives are intended;
>
> B—the behavior that indicates learning;
>
> C—the conditions under which the behavior is to appear;
>
> D—the degree of competency that will be accepted.

Though these elements are similar to those already discussed, the familiar ABCD format provides a helpful reminder. For example, in the following objective—each student will be able to define eight of the ten items in the reading passage of the unit test—A refers to the audience (each student), B defines the behavior, C refers to the condition (in the reading passage of the unit test), and D establishes the degree of competency (eight of ten items or 80 percent). (The order in which these elements appear can vary; the important thing is that all four elements must be present.)

Table 11.6 illustrates the manner in which an objective by the use of an action verb, can specify a student response.

Sources of Objectives

As you begin to consider the importance of good objectives for your teaching, you may want to turn to established sources of objectives and then commence writing your own. Among the many sources you can use are the following:

1. *Published materials.* Look at your own texts and the instructor manuals that accompany them. They usually contain a wealth of valuable materials. You might also consider the annual yearbooks published by the national associations of teachers of your subjects. *The Encyclopedia of Educational Research* is another excellent source.
2. *Your colleagues.* Teachers of the same subject or grade can often complement each other, thinking of outcomes you could forget.
3. *Specialized sources,* such as *The Taxonomy of Educational Objectives.*

Table 11.6

How Verbs Specify Response

Action Verb	Types of Response	Sample Test Task
Identify*	Point to, touch, mark, encircle, match, pick up.	"Put an X under the right triangle."
Name*	Supply verbal label (orally or in writing).	"What is this type of angle called?"
Distinguish	Identify as separate or different by marking, separating into classes, or selecting out a common kind.	"Which of the following statements are *facts* (encircle F) and which are opinions (encircle O)?"
Define	Supply a verbal description (orally or in writing) that gives the precise meaning or essential qualities.	"Define each of the following terms."
Describe*	Supply a verbal account (orally or in writing) that gives the essential categories, properties, and relationships.	"Describe a procedure for measuring relative humidity in the atmosphere."
Classify	Place into groups having common characteristics, assign to a particular category.	"Write the name of the type of pronoun used in each of the following sentences."
Order*	List in order, place in sequence, arrange, rearrange.	"Arrange the following historical events in chronological order."
Construct*	Draw, make, design, assemble, prepare, build.	"Draw a bar graph using the following data."
Demonstrate*	Perform a set of procedures with or without a verbal explanation.	"Set up the laboratory equipment for this experiment."

*Sullivan states that these six action verbs (and their synonyms) encompass nearly all cognitive learning outcomes in the school. See H. J. Sullivan, "Objectives, Evaluation, and Improved Learner Achievement," in *Instructional Objectives.* AERA Monograph Series on Curriculum Evaluation, No. 3 (Chicago: Rand McNally, 1969).

Reprinted with the permission of Macmillan Publishing Company, Inc. from *Measurement and Evaluation in Teaching*, Sixth Edition by Norman E. Gronlund and Robert L. Linn. Copyright © 1990 by Macmillan Publishing Company. © 1985, 1981, 1976, 1971, 1965 by Norman E. Gronlund.

The Taxonomy of Educational Objectives

Long interested in taxonomies of educational objectives, Benjamin Bloom and his colleagues devised the **Taxonomy of Educational Objectives,** which is an endeavor to clarify some of the vague terminology often used in the social sciences (Bloom et al., 1956). Bloom (1913–) is the Charles H. Swift distinguished professor emeritus of education at the University of Chicago. The main purpose of the taxonomy is to provide a classification of the goals of our educational system (Bloom et al., 1956, p. 1). There are three taxonomies: *cognitive, affective,* and *psychomotor.* The cognitive taxonomy, which has greatly influenced American education, is divided into six major classes:

- *Knowledge*—the recall of pertinent facts when needed—for example, who were the first astronauts to reach the moon?
- *Comprehension*—understanding the meaning of what is presented—for example, can you explain the causes of World War II?
- *Application*—use of ideas and rules where needed—for example, final e makes the preceding vowel long.
- *Analysis*—separating a unit into its parts—for example, how many parts make up educational psychology?
- *Synthesis*—constructing a whole from parts—for example, write a paper about a topic combining class work, films, and a field visit.

• *Evaluation*—making judgments—for example, can you justify, or not justify, a particular nation's aggressive policies?

Each category is further subdivided into other, more specific objectives. The authors state that these six classes represent a hierarchical order of the different classes of objectives. The objectives of each class usually depend on the preceding classes (Bloom Ed., 1956, p. 18).

The great value of the taxonomy is its general application. Experts in curriculum construction can study it for a refinement of the objectives of any school. Inexperienced teachers can turn to the taxonomy as a guide to the kind of objectives for which students should be striving. Both expert and neophyte can profit by the wide range of test items that the authors present to ascertain if students are actually achieving these goals.

When the authors suggest typical objectives and test items, they offer an invaluable service to teachers. For example, in the main class of *knowledge,* one of the objectives is *knowledge of specific facts.* This is followed by an explanation of what is meant by the heading, and then the authors present illustrative educational objectives for this category.

*Knowledge of specific facts—**Illustrative Educational Objectives:***

• the recall of major facts about particular cultures
• the possession of a minimum knowledge about the organisms studied in the laboratory
• knowledge of biological facts important to a systematic understanding of biological processes
• recall and recognition of factual information about contemporary society
• knowledge of practical biological facts important to health, citizenship, and other human needs
• acquiring information about major natural resources
• acquiring information about various important aspects of nutrition
• recall and recognition of what is characteristic of particular periods
• knowledge of physical and chemical properties of common elements and their compounds
• an acquaintance with the more significant names, places, and events in the news
• a knowledge of the reputation of a given author for presenting and interpreting facts on governmental problems
• knowledge of reliable sources of information for wise purchasing (Bloom et al., 1956, pp. 66–67).

The Taxonomy (often referred to as Bloom's Taxonomy) is a remarkably flexible tool. Not only does it offer reliable insights into the formation of acceptable objectives, but it can also be used as the basis for teaching thinking skills (see chapter 10). To support the contention that properly stated instructional objectives are well worth it, consider the research of Boulanger (1981). Examining eleven preinstructional strategies used with science classes, he found that eight of these strategies produced statistically significant cognitive effects, and among the most powerful contributions to the positive effects were the five studies that used behavioral objectives.

Finally, we return to the broader themes with which we initiated our discussion of objectives. Combining your knowledge of development and learning, remember those basic principles that will guide you in your selection and formulation of specific objectives suited for your students. Table 11.7 illustrates these features.

Instructional Objectives and School Subjects

One of the objectives (general) of educational psychology is to help you identify those obstacles that are inherent in teaching any subject. Once you identify these problems you can formulate specific instructional objectives that reflect the guidelines just presented.

The subjects we shall examine, from the perspective of educational psychology, are reading, mathematics, and science.

Reading

In a widely read report, *Becoming a Nation of Readers* (1984), reading was compared to the performance of a symphony orchestra. This analogy illustrates three points. First, like the performance of a symphony, reading is a holistic act. In other words, although reading can be analyzed into subskills such as discriminating letters and identifying words, performing the subskills one at a time does not constitute reading. Reading can be said to take place only when the parts are put together in a smooth, integrated performance. Second, success in reading comes from practice over long periods of time. Third, readers interpret text differently, depending on their background, the purpose for reading, and the context in which reading occurs.

A topic that seems to be in a constant state of crisis, the teaching of reading has probably attracted more speculation, research, attacks, and apparent "breakthroughs" than any other school subject. No one questions its

Table 11.7

Guidelines for Achieving Educational Objectives

Knowledge of the Learner	Educational Import
1. The learner possesses a unique capacity for achievement.	Schools must recognize and provide for individual differences among students.
2. The learner's achievement is affected by the nature of the environmental contacts.	Learning experiences furnished by the school must enhance, or enrich, the learner's background.
3. The learner's developmental pattern should suggest classroom materials and methods.	A wide assortment of learning experiences should afford maximum opportunity for achievement at all ages.
4. The learner's intellectual level is not fixed and is capable of change.	Administrative procedures and organization should account for a variable expression of intellectual capacity.
5. The learner's emotions exercise a decisive effect, either positive or negative, upon learning.	The classroom atmosphere should be sufficiently stable to afford security and sufficiently stimulating to offer challenge.
6. The learner is a social being who requires satisfactory relations with other humans.	Emphasis upon the individual should not cause neglect of the interaction with peers, which is necessary to develop the mature personality.
7. The learner is an active, motivated individual who is capable of responses that range from the concrete to the abstract.	Self-activity in pursuit of an attainable goal is essential for learning. The learner should have educational experiences that require motor responses, thinking, problem solving, and creative thought.

primacy in school, or, indeed, its critical function in an individual's adaptation to a technological society. What is questioned is the best technique to produce the best results for the most children. Determining the most suitable methods leads to a consideration of objectives.

The latest report of The National Assessment of Educational Progress (1988), identified five levels of proficiency to describe students' reading skills and strategies.

1. *Rudimentary skills and strategies.* Students can follow brief written directions, use appropriate words to describe a simple picture, and interpret clues to identify a common object.
2. *Basic skills and strategies.* Locate and identify facts taken from simple paragraphs and stories. They can combine ideas and make inferences from short, simple passages.
3. *Intermediate skills and strategies.* Students can search for, locate, and organize information from a fairly lengthy passage. They can also detect the main ideas and the author's purpose.
4. *Adept skills and strategies.* Students can understand difficult passages. They can react to and explain the story as a whole.

5. *Advanced skills and strategies.* These students can extend and restructure the ideas in complex passages and texts.

If we examine several of the key elements of reading within the context of these objectives, we can see more clearly how the use of objectives—both general and specific—can both aid your teaching and help your students to avoid reading problems.

As we summarize the research of the last decade, several generalizations become possible.

• *Reading is a constructive process,* which clearly implies that readers construct meaning from what they read (Mason & Au, 1990). The meaning that your students glean from their reading also depends upon their previous experiences, which may be rich or deficient. A related problem here is that even if your students possess relevant knowledge about what they are reading, they may not use it.
• *Reading must be fluent,* which means that your students must be able to decode quickly and accurately. Are you sufficiently familiar with the coding process to determine where your students may

TEACHER ⟷ STUDENT
INTERACTIONS

Thinking About Objectives

1. Be sure you understand the distinction between goals and instructional objectives.
   - Write down what you think are the goals of a course that you are teaching now or will teach. Discuss them in class and then compare them with those of your classmates.
   - Within the framework of the general goals for this course, narrow your aims and write several general instructional objectives as defined by Gronlund.
   - Finally, write several specific objectives that you think you want your students to attain in your course.

2. Good objectives should be clearly written and expressed in behavioral terms.
   - Do the texts that you use in your teaching present objectives for the chapter or unit?
   - If objectives have been written, are they phrased in a way that your students find helpful? Be sure that your students understand them and use them as guides for their reading.
   - If objectives have not been written for chapters or units, then write your own, beginning with general instructional objectives and then moving to those specific objectives that reflect your students' needs.

3. In writing objectives, be sure that you include the student behavior that should result, the conditions under which the behavior should appear, and the criteria that satisfy the objective.
   - When your work in this course is complete, you should be able to write instructional objectives for this text. For example:
     a. Identify three learning strategies discussed in chapter 7, and give examples of each.
     b. Name the stages of development in Piaget's cognitive theory, and give four characteristics of each stage.
     c. Identify three motivational theorists, and list two essential concepts for each theory.
   - Now, using the same format, write four or five objectives for the subject(s) you teach.

be having difficulties? Does your knowledge of attention help here?

- *Reading must be strategic,* which means that good readers adapt their reading techniques to the difficulty of the text and the purpose of their reading (Mason & Au, 1990). What do you see as the role of pre-reading suggestions? Can you treat a reading assignment as

problem solving and adjust your teaching accordingly?

- *Reading requires motivation,* which demands that your teaching be innovative and challenging. See if you can apply ideas from the motivation chapter to reading instruction. For example, can you suggest reading materials that help to satisfy the needs of a particular student?
- *Reading is a continuously developing skill,* which suggests that your instruction and materials must match the changing abilities and skills of students.

These generalizations are appropriate for all teachers, even teachers of older students who are not enrolled in a specific reading class. The relationship between reading ability and academic success is so well-documented that you probably need few reminders of this truism. Given these facts about reading, how are our students doing today?

If we now examine several specific findings of the National Assessment of Educational Progress (1988) in reading, we find that:

- nine-year-old students were better readers in 1988 than students of the same age in 1971.
- thirteen-year-olds have shown little change in their reading abilities since 1971.
- seventeen-year-olds showed slight gains in reading proficiency from 1971 to 1988.
- African-American and Hispanic students made substantial improvements.
- although African-American and Hispanic students have shown gains, more improvement is necessary. For example, the average reading proficiency of black and Hispanic seventeen-year-olds remains substantially below that of same age white students.
- almost all thirteen- and seventeen-year-old students can read basic materials and 84 percent of the seventeen-year-olds still in school have acquired intermediate reading skills and strategies necessary to understand information in relatively lengthy reading passages.
- seven percent of nine-year-olds in 1988 still could not do basic reading exercises, signalling future school failure.

These ideas help us to understand more easily why students experience difficulties, and we can begin to identify problems that should guide teaching. Since reading is an active, constructive process, the cognitive work we have discussed would seem to offer insights into methodology. For example, recent analyses of reading processes have viewed reading within the framework of **parallel distributed processing.** That is, skillful reading depends not just on the appearance of words but also on their meaning and pronunciation. These three sources of information are not processed independently. Rather, skillful reading results from the coordinated and interactive processing of all three: spelling + sound + meaning (Adams, 1990).

Teaching Reading

Calfee and Drum (1986), summarizing the general objective of reading instruction, noted that teaching reading does not simply teach a child a system for translating speech into print, but instills an understanding of the conventions for thinking and communicating in the modern world. Among the topics occupying the time and attention of reading researchers are the following:

- Decoding, a controversial and elusive topic, refers to the technique by which we recognize words. Two interpretations divide reading theorists: those who argue that instruction should focus on the whole word and those who fervently believe that individual letters must be taught—the phonics method. Research today indicates that early phonics instruction produces the most satisfactory results.
- Vocabulary, or word meaning, refers to teaching the meaning of a word, and not merely how to pronounce it. It is interesting to pause for a moment and consider the ramifications of this statement. Knowledge of vocabulary is highly correlated with intelligence, which is highly correlated with reading performance and school success. Is it any wonder, then, that the acquisition of vocabulary rates high on any list of reading priorities?
- Reading comprehension, which is the ultimate objective in any type of reading instruction, means that a reader recognizes not only words but understands the concepts that words represent. Reading a text, comprehending it, and later recalling it involve complex strategies (perceptual, linguistic, and conceptual operations) that take years to develop (Mason & Au, 1990). Letters on the printed page must be encoded, text references must be comprehended, and the theme of the content must be followed (Beck & Carpenter, 1986, p. 1098).

Here is an example of achieving a general objective—identifying problems in a critical school subject—and offering opportunities for you to identify specific instructional objectives that meet your (and your students') individual needs.

Mathematics

The public's persistent concern with mathematics has been well-documented and needs no additional support here. Some individuals experience problems with num-

Focus on Teachers

How Clear Objectives Can Help

As an example of the efforts being made to aid students with comprehension problems, Palincsar and Brown (1984), working with junior high school students, identified six major objectives that reflect Gronlund's general instructional objectives:

- understanding the purposes of reading, both explicit and implicit;
- activating relevant background knowledge;
- allocating attention so that concentration can be focused on the major content at the expense of trivia;
- evaluating content critically for internal consistency and compatibility with prior knowledge and common sense;
- monitoring ongoing activities to see if comprehension is occurring, by engaging in such activities as periodic review and self-interrogation;
- drawing and testing inferences of many kinds, including interpretations, predictions, and conclusions.

They then selected four procedures that would enable the students to focus on these objectives: *summarizing, questioning, clarifying, and predicting.* This instructional technique began with modeling the activity; then each student performed the activity with a teacher, and, finally, the student performs independently of any teacher.

Note the attempt to engage many of the processes discussed in the learning section: attending, monitoring, predicting, evaluating. The results were impressive: from low comprehension levels to about the 70th percentile on standardized comprehension tests. Most noteworthy about this study, however, has been its lasting effect and transfer to new tasks.

bers as early as the first grade and develop an anxiety, even a phobia, about mathematics that remains with them throughout their lives. Given the pervasive role of mathematics in modern life, such individuals will probably encounter constant frustration.

There are also cultural differences in math achievement scores. Comparing the mathematical performance of Chinese students in Beijing and American students in Chicago, Stevenson and his colleagues (1990) found that American students did more poorly *but that neither the children nor their mothers realized it.* Both mothers and students viewed their performance favorably. The investigators speculate that the reasons for this discrepancy may be the result of lower standards for the American youngsters and teachers' deemphasis of mathematics.

Gaps also appear between the scores of African-Americans and whites, and the causes are unclear. Since mathematics is a hierarchical system, Entwisle and

Alexander (1990) examined the mathematical abilities of 785 black and white students at school entrance in Baltimore and found little difference, which doesn't necessarily mean that these abilities developed in the same way. The students were, nevertheless, of similar ability when they started school.

By the end of the first grade, differences had appeared, with the white students showing superior scores and black males surpassing black females. The authors conclude that though family type was not a factor, parental expectations and social class were both influential. Thus, important differences were appearing in the first year of school.

How can educational psychology help? If we follow the same procedure as with the reading section, we should be able to identify key functions in mathematics learning, point out potential trouble spots, and suggest ways in which instruction can utilize this psychological probing, beginning with the formulation of clear objectives. Remember: what do you want your students to acquire? Under what conditions? What criteria will you use to determine that they have acquired this desired behavior?

Skill and/or Understanding

Three themes characterize recent work in the psychology of mathematics:

1. the relationship between computational skills and understanding;
2. the role of mental representations in learning; and
3. the way in which new knowledge is constructed by learners.

The relationship between computational skill and understanding has intrigued psychologists, who have urged, for example, that procedural errors should be examined more closely than simply dividing them into "right" or "wrong." If you recall from our previous discussions of both development and learning, we are rule-learners. We learn rules and apply them as widely as possible to solve routine problems, but we also adapt our rules searching for innovative solutions when needed.

Our repeated use of arithmetic procedures (also called algorithms) can be good or bad, depending on the purpose for which the procedure is used. For example, try these simple problems.

33	58	314	8,218
−19	−24	−182	−4,742

What were your answers? Assuming that you refuse to panic, you undoubtedly answered

| 14 | 34 | 132 | 3,476 |

But some students, given the identical subtraction problems, will respond:

| 26 | 34 | 272 | 4,536 |

What has happened? Can you identify the student's problem? Here we have an example of a fairly common mathematical problem that, upon analysis, clearly signals that many such errors are rule-governed.

Note the repeated mistake; the student, in each example, subtracted the smaller number from the larger, regardless of position. It is not that this student failed to learn an algorithm but rather that the algorithm was misapplied. Called "buggy algorithms," they indicate that students do not recognize the limitations of applications. (The name comes from a computer program (Buggy) devised by Brown and Burton (1978) to aid teachers with their diagnosis.)

As Romberg and Carpenter (1986) stated, the reasons for using the common buggy algorithms are to discover how and why these misapplications are acquired. Note how this objective will guide the instruction to follow. What seems to happen is that students are confronted with problems for which their learned algorithms are incorrect. But if they don't understand the mismatch and have nothing else to use, they apply the algorithm anyway. Thus, understanding does not match the skills, which they learned mechanically. Teach your students to avoid mechanical application of the procedures; otherwise they cannot use their knowledge.

Using Mathematical Knowledge

Students too frequently cannot transform the mathematical meaning from concrete to abstract. A similar difficulty exists with word problems, which link mathematics with language understanding. Nesher (1986) summarizes the issue by noting that word problems should occupy a unique category since they require employment of a student's language knowledge as well as a special interpretation in mathematical contexts. Often the text's complexity obscures the needed mathematical processing.

Students can experience difficulties when they are forced to use their mathematical skills either in practical, everyday situations, or to solve word problems (Hughes, 1986). For example, asking an eleven-year-old to solve a simple division problem proved fairly simple.

A bar of chocolate can be broken into 18 squares. There are 6 squares in each row. How many rows are there?

Seventy-three percent of the students answered correctly.

But if you take a slightly different approach, the results change dramatically. Ask students of this age to determine your batting average.

To determine batting average, divide the number of times at bat into the number of base hits.

Name	Times at bat	Base hits	Average
Travers	40	12	?

Reporting a similar problem, Hughes stated that only 25 percent of the students answered correctly, while 38 percent wouldn't even attempt the problem.

Perhaps even more startling were the results of this problem presented to eleven- to thirteen-year-old students.

> The Green family has to drive the 252 miles from Boston to New York. After driving 98 miles, they stopped for lunch. How do you figure the remaining distance they have to drive?

84 x 3	252 + 98	252 – 98
252 x 98	154 + 98	252 ÷ 98

Note: The youngsters are asked only to select the correct calculation, not to compute it. Only 60 percent of the students selected the correct answer.

There is nothing startling in these results. If students are not expected to apply their learned behavior under real conditions, many, if not most, will react as the students in this study did.

We must face reality when facts such as these are presented. Nesher (1986) suggests that we turn to the notion of schema for help. (Recall that a schema is hypothesized to be a cognitive structure, a way of organizing knowledge.) She identified three types of schema: (a) *the dynamic schema,* in which changes in the initial situation are described: John had 9 marbles. He lost 3 of them. How many are left? (b) *the static schema,* in which relationships, involving no action, are described: There are 6 oranges and 3 apples on the table. How many pieces of fruit are there? (c) *the comparative schema,* in which one situation is described in relation to another: John has 9 marbles and Jim has 5. How many more marbles does John have than Jim? Interestingly, children experience different degrees of difficulty with each of these; success rates are highest for the dynamic schema, followed by the static and, finally, the comparative.

Mathematics and the Schools

What is the status of math in our schools today? In a series of reports entitled *The Nation's Report Card,* Educational Testing Service has assessed the progress of students in mathematics (Dossey, Mullis Lindquist, & Charbos, 1988). This *National Assessment of Educational Progress* in mathematics offers both hope and frustration. Here are some of their general findings.

- The most recent international survey shows that average Japanese students exhibit higher levels of achievement than the top five percent of American students enrolled in college preparatory mathematics courses.
- One of three major American corporations is forced to offer basic reading, writing, and arithmetic courses.
- American colleges report a 10 to 30 percent increase in the need for remedial mathematics courses.
- In the coming century, the fastest growing occupations will require higher levels of mathematic proficiency than do current occupations.

How are our students positioned to meet these challenges? We can be encouraged by the performance of nine- and seventeen-year-olds, who show better achievement in lower order skills. For example:

- Nine-year-olds showed marked improvement in the years from 1978 to 1986,
- Thirteen-year-olds showed similar improvement but a slightly different pattern. Scores declined between 1973 and 1978, improved between 1978 and 1982, and then leveled off in 1983.
- Seventeen-year-olds showed declining levels from 1973 to 1978, a continuing, though lesser decline into the 1980s, and a slight upturn between 1982 and 1986.
- Mathematics instruction remains traditional—teacher explanations at the board, coupled with texts and workbooks. Innovation is disappointingly rare.
- Students are given basic mathematical knowledge and skills in numbers and operations between grades three and seven, with higher level applications appearing across all levels. Girls are superior to boys in basic knowledge and skills while males surpass females in higher level applications.

Finally, the authors concluded that to improve our ability to compete internationally, our country must increase the number of secondary school students taking advanced math courses. Reform, however, should be initiated at all educational levels, not just in high schools.

From this brief review of some of the issues facing mathematics educators, it may be possible for you to formulate specific objectives that meet your needs. Several instructional implications seem to arise from our discussion.

- The mathematical knowledge that students bring to your classroom must be more carefully evaluated. As we have repeatedly seen, prior knowledge can be a potent influence on later learning.
- Careful diagnosis for the meaning of error seems to be a likely source of objectives.

- Assess carefully the relationship between understanding and skill usage in your class; the results may more accurately shape your instruction (Ball, 1986).
- Familiarity with developmental changes and levels of cognitive development can help you more appropriately match instruction with ability level.
- Encourage efforts to integrate mathematics with other subjects—"mathematics across the curriculum" (Kleiman, 1991).

Science

The contribution of educational psychology to science instruction parallels that of its input to the other subjects discussed. As you have probably discerned by now, understanding as an objective is the critical component stressed. Carey (1986) notes that students reading a science text or listening to a science teacher must gain understanding by relating what they read to what they know, in an interactive process. But, as she points out, students may experience more problems with science because they lack the necessary schema that is at the heart of understanding.

Science and the Schools

What is the status of science in our schools today? Assessing the current level of scientific proficiency as part of the series of reports entitled *The Nation's Report Card,* Educational Testing Service reports that science learning suffered a sharp decline in the 1970s, followed by a slight gain since then (Mullis & Jenkins, 1988).

Here is a summary of several of the findings.

- At age seventeen, students remained below 1969–1970 in science achievement. Performance has improved somewhat between 1982 and 1986.
- At age thirteen, students remained below the average achievement of 1969–1970. At age nine, students tested merely returned to the initial level of achievement.
- The average proficiency of thirteen- and seventeen-year-old African-Americans and Hispanic students remains at least four years below that of their white peers.
- At age seventeen, about one-half of the males but only one-third of the females demonstrated an ability to analyze scientific procedures and data.
- Approximately one-half of the teachers in grades seven and eleven reported spending three hours or less providing science instruction each week.

These findings are derived from five assessments conducted since 1969–1970. Based on assessment results, five levels of proficiency were identified.

"He's a little strange, but I understand he's an outstanding science teacher."

© James Estes.

- Level 150—knows everyday science facts
- Level 200—understands simple scientific principles
- Level 250—applies basic scientific information
- Level 300—analyzes scientific procedures and data
- Level 350—integrates specialized scientific information

Specifically, the most recent assessment found the following:

Nine-year-olds. This age group showed small but steady gains from 1977 to 1986. They are now at the level of the first assessment in 1969–1970.

Thirteen-year-olds. This age group has declined more and recovered less than the nine-year-olds. They are now below the level of assessment in 1969–1970.

Seventeen-year-olds. The performance of this age group dropped steadily from 1969–1970 to 1982 but has improved since. They are now still below the level of assessment in 1969–1970.

We are rightly concerned about the scientific skills of our students in a time when understanding of science and technology is needed for decision-making, such as voting on environmental and technical matters. Unless conditions in the nation's schools change radically, it is unlikely that today's nine- and thirteen-year-olds will perform much better as the seventeen-year-olds of tomorrow (Mullis and Jenkins, 1988, p. 7).

If the task of science is to develop new schemata, what can be used as a basis for understanding? Here is the source of many of the difficulties that students experience with science. Carey (1986) indicated that a typical junior or senior high school text often contains more new words per page than a foreign language text. But with foreign language words students at least understand the concepts they represent, which is not the case in science. Carey concludes that the full force of what students *do not understand* has just begun to be appreciated.

Research into science instruction has focused on the manner in which scientific knowledge is organized and accessed. Science educators have also concentrated on the relationship between the ability to reason scientifically and the development of Piaget's stages of cognitive growth.

Your identification of *specific instructional objectives* in your science classes would probably benefit from close scrutiny of the developmental sequence discussed earlier in this text; what cognitive abilities do your students require if they are to master needed scientific concepts? If these abilities are lacking, how will you alter your objectives? When an elementary school student asks, "If the earth is round, why don't the people in Australia fall off?" developmental knowledge will help to shape a teacher's answer and methods.

Also, the pertinent features of the learning work discussed in this text—proper use of reinforcement, rule learning, memory cues, the interactive role of the learner during problem solving—will help you to form pertinent objectives. A field trip designed to obtain seeds from trees and bushes provides opportunities for students to recall, interact with the teacher and other students, and to be reinforced.

Finally, suggestions to improve science education include the following objectives (Hurd, 1991):

- Integrate the findings from science and technology.
- Modernize content and stress the application of scientific knowledge to everyday life.
- Introduce higher order thinking skills into science instruction (see chapter 9).
- Use more meaningful texts with less jargon.
- Teach students to adapt to scientific change.

Instructional Objectives and Computers

Finally, we turn to the last question asked in the introductory section of this chapter: what are your objectives with regard to computer usage, both for yourselves and your students? It is a difficult question to answer because of the various views that school systems have of computer usage. Does formal instruction begin at kindergarten and continue each year as the responsibility of the classroom teacher? Or are the teachers of certain levels (for example, grades four and six) responsible for instruction with all other teachers encouraged to utilize computers as much as possible? Or does instruction remain informal until the secondary level?

For the purposes of this discussion, we'll assume that you are not directly responsible for computer instruction but have computers available for your classroom use. Take advantage of them! Resistance to computer usage among teachers is still strong to the extent that not all teachers use them, and even when they do, the computers are utilized about 25 percent of the available time (Reith, et al., 1988). Possible reasons for this include:

- lack of teacher training
- lack of support for computer usage
- poor scheduling
- lack of appropriate software.

To help you avoid a similar reaction, what should you know, and urge your students to know, in order that you, and they, may view computers as "friendly"? Before beginning our discussion, however, remember that although computer usage in the classroom has been widely applauded, techniques for aiding learning have not been clearly identified. The potential of these new technologies rests not only in the technology itself but also in an instructor's ability to vary methods and media according to the students' needs and the demands of the task (Hooper & Hannafin, 1991).

Why Bother with Computers?

Today's students are required to deal with complex activities on a daily basis, and frequently the computer is the key to successful performance. When you go to your bank to cash your check, the cashier punches in a magic series of numbers, and figures appear on a screen indicating, that yes, indeed, you do have enough money to cover this transaction. Your modern car is a technological marvel, forcing you to study carefully the accompanying owner's manual.

With the advent of the personal computer, avoiding its constant impact has become almost impossible. At home, at work, at school, computer knowledge has become almost mandatory for achievement and success. How can we do otherwise than prepare our students to meet this demand? Far too many people remain illiterate, scientifically backward, and mathematically deficient, and these same people typically experience extreme

Computers can play a valuable role in the teaching-learning process. They increase opportunities to respond, expand academic engaged time, and often provide specific feedback and reinforcement—all of which are fundamental activities for effective teaching and effective learning.

difficulty in coping with our society. It seems that we are at the point where computer illiteracy will produce the same outcome as a deficiency in reading or mathematics. Times are changing, however.

A Look Back

Most teachers have arrived at their present state of computer competence in much the same manner. Usually one curious teacher in a building became intrigued by this new technology and "learned computers" (Goodson, 1990). When school systems made computers available to teachers, this teacher became a mentor to the rest of the faculty. Teachers have their levels of readiness (much like our students) and, after initial wariness, many were surprised to discover that they had most of the skills needed to master this new technology.

They could type, so they had familiarity with a key board. They were accustomed to using teachers' manuals, so they weren't overwhelmed by the computer manuals. They constantly used blackboards and overheads, so seeing their ideas on a screen came as no surprise.

"I feel pretty silly putting pegs in holes when I have a personal computer at home."

© 1988; Reprinted courtesy of Bunny Hoest and Parade Magazine.

Table 11.8

Focus on Classrooms: Technological Competencies in Computer Use

Awareness Level

Introduction to technology for individuals who know little about it, especially as an educational tool, and who may need to acquire a positive attitude about the use of technology in special and general education. At this level, the user will:

1. Recognize component parts, functions, and appropriate care.
2. Use and understand terms.
3. Recognize need to utilize technology to assist persons to compensate, remediate, communicate, and control environments.
4. Recognize need to integrate technology into instructional curriculum of all students.
5. Identify general uses of storage and manipulation of data.
6. Be aware of questions for and sources of external evaluation of technology.
7. Recognize need for planning and cost effectiveness.
8. Understand purchasing guidelines and sources.
9. Recognize need for telecommunications and networks.
10. Identify present uses of technology in the workplace and for effective living for the handicapped.
11. Recognize need to be familiar with documentation for hardware, software, and adaptive devices.
12. Understand input-output information-processing model, including impact that sensory deficits have on learners and how technology can be used to compensate for these deficits.

Knowledge Level

At this level, the goal is to provide a personal orientation so that the user can approach the computer with relative com-

fort and have a broad understanding of its capacity. The user will have knowledge of:

1. Appropriate uses of:
   a. CAI (computer assisted instruction).
   b. CMI (computer managed instruction).
   c. applications software, e.g., word processing, spreadsheet, data base management.
   d. emerging technologies, e.g., videodisk, telecommunication networks, adaptive devices.
2. Integrating computers/technology into curriculum.
3. Research on special education applications.
4. Implications of FERPA, copyright laws, and licensing on school setting applications.
5. Basic operations of computers.
6. Funding sources for special education technology.
7. Evaluation components of instructional and administrative software.
8. Special education applications information and assistance resources.
9. Professional development resources.
10. Technology used to compensate in:
    a. environmental control.
    b. communication.
    c. mobility.
    d. skills in learning, leisure activities, vocational activities, and basic living skills.
11. Software evaluation components:
    a. instructional information.
    b. educational adequacy.
    c. technical adequacy.
    d. hardware/adaptive device compatibility.
    e. appropriateness in meeting special needs.
12. Purchasing questions to ask for adaptive devices.

With these more comfortable feelings came the realization that computers could never replace teachers.

One of the major changes in thinking about computers was the move away from the belief that everyone had to be a programmer. Teachers now realize that they don't have to write their own software; excellent commercial programs can meet their needs.

Schools next had to decide on a plan that would fit the needs of their students and *not* just focus on teacher expertise. For example, students will be able to use an expanding technology to create, explore, and reinforce

their ideas. Teachers who are at ease with the technology will apply it to their own needs and meet student needs more efficiently, emphasizing skills and problem solving (Goodson, 1990). Table 11.8 presents several competencies that should allow you to assess your own level of proficiency.

To acquire **computer literacy** students should actually work with a computer to gain performance proficiency, as well as obtaining knowledge about the history and nature of computers and their use in our society. The performance skills they acquire should en-

13. Adaptive devices evaluation components:
    a. alternative switches.
    b. touch-sensitive input devices.
    c. speech output.
    d. modified displays.
    e. tactile output.
    f. special needs software.
14. Developing a team approach and the available resources for information and assistance with uses and evaluation of adaptive devices.
15. Resources for information and assistance with the uses of technology with students through user groups, and other human resources, banks, data bases, etc.

Utilization Level

At this level, the user will develop the skills needed to implement computer applications for case management and to understand the computer's instructional value. The user will:

1. Organize and manage technology for effective educational use in the classroom and/or label situation.
2. Select software for specific uses and needs in case management and assessment.
3. Communicate effectively with others using appropriate technological/computer terminology.
4. Identify and remedy common problems with hardware, software, and adaptive devices.
5. Use hardware and appropriate software for basic computer operations, including "booting" a program, formatting a disk, backing up (copying) a disk, and copying selected files to another disk.
6. Access and use of software for:
    a. CAI (computer assisted instruction):
       (1) drill and practice.
       (2) tutorial.
       (3) simulation.
       (4) problem solving.
       (5) utilities.
    b. shell programs adaptive to individualized content material.
    c. CMI (computer managed instruction).
    d. word processing, data base management, telecommunications and networks, adaptive devices.

Proficiency Level

At this level, skills will be developed that are necessary for the user to be more innovative in the delivery of professional and educational services. The technology proficient user will:

1. Use application software to complete case management and assessment tasks.
2. Be a resource to instructional staff in the selection, use, and evaluation of appropriate hardware and software.
3. Write goals and objectives that integrate technology into teaching specific skills to students.
4. Evaluate the appropriateness of hardware, software, and adaptive devices.
5. Evaluate hardware, software, and adaptive devices for instructional, educational, and technical adequacy.
6. Develop evaluation plans for hardware, software, adaptive devices, etc. that are applicable to specific populations and specific situations and/or educational systems.
7. Have a directed experience utilizing adaptive devices that compensate for specific student deficits.

Adapted from Basic technological competencies by C. Deupree, 1988, NASP CTASP Newsletter, 7(1), p. 6. Copyright 1988 by National Association of School Psychologists. Adapted from COMPUTE (Coalition of Organizations in Michigan Promoting the Use of Technology in Special Education) and the Michigan Association of School Psychologists Proposed Technological Competency Standards.

able them to use a computer for assistance with their school work. Again, whether or not students should become involved in programming is an issue the local school board should decide.

Computer Assisted Instruction (CAI)

Think of **computer assisted instruction** as an instructional aid that can help you to attain previously formulated objectives. In other words, you use a computer to improve, to facilitate, or to supplement your normal work. You may decide that by having your students use computers you can improve practice sessions, demonstrate the steps leading to problem solutions more clearly, or utilize the computer as a tutor.

Among the benefits attributed to computer usage in the classroom is the flexibility it provides teachers, especially its ability to meet the individual needs of students. Using a computer enables a student to spend as much time as needed to master a task, either lingering when difficulty is encountered or moving quickly through

A Computer Glossary

You may find it helpful to pause here and consider some of the more common terms associated with computer usage.

ASCII—American Standard Code for Information Interchange, a code whereby numbers are used to represent letters and symbols.

Bit—Acronym for binary digit, the smallest unit of information used by the computer (either 0 or 1)

Byte—the number of bits required to store one character, usually made up of eight bits

Cathode Ray Tube (CRT)—the monitor

Central Processing Unit (CPU)—the heart of the computer, controls operations

Computer Assisted Instruction (CAI)—use of computer to aid classroom instruction

Computer Managed Instruction (CMI)—use of computer to aid in classroom management, record keeping, for example

Disk drive—a peripheral that stores information on disks, which you can then use or save; transmits information on the disk to and from the computer

Hardware—the collection of devices that constitute the computer system

Microcomputer—those computers whose CPU is a microprocessor

Microprocessor—silicon chip containing computer's basic control functions

Modem—enables you to transmit computer signals over telephone lines

Networking—communication among two or more computers

Peripherals—devices that enable you to communicate with computer (disk drive, printer, keyboard)

Printer—the output peripheral that enables you to put characters on paper

Random Access Memory (RAM)—information presented to or read from computer, non-permanent, and may be lost when computer is shut off unless previously saved to tape or disk

Read Only Memory (ROM)—information locked into computer, which is stored permanently. It cannot be changed.

Software—computer programs; those instructions that tell the computer to perform a specific task.

"easy" material. (Note the similarity to our previous discussion of the advantages of the time-on-task concept.)

Over the past few years there has been a growing literature on evaluating the effectiveness of CAI. Since an examination of individual studies may convey different conclusions, educational researchers have reviewed this literature in a variety of ways. Most recently, meta-analysis has been used (remember our discussion of this technique in chapter 2?). Kulik and Kulik (1991) conducted a meta-analysis of CAI of findings from 254 research studies. The research that they included in their review covered students ranging from kindergarten age to adults. They found that the CAI raised final examination scores in the typical study by .30 standard deviations (approximately from the 50th to the 62nd percentile). The findings were in agreement with previous research in the field. Interestingly, the CAI was very effective when the duration of treatments was limited to four weeks or less. When treatments were continued for several months or longer, the effects were less robust. Their study did not provide any information on whether the use of CAI was cost effective when compared to other successful treatments such as tutoring.

Here are several examples of the more common classroom usages of computers.

Drill and Practice. As the name implies, programs designed for this purpose have as their objective helping students master the basic elements in mathematics, reading, spelling, and any other subject in which they must acquire fundamental facts. Used in this manner, computers resemble a teaching machine in that they present a stimulus, elicit a response, and provide reinforcement. Surprisingly, in a study of 200 primary schools involving over 600 teachers in which computers were used for drill and practice, the students, (five to eleven years) showed an increase in cooperative behavior when they worked in small groups (Jackson, Fletcher, & Messer, 1988).

Lockard, Abrams, and Many (1987) use arithmetic as an example to describe several types of programs that are available. At the basic level a program may offer students a fixed number of problems to solve. All students face the same tasks, and only after successful completion can they move on to a higher level. They spend as much time as needed to work to mastery.

Next is the program that has an arbitrary mastery criterion—six successive successful completions may be required. Note that some students may well meet this criterion on their initial effort, while others might need several attempts.

A more adaptive program could require students to reach mastery after a relatively few responses, or increase the difficulty of the materials, or even force students to switch the operations needed—for example, from multiplication to division. For a student experiencing difficulty, the program would then branch to less difficult context, or return the user to a lower level. As Lockard et al. (1987, p. 150) note, such constant adjustments are intended to assume mastery without causing either boredom or frustration.

As you can well imagine, there are opponents as well as proponents, of using computers for drill. They argue that:

- programs are boring;
- all students receive the same content, regardless of ability;
- programs may provide undesirable feedback;
- some teachers use computers for primary instruction;
- computers used for drill is an expensive waste of money.

On the other hand, proponents argue that:

- extra practice is provided where needed most;
- attention can be maintained during practice sessions;
- where problems exist, they are usually the result of poorly designed programs;
- unexpected bonuses, such as a student's fascination with the computer itself or interest in programming, can often result.

We can perhaps best conclude that the question to be faced is not whether computers should be used in this manner, but what the objectives for such use should be.

Tutorials. The major difference between computers used for drill and as a tutor is that, in the tutorial, new material is introduced. The computer, in a sense, is acting as a one-on-one instructor. Two types of tutorials seem most popular: *linear* and *branching*.

With a *linear* program, all students receive the identical material and must respond to each item. The only concession to individual differences is the amount of time taken to respond successfully.

In a *branching* program, however, all students do not necessarily have to go through the same content. Alternate paths are available so that successful students are "branched" to new material, while the less successful are routed to remedial work.

Opponents argue that tutorial programs "trivialize" important concepts by breaking them into such minute elements that students fail to grasp the relationships that make up the total concept. Proponents argue that this criticism applies to any type of teaching. When tutorials are combined with teacher instruction, they afford a basic dimension that enables an instructor to present a broader perspective of a topic than might otherwise be possible.

Problem Solving. In an attempt to involve higher cognitive processes, sophisticated programs have been designed that present students with identifiable problems. The process entails exactly the same steps discussed in chapter 9, Learning: Strategies and Skills. An attractive feature of these programs is the strong motivational appeal that they exercise for students.

Among the major claims for the use of problem solving software has been that in a time of growing concern about the thinking skills of our students, computer usage devoted to problem solving results in enhancing students' abilities, especially with regard to memory, use of learning strategies, and creative thinking.

The chief problem seems to be in curriculum placement. These abilities require time to develop, and since they are not confined to any one subject, they have an impact across the curriculum. Decisions must be made, then, about teaching these skills in separate courses or encouraging individual instructors to present them in their courses.

Although these are some of the main interpretations of CAI, other computer uses also aid instruction. For example, both the use of word processing and data base programs are gaining in popularity.

Computer Managed Instruction (CMI)

To say that teachers spend considerable time in keeping track of student activities, grades, and records is a mammoth understatement. Grades, attendance records, text assignments, and auxiliary equipment are but a few of the records that teachers must keep. It is precisely here that **Computer Managed Instruction** (CMI) can help: tracking and documenting classroom activities, thus making manageable the necessary paper work.

Computer managed instruction is usually thought of as the use of the computer to collect, analyze, and report information concerning the performance of students in an educational program. For example, you may decide to create a file for each student in your class, beginning with the student's name. You then continually add data to the file: test scores, results of standardized tests, any special work, pertinent health data, need for any type of special attention (e.g., medication). As you can see, the list could become endless, but you have created an invaluable tool for instantly attaining information on every student in your class—all of this on one small disk.

By this time you have probably anticipated the next trend in CAI-CMI, which is to include a CMI element in CAI to provide constant evaluation of a student's progress. There are five major functions in this usage:

- Assessment—collecting vital information
- Diagnosis—a continuing evaluation of learner needs
- Learning prescription—matching students' needs with appropriate instruction
- Record keeping—maintaining all kinds of student records

TEACHER ⟷ STUDENT INTERACTIONS

Objectives in the Classroom

1. Educational psychology can help in identifying desirable objectives in the various subjects.

   • Try to discover what your students think about reading. In your discussion with your students, ask questions similar to the following: (By using appropriate language, you can do this at almost any level.)

      1. Why is it important to read well?
      2. What do people do when they read?
      3. When you're reading and you come to something you don't know, what do you do? Does everyone here do the same thing?
      4. Do you know anyone who is a good reader?
      5. What makes someone a good reader?
      6. Do you think you are a good reader? Why?
      7. What would you like to improve in your reading?

   • Now that you have some idea of how your students feel about reading, use the ABCD format to write objectives for the subject(s) that you teach. Discuss them in class to determine if there is agreement about what you have designated audience, behavior, conditions, and degree of competence.

   • Knowing that repeated mathematical errors produce frustration, a lack of a willingness to apply mathematical principles, and decreasing motivation, use the ABCD method to write specific objectives that are realistic for your students. For example, each student (A) will solve (B) eight of ten word problems (D) on the weekly test (C).

   • Since some students have nothing in their background to which they can relate any given scientific concept, consider whether you want to teach a concept in isolation before they meet it in context, or treat it as it appears in the flow of your lesson. Whatever you decide, write specific objectives that indicate what you expect from your students; be sure to specify behavior, conditions, and criteria.

2. Teachers are often uncertain as what to expect from their students with regard to computer knowledge. Try using the cognitive domain of Bloom's *Taxonomy of Educational Objectives* to help you refine your thinking (depending, of course, on the grade level).

   • Try something like this. In a practical demonstration of word processing skills, each student will write one paragraph including six commands (knowledge).

   • Now write objectives for your computer work, using the other categories of the taxonomy.

• Reporting—supplying needed information for both teachers and students.

As you can see, then, the goals of CMI are not solely restricted to course management but also apply to learner performance, the learning sequence, and selection of appropriate learning activities (Soulier, 1988).

Using the Technology

Computer usage continues to increase at a steady rate until now the estimated number of computers in our elementary and secondary schools has reached into the millions. Most elementary schools have five or more computers, while 50 percent of our high schools have at least fifteen computers. These figures alone testify to the need for you to be sufficiently comfortable with computers so that you can at least knowledgeably help your students. Research also suggests that computer usage is positively correlated with higher achievement. (For a more detailed discussion of this topic see Lockard et al., 1987.)

When we couple these facts with the global objective that we all share, that of adequately preparing our students to participate meaningfully in our society, you can understand the urgency of insuring that both teachers and students are competent computer users. We can perhaps best summarize our discussion by paraphrasing Lesgold's (1986) answers to these questions:

• How will the massive use of computers change the occupational roles in our society? Any technological change is inevitably accompanied by a shift in the value placed upon certain skills. As computer usage has extended even farther into our society, we have seen computers manage routine tasks, displacing thousands of workers and moving them into a rapidly proliferating service economy. This trend has also freed others to engage in more innovative design and problem solving activities.

• What are the implications for curriculum change? A computer era would seem to require more complex schooling, which is one of the reasons that chapter 11 is devoted to thinking skills. Students should possess those skills that enable them to adapt to the swift and unexpected changes that we all can anticipate facing. If computer usage helps students to extend learning and solve problems, you will have done much to ready them for a high technology future.

Conclusion

In this chapter, you examined the key role that instructional objectives play in both teaching and learning. Instruction improves because you have decided exactly what it is you want your students to accomplish. Learning improves because students know exactly what is expected of them, and they understand the basis of their marks and grades.

If there is one indispensable guideline for formulating objectives, it is to be precise. But, as we all know, precision is frequently easier to talk about than to accomplish, so specific suggestions were made to help you state desirable instructional objectives. These were based on Mager's (1975) work and are as follows:

- What behavior do you wish your students to acquire?
- Under what conditions should students be able to demonstrate that behavior?

- What are the criteria you will adopt to insure that your students have acquired that behavior satisfactorily?

We then turned our attention to specific topics that are critical for educated individuals—reading, science, mathematics, and computer usage. You were urged to use instructional objectives to help in identifying those stumbling blocks that inhibit student achievement. We conclude this chapter, then, by stressing the importance of instructional objectives in the classroom, both to improve teaching and learning and to identify potential problems for your students.

Chapter Highlights

Deciding on Educational Objectives

- Clearly articulated objectives make learning more meaningful and useful.
- Models such as Adler's Paideia Proposal stress the quality of education by focusing on self-improvement, enlightened citizenship, and career productivity.
- The public's expectations for its schools—that is, achievement of goals—reflect a concern for the fulfillment of its products. Are our graduates as well-prepared as possible for the life of their choosing?

The Role of Objectives in Instruction

- Objectives guide your classroom work with regard to planning, teaching, and testing.
- Writing clear, behavioral objectives forces you to think about what exactly you want to accomplish.
- When you begin to concentrate on what you want to accomplish, distinguish among description, goals, and objectives.
- As you think about your objectives, remember the difference between general and specific instructional objectives, deciding what you wish to use and when each type seems more appropriate.
- Your objectives must be clear and realistic, indicating exactly what students must accomplish and at what level.
- You should specify the behavior to be acquired, the conditions under which the behavior occurs, and the criteria informing an observer that the objective has been achieved.
- Don't hesitate to use established sources of objectives that you can readily apply to your work.

Instructional Objectives and School Subjects

- Educational psychology is particularly well-suited to help you devise appropriate objectives because of the insights it offers into the teaching and learning processes. In this chapter, three subjects were used to illustrate educational psychology's role: reading, mathematics, science.
- The National Assessment of Educational Progress reports can help in identifying those topics that need special attention.

Instructional Objectives and Computers

- Increased interest in the instructional use of computers has intensified the need to articulate precise objectives for computer usage in the classroom.
- Developmental considerations must be accounted for to insure that objectives are biologically and psychologically appropriate.
- Perhaps the first task that schools must set themselves as they begin to formulate objectives for computer instruction is to define as accurately as possible—given the needs of their students—the meaning of computer literacy.

Key Terms

Computer Assisted Instruction
Computer literacy
Computer Managed Instruction
Expected Learner Outcomes (ELO)
General instructional objective
Illustrative instructional objectives
Instructional objectives
Microcomputer

Microprocessor
Networking
Parallel distributed processing
Specific instructional objective
Task analysis
Taxonomy of educational objectives

Suggested Readings

Bloom, B. (Ed.). (1956). *Taxonomy of educational objectives. Handbook 1: Cognitive domain.* New York: McKay. For anyone interested in education and particularly for those concerned with goals and objectives, this wonderful little book is a must. Carefully reasoned, thoughtfully presented, and full of pertinent examples, it is a storehouse of valuable suggestions for identifying objectives and then testing to determine if the objectives were obtained.

Cooper, J. (Ed.). (1986). *Classroom teaching skills.* Lexington, MA: Heath. An excellent manual that presents practical guidelines for formulating objectives and the means of reaching them.

Gagne, R. (1988). *Essentials of learning for instruction.* Englewood Cliffs, NJ: Prentice-Hall. Gagne's continuing efforts to link the conditions of learning with types of learning and learning outcomes are well-presented in this little book. This is an integrated model, one that you would find both interesting and helpful.

Ramsey, P. (1987). *Teaching and learning in a diverse world.* New York: Teachers College Press. If you were to choose one source to attempt to grasp the realities of multicultural education, this would be it. A sensitive appraisal of the needs of these students.

Effective Teaching Strategies and the Design of Instruction

There are still those who labor under the illusion that teaching is a relatively simple task. Teachers talk; students listen. This stereotype of teaching ignores the complicated interactions that occur between teacher and student. In his charming little classic, *The Teacher in America*, Jacques Barzun (1954), however, presents a different picture.

Assigned to teach a class in naval history, Barzun describes the admiral who gave him a friendly and reassuring pat on the shoulder, saying "Any damn fool can teach naval history." Barzun admits to being encouraged by this display of support, but deep within his psyche he knew the admiral was wrong.

"I had visited a midshipmen's school and heard a petty officer who was not a damn fool but not a teacher either, instruct in the subject. He had his nose in a book and was reading aloud: `On the eleventh of February, Commodore Perry made for an anchorage twelve miles farther up Yedo Bay. This is important; take it down: On—the—eleventh—of—February—Commodore—Perry—made—for—an—unchorage. . . .'

This surely was not the most enticing of classes; the petty officer was out of his element. As Barzun notes, if Charles Dickens, famous for his public readings, had held that textbook of naval history in his hands, the class would have **seen** Commodore Perry steaming up the bay in defiance of Japanese orders. They wouldn't need to be told what's important.

When you are in the classroom working with students, you will discover a strong emotional commitment on both your parts. Regardless of the teaching method, regardless of the subject, and regardless of any auxiliary aids, certain intangibles exert a subtle though powerful influence upon learning and performance.

For example, personality studies suggest that personal characteristics affect both teacher performance and student learning. Students also react in an individual and often contrary manner. Some students may resent the exciting lecturer who dominates every moment of a class; others may achieve admirably under such stimulation. Some students thrive in an atmosphere where discussion is the technique; others, as a result of their individual personalities, avoid participation.

Students bring their attitudes, interests, prejudices, values, and opinions into the classroom with them. So do teachers. Realizing that these variables combine in the teaching-learning process, you can more readily appreciate the complicated nature of teaching.

To help you understand the intricacies of teaching, in this chapter we'll discuss "teaching" as the public thinks of it and teaching as it really is. Next we'll examine various theories and designs of instruction that reveal how teaching can be analyzed. This should help you to adopt, and adapt, different strategies for your purposes. But you should make these adaptations in light of the individual differences of your students, which will occupy us in the final section of the chapter.

When you complete this chapter, you should be able to:

- identify the common features of teaching.
- distinguish between direct and inquiry teaching.
- use praise in the classroom more effectively.
- apply the research findings concerning teaching to improve your own instruction.
- distinguish instructional theory from instructional design and apply the appropriate features of both to your own teaching.
- furnish examples of how you could adapt your teaching to the needs of your students.

First, let's try to grasp the meaning of "teaching."

The Meaning of Teaching

The moment of truth is at hand. You have closed the classroom door behind you, and as you slowly turn to meet the eager (and perhaps not so eager) faces watching your every move, you're probably wondering: How to begin? Nervous? Right. Uncertain? Right. Never have done this before? Wrong!

As a reminder that we all have had more teaching experience than we realize, try answering these questions.

- Have you ever been a babysitter? If so, you had to give directions, explain a word, show a child how to do something.
- Have you ever coached? If so, you instructed, explained, demonstrated, and evaluated.
- Have you ever been a summer counselor? If so, you managed, directed, lectured, demonstrated, and led group discussions.
- Have you ever worked? If so, at some time you undoubtedly explained procedures to a new employee.

Consequently, you have experience with the four "common features" of teaching: teachers, learners, subject matter, and context (Posner, 1989). Let's briefly examine each of these features of teaching.

Teachers. What kind of person were you in whatever teaching experience you had? Were you permissive or authoritarian? What did you see as the best role for you? What were the tasks you faced? When you enter a typical classroom, you must answer the same questions. Think about the circumstances in which you expect to teach (elementary, secondary, which subject(s), the kind of community) and try to determine how well your perspective of teaching "fits" these circumstances.

Learners. Everyone is a learner, but age, objectives, backgrounds, and experiences vary enormously. We have discussed learning in several of the preceding chapters, so here we'll just note that one of the most important considerations for student learning is to discover what they already know and use this as building blocks for your new work.

Subject matter. How much material do you think your students should cover? How much time should you devote to a particular topic? Are you going to emphasize facts, comprehension, or both in this particular unit?

Context. Any analysis of the impact of teaching must account for more than the immediate classroom. Parents, community, and a changing cultural blend all influence the success of the teaching-learning interaction.

That's a Good Teacher

What precisely is it that effective teachers do in the classroom that enables us to say, "That's a good teacher!"? Here are several findings from the vast research on teacher effectiveness that you may find helpful (Wittrock, 1986).

(a)

(b)

(c)

(d)

Effective teaching takes place throughout a school and requires flexibility on the part of teachers and students.

- *Quantity and pacing of instruction.* The most consistently replicated findings link students' achievement to their opportunities to learn the material. Have you allowed them enough time to master the material, given their abilities? The following seem particularly relevant:

  a. *Content covered.* Whether you teach pages of a curriculum or test material, the amount learned is related to opportunity to learn. For example, if you are teaching about the Civil War, your students must understand the views of the leading political and military figures, the causes of the war, the battles, and the role of European powers if they are to grasp the complexity of this topic. Though you personally may be fascinated by Lincoln, you can't spend all of your time on his personality. Your students must have the opportunity to study the entire range of topics.

  b. *Role definition/expectations/time allocation.* Achievement is greatest when teachers focus on instruction, expect students to master the curriculum, and allocate most available time to academic activities. Our concern here is with quality time (Blair, 1988). The *amount* of time that students have to learn affects *how much* they learn. Also, the way that teachers use this time affects student achievement. Allocation of time alone, of course, doesn't guarantee learning; your students must be *engaged* in their work during this time. Try to have your students as actively involved as possible. Carefully observe how they react to material; vary your pace accordingly; provide appropriate feedback.

c. *Classroom management/student-engaged time.* Maximum achievement is related to a teacher's ability to organize the classroom as an efficient learning environment. Effective organization includes good preparation of the physical environment with recognized rules and procedures, continuous monitoring of the entire class, good lesson pacing, variety of assignments, clear accountability, and recognized procedures when students need help (Gettinger, 1988). We'll discuss classroom management in greater detail in chapter 13, but for now remember that students learn best in an environment in which they know exactly what is expected of them regarding both their behavior and achievement.

d. *Consistent success/academic learning time.* When students' academic learning time is increased, a concomitant increase in achievement will likely occur, especially for low-achieving or at risk students (Berliner, 1988). Students must be engaged in appropriate academic activities with a good probability of success. For example, **The Beginning Teacher Evaluation Studies (BTES)**, inspired by John Carroll's model of school learning (1963), represented an effort to identify a mediating variable between teaching behavior and student performance (Shulman, 1986). Carroll's model shifted the research emphasis from teacher behavior to student activities—what were students doing with their task? Explanations of student achievement that focused solely on teachers seemed lacking in predictive power. For example, how could the number and quality of teacher praise statements in the fall influence student achievement in spring examinations? Researchers raising such questions then turned their attention to a more meaningful subject—the time that a student spent on particular content. Figure 12.1 illustrates the various time—allocated time, instructional time, engaged time, academic learning time—that teachers need to be aware of and manage.

e. *Active teaching.* Students achieve to a higher level in classes where they are directly taught by their teachers rather than working on their own. Active teaching can take two forms: direct

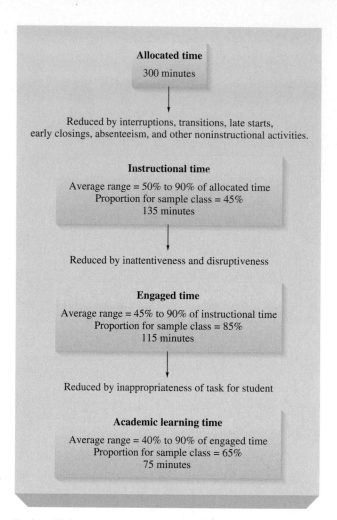

Figure 12.1
Components of academic learning time.

instruction and inquiry (Blair, 1988). With direct instruction, teachers tell, demonstrate, explain, and assume the major responsibility for the lesson's progress and adapt the work to their students' ages and abilities. Student achievement seems to be superior with direct instruction. Table 12.1 summarizes many of the activities involved in direct instruction. These include class presentations, guiding practice, grading of work, providing feedback, and monitoring students' work.

Teaching that encourages inquiry learning (i.e., inquiry teaching) is less structured and more informal. You will find yourself arranging classroom conditions in a way that encourages students to think about the means of solving problems. Since chapter 9 was devoted to an analysis of the teaching of thinking skills, our concern here is to emphasize that both types of instruction are

Table 12.1

Instructional Functions

1. Daily Review and Checking Homework

   Checking homework (routines for students to check each other's papers)

   Reteaching when necessary

   Reviewing relevant past learning (may include questioning)

   Review prerequisite skills (if applicable)

2. Presentation

   Provide short statement of objectives

   Provide overview and structuring

   Proceed in small steps but at a rapid pace

   Intersperse questions within the demonstration to check for understanding

   Highlight main points

   Provide sufficient illustrations and concrete examples

   Provide demonstrations and models

   When necessary, give detailed and redundant instructions and examples

3. Guided Practice

   Initial student practice takes place with teacher guidance

   High frequency of questions and overt student practice (from teacher and/or materials)

   Questions are directly relevant to the new content or skill

   Teacher checks for understanding (CFU) by evaluating student responses

   During CFU teacher gives additional explanation, process feedback, or repeats explanation—where necessary

   All students have a chance to respond and receive feedback; teacher insures that all students participate

   Prompts are provided during guided practice (where appropriate)

   Initial student practice is *sufficient* so that students can work independently

   Guided practice continues until students are firm

   Guided practice is continued (usually) until a success rate of 80% is achieved

4. Correctives and Feedback

   Quick, firm, and correct responses can be followed by a question or a short acknowledgement of correctness ("That's right").

   Hesitant correct answers might be followed by process feedback (i.e., "Yes, Linda, that's right because. . . .")

   Student errors indicate a need for more practice.

   Monitor students for systematic errors.

   Try to obtain a substantive response to each question.

   Corrections can include sustaining feedback (i.e., simplifying the question, giving clues), explaining or reviewing steps, giving process feedback, or reteaching the last steps.

   Try to elicit an improved response when the first one is incorrect.

   Guided practice and corrections continue until the teacher feels that the group can meet the objectives of the lesson.

   Praise should be used in moderation, and specific praise is more effective than general praise.

5. Independent Practice (Seatwork)

   Sufficient practice

   Practice is directly relevant to skills/content taught

   Practice to overlearning

   Practice until responses are firm, quick, and automatic

   Ninety-five percent correct rate during independent practice

   Students alerted that seatwork will be checked

   Student held accountable for seatwork

   Actively supervise students, when possible

6. Weekly and Monthly Reviews

   Systematic review of previously learned material

   Include review in homework

   Frequent tests

   Reteaching of material missed in tests

Note. With older, more mature learners, or learners with more knowledge of the subject, the following adjustments can be made: (1) the size of the step in presentation can be larger (more material is presented at one time), (2) there is less time spent on teacher-guided practice and (3) the amount of overt practice can be decreased, replacing it with covert rehearsal, restating and reviewing.

From Barak Rosenshine and Robert Stevens, "Teaching Functions." Reprinted with permission of Macmillan Publishing Company from *Handbook of Research on Teaching*, Third Edition, Merlin C. Wittrock, Editor. Copyright © 1986 by the American Educational Research Association.

necessary. Both types of instruction also are examples of direct instruction. That is, student must acquire facts before they attempt to solve problems, but teachers must also urge them to learn those adaptive skills that carry beyond the classroom.

- **Quality of instruction.** The second major category focuses on the quality of teaching. Major findings include the following:

  a. *Giving information.* Students achieve better when teachers' presentations are clear and not vague or rambling, when the information is well-structured, sufficiently redundant, and well-sequenced.

  b. *Questioning students.* Estimates are that 75 percent of questions should elicit the correct response, but good questions also relate to timing, quality, cognitive content, clarity, and selection of respondents (Brophy & Evertson, 1976).

  c. *Reacting to student responses.* Although findings on feedback are weaker, the basic conclusion remains that correct responses be acknowledged as such. If the response is incorrect, your reaction should be confined to the response and not include any personal criticism, followed by attempts to ensure that students give the correct response. Insist that your students give some response, even "I don't know," so that both you and your students have overt behavior as a guide to appropriate follow-up. Be careful about the use of praise, which research has shown to be carelessly employed by many teachers (Brophy, 1981).

Teacher praise, as a function of teacher effectiveness, has recently received mixed reviews as a means of facilitating student achievement. Praise has a more intense meaning than feedback, conveying as it does an affective commitment by the instructor; in other words we go beyond "that's right" to "right, good thinking, John; keep up the good work." Examining the praise research, Brophy and Good (1986) found that teacher praise usually is infrequent, noncontingent (not always based on a student's appropriate behavior), global rather than specific, and determined more by students' personal qualities than by students' achievement. To help you in your use of praise, consider the guidelines for the effective use of praise as presented in Table 12.2.

- *Context-specific effects.* The third category of effective teaching behaviors is referred to as context-specific effects and includes aspects of the environment as well as student characteristics. There are three critical context-specifics effects.

  a. *Grade level.* In the early grades, classroom management entails considerable instruction in

"Excellent Communication skills. Poor choice of words."

© Martha F. Campbell.

rules and procedures, basic skills, and overt student participation. These techniques change with increasing grade level, where overt participation is less important than teacher clarity, enthusiasm, and a well-structured classroom.

  b. *Student socioeconomic status (SES), ability and affect.* Students of lower socioeconomic status (SES) and/or low ability often benefit most from structured instruction, considerable feedback and redundancy, and information provided in smaller steps. These students also achieve at a higher level in an atmosphere in which they feel comfortable and secure.

  c. *Teachers' intentions/objectives.* The best way to summarize this category is to state that appropriate instruction varies with objectives. What do these findings mean for you? As we have seen, achievement is influenced by the amount of time that students spend engaged with appropriate academic tasks. Also, studies of direct instruction indicate that students learn more efficiently when you structure new information for them and help relate it to what they already know, and then monitor their performance and provide corrective feedback during recitation, drill, practice, and application activities (Brophy, 1986). (See Table 12.3 for a summary of the three categories.)

Table 12.2

Guidelines for Effective Praise

Effective Praise	Ineffective Praise
1. Is delivered contingently	1. Is delivered randomly or unsystematically
2. Specifies the particulars of the accomplishment	2. Is restricted to global positive reactions
3. Shows spontaneity, variety, and other signs of credibility; suggests clear attention to the student's accomplishment	3. Shows a bland uniformity, which suggests a conditioned response made with minimal attention
4. Rewards attainment of specified performance criteria (which can include effort criteria, however)	4. Rewards mere participation, without consideration of performance processes or outcomes
5. Provides information to students about their competence or the value of their accomplishments	5. Provides no information at all or gives students information about their status
6. Orients students towards better appreciation of their own task-related behavior and thinking about problem solving	6. Orients students toward comparing themselves with others and thinking about competing
7. Uses students' own prior accomplishments as the context for describing present accomplishments	7. Uses the accomplishments of peers as the context for describing students' present accomplishments
8. Is given in recognition of noteworthy effort or success at difficult (for *this* student) tasks	8. Is given without regard to the effort expended or the meaning of the accomplishment (for *this* student)
9. Attributes success to effort and ability, implying that similar successes can be expected in the future	9. Attributes success to ability alone or to external factors such as luck or easy task
10. Fosters endogenous attributions (students believe that they expend effort on the task because they enjoy the task and/or want to develop task-relevant skills)	10. Fosters exogenous attributions (students believe that they expend effort on the task for external reasons—to please the teacher, win a competition or reward, etc.)
11. Focuses students' attention on their own task-relevant behavior	11. Focuses students' attention on the teacher as an external authority figure who is manipulating them
12. Fosters appreciation of and desirable attributions about task relevant behavior after the process is completed	12. Intrudes into the ongoing process, distracting attention from task relevant behavior

From Jere Brophy, "Teacher Praise: A Functional Analysis" in *Review of Educational Research,* Spring 1981, 51, pages 5–32. Copyright 1981 by the American Educational Research Association. Reprinted by permission of the publisher.

Teaching and Subject Matter

Along with these ideas about good teaching is the need to be confident about the subject you are teaching. Shulman (1986) distinguished three types of content knowledge: subject matter knowledge, pedagogical knowledge, and curriculum.

Subject matter knowledge refers to a teacher's comprehension of a subject when compared to that of a specialist. How comfortable am I with this subject? Can I answer students' questions accurately and in a relaxed manner?

Pedagogical knowledge refers to how the basic principles and strategies of a subject are best acquired and retained. Am I sufficiently prepared in this subject to know the best way to introduce it? What is the best way to teach its core elements? What is the best way to evaluate my students?

Curriculum knowledge refers to the optimal manner in which knowledge of a subject can be best organized and presented—in texts, programs, media, and workbooks. Am I aware of the supplementary materials that can broaden my students' knowledge of this subject?

For example, let's assume that you are teaching one of Faulkner's stories and that students are having difficulty. What do you do? Do you turn to the story and attempt to clarify themes, or do you search for an outside interpretation?

Does your knowledge of a subject affect the manner in which you teach it? Subject matter knowledge can work in two ways. If you feel shaky about material, you may attempt to brush by it quickly. Conversely, if you have depth of knowledge, you may do too much with your students.

Table 12.3

Teaching Behaviors that Affect Student Achievement: A Summary

Category	Meaning
Quantity and pacing of instruction	1. Content covered 2. Role definition, expectations, time allocations 3. Classroom management—student-engaged time 4. Consistent success—academic learning time 5. Active teaching
Quality of Instruction	1. Giving information 2. Questioning students 3. Reacting to student response 4. Other correlates (homework, emotional climate)
Context-specific effects	1. Grade level 2. Student SES, ability, affect 3. Teachers' intentions, objectives

In attempting to answer the question of how much and what should teachers know of what they teach, researchers are just beginning the task of unraveling teacher cognition. Shulman's three categories help us to discover where teachers turn when students experience difficulty, and if differences in the knowledge that students bring to a subject produce differences in the way that they organize that topic.

Nevertheless, it all comes down to one fundamental question: *How much and what should teachers know of what they teach* (Shulman, 1986, p. 26)? The best advice is to know as much as possible about your subject, present it as dynamically as possible, and be prepared to answer all kinds of questions about what you teach.

What does all of this mean for you? You should remember one guiding principle: *Your task is to help your students learn as much as their potential permits.* To help you comprehend the relevance of the remaining work of this chapter, here are several principles of learning proposed by Bower and Hilgard (1981) that have direct instructional implications.

- Be sure you know what you want to accomplish; that is, keep clearly defined objectives in sight at all times (see chapter 10).

Focus on Classrooms

The Instructional Environment

Many educational psychologists have turned their attention toward a more complete understanding of the instructional environment than has been possible in the past. In fact, methods have been devised to measure specific components of the instructional environment. One of these techniques is the *TIES* or *The Instructional Environment Scale* developed by Ysseldyke and Christenson (1987) at the University of Minnesota. Teachers and other school professionals can use the scale to aid them in designing effective instruction in their classroom. A teacher can work with colleagues or can request the assistance of a master or resource teacher or psychologist to better understand their contribution to the instructional environment. Basically, the TIES assesses various domains of instruction in the classroom.

Twelve components were selected for inclusion in the TIES, and they are presented in Box Figure 12.1. The twelve components are said to be relevant across different types of classrooms (e.g. regular and special education) and across different grades (e.g. K through high school).

The meaning of each of the twelve components is as follows:

1. *Instructional presentation.* Instructional presentation greatly influences quality teaching with lesson development being most important.
2. *Classroom environment.* Effective classroom management, which incorporates behavioral rules and organizational routines, is essential to quality teaching.
3. *Teacher expectations.* Teachers should have high academic expectations and accountability for academic performance for their students; they should also make these standards clear to students.
4. *Cognitive emphasis.* By cognitive emphasis, the authors mean that students should understand how to solve problems and how to approach a task.
5. *Motivational strategies.* Effective instruction depends upon motivated instructional lessons or other strategies (e.g. praise).
6. *Relevant practice.* Two types of practice are necessary, controlled (guided) and independent (seat work), which must be present to promote student achievement; practice must be on appropriate tasks.
7. *Academic engaged time.* The time that students spend engaged in learning predicts academic achievement moderately; other components noted above are designed to increase academic engaged time.

8. *Informed feedback.* Feedback that is task specific and explicit as well as that which provides students with increased opportunity to respond is important to student achievement.

9. *Adaptive instruction.* Based on application with handicapped children, adaptive instruction that incorporates clearly communicated instructional goals at an appropriate difficulty level, careful monitoring of feedback, a comprehensive feedback system, and student responsibility for task completion have all been found to increase student achievement.

10. *Progress evaluation.* Monitoring student performance with the explicit purpose of providing student correction opportunities and time needed to achieve mastery all aid student achievement.

11. *Instructional planning.* It is essential that the teacher match student characteristics with the instruction delivered in the classroom.

12. *Student understanding.* Student's accurate perception of tasks and directions is critical for increasing engaged time and achievement.

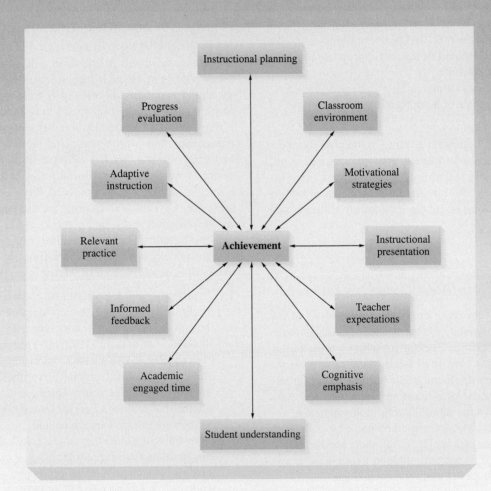

Box Figure 12.1
Important components of an instructional environment as conceptualized in The Instructional Environment Scale.

- Recognize the stages in any task that are necessary for mastery. If you know your subject, you are aware of the sequence of the content that students need to progress at their level. For example, students can't do long division until they can add, subtract, and do short division.
- Encourage as much student activity as possible. Student involvement may range from reading a text with comprehension to class discussion of research projects.
- Provide reinforcement, but be sure it is both specific and deserved. Students need encouragement; just be sure it is appropriate, and don't use praise carelessly.
- Be on guard against student anxiety, which can result from many causes. Constantly monitor the classroom atmosphere so that it remains challenging but not overwhelming. Remember that tried-and-true cliche—match the mix; that is, use teaching techniques and materials that are appropriate for the level of your students.
- Teach for understanding.
- Encourage the use of learning strategies (see chapter 9).

As you proceed with your reading, remember these established principles and keep these questions in mind: Will they help me teach more effectively and my students learn better? Which teaching theories and models best fit my teaching style, the level of my students, and the subject(s) I teach?

Instructional Theory and Design

Instructional theory represents a detailed analysis of the personalities involved, while instructional design concentrates on the steps needed to achieve a particular learning objective. We shall begin with those theorists who have made significant contributions to our understanding of the teaching-learning interaction and who have also made what amounts to a philosophical statement about their views of human nature, especially how we learn: Jerome Bruner, B. F. Skinner, and Benjamin Bloom. Then we'll turn our attention to two leading exponents of instructional design: Robert Gagne and Susan Markle.

Bruner and Instructional Theory

In a wide-ranging series of essays from the cognitive perspective, Bruner (1960, 1966b, 1971) has afforded us penetrating insights into both **inquiry teaching** and learning. Examining the classroom functions of the instructor, he sees three sources of teacher behavior. *First,* teachers are communicators of knowledge, which implies mastery of both the knowledge to be communicated and the effective methods of its communication; you must know what to teach and how to teach it. *Second,* teachers are models; they should be competent and exciting individuals who will inspire in students a love of learning. Your behavior in the classroom is an important source of knowledge, guidance, and motivation for your students. We saw this clearly demonstrated in Bandura's work on modeling in chapters 4 and 10. *Third,* teachers are symbols, the immediate representative of "education," and can be particularly persuasive figures in shaping a youth's attitudes, interests, opinions, and values, let alone intellectual achievement.

Principles of Instructional Theory

Bruner noted that learning is closely linked to cognitive structures, readiness, motivation, and interaction with the environment. He raised the question: Since psychology already contains theories of learning and development, why is a theory of instruction needed? His answer is that theories of learning and development are *descriptive rather than prescriptive;* that is, they tell us what happened after the fact. For example, from Piaget's theory we know a child of six usually has not achieved the cognitive ability of reversibility. A theory of instruction prescribes how teachers can help a child acquire it. What are the materials and what are the methods best suited to help these students move to a higher cognitive level?

Bruner believes that there are four elements in any theory of instruction or inquiry teaching. These are:

1. The theory should specify those experiences that *predispose* a youngster toward learning. What is there in the classroom or materials that will make students want to learn? How can I get my students to want to learn long division?
2. The theory should clearly delineate the structure of any subject to aid learning. Teachers must determine whether the subject is best presented enactively (you might want preschoolers to actually mix the ingredients of a cake they are to bake), that is, by emphasizing psychomotor learning; iconically (show a picture of a Civil War battlefield and ask your students to picture a row of Confederate soldiers behind the stone wall), by using images and other visuals to represent concepts; or symbolically, that is by using rules, logic, and propositions. Here you act as a decision maker; deciding whether the materials and methods are appropriate for a youngster's developmental level.

3. The theory should specify the *optimal sequence* for presenting materials. Is it always better to proceed from concrete to abstract, simple to complex, part to whole? Or is it better to present the entire structure and then fill in pieces? Since teachers must lead students through a predetermined sequence, they again act as decision makers. Your decision may have a powerful influence on the ease or difficulty with which a student learns.

4. The theory should specify the *nature and pacing of rewards and punishments.* Learning depends on knowledge of results, and the theory should indicate where, when, and under what circumstance correction and praise occur. Teachers then become actively engaged in instructing students to use error and to apply information correctly.

Bruner concluded that a theory of instruction must accept that a curriculum reflects the nature of knowledge, the nature of the learner, and the learning process. To be successful, a teaching theory must erase the lines of distinction between these three dimensions. The theory should have as its ultimate goal teaching students to participate in the entire process of acquiring and using knowledge.

The Scope of Teaching

One of Bruner's major assumptions is that teaching is an effort to assist growth. He believes that intellectual growth has several discernible characteristics.

*   *Increasing independence of a response from an immediate stimulus distinguishes mental growth.* We can predict much of young children's behavior from knowing the stimuli around them. As students grow mentally, they are able to maintain a desired response, although conditions (stimuli) change. A good example is the ability to give the right response in a multiple-choice examination—students maintain the response in spite of assorted stimuli.
*   *Students also can change their responses to meet unchanging environmental demands.* For example, if an answer is incorrect, and students know it is incorrect, they change their answer (response) to the same question (stimulus).
*   *Intellectual growth depends upon a student's mental construction of a model of the world.* (Recall Piaget's insistence on "operations" to form psychological structures.) The child actively constructs a mental picture of the world. Building this mental image of the world permits a student to use the information to compare, judge, and predict. It is similar to Piaget's explanation of a child's ability to go from the real to the possible.

*   *Developing skill in symbolic activity features intellectual development.* Youngsters can say what they have done or will do; they begin to use propositions or statements and thus reflect a logicomathematical capacity that did not previously exist.
*   *Intellectual development depends on a close interaction between a teacher and a learner.* There are many tutors in a child's environment—school teachers, fathers, mothers, friends, heroes—and considerable uncertainty exists about the details of the different relationships. For example, different individuals possess different personalities and thus do things differently. Is the relationship between a permissive teacher and students radically different from the relationship between a firm teacher and students? What is the ideal learning environment for these two examples? Are they identical?
*   *Finally, intellectual development is marked by increasing competence in attending to several possibilities.* For example, in Piaget's conservation experiments, when youngsters are no longer distracted by the length or width of the glass but realize that the liquid remains intact, they are attending to several things.

Bruner and the Process of Education

Bruner developed four major themes in analyzing learning: structure, readiness, intuition, and motivation.

Understanding a subject's structure is central to Bruner's thinking. The first object of any act of learning, over and beyond the pleasure it may give, is that it should serve us in the future. Learning should not only take us somewhere, but it should also allow us later to go further more easily (Bruner, 1960, p. 17).

As Bruner noted, grasping a subject's structure is understanding it so that many other things can be related to it meaningfully—to learn structure is to learn how things are related. Students can grasp a subject's structure only if they understand its basic ideas. The more basic the idea that students learn, the more they can apply it to other topics. If students understand a subject's fundamental structure, the subject itself becomes more comprehensible, aids memory, facilitates transfer, and helps to build the "spiral curriculum." For example, identifying and understanding the causes of the Civil War can help your students to look beyond the names of the battles in any other war they study.

The **spiral curriculum** *is closely linked to Bruner's second theme—readiness—*and is an excellent example of an attempt to develop structure. For example, World War II has become a major topic in contemporary history. Using the principles of the spiral curriculum, students learn about WW II at successively higher grade levels in

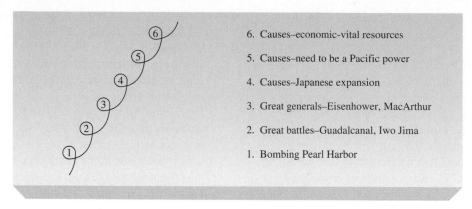

6. Causes–economic–vital resources

5. Causes–need to be a Pacific power

4. Causes–Japanese expansion

3. Great generals–Eisenhower, MacArthur

2. Great battles–Guadalcanal, Iwo Jima

1. Bombing Pearl Harbor

Figure 12.2
The spiral curriculum illustrated with an example—content concerning World War II.

an increasingly abstract manner. Figure 12.2 illustrates the process. Note the increasing abstraction and complexity of the presentation. Completing their study, students should have a good grasp of the subject.

His famous statement that any subject can be taught effectively in some intellectually honest form to any child at any stage of development implies that the basic ideas of science, mathematics, and literature are as simple as they are powerful. If teachers begin teaching the foundations of these subjects in an appropriate manner consistent with students' intellectual level, as described by Piaget, students can learn important basics at any stage of mental development. Then, by applying the principles of the spiral curriculum, they can steadily proceed to more complex forms of the subject.

Once students obtain a detailed knowledge of a subject, they can begin to expand their hypothetical abilities; that is, they can make an informed guess. Knowing a topic deeply and widely enables them to proceed by implicit perception; they can grasp something without detailed analysis. They can make their informed guess and then subject it to critical analysis, thus fostering both problem-solving and creative behavior. Understanding the geography and history of the countries of Eastern Europe can help students speculate about the reasons for their independence movements.

Motivation is Bruner's final indispensable learning ingredient. He questions the value of excessive emphasis upon examinations, grades, and promotions with respect to a desirable lifetime commitment to learning. Children always have mixed motives for learning: pleasing parents and teachers, competing with peers, and acquiring a sense of self-mastery. Inspiring intrinsic motivation is difficult in children, so Bruner realistically states that, if you teach well and what you teach is worth learning,

forces at work in our society will provide the external prod to have students become more involved in their learning processes.

Modes of Representation

How can these ideas of Bruner's help us in teaching? Bruner believes that if teachers understand the mental stages that a child passes through, they can adapt their teaching accordingly. He calls these **modes of representation.** The first level is the **enactive** mode of representation. The infant knows the world only by acting on it; otherwise the object does not exist. As Bruner notes, even in an adult's life, there are times when words simply cannot express what is meant (1966, p. 10). For example, how can you tell someone about the "feel of" the golf or tennis swing?

The second level is the **iconic** mode of representation, Bruner's expression for perceptual organization. When we face a series of apparently unrelated tasks, discovering a pattern makes the work easier. Word problems are a good example. Once students see the steps necessary to solve the problem (the pattern), the problem then becomes more realistic and easier to solve.

The third level is the **symbolic** mode of representation. Here the child engages in symbolic activities, such as language and mathematics. Bruner (1966, p. 14) stated that when children translate experience into language, they enter the world of possibilities, enabling them to solve problems and engage in creative thinking.

Students learn according to their mode of representation, and for Bruner, learning a subject involves three almost simultaneous processes: acquisition of new information, transformation, and evaluation.

• *Acquisition of new information,* which replaces or expands what the student already knows, is the initial phase. Here the child incorporates environmental stimuli according to the existing mode of representation: by physical action, by forming images, or by abstracting, comparing, and judging. Before students can understand the surge toward freedom and independence among the countries of Eastern Europe, they must know the history of these countries, especially since World War II.

- *Transformation* is the second phase. Once youngsters or adults acquire new information, then they must manipulate or change it to meet new tasks. Bruner often uses the illustration, *going beyond the information given.* For example, your friend passes by the door and says, "Hi, Janie." You do not see her, but immediately think, "There goes Liz." You manipulated verbal stimuli to form the idea of your friend.
- *Evaluation* is the final phase. Have they successfully manipulated the information? Was it adequate? Correct?

Bruner joins mental growth, modes of representation, and learning processes to support his idea of the spiral curriculum. He stated (1960) that if teachers respect a student's thinking process and translate material into meaningful units (that is, if they match the subject matter to the student's mode of representation), they can introduce great ideas to children at different times and with increasing abstractness. For example, freedom discussed in the first grade differs from a junior high school discussion of slavery, which differs from a high school discussion of the meaning of the Constitution—hence the spiral curriculum.

Bruner also makes specific teaching recommendations, especially those relating to the continued use of discovery teaching and learning (Wilcox, 1987). He noted that there are many mechanical aids for teachers (films, tv, programmed instruction), but that the chief facilitator of learning remains the teacher. If you believe in cognitive learning principles, consider the following:

First, if you desire to teach effectively, you must master the material to be taught. (There probably is no better way to learn a subject than to teach it.) *Second,* remember that you are a model. Unimaginative, uninspiring, and insecure teachers are hardly likely to spark a love of learning, especially since students quickly sense a lack of commitment. *Third,* as a model, you will find that students will identify with you and often compare themselves with you. It is a sobering thought, but it can motivate you to search constantly for ways to better your teaching and furnish a stimulating classroom atmosphere.

Focus on Classrooms

Teaching and Learning: Bruner in the Classroom

Bruner described a junior high school course he taught that illustrates these principles (1966b, p. 109). One unit related Caesar's decision to cross the Rubicon and drive for Rome. The class had Caesar's commentaries, nothing about his opponent Pompey, and some letters from Cicero. The class immediately divided into Caesarians and Pompeyans and tried to obtain more information about strategy. Would Caesar move his army through a narrow valley unless he had previous reassurance that the inhabitants were friendly? Bruner states that the students reasoned like politicians.

One group of troublesome students provided an excellent analysis of the corrupt Roman political system and sympathized totally with Caesar. Pompey "had no guts." When these students compared Romans to current politicians and equated Roman governmental problems with current difficulties, the course came alive.

Here you see an excellent example of theory translated into practice. Remember: Bruner believes that any act of learning involves three processes:

1. *The acquisition of new information.* What was the political situation in the valley?
2. *Transformation, or manipulation,* of existing knowledge to make it fit new tasks. Was the Roman political situation similar to contemporary American politics?
3. *Evaluation,* or determining if the manipulated knowledge is adequate. Does understanding and applying current information help to comprehend the Roman issues?

Learning occurred that reflected what had gone before it and that permitted generalization beyond it. Anyone at any age is ready to learn; allow children to explore and make educated guesses; allow them to make mistakes; teach them the structure of a subject, not minute and isolated facts.

Skinner and the Technology of Teaching

You previously examined Skinner's presentation of instrumental learning in chapter 6. Now we'll follow his theoretical beliefs into the classroom and see how he has steadfastly applied the principles of operant conditioning to both learning and teaching, a procedure called **programmed instruction.**

Recall that Skinner argued that teachers depend too heavily upon punishment while neglecting their use of positive reinforcement. Arguing that there are special techniques to arrange contingencies of reinforcement—the relationship between behavior and the consequences of that behavior—Skinner stated that teachers now can effectively control behavior. This assumption is the basis of operant conditioning (Skinner, 1968).

Skinner in the Classroom

In education—where control of behavior is critical—Skinner believed all is chaos. As an example, he turns to one of his favorite subjects: the teaching of arithmetic. Here the responses are verbal—speaking and writing figures, words, and signs—and it is necessary to bring them under stimulus control. How do teachers accomplish this? They should use reinforcers, which traditionally has meant reliance on negative consequences. Skinner noted that although yesterday's physical punishment is mostly gone, teachers still rely too much on sarcasm, ridicule, and low marks. So arithmetic, as most subjects, becomes mired in a maze of dislike, anxiety, and, ultimately, boredom.

Improvement is possible since there are general characteristics of teaching that, if practiced, cultivate both teaching and learning. These would include the following (Skinner, 1968, p. 199):

- *Define the* **terminal behavior.** Decide what students should be able to do after your teaching. Proclaiming the citizen enlightened is both inadequate and unworthy; it does not describe behavior. "Knowledge" is another deceptive goal of education. Students have learned something when they behave; that is, they respond to stimuli differently than they did before instruction. Students "know" when teachers can specifically identify their behavior; that is, teachers have taught them to behave in certain ways. What they know is what they do, so teachers must objectively and concretely state their objectives.
- *Solve the problem of the* **first instance.** Once you have determined the terminal behavior (what you want students to do after teaching), you must strengthen it by reinforcement. But you cannot reinforce what does not appear. The problem of the first instance means that students must exhibit some aspect of the desired behavior. One option is to induce it, such as physically taking a child's hand and guiding it to form letters. Another option is to have students imitate the teacher or some example of excellent work. Simply telling students what to do and then reinforcing them when they do it is yet another possibility. Learning, however, does not

occur because you have primed the behavior; it occurs only when behavior is reinforced. The above examples are only the first step in the process.
- *Decide what you will use to prompt behavior.* One reinforcement will hardly free a response from priming stimuli. When do you stop priming students? If you continue too long, you are inefficient; if you stop too soon, you may cause error. Use only as much as is necessary. For example, you may wish students to be able to identify the Midwestern states, their major cities, and principal industries. You may begin by using maps and reading materials. Some cities may be near water and be port cities. Later, when students should know which cities do what, you may ask them to locate the city without using maps or texts. You have supplied a prompt, which is part of the original priming behavior.
- *Program complex behavior.* Priming and prompting evoke a behavior to be reinforced in the presence of required stimuli. But some behavior is so complex that you cannot reinforce it as a unit. You must program it, which does not mean teaching one thing at a time as a collection of responses. What a student does halfway through a program may not be a part of the terminal behavior. Small steps are needed to insure constant reinforcement.
- *Decide not only the proper size but the most effective sequence of steps for your program.* You must insure not only an orderly arrangement of steps but also that students are properly prepared for each step. You cannot always depend upon a subject's inherent logic. A good example is our work with Piaget. Usually students are well-advised to read original sources and trace the author's work. This may not work with Piaget because his ideas are so complex and his writing so tortuous that students, proceeding logically, may become hopelessly confused. Instructors are better advised to select basic ideas and test them before presenting the entire system. For example, you should understand Piaget's notion of the functional invariants before you plunge into his theory of cognitive development.

An example that reflects many of these principles is the highly structured Bereiter-Englemann program, designed to prescribe teaching procedures for disadvantaged children. The authors (1966) stated that new teachers like to work with "ideas." Good teaching, however, uses much smaller and more intricate units than ideas; it involves specific information modules and specific techniques. Teaching is the interplay between information, pace, discipline, rewards, and drama as they relate to curriculum (1966, p. 105).

Acquiring these techniques comes gradually—a motivational trick here, an attention-getting device there. Bereiter and Englemann believed that teachers are good not because of what they are but because of what they do. Good teachers do the "right thing" because they have learned slowly, even painfully. They were not naturally proficient; they achieved proficiency through practice.

Here are some of Bereiter and Englemann's teaching strategies. They are intended for use in an intensive preschool program for disadvantaged children, but they have broad applicability.

• *Be careful when you vary your presentation methods.* Variations may confuse the culturally disadvantaged child who ordinarily experiences considerable language difficulty. Excessive variation bothers and bewilders all children who need to feel psychologically secure in the classroom. Still, youngsters, disadvantaged or not, must respond in a variety of situations and should be ready to respond to variation outside the classroom. The authors' suggestion is pertinent, but remember: Consider variation in relation to the readiness of your students.

• *Give children sufficient time to respond.* Time has been a recurring theme in this text. You previously encountered it in Bloom's work on mastery learning and in Martin's analysis of praise. Here Bereiter and Englemann urge that the lesson's tempo be such that the youngster can respond thoughtfully.

• *Use questions liberally.* Questions are important because they help a child to attend to relevant cues. You must consider the question's difficulty: Is the child capable of answering it? The value of questioning is clear from countless studies: Subjects tend to remember more about the material on which they are questioned, and they retain it longer. The direct instructional effect of questioning is substantial.

•*Use multiple examples.* When presenting a new concept, avoid talking too much about it. The authors advise that you "stretch" the concept; that is, if you are teaching the concept of "red," give numerous examples of different objects, sizes, shapes, all of which are different with one exception—the color red.

•*As far as possible, prevent incorrect responses.* Helping children avoid error will help them to avoid mistake patterns. Always assume that children will repeat mistakes in similar situations and try to forestall them. Use prevention techniques.

•*Be clear in responding to correct and incorrect answers.* If a child brings a blue crayon when asked to bring a red, do not praise the youngster for

The use of time in the classroom is a critical element in effective teaching and effective learning.

bringing a crayon. Youngsters cannot understand the subtle distinction. Teachers should provide nonthreatening but clear feedback. This suggestion is similar to warnings about nonpertinent praise. Bereiter and Englemann furnish several more suggestions that indicate the nature of the program: carefully controlled stimuli, judicious application of reinforcement, and the avoidance of error. The Bereiter-Englemann program is an example of behavioral principles put to action.

Some recent work derived from the Bereiter-Englemann program that has focused on curricular interventions has been applied to all students with great promise, especially with regard to higher order thinking skills (Carnine, 1991). Table 12.4 presents research that may close the gap between special and regular education and, as Carnine (1991) argues, should encourage educators to teach higher order thinking skills in reasoning, science, and problem solving through curricular interventions.

Bloom and School Learning

Benjamin Bloom's ideas on learning have received the careful attention of psychologists and educators. Bloom, long a leader in American education and a fervent advocate of educational research guiding classroom policy, has devised an explanation of school learning that is a sophisticated mix of theory and research. Noting that educational research has moved in new directions, Bloom (1981) stated that recent studies have shifted from analyzing teacher and student characteristics to direct observation of the interactions between the two. Bloom, however, believes that the most important change is the movement away

Table 12.4

Research on Closing the Gap between Special Education and General Education Students

Reasoning

1. On a variety of measures of argument construction and critiquing, high school students with mild handicaps in a higher-order-thinking intervention scored as high as or higher than high school students in an honors English class and college students enrolled in a teacher certification program (Grossen & Carnine, 1990b).

2. In constructing arguments, high school students with learning disabilities in a higher-order-thinking intervention scored significantly higher than college students enrolled in a teacher certification program and scored at the same level as general education high school students and college students enrolled in a logic course. In critiquing arguments, the students with learning disabilities scored at the same level as the general education high school students and the college students enrolled in a teacher certification program. All of these groups had scores significantly lower than those of the college students enrolled in a logic course (Collins & Carnine, 1988).

Understanding Science Concepts

1. High school students with learning disabilities were mainstreamed for a higher-order-thinking intervention in science. On a chemistry test that required applying concepts such as bonding, equilibrium, energy of activation, atomic structure, and organic compounds, the students' scores did not differ significantly from control students' in an advanced placement chemistry course (Hofmeister, Englemann, & Carnine, 1989).

2. Middle school students with learning disabilities were mainstreamed for a higher-order-thinking intervention in science. On a test of misconceptions in earth science, the students showed better conceptual understanding than Harvard graduates interviewed in Schnep's 1987 film, *A Private Universe* (Muthukrishna, Carnine, Grossen, & Miller, 1990).

Problem Solving

1. On a test of problem solving in health promotion, high school students with mild handicaps in a higher-order-thinking intervention scored significantly higher than nonhandicapped students who had completed a traditional high school health class (Woodward, Carnine, & Gersten, 1988).

2. Middle school students with learning disabilities were mainstreamed for a higher-order-thinking intervention in science. On a test of earth science problem solving, the students scored significantly higher than nonhandicapped students who received traditional science instruction (Woodward & Noell, this series).

3. High school special education students were mainstreamed for a higher-order-thinking intervention in math. On a test of problem solving requiring the use of ratios and proportions, the students scored as well as nonhandicapped high school students who received traditional math instruction (Moore & Carnine, 1989).

4. Middle school students with mild handicaps were mainstreamed for a higher-order-thinking intervention in earth science. Most of the students with handicaps scored higher than the nonhandicapped control students in problem solving involving earth science content (Niedelman, 1991).

From "Curricular Interventions for Teaching Higher Order Thinking to all Students: Introduction to the Special Series" by D. Carnine, 1991, in *Journal of Learning Disabilities*, Vol. No. 24, pp.261–269. Copyright 1991 by PRO-ED, Inc. Reprinted by permission.

from studying fixed variables toward analyzing more productive variables such as the following:

- **Time-on-task.** Time has always been recognized as a critical factor in learning, whether it is years a subject appears in a curriculum, number of days in the school year, number of hours per day, or the number of minutes per class. These are relatively fixed times, which tell us little about how much time students are actively engaged in learning. As Bloom stated (1981, p. 3), if one student is actively engaged 90 percent of the time as opposed to 30 percent for another student,

we should not be surprised at different achievement levels. Time-on-task appears to be closely related to quality of instruction and prerequisite knowledge. Bloom stresses that time-on-task can be altered.

Working from an applied perspective, Gettinger (1990) identified three aspects of learning time that could be increased: first is the time used for instruction; second is engaged time; and the third is productive learning time. Table 12.5 summarizes the methods Gettinger reviewed that have been found to increase the various aspects of time.

Table 12.5

Best Practices to Increase Academic Learning Time

Increase time used for instruction:
Establish contingencies for school attendance and
      punctuality.
Minimize interruptions.
Program for smooth transitions.
Maintain an academic focus.

Increase engaged time:
Clarity instructions and expectations regarding
      performance.
Keep instruction fast-paced.
Maintain an interactive teaching style and frequent
      student responding.
Adopt seating arrangements to maximize attending.

Increase productive learning time:
Use seatwork effectively.
Provide immediate, appropriate feedback.
Diagnose, prescribe, and monitor performance
      accurately.

From Maribeth Gettinger, *Best Practices—II*. Copyright 1990 by the National Association of School Psychologists. Reprinted by permission of the publisher.

• *Intelligence versus cognitive entry behaviors.*
Although researchers repeatedly have demonstrated a
link between intelligence and aptitude tests and later
achievement, Bloom argues that these findings do not
determine a student's potential for learning. Cognitive
entry characteristics (that knowledge essential for
learning a particular subject) also show a close
relationship with achievement and can be altered.
These characteristics are subject to change because
they contain specific content and skills that can be
learned.

• *Summative versus formative testing.* Although the
customary use of classroom tests has been to measure
a student's achievement at the completion of a block
of work (**summative evaluation**), they have also
long been used to assess the quality of learning as
well as the quality of the learner. **Formative
evaluation,** on the other hand, is primarily intended
to aid in the formation of learning by providing
feedback about what has been learned and what
remains to be learned. Bloom believes that when tests
are used in this manner, the number of students who
achieve mastery increases dramatically, chiefly

because the necessary prerequisite skills have been
identified for each student, student motivation
intensifies, and more time is spent on task.

• *Teacher characteristics versus qualities of teaching.*
Bloom believes that studies devoted to the impact
that teacher characteristics have on student learning
(to be reviewed later in this chapter) have shown
negligible results. More recent studies have focused
on the qualities of teaching (teachers interacting with
students) and shown a direct causal relation with
student learning. Studies of cues (what is to be
learned), reinforcement (rewards for learning), and
participation (active student engagement in learning)
provide valuable clues as to just what teachers are
doing with their time.

• *Parent status versus home environment processes.*
Educators are keenly aware of the influence that
socioeconomic status (SES) exerts on learning.
Knowing about SES, however, adds little to your
ability to aid student achievement. What parents do
when they are interacting with their children is
another story. For example, language in the home
may powerfully affect language and reading in
school. Once you determine this, you can use special
courses, remedial reading materials, and prerequisite
knowledge to change the outcome.

Bloom and Mastery Learning

Mastery learning is probably the key element in
Bloom's work, for it is this goal that all other means are
intended to achieve. As Bloom noted (1981), most teachers begin a school year with the entrenched expectation
that about a third of the students will adequately learn, a
third will pass, and a third will achieve a marginal pass
or fail. Bloom finds this condition one of the most waste-
ful in all of education, especially since he believes that
about 90 percent of all students can learn to mastery if
properly instructed.

• *Aptitude for particular learning.* A few students (1–
5 percent) will show special talent for any subject;
another small group (1-5 percent) will show a special
disability for a given subject, which leaves the
majority 90 percent. Here is the basis for Bloom's
belief that 95 percent of our students can achieve
mastery, some requiring more time, effort, and help
than others.

• *Quality of instruction.* We begin with the
assumption that individual students need individual
instruction to reach mastery. You may argue that
teachers have always attempted to adapt their
teaching to individuals. In a 30 student to 1 teacher
classroom, this goal often remains elusive. We are

beginning to understand how individual differences can be best served in the average classroom. The quality of instruction must be considered in light of individual learners and not groups.

• *Ability to understand instruction.* Do your students understand what they are to learn and how they are to learn it? It is precisely here that student ability interacts with quality of instruction and curricular material. Since our schools are highly verbal, ability to understand is linked to language ability and reading comprehension. Modifying your instruction by using a variety of techniques—tutorial, group, text, media—can benefit their comprehension.

• *Perseverance.* How much time is a student willing to spend in learning? Studies have shown that student perseverance varies from subject to subject. Adapting instruction and using appropriate content have been shown to increase perseverance. Bloom emphasizes the significance of perseverance by commenting on students' variability in the amount of time they are willing to spend on a task. Some students give up quickly on math problems but will work indefinitely on a faulty automobile engine. Bloom also believes that the key to increasing perseverance is appropriately designed instruction and learning materials.

• *Time allowed for learning.* If aptitude determines the rate of learning, then time on task can produce mastery. Bloom believes that some students spend as much as six times longer on homework than others, yet time spent on homework often has little relationship to final grades. Homework with the correct structure and conditions for learning, however, can be quite effective. Teachers can alter the time spent on task by following mastery principles and allowing students the time they need to reach mastery in a particular subject, which in turn depends on aptitude, verbal ability, quality of instruction, and quality of help received outside the school.

If you are to help your students achieve mastery, first be certain what you mean by mastery and know when students reach it. Use formative evaluation techniques as frequently as you think they are needed: divide a subject into meaningful sections, and then construct a diagnostic test to discover if a student has mastered the material. You now know where specific weaknesses lie and what steps students must take to overcome any difficulties.

Not only does Bloom's work on mastery learning recommend itself for its obvious cognitive benefits, but students usually show an increased interest in subject matter, and, perhaps most important of all, an increased sense of self-worth. For example, they do better on teacher-made tests, earn higher grades, and attain higher scores on standardized tests. Their retention and transfer of material learned under mastery learning conditions improves substantially (Guskey, 1986).

Teachers also experience positive effects. When they see the improvement in their students' learning, they gain a sense of professional renewal; they feel better about themselves and their work. Teachers tend to see learning as a cooperative venture in which their role is more of a facilitator in helping their students reach the highest level of learning possible for each student (Guskey, 1986).

A Model of School Learning

How can Bloom's basic ideas help to improve classroom learning? Individual differences in learning ability may not be alterable, but individual differences in learning *can* be predicted, explained, and improved. For example, much of the variation in school learning can be traced to environmental conditions in the home and school, both of which are subject to modification if teachers work closely with parents.

Three interdependent variables, which can be phrased as questions, form the foundation of Bloom's theory.

• To what extent has a student learned the necessary prerequisites for the new learning to be attempted?
• To what extent can a student be motivated to engage in the learning process?
• To what extent is instruction appropriate to the learner?

Consequently the theory treats student characteristics, instruction, and learning outcomes (Bloom, 1976b). The student characteristics deemed to be most significant for learning are **cognitive entry behaviors** (the necessary prerequisite skills), and **affective entry characteristics** (motivation to learn new material). **Quality of instruction,** as we have seen, refers to needed cues, practice, and reinforcement. Learning outcomes can be designated by level and type of achievement, rate of learning, and affective results. The interaction of these variables can be seen in Figure 12.3. By *learning task* Bloom means a learning unit in a course, a chapter in a textbook, or some topic in the curriculum. Such a task usually takes from one to five hours to master.

Cognitive entry behavior is the prerequisite learning needed for mastery of new tasks and, as such, represents one aspect of a student's history. Though it is possible that all the students have had an opportunity to acquire the prerequisite learning, and it is even possible that all the students did acquire it, the critical point is the availability of the prerequisite learning at the time it is required in the

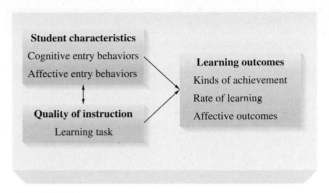

Figure 12.3
Bloom's theory of school learning.

specific new learning task (Bloom, 1976, p. 33). That is, the student remembers and can use these prior learnings when and where they are required in a specific new task. (How much of the background of the Eastern European countries does a student bring to an analysis of the independence movement?)

Cognitive entry behaviors fall into two categories: those that are *specific* for a specific subject (addition, subtraction, and multiplication are necessary prerequisites for division), and those that are *general,* such as verbal ability and reading comprehension. Both types of entry behaviors are alterable.

Affective entry characteristics refer to the differences among students in what they are emotionally prepared to learn as expressed in their interests, attitudes, and self-views (Bloom, 1976b, p. 74). All students have different histories that color their reactions to a specific subject and to school in general. A brother or sister may have been unhappy in school or disliked a particular teacher. Such feelings often affect younger students.

Especially interesting in Bloom's analysis of affect is the notion of age-change: correlations between affect toward school and achievement in a particular subject is relatively low up to grade five but increases sharply at the junior and senior high levels. Bloom estimates that affect toward school will account for as much as 25 percent of the variation in achievement. Again affect toward both school and subject can be altered.

As indicated earlier, Bloom's interest lies in teaching and not the teacher; thus his analysis of quality of instruction focuses on the interactions that occur in the classroom. Cognitive entry behaviors and affective entry characteristics can account for about 65 percent of the achievement variation on a new learning task.

Bloom believes that quality of instruction can do little to overcome the input of cognitive entry behaviors unless it is remedial, which is not usually the case. Affective

entry characteristics can be altered by the quality of instruction, and, in spite of the significant contribution made by cognitive entry behaviors, quality of instruction can have a powerful effect on learning a particular task.

We can perhaps best conclude Bloom's excellent analysis of school learning by noting that with this system most students become quite similar with regard to learning ability, rate of learning, and motivation for further learning when provided with favorable learning conditions (Bloom, 1981, p. 135).

The three theorists—Bruner, Skinner, and Bloom—have examined teaching from a definite theoretical perspective that led them to formulate a specific instructional theory. Each of them has much to offer, and you probably would be well-advised to take from each theorist those aspects that are best suited for your beliefs and objectives. That is, you may analyze a task from a cognitive perspective, but yet you can find much to use in the work of Skinner concerning the best means of using reinforcement, or in Bloom's concern about cognitive entry behavior. To help you separate and compare the various components of these theories, see Table 12.6.

The Design of Instruction

As you read the accounts of the preceding theories, you probably became aware that each theorist attempted to relate ideas of teaching and instructional outcomes to definite views of how students develop and learn. This perceived relationship defines a particular instructional theory. The instructional design explanations follow a different path. They are intended to identify efficient procedures by which instruction may be designed. These models begin with needs assessment and specify a number of steps to reach a predetermined goal.

Reigeluth (1983) defined instructional design quite simply: concern with understanding, improving and applying methods of instruction. The relationship between instruction and its component parts can be visualized as the five interrelated and interdependent aspects of instruction seen in Figure 12.4.

Since the remainder of the chapter is devoted to specific and highly objective components of teaching, keep in mind the instructional theories just discussed. Try to fit the more practical design aspects you will read about into your own theoretical framework. As mentioned, you can be quite eclectic in so doing, but you should be consistent. One of a beginning teacher's major causes of discipline problems is switching from a tightly controlled technique to a policy of discovery and variation, without first preparing the students. Remember: Changes in classroom conditions cause changes in behavior.

Table 12.6

Instructional Theories—A Summary

Name	Basis	Emphasis	Application
Bruner	Cognitive development	Theoretical base Optimal sequence Structure Modes of representation	Readiness Motivation Acquisition, transformation, evaluation Spiral curriculum
Skinner	Operant conditioning	Defined objectives First instance Sequential steps Controlled responses Reinforcement	Programmed instruction All aspects of behavior
Bloom	Educational research	Alterable variables Mastery learning Entry behaviors Time-on-task Learning outcomes	Prerequisite skills Learning tasks Achievement levels Teaching (not the teacher)

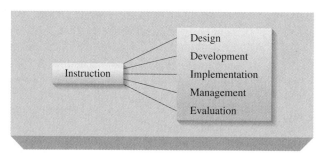

Figure 12.4
Interrelated aspects of instruction.

To help you understand the intricacies of instructional design, the works of Robert Gagne and Susan Markle are presented next.

Gagne and Instructional Design

In 1979, Gagne and Briggs published one of the first major entries in the field of instructional design, *Principles of Instructional Design.* This influential work was based upon Gagne's views of five learning outcomes: *verbal information, intellectual skills, cognitive strategies, attitudes,* and *motor skills.* Each of these five learning outcomes demands a different set of conditions for optimizing learning, retention, and transferability. The

"optimal conditions" refer to a particular set of external events surrounding the learner: The instruction that students receive. Table 12.7 summarizes the meaning of Gagne's learning outcomes.

According to Gagne, instruction determines the extent of a student's learning. There are nine instructional events that Gagne believes occur in an ordered sequence similar to the following:

1. *Gaining attention.* Instruction terminates immediately if attention falters. What you previously read in the learning chapters applies here: Vary stimuli, use a multi-sensory approach, and be sure that stimuli are biologically and psychologically appropriate.
2. *Inform learners of the objective.* What precisely is to be learned? Students should know the criteria for mastery and when they have achieved it. (Note the similarity to Bloom's work we previously discussed.)
3. *Stimulate recall of prerequisites.* Students may need a simple reminder of previous learning, or they might require detailed help. Recall Bloom's emphasis on the importance of *entry* behaviors and their relationship to achievement.
4. *Present the stimulus material.* Use techniques that are as stimulating as possible, whether verbal, demonstrative, or media-related. Make the material

Table 12.7

Gagne's Learning Outcomes

Learning Outcomes	Meaning
Verbal information	Names, facts, generalizations that students can state
Intellectual skills	"Knowing how" rather than "knowing what"—knowledge and use of concepts and rules
Cognitive strategies	Internally organized skills—techniques used to aid attention, learning, remembering, and problem solving
Attitudes	Previous learning that influences choice about behavior
Motor skills	Skillful execution of bodily movements

From R. Gagne and L. Briggs, *Principles of Instructional Design*. Copyright © 1979 Holt Rinehart and Winston, Inc., Orlando, FL.

interesting and pertinent to facilitate attention and to spark inquiry.

5. *Provide learning guidance.* Your task here is to ensure that students acquire the details involved in the learning objective; if a series of steps are needed for mastery, then students must know what these steps are and how to master them. Learn the geography; learn the history; only now speculate about politics.

6. *Elicit the performance.* You cannot be certain that your students have learned unless they perform the behavior. (Recall the discussion at the beginning of the learning section concerning learning versus performance.) Be certain students' behavior is that demanded in the objective. Can your students specify the specific causes of the independence movement?

7. *Provide feedback.* Your reinforcement should be carefully considered. Provide students with accurate, detailed comments or notes about their performance, specifying what was done well and what needs improvement. Does it match a specific response? Is it appropriate for the quality of the response? Again, do not over praise. Finally, check to see if students understand the feedback and are able to use it to improve future performance.

8. *Assess the performance.* Your method of assessment should be well-planned to determine if your students attained the objectives of the work. Assessment of student performance can occur in several ways. Assessment and testing of classroom performance are discussed in detail in chapters 15 and 16.

9. *Enhance retention and transfer.* You simply cannot assume that students will automatically transfer their learning from one class to another; in your instructional plans you must include provisions for both review and the use of the material in novel situations.

Gagne believes that the distinguishing characteristics of this nine-step model generate a new theory of learning and memory. It also utilizes existing theory as a basis for designing instruction and attempts to include all types of learning outcomes that are typically the objectives of instruction. Finally, the model provides an instructional basis for analyzing the interaction of internal events with external events, which makes the model applicable to instruction of many forms in a wide variety of settings.

Markle's Programmed Instruction Model

Adapting Skinner's technology of teaching and yet remaining faithful to the basic principles of operant conditioning, Susan Markle (1978) built her concept of programmed instruction around the principle of active responding. Noting that the programmed instruction movement almost succumbed to its initial success, Markle believes that rigid adherence to these early views—small steps, heavy prompting, verbatim student responses to oft repeated sentences—all contributed to criticism of the system as being excessively sterile.

The Basic Programing Principles

Three programing principles—active responding, errorless learning, and immediate feedback—form the basis of Markle's model of instructional design (Markle, 1978).

The Principle of Active Responding. Here Markle refers not to random student activity but rather to meaningful responses that are covert, overt, psychomotor, or verbal. Students who think through an answer are active in the sense that Markle intends. To indicate how meaningful activity can be incorporated into programmed instruction, Markle uses the following example:

The symbol for "less than" is <, and the symbol for "greater than" is >. Which of these questions is more meaningful, a or b?

a. Write the symbol for "less than."_____

Write the symbol for "greater than."_____

b. Make these arithmetic statements true by writing the correct symbol: _____

   1. 8 ? 3   2. 2 x 2 ? 5   3. 3 + 7 ? 8

The second response (b) is more meaningful. Each of these frames requires student activity, but in the second (meaningful) frame the student reads the instruction, examines the problems, decides which quantities are greater (making computations, if necessary) and writes the symbol in the blank space.

Note that the amount of processing required and the amount of overt activity needed are not identical. If you return to the two math frames, you notice immediately that task b requires far more thought. As Markle noted (1978, p. 9), the response request—what the student is asked to do—determines what information the student will notice and retain. Information that isn't needed, that is not processed at a meaningful level, is likely to go unnoticed. Telling the student and causing the student to process are not the same.

Must students respond overtly? Note: The question does not eliminate the necessity of responding but of responding overtly. As Markle notes, when organizing and responding are required, students should probably write their responses.

Overt or Covert Responses?

No one questions the need for active responding, but if a response remains covert (that is, inside a student's head), how can you be sure that the student knows the correct answer? Programmers are often split on this issue, and what you decide will reflect your personal preference. Incidentally, this issue by no means is restricted to programmed instruction; all instructional theories and designs face the same question.

To illustrate the problem, examine the following statements and decide if you would want your students to respond covertly or overtly.

1. The student is learning how to write numbers.
2. The student is learning to sing the notes of the scale.
3. The student is learning how to play first base.
4. The student is learning Spanish names for familiar objects.
5. The student is learning to distinguish the music of Handel from that of Mozart.

You may decide that all statements require an overt response, but most readers would agree that 1, 2, and 3 demand overt activity; most would agree that learning is probably enhanced by overt responses in number 4; there would be less agreement about the last statement. Active responding, yes; overt responding, maybe. Note that active, overt responding provides rich opportunities for feedback and reinforcement, which are particularly important in the beginning stages of acquiring new knowledge or skills.

The Principle of Errorless Learning. Markle attempted to define more precisely the meaning of error. As we have seen in the learning section, Skinner was urgently concerned with the control exerted by the environment, stating that lack of control and not the theory itself is responsible for unexpected results. Although we all make mistakes, the goal of instruction should be to reduce error as much as possible.

If learners respond actively, they tend to remember the circumstances surrounding the learning—your teaching, the stimuli, the response, any feedback that was provided. If they give an incorrect response, what do they learn? They learn the error. Markle then questions the manner in which we treat error. If we tell students "No, that's wrong" or make a red x on the paper, will they suppress the mistake? No. Students will simply try some other response, but nothing has been done to reinforce the correct answers, which argues for errorless learning. If you say, "No, John, 9 x 7 is not 56, it's 63," then the student does not respond actively. Does it follow, then, that students should never be allowed to make mistakes? Not in this system.

There may be a good reason for getting a mistake out in the open, such as diagnosing a lack of background information that is needed for a topic. Students should also be permitted to "mess around" with the subject matter, as in a lab or in simulated lab situations in computer-assisted instruction (Markle, 1978, p. 23).

Errors serve many functions. They can be a signal that instruction needs improvement; they are a reliable guide for diagnosis; they aid programmers in shaping the final form of a program.

The Principle of Immediate Feedback. Markle links the need for feedback to the manner in which the statement is framed. For example, there are instances where feedback would add nothing to the learning. If I should ask you how much is 2 + 2, you don't need me or the text to tell you that you are right. You have that information from your personal knowledge. Challenging situations, however, cause students to make more errors and learn less when feedback is lacking (Markle, 1978, p. 32).

The Functions of Teaching

1. Any type of instruction involves the four functions of teaching.
   - To help you diversify your instruction, describe, in concrete terms, the kinds of students and type of content that you think require direct instruction. Do the same for inquiry instruction.
   - To determine your students' prior knowledge in a subject, devise a brief (6 to 10 items) diagnostic pretest that assesses what you think is needed for a successful introduction to new work. This type of device can be used at all levels and for almost any subject.
   - Analyze the texts that you are using to determine if they present subject matter effectively. Use questions such as these as a guide:
     a. What is the main purpose of the text?
     b. Is the reading level appropriate for my students?
     c. Is the format designed to hold a student's attention and to sustain motivation?
     d. Is the subject matter presented in a clear and orderly manner?
     e. Is there adequate subject matter coverage?

These five points will also serve as guidelines if you serve on curriculum committees or textbook evaluation committees.

   - Keep a journal in which you list the community resources that you could use: social agencies, recreational facilities, businesses that offer field trips, cultural organizations that offer speakers.

2. One of the major findings regarding teaching relates to the quantity and pacing of instruction.
   - Be sure that you remain involved with your students, which is the key to successful time-on-task and which enables you to furnish necessary feedback.
   - For a quick check of how your students spend their time during any lesson or with any subject, have an observer (even one of your students) make two observations. Give your observer a list of your students' names next to two columns: off-task, on-task. At each observation point, the observer puts a check in the appropriate box.
   - To review your own use of class time, make a list of the functions that you perform in the classroom (direct instruction, monitoring seatwork, checking homework, conducting drills, encouraging student inquiry). For each lesson taught, put a check next to the appropriate function. Are you making the best use of your time?
   - It is an excellent idea to tape some of your classes occasionally. When you listen to the tape, use a device such as the Bloom's Taxonomy to evaluate your questions.

   Did they mainly demand facts?

Did they pursue students' comprehension of their work? Did they prod students to use their facts to solve problems? Did they urge students to think about relations? Did they require students to integrate facts and then make a judgment?

3. Other major findings about teaching focus on the quality of instruction.
   - Once you decide on your objectives, apply the main features of direct instruction by listing them on the board, explaining them to your students, and then acting on them. For example:
     a. Be sure that all students are actively engaged on task.
     b. Use several concrete examples to illustrate your lesson.
     c. Be sure that your vocabulary and level of difficulty are correct for your students.
     d. Monitor your pace by watching your students, and slow down or pick up accordingly.
     e. Stop to ask questions and provide appropriate feedback.
     f. Give a clear summary.

   - If you have taped any of your lessons, listen to them again and evaluate the way that you use praise. A good technique is to have the *Guidelines for Effective Praise* (see Table 11.2 on page 324) in front of you as you listen to the tape and check your responses against the criteria for effective and ineffective praise.
   - Once students have acquired needed information—by either direct or inquiry instruction—you will want to question them about their knowledge. Pick one topic that you will teach (for example, photosynthesis). Now decide:
     a. how you will respond to correct answers. "What does a green plant make from water and gas?" "Sugar." If you find yourself frequently saying, "That's right," you're probably asking too many factual questions.
     b. how you will respond to incorrect answers. You must tell students immediately that they are wrong. If they can't answer a factual question, tell them what they need to know. If they are wrong on a higher level question (synthesis, evaluation), say something like, "You're almost right but. . . ." At this point you can either give them the needed information or use additional questioning to lead them to the correct answer.
     c. how you will respond to an incomplete answer. You may ask another question that acts as a probe to the student, thus requiring the student to answer. You may also ask another student to complete the first student's answer.

The Individual Differences of Learners

Although our focus has been on teachers and teaching strategies, we should not overlook the necessity of adapting our teaching to the characteristics of our learners. One way of accomplishing this goal is to help them to develop efficient study skills.

Students and Study Skills

Being able to study effectively is important for a student's success in school. Many capable students at all grade levels may experience frustration and even failure in school *not* because they lack ability but because they do not have adequate study skills. Good study skills benefit students beyond improving their academic performance. Children who have developed good study skills are also more likely to increase their feelings of competence and confidence as they learn. They tend to approach their school work with a positive attitude, rather than a negative and anxious one.

Developing Study Skills

Study skills may be viewed as basic learning tools; they enable students to acquire and retain information presented in textbooks and classrooms. More specifically, study skills include listening and reading, notetaking, outlining, managing time, and taking tests. Study skills may be organized into four general stages of learning that are common to all students. The first stage of studying involves taking in information from books, lectures, or presentations. Study behaviors that are associated with success at this stage include listening and reading. The second stage entails some organization of the information. Study behaviors that facilitate organization of the information include underlining, notetaking, outlining, making lists, or asking oneself questions about the material. Stage three involves practicing or rehearsing the organized material and requires some type of review or discussion on the part of the learner. The final stage is the actual remembering or application of information. Skills in taking tests, writing, or preparing reports are used in this stage.

How Parents Can Help

Parents must remember that there is no simple formula for improving study skills for all children. More important than following any one particular method are building good habits, developing a system that works for them, and using the system effectively and consistently. Learning styles vary from student to student. Study habits that work for one person may not work well for another person—even for two children who come from the same family! Students must discover how they learn and then work out a study system that fits in best with the way they learn things. Here are some tips parents can pass on to their children for helping them develop good study skills. Without pressuring, parents may encourage children to:

- *Establish a study routine.* Children should pick a place, find a time, and build a routine. Studying should be a part of the daily family routine. Students find that they learn more if they get into the habit of studying at the same time and in the same place each day. Of course, special family events or sudden demands will force them to break that routine from time to time, but they should try to stay in the routine as much as possible.
- *Make sure study surroundings allow children to concentrate.* To concentrate on studies, some children may require total quiet, while others may need a little background noise (such as music). Children should find the atmosphere that helps them focus on what they have to study without being distracted by other activities or being so relaxed that they fall asleep. Children may need some cooperation from the family to do this (not disturbing them, taking phone messages, etc.).
- *Keep assignments in one folder.* Students may have a separate notebook for each class, but they should keep all homework assignments in one folder. That way, they will be able to see all of the things they have to do and divide their study time accordingly.
- *Work out a study system.* Rather than just reading straight through an assignment, most students find that they learn more if they work out a systematic method. This may involve skimming the material, underlining or taking notes, reviewing major ideas, and so on. Two key elements are *to read with a question in mind* and take *notes in their own words.* One popular system known as the **SQ3R** method involves these steps: (a) *Survey:* Quickly scan the reading assignment (look at headings, graphs, summaries, etc.); (b) *Question:* Make up a question to keep in mind as they read; (c) *Read:* Then, read to answer the questions they formulated; (d) *Recite:* Try to answer questions without looking at the reading assignment; and (e) *Review:* Immediately review the material to make certain notes are organized and major ideas are understood.
- *Expand concentration time.* At first, children may be able to concentrate for only short time periods (ten minutes is typical, since it is the time between

Parents can play an important role in effective learning by helping children develop study routines and possible reinforcement for their efforts and products.

commercials on tv programs). Parents can help children work on expanding this to longer stretches without breaks, so that getting through assignments will not take as long. Most children must work up slowly and steadily, just like one does in weight training or aerobics.

• *Develop time estimation skill.* One key to good studying is being able to estimate how long it will take to complete each assignment. Start by having children make an estimate on each assignment, then note how long it really takes to do the work, and note how well they do on the assignment (or how they do on the test for which they studied). Most students must keep adjusting and evaluating estimates until they become routinely accurate.

• *Plan ahead.* Athletes cannot get into shape in one or two nights; they need to "work out" for several weeks. Studying works the same way. Students should start working on major assignments or reviewing for major tests well ahead and plan their strategy for finishing the assignment on time.

• *Set goals.* Before beginning work on an assignment, help children decide how well they want to do on it and how much effort it will take to do that well. This will help them learn to divide study time effectively so that they do not spend too much time on relatively unimportant assignments.

• *Reward achievements.* When children achieve one of their study goals, give them a little reward: make a snack, allow them to call a friend, or whatever. Often children will want someone (parent or friend) who can congratulate them on their achievements and with whom they can share what they have learned.

The Role of Homework

Another means of adapting your instruction to the needs of your students is by the use of carefully assigned homework. Homework engenders many different responses from students, teachers, and parents. Many students hate it; still a significant number think it's important; some teachers think it is useless; others see it as essential. Some parents think it is just busy work, yet

Copyright © 1991 Joel Pett, Lexington Herald Leader. Reprinted by permission.

Table 12.8

Suggested Effects of Homework

Positive Effects

Immediate achievement and learning
 Better retention of factual knowledge
 Increased understanding
 Better critical thinking, concept information,
  information processing
 Curriculum enrichment

Long-term academic effects
 Willingness to learn during leisure time
 Improved attitude toward school
 Better study habits and skills

Nonacademic effects
 Greater self-direction
 Greater self-discipline
 Better time organization
 Better time organization
 More inquisitiveness
 More independent problem solving

Greater parental appreciation of and involvement
in schooling

Negative Effects

Satiation
 Loss of interest in academic material
 Physical and emotional fatigue

Denial of access to leisure-time and community
activities

Parental interference
 Pressure to complete assignments and perform well
 Confusion of instructional techniques

Cheating
 Copying from other students
 Help beyond tutoring

Increased differences between high and low
achievers

Reprinted by permission of Longman Publications. *Homework.* by Harris Cooper.
Copyright © 1989 by Longman Publishing Group.

many think that it is an indication of the quality of the school and that it is critical for their child. By homework, we mean "tasks assigned to students by school teachers that are meant to be carried out during non-school hours" (Cooper, 1989, p. 86).

In a recent and thorough review of research on homework, Cooper (1989) concluded that homework has positive effects on achievement, especially for junior and senior high school students. Several other authors, although with far less an empirical orientation than that of Cooper, have touted the benefits of homework for children in the 1980s and 90s. Books such as *Homework Without Tears* (Canter & Hausner, 1987) and *Hassle Free Homework* (Clark & Clark, 1989) have been promoted in bookstores across the country to parents as guides for helping their children. Thus, homework, currently seems to be perceived positively and as an important instructional adjunct that can affect students, teachers, and parents. Homework deserves your attention, so let's scrutinize some of the points that Cooper (1989) made in his synthesis of research on homework.

Cooper's review of the research literature identified numerous potential positive and negative effects of homework on students. Table 12.8 documents many of the suggested effects resulting from homework. Note that homework is seen as having some important "side effects" on student-parent relations and self-management. Based on your own experiences with homework, can you add possible positive or negative effects to the list in Table 12.8?

In addition to examining the effects of homework, Cooper formulated a "model" of the factors that influence homework outcomes. He identified over twenty specific factors (e.g., student characteristics, home environment, testing related work, parents' involvement) and organized these specific factors into six general factors.

The general and specific factors that influence the effects of homework are displayed in Figure 12.5. Of all factors, grade level was perhaps the most significant. Specifically, Cooper found the effect of homework on achievement was only negligible for elementary students, moderately important for junior high students, and very important for high school students. Although the effects of homework

Exogenous factors	Assignment characteristics	Initial classroom factors	Home-Community factors	Classroom follow-up	Outcomes or effects
Student characteristics Ability Motivation Study habits Subject matter Grade level	Amount Purpose Skill area utilized Degree of individualization Degree of student choice Completion deadlines Social content	Provision of materials Facilitators Suggested approaches Links to Curriculum Other rationales	Competitors for student time Home environment Space Light Quiet Materials Others' involvement Parents Siblings Other students	Feedback Written comments Grading Incentives Testing or related content Use in class discussion	Assignment completion Assignment performance Positive effects Immediate academic Long-term academic Nonacademic Parental Negative effects Satiation Denial of leisure time Parental interference Cheating Increased student differences

Figure 12.5
A model of factors influencing the effect of homework.

on elementary students' achievement were small or nonexistent, Cooper still recommends some homework for elementary students. He believes it can help them to develop good study habits, fosters positive attitudes toward school, and communicates the idea that learning takes place at home as well as school.

Cooper also concluded that in-class study supervised by a teacher was as good or better than homework, especially for younger students. As noted by Cooper, however, the allocation of time for in-class study versus other learning activities becomes the issue. As a conclusion to his work on homework, Cooper generated a policy statement on homework for school districts and teachers. We believe that this policy statement (see Figure 12.6) serves as a summary of best practices with regard to homework and have reprinted it here for your review and use.

Adapting Your Teaching

When you attempt to adapt instruction, you try to match instructional method and material with your student's aptitudes. Commonly called "matching the mix," it is more technically referred to as **aptitude-treatment interaction.** Though research has not supplied the data needed to prescribe exactly the needed adaptive measures, the concept maintains its appeal for many teachers. (See Cronbach & Snow, 1977, for more details.)

Individual differences in aptitude require adaptive teaching that either focuses directly on developing aptitudes or compensates for a particular aptitude level (Corno & Snow, 1986, p. 606). Such adaptation takes two forms: **macroadaptation,** which refers to long range decisions (perhaps involving program change), and **microadaptation**, which refers to the moment-by-moment changes you make in your daily classroom activities.

Macroadaptation

Instructional designers, given the state of the art, have usually confined their efforts to programs that affect cognitive aptitude differences, especially differences in learning rates. Two of the more popular of these programs are **I**ndividually Prescribed Instruction and Individually Guided Education (Corno & Snow, 1986). As you read about these programs, note how many elements of effective teaching are incorporated in their suggestions.

Individually Prescribed Instruction (**IPI**) is a popular form of individualized instruction utilizing precise program specification. The planning for each student's program is as painstaking as that for producing a teaching machine program. Individually Prescribed Instruction has these major features.

For districts

Homework is a cost-effective instructional technique. It can have positive effects on achievement and character development and can serve as a vital link between the school and family.

Homework should have different purposes at different grades. For younger students, it should foster positive attitudes, habits, and character traits. For older students, it should facilitate knowledge acquisition in specific topics.

Homework should be required at all grade levels, but a mixture of mandatory and voluntary homework is most beneficial.

The frequency and duration of mandatory assignments should be:

1. Grades 1 to 3—one to three assignments a week, each lasting no more than 15 minutes
2. Grades 4 to 6—two to four assignments a week, each lasting 15 to 45 minutes
3. Grades 7 to 9—three to five assignments a week, each lasting 45 to 75 minutes
4. Grades 10 to 12—four to five assignments a week, each lasting 75 to 120 minutes

For schools

The frequency and duration of homework assignments should be further specified to reflect local school and community circumstances.

In schools where different subjects are taught by different teachers, teachers should know:

1. What days of the week are available to them for assignments
2. How much daily homework time should be spent on their subject

Administrators should:

1. Communicate the district and school homework policies to parents
2. Monitor the implementation of the policy
3. Coordinate the scheduling of homework among different subjects, if needed

Teachers should state clearly:

1. How the assignment is related to the topic under study
2. The purpose of the assignment
3. How the assignment might best be carried out
4. What the student needs to do to demonstrate that the assignment has been completed

For teachers

All students in a class will be responsible for the same assignments, with only rare exceptions.

Homework will include mandatory assignments. Failure to turn in mandatory assignments will necessitate remedial activities.

Homework will also include voluntary assignments meant to meet the needs of individual students or groups of students.

All homework assignments will *not* be formally evaluated. They will be used to locate problems in student progress and to individualize instruction.

Topics will appear in assignments before and after they are covered in class, not just on the day they are discussed.

Homework will not be used to teach complex skills. It will generally focus on simple skills and material or on the integration of skills already possessed by the student.

Parents will rarely be asked to play a formal instructional role in homework. Instead, they should be asked to create a home environment that facilitates student self-study.

Figure 12.6
A recommended homework policy.

- *Objectives are characterized as student behaviors.* Since IPI entails the extensive use of self-teaching materials, educators must devise materials that permit attainment of specific objectives.
- *Objectives must encourage student progress with little unnecessary repetition.* Though a logical sequence of steps is vital, the program must also provide for branching or "break points." For example, in teaching addition, there are desirable spots to introduce subtraction skills.
- *The materials must permit the students to learn from them independently without constant help from the teacher.* Since many students will be at different levels, the materials must allow students to profit from their own study. The behavioral objectives are the main guide: "What materials will enable students to attain this ability?"
- *There must be a detailed diagnosis of the learner to determine existing skills and knowledge and the ideal starting point in the sequence.* If instruction is to be efficient and challenging, it must account for individual differences upon entering the program; it must place the learner at an appropriate level in the learning sequence, and it must accommodate the program to students' needs.
- *The learner establishes a personal pace.* Most students need little teacher assistance; usually two or three teachers, with three or four teacher aides, will provide individual help. There are tests for each objective and a test on all the unit's objectives. If students demonstrate sufficient mastery, then they move to the next unit. If not, additional work is provided to overcome deficiencies. Such continuous monitoring ensures that each student works with suitable materials.
- *Instruction must provide opportunities for students to practice the desirable behaviors.* Reading about or being told something is inadequate. Activities must allow practice in what is to be learned.
- *Learning is enhanced through immediate feedback.* Students should not have to wait days to see if they are correct. The IPI procedure attempts to keep students fully and immediately informed of their progress.
- *Success or failure in changing student behavior is continuously used to modify the program.* Constant monitoring of student programs allows constant change in the program. Material is revised depending on the feedback from students.

Children get their folders at the beginning of each period. These contain information on past performance and current assignments (additional work, test). If they need

Herbert J. Klausmeier, V. A. C. Henmon Professor Emeritus, Department of Educational Psychology, University of Wisconsin-Madison.

Source: University of Wisconsin-Madison

help, they raise their hands, and teachers come to them. Children's work is immediately checked on completion, and tests are administered by teachers' aides. At the end of class, the children return the folders; teachers then evaluate them and make new assignments.

These principles are attractive because of their individually prescribed learning tasks and the organization of curriculum into predictable teaching techniques.

Individually Guided Education (IGE). For many years Herbert Klausmeier (1976) and several of his associates at the University of Wisconsin have worked on a new form of schooling—**individually guided education.** It is a comprehensive design intended to achieve certain objectives through individualized instruction. But it is not individualized instruction in which students use programmed instructional materials with little teacher assistance. Klausmeier's interpretation of individualized instruction is that in which self-instructional material is only one aspect of the program.

IGE involves planning individual institutional programs for students as well as providing instructional materials (books, audiovisual materials, demonstrations) that suit individual learning styles. It also provides different methods of instruction (small group, large group, tutoring, independent study) while attempting to match teachers and students. It is a comprehensive system of schooling that focuses on the individual not by age and not by classroom group. It is a nongraded system in which teachers work with students whose ages may vary as much as four years. IGE demands a new organization, team teaching, and differential staffing, as well as nongrading. There is a clear statement of objectives, assessment of students' readiness, constant evaluation of progress, varied teaching techniques and materials, measurement of final achievement, and a decision about future progress or remedial work.

Klausmeier makes an interesting distinction between teachers in IGE and those in self-contained classrooms: The IGE teacher is engaged in all aspects of teaching-learning, such as setting goals and assessing students' characteristics, and in formulating instructional programs, using new material and experimenting with new techniques. IGE teachers have a more encompassing role.

Efforts to individualize instruction will continue and will be similar to tutoring or the elaborate programs we have just seen. Students can only benefit from your attempt to adapt your methods because the spread of the principles of individual instruction will gradually affect all teachers. Try to study some of the major programs and determine how you can adapt any attractive suggestions to your work. Remember these principles in your teaching:

- *Be sure students understand what they are doing and why.* No matter how you phrase your objectives, be sure that they are clear to guide your teaching and provide students with a sense of direction.
- *Be positive that your students can assimilate the material you are presenting.* Lack of maturity and experience are powerful obstacles to learning. Think of this physical example as a guide; forcing a five-year-old to throw a regulation size basketball at a basket ten feet above the ground will probably cause frustration and a dislike of the game. The same is true of presenting abstract material to youngsters at a preoperational cognitive level.
- *Understand the logic of your subject.* Know where it is more practical to divide a subject into manageable units. Know where there are opportunities to "branch" to introduce related material that will broaden learning. If you are teaching about methods of transportation, ask your students why businesses

cluster around major roadways. (Select an obvious example in your state.)
- *Adapt your instruction to the learner's pace.* Though this requires effort, perhaps extra work, it will result in solid learning, enhanced motivation, and steady progress.
- *Provide constant feedback.* Students should know as soon as possible whether they are right or wrong, what comes next, or what needs to be remedied. This demands continuous evaluation, which is a desirable legacy of individualized instruction since it encourages progress and also prevents students from falling too far behind.

Microadaptation

Here we see teachers adapting at the level of individual students. Teachers will vary the organizational pattern of their classrooms—whole class, groups, learning centers, one-on-one. They will also vary the materials they present—reviews, summaries, analogies—and the way they present it: verbally, filmstrips, slides, overheads, videotapes, and films. They alter their reinforcement patterns, perhaps slowly limiting praise as the percentage of correct responses increases.

These techniques reflect the work presented in the theory and design sections and are intended to develop student aptitude or circumvent inaptitude. Madeline Hunter's theory provides an excellent example of microadaptation.

Madeline Hunter's Clinical Theory of Instruction

Working on the assumption that the teacher is a decision making professional, Hunter's **Clinical Theory of Instruction** (CTI) claims universal application, regardless of content, school organization, learner's age, or socioeconomic status. Hunter and Russell (1981) stated that CTI is derived from research on human learning and based on the notion that instructional decisions are made consciously or by default.

Defining instruction as the teacher's decisions and actions deliberately designed to increase the probability of learning, Hunter's work rests upon several assumptions. These include:

- Though learning is our major concern, instructional decisions and actions are what we control.
- If teacher and student behavior are not random but directed at specific learning objectives, student achievement will increase.

Madeline Hunter.

- All students can learn the next thing beyond that which they now know.
- Achievement is enhanced if teachers constantly adjust instruction in light of emerging student behaviors.
- Established principles of learning can guide teachers' decisions and actions when they understand their own behavior.
- Most teachers want to improve their performance.

Planning for Effective Instruction

The careful design of lessons continues to be one of the most important elements in successful teaching. Hunter and Russell (1981) suggest the following steps to achieve your objectives:

Step 1. Anticipatory set. Here Hunter is chiefly concerned with readiness and attention and suggests using a brief practice period of previous learning and then focusing your students' attention on what is to be learned. You should not continue this activity beyond the time to "set" your students, to make sure that they are ready for the new learning.

> You probably will use verbal cues quite frequently as a means of focusing attention and leading your students to the new learning.
> Do you remember the instructional theories that we previously discussed?
> How does the instructional design work differ from these theories?
> Today we want to talk about Madeline Hunter's work as an example of instructional design. She believes that. . . .

Step 2. The objective and its purpose. Hunter believes that you must clearly inform students of what they should be able to do by the end of the instruction and why it is important that they master the lesson's content.

> You had difficulty yesterday in distinguishing Skinner's theory from Markle's design. During this class we'll concentrate on active responding and meaningfulness to help you separate the two.

Step 3. Instructional input. You must decide just what information your students need to attain the lesson's objective. How are you going to do this? The content of this chapter should be helpful: readiness of students, reinforcements needed, degree of understanding, the necessary design, specific steps.

1. Today you are going to see a film of a teacher using Hunter's steps for presenting a lesson.
2. To help you see the application of Markle's work, complete this lesson on programmed instruction.
3. For the next few minutes, apply Bruner's spiral curriculum to examples of instructional design.

Step 4. Modeling. We have discussed modeling in several preceding chapters sufficiently for you to realize its value to students in actually seeing examples of an acceptable finished product. Whenever you model, be sure that you combine both visual and verbal stimuli so that your students will concentrate on the essential features that you wish them to learn.

> I'm going to teach today's class in instructional design according to the steps proposed by Hunter. During the presentation, I want you to identify each of the seven steps of the lesson.

Step 5. Checking for understanding. If you are to make accurate adjustments in your instruction, you must continuously assess your students' level of understanding. Hunter states that you can use several methods to accomplish this assessment: *sampling,* which consists of questions to the total group to focus on the problem and assess readiness; *signaled responses,* having each group member signal, in some predetermined manner, if they agree or disagree; *individual private responses.*

1. Write the name of the person who advocated mastery learning in this chapter.
2. Thumbs up if you agree with this answer; thumbs down if you disagree.
3. Who based a theory of instruction on Piaget's work?

Step 6. Guided practice. Be careful of your students' efforts in their initial attempts at new learning. Circulate among your students to be sure that students are performing satisfactorily. Students must practice their skills, but they require monitoring if they need clarification or remediation.

Step 7. Independent practice. Once students have eliminated major errors, they can then apply the skills in some appropriate task: homework, research papers, reading assignments.

> Hunter's ideas have proven to be extremely popular with classroom teachers. Workshops explaining her methods are given frequently around the country. Not all educators, however, support her work.

Adapting Instruction in a Multicultural Classroom

Multicultural education is a perspective appearing in every phase and aspect of teaching, which enables teachers to scrutinize their options and choices to clarify what social information they are conveying overtly and covertly to their students. It also is a means of challenging and expanding the goals and values that underlie the curriculum, materials, and activities (Ramsey, 1987, p. 6).

In a multicultural curriculum, students learn about themselves and others as they study various cultures. They analyze the beliefs, attitudes, values, and behavior that are characteristic of a particular culture. As they do, those of that culture should increase their sense of self-esteem and simultaneously develop an appreciation and understanding of other cultures.

In presenting multicultural topics, teachers proceed in exactly the same manner as with their other subjects (Tiedt & Tiedt, 1990). That is, they establish the necessary knowledge base, utilize effective instructional methods, and base their instruction on their students' needs.

Focus on Teachers

To Be "Hunterized" or Not?

In an article entitled "Teachers Ask: Is There Life After Madeline Hunter?" (Garman & Hazi, 1988), the authors identify several pros and cons of Hunter's system. Examining the movement in Pennsylvania, the authors note that state officials, responding to national concerns about education, turned to a search for some means of evaluating and rewarding good teaching. Impressed by the seven identifiable steps, the Pennsylvania State Department of Education proposed a series of workshops featuring the Hunter model.

Interviewing more than 200 Pennsylvania teachers who were involved in the Hunter training program, the authors first mention "the good news." For example, there is no denying the attention that the model has brought to teaching nor the sense of professionalism that accompanies such attention. Teachers also felt that careers were enhanced by participating (financial rewards, promotions). Finally, by standardization of the seven steps, teachers could be held more accountable.

"The bad news" (expressed by about two-thirds of the teachers) focused on such negative features as being forced to adopt a single method, whether you agreed with it or not. Many teachers were angry. If you didn't use Hunter, you weren't rewarded; the seven steps seemed more like a game; many felt the charges for the workshops were excessive. Most of the teachers interviewed rejected the notion that the Hunter model made them better teachers.

One major criticism from participants and observers alike was the increasing rigidity of the system. Regardless of the technique adopted, teachers must have the freedom to experiment and to explore, adapting methods to their own personalities.

Responding to these and similar criticisms, Hunter (1987) denies that her model is a recipe for successful teaching; rather she considers it a decision-making model. Where her model has not produced any different effects than other techniques, Hunter believes that CTI has been used poorly. She insists that there is no such thing as a "Madeline Hunter-type lesson," no one way to teach. She argues that her work presents basic instructional knowledge that teachers can use to make their classroom decisions.

Our purpose here is actually a continuation of a theme initially presented in chapter 1—the need to be sensitive to the unique needs of multicultural students (Rogoff, 1990). Although your recognition of students' individual differences is not confined to multicultural students, nevertheless, their classroom challenges may have quite different roots from those of your other students.

As a dramatic illustration of these differences, consider the following:

> In a San Francisco elementary school, a teacher plays hangman with her students to enliven a spelling lesson. As the class eagerly shouts out letters, one child bursts into tears. A Cambodian immigrant recently arrived from a Thai refugee camp, the child speaks little English. Another child is found who can interpret, and the hysterical child finally manages to communicate that she had witnessed the hanging of her father in Cambodia (Olsen, 1988, p. 211).

It's not difficult to envision this student's having learning difficulties may well be linked to the emotional trauma she is experiencing.

Though you may not have the language skills to communicate fully with some of your students, you can nevertheless be sensitive to their origins and customs, help students to see themselves as part of the larger society, encourage respect and appreciation for the ways of others, urge students to develop positive relationships with children of all cultures, and learn as much as possible about the heritage of your students.

Teacher Expectancies

In adapting your instruction, you must avoid certain pitfalls, particularly being blinded by your expectations for any student since it may have powerful effects on a student's achievement. In 1968, Rosenthal and Jacobson reported the results of a study that fascinated both educators and psychologists. Beginning in 1964, the authors had teachers in an elementary school administer an imposing test, the *Harvard Test of Inflected Acquisition*, that actually was a nonverbal IQ test. It was administered to youngsters who would return in the fall. Teachers were told that the test would predict which youngsters would show an academic spurt in the coming year. These would be the "intellectual bloomers." The tests supposed predictive value, and the youngsters so identified were imaginary. Teachers believed that they were taking part in a study to validate a test predicting the likelihood that a child will show an inflection point or "spurt" within the near future. The top 20 percent (approximately) of the scores on these tests will probably be found at various levels of academic functioning (Rosenthal & Jacobson, 1968, p. 66).

In the fall, the teachers were told which youngsters had scored in the top 20 percent, and the investigators suggested that these children would probably show remarkable progress during the year. Actually, there was no difference between them and the control group. All the youngsters were retested at the end of the school year, using the same test. The experimental group (the late bloomers) all scored higher than the control group. The investigators interpreted the results to indicate that when teachers expected more of children, the youngsters met their expectations—a **self-fulfilling prophecy** referred to as *Pygmalion in the classroom* was the result.

The news media and the general public seized upon the results, and the study received enormous publicity. Uncritically accepted, the results were interpreted as heralding a breakthrough in the classroom. Many educators and investigators remained skeptical, and their skepticism was confirmed when attempts to replicate the Rosenthal and Jacobson findings produced conflicting evidence. Other critics attacked the study's methodology. Carefully controlled studies, in which teachers received varied information (IQ scores, no IQ scores, IQ scores inflated by 16 points, or designating some students academic bloomers) did not duplicate Rosenthal's findings. Kerlinger (1973) believed that these findings cast serious doubt on the Rosenthal hypothesis.

Perhaps it is safest to conclude that teachers' expectations make a difference, but not as uniformly and in a much more complex manner than originally believed. Answering his critics, Rosenthal stated that expectations produce effects because teachers provide a favorable social and emotional atmosphere for the selected students. These students receive more attention, thus furnishing carefully controlled reinforcement. Teachers spend more time with them, demand more from these students, and usually receive it.

If teacher expectations produce differences in a student's achievement, the process may be as follows. Because of what they have heard or read about these students, teachers develop certain expectations about them. Teachers then behave differently with these students. Students infer from a teacher's behavior that they are or are not good achievers and frequently behave accordingly. If a student understands the meaning of a teacher's behavior, achievement may follow the direction of the teacher's expectations (Hamachek, 1987).

How do these expectations translate into teacher behavior in the classroom? Teachers often tend to:

- seat low-expectation students farther from the teacher.
- pay less attention to low-expectation students in academic activities.
- less often call on these students to answer questions.
- wait less time and then interrupt those students whom they perceive as less capable.
- criticize more frequently those students for whom they have low expectations, praising them less often.

TEACHER ⟷ STUDENT
INTERACTIONS

Adapting Your Teaching

1. When you attempt to adapt your teaching, you are "matching the mix," which introduces the notion of aptitude-treatment interaction.

   • One way of helping both you and your students to adapt classroom materials is to be sure that your students have good study habits. Prepare a chart that you distribute to your students (using appropriate language) on which you have listed those habits that you think are important for the success of your students. Then have them check one of two columns marked *always* or *seldom*. (Use terms with which your students are comfortable.) For example:

	Always	Seldom
Have a regular place to study		
Do my homework at the same time		
TV on when studying		

   • Be sure you know what your students are capable of before introducing a new topic. Use a pretest to assess their current level of knowledge. Once you know the extent of their prior knowledge, make a simple chart of each student's weaknesses. For example, on a scale of 1–10, rate each student on key topics.

   ### American History-The Civil War
	Politicians	Geography	Products	Battles
John	4	2	1	8
Heather	4	4	3	6
Tim	2	1	0	2
Diana	1	1	1	5

   You can then individualize your instruction and help each student to attain the unit's objectives.

   • Try independent work with some of those students whose weaknesses you have identified. (These students must be able to work without constant supervision; not all students can do this, but selected students are capable of it.) Be sure they understand exactly what they are to do and provide, or direct them to, the proper materials that will bring them up to class level. You may want to set up a learning center in your classroom or enlist the school librarian's aid, or have your students go to the community's library.

   • Link the assessment of your students' prior knowledge with both the current topic and future work. Ask yourself these questions:

   Am I assuming that my students have enough background data to begin work or must I pretest?

   Does the difficulty level of the subject matter, the materials, and activities match the ability level of my students?

   Am I sufficiently familiar with the subject's content, the materials, and activities to adapt them to meet the needs of my students?

   Do my students understand that what they are doing now is related to the unit's objectives?

2. Teachers' decisions and actions are deliberately designed to increase the probability of student learning.

   • Here are some decisions you must make:

   Shall I lecture, assign teams to projects, use class activities such as debates, or set up independent work assignments?

   Shall I have one group compete against another?

   Shall I have groups cooperate?

   Shall I try to prevent my students from making any mistakes by breaking the material into small, easy-to-master steps?

   Shall I encourage students to use their mistakes as a means of teaching problem solving?

   • Remember: The activities that you use are those in which the *learners* are engaged. Among student activities that lead to learning are the following:

   Have your students solve problems, not just memorize facts.

   Have them play roles in various classes.

   Have them debate various issues.

   Have them look up information.

   Have them *read, read, read!*

   Have them *write, write, write!*

- provide lower quality feedback to their low-expectation students.

Not all teachers, of course, treat low- and high-expectation students differently. Yet the evidence continues to indicate the existence of expectations that influence teacher behavior. The solution is not to form expectations but to have a reliable and valid process for assessing students so that one's expectations are accurate.

Conclusion

After reading this chapter, you should be convinced of the complexity of teaching. Attempting to identify and control the many variables that affect both teaching and learning requires knowledge, insight, and sensitivity. Among those who have grappled with this problem are both theorists and practitioners.

Bruner, with his perceptive analysis of teaching and learning, has afforded us a unified picture of how both can be fused into one meaningful act. One—teaching—cannot be divorced from the other—learning. It is the graceful blend of the two that defines successful teaching.

Skinner, on the other hand, faithful to behavioristic views, has translated the principles of operant conditioning into a technology of classroom management. By the careful selection of controlled amounts of material and the proper application of positive reinforcement, learning can proceed unhindered by fruitless detours.

Bloom, with his concern for mastery learning, has devised a model of school learning that incorporates cognitive entry characteristics, affective entry characteristics, and quality of instruction. When these features are coupled with the judicious use of time, Bloom believes that almost all students can learn to mastery.

These theorists link their sweeping views of human behavior to the practical dictates of the classroom, unlike those who advocate instructional design. Gagne and Markle, for example, focus on stages or steps that produce efficient instruction.

Regardless of the theory or design, instruction must be adapted to the needs of the learner. Whether general curriculum changes or programs are tailored to the individual student, adaptation is at the heart of successful teaching.

Chapter Highlights

The Meaning of Teaching

- Recent analyses of teaching have several pertinent findings, such as the importance of pacing (especially the need for quality student-engaged time).
- The study of how teaching methods interact with student characteristics is known as **attribute-treatment interaction.**
- John Carroll's model of school learning has guided several research efforts into the variables of teaching behavior and student performance.
- Both direct and inquiry instruction are aspects of active teaching.
- Teachers' use of praise has been carefully analyzed in attempts to make it a more meaningful and forceful element in the classroom.

Instructional Theory and Design

- Jerome Bruner's work has caused investigators to examine more closely the role of cognition in instruction.
- By understanding the intellectual growth of their students—how they utilize the modes of representation—teachers can more effectively facilitate learning.

- B. F. Skinner has applied the principles of operant conditioning (see chapter 5) to the classroom as he has consistently advocated a technology of teaching.
- Skinner urges that teachers first decide what their students should be able to do after instruction, carefully determine the steps needed to achieve that behavior, and skillfully use appropriate reinforcers.
- Benjamin Bloom believes that studies of teaching must take into account the time students need for a task, their cognitive-entry behaviors, and the proper use of testing, among other aspects.
- Bloom's concern with mastery learning has led him to propose a model of school learning with such core concepts as cognitive-entry behaviors, affective entry characteristics, and quality of instruction.
- Instructional design refers to those techniques that analyze teaching according to its component parts.
- Robert Gagne, employing an instructional design technique, has formulated a plan that accounts for learning outcomes as they are related to specific conditions for that learning.
- Susan Markle, using a programmed instruction model (programmed with one m), has concentrated on a student's active responding.

The Individual Differences of Learners

- Your teaching success will depend on how successfully you adapt your instruction to the individual differences of the learners in your class.
- Among the more well-known of several plans to help you adapt your teaching to the needs of your students is Madeline Hunter's Clinical Theory of Instruction.
- The "Pygmalion in the classroom" effect—letting your expectations about students affect your assessment of them—is a danger to be aware of and avoid.
- Your students' behavior must be your sole concern in the judgments you make.

Key Terms

Affective entry characteristics
Aptitude-treatment interaction
Attribute-treatment interaction
Beginning Teacher Evaluation Studies (BTES)
Clinical theory of instruction (CTI)
Cognitive entry behaviors
Enactive
Formative evaluation
Iconic
Individual guided education
Individually Prescribed Instruction (IPI)
Inquiry teaching
Macroadaptation
Mastery learning
Microadaptation
Modes of representation
Programmed instruction
Quality of instruction
SQ3R
Self-fulfilling prophecy
Spiral curriculum
Summative evaluation
Symbolic
Teacher expectancies
Terminal behavior
Time-on-task

Suggested Readings

Bloom, B. (Ed.). (1981). *All our children learning.* New York: McGraw-Hill. In this collection of essays, Bloom's ideas of teaching and learning are nicely summarized. His model of mastery learning, coupled with his views of schools and society, provide insights into the teaching-learning process.

Brophy, J. (1987). Teacher influences on student achievement. *American Psychologist, 41,* 1069. An excellent article that will give you a better understanding of a teacher's role and the impact that a teacher can make.

Bruner, J. (1960). *The process of education.* Cambridge, MA: Harvard. This charming classic is a must reading for any student of teaching and learning. Writing with grace and style, Bruner presents his ideas on the spiral curriculum together with a rationale for development and learning.

Shulman, L. (1986). Paradigms and research programs in the study of teaching. In M. Wittrock (Ed.). *The Handbook of Research on Teaching.* New York: Macmillan. Probably the best current analysis of the research that has guided the development of teaching methods. Shulman's work is careful, thoughtful, and provides the reader with a fine overview of the many variables that affect classroom performance.

Classroom Management: Organization and Control

I t was 8:15 a.m. on an October morning, and Virginia Allan's fifth grade class came swirling into her classroom. Some went to hang up their jackets, others went immediately to their desks, and others remained talking at the back of the room. Jimmy, an energetic, likeable eleven-year-old boy came through the doorway and bumped into Tommy, one of the boys who were talking at the back of the room. The boys began to shout and push each other.

"Stop that, Jimmy!" shouted Mrs. Allan. "Don't do any more pushing and shoving."

Suddenly, Jimmy turned and shouted back, "Don't yell at me! Don't blame me! You're always picking on me."

Mrs. Allan was stunned. She had encountered cases of misbehavior from the first day, but this was the most flagrant. Also, Jimmy hadn't caused any previous serious problems.

After Mrs. Allan separated the boys and told Jimmy to see her after school, the incident still bothered her throughout the day. Was it something she had done, or not done? Had she missed or misread clues that Jimmy might have given?

Oow would you answer these questions? Before you answer, however, look at the choice of words that were used to describe the behavior: swirling, standing around talking, no previous serious problems. If you were to advise this teacher, you would probably direct her attention to the manner in which she was managing her classroom.

Do students know what they are to do when they enter the classroom? Do they have work that should occupy them immediately? Had she been attentive enough to the individual students? Jimmy may, indeed, have given earlier warnings that something was bothering him. This incident reinforces the belief that a smoothly running classroom will do much to cut down on discipline problems.

To help you understand the importance of classroom management, this chapter opens by describing what most concerns teachers, then turns to an analysis of life in the classroom—what really happens when you close the classroom door. We'll next examine models such as QAIT to help you identify critical classroom features that lead to successful classroom management. We then move to specific techniques for organizing the classroom—what rules help, what kinds of behavior you can expect at different age levels.

Finally, we turn to clear and specific suggestions for maintaining control in your classroom by analyzing three well-known methods. Each of these techniques differs in philosophy and in efficiency. Consequently, you may want to select those that have the most support for effective classroom management.

When you finish reading this chapter, you should be able to:

- describe the significance of time to master classroom material.
- match developmental tasks with appropriate management techniques.
- identify those rules that are needed for a smoothly functioning classroom.
- use methods that maintain a productive classroom control.

Management Concerns in the Classroom

Many readers may believe that this is the most important chapter in the book. Managing a classroom means more than avoiding chaos; it means establishing a routine that enables learning activities to proceed smoothly. It also

"Sure there's a way to discipline them. Yell at them."

There are, however, better ways of guiding student behavior.

© 1990 by Sidney Harris—*Phi Delta Kappan.*

helps to prevent many unnecessary discipline problems. We can only guess at the amount of learning that was lost after the boys' fight that was described in the chapter's opening.

Students must know what is expected of them; they must know what various signals (fire drills, assemblies, bells, whistles) mean and what they should do. Do not minimize the importance of routine: a smoothly running classroom can prevent discipline problems. Teachers who give the impression of knowing what they are doing and who act decisively also give the impression of being in control.

Learning can occur only in an orderly classroom. Orderly, however, does not imply quiet or rigid. The hum and flow of youngsters engaged in meaningful activity in one classroom can be more orderly than the classroom in which you can hear a clock tick: students in various groups around the classroom, perhaps talking over a project, or moving to the library area for research materials, or reading or writing in the group area. An orderly environment is one in which everyone—teacher and students—knows exactly what is going on.

Although management issues most concern beginning teachers, it is one that actually keeps us all on the alert, regardless of experience, and that is by no means confined to discipline. In defining classroom management as those rules and procedures that maintain order so that learning may result, you will notice that *organizing your classroom is the first step in effective classroom management.*

Focus on Classrooms

Classroom Activities to Manage

Stop for a moment and think what you mean by "classroom management." List six activities that you believe fall into this category.

1.

2.

3.

4.

5.

6.

Did you include discipline as one of your topics? You probably did and rightly so. But consider any of the routine procedures that, if not closely monitored, can lead to discipline problems. For example, do your students have assigned seats? If not, the ensuing "musical chairs" could likely lead to pandemonium at any given moment. Who is in charge of attendance, you or a designated student?

At the elementary school level, do students know their groups for various subjects? Did you assign seats for each group? Does each student have paper? pencil? crayons? How did students get them? Do students have a clear understanding of what they are to do while you work with one of the groups?

Though you may initially react to these examples as trivial, remember that mastery of the simple routine of your classroom will save you countless problems in the future. If you have a well-ordered classroom, you will keep your discipline problems to a minimum. These examples also point to a basic distinction that is made throughout the remainder of the chapter: Classroom management consists of two parts, organization and control.

Proactive classroom management means that you should have a program that includes reactive responding to problems and a plan for productive learning.

Preventing Classroom Problems

Educational psychologists have recently begun to shift their focus from merely managing student behavior in the classroom to the *prevention* of behavioral problems by using instructional and managerial procedures. Increasingly, psychologists and educators have realized that the prevention of problems should be a national priority, not just in schools but across the life-span in all types of community settings. Reflecting this perspective, The American Psychological Association commissioned a task force to examine existing prevention programs and identify those that could be considered outstanding (Price, Cowen, Lorion, & Ramos-McKay, 1988).

In this chapter, we have adopted a dual focus on strategies that you can use to respond to problems as they occur in your classroom and techniques to prevent problems from occurring. A comprehensive classroom management program includes reactive responding to problems and proactive planning for productive behavior, a strategy that has been labeled **proactive classroom management** (Gettinger, 1988). Proactive classroom management has three characteristics that distinguish it from other management techniques (Gettinger, 1988):

- It is preventative rather than reactive.
- It integrates methods that facilitate appropriate student behavior with procedures that promote achievement, using effective classroom instructional techniques.
- It emphasizes the group dimensions of classroom management.

Maintaining sufficient order requires that you have students enter your classroom and move to their seats with no disruption. Once there, be certain that they have the needed materials and understand what they are to do with them. Your plan for any lesson must provide for engaged time for all your students. Finally, see that your students leave in an orderly fashion.

Let's take a general example here. Your students enter your room. They immediately check the board to see what they are to do for the first part of the period. Two assigned students may move around the room collecting homework. Note: The students know what is expected of them; they know the rules (classroom organization). While this is going on, you may devote your time to individuals, checking one or two students who could have problems. Notice how you are heading off potential trouble, a practice that in itself is a form of classroom control. At the same time, all of your students are productively engaged. Remember: Engaged time is not the time allotted to any class; it is the time during which students are actively involved in their work.

Thus, effective teaching and fruitful learning are tightly linked to classroom organization and management. Doyle (1986) notes that although *learning* is served by an *instructional* function, *order* is served by a *managerial* function: forming groups, establishing rules and procedures, reacting to misbehavior, and in general, monitoring classroom activities. Individuals learn; order applies to groups.

Using Students' Learning Styles to Prevent Problems

Educational researchers have concentrated on students' learning styles when they learn academic material. If you think about the ways that you learn best and the kind of setting you prefer, you will probably list such variables as noise level, degree of light illumination, type of furniture, time of day, amount of movement, and temperature (Dunn, 1987). Your students react in the same manner. To help teachers adjust to these different preferences of their students, Dunn and her associates (1987) have devised a learning style model in which they define learning style by student reactions to twenty-three classroom elements. Among these are the following:

- The immediate environment (noise level, temperature, light, and design)
- The emotional atmosphere (motivation by parents, teachers, or self, persistence, responsibility, and structure)
- Sociological preferences (learning alone or with peers, learning with adults present, learning in combined ways)
- Physical characteristics (auditory, visual, tactile, and kinesthetic preferences, time of day, mobility)
- Psychological inclinations (global/analytic, hemispheric preference, impulsive/reflective).

You may be able to manipulate several of these to help students with their learning. For example, you could change the seats of those students who are bothered by

noise to a part of the room removed from corridors. Or those students who prefer bright light could move next to the windows. These are simple steps to take, but frequently they are all that is needed to avoid a classroom problem.

Each reader, however, will have a different interpretation of order. For some, a silent, smoothly functioning classroom is the key to learning, but for others, controlled movement and an acceptable noise level signify the ideal classroom atmosphere. The rules that you establish for your classroom will define your interpretation of order. To help you think about the importance of classroom management, let's turn to John Carroll's views of the use of time.

Time and Teachers: The Carroll Model

In chapter 12, we mentioned the pervasive influence that John Carroll has exercised over recent research into the improvement of students' achievement. (His 1963 article, "A Model of School Learning," was the basis of Bloom's work on school learning.) Discussing classroom organization and management, Carroll noted that the primary job of the educational psychologist is to develop and apply knowledge concerning why students succeed or fail in their learning at school, and to assist in the prevention and remediation of learning difficulties (1963, p. 723).

With this guideline, Carroll states that a learner will succeed in learning a task to the extent that the needed time is spent for that student to learn the task. Time (actual time spent on learning) becomes the key feature. Carroll uses two categories to analyze time.

1. *The determinants of time needed for learning.* There are three important aspects in this category:
   (a) *aptitude,* which refers to the amount of time any student will need to learn a task. Be on the watch for those students who do well except perhaps for one exception (science, math, art, music); be sure to give them additional time in the subject that's causing them difficulty; (b) *ability to understand instruction,* which refers to the effects of general intelligence and verbal ability. Not only should you be aware of a student's understanding, but think of your own teaching: Was it clear? Was it to the point? How many failed to understand? Be honest with yourself; and (c) *quality of instruction,* which refers to a teacher's ability to present appropriate material in an interesting manner.

2. *Time spent in learning.* Carroll focused on two important features of this category: (a) *the time*

allowed for learning, which refers to the opportunity that individual schools allow for learning; and
(b) *perseverance,* which refers to the amount of time students are willing to spend in learning.

We may also divide the five features of these two categories by identifying those that reside within the student, those that stem from external conditions, and one that results from the interplay of external with internal. Those conditions over which a teacher has little control are aptitude and ability to understand instruction; time allowed for learning and quality of instruction are both under the control of the instructor; perseverance or the motivational aspect, reflects both student characteristics and the classroom situation.

If we now link Carroll's model of school learning to an effectively managed classroom, we can draw three conclusions. First, is the inescapable link between learning and order. Simply put, learning rarely emerges from chaos. Second, a disorganized classroom substantially reduces time for learning; too much time is spent in trying to achieve order. Third, the quality of your instruction is tightly bound to the efficiency of your classroom management. In this instance, good intentions are not enough; you cannot teach effectively if students are out of control.

A strong relationship exists between the way in which you manage your classroom and the effectiveness of your teaching, which means that your instruction must be appropriate for the age and level at which you teach. Let's use the developmental task model to review important developmental principles.

Developmental Tasks and Classroom Management

The developmental changes that your students experience will require teachers of different grade levels to adopt different types of management techniques. You have to stop for only a moment and think of the developmental characteristics of the elementary school child that we discussed in chapter 3 and compare them with those of the adolescent. The developmental sequence alone dictates changing management techniques.

As we have seen in the chapter on motivation, when natural motivators can be linked with educational requirements, tasks are more easily mastered. If you examine Table 13.1 carefully, you can distinguish those tasks that are significant for the different age groups. Now think about the classroom techniques you would use in teaching five-year-olds to read compared to those you

would use in working with adolescents in a current events class. (Note the appearance of developmental tasks in more than one category, emphasizing the integrated nature of development.)

Assuming that schools are different social contexts at preschool, elementary, and secondary levels, Minuchin and Shapiro (1983) stated that they are organized differently, children perceive them differently, and different aspects of social behavior appear to meet students' changing needs. *Preschool experiences* are more protective and caring than educational, with children interacting with one or two teachers, perhaps an equal number of aides, and several peers. Socialization and communication needs are paramount and are shaped by adults with an important, often unarticulated goal: desirable socialization (necessary conformity) and individuation (self-expression).

The *elementary school classroom* becomes more of a true social unit with more intense interactions between teacher and student and among peers. Teachers, as authority figures, establish the climate of the classroom and the kind of relationships permitted. Peer group relationships stress friendship, belongingness, and status.

In *high school,* the entire school, rather than a particular classroom, becomes the social context. Heterosexual relationships assume considerable importance, and social behavior becomes the standard of acceptance. Extracurricular activities now are a greater and more significant part of adolescent life.

With age, then, the school environment broadens in scope and complexity, producing changes in self-concept, gender differentiation, and interpersonal relationships. With these inevitable changes, it is little wonder that management techniques change accordingly.

For example, during the kindergarten and elementary school grades, students are being socialized—they are learning to respond to teachers and get along with their peers—and instructed in the basic skills. Discipline is typically not a major concern since youngsters of this age usually react well to authority and seek teacher praise and rewards. Adjustment to the school as a major socializing agent and mastery of the fundamentals are the two chief tasks that you should incorporate into your classroom management.

Students in the middle elementary school grades know a school's routine and have worked out their relationships with their peers. You should be able to concentrate on curricular tasks provided that you maintain a clearly defined classroom atmosphere.

The upper elementary and lower high school years are times when peer pressure mounts, and most students

Table 13.1

Developmental Tasks—Guidelines for Teachers

	Infancy-Early Childhood	Middle Childhood	Adolescence
Physical	Learning to walk Learning to take solid foods Learning to talk Learning to control eliminations	Learning physical skills necessary for games	Accepting one's physique
Cognitive	Learning to talk Acquiring concepts Readiness for reading Learning to distinguish right from wrong Learning sex differences	Building a healthy self-concept Learning an appropriate sex role Developing the fundamental skills—reading, writing, arithmetic Developing concepts for everyday living	Preparing for a career
Social	Learning to distinguish right from wrong Learning sex differences	Learning to get along with others Learning an appropriate sex role Developing acceptable attitudes toward society	Developing a satisfactory social role Achieving mature relations with both sexes Preparing for marriage and family
Personal-Emotional	Learning to distinguish right from wrong Learning sex differences	Building a healthy self-concept Developing attitudes and values Achieving independence	Preparing for a career Achieving emotional independence from adults Preparing for marriage and family Acquiring systems to guide behavior Achieving socially responsible behavior

are more concerned with pleasing friends than teachers. Your role as an authority figure becomes more challenging to students, and classroom control becomes more of an issue. Students should have mastered the basics and can function, to a certain extent, independently. Classroom procedures and rules should be distinct, understandable, and fair. When students of these ages know the boundaries and what is expected of them, your major tasks will include subject matter expertise and motivation.

In the upper high school grades, you are working with more mature students, the vast majority of whom are beginning to think of college and/or careers. Thus, these students are more responsible, and your concern with management decreases after the beginning of the year when you inform students what you expect of them in your class. Those wildly disruptive students, a small minority, often have either dropped out of school by these years or have been placed elsewhere.

The developmental characteristics that affect teacher management techniques should influence your decision as to what age group you would like to teach. Table 13.2 summarizes these features.

Classrooms are remarkably complex settings, and the activities that occur within them are subject to the likes and dislikes, feelings, and motivations of a large number of people. Many students have a tendency to "fool around" when their attention wavers; they require a task to prevent classroom problems and loss of learning. What are some of these problems?

Table 13.2	
Management and Development	
Level	Desirable Qualities
Lower elementary	Patience Nurturance skills Socialization skills Instructional skills
Middle elementary	Patience Diagnostic skills Instructional skills Understanding Developmental awareness
Upper elementary– junior high	Good motivator Firm Good manager Patience Understands concern of early adolescence
Senior high	Subject matter expertise Good relationships Control plus freedom

"Heckuva day, wasn't it, Ms. Carpenter? No hard feelings?"

© James Estes.

Management and Control of Problem Students

We have stressed that any analysis of classroom management cannot be confined to a discussion of discipline alone. For example, in the chapter's opening vignette, if the students had known exactly what they had to do when they came into the classroom, no one would have been standing in the back of the room, and the incident may have been avoided.

Throughout the remainder of this chapter, we'll mention a wide variety of factors that contribute to good classroom management, yet control remains central to our discussion. To help you put this issue in perspective, examples of student behavior problems (based on empirical classification studies) will be identified. Thus, you will have a frame of reference to determine what kinds of management techniques may be most effective with each type of problem.

In thinking about managing classrooms, it is useful to know something about the kinds of students who will be exhibiting problem behaviors. Over the years researchers have used a variety of checklists and rating scales to measure the types of problems that parents and teachers report that children experience. Table 13.3 displays some of the various patterns of child problems that have emerged. Remember, however, although each category is presented separately, any one student may have more than one particular behavior problem. As you read through the categories, try to answer the following questions:

- What do you see as the core of each of these problems?
- How would this problem affect the rest of the class?
- How would you handle each of these problems?
- Do you need help in working with this student?

Remember your answers; we'll return to them at the end of the chapter. Now let's examine what is actually going on in the classroom.

Table 13.3

Dimensions of Behavior Arising in Multivariate Statistical Analysis with Frequently Associated Characteristics of Each

Conduct
    Fighting, hitting
    Disobedient, defiant
    Temper tantrums
    Destructiveness
    Impertinent, impudent
    Uncooperative, resistant

Attention Problems
    Poor concentration, short attention span
    Daydreaming
    Clumsy, poor coordination
    Preoccupied, stares into space
    Fails to finish, lacks perseverance
    Impulsive

Motor Overactivity
    Restless, overactive
    Excitable, impulsive
    Squirmy, jittery
    Overtalkative
    Hums and makes other odd noises

Socialized Aggression
    Has "bad" companions
    Truant from home
    Truant from school
    Steals in company of others
    Loyal to delinquent friends
    Belongs to a gang

Anxious-Depressed Withdrawal
    Anxious, fearful, tense
    Shy, timid, bashful
    Withdrawn, seclusive
    Depressed, sad, disturbed
    Hypersensitive, easily hurt
    Feels inferior, worthless

Schizoid-Unresponsive
    Will not talk
    Withdrawn
    Sad
    Stares blankly
    Confused

Adapted from Herbert C. Quay, "A Critical Analysis of DSM III as a Taxonomy of Psychopathology in Childhood and Adolescence" in *Contemporary Directions in Psychopathology*, edited by T. Millon and G. Klerman. Copyright © 1986 Guilford Press, New York, NY. Used with permission.

Life in the Classroom

Much has been written about the necessity of adapting general management techniques for classroom use. Management is an essential function of all organizations for goal attainment, which involves three basic functions: *planning*, by which objectives and procedures are selected; *communication*, by which information is transferred; *control*, by which performance is matched to plans.

Note how these three basic functions identify the major topics in the remainder of the chapter.

1. *Planning* concerns what activities are ongoing; how can they best be organized?
2. *Communication* underscores the necessity to tell students what is expected of them and thus is a major element in effective management.
3. *Control* dramatizes the need to maintain a classroom atmosphere conducive to learning. Although planning, communication, and control are essentials for all classrooms, they appear in different guises in different classrooms. The chief reason for this is the uniqueness of the classroom environment.

When You Close the Classroom Door

Philip Jackson, in his *Life in Classrooms* (1968), has written a charming and enduring essay on "life as it is" in the classroom. Noting that although schools are places where skills are acquired, tests given, and amusing and maddening things happen, they are also places where young people come together, make friends, learn, and engage in all sorts of routine activities. Jackson adds that if we total the number of hours that a youngster spends in kindergarten and elementary school, we obtain a figure of 7,000 hours. If you were to spend an equal amount of time in church, you would have to attend a one-hour service one day a week for 150 years.

Shouldn't this amount of time be translated into meaningful outcomes? Although the classroom is a stable environment and its activities are spinoffs of certain set procedures—seatwork, group discussion, teacher demonstration, question-answers—we must also remember that young people are in school because they must be.

Given the reality of time and coercion, Jackson turns to three features of classroom life not typically mentioned: *crowds*, *praise*, and *power*.

Spending time in a classroom means learning to live with others, which can entail delay, denial, interruptions, and social distraction. During this time, and in the presence of others, a student experiences the pain of failure and the joy of success, which then become part of that student's official record. Finally, there is a vast gulf between a powerful teacher and students; how that authority is used tells us much about the atmosphere of any classroom.

It is difficult to determine how students react to classroom conditions. Realistically, everyone can be temporarily unhappy, even achieving, seemingly happy students. Jackson (1968) stated that students' attitudes toward school are complicated and puzzling. Summarizing data from previous studies, he demonstrated considerable negative feelings among basically satisfied students. The following are some of the negative items that students used to describe their feelings toward classroom life:

bored

uncertain

dull

restless

inadequate

unnoticed

unhelped

angry

restrained

misunderstood

rejected

Jackson summarized student feelings nicely when he stated:

> The number of students who become ecstatic when the school bell rings and who remain that way all day is probably very small, as is the number who sit in the back of the room and grind their teeth in anger from opening exercise to dismissal. One way of interpreting the data we have reviewed so far is to suggest that most students do not feel too strongly about their classroom experience, one way or the other (Jackson, 1968, p. 60).

You can see how the adjectives that students used reflect not only the common characteristics of a classroom but also planning, communication, and control. For example, bored and uncertain probably refer to poor planning and communication, as well as uncertainty about what is expected of them.

Students' feelings about school have not changed much since Jackson's report in 1968. Asking junior high school students about their thoughts on good teaching produced the following responses:

> Don't assign extra work to students who finish their work early.
>
> Don't be overconfident.
>
> Correct papers with appropriate comments.
>
> Be versatile.
>
> Don't yell.
>
> Be patient.
>
> Don't give up on students.
>
> Let students go to the bathroom.
>
> Be supportive and reassuring.
>
> Have a sense of humor.
>
> Don't leave the classroom.
>
> Check on students while they work.
>
> Be qualified in your subject area.
>
> Teach at our level.
>
> Use textbooks.
>
> Don't have class favorites.
>
> Don't complain.
>
> Dress neatly and stay young.

Classroom Activities

If we now attempt to analyze the classroom more formally, classroom activities emerge as the basic unit of organization. Doyle (1986) described activities as relatively short blocks of classroom time (about ten to twenty minutes) during which students are arranged and taught in a particular way.

For example, most activities involve seatwork, recitation, small groups, and presentations. Again we note the importance of engaged time. If students aren't "hooked" immediately, valuable learning time is lost.

Types of Activities

Berliner (1983), studying seventy-five classrooms from kindergarten to grade six, identified eleven activities that consistently appeared:

• reading circle
• seatwork
• one-way presentation
• two-way presentation
• use of media
• silent reading

- construction
- games
- play
- transitions
- housekeeping.

You can probably determine at a glance that some of these activities consume most of the time: About 65 percent of classroom time is spent in seatwork, 35 percent in recitation or whole class presentations. These numbers will change because at any given time transitions and housekeeping intrude.

Note that activities with different labels have a similar structure. Seatwork, for example, is quite alike regardless of subject matter. Also, lectures, demonstrations, and audiovisual presentations share many similarities. Doyle (1986) estimated that a teacher's involvement during a class seems to consist mainly of:

- actual instruction (questions, feedback, imparting knowledge)—about 51 percent
- organizing students—about 23 percent;
- dealing with deviant behavior—about 14 percent;
- handling individual problems and social tasks—about 12 percent;

The findings we have been discussing are consistent with the emphasis placed on such topics as time on task and student engagement in the learning and teaching sections. School outcome variables are not divorced from "climate variables," the atmosphere to which students are exposed. For example, Brookover et al. (1979) studied sixty-eight schools drawn from a state pool of Michigan fourth and fifth grades. Using a variety of assessment techniques, they examined such variables as the social composition of the student body, the school's social structure, and the school's climate. They assessed as outcomes student achievement, self-concept with regard to academic ability, and self-reliance.

The investigators discovered that many of the outcome differences could be attributed to the school's social characteristics. Teachers in the higher achieving schools spent more time on instruction and had more academic interactions with their students than those in the low-achieving schools. The authors concluded that student characteristics do not predict outcome independent of classroom processes. Schools with comparable resources may have very different climates and quite different student outcomes. With this brief glimpse of the varied and complex life of the classroom, you can understand the need for careful organization of these activities.

Focus on Classrooms

Student Engagement During Class

Considerable research has been done on student behavior during classroom activities. You should find these data pertinent when planning activities for a class. In one of the most comprehensive studies yet undertaken, Gump (1982) studied third graders by using time-lapse photography. He found that student involvement (time on task) was highest in teacher-led small groups and lowest during student presentations.

Between these two extremes, engagement was high during whole class recitations, tests, and teacher presentations but dropped during independent seat work and supervised study. Research has continued to support this study, with studies indicating student involvement during recitation at 85 percent and 65 percent for seatwork.

Student involvement during the beginning phases of a lesson seems to be significantly lower than during the remainder of the activity. The lowest involvement scores of all occur during the beginning phase of seatwork, while highest involvement occurs during the remaining phase of recitations.

Remember that your students will be most actively engaged when you lead small groups and least actively engaged during student presentations. These results have received tentative support in high school studies as well as in the elementary grades. (For further information, see Doyle, 1986)

Organizing Classroom Activities

Recall the distinctions that have been made throughout the chapter thus far: good classroom management entails more than gimmicks or entertainment devices to keep students under control. The first element to consider is that of classroom atmosphere. What is the "climate" of your classroom like? Is it conducive to learning?

High work involvement with a minimum of deviant behaviors does not appear by accident. Laslett and Smith (1984) have identified four "rules"—actually skills— that should help your classroom organization.

1. *Get them in.* Lessons should start on time, and teacher attention should not be diverted by routines that should have been attended to earlier. The authors believe that classwork begins smoothly when teachers are present before the class arrives

and have checked that everything is in proper order. Your being there early simply reinforces your authority by deciding when you want the class to enter, by assigning seats, and by having immediate work to occupy each student.

2. *Get them out.* Before deciding what you will teach, Laslett and Smith (1984) recommend that you consider what would be the ideal method for concluding the lesson and dismissing the class. They argue that there is nothing strange about these priorities when you consider that carefully won and maintained control can be quickly lost at the conclusion of a lesson. Such planning is only part of the smooth transitional processes constantly needed. Control is not the only reason for thinking about concluding your lesson. If you do not provide time for some reinforcement at the end of the lesson, learning can be lost in the rush toward dismissal.

3. *Get on with it.* Here your focus should be on the lesson itself: content, manner, and organization. To maintain motivation, assure that class activities are complete, well-structured, and as interesting as you can make them. Balance your work by making your classes as varied as possible. Mix the familiar with the new, the interesting with what you know might be boring but necessary, seatwork with recitation. As these authors note, however, be sure that variety does not become confusion.

4. *Get on with them.* Classroom disruptions are infrequent when positive interactions characterize the teacher-student interactions. Success as a teacher hinges on your relationship with your students. Several techniques to further these relationships will be suggested throughout the chapter, but for now remember to know your students as well as you can, both their in-and-out-of-school lives. Constantly be aware of what is going on in your class.

Though these four "rules" will not guarantee the absence of discipline problems, following them carefully should help to eliminate misbehaviors that result from classroom disorganization. Let's now consider a technique for integrating the many ideas we have discussed. One way is by referring to the **QAIT** model developed by Slavin (1987d).

The QAIT Model

Teachers must adapt instruction to students' levels of knowledge, motivate students to learn, manage student behavior, group students for instruction, and test and evaluate students. These functions are carried out at two levels. At the school level, the principal and/or central administrators may establish policies concerning grouping of students (e.g. tracking), provision and allocation of special education and remedial resources, and grading, evaluation, and promotion practices. At the classroom level, teachers control the grouping of students within the class, teaching techniques, classroom management methods, informal incentives, frequency and form of quizzes and tests, and so on. These elements of school and classroom organization are at least as important for student achievement as the quality of teachers' lessons (Slavin, 1987d, p. 90).

Building on Carroll's model of school learning (see chapter introduction), Slavin (1987d) proposed an instructional model focused on the alterable elements of Carroll's model. Called QAIT, the model encompasses the following four components: quality of instruction, appropriate levels of instruction, incentive, and time.

Quality of instruction depends both on the curriculum and the lesson presentation. Slavin stated that when quality instruction occurs, the information presented makes sense to students, is interesting, and is both easy to remember and to apply. Above all else, however, Slavin argues that instruction must make sense to students. For this to happen: (a) you must present information in an orderly systematic fashion; (b) you must provide smooth transitions to new topics; (c) you must use vivid images and concrete examples; and (d) you must insure necessary repetition and reinforcement.

Appropriate levels of instruction implies that you know that your students are ready to learn new material. The lesson cannot be either too easy or too difficult. One of your most challenging tasks will be to accommodate your teaching to the individual differences and needs of your students. Though most of the methods schools and teachers use to provide appropriate levels of instruction (remedial grouping, tracking, special education) have serious drawbacks, given the diversity of your students, there can be no avoiding the issue. Slavin (1987d) identifies the following methods as most common:

1. *Ability groups* (elementary schools), in which students remain in heterogeneous classes most of the day but are grouped for certain subjects such as reading and mathematics, can be effective.

2. *Group-based mastery learning* (see chapter 12) does not require permanent ability groups; students regroup after each skill is taught. The danger here is that in the traditional class period corrective instruction can slow the entire class.

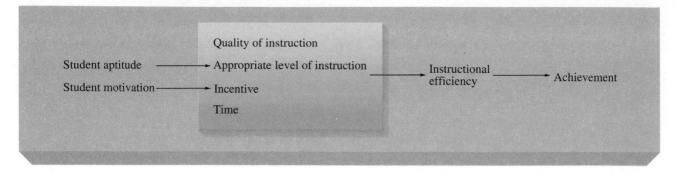

Figure 13.1
The QAIT model.

3. *Individualized instruction* (see chapter 11) provides for accommodation and can be effective if coupled with personalized contact with an instructor and some group work.

Summarizing what is currently known about the results of grouping practices, Slavin (1988a) separates the results into two categories:

- within-class groupings—the research suggests that the evidence for the value of mastery learning remains inconclusive, while analyses of cooperative learning methods indicate consistent gains in student achievement if properly managed.
- between-class groupings (ability groups, special classes)—have little effect on student achievement although acceleration may possibly benefit some gifted students; departmentalization at the upper elementary and middle school levels probably should be avoided; regrouping strategies (regroup for certain subjects such as math and/or reading) can be effective.
- *Incentive* refers to the degree of student motivation. As much as we desire intrinsic motivation for our students (see chapter 10), not all students will be ecstatic about all subjects all the time. One of the best incentives you can offer is to ensure that students be held accountable for what they do. Give them time to respond to your questions; check their homework. Don't rely solely on individual praise and reward; cooperative learning methods in which groups are rewarded because of their learning have consistently shown increased student achievement.
- *Time* refers to sufficient time for learning to occur. But don't be satisfied with "time" as a global concept. Remember the distinction between allocated time and engaged time.

These four elements of QAIT (quality, appropriateness, incentive, time) share one critical characteristic: Each element must be adequate if instruction is to be ef-

fective (Slavin, 1987d, p. 92). Figure 13.1 illustrates the QAIT model.

Note the independent variables in Figure 13.1. Students bring to your classroom certain abilities and motivational dispositions over which the school has little control. The alterable variables are QAIT, and they influence achievement by two time-related variables seen in the middle column—instructional efficiency and engaged time. Note how instructional efficiency in turn is related to quality of instruction, appropriate levels of instruction, and incentive.

Slavin argues that his model accounts for many of the variables that help us to understand how classroom organization affects learning outcomes. The QAIT model is not bound by any particular theory but can be adopted as a method to understand instruction and learning in any classroom context.

Classroom Contexts

We have identified several common classroom activities and examined ways to improve performance in many of them. Now let us consider two of these activities in greater detail.

Recitation

Recitation entails calling on individual students who give answers publicly before the rest of the class, usually for a brief time. Recitation has several purposes: review, introducing new material, checking assigned work, practice, and comprehension (Doyle, 1986). Consequently, the purpose of the recitation dictates the type of question and opportunity for participation.

Since recitation involves your use of questions, you must ask them in a manner calculated to sustain the attention of the entire class. Try to systematize your questions so that all members have the chance to participate. Think about your questions. Do you intend them for

Focus on Students

The Native American Student: Core Values and the Teaching Process

Disproportionate numbers of Native American students have experienced difficulties with school. The dropout rate remains alarmingly high, enrollment in higher education is low, and teen pregnancy, suicide, and substance abuse continue at rates significantly higher than their Anglo peers. Many educators have observed that Native American students often have poor self-esteem and lack pride in being "Indian."

In a recent article in *Phi Delta Kappan* (1989) a leading educational publication, Lee Little Soldier reviewed some of the major core values of Native Americans that he believed educators should recognize and use constructively. Noting some vast differences among the many North American tribes of Native Americans, Soldier cited the following five core values as being relevant to the education of Native American students:

1. Native Americans respect and value the dignity of the individual, and (subsequently) children are afforded the same respect as adults.

2. Traditional Indian families encourage children to develop independence, to make wise decisions, and to abide by them. Thus, the locus of control of Indian children is (more) internal, than external, and they are not accustomed to viewing adults as authorities who impose their will on others.

3. Cooperation and sharing are important values. Native Americans are thought to be more group-centered than self-centered. They are accustomed to sharing whatever they have with many family members. Soldier perceives sharing as a habit that often bothers teachers who emphasize labeling possessions and taking care of one's own belongings.

4. Harmony is another core value of Native Americans according to Soldier: harmony with self, with others, and with nature.

5. The perception of time by Native Americans traditionally differs from that of the Anglo world. It appears that Native Americans view time as a continuum with no real beginning or end. There is an emphasis on living in the present and not worrying much about the future. Native Americans generally are patient individuals. Strict adherence to rigid schedules may prove to be difficult for many native Americans.

Thus, a significant problem facing educators who wish to teach Native American students effectively is to develop supportive learning environments without compromising educational goals. According to Soldier, the answer to this problem may lie partly in the concept of instruction that is currently being characterized as cooperative learning. Instructional approaches that emphasize the group and the values of sharing and cooperating are consistent with many Native Americans' basic values.

Note. From "Cooperative Learning and the Native American Student" by L. L. Soldier, (1989, October) *Phi Delta Kappan*, 161–163.

review? Will you be satisfied with a yes or no answer, or are you looking for a thoughtful reply? Remember:

- *Ask your question of the entire class,* give them time to think of the answer, and then call on an individual student. Do not indicate a student and then ask your question.
- *Wait for the answer.* Give the student time to think and respond. Use your best judgment, and if the delay continues, rephrase the question, perhaps supplying prompts. If a student answers incorrectly, correct the answer impersonally, explaining as you do. Discourage any type of student calling-out while another student is thinking of an answer, as this behavior can quickly produce chaos.

Seatwork

Two types of seatwork are most commonly used. First is *supervised study* during which all students are assigned independent work and the teacher moves around the room, monitoring each student's work. Second is *independent work*, when the teacher is busy with another group and does not monitor each student's work.

Estimates are that students in grades one through seven spend from 50 percent to 75 percent of their time working alone on seatwork. Since students are less engaged during seatwork than they are in group or individual work with teachers, you should be alert to techniques that improve engaged time. Here are several suggestions to guide seatwork:

- Spend sufficient time explaining, discussing, and even practicing before your students commence work on their own.
- Practicing should immediately precede the seatwork.
- The exercises assigned to your students should flow directly from your explanations and the practice.
- Guide your students through the first few exercises.

A good clue to the success you can expect from assignments lies in the number of questions you receive during the actual seatwork. If you find yourself giving multiple explanations during the seatwork, you can anticipate multiple errors (Rosenshine & Stevens, 1986).

Establish a set routine that your students are to follow any time they engage in seatwork. In this way, they will know what to do when they have questions, when they finish, and how to get help. Even if you are working with another group, arrange seating so that you can adequately monitor both groups. If possible, try to move around the seatwork group. Teacher contact greatly increases engaged time since feedback and follow-up are as related to achievement as praise or reward.

Although teachers can easily overuse seatwork, if the assignment is interesting, clearly explained, and not just busy work, seatwork can be a valuable classroom tool—as it should be, given the amount of time students spend at it.

Managing the Classroom

These next two sections, Managing the Classroom and Methods of Control, are actually subdivisions of the same topic. They are separated here because of their unique importance and to give you the perspective of general and specific measures that apply directly to control. Remember: The initial meetings that you have with your class during the first two weeks of school are probably the most important with regard to classroom control. During these sessions you will have set the classroom atmosphere by the rules and procedures you establish.

Rule Setting and Classroom Procedures

Any time people—adults or students—come together to achieve a particular goal, their behavior must be subject to rules. Otherwise goal attainment is doomed. You may have had experience in attempting to learn in a setting where individual misbehavior constantly disrupted the class. If you were intent on learning, you probably became frustrated very quickly.

Many rules are explicit and openly discussed. Behaviors such as tardiness, fighting, talking in class, and other similar activities cannot be tolerated for the good of the entire group. Other behaviors such as leaving the room, sharpening pencils, or getting a drink of water are more implicit; that is, they are known and require little discussion once rules are established. For leaving the room, you may require hand-raising or some other technique such as a student's walking to a chalkboard, writing his/her name on the board, leaving the room, and upon re-entering, erasing the name from the board.

Good class management begins with a clear understanding of rules, preferably rules that are worded positively.

Good Managers

Emmer et al. (1980), studying elementary school teachers designated as "good managers," stated that all these teachers made known their rules and procedures on the first day of class but quite deliberately integrated them into a system, which they taught. Their rules were explicit, concrete, and functional, and these teachers gave examples of the signals they would use for various activities.

The "good" managers did not initially overburden their students with rules—a tendency of many beginning teachers—but began with those that they considered basic and then gradually introduced more as they were needed. They also periodically reminded their students of the rules. By monitoring their classes closely, they were able to notice any rule violations almost instantly and attempt to correct them before minor violations developed into major problems.

Secondary school teachers also clearly and unmistakably stated the desired behaviors for their classes, gave precise indications of the expected work standards in their classes, and acted immediately to check disruptive behavior (Evortson & Emmer, 1982). Less effective managers, soon after the opening of school, experienced more talking-out in class and unapproved movement around the room. The main difference between the elementary and secondary "good" managers was that the secondary school instructors spent less time teaching and rehearsing the rules and procedures. Remember:

- Decide on as few important rules as possible.
- Make rules absolutely clear to all.

- Enforce rules for all.
- Avoid playing favorites.

Rules and Classroom Activities

As we have seen, classroom activities run in cycles in which students' behaviors are defined by rules. Once teacher and other students repeatedly perform and reinforce behaviors specified by the rules, the rules become a part of the regular classroom routine. When this happens, the pieces are in place for efficient instruction. Medland and Vitale (1984) suggest that the following five steps will help you to formulate meaningful rules for your many classroom activities:

1. *Define the class activity.* We have previously commented on general classroom rules (for example, no calling out) but specific activities require specific rules. When you are working with one reading group, other group members must occupy themselves with seatwork. Efficient laboratory sessions demand orderly retrieving and storing of equipment. Physical education classes necessitate proper dress, equipment, and warm-up, certainly activities that need structure and rules.

2. *Determine the social behaviors necessary for activities.* What is it that you want your students to accomplish during the activity? How should they go about it? Answering these two questions should help you to identify the needed behaviors. Also, consider what is inappropriate for the activity.

3. *Determine which activities need a list of rules.* Several guidelines can help you here (Medland & Vitale, 1984).

   a. Are there many social behaviors associated with the activity?

   b. Does the activity require considerable time?

   c. Are special classroom rules needed to cover the activity's behaviors?

   d. Have misbehaviors been associated with this activity?

Answering any of these questions in the affirmative would seem to suggest the need for appropriate rules.

4. *Make a set of rules for the selected activities.* Rules add structure to any activity and enhance learning by providing a means of coordinated movement. If you think for a moment about the rules that function when you are with one group, and the rules that apply to those doing seatwork, you can understand the necessity for coordination.

Since rules describe the behaviors necessary to accomplish an activity, try these suggestions:

- Keep your rules short.
- Phrase rules in a positive way.
- Don't use too many rules.

5. *Be sure you formulate a set of general activity rules.* We have previously commented on the need for such rules, and you can understand the necessity for being certain that your activity rules are consistent with the general rules. Otherwise, students become confused, and any contradiction could lead to misbehavior.

From this discussion it should be clear that successful teachers establish a classroom work system with rules and procedures designed to keep the system in good order. Successful teachers set these rules at the beginning of the school year, even though their students previously have learned those general rules that apply to school behavior. Experience has shown that unless rules are reinforced, student behavior deteriorates. The quality of rule setting, even at the secondary level, determines the order that will prevail in any class for its duration (Doyle, 1986).

Finally, although classroom order depends on your ability to have your students understand classroom procedures, you must also be ready to cope with rule violations. Your students expect a certain minimum level of competence in making the system work.

Management and Control

You should also take into account several developmental considerations in managing your classroom. Students exhibit a wide range of difficulties in development, but many problems are not serious enough to be of great concern. Kazdin (1988), however, noted that the following developmental issues are noteworthy in considering students' problems.

- Some of the behaviors that characterize maladjustment are relatively common in childhood. As most students mature, they do not experience severe problems.
- As students develop and undergo rapid changes, problem behaviors wax and wane at different ages. Such behaviors as lying and destructiveness are frequent from four to nine years of age but decline by ten to eleven years of age.
- As a result of rapid changes across development, a problem of one type may be replaced by another problem at a later age.

There probably is no such thing as the "normal" youngster; all students usually exhibit troublesome behavior during development. They are anxious, insecure, and aggressive, but only when these traits persist and become severe do they bother teachers. For most children, problems do not persist. Youngsters typically outgrow such behavior and progress to more mature stages of development.

Be alert to developmental problems and know when and where to refer them. Remember, however, that all children experience stress, and their reaction may be to exhibit maladaptive behavior. Your role (shared with parents) in helping your students to master developmental crises is vital because the manner in which they meet these difficulties shapes the way that they face future dilemmas.

You are teaching your students problem solving behavior, and what they learn may last a lifetime. Constant failure, punishment and ridicule destroy confidence and can cause a low self-concept that may result in a worrisome elementary school student who becomes a sullen, rebellious secondary school student. Estimates are that about 5 percent of all school-age youngsters show serious symptoms, and about 10 percent manifest milder behavioral disturbances. Thus, 85 percent of students proceed normally, perhaps causing teachers some anxieties with temporary maladaptive behavior (J. Travers, 1982).

Your students, then, will inevitably experience growth problems and bring them to the classroom. They usually pass fairly quickly; only when they persist should you become concerned.

Aggression in the Classroom

An aggressive student not only can be a classroom problem but also may require special treatment. You may also find it helpful to consider this problem developmentally so that you can identify those classroom situations that could trigger an outburst.

Since a completely satisfactory theory of aggression still eludes us, research interest has recently turned to the social encounters of infancy and early childhood to discover the roots of aggression. (See Parke & Slaby, 1983 for a particularly thoughtful analysis of aggressive behavior.) Investigators have discovered that as early as twelve to eighteen months, half of the interchanges among children in a nursery involved conflict. By 2 1/2 years, such disruptive interchanges had dropped to 20 percent, and by 42 months to 5 percent. Between two and four years, physical aggression decreases and verbal aggression increases, and by seven years, aggressive behavior becomes much more person-oriented. Aggressive students present behaviors that are typically classified as externalizing.

As students continue to age and greater cognitive ability develops, their understanding of another student's intentions becomes important. There seems to be clear developmental changes involved. Seven-year-olds respond aggressively to both accidental and intentional provocation, while nine- and twelve-year-olds react less aggressively to accidental provocation. Twelve-year-olds also responded less aggressively to intentional verbal than to intentional physical provocations than did the seven- and nine-year-olds. Box Table 13.1 illustrates a general developmental sequence of aggressive behavior.

Remember that there are clear sex differences in aggression, with boys generally being much more aggressive. Impressive evidence exists that aggression in males is remarkably stable. Studying subjects from two to eighteen years of age, Olweus (1982) reports that male aggression and acting-out behaviors show substantial persistence over long periods of time.

Some students who exhibit aggressive behavior may need professional services focused on the school and family (Horne & Sayger, 1990). In dealing with most cases of aggression, however, try these suggestions:

- *Stop trouble before it starts.* Knowing when to interrupt behavior is a valuable asset—too soon makes a teacher appear fussy, too late may produce an uproar. If a youngster is not going to stop voluntarily, then a teacher should act decisively.
- *Use **signal interference.*** A skillful teacher instantly notices the signs that lead to trouble: fidgeting in one youngster, rigidity in another. Watch youngsters and then act. Let the student know you are aware by moving closer, staring, coughing. Discover those mannerisms that signal difficulty. Whatever the time, whatever the exertion, the results will make your efforts worthwhile.
- *Avoid the **tribal dance,*** which usually involves a dare. Trouble starts; the teacher acts; the student reacts to protect status. The tribal dance has started. The student dares the teacher to do something, and the teacher must accept the dare or retreat and lose status. Teachers must act quickly to avoid the tribal dance either by ignoring the behavior or by instantly suppressing it, and by knowing those students who are susceptible to the ritual. The truly tough youngsters are not usually susceptible; they are not forced to prove their courage. The lesson here is that you should know the danger signals and not put yourself in an impossible situation.

The Bully

Is there any reader who did not have nightmares sometime during school about that "monster" who loved to tease, humiliate, threaten, and fight? Even today most middle school principals will list bullying among their major worries.

Who is the bully? Most bullies seem to be students who have been treated violently themselves, attend schools that treat violence ineffectively, or are members of a peer group that encourages aggression. When we couple this kind of student with others who are almost "natural victims" (small, underweight, perhaps differently dressed, or having an obvious personal problem, such as anxiety), then conditions are ripe for bullying.

Olweus (1982) has identified four causes in the development of a bully:

1. **indifference** (usually by the mother), which Olweus terms silent violence;
2. parents who are **permissive** with an aggressive child;
3. parents who typically resort to **physical punishment**;
4. a **temperamentally** aggressive child.

Be alert for this type of behavior; often teachers and parents are the last to know since the victim is reluctant to talk about it. Among Olweus's suggestions for dealing with bullies are the following:

- Supervise recreation periods more closely.
- Intervene immediately to stop bullying.
- Talk to both bully and victim privately, and insist if such behavior does not stop, both school and parents will become involved.
- If the problem persists, therapy may be needed.

It is interesting to note that bullying is not just a concern in the United States. In Japan, bullying (or ijime) is a major social problem of concern to the entire nation (Prewitt, 1988). Remember: Prevent bullying, reinforce a child for not acting as a bully, and work with the victim to build self-confidence and success.

Box Table 13.1

Development and Aggression

Age	Type of Aggression	Cause
birth–2 yrs.	General upset	Possession of object
2–4	Physical Some verbal	Frustration
4–8	Verbal Physical	Hostility towards others
8–12	Verbal Some physical	Peers Authority Insecurity

- *Watch for hidden effects.* Though a student may do what you want, there are usually side effects, and the wise teacher will work with a disciplined youngster to prevent feelings of hostility and isolation. We may have to live with aggression, but don't breed it by exposing normal youngsters to classroom experiences that produce frustration.
- *Recognize your own aggression.* Though your hostility may be justified, your maturity and your professional obligation demand that your behavior reduce classroom tension and lessen the opportunities for student aggression.
- *Evaluate your classroom procedures.* Emmer et al. (1984) suggested that you frequently check your classroom's organization and decide if you should make changes in your management procedures.

TEACHER ⬌ STUDENT
INTERACTIONS

Managing Classroom Activities

1. Time, for both students and teachers, is a critical factor in learning.
   - Be careful of the way that you allocate time. You may like math and enjoy teaching it, but if you find that you are spending ninety minutes on math and twenty minutes on language, re-examine your time commitment. Ask yourself about the consistency and rationale for your time allotment.
   - Try to assess the time that your students are actively engaged; estimates are that students, on the average, are attentive about 75 percent of the time, but the range is quite large, from 50 to 90 percent. Ask someone (perhaps a student teacher) to observe one of your classes (at different times of the day) and at five-minute intervals record what each student was doing. Check the results. This strategy will give you helpful insights into the time that your students (and you) are engaged in various tasks.
   - Check your behavior to make sure that you're not spending too much time on mechanical tasks: arranging furniture, passing out papers, getting students in, getting them out. Try to keep students engaged until the last minute; you may want to close a class by asking an open-ended question to be picked up at the beginning of the next class. With regard to time, remember this educational guideline: Use it; don't lose it.
   - Try to identify the time of the day when your students are more energetic than others. Is it at the beginning of the school day? After the students settle in? Toward the end of the day? Once you have discovered these optimal times for engagement, capitalize on them for more intensive work.

2. Classroom activities are the basic unit of organization.
   - In planning a particular activity (soon after school opens in the fall), arrange to have it videotaped. Watch yourself. Have you arranged things so that there is a minimum of confusion (seating arrangements, grouping, availability of materials, etc.)?
   - Design activities so that students clearly understand not only what they are to do but also why they are doing it. To further cultural understanding, you could

have your students trace their family roots through three or four generations. This activity helps them to appreciate the reasons that people leave their lands of origin and the problems that recently-arrived immigrants can experience. This activity should minimize any misunderstandings that may arise.
   - Be sure you know how to use audiovisual materials. Fumbling for the right switch or adjustment only provides time for misbehavior.
   - If you are planning an out-of-class activity, involve your class in the planning. What should they bring? Do they need money? How are they to get there? What kinds of behavior are acceptable? How should they act when they get there (staying together, free time, etc.)?
   - Don't hesitate to use educational games. Many excellent types are available (don't hesitate to create your own—perhaps with the help of your students). They are useful for socializing, for motivation, for a change of pace, and as stimuli for thinking.

3. Sensible rules are at the core of every well-managed classroom.
   - At the beginning of the year, post your classroom rules; keep them simple and list as few as possible, but make sure your students understand them; they should know exactly what's expected of them with regard to routines, transitions, and acceptable behavior.
   - Decide how you will use the time at the beginning and end of a class or day so that it has important learning outcomes. Don't be in the position of talking to students as they leave the classroom. Immediately tell students what you expect of them.
   - Carefully examine the physical facilities of your classroom, and decide on rules that expedite learning. Is the room neat? Do posters reflect a theme or topics under class discussion? What does the physical layout of the classroom suggest for traffic patterns? How will you provide for handicapped students? Do you have a safe and effective plan for storing materials? Do you have a plan for distributing materials? Is your classroom physically safe for students?

Searching for the Causes of Classroom Problems

Once you recognize that a problem exists, the next step is to identify what is causing it. If you answer these questions objectively, you may well discover significant clues.

- Is your room arrangement causing any problems, such as congestion, bumping, limited visibility for some students?
- Are your rules and procedures clear? Some disruptive behavior may not be included under your rules, or you may be forgetting to enforce one or more rules.

- Are you managing student work carefully? Be sure that your directions are clear and understood by all and that students realize that they will be accountable for their work.
- Are you satisfied with the consequences of appropriate and inappropriate behavior? Review your own behavior to be sure that your rewards and penalties are still effective and that you are not punishing or praising students too freely.
- Are you detecting any misbehavior in its early stages? You may need to work on your monitoring ability for dealing with misbehaviors in their early stages, before they become major problems.
- Is your teaching effective? Check to be certain that students are not confused during your instruction and that transitions from one activity to another are smooth and uneventful.

Methods of Control

You have now reached the point where you can better understand the specific suggestions about to be made. All the topics discussed in this chapter point to one basic conclusion: A smoothly running classroom blocks most problems before they can get started. You must always relate your present classroom situation to your students' needs and developmental changes. If your classroom is well-organized, and you have followed the management ideas presented here, and you're still not satisfied, you may want to adopt specific control techniques.

Misbehavior in the Classroom

The acts of school violence that you read or hear about in the news are infrequent and seldom occur in most effective schools. We do not wish to minimize, however, the growing concern in this country with crime and violence in the schools. Several years ago, the National Institute of Education (1978) conducted a survey of principals, teachers, and students in secondary schools. Although the study is dated, it remains the only representative analysis of crime and violence in schools and is methodologically sound. The results of the study (called the "Safe Schools Study") indicated that only one of fifty-eight crimes that occur in schools are reported. The following figures described what happened during a typical month in America's secondary schools:

- 282,000 students were physically attacked.
- 112,000 students were robbed through force or weapons.
- 2.4 million students had their personal property stolen.
- 800,000 students stayed home from school because they were afraid to go to school.
- 6,000 teachers were robbed.
- 1,000 teachers were assaulted seriously enough to require medical attention.
- 125,000 teachers were threatened with physical harm.
- More than 125,000 teachers encountered at least one situation in which they were afraid to confront misbehaving students.
- One out of two teachers was the victim of an insult or obscene gesture.
- 2,400 school fires were set.
- 13,000 thefts of school property occurred.
- 24,000 incidents of vandalism occurred.
- 42,000 cases of damage to school property occurred.

Despite these findings, the typical classroom acts of misbehavior are calling-out, refusals, tardiness, and missing class. Make no mistake—they are annoying and, if left unchecked, will lead to major classroom disruptions.

The key to understanding misbehavior is to be alert to what students do while in the classroom. What may appear to be misbehavior may actually aid a class. For example, the student who, in eagerness, talks out may generate an enthusiasm and motivation that spreads to other class members; but a student who refuses to do what you request or answers you back constitutes true misbehavior (Doyle, 1986).

You must also be aware of any change in your behavior when different students demonstrate the same behavior. Some students seem to be particularly skilled in irritating and frustrating teachers. These are not usually the overtly unruly but those who walk the thin line between acceptable behavior and insolence. Others see any teacher as an authority figure who must be challenged.

Some readers will ignore the student who practices that studied insolence and concentrate on any unruliness; others will see both types of behavior as inappropriate. Remember, however, that you and you alone will establish the rules of acceptable behavior in your classroom. As long as your students do not violate school codes, you are responsible for setting standards. You should never become a teacher who intervenes frequently to check misbehavior. Such behavior characterizes least effective teachers and is a clear signal that something is wrong.

Multicultural Students and Discipline

There must be order in a classroom. Otherwise, chaos prevails and learning suffers. It makes no difference which students are involved in disruptive behavior; you must determine the degree of control necessary for efficient learning.

Our discussion is intended to remind you to treat all students fairly and equally. Evidence indicates that larger numbers of minority students are disciplined and suspended, which causes additional problems since the time lost from school hurts both motivation and achievement (Children's Defense Fund, 1975).

About two million students are suspended from school each year, with African-American and Hispanic students more than twice as likely as white students to be suspended. The dropout rate for all Hispanics remains high (80 percent in New York, 70 percent in Chicago, and 50 percent in Los Angeles (Grossman, 1984). Dropouts are likely the result, in part, of discipline problems that are related to academic skill difficulties (Casas, Furlong, Solberg, & Carranza, 1990).

Think about this statement.

> Teachers have absolutely no knowledge, not only of the language but about the culture of the children that they are working with . . . Haitian children are very physical. We express . . . we use our hands . . . we talk. This doesn't mean that we are creating a scene or disrupting. If the child wants to speak, instead of saying: "Hi, Johnny," he will touch the other child automatically. In the classroom, if the teacher said you were supposed to be quiet, or "You don't move," it quickly turns into a discipline thing. They don't understand that we use a lot of body language (New Voices, 1988, p. 62).

You must keep order in your classroom—that's a given. Some behavior, however, that is natural for particular students could lead to problems. Take these students aside, explain what could happen if the entire class acted like this, and work out some signal that would let you know when they need help.

Occasionally a minority student may have difficulty understanding what is going on in the classroom and, in his/her efforts to keep up with others, may appear to act in a disruptive fashion. "Calling out" is a good example of this situation. For example, a Spanish-speaking student may call out for a translation. If intervention programs are available for minority students during the elementary school years, these students may acquire those academic skills that will ultimately reduce discipline problems (Miranda & Santos de Barona, 1990).

The point here is to make a concerted effort to understand your students. To help you to understand your students better, use the following questions as a guideline (Grossman, 1990):

- How much reinforcement and punishment are students accustomed to receive from the adults in their culture? For example, Hawaiian children

respond well to considerable attention while Navajo students prefer to work independently.
- What kinds of consequences work best for a particular student? Is this student used to physical punishment, loss of attention, removal (such as being sent to their rooms), or loss of privileges? Mexican-American students, for example, do not react well to persistent questioning by a well-intentioned teacher intent on having them give a correct answer. This technique violates their sense of tolerance.
- How much initiative can you expect a newly-arrived student to display? Japanese students may at first be reluctant to express their opinions and resist answering questions or raising issues for discussion. They may depend solely on memorization and be confused by attempts to have them solve problems on their own.

If you think about these situations, and others that you may encounter, you become more sensitive to the relationship between cultural background and classroom behavior.

Maintaining Classroom Control

While teaching a college mental hygiene course, Kounin (1970) noticed a student reading a newspaper in the back of the room. He immediately and angrily reprimanded him. The discipline succeeded; the student's attention returned to the lecturer. But the reprimand also affected other class members. Attention was rigid, and a depressing silence settled on the room. This was Kounin's first experience with **the ripple effect.** Punishment was not confined to one student; its effects spread to other class members. Kounin decided to study ripple effects and what he calls **desists**—a teacher's actions to stop misbehavior.

To avoid experimental contamination, Kounin and his colleagues videotaped thirty actual classrooms. They analyzed the tapes and coded teachers' desist techniques for clarity, firmness, intensity, focus, and student treatment. They then attempted to relate the desist techniques to managerial success, which they defined as the degree of student work involvement in that teacher's class, the amount of student deviancy in that class, and to what degree deviancy spread to other class members. There was no relationship between the qualities of a teacher's desists and success in handling deviant behavior.

Does this mean that misbehavior is insignificant and of no concern to others? Absolutely not—discipline heads any list of teachers', administrators' and parents' educational concerns. The problem is to isolate those techniques that contain misbehavior and prevent them from spreading. The question should be: What is it that teachers do that makes a difference in how students behave?

Effective Teacher Behaviors

Additional study convinced Kounin that some teachers' behaviors correlated highly with managerial success. These behaviors were effective not only with specific children but also with an entire class. In this second study, Kounin videotaped fifty first and second grade classes for a full day each. Realizing that the clarity, firmness, intensity, and focus of a teacher's desist are not critical in maintaining classroom control, Kounin searched for something else. From continued replaying of the tapes, certain characteristics emerged.

1. *Withitness.* The first was **withitness,** which means that teachers know and understand what's occurring in their classrooms. Some teachers clearly demonstrated they knew what was going on in their classrooms. These teachers select the correct targets for their desists; that is, they know who misbehaved and how serious it was. They also timed their intervention so that the misbehavior did not spread and become more serious.

2. *Overlapping.* Some teachers had no difficulty in attending to two issues simultaneously. For example, what would you do in the following situation? You are with a group in which one youngster is reading aloud when two other youngsters in another group, who are supposedly doing seatwork, become noisy. Do you leave the reading group and attempt to check the noisy twosome? Or do you tell the youngster to continue reading, while simultaneously telling the other youngsters to stop talking and get to work. Kounin refers to the latter technique as **overlapping**: A teacher demonstrates the ability to handle two events simultaneously. As he notes, a learning event and misbehavior simultaneously present a teacher with two issues; the two events overlap.

   Although both withitness and overlapping are associated with managerial success, Kounin believed that withitness seems to be more important. Teachers who demonstrate withitness can simultaneously handle two issues (overlapping). What can you learn from Kounin's discussion of these two topics? Work at widening your attention; force yourself to try to know everything that is occurring in your classroom so that you acquire withitness. When this happens, you are almost compelled to attend to multiple events (overlapping). Since these teacher behaviors relate closely to managerial success, they are well worth the effort.

3. *Transition smoothness.* The next characteristic Kounin discovered was **transition smoothness.** Some teachers had no trouble in handling activity and movement in their classes. The classes he videotaped averaged 33.2 major changes in learning activities during the day. If these transitions are not handled smoothly, chaos can result. Teachers must initiate, sustain, and terminate many activities involving many materials. If you are to maintain smooth movement, you must avoid jerkiness and slowdowns, those teacher behaviors that abruptly introduce one activity by interrupting another: "Close your books, return to your desks, and do your arithmetic." There is no smoothness here; the youngsters are unready to interpret and act on the teacher's directions. Also avoid **dangles**—leaving some direction unfinished—and **flip-flops**—changing from one activity to another and then back again.

   Slowdowns occur when a teacher's behavior slows an activity's movement. Kounin identified two kinds of slowdown: **overdwelling,** when a teacher spends excessive time—beyond that needed for student understanding—on a topic, and **fragmentation,** when a teacher has individual students do something it would be better to have the group do—for example, having children come to the reading group one by one instead of as a group. Kounin concluded that avoiding jerkiness and slowdowns is a significant aspect of successful classroom management.

4. *Group alertness.* In Kounin's terms, **group alertness** refers to programming for "learning-related" variety. As mentioned previously, be honest with yourself. Am I an interesting teacher? Are my classes lively? Do I keep all of my students involved? To help you minimize misbehavior, remember to:

   • watch all of your students while one is responding.
   • keep on the move; don't stay in one spot; let students know that you are interested in what they are doing.
   • call on students randomly; avoid any set patterns.
   • keep interest high by leading up to a question—"you haven't heard about this before, but I think you can answer it."

Finally, Kounin emphasized that teachers are not tutors; that is, they work with groups, either the class as a whole, or subunits within the class. How then, can you keep your classes alert? Kounin observed teacher behaviors that he designated as *positive group alerting cues,* such as creating suspense before calling on a student, and consistently calling on different students. *Negative group alerting cues* had teachers concentrating on only one student, designating a student to answer before asking the question, or having youngsters recite in a predetermined sequence.

Table 13.4

Procedures for Appropriate Social and Academic Behavior: Percentage of Teachers Reporting Use and Mean Frequency of Reported Use

Procedure	Inappropriate social behavior		Inappropriate academic behavior	
	% Reporting (SD)	Mean freq. (SD)	% Reporting (SD)	Mean freq. (SD)
1. Praise or compliment	100 (0.0)	2.5 (0.18)	100 (0.0)	2.6 (0.11)
2. Hug, pat on back, wink, etc.	92 (8.2)	1.9 (0.27)	89 (10.9)	1.8 (0.31)
3. Friendly/encouraging teasing	84 (11.8)	1.7 (0.34)	85 (13.3)	1.7 (0.35)
4. Show others the good work	78 (9.5)	1.5 (0.19)	87 (4.4)	1.5 (0.17)
5. Send note or call parents	72 (15.8)	1.3 (0.36)	79 (9.8)	1.3 (0.28)
6. Special time with teacher	69 (6.0)	1.1 (0.17)	76 (9.7)	1.1 (0.24)
7. Use special materials/objects	67 (13.7)	1.2 (0.27)	66 (16.6)	1.2 (0.32)
8. Give happy face, star, or other symbolic reward	65 (22.5)	1.5 (0.64)	82 (20.6)	1.9 (0.69)
9. Give sticker, food, or other material reward	63 (17.4)	1.3 (0.49)	71 (13.6)	1.5 (0.48)
10. Allow to run errands	63 (11.0)	1.1 (0.29)	59 (12.5)	1.0 (0.21)
11. Allow child to tutor	55 (12.2)	0.9 (0.27)	78 (11.7)	1.2 (0.24)
12. Stories, movies, parties	50 (8.5)	0.9 (0.26)	42 (10.7)	0.8 (0.24)
13. Give free time, less classwork or homework	49 (11.4)	0.8 (0.28)	51 (13.1)	0.7 (0.25)
14. Post progress/work	48 (9.8)	0.9 (0.28)	93 (4.7)	1.9 (0.23)
15. Assign as monitor/line leader	41 (14.4)	0.8 (0.28)	37 (11.3)	0.7 (0.21)
16 Do nothing special (ignore)	39 (12.0)	0.7 (0.27)	32 (7.0)	0.5 (0.08)
17. Bonus points/extra credit	38 (11.2)	0.7 (0.23)	61 (20.3)	1.1 (0.43)
18 Eat in room/talk to neighbor	36 (10.6)	0.6 (0.14)	31 (9.1)	0.5 (0.12)
19. Allow to choose own seat	34 (12.8)	0.6 (0.26)	34 (8.3)	0.5 (0.21)
20. Allow to skip ahead in work	29 (7.5)	0.4 (0.12)	56 (6.8)	0.9 (0.22)
21. Points given toward earning privileges	28 (12.6)	0.5 (0.23)	32 (8.9)	0.5 (0.24)

Note. Percentages are averages of responses across all grades, K-6.
Reprinted with permission from *Journal of School Psychology,* Vol. 28, L. A. Rosen, et al., "A Survey of Classroom Management Practices" Pub. 1991, Pergamon Press Ltd. Oxford, England.

Using Behavior Modification

As we now focus our discussion on specific techniques for handling misbehavior, you must make a decision concerning the nature of the method with which you feel most comfortable. In a survey of teachers' classroom management techniques, Rosen et al. (1990) found distinctions between teachers' responses to appropriate and inappropriate academic and social behaviors. Note in Tables 13.4 and 13.5 that more teachers reported using management techniques to control inappropriate social behavior than inappropriate academic behavior.

Although there were a few exceptions, the percentage of teachers using management techniques addressing appropriate social behaviors was equivalent to the percentage using the same technique for appropriate academic behavior. Moreover, verbal management techniques (for example, praise or reprimands) were used more than techniques based on concrete consequences (for example, a pat on the back or sending a note home). A second study by the authors using direct observations of the teachers also verified that the teachers used more verbal techniques than those based on concrete consequences.

Table 13.5

Procedures for Inappropriate Social and Academic Behavior: Percentage of Teachers Reporting Use and Mean Frequency of Reported Use

Procedure	Appropriate social behavior		Appropriate academic behavior	
	% Reporting (SD)	Mean freq. (SD)	% Reporting (SD)	Mean freq. (SD)
1. Reprimand privately	99 (1.9)	2.4 (0.18)	94 (5.9)	2.0 (0.27)
2. Send notice or call parents	95 (4.3)	2.1 (0.18)	96 (4.1)	2.0 (0.16)
3. Reassure/discuss with child	94 (3.9)	2.2 (0.29)	97 (3.1)	2.3 (0.13)
4. Take away a privilege	83 (6.3)	1.5 (0.34)	62 (9.1)	1.0 (0.22)
5. Reprimand loudly in class	77 (13.5)	1.1 (0.26)	48 (12.4)	0.5 (0.16)
6. Move desk by teacher, in corner, in hall	72 (7.6)	1.2 (0.22)	56 (7.8)	0.8 (0.31)
7. Threaten to punish	63 (13.3)	0.9 (0.24)	39 (9.5)	0.5 (0.12)
8. Take away snack or recess	47 (12.7)	0.8 (0.33)	46 (13.1)	0.7 (0.25)
9. Tell child to put work away or head down	46 (16.8)	0.7 (0.33)	25 (16.1)	0.3 (0.20)
10. Send to principal	45 (8.8)	0.5 (0.15)	18 (10.4)	0.2 (0.13)
11. Do nothing special (ignore)	43 (15.8)	0.5 (0.21)	29 (14.9)	0.4 (0.19)
12. Detention/stay after school	42 (21.1)	0.8 (0.39)	36 (23.5)	0.6 (0.41)
13. Assign extra work or sentences to write	32 (15.8)	0.4 (0.24)	30 (10.9)	0.4 (0.18)
14. Bang book/ruler on desk	29 (9.9)	0.4 (0.16)	N/A	N/A
15. Write negative comment on academic work	23 (6.7)	0.4 (0.14)	61 (4.3)	0.8 (0.23)
16. Take chair away	23 (12.4)	0.3 (0.15)	9 (8.7)	0.1 (0.10)
17. Rip up papers, work, etc.	18 (6.0)	0.2 (0.08)	28 (10.7)	0.3 (0.10)
18. Shake or use other firm physical contact	16 (9.7)	0.2 (0.12)	4 (3.2)	0.1 (0.05)
19. Send to different or lower classroom	13 (8.9)	0.2 (0.15)	8 (4.6)	0.1 (0.04)
20. Take points off grade	7 (2.4)	0.1 (0.08)	43 (18.3)	0.8 (0.39)
21. Publically post demerits	7 (8.9)	0.1 (0.14)	3 (3.2)	0.0 (0.0)
22. Take away gym, art, etc.	6 (5.7)	0.1 (0.08)	4 (4.0)	0.1 (0.05)

Note. Percentages are averages of responses across all grades, K-6.
Reprinted with permission from *Journal of School Psychology*, Vol. 28, L. A. Rosen, et al., "A Survey of Classroom Management Practices" Pub. 1991, Pergamon Press Ltd. Oxford, England.

Interestingly, most of the interactions that teachers had with their students were classified as neutral and were not designed to control behavior. The authors concluded that the choice of a management technique appears to depend greatly on the teacher's acceptance of the procedure.

In a sense, the control section of this chapter reflects many of the choices that you faced in the learning section (see especially chapters 6 and 7). Which basic theoretical position should I follow: cognitive, behavioral, or some combination of both? Most of us are not bound by any rigid adherence to a particular belief; nevertheless, we tend to favor one while incorporating material from others.

You may well believe that behavioral techniques are best suited for all aspects of the classroom, or decide that certain types of student behavior (perhaps hyperactivity or aggression) are better met by behavior modification. In fact, behavioral techniques are among the most widely evaluated procedures in psychology and education.

Table 13.6

Summary of Basic Principles of Operant Conditioning

Principle	Characteristic Procedure and Its Effect on Behavior
Reinforcement	Presentation or removal of an event after a response that increases the frequency of the response.
Punishment	Presentation or removal of an event after a response that decreases the frequency of the response.
Extinction	No longer presenting a reinforcing event after a response that decreases the frequency of the previously reinforced response.
Stimulus control and discrimination training	Reinforcing the response in the presence of one stimulus but not in the presence of another. This procedure increases the frequency of the response in the presence of the former stimulus and decreases the frequency of the response in the presence of the latter stimulus.

From *Behavior Modification in Applied Settings*, 4th Ed. by A. E. Kazdin. Copyright © 1989, 1984, 1980, 1975 by Wadsworth, Inc. Reprinted by permission of Brooks/Cole Publishing Company, Pacific Grove, CA 93950.

Remember that behaviorism's basic assumptions are that both adaptive and maladaptive behavior are learned, and that the best means for treating problems is to structure a student's classroom environment so that you can reinforce desirable behavior. (Here you may want to re-read chapter 6 to refresh your knowledge of behaviorism.)

Definition of Terms

Although behavior modification is the general label that identifies those management techniques emerging from behavioral theory, certain distinctions should be made.

- **Behavior influence.** This occurs whenever one person exercises some control over another. It is a constant occurrence in home, work, politics, and schools where teachers are constantly involved with behavior.
- **Behavior modification.** Behavior modification is a deliberate attempt to apply certain principles derived from experimental research to enhance human functioning. These techniques are designed to better a student's self-control by improving skills, abilities, and independence. One basic rule guides the total process: People are influenced by the consequence of their behavior. A critical assumption is that the current environment controls behavior more directly than an individual's early experience, internal conflicts, or personality structure.
- **Behavior therapy.** Behavior modification and behavior therapy are often used synonymously, but behavior modification is the more general term.

Behavior therapy usually applies to a one-to-one client-therapist relationship. So, technically, behavior therapy is only one aspect of behavior modification.

Teachers using behavior modification attempt to influence their students' behavior by changing the environment and the way that youngsters interact with their environment, rather than by probing into backgrounds, or referring a child for medical treatment (usually medications), or expulsion. To be successful you must clearly specify the problem behavior. What is it, precisely, that you wish a student to do, or not to do? Try to determine the consequences of children's behavior; that is, what do they obtain by it? Then decide what you are going to do. Will you ignore it, hoping for extinction; or will you punish it; or will you reward some other form of behavior?

Decisions about how to manage behavior (for example, punish an undesired behavior or reinforce a desired behavior) and which behavioral techniques to use are important and often complex decisions. Table 13.6 summarizes much of what was stated in chapter 6 by highlighting the critical dimensions of applied behavioral techniques.

- *Positive reinforcement.* As we have seen in chapter 6, positive reinforcement means, approximately, reward and can be defined as any event following a response that increases the possibility of recurrence of that response. Good examples would be money, food, praise, attention, and pleasurable activities. You must be careful in using positive reinforcement with your students; what may be pleasurable (positive reinforcement) for one student may not be for another. Rewards for secondary students will not be the same as those for elementary or preschool students. Table 13.7 provides examples of rewards that are effective with secondary school students.

Here is the value of knowing your students—what they like and dislike. Students will have different preferences among the items in the table. Positive reinforcement is a powerful tool in changing behavior; presenting youngsters with something they like can consistently produce desirable results.

- **Token economy.** Token economies have been widely used in managing groups. For example, students, patients, and other group members receive tokens when they exhibit desirable behavior, collect them, and when they attain an accepted number, exchange them for something pleasurable. For example, talkative students may receive tokens for every fifteen or twenty minutes they are silent; when they have enough tokens, they may trade them for extra recreation or something else they like.
- **Shaping.** You first determine the successive steps in the desired behavior and teach them separately, reinforcing each until students master it. The students then move to the next phase where the procedure is repeated. Finally, they acquire the total behavior by these progressive approximations.
- **Contingency contracting.** A teacher and student decide on a behavioral goal and what the student will receive when he/she attains the goal. For example, the goal may be successfully completing twenty division problems; the positive reinforcement may be an extra art period if this is the child's favorite school activity. Contracts involve an exchange—both teacher and student agree on what each will do.
- **Aversive control.** Students maintain some undesirable behavior because the consequences are reinforcing. To eliminate the behavior, a teacher might apply an aversive stimulus (for example, remaining after school). The removal of positive reinforcement is another example of aversive control. (Recall the definition of punishment: the introduction of aversive stimuli or the withdrawal of positive reinforcement.) You have read about the possible consequences of punishment's effect; but again, use care in the selection of an aversive stimulus, and try to have students do something desirable so that you can positively reinforce them.
- **Overcorrection.** Overcorrection combines both restitution and positive practice. For example, a girl may deliberately knock things off another student's desk as she moves about the room. The teacher not

only has her remedy the situation (put the things back on the desk)—restitution—but also straighten all the other desks in the room—positive practice.

Behavior Modification and the Causes of Behavior

As noted in previous chapters, behavioral techniques are often called applied behavior analysis when used in educational settings. Applied behavior analysis involves a "systematic performance-based, self-evaluative method of studying and changing socially important behavior" (Sulzer-Azaroff & Mayer, 1991, p. 4). Table 13.8 provides a list of the characteristics of applied behavior analysis. As you examine this table, note the emphasis on the environment as the cause of behavior.

Why should teachers concentrate on student behavior and not the causes of the behavior? Behaviorists argue that teachers are not analysts. They are not trained to explore the special circumstances that influence behavior. Since the multiple and interactive causes of behavior can elude detection by highly trained and skilled professional psychologists and counselors, busy teachers, who

Table 13.7

Intermittent Rewards Suitable for Secondary Students

- Writing a note to the student's parents
- Writing a note to the student
- Calling the student's parents
- Calling the student
- Complimenting the student in front of another staff member
- Asking one of the administrators to reward the student's behavior
- Privately praising the student's classroom performance in a nonclassroom setting such as in the hall after school
- Give the student a responsibility
- Tokens for a video arcade
- Tickets to a school activity
- Food
- Coupon to rent a movie
- Let the student choose an activity for the class
- Check out a book the student might be interested in

From R.S. Sprick and V. Nolet, "Prevention and Management of Secondary-Level Behavior Problems" in *Interventions for Achievement and Behavior Problems* edited by G. Stoner, et al. Copyright 1991 by the National Association of School Psychologists. Reprinted by permission of the publisher.

Table 13.8

Characteristics of Applied Behavior Analysis

Characteristics

- Focus on behaviors of applied (social or clinical) significance.
- Search for marked intervention effects that make a clear difference to the everyday functioning of the individual.
- Focus on overt behaviors.
- Focus on the behaviors of one or a small number of individuals over time.
- Assessment of behavior through direct observation, as in counting the frequency of responses.
- Assessment continuously over time for extended periods (hours, days, weeks).
- Use of environmental (and observable) events to influence the frequency of behavior.
- Evaluation and demonstration of the factors (e.g., events) that are responsible for behavior change.

From *Behavior Modification in Applied Settings*, 4th Ed. by A. E. Kazdin. Copyright © 1989, 1984, 1980, 1975 by Wadsworth, Inc. Reprinted by permission of Brooks/Cole Publishing Company, Pacific Grove, CA 93950.

have neither the time, training, or experience, are less likely to detect them.

Even if teachers can identify the cause of maladaptive behavior, they frequently can do little about it. If the trouble lies in the home, a teacher's options are limited. Consequently, teachers must focus on the child's behavior and, if necessary, obtain professional consultation. Occasionally, however, the causes of maladaptive behavior are discernible and treatable, but the behavior remains. An example is a reading problem caused by poor vision; when the physical difficulty is corrected, the reading deficiency remains.

Noting the concern that all teachers share in maintaining discipline, Wielkiewicz (1986) suggested the need for several steps in any behavior management program.

- *Identify the problem.* Usually a general problem is identified—this boy is hostile—and then additional assessment helps to identify the circumstances that trigger the hostility.
- *Refine the target behavior.* A general label such as "hostility" is not much help. If you recall that one of the major objectives of applied behavior analysis is the accurate presentation of reinforcement, then you

must identify precise behavior (the target behavior) if reinforcement is to be effective. What behavior? Under what circumstances is the behavior to be reinforced?

- *Assess the baseline rate.* What is the rate of occurrence when behavior management is not in effect? How does it compare to intervals when behavioral techniques are at work? If you obtain a baseline rate before intervention, then you can assess the success of the program.
- *Identify the reinforcer and contingency.* You must know your students well to discover just what reinforces them, not always an easy task with some students in a classroom setting. You may have to link tokens earned at school with reinforcement at home.
- *Begin the program.* In a manner they can understand, tell students what they need to know.
- *Modify the program when necessary.* If the program does not appear to be as successful as you anticipated, step back and evaluate your steps. Perhaps more time is necessary, or some other element interferes, such as a brother or sister who attempts to subvert the program when at home.
- *Fade out the program.* The good program puts itself out of business. The desired behavior appears at a steady rate with ever increasing frequency between reinforcements.
- *Ensure generalization.* A good program includes procedures that will facilitate transfer and maintenance of behavior change over time and across settings.

Understanding the Causes of Behavior

Our third and final explanation of maintaining classroom control differs distinctly from Kounin's work, which focused on teachers' behaviors and behavior modification, which focused on the careful application of reinforcers. Here the search concentrates more on the cognitive than on overt behavior. The classic work of Dreikurs et al. (1971) and Redl and Wattenberg (1959) are good examples of this kind of analysis.

Social Discipline and Goal-Seeking

Students, like all of us, are constantly searching for something—the goals that they have identified for satisfying their needs. Goal seeking, a frequent theme in the motivational literature, is especially important for teachers since a student seeking a positive goal is a joy in the classroom. Dreikurs et al. (1971) have raised several provocative issues about discipline, and their discussion of goals is especially pertinent here. Their basic premise states that behavior is purposive and that correcting goals

Focus on Classrooms

Using Behavior Modification

Below are several widely accepted strategies for using behavior modification:

- *Know your target.* Just what behaviors do you wish to change? Specify precisely what the behavior is and what you want it to become. Do not attempt too much. For example, some students may be unable to tolerate inattention too long; consequently, they frequently use maladaptive, disruptive behavior to secure attention. You will not immediately change that behavior for an entire day, but you may quickly change it for a period and gradually extend it for an entire school day.
- *Know the circumstances surrounding the behavior.* When maladaptive behavior occurs, try to discover what happened immediately preceding and following it. A girl may consistently misbehave just before reading period. She has a reading problem, but her friends read smoothly and effortlessly. By being disruptive, she secures satisfaction and successfully directs attention from her difficulty. The teacher should strive for Kounin's "transition smoothness" by providing positive reinforcement just before the reading class, and then either ignoring (if possible) her behavior in reading or planning that she has some reading task that ensures positive reinforcement.

Many teachers and parents have found helpful the use of a simple model—referred to as the ABC model—to organize information about the events surrounding a target behavior. The A in the model refers to antecedents, the B to behavior, and the C to consequences. By focusing on those events that surround the target behavior—both antecedent and consequence—we gain knowledge about events that are likely to

influence a student's behavior. Box Table 13.2 illustrates the use of the ABC model by a school psychologist who was trying to understand the events that controlled an aggressive third grader's behavior.

You can see that Jim, the classmate on the other team, and the teacher influenced John's behavior. Jim's successes served to stimulate negative comments from John, but the teacher's close physical proximity to John appeared to reduce/stop John's teasing. One can conclude from this analysis that teacher proximity is an important element in managing John's behavior.

- *Know your students so that you know what reinforces them.* Although the primary reinforcers, such as food and physical stimulation, are powerful shapers of behavior, they are hardly appropriate for the classroom. Teachers must search for those things, objects, events, that individual students find reinforcing. For example, some students find adult attention a strong positive reinforcement. Other youngsters, because of unpleasant experiences with adults, think their attention is aversive. You must know your students to use reinforcers effectively.
- *Select appropriate strategies.* Select techniques that effectively encourage desirable behavior and discourage undesirable behavior.
- *Use feedback wisely.* Make sure that students understand the link between behavior and reinforcement. Your goal should be a gradual reduction in external reinforcement and increasing self-control.

Thoughtfully used, behavior modification techniques can help you attain a constructive classroom atmosphere.

Box Table 13.2

The ABC Model Used To Understand Aggressive Behavior

Antecedents	Behavior	Consequences
Jim makes a good play.	John calls Jim a bad name.	Jim ignores John.
Jim's teammates congratulate him.	John calls Jim another name and challenges him with the statement, "I can beat you any day."	Jim says, "Not today," in response.
Teacher moves close to John.	John stops teasing Jim.	Teacher praises John for controlling his temper.

is possible, while correcting deficiencies is fantasy. They believe that the force behind every human action is its goal and that all our actions are an effort to find a place for ourselves. Students are not driven through life; they seek their own goals.

The following assumptions are associated with the Dreikurs' **social discipline** model:

- Students are social beings and desire to belong to a social group.
- Students are decision-makers.
- All behavior is purposeful and directed toward social goals.
- Students see reality as they perceive it to be.
- A student is a whole being who cannot be understood by isolated characteristics.
- A student's misbehavior results from faulty reasoning on how to achieve social recognition (Wolfgang & Glickman, 1986, p. 190).

Once students establish goals, their behavior manifests a certain consistency and stability that crises and frustrations threaten. All youngsters want attention and when they do not receive it through socially acceptable means, they try anything to obtain it. Punishment is preferable to being ignored; it reinforces one's presence. Some children feel accepted only when they do what they want, and not what they are supposed to do.

Parents and teachers who engage in a power struggle with children are eventually doomed to failure. Once a power struggle begins, youngsters want to get even with those who punish them. They seek revenge, and the turmoil they create provides feelings of satisfaction. If students experience constant struggle and failure, they finally withdraw, desiring only to be left alone.

Discipline should not be considered an either-or proposition—either students obey instantly or they rule the classroom, causing chaos. Discipline does not mean control by punishment. The authors believe that self-discipline comes from freedom with responsibility, while forced discipline comes only from force, power, and fear (Dreikurs et al., 1971).

The classroom atmosphere must be positive, accepting, and nonthreatening. Students need limits, however, and discipline means teaching them that certain rules exist that everyone must follow. Students and teachers should agree on the rules for classroom behavior, which increases their appreciation of the necessity for rules, especially when they have cooperated in formulating them. Discussing rules on borrowing, using equipment, name calling, or classroom manners is excellent training in discipline. (You can find further information on Dreikur's social discipline model in Wolfgang & Glickman, 1986.)

Good class management requires direct communication characterized by attention, a soft controlled voice, and specific feedback about the student's misbehavior.

Mutual Respect in the Classroom

Dreikurs and his colleagues state that both teachers and students need inner freedom, which results from cooperating with each other, accepting responsibility for behavior, speaking truthfully, respecting each other, and agreeing on common behavioral rules. Here are some of their practical suggestions.

- *Do not nag or scold.* Frequently this response gives students just the attention they want.
- *Do not ask a student to promise anything.* Children will agree to almost anything to extricate themselves from an uncomfortable situation. You just waste your time.
- *Do not reward good behavior.* The child may work only for the reward and stop immediately. Also children expect something whenever they behave correctly. (Note how this differs from behavior modification techniques.)
- *Avoid double standards.* What is right for the student (politeness, punctuality) is right for the teacher. (Here Dreikurs' work approximates the modeling of social learning theory.)
- *Avoid threats and intimidation.* Students cannot learn or acquire self-discipline in a tense, hostile environment.

• *Try to understand the purpose of misbehavior.* Why do students clown during arithmetic? Is it to get attention, or to demonstrate to peers that they are powerful since they dare to defy adult pressure?
• *Establish a relationship based on trust and mutual respect.* If you treat your students as "nearly equal," they soon respect you and believe that you truly want to help them. Thus, they often will discuss their problem with you, which will help you devise ways to correct it.
• *Emphasize the positive.* Refuse to take misbehavior personally to avoid causing a ripple effect to permeate the classroom. Try to make your behavior kind but firm.

These techniques of control reflect the theme of teacher-student cooperation that has been a thread of continuity throughout our work. What happens between a teacher and student constitutes a relationship, one that must be positive if teaching and learning are to attain desired objectives.

Using Influence Techniques

Redl and Wattenberg (1959) in their classic statement about discipline, teaching, and techniques of control, believe that a student's mental health affects learning just as academic efficiency enables a student to adjust more satisfactorily. Emotional problems inevitably impair learning, although a minority of disturbed children try to compensate for their problems by overachieving academically. As the authors note, success in any phase of life is an emotional tonic.

What techniques can teachers use to guide behavior toward desirable goals? To be practically helpful, Redl and Wattenberg urge you to be totally realistic. That is, you must accept certain administrative procedures. Will a principal support you if you send a student to the office? Another consideration is your personality. Do you think that sending a youngster to someone else for discipline is your failure and a sign of weakness to the class? Here are their four categories of **influence techniques.** Although born from a psychoanalytic approach to behavior, many of these methods of influence have an established empirical basis in the effective teaching literature. Recent work by Gettinger (1988) on proactive classrooms incorporates many of the techniques discussed below in the sections on Supporting Self-Control and Situational Assistance.

• *Supporting self-control.* The basic assumption underlying this category is that students want to do the right thing. Problems occur when they forget the rules or when impulse overpowers self-control. These youngsters recover quickly if a discerning teacher, quietly mentioning their misbehavior, reinforces their self-control. Here are several supporting self-control techniques.
• *Signals.* When a student begins to misbehave, using a signal, such as shaking your head, raising a warning hand, or even just looking sometimes may stop trouble for a typically well-controlled youngster. The student retains control if the teacher acts immediately, that is, at the first signs of trouble. Do not hesitate; even well-controlled students become problems if their misbehavior goes unchecked.
• *Proximity control.* Students begin to misbehave; the teacher simply stands by them; often a teacher's immediate presence will stifle trouble before it becomes serious. Many teachers are unaware of using the technique of **proximity control** when they move troublesome youngsters close to them, to a front-row chair, or to an aisle where they can get to them quickly.
• *Interest boosting.* When students become bored, they become restless. Occasionally going to such students and expressing interest in their work will help them renew their attention. **Interest boosting** is usually successful with a well-controlled youngster who is experiencing momentary restlessness. You must know your students for this technique to be effective.
• *Planful ignoring.* Sometimes it is better to ignore an incident if youngsters can themselves regain their poise. Be careful about this. If students interpret your behavior as weakness, you must abandon **planful ignoring**. If you notice that well-disciplined children are becoming troublesome, you must act decisively. Only you can decide, and your decision comes from knowledge of your students.

Redl and Wattenberg stated that supportive techniques have the advantage of immediately checking misbehavior, thus preventing serious trouble. They also reinforce a child's sense of self-control. Remember, however, that these techniques are chiefly effective with those students who are usually well-behaved. Do not overuse them since there is a danger that students can think you are unfair by expecting too much of them, particularly if you ignore similar behavior in more troublesome youngsters. Redl and Wattenberg believe that these are the methods of "first choice"; that is, when they work little else is needed. If they fail, more direct efforts are necessary.

• *Situational assistance.* The second class of techniques helps to remove those difficulties that students themselves cannot master. Teachers have a more active role. Since they change a program, they restructure the situation; that is, teachers have the responsibility of modifying the circumstances that seem to be causing the problem. Here are several situational assistance techniques.

- *Helping over hurdles.* Teachers can avoid many problems by providing timely assistance. Students, both elementary and secondary, must know precisely what they are doing if they are not to misbehave. First graders left to their own devices, or senior high students engaged in a project they cannot understand, are headed for trouble. Give clear directions to "help them over the hurdles."

- *Restructuring the situation.* Change the pace of the classroom occasionally; vary the routine and shift activities so that there can be some physical release after verbal learning.

- *Removing seductive objects.* You can be certain that there are some objects that attract students' attention, producing restlessness and problems. For example, setting up audiovisual equipment you will not use until much later will distract your students. Occasionally classroom projects have objects that tempt some youngsters to mischief.

- *Anticipating planning.* Redl and Wattenberg succinctly summarized this category's meaning: To wait for trouble to arise is to look for trouble. Before a field trip, for example, tell your group what to expect and what behavior is acceptable.

- *Reality and value appraisal.* Helping youngsters to cope realistically with their problem is the third of the influence techniques. Although many cases of misbehavior are obscure, there still is a need for youngsters to develop a sense of cause and effect. The following techniques may help students to view behavior in a different perspective:

- *Direct appeal.* Sometimes students can improve their behavior if you show them the connection between their behavior and its consequences. Telling a student that his talking is disturbing others may help. You also must be realistic; some students simply do not care.

- *Defining limits.* Students must know exactly what is expected of them. How you do this extends from posting a list of classroom rules (probably in the elementary school) to a simple yes or no at the secondary level. The fewer the rules, the fewer the violations. But those you insist on, enforce. Youngsters expect limits; they want them. Rules provide them with security while simultaneously giving them something to test. We have previously discussed this topic, but we cannot overlook its importance.

"I'm your teacher, Mrs. Gridley. Learn to read, write, and do arithmetic, and nobody will get hurt."

Avoid using threats to control or motivate students.
Reprinted courtesy *Kappan* and Stan Fine.

Invoking the Pleasure-Pain Principle

The final category from Redl and Wattenberg's work is somewhat similar to behavior modification. What you do to students because of their behavior will guide their future actions. Redl and Wattenberg's interpretation of the pleasure-pain principle differs from behavior modification in that teachers deliberately produce pleasant or unpleasant feelings. Rewards, threats, praise, and blame are all used to produce these feelings, to cause a fear of consequences, or to create inner anxiety that will help students to maintain control over their behavior. Here are some of the techniques.

- *Rewards and promises.* If possible use positive techniques to influence behavior; they not only inform students that their actions are acceptable, but they are also a powerful force in developing a satisfactory self-concept. You should be aware that students may work for the reward alone, circumventing intrinsic motivation. Also, be sure that all youngsters receive either a reward or a promise of one for their effort. These are not insurmountable obstacles, so you should use positive techniques as much as possible.

- *Threats.* Pointing out undesirable consequences sometimes helps certain students to behave properly. The authors believe that threats should be used sparingly, if at all. They may cause cheating, lying, excessive anxiety, or overt challenges by students. There is also a danger for teachers. You undoubtedly chose teaching as a career because you like young people; consequently, you may not follow through on your threat. Students see this as a sign of weakness; you may inadvertently cause yourself discipline problems by the careless use of threats.

Focus on Classrooms

Glasser's Control Theory

Recently, the work of William Glasser (1986) has attracted considerable attention. Advocating a similar perspective to that of Redl and Wattenberg—searching for the causes of misbehavior—Glasser argues that under the best of conditions, teaching is a hard job, but when students make no effort to learn, it becomes an impossible task.

Glasser's beliefs, which he calls **control theory,** attempt to explain how our behavior is always our best attempt to satisfy powerful forces at work within us. If nothing outside us, including school, can ever fulfill our needs, a good school could be defined as a place where almost all students believe that if they do some work, they will be able to satisfy their needs enough so that it makes sense to keep working (Glasser, 1986, p.15).

The following basic assumptions, which are derived from Glasser's Reality Therapy, help to explain his views on discipline:

- Relevance, responsibility, and reality are necessary for schools without failure.
- A student is rational and capable of responsibility.
- Students must meet their own needs in a way that does not infringe on the rights of others.
- Each student has two basic needs, a need for love and a need for self-worth.
- Misbehavior results from these two basic needs not being met.
- Students must make their own behavior logical and productive and behave in a responsible manner (Wolfgang & Glickman, 1986).

Arguing that we attempt to satisfy five basic needs—to survive and reproduce, to belong and love, to gain power, to be free, to have fun—Glasser believes that we (and our students) always choose to do what is most satisfying to us at the time. Immediately after birth we begin to learn what satisfies our needs and then form pictures of what produces need satisfaction. Glasser then states that the pictures in students' heads determine what they do in school.

None of us satisfies our needs directly; rather we behave to satisfy the "pictures in our heads," as Glasser says. *When we act it is always our best effort to gain effective control of our lives.* Glasser believes that students have a much greater opportunity to satisfy the pictures in their heads during school time if they are taught by a *learning-*

William Glasser, M.D., President, Institute for Reality Therapy, Los Angeles.

Photograph courtesy of the Institute for Reality Therapy.

team model. The team concept can be a powerful motivator because:

- students gain a sense of belonging by working together in learning teams of two to five students.
- a sense of belongingness provides the initial impetus to work, and successful students become excellent role models.
- stronger students find need-fulfillment in helping weaker peers; power and friendship become a united force.
- weaker students find need fulfillment by contributing as much as possible.
- students learn to work together and apart from the teacher, giving a sense of power and freedom.
- learning teams offer meaningful structure.

Notice that each of these statements refers to satisfaction of the pictures that fulfill needs and to an ever increasing degree of control. Glasser's work is thoughtful and could furnish you with practical techniques for improving classroom control.

- *Praise and blame.* These techniques make people feel good or bad about themselves. Positive adult attention enhances students' self-concepts; blame may produce inner anxiety and a desire to change conduct. Praise and blame are effective only when a class respects you. Be careful not always to blame or praise the same students.
- *Punishment.* The authors define punishment as the planned infliction of an unpleasant experience to modify future behavior. It is always unpleasant, and students always suffer some kind of hurt or loss. Punishment is constructive only under certain conditions: children know their behavior is wrong and the punishment fits the misbehavior. Otherwise, students interpret your action as revenge, which causes a lingering resentment that can only bode ill for the future.

Time your intervention carefully; do not delay because children will have forgotten why you are punishing them. Try to avoid mass punishment; if an entire class has misbehaved, you may have no alternative, but do not punish an entire class because you cannot identify a culprit. Enough has been said about the ramifications of punishment to cause you to apply it cautiously.

Redl and Wattenberg argue strongly that teachers should strive to understand the causes of misbehavior to respond effectively. The various methods of control that we have discussed are not mutually exclusive. You will probably select those features of each that appeal to you and adapt them to your method of classroom management.

Don't Cause Any Problems Yourself

Your first task in establishing a desirable classroom atmosphere is not to cause any problem yourself. Your initial reaction undoubtedly is to place all responsibility for discipline problems on students, but closer inspection may suggest that some responsibility falls "behind the infallible side of the desk." Though experience may eliminate many of the self-generated problems, to be aware of them early is to minimize their repercussions. How would you honestly answer the following seven questions?

- *Are you unfair?* Students probably react more intensely to this issue than any other. You must treat all students equally, which may be difficult because some students will seem to provoke you deliberately. But if you punish this student for disrespect, then you must punish all for disrespect. If you equivocate, a student's attitude toward you will quickly degenerate into personal resentment, with serious consequences.
- *Are you inconsistent?* Do you react to similar conditions in a similar manner? If you scold or punish students for talking one day, then ignore them the next, you are inconsistent. If you expect students to do papers or reports carefully in October or November, and then ignore these standards in January and February, you are inconsistent. Students are bewildered; they do not know how to act; their behavior and work soon become erratic, and these conditions encourage trouble.
- *Are you boring?* This is a blunt question that deserves a frank answer. If you maintain the same pace and procedure every day, students eventually search for excitement. Break your routine; use games, stories, the playground, audiovisual techniques, discussions, lectures, group work, guests, and any relevant source or technique that will make your classroom exciting and inviting.
- *Have you established routine?* You cannot break routine unless you have established it. Make no mistake; routine is one of your best safeguards against discipline problems. Students must know what they are to do, when they are to do it, and where they are to do it. If you betray uncertainty about school rules, classroom procedures, location of materials, meaning of bells, function of machinery, or poor daily planning, you only invite trouble. Master routine; when you break it, your students perceive change as a real treat.
- *Do you know your subject?* Woe to the teacher who consistently cannot answer questions, who demonstrates a lesson and arrives at the wrong answer. Students quickly sense incompetence and lose respect for you.
- *Can you control your temper?* A common mistake is to interpret all challenges personally. Some problems are personal attacks, but these are usually infrequent; most arise from the daily give and take of the classroom. If you respond spitefully, you create a sharp personal confrontation. Although it is difficult not to see misbehavior as a personal challenge, work at it; eventually an objective perspective will serve you well.
- *Have you considered how you should best respond?* If you require considerable personal control, your disciplinary methods should focus on students' behavior, either rewarding, ignoring, or punishing it. If you are less concerned about control, you probably are more interested in a search for the causes of problems, in an understanding of the behavior. Adapt

your techniques to your personality and beliefs; do what you do best.

If you are still concerned about classroom control and want to be certain that you are not responsible for any upsets, try the following exercise. You can see it is a means of quickly examining your behavior. Can you identify the problem? What were you teaching? How were you doing it? What was the time of day? If you honestly and objectively conclude that there was trouble, but that you were not the cause (as a result of evaluating your answers to the seven questions), then you search elsewhere: specific control techniques, one or two particularly disruptive students, a topic that didn't interest students, a restless class at a particular time of the day. Even if you're tired and unhappy after a class, try it, and be ruthlessly honest with yourself. You may want to do it for a full week, thus capturing all times and all classes.

Class	On-Task Engaged	On-Task Not Engaged	Off-Task Distracted	Off-Task Disruptive
One (Arithmetic)				
Two (Reading)				
Three (Social Science)				
Four (Art)				
Five (Music)				

After checking your students' behavior for each class, assess how much you contributed to that behavior.

Your Behavior	**Yes**	**No**
Fair		
Boring		
Knowledge		
Temper		
Appropriate responses		
Routine established		

List your classes (1-5 for secondary school subjects, subject name for elementary). Check the box that best describes students' behavior during each class. Now focus on the class that you're concerned about. Go to the second checklist and objectively analyze your behavior. You can use this technique both for classes and individual students.

Now return to p. 396 and re-examine the problem types discussed there. As a result of your reading, would you now handle any of these problems differently? Compare your answers now and those you gave when you first read them.

Teacher-Parent Collaboration

Virtually all of the management strategies that we have introduced in this chapter involve what you as a teacher can do in the school setting. But students also spend a considerable amount of time at home and in the community. Parents still greatly influence elementary students, and some parents can have a major role in establishing effective management programs in the classroom. In fact, there is a considerable amount of research to support the successful outcomes that occur with students when parents are involved in academic and behavioral programs (Kramer, 1990).

What are some examples of the way that parents can be involved? One illustration of how parent involvement can make a difference is a project by Sherridan, Kratochwill, and Elliott (1990). In the study, two forms of consultation with teachers for the purpose of establishing an intervention program for students demonstrating social withdrawal were implemented. In one form of consultation, the teacher and psychologist developed a program to improve social interaction skills in the school only. In the second form of consultation, the teacher met with the psychologist and the parent. The parent established the same program in the home setting as the teacher did in the classroom.

What do you think the outcome of this program was? Results indicated that the students who received the teacher only services improved only in the classroom. Students who received the services of both the teacher and the parent improved in both the home and the school. Also, the changes in the students in both home and school settings were maintained better in the dual teacher and parent program. Thus, there were direct benefits to the students in the intervention when it was implemented by the teacher, but the program had greater impact when both the teacher and the parent were involved.

Similar programs have been established with teachers making contact with parents in the hopes of improving behavior in school. Many of these programs involve home-based reinforcement delivered by the parent (Kelley & Carper, 1988) or programs that involve a combination of a home note system with back-up contingencies administered by the parent. Figure 13.2 provides an example of a home note for use with adolescents and older students. Such a note system is designed to be used by the teacher to

SCHOOL–HOME NOTE

Name_____   Date_____

CLASS _____   Assignment:

Completed Classwork	Yes	So-So	No	NA
Obeyed Classroom Rules	Yes	So-So	No	NA
Handed in Homework	Yes	So-So	No	NA

Comments: Initials _____
_____

CLASS _____   Assignment:

Completed Classwork	Yes	So-So	No	NA
Obeyed Classroom Rules	Yes	So-So	No	NA
Handed in Homework	Yes	So-So	No	NA

Comments: Initials _____
_____

CLASS _____   Assignment:

Completed Classwork	Yes	So-So	No	NA
Obeyed Classroom Rules	Yes	So-So	No	NA
Handed in Homework	Yes	So-So	No	NA

Comments: Initials _____
_____

CLASS _____   Assignment:

Completed Classwork	Yes	So-So	No	NA
Obeyed Classroom Rules	Yes	So-So	No	NA
Handed in Homework	Yes	So-So	No	NA

Comments: Initials _____
_____

Parent Comments:
_____

Figure 13.2

To improve school-home relations and to keep parents informed of progress, many schools have adopted home notes as a means of communication.

monitor certain classroom behaviors and to communicate the information to the parents. Parents are responsible for establishing and delivering the consequences.

Here are several guidelines for implementing a school-home note system that will be useful to you. It includes the following components:

- Plan a parent-teacher conference to communicate your concerns, agree on the nature of the problem, and secure the commitment of the parent.
- Define the problem behaviors that both you and the parent agree need to be changed, and be as specific as possible.
- Set small goals to change the problem behavior.
- Design the school-home note (like the example in Figure 13.2).
- Establish responsibilities for you and the parent(s). The parent will complete the note, and it is the responsibility of the student to return the note to you.
- Collect baseline information to determine the nature of the problem.
- Establish the reward system and how consequences will be delivered.
- Implement the program with the stipulated consequences.
- Fade out the note system as the student's behavior improves.

TEACHER ⬌ STUDENT
INTERACTIONS

Maintaining Order in the Classroom

1. Be alert to what your students are doing in the classroom.

   - Watch your students carefully during class, and when you sense their attention is wandering, pose unexpected questions, stop and have students question each other, or suddenly become quiet to regain their attention.
   - Involve the group; "who'll get this first?" Look at one student, then another, and then another, creating the impression that you expect them all to be first.
   - When you detect student restlessness or fading attention, act immediately; stare at the student; use the student's name. Build a repertoire of these mild behavioral countermeasures to prevent, if possible, serious misbehavior.
   - Make this repertoire a sequence of responses that ranges from lesser to more serious: standing next to the student, staring at him/her, calling attention to the behavior by using the student's name, reprimanding more sharply, talking to the student after school, holding a conference with the parents (perhaps including the principal), making a referral, and finally, recommending formal school action.
   - Know your students well enough so that you can detect something outside the class that may be influencing a student's behavior in class. This could include family financial problems, family illness, or a pending parental divorce. By talking to such students, you may be able to help them adjust to the stress and to prevent any emotional spillover to the classroom.

2. Certain teacher behaviors lead to a smoothly running classroom.

   - Communicate with the entire class even while you are working with one student; use body language, facial expressions, and verbal statement and questions.
   - Be sensitive to your students' span of interest and when it's lost, shift to another medium (perhaps discussion, watch a filmstrip, listen to a tape recording) or another activity ("OK, stand up and let's stretch"), or another subject.
   - Don't overdwell; sometimes teachers are so concerned about learning that they continue to the point of boredom; watch for the signs.

   - Act immediately when you detect the first signs of misbehavior, no matter how small; be sure that your reaction is appropriate for the seriousness of the misbehavior.
   - Make sure that your behavior is consistent with what you expect from your students; in this respect you are a constant model: speech, dress, clarity, courtesy, promptness.
   - Don't be afraid to use humor; when appropriate, it can be an effective change of pace in the classroom. Be careful, however; don't let it become sarcastic, don't let any one student become the butt of jokes, and don't overdo it.

3. Use those control techniques that are best suited for you and a particular class.

   - Be natural; keep your voice and body movements as relaxed as possible. In this way, you can create a positive learning environment. Occasionally teachers, by the shrillness of their voices and tense, rapid movements, can overstimulate a class.
   - Use as much positive reinforcement as possible; identify desirable student behavior and respond to it immediately. If you "get along" with your students, most of them will want to receive similar recognition from you.
   - At times it may be difficult not to take misbehavior personally, but make every effort to understand why students respond as they do. Sometimes students can misinterpret your behavior and can't understand why they are punished.
   - Try to help your students to develop inner controls. After students have misbehaved and you have reacted, talk to them to discover why the misbehavior occurred. Do they know why they acted as they did? Were they angry for some reason? Did some classmates urge them on? Help them to recognize the signs of trouble and suggest ways of avoiding it: remind them that they can always talk to you if something is bothering them; if you know your students well, you can use those that they admire as models for handling difficult situations.
   - Rules, control measures, and appropriate disciplinary techniques all add up to good classroom management and a minimum of problems.

Kelley and Carper (1988) suggested that cooperation is the key to success in any program when school-home notes are used. It is important for teachers to communicate with parents and urge them to assist with their child since parents can be extremely helpful in a comprehensive classroom management program.

You Are Not Alone

In thinking about the task of managing your classroom, don't feel overwhelmed. In this chapter we have presented new information that can have a bearing on effective classroom management. You will need time, however, to think about the issues in classroom management, and you will need experience in putting the various techniques into practice. Here are some ways that will make the task of classroom management easier.

- Read more about classroom management techniques. We have provided several resources at the end of the chapter for you to consider.
- Take courses that focus on classroom management techniques. Typically, courses in classroom management are offered in schools of education through the departments of educational psychology or special education.
- Use your time in practice teaching to sharpen your classroom management skills. Seek out effective teachers and visit their classrooms to observe skillful classroom management in action.
- Participate in preservice and inservice experiences that focus on developing successful classroom management skills.
- Discuss a student's problem with the parents when possible. Sometimes the parents can provide insights into the problem and may be able to assist in a discipline program (as noted above).
- Seek out the consultation of other professionals who will be able to offer you advice on solving specific

discipline problems and suggest ways to improve your classroom management tactics. Individuals in the school who may be able to assist you include lead teachers, special education resource teachers, school psychologists, and counselors.

Conclusion

In this chapter you examined one of the critical elements that contribute to successful teaching: classroom management. A well-run classroom is a must if both teachers and students are to reach their goals. Not much can be accomplished in chaos.

You identified problem behaviors to keep in mind as you read about the organization of classroom activities. These classroom activities require management: establishing rules and procedures, and introducing a sense of order and control into your classroom.

Specific techniques of control were discussed in detail. You will find one of these methods best suited to you, which means that you will follow its suggestions for the most part. You will also, however, adapt features from the other techniques while remaining consistent in how you handle problems.

Chapter Highlights

Management Concerns in the Classroom

- Your students' learning depends on the orderly routine that you establish in the classroom. Remember that orderly does not imply an atmosphere of quiet terror. It means an atmosphere in which all students (and teachers) know exactly what is expected of them.
- Organizing your classroom in a way that satisfies you and that your students understand is the first step in providing effective teaching and learning.
- John Carroll's ideas on the use of time has had a significant impact on the way that we structure our classrooms. His basic thesis is that students will learn to the extent that time is available (that is, time on task) for learning.
- The developmental characteristics of your students affect the management techniques you use and influence your decision about the age group you would like to teach.

Life in the Classroom

- Students' attitudes toward school seem to be a mixture of happiness and unhappiness. The causes of these mixed feelings seem to be rooted in the

conditions of the individual classrooms, that is, how you manage your work.

- Student engagement, that is, what students are doing at any time, is related to your activity. Student engagement seems to be highest when teachers lead small groups and lowest during student presentations.
- Teachers in "higher achieving schools" spend more time in actual teaching and in academic interactions with their students than do teachers in "lower achieving schools."
- As you decide how to organize your classroom, what to teach, and how to teach it, remember that you must adapt your techniques—both instructional and organizational—to the needs of your students.

Managing the Classroom

- The rules you establish for organizing your classroom, since they establish the conduct that you think is important, are critical. Unless your students' behavior conforms to these rules, learning will be negatively affected.
- Good managers make their rules known on the first day of class and combine the teaching of the rules with a demonstration of the signals they would use for various activities.

- Good managers use as few rules as possible and then introduce others as needed. They also occasionally remind their students of these rules and act immediately when they see a rule violation. This action usually prevents minor difficulties from becoming major problems.
- By understanding the developmental characteristics of the students you are teaching, you can anticipate many of the sources of potential problems and formulate rules that will help you to prevent them.

Methods of Control

- You and you alone can determine what is misbehavior, since individual differences apply to teachers as well as students. What one teacher may judge to be misbehavior, another may ignore.
- Among teacher behaviors that contribute to the successful management of their classrooms are withitness, overlapping, transition smoothness, and group alertness.
- Behavior modification, as a means of classroom control, relies on changing the classroom environment and the manner in which students interact with the environment to influence students' behavior.
- Understanding the causes of a student's misbehavior requires that teachers realize that their students' behavior has a purpose. Consequently, if teachers can identify the goal that a particular behavior is intended to achieve, they can correct problem behavior.
- Most teachers are eclectic in the manner in which they manage their classes, selecting and choosing from all of the techniques discussed in this chapter as the need requires.

Key Terms

Aversive control
Behavior influence
Behavior modification
Behavior therapy
Carroll model
Contingency contracting
Control theory
Dangles
Desists
Developmental task
Flip-flops
Fragmentation
Group alertness
Influence techniques

Interest boosting
Overcorrection
Overdwelling
Overlapping
Planful ignoring
Proactive classroom management
Progessive approximations
Proximity control
QAIT
Ripple effect
Shaping
Signal interference
Signals
Slowdowns
Social discipline
Token economy
Transition smoothness
Tribal dance
Withitness

Suggested Readings

Emmer, E., Evertson, C., Sanford, J., Clements, B., & Worsham, M. (1989). *Classroom management for secondary teachers.* (2nd ed.). Englewood Cliffs, NJ: Prentice-Hall.

Evertson, C., Emmer, E., Sanford, J., Clements, B., and Worsham, M. (1984). *Classroom management for elementary teachers.* Englewood Cliffs, NJ: Prentice-Hall. These two references are among the best that you will read about the realities of classroom management and the need for meaningful classroom rules to maintain order and to aid student learning.

Glasser, W. (1986). *Control theory in the classroom.* New York: Harper and Row. Glasser's attempt to explain students' behavior as an effort to satisfy their needs: they act to satisfy "the picture in their heads," and Glasser believes that teachers should adopt techniques to meet that need.

Jackson, P. (1968). *Life in classrooms.* New York: Holt, Rinehart and Winston. This little classic should be a "must" in your reading. It is still probably unrivaled in its presentation of classroom activities—teachers' and students'.

Sulzer-Azaroff, B., & Mayer, G. R. (1991). *Behavior analysis for lasting change.* Fort Worth: Holt, Rinehart and Winston, Inc. This text presents a comprehensive review of behavior modification techniques in educational and applied settings. Special emphasis is placed on procedures for maintenance of student behavior change.

Individual Differences and Diversity in the Classroom

Mrs. Allan, principal of the Brackett school, had detected an underlying current of unrest among her teachers and decided to bring it out into the open. She knew what was bothering them: they were concerned about the mainstreamed students in their classes.

At the next scheduled faculty meeting, she reviewed how the mainstreamed students had been assessed and said she felt that they were progressing nicely.

Dolores Amico, a third-grade teacher, grumbled a little. "With all we have to do—and remember, you asked us to get additional information on our students this year—I'm not sure I'm helping Joey as much as possible."

"Dolores, just having Joey in class and doing what you can to help is a tremendous boost for him. With the aid he gets from Mary Powers (learning resource) and Ann Kline (reading specialist), do you think he'll get through the year?"

"I suppose so, if we can keep up this level of support."

"Of course we can," snapped Mary Powers impatiently. "When he comes to me, he's happy and seems to be getting along with everyone else in the class."

"Not only that," Ann Kline joined in, "we don't have any choice; legislation provides for students like Joey."

Mrs. Allan now wanted to move the discussion to a different level. "I know you're worried that you feel you might not be prepared to do all you can. Many teachers feel this way but your concern, your efforts, together with specialized support can make a big difference in the lives of students like Joey."

Mrs. Allan was reflecting a concern of all the staff to be aware of the needs of students like Joey who with help can probably meet the learning standards for his grade level.

We have previously described (chapters 3, 4, and 5) the typical course of development for most students and traced the manner in which they learn and best respond to instruction. We know, however, that although all students exhibit individual differences, some have been identified as *students who are exceptional.* (Note: Exceptional is a general term that refers to one or more kinds of exceptionality.) Consequently, this chapter is devoted to an analysis of exceptional students and their classroom activities.

Phyllis Allan, the principal of Brackett school, was worried about both her teachers and the exceptional students in her school. Like many educators, she realized that her teachers wanted to be sure that these students received the best education possible but were worried about their ability to provide it.

Before addressing the specific categories of exceptionality, we'll first explore the implications of mainstreaming, which means that students who are exceptional should be in regular classrooms whenever possible. Mrs. Allan's concern (in the opening vignette) that her teachers felt uncertain about their work with mainstreamed children (exceptional students who are in regular classrooms) is quite real and is mirrored in schools—both elementary and secondary—across the country.

To help you become more familiar with this topic, we'll first review typical developmental milestones and then turn our attention to types of exceptionality, with the remainder of the chapter organized around the following categories:

> gifted/talented
>
> sensory handicaps
>
> communication disorders
>
> physical and health impairments
>
> behavior disorders
>
> learning disabilities
>
> mental retardation

When you have completed reading this chapter, you should be able to:

- identify the various types of exceptionalities.
- appraise the progress of mainstreamed students in your class.
- discriminate the range of individual differences among your students.
- contrast educational programs for specific exceptionalities.
- formulate appropriate classroom techniques for students to address their specific exceptionalities.

Individual Differences in the Classroom

Individual differences fascinate and challenge the instructional skills of every teacher. The individual differences of students who have been identified as exceptional learners with exceptional needs illustrate how developmental characteristics can guide us when they are matched with appropriate curriculum materials and a supportive classroom atmosphere. Instruction in any subject must be adapted to students who differ in a wide range of abilities: intellectual, motor, and behavioral (Snow, 1986).

Students at Risk

Although we will focus on students that meet the criteria for categories of exceptionality, there is a group of students who are considered **at risk.** These children are not currently identified as handicapped under various criteria but they are considered to have a high probability of becoming handicapped (Heward & Orlansky, 1988). Many of the children who fall into the at risk group are preschoolers. Another way of characterizing these students is that they are in danger of failing to complete their education with an adequate level of academic skills (Slavin & Madden, 1989). In fact, a number of variables lead us to predict that such students would be at risk for dropping out of school. These risk factors include low academic achievement, grade retention, low socioeconomic status, social behavior problems, and poor school attendance (Slavin, 1989).

As you can imagine, a large number of programs have been designed for exceptional children. In a comprehensive review of programs designed to help these children succeed in school, Slavin and Madden (1989) provided the following research synthesis for what works (and what does not work) with students at risk. Does it challenge any of your beliefs?

- First grade prevention programs that include intensive resources, tutors, and small-group instruction increase students' reading achievement.
- Cooperative learning programs and continuous progress models accelerate the achievement of students at risk.

Focus on Students

Thinking About Individual Differences

Stop for a moment to consider the possible range of individual differences you can expect to find in the classroom. To help shape your thinking, use the following questions as a guide:

1. What kinds of student differences can you expect to find in your classroom? Try to answer the question by placing each difference under the following categories:

   Physical   Behavioral   Cognitive

2. Assume that you are a teacher in either an elementary or secondary school and have just been asked by the school psychologist if there are some students who you think should not be in your classroom? Why? What are your reasons for excluding them? Where should they be placed?

3. Can you identify those students who could do well in a regular classroom but who will need some specific help? Are there students who you think should not be in a regular classroom if they are to receive the best education possible? Can you give specific examples?

When you finish your reading of this chapter, return to these questions and ask yourself if you would answer them in the same manner. If not, what would you change? Why?

You can expect to find a wide range of individual differences in schools.

- Frequent assessment of student progress that results in a restructuring of instructional content characterize effective programs.
- Effective programs are comprehensive and include teachers' manuals, curriculum guides, lesson plans, and many other supportive materials.
- Ineffective strategies include failing, which negatively affects achievement, and pullout programs, which only keep students in the early grades from falling further behind their peers.

Many of the instructional and behavior management procedures that have been found to be effective with at-risk students can and should be used with exceptional students. Keep these points in mind as you read the remainder of this chapter.

Ability Grouping

The task that you face in dealing with a wide range of individual differences reflects the common goal that all citizens will be brought to minimally acceptable levels in reading, writing, mathematics, and citizenship, for example. As a teacher, however, you are also expected to help students achieve those individual goals in which all citizens realize their own maximal potential for individual development and for specialized contribution to society (Snow, 1986, p. 1034).

One way of achieving these goals is to use skillfully the concept of **ability grouping.** There are several means of forming ability groups.

- Assign students to classes depending on their abilities; good examples of this technique would be high school "tracks," in which students are placed in "college prep" or general classes; another example is placing students in special education classes;
- Create ability groups within a single class; a good example of this technique would be assigning students to reading groups based upon their reading ability.
- Form small, mixed-ability groups in which higher ability students serve as peer tutors, a form of cooperative learning. (See chapter 11.)

Research indicates that although teaching homogeneous classes may be easier with regard to planning, it is more demanding than teaching a small group. Small group instruction, involving different ability levels, requires more differentiated instruction, well-chosen assignments, and rules of conduct that all group members understand (Brophy & Good, 1986). Teachers have many ways of manipulating the organizational structure of the class as long as grouping is short-term and does not label (Corno & Snow, 1986).

A teacher's task is clear: to establish educational environments that permit the greatest number of students to flourish to the fullest extent of their abilities. *P.L. 94–142, The Education for All Handicapped Children Act*—(now called **IDEA**—Individuals with Disabilities Education Act)—provides services for handicapped students in the least restrictive environment, which in many cases is the classroom.

To give you an idea of the dimensions of the issue, Ysseldyke and Algozzine (1990) have identified the following ten categories used to provide services to exceptional students:

- *Blind or visually handicapped.* Less than 1 percent of the school-age population is classified in this category.
- *Deaf or hard of hearing.* Less than 1 percent of the school age population is classified in this category.
- *Deaf and blind.* Less than 1 percent of the school age population is classified in this category.
- *Orthopedically or other health impaired.* Less than 1 percent of the school age population is classified in these two categories.
- *Mentally retarded.* About 1.4 percent of the school age population is classified in this category.
- *Gifted and talented.* About 3 percent of the school age population is classified in this category.
- *Learning disabled.* About 5 percent of the school age population is classified in this category.
- *Emotionally disturbed.* About 1 percent of the school age population is classified in this category.
- *Language impaired.* About 2.5 percent of the school age population is classified in this category.
- *Multihandicapped or severely impaired.* Less than 1 percent of the school age population is classified in this category.

Categories of exceptionality, however, vary across the states. (For example, Massachusetts and South Dakota do not use categories for providing special education services.) Other states also are moving away from this system. (We'll say more about this change later in the chapter.)

Focus on Schools

Pioneers in Special Education

Samuel A. Kirk.

One of the outstanding individuals credited with furthering the field of special education has been Samuel Kirk (1904–). He received his doctorate from the University of Michigan, specializing in physiological and clinical psychology. Kirk has been a staunch believer in the power of the environment and consistently challenges the idea of an unchanging IQ. His work contributed to an increasing interest in the plight of disadvantaged children and influenced the nature of the Head Start program. His research into psycholinguistic deficits and learning disabilities did much to advance both fields.

Source: University of Arizona (professor of special education) courtesy of Samuel A. Kirk.

As we noted, federal law also mandates that these students be placed in the **least restrictive environment** in which they can achieve success. Least restrictive means that students are to be removed from the regular classroom, home, and family as infrequently as possible. Their lives should be as "normal" as possible, and intervention should be consistent with individual needs and not interfere with individual freedom any more than is absolutely necessary. For example, children should not be placed in a special class if they can be served adequately by a resource teacher, and they should not be placed in an institution if a special class will serve their needs just as well (Hallahan & Kaufmann, 1988, p. 8). Given the importance of serving handicapped students in the least restrictive environment, we offer Table 14.1 as a concise summary of guidelines for implementing least restrictive services.

Let us now consider how these students are identified as exceptional.

The Assessment of Students

Assessment is an information-gathering process central to decision making about exceptional children. It can be a complex process and is given detailed consideration in

Table 14.1

Implementing Least Restrictive Environment Placements

1. Not all handicapped children benefit from being placed in the "mainstream." So-called restrictive environments such as residential institutions, resource centers, and self-contained special education classrooms in many cases offer the child developmental opportunities that would be impossible to achieve in a "less restrictive" setting.

2. Placement of handicapped children should be decided on an individual basis, based on the readiness of the special student and the preparedness of the receiving classroom to meet individual children's special needs.

3. Placement decisions should take into consideration a child's social and emotional developmental opportunities, as well as intellectual and physical development.

4. Teachers should be involved in placement decisions to ensure acceptance of the exceptional child in the classroom and to evaluate the capability of the classroom to accommodate the individual child's special needs. Regular teachers should be informed of special placements in their classes.

5. Transitional periods are often necessary to prepare both handicapped and nonhandicapped students to adjust to new situations.

6. Staff development programs to prepare teachers to work with exceptional children in their classes must be available prior to such placements, and continuous support and training are necessary to meet problems as they arise. Special education teachers specialize in certain areas and may require in-service training when assigned children with disabilities in which they have little or no expertise. In-service training also is needed for paraprofessionals and other support personnel.

7. Class sizes must be kept low in special education, whether in a "restrictive" environment or in the regular classroom, to ensure the necessary individualization of instruction.

8. Certified special education teachers must be retained to continue to meet the needs of children in special classes and to work with regular teachers in developing appropriate instructional programs for exceptional children.

9. Counselors, psychologists, psychiatrists, and other auxiliary personnel must be readily available to special and regular teachers.

10. Teachers should have regularly scheduled release time for consultations with support personnel.

11. Instructional materials, equipment, and facilities must be adapted to the needs of exceptional children in the regular classroom and throughout the school.

12. Scheduling of the educational program and buses should conform to the needs of exceptional children rather than vice versa.

13. Safeguards should exist to see that funds designated in special education follow the child, even if in a less restrictive environment, including the regular classroom.

From "What Can Be Expected of the Regular Teacher? Ideals and Realities" by M. Rauth, 1981, in *Exceptional Education Quarterly*, Vol. No. 2, pp. 27–36. Copyright 1981 by PRO-ED, Inc. Reprinted by permission.

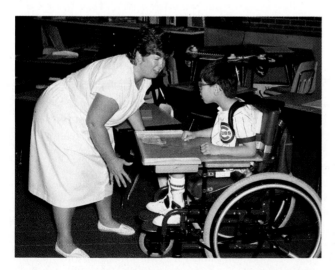

What are some of the most important issues in the special education of the handicapped?

chapters 15 and 16. The discussion of assessment in this chapter focuses on children who are exceptional. Before you commence an evaluation of a student, several issues require attention. These issues are those that school professionals take into account in the decision making process and include the following (Rutter, 1975).

1. *Children are developing organisms.* Any evaluation must consider the student's developmental level, since one of the major criteria in judging the abnormality of behavior is its age appropriateness. Since students behave differently at different ages, it is important to know what behavior is typical of the various ages. Students are vulnerable to different stresses at different ages. At some ages they may be particularly susceptible to an interruption of physical development whose consequences are both physical and psychological (anorexia nervosa in adolescents,

for example). At an earlier age, interference with psychological development may have physical and psychological consequences (separation from the mother during the first months of life, for example).

2. *Epidemiological considerations.* Since any information concerning the nature and dimensions of a problem will facilitate evaluation (How often? When? In the classroom or schoolyard?), studies that examine the distribution of the problem in the general population are usually helpful. These studies show that from 5 percent to 15 percent of children experience sufficiently severe disorders to handicap them in daily living. Though the precise number may vary, it is clear that except for a minority of cases, students with these disorders are not qualitatively different from their classmates.

3. *The abnormality and severity of the handicap.* Several criteria are used in assessing abnormality, the first of which is the age and sex appropriateness of the behavior. For example, certain behavior is normal at one age and not another; bedwetting is common until four or five years of age, but uncommon by ten years of age. Persistence of a problem is another criterion; a reluctance to leave home and attend school is normal in the early years, but abnormal in the later grades. Other criteria that cluster and indicate a problem are the extent of the disturbance and the intensity of the symptoms under different circumstances.

The severity of a problem can be judged by four criteria. First is the degree of personal suffering that a student experiences (can the student function in the classroom?); second is the social restriction involved (does it prevent a student from doing what is desired, such as actively participating in the classroom?); third is there any interference with development (for example, does dependency on the parents become so intense that a student finds it impossible to form normal peer relationships?); fourth, is there an effect on others (has a student's behavior become so maladaptive that interpersonal relationships in the classroom deteriorate?).

Guidelines for Diagnosis/Classification

Using these criteria to determine that assessment is needed, we next face the issue of classification. Remember: Most problems are too intricate to be explained by one cause and can respond only to a search for multiple causes. The diagnostic process is both complex and controversial given the unreliability of the diagnostic and classification systems now available. For example, the widely used Diagnostic and Statistical Manual of the American Psychiatric Association (DSM-II-R, 1987) has

Table 14.2
Phases of Assessment

Phase	Meaning
Screening	Identifying students with suspected handicaps—varied methods used (tests, ratings, checklists, interviews, among others)
Eligibility	Determining whether a student is eligible for special education. Deciding if a problem is related to a handicap
Program planning	Using demonstrated skill deficits as a basis for planning and organizing a remedial program
Monitoring student progress	Teachers gather data about the effects of the program—use varied techniques to modify the program as needed
Evaluating the program	Programs are evaluated annually (at least) Should the program be continued, terminated or modified?

been faulted for yielding unreliable results in the classification of children and youth. The categories of exceptionality used in education (from P.L. 94–142) are even more unreliable, and the labels used to classify students do not convey accurate information.

For example, Rutter uses the term "minimal brain damage" to illustrate how a diagnosis can be misleading, even dangerous. There are several, not one, brain damage syndromes, and the form they take is often indistinguishable from the behavior of students without brain damage. Furthermore, brain damage does not directly lead to psychiatric disorder, although it may increase a student's vulnerability to environmental stress. For example, parental pressure to excel may precipitate a latent problem.

Assessment and Decision Making

Assessment is the process of collecting data for the purpose of specifying and verifying problems and making decisions about students. Table 14.2 illustrates the various phases of assessment in the evaluation of students for special education programs.

Your major concerns about students with any type of deficit will be to identify the nature of the problem and how that deficit can best be treated. Decisions about these students follow these guidelines:

- When you make a referral decision, you are seeking information and assistance from others. You are asking for professional help with students who are displaying worrisome behavior.
- Since schools must detect problems before they become limiting, and since there may be deficits that teachers find difficult to detect (such as a hearing impairment), screening devices may be used. All students in a school or district are examined.
- Schools also must classify students with problems to make them eligible for special services. As you can well imagine, there are various classification schemes, with decisions following federal and state guidelines. (We shall explain these in detail later in the chapter.) These are critical decisions because once classified, many students remain in that category (learning disabled, behavioral disorder) for their academic lives. Federal and state regulations require that classification decisions include formal assessment data to avoid subjective impressions.
- Assessment data should help determine how and where a student is to be taught. Today there is a strong movement among special educators for curriculum-based assessment procedures to facilitate instructional decisions (Shinn, 1989).
- Assessment procedures are also used to discover what progress a student has made and whether he/she has obtained predetermined objectives. Whatever the evaluation technique used, assessment must match the curriculum.

Remember: Before reaching any decision about a student, be aware of the problems of labeling students. Once you become involved in the assessment of students, you and other professionals must accept the responsibility for your decision.

Problems with Labeling Students

"Exceptional" includes both persons who are talented and those who are handicapped. These students have some characteristic—physical, mental, behavioral, social—that requires special attention for them to achieve to their potentials. Awareness of the characteristics and needs of exceptional students point to an important conclusion: A student may be handicapped in one situation but not another. A student who appears at your classroom door in a wheelchair may be an outstanding scholar; a physical handicap does not imply cognitive difficulties. Avoid the pitfall of stereotyping students who are exceptional.

Although labels sometimes may be necessary for identifying exceptional students and making available appropriate services, problems result from a rigid classification system. These pitfalls range from indiscriminate exclusion from a regular classroom to the very real dangers that the label itself becomes a self-fulfilling prophecy. Sensitive to these problems, today's educators emphasize the skills that a child who is exceptional possesses and attempt to improve inadequate skills.

The Role of Support Systems

With the mandate to place exceptional children in regular classrooms whenever possible, school systems have had to make major adaptations. Most teachers will frequently find themselves working with students who have some limiting characteristic but not sufficiently severe to affect the work of the regular classroom teacher. Teachers will also have the able support of a wide range of specialized help. Among these will be the following:

- paraprofessionals to assist in clerical and non-technical tasks;
- reading specialists, who are particularly helpful with those designated as learning disabled—reading;
- physical and occupational therapists;
- social workers;
- speech and language specialists; and
- psychologists.

Families as Support Systems

An additional change in our thinking about the education of exceptional children has been the role of parents. As family members have become more involved, there has been a corresponding need for classroom teachers to become even more sensitive to teacher-parent relations. In working with parents, remember that families have a legal right to be included in planning, and that parents can and do help in reinforcing the skills that you are attempting to instill in a child who is exceptional. Family members may require some form of intervention to cope with the stress of a child who is exceptional (Bailey & Simeonsson, 1984).

If parents of an exceptional student cooperate and want to help in educating their child (helping him/her at home, for example) you should remember that parents may not be good teachers and may need careful and detailed assistance. For example, teachers, as trained professionals, generally give more useful information, structure tasks to a greater degree, provide better feedback, and require more independent activities from the child. Probably the best advice you can follow is:

- provide clear guidance;
- use simple, non-technical language;

Parent involvement is an important ingredient in the education of all children, but for many handicapped children it is essential. School personnel need to recognize the role of parents and provide support and encouragement to them.

• observe the interaction between parents and child for signs of excessive dominance;
• establish attainable goals;
• be sure the parents fully understand what the completed task should be;
• be sure the work you assign causes no conflict in the home (time, television, family activities); and
• finally, reinforce parents as well as children.

To help teachers in their work with children who are exceptional, the remainder of the chapter will be devoted to an analysis of the mainstreaming movement, followed by a discussion of a model that traces those developmental paths that extend from normalcy to exceptionality. We will then explore many of the categories of exceptionality that you may find in your classroom.

Mainstreaming

Mainstreaming means that, for some youngsters, your classroom could be their least restrictive environment. Mainstreaming's admirers praise it as the single greatest educational change since school integration. Its critics question it as a headlong plunge into chaos in the classroom. Typically, reality lies somewhere between these two extremes.

What Is Mainstreaming?

Mainstreaming means integrating physically, mentally, and behaviorally handicapped children into regular classes. In the past, these students were educated apart from their peers, but in 1975, Congress passed the *Education for All Handicapped Children Act of 1975 (P.L. 94-142),* which ensures every child some form of public education. If possible, integration into regular classes as soon as possible is desirable for all but the most severely handicapped.

Mainstreaming, however, may be a mixed blessing for some exceptional children. **Insensitive classmates** can make life miserable for the handicapped. Teachers' organizations generally favor mainstreaming with reservations, but, as we saw in Mrs. Allan's remarks about mainstreaming in the chapter opening, individual teachers feel uneasy. Administrators must designate funds to

Focus on Teachers

Teachers and the Referral Process

By now you realize that the teacher's role is critical in working with students who are handicapped. A teacher's responsibility often will extend to determining who is handicapped. Teachers are frequently pivotal in the identification process since once a teacher initiates the referral process, such students are assessed and often receive some form of special help (Pugach, 1985).

Pugach investigated the referral practices of classroom teachers. She personally interviewed 39 teachers (21 elementary, 18 junior high) in a Midwest school system of 5,000 students. She divided the teachers into three groups: those making no referrals that year, the second making one to three referrals, and the third making four or more. The interviews focused on demographic information, problems of a particular student, and the general efficiency of the school system.

Pugach found that elementary level teachers were more likely to attempt serious intervention before referral, feeling a professional obligation to attempt to find a solution. Junior high teachers made more casual intervention efforts. Only 36 percent of the teachers used specialized help before referral, although it was available. Over 50 percent of the teachers who referred students felt it was their only choice, although they believed special placement was unnecessary. Only 27 percent referred students for the expressed purpose of removing them from the classroom. Of the 28 teachers who had made referrals, 64 percent cited behavioral problems as the cause; 61 percent believed that the student referred had abilities within a normal range for their age.

Two aspects of this study deserve our added attention. First, teachers often feel frustrated when they decide that a student needs short-term remediation. Where do they turn? In this study, we have seen that they believe they have no recourse other than to initiate a referral process that typically results in some form of special education treatment. *Know your system and the professionals who work in it. Know the services that are available before you initiate specialized procedures.* Second, be extremely sensitive to the delicate role you play in identification. As this study clearly shows, teachers often exercise a decisive role in a student's future educational path.

install ramps, elevators, and other special equipment; otherwise, school life could become excessively difficult for a physically handicapped youngster.

This attitude toward mainstreaming, favorable but cautious, reflects an awareness of the dangers of pendulum swings in education—for example, from enthusiasm for special classes to a rush away from them. Some be-

lieve that the current zeal for mainstreaming, resulting from excessive expectations for special classes, may in turn lead to excessive expectations for mainstreaming. Others believe that mainstreaming has been oversold and underfunded. We need both quality special education and appropriate integration of exceptional children into regular classes.

The Education for All Handicapped Children Act

Among the chief requirements of the mainstreaming legislation are the following (Haring & McCormick, 1986):

1. *All children must be provided with a free, appropriate public education no matter the severity of their handicap.* The rationale for this requirement lies in our national commitment to education for all. One important feature of this stipulation addresses the financial responsibility of government at all levels: Not only must an exceptional child's program be supported but also any specialized service deemed vital.

2. *All children who are handicapped must be fairly and accurately evaluated.* Historically, these children have suffered unnecessary burdens because of poor evaluation procedures that led to faulty labeling and improper program placement. One outcome of these practices was that the minority student, often experiencing language difficulties and cultural bewilderment, would be placed in classes for the mildly mentally retarded.

3. *The education of children who are exceptional must "match" individual capacities and needs.* One of the main features of the changed legislation was the demand that each exceptional child receive an individualized educational plan—the IEP. The IEP, based on the student's needs, is prepared annually by a committee that includes any needed special education teacher, a school representative, an expert on the student's disability, and the child's parents. The IEP must incorporate a statement about the student's present level of functioning, long-term goals, short-term objectives, special services needed, and any other pertinent information. Figure 14.1 illustrates a typical IEP.

4. *Children who are exceptional must be educated in the least restrictive, most normal educational environment possible.* We have previously commented on this requirement, but there is also the added task of insuring that those students who need separate placement be brought together with non-handicapped students for physical education (where appropriate), assemblies, and lunch periods.

INDIVIDUALIZED EDUCATION PROGRAM

_11/11/90_
Date

Student: _Smith_ _Tom_ _H._

Last Name   First   Middle

_5.3_   _8-4-80_

School of Attendance   Home School   Grade Level   Birthdate/Age

School Address   School Telephone Number

Child Study Team Members

LD Teacher

Case Manager

Homeroom   _Parents_

Name   Title   Name   Title

Facilitator

Name   Title   Name   Title

Speech

Name   Title   Name   Title

Summary of Assessment Results
IDENTIFIED STUDENT NEEDS: _Reading from last half of_
DISTAR II — present performance level

LONG-TERM GOALS: _To improve reading achievement level by at_
least one year's gain. To improve math achievement to
grade level. To improve language skills by one year's gain.

SHORT-TERM GOALS: _Master Level 4 vocabulary and reading skills._
Master math skills in basic curriculum. Master spelling
words from Level 3 list. Complete Units 1-9 from
Level 3 curriculum.

MAINSTREAM MODIFICATIONS

White copy–Cumulative folder   Goldenrod–Case manager
Pink copy–Special teacher   Yellow copy–Parent

(a)

Figure 14.1

(a) An individualized education program; (b) description of services to be provided.

DESCRIPTION OF SERVICES TO BE PROVIDED

Type of Service	Teacher	Starting Date	Amt. of time per day	OBJECTIVES AND CRITERIA FOR ATTAINMENT
SLD Level III	LD Teacher	11-11-90	2½ hrs.	Reading: will know all vocabulary through the "Honeycomb" level. Will master skills as presented through DISTAR II. Will know 123 sound-symbols presented in "Sound Way to Reading." Math: will pass all tests at basic 4 level. Spelling: 5 words each week from Level 3 list. Language: will complete Units 1-9 of the grade 4 language program. Will also complete supplemental units from "Language Step by Step."

Mainstream Classes	Teacher	Amt. of time per day	OBJECTIVES AND CRITERIA FOR ATTAINMENT
		3½ hrs.	Out-of-seat behavior: sit attentively and listen during mainstream class discussions. A simple management plan will be implemented if he does not meet this expectation. Mainstream modifications of Social Studies: will keep a folder in which he expresses through drawing the topics his class will cover. Modified district social studies curriculum. No formal testing will be made. An oral reader will read text to him, and oral questions will be asked.

The following equipment, and other changes in personnel, transportation, curriculum, methods, and educational services will be made:

DISTAR II Reading Program, Spelling Level 3, "Sound Way to Reading" Program, vocabulary tapes

Substantiation of least restrictive alternatives: _The planning team has determined the student's academic needs are best met with direct SLD support in reading, math, language, and spelling._

ANTICIPATED LENGTH OF PLAN _1 yr._ The next periodic review will be held: _May 1991_
DATE/TIME/PLACE

☒ I do approve this program placement and the above IEP
☐ I do not approve this program placement and/or the above IEP
☐ I request a conciliation conference

_____
PARENT/GUARDIAN

_____
Principal or Designee

(b)

Figure 14.1 continued

Focus on Teachers

The Special Education Process

Traditionally, when a teacher was concerned about a student who was experiencing an academic or behavioral problem, the first step was to refer that student for a special education evaluation. This process has changed dramatically in recent years. Due to the increasing emphasis on mainstreaming exceptional students and the concept of least restrictive environment, more and more students are being maintained in the regular classroom through prereferral intervention. Box Figure 14.2 illustrates the prereferral process as it would be typically implemented in a school setting.

What is a teacher's role both prior to and after the referral? The role of the regular education teacher in this decision making process is demonstrated in Box Table 14.1.

Note in Box Table the central role of the teacher in providing services to the exceptional student at the prereferral stage. In this phase, teachers have the consultation support of various school professionals in developing the prereferral intervention program.

Box Table 14.1

How the Regular Classroom Teacher Participates in Special Education Decision Making

Prereferral Stage: Regular Education Process
The teacher notices that a student is performing differently from most of the other students in the class.

The teacher checks with other teachers to verify his or her observations, then checks with the student's parents to eliminate special circumstances at home that might explain the exceptional performance.

The teacher tries different methods of instruction (prereferral interventions) to identify the nature of the problem, and gathers information about the student's performance in other areas.

The teacher decides the prereferral intervention was effective and continues to use instructional modifications to provide special education in the regular classroom.

The teacher decides the student's performance is sufficiently different to warrant special services, and refers the student to the school's special education support team.

Postreferral Stage: Special Education Process
The teacher reviews the results of individual psychological and educational testing, then consults with other team members and compares the student's performance to established criteria for eligibility for special education.

The teacher offers an opinion about the appropriate placement for the student.

The teacher cooperates with other team members in providing special services and evaluating their effectiveness.

Box Figure 14.1
Flow chart for prereferral consultation process.

5. *Students' and parents' rights must be protected throughout all stages of evaluation, referral, and placement.* Parental involvement and consent have become an integral part of the entire process. To give you an idea of the role envisioned for parents in the process, consider several measures relating to need assessment and parental involvement.

Parents are to receive a written notice in their native language about any change identification, evaluation, or placement of their child. The legislation defines native language as the language normally used by a person with limited English-speaking ability. If parents remain dissatisfied with placement and education, they may initiate a due process hearing, which is to be conducted by someone not presently responsible for the child's education.

All participants will receive a verbatim record of the hearing. If still dissatisfied, parents or guardians may carry their grievance to the appropriate state agency and, ultimately, to the courts. While a decision is pending, children remain where they were before the appeal.

The legislation, sweeping in its scope, illustrates why some observers believe that it has and will continue to produce radical changes in education. Of importance here is the teacher's role in the process. Somewhere in the identification, evaluation, and placement procedure, teachers will be asked to comment on the child's classroom performance. (Some states have the teacher play a key role in presenting current and past educational information.)

Since the legislation also requires each state to develop and implement a comprehensive system of personnel development, teachers will experience changes in preservice education and in-service training. Sooner or later you will encounter the ramifications of P.L. 94-142. Mainstreaming is here to stay. Table 14.3 is a summary of the major provisions of P.L. 94-142.

Classroom Support for Mainstreamed Students

Mainstreaming, or integration of exceptional children into regular classrooms, means that the mildly handicapped—of all categories—will require additional classroom support. Special education teachers will function as resource personnel, helping regular teachers to plan a student's schooling.

The scope of the federal and state special education legislation has caused educators to realize that almost 50 percent of school children experience problems, some of which require special help. Unless teachers possess both competence and understanding, mainstreaming simply will not achieve its desired objectives. Ultimately, then, much of the responsibility rests with teachers. Faced with this assignment, teachers may have many questions, several of which probably are similar to the following:

How can I lessen the anxieties of exceptional students and their classmates?

Exactly what are my obligations under mainstreaming?

How many students who are handicapped will be in my class?

Will I receive help in planning programs?

What is the responsibility of resource personnel?

How can I spare the time?

How can I learn more about special needs?

Though most teacher-preparation institutions have incorporated planning for exceptional children in their courses, you may find several professional activities helpful.

- Classroom visitation. Observation and demonstration by others can be invaluable. Having a skilled expert observe you, make constructive suggestions, and actively demonstrate techniques for you can substantially enhance your own expertise.

- Teacher demonstrations. Administrators and supervisors can schedule visits to other schools and classrooms where master teachers offer demonstration lessons. Learning theorists have amply demonstrated the persuasiveness of observational learning.

- Meetings, institutes, and conferences. These assemblies can be helpful if they are planned to discuss pertinent problems and permit meaningful participation.

- Professional library. Since the vast special-education literature and the rapidly accumulating mainstreaming data often provide profitable suggestions, sample as many bibliographies, articles, books, and government pamphlets as possible. You would find the following journals particularly helpful:

Journal of Learning Disabilities

Teaching Exceptional Children

Exceptional Children

Mental Retardation

Table 14.3

Major Provisions of PL 94-142

Each state and locality must have a plan to ensure:

Child identification	Extensive efforts must be made to screen and identify all handicapped children.
Full service, at no cost	Every handicapped child must be assured an appropriate public education at no cost to the parents or guardians.
Due process	The child's and parents' rights to information and informed consent must be assured before the child is evaluated, labeled, or placed, and they have a right to an impartial due process hearing if they disagree with the school's decisions.
Parent/parent surrogate consultation	The child's parents or guardian must be informed about the child's evaluation and placement and the educational plan; if the parents or guardian are unknown or unavailable, a surrogate parent to act for the child must be found.
LRE	The child must be educated in the least restrictive environment that is consistent with his or her educational needs and, insofar as possible, with nonhandicapped children.
IEP	A written individualized education program must be prepared for each handicapped child. The plan must state present levels of functioning, long- and short-term goals, services to be provided, and plans for initiating and evaluating the services.
Nondiscriminatory evaluation	The child must be evaluated in all areas of suspected disability and in a way that is not biased by the child's language or cultural characteristics or handicaps. Evaluation must be by a multidisciplinary team, and no single evaluation procedure may be used as the sole criterion for placement or planning.
Confidentiality	The results of evaluation and placement must be kept confidential, though the child's parents or guardian may have access to the records.
Personnel development, in-service	Training must be provided for teachers and other professional personnel, including in-service training for regular teachers in meeting the needs of the handicapped.

There are detailed federal rules and regulations regarding the implementation of each of these major provisions. The definitions of some of these provisions—LRE and nondiscriminatory evaluation, for example—are still being clarified by federal officials and court decisions.

From D. P. Hallahan and J. M. Kauffman, *Exceptional Children: Introduction to Special Education,* 4th ed. Copyright © 1988 Prentice-Hall, Inc., Englewood Cliffs, NJ., Allyn & Bacon Inc., Needham Heights, MA.

Remedial and Special Education

American Journal of Orthopsychiatry

Exceptional Children

Educational Leadership

Behavioral Disorders

Journal of Special Education

• Curriculum and research. Thoughtful school officials may encourage teachers to publish bulletins, to prepare curriculum alterations, and to cooperate in writing course objectives. Scholarships may be available; universities may offer course vouchers as a courtesy for student-teacher placement; some teachers may conduct research with their classes. All of these activities promote professional growth and furnish information that may produce more efficient teaching and learning.

Some Results of Mainstreaming

In the years that have passed since P.L. 94-142 took effect, the reactions of educators and the results of a wide variety of studies have been used to evaluate its effectiveness. The results are mixed. For example, Wang and Baker (1985/1986), in a study intended to assess the sources of mainstreaming in educating disabled students, summarized the results of eleven empirical studies.

The eleven studies contained a total of 541 students highly diverse in socioeconomic status, sex, race, and geographic location. Thirty-nine percent of the comparisons were of primary and elementary school students, 16 percent involved middle school students, 1 percent were preschool children, and in 44 percent of the comparisons no information or grade level was provided. The categories of exceptionality broke down as follows:

- 53 percent of the students were classified as mentally retarded;
- 3 percent were learning disabled;
- 19 percent were hearing impaired;
- 25 percent were classified as "mixed category."

Though the authors found that the mainstreamed students with disabilities outperformed nonmainstreamed students with similar educational classifications, the results were not statistically significant. Nevertheless, the positive outcomes on all measures caused the authors to conclude that mainstreaming improves performance, attitudes, and process outcomes for exceptional students.

We must be cautious in interpreting the results of studies investigating differences between segregated and mainstreamed students particularly with regard to:

- *the nature of the disability*; emotionally disturbed students find greater difficulty in adjustment and peer acceptance in regular classes than those students with other disabilities, such as a youngster experiencing vision and hearing difficulties;
- *parental warmth, acceptance, and cooperation,* which have a powerful impact on a student's locus of control and achievement;
- *uncontrolled, multiple variables,* such as sibling reaction, self-esteem, and teacher behavior.

Consequently, care must be taken before interpreting these conflicting results; the final verdict on mainstreaming has yet to be rendered. Perhaps the safest route is for our schools to follow such general guidelines as:

- Students should be capable of doing some work at grade level.
- Students should be capable of doing some work without requiring special materials, adaptive equipment, or extensive assistance from the regular classroom teacher.
- Students should be capable of "staying on task" in the regular classroom without as much help and attention as they would receive in the special classroom or resource room.

Focus on Classrooms

The Regular Education Initiative

A recent movement among many special educators has raised questions about the extent to which P.L. 94–142 has been fully realized. Called the **Regular Education Initiative (REI)**, its thrust has been to call into question the exclusion of students who are mildly handicapped (identified as the learning disabled, the seriously emotionally disturbed, and educable mentally retarded). Supporters of REI argue that most of these students can and should receive all of their education in the regular classroom.

Descriptions of REI contain many statements with which few educators could or would disagree, such as the following:

- Better integration and coordination of services for students with handicaps is needed.
- Effective and economical methods of educating these students should be a priority.
- Students should be identified as needing special services only when necessary.
- Special education should be reserved for those students needing the most specialized help.
- Some students are labelled because of the inadequacies of regular classroom teachers (Kauffman, Gerber, & Semmel, 1988).

As the implications of REI spread throughout the educational community, it received a more searching examination, and several important issues were identified.

1. Can regular classroom teachers distribute instructional resources for all?
2. Does REI distinguish sufficiently between elementary and secondary levels?
3. Research does not support the belief that all students with handicaps should be in regular classrooms.
4. Although there are problems with identifying (labelling) such students, they nevertheless exist.

You can see, then, that REI is a hotly debated topic that cuts to the core of the controversy surrounding the effectiveness of special education services.

Services across the categories of exceptionality that we have identified do not always demonstrate the individualized instructional strategies needed for these students. Frequently, the same instructional tasks are being used with non-handicapped students and with different types of handicapped students, which ignores the need to individualize instruction for students (Ysseldyke et al., 1989).

The issues have been defined; the lines have been drawn; the implications are far-reaching. You should be alert to the direction this controversy takes since it can affect all classrooms. (See Lloyd, Singh, & Repp, 1991, for a review of these issues.)

Table 14.4

Milestones in Development and Learning

Developmental Domains

	Physical	Cognitive	Social	Emotional	Language
Infancy (0-2)	1. Can hear and see at birth 2. Rapid growth in height and weight 3. Rapid neurological development 4. Motor development proceeds steadily (crawling, standing, walking)	1. Seek stimulation 2. An egocentric view of the world begins to decrease 3. Demonstrates considerable memory ability 4. Begins to process information	1. Need for interaction 2. Smiling appears 3. Reciprocal interactions begin immediately 4. Attachment develops	1. Beginnings of emotions discernible in first months 2. Infant passes through emotional milestones	1. Proceeds from cooing and babbling to words and sentences 2. Word order and inflection appear 3. Vocabulary begins to increase rapidly
Preschool (2-6)	1. Extremely active 2. Mastery of gross motor behavior 3. Refinement of fine motor behavior	1. Perceptual discrimination becomes sharper 2. Attention more focused 3. Noticeable improvement in memory 4. Easily motivated	1. Attachment 2. Beginning of interpersonal relationships a. parents b. siblings c. peers d. teachers 3. Play highly significant	1. Still becomes angry at frustration 2. Prone to emotional outbursts 3. Emotional control slowly appearing 4. Aware of gender 5. Fantasies conform more to reality 6. May begin to suppress emotionally unpleasant memories	1. From first speech sounds (cooing, babbling) to use of sentences with conjunctions and prepositions 2. Acquires basic framework of native language
Middle Childhood (7–11)	1. Mastery of motor skills 2. Considerable physical and motor skills	1. Attention becomes selective 2. Begins to devise memory strategies 3. Begins to evaluate behavior 4. Problem solving behavior shows marked improvement	1. Organized activities more frequent 2. Member of same sex group 3. Peer influence growing 4. Usually have "best" friend	1. Pride in competence 2. Confident 3. Growing sensitivity 4. Volatile 5. Striving, competitive 6. Growing sexual awareness	1. Rapid growth of vocabularly 2. Uses and understands complex sentences 3. Can use sentence content to determine word meaning 4. Good sense of grammar 5. Can write fairly lengthy essays

- Students should be capable of fitting into the routine of the regular classroom.
- Students should be able to function socially in the regular classroom and profit from the modeling or appropriate behavior of their classmates.
- The physical setting of the classroom should not interfere with the student's functioning (or it should be adapted to their needs).
- It should be possible to work out scheduling to accommodate the students' various classes, and the schedules should be kept flexible and be easy to change as students progress.

Neverstreaming: A New Concept

In this chapter, we introduced you to the concept of mainstreaming. Many proposals have been offered to implement the concept of mainstreaming, including consultation by the teacher with a professional (e.g. resource teacher, school psychologist), individualized instruction, and cooperative learning, just to name a few. Nevertheless, many educators in both regular and special education are not comfortable with the concept when it is put into practice. As an alternative to mainstreaming, Robert Slavin and his associates (1991) have proposed a new concept called **neverstreaming.** According to the authors, "The key

Developmental		
Piaget	**Erikson**	**Kohlberg**
Sensorimotor 1. Use of reflexes 2. Primary circular reactions 3. Secondary circular reactions 4. Coordination of secondary schemata 5. Tertiary circular reactions 6. Representation	1. Development of trust	1. Begins to learn wrong from right
Preoperational 1. Deferred imitation 2. Symbolic play 3. Mental imagery 4. Drawing 5. Language	1. Growing competence and autonomy 2. Initiative and purpose	1. Beginning of preconventional moral reasoning
Concrete Operations 1. Conservation 2. Seriation 3. Classification 4. Number 5. Reversibility	Industry and competence	1. Continued development of preconventional moral reasoning to 2. Conventional moral reasoning

Education and Exceptionality: A Model

It is important to associate a student's characteristics with typical developmental characteristics. How much does a student vary from the norm? How does this affect adjustment? What are the educational implications of a particular student's developmental path?

We previously discussed in some detail the developmental paths that most children take, the theories that attempt to explain the various phenomena, and the research that either verifies or challenges the theories and conclusions. It might be wise at this point to review quickly the developmental norms presented in chapters 3, 4, and 5. (See Table 14.4.)

Although we can arbitrarily divide development into many parts, the following categories will help you to relate these developmental accomplishments to the potential damage resulting from a deficit in any one aspect. For example, extremes in cognitive development may well mean that you can have in your classroom students who are mildly mentally retarded and students who are gifted.

Study any of the eight columns of Table 14.4, and you see how deviation from these milestones can cause varied problems. For example, examining the sequence of social development and learning, you can visualize a student—for whatever reason—having problems with peers, causing classroom difficulties, and experiencing learning problems. How severe is the underlying problem? Who makes the diagnosis of the problem? Should the student be formally referred or is consultation possible? Could there be long-term effects of the problem?

These questions cannot be taken lightly since they involve a teacher's role in the prereferral and referral process. With mainstreamed students assigned to regular classes, the questions are similar but follow a slightly different path. A student's problem will have been previously diagnosed, specialized help will be available, and a teacher's task will be to determine the extent to which that student can flourish in a regular classroom despite the handicap.

Your involvement with mainstreamed students will occur either with the referral process and/or with actual instruction. By attempting to match average development with a problem in any of the developmental phases seen in Table 14.4, you can better understand both a student's problem and the need for an appropriate remedial program.

focus of this approach is an emphasis on prevention and early, intensive, and continuing intervention to keep student performance within normal limits" (p. 373). The focus is designed to keep nearly all children in the mainstream by trying to prevent academic problems. Neverstreaming is designed to be a comprehensive approach to academic skill development. One such approach that Slavin and his co-workers are investigating is teacher-tutoring with children who have reading problems. Although the neverstreaming approach is just being investigated, this model is one that may have the potential to change your role as a teacher. Think about it!

Multicultural Students and Special Education

Of growing concern to U.S. educators is the large number of multicultural students in special education classes. Faced with standardized tests in a language that may cause them difficulty and adjustment to a new culture, many of these students experience achievement problems. Too often they are labelled as failures and assigned to a special education class.

Difficulty in identifying students in need of services remains the culprit. Is it limited ability in the new language? Is it the assessment strategies used by professionals? Is it uneasiness with a new culture? Is it sheer unfamiliarity with American schools? Or is it actually some handicapping condition? If you examine these questions objectively, you probably would agree that there is a real risk that some immigrant students will be inappropriately placed in special education classes.

Students from different ethnic groups reflect their distribution in the general population most closely in the learning disability, emotional disturbances, and speech impaired categories, but Asian students are underrepresented in each of the categories. White and Asian students are underrepresented in the mental retardation category, and African Americans are overrepresented. Asian students are overrepresented in gifted and talented programs while African American, Hispanic, and Native American students are underrepresented (Ysseldyke & Algozzine, 1990).

Frequently, a physical problem may be at the root of a student's difficulties, particularly since many of these students have undetected health problems. Occasionally, emotional problems follow the traumatic experiences of some of these students. Many school systems, wishing to avoid unwarranted special education placement, have attempted an immediate evaluation of these students.

Few linguistically and culturally appropriate assessment instruments exist for the students who speak languages other than English or Spanish, and there seems to be a limited understanding of many of the different cultures from which students come. Consequently, educators hesitate to place a newly arrived immigrant student who does not present a physical handicap into special education (New Voices, 1988). Nevertheless, through no fault of their own, many of these students seem to be candidates for special education. As a teacher, or potential teacher of such students, try to determine just what is the source of any problem so that your judgment is based as much on knowledge of a student as on immediate behavior.

After implementation of a mutually acceptable plan (by the family, school, and specialists), the student begins the specified program. The process does not cease here but provides continuous evaluation to determine the program's effectiveness, and, if necessary, to devise a new plan. As we have emphasized throughout this chapter, you should prepare for involvement at two key points: helping to identify a student's needs by reporting on educational status, and working with the student and specialized personnel to implement the educational plan.

Bilingual Education

Today there are over 30 million Americans for whom English is not the primary language. Estimates are that there will be about 6 million American school children with "limited English proficiency" (LEP) by the year 2,000. In some states (California, Texas, Florida), the linguistic-minority school population is about 25 percent and in some large urban school districts, 50 percent of the students come from non-English-speaking homes.

What happens to students who do not speak the language of the school? Unfortunately, many will achieve below their potential and drop out of school. In an effort to combat this problem, The Bilingual Act of 1988 stipulates that students with limited English proficiency receive **bilingual education** for three years and up to five years if needed until they can use English to succeed in school.

America, as a nation of immigrant people, has long faced this problem, with our schools playing a special role in the naturalization process (Fillmore & Valadez, 1986). Schools are where minority children are exposed to the majority language, usually with the assumption that "they'll pick it up." Little, if any, special help was provided to these students, and drop-out rates remained high. In a technological society, a lack of education and poor language combine to produce a bleak future; hence increased attention has been given to this issue.

Bilingual Children

As research begins to accumulate about bilingual education programs, more knowledge about the students themselves is becoming available. For example, the higher the degree of bilingualism, the better the level of cognitive attainment (Hakuta, 1986). This is especially true when the native language is retained, the social climate is positive, and minority-language children are not negatively labeled.

Recent research, however, indicates that the native language does not interfere with second language development. Both first and second language acquisition seem to be guided by similar principles; the acquisition of languages is a natural part of our cognitive system. Also, the rate of acquisition of the second language seems to be related to the level of proficiency of the first (Hakuta, 1986). With these ideas in mind, what programs have been devised to help these students?

Bilingual Education Programs

In a landmark decision in 1974 (Lau v. Nichols, 414, U.S. 563), the U.S. Supreme Court ruled that LEP students in San Francisco were being discriminated against since they were not receiving the same education as their English-speaking classmates. The school district was ordered to provide means for LEP students to participate in all instructional programs. The manner of implementing the decision was left to the school district under the guidance of the lower courts. This decision provided the impetus for the implementation of bilingual education programs in the United States.

Two different techniques for aiding LEP students emerged from this decision. The *English as a second language program* (ESL) usually has students removed from class and given special English instruction. The intent is to have these students acquire enough English to allow them to learn in their regular classes that are taught in English. With the *bilingual* technique, students are taught partly in English and partly in their native language. The objective here is to help students to learn English by subject matter instruction in their own language and in English. Thus, they acquire subject matter knowledge simultaneously with English.

In today's schools, bilingual education has become the program of choice. It is important to remember that programs for LEP students have two main objectives:

- Provide these students with the same education that all children in our society have.
- Help them to learn English, the language of the school and society (Fillmore & Valadez, 1986).

Bilingual education programs can be divided into two categories. First are those programs (sometimes called "transitional" programs) in which the rapid development of English is to occur so that students may switch as soon as possible to an all-English program. Second are those programs (sometimes referred to as "maintenance" programs) that permit LEP students to remain in them even after they have become proficient in English. The rationale for such programs is that students can use both languages to develop mature skills and to become fully bilingual.

The difference between these two programs lies in their objectives. Transitional programs are basically compensatory—use the students' native language only to compensate for their lack of English. Maintenance programs, however, are intended to bring students to the

fullest use of both languages. As you can well imagine, transitional programs are the most widely used in the schools.

Since the use of two languages in classroom instruction actually defines bilingual education, several important questions must be answered.

- What is an acceptable level of English that signals the end of a student's participation?
- What subjects should be taught in each language?
- How can each language be used most effectively? (That is, how much of each language is to be used to help a student's progress with school subjects?)
- Should English be gradually phased in, or should students be totally immersed in the second language (which, for most of the students we are discussing, would be English)?

One reason for the controversy surrounding these programs is that research has yet to grapple with many of the important variables. For example, what should be evaluated, English proficiency or subject matter success? How can the quality of the program be assessed? How alike are the children in any program (ability, SES, proficiency in their native languages, the level of English on entering the program)?

Although the answers to these and other questions continue to spark controversy, bilingual programs allow students to retain their cultural identities while simultaneously progressing in their school subjects. It also offers the opportunity for students to become truly bilingual, especially if programs begin early.

Who are the exceptional students who will appear in your classroom? As we have noted, we'll use the seven categories of exceptionality mentioned at the opening of the chapter, beginning with the gifted and talented. Each of these categories will be described and analyzed in the remainder of the chapter. We must again emphasize, however, that our use of the "categories" is only to help organize the information available on exceptional children. Finally, remember that most exceptional students are more like "normal" students than they are different.

The Categories of Exceptionality

You might wonder what types of exceptional students you will encounter in school. Researchers have reported the incidence and prevalence of various categories of exceptionality to give us some idea about the frequency of these students. The terms incidence and prevalence are sometimes used interchangeably in discussions of exceptional children; however, they should be differentiated

TEACHER ⬌ STUDENT
INTERACTIONS

Students Who Are Exceptional

Students who are exceptional will display behaviors that require your special attention. You should evaluate their behavior to design a better instructional environment.

1. Those students who are exceptional and who spend time in a typical classroom may display behaviors that require your careful attention. For example, students with learning and behavior problems may exhibit:

   • poor academic performance
   • attention difficulties
   • hyperactivity
   • difficulty with memory of symbols
   • lack of coordination
   • perceptive problems
   • language difficulties
   • aggression
   • withdrawn behavior

2. Watch your students; listen to them; evaluate their behavior. Then, if you're still unhappy with their performance, analyze your instruction by using the following criteria:

   • *Student motivation.* Does the classroom environment make students want to learn?
   • *Student attention.* Does the learning environment attract students so that they will attend to the task?
   • *Positive reinforcement.* Does the classroom setting challenge students and provide satisfactory rewards and feedback?
   • *Modeling.* Do the students see good examples of how learning should occur?
   • *Practice.* Are the students given sufficient opportunity to practice?
   • *Time-on-task.* Are the students given the chance to learn skills until they are comfortable with them?
   • *Pacing.* Am I setting the right tempo in class so that the rate and amount of material taught provide time and incentive?
   • *Generalization.* Do the students have a chance to transfer their learning to other settings?

3. You may want to monitor mainstreamed students more carefully when they are in class, so you could try something like this (Bos & Vaughn, 1988):

   Put the student's name on a card that says:

   Student Helped—Name

Date	Time	Comments

   Carefully mark the date and time and use appropriate comments, such as:

   difficulty with long and short vowels
   trouble with two-place multiplication

4. You can use this technique with behavioral problems as well. Keep a close check on dates to determine if the time between incidents is improving.

   • What was the time of day?
   • Was it the same each time the incident occurred?
   • What was the subject matter when the incident occurred?

   With these and other simple techniques, you can keep a close check on the progress of your students who are exceptional.

(Hallahan & Kauffman, 1988). Incidence refers to the number of new cases of exceptionality during a period such as one year. In contrast, prevalence refers to the total number of existing cases (new and old) in the population at a particular time.

When discussing students with exceptional needs, considering prevalence by three broad categories is useful. First, there are *high-prevalence* categories, which typically include students with learning disabilities, gifted and talented, and those with speech and language problems. In the *moderate-prevalence* category are those with mental retardation and those who are emotionally disturbed. A number of categories of exceptionality are considered *low-prevalence,* such as students with hearing and visual

The Mentally Gifted. Children who are mentally gifted, like those who are mentally retarded, benefit from special educational programs to help them develop their abilities.

problems, health and orthopedic handicaps, and multiple handicaps. In the following section we will provide you with some prevalence information on the various categories of exceptionality.

The range of exceptional abilities varies widely, and any particular difficulty will affect performance in some subjects more than others. A student confined to a wheelchair, for example, may do quite well in academic subjects but be prevented from full participation in certain motor activities. Visual problems, depending on severity, can cause major problems in adaptive behavior or be erased quite simply by eyeglasses. Note also that we have included the talented and gifted among the categories since they are unquestionably exceptional.

The Gifted/Talented

What to do with gifted and/or talented students has perplexed educators for as long as these children were recognized as exceptional. Even defining **gifted** has caused considerable controversy. Initially, the results of IQ were used with some arbitrary figure such as 120 or 140 signifying the cut-off point. This definition, however, was too restrictive; youngsters who had exceptional talent in painting or music, or who

seemed unusually creative were also gifted (Reis, 1989). As a result, the *Gifted and Talented Children's Education Act of 1978* defined these students as follows:

> The term gifted and talented children means children, and, whenever applicable, youth who are identified at the preschool, elementary, or secondary level as possessing demonstrated or potential abilities that give evidence of high performance capabilities in areas such as intellectual, creative, specific academic, or leadership ability, or in the performing and visual arts, and who by reason thereof, require services or activities not ordinarily provided by the school.

Who Are the Gifted and Talented?

Estimates are that about 3 percent to 5 percent of the school population fits the above definition. Recent United States government reports reflect this interest in the gifted, stating that the gifted are a minority who need special attention. They are a minority, characterized by their exceptional ability, who come from all levels of society, all races, and all national origins, and who represent both sexes equally (Sternberg & Davidson, 1986).

If these children are so talented, why do they require special attention? For every Einstein who is identified and flourishes, there are probably dozens of others whose gifts are obscured. Thomas Edison's mother withdrew him from first grade because he was having so much trouble; Gregor Mendel, the founder of scientific genetics, failed his teacher's test four times; Isaac Newton was considered a poor student in grammar school; Winston Churchill had a terrible academic record; Charles Darwin left medical school.

Schools frequently fail to challenge the gifted, and their talents are lost to themselves, professions, and society. You may wonder why extraordinary children fail with ordinary educational programs. Most schools are designed for the average; as the slow learner has difficulty keeping up with average classmates, so the gifted has difficulty staying behind with average classmates. The gifted lose their motivation and either reconcile themselves to mediocrity or become discipline problems (Borland, 1990).

But the curriculum is not the only issue facing these students; there are several others.

- *Failure to be identified.* In a recent survey, the U.S. Office of Education reports that 60 percent of schools reported no gifted students. Teachers and administrators simply fail or refuse to recognize them.
- *Hostility of school personnel.* Hostility traditionally has been a problem for the gifted. Resentment that they are smarter than teachers, dislike for an "intellectual elite," and antagonism toward their often obvious boredom or even disruptive behavior have all occasionally produced a hostile atmosphere for the gifted.
- *Lack of attention.* The "in- and out-of-favor" phenomenon that we described causes this condition. Estimates are that only 3 or 4 percent of the nation's gifted have access to special programs.
- *Lack of trained teachers.* There are remarkably few university programs to train teachers for these children.

Gifted Multicultural Students

In spite of a concentrated effort to insure equality in our schools, minority students remain woefully underrepresented in programs for the gifted (Frasier, 1989). Many explanations have been offered for this phenomenon: low IQ test scores, or lack of a stimulating socioeconomic background, among others. Some writers have speculated that problems in identifying minority gifted adolescents, for example, are the major cause of underrepresentation of these groups (Genshaft, 1991).

Yet we are now seeing a reconsideration of the role of a student's homelife in intellectual development. Research has shown that the quality of those homes that foster intellectual achievement are quite similar, regardless of income level (Frasier, 1989). R. Brown (1988), examining model youth, pointed out the considerable support for intellectual development in the African-American community.

In an interesting analysis, Sue and Okazaki (1990), arguing against either heredity or environment as the explanation of high levels of achievement, turn to the concept of relative functionalism. For example, they suggest that the behavior patterns of Asian-Americans (including achievement) result from a combination of cultural values and status in society. That is, education provides an opportunity for upward mobility—it becomes increasingly functional when other avenues are blocked.

Frasier (1989) suggested that we change the screening procedures that have inherent limitations built into them for multicultural students. Why not use behavioral traits indicating giftedness, such as the *use* of language rather than a test question *about* language? Parents of multicultural students can help educators reword items on rating scales. Vignettes of successful multicultural students can be used for motivational purposes.

These and similar techniques broaden the concept of giftedness in multicultural populations. Different concepts of intelligence (such as Sternberg's Triarchic Model or Gardner's Multiple Intelligences, see chapter 3) can enrich the use of intelligence as a criterion for a gifted program. Other attempts to identify potential for a gifted program could include:

- seeking nominations from knowledgeable professional and non-professionals.
- use of behavioral indicators to identify those students who show giftedness in their cultural tradition.
- collecting data from multiple sources.
- delaying decision making until all pertinent data can be collected in a case study.

Remember: The gifted in our schools are a diverse group.

How have the schools treated gifted students once they have been identified? Usually one of three different techniques has been adopted: acceleration, enrichment, or some form of special grouping (Eby & Smutny, 1990).

Acceleration. **Acceleration** means some modification in the regular school program that permits a gifted student to complete the program in less time or at an earlier age than usual. Acceleration can take many forms: school admission based on mental rather than chronological age,

Focus on Students

Genetic Studies of Genius

In 1921, Lewis Terman began one of the most ambitious studies of the gifted ever undertaken, known as the **Genetic Studies of Genius.** Terman wished to identify over 1,000 children in the California schools whose IQ was so high that it placed them within the highest one percent of the nation's child population. Teachers were asked to name their school's brightest children, who were then given a group intelligence test. Those who scored highest were administered an individual Stanford-Binet test. The original criterion for inclusion in the study was an IQ of 140.

This phase of the study yielded 661 subjects (354 boys and 307 girls). An additional 365 subjects came from volunteer testers in schools outside the main survey. Both of these groups consisted of subjects from eighth grade or lower. Another 444 subjects, all junior and senior high school students, were selected by their scores on group intelligence tests. These 1,470 subjects were selected from a school population of one-quarter million. Fifty-eight more subjects were added during the first follow-up in 1927-1928, providing a grand total of 1,528 subjects.

Terman and his associates collected additional information about the subjects: developmental histories, school information, medical data, anthropometrical measurements, achievement test data, character test data, interests, books read over a two-month period, data on the nature of their play, word association tests, and, finally, home ratings. These data were eventually used to supply information about the characteristics of the gifted compared with their average peers (Terman & Oden, 1959).

What is especially interesting about Terman's work was his method of identifying the gifted—by almost sole reliance upon intelligence tests. Today, as indicated, we have broadened our definition of these children to include those who demonstrate talent across many fields.

skipping grades, combining two years' work into one, eliminating more basic courses, and early admission to high school and college. To say that reactions to acceleration are mixed would be an understatement. Recent reactions, however, have turned more positive.

Learning for the gifted is inadequate if it omits acceleration, according to Stanley and Davidson (1986), who have worked with the mathematically precocious. Concluding that most of the gifted child research was buried with Lewis Terman in 1956, they stated that acceleration is vastly preferable to various enrichments that frequently degenerate into busywork (unrelated to the student's

specific talent) or merely present advanced material earlier, guaranteeing future boredom.

Grade acceleration and subject matter acceleration should proceed simultaneously (Stanley & Davidson, 1986). Using an example from the Johns Hopkins program, they describe a verbally and mathematically brilliant boy who took one course each semester and summer from age twelve to fifteen. He also skipped the second, eleventh, and twelfth grades, which combined with subject matter acceleration, enabled him to enter Johns Hopkins at fifteen years, two months.

Most gifted boys and girls want to accelerate, which they do with ease and pleasure (Stanley & Davidson, 1986). Of their forty-four early college entrants, only one experienced initial difficulty, which he quickly conquered. Such procedures are relatively inexpensive and may actually save a school system time and money. For example, identification of the gifted, grade skipping, some special courses, early high school graduation, and arrangement for early college placement require little extra funding. Those gifted students who desired to accelerate had few social or emotional problems.

Enrichment. **Enrichment** is a term designating different learning experiences in the regular classroom. Enrichment techniques usually follow one or more of these procedures:

- Attempt to challenge gifted students by assigning extra readings and assignments, and permit them to participate in related extracurricular activities. For example, if parents can arrange the time, they could take a scientifically advanced student to special classes at an institution such as the New England Aquarium.
- Group the schools' gifted so that they are together occasionally, enabling interested teachers to challenge their abilities by group discussions and independent research.
- Provide special offerings, such as extra language or advanced science.
- Employ for each school system a special teacher who could move from school to school, identify the gifted, aid regular teachers, and actually work with the gifted in seminars or group discussions.

Enrichment has its advantages and disadvantages. The major disadvantage is the tendency to provide the gifted with busy-work and call it enrichment. More of the same is not enrichment. Another disadvantage is that extra work, discussions, or classes may not match the talent and interests of the gifted child.

The chief advantages are that it should provide challenging, meaningful work for gifted youngsters while they remain with their peers. If teachers can satisfactorily adjust their instruction, enrichment can deter gifted youngsters from social and emotional maladjustment that could accompany acceleration.

In an attempt to avoid these pitfalls, Renzulli (1986) has devised the enrichment **Triad Model,** which entails three components: exploration, skill building, and research into real problems. *Exploration* helps students find topics and subjects that are commensurate with both a student's interests and skills and which are not in the basic curriculum. *Skill building* focuses on the research, data, and communication skills in particular disciplines, an introduction to problem solving strategies and creative thinking. *Research into real problems* has the student investigate some actual consequence and propose a novel solution.

Students involved in the Triad Model have been identified by Renzulli's three-ring model of giftedness: above-average ability in a subject or field (music, art), creative potential, and task commitment. Though Renzulli's model has proven to be popular with classroom teachers, little research is available to testify to its effectiveness.

Special groups. Special grouping implies self-contained special classes, or even special schools, and not to the temporary groupings mentioned under enrichment. Considerable controversy swirls around self-contained units for the gifted, some of which relate to the Jeffersonian versus Jacksonian concepts of equality. Should a democracy encourage and establish an intellectual elite? Aside from the philosophical issue, no evidence exists indicating a clear superiority of special grouping over other techniques. Research is inconclusive, and experts remain uncertain as to the social desirability of grouping or its effect on achievement.

Developing Talent

Defining talent as an unusually high level of demonstrated ability, achievement, or skill in some special field of study or interest, Bloom and his colleagues (1985) investigated the development of talent in several fields: psychomotor (including athletic), aesthetic (including musical and artistic), and cognitive. Selecting Olympic swimmers and world class tennis players, concert pianists and sculptors, and finally research mathematicians and research neurologists, Bloom and his team subjected the participants to intensive interviewing. The team also interviewed the parents and teachers of these individuals, with the subjects' permission.

From these interviews, Bloom and his colleagues reached the following general conclusions:

- Young children initially view their talent as play and recreation, followed by a long period of learning and hard work, eventually focusing on one particular learning activity (math, science).
- The home environment structured the work ethic and encouraged a youngster's determination to do the best at all times.
- Parents strongly encourage children in a specialized endeavor in which a youngster showed talent.
- No one "made it alone;" families and teachers or coaches were crucial at different times in the development of a youngster's talent.
- Clear evidence of achievement and progress was necessary for the individual to continue learning even more difficult skills.

If talent is to flourish, strong interest and emotional commitments to a particular talent field must be accompanied by a desire to reach a high level of attainment and a willingness to expend great amounts of time and effort to reach high levels of achievement in the talent field.

Three recent trends augur well for the future of students who are gifted and talented: (a) the movement throughout the special education field for greater individualized instruction could, if also applied to the gifted, allow them to move more rapidly through both the elementary and secondary curriculum; (b) the greater interest in the gifted on the part of colleges and universities should bring more substantial financial support, more widespread academic encouragement, and better continuity to programs; and (c) multicultural efforts to identify talented men and women should help to dispel charges of elitism (Fox & Washington, 1985).

Finally, if you discover talented students in your class, you may find these suggestions helpful.

- *Learn to recognize the signs of giftedness.* Terman's discouraging conclusions about the failure of parents and teachers to recognize unusual talent should be a warning to everyone. As the gifted return to educational prominence, you will probably be more sensitive to these youngsters and become more capable of discovering hidden talent. If you suspect unique talent, arrange for a referral to the school psychologist or counselor. Avoid guesses; confirm your intuition.
- *Help the gifted; do not reject them.* Once you have identified gifted students, plan to help them. This task is easier said than done because teachers busy with twenty or thirty students can consider extra work with a gifted student an imposition. Try to control such feelings and recall that they are exceptional students with deep, often, unmet needs. They may be personally difficult because school bores them, or you may feel intimidated by their quickness. Be honest with yourself; recognize the reasons for your feelings;

TEACHER ←→ STUDENT
INTERACTIONS

Working with the Gifted and Talented

1. The gifted are excellent readers.
   - Outline a reading program that challenges them, keeps them interested, and encourages them in any special talent they possess.
   - Do not use reading materials that they will meet in the next grade; you only ensure future, more serious, problems, and do later teachers a disservice.

2. The gifted enjoy working with abstract materials and complex relationships.
   - Provide situations where they work with other gifted students on some complex problem or project you have devised.
   - Encourage discussions and seminars where they can express and support their beliefs and yet be challenged by equally inquiring minds.
   - Search the Educational Resources Information Center (ERIC) for possible programs and techniques.

3. The gifted are insatiably curious.
   - Be sure to fill their free time productively when they complete assignments before their classmates; urge them to build collections—books, rocks, fish, whatever they enjoy that is educationally profitable.
   - Permit them to go on field trips with parents, other classes, or by special arrangement. Combine this activity with both written and oral reports. (You must treat judiciously their use of free time; otherwise classmates may become envious, and the gifted student soon feels different and isolated.)
   - Although they have similar interests in games and sports, their interests are more mature. For example, when most youngsters quickly acquire an interest in baseball, it centers on the physical aspects of the game. It is the gifted child who wants to know rules, who interprets disputes, or who quotes batting averages. Use this interest to motivate them to read, calculate, or even invent a board game.

4. Know what your state department of education is doing. Is anyone coordinating efforts for the gifted? Those states that have such coordinators will offer excellent suggestions for programs, teaching techniques, and related literature.

try to challenge them. If you succeed and follow their progress, you can take pride in a job well done.
- *Avoid hostility toward the gifted.* Discipline problems and feelings of inadequacy can often produce open hostility toward these students. Realize that feelings may exist; try to realize why you feel this way, and determine to recognize these students for what they are: youths with real needs who require help.
- *Remember that gifted students are similar to other students.* You should help to bring together the talented with the other students to remove feelings of isolation, or of "being different." Terman's findings that the gifted have the same interest in games and sports should be a definite help to you. Also, remember that the intellectually gifted student is not necessarily physically gifted, or that the artistically talented may not be mathematically superior. These facts should help you guide the gifted's social and emotional development.
- *Recognize where your talents lie.* As someone who has survived many years of academic trial, you possess certain talents. Recognize them and use them in your work. For example, if you like to excel in literature, you can be of enormous help in arranging reading programs for gifted students; your knowledge of books will permit you to make pertinent suggestions for those with other talents—the artistic, the scientific.
- *Watch for signs of boredom.* Recall Terman's guidelines: The gifted are usually at least two years beyond grade placement, sometimes three or four. Gifted youngsters may quickly become restless if immersed in a regular curriculum.

Sensory Handicaps

Some students will enter your classroom with visual and hearing problems, but educational and psychological assessments have shown that they are at or above grade level in cognitive, general psychomotor, and auditory skills. Consequently, these students will spend most, if not all, of the day in a regular classroom (depending on the severity of the impairment). The visually handicapped are a good example.

Visual Impairment
The following definitions of visual impairment (Livingston, 1986) are widely used today:

- **Visual impairment.** Any type of reduction in vision fits into this general classification. When vision remains limited following intervention (prescription lenses, surgery), special services are required for these students to benefit from instruction, and they are considered the visually impaired.
- **Visually limited.** When students have difficulty seeing under average conditions but adaptation

(glasses) corrects the condition, they are classified as sighted for educational purposes.

- **Legally blind.** You probably recall from any eye examinations you may have had that normal vision is 20/20. The numerator of this fraction indicates the distance at which you can read figures on a chart (usually the Snellen). The denominator indicates the distance at which a person with normal vision could read those same letters. If for example, your vision is 20/60, that means you can read at 20 feet what the person with average vision can read at 60 feet. Legal blindness refers to those individuals with vision of 20/200 or less in the better eye (after correction).

The National Society for the Prevention of Blindness recommends that children be referred for an eye examination if they are unable to read lines on the Snellen Chart as follows:

three-year-olds	20/50 or less
four-year-olds through third grade	20/40 or less
fourth grade and above	20/30 or less

An accurate count of visually impaired children remains elusive since data collection varies from state to state. The most widely used figure suggests that one in every 1,000 children is either visually impaired or blind, which translates into 55,000 visually impaired children in the United States.

Myths of the Visually Impaired

We should dispel some of the myths surrounding persons who are visually impaired. They are not born with greater auditory acuity, tactile sense, or musical talent. Superior performance may result from more constant use. Visual problems do not adversely affect cognitive, language, motor, and social abilities. Such views represent the stereotypes of society.

For example, though concept development may initially be delayed, visually impaired students demonstrate normal performance during the elementary years. It is understandable, then, that their achievement suffers. Language development may also be delayed, but again, most youngsters progress to normal levels of usage during the school years. Any social problems that may arise seem to be more the result of the attitudes of others. Perhaps the best way to summarize the developmental characteristics of visually impaired children is to note that they are like other children in many more ways than they are different from them.

If your classroom is the least restrictive environment for a visually impaired student, then that student should be taught the same sequence of topics as students with

---

TEACHER ⟷ STUDENT INTERACTIONS

Working with the Visually Impaired

1. The National Society's publication, *Vision Screening in Schools,* recommends that teachers can help in identifying vision problems by being aware of several symptoms.
   - Clumsiness; difficulty in walking in a new environment
   - Awkward head positions to see
   - "Tuning out" on information written on blackboard
   - Constantly asking others to tell them what is written at a distance
   - Constant squinting
   - Constant rubbing of eyes
   - Obvious eye problems: red, swollen, crusted

2. Be alert for those youngsters who complain of itchy or scratchy eyes, dizziness, headaches, or feelings of nausea following eye work.
   - Urge normally sighted classmates to respect and encourage students who are visually impaired.
   - If you have any of these students in class, remember to say aloud what you are writing on the board.
   - With regard to content, your expectations should match the potential of these students; in other words, treat them like their classmates in academic matters.

---

normal vision. They should be monitored carefully so that they acquire appropriate non-academic skills, enabling them to interact with and be accepted by their peers.

Hearing Impairment

Hearing is the sense that developing students use to learn those language and speech skills necessary for social interaction and academic success. Hearing impaired students possess the same potential for acquiring language as other children, but they lack linguistic input, the raw material of language acquisition (Lowenbraun & Thompson, 1986).

The following definitions are widely used today:

- **Hearing impairment** refers to any type of hearing loss that ranges in severity from mild to profound. There are two subdivisions of hearing impaired: (a) deaf—deafness defines a hearing disability so acute that an individual is prevented from processing

TEACHER ⬌ STUDENT INTERACTIONS

Working with the Hearing Impaired

1. Be on the lookout for those students who:
   - have trouble following directions.
   - seem to be at a loss with other students.
   - do not pay attention to noises (halls, classroom sounds, voices from the corridor).
2. Be careful of seating.
   - If you tend to remain at the front of the classroom, seat students with a hearing deficit in the front row so that they can hear better and perhaps read your lips, if necessary.
   - Encourage these students to watch your face carefully.
   - Do not exaggerate your speech.
   - Discourage their use of distorted positions to hear better.
   - Urge the remainder of the class to speak clearly and distinctly but, again, not in any exaggerated fashion.
3. Be especially alert to the kinds of social interactions in which these students engage.
   - Don't let these students depend solely on you for social interactions.
   - Encourage other students to interact with a hearing impaired student.
   - Arrange classroom activities in which hearing impaired students can actively participate (projects entailing art, data collection, etc.).

linguistic information through audition with or without a hearing aid; and (b) **hard of hearing**—these individuals have sufficient hearing potential that, with the use of a hearing aid, they can process linguistic information through audition. (Note: Be sure to make a clear distinction between "deaf" and "hearing loss" since deafness implies a hearing loss so severe that normal activity is impossible.)

Estimates are that about 8 percent, or over 17 million Americans, experience some form of hearing difficulty. Within this group, approximately 100,000 preschool youngsters, 600,000 elementary and junior high students, and almost 1,000,000 high school and college students have some degree of hearing loss. About 50,000 children and youth have been educated under the conditions of P.L. 94–142.

Since most classrooms rely heavily on both spoken and written language, students with any type of hearing

impairment remain at a distinct disadvantage in their learning. One of the most realistic dangers these students face reflects the dangers of labeling that we previously discussed. If initially we lack hard evidence of a problem, we could too easily label such a student as slow or difficult, with all the attendant problems that accompany such categorizing.

For the hearing impaired, controversy surrounds the meaning of least restrictive environment (Lowenbraun & Thompson, 1986). If interaction with peers is deemed vital, a regular classroom would seem most suitable, but also most fraught with potential communication pitfalls. Most experts agree, however, that a regular classroom is most beneficial if specialized support is available.

Try to detect students with hearing impairments as soon as possible. Students with a mild hearing loss (and even for some with a more severe loss) often adapt sufficiently to go several years in school without being identified. They compensate in ways that cause teachers to miss the problem. But these students suffer because they cannot work to full potential and frequently become frustrated and anxious.

Communication Disorders

Some students have speech and language problems that are unrelated to sensory handicaps or cognitive difficulty. (Speech and language problems are high-prevalence categories of exceptionality.) They are delayed in demonstrating language or have difficulty in expressing themselves. Under P.L. 94–142, "Speech Impaired" is defined as a communication disorder, such as stuttering, impaired articulation, language impairment, or voice impairment that affects educational performance.

Use of the terms communication, language, and speech still require classification, for although they are often used synonymously, they technically have different meanings. (See chapters 2 and 3 for language discussion.)

Communication refers to any process that transmits information (language, speech, telephone, computer). **Language,** a more restricted term, refers to verbal or nonverbal communication between individuals. **Speech,** an even more restrictive term, refers to human usage; sound is the vehicle for conveying meaning.

What happens when students talk? Three major accomplishments are necessary. First is **encoding,** in which speaker A wishes to convey some meaning to receiver B and must fit the message to the language. The message must also fit the grammar of the language before it becomes part of the sound system. This phase is referred to as "encoding." Second is **transmission** of the message, which commences when the brain activates the speech organs. The speech organs now produce a speech sound that generates sound waves. These reach listener B, cause ear vibrations, and eventually stimulate B's brain. Third is **decoding,** in which the listener uses the sound and grammar of the message to interpret it. Assume that phonologically you decode a message such as "I'd like the sand which you ate," which is semantically illogical. We return to phonological decoding—the sounds are the same. But grammatically, two arrangements are possible:

1. I'd like the sand, which you ate.
2. I'd like the sandwich you ate.

Now all aspects of decoding—phonological, grammatical, and semantic—are complete, and you accept the message.

You will better understand communication disorders if you remember that language consists of three major elements: *sounds* (phonology), *meaning* (morphology), and *grammar* (syntax). Any language possesses certain fundamental distinctive sounds: the phonemes of that language. Think of two similar sounding words: thin, shin. The initial sounds differ sufficiently so that they are distinctive and thus qualify as phonemes.

Although phonemes affect meaning (for example, adding an s can change a singular to a plural), they possess no meaning themselves. Morphemes, however, introduce meaning. The morpheme may be a word (free morphemes) or part of a word (bound morphemes). For example, *cat* and *be* are free morphemes; *s* and *ed* are bound morphemes. Morphemes allow a speaker to signal relationships: Jack is older than Jill. Morphemes also permit the speaker to indicate numbers, an important consideration in English—for example, cats, pails, roses.

Linguists believe that morphemes carry a considerable burden in the English language. Cat, for example, tells us that there are three phonemes, so arranged that they convey the meaning of an animal. Consider also the string of morphemes: Jack fetch pail water. It is not grammatical because it lacks those morphemes necessary to signal relationship: ed, a, of. "Jack fetched a pail of water" is a grammatical sentence.

Morphemes are meaningfully arranged in the grammar or construction of a language, forming acceptable constructions of a language, the syntax of that language. Syntax arranges morphemes in meaningful sentences. Recent grammatical studies have shown that any speaker can say, and any listener can understand, an infinite number of sentences. Thanks to grammar, no two sentences you speak, hear, or read are identical (excluding trivia, such as "How are you?").

Students with problems in any or all of these three aspects of language will experience communication disorders, which may be divided into two categories: (a)

speech disorders, such as misarticulation, which refers to difficulty with phonemes; *apraxia,* which refers to difficulty with commands to the muscles controlling speech; *voice disorders*, which are deviations of pitch, loudness, or quality; *fluency disorders*, which usually take the form of stuttering; and (b) *language disorders,* which usually refer to the difficulty in learning the native language with respect to content, form, and usage, and possibly those students with delayed language development.

What are possible causes of communication disorders? They may range from neuropsychological elements that interfere with cognitive development and information-processing strategies, structural and physiological elements (such as the hearing problems just discussed), and environmental causes such as a deprived socio-cultural condition. These elements rarely act in isolation, and your instruction must accept the reality of interaction among the causative elements. For example, hearing impairments may adversely affect peer interactions, causing a student to engage in limited attempts at communication.

Among the characteristics you should be on the alert for are the following:

1. Is there any kind of articulation delay or disorder?
2. Is there anything unusual about a student's voice (loud, uneven pitch)?
3. Is there a smooth flow of speech?
4. Does a student use the same type of speech (similar words to describe actions, people, objects) with the same meanings as typical students?
5. Does a student use speech to achieve goals in the same manner as other students?

To aid students with communication disorders, Bailey and Wolery (1984) suggest that you reinforce both verbal and nonverbal forms of communication. Encourage nonhandicapped classmates to talk to these students as much as possible and reinforce them for doing so. Also urge their peers to play with them frequently, thus increasing all forms of interaction. You yourself should be a clear and positive model to students with communication problems as you have them use increasingly more complex speech patterns.

Physical and Health Impairment

Under the definitions used in P.L. 94–142, physical disabilities are grouped into two classes: (a) those involving *orthopedic impairment* such as cerebral palsy, amputations, muscular dystrophy, polio, spinal cord injuries, and multiple sclerosis; and (b) those affecting *vitality* such as heart problems, asthma, epilepsy, diabetes, and leukemia. Many of these students can function in a regu-

Working with Students Who Are Physically or Health Impaired

1. Consider the following specific suggestions for integrating these students into your classroom:

   • Ask students what adaptations, special equipment, or teaching procedures work best for them.
   • Ask parents, therapists, or education specialists what special devices or procedures are needed to assist students.
   • Allow disabled students, if possible, the opportunity to do what their peers do, even though their physical disability may cause them to seem uncoordinated.
   • Have volunteers assist with physical management so that students with disabilities can go on field trips and participate in special events and projects.
   • Work with nondisabled students so that they understand that characteristics such as drooling, unusual ways of talking, and physical awkwardness cannot be helped and should not be ridiculed.
   • Prepare yourself and your class for helping students with special needs.
   • Treat students with disabilities as normally as possible. Do not overprotect them; make them assume responsibility for themselves.

lar classroom once they have mastered supportive equipment such as crutches or an artificial limb. For others, transition into a regular classroom depends on other circumstances such as the quality of support services, the availability of transportation, accessibility within and without the school, and the opportunity for individualized programs.

Once your initial anxiety is over, you will be concerned mainly with insuring that these students are able to share fully in class activities without lowering your expectations for them. Familiarize yourself as fully as possible with any equipment being used (braces, wheelchairs) and be aware of the characteristics of some of the more common handicaps such as the following:

• *Asthma.* Treat students with asthma as normally as possible since the asthma is unlikely to interfere with education.
• *Amputation.* Students with a prosthesis will usually function at normal levels and require little support once they have overcome the immediate effects of the trauma.

• *Epilepsy.* Seizures are serious, and you should be alert to their possibility. If medication used to control seizures is particularly potent it may affect learning.
• *Cerebral palsy.* One of the most common handicaps in this category, its severity will determine placement, either in a regular or special class.
• *Muscular dystrophy.* The education goal for these students, again depending on the initial severity of the condition, is to maintain them in an ordinary class for as long as possible.

Behavior Disorders

Here we encounter a particularly baffling cluster of problems whose exact definition and prevalence have continually frustrated investigators. You will find some students who are unusually restless and active, to the point of disrupting a classroom; others seem to explode into tantrums at the slightest provocation; still others may be terrified of the most simple situations (for example, the student who will not enter a classroom unless the lights are on). These few examples should give you a sense of the wide range of problems encompassed by the label **behavior disorders** or emotionally disturbed.

Characteristics of Behavior Disorders

Behavior disorders include any condition in which one or more of the following characteristics are exhibited over a long period of time and to a marked degree, which adversely affects educational performance:

• *an inability to learn* that cannot be explained by intellectual, sensory, or health factors;
• *an inability to build or maintain satisfactory interpersonal relationships* with peers or teachers;
• *inappropriate types of behavior or feelings* under normal circumstances;
• *a general pervasive mood of unhappiness or depression;*
• *a tendency to develop physical symptoms or fears* associated with personal or school problems (Rutter & Garmezy, 1983).

These problems can be grouped into two general categories: environmental conflict and personal disturbance. Environmental conflict encompasses aggressive-disruptive behavior, hyperactivity, and social maladjustment; personal disturbance includes anxiety and withdrawal.

As you can well imagine, determining the causes of the problem are difficult, with assessments incorporating biological and environmental elements. These youngsters are difficult to work with, and teachers may be enormously relieved when students with behavior disorders are removed from regular classrooms. But before

Table 14.5

Classification Criteria for Attention–Deficit Hyperactivity Disorder

Note: Consider a criterion met only if the behavior is considerably more frequent than that of most people of the same mental age.

A. A disturbance of at least six months during which at least eight of the following are present:

(1) often fidgets with hands or feet or squirms in seat (in adolescents, may be limited to subjective feelings of restlessness)

(2) has difficulty remaining seated when required to do so

(3) is easily distracted by extraneous stimuli

(4) has difficulty awaiting turn in games or group situations

(5) often blurts out answers to questions before they have been completed

(6) has difficulty following through on instructions from others (not due to oppositional behavior or failure of comprehension), e.g., fails to finish chores

(7) has difficulty sustaining attention in tasks or play activities

(8) often shifts from one uncompleted activity to another

(9) has difficulty playing quietly

(10) often talks excessively

(11) often interrupts or intrudes on others, e.g., butts into other children's games

(12) often does not seem to listen to what is being said to him or her

(13) often loses things necessary for tasks or activities at school or at home (e.g., toys, pencils, books, assignments)

(14) often engages in physically dangerous activities without considering possible consequences (not for the purpose of thrill-seeking), e.g., runs into street without looking

Note: The above items are listed in descending order of discriminating power based on data from a national field trial of the DSM-III-R criteria for Disruptive Behavior Disorders.

B. Onset before the age of seven.

C. Does not meet the criteria for a Pervasive Developmental Disorder.

Criteria for severity of Attention-Deficit Hyperactivity Disorder:

Mild: Few, if any, symptoms in excess of those required to make the diagnosis *and* only minimal or no impairment in school and social functioning.

Moderate: Symptoms or functional impairment intermediate between "mild" and "severe."

Severe: Many symptoms in excess of those required to make the diagnosis *and* significant and pervasive impairment in functioning at home and school and with peers.

Reprinted with permission from the *Diagnostic and Statistical Manual of Mental Disorders, Third Edition.* Copyright 1987 American Psychiatric Association.

rendering judgment, you should keep firmly in mind the interactive nature of the factors involved.

Attention-Deficit Hyperactivity Disorder

One of the more challenging problems that you may experience in school settings are those students diagnosed as having Attention-deficit Hyperactivity Disorder (ADHD). Research shows that ADHD occurs in approximately 3 percent to 5 percent of U.S. elementary school students and is three times more common in boys than girls (Braswell & Bloomquist, 1991). Although there is considerable controversy over the diagnosis of this problem (some authors discuss it as primarily a language disorder—see Lovinger, Brandell, & Seestedt-Stanford, 1991), most researchers rely on the diagnostic criteria presented by the American Psychiatric Association in their Diagnostic and Statistical Manual of Mental Disor-

ders (DSM-III-R, 1987). Table 14.5 presents the diagnostic criteria for ADHD from the DSM-III-R.

ADHD (sometimes simply called hyperactivity) seems to be caused by a variety of factors—neurological, emotional, dietary, and/or environmental—and can encompass a range of behaviors (Greene, 1987). For example, some students may exhibit only mild and infrequent episodes while others are chronically disruptive. Among the methods used with these students are medication, behavior modification, perceptual-motor training, and special diets.

School can become a problem for these children since it may be the first time that they are required to demonstrate self-control and adjustment to a structured environment. In fact, parents may realize at the time of school entrance that their child suffers from ADHD. Previously they may have dismissed such behavior as just "growing up." These students have a tendency to shout things out in class, demand a teacher's immediate attention, and not to wait their turn. If this behavior is accompanied by emotional outbursts, those around such children may begin to suspect that they are seriously emotionally disturbed.

What can you do to help these students? Here are a few suggestions you may find helpful (Ingersoll, 1988):

- Keep your own emotions under control. Though this may be easier said than done given the demands that these students will make upon you, it's nevertheless true that you only add to the problem if you respond in anger. Remember: It's not the student who so aggravates you; it's the disorder.
- Provide structure and feedback. Because these students cannot organize their own world, you have to do it for them (Ingersoll, 1988, p. 167). These students should know exactly where they are to be at all times and where things are to go, and perhaps most important of all, they must receive clear, precise instructions from you.
- Use feedback to improve their behavior. Positive feedback can be a major force in helping to improve this behavior. Reinforce often, reinforce small steps, and vary the reinforcers.
- Help these students with their peer problems. Reinforce peers for including ADHD students in their activities, but you must be subtle with older students. Also try to plan activities that require mutual cooperation for success.*

Most students, however, develop normally, that is, with a minimum of difficulties. Even those who experience some emotional and behavioral problems usually do not experience serious psychiatric illness. Their roots may be traced to many sources—the student, family, school, society—and again dramatically illustrate the importance of an interactive analysis.

It is deceptively simple to classify a student's problem along a single dimension: a disturbed personality, parental separation, or the school. But a student's behavior represents the interaction of many causal points. There is no avoiding the biological, psychological, and social consequences of a problem, either physical, emotional, or behavioral. For example, it is possible to classify many of the disorders discussed in this section as emotional. To do so is a disservice to the student who is experiencing the problem. There may well be a physical cause behind an apparent emotional problem such as anxiety; any physical difficulty, such as asthma, can have definite, even serious emotional consequences.

*For further practical guidelines for working with these students see Ingersoll, Barbara. (1991). *Your Hyperactive Child*. New York: Doubleday.

TEACHER ⟷ STUDENT INTERACTIONS

Working with Students with Behavior Disorders

1. The term *behavior disorders* encompasses a wide variety of problems that require diversified classroom strategies.

   - When possible, change pace, or even your schedule, when you detect a possible eruption.
   - Be sure that these students understand classroom rules. Try listing the rules on the board and reinforcing (by praise or token) when the student follows the posted rules.
   - Remove as many distractions as possible from these students so that they may focus more fully on their work.
   - These students need structure, with their learning tasks carefully arranged in small, concrete steps.
   - Select several peers and ask them to ignore any disruptive behavior and reinforce positive behavior. Elementary school students are particularly good at this.
   - Above all, be consistent in your interactions with these students, which will differ according to the behavior. Ignoring acting out behavior may be impossible because it could become disruptive; it may be quite effective, however, with withdrawn students.

2. There are several behaviors to avoid in working with these students.

   - Don't use sarcasm or ridicule.
   - Don't use force.
   - Don't make an issue of minor problems.
   - Don't compare one student's behavior with another.

Working with students who display behavior disorders requires both knowledge and patience, characteristics not always in plentiful supply. Although most educators believe that mainstreaming these students is positive, good guidelines for the best way to handle them in a regular class are still lacking. Figure 14.2 illustrates several behavior patterns that students might display in the classroom; some of these are teacher-related; others are peer-related. Students who demonstrate externalizing patterns typically have more difficulty in their adjustment to the expectations of teachers. In contrast, internalizing students may not have as much difficulty with teachers but will likely have considerable difficulty with peers who may neglect or reject them.

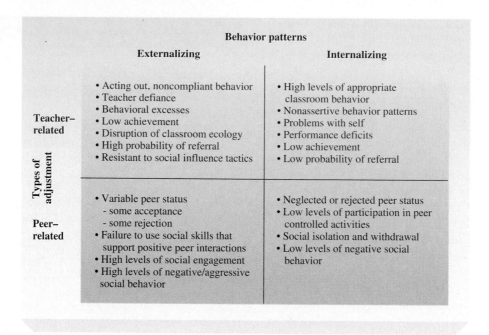

Figure 14.2
Interrelationships of bipolar behavior patterns and school adjustment types.

Learning Disabilities

Of all the categories of exceptionality we have discussed, perhaps none has caused as much difficulty in definition as **learning disabilities** or learning disorders. Dissatisfaction with existing definitions (including that offered by the Office of Education in 1977) caused representatives of several organizations to meet and propose a new definition that has become more widely accepted.

In 1981, *The National Joint Committee for Learning Disabilities* (NJCLD) proposed the following definition of learning disabilities:

> Learning disabilities is a generic term that refers to a heterogeneous group of disorders manifested by significant difficulties in the acquisition and use of reading, writing, reasoning, or mathematical abilities. These disorders are intrinsic to the individual and presumed to be due to central nervous system dysfunction. Even though a learning disability may occur concomitantly with other handicapping conditions (e.g., sensory impairment, mental retardation, social and emotional disturbance) or environmental influences (e.g., cultural differences, insufficient-inappropriate instruction, psychogenic factors), it is not the direct result of the conditions or influences (Hammill, Leigh, McNutt, and Larsen, 1981, p. 336).

Recently, a special study group of the National Institute of Health expanded this definition to encompass social skills and the relationship between learning disabilities and attention-deficit disorder.

Though controversy may swirl around definitions, professionals working with these students are in general agreement about the following aspects of the problem (Morsink, 1985):

- *Discrepancy.* There is a difference between what these students should be able to do and what they are actually doing.
- *Deficit.* There is some task others can do that an LD child can't do (such as listen, read, or do arithmetic).
- *Focus.* The child's problem is centered on one or more of the basic psychological processes involved in using or understanding language.
- *Exclusions.* Learning disabilities are not the direct result of poor vision or hearing, disadvantage, or retardation, but these students still aren't learning.

Development and Learning Disabilities

An **exclusion component** is now used to identify as accurately as possible students with learning disabilities. This component means that the problems are not a result of mental retardation, visual or hearing impairment, motor handicaps, or environmental disadvantage. You have probably concluded that learning disabilities characterize the school-age child; they are difficult to detect in young children. Reading, mathematics, and language are the vulnerable subjects, with research focusing on the psychological processes that may cause the problem. Symbolic activity seems to be the basic weakness. To help you separate myth from fact, Table 14.6 presents several misconceptions about learning disabilities.

Learning Disabilities—A Clinical Interpretation

Levine, Brooks, and Shonkoff (1980) attempted to link developmental characteristics and milestones with clinical dysfunction in children who evidence learning problems. They used the following categories:

- *Selective attention and activity.* Students labeled "hyperactive" or having "minimal brain dysfunction" are increasingly identified as having attention difficulties. Unless they can focus on meaningful stimuli, they will encounter adjustment problems from birth. As we have seen, infants can discriminate detail and detect differences between the familiar and the discrepant, thus facilitating cognitive development. During the preschool years attention becomes more efficient, preparing the child for more formal schooling. It is during these years that attentional problems become apparent, a fact that is disturbing because early academic success depends upon the capacity to select and sustain a focus.

    Attention deficits are associated with academic, social, and behavioral problems, especially for boys. Some of the signs of an attention deficit are easy distractibility, impulsivity, task impersistence, insatiability (never satisfied), and the ineffectiveness of rewards and punishments for these children.

- *Visual-spatial and gestalt processing.* Some students have difficulty with spatial relations, which affects their performance in activities ranging from catching a ball to reading. They have difficulty in discriminating patterns, or shapes, which is critical for comprehending the physical world. This is especially true in attempting to master the symbols used in reading and mathematics.

- *Temporal-sequential organization and segmental processing.* It is difficult to learn something unless you place it in the right order. Words, numbers, and the steps in a task (learning to tie shoes) involve order. Most of a student's classroom activities demand sequential organization. Storage and retrieval of information is a particular problem for these youngsters, as is following directions. "Open your book to page 20, do the first three problems, and then check the answers on page 132." Since an attention

Table 14.6

Myths and Facts About Learning Disabilities

Myth	Fact
All LD students are brain-damaged.	Learning problems occur without brain damage.
All LD students have perceptual problems.	Many students with learning disabilities show no such evidence.
Perceptual training will lead to academic gains.	Perceptual training improves perceptual skills, which may lead to academic gain.
Hyperactivity is easily controlled by drugs.	The effective use of drugs is complicated and requires the cooperation of students, teachers, parents, and physician.
LD students do not have math problems.	Two out of three students with learning disabilities receive special instruction in math.
Knowing a student's learning disability is the result of brain damage helps a teacher.	Such a diagnosis is of little help to a teacher (it may help staff or medical personnel).

Adapted from Hallahan and Kauffman, 1988.

deficit may be involved, teachers should offer help in focusing upon steps, accompanied by reinforcement.

- *Perceptive language function.* Some students have difficulty in interpreting auditory stimuli and in obtaining meaning from words and sentences. The strong link between language development and academic success poses obstacles that these students must quickly overcome, or educational failure can result.

- *Expressive language function.* Competent spoken language depends on a number of factors, including the capacity to retrieve relevant words from memory, arrange these words in phrases or sentences that conform to linguistic rules, develop ideas in meaningful sequence or narrative, and plan and execute the highly complex motor act of speech (Levine, Brooks, & Shonkoff, 1980, p. 77).

Acquiring these abilities also carries with it the potential for difficulty: poor articulation, lack of ability to convey symbolic meaning, and stuttering, all of which affect oral work in the classroom.

- *Memory.* Smooth developmental progression relies on the storage of data, experience, and acquired skill. Retention and retrieval of this accumulated content is basic for meaningful learning. Students can't read meaningfully if they can't recall the order and meaning of words. Students with memory deficits frequently show a wide range of clinical symptoms, both behavioral and academic. For example, such students may be unable to retain directions and then appear lazy or poorly motivated. Weak visual memory may result in shaky word configurations, thus slowing the rate of reading.

- *Voluntary motor function.* Typical of this category are those students who say, "I know what you mean, but my body won't do what I tell it." Problems in this category include both gross and fine motor functioning, which may or may not be associated with learning difficulties. In many cases a cycle is established in which motor difficulties lead to embarrassment, lowered self-esteem, and social withdrawal, all of which can contribute to the formation of learning disabilities. Lack of control of the fingers and hand in writing or an inability to move correctly in classroom games or physical activities could possibly cause a tendency to avoid these potentially embarrassing situations.

- *Developmental implications.* Learning disabilities affect from 4 percent to 20 percent of school age children with a boy-girl ratio of between 6 and 8 to 1. Learning disorders are probably the most common of the problems that plague children. Parents and teachers are usually involved immediately, but frequently counseling is needed because of accompanying emotional or behavioral difficulties.

The Role of Previous Knowledge

Studies of students with learning disabilities have underscored the key role of specific knowledge and skills in learning (Brown & Campione, 1986). As psychological theory has shifted to a greater cognitive emphasis, the role of previous knowledge, the knowledge that a student brings to any topic, is critical. Consequently, it is essential to determine the extent to which a student can function effectively with the knowledge needed to perform a specific academic task. Rather than seeking underlying mental problems, teachers can help these students to acquire the

necessary pre-requisite knowledge and skills. Can this student move on to fractions? Does that student understand the logic behind the experiment?

Instruction, then, should focus on where the student is now and appropriate methods that match a particular level of competence. If possible, you could have students with learning disabilities work with expert peers who guide their efforts and carefully structure the environment for them. This strategy may help these students to adopt regulatory and structuring activities of their own. If successful, you have provided considerable social support for students who are disabled.

Mental Retardation

Much of the dramatic change in our thinking about exceptionality can be traced to the relatively recent surge of interest in **mental retardation.** After decades of neglect, the public has willingly supported programs designed to educate, rehabilitate, and care for exceptional children, a large number of whom are mentally retarded.

Who are the mentally retarded? A widely accepted definition has been proposed by the American Association on Mental Retardation.

> Mental retardation refers to significantly subaverage general intellectual functioning resulting in or associated with concurrent impairments in adaptive behavior and manifested during the development period (Grossman, 1983, p. 11).

Obviously, some individuals are more severely mentally retarded than others. Table 14.7 should help you to sort out these differences.

1. *Those who are moderately mentally retarded* constitute about 6 percent of the mentally retarded. Although many reside in institutions, some adults may live with their families and can do household chores. Brain damage and Down's syndrome are the chief causes of moderate mental retardation.

2. *Those who are severely mentally retarded* encompass about 3.5 percent of this population. They have historically been institutionalized, requiring constant supervision; they may acquire language and self-care skills only after extensive training. Genetic problems and neurological damage usually cause severe mental retardation.

3. *Persons who are profoundly mentally retarded* represent about 1.5 percent of the mentally retarded population. They require total care. Infant mortality is high in this group.

Table 14.7

Developmental Characteristics of Mentally Retarded Persons

Degrees of Mental Retardation	Preschool Age (0–5) Maturation and Development	School Age (6–20) Training and Education	Adult (21 and over) Social and Vocational Adequacy
Mild	Can develop social and communication skills; minimal retardation in sensorimotor areas; often not distinguished from normal until later age.	Can learn academic skills up to approximately sixth-grade level by late teens. Can be guided toward social conformity. "Educable."	Can usually achieve social and vocational skills adequate to minimum self-support but may need guidance and assistance when under unusual social or economic stress.
Moderate	Can talk or learn to communicate; poor social awareness; fair motor development; profits from training in self-help; can be managed with moderate supervision.	Can profit from training in social and occupational skills; unlikely to progress beyond second-grade level in academic subjects; may learn to travel alone in familiar places.	May achieve self-maintenance in unskilled or semiskilled work under sheltered conditions; needs supervision and guidance when under mild social or economic stress.
Severe	Poor motor development; speech is minimal; generally unable to profit from training in self-help; little or no communication skills.	Can talk or learn to communicate; can be trained in elemental health habits; profits from systematic habit training.	May contribute partially to self-maintenance under complete supervision; can develop self-protection skills to a minimal useful level in controlled environment.
Profound	Gross retardation; minimal capacity for functioning in sensorimotor areas; needs nursing care.	Some motor development present; may respond to minimal or limited training in self-help.	Some motor and speech development; may achieve very limited self-care; needs nursing care.

Source: *The Problem of Mental Retardation*, U.S. Department of Health, Education, and Welfare, Office for Handicapped Individuals. Washington, D.C.: U.S. Government Printing Office, 1975.

Those students who are mentally retarded and who might be mainstreamed (approximately 89% of all retarded students) into regular classrooms usually fall into the 70–85 IQ bracket. You infrequently find extremely mentally retarded students in regular classes. More typical of the type of mentally retarded student who is mainstreamed is the following:

A Mentally Retarded Student Who Is Adapting

Today Eddie is nineteen years old, physically strong, and works in a local gas station. Usually pleasant, Eddie is perfectly capable of pumping gas, cleaning windshields, and getting coffee and donuts. It is only when you await change from a $20.00 bill that you notice Eddie's difficulty. If you are a new customer, one of the other attendants immediately helps; if you are known and trusted, you tell Eddie what change to give you.

Eddie is a good example of a young mentally retarded person who is functioning satisfactorily. Experiencing immediate difficulty in school, he was placed in a special class when he was eleven. Learning rudimentary skills, he acquired sufficient knowledge to enable him to service cars—gas, water, battery, washing. The station owner feels strongly about him and has given him an opportunity that many other similar youths never receive.

There is one problem—Eddie is usually pleasant, but several mechanics mock him and send him on foolish errands, which infuriates him when he realizes what they have done. Human nature being human, these conditions are perhaps inevitable. Still, given this one drawback, Eddie enjoys a unique situation where he has proven himself a valuable asset and shown the wisdom of attempts to bring youths like him as close as possible to normal lives. Many individuals such as Eddie blend into society, leading lives that are not dramatically different from those who hold similar jobs. (Note that Eddie fits the behavioral classification of mildly mentally retarded described in Table 14.7.)

Common Problems of Mentally Retarded Students

Mental retardation can result from many causes: genetic, prenatal, perinatal, postnatal, and cultural. These general categories encompass specific causes such as PKU (phenylketonuria), rubella, oxygen deprivation at birth, brain injury, drugs, and economic deprivation. In spite of being mentally handicapped, you should remember that mentally retarded students have the same basic needs as the nonretarded and demonstrate considerable individual differences.

The student who is mildly mentally retarded will exhibit difficulties at specific levels of learning. For example, among the more common problems are the following:

- *attention,* which may be both limited and non-selective;
- *cognitive processing,* especially with regard to organization, classification, and strategies;
- *memory,* which may be poor for short term retention;
- *transfer,* which may be a particularly difficult task;
- *distractibility,* which results in excessive attention to incidental information.

Conclusion

In this chapter, you read about the influence that P.L. 94–142 has had on the placement of students who are exceptional. Today students who are designated as exceptional must be in the environment that is least restrictive for them, which may or may not be the regular classroom. This placement is to ensure that such students have the fullest opportunity to learn and to develop.

Mainstreaming is the attempt to have students who are exceptional spend as much time as possible in a regular classroom. For many students, this arrangement is the least restrictive environment in which they can function successfully.

You also examined the seven types of exceptionality, their characteristics, and the type of environment that

TEACHER ⟷ STUDENT INTERACTIONS

Working with Students Who Are Mildly Mentally Retarded

1. Students who are mildly mentally retarded are mainstreamed into many classes. To facilitate their adjustment and progress, teachers are encouraged to consider the following:

   1. *Provide carefully guided instruction.* This strategy will help avoid failure, and their performance will enable you to emphasize positive features. These youngsters work best with a carefully designed, step-by-step technique, similar to previous suggestions for mastery learning. Considerable repetition is usually necessary, and you should adapt material appropriately for the slow learner. Use as much positive reinforcement as possible.

   2. *Avoid any kind of competition or comparison* between mentally retarded students and their classmates. Constant failure has a damaging impact on anyone's self-concept. Cooperative groups where handicapped students work on teams with nonhandicapped peers is desirable.

   3. *Discover the specific skills mentally retarded students may possess.* If possible, let them demonstrate these skills for other students.

   4. *Be careful of environmental stimuli.* Too many stimuli, especially if they are similar, confuse these children. For example, "ough" in through, thought, trough. Here similar letters demand different responses.

   5. *Be careful of both the number of things taught and the abstractness of the material.* Sheer numbers can overwhelm anyone, especially these youngsters. The more abstract the material, the greater the difficulty the low ability youngster will have with it.

seems to be best suited for their purpose. But you also read about the danger of labels and were urged not to let any label become a self-fulfilling prophecy.

Finally, remember the theme that permeated this chapter: Do everything possible to help all students to learn as well as they can and to flourish as fully as possible in the educational environment.

Chapter Highlights

Individual Differences in the Classroom

- You can expect to find a wide range of individual differences in your classroom: physical, cognitive, and behavioral.
- Federal law (P.L. 94–142) requires that students with handicaps be placed in the environment that is "least restrictive" for them.
- Assessment plays a critical role for making placement decisions about students.
- Any classification system of students with handicaps must avoid the dangers of labeling.
- Several support systems, ranging from a student's family to professional staff, operate to help students adjust to their placement.

Mainstreaming

- Mainstreaming means that, whenever possible, students with handicaps are to be placed into regular classrooms.
- You will undoubtedly be involved somewhere in educational decisions about these students: identification, evaluation, and placement.
- Your informed input requires knowledge from reading, classroom visits, and workshops (among other sources).

Education and Exceptionality: A Model

- A thorough familiarity with normal development can provide developmental milestones to use as an aid in judging student behavior.
- Considerable sensitivity is needed in making decisions about multicultural students since many factors may affect their performance.

The Categories of Exceptionality

- Students who are gifted/talented have often been overlooked in our classrooms, but today we realize they deserve special attention to further their abilities in a manner calculated to provide normal social and emotional development.
- Students with visual and hearing impairments require early detection to prevent lingering problems that may affect performance. The cognitive ability of these students will follow a normal range, so your expectations for them should be similar to those for the rest of the class.
- Students with communication disorders may experience a developmental delay in language acquisition or find difficulty in expressing themselves. Your knowledge of language development should help you to identify these students.

- Students with physical and health impairments need your help in physically adjusting to the classroom and participating in all class activities.
- Students with behavior disorders present a range of problems that can be classified as being caused by either personal or environmental reasons. You will need considerable sensitivity in working with these students to help them achieve as fully as possible.
- Students with learning disabilities are now identified by applying an exclusion component; that is, the difficulty is not attributed to some other cause such as mental retardation or a physical problem. In your work with these students, be careful that some other surface difficulty does not mask the learning disability.
- Students who are mentally retarded will be in your class; they require a carefully sequenced program and a lack of stress in their work.

Key Terms

Ability grouping
Acceleration
At risk
Behavior disorders
Bilingual education
Communication
Decoding
Encoding
Enrichment
Exclusion component
Gifted
Hard of hearing
Hearing impairment
High-prevalence
Incidence
Insensitive classmates
Language
Learning disabilities
Least restrictive environment
Legally blind
Mainstreaming
Mental retardation
Neverstreaming
Prevalence
Regular Education Initiative (REI)
Speech
Transmission
Triad model
Visual impairment
Visually limited

Suggested Readings

Bloom, B. (1985). *Developing talent in young people.* New York: McGraw-Hill. A fascinating account of how talented youth can be encouraged to develop fully their unusual potential. As might be expected of Bloom—thorough, readable, and practical.

Brown, A., and Campione, J. (1986, October). Psychological theory and the study of learning disabilities. *American Psychologist, 41,* 1059–1068. An excellent article that nicely blends theory and research. You should find this in your school library.

New Voices. *Immigrant students in U.S. public schools.* (1988). Boston: The National Coalition of Advocates for Students. One of the best descriptions currently available of the problems that immigrant students face.

Sroufe, L. A., and Rutter, M. (1984). The domain of developmental psychopathology. *Child Development, 55,* 17–29. A fine overview of the psychosocial problems that children of all ages can encounter. Provides a fine framework for the analysis of psychopathological problems.

Assessing Educational Outcomes

Classroom Tests and the Assessment of Students

Barbara Cotter, the junior high school English teacher we met earlier, was puzzled by the lack of achievement of one of her students, Sheilah Johnson. During class time, she usually seemed to know and understand the material; when called on, she responded with correct answers, and her interpretation of a story's theme seemed superior to the rest of the class. Her records indicated that she was healthy, well-adjusted, had above average intelligence, and had no discernible problems. Yet academically, she seemed to be lagging behind her classmates.

Trying to discover more about the reasons for her poor academic record, the teacher managed to talk to her after class. "Well, Sheilah, we've got that test coming up Friday. From listening to you in class, you'll probably do quite well."

"Thanks a lot, Ms. Cotter, but you know I'll foul up."

"Why do you say that, Sheilah? You've done the reading; I can tell you're comfortable with the material from your answers in class. Why do you think you'll do poorly?"

"I always do," Sheilah replied. "I get all confused with multiple-choice questions and then run out of time on the essay questions. I want to do well but get pretty frustrated with tests."

The process of assessing students' learning is central to instruction and is most frequently accomplished with either teacher-made or commercially published standardized tests. To help you construct or select fair tests and at the same time to help your students prepare for them, we'll explore the world of testing and measurement in this chapter. A major theme will be the role of testing and assessment in the teaching-learning process. In other words, testing is not an isolated activity to be done because students "need a grade"; sound instruction requires sound classroom-level assessment of students' achievement and behavior. A second theme highlights students' need to be helped in taking tests so that their performance accurately reflects their learning.

To understand these themes and integrate them into your thinking about testing, you'll read about the terminology of testing and assessment, examine basic issues in measuring human performance, and confront several of the issues that you will face in constructing your own tests. You must plan assessments carefully and give thoughts to the kinds of tests and the kinds of items that will best sample your students' learning. Finally, you also use test data to give marks, assign grades, and report on the progress of your students. You should feel much more comfortable discussing grades with students, parents, and school officials if your grades are based on well-constructed tests.

When you have completed reading this chapter, you should be able to:

- plan for tests that serve specific purposes.
- write appropriate test items.
- assess the role of testing in your classroom.
- evaluate how successfully students attained desired objectives.
- evaluate your instructional effectiveness by the results of your testing.
- discuss the use of authentic assessment methods to guide instruction and document students' learning.

Assessment: Terminology and Assumptions

Effective communication about tests and the assessment process requires us to distinguish between terms such as assessment, testing, tests, measurement, and grading. These are *not* synonymous terms. By **assessment** we mean the process of gathering information about a student's abilities or behavior for the purpose of making decisions about the student. There are many tools or methods a teacher can use to assess a student, such as paper-and-pencil tests, rating scales or checklists, interviews, observations, and published tests. Thus, assessment is more than testing.

Testing is simply one procedure through which we obtain evidence about a student's learning or behavior. **Teacher-constructed tests**, as well as commercially published tests, have and will continue to play a major role in the education of students. Such tests are assumed to provide reliable and valid means to measure students' progress. A test is a sample of behavior. It tells us something, not everything, about some class or type of behavior. Well-designed tests provide representative samples of knowledge or behavior.

To **measure** means to quantify or to place a number on a student's performance. Not all performances demonstrating learning can or need to be quantified (for example, art or musical exhibitions). The science of measurement in itself includes many important concepts—reliability, validity, standard scores—for teachers and others responsible for assessing students. We'll consider these psychometric concepts later in this chapter.

A final term that deserves definition is **grading.** Grading is the assignment of a symbol to a student's performance. Grading is not assessment; rather it is often an interpretation of the assessment process. As you well know, it most frequently takes the form of a letter (A, B, C) and indicates some relative level of performance to other students or stated criteria. Remember: You can assess your students' work, effort, attitude, and a host of behaviors without ever assigning a grade.

Now that we have defined key assessment terms, here are four assumptions that we believe are fundamental to the assessment of students. Read them carefully and think about the implications of these fundamental assumptions.

1. Tests are samples of behavior and serve as aids to decision making.
2. A primary reason to conduct an assessment is to improve instructional activities for a student.
3. The person conducting the assessment is properly trained.
4. All forms of assessment contain error.

These assumptions are rather straightforward; however, each deserves additional commentary. The first assumption stresses that tests do not reveal everything a student does or does not know; they provide snapshots of a student's knowledge or behavior. When a test is well-constructed, it can give us representative and useful information about a student, which in turn can be helpful in making decisions about the student.

This information leads us to the second assumption, which emphasizes that the primary educational reason for using tests is to guide instructional activities. Good tests can furnish teachers with information about what to teach next and under what conditions the content might best be taught.

This point leads to the third assumption: A teacher must be properly trained to use tests and the information they yield. A poor test or the misuse of a well-constructed test can significantly damage the teaching-learning process.

The final assumption—all forms of assessment contain some error—is a cautionary note to all persons involved in assessing human performance and stresses the need for frequent assessment of students with a variety of methods. This final assumption also emphasizes that teachers are entrusted to make important and difficult decisions about all of their students.

Uses and Users of Classroom Assessment Information

Research suggests that teachers spend as much as a third of their time involved in some type of assessment. Teachers are continually making decisions about the most effective means of interacting with their students. These decisions are usually based on information they have gathered from observing their students' behavior and performances on learning tasks in the classroom (Witt, Elliott, Gresham, & Kramer, 1988).

Many individuals have a vested interest in student learning and assessment information about such learning. Clearly, teachers, students, and parents should have great interest in the results of student assessments. School administrators and community leaders also voice keen interest in assessment results that document students' performances. No single assessment technique or testing procedure can serve all these potential users of assessment results. Thus, the purpose of one's assessment must be clear, for it influences assessment activities and, consequently, the interpretation of any results.

Teachers have three main purposes for assessing students: (a) to form specific decisions about a student or a group of students, (b) to guide their own instructional planning and subsequent activities with students, and (c) to control student behavior. Teachers use assessment results for specific decisions, including diagnosing student strengths and weaknesses, grouping students for instruction, identifying students who might benefit from special services, and grading student performances.

Teachers can also use assessment activities and results to inform students about teacher expectations. In other words, the assessment process can provide students with information about the kind of performance that they need to be successful in a given classroom. Tests become a critical link in teaching when teachers provide to students clear feedback about results.

Teachers can also use tests and the assessment of students to facilitate classroom management. For example, the anticipation of a forthcoming assessment can serve to encourage students to increase their studying and classroom participation. Assessments likewise provide teachers valuable feedback about how successful they have been in achieving their instructional objectives, and thus help them chart the sequence and pace of future instructional activities.

Students also are decision makers and use classroom assessment information to influence many of their decisions. For example, many students set personal academic expectations for themselves based on teachers' assessments of prior achievement. Feedback they receive from teachers about their performances on classroom tests directly affects other students' decisions about if, what, when, and with whom to study.

The assessment activities and decisions of teachers affect parents as well as students. For example, many parents communicate educational and behavior expectations to their children. Some parents also plan educational resources and establish home study environments to assist their children. Feedback from teachers about daily achievement, communicated via homework, classroom tests, annual standardized tests, report cards, and school conferences often significantly influence these parental actions.

Testing results also provide parents and others in the community with information about the school's performance. That is, does the school prepare students for the basic skills of reading, writing, and calculating? In sum, teachers' assessments of children greatly influence parents' attitudes about their children and schooling. Clearly, the enterprise of assessing students is crucial in the lives of teachers, students, and many parents.

Multicultural Students and Testing

Of all the topics discussed in these next two chapters, none is more practically important than your ability to help students to take tests. Tests often scare students or cause them anxiety. Whatever the reason for test anxiety—parental pressure, their own anxieties, the testing atmosphere—merely taking a test can affect a student's

Focus on Students

What They Think About Tests

To give you an idea of what students think about tests, here is a tape-recorded conversation that took place between a high school history teacher and several members of his class.

Teacher: What do you see as the value of tests?

Student 1: If they're any good, they have to be fair.

Student 2: Yeah, they can't be all essay.

Teacher: Why do you say that?

Student 1: You never have enough time to finish if they're all essay.

Student 2: That's right; it should be a mix of essay and objective.

Teacher: Well, you people study a lot. What's the best way of finding out what you know?

Student 1: Objective tests are best; they have more questions.

Student 2: Yeah, they're more straightforward.

Student 3: I hate objective tests; they're always so tricky.

Student 1: I don't agree; they're a good way of covering everything.

Student 3: There are other good ways to find out what I've learned. I can tell you, I can show you by using what I've learned. I could write a story about what I've learned.

Teacher: Well, is it the kind of question—you know, for example, multiple choice?

Student 3: They're so misleading.

Student 2: Especially if they have those "none of the above."

Student 1: The only time I think they're unfair is when the teacher asks about things we didn't do in class.

Student 2: Yeah, I hate to study things and then not get asked about them.

Teacher: Should every test have an essay part?

Student 1: Well, I don't like them, but I guess it depends on the subject.

Student 3: I don't mind them, but I found them tough at first. You never know what the teacher really wants.

Teacher: How much should tests count toward your grade?

Student 3: Not everything because there are other ways of showing what you've learned.

Student 1: Well, they're the best means of finding out if you studied and how you're doing—as long as there's not too much pressure.

Student 2: They should count more than anything else.

This is a fair summary of what these students think about tests and actually is quite revealing. Obviously, there is a good relationship between these students and their teacher, and they were willing to speak quite frankly. Their reactions seem fair, and through it all, they seem to accept tests as a major part of their evaluation. What else would you conclude from this conversation?

performance. This is especially true for those students who find your classroom a different cultural experience. Language, reading, expectations, and behavior all may be different and influence test performance (Stigler et al., 1990). One publication, *New Voices: Immigrant Students in U.S. Public Schools (1988),* describes many of these students as having experienced wars, political oppression, economic deprivation, and long, difficult journeys to come to the United States.

These students want to succeed. Interviews with many of these immigrant students showed that almost 50 percent were doing one to two hours' homework every night (25 percent of the Southeastern Asian students reported more than three hours' homework each night). We have mentioned throughout our work of the need for sensitive responsiveness. Here is an instance where being sensitive to the needs of multicultural students can only aid both teaching and learning.

We have commented earlier on the positive and receptive nature of the classroom environment. When students feel comfortable, they do better. When students are prepared adequately to take a test, they do better. Try to help any student who is uncertain about the "test." Provide information about why the test is being given, when it is being given, what material will be tested, and what kind of items will be used. These are just a few topics to consider. You also want to be sure that language is not a barrier to performance. Take some time to explain the terms in the directions of your test. Tell them or illustrate what "analyze" means, what you are looking for when you ask them to "compare," what "discuss" means.

Helping multicultural students in this way will take extra time and effort. But it is teaching just as teaching English or history. As more and more multicultural students take classroom tests, you want them to do well and not be limited by the mechanics of the test.

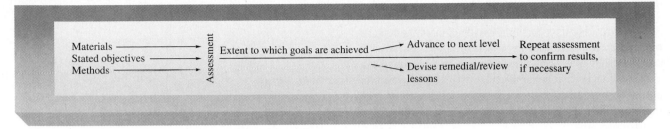

Figure 15.1
The integration of teaching and assessment activities.

Integrating Learning and Assessment

Assessment of students' learning traditionally has been conducted with tests. Tests don't exist in a vacuum. Good tests are designed and used to discover if objectives have been met, if learning has occurred, and as a means of communication. They are a valuable and powerful tool, not only in assessing student progress, but also as a means of examining teaching efforts. Today other techniques, such as teacher observation, student portfolios, and student exhibits also have been proposed as a means of evaluating student performance (Archbald & Newmann, 1988). This collection of techniques is now referred to as authentic assessment.

Educators can defend the success of teaching, the value of curriculum, or the amount of learning only by some demonstrable proof. Proof, however, requires evidence. In education such evidence is obtained through assessment, often by testing. Our preceding work in chapters 11 and 12 was concerned with identifying and attaining worthwhile objectives and instructional methods. Here is your third major task: assessing students' learning. Figure 15.1 illustrates the integrated nature of the three enterprises of identifying learning objectives, selecting teaching methods, and assessing learning.

Figure 15.1 graphically illustrates the key position of assessing students' learning in the teaching-learning process. You have formulated desirable objectives, selected methods and materials to attain these objectives, and used the results of assessment to indicate whether learning has occurred. If it has, students advance to more difficult materials; if it has not, then you should initiate review and repetition.

The above procedure, which is most commonly completed by using a classroom test, focuses upon student achievement. What have students learned as manifested on the test? Have they achieved enough objectives to move on to the next level? The vital role of objectives is clear once more. That is, objectives must be sharply defined and stated in language that permits measurement and specifies behavioral change.

Testing, however, also has a guidance function. Depending upon the nature of the test scores, the results will portray the specific type of remedial work required, or the kind of advanced material that would be most suitable for continued growth. Careful interpretation of test scores also furthers the diagnosis of learning difficulties, both for an individual and a class. If an individual, or class, has failed to attain objectives, teachers search for the cause. There are three immediate possibilities: *the student* (e.g., physically ill at the time of testing, bothered by a personal problem), *the difficulty of the material, or your methods.* If the class is typical, if the material has been proven to be successful with other similar groups, then you can consider several possibilities: lack of background information, too rapid a presentation, or limited student activity when the material demanded more personal involvement. There is another lesson here: Professional teachers will also use test results as a form of self-evaluation; that is, testing results inform teaching.

Testing can likewise help teachers and administrators in their search for appropriate subject matter. If students consistently fail, or experience difficulty, or score unusually high, you may question the nature of the subject matter. Objectives, methods, and materials all reinforce the belief that the assessment of students is at the vital core of education.

Tests and other assessment activities also provide information about the conditions of learning. What do you know about the motivation of the class? Do your students realize they are faced with a problem? Are you providing the opportunity for them to practice the desired behavior? Have they been given sufficient time? Are they deriving satisfaction from their work? How much direction is necessary? Are they obtaining feedback? Both learning and teaching become more efficient as you acquire additional knowledge about the conditions of learning.

Teachers and Testing

Surprisingly, theorists concerned with education often are more aware of the importance of testing and assessment activities than many practitioners who are inherently suspicious of testing. Teachers frequently feel that testing is an added burden that interferes with real teaching and learning. It frequently is, unless the tests are carefully constructed and the content is relevant. Can you assess the quality of materials, the effectiveness of your teaching, and the worthiness of objectives without testing?

If teachers avoid, or merely tolerate testing, it is impossible to judge these issues without resorting to guessing. When one realizes that tests, both teacher-made and standardized, may alter a student's future, it is apparent that poorly made and questionably interpreted tests can cause lasting damage. Grades, promotion, college acceptance, and employment opportunities all reflect the results of testing. Why then are teachers frequently careless in the construction of tests and the interpretation of test results?

One reason may be that teachers are confident about their judgment of students (Marso & Pigge, 1989). They "know" what their students can do; in many instances they view testing as superfluous. Another reason is that a good test is extremely difficult and time consuming to construct. What are the objectives I wish to sample? How are they related to this particular context? Will these items adequately measure the objectives? Still another reason is the dependability of the score: Was the student ill? Was there trouble at home? There may have been a discipline problem in class just before the test; the test itself may have left much to be desired.

Admittedly, each and all of these events can influence the test score. The primary purpose of this chapter is to alert you to these obstacles and to suggest techniques for limiting any negative effect they could have on students' performance. Let's now examine some of the various methods teachers use to assess students.

Methods of Assessing Students

The assessment of students' classroom performances can take many forms. Some assessment methods are formal, others informal; some are administered to an individual, others to a group; some are standardized for all classrooms, others designed for a specific classroom context. Typically, educators have used four primary methods for assessing students' classroom performances: paper-and-pencil tests, oral questions, **performance tests**, and standardized tests. The first three methods are teacher-constructed, whereas **standardized tests** usually are commercially constructed.

"But isn't it more important to learn how to be a decent human being?"

H. Schwadron in *Phi Delta Kappan.*

In this chapter, we'll focus on teacher-constructed tests, which are the most frequently used methods for assessing students. Chapter 16 will be devoted to an analysis of standardized tests and will examine some emerging alternative assessment strategies (that is, authentic/performance assessment) that are assuming a more salient role in the classroom. Before examining details of both teacher-constructed and standardized tests, note the major advantages of each as summarized in Table 15.1.

Teacher-Constructed Tests

Although teachers use many techniques in evaluating students, probably the most popular is the written paper-and-pencil test that they construct. These usually consist of essay or **multiple-choice items.**

The multiple-choice pencil-and-paper test is probably the most frequently used kind of test, with other types such as **true-false,** essay, and performance tests also quite popular with teachers. Good multiple-choice items are difficult to prepare but can be scored easily and objectively. **Essay tests,** on the other hand, are relatively easy to prepare but extremely difficult to score.

Tests, measurements, and **evaluations** are needed for successful education, but that need should not blind you to several difficulties. All measurement is subject to error. The testing conditions, the person giving the test, the person taking the test, and the test itself are all potential sources of error. These reservations should not discourage you; test making has become quite precise, and statistical techniques have become more sophisticated and yield more information from test scores. Yet, realistically, problems remain. For example, when you consider the limitations of the test itself, the lack of a true zero is

Table 15.1

Comparative Advantages of Standardized and Informal Classroom Tests of Achievement

	Standardized Achievement Tests	Informal Achievement Tests
Learning outcomes and content measured	Measure outcomes and content common to majority of United States schools. Tests of basic skills and complex outcomes adaptable to many local situations; content-oriented tests seldom reflect emphasis or timeliness of local curriculum.	Well-adapted to outcomes and content of local curriculum. Flexibility affords continuous adaptation of measurement to new materials and changes in procedure. Adaptable to various-sized work units. Tend to neglect complex learning outcomes.
Quality of test items	General quality of items high. Written by specialists, pretested, and selected on basis of effectiveness.	Quality of items is unknown unless test item file is used. Quality typically lower than standardized because of teacher's limited time and skill.
Reliability	Reliability high, commonly between .80 and .95; frequently is above .90.	Reliability usually unknown; can be high if carefully constructed.
Administration and scoring	Procedures *standardized*; specific instructions provided.	Uniform procedures favored but may be flexible.
Interpretation of scores	Scores can be compared with those of norm groups. Test manual and other guides aid interpretation and use.	Score comparisons and interpretations limited to local school situation.

Reprinted with the permission of Macmillan Publishing Company, Inc. from *Measurement and Evaluation In Teaching*, Sixth Edition by Norman E. Gronlund and Robert L. Linn. Copyright © 1990 by Macmillan Publishing Company. © 1985, 1981, 1976, 1971, 1965 by Norman E. Gronlund.

apparent. If a student scores zero on a geography test, does this imply no geographical knowledge? Obviously not. It means that knowledge is zero on the geographical material that the particular test was measuring, but it tells us nothing more about the student's knowledge of geography.

Again, how much does the teacher influence the results of any examination? The disciplinary attitude toward assessment, the "life or death" view, or the indifferent approach, affect results. Testing has not yet been subjected to the complete control that measurement experts desire. As continued efforts add to knowledge of the classroom's psychological atmosphere, testing itself will undoubtedly improve.

The individual student, however, remains the chief variable in our analysis of measurement problems. A student's knowledge is not the primary concern. The most worrisome element is the opportunity to demonstrate knowledge. In teacher-made tests, the student's outlook on testing is important. If a test is only the measure of achievement, the learning process is distorted. Tests that tell what should be reviewed, or where the student can next progress, are constructive and serve a valuable motivational purpose.

Issues in Constructing Tests

Individuals interested in constructing a test are confronted with challenges concerning *what* to assess, *how* to assess it, and whether they measured it in a reliable and valid manner. These are fundamental challenges to teachers who construct their own tests and to professionals who design standardized tests. Consequently, these topics now deserve our attention.

What to Test

For teachers, the question of what to test implies that *the test must measure what was taught*. Tests will be reliable and valid to the same degree that test constructors are successful in relating test items to what was taught. For teacher-made tests, you may question whether there is any difficulty in testing what was taught. After all, students were exposed to the same teacher, methods, and materials. The answer is not that simple.

Temporarily ignoring the conditions of testing—classroom atmosphere, student health, and related factors—the test itself may fail to assess a student's learning. Did you know why you were teaching; that is, were the objectives stated in objective terms that permitted measurement? Did the test adequately sample the material that was taught? Did it stress the content that you emphasized as important?

Teachers occasionally stress certain aspects of a subject and then test other sections. This strategy supposedly insures broader coverage. Yet it is obviously unfair to the student. Did you construct items that concentrated only upon a small amount of the material that was taught? Are the items comprehensible to the student?

You should also be alert to other issues. The essay test, for example, allows students to express their own ideas in a creative fashion and permits them to demonstrate such elements as organization and grasp of a subject and its application to a particular problem. It also is deceptively easy to construct. But it samples only a limited amount of material (unless you increase the time for assessment), favors the articulate student, and is difficult to mark. Conversely, an objective or multiple choice test samples much more subject matter than the essay examination, has greater objectivity of scoring, and reduces the verbal element in a student's response. Measuring problem-solving and creative behavior, however, is difficult. These tests also emphasize factual information, frequently promote guessing, and are time consuming to prepare.

Determining what to measure and deciding how to measure it are genuine concerns for teachers. Avoid absolute standards. If most students receive an A on a test, or almost all fail another test, you can assume that the test is at fault. Often teachers postpone constructing a test until the last moment, with the result that the test is hastily written and inadequate to sample a student's attainment of objectives. Also be aware of the trivial and ambiguous. Examine Figure 15.2 and see the key role that assessment plays in the teaching-learning process, a role that incorporates all that we have examined thus far in our work. With these ideas in mind, let's now examine the important topics of reliability and validity.

Reliability

A test is reliable to the extent that a student's scores are nearly the same in repeated measurements. A test is reliable if it is consistent (Frisbie, 1988). Do two forms of a test yield similar results? If the test is repeated after a certain interval, how consistent are the results? Some error always exists in any test since fluctuations in human behavior are uncontrollable, and the test itself may contain possibilities of error (Matarazzo, 1990). For example, its

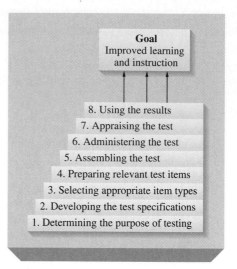

Figure 15.2
Planning your test.

language may be so ambiguous as to be misleading; correcting essay examinations also introduces the chance of error (Griswold, 1990).

You should note carefully the distinction between **reliability** (consistency) and **validity** (meaningfulness). A valid test must be reliable, but a reliable test need not be valid. In other words, reliability is a necessary but not sufficient condition for validity. For example, a test may have an error built into it. Giving an algebra test to first-graders will produce consistent results, but the results are not meaningful for six-year-olds. Thus, the test would be reliable, but would not be valid.

> Suppose, for instance, Miss Jones had just given an achievement test to her students. How similar would the students' scores have been if she had tested them yesterday, or tomorrow, or next week? How would the scores have varied had she selected a different sample of equivalent items? If it were an essay test, how much would the scores have differed had a different teacher scored it? These are the types of questions with which reliability is concerned (Gronlund, 1985, p. 87).

We may conclude, then, that unless a test is reasonably consistent on different occasions or with different samples of the same behavior, we can have very little confidence in its results (Griswold, 1990).

A variety of factors, some concerning the individual taking the test and others inherent in the design and content of the test itself can affect the reliability of a test. Student characteristics affecting a test's reliability include guessing, test anxiety, and practice in answering items like those on the test (Witt et al., 1988). Characteristics of the test that can influence reliability include its length (longer tests are generally more reliable), the homogeneity or similarity of items (more homogeneous tests are usually more reliable), and time to take the test (speed tests are typically more reliable than unbound tests).

Validity

When you test a student in arithmetic, you are testing a sample of that student's arithmetic knowledge. From the test score (for example, on subtraction), you infer that a student knows how to subtract or not. *Your inference depends on the truthfulness or meaning of the test, its validity.* Validity is the extent to which a test measures what it is supposed to measure. Of all the essential characteristics of a good test, none surpasses validity. If a test is not valid for the purpose used, it has no value. For example, if a test designed to measure academic achievement in a particular subject uses questions that are phrased in difficult language, it does not test geography or history as much as it does reading. The test does not measure what it claims. Validity is specific. A test may be valid for one purpose and no other. To administer a spelling test for the purpose of determining a student's achievement in grammar is invalid.

There are three major kinds of validity: content validity, criterion-related validity, and construct validity.

1. A test has **content validity** if it adequately samples behavior that has been the goal of instruction. Does the test adequately represent the material that was taught? Testing a minor portion of a unit on Hamlet after stressing the unity of the total play violates content validity. Determining whether a test has content validity is somewhat subjective. It usually is established when subject-matter experts agree that the content covered is representative of the tested domain of knowledge. Content validity also is referred to as face validity because judgments about content are based on reading or looking at the content.

2. A test has **criterion-related validity** if its results parallel some other, external criteria. Thus, test results are similar or not similar to another sample of a student's behavior (some other criterion for comparison). If students do well on a standardized reading test that measures all aspects of reading, they should likewise do well in completing and understanding geography and history assignments. Some authors refer to this type of validity as predictive validity. You can understand how this kind of validity is valuable for the teacher, particularly in assessing the validity of teacher-made achievement tests. Some other measure is taken as the criterion of success.

3. A test has **construct validity** when the particular knowledge domain or behavior purported to be measured is actually measured. For example, you may claim that your test measures understanding and not facts. If the results of your test agree with ratings of your students on understanding, then your test is, indeed, measuring the construct of understanding. If a test claims to measure anxiety, then its results should match judgments of people identified as anxious. Construct validity is a complex issue and is increasingly coming to refer to the entire body of research about what a test measures (Lyman, 1986).

It makes no sense to prepare or select a classroom test designed to measure something other than what has been taught. We don't measure height by using a bathroom scale. Therefore teachers and others should work hard to ensure that a test does the job it's designed to do.

Planning a Teacher-Constructed Test

With these basic notions of testing in mind, we turn now to the process of constructing those tests that you need to devise for your students. The first step in the process is planning. Constructing a "good" test remains a formidable challenge, one that demands time and effort. Teachers are busy and may well be tempted to ask, "Why bother?" Nitko (1983) summarized well the importance of developing skill in test construction.

- Developing a test helps you to identify more precisely those behaviors important for students to learn.
- As you develop a test, your perspective on both teaching and learning broaden as you distinguish conditions and sequences of learning.
- As you gain skill in constructing your own tests, you become more critical of published testing material.
- A carefully constructed test furnishes you with fair and objective information for the evaluation of students.

Test Planning and Objectives

The first step in planning the test is to review the objectives of the unit or subject. A clear understanding and statement of your specific instructional objectives will significantly improve the quality of the tests that you construct (Gentry, 1989). At this point you might want to review the objectives section of chapter 11.

Table 15.2

Action Words: Keys to Assessment

If You Want to Measure:	Use These Key Words in the Exercise:		Illustration
Recall	define identify label list name	repeat what when who	List the names of the main characters in the story.
Analysis	subdivide breakdown separate	categorize sort	Break the story down into different parts.
Comparison	compare contrast relate	differentiate distinguish	Compare themes of these two stories.
Inference	deduce predict infer speculate	anticipate what if apply conclude	If I wanted to make this character more believable, how might I do it?
Evaluation	evaluate judge assess appraise defend	argue recommend debate critique	Evaluate this story. Is it well written? Why or why not?

Some of the questions that you should answer in this planning stage include the following: Will your test give evidence of the degree to which the students have achieved these goals? What exactly is the purpose of this test? Is it a pretest to discover weaknesses and strengths, or will the results be used as a basis for evaluating a student's academic achievement? How many and what kind of questions should be used? Does the test reflect the emphasis of instruction? Figure 15.2 summarizes the various steps in the process of planning a test and again emphasizes that the goal of classroom testing is improved instruction.

As you plan your tests, be guided by several considerations:

• Be sure you know why you are testing, that is, the purpose of your test. For example, "giving a test" merely because you need marks for your students lacks a clear rationale for testing.
• What type of item will best serve your purposes? Should you use essay or objective items?
• Devote time to preparing relevant items.

Earlier in this book (in chapter 8), the importance of teaching thinking skills was stressed. It logically follows that the assessment of a student's knowledge should be sensitive to the various levels of thinking skills that can be used to solve problems. Both multiple-choice and essay test items can be written to assess recall, analysis, comparison, inference, or evaluation skills. By carefully wording your questions, you can influence the level of thinking skill needed to answer the question. Table 15.2 illustrates action words to consider when you want to assess various levels of thinking skills in your students.

Selecting Test Items

You should consider carefully those aspects of testing that need your pre-test attention. Once you have determined the purpose of your test and identified those behaviors that are critical for mastery, you want to give thought to those items that will best serve your purpose.

What type of test item should you use? Although some readers will use performance items or interviews,

Focus on Teachers

Thinking About Your Test

A major goal of testing is the attempt to secure as much valuable information about your students as possible. Teachers who are concerned about their tests follow these steps:

- They plan the test.
- They obtain crucial information.
- They use the data to form judgments.
- They use these judgments to make decisions about students and to prepare evaluation reports.

In the first phase—planning the test—you will want to avoid two major mistakes:

1. making hasty judgments based on inadequate data;
2. testing with no definite purpose in mind.

The danger of snap decisions is all too real and can have long-term consequences with serious effects on a student's future. If you have no purpose for your testing other than giving the test, perhaps you should rethink your objectives.

Think first of what you want to obtain. For example, you may decide you need achievement data about your students, either to determine current progress or as a means of formulating a grade. Now consider how you will obtain this information. You have decided upon a test as the best means of obtaining data. What types of test items best serve your purpose? You may find these guidelines helpful.

- *Be sure your students are ready*, both cognitively and emotionally, so that you gain legitimate information about their achievement. When students are ready, they will perform better and gain more from the test as a learning experience.
- *Be consistent in everything you do in testing*. Items should reflect what has been taught; scoring should be identical for all students. All students should take the test under similar conditions, and you must record test results for all students in exactly the same manner.
- *Be fair in your treatment of all students*. Be aware of your personal biases. Some students are more likeable than others, but you can't let that influence your scoring and interpretation of test results.
- *Be aware of any discrepancies among your students*. For example, someone may be sick; another may have misinterpreted the test directions.

most will be concerned with either objective or essay items. We'll discuss these in some detail, but here are a few distinguishing characteristics of each.

- Objective test items are usually separated into two classes: **supply items** that require students to give an answer, and **selection items** that require students to choose from among several alternatives. Selection items are more highly structured and restrict the type of response students can make.
- *Essay questions* permit students greater latitude of expression and are divided into two types. The **extended response** type furnishes students with complete freedom to make any kind of response they choose. The **restricted response** type asks for specific information, thus restricting somewhat students' responses.

Be careful of the number of items you use. How much time have you allotted for testing? Here you face a rather delicate issue since an increase in the number of items increases your test's reliability. But students should have enough time to answer each item. These are decisions you have to make. Also, be conscious of the difficulty of the items you write since complexity obviously affects time and number of items.

Before we consider the specifics of writing both types of items, examine Table 15.3. This table provides a comparative summary of teacher-constructed tests and may help you to decide which type of item would best suit your purposes.

Writing Essay Tests

Teachers have long claimed advantages for the essay examination that are not subject to either proof or disproof. Whether they evaluate higher thought processes more effectively than the objective test is an unanswered question. Essay tests have both advantages and disadvantages. Since teachers place so much value on essay tests, they remain the most widely used classroom test and deserve your careful study and thought.

Here are some general considerations you may find helpful.

- *Determine the level of thought you want the students to use.* For example, if a political science teacher wants students to think critically about election processes, then an essay question should force students to weigh TV commercials against fact, to question emotional appeals to an electorate, and to examine conflicting interpretations of issues. Responses should reflect these criteria.

Table 15.3

Characteristics of Test Items

	Objective Test	Essay Test
Learning outcomes measured	Is efficient for measuring knowledge of facts. Some types (e.g., multiple-choice) can also measure understanding, thinking skills, and other complex outcomes. Inefficient or inappropriate for measuring ability to select and organize ideas, writing abilities, and some types of problem-solving skills.	Is inefficient for measuring knowledge of facts. Can measure understanding, thinking skills, and other complex learning outcomes (especially useful where originality of response is desired). Appropriate for measuring ability to select and organize ideas, writing abilities, and problem-solving skills requiring originality.
Preparation of questions	A relatively large number of questions is needed for a test. Preparation is difficult and time-consuming.	Only a few questions are needed for a test. Preparation is relatively easy (but more difficult than generally assumed).
Sampling of course content	Provides an extensive sampling of course content because of the large number of questions that can be included in a test.	Sampling of course content is usually limited because of the small number of questions that can be included in a test.
Control of student's response	Complete structuring of task limits student to type of response called for. Prevents bluffing and avoids influence of writing skill, though selection-type items are subject to guessing.	Freedom to respond in own words enables bluffing and writing skill to influence the score, though guessing is minimized.
Scoring	Objective scoring that is quick, easy, and consistent.	Subjective scoring that is slow, difficult, and inconsistent.
Influence on learning	Usually encourages student to develop a comprehensive knowledge of specific facts and the ability to make fine discriminations among them. Can encourage the development of understanding, thinking skills, and other complex outcomes if properly constructed.	Encourages students to concentrate on larger units of subject matter, with special emphasis on the ability to organize, integrate, and express ideas effectively. May encourage poor writing habits if time pressure is a factor (it almost always is).
Reliability	High reliability is possible and is typically obtained with well-constructed tests.	Reliability is typically low, primarily because of inconsistent scoring.

- *Phrase your questions so that they demand some novelty in students' responses.* Students often complain that essay questions make them reproduce material. Novel questions enable them to integrate and apply their knowledge. If you begin questions with "compare, contrast, predict, illustrate," you are asking students to select, organize, and use their knowledge.

- *Write essay questions that clearly and unambiguously define the students' task.* For example, *Discuss the organizations that contribute to the health of the community* is poorly phrased. What does "discuss" mean? Does it mean list, criticize, or evaluate? What kind of organizations? What type of contributions? This and similar items force students to guess.

Focus on Classrooms

Essay Tests—Pros and Cons

There are pros and cons about the essay test. Among the advantages are:

- It is fairly easy to construct.
- It may be administered simply; questions may be written on the blackboard.
- It emphasizes wholes rather than parts.
- It better illustrates a student's ability to recall, organize, reorganize, and apply knowledge. Also, a student's expression of ideas may well reflect learning that is impossible to measure objectively.

Among the disadvantages are:

- Its validity is questionable because of the small amount of material it samples.
- Teachers are often tempted to grade other factors than content, for example, spelling or grammar. Also, if a student is more articulate than his or her classmates, it is often troublesome to distinguish between fact and form.
- Scoring answers to essay questions can be difficult. Study after study has shown the wide difference among teachers in grading essay tests. It is a true saying that students often pass or fail essay tests depending on who marks the paper and who takes the test.

Essay tests will continue to be used widely, so you should be aware of several precautions that you can take to improve your essay questions. Here are examples of the various kinds of essay questions and the purposes they serve. A classic, yet still valid source is Weidmann (1933, 1941), who classified essay questions as follows:

1. Who, what, when, which, where
2. List
3. Outline
4. Describe
5. Contrast
6. Compare
7. Explain
8. Discuss
9. Develop
10. Summarize
11. Evaluate

Give your test plenty of thought; your students deserve a fair opportunity to display what they have learned.

- *Be certain that your question specifies the behavior you want.* If you phrase your questions accurately, you will help your students to display what they really know, and you will make your scoring of the

answers easier and more exact. The pertinence and phrasing of the question is critical in an essay test, which is one of the reasons that the construction of such a test is deceptively simple.

Suggestions for Writing Essay Questions

In this section, we'll discuss several guidelines that will help you write more precise essay questions. Remember, however, that students take these tests, bringing with them their fears and anxieties about test-taking. Their perceptions of what it means to take your tests will affect their performance. Perhaps you can help them by acting on some of the suggestions that focus on students in this section.

Here are some general suggestions that you may find helpful for writing essay questions.

- Be sure that your questions reflect the material that you taught and that your students have read.
- Be precise in your wording so that your students clearly understand what is expected of them. Vague, ambiguous questions are not only unfair to students, but they can only add to the difficulty of scoring.
- Use your questions, when possible and when you deem advisable, to have students explain new situations or to solve problems; do not restrict them to purely factual material.
- Avoid optional questions. If you provide such an alternative—for extra credit or whatever reason—not all students take the same test, so it is almost impossible for you to compare them.
- Write sensible questions that permit your students to read, interpret, and answer them in the allotted time.

Writing clear and purposeful essay questions should enable you to assess your students' factual knowledge and their ability to organize, interpret, and apply their learning.

Suggestions for Scoring Essay Tests

You can increase the reliability of your test before you actually administer it by giving thought to your scoring. We have previously touched on several important, but general considerations: Are you assessing objectives? How wide a range of responses will you accept? Specifically, you might consider the following:

- Decide what major points must be in an answer for full credit. Must they all be there? If not, how many? How many points will you assign to each? How much weight will you give to each question?
- Read all answers to one question; do not read all the answers on a single student's test. By reading all

TEACHER ←→ STUDENT
INTERACTIONS

Helping Students Prepare for Essay Tests

1. Some students, when faced with questions and a blank piece of paper, have no idea how to begin. First, tell them to read the question carefully, not only for what content is called for but also for the exact meaning of what's asked. For example, you are taking an educational psychology exam and one of the questions is: *Compare the basics of essay tests with those of objective tests.* Your instructor has asked you to examine the qualities or characteristics of both types of tests and show similarities and differences.

   • To help your students, teach them what certain words mean:

     compare—show similarities and differences
     classify—assign to a category
     evaluate—make a value judgment
     summarize—to present the main points briefly.

   You know what words will appear most frequently in your questions, so be sure that your students know exactly what you're asking for.

2. If you can impress the following guidelines on your students, you can help them to relax a little more and focus on the test itself, thus giving you a better idea of their actual knowledge.

   • Read all of the questions carefully. If you have to choose, *think before you choose.* Pick those questions you are comfortable answering. As you read each question, jot down next to the question the ideas that you think of immediately. In this way you won't forget what's important for question 4 after you've spent time on the first three.
   • Indicate clearly what question you're answering.
   • Plan the amount of time you'll spend on each question. If the period is one hour and there are four questions, you should spend about fifteen minutes on each. The "about" is cautionary; leave some time at the end to check your work.
   • General suggestions: write as clearly as possible; use complete sentences; try to use words you know (so you can spell them correctly); devote one topic to each paragraph.

either the question was at fault, or your teaching was misinterpreted or not understood at all.

• Do not associate a name with a test, since your previous knowledge and feelings about a student could possibly bias your scoring. If possible, have students use an identification number instead of their names. You can match names to numbers after you have finished scoring the tests.

Finally, remember that essays are a good means of obtaining more than factual material from your students: How do they organize, interpret, and apply data? Can they use data they know to solve problems? But also remember that scoring can be unreliable unless you're careful.

Writing Objective Tests

There are purposes for which objective tests are better suited than the essay examination. Their range of coverage in a relatively brief period and the objectivity of scoring make them an attractive tool, although you must consider the time and care that go into the construction of the items.

One of the major criticisms constantly directed at the objective test is its apparent emphasis on fragmented, factual knowledge. Consequently, psychologists and educators have labored to devise test items that sample a student's depth and understanding of knowledge. Objective items fall into two general categories: supply type (free response, simple recall, completion), and the selection type (alternative response, multiple-choice, matching).

Suggestions for Writing Supply Items

Simple recall and completion items are fundamentally the same. In both instances, the subject responds with either one or a few words. The simple recall type usually takes the form of a direct question, while the completion item normally uses a sentence with one or several key words missing. For example:

1. Who is the present president of the United States? (simple recall)
2. The next election for president of the United States will be held in the year _____. (completion)

Care is needed to have directions sufficiently clear so that students know exactly what is expected without "leading" them. Remember: Avoid textbook language, phrase questions to offer only one possible correct answer, and avoid excessive blanks in completion items.

answers to a single question, you increase the reliability of your scoring. You are more accurately comparing your students' responses, thus giving you a sense of how your class achieved as a group. If all or most of your students—bright, average, slow—failed one question, then you can be quite sure that

Taking tests involves both subject-matter knowledge and knowledge of test-taking skills. Teachers can do much to facilitate students' test-taking.

Although supply items appear to be easy to write, you must be sure that the items serve the purpose for which they are intended.

- *Don't be fancy with the wording of items.* Since only one response can be correct, your phrasing must be sufficiently precise so that students understand its intent.
- *Avoid using the exact wording from a text in your item* since they often become vague when removed from context.
- *Avoid giving clues.* Giving clues is almost always inadvertent because of phrasing, answers from preceding questions, or the format of the item (using the exact number of blanks as letters in the correct response).

Suggestions for Writing Selection Items

The selection type (alternative response, multiple-choice, matching) restricts the student's answers to those that are presented in the item.

Writing True-False Items

The more common alternative response item is the true-false, right-wrong, yes-no variety. A declarative sentence is the usual form of a true-false item, and the subject indicates whether the statement is T (true) or F (false).

Directions: Mark each of the following statements true or false. If the statement is true, circle the T; if it is false, circle the F.

T F   Jimmy Carter became president of the United States in 1977.

As you can see, you are asking students to judge the correctness of a statement. Try to avoid opinion statements since students are unaware if it is your opinion or not. Attribute the opinion to a definite source.

T F   Ronald Reagan supported aid to the Contras

Since your chief objective in writing true-false items will be to state them in clear and unambiguous terms, try to remember these guidelines:

- Be certain that the statement is definitely true or definitely false.
- Avoid writing irrelevant and trivial items.
- Avoid any obvious patterns: two true and then two false statements.
- Avoid using negative statements.
- Avoid textbook phrasing.
- Avoid terms such as *always* and *never.*
- Keep the length of true statements about the same length as false statements.

Writing Multiple-Choice Items

The multiple-choice item presents students with a question or incomplete statement and several possible responses, one of which is correct (unless more than one response to each item is permitted, which is the multiple-response type). The typical multiple-choice item reads as follows:

Directions: For each of the following questions, there are several possible answers. Select the response that you think is correct for each question, and write the number of that answer in the blank space to the right of the question.

1. Who is considered to be the "founder" of operant conditioning?
    a. Lewin
    b. Watson
    c. Skinner
    d. Thorndike

TEACHER ←→ STUDENT
INTERACTIONS

Helping Students to Prepare for Objective Tests

1. You can help your students prepare for objective tests by impressing on them how searching and analytical objective items can be. You can use the *Taxonomy of Educational Objectives* (Bloom (Ed.), 1956, p. 156), for example, to assess the complexity of your questions. (See chapter 9 for a detailed explanation of the Taxonomy.)

   - Questions reflecting *knowledge* search for:
     facts
     definitions
     results
     techniques.
   Start your questions with words such as list, write, recall, or name.

   - Questions reflecting *comprehension* search for:
     understanding
     interpretation
     explanation.
   Start your questions with words such as explain, transform, retell, or expand.

   - Questions reflecting *application* search for:
     usage
     demonstration
     specification
     prediction.
   Start your questions with words such as use, construct, apply, or utilize.

   - Questions reflecting *analysis* search for:
     identification
     recognition
     classification
     inference.
   Start your questions with words such as divide, examine, simplify, or classify.

   - Questions reflecting *synthesis* search for:
     integration
     realignment
     novelty.
   Start your questions with words such as create, design, develop, or compare.

   - Questions reflecting *evaluation* search for:
     decisions
     judgments.
   Start your questions with words such as rank, award, justify, evaluate.

2. Here are some specific suggestions for helping students to prepare for objective tests.

   - If it's to be a machine-scored test, be sure they understand the mechanics of taking this kind of test: name in the right place, filling in the blocks carefully, correct type of pencil.
   - Read all the possible answers to each question; don't jump at the response you think is right.
   - Go through the test quickly, answering those items you're sure about; then go back to those you're doubtful about.
   - On those items giving you trouble, try to eliminate any response you know is wrong. Then use any clues (wording, contradictions) to eliminate any other false responses.
   - Find out if you're to be penalized for guessing.
   - True-false items that use such terms as "always" or "never" are usually false.
   - If a true-false statement is lengthy, it's usually true.
   - Be sure to understand the directions in matching items, and look for any theme between the question list and the answer list.
   - Always look for verbal clues.

You present your students a problem followed by several solutions. Note in the above, there is one correct answer (which one?) and three distractions. The manner in which the problem is stated (called the stem) may be either a question or an incomplete statement. The multiple-choice item is thought to be the best of the objective items. When it is used, the direct question is the preferred form. At least four possible responses are needed (all of which should be plausible); all answers require consistency and equal length.

Here are some suggestions for writing multiple-choice items:

- The stem should present the problem in a clear and definite manner.
- Again, avoid negative statements where possible.
- Be sure that all distractors are plausible.
- The correct answer should be clearly distinguished from the incorrect distractors.
- Be sure that the correct answer appears in a different position from item to item.

- Avoid using "all of the above" or "none of the above" responses.
- Avoid clues, that is, words such as *always* or *never.*

Writing Matching Items

The **matching item** usually utilizes two columns, each item in the first column to be matched with an item in the second column. Here is a typical matching item.

> Directions: Below are two lists, one containing the names of individual psychologists, the other the names of schools of psychology. Match the individual with a school of psychology by writing the number of the school before the name of the appropriate individual in the space provided.

____	Watson	1. Gestalt
____	Skinner	2. Functionalism
____	Thorndike	3. Dynamic psychology
____	Koffka	4. Behaviorism
____	Woodworth	5. Topological
		6. Connectionism
		7. Programming
		8. Structuralism
		9. Contiguity

In writing the matching item, the instructions should be simple, clear, and precise; otherwise they can confuse students. Also include more than the required number of responses, keep homogeneous material in both columns, and keep the list of responses fairly short. The matching item is best suited for a test of factual material.

Here are some suggestions for writing matching items.

- Use more possible responses than items to be matched, thus reducing the likelihood of successful guessing.
- Arrange the list of responses logically.
- Be sure your students know the reasons for matching specific items.

Objective items should be selected for a particular purpose, carefully written to suit the appropriate reading level of a class, and free from ambiguity. You must rely on your own judgment, based on your knowledge of a class, to allot sufficient time for the objective test. There is no other reliable guide, although a rule of thumb is 100 true-false items or 75 multiple-choice items are appropriate for a 50-minute period.

Using Data from Teacher-Constructed Tests

Some of the purposes of classroom testing and assessment have been mentioned: assessing ability, measuring achievement, determining the degree to which objectives have been attained, and guiding educational decisions. But you also use test data in marking, grading, and reporting. **Marking** refers to your assessment of a test or an oral or written report; **grading** refers to your evaluation of tests, reports, essays; **reporting** refers to the manner in which you communicate these results to children and parents. Let's examine each of these in detail.

Marking

A mark—no matter what the educational level—is a judgment of one person by another. Sometimes your judgment may be informal, as when you discuss an oral report with a student, or mark and comment on an essay examination. Occasionally your mark may be quite mechanical as when you simply total the number of correct items in an objective test and assign marks on the basis of number right. A certain percentage of your class receives an A, B, C, D, E or 70, 80, 90.

Remember: Our concern here is with the mark you assign to a test or report. Are you more comfortable with percentage figures or letters? How will you use this mark? Will your students understand a letter grade if they've taken an objective test? How will you connect numbers to letters? What contributes to a letter grade?

Although students understand both A or 95 as a judgment of how they performed, they may better understand a number as reflecting exactly what they did on a test. Letter grades may include many variables, such as spelling or writing ability. Depending on your likes and dislikes you may discriminate more fairly by using numbers: 66, 68, 71, as opposed to C+, C, C–.

What can you do to improve your marking technique?

- *Be sure to mark (or somehow indicate) any work you assign.* Nothing frustrates students more than spending substantial time on a project and not having teachers react to it. Your assignments are quickly labeled "busy work" and, if done at all, contribute little to learning. The best rule of thumb is if you assign written work, mark it. If you assign readings, discuss them, so all students feel involved and realize that you always respond to assignments.

• *Return work promptly or as soon as possible.* Unless students receive feedback, they often forget, or worse, remember error. Giving a test one day and not returning it for a week or two is poor teaching. If you believe that tests aid teaching and learning, they become an integral part of your work, not something added at the end of a unit or course. If you delay furnishing test results, students find it difficult to use your corrections; too much has happened since the tests. If serious weaknesses are uncovered, but the test was some two weeks ago, students probably should not have commenced new work. If they did well, they could possibly have bypassed the introductory work of the next topic.

• *If possible, personally comment on the test.* If it is an objective test, students will appreciate some remark even if only "You did quite well on this test." Essay tests provide more freedom to comment.

• *Be specific in your comments*; telling students they are wrong has little effect. Your comments should indicate precisely where the error is and, if necessary, how to correct it. Tell students exactly where their answers are superior so that they can capitalize on their strengths.

• *Mark the student's work, not the student.* In this chapter, we have constantly cautioned against using tests for personal reasons, which is especially dangerous for objective marking.

• *Avoid sarcasm and belittling or ridiculing remarks.* You have the experience, the authority, and power in the classroom. Use it wisely and not to enhance self-importance. A successful teacher works with students, so be careful of your remarks; they can hurt and discourage sensitive, developing personalities.

• *You must make a personal decision,* which is often based on available time, whether to have students repeat their work and correct errors. Merely mentioning mistakes does not remedy them. If possible, have students actually rework their errors after they have determined where they blundered.

Grading

Most schools insist that teachers periodically grade their students, which means that you must judge a student's work for two or three months and decide upon A or B, 90 or 72. What contributes to the grade? Is it the mere average of all test scores, or should it also include students' attitude, improvement, or participation? Only you can answer this question by determining the purpose of grading.

If a grade is intended to indicate competence in algebra, then it should probably consist essentially of marks assigned to subject matter: tests, reports, final examina-

Focus on Teachers

Writing Comments on Tests

Ellis Page (1958) conducted a famous study of marks and the effects of teacher comments. He wanted to determine if teachers' comments improve student performance and which comments were effective. Previous similar studies had inherent difficulties: Outsiders conducted the experiment, tests were contrived to mask the treatment, and praise or reproof was often random (classroom comments are definite and specific). Page's study eliminated these problems by leaving classroom procedures untouched, except for written comments upon the test.

Seventy-four teachers randomly selected one of their classes as an experimental group. The total student group consisted of 2,139 secondary school students. The teachers initially administered whatever test came next in the course. They then scored the tests as usual—A, B, C, D, or F—and then randomly assigned each paper to one of three groups. The *no comment* group received a mark and nothing else. The *free comment* group received whatever comment the teacher deemed appropriate. The *specified comment* group received uniform comments previously designated for each mark:

A. Excellent! Keep it up.
B. Good Work. Keep at it.
C. Perhaps try to do still better?
D. Let's bring this up.
F. Let's raise this grade.

The teachers returned the tests with no unusual attention. The effects of these comments were judged by the scores the same students achieved on the next scheduled test. The results were:

• The free comment students achieved higher scores than the specified comment group, which did better than the no comment students.

• The results were consistent for all schools in the sample.

• Although teachers had expected the better students to profit more from their comments, no evidence supported their expectations.

Page concluded that when secondary school teachers write truthful but encouraging remarks on student papers, they have a measurable and potent effect on students so that learning improves.

tion. Specialized schools or programs can then strictly interpret a grade and judge a student's readiness for a course or program. Such grades characterize most secondary schools, while elementary school grades often represent some combination of competence, effort, and general attitude. A combination is difficult to interpret, and even at the elementary level it is better to assign a competence grade and to report on attitude, interest, or comprehension in some other way.

One danger in assigning grades, both at the elementary and secondary levels, is using grades to discipline or punish the unruly student. It can be more subtly done in grading than in marking. If you mark harshly on a test, it is obvious that you are not marking content. Something else is influencing the mark. But unless a grade represents competence—and students, parents, teachers, and administrators have agreed on this—many other forces will affect the final grade.

As you can see from this brief discussion, the more variables that are included in a grade, the less effective it is as an indication of achievement. Your grades will represent true achievement to the extent that they reflect objectives and satisfactory test construction.

In a perceptive and now classic essay, Palmer (1962) identified several dishonest grading habits.

- *Abdicating.* The first, and most indefensible, way of grading dishonestly is by abdication. Some teachers may doubt the role of testing in teaching and learning. Consequently they either use hastily devised tests or none at all. It is hard to decide which is more harmful to students. With no testing, everyone understands that a course represents a teacher's personal opinion. No one is sure of what a disorganized collection of test scores represents.
- *The "carrots and clubs" system.* This is another dishonest method, wherein grades represent many different things for different teachers: tests, entire course work, spelling mistakes in history tests, personal likes and dislikes. Enough has been said of the purpose of grading to alert you to the dangers of marking something other than merit.
- *Defaulting.* Grading by default was briefly popular in the 1960s when many instructors and schools were reluctant to grade students. Many college professors refused to give tests and assigned everyone an A. Secondary and elementary teachers gave as few tests as possible. Academic dishonesty soon became apparent because no one could determine how students were prepared for new, more difficult, work. Many students, at all levels, found themselves progressing into programs or schools for which they had neither the interest, competence, or ability. Today there is intense national interest in improving tests, marks, and grades.
- *Being a zealot.* Test, test, test! These teachers turn their classes into a nightmarish endurance contest. The danger here is so obvious it needs little comment, but consider the possible outcome: student dislike of the course, teacher, and school.
- *Changing rules in midstream.* The "tough" teacher eases standards. Easy markers panic when the principal mentions how well their students are doing. The pattern is reversed; students are bewildered; the learning atmosphere becomes tense and mistrustful.
- *Psychic testing.* This is an alarming extension of abdication and default. "They do not require tests; they know who will receive A's or F's." Most students are frightened by this type of teacher, and, in college, especially, they will shun the course.
- *Being a perfectionist.* Some teachers, striving for impossible perfection, inform their class that no one receives an A and only geniuses need expect B. Failure is rampant.

Unfortunately you have probably experienced one, or several, of the above. To avoid these pitfalls, remember: Decide specifically what the grade is to represent and have it firmly in mind when you assign grades. You should share this information, or whatever criteria you use, with your students and your decision should be accepted by teachers and administrators and communicated to parents.

Reporting

Parents wish to be informed of their children's educational progress, which is one rationale for report cards. Teachers know how their students are progressing. Students and parents, however, need extra communication. You can use reports to strengthen the link between home and school, which is the main benefit of any reporting system. Schools and teachers should know how much support they will receive from parents, what advantages or disadvantages the child has, what the parents' attitude is toward education. Parents should know what the objectives of teachers and schools are, how their child meets these objectives, and what they should reasonably expect their child to attain.

Other than informing parents and students of progress, a reporting system should bring together parents and teachers so that they can combine efforts to encourage and help children. Unfortunately, most new teachers dread these conferences. They often report feeling insecure and defensive, especially if the child has earned poor grades. To evade or to be vague can be disastrous. Honest and hopeful evaluation, based on student work and observation of behavior, is the only rule. To portray an average child as superior in both ability and performance frustrates everyone. Parents' expectations are unduly heightened; children quickly sense adult dishonesty; teachers avoid a crucial task. If home and school are to work together, there must be honesty, tempered by mature judgment.

"Now, now, Mr. and Mrs. Swenson, your son's grades aren't that bad."

© Art Bouthillier.

What to Report

No reporting system is completely satisfactory. Either the report of academic progress is slighted (John is doing very nicely), or there is excessive emphasis upon a grade (John—C⁻). For example, the traditional report card supplies letter or numerical grades with little interpretation—A, B, C, 95, 85, 75. There may be a column where teachers check attitudes as satisfactory or unsatisfactory. Such cards are more typical of elementary than secondary schools.

A less rigid system may use two categories: satisfactory or unsatisfactory, which provides a less rigid classification. Doubts persist about such reports. Satisfactory or unsatisfactory—compared to what? How much realistic information is conveyed to parents in this system?

A third, equally unsatisfactory, technique is to use even broader categories: John is progressing. John has shown improvement since the last report. It is necessary to discuss John's progress, so please arrange a conference.

Given these conditions, what can you do?

• *It makes little difference what system you prefer; you probably will be requested to use the school's system.* The best advice is to study it thoroughly so that you can report objectively and carefully.

• *Know exactly what constitutes your evaluation of a student.* If you assign a C or 75, or satisfactory, or progressing normally, be sure that you realize exactly what contributes to the grade: tests, homework assignments, class participation, library research, and reports.

• *Beware of personal opinion in any objective reporting.* When you judge a student's work unsatisfactory, or nonprogressing, or even C, avoid any personal prejudices. Separate the subjective from the objective, even if the report is just a comment. For example, state precisely what the student has accomplished, and then relate it to ability or aptitude. Answer the question: Can you objectively defend your grade as free from bias?

• *Use any subjective evaluation cautiously but honestly.* Whether it is a written comment, or an attitude checklist, make your judgment as fair as possible, but tell parents exactly what you think. For example, if a student is not working up to ability, tell the student; if a student's classroom behavior is damaging achievement, tell the student.

• *Use a parent-teacher conference wisely.* Here you have a unique opportunity to improve home-school cooperation. If you are prepared, if you can justify your grades and comments, then the conference no longer becomes something to dread, but a tool to help students. But you must be able to produce test scores, marks, or essays and reports, and a record of completed assignments to support objective grades. You must be prepared to furnish detailed reasons for your personal evaluation. There is no greater persuasive argument than facts.

Gronlund (1985) suggested that schools and teachers adopt guidelines for their grading and reporting practices and then follow these procedures. For example, a grading and reporting system functions effectively when it results from the efforts of students, parents, and school personnel. The system itself should be sufficiently detailed to be helpful in diagnosis, yet not overly complicated. It should also reflect those educational objectives that guide learning, grading, and reporting.

Now that you have an understanding of traditional assessment techniques, you can better appreciate the ongoing search for "truer," more meaningful, assessment methods, which historically has been a common theme in both the fields of education and psychology. Let's turn our attention to these new features.

Alternative Methods and New Assessment Trends

During the past decade we have witnessed an immense growth in the application of behavioral assessment methods. These methods emphasize observation techniques to characterize a person's overt behavior and are useful in linking assessment results to interventions (Kratochwill & Sheridan, 1990; Shapiro, 1988). Progress in the application of behavioral assessment methods in psychology, along with the school restructuring movement, have fostered the development of two new (and related) assessment methods for evaluating students' learning. These techniques are referred to as **curriculum-based assessment** (CBA) and authentic assessment. Before examining these new techniques in detail, we want to discuss the basic assumptions underlying behavioral assessment and highlight their practicality in assessing students' academic and social behavior.

Behavioral Assessment Fundamentals

In behavioral assessment it is assumed that assessment of people's behavior at any time is merely a sample of their behavior that may or may not be representative of their behavior in other situations or at other times. Therefore, repeated assessments of a person's behavior over time and in different assessments is typical of behavior assess-

ment. As stated earlier, observation is the primary method used to conduct a behavioral assessment. There are, however, several forms of observation and related techniques that are used to conduct a behavioral assessment (Gresham, 1985). These techniques include interviews, self-reports, ratings by others, role plays or performances, in addition to naturalistic observations (at home, in the schoolyard, in the classroom). Gresham used a directness continuum to classify these various assessment methods, whereby direct methods are those used at the same time and in the same place as the actual behavior. Methods such as naturalistic observations and self-monitoring are considered to be direct assessment methods. Indirect methods are removed in time and place from the actual occurrence of the target behavior. Interviews with students, self-reports from students, ratings by others (i.e., parents, teachers), and behavioral role-plays are all examples of indirect methods of behavioral assessment (Witt, Elliott, Gresham, & Kramer, 1988).

During the past several years much has been written about behavioral assessment and its application in schools to assess the academic and behavior functioning of children (Kratochwill & Sheridan, 1990). Interested readers are encouraged to consult these basic sources for more information. With this as background on behavioral assessment, let's now turn to an examination of CBA.

Curriculum-Based Assessment (CBA)

Curriculum-based assessment is a relatively new approach to educational assessment, although as noted by Shapiro and Derr (1990), "Its basic idea is as old as education itself: using the curricula to assess student learning." CBA may be defined as a methodology whereby (a) assessment is linked to the curriculum and instruction, (b) educational success is evaluated by student progress in the curriculum, and (c) the purpose is to determine students' instructional needs (p. 365). The impetus for the acceptance of CBA is the growing dissatisfaction among educators with the incongruence between what is taught in the classroom and what is tested by standardized achievement tests. If assessment results are to guide instructional intervention, then the assessment method must cover material and tasks representative of what has been or will be taught. Unfortunately, the content of many standardized **achievement tests** does not adequately assess what is taught in basal curricula (Jenkins & Pany, 1978; Shapiro & Derr, 1990). So CBA was born and has been developed by several researchers around the country.

Several forms of CBA have developed concurrently (e.g., *Curriculum-Based Evaluation* by Howell, 1986;

Curriculum-Based Measurement by Deno, 1985; and *Criterion-Referenced-Curriculum-Based Assessment* by Blankenship, 1985). Although each form of CBA has some unique characteristic, they are more alike than different. Basically, CBA has been primarily used at the elementary level for the basal curricula in reading and math. The heart of a CBA assessment is the development of brief (three to five minutes), frequent (weekly) "tests" or probes on material that has come directly from the curriculum. Most of these tests or samples of behavior will be of the pencil-and-paper variety.

The results of several CBA assessments will yield (a) information about what material from the curriculum students know and what material they do not know (or at least have not mastered) and (b) the rate at which a student is acquiring new information. With this kind of information, the content of a remedial program can be readily identified and some reasonable prediction about the amount of time needed to master the material can be rendered. These are essential ingredients in the development of an intervention for a student who is experiencing academic problems.

The logic of CBA, using specific curriculum content for assessing what students know, is very appealing to many teachers and school psychologists who evaluate children. Yet CBA is hard work and still must address the criteria for being reliable and valid. At this time, CBA is enjoying increasing popularity among school practitioners, especially school psychologists who often are responsible for assessing students with academic difficulties (Rosenfield & Shinn, 1989). When considering teacher-directed assessments, however, the trend in classroom assessment is toward authentic assessment, a more comprehensive and flexible approach to assessment than offered by CBA approaches.

Authentic Assessment

Authentic assessment is a philosophy about classroom assessment as well as a combination of practical data collection techniques. As such, it is a central piece of the outcome-oriented education and school restructuring movements in the United States. Consequently, authentic assessment methods are being proposed as replacements for both standardized tests and typical pencil-and-paper classroom tests.

What exactly is authentic assessment? Although no standard definition of authentic assessment has been offered, perhaps the statement by Archbald and Newmann (1988) will serve as a beginning: "A valid assessment system provides information about particular tasks on which students succeed or fail, but more important, it also presents tasks that are worthwhile, significant, and

Assessing children's understanding of common school situations and their problem-solving strategies for dealing with these situations is an important focus for educators interested in the social emotional functioning of students.

meaningful—in short, authentic" (p. 1). Performance assessment is a closely related approach, and in fact, often is conceptualized as a subset of authentic assessment. Thus, the definition of performance assessment is also offered to facilitate understanding of the nature of authentic assessment. Specifically, Airasian (1991) defines performance assessment as "assessments in which the teacher observes and makes a judgment about a pupil's skill in carrying out an activity or producing a product" (p. 252). Table 15.4 illustrates the dimensions on which performance-based assessments differ from the typical classroom objective test, essay test, and oral questioning by a teacher. A careful review of this table should give you a clear understanding of the types of activities expected of teachers in an authentic assessment-oriented classroom.

Authentic assessment involves assessment activities like those commonly used in the world outside the classroom: work samples, performances, exhibitions, and self-evaluation reports. With an authentic assessment, the learner must produce something new, rather than simply reproduce prior knowledge. Authentic assessments can guide teaching and provide evidence that a student has achieved significant learning objectives. Multiple-choice and many **standardized tests** rarely accomplish these goals and in most cases are inconsistent with the spirit of authentic assessment.

Table 15.4

Comparison of Various Types of Assessment

	Objective Test	Essay Test	Oral Question	Performance Assessment
Purpose	Sample knowledge with maximum efficiency and reliability	Assess thinking skills and/or mastery of a structure of knowledge	Assess knowledge during instruction	Assess ability to translate knowledge and understanding into action
Typical Exercise	Test items: Multiple-choice True/false Fill-in Matching	Writing task	Open-ended question	Written prompt or natural event framing the kind of performance required
Student's Response	Read, evaluate, select	Organize, compose	Oral answer	Plan, construct, and deliver original response
Scoring	Count correct answers	Judge understanding	Determine correctness of answer	Check attributes present, rate proficiency demonstrated, or describe performance via anecdote
Major Advantage	Efficiency—can administer many items per unit of testing time	Can measure complex cognitive outcomes	Joins assessment and instruction	Provides rich evidence of performance skills
Potential Sources of Inaccurate Assessment	Poorly written items, overemphasis on recall of facts, poor test-taking skills, failure to sample content representatively	Poorly written exercises, writing skill confounded with knowledge of content, poor scoring procedures	Poor questions, students' lack of willingness to respond, too few questions	Poor exercises, too few samples of performance, vague criteria, poor rating procedures, poor test conditions
Influence on Learning	Overemphasis on recall encourages memorization; can encourage thinking skills if properly constructed	Encourages thinking and development of writing skills	Stimulates participation in instruction, provides teacher immediate feedback on effectiveness of teaching	Emphasizes use or available skill and knowledge in relevant problem contexts
Keys to Success	Clear test blueprint or specifications that match instruction, skill in item writing, time to write items	Carefully prepared writing exercises, preparation of model answers, time to read and score	Clear questions, representative sample of questions to each student, adequate time provided for student response	Carefully prepared performance exercises; clear performance expectations; careful, thoughtful rating; time to rate performance

From R. J. Stiggins, "Design and Development of Performance Assessments" in *Educational Measurement: Issues and Practice*, 6:35, 1987. Copyright 1987 by National Council on Measurement in Education, Washington, DC. Reprinted by permission of the publisher.

Some educational subjects have a long history of using authentic performances or products as a means of assessing students' learning. For example, physical education, art, music, and vocational and technological arts all use, to a large extent, students' products or performances to determine whether the learning objectives of a class have been met. Thus many educators are already aware of the importance of authentic assessment and are actively using it.

Authentic assessment often requires students to apply knowledge and skills resulting in some type of *performance* or *demonstration* (Coalition of Essential Schools, 1990). A performance is a recital, a debate, a play, a game, an oral report in front of a class, or any event where a student can be observed using acquired knowledge or skills. Some performances may be videotaped to provide feedback to students and to allow others to evaluate the performance.

Portfolios are another common feature of an authentic approach to assessment (referred to as **portfolio assessment**). A portfolio is a revealing collection of a student's work that a teacher and/or a student judges to be important evidence of the student's learning (Paulson, Paulson, & Meyer, 1991). A portfolio often serves two purposes, documentation and evaluation. Some teachers, particularly those involved with language and communication arts, already use writing portfolios as a means of collecting and analyzing students' growth in written communication skills.

Exhibitions are one of the most frequently discussed components of an authentic assessment system. Exhibitions require integration of a broad range of competencies and ever-increasing student initiative and responsibility. Gibbons (1974, 1984) is credited with stimulating educators to apply to schooling the philosophy of the "Walkabout," an Australian aborigine rite of passage to adulthood. In many cases, the educational application of the Walkabout has been the development of rite of passage or exit exhibitions where students are required to demonstrate the integration and application of knowledge and skills in targeted areas of outcome competencies. In some school systems, rite of passage exhibitions serve as gateways to the next level (i.e., an exhibition of essential skills must be demonstrated to move to junior high school; another exhibition of even more sophisticated skills must be passed to earn a diploma). Figure 15.3 illustrates the content and activities required in a twelfth grade exhibition referred to as a ROPE or Rite of Passage Experience.

Performances, portfolios, and exhibitions all can be rich sources of information about a student and the teaching-learning process. To interpret the results of these assessment methods, an evaluation scheme is required that provides meaningful feedback about a student's academic and behavioral strengths and weaknesses. In an authentic assessment approach, evaluative schemes are referred to as **profiles.** Meaningful profiles are developed by expert teachers and provide clearly articulated criteria that allow reliable judgments about the student's demonstrated level of proficiency. The development of schemes to evaluate and score students' performances is perhaps the most challenging implementation aspect of authentic assessment. An example of an evaluation and scoring scheme for students' written reports is provided in Figure 15.4.

Profiles are useful for evaluating discrete performances and products of students; however, a comprehensive system for evaluating students' progress is also needed. Grades traditionally have been used to accomplish this goal. In an authentic assessment system, **performance-based grading benchmarks** provide the standards by which students' accomplishments are evaluated. Grading is unnecessary, if not inconsistent, in an authentic assessment system. Instead, students' progress toward mastery of the agreed upon learning outcomes is evaluated by comparing their work to the terminal learning objectives for any given subject or school year. Students' work and accomplishments are compared to a standard of performance, as opposed to other students (that is, a **criterion-referenced** or mastery approach).

A final common component of an authentic assessment system is **student self-assessment.** In theory, self-assessments by students could be part of any approach to assessment. In practice, they are infrequently used because the evaluation criterion and the expected learning outcomes rarely are explained to students. In an authentic assessment system, learning outcomes are made explicit, and students are encouraged to review and analyze their performances, portfolios, and other activities that provide feedback about their learning. Thus, understanding one's strengths and weaknesses is an important outcome of this form of assessment and schooling.

In conclusion, authentic assessment is an ambitious approach to both assessing and teaching students that places heavy emphasis on teachers' judgments. Few teachers will use all the procedural components reviewed here for any given class, yet some of the procedures would appear to be very useful and easily can be integrated into almost any class—elementary through high school.

Research on Teachers' Judgments of Students' Achievement

In 1989, Robert Hoge and Theodore Coladarci published a data-based review of research examining the match between teacher-based assessments of student achievement

All seniors must demonstrate mastery in fifteen areas of knowledge and competence by completing a portfolio, a project, and six other presentations before a ROPE committee consisting of staff members (including the student's home room teacher), a student from the grade below, and an adult from the community. Nine of the presentations are based on the materials in the portfolio and the project; the remaining six presentations are developed especially for the presentation process.

The Portfolio. The portfolio, developed during the first semester of the senior year, is intended to be "a reflection and analysis of the graduating senior's own life and times." Its requirements are:

1. *A written autobiography,* descriptive, introspective, and analytical. School records and other indicators of participation may be included.

2. *A reflection on work,* including an analysis of the significance of the work experiences for the graduating senior's life. A resume can be included.

3. *Two letters of recommendation* (at minimum) from any sources chosen by the student.

4. *A reading record* including a bibliography, annotated if desired, and two mini-book reports. Reading test scores may be included.

5. *An essay of ethics* exhibiting contemplation of the subject and describing the student's own ethical code.

6. *An artistic product* or written report on art and an essay on artistic standards for judging quality in a chosen area of art.

7. *A written report analyzing mass media:* who or what controls mass media, toward what ends, and with what effects. Evidence of experience with mass media may be included.

8. *A written summary and evaluation of the student's course work in science/technology; a written description of a scientific experiment* illustrating the application of the scientific method; an *analytical essay* (with examples) on social consequences of science and technology; and *an essay on the nature and use of computers* in modern society.

The Project. Every graduating senior must write a library research-based paper that analyzes an event, set of events, or theme in American history. A national comparative approach can be used in the analysis. The student must be prepared to field questions about both the paper and an overview of American history during the presentations, which are given in the second semester of the senior year.

> *To graduate from Walden III you must complete a portfolio, a written project, and fifteen oral presentations before two teachers, a peer, and an outside adult.*

The Presentations. Each of the eight components of the portfolio, plus the project, must be presented orally and in writing to the ROPE committee.

Six additional oral presentations are also required. For these, however, no written reports or new products are required by the committee. Supporting documents or other forms of evidence may be used. Assessment of proficiency is based on the demonstration of knowledge and skills during the presentations in each of the following areas:

1. *Mathematics knowledge and skills* is demonstrated by a combination of course evaluations, test results, and work sheets presented before the committee, and by the ability to competently field mathematics questions asked during the demonstration.

2. *Knowledge of American government* should be demonstrated by discussion of the purpose of government; the individual's relation to the state; the ideals, functions, and problems of American political institutions; and selected contemporary issues and political events. Supporting materials can be used.

3. The *personal proficiency* demonstration requires the student to think about and organize a presentation about the requirements of adult living in our society in terms of personal fulfillment, social skills, and practical competencies; and to discuss his or her own strengths and weaknesses in everyday living skills (health, home economics, mechanics, etc.) and interpersonal relations.

4. *Knowledge of geography* should be demonstrated in a presentation that covers the basic principles and questions of the discipline; identification of basic landforms, places, and names; and the scientific and social significance of geographical information.

5. Evidence of the graduating senior's successful *completion of a physical challenge* must be presented to the ROPE committee.

6. A demonstration of *competency in English (written and spoken)* is provided in virtually all the portfolio and project requirements. These, and any additional evidence the graduating senior may wish to present to the committee, fulfill the requirements of the presentation in the English competency area.

The above is drawn from the 1984 student handbook, "Walden III's Rite of Passage Experience," by Thomas Feeney, a teacher at Walden III, an alternative public school in Racine, Wisconsin. Preliminary annotations are by Grant Wiggins.

Figure 15.3
Walden III's rite of passage experience (ROPE).

	1	2	3	4	5	
O	Little or nothing is written. Essay is disorganized and poorly developed. Does not stay on topic		Essay is incomplete. It lacks an intro, well-developed body, or conclusion. Coherence and logic are attempted but inadequate		The essay is well-organized. It is coherent, ordered logically, and fully developed	×6
S	The student writes frequent run-ons or fragments		Occasional errors in sentence structure. Little variety in sentence length structure		Sentences are complete and varied in length and structure	×5
U	Student makes frequent errors in word choice and agreement		Student makes occasional errors in word choice and agreement		Usage is correct. Word choice is appropriate	×4
M	Student makes frequent errors in spelling, punctuation and capitalization		Student makes an occasional error in mechanics		Spelling, capitalization, and punctuation are correct	×4
F	Format is sloppy. There are no margins or indents. Handwriting is inconsistent		The margins and indents have inconsistencies—no title or inappropriate title		The format is correct. The title is appropriate. The margins and indents are consistent	×1

O = Organization
S = Sentence structure
U = Usage
M = Mechanics
F = Format

The essays are scored using a 1-5 scale. The numbers in the boxes to the far right indicate the relative importance of each factor in the overall grade. Thus, organization is valued most, and counts 30% of the grade; format counts 5% of the grade.

Figure 15.4
A grading grid for essays: Adams county schools, CO.
Source: Adams County Schools, Adams, CO.

levels and objective measures of student learning. As a rationale for their work, they noted (a) that many decisions about students are influenced by a teacher's judgments of the student's academic functioning and (b) historically there seems to be a widespread assumption that teachers generally are poor judges of the attributes of their students.

Hoge and Coladarci identified sixteen studies that were methodologically sound and featured a comparison between teachers' judgments of their students' academic performance and the students' actual performance on an achievement criterion. They found generally "high levels of agreement between teachers' judgmental measures and the standardized achievement test scores" (p. 308). The range of correlations was from a low of .28 to a high of .92, with the median being .65. (Note: A perfect correlation would be 1.00.) The median correlation certainly exceeds the convergent and concurrent validity coefficients typically reported for psychological tests.

This review of research has an important implication for practitioners and researchers alike: Teachers, in general, can provide valid performance judgments of their students. This result is comforting and shouldn't be surprising given the number of hours that teachers have to observe their students' performances.

Helping Students Take Tests

Let's turn for a moment to the concept of **test-wiseness,** which refers to teaching students how to take tests. Think of the conversation between the teacher and Sheliah, the student at the chapter's opening. Could Sheliah's performance have been improved if she had been taught techniques to improve test-taking? Don't confuse test-wiseness with coaching. Coaching means preparing students to take a specific test, that is, familiarizing them with the content of a particular test. Test-wiseness, however, means helping students to take all kinds of tests.

TEACHER ⬌ STUDENT INTERACTIONS

Testing: A Review

1. At the start of the year, when you talk with your class about your tests and grades, emphasize that you want to find out what they've learned so that you can help them on anything they still must master.

   - Point out that counselors need tests and grades to help them to make decisions about what they want to do.
   - Admissions offices and employers will want to know about their skills so that they can place them correctly.
   - Stress that tests let teachers and others know how much they have learned and how helpful tests can be.
   - Emphasize that you will review the test after it's taken to discuss their strengths and weaknesses and to help them with future tests.

2. How students perceive tests affects their performance. Consequently, you owe it to them—and yourself as well—to prepare the test carefully and to prepare your students psychologically.

   - Inform students in advance of the test. You may have very good reasons for occasionally resorting to surprise quizzes, but let these surprises remain occasional.
   - Students should understand exactly what material will be covered.
   - Students may find it helpful to know how you're scoring the test.
   - You should inform students about the kind of test they will take.

- Keep your directions simple and obvious. You probably remember how frustrated you were when directions were unclear, costing you valuable test time before you could decode them.
- When your class is to take an essay test, urge them to underline key words and phrases to help them understand just what is asked.
- Once they have completed their underlining, urge them to stop for a moment and judge how much time they should allot to each question. (They will be able to answer some more quickly than others.)
- If they have difficulty in determining just what is required, suggest to them that they think about the class work and reading material for the test and attempt to make any pertinent association.
- With objective tests, tell your students to read through the entire test, again judging time and potential difficulty with particular items.
- Have them answer immediately those items they positively know.
- With those items they feel uncertain about, have them eliminate any responses they know are incorrect. This frequently leaves only two responses, and by eliminating unnecessary distractors, they may better be able to make a final decision.
- With these suggestions in mind, most students will be able to relax a little more and thus be capable of a better performance.

If you think of test-wiseness as providing an opportunity for students to demonstrate what they know, then you become more sensitive to the importance of testing. You can help students to improve their test-taking skills by having them consider these suggestions (Dobbin, 1984):

- *One of the most productive strategies is to find out what the test is like beforehand.* There is a lot of information and practice material available about such exams as the Scholastic Aptitude. If it is a teacher-made test, *ask the teacher any questions you may have.* There's no better source. For example, what will the test cover? Where will it begin? Where will it end? Will it be multiple-choice or essay? How long will it be? (Students should know if they're expected to finish it. Speed can be a factor in a mark.) Should I guess? (Some tests penalize students for guessing.) Will anything else other than content be scored? Students have a right to know if handwriting and spelling will count.

- *Decide how to study for the test.* What are you going to study? If you have a good idea of what the test will be like, then concentrate on that content and any needed skills. Get all the relevant material together and try to remember what the teacher emphasized in class. You could even make an outline of these topics. Combine reading your notes with reading the text; underline anything you think is critical. As Dobbin (1984) noted, *cram with a plan!*

You have identified the critical content, the necessary facts and meanings; now you have to study

Talking to students about their test-taking strategies and coaching them to use good problem-solving skills are important teaching activities that enhance student performances on tests.

with intensity. Since cramming is best done with facts—Who was the U.S. president during the first World War—why not make out questions about the facts? Put one question on a card. Vary the cards; get someone else to ask you the questions. After awhile, close your eyes and try to visualize the card with both question and answer. Finish up the night before the exam, if possible.

• *Make sure you're physically prepared to take the test.* This includes your physical condition: Get plenty of sleep, don't take any stimulants, don't eat too much before the test (you could get drowsy). Give yourself plenty of time; try to get to the test early.

Conclusion

This chapter focused on teacher-made tests, both essay and objective, and introduced several new suggestions for assessing students, particularly authentic assessment. After the basic elements of each were identified, sugges-

tions were made to help you write, mark, grade, and report. To determine the real purposes of a unit of work, you may want to write them out to aid teaching and testing. You can then decide what specific kinds of behavior can be measured to indicate attainment of these objectives.

You were asked to familiarize yourself with the different types of test items and with the principles of test construction. This helps you to decide what kind of test would be best suited for your students.

Don't throw away your tests. Look at the results and decide what items worked for you. You can then begin a collection of good, discriminatory items. Finally, keep an open mind about the first form of the test. There is no way of telling how easy or difficult a test is until it has been used.

Constructing a good test is not an easy task; it is time-consuming, difficult, and even frustrating. But you cannot obtain an accurate appraisal of your students without accurate measurement.

Chapter Highlights

Assessment: Terminology and Assumptions

- Assessment refers to the process of gathering pertinent information to help make decisions about students.
- Testing is one means of obtaining evidence about a student's learning or behavior.
- Measurement means to place a number on a student's performance.
- Grading is the assignment of a symbol to a student's performance.
- Careful analysis of testing results aids educators in improving their instruction, revising curricula, guiding students to realistic decisions, judging the appropriateness of subject matter, and assessing the conditions of learning.
- Educators today are sensitive to the needs of multicultural students in taking tests. In giving tests to these students, teachers should be aware of their test-taking skills, such as language comprehension, that could influence the test results.
- All forms of assessment contain error, which implies that we must assess students frequently and with a variety of methods.

Integrating Learning and Assessment

- Assessment techniques should help you to determine if your objectives have been met.
- If objectives remain unattained, then you must search for the cause and attempt to discover whether it is in the student(s), the material, or your methods.
- The evidence provided by assessment enables teachers and administrators to present appropriate materials that serve the needs of their students.
- Test-wiseness refers to familiarity with test-taking procedures that students can learn.

Methods of Assessing Students

- Assessing classroom performance typically entails four methods: pencil-and-paper tests, oral questions, performance tests, and standardized tests.
- Teacher-constructed tests usually consist of essay questions or multiple-choice items.
- There are two general categories of standardized tests: aptitude and achievement.
- A norm-referenced test enables you to compare a student with a representative group.

- A criterion-referenced test enables you to determine if a student has achieved competence at one level before moving on to a new, higher level of content.

Issues in Constructing Tests

- Reliability refers to a test's consistency, which can be affected by an individual's characteristics and by the design of the test.
- Validity refers to a test's meaningfulness, that is, its ability to measure what it is supposed to measure.

Planning Teacher-Constructed Tests

- Test items should reflect the objectives of the subject or unit.
- Think about the test; take the time to construct relevant items. Avoid the habit of hastily throwing a few questions together. This isn't fair to you, given the amount of time you have spent teaching, and it certainly isn't fair to your students, who deserve a thoughtful assessment of their achievement.
- Next you must decide what kind of test best serves your purpose—essay or objective—both of which have strengths and weaknesses. Consider carefully which type of test is better suited to obtain the information you need to evaluate your students' achievement.

Writing Essay Tests

- Writing essay questions is more difficult than it initially appears. Clarity, level, and a necessary degree of objectivity are required.
- Scoring the answers to essay questions requires a clear understanding of the major points in the answer. Try to insure that you do not know which student's paper you're marking. Also read all answers to one question rather than reading all of a student's answers at one time.

Writing Objective Tests

- Objective tests sample a wide range of material and, if carefully formulated, can also assess comprehension as well as knowledge.
- Be sure your students are ready for an objective test: Are there any mechanics they should be familiar with? Do they have a strategy for taking the test? What clues does the item furnish? What are the rules for guessing?

Using Data from Teacher-Constructed Tests

- If you assign work, mark it and return it as soon as possible with appropriate remarks.
- When you grade students (that is, judge their work over a period of time) be sure that your grade represents their work, not their behavior.
- One of the main reasons for reporting, if not the main reason, is to strengthen the association between home and school.

Alternative Methods and New Assessment Trends

- Advances in behavioral assessment and the school restructuring movement have led to the development of two new assessment approaches: curriculum-based assessment and authentic assessment.
- Behavioral assessment emphasizes observational techniques to characterize a student's overt behavior or performance.
- Behavioral assessment assumes that a student's behavior may be merely a sample of his/her behavior. Therefore, repeated assessments over time and in different situations is typical of a behavioral approach to assessment.
- Curriculum-based assessment (CBA) grew out of the concern that many standardized tests do not adequately test what is taught in a student's curriculum.
- Although several approaches to CBA have been developed, they all use the content from the curriculum in the classroom to develop brief probes or tests that provide information on what a student knows or doesn't know and the rate at which students are acquiring new information.
- Authentic assessment is a collection of assessment techniques (i.e., portfolios, performances, exhibitions) and interpretative tools (i.e., profiles and self-ratings) that are designed to link teaching and assessment.
- Authentic assessment focuses on authentic classroom performances rather than typical multiple-choice or pencil-and-paper essays. The integration of "real" world skills is stressed.
- Authentic assessment places a heavy emphasis on teacher judgments of student's performances.

Key Terms

Achievement tests
Application
Assessment
Authentic assessment
Comprehension
Construct validity
Content validity
Criterion-referenced tests
Criterion-related validity
Curriculum-based assessment (CBA)
Essay test
Evaluation
Exhibitions
Extended response
Grading
Knowledge
Marking
Matching items
Measure
Multiple-choice items
Performance-based grading benchmarks
Performance test
Portfolio assessment
Profiles
Reliability
Reporting
Restricted response
Selection
Standardized tests
Student self-assessment
Supply items
Teacher-constructed tests
Test-wiseness
True-false question
Validity

Suggested Readings

Bloom, B., Madaus, G., and Hastings, Thomas, J. (1981). *Evaluation to improve learning.* New York: McGraw-Hill. An insightful look at the testing field with emphasis on formative and summative evaluation. Tightly linked to objectives, this text is a highly valuable source.

Dobbin, J. (1984). *How to take a test: Doing your best.* Princeton, NJ: Educational Testing Service. One of the best single sources for suggestions to help your students prepare for tests; contains many tips for improving test performance.

Green, B. (1981). A primer of testing. *American Psychologist, 36,* 1001–1011. The entire issue is devoted to testing, while Green's article discusses basic terminology and concepts.

Gronlund, N. (1985). *Measurement and evaluation in learning.* New York: Macmillan. One of the best basic texts that presents a comprehensive and searching examination of the testing field.

Standardized Tests in the Classroom

It was that time of the year again and Hugh Taylor, who taught the sixth grade at Bailey School, knew that his students were about to take their standardized achievement tests. He always worried that any students who were not "test-wise" might not do as well as they could. So this year he decided to discuss these tests with his class.

He started by asking them, "Why do you have to take these tests anyway?"

"So the teachers can have a day off, Mr. Taylor," laughed Phil, a happy-go-lucky twelve-year-old.

"Hardly that, Phil. We're here with you all the way. But seriously, what good comes from them? Alice?"

"Well, Mr. Taylor, I suppose it helps you to find out what we're not good at."

"Good, Alice. That's probably the most important reason—to discover what you have to do to improve."

"For example, if anyone seemed to have trouble finding out what the main idea of a story or passage was,

we could zero right in on it. If you work on it now, you'll lessen the possibility of having any trouble in junior high school." He knew that his students were looking ahead to junior high school with a little anxiety.

He then turned to Phil. "OK, Phil. You were being funny a little while ago. Now, seriously, tell us what you do when you take one of these tests—what you look for, what you skip, and what you think is important."

Phil grinned sheepishly and said, "Well, Mr. Taylor, I look for give-aways."

"That's interesting, Phil. What do you mean?"

"Little clues that tip the answer; words like always or never."

"Good, Phil. That will help anybody taking a standardized test. Any other tips? Anybody have any ideas to add?"

The discussion between Mr. Taylor and his students demonstrates the concern that many teachers and students have about taking standardized tests.

With the basics of assessment and test-construction behind us, we turn now to the world of standardized tests. Though teachers may occasionally have the responsibility of selecting a standardized test for a particular purpose, the chances are that their major task with regard to these tests will be as an advisor in the selection process. Standardized tests have become a major part of many schools' testing program, and teachers must be informed professionals. It should be noted, however, that some school systems are seriously questioning the value of standardized testing today. Yet at a national level many educational leaders are urging a national examination to assess students' academic progress (Gawronski, 1991). Thus, the advantages and disadvantages of standardized tests will be examined in this section of the chapter.

Standardized tests have become "big business." When you consider that about 45 million students are enrolled in kindergarten through grade twelve, you begin to sense the enormous dimensions of "testing." If we now include the multibattery nature of most standardized tests, the need for prudent and knowledgeable guardians of students' interest become apparent.

Standardized tests, as classroom tests, must be appropriate for the educational purposes of the system, the school, and your students. Giving tests simply because it is "the thing to do" represents a futile and expensive exercise. The best, and perhaps the only, safeguard against such a practice is knowledge: knowledge of test construction in general, of specific tests, of your students, and of the educational goals of your school.

First, we'll discuss the objectives of a school's testing program, and then begin our examination of standardized tests with a description of what these tests are like. Next we'll examine how the results of standardized tests can help teachers in the classroom. As with most topics about education, controversy exists about these tests, so both pros and cons will be presented. Since there are several types of standardized tests, we'll sort out the differences. Finally, we'll examine several current issues that are swirling about standardized testing.

When you finish reading this chapter, you should be able to:

- distinguish between the purposes of standardized tests and teacher-made tests.
- appraise the various interpretations of intelligence and intelligence tests.
- use basic statistical techniques to interpret test results.
- evaluate standardized test scores.
- apply the results of standardized testing to improve teaching and learning.
- make informed decisions concerning current testing issues.

A School's Testing Program

Before beginning a specific analysis of standardized tests, however, let's again recall how significant the relationship is between learning objectives and testing. Schools are designed to change students' behavior. The ideal means of accomplishing this change largely determines the choice of administrative structure (self-contained classroom versus team teaching, for example), methods, materials, and curriculum. We can't make reliable decisions about these matters unless they are based upon an accurate assessment of student capacity. All of these issues—administration, assessment, counseling, teaching, learning—involve educational objectives.

What do we need to know about a student, and how can we acquire this knowledge? Once we have the needed information, what does it mean? Little value is derived from a series of achievement tests unless the results can be used to improve the instruction offered students. Unless you understand exactly what a test score does and does not mean, tests are of little value and may, in fact, be detrimental.

The results of group intelligence testing during World War I, the more sophisticated selection tests developed during World War II, and both state and federal legislation (P.L. 94–142; the Individuals with Disabilities Act) have combined to establish an important place for testing at all levels of education. As a guide for the selection and use of instruments in a school testing program, remember that any program implies the systematic use at all levels, and in all disciplines, of several tests.

The selection, administration, and interpretation of standardized tests should be linked closely to the educational objectives of a particular school system. The testing program usually involves *readiness tests* before school entrance, *subject-matter achievement tests* throughout all levels, occasionally *cognitive tests* for students with special needs, and other tests, such as *interest inventories, personality questionnaires,* and *academic diagnostic tests* as needed in individual cases. (See Table 16.1.) Thus, a variety of tests are available to educators. In some cases, these tests are administered to individual students by specialists such as counselors or school psychologists.

Table 16.1	
School Testing Programs	
Level	Type of Test
Preschool	Psychomotor and readiness
Primary	Basic skills Reading
Elementary	Achievement Basic skills Personality/behavior
Junior high	Aptitude Achievement Basic skills Personality/behavior
Senior high	Aptitude Achievement Basic skills College entrance Vocational/interests Personality/behavior

Standardized tests often are directly administered to students in a one to one situation. However some standardized rating scales are administered through an interview with an adult who knows the student well.

Knowledge of the nature of standardized tests and how they aid in the attainment of educational objectives is a basic requirement for an appropriate testing program. Testing programs generally have three major purposes: instructional, guidance, and administrative.

1. *Instructional.* Achievement tests administered in the fall help teachers to commence instruction where students can logically expect both challenge and success. In other words, some achievement tests answer the questions: Where are my students right now? Where can I begin instruction?
2. *Guidance.* The results of some testing programs enable instructors to adapt the curriculum more efficiently to the student, and to aid students in choosing specialized courses, thus serving a guidance function by helping to answer such questions as: What do they need? Are special services, such as gifted/talented programs, remedial reading programs, or special education programs needed?
3. *Administrative.* Administrators are often interested in how groups of students are performing. Good tests can help them to make more suitable decisions about curriculum, placement, and how their students compare to others in the region or nation on the basis of substantial data.

Remember: Achievement tests are designed to indicate how much one has accomplished because of training. Aptitude tests reveal an individual's potential for learning, such as general intelligence, or specific abilities such as music or art. These are the basic ingredients of a school's testing program. The next question to be answered is: What is meant by standardized tests?

Standardized Tests

Standardized tests are commercially prepared and sample behavior under uniform procedures. Uniform procedures means that the same fixed set of questions is administered to all students; the directions are the same; the time requirement is the same; the scoring procedure is the same. Testing experts usually administer the test to a norm group (usually a large, national sample) so that any one student's performance can be compared to others throughout the country. Standardized tests are usually classified according to what they measure. There are two general categories: aptitude and achievement tests.

1. **Aptitude tests** are intended to assess students' general or specific abilities; for example, intelligence tests supposedly assess a student's total ability. (The current controversy concerning what intelligence tests measure will be discussed later.) There are other, more specific aptitude tests that measure mechanical, musical, artistic, and many other aptitudes.

2. **Achievement tests** measure accomplishment in such subjects as reading, arithmetic, language, and science. Gronlund (1985) noted that carefully constructed standardized achievement tests possess the following characteristics:

   • the test items are of high technical quality, developed by test specialists, pretested, and selected according to precise requirements;
   • directions for administering and scoring are rigidly controlled to ensure uniformity;
   • norms are provided to help interpret test scores;
   • equivalent forms of the test are typically available;
   • a variety of materials, including a test manual, are included to aid in administering, scoring, and interpreting scores.

You can see, then, that uniformity is a critical element in these tests so that legitimate comparisons can be made. How does a fourth-grade student in Maine compare to a fourth-grade student in California? Standardization means the degree to which the observational procedures, administrative procedures, equipment and materials, and scoring rules have been fixed so that exactly the same testing procedure occurs at different times and places.

Many standardized tests will allow you to compare a given student with a representative group (referred to as a norm group) of students. Such tests are called norm-referenced tests. A norm-referenced test (NRT) yields a score that enables you to compare it with the scores of others who took the same test. For example, when you grade an essay test, you compare each student's answers to those of other students and decide that the answers, compared to the others, warrant a B. A score on a standardized achievement test informs you how a student compares to some national group that took the test.

There are several advantages of norm-referenced tests.

• They can assess a broad range of knowledge and understanding.
• They reflect common goals for learning.
• They can assess achievement at all levels of attainment—high, medium, low.
• They can sample achievement more widely.
• They reflect the belief that achievement is more or less, not all or nothing.
• They furnish a single score that summarizes a student's general level of achievement.
• They provide summative evaluation information.
• They identify learning as the primary responsibility of the student.

Madaus (1989) tells of a student's bringing home a score of 38 on an English test. The parents are upset until they discover that the highest score was 58 and that their child's score ranked tenth highest in a class of 40.

There are other tests that provide a score informing us of the extent to which a student has achieved predetermined objectives. These are called criterion-referenced tests (CRT). Criterion-referenced tests are increasingly popular because of renewed emphasis on individualized instruction, behavior objectives, and mastery learning. No question arises as to whether one student is better or worse than another; the focus is on reaching a particular standard of performance.

Typically skills within a subject are hierarchically arranged so that the skills that are learned initially are tested first. In math, for example, addition skills would be taught and evaluated before multiplication skills. These tests are usually criterion-referenced because a student must achieve competence at one level before being taught at a higher level. Thus, criterion-referenced tests help teachers to determine if a student is ready to move on to the next level. The major characteristics of criterion-referenced and norm-referenced tests are presented in Table 16.2.

Developing a Standardized Test

Standardization implies consistency or sameness, which is the greatest contribution of the standardized test. If students' scores are to be compared, the test and the testing circumstances must remain uniform at any and all test administrations. The standardized test contains detailed directions that the tester must follow faithfully. If

Table 16.2

Comparison of Norm-Referenced Tests (NRTs) and Criterion-Referenced Tests (CRTs)*

Common Characteristics of NRTs and CRTs

1. Both require specification of the achievement domain to be measured.
2. Both require a relevant and representative sample of test items.
3. Both use the same types of test items.
4. Both use the same rules for item writing (except for item difficulty).
5. Both are judged by the same qualities of goodness (reliability and validity).
6. Both are useful in educational measurement.

Differences between NRTs and CRTs (but it is only a matter of emphasis)

1. NRT—Typically covers a *large* domain of learning tasks, with just a few items measuring each specific task.
   CRT—Typically focuses on a *delimited* domain of learning tasks, with a relatively large number of items measuring each specific task.
2. NRT—Emphasizes *discrimination* among individuals in terms of relative level of learning.
   CRT—Emphasizes *description* of what learning tasks individuals can and cannot perform.
3. NRT—Favors items of average difficulty and typically omits easy items.
   CRT—Matches item difficulty to learning tasks, without altering item difficulty or omitting easy items.
4. NRT—Used primarily (but not exclusively) for *survey* testing.
   CRT—Used primarily (but not exclusively) for *mastery* testing.
5. NRT—Interpretation requires a clearly defined group.
   CRT—Interpretation requires a clearly defined and delimited achievement domain.

Reprinted with the permission of Macmillan Publishing Company, Inc. from *Measurement and Evaluation In Teaching*, Sixth Edition by Norman E. Gronlund and Robert L. Linn. Copyright © 1990 Macmillan Publishing Company, © 1985, 1981, 1976, 1971, 1965 by Norman E. Gronlund.

test administrators should vary the testing conditions, they introduce an unaccountable source of error, and comparison of these scores with others becomes meaningless.

These tests include identical material, oral directions, time, or demonstrations. Testing conditions should be as comfortable as possible, with adequate seating, lighting, and ventilation. The tester should, as much as possible, establish rapport with the subjects to reduce the inevitable tension and anxiety that accompany any test.

The construction of the standardized test is an involved and complicated process (Nitko, 1983). Unlike the teacher-made test, a standardized test is usually fashioned by a measurement expert, or a team of experts, in a particular field. A team usually includes both subject-matter and testing specialists. Considerable care is taken to insure a comprehensive coverage of a subject (content validity) and to avoid ambiguity in the writing of the individual items. The test is initially given an experimental trial with representative groups to ascertain its suitability, reliability, and validity. As a result of these trials, revisions are made that should result in a highly accurate instrument. Authors of good tests may spend from four to five years developing and refining a test.

Probably the most desirable aspect of standardized tests are the **norms** supplied with them. Norms enable you to interpret the test scores of your class by comparing them with many other scores derived from a national sample. In standardizing a test, it is given to large numbers of subjects who represent the population of students for whom it is ultimately intended. These norm groups should represent the total population with regard to age, sex, and socioeconomic status.

If a test is intended as a fifth-grade arithmetic achievement instrument, then it is tried upon as many fifth-graders as possible who represent the age range of the typical fifth-grade population, and who also represent urban and rural populations, multicultural students, and the like. *Norms, then, provide the normal range of scores for a given population.* If a test consists of 100 items, and the typical twelve-year-old correctly answers 60 of these items, the twelve-year-old's average on this test is 60.

When selecting a standardized test, ask questions such as: Why is testing necessary? What objective information is known about the test being examined? What technical information about the test is provided?

Table 16.3 summarizes the main aspects of test selection.

Types of Standardized Tests

Standardized tests are classified according to what they measure and teachers generally are concerned with two general categories: achievement and aptitude tests. As we noted in chapter 15, achievement tests measure accomplishment in a subject such as reading, arithmetic, language, or science. Aptitude tests are designed to

TEACHER ←→ STUDENT
INTERACTIONS

Selecting and Using Standardized Tests

1. At some point in your career you may be a member of a test selection committee. Here are some guidelines to consider when reviewing tests for possible use with your students.

   - Be sure the test is a fair assessment of those objectives that teacher-made tests cannot effectively measure.
   - Study the test literature, such as *The Mental Measurements Yearbook* (Mitchell, 1985), to determine the most promising tests.
   - Carefully analyze the specimen sets (inexpensive or free samples of test items) that many publishers provide potential purchasers.
   - Select those tests that most closely approximate the school's goals.
   - Consider cost, time for administration, and ease of administration, scoring, and interpretation.
   - Remember, any test battery may only partially assess the objectives formulated for your classroom.
   - Test material can become quickly outdated, especially in subjects such as science and social studies.
   - Examine format, content, the manual, and instructional suggestions carefully.
   - Combine test results with other means of student evaluation (teacher-made tests, observation, and aptitude assessment).

2. To help achieve positive outcomes with a testing program, you must treat the test properly.

   - Take into consideration such general characteristics as student worry and anxiety, motivation, and rapport.
   - Standardized achievement tests of students should not be used to evaluate teachers. Too many conditions elude control, and more direct methods for evaluating teachers are recommended.
   - Don't make the test the intentional objective of instruction. If teachers teach for the test, a desired breadth of learning may be lost.
   - Be careful in how you interpret test scores, particularly intelligence test scores. Again we see the value of norms, and you are urged to look to these and not compare the scores of students on different IQ tests. If similar misuses are shunned, and if test scores are interpreted properly, they are useful tools in the guidance of learning.

Table 16.3

Steps in Test Selection

1. Why is testing necessary?
   a. Purpose of testing
   b. Characteristics of the group being tested
   c. Uses of the test

2. What tests are pertinent?
   a. Needed data from test
   b. Types of suitable tests
   c. Description of test's content

3. What information about the test is available?
   a. Texts
   b. Journals
   c. Reference books

4. Does the test meet your needs?
   a. Appropriate for your purposes
   b. Suitable content
   c. Easy to administer
   d. Clarity of instructions and items
   e. Technically adequate (reliability and validity information)
   f. Cost effective

5. What is your overall evaluation?

assess students' general and specific abilities. We'll examine both types of test in some detail.

Standardized Achievement Tests

Achievement tests attempt to assess the knowledge and skills taught by the school. A standardized achievement test has certain distinctive features, including a fixed set of test items designed to measure a clearly defined achievement domain, specific directions for administering and scoring the test, and norms based on representative groups of individuals like those for whom the test was designed (Gronlund, 1985, p. 264). Thus, the same content and procedure permit the identical testing of individuals in different places at different times. Students tested in Madison, Wisconsin, can be compared on the same test to students in Boston or San Francisco. Norms then enable us to compare an individual's score with those of known groups who also have taken the test.

Achievement tests have one main objective: to discover how much an individual has learned from educational experiences. They may be prepared for use throughout the entire system (for example, everyone studying American history takes the same examination, most likely at the end of the school year) or prepared by specialists and standardized for national use. Thus, there are achievement tests that cover a number of subjects like reading, mathematics, or social studies, and tests in specific subjects such as French or American history.

When achievement tests fit the goals of learning and measure with acceptable accuracy, they have many desirable uses. Probably the most important of these is to assess the development of individual learners. Once you determine students' potential and decide on the objectives of instruction, you should check your students' learning progress, mainly with teacher-made tests and occasionally with standardized tests.

Standardized achievement tests aid both in the academic guidance of students and in planning curriculum changes. Standardized achievement tests likewise help in decisions about promotion and admission, since they yield additional evidence from objective sources and influence institutional decisions about advancement and admission.

The value of the standardized achievement test lies in the strength of all standardized tests: It samples an extensive range of subject matter, and it affords norms that enable school systems to evaluate themselves. If these tests are selected in accordance with learning objectives, they can be a helpful tool for any school system because they can stimulate creative thinking about the effectiveness of the curriculum, materials, and instruction.

Types of Standardized Achievement Tests

Two types of standardized achievement tests are currently popular: **multilevel survey batteries** that assess separate curricular topics over a wide range of grades, and those designed to measure specific subjects, such as reading or mathematics (see Witt et al., 1988).

Among the most popular of the achievement test batteries are the Metropolitan Achievement Tests, which range from grade one to grade twelve. These tests, available in alternate forms, measure achievement in reading, arithmetic, language, social studies, science, and study skills. The format is attractive, the test content adequate, and the test items carefully written.

Another example of a multilevel survey battery is the California Achievement Tests, which are applicable to kindergarten through grade twelve. These tests measure reading, arithmetic, language, spelling, and reference skills. Reliabilities of total scores are good, and the difficulty of the items is appropriate for the level. Table 16.4 describes several other widely used and well-regarded batteries.

Other types of standardized achievement tests measure readiness, or achievement in a specific subject, or assess an individual's readiness for instruction, or measure vocational achievement, or determine a person's qualifications for graduate training. For example, The Metropolitan Readiness Tests are a good illustration of these more specific measures. They measure a child's ability to acquire first-grade skills and include items that assess auditory memory, letter recognition, and visual matching among others.

Achievement in reading represents a particularly popular type of specific standardized test. They are typically used to assess the efficiency of reading instruction in a system, for diagnostic purposes, and to identify underachievement in related subjects. The Iowa Silent Reading Tests have been widely adopted for both elementary and secondary usage. These assess a subject's rate of reading, comprehension, vocabulary, word and sentence meaning, and ability to locate information. The advanced level also includes tests on poetry comprehension and directed reading. These tests encompass the various skills needed in reading, and a weakness in any one of them could conceivably cause reading difficulties.

Standardized Aptitude Tests

Aptitude tests (both individual and group) are used to predict what a student can learn. Aptitude tests do not measure native capacity or learning potential directly; rather they measure performance based on learning abilities (Gronlund, 1985, p. 295).

It is interesting to note some differences between aptitude and achievement tests. Aptitude tests predict an individual's performance in a certain task or in a particular job by sampling the cumulative effect of many experiences in daily living, including definite educational experiences. Make no assumption, however, that aptitude tests measure only innate capacity, while achievement tests measure only the effects of learning. Any psychological test reflects the influence of past experiences upon present performance. Memory and transfer ensure that there is no escape from the past.

While supporting the relationship between intelligence and achievement (general measures of ability predict learning performance), remember that specific abilities (mathematics, for example) differ within the individual. It is a truism with which we can readily agree. Our personal experience testifies to specific strengths and weaknesses. Some readers of this chapter undoubtedly freeze at the sight of numbers while others possess little, if any, artistic ability. It is the totality or pattern of performance on measures of general ability that is significant for understanding the achievement-intelligence relationship.

Table 16.4

Widely Used and Highly Regarded Group–Administered Comprehensive Achievement Batteries

Battery	Grades	Subject Areas Assessed
Iowa Tests of Basic Skills (Forms 7 and 8) (Hieronymous et al., 1983)	K.1–1.5	Listening, vocabulary, word analysis, language, mathematics
	K.8–1.9	Listening, vocabulary, word analysis, reading, language, mathematics
	1.7–2.6	Vocabulary, word analysis, reading comprehension, spelling, mathematics skills, listening, language skills, work study skills
	2.7–3.5	Vocabulary, word analysis, reading comprehension, spelling, mathematics skills, listening, language skills, work study skills
	3–9	Vocabulary, reading, spelling, math, capitalization, punctuation, usage, visual materials, reference materials
Iowa Tests of Educational Development (7th edition) (Iowa Tests of Educational Development, 1982)	9–12	Correctness and appropriateness of expression, ability to do quantitative thinking, social studies, natural sciences, literacy materials, vocabulary, sources of information total, reading total
Metropolitan Achievement Tests (Survey Battery) (5th edition) (Balow, Farr, Hogan, and Prescott, 1978)	K.0–K.5	Reading, mathematics, language total
	K.5–1.4	Reading, mathematics, language, total
	1.5–2.4	Reading, mathematics, language, basics total, science, social studies, complete total
	2.5–3.4	Reading, mathematics, language, basics total, science, social studies, complete total
	3.5–4.9	Reading, mathematics, language, basics total, science, social studies, complete total
	5.0–6.9	Reading, mathematics, language, basics total, science, social studies, complete total
	7.0–9.9	Reading, mathematics, language, basics total, science, social studies, complete total
	10.0–12.9	Reading, mathematics, language total
Metropolitan Achievement Tests (Instructional Battery) (5th edition) (Balow, Farr, Hogan, and Prescott, 1978)	K.5–9.9	Reading, language, mathematics

Battery	Grades	Subject Areas Assessed
SRA Achievement Series (Naslund, Thorpe, and Lefever, 1981)	K–1	Reading, mathematics, composite, verbal, nonverbal, total
	1–2	Reading, mathematics, composite, verbal, nonverbal, total
	2–3	Reading, mathematics, language arts, composite, verbal, nonverbal, total
	3–4	Reading, mathematics, language arts, composite, verbal, nonverbal, total
	4–6	Reading, mathematics, language arts, reference materials, social studies, science, composite, verbal, nonverbal, total
	6–8	Reading, mathematics, language arts, reference materials, social studies, science, composite, verbal, nonverbal, total
	8–9	Reading, mathematics, language arts, reference materials, social studies, science, composite, verbal, nonverbal, total
	9–12	Reading, mathematics, language arts, reference materials, social studies, science, survey of applied skills, composite, verbal, nonverbal, total
Stanford Achievement Test (1982 edition) (Gardner, Rudman, Karlen, and Merwin, 1982)	1.5–2.9	Reading, word study skills, total, mathematics, listening, spelling, environment
	2.5–3.9	Reading, word study skills, total, mathematics, listening, spelling, environment
	3.5–4.9	Reading, mathematics, language, listening, science, social science, using information
	4.5–5.9	Reading, mathematics, language, listening, science, social science, using information
	5.5–7.9	Reading, mathematics, language, listening, science, social science, using information
	7.0–9.9	Reading comprehension, mathematics, language, listening, social science, science, using information
Stanford Test of Academic Skills (1982 edition) (Gardner, Callis, Merwin, and Rudman, 1982)	8.0–12.9	Reading comprehension, reading vocabulary, reading, total, spelling, english, english total, mathematics, science, social science, using information
	9.0–13	Reading comprehension, reading vocabulary, reading, total, spelling, english, english total, mathematics, science, social science, using information

From *Preschool Screening: Identifying Young Children with Developmental and Educational Problems* (pp. 126–129) by Robert Lichtenstein and Harry Ireton, 1984. Copyright © 1984 Grune & Stratton, Inc., Orlando, FL., Allyn & Bacon, Inc. Needham Heights, MA.

Focus on Students

Testing Young Children

If you administer standardized achievement tests to young children, remember certain developmental considerations. In a thoughtful essay, Ludlow (in press) notes that youngsters from kindergarten to grade two (about 4 1/2 to 7 years of age) interpret assessment tasks in a highly personal manner. (Recall that children of this age are struggling to overcome egocentrism—see chapter 3.) Developmental factors, then, may influence how such children interpret a question. The younger the child, the greater the measurement problem. Several questions must be considered when testing young children.

- Are these tests technically inadequate? No, the tests are constructed following the same safeguards as tests for older subjects, but they cannot control for an important source of variation: The manner in which a child's cognitive, social, and affective development may interact and influence test scores.

- Do young children possess the skills necessary to answer the range of questions presented? Not always. For some children, a picture as part of a question may elicit highly individual responses because of a child's experiences. Other youngsters may lack such test-taking skills as patience, task persistence, or reading ability. You should also be careful in interpreting test norms since your system may vary significantly from national norms.

- Do youngsters interpret test instructions similarly? Obviously not, given several of the developmental characteristics just mentioned: lack of attention, reading difficulties, lack of ability to make the correct written response (especially important if the test is machine-scored).

  Nevertheless, carefully selected, properly administered, judiciously interpreted standardized achievement tests for young children may yield needed data. More will be said about assessing preschoolers later in this chapter.

"After 20 years of schooling, your aptitude test shows that you're skilled at just one thing — taking tests."

H. Schwadron in *Phi Delta Kappan.*

intelligence is that our experience is not with intelligence in the abstract but with intelligent behavior. Some individuals can solve problems rapidly; others master certain kinds of tasks easily; still others are remarkably well-adjusted. Each of these examples represents a form of intelligence and explains why there are so many different definitions of intelligence.

Definitions of Intelligence

L. M. Terman (1921) characterized intelligence as the ability to carry on abstract thinking. David Wechsler (1958) characterized it as the aggregate or global capacity of the individual to act purposefully, to think rationally and to deal effectively with the environment. These statements represent the most widely held class of definitions that describe intelligence as unitary. Other theoretical explanations define intelligence quite differently. Researchers view it not as an all-inclusive, global concept, but as a cluster of several factors or abilities. J. P. Guilford (1967), for example, stated that although some psychologists still view intelligence as a monolith, there is overwhelming evidence to indicate that many elements or factors are involved. Differences within one person's abilities, differing patterns of intellectual growth and decline, the instability of individual IQ scores over the years, and the different symptoms of brain damage all suggest that intelligence may be multifaceted.

B. F. Skinner (1953) offered an even more radical analysis. He noted that we can designate almost any characteristic as a dimension of personality, but that this

---

Before discussing the various intelligence tests, we'll examine the conditions that led to their use and general acceptance.

The Measurement of Intelligence

Any attempt to analyze an issue or problem should commence with a clear definition of terms. A satisfactory definition of intelligence or cognitive ability, however, has always been elusive. Another obstacle to understanding

adds little to our knowledge until something beyond mere naming is achieved. We may easily coin the term "intelligence" or even neatly define it, but this alone does little to increase our practical understanding of the concept. Skinner stated that we must define intelligence by its behavior.

More recent attempts to analyze intelligence have likewise moved away from accepting intelligence as a unitary concept. Intelligence as a dynamic process involving individual competences (musical, artistic, logical) has been proposed by Kornhaber, Krechevsky, and Gardner (1990). They also stress the interactions between individuals and the societies in which they function, a contextual interpretation. (Gardner's belief in multiple intelligences and Sternberg's triarchic interpretation of intelligence were discussed in detail in chapter 8.)

Urging that an all-purpose intelligence test should be a thing of the past, Hunt (1990) argued that three different views of intelligence are necessary to understand intellectual functioning: intelligence as general reasoning ability, intelligence as domain-specific skills, and intelligence as information processing. Thus, there is no universally accepted definition of intelligence, although, as we have seen, current efforts (e.g., Sternberg and Gardner) stress the multiple qualities of intelligence and the role of context (Davidson, 1990).

Individuals have intelligence to the extent that they behave intelligently. This statement resembles the definition of intelligence that many psychologists feel is the only one acceptable: Intelligence is that quantity that the intelligence test measures. But this is unsatisfactory as well. Before constructing a test, decisions must be made about the nature of what is to be measured. In the instance of intelligence testing, what is to be measured obviously is intelligence. Consequently, items are chosen that are best suited to measure the author's concept of intelligence.

Background of the Intelligence Testing Movement

Intelligence, that fascinating yet enigmatic "something" that promised to discriminate the able from the less able, defied definition but perhaps could be quantified. With the advent of the twentieth century and the influx of immigrants to American shores, there appeared to be a need to devise some means of classifying individuals for education, for work, and ultimately for military service. This social context helps to explain the ready, almost eager, acceptance that the mental testing movement received. Here at last was a tool, so went the claim, that cut through the outer psychological barriers and laid bare the untarnished portrait of a person's innate capacity. The circumstances that led to the development and acceptance of the Binet and Wechsler tests illustrate the methods that investigators adopted to assess native ability by individual intelligence tests.

Binet and Mental Tests

The story of Alfred Binet and his search for the meaning and measurement of intelligence is chronicled as a major event in the history of psychology. Binet, who was born on July 8, 1857, and died in Paris on October 18, 1911, was originally trained for law. A time-consuming hobby, one that lasted throughout his life, was writing plays for the theaters of Paris. Later, as his interests changed, he received a doctorate in science from the Sorbonne, where he remained as director of the psychological laboratory. Much of his early work on the intellectual and emotional lives of children was the result of studies of his daughters. He was cofounder, in 1895, of *L'Annee Psychologique,* the journal in which his early studies on intelligence were published.

In 1904, Binet was asked by the Parisian Minister of Public Instruction to formulate techniques for identifying the children most likely to fail in school. A different problem, it meant finding some means of separating the normal from the truly retarded, of determining the lazy but bright who were simply poor achievers, and of eliminating the halo effect, which means assigning an unwarranted high rating to youngsters because they are neat or attractive (Gould, 1981).

Devising such an instrument meant that Binet had to begin with a preconceived notion of intelligence, since you cannot measure something unless you know what that something is. In a series of articles published in *L'Annee Psychologique,* Binet therefore outlined his idea of the nature of intelligence. It consisted of three elements:

1. *Any mental process possesses direction*; it is directed toward achievement of a particular goal and to the discovery of adequate means of attaining the goal. In the preparation of a term paper, for example, you select a suitable topic and the books and journals necessary to complete it.
2. *The ability to adapt by the use of tentative solutions.* Here you select and utilize some stimuli and test their relevance as you proceed toward the goal. Before writing your term paper, you may make a field trip to the area you are discussing, or to save time, you may decide to use library resources.
3. *The ability to make judgments and to criticize solutions.* Frequently called "autocriticism," this implies an objective evaluation of solutions. You may complete your paper, reread it, decide that one topic included is irrelevant, and exclude it.

The items in Binet's early test reflected these beliefs. When an item seemed to differentiate between normal and subnormal, he retained it; if no discrimination appeared, he rejected it. Binet defined normality as the ability to do the things that others of the same age usually do. Fortunately for the children of Paris, Binet was devoted to his task. The fruits of his and his coworkers' endeavors was the publication in 1905 of the *Metrical Scale of Intelligence.*

Since their publication, Binet's mental age scales have pointed the way for intelligence testing, and its success led a leading American psychologist, Lewis Terman, to adapt it for American usage. Terman's revision, called the **Stanford-Binet,** first appeared in 1916 and was revised in 1937, 1960, 1972, and recently revised and renormed in 1986 by Hagan, Sattler, and Thorndike.

As a result of his studies, Binet arrived at certain conclusions about the nature of intelligence. One such idea was that nearly all of psychology's data relate to intelligence. Another was that intelligence involves the fundamental faculty of judgment (call it common sense or adaptation). To judge well, to comprehend well, and to reason well are the essential functions of intelligence.

Binet's orientation was practical; he did not become entangled in problems of definition. For Binet, children and adults simply had something that distinguished them from one another and that enabled them to perform well or poorly on any given task. Call it what you will, it existed and therefore could be measured. Here Binet's practical side again manifested itself. Age must be a key element, he reasoned, since older children generally do better than younger children on the same task. So one must find tasks that are appropriate for a given age and determine if a youngster does about the same, better, or worse on these tasks than others of his age.

But even if we can measure it on a scale, exactly what meaning are we to give intelligence? Since Binet considered almost all psychological data as intellectual phenomena, to him the fundamental faculty of judgment was critical. All other intellectual faculties were of little importance in comparison with judgment. What was of utmost significance to him in the measurement of intelligence was not that the youngsters made mistakes, but the kind of mistakes that they made; the absurd error resulting from a lack of judgment tells much about the student.

Wechsler's Measures of Intelligence

Dissatisfied with previous attempts to measure *adult intelligence,* David Wechsler, a clinical psychologist at New York's Bellevue Hospital, left a lasting imprint on the nature and measurement of intelligence. As part of his hospital work, Wechsler needed some reliable means for identifying the truly subnormal in his examination of criminals, neurotics, and psychotics. The Binet scales, effective through the early teens, did not accurately assess adult intelligence.

Sympathetic to Binet's views of intelligence, Wechsler likewise considered intelligence a general capacity. He defined intelligence as the aggregate or global capacity of the individual to act purposefully, to think rationally, and to deal effectively with his environment (Wechsler, 1958), a definition that closely approximates Binet's reasoning.

Wechsler made a classic comparison of electricity and intelligence. We do not confuse the nature of electricity with our techniques for measuring it; exactly the same holds true for intelligence. General intelligence, like electricity, is a kind of energy. We do not fully understand its ultimate nature; we understand it by the things it does and enables us to do. According to Wechsler, electricity produces heat and magnetic fields in much the same way as intelligence produces associations, understandings, and problem solving abilities. Consequently, we know intelligence by what it enables us to do.

As we have noted, once a definition of intelligence is formulated, then a researcher can devise tests to meet those criteria. Wechsler first stated that intelligence is a global concept composed of interdependent elements, which led him to construct a test that best measured the various elements and that jointly gave a comprehensive view of intelligence.

After years of investigation, Wechsler reached the conclusion that intelligence tests measure a quantity that is far from simple. It cannot be expressed in a single figure (a general factor), since it includes more than just a single ability. Intelligence is the ability to utilize the previously mentioned energy in a context that has form, meaning, content, and purpose.

There are three forms of the Wechsler test, designed to measure the intelligence of human beings throughout the life span, beginning at the age of four. These are:

1. **The Wechsler Adult Intelligence Scale-Revised, WAIS-III,** which is a revised form of his first test, published in 1939, 1955, and 1980. It consists of eleven subtests, six comprising the verbal scale and five forming the performance scale. Consequently, there are three possible intelligence scores: *verbal, performance,* and *total IQ.* Many clinicians have found the separation into verbal and performance assessments to be particularly valuable for diagnostic purposes.

2. **The Wechsler Intelligence Scale for Children— III,** first appeared in 1949, was renormed in 1974, and again in 1991. It attempts to assess the intelligence of children from five to fifteen.

3. **The Wechsler Preschool and Primary Scale of Intelligence, WPPSI-R,** which is designed to measure the intelligence of children from four to six and one-half years of age.

Particularly significant in Wechsler's speculation (1958) is his firm belief that the definition of general intelligence, far from being merely interesting theorizing, is at the heart of the measurement of intelligence. Although a firm adherent of intelligence as a general capacity (as his definition shows), he stated that there are other important aspects of intelligence, such as *motivation and persistence at a task.* For example, individuals achieving precisely the same score on the same intelligence test defy identical classification. One youngster with a Binet IQ of 75 may require institutional care, while another child with the same IQ of 75 may function adequately in the home. Clearly, other elements such as behavior adaptation and persistence are significant in assessing intelligence.

The Wechsler and Binet scales were the forerunners of a movement that caught, and held, the attention of psychologists and educators for decades. Only gradually, as the claims of these test makers were weighed against growing insights into learning and development and concerns about racial bias, did doubts arise about their efficacy.

Problems in Measuring Intelligence

Measurement difficulties have plagued the testing movement from its inception. Intrigued by numbers, investigators have long felt that if it is possible to quantify a given concept, then the results must be precise and beyond challenge. Applying such a rationale to the measurement of intelligence—a concept that has staunchly resisted definition for over a century—has produced some insights, some moments of comic relief, but also much damage.

In a biting criticism, Gould (1981) noted that mental tests evolved from an hereditarian belief that an individual's head size was an excellent indication of intelligence. In the latter part of the nineteenth century, brain size was also thought to be directly related to intelligence, and Paul Broca's work was an outstanding example of efforts to measure cranial capacity. If at all possible, Broca attempted to remove the brain after autopsy and weigh it.

Interpreting his results, he carefully allowed for an increase in brain size with body size and a decrease with age and disease. Broca's data have rarely been questioned; his assumptions, however, are another story. White males, especially French white males, were assumed to be superior intellectually with brain size greater than any others. Embarrassing results almost immediately posed a challenge to these assumptions: Many eminent men were found to have quite small brains (Broca's brain later was discovered to be only slightly above normal; it is interesting to speculate how he would have explained this finding). Another embarrassment was that many criminals were found to have large brains.

Perhaps the most intriguing of his methods was the excavation of cemeteries to exhume bodies buried during different centuries. Broca hypothesized that brain size should increase as civilization progressed. His arduous efforts produced yet another embarrassment. Obtaining twelfth, eighteenth, and nineteenth century samples from Parisian cemeteries, Broca was initially chagrined to find the cranial capacities of the twelfth century sample to be larger than that of the eighteenth century. There was actually little difference among the three samples. Undaunted, Broca explained away his finding by that convenient variable: socio-economic status. The twelfth century sample was from a churchyard; therefore, its occupants must have been high on the social ladder. The eighteenth century sample was from a common grave; consequently the cranial capacity of its occupants was naturally smaller. So much for science.

Binet's Lost Legacy

Originally Binet followed Broca's methods, believing that skull measurement was the surest way to assess intelligence. But Binet was a scholar, not intent on forcing data to match assumptions, and he quickly dismissed Broca's techniques, turning to the scales just described.

If the followers of Binet had remained faithful to his rationale, considerable anguish would have been avoided. Binet never defined intelligence; he felt intelligence was too complex to be defined by a single number; he flatly refused to label individuals. Binet's intent was clear: to provide a means of identifying those Parisian students who needed help.

It was during the early decades of the twentieth century that Binet's objectives were subverted, that IQ scores were seen as an unchanging figure that precisely portrayed innate ability. *Individuals were labelled, and the IQ label was fixed forever*; heredity had become destiny. As concern grew about America's swelling immigration population and their supposed mental deficiency (unfortunately, language differences were rarely considered), Henry Goddard visited Ellis Island in 1912 armed with translations of Binet's scale, and as immigrants came ashore, Goddard and his colleagues visually inspected them and instantly identified those who might be defective and tested them on the spot. Needless to say, few if any, of the subjects did well; the vast majority were rated as "feeble-minded." The disregard for language and cultural differences was not an issue then but is a serious concern today. Tests must be nonbiased and used by well-trained professionals.

Similar results were obtained when group intelligence tests, based on the Binet scales, were given during World War I. The average mental age of white American males barely surpassed moronic—13 years. The results puzzled the test designers, but rather than admit that these tests were powerfully influenced by education and environment, they confessed uncertainty as to their true meaning.

In the never-ending heredity versus environment struggle (often referred to as the nature vs. nurture controversy), the test makers clearly sided with the hereditarians, an important realization for those attempting to link intelligence to learning: If an individual does poorly on a mental test, what does this suggest for learning ability? Today the answer to such a question would address the contributions of both heredity and environment to mental test performance. Thus, a low score on an aptitude test may not be a precise indication of poor education, poor motivation, or difficulty with specific topics (math, reading). Most likely it is the result of a combination of these and other causes.

Stability of the IQ

One of the most pervasive ideas about intelligence that has become entrenched in the minds of many is that infants are born with a certain amount of "intelligence," which does not change as the child grows. Misinterpreting research on the stability of performances on intelligence tests has fed this misconception. In general, most research has suggested that IQ tests tend to yield scores that are fairly stable (Elliott, Piersel, Witt, Argulewicz, Gutkin, & Galvin, 1985). However, this same research indicates that IQs are more stable over shorter as opposed to longer periods and more stable for older children and adults than for children under six years of age. There is a good deal of evidence to indicate that IQ scores obtained before children enter kindergarten or first grade are not highly reliable.

Data on the relative stability of IQ can be deceiving and must be interpreted with care. When looking at the IQ scores of large groups of individuals, we can make the general statement that most of those within the group would receive similar scores if retested. It is not unusual, however, for particular individuals to show a great deal of variability in their scores. Changes of 8, 10, 15, or even 30 IQ points are not unheard of results.

Bias in Cognitive Abilities Testing

No issue related to the assessment of cognitive abilities has generated as much heated debate as the question of whether IQ tests are biased against individuals from minority cultures. Though there is no universally accepted definition of bias, Brown and Campione (1986) stressed most definitions hold that a test can be considered biased if it differentiates between members of various groups on bases other than the characteristic being measured (p. 224). Discussions in the popular press have vehemently assailed most aptitude and achievement tests as being unfair to children from backgrounds different from those of most middle-class white Americans. Numerous researchers have investigated the issue of bias in mental tests, with the greatest amount of attention focused on the differences between the performance of blacks and whites (e.g., Jensen, 1981). Some have turned to the courts for help in determining whether IQ tests are biased and whether they should be used in the assessment of minority children. Courts, however, have not been consistent in their findings (Larry P. v. Riles, 1977; PASE v. Hannon, 1980).

The technical evidence overwhelmingly indicates that the vast majority of items used on tests like the WISC-R and Binet are not biased; these tests tend to measure the same factors (verbal, perceptual, performance, etc.), and predict success equally well for all racial groups (Reynolds & Kaiser, 1990). This last point is critical, for it is important to remember that IQ tests do *not* measure the amount of some innate, immutable ability that we all possess, but *provide a general measure of* expe*cted school achievement,* just as they were designed to do in the early 1900s. The predictive validity evidence suggests that race does not really matter. An individual with an IQ score of 60 from a reliable test is at risk of failing in almost every public educational system, and an individual with a score of 140 is likely to do well in that same system. It is worth repeating that these tests do not measure innate ability but attempt to predict school achievement.

Preschool Screening

Throughout this chapter, we have noted that the primary purpose of assessment is to determine if a problem exists and how it should be resolved. In other words, assessment stimulates and guides actions. Given that substantial numbers of young children are struggling and even failing in school, **preschool assessment** methods are needed to identify these children early and to establish intervention methods to improve their lives at school.

Many different sets of developmental categories or skills, such as perceptual processing, cognitive, language, speech/articulation, gross motor, fine motor, self-help, social-emotional, and school readiness are important targets of assessment (Lichtenstein & Ireton, 1984). Researchers have developed a variety of standardized tests, both multidimensional and unidimensional in nature, that can be used to assess skills and abilities of preschoolers. Though space does not allow us to describe such tests in detail, we have reprinted two useful tables from Witt et al. (1988) that document over fifty tests that have been designed to provide meaningful information about the functioning of young children at school and home. (See Tables 16.5 and 16.6.)

In theory, preschool screening should aim to recognize early problem warning signs to make a comprehensive assessment for identification and treatment. The utility of preschool screening, however, is influenced by several factors, including the provision of follow-up services, timing of screening, and involvement of parents. Before concluding this section, let's examine each of these factors briefly.

Provision of follow-up services. Implementation of a screening program without the provision of follow-up assessment and treatment services is an irresponsible policy and poor educational practice. We believe the development of preschool screening procedures should be concurrently coordinated with a comprehensive assessment and treatment program. In fact, the instructional objectives of a treatment program provide the primary basis for determining the content validity of assessment procedures.

Timing of screening. The issue of timing of screening has two components: (a) the age of the child and (b) the time of year when screening is done. A guiding principle in all assessment activities is that the more recent an assessment, the more accurately it predicts behavior. This is particularly true with preschoolers because within a few months, a child may demonstrate quantitative and qualitative advances in development across several domains. A corollary principle of preschool assessment is that identification must be made soon enough to permit early intervention, especially for sensory problems and "disadvantaged" children. Thus, the critical question becomes: At what age can reliable and valid measures of

skills and abilities that are relevant to successful performance in school first be obtained?

Generally, research indicates that by the ages of four or five, developmental gains in language, fine motor, and cognitive skills begin to stabilize and correlate significantly with school age measures of achievement. Earlier assessments, except in cases of severe handicaps, generally do not have substantial predictive validity. Thus, there exists a dilemma in wanting to intervene as early as possible but being limited by the reliability and validity of the assessment tools that exist for preschoolers.

Several schedules for preschool screening programs exist, including testing children (a) once in the spring or fall prior to school entry, (b) more than once during the years preceding school or kindergarten, or (c) once immediately before or during the first few weeks of kindergarten. Each of these schedules for testing has some advantages. In general, however, periodic, repeated assessments offer greater reliability and more information than a one-time annual approach.

Involvement of parents. Although parental involvement is the last topic discussed here, it is by no means the least important. Parents play a critical role in the assessment and treatment of young, at-risk or handicapped children. Also, as a result of recent amendments to the Public Law 94–142 (such as P.L. 99–457), working with parents is not only considered good educational practice, it is the law.

Entire books have been written to describe standardized tests. We have obviously provided you with only a sample of tests in our discussion of achievement, intelligence, and preschool tests. With this as background information, we turn now to the important topic of test interpretation.

Interpreting Standardized Test Scores

Let's assume that your students have recently taken a standardized achievement test, and a copy of the results are sent to you. You will receive several kinds of scores: raw scores, percentiles, grade equivalents, and standard scores. Since these scores are probably unfamiliar to most readers, this section will examine the meaning of the various scores and the uses to which they can be put.

If these results are to provide the best information possible, then you must have some means of telling

Table 16.5

Multidimensional Preschool Screening Instruments

Name of Instrument	Age Range	Administration Time	T = Test	P = Parent Record	E = Professional Examiner	Cognitive	Language	Speech	Fine Motor	Gross Motor	Self-Help	Social-Emotional	Reliability Data	Validity Data	Normative Data
ABC Inventory	3–6 to 6–6	10 min.	T			x			x				−	+	+
Brigance Diagnostic Inventory of Basic Skills	4–5 to 12–0	15 min.	T		E	x	x	x	x	x			−	−	−
Brigance Diagnostic Inventory of Early Development	0–1 to 6–0	30–45 min.	T	P	E	x	x	x	x	x	x		−	−	−
Comprehensive Identification Process	2–6 to 5–6	30 min.	T	P		x	x	x	x	x		x	−	−	−
Cooperative Preschool Inventory, Revised Edition	3–0 to 6–0	15–20 min.	T			x	x		x				+	+	+
Daberon: A Screening Device for School Readiness	4–0 to 6–0	20–40 min.	T			x	x		x	x			+	+	+
Dallas Preschool Screening Test	3–0 to 6–0	15 min.	T			x	x	x	x	x			+	+	+
Denver Developmental Screening Test	0–1 to 6–0	15–20 min.	T	P		x	x		x	x	x		+	+	+
Denver Prescreening Developmental Questionnaire	0–3 to 6–0	5 min.		P		x	x		x	x	x		−	+	+
Developmental Indicators for the Assessment of Learning (DIAL)	2–6 to 5–6	25–30 min.	T			x	x		x	x		x	+	+	+
Developmental Profile II (Developmental Profile)	0–0 to 9–0	30–40 min.		P		x	x		x	x	x	x	+	+	+
Developmental Tasks for Kindergarten Readiness	4–6 to 6–2	20–30 min.	T			x	x		x			x	+	+	+
Early Detection Inventory	3–6 to 7–6	15–30 min.	T	P		x	x	x	x	x		x	−	+	+
Early Screening Inventory (Eliot-Pearson Screening Inventory)	4–0 to 6–0	15 min.	T			x	x	x	x	x			+	+	+
Hannah-Gardner Test of Verbal and Nonverbal Language Functioning	3–6 to 5–6	25–35 min.	T			x	x	x					+	+	+
Kaufman Infant and Preschool Scale	0–1 to 4–0	25–30 min.	T	P		x	x						−	−	+
Kindergarten Questionnaire	4–0 to 6–0	20–30 min.	T	P		x	x		x	x		x	−	+	−
Lexington Developmental Scale, Short Form	0–3 to 6–0	30–45 min.	T			x	x		x	x		x	+	+	−
Lollipop Test: A Diagnostic Screening Test of School Readiness	4–0 to 6–0	15–20 min.	T		E	x	x		x				+	+	+
McCarthy Screening Test	4–0 to 6–5	20 min.	T			x	x		x	x			+	+	+
Minneapolis Preschool Screening Instrument	3–7 to 5–4	10–15 min.	T			x	x	x	x	x			+	+	+
Minnesota Preschool Inventory	4–8 to 5–7	15 min.		P		x	x	x	x	x	x	x	−	+	+
Preschool Attainment Record, Research Edition	0–6 to 7–0	20–30 min.		P	E	x	x		x	x	x	x	−	−	−
Preschool Screening Instrument	4–0 to 5–0	5–10 min.	T	P		x	x		x	x			+	+	−
Preschool Screening System (PSS Field Trial Edition)	2–6 to 5–9	15–20 min.	T	P		x	x		x	x	x		+	+	+
Riley Preschool Developmental Screening Inventory	3–0 to 6–0	5–10 min.	T			x			x				−	−	+
School Readiness Checklist—Ready or Not?	4–0 to 7–0	10–15 min.		P		x	x		x	x	x	x	−	+	+
School Readiness Survey	4–0 to 6–0	25–35 min.	T	P		x	x						+	+	+
Slosson Intelligence Test	0–1 to adult	10–20 min.	T			x	x						−	+	+

Table 16.6

Selected Unidimensional Preschool Screening Measures

Name of Instrument	Age Range	Administration Time	T = Test	P = Parent Record	E = Professional Examiner	Reliability Data	Validity Data	Normative Data
Language and Vocabulary Measures								
Assessment of Children's Language Comprehension[a]	3-0 to 6-6	10-20 min.	T		E	-	-	+
Bankson Language Screening Test[c]	4-1 to 8-0	25 min.	T			+	+	+
Del Rio Language Screening Test[c]	3-0 to 6-11		T			-	+	+
Peabody Picture Vocabulary Test—Revised[a]	2-6 to adult	10-20 min.	T		E	+	+	+
Pictorial Test of Bilingualism and Language Development[b]	4-0 to 8-0	15 min.	T			+	+	-
Preschool Language Assessment Instrument[c]	3-0 to 6-0	20 min.	T			+	-	+
Screening Test for Auditory Comprehension of Language[a]	3-0 to 6-0	5-10 min.	T		E	+	-	+
Test of Early Language Development[c]	3-0 to 7-11	15-20 min.	T			+	+	+
Verbal Language Development Scale[c]	0-1 to 16-0	20 min.		P	E	+	+	-
Social-Emotional Measures								
Burks' Behavior Rating Scales: Preschool and Kindergarten	3-0 to 6-11	10 min.		P	E	+	-	-
Child Behavior Rating Scale	4-0 to 9-0	10 min.		P		+	+	+
Children's Self-Social Construct Tests: Preschool Form	3-6 to 10-0	10-15 min.	T			-	-	-
Joseph Preschool and Primary Self Concept Screening Test	3-6 to 9-11	5-7 min.	T			+	+	+
Speech/Articulation Measures								
Denver Articulation Screening Test	2-6 to 7-0	5 min.	T			+	+	+
Photo Articulation	3-0 to 12-0	5 min.	T		E	+	+	+
Perceptual-Motor Measures								
Developmental Test of Visual-Motor Integration	2-0 to 15-0	5-10 min.	T			+	+	+
Riley Motor Problems Inventory	4-0 to 9-0	10 min.	T		E	+	+	-
Tree/Bee Test of Auditory Discrimination	3-0 to adult	10-15 min.	T			+	+	+
Observational Instruments for Classroom Use								
Basic School Skills Inventory—Screen	4-0 to 6-11	5-10 min.				+	+	+
Preschool Behavior Rating Scale	3-0 to 5-11	5-10 min.				+	+	+
Classroom Behavior Inventory, Preschool Form	2-0 to 6-0	10-15 min.				-	+	-

From *Preschool Screening: Identifying Young Children with Developmental and Educational Problems* (pp. 132–136, 138–139) by Robert Lichtenstein and Harry Ireton, 1984. Copyright © 1984 Grune & Stratton, Inc., Orlando, FL.

[a] Measures receptive language only.

[b] Measures expressive language only.

[c] Measures both expressive and receptive language.

whether a score is good or poor. You usually can't do this by looking at the raw score (the number of correct items on each of the subtests), although these give some information as we shall see. Raw scores are converted into derived scores, which are more meaningful and tell you more about a student's performance.

Kinds of Scores

Raw scores. **Raw scores** may be difficult to interpret. If an arithmetic test contains 50 items and a student scores 32, that student's raw score is 32. What does this tell you? You probably think immediately that at least this student knew more than half the answers. But how did the other students do? You don't know. Was it an easy or difficult test? You don't know unless you can compare scores. To help you make sense of your students' raw scores, *you could rank them from highest to lowest.* This ranking enables you to interpret a score in relationship to other scores.

Another possibility is to assume that the score of 32 is the average raw score for the group taking this test. These are fifth-grade students. The month is September. Thus 32 is the **grade equivalent** score of 5.0 for that test. Don't assume that a student who has a grade equivalent score of 7.2 on this test should be working at a seventh grade level. It means that this student's performance on fifth grade material is equal to the performance of a student in the second month of the seventh grade on fifth grade material (Bloom, Madaus, & Hastings, 1981). The score tells you that your fifth-grade student knows this subject thoroughly. It does not say that this same student has mastered seventh grade or even sixth grade material. These scores seem easy to interpret, but they are just as easily and often misinterpreted. Of greater interpretative value are derived standard scores, which we'll examine shortly.

Percentiles and measures of central tendency. You are probably comfortable with a scoring system that assigns the highest score a rank of one, the second highest two, and the like. **Percentiles** are similar to this except that the lowest percentile rank appears at the bottom of the scores. For example, a percentile rank of 74 means that this student did as well as or better than 74 percent of the other students. If the student's raw score mentioned earlier—32—placed that student 40th from the bottom in a class of 50, the percentile rank would be:

$$\frac{40}{50} \times 100 = 80$$

Table 16.7

A Typical Frequency Distribution

Scores	Frequency
21	2
20	1
19	6
18	10
17	20
16	19
15	16
14	22
13	5
12	27
11	36
10	27

This student is at the 80th percentile: He/she did as well as or better than 80 percent of the students. Be careful how you use this score with parents who may interpret it as a score of 80.

Working with many numbers is cumbersome, time-consuming, and prone to misinterpretation. Consequently, we should search for techniques to organize our data. A good way to begin is with a **frequency distribution.**

You often want to organize and summarize data. The first step usually entails constructing a frequency distribution, which tells us the frequency with which a particular score appears in a score category. To prepare a frequency distribution, the scores typically are grouped by intervals, and each test score is assigned to the proper interval. Table 16.7 illustrates this procedure in which the scores range from a low of 10 to a high of 21 and the number of individuals achieving each score is provided—the frequency column.

Now that we have grouped our data, we want to use the groupings. A basic way of describing the scores is to give the average score. Are you of average height? Although most people understand the meaning of average, there are three measures of central tendency (average): mode, median, mean.

The **mode** is that score obtained by the largest number of students. Once you have finished a frequency distribution, you can determine the mode simply by looking at the frequency column. In Table 16.7 the mode is 11, which 36 individuals earned.

The **median** is that point in the distribution above which and below which exactly 50 percent of the cases lie. In Table 16.7 look up the frequency column until you find half the scores accounted for. What is the median score? (Answer 13.5.)

The **mean** is the average of the raw scores; add all the scores and divide by the number of scores. The formula for calculating the mean is:

$$\overline{X} = \frac{\Sigma X}{N}$$

where $\overline{X}$ is the mean score, Σ is the sum of all the scores, and N is the total number of scores. Table 16.8 illustrates the process with a sample data set.

These measures of central tendency give a good idea of how any student did in relation to the average score of the group. When the distribution of scores is normally distributed, all three measures of central tendency are equal. When the distribution of scores is skewed or unbalanced (for example, if there are two or three very high scores and the remainder in a typical class are much lower), then the median is a more representative score than the mean.

Standard scores. To further our understanding of any score we need some method that will provide constancy, that is, a score not affected by the length of the test or the difficulty of the items. Glasnapp and Poggio (1985) define standard as constancy across different times and situations. Standard scores do this for us; they offer a constant definition and interpretation. How is this possible? Standard scores relate to the normal curve, a theoretical mathematical model based on the assumption that most human characteristics are distributed normally. So the normal curve is a representation showing the normal distribution of a particular trait. Figure 16.1 illustrates the normal curve.

Look at the baseline of the normal curve. You see a series of numbers ranging from +1 to +3, –1 to –3. These are **standard deviation units,** which tell us how much a score varies from the mean. Look again at Figure 16.1 and note that +1 and –1 standard deviation units from the mean will include about 68 percent of the scores; +2 and –2 standard deviation units will include 95 percent of the

Table 16.8

Calculating the Mean

9
4
4
3
3
3
1
9
7
7
50

Using the formula for the mean:

$$\Sigma\,\frac{X}{N} = \overline{X}$$

$$\text{then } \overline{X} = \Sigma\,\frac{X}{N} = \frac{50}{10} = 5$$

scores. Once the mean and standard deviation are computed, we can use them to derive several standard scores: Z scores, T scores, and stanine scores.

Z scores are the fundamental standard scores, which tell us the distance of a student's raw score from the mean in standard deviation units. Here is an example: raw score on a reading test—78, mean—72, standard deviation—24, raw score minus the mean—6, divided by a standard deviation of 24 = +.25. This student has a Z score of +.25, informing us that the raw score was a little above average (1/4 of a standard deviation unit). Thus by looking at a Z score, you can quickly tell how a student has done on a test and can compare students across classes.

T scores offer an alternative method of computing standard scores that avoid negative Z scores and decimals. T scores are computed by multiplying the standard score by 10 and adding 50. Let's take a Z score of –1.5. The result would be: 10 x (–1.5) + 50 = 35.

Stanine scores (a word derived from standard nine) were devised during World War II to classify pilots as quickly as possible. Those taking the tests would be classified into one of nine groups. A stanine has a mean of 5 and a standard deviation of 2. Stanine 5 includes the

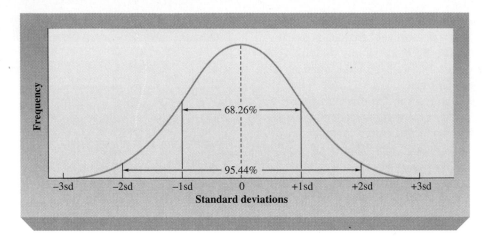

Figure 16.1
The normal curve.

"I thought there was supposed to be safety in numbers."

© James Warren. Reprinted by permission.

middle 20 percent of the scores. The ideal percentage for each stanine is as follows (Lyman, 1986):

Lowest	Next	Next	Next	Middle	Next	Next	Next	Highest
4%	7%	12%	17%	20%	17%	12%	7%	4%
Stanine 1	2	3	4	5	6	7	8	9

As you can see, it is a quick means of classification and is easily understood. If you tell parents that their child is in the ninth stanine, with nine as the highest, they can readily grasp the meaning. Figure 16.2 illustrates how these various scores relate to each other.

Let's assume that one of your students has a raw score of 300 on a particular test and the mean for the test is also 300. This can be transformed into a percentile rank of 50, a Z score of 0.00, a T score of 50, and a stanine of 5. You would do well to familiarize yourself with these scores since almost all standardized tests use one or more of them.

Using Standardized Tests

A major concern about standardized tests should be how to obtain the most helpful information from them to aid your students. One way of accomplishing this is to compare the results with the learning objectives of your school or classroom. Understanding the potential uses of test results is a major step in actively applying their results to your classroom.

We have previously seen how standardized tests such as the Scholastic Aptitude Test are used to form opinions about the state of education. Currently, the SAT is being revised to include longer reading passages, vocabulary testing in the context of reading, interpretation of mathematical data, and the opportunity to work out mathematical problems rather than select options from a multiple choice format among other changes (Moses, 1991b). Yet, standardized tests themselves have changed very little in spite of widespread usage, continuing controversy about usage and interpretation, advances in statistical techniques, and improved test construction (Linn, 1986).

Educational Applications of Standardized Testing

Other forces, such as institutional concerns about efficiency, tracking, and selection have been mainly responsible for the popularity of standardized tests. One of the more prominent influences on the acceptance of standardized

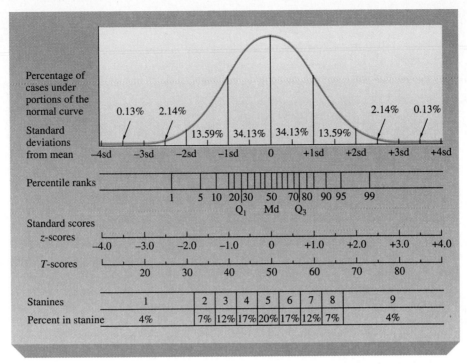

Figure 16.2
Relationship among standardized test scores.

tests has been their educational application. Five major uses have been identified (Linn, 1986).

1. *Special education placement.* Tests that predict academic achievement (IQ tests) have played central roles in the decision making about student placement. Though many questions have been raised about this policy, particular concern has been expressed about the large number of minorities in special education classes. Do these tests lead to bias in decision making about minorities? Recent court decisions have both affirmed (Larry P. v. Riles, 1980) and denied (PASE v. Hannon, 1980) that IQ tests are biased, which still leaves the question unanswered.

2. *Student certification.* When students received a high school diploma it was a signal that, based on teacher grades and the satisfaction of course requirements, the school testified to their ability to perform adequately at a satisfactory level. Now, more and more states are turning to **Minimum Competency Tests** to provide evidence for certification. We shall discuss these tests in greater detail, but here our interest lies in their ability to furnish convincing evidence concerning a student's minimal satisfactory performance. Although student scores in those states using minimum competency tests (MCTs) have risen

rather dramatically, several questions remain: Would other tests of the same content produce the same results? Have thinking skills improved similarly? Are teachers teaching for the test?

3. *Teacher testing.* Recently, national concern has been expressed over teacher competency, not only with regard to initial certification but also for continued employment. Heated political debates have emerged in the wake of questions about teacher competency, which are not our concern here. Our interest focuses on the means used to judge instructional ability: Should the means be a national test, or the judgment of others? In both instances, the key requirement must be that the knowledge and skills assessed are actually those required for competent job performance.

4. *Educational assessment.* This idea—making decisions about schools based on testing students— is far from new. Comparing students from a particular school to national norms traditionally has appealed to many educators. Though student scores may seem a fragile foundation on which to make judgments, sophisticated item analysis techniques have greatly enhanced and lent support to such a use of test scores.

As students get older, they often take tests that help them identify vocational or career interests.

5. *Instructional guidance.* As testing technology has improved, standardized tests have more frequently been used as diagnostic guides. When a combination of tests providing more detailed information are enriched with insights derived from cognitive psychology (see chapter 7), sharper diagnostic distinctions are possible.

Multicultural Students and Standardized Testing

We previously have commented on the importance of style for both teaching and learning. Cognitive style is thought to be rooted at a deep structural level and influences the way in which we organize and use the environment (Hilliard, 1983). Cognitive style, in turn, leads to expectations, and if teachers are unaware of the significance of style to learning, educational outcomes—as measured by tests—can be negatively affected. What does cognitive style, especially those of multicultural students, have to do with standardized testing? Our concern is with the response of these students to such tests.

Probably no one has more thoughtfully considered how multicultural students react to standardized testing than Anastasi (1982). Noting that cultural conditions may produce low scores, she states that test results can have a negative influence on motivation, interests, and attitudes.

Distinguishing between cultural factors that can affect test performance and test elements that also influence test results, Anastasi states that it is the test-related elements that reduce validity. Among these elements are:

- previous testing experience;
- motivation to do well on a particular type of test;
- rapport with the examiner.

Every effort should be made with all students, especially minority students, to familiarize them with the test-taking procedures previously described and those that appear throughout this chapter.

Cultural context also must be taken into consideration. If a test uses names or pictures unfamiliar to a student, or the portrayal of an affluent middle-class family, or the representation of a single racial type, they may have adverse effects on a student. Students benefit from the evaluations of those who have common ground with them (Rogoff, 1990). Most test publishers are working diligently to consider minority implications as they construct their tests.

The interpretation and use of standardized test scores—a major consideration in this chapter—need sensitive attention for minority students (Jones, 1988). If a student's scores are quite low, we should investigate why this happened. Does it reflect what was just mentioned: motivation, reading ability, or lack of familiarity with test-taking?

But our discussion should not be all negative. Standardized tests can be a safeguard against racism or favoritism. The tests can't see color or hear language. Also, if a disproportionate number of a minority group do poorly, a clear warning flag is raised, and steps must be taken to improve conditions contributing to these scores. As Anastasi noted (1982, p. 62) affirmative action implies that an organization does more than merely avoid discriminating practices.

Common Criticisms of Standardized Tests

Though we have emphasized the positive aspects of these tests, standardized testing has had its share of criticism. The most common criticisms of standardized tests come from classroom teachers. These criticisms seem to focus on the pressure that tests exert on the curriculum, the danger of labeling students, and the accompanying side effects of worry and anxiety. Criticisms of standardized tests in the classroom can be summarized by eight statements (Kellaghan, Madaus, & Airasian, 1980).

1. *Testing limits teaching,* in the sense that instructors teach for the test, thus restricting students' experiences.
2. *Testing produces rigid grouping practices.* Students are assessed, and the resulting label causes an inflexible classification.
3. *Testing lowers student achievement.* Testing takes time from instruction, especially if time is taken to practice for the test. Some teachers also have a tendency to concentrate on bright students since their scores appear easier to raise.
4. *Tests lead to labeling students.* This common danger can easily influence teacher expectations and leads also to the difficulties posed in statement #2.
5. *Testing arouses negative emotional feelings.* We have commented frequently on such test accompaniments as fear, anxiety, and competitiveness for some students.

6. *Testing may negatively affect a student's self-concept.* Given the reality of students who "freeze" during testing, test results may not reflect actual ability. Yet students will believe "the score," causing lowered self-esteem with all its attendant consequences.
7. *Test scores do not directly influence teaching.* Test scores provide little relevant information about individual students, only how they relate to other similar students. We have mentioned this previously when noting the efforts of test publishers to provide more penetrating diagnostic tools.
8. *Tests often do not measure what was taught.* This statement, which is a common criticism by teachers, reinforces criticism #1 since teachers frequently feel compelled to teach for the test.

Given the advantages and disadvantages of standardized tests that we have reviewed in this chapter, it is now time to focus on the resulting "best practices." We believe that standardized tests have a significant role in educational psychology and effective teaching. Like most anything else, however, one must be cautious and use good judgment to achieve maximum results from the use of standardized tests.

Best Practices

Standardized tests have generated concerns for many educators. We, believe, however, that many of the concerns are the result of poor testing practices or misunderstanding of the purposes and that standardized tests will continue to have a central place in our students' education. Recognizing this, a joint committee on testing practices from major educational and psychological associations developed the *Code of Fair Testing Practices in Education* (1988). The Code contains standards for educational test developers and users in four categories: developing/selecting tests, interpreting scores, striving for fairness, and informing test takers.

The Code is meant for the general public and is limited to educational tests. It supplements the more technical *Standards for Educational and Psychological Testing* (AERA, APA, NCME, 1985). We have reprinted the four sections of the Code in their entirety in an appendix to this chapter. This code serves as an appropriate conclusion to this chapter on standardized testing, for it reminds us that tests affect everybody (developers, users, and students) and that their use requires significant knowledge and skill on the part of educators.

TEACHER ⟷ STUDENT
INTERACTIONS

Communicating Test Results

1. Your first concern is with the kinds of people who have a right to receive test information. As mentioned previously, the Buckley amendment (The Family Education Rights and Privacy Act of 1975) provides that adult students and the parents of minors have access to test results. Your school may also have its own policy with regard to those who have access to test results, who can release test scores, and who can interpret scores to students and parents. You may find these suggestions helpful in discussing test results.

- Try to link the test score to an educational objective such as improving reading skills or class placement.

- Know what you're talking about. What do the scores mean? How do they relate to the school? the class? a particular student?

- If you're discussing test results with parents, try to establish a comfortable basis for your talk; tie it specifically to improving their child's achievement.

- Be careful what you say; choose your words carefully. Explain results in terms that others can understand. We have mentioned how easy it is to misunderstand a score if you don't describe it precisely yet simply.

- If you think it's called for, explain what the score means in relation to others who took the test—the norm group.

- You could ask parents how they think their child is doing and then link their answer to test results to show that the student should be doing better, or is currently doing well.

- If you tell parents, or a student, about a low score, you need considerable sensitivity. Try something like this.

This grade is low and could keep you from being promoted. But I think if you work hard, you still have time to bring it up.

2. One way of helping your students to do well is to be sure that they are prepared to take the test, specifically a standardized test. By combining many of the features that we have discussed, you can devise a quick checklist that helps your students prepare for the test. Ask yourself:

"Did I remind them . . .

Yes   No

1. to get a good night's sleep.
2. to be careful of what they eat.
3. to be on time.
4. to listen to directions.
5. to be sure they understand the directions.
6. to ask questions if the directions are unclear.
7. to plan their time.
8. to "psych" themselves: I can do well.
9. that there will be different types of questions.
10. to look at the test materials immediately.
11. to skip a difficult item and return to it later.
12. to use the test-taking strategies that were taught in class.
13. to be sure that the item number and answer number match.
14. not to rush but pace themselves.
15. to go back and complete unanswered questions if time permits.

Conclusion

In this chapter many standardized tests used most frequently in schools were described. But most importantly, suggestions were made regarding the interpretation and use of standardized test scores.

When you are presented with an array of test results, you must be able to understand what those scores mean. Only then can you use them appropriately in planning for instruction and altering the curriculum in the best interests of a particular student.

Test results do not remain hidden, however. They are communicated with others: students (if appropriate), parents, administrators, and colleagues (other teachers working with a student, counselors, special teachers). To communicate results meaningfully, you have to be able to tell others what the score signifies with regard to student standing, comparison with others, and future plans for a student.

You may be called upon to help in selecting standardized tests for your school. You certainly will be called upon to interpret and use the test scores of your students. The basic rule to remember—regardless of the type of test—is to use test scores in a manner calculated to improve instruction and learning.

Although the place and function of standardized testing on the national scene has raised questions, it seems some standardized tests are likely to be used to assess students' achievement and other types of behavior. Consequently, knowledge of their strengths and weaknesses and professional best practices is an essential of good teaching.

Chapter Highlights

A School's Testing Program

- The use of standardized tests is an integral part of the educational purposes of the entire school system and should serve the needs of its students at all levels.
- A well-designed standardized testing program serves three purposes: instructional, guidance, and administrative.
- The value of standardized tests lies in their consistency or sameness that provides a means of comparing students.
- The norms that accompany standardized tests enable teachers, counselors, and educators to interpret test scores by comparing them to the scores of other students taken from a national sample.
- A norm-referenced test enables you to compare a student with a representative group of students who have already taken the test.
- A criterion-referenced test enables you to determine if a student has achieved competence at one level of knowledge or skills before moving on to the next higher level of content.

Types of Standardized Tests

- Standardized achievement tests are designed to assess the knowledge and skills taught by the schools. The value of these tests is in their assessment of the development of individual learners at different ages and in different subjects.
- Standardized aptitude tests are used to predict what a student can learn; they are an assessment of performance based on learning abilities.
- Although any clear definition of intelligence has remained elusive, attempts to measure it have produced some of psychology's most colorful, damaging, and useful insights into human behavior.
- Given the problems that have been encountered in attempts to measure intelligence, several reasonable suggestions have been made as to fruitful uses of the results of intelligence testing:
- Properly interpreted, these scores can help teachers to improve their instruction;
- They are a good guide for initial efforts at grouping your students;
- Several of these tests can be used to identify students' needs;
- Teachers can use test results to monitor school progress: are these students doing as well as possible given what you know about their abilities?

Interpreting Standardized Test Scores

- To utilize the results of standardized testing as fully as possible, you must have some means of interpreting students' scores.
- Several meaningful techniques are available that can help you to analyze scores and organize data so that the results of testing can be applied to your classroom work. These include standard scores, percentile ranks, and knowledge of the normal distribution.

Using Standardized Tests

- The possible uses of standardized tests include instructional assistance, certification purposes, special education placement, the testing of teachers, and assessing the success of a school.
- Many warnings have appeared about the potential negative effects of standardized testing on multicultural students (language, previous testing experience, maturation). Standardized tests, however, are not necessarily a negative experience for these students; they can be a safeguard against racism or favoritism.
- Standards as a guide to the best practices in test construction have been proposed for test developers.

Key Terms

Achievement test
Aptitude test
Assessment
Frequency distribution
Mean
Median
Minimum competency tests
Mode
Multilevel survey batteries
Norms
Percentile score
Preschool assessment
Raw score
Standard deviation units
Standardized tests
Standard scores
Stanford-Binet
Stanine scores
T scores
WAIS-III (the Wechsler Adult Intelligence Scale III)
WISC-III (the Wechsler Intelligence Scale for Children III)
WPPSI-R (the Wechsler Preschool and Primary Scale of Intelligence-Revised)
Z scores

Suggested Readings

Gould, S. (1980). *The mismeasure of man.* Cambridge, MA: Harvard. A witty, devastating account of how intelligence tests have been misused and the mischief that has resulted.

Linn, R. (1986). Educational testing and assessment. *American Psychologist, 41,* 1153–1160. This fine article presents the pros and cons of recent measurement strategies. It is easy to read and valuable.

Lyman, H. (1986). *Test scores and what they mean.* Englewood Cliffs, NJ: Prentice-Hall. It is simply not enough to obtain test scores; they must be interpreted and used. Lyman's brief work is a valuable tool for using test scores to improve student performance and for helping you to improve your teaching.

The Code of Fair Testing Practices in Education

Prepared by the Joint Committee on Testing Practices

The Code of Fair Testing Practices in Education states the major obligations to test takers and professionals who develop or use educational tests. The Code is meant to apply broadly to the use of tests in education (admissions, educational assessment, education diagnosis, and student placement). The Code is not designed to cover employment testing, licensure or certification testing, or other types of testing. Although the Code has relevance to many types of educational tests, it is directed primarily at professionally developed tests such as those sold by commercial test publishers or used in formally administered testing programs. The Code is not intended to cover tests made by individual teachers for use in their own classrooms.

The Code addresses the roles of test developers and test users separately. Test users are people who select tests, commission test development services, or make decisions on the basis of test scores. Test developers are people who actually construct tests as well as those who set policies for particular testing programs. The roles may, of course, overlap as when a state education agency commissions test development services, sets policies that control the test development process, and makes decisions on the basis of the test scores.

The Code presents standards for educational test developers and users in four areas:

A. Developing/Selecting Tests
B. Interpreting Scores
C. Striving for Fairness
D. Informing Test Takers

The Code has been developed by the Joint Committee on Testing Practices, a cooperative effort of several professional organizations, that has as its aim the advancement, in the public interest, of the quality of testing practices. The Joint Committee was initiated by the American Educational Research Association, the American Psychological Association, and the National Council on Measurement in Education. In addition to these three groups, the American Association for Counseling and Development/Association for Measurement and Evaluation in Counseling and Development, and the American Speech-Language-Hearing Association are now also sponsors of the Joint Committee. This is not copyrighted material. Reproduction and dissemination are encouraged. Please cite this document as follows:
Code of Fair Testing Practices in Education. (1988) Washington, D.C.: Joint Committee on Testing Practices.
(Mailing Address: Joint Committee on Testing Practices, American Psychological Association, 1200 17th Street, NW, Washington, D.C. 20036.)

Organizations, institutions, and individual professionals who endorse the Code commit themselves to safeguarding the rights of test takers by following the principles listed. The Code is intended to be consistent with the relevant parts of the *Standards for Educational and Psychological Testing* (AERA, APA, NCME, 1985). However, the Code differs from the Standards in both audience and purpose. The Code is meant to be understood by the general public; it is limited to educational tests; and the primary focus is on those issues that affect the proper use of tests. The Code is not meant to add new principles over and above those in the Standards or to change the meaning of the Standards. The goal is rather to represent the spirit of a selected portion of the Standards in a way that is meaningful to test takers and/or their parents or guardians. It is the hope of the Joint Committee that the Code will also be judged to be consistent with existing codes of conduct and standards of other professional groups who use education tests.

A Developing/Selecting Appropriate Tests*

Test developers should provide the information that test users need to select appropriate tests.

Test Developers Should:

1. Define what each test measures and what the test should be used for. Describe the population(s) for which the test is appropriate.
2. Accurately represent the characteristics, usefulness, and limitations of tests for their intended purposes.
3. Explain relevant measurement concepts as necessary for clarity at the level of detail that is appropriate for the intended audience(s).
4. Describe the process of test development. Explain how the content and skills to be tested were selected.
5. Provide evidence that the test meets its intended purpose(s).
6. Provide either representative samples or complete copies of test questions, answer sheets, manuals, and score reports to qualified users.

---

*Many of the statements in the Code refer to the selection of existing tests. However, in customized testing programs test developers are engaged to construct new tests. In those situations, the test development process should be designed to help ensure that the completed tests will be in compliance with the Code.

7. Indicate the nature of the evidence obtained concerning the appropriateness of each test for groups of different racial, ethnic, or linguistic backgrounds who are likely to be tested.
8. Identify and publish any specialized skills needed to administer each test and to interpret scores correctly.

Test users should select tests that meet the purpose for which they are to be used and that are appropriate for the intended test-taking populations.

Test Users Should:

1. First define the purpose for testing and the population to be tested. Then, select a test for that purpose and that population based on a thorough review of the available information.
2. Investigate potentially useful sources of information, in addition to test scores, to corroborate the information provided by tests.
3. Read the materials provided by test developers and avoid using tests for which unclear or incomplete information is provided.
4. Become familiar with how and when the test was developed and tried out.
5. Read independent evaluations of a test and of possible alternative measures. Look for evidence required to support the claims of test developers.
6. Examine specimen sets, disclosed tests or samples of questions, directions, answer sheets, manuals, and score reports before selecting a test.
7. Ascertain whether the test content and norms group(s) or comparison group(s) are appropriate for the intended test takers.
8. Select and use only those tests for which the skills needed to administer the test and interpret scores correctly are available.

B Interpreting Scores

Test developers should help users interpret scores correctly.

Test Developers Should:

9. Provide timely and easily understood score reports that describe test performance clearly and accurately. Also explain the meaning and limitations of reported scores.

10. Describe the population(s) represented by any norms or comparison group(s), the dates the data were gathered, and the process used to select the samples of test takers.
11. Warn users to avoid specific, reasonably anticipated misuses of test scores.
12. Provide information that will help users follow reasonable procedures for setting passing scores when it is appropriate to use such scores with the test.
13. Provide information that will help users gather evidence to show that the test is meeting its intended purpose(s).

Test users should interpret scores correctly.

Test Users Should:

9. Obtain information about the scale used for reporting scores, the characteristics of any norms or comparison group(s), and the limitations of the scores.
10. Interpret scores taking into account any major differences between the norms or comparison groups and the actual test takers. Also take into account any differences in test administration practices or familiarity with the specific questions in the test.
11. Avoid using tests for purposes not specifically recommended by the test developer unless evidence is obtained to support the intended use.
12. Explain how any passing scores were set and gather evidence to support the appropriateness of the scores.
13. Obtain evidence to help show that the test is meeting its intended purpose(s).

C Striving for Fairness

Test developers should strive to make tests that are as fair as possible for test takers of different races, gender, ethnic backgrounds, or handicapping conditions.

Test Developers Should:

14. Review and revise test questions and related materials to avoid potentially insensitive content or language.
15. Investigate the performance of test takers of different races, gender, and ethnic backgrounds

when samples of sufficient size are available. Enact procedures that help to ensure that differences in performance are related primarily to the skills under assessment rather than to irrelevant factors.

16. When feasible, make appropriately modified forms of tests or administration procedures available for test takers with handicapping conditions. Warn test users of potential problems in using standard norms with modified tests or administration procedures that result in non-comparable scores.

Test users should select tests that have been developed in ways that attempt to make them as fair as possible for test takers of different races, gender, ethnic backgrounds, or handicapping conditions.

Test Users Should:

14. Evaluate the procedures used by test developers to avoid potentially insensitive content or language.

15. Review the performance of test takers of different races, gender, and ethnic backgrounds when samples of sufficient size are available. Evaluate the extent to which performance differences may have been caused by inappropriate characteristics of the test.

16. When necessary and feasible, use appropriately modified forms of tests or administration procedures for test takers with handicapping conditions. Interpret standard norms with care in the light of the modifications that were made.

Bibliography

A

A nation at risk. (1983). Arlington, VA: American Association of School Administrators.

A nation prepared. (1986). New York: Carnegie Corporation.

Ada, A. (1986). Creative education for bilingual teachers. *Harvard Educational Review, 56,* 386-394.

Adams, J. (1986). *Conceptual blockbusting.* San Francisco: Freeman.

Adams, M. J. (1990). *Beginning to read: Thinking and learning about print.* Cambridge, MA: MIT Press.

Adler, M. (1982). *The Paideia proposal.* New York: Macmillan.

Ainsworth, M. (1973). The development of infant-mother attachment. In Bettye Caldwell and Henry Ricciuti (Eds.), *Review of Child Development Research.* Chicago: U. of Chicago Press.

Ainsworth, M. (1979). Infant-mother attachment. *American Psychologist, 34,* 932-937.

Airasian, P. (1988). *Educational testing in public policy.* Talk given at the U. of Chicago. "The Individual, the Environment, and Education." A Conference in honor of Benjamin Bloom.

Airasian, P. W. (1991). *Classroom assessment.* New York: McGraw Hill, Inc.

Alberto, P., & Troutman, A. (1986). *Applied behavioral analysis for teachers.* Columbus, Ohio: Merrill.

Alderman, M. K. (1990, September). Motivation for at-risk students. *Educational Leadership,* 27-30.

Altwerger, B., Edelsky, C., & Flores, B. (1987). Whole language: What's new? *Reading Teacher, 41,* 144-154.

Ames, C. (1984). Competitive, cooperative, and individualistic goal structures: A cognitive-motivational analysis. In R. Ames and C. Ames (Eds.), *Research on Motivation in Education: Vol. 1. Student Motivation* (pp. 177-207). San Diego, CA: Academic Press.

Ames, C., & Ames, R. (Eds.). (1985). *Research on motivation in education: Vol. 2. The classroom milieu.* San Diego, CA: Academic Press.

Ames, C., & Ames, R. (Eds.). (1989). *Research on motivation in education: Vol. 3. Goals and cognitions.* San Diego, CA: Academic Press.

Ames, R. (1983). Teachers' attributions for their own teaching. In J. Levine and M. Wang (Eds.), *Teacher and Student Perceptions: Implications for Learning.* Hillsdale, NJ: Erlbaum.

Anastasi, A. (1982). *Psychological testing.* New York: Macmillan.

Anderson, B. (1982). Test use today in elementary and secondary schools. In A. Wigdor & W. Garner (Eds.), *Ability Testing.* Washington, DC: National Academy Press.

Anderson, J. (1985). *Cognitive psychology and its implications.* San Francisco: W.H. Freeman.

Anderson, J. R., & Bower, G. (1983). *Human associative memory.* Washington, DC: Winston.

Anderson, L. W., & Burns, R. B. (1989). *Research in classrooms: The study of teachers, teaching, and instruction.* New York: Pergamon.

Anderson, L. W., & Pellicer, L. O. (1990). Synthesis of research on compensatory and remedial education. *Educational Leadership, 10.*

Anglin, J. M. (1973). *Beyond the information given.* New York: Norton.

Annis, L. (1978). *The child before birth.* New York: Cornell U. Press.

Anselmo, S. (1987). *Early childhood development.* Columbus, Ohio: Merrill.

Archbald, D. A., & Newmann, F. M. (1988). Beyond standardized testing: Assessing authentic academic achievement in the secondary school. Reston, VA: National Association of Secondary School Principals.

Arkes, H., & Garske, J. (1982). *Psychological theories of motivation.* Belmont, CA: Brooks/Cole.

Armstrong, D., & Savage, T. (1983). *Secondary education: An introduction.* New York: Macmillan.

ASCD Panel on Moral Education. (1988). Moral education in the life of the school. *Educational Leadership.* Volume 45.

Asher, W. (1990). Educational psychology, research methodology, and meta-analysis. *Educational Psychologist, 25,* 143-158.

Atkinson, J. W. (1964). *An introduction to motivation.* Princeton, NJ: Van Nostrand.

Atkinson, R. (1975). Mnemonic techniques in second-language learning. *American Psychologist, 30,* 821-828.

Atkinson, R. C., & Shiffrin, R. M. (1968). Human memory: A proposed system and its control processes, In K. W. Spence & J. T. Spence (Eds.), *The psychology of learning and motivation.* New York: Academic Press.

Ausubel, D. (1960). The use of advance organizers in the learning and retention of meaningful verbal material. *Journal of Educational Psychology, 51,* 267-272.

Ausubel, D. (1968). *Educational psychology: A cognitive view.* New York: Holt, Rinehart and Winston.

Ausubel, D. (1977). The facilitation of meaningful verbal learning in the classroom. *Educational Psychologist, 12,* 162-178.

Ausubel, D. (1980). Schemata, cognitive structures, and advance organizers: A reply to Anderson, Spiro, and Anderson. *American Educational Research Journal, 17,* 400-404.

Ausubel, D., Novak, J., & Hanesian, H. (1978). *Educational psychology: A cognitive view.* New York: Holt, Rinehart and Winston.

Ausubel, D., & Robinson, F. (1969). *School learning.* New York: Holt, Rinehart and Winston.

Azrin, N. H., & Holz, W. C. (1966). Punishment. In W. Honig (Ed.), *Operant Behavior: Areas of Research and Application*. New York: Appleton-Century-Crofts.

B

Babkin, B. R. (1949). *Pavlov*. Chicago: U. of Chicago Press.

Baddeley, A. (1988). Cognitive psychology and human memory. *Trends in Neurosciences, 11,* 176-181.

Baddeley, A. (1990). *Human memory: Theory and practice*. Boston: Allyn & Bacon.

Bailey, D. B., & Simeonsson, R. J. (1984). Critical issues underlying research and intervention. *Journal of the Division for Early Childhood, 9,* 38-48.

Bailey, D. B., & Wolery, W. (1984). *Teaching infants and preschoolers with handicaps*. Columbus, Ohio: Merrill.

Bakeman, R. (1977). Behavioral dialogues: An approach to the assessment of mother-infant interaction. *Child Development, 48,* 195-203.

Bakeman, R., & Brown, J. (1980). Early intervention: Consequences for social and mental development at three years. *Child Development, 51* 437-447.

Baker, K. (1986). Crime and violence in schools: A challenge to educators. In T. R. Kratochwill (Ed.), *Advances in School Psychology*. (Volume 5, pp. 51-85). Hillsdale, NJ: Lawrence Erlbaum.

Bales, J. (1990). Skinner gets award, ovations at APA talk. *The APA Monitor, 21,* 10, 1, 6.

Ball, D. (1986). Level of teacher objectives and their classroom tests: Match or mismatch. *Journal of Social Studies Research, 10,* 27-31.

Ball, S. (1977). *Motivation in education*. New York: Academic.

Bandura, A. (1977). *Social learning theory*. Englewood Cliffs, NJ: Prentice-Hall.

Bandura, A. (1978). The self system in reciprocal determinism. *American Psychologist, 33,* 344-358.

Bandura, A. (1981). Self-referent thought: A developmental analysis of self-efficacy. In J. Flavell & L. Ross (Eds.), *Social Cognitive Development*. New York: Cambridge U. Press.

Bandura, A. (1986) *Social foundations of thought and action: A social-cognitive theory*. Englewood Cliffs, NJ: Prentice-Hall.

Bandura, A., Ross, D., & Ross, S. (1963). Imitation of film-mediated aggressive models. *Journal of Abnormal and Social Psychology, 66,* 3-11.

Bandura, A., & Schunk, D. (1981). Cultivating confidence, self-efficacy, and intrinsic motivation. *Journal of Personality and Social Psychology, 41,* 586-598.

Bandura, A., & Walters, R. (1963). *Social learning and personality development*. New York: Holt, Rinehart and Winston.

Banks, J., & Banks, C. A. (1989). *Multicultural education: Issues and perspectives*. Boston: Allyn and Bacon.

Barba, M. (1985). Portfolio assessment: An alternate strategy for placement of the RN Student in a baccalaureate program. *Innovative Higher Education, 9,* 121-127.

Bardon, J. (1983). Psychology applied to education: A specialty in search of an identity. *American Psychologist, 38,* 185-196.

Barker, R. G. (1968). *Ecological psychology*. Stanford: Stanford University Press.

Barker, R. G., & Associates. (1978). *Habitats, environments, and human behavior*. San Francisco: Jossey-Bass.

Barlow, D. H., & Hersen, M. (1984). *Single case experimental designs: Strategies for studying behavior change* (2nd ed.). New York: Pergamon Press.

Bartlett, F. C. (1932). *Remembering: A study in experimental and social psychology*. London: Cambridge University Press.

Barzun, J. (1954) *The teacher in America*. Boston: Little, Brown.

Beck, I., & Carpenter, P. (1986). Cognitive approaches to understanding reading: Implications for instructional practice. *American Psychologist, 41,* 1098-1105.

Beck, R. (1983). *Motivation: Theories and principles*. Englewood Cliffs, NJ: Prentice-Hall.

Becker, H., & Epstein, J. (1982). Parent involvement: A survey of teacher practices. *The Elementary School Journal, 83,* 85-102.

Becoming a nation of readers: The report of the commission on reading. Washington: National Academy of Education, National Institute of Education, and Center for the Study of Reading, 1985.

Bell, S. (Ed.). (1977). *Motivation in education*. New York: Academic.

Bennett, C. (1990). *Comprehensive multicultural education*. Boston: Allyn and Bacon.

Benninga, J. (1988, February). An emerging synthesis in moral education. *Phi Delta Kappan, 69,* 415-418.

Benson, D. F., & Greenberg, J. (1969). Visual form agnosia. *Archives of Neurology, 20,* 82-89.

Berdine, W., & Blackhurst, A. E. (Eds.). (1985). *An introduction to special education*. Boston: Little, Brown.

Bereiter, C., & Englemann, S. (1966). *Teaching disadvantaged children in the preschool*. Englewood Cliffs, NJ: Prentice-Hall.

Berk, L. (1992). *Child development*. Boston: Allyn & Bacon.

Berliner, D. (1983). Developing conceptions of classroom environments. *Educational Psychologist, 18,* 1-13.

Berliner, D. (1987). Knowledge is power. In David Berliner and Barak Rosenshine (Eds.), *Talks to Teachers*. New York: Random House.

Berliner, D. C. (1988). The half-full glass: A review of research on teaching. In E. L. Meyer, G. V. Vergason, & R. L. Whelan (Eds.), *Effective instructional strategies for exceptional children* (pp. 7-31). Denver: Love.

Berlyne, D. E. (1974). Attention. In E. C. Caterette and M. Friedman (Eds.), *Handbook of Perception*. New York: Academic.

Bersoff, D. N. (1978). Legal and ethical concerns in research. In L. Goldman (Ed.), *Research methods for counselors: Practical approaches in field settings*. New York: John Wiley.

Bettleheim, B. (1987, March). The importance of play. *Atlantic,* 35-46.

Birely, M., & Genshaft, J. (Eds.). (1991). *Understanding the gifted adolescent: Educational development and multicultural issues*. New York: Teachers College Press.

Blair, T. (1988). *Emerging patterns of teaching*. Columbus, Ohio: Merrill.

Blankenship, C. (1985). Using curriculum-based assessment data to make instructional decisions. *Exceptional Children, 52*, 233-238.

Blatt, M. (1975). Studies of the effects of classroom discussions upon children's moral development. *Journal of Moral Development, 42*, 129-161.

Blatt, M., & Kohlberg, L. (1978). Effects of classroom discussions upon children's level of moral development. In L. Kohlberg, (Ed.), *Recent Research in Moral Development*. New York: Holt, Rinehart and Winston.

Blehar, M., Lieberman, A., & Ainsworth, M. (1977). Early face-to-face interaction and its relation to later infant-mother attachment. *Child Development, 48*, 182-194.

Bloom, Benjamin (Ed.). (1956). *Taxonomy of educational objectives. Handbook 1: Cognitive domain*. New York: McKay.

Bloom, B. (1976a). *Language, memory, and thought*. Hillsdale, NJ: Erlbaum.

Bloom, B. (1976b). *Human characteristics and school learning*. New York: McGraw Hill.

Bloom, B. (1981). *All our children learning*. New York: McGraw Hill.

Bloom, B. (1985). *Developing talent in young people*. New York: McGraw Hill.

Bloom, Benjamin, Madaus, G., & Hastings, J. T. (1981). *Evaluation to improve learning*. New York: McGraw Hill.

Boateng, F. (1990). Combatting deculturalization of the African-American child in the public school system: A multicultural approach. In Lomotey, K. (Ed.), *Going to School: The African-American Experience*. New York: State University of New York Press.

Boden, M. (1977). *Artificial intelligence and natural man*. New York: McGraw Hill.

Borland, J. (1989). *Planning and implementing programs for the gifted*. New York: Teachers College Press, Columbia U.

Bos, C., & Vaughn, S. (1988). *Strategies for teaching students with learning and behavior problems*. Boston: Allyn and Bacon.

Boulanger, F. D. (1981). Instruction and science learning: A quantitative synthesis. *Journal of Research in Science Teaching, 18*, 311-327.

Bourne, L., Dominowski, R., & Loftus, E. (1987). *Cognitive processes*. Englewood Cliffs, NJ: Prentice-Hall.

Bower, G., & Hilgard, E. (1981). *Theories of learning*. New York: Appleton-Century.

Bowlby, J. (1969). *Attachment*. New York: Basic.

Brabeck, M. (1983). Moral judgment: Theory and research on differences between males and females. *Developmental Review, 3*, 274-291.

Bragstad, B. J., & Stumpf, S. (1984). *A guidebook for teaching study skills and motivation*. Boston: Allyn & Bacon.

Bransford, J. D., Sherwood, R., Vye, N., & Rieser, J. (1986). Teaching thinking and problem solving. *American Psychologist, 41*, 1078-1089.

Bransford, J., & Stein, B. (1984). *The IDEAL problem solver*. New York: Freeman.

Braswell, L., & Bloomquist, M. L. (1991). *Cognitive-behavioral therapy with ADHD children*. New York: Guilford Press.

Brazelton, T. B. (1984). *Neonatal behavioral assessment scale*. London: William Heinemann Medical Books.

Brazelton, T. B. (1990). Saving the bathwater. *Child Development, 61*, 1672-1681.

Brazelton, T. B., & Als, H. (1979). Four early stages in the development of mother-infant interaction. *The Psychoanalytic Study of the Child, 34*, 349-369.

Brazelton, T. B., & Cramer, B. (1990). *The earliest relationship*. Reading, MA: Addison-Wesley.

Breland, K., & Breland, M. (1961). The misbehavior of organisms. *American Psychologist, 16*, 681-684.

Broadbent, D. E. (1958). *Perception and communication*. London: Pergamon.

Broadbent, D. E. (1954). The role of auditory localization in attention and memory span. *Journal of Experimental Psychology, 47*, 191-196.

Bronson, M., Pierson, D., & Tivnan, T. (1984). The effects of early education on children's competence in elementary school. *Evaluation Review, 8*, 615-627.

Brookover, W. B., Beady, C., Flood, P., Schweitzer, J., & Weisenbaker, J. (1979). *School social systems and student achievement*. New York: Praeger.

Brophy, J. (1981). Teacher praise: A functional analysis. *Review of Educational Research, 51*, 5-32.

Brophy, J. (1983a). Fostering student learning and motivation in the elementary school classroom. In Scott Paris, Gary Olson, and Harold Stevenson (Eds.), *Learning and motivation in the classroom*. Hillsdale, NJ: Erlbaum.

Brophy, J. (1983b). If only it were true: A response to Greer. *Educational Researcher, 12*, 10-12.

Brophy, J. (1986). Teacher praise: A functional analysis. In Merlin Wittrock (Ed.), *Handbook of Research on Teaching*. New York: Macmillan.

Brophy, J. (1987a, October). Synthesis of research on strategies for motivating students to learn. *Educational Leadership*, 40-48.

Brophy, J. (1987b). Teacher influences on student achievement. *American Psychologist, 41*, 1069-1077.

Brophy, J. (1988, September). Research on teacher effects: Uses and abuses. *The Elementary School Journal*, 3-21.

Brophy. J., & Evertson, C. (1976). *Learning from teaching: A developmental perspective*. Boston: Allyn & Bacon.

Brophy, J. & Good, T. (1974). *Teacher-Student relationships: Cause and consequences*. New York: Holt, Rinehart and Winston.

Brophy, J., & Good, T. (1986). Teacher behavior and student achievement. In Merlin Wittrock (Ed.), *Handbook of Research on Teaching*. New York: Macmillan.

Brophy, J., & Putnam, J. (1979.) Classroom management. In Daniel Duke (Ed.), *The Seventy-eighth Yearbook of The National Society for the Study of Education*. Chicago: U. of Chicago Press.

Brown, A., & Campione, J. (1986). Psychological theory and the study of learning disabilities. *American Psychologist, 41*, 1059-1068.

Brown, D. S. (1988). Twelve middle-school teachers' planning. *The Elementary School Journal, 89*, 69-87.

Brown, F. G. (1983). *Principles of educational and psychological testing.* (3rd ed.). New York: Holt, Rinehart & Winston.

Brown, J. S., & Burton, R. R. (1978). Diagnostic models for procedural bugs in basic mathematical skills. *Cognitive Science, 2,* 153-192.

Brown, R. (1988). Model youth: Excelling despite the odds. *Ebony, 43,* 40-48.

Brown, R., & Lennenberg, E. (1954). A study in language and cognition. *Journal of Abnormal and Social Psychology, 44,* 454-462.

Brown, R., & McNeil, D. (1966). The 'tip of the tongue' phenomenon. *Journal of Verbal Learning and Verbal Behavior, 5,* 325-337.

Brownell, G. (1987). *Computers and teaching.* St. Paul: West.

Bruner, J. (1960). *The process of education.* Cambridge, MA: Harvard U. Press.

Bruner, J. (1962). *On knowing: Essays for the left hand.* Cambridge, MA: Harvard U. Press.

Bruner, J. (1966a). *Studies in cognitive growth.* New York: Wiley.

Bruner, J. (1966b). *Toward a theory of instruction.* Cambridge, MA: Harvard U. Press.

Bruner, J. (1969). Processes of growth in infancy. In J. Ambrose (Ed.), *Stimulation in Early Infancy.* New York: Academic.

Bruner, J. (1971). *The relevance of education.* New York: Norton.

Bruner, J. (1978.) *Human growth and development.* New York: Oxford.

Bruner, J. (1983). *In search of mind.* New York: Harper.

Bruner, J. (1986). *Actual minds, possible worlds.* Cambridge, MA: Harvard University Press.

Bruner, J., & Goodman, C. (1947). Value and need as organizing factors in perception. *Journal of Abnormal and Social Psychology, 42,* 33-44.

Bruner, J., Goodnow, J., & Austin, G. (1956). *A study of thinking.* New York: Wiley.

Bruner, J., Jolly, A., & Sylva, K. (1978). *Play: Its role in development and evolution.* New York: Basic.

Brunner, C., & Majewski, W. (1990). Mildly handicapped students can succeed with learning styles. *Educational Leadership, 48,* 21-23.

Buck, R. (1988). *Motivation and emotion.* New York: Cambridge U. Press.

Bullinger, A., & Chatillon, J. (1983). Recent theory and research of the Genevan school. In Paul Mussen (Ed.), *Handbook of Child Psychology.* New York: Wiley.

Buss, A., & Plomin, R. (1985). *Early developing personality traits.* Hillsdale, NJ: Erlbaum.

C

Caine, R., & Caine, G. (1990). Understanding a brain-based approach to learning and teaching. *Educational Leadership, 48,* 66-70.

Calfee, R. C. (1984). Applying cognitive psychology to educational practice: The mind of the reading teacher. *Annals of Dyslexia, 34,* 219-240.

Calfee, R., & Drum, P. (1986). Research on teaching reading. In Merlin Wittrock (Ed.), *Handbook of Research on Teaching.* New York: Macmillan.

Calvert, P. (1986). Responses to guidelines for developmentally appropriate practice for young children and Montessori. Paper presented at the Annual Meeting of the National Association for the Education of Young Children. Washington, DC.

Camp, B. W., & Bosh, M. A. (1981). *Think aloud.* Champaign, IL: Research Press.

Camp, D. S., Raymond, G., & Church, R. (1967). Temporal relationship between response and punishment. *Journal of Experimental Psychology, 74,* 114-123.

Campbell, D., & Stanley, J. (1963). Experimental and quasi-experimental designs for research on teaching. In N. L. Gage (Ed.), *Handbook of Research on Teaching.* Chicago: Rand McNally.

Canter, L., & Hausner, L. (1987). *Homework without tears: A parents' guide for motivating children to do homework and to succeed in school.* New York. Harper & Row.

Capelli, C., Nakagawa, N., & Madden, C. How children understand sarcasm: The role of context and intonation. *Child Development, 61,* 1824-1841.

Caplan, T., & Caplan, F. (1983). *The early childhood years.* New York: Bantam.

Carden-Smith, L. K., & Fowler, S. (1984). Positive peer pressure: The effects of peer monitoring on children's disruptive behavior. *Journal of Applied Behavior Analysis, 17,* 213-217.

Carey, S. (1986). Cognitive science and science education. *American Psychologist, 41,* 1123-1130.

Carey, W. (1981). The importance of temperament-environment interaction for child health and development. In Michael Lewis and Leonard Rosenblum (Eds.), *The Uncommon Child.* New York: Plenum.

Carroll, J. (1963). A model of school learning. *Teachers College Record, 64,* 723-733.

Cartledge, G., & Milburn, J. (1986). The case for teaching social skills in the classroom: A review. *Review of Educational Research, 48,* 133-156.

Catledge, G., & Milburn, J. F. (1986). *Teaching social skills to children: Innovative approaches.* (2nd ed.). New York: Pergamon.

Casas, J. M., Furlong, M., Solberg, U. S., & Carranza, O. (1990). An examination of individual factors associated with the academic success and failure of Mexican-Americans and Anglo students. In D. Barona and E. E. Garcia (Eds.), *Children at risk: poverty, minority status, and other issues in educational equity* (pp. 103-118). Washington, DC: National Association of School Psychologists.

Case, R. (1978). A developmentally based theory and technology of instruction. *Review of Educational Research, 48,* 439-463.

Case, R. (1985). *Intellectual development: Birth to adulthood.* New York: Academic.

Ceci, S., & Bronfenbrenner, U. (1991). On the demise of everyday memory: "The rumors of my death are much exaggerated" (Mark Twain). *American Psychologist, 46,* 27-31.

Chase, W., & Simon, H. (1973). Perception in chess. *Cognitive Psychology, 4,* 55-81.

Chess, S., & Hassibi, M. (1978). *Principles and practices in child psychiatry.* New York: Plenum.

Children's Defense Fund. (1975). *School supervisors: Are they helping children?*

Chomsky, N. (1957). *Syntactic structures.* The Hague: Mouton.

Clabby, J. F., & Elias, M. J. (1987). *Teaching your child decision making.* Garden City, NY: Doubleday & Co.

Clark, C. (1983). *Family life and school achievement.* Chicago: U. of Chicago Press.

Clark, C., & Peterson, P. (1986). Teachers' thought processes. In Merlin Wittrock (Ed.), *Handbook of research on teaching*. New York: Macmillan.

Clark, F., & Clark, C. (1989). *Hassle-free homework: A six-week plan for parents and children to take the pain out of homework*. New York: Doubleday.

Clarke, A., & Clarke, A. D. (1977). *Early experience: Myth and evidence*. New York: The Free Press.

Clarke, B. R., & Stewart, D. A. (1986). Reflections on language programs for the hearing impaired. *The Journal of Special Education, 20*, 153-165.

Coalition of Essential Schools (1990). Performances and exhibitions: The demonstration of mastery. *Horace, 6*, 1-9.

Coie, J. D., Dodge, K. A., & Cappotelli, H. (1982). Dimensions and types of social status: A cross-age perspective. *Developmental Psychology, 18*, 557-570.

Colby, A., Kohlberg, L., Gibbs, J., & Lieberman, A. (1983). A longitudinal study of moral judgment. *Monographs of the Society for Research in Child Development, 48*, Serial No. 200.

Cole, M., and Scribner, S. (1974). *Culture and thought*. New York: Wiley.

Coleman, J. (1978). Current contradictions in adolescent theory. *Journal of Youth and Adolescence, 7*, 1-11.

Collins, A. M., & Loftus, J. (1975). A spreading-activation theory of semantic processing. *Psychological Review, 82*, 407-428.

Collins, A. M., & Quillian, M. R. (1969). Retrieval time from semantic memory. *Journal of Learning and Verbal Behavior, 8*, 240-247.

Collins, M., & Cornine, D. (1988). Evaluating the field test process by comparing two versions of a reasoning skills CAI program. *Journal of Learning Disabilities, 21*, 375-379.

Colmar, Susan. (1988). A perspective on behavior checklists. *Educational Psychology—An International Journal of Experimental Educational Psychology, 8*, 117-121.

Conrad, R. (1964). Acoustic confusion in immediate memory. *British Journal of Psychology, 55*, 75-84.

Conway, M. (1991). In defense of everyday memory. *American Psychologist, 46*, 19-26.

Cook, T. D. (1974). The potential and limitations of secondary evaluations. In M. W. Apple, H. C. Subkoviok, & J. R. Lufler (Eds.), *Educational Evaluation: Analysis and Responsibilities*. Berkeley, CA: McCutchan.

Cooley, W. W., & Lohnes, P. R., (1968). *Predicting development of young adults*. Pittsburg: American Institute for Research.

Cooper, H. (1989, November). Synthesis of research on homework. *Educational Leadership*, 85-91.

Cooper, H., & Brophy, J. (1983). *Pygmalion grows up*. Hillsdale, NY: Erlbaum.

Cooper, J. (Ed.). (1986). *Classroom teaching skills*. Lexington, MA: D.C. Heath.

Corkill, A. J., Glover, J. A., Bruning, R. H., & Krug, D. (1989). Advance organizers: Retrieval hypotheses. *Journal of Educational Psychology, 81*, 43-51.

Cornine, D. (1991). Curricular interventions for teaching higher order thinking to all students: Introduction to the special series. *Journal of Learning Disabilities, 24*, 261-269.

Corno, L., & Snow, R. (1986). Adapting teaching to individual differences. In Merlin Wittrock (Ed.), *Handbook of research on teaching*.

Costa, A. (Ed.). (1985). *Developing minds*. Alexandria, VA: ASCD.

Costa, A., Hanson, R., Silver, H., & Strong, R. (1985). Building a repertoire of strategies. In A. Costa (Ed.), *Developing minds*. Alexandria, VA: ASCD.

Cote, J. D. (1985). Fitting social skills interventions to the target group. In B. H. Schnerder, Rubin, K. H., and Ledingham, J. E. (Eds.), *Children's peer relations: Issues in assessment and intervention* (pp. 141-156). New York: Springer-Verlag.

Cote, J. D., Dodge, K. A., & Coppotelli, H. (1982). Dimensions and types of social status: A cross-age perspective. *Developmental Psychology, 18*, 557-570.

Covington, M. O., & Onelich, C. (1980). Are causal attributions causal? A path analysis of the cognitive model of achievement motivation. *Journal of Personality and Social Psychology, 37*, 1487-1504.

Craik, F. I., & Lockhart, R. S. (1972). Levels of processing: A framework for memory research. *Journal of Verbal Learning and Verbal Behavior, 11*, 671-684.

Craske, M. L. (1985). Improving persistence through observational learning and attribution retraining. *British Journal of Educational Psychology, 55*, 138-147.

Cronbach, L. (1970). *Essentials of psychological testing*. New York: Harper and Row.

Cronbach, L., & Snow, R. (1977). *Aptitudes and instructional methods*. New York: Irvington.

Cruickshank, D. (1986). Profile of an effective teacher. *Educational Horizons*, 90-92.

Cullinan, D., & Epstein, M. (1986). Behavior disorders. In Hoving Norris and Linda McCormack (Eds.), *Exceptional children and youth*. Columbus, Ohio: Charles Merrill.

Curriel, H., Rosenthal, J., & and Richek, H. (1986). Impacts of bilingual education on secondary school grades, attendance, retentions, and drop-out. *Hispanic Journal of Behavioral Sciences, 8*, 357-367.

D

Dacey, J. (1989a). Discriminating characteristics of the families of highly creative adolescents. *The Journal of Creative Behavior, 23*, 263-273.

Dacey, J. (1989b). Peak periods of creative growth across the lifespan. *The Journal of Creative Behavior, 23*(4), 224-247.

Dacey, J., & Kenny, M. (in press). *Adolescents today*. Dubuque, IA: Brown/Benchmark.

Damico, S. (1985). The two worlds of school differences in the photographs of black and white adolescents. *The Urban Review, 17*, 210-222.

Damon, W. (1983). *Social and personality development*. New York: Norton.

Damon, W. (1988). *The moral child: Nurturing children's natural moral growth.* New York: Free Press.

Daniels, L. (1990, January 10). Tests show reading and writing lag continues. *New York Times,* B8.

Davidson, J. (1990). Intelligence recreated. *Educational Psychologist, 25,* 337-354.

Davis, D. (1982). Determinants of responsiveness in dyadic interaction. In William Ickes and Eric Knowles (Eds.), *Personality, roles, and social behavior.* New York: Springer-Verlag.

deBono, E. (1970). *Lateral thinking.* New York: Harper & Row.

deBono, E. (1984). *The art and science of success.* Boston: Little, Brown.

deBono, E. (1985). The CoRT thinking program. In Arthur Costa (Ed.), *Developing minds.* Alexandria, VA: ASCP.

deBono, E. (1985). The CoRT thinking program. In J. Segal, S. Chipinaw, & R. Glaser (Eds.), *Thinking and learning skills,* Vol. I. Hillsdale, NJ: Erlbaum.

de Charms, R. (1976). *Enhancing motivation: Change in the classroom.* New York: Irvington.

de Groot, A. (1965). *Thought and choice in chess.* The Hague: Mouton.

de Jong, T., & Ferguson-Hassler, M. (1986). Cognitive structures of good and poor novice problem solvers in physics. *Journal of Educational Psychology, 78,* 279-288.

Denham, S., McKinley, M., Couchoud, E., & Holt, R. (1990). Emotional and behavioral predictors of preschool peer ratings. *Child Development, 61,* 1145-1152.

Deno, S. (1985). Curriculum-based measurement: The emerging alternative. *Exceptional Children, 52,* 219-232.

Derry, S. J. (1989, December/January). Putting learning strategies to work. *Educational Leadership,* 4-10.

Devilliers, J., & Devilliers, P. (1978). *Language acquisition.* Cambridge, MA: Harvard University Press.

Dewey, J. (1916). *Democracy and education.* New York: Macmillan.

Dewey, J. (1933). *How we think.* Boston: Heath.

Dick, W., & Carey, L. (1978). *The systematic design of instruction.* Glenview, IL: Scott, Foresman.

Diener, C., & Dweck, C. (1978). An analysis of learned helplessness: Continuous changes in performance, strategy, and achievement cognitions following failure. *Journal of Personality and Social Psychology, 36,* 451-462.

Dill, D. (1990). *What teachers need to know.* San Francisco: Jossey Bass.

Dobbin, J. (1984). *How to take a test: Doing your best.* Princeton, NJ: Educational Testing Service.

Dodge, K., Coie, J., Pettit, G., & Price, J. (1990). Peer status and aggression in boys' groups: Developmental and contextual analyses. *Child Development, 61,* 1289-1309.

Donaldson, M. (1986) Introduction. In Martin Hughes (Ed.), *Children and number.* New York: Blackwell.

Donnellan, A. M., & LaVigna, G. W. (1990). Myths about punishment. In A. C. Repp and N. N. Singh (Eds.), *Perspectives on the use of nonaversive and aversive interventions for persons with developmental disabilities* (pp. 33-57). Sycamore, IL: Sycamore Publishing Co.

Doris, J. (Ed.). (1991). *The suggestibility of children's recollections: Implications for eyewitness testimony.* Washington, DC: American Psychological Association.

Dossey, J., Mullis, I., Lindquist, M., & Chambers, D. (1988). *The mathematics report card.* Princeton, NJ: Educational Testing Service.

Doyle, W. (1983). Paradigms for research on teacher effectiveness. In L. S. Shulman (Ed.), *Review of Research in Education.* Vol. V. Itasca, IL: F.E. Peacock.

Doyle, W. (1986). Classroom organization and management. In Merlin Wittrock (Ed.), *Handbook of Research on Teaching.* New York: Macmillan.

Dreikurs, R., Grunwald, B., & Pepper, F. (1971). *Maintaining sanity in the classroom.* New York: Harper & Row.

Dukes, W. F. (1965). N-1. *Psychological Bulletin, 64,* 74-79.

Dulit, E. (1972). Adolescent thinking a la Piaget: The formal stage. *Journal of Youth and Adolescence, 4,* 281-301.

Dunkin, M. J., & Biddle, B. J. (1974). *The study of teaching.* New York: Holt, Rinehart, and Winston.

Dunn, R. (1987). Research on instructional environments: Implications for student achievement and attitudes. *Professional School Psychology, 3,* 43-52.

Dunn, R. (1990). Rita Dunn answers questions on learning styles. *Educational Leadership, 48(2),* 15-18.

Dweck, C. (1975). The role of expectations and attributions in the alleviation of learned helplessness. *Journal of Personality and Social Psychology, 31,* 674-685.

Dweck, C., & Elliot, E. (1983). Achievement motivation. In Paul Mussen (Ed.), *Handbook of child psychology.* New York: Wiley.

Dweck, C., & Repucci, N. D. (1973). Learned helplessness and reinforcement of responsibility in children. *Journal of Personality and Social Psychology, 25,* 109-116.

E

Ebbinghaus, H. (1885). *On memory.* New York: Teachers College Press.

Ebel, R. (1979). *Essentials of educational measurement.* Englewood Cliffs, NJ: Prentice-Hall.

Eby, J., & Smutny, J. (1990). *A thoughtful overview of gifted education.* New York: Longman.

Eccles, J. (1985). The human brain and the human person. In John Eccles (Ed.), *Mind and Brain.* New York: Pergamon.

Edelbrock, C. (1988). Informant reports. In E. S. Shapiro and T. R. Kratochwill (Eds.), *Behavioral Assessment in Schools: Conceptual Foundations and Practical Applications* (pp. 351-383). New York: Guilford Press.

Edwards, B. (1979). *Drawing on the right side of the brain.* Los Angeles: Tarcher.

Einon, D. (1985). *Play with a purpose.* New York: Pantheon.

Eisenberg, L. (1979). Perspectives on psychosomatics as a concept. In L. Jarvik, C. Eisdorfer, and J. Blum (Eds.), *Intellectual functioning in adults.* New York: Sprinzer.

Eisenberg, N., & Mussen, P. (1989). *The roots of prosocial behavior in children.* Cambridge: Cambridge U. Press.

Eisenson, J. (1986). *Language and speech disorders in children*. New York: Pergamon Press.

Elkind, D. (1970, April 5). Erik Erikson's eight ages of man. *New York Times Magazine,* 1970.

Elkind, D. (1981). *The hurried child.* Reading, MA: Addison-Wesley.

Elkind, D. (1987). *Miseducation: Preschoolers at risk.* New York: Knopf.

Elliott S. N., & Gresham, F. M. (1991). *Social skills intervention guide.* Circle Pines, MN: AGS.

Elliott, S. N., Piersel, W., Witt, J. C., Argulewicz, E., Gutkin, T. B., & Galvin, G. (1985). Three year stability of WISC-R IQs for handicapped children from three racial/ethnic groups. *Journal of Psychoeducational Assessment, 3,* 233-244.

Ellis, H., & Hunt, R. (1989). *Fundamentals of human memory and cognition.* Dubuque, IA: Brown.

Emde, R. (1980). Emotional availability. In P. M. Taylor (Ed.), *Parent-infant relationships.* New York: Grune and Stratton.

Emmer, E., Evertson, C., & Anderson, L. (1980). Effective classroom management at the beginning of the school year. *Elementary School Journal, 80,* 219-231.

Emmer, E., Evertson, C, Sanford, J., Clements, B., & Worsham, M. (1984). *Classroom management for secondary teachers.* Englewood Cliffs, NJ: Prentice-Hall.

Endler, N. S., Boulter, L. R., & Osser, H. (Eds.). (1976). *Contemporary issues in developmental psychology.* New York: Holt, Rinehart, & Winston.

Engle, G. (1977). The need for a new medical model: A challenge for biomedicine. *Science, 196,* 129-135.

Ennis, R. (1987). A taxonomy of critical thinking dispositions and abilities. In J. Barron and R. Sternberg (Eds.), *Teaching thinking skills.* New York: Freeman.

Enright, R. D. & the Human Development Study Group. (in press). The moral development of forgiveness. In W. Kurtines & J. Gewitz (Eds.), *Handbook of moral development.* (Volume 1, 123-152). Hillsdale, NJ: Erlbaum.

Entwiste, D., & Alexander, K. (1990). Beginning school math competence: Minority and majority comparisons. *Child Development, 61,* 454-471.

Entwistle, N., & Waterson, S. (1988). Approaches to studying and levels of processing in university students. *British Journal of Educational Psychology, 58,* 258-265.

Epstein, J. (1988). Effects on student achievement of teachers' practices of parent involvement. In S. Silvern (Ed.), *Literacy through family, community, and school interaction.* Greenwich, CT: JAI Press.

Epstein, J., & Becker, H. (1982). Teachers' reported practices of parent involvement: Problems and possibilities. *The Elementary School Journal, 83,* 103-113.

Epstein, R. (1985). The case for praxics. *The Behavior Analyst, 7,* 101-119.

Erickson, F. (1986). Qualitative methods in research on teaching. In M. Wittrock (Ed.), *Handbook of research on teaching.* New York: Macmillan.

Erikson, E. (1950). *Childhood and society.* New York: Norton.

Erikson, E. (1959). Growth and crises of the healthy personality. *Psychological Issues, 1.*

Erikson, E. (1968). *Identity: Youth and crisis.* New York: Norton.

Esveldt-Dawson, K. & Kazdin, A. E. (1982). *How to use self-control.* Lawrence, KS: H & H Enterprises.

Evertson, C., Emmer, E., Sanford, J., Clements, B., & Worsham, M. (1984). *Classroom management for elementary teachers.* Englewood Cliffs, NJ: Prentice-Hall.

Evertson, C., & Green, J. (1986). Observation as inquiry and method. In Merlin Wittrock (Ed.), *Handbook of research on teaching.* New York: Macmillan.

Evortson, C., & Emmer, E. (1982). Effective management at the beginning of the school year in junior high classes. *Journal of Educational Research, 74,* 485-498.

F

Falkof, L., & Moss, J. (1984). When teachers tackle thinking skills. *Educational Leadership, 42,* 4-10.

Fanelli, G. (1977). Locus of control. In Samuel Ball (Ed.), *Motivation in education.* New York: Academic Press.

Fantz, R. (1961). The origin of form perception. *Scientific American, 204,* 66-72.

Fantz, R. (1963). Pattern vision in newborn infants. *Science, 140,* 296-297.

Fantz, R., & Nevis, S. (1967). Pattern preferences and perceptual-cognitive development in early infancy. *Merrill-Palmer Quarterly, 13,* 77-108.

Feiman-Nemser, S., & Floden, R. (1986). The cultures of teaching. In Merlin Wittrock (Ed.), *Handbook of research on teaching.* New York: Macmillan.

Feldhusen, J. F. (1989). Synthesis of research on gifted youth. *Educational Leadership,* 6-11.

Ferster, C. B., & Skinner, B. F. (1957). *Schedules of reinforcement.* New York: Appleton-Century-Crofts.

Feuerstein, R. (1980). *Instrumental enrichment.* Baltimore: University Park Press.

Feuerstein, R., Jensen, M., Hoffman, M. & Yaacou, R. (1985). Instrumental enrichment: An intervention program for structural cognitive modifiability. In J. Segal, S. Chipman, and R. Glaser (Eds.), *Thinking and learning skills,* Vol. 1. Hillsdale, NJ: Erlbaum.

Fillmore, L., & Valadez, C. (1986). Teaching bilingual learners. In Merlin Wittrock (Ed.), *Handbook of research on teaching.* New York: Macmillan.

First, J. (1988). Immigrant students in U.S. public schools: Challenges with solutions. *Phi Delta Kappan, 70,* 205-210.

Fischer, K., & Silvern, L. (1985). Stages and individual differences in cognitive development. In Mark Rosenzweig and Pyman Porter (Eds.), *Annual review of psychology.* Palo Alto: Annual Reviews.

Flavell, J. H. (1963). *The developmental psychology of Jean Piaget.* Princeton: Van Nostrand.

Flavell, J. (1985). *Cognitive development.* Englewood Cliffs, NJ: Prentice-Hall.

Flinders, D. (1989, May). Does the "Art of Teaching" have a future? *Educational Leadership,* 16-22.

Ford, M., & Ohlhausen, M. (1988, April). Classroom reading incentive programs: Removing the obstacles and hurdles for disabled readers. *Reading Teacher,* 796-798.

Forness, S. R., & Kavale, K. A. (1991). School psychologists' roles and functions: Integration into the regular classroom. In G. Stoner, M. R. Shinn, and H. M. Walker (Eds.), *Interventions for achievement and behavior problems* (pp. 21-36). Washington, DC: National Association of School Psychologists.

Foster, S. (1986). Ten principles of learning revised in accordance with cognitive psychology: With implications for teaching. *Educational Psychologist, 21,* 235-243.

Fox, L. H., & Washington, J. (1985). Programs for the gifted and talented: Past, present, and future. In F. D. Horowitz and M. O'Brien (Eds.), *The Gifted and talented.* Washington, DC: American Psychological Association.

Fraenkel, J. R., & Wallen, N. E. (1990). *How to design and evaluate research in education.* New York: McGraw-Hill.

Frasier, M. (1989). Poor and minority students can be gifted, too. *Educational Leadership, 46,* 16-18.

Frederiksen, N. (1984). Implications of cognitive theory for instruction in problem solving. *Review of Educational Research, 54,* 363-408.

Frentz, C., Greshman, F. M., & Elliott, S. N. (1991). Popular, controversial, neglected, and rejected adolescents: Contrasts of social competence and achievement differences. *Journal of School Psychology, 29,* 109-120.

Frisbie, D. (1988). NCME instructional module on reliability of scores from teacher-made tests. *Educational Measurement, 7,* 25-33.

From gatekeeper to gateway: Transforming testing in America. *Report of the National Commission on Testing and Public Policy.* Chestnut Hill, MA: Boston College.

Fromberg, D., & Driscoll, M. (1985). *The successful classroom.* New York: Teachers College.

G

Gage, N. L. (1977). *The scientific basis of the art of teaching.* New York: Teachers College Press.

Gage, N. L. (1985). *Hard gains in the soft sciences: The case of pedagogy.* Bloomington, IN: Phi Delta Kappan.

Gagne, R. (1977). *The conditions of learning.* New York: Holt.

Gagne, R. (1988). *Essentials of learning for instruction.* Englewood Cliffs, NJ: Prentice-Hall.

Gagne, R., & Briggs, L. (1979). *Principles of instructional design.* New York: Holt, Rinehart and Winston.

Gandry, E., & Spielberger, C. (1971). *Anxiety and educational achievement.* New York: John Wiley.

Garcia, E. E. (1990). Language-minority education litigation policy: "The law of the land." In S. Barona & E. E. Garcia (Eds.), *Children at risk: Poverty, minority status, and other issues in educational equity* (pp. 53-63). Washington, DC: National Association of School Psychologists.

Garcia, J., Kimmedorf, D. J., & Kolling, R. A. (1955). Conditioned aversion to saccharin resulting from exposure to gamma radiation. *Science, 122,* 157-158.

Gardner, H. (1982). *Developmental psychology.* Boston: Little Brown.

Gardner, H. (1983). *Frames of mind.* New York: Basic.

Gardner, H. (1985). *The mind's new science.* New York: Basic Books.

Gardner, H. (1987). Developing the spectrum of human intelligences. *Harvard Educational Review, 57,* 187-193.

Gardner, H. (1991). *The unschooled mind.* New York: Basic Books.

Gardner, L. (1972). Deprivation dwarfism. *Scientific American, 2277,* 76-82.

Garger, S. (1990). Is there a link between learning style and neurophysiology? *Educational Leadership, 48,* 63-65.

Garman, N., & Hazi, H. (1988). Is there life after Madeline Hunter? *Phi Delta Kappan, 69,* 669-672.

Gawronski, J. D. (1991, October). National assessment: Ready or not—here it comes. *Thrust for Educational Leadership,* 12-16.

Gay, G. Ethnic minorities and educational equality. In J. Banks & C. A. Banks (Eds.), *Multicultural Education: Issues and Perspectives.* Boston: Allyn and Bacon.

Gelfand, D. M., & Hartmann, D. P. (1986). *Child behavior analysis and therapy* (2nd ed.). New York: Pergamon.

Gelman, R. (1969). Conservation acquisition: A problem of learning to attend to relevant attributes.

Journal of Experimental Child Psychology, 7, 167-187.

Gelman, R., & Baillargeon, P. (1983). A review of some Piagetian concepts. In P. Mussen (Ed.), *Handbook of Child Psychology.* New York: Wiley.

Genshaft, J. (1991). The gifted adolescent in perspective. In M. Birely and J. Genshaft (Eds.), *Understanding the gifted adolescent: Educational development and multicultural issues.* (pp. 259-262). New York: Teachers College Press.

Gentry, D. (1989). Teacher-made test construction. Paper presented at the annual meeting of the Mid-South Educational Research Association, Little Rock, Arkansas.

Geschwind, N. (1979). Specializations of the human brain. *Scientific American, 241,* 180-201.

Gettinger, M. (1988). Methods of proactive classroom management. *School Psychology Review, 17,* 227-242.

Gettinger, M. (1990). Best practices in increasing academic learning time. In A. Thomas and J. Grimes (Eds.), *Best practices in school psychology-II.* (pp. 393-405). Washington, DC: National Association of School Psychologists.

Getzels, J. W., & Cslkszentmihalyi, M. (1976). *The creative vision: A longitudinal study of problem finding in art.* New York: John Wiley & Son.

Getzels, J. W., & Dillon, J. T. (1973). The nature of giftedness and the education of the gifted. In R. Travers (Ed.), *Second handbook of research on teaching.* Chicago: Rand McNally.

Ghatala, E., Levin, J., Pressley, M., & Ledico, M. (1985). Training cognitive strategy monitoring in children. *American Educational Research Journal 22,* 199-215.

Gibbons, M. (1974). Walkabout: Searching for the right of passage from childhood and school. *Phi Delta Kappan, 9,* 596-602.

Gibbons, M. (1984). Walkabout ten years later: Searching for a renewed vision of education. *Phi Delta Kappan, 9,* 591-600.

Gibson, J. J. (1979). *The ecological approach to visual perception.* Boston: Houghton Mifflin.

Gilligan, C. (1977). In a different voice: Women's conception of self and of morality. *Harvard Educational Review, 47,* 481-517.

Gilligan, C. *In a different voice.* (1982). Cambridge, MA: Harvard University Press.

Ginsberg, H., & Opper, S. (1988). *Piaget's theory of intellectual development.* Englewood Cliffs, NJ: Prentice-Hall.

Glaser, R. (1979). Trends and research questions in psychological research on learning and schooling. *Educational Research, 8,* 6-13.

Glaser, R. (1991). The reemergence of learning theory within instructional research. *American Psychologist, 45,* 29-39.

Glasnhapp, D., & Poggio, J. (1985). *Essentials of statistical analysis for the behavioral sciences.* Columbus, Ohio: Merrill.

Glass, A., Holyoak, K., & Santa, J. (1987). *Cognition.* Reading, MA: Addison-Wesley.

Glass, G., McGaw, V., & Smith, M. L. (1981). *Meta-analysis in social research.* Beverly Hills: Sage.

Glasser, W. (1986). *Control Theory in the Classroom.* New York: Harper and Row.

Gloeckler, T., & Simpson, C. (1988). *Exceptional students in regular classrooms.* Mountain View, CA: Mayfield.

Glover, J. A. & Ronning, R. R. (1987). Introduction. In J. A. Glover and R. R. Ronning (Eds.), *Historical foundations of educational psychology* (pp. 3-15). New York: Plenum Press.

Glover, J. A., Ronning, R. R., & Bruning, R. H. (1990). *Cognitive psychology for teachers.* New York: Macmillan.

Goetz, T., & Dweck, C. (1980). Learned helplessness in social situations. *Journal of Personality and Social Psychology, 39,* 246-255.

Goldsmith, H. H. (1983). Genetic influences on personality from infancy to adulthood. *Child Development, 54,* 331-355.

Goldstein, A. P. (1988). The prepare curriculum: Teaching prosocial competencies. Champaign, IL: Research Press.

Good, T., & Weinstein, R. (1986). Schools make a difference: Evidence, criticisms, and new directions. *American Psychologist, 41,* 1090-1097.

Goodlad, J. (1984). *A place called school.* New York: McGraw-Hill.

Goodman, K. (1986). *What's whole in whole language?* Ontario, Canada: Scholastic.

Goodman, Y. (1989). Roots of the whole language movement. *Elementary School Journal, 90,* 113-127.

Goodnow, J. (1990). The socialization of cognition. In J. Stigler, R. Shweder, & G. Herdt (Eds.), *Cultural psychology.* New York: Cambridge U. Press.

Goodson, B. (1990). Looking into the 1990s. *Teaching and Computers, 7,* 18-21.

Gordon, I. J. (1977). Parent education and parent involvement. *Childhood Education, 54,* 71-78.

Gordon, T. (1974). Teacher effectiveness training. New York: Peter Wyden.

Gorman, R. (1972). *Discovering Piaget: A guide for teachers.* Columbus, Ohio: Charles Merrill.

Gould, S. (1981). *The mismeasure of man.* Cambridge: Harvard University Press.

Grady, M. (1984). *Teaching and brain research.* New York: Longman.

Graham, P., & Rutter, M. (1977). Psychiatric disorder in the young adolescent. *Proceedings of the Royal Society of Medicine, 66,* 1226-1229.

Graham, S., & Barker, G. (1990). The down side of help: An attributional-developmental analysis of helping behavior as a low-ability cue. *Journal of Educational Psychology, 82,* 7-14.

Grant, C., & Sleeter, C. (1989). *Turning on learning: Five approaches for multicultural teaching.* Columbus, Ohio: Merrill.

Grant, N. (1988). The education of minority and peripheral cultures: Introduction. *Comparative Education, 24,* 155-166.

Gray, J. A., & Wedderburn, A. (1960). Grouping strategies with simultaneous stimuli. *Quarterly Journal of Experimental Psychology, 12,* 180-184.

Green, B. (1981). A primer of testing. *American Psychologist, 36,* 1001-1011.

Green, D. Attitudes. In Samuel Bell (Ed.), *Motivation in education.* New York: Academic Press.

Green, W. Hearing disorders. In W. Bendine and A. E. Blackhurst (Eds.), *An introduction to special education.* Boston: Little Brown.

Greene, L. (1987). *Learning disabilities and your child.* New York: Fawcett Columbine.

Greenfield, P. (1966). On culture and conservation. In J. Bruner, R. Oliver, and P. Greenfield (Eds.), *Studies in cognitive growth.* New York: Wiley.

Greeno, J. (1980). Trends in the theory of knowledge for problem solving. In D. Tiema and F. Reif (Eds.), *Problem solving education.* Englewood Cliffs, NJ: Prentice-Hall.

Greeno, J. G., & Bjork, R. A. (1989). Mathematical learning theory and the new `mental forestry'. *American Review of Psychology, 24,* 81-116.

Greer, R. D. (in press). The teacher as strategic scientist: A solution to the educational crisis? *Behavior and Social Issues.*

Gresham, F. M. (1985). Behavior disorder assessment: Conceptual, dysfunctional, and practical considerations. *School Psychology Review, 14,* 495-509.

Gresham, F. M., & Elliott, S. N. (1984) Assessment and classification of children's social skills: A review of methods and issues. *School Psychology Review, 13,* 292-301.

Gresham, F. M., & Elliott, S. N. (1988). Teachers' social validity ratings of social skills: Comparisons between mildly handicapped and nonhandicapped children. *Journal of Psychoeducational Measurement, 6,* 225-234.

Gresham, F. M., & Elliott, S. N., (1990). *Social Skills Rating System.* Circle Pines, MN: AGS.

Gresham, F. M., & Elliott, S. N., & Black, F. (1987). Social skills comparisons across diagnostic subgroups of children. *School Psychology Review, 16,* 78-88.

Gresham, F. M., Evans, S., & Elliott, S. N. (1988). Self-efficacy differences among mildly handicapped, gifted, and nonhandicapped students. *The Journal of Special Education, 22,* 231-241.

Grice, G. R., & Hunter, J. J. (1964). Stimulus intensity effects depend upon the type of experimental design. *Psychological Review, 71,* 247-256.

Griswold, P. (1990). Assessing relevance and reliability to improve the quality of teacher-made tests. *NASSP Bulletin, 74,* 18-24.

Gronlund, N. (1985). *Measurement and evaluation in learning.* New York: Macmillan.

Grossen, B., & Cornine, D. (1990). Diagramming a logical strategy: Effects in difficult problems types and transfer. *Learning Disability Quarterly, 13,* 168-182.

Grossman, H. (1983). *Classification in mental retardation.* Washington, DC: American Association on Mental Deficiency.

Grossman, H. (1984). *Educating Hispanic students: Cultural implications for instruction, classroom management, counseling, and assessment.* Springfield, IL: Charles Thomas.

Grossman, H. (1990). *Trouble-free teaching.* Mountain View, CA: Mayfield.

Grossnickle, D. R., & Thiel, W. B. (1988). *Promoting effective student motivation in school and classrooms: A practitioner's perspective.* Reston, VA: National Association of Secondary School Principals.

Guilford, J. (1967). *The nature of human intelligence.* New York: McGraw-Hill.

Gump, P. (1982). School settings and their keeping. In D. L. Duke (Ed.), *Helping teachers manage classrooms.* Alexandria, VA: ASCD.

Gursky, D. (1991, April). Ambitious measures. *Teacher,* 50-56.

Guskey, T. (1986, Winter). Bloom's mastery learning: A legacy of effectiveness. *Educational Horizons,* 80-86.

Guttman, N., & Kalish, H. (1956). Discriminability and stimulus generalization. *Journal of Experimental Psychology, 51,* 79-88.

H

Hakuta, K. (1986). *Mirror of language: The debate of bilingualism.* New York: Basic Books.

Hall, R. V., & Hall, M. C. (1980). *How to select reinforcers.* Lawrence, KS: H & H Enterprises.

Hallahan, D., & Kauffman, J. (1988). *Exceptional children: Introduction to special education.* Englewood Cliffs, NJ: Prentice-Hall.

Hallahan, D., Kauffman, J., Lloyd, J.W., & McKinney, J. (1988). Questions about the regular education initiative. *Journal of Learning Disabilities, 21,* 3-5.

Hamachek, D. (1987). *Encounters with the self.* New York: Holt, Rinehart, and Winston.

Hammill, D., Leigh, J., McNutt, G., & Larsen, S. A new definition of learning disabilities. *Learning Disability Quarterly, 4,* 336-342.

Haney, C., Banks, C., & Zimbardo, P. (1973). Interpersonal dynamics in a simulated prison. *International Journal of Criminology and Penology, 1,* 69-97.

Haney, W., & Madaus, G. (1978). Making sense of the competency testing movement. *Harvard Educational Review, 48,* 462-484.

Haney, W., & Madaus, G. (1989). Searching for alternatives to standardized tests: Why, what, and whither. *Phi Delta Kappan, 70,* 683-687.

Hansen, R. Anxiety. In Samuel Bell (Ed.). (1977). *Motivation in education.* New York: Academic Press.

Haring, N., & McCormick, L. (1986). *Exceptional children and youth.* Columbus, Ohio: Merrill.

Harmin, M. (1988). Value clarity, high morality: Let's go for both. *Educational Leadership, 45,* 24-30.

Harre, R., & Lamb, R. (1983). The encyclopedic dictionary of psychology. Cambridge, MA: The MIT Press.

Hart, L. (1983). *Human brain and human learning.* New York: Longman.

Hartup, W. (1983). Peer relations. In Paul Mussen (Ed.), *Handbook of child psychology.* New York: Wiley.

Hartup, W., Laursen, B., Stewart, M. I., & Eastenson, A. (1988). Conflict and friendship relations of young children. *Child Development, 59,* 1590-1600.

Havighurst, N. B. (1957). *Society and education.* Boston: Allyn and Bacon.

Havighurst, R. (1972). *Developmental tasks and education.* New York: David McKay.

Hayes, J. (1989). *The complete problem solver.* Philadelphia: The Franklin Institute Press.

Hazen, N., Black, B., & Fleming-Johnson, F. (1984). Social acceptance: Strategies children use and how teachers can help children learn. *Young Children, 39,* 26-36.

Heath, S. B., & McLaughlin, M. B. (1987). A child resource policy: Moving beyond dependence on school and family. *Phi Delta Kappan, 68,* 576-580.

Hembree, H. (1988). Correlates, causes, effects, and treatment of test anxiety. *Review of Educational Research, 58,* 41-77.

Hergenhahn, B. R. (1988). *An introduction to theories of learning.* Englewood Cliffs, NJ: Prentice-Hall.

Heron, W. (1957). The pathology of boredom. *Scientific American, 30,* 52-56.

Herrnstein, R. J. (1961). Relative and absolute strength of response as a function of frequency of reinforcement. *Journal of the Experimental Analysis of Behavior, 4,* 267-272.

Hess, R., Chih-Mei, C., & McDevitt, T. (1987). Cultural variations in family beliefs about children's performance in mathematics: Comparisons among People's Republic of China, Chinese-American, and Caucasian-American families. *Journal of Educational Psychology, 79,* 179-188.

Heward, D. P. & Kaufmann, J. M. (1988). *Exceptional children* (3rd ed.). Columbus, Ohio: Merrill.

Heward, W. L., & Orlansky, M. D. (1988). *Exceptional children.* Columbus, Ohio: Merrill.

Highet, G. (1950). *The art of teaching.* New York: Knopf.

Hilgard, E., & Bower, G. (1981). *Theories of learning.* New York: Appleton-Century.

Hill, J. (1980). *Understanding early adolescence.* Chapel Hill, NC: U. of North Carolina Press.

Hill, K. T., & Wigfield, A. (1984). Test anxiety: A major educational problem and what can be done about it. *Elementary School Journal, 85,* 105-126.

Hillerbrand, E. (1989). Cognitive differences between experts and novices: Implications for group supervision. *Journal of Counseling and Development, 67,* 293-296.

Hilliard, A. (1983). Psychological factors associated with language in the education of the African-American child. *Journal of Negro Education, 52,* 24-34.

Hinde, R. A. (1979). *Towards understanding relationships.* New York: Academic Press.

Hinde, R. A. (1987). *Individuals, relationships and culture.* Cambridge: Cambridge University Press.

Hiroto, D. S. (1974). Locus of control and learned helplessness. *Journal of Experimental Psychology, 102,* 187-193.

Hirsch, E. D. (1987). *Cultural literacy: What every American needs to know.* Boston: Houghton Mifflin.

Hochhauser, M., & Rothenberger, J. (1992). *AIDS Education.* Dubuque, IA: Wm. C. Brown.

Hodgson, A. (1986). Integrating physically handicapped pupils. *Special Education: Forward Trends, 11,* 27-30.

Hofmeister, A., Engelmann, S., & Cornine, D. (1989). Developing and validating science education videodiscs. *Journal of Research in Science Teaching, 26,* 665-677.

Hofstadter, D. (1979). *Godel, Escher, Bach: A golden braid.* New York: Basic Books.

Hoge, R. D., & Coladarci, T. (1989). Teacher based judgment of academic achievement: A review of the literature: *Review of Educational Research,* 297-313.

Holmes, C. T. (1990). Grade level retention efforts. A meta-analysis of research studies. In L. A. Shepard and M. L. Smith (Eds.), *Flunking grades: Research and policies on retention.* New York: The Falmer Press.

Holz, W. C., & Azrin, N. H. (1961). Discriminative properties of punishment. *Journal of the Experimental Analysis of Behavior, 4,* 225-232.

Hooper, S., & Hannafin, M. (1991). Psychological perspectives on emerging instructional technologies: A critical analysis. *Educational Psychologist, 26,* 69-95.

Horne, A. M., & Sayger, T. V. (1990). *Treating conduct and oppositional defiant disorders in children.* New York: Pergamon Press.

Houston, J. (1981). *Fundamentals of learning and memory.* New York: Academic Press.

Houston, J. (1985). *Motivation.* New York: Macmillan.

Hovland, C. (1953). *Communication and persuasion: Psychological studies of opinion change.* New Haven: Yale University Press.

Howard, G. (1991). Culture tales: A narrative approach to thinking, cross-cultural psychology, and psychotherapy. *American Psychologist, 46,* 187-197.

Howell, K. W. (1986). Direct assessment of academic performance. *School Psychology Review, 15,* 324-335.

Howell, K., & Morehead, M. (1987). *Curriculum-based evaluation for special and remedial education.* Columbus, Ohio: Merrill.

Hubel, D. (1979). The brain. *Scientific American, 241,* 44-53.

Hubel, D. H., & Wiesel, T. N. (1968). Perceptive fields and functional architecture of monkey striate cortex. *Journal of Physiology, 195,* 215-243.

Huck, S. W., & Sandler, H. M. (1979). *Rival hypotheses: Alternative interpretations of data based conclusions.* New York: Harper & Row.

Hughes, M. (1986). *Children and number.* New York: Blackwell.

Hulse, S., Egeth, H., & Deese, J. (1980). *The psychology of learning.* New York: McGraw Hill.

Hunt, E. (1990). A modern arsenal for mental assessment. *Educational Psychologist, 25,* 223-242.

Hunt, E., Lunneborg, C., & Lewis, J. (1975). What does it mean to be high verbal? *Cognitive Psychology, 7,* 194-227.

Hunter, B. (1983). *My students use computers.* Reston, VA: Reston Publishing Company.

Hunter, M. (1987, April). The Hunterization of America's schools. *Instructor,* 56-58, 60.

Hunter, M., & Russell, D. (1981). Planning for effective instruction: Lesson design. *Increasing your teaching effectiveness.* Palo Alto, CA: The Learning Institute.

Hurd, P. (1991). Why we must transform science education. *Educational Leadership, 49,* 33-35.

Hyden, H. (1985). The brain, learning and values. In John Eccles (Ed.), *Mind and brain.* New York: Pergamon.

Ingersoll, B. (1988). *Your hyperactive child.* New York: Doubleday.

Isenberg, J. (1987, June). Societal influences on children. *Childhood Education,* 341-348.

J

Jackson, A., Fletcher, B., & Messer, D. (1988). Effects of experience on microcomputer use in primary schools: Results of a second survey. *Journal of Computer-Assisted Learning, 4,* 214-226.

Jackson, P. (1968). *Life in classrooms.* New York: Holt, Rinehart, and Winston.

Jenkins, J., & Pany, D. (1978). Standardized achievement tests: How useful for special education? *Exceptional Children, 44,* 448-453.

Jensen, A. (1981). *Bias in mental testing.* San Francisco: Free Press.

Johnson, D. (1981). Student-student interaction: The neglected variable in education. *The Educational Researcher,* 5-10.

Johnson, D., & Johnson, R. (1986, January 6). Computer-assisted cooperative learning, *Educational Technology.*

Johnson, M., & Brooks, H. (1979). Conceptualizing classroom management. In Daniel Duke (Ed.), *Classroom Management. The Seventy-eighth Yearbook of the National Society for the Study of Education.* Chicago: University of Chicago Press.

Jones, B. F., Pierce, J., & Hunter, B. (1988-1989, December/January). Teaching students to construct graphic representations. *Educational Leadership,* 20-25.

Jones, R. L. (Ed.). (1988). *Psychological assessment of minority group children: A casebook.* Berkeley, CA: Cobb & Henry Publishers.

K

Kagan, J. (1989). *Unstable ideas.* Cambridge, MA: Harvard U. Press.

Kagan, J., & Moss, H. (1962). *Birth to maturity.* New York: Wiley.

Kail, R. (1984). *The development of memory in children* (2nd ed.). San Francisco: Freeman.

Kail, R. V., Jr., & Hagen, J. W. (Eds.). (1977). *Perspectives on the development of memory and cognition.* Hillsdale, NJ: Erlbaum.

Kaiser, A. P., Hemmeter, M. L., & Alpert, C. L. (in press). Alternative intervention strategies for treatment of communication disorders in young children with developmental disabilities. In T. R. Kratochwill, S. N. Elliott, & M. Gettinger (Eds.), *Advances in school psychology.* (Vol. 8). Hillsdale, NJ: Erlbaum.

Kalish, H. (1981). *From behavioral science to behavior modification.* New York: McGraw-Hill.

Kauffman, J., Gerber, M., & Semmel, M. (1988). Arguable assumptions underlying the regular education initiative. *Journal of Learning Disabilities, 21,* 6-11.

Kaufman, M., Agard, J. A., & Semmel, M. I. (1985). *Mainstreaming: Learners and their environments.* Cambridge, MA: Brookline Books.

Kazdin, A. (1988). *Child psychotherapy: Developing and evaluating effective treatments.* New York: Pergamon Press.

Kazdin, A. (1989). *Behavior modification in applied settings.* (4th ed.). Pacific Groves, CA: Brooks/Cole.

Kazdin, A. (1992). Research design in clinical psychology. (2nd ed.). New York: Pergamon.

Keil, F. (1979). *Semantic and conceptual development.* Cambridge, MA: Harvard University Press, 1979.

Keith, T. Z. (1987). Children and homework. In D. Thomas and J. Grimes (Eds.), *Children's needs: Psychological perceptions* (pp. 275-282). Washington, DC: National Association of School Psychologists.

Kellaghan, T., Madaus, G., & Airasian, P. (1980). *Standardized testing in elementary schools: Effect on schools, teachers, and students.* Washington, DC: N.E.A.

Keller, F. S. (1968). Good-bye teacher. *Journal of Applied Behavior Analysis, 1,* 69-89.

Keller, & Sherman, J. (1974). *The Keller plan handbook.* Menlo Park, CA: W. A. Benjamin.

Kelley, M. L. (1990). *School-home notes: Promoting children's classroom success.* New York: Guilford Press.

Kelley, M. L. & Carper, L. B. (1988). Home-based reinforcement procedures. In J. C. Witt, S. N. Elliott, and F. M. Greshman (Eds.), *Handbook of behavior therapy in education* (pp. 419-438). New York: Plenum.

Kellogg, J. (1988). Forces of change. *Phi Delta Kappan, 70,* 109-204.

Kerlinger, F. (1973). *Foundations of behavioral research.* New York: Holt, Rinehart and Winston.

Kety, S. (1979). Disorders of the human brain. *Scientific American, 244,* 202-218.

Kim, E., & Kellough, R. (1991). *A resource guide for secondary school teaching.* New York: Macmillan.

Kimble, G. (1981). Biological and cognitive constraints on learning. In L. T. Benjamin (Ed.), *The G. Stanley Hall Lecture Series.* Washington, DC: American Psychological Association.

Kimble, G., & Hilgard, E. (1961). *Marquis' conditioning and learning.* New York: Appleton-Century-Crofts.

Kinsbourne, M. (1986). Systematizing cognitive psychology. *Behavioral and Brain Sciences, 9,* 567.

Klausmeier, H. (1976). Instructional design and the teaching of concepts. In J. Levin and V. Allen (Eds.), *Cognitive learning in children.* New York: Academic.

Kleiman, G. (1991). Mathematics across the curriculum. *Educational Leadership, 49-51.*

Kohlberg, L. (1975). The cognitive-developmental approach to moral education. *Phi Delta Kappan, 56,* 670-677.

Kohlberg, L. (1976). Moral stages and moralization: The cognitive developmental approach. In T. Lickona (Ed.), *Moral development and behavior: Theory, research, and social issues.* New York: Holt, Rinehart and Winston.

Kohlberg, L., & Hersh, R. (1977). Moral development: A review of the theory. *Moral Development, 2,* 53-59.

Kolesnik, W. (1978). *Motivation.* Boston: Allyn and Bacon.

Koretz, D. (1989). The new national assessment: What it can and cannot do. *NEA Today, 7,* 32-37.

Kornhaber, M., Krechevsky, M., & Gardner, H. (1990). Engaging intelligence. *Educational Psychologist, 25,* 177-200.

Kosslyn, S. (1980). *Image and mind.* Cambridge, MA: Harvard University Press.

Kounin, J. (1970). *Discipline and group management in classrooms.* New York: Holt, Rinehart and Winston.

Kramer, J. J. (1990). Training parents as behavior change agents: Successes, failures and suggestions for school psychologists. In T. B. Gutkin and C. R. Reynolds (Eds.), *Handbook of school psychology* (2nd ed.). (pp. 683-702). New York: Wiley.

Kratochwill, T. R. (Ed.). (1978). *Single subject research: Strategies for evaluating change.* New York: Academic.

Kratochwill, T. R., & Bijou, S. W. (1987). The impact of behaviorism on educational psychology. In John A. Glover & R. R. Rouning (Eds.), *Historical foundations of educational psychology* (pp. 131-157). New York: Plenum Press.

Kratochwill, T. R., & Goldman, J. A. (1973). Developmental changes in children's judgments of age. *Developmental Psychology, 9,* 358-362.

Kratochwill, T. R., & Levin, J. R. (Eds.). (1992). *Single-case design and analysis: New developments for psychology and education.* Hillsdale, NJ: Erlbaum.

Kratochwill, T. R. & Morris, R. J. (Eds.). (1991). *The practice of child therapy* (2nd ed.). New York: Pergamon.

Kratochwill, T. K., & Sheridan, S. (1990). Advances in behavioral assessment. In T. B. Gutkin and C. R. Reynolds (Eds.), *The Handbook of school psychology* (2nd ed.). (pp. 328-369). New York: John Wiley & Sons.

Krouse, H. (1986). Use of decision frames by elementary school children. *Perceptual and Motor Skills. 63,* 1107-1112.

Kubiszyn, T., & Borich, G. (1984). *Educational testing and measurement.* Glenview, IL: Scott Foresman.

Kulik, C. C., & Kulik, J. A. (1991). Effectiveness of computer-based instruction: An upgraded analysis. *Computers in Human Behavior, 7,* 75-94.

L

Lachman, R., Lachman, J., & Butterfield, E. *Cognitive psychology and information processing.* Hillsdale, NJ: Lawrence Erlbaum.

Lamb, M. E., & Baumrind, D. (1978). Socialization and personality development in the preschool years. In M. E. Lamb (Ed.), *Social and personality development.* New York: Holt, Rinehart and Winston.

Langlois, J., & Downs, A. C. (1979). Peer relations as a function of physical attractiveness: The eye of the beholder or behavioral reality? *Child Development, 50,* 409-418.

Langone, J. (1991). *AIDS: The facts.* Boston: Little, Brown.

Larkin, J. (1980). Teaching problem solving in physics. In D. Tuma and F. Reif (Eds.), *Problem solving and education.* Englewood Cliffs, NJ: Prentice-Hall.

Laslett, R., & Smith, C. (1984). *Effective Classroom Management.* New York: Nichols. *Lau v. Nichols,* 414, U.S. 563, (1974).

LaVigna, G. W., & Donnellan, A. M. (1986). *Alternatives to punishment: Solving behavior problems with non-aversive strategies.* New York: Irvington Publishers.

Lawrence, D. (1963). The nature of a stimulus. In Sigmund Koch (Ed.), *Psychology: A study of a science: Vol. 5.* New York: McGraw-Hill.

Lazar, I., & Darlington, R. (1982). Lasting effects of early education: A report from the consortium for longitudinal studies. *Monographs of the Society for Research in Child Development, 47,* Serial No. 195.

Leahey, D., & Harris, T. (1985). *Human Learning.* Englewood Cliffs, NJ: Prentice-Hall.

Lee, M. (1986). The match: Learning styles of black children and microcomputer programming. *Journal of Negro Education, 55,* 78-90.

Leinhardt, G., & Greeno, J. (1986). The cognitive skill of teaching. *Journal of Educational Psychology, 768,* 75-95.

Leiter, M. P. (1977). A study of reciprocity in preschool play groups. *Child Development, 48,* 1288-1295.

Lenneberg, E. (1967). *Biological Foundations of Language.* New York: Wiley.

Lesgold, A. (1986). Preparing children for a computer-rich world. *Educational Leadership, 43,* 7-11.

Lesner, W. J., & Hillman, D. (1983). A developmental schema of creativity. *The Journal of Creative Behavior, 17,* 1-11.

Levin, J. (1981). The mnemonic '80s: Keyword in the classroom. *Educational Psychologist, 167,* 65-82.

Levine, M., Brooks, R., & Shonkoff, J. (1980). *A pediatric approach to learning disorders.* New York: Wiley.

Levine, M., Carey, W., Crocker, A., & Gross, R. (Eds.). (1983). *Developmental-behavioral pediatrics.* Philadelphia: Saunder.

Levine, R. (1977). Child rearing as cultural adaptation. In P. Leiderman, S. Tulkin, and A. Rosenfeld (Eds.), *Culture and infancy.* New York: Academic.

Lewin, K. (1935). *A dynamic theory of personality.* New York: McGraw-Hill.

Lewis, D., & Greene, J. (1982). *Thinking better.* New York: Holt.

Lichtenstein, R., & Ireton, H. (1984). *Preschool screening: Identifying young children with developmental and educational problems.* New York: Grune and Stratton.

Lickona, T. (1977). How to encourage moral development. *Learning, 5,* 36-44.

Lickona, T. (1983). *Raising good children.* New York: Bantam.

Lindholm, K. J. (1990). Bilingual immersion education: Educational equity for language minority students. In A. Barona and E. E. Garcia (Eds.), *Children at risk: Poverty, minority status, and other issues in educational equity* (pp. 77-89). Washington, DC: National Association of School Psychologists.

Linn, R. (1986). Educational testing and assessment. *American Psychologist, 41,* 1153-1160.

Lipman, M. (1987, September). Critical thinking: What can it be? *Educational Leadership,* 38-43.

Lipman, M. (1987). Some thoughts on the foundations of reflective education. In J. Baron and R. Sternberg (Eds.), *Teaching thinking skills.* New York: Freeman.

Lisina, M. I. (1982). The development of interaction in the first seven years of life. In W. Hartup (Ed.), *Review of child development research.* Chicago: University of Chicago Press.

Livingston, R. (1986). Visual impairments. In N. Haring and L. McCormick (Eds.), *Exceptional children and youth.* Columbus, Ohio: Charles Merrill.

Lloyd, J. W., Singh, N. N., & Repp, A. C. (Eds.). (1991). *The regular education initiative: Alternative perspectives on concepts, issues, and models.* Sycamore, IL: Sycamore Publishing Co.

Lockard, J., Abrams, P., & Many, W. (1987). *Microcomputers for educators.* Boston: Little, Brown.

Loftus, E. F., & Palmer, J. C. (1974). Reconstruction of automobile destruction: An example of the interaction between language and memory. *Journal of Verbal Learning and Verbal Behavior, 13,* 585-589.

Lombana, J. (1983). *Home-school partnerships.* New York: Gruene and Stratton.

Lomotey, K. (1990). *Going to school: The African-American experience.* New York: State University of New York Press.

Looft, W. R. (1971). Children's judgments of age. *Child Development, 42,* 1282-1284.

Looft, W. R., Raymond, J. R., & Raymond, B. B. (1972). Children's judgments of age in Sarawak. *Journal of Social Psychology, 86,* 181-185.

Lovell-Troy, L. (1989). Teaching techniques for instructional goals: A partial review of the literature. *Teaching Sociology, 17,* 28-37.

Lovinger, S. L., Brandell, M. E., & Seesdedt-Stanford, L. (1991). *Language learning disabilities: A new and practical approach for those who work with children and their families.* New York: Continuum.

Lowenbraun, S., & Thompson, M. (1986). Hearing impairments. In N. Haring and L. McCormick (Eds.), *Exceptional children and youth.* Columbus, Ohio: Merrill.

Ludlow, L. (1989). *Testing young children.* Unpublished manuscript.

Luria, A. (1973). *The working brain.* New York: Basic.

Luria, A. (1980). *Higher cortical functions in man.* New York: Basic.

Lyman, H. (1986). *Test scores and what they mean.* Englewood Cliffs, NJ: Prentice Hall.

Lynn, S. (1985). A twinkle in the teacher's eye. *Instructor, 74,* 76.

M

Maccoby, E. (1990). Gender and relationships. *American Psychologist, 45,* 513-520.

Madaus, G. (1989). *Teach them well.* Boston: Allyn and Bacon

Maehr, M. (1984). Meaning and motivation: Toward a theory of personal investment. In R. Ames & C. Ames (Eds.), *Research on motivation in education: Vol. 1.* New York: Academic Press.

Mager, R. (1975). *Preparing instructional objectives.* Palo Alto, CA: Fearon.

Malone, M. (1984). An analysis of difference in cognitive development in selected African and Western societies. Unpublished Manuscript.

Manaster, G. J. (1989). *Adolescent development.* Itasca, IL: Peacock.

Mann, L. (1979). *On the trail of process: A historical perspective on cognitive processes and their training.* New York: Grune & Stratton.

Marcia, J. (1966). Development and validation of ego identity status. *Journal of Personality and Social Psychology, 3,* 551-558.

Marcia, J. (1980). Identity formation in adolescence. In J. Adelson (Ed.), *Handbook of Adolescent Psychology.* New York: Wiley.

Marjoribanks, K. (1986). Cognitive and environmental correlates of aspiration: Attitude-group differences. *Journal of Research in Childhood Education, 1,* 95-103.

Marjoribanks, K. (1988). Cognitive and environmental correlates of adolescents' achievement ambitions. *Alberta Journal of Educational Research, 2,* 166-178.

Markle, S. (1978). *Designs for instructional designers.* Champaign, IL: Stipes Publishing Co.

Marland, R. W. (1986). A study of teachers' interactive thoughts. Unpublished Dissertation.

Marr, D. (1982). *Vision.* San Francisco: Freeman.

Marso, R., & Pigge, F. (1989). The status of classroom teachers' test construction proficiencies. Paper presented at the annual meeting of the National Council of Measurement in Education. San Francisco.

Martin, G., & Pear, J. (1978). *Behavior modification.* Englewood Cliffs, NJ: Prentice-Hall.

Maslow, A. (1987). *Motivation and personality.* New York: Harper & Row.

Mason, J., & Au, K. (1990). *Reading instruction for today.* Glenview, IL: Scott, Foresman/Little, Brown.

Matarazzo, J. (1990). Psychological assessment versus psychological testing: Validation from Binet to the school, clinic, and courtroom. *American Psychologist, 45,* 999-1017.

Matheney, A. P., Jr. (1980). Bayley's infant behavior record: Behavioral components and twin analyses. *Child Development, 51,* 1157-1167.

Mayer, R. (1981). *The promise of cognitive psychology.* San Francisco: W. H. Freeman.

McBay, S. (1990, January 10). Plan unveiled for improving minority education. *New York Times,* B8.

McCaslin, M. (1989). Theory, instruction, and future implementation. *Elementary School Journal, 90,* 223-229.

McClelland, D. (1973). Sources of achievement. In D. C. McClelland and R. S. Steele (Eds.), *Human motivation: A book of readings.* Morristown, NJ: General Learning Press.

McClelland, D. (1987). *Human motivation.* New York: Cambridge, U. Press.

McClelland, D., & Pilon, D. A. (1983). Sources of adult motives in patterns of parent behavior in early childhood. *Journal of Personality and Social Psychology, 44,* 564-574.

McClelland, D., & Steele, R. (1973). *Human motivation.* Morristown, NJ: General Learning Press.

McConnell, J. V. (1980). *Understanding human behavior. An introduction to psychology* (3rd ed.). New York: Holt, Rinehart and Winston.

McConnell, S. R., & Odom, S. L. (1986). Sociometrics: Peer-referenced measures and assessment of social competence. In P. S. Strain, M. J. Guralnick, and H. M. Walker (Eds.), *Children's social behavior: Development, assessment, and modification* (pp. 215-284). Orlando, FL: Academic Press.

McDevitt, T., Spivey, N., Sheehan, E., Lennon, R., & Story, R. (1990). Children's beliefs about listening: Is it enough to be still and quiet? *Child Development, 61,* 713-721.

McKeachie, W., Pintrich, P. R., & Lin, Y. (1985). Teaching learning strategies. *Educational Psychologist, 20,* 153-160.

McLaughlin, B. (1990). Development of bilingualism: Myth and reality. In A. Barona and E. E. Garcia (Eds.), *Children at risk: Poverty, minority status, and other issues in educational equity* (pp. 77-89). Washington, DC: National Association of School Psychologists.

McLoyd, V. (1990). Minority children. *Child Development, 61,* 263-266.

McNamara, E., Evans, M., & Hill, W. (1986). The reduction of disruptive behavior in two secondary school classes. *British Journal of Educational Psychology, 36,* 209-215.

McTighe, J., & Lyman, F. T. (1988). Aiding thinking in the classroom: The promise of theory-embedded tools. *Educational Leadership, 47,* 18-24.

Medland, M. & Vitale, M. (1984). *Management of classrooms.* New York: Holt, Rinehart and Winston.

Medley, D. (1979). The effectiveness of teachers. In P. Peterson and H. Walberg (Eds.), *Research on teaching: Concepts, findings, and implications.* Berkeley, CA: McCutchan.

Medway, F. J., & Rose, J. S. (1986). Grade retention. In T. R. Kratochwill (Ed.), *Advances in school psychology* (Vol. 5, pp. 141-175). Hillsdale, NJ: Erlbaum.

Mensh, E., & Mensh, H. (1991). *The IQ mythology: Class, race, gender.* Carbondale, IL: Southern Illinois University Press.

Menzel, E. W. (1978). Cognitive mapping in chimpanzees. In S. H. Hulse, H. Fowler, and W. K. Honig (Eds.), *Cognitive processes in animal behavior.* New Jersey: Erlbaum.

Mercer, C. (1986). Learning disabilities. In N. Hoving and L. McCormick (Eds.), *Exceptional children and youth.* Columbus, Ohio: Charles Merrill.

Mercer, J. (1979). *SOMPA Assessment Manual.* New York: The Psychological Corporation.

Mervis, C. B., & Rosch, E. (1981). Categorization of natural objects. *Annual Review of Psychology, 32,* 89-115.

Messick, S. (1979). Potential uses of noncognitive measurement in education. *Journal of Educational Psychology, 71,* 281-289.

Messick, S., Beaton, A., & Lord, F. (1983). A design for a new era. *National Assessment of Educational Programs.*

Miller, G. A. (1956). The magical number seven, plus or minus two: Some limits on our capacity for processing information. *Psychological Review, 63,* 81-97.

Miller, P. (1989). *Theories of developmental psychology.* New York: Freeman.

Miller-Jones, D. (1989). Culture and testing. *American Psychologist, 4,* 360-367.

Millman, J., Bishop, C., & Ebel, R. (1965). An analysis of test-wiseness. *Educational and Psychological Measurement, 710.*

Minner, S. (1989). Informal assessment of written expression. *Teaching Exceptional Children, 21,* 76-79.

Minuchin, P., & Shapiro, E. (1983). The school as a context for social development. In Paul Mussen (Ed.), *Handbook of child psychology.* New York; Wiley.

Miranda, A. H., & Santos de Barona, M. (1990). A model for interventions with low achieving minority students. In A. Barona and E. E. Garcia (Eds.), *Children at risk: Poverty, minority students, and other issues in educational equity.* (pp. 119-134). Washington, DC: National Association of School Psychologists.

Mishkin, M. (1987). The anatomy of memory. *Scientific American, 256,* 80-89.

Mitchell, J. (Ed.). (1985). *The ninth mental measurements yearbook.* Lincoln: University of Nebraska Press.

Monk, D. (1987). *Motivation: The organization of action.* New York: Norton.

Moore, B., & Parker, R. (1986). *Critical thinking.* Palo Alto: Mayfield.

Moore, G. (1983). *Developing and evaluating educational research.* Boston: Little, Brown.

Moore, L., & Cornine, D. (1989). Evaluating curriculum design in the context of active teaching. *Remedial and Special Education, 10,* 28-37.

Morgan, S. (1986). Locus of control and achievement in emotionally disturbed children in segregated classes. *Journal of Child and Adolescent Psychotherapy, 3,* 17-21.

Morris, R. J., & Kratochwill, T. R. (1983). *Treating children's fears and phobias.* New York: Pergamon.

Morsink, C. (1985). Learning disabilities. In W. Berdine and A. E. Blackhurst (Eds.), *An introduction to special education.* Boston: Little, Brown.

Morsink, C. V. (1983). *Teaching special needs students in regular classrooms.* Boston: Little, Brown.

Moses, S. (1990). Assessors seek test that teaches. *The APA Monitor, 21,* 1, 37.

Moses, S. (1991 a). Major revision of SAT goes into effect in 1994. *The APA Monitor, 22,* 1.

Moses, S. (1991 b). Motivation neglected in educational reform. *The APA Monitor, 22,* 1.

Moses, S. (1991 c). Questions surround idea of national exam. *The APA Monitor, 22,* 34-35.

Mosher, R. (1979). *Adolescents' development and education.* Berkeley, CA: McCutchan.

Montagu, E., Huntsberger, J., & Hoffman, J. (1989). *Beginning teaching in the elementary and middle schools.* Columbus, Ohio: Merrill.

Mountcastle, V. (1978). An organizing principle for cerebral function. In G. Edelman and V. Mountcastle (Eds.), *The mindful brain.* Cambridge, MA: MIT Press.

Mullis, I., & Jenkins, L. (1988). *The science report card.* Princeton NJ: Educational Testing Service.

Murnane, R., Singer, J., Willett, J., Kemple, J., & Olsen, R. (1991). *Who will teach: Policies that matter.* Cambridge, MA: Harvard University Press.

Muth, D., Glynn, S., Britton, B., & Graves, M. (1988). Thinking out loud while studying text: Rehearsing new ideas. *Journal of Educational Psychology, 80,* 315-318.

Muthukvishna, N., Cornine, D., Grossen, B., & Miller, S. (1990). *Children's alternative frameworks: Should they be directly addressed in science?* Unpublished manuscript, University of Oregon, Eugene.

Myers, P. I. & Hammill, D. D. (1990). *Learning disabilities: Basic concepts, assessment practices, and instructional strategies* (4th ed.). Austin, TX: U. of Texas Press.

N

Naragan, J., Heward, W. L., & Gardner, R. (1990). Using response cards to increase student participation in an elementary classroom. *Journal of Applied Behavior Analysis, 23,* 483-490.

National Education Association (1982). *Status of the American public school teacher 1980-1981.* Washington, DC: NEA.

National Institute of Education. (1978). *Violent schools—safe schools: The safe school study report to Congress.* Vol. 1. Washington, DC: National Institute of Education.

Natriello, G. (1987). The impact of evaluation processes on students. *Educational Psychologist, 22,* 155-175.

Neisser, U. (1967). *Cognitive psychology.* New York: Appleton-Century-Crofts.

Neisser, U. (1982). *Memory observed.* San Francisco: Freeman.

Nesbit, J., & Hunka, S. (1987). A method for sequencing instructional objectives which minimizes memory load. *Instructional Science, 16,* 137-150.

Nesher, P. (1986). Learning mathematics: A cognitive perspective. *American Psychologist, 41,* 1114-1122.

New Voices. (1988). *Immigrant students in U.S. public schools.* Boston: The National Coalition of Advocates for Students.

Newell, A. (1980). One final word. In D. Tuma and F. Reif (Eds.), *Problem solving and education.* Englewood Cliffs, NJ: Prentice-Hall.

Newman, R. S. (1990). Children's help-seeking in the classroom: The role of motivational factors and attitudes. *Journal of Educational Psychology, 82,* 71-80.

Nicaise, M. (1991). *A cognitive-attentional treatment program for the reduction of test anxiety in secondary students.* Master's Thesis, University of Wisconsin-Madison.

Nickerson, R. (1987). Why teach thinking? In J. Baron and R. Sternberg (Eds.), *Teaching thinking skills.* New York: Freeman.

Nielsen, L. (1987). *Adolescent psychology.* New York: Holt, Rinehart and Winston.

Nitko, A. (1983). *Educational tests and measurement: An introduction.* New York: Macmillan.

Noel, M. (1984, March/April). Federal regulation: Its reach exceeds its grasp. *Remedial and Special Education, 5,* 32-35.

O

Ogbu, J. (1990). Literacy and schooling in subordinate cultures: The case of Black Americans. In K. Lomotey (Ed.), *Going to School: The African-American experience.* New York: State University of New York Press.

Ollendick, T. H., Oswald, D. P., & Francis, G. (1989). Validity of teacher nominations in identifying aggressive, withdrawn, and popular children. *Journal of Clinical Child Psychology, 18,* 221-229.

Olsen, L. (1988). Crossing the school-house border: Immigrant children in California. *Phi Delta Kappan, 70,* 211-218.

Olweus, D. (1982). Development of stable aggressive reaction patterns in males. In R. Blanchard and C. Blanchard (Eds.), *Advances in the study of aggression.* Vol. 1. New York: Academic.

Ornstein, A., & Levine, D. (1982, March/April). Multicultural education: Trends and issues. *Childhood Education, 58,* 241-245.

Osofsky, J. (1976). Neonatal characteristics and mother-infant interactions in two obstetrical situations. *Child Development, 47,* 1138-1147.

Osofsky, J. (Ed.). (1979). *Handbook of infant development.* New York: Wiley.

Osofsky, J. (Ed.). (1986). *Handbook of infant development* (2nd ed.). New York: Wiley.

Osofsky, J., & Connors, K. (1979). Mother-infant interaction: An integrative view of a complex system. In J. Osofsky (Ed.), *Handbook of infant development.* New York: Wiley.

P

Page, E. (1958). Teacher comments and student performance. *Journal of Educational Psychology, 49,* 173-181.

Paivio, A. (1974). Comparisons of mental clocks. *Journal of Experimental Psychology, 4,* 61-71.

Paivio, A. (1979). *Imagery and verbal processes.* Hillsdale, NJ: Erlbaum.

Palincer, A. S., & Brown, A. (1984). Reciprocal teaching of comprehension-fostering and monitoring activities. *Cognition and Instruction, 1,* 117-175.

Palmer, O. (1962) Seven classic ways of grading dishonestly. *The English Journal,* 464-467.

Paolitto, D., & Hersh, D. R. (1976). Pedagogical implications for stimulating moral development in the classroom. In J. Meyer (Ed.), *Reflections on values education.* Ontario: Wilfred Laurier Press.

Paris, S., Cross, D., & Lipson, M. (1984). Informed strategies for learning: A program to improve children's reading awareness and comprehension. *Journal of Educational Psychology, 76,* 1239-1252.

Parke, R., & Slaby, R. (1983). The development of aggression. In Paul Mussen (Ed.), *Handbook of child psychology.* New York: Wiley.

Parten, M. (1932). Social participation among preschool children. *Journal of Abnormal and Social Psychology, 27,* 243-268.

Pask, G. (1976). Styles and strategies of learning. *British Journal of Educational Psychology, 46,* 128-408.

Paulos, J. (1988). *Innumeracy.* New York: Hill & Wang.

Paulson, F. L., Paulson, P. R., & Meyer, C. A. (1991, February). What makes a portfolio a portfolio? *Educational Leadership,* 60-63.

Pavlov, I. P. (1927). *Conditioned reflexes.* London: Oxford University Press.

Pavlov, I. P. (1928). *Lectures on conditioned reflexes.* London: Oxford University Press.

Pendarvis, E. (1985). Gifted and talented children. In W. Berdine and A. E. Blackhurst (Eds.), *An introduction to special education.* Boston: Little, Brown.

Perkins, D. N. (1981). *The mind's best work.* Cambridge: Harvard University Press.

Perkins, D. N. (1986). Thinking frames. *Educational Leadership, 43,* 4-10.

Perkins, D. N. (1987). Thinking frames. In J. Baron and R. Sternberg (Eds.), *Teaching thinking skills.* New York: Freeman.

Perkins, M. (1982). Minimum competency testing: What? why? why not? *Educational Measurement: Issues and Practices, 1,* 5-9, 26.

Peterson, L. R., & Peterson, M. J. (1959). Short-term retention of individual verbal items. *Journal of Experimental Psychology, 58,* 193-198.

Peterson, P., & Barger, S. A. (1984). Attribution theory and teacher expectancy. In J. B. Dusek (Ed.), *Teacher expectancies.* Hillsdale, NJ: Erlbaum.

Petri, H. (1991). *Motivation: Theory and research.* Belmont, CA: Wadsworth.

Pfiffner, L., Rosen, L., & O'Leary, S. (1985). The efficacy of an all-positive approach to classroom management. *Journal of Applied Behavior Analysis, 18,* 257-261.

Phares, E. J. (1973). *Locus of control: A personality determinant of behavior.* Morristown, NJ: General Learning Press.

Phillips, D. C. (1983). On describing a student's cognitive structure. *Educational Psychologist, 18,* 59-74.

Phillips, J. (1979). *The origin of intellect: Piaget's theory.* San Francisco: Freeman.

Phye, G., & Andre, T. (1986). *Classroom cognitive learning.* New York: Academic.

Piaget, J. (1936). *The language and thought of the child.* New York: Harcourt, Brace, and World.

Piaget, J. (1952). *The origin of intelligence in children.* New York: International Universities Press.

Piaget, J. (1964). Development and learning. In R. Ripple and V. Rockcastle (Eds.), *Piaget rediscovered.* Washington, DC: U.S. Office of Education, National Science Foundation.

Piaget, J. (1967). *Six psychological studies.* New York: Random House.

Piaget, J. (1969). *Science of education and the psychology of the child.* New York: Viking.

Piaget, J. (1971). *Biology and knowledge.* Chicago: University of Chicago Press.

Piaget, J. (1973). *The child and reality.* New York: Grossman.

Piaget, J., & Inhelder, B. (1969). *The psychology of the child.* New York: Basic Books.

Piersel, W., & Kratochwill, T. R. (1979). Self-observation and behavior change: Applications to academic and adjustment problems through behavioral consultation. *Journal of School Psychology, 17,* 151-161.

Pintrich, P., Cross, D., Kozma, R., & McKeachie, W. (1986). Instructional psychology. In M. Rosenzweig and L. Porter (Eds.), *Annual review of psychology.* Palo Alto, CA: Annual Reviews.

Pintrich, P., McKeachie, W. & Lin, Y. (1987). Teaching a course in learning to learn. *Teaching of Psychology, 14,* 81-86.

Pirozzolo, F., & Wittrock, M. (Eds.). (1981). *Neuropsychological and Cognitive Processes in Reading.* New York: Academic Press.

Polya, G. (1957). *How to solve it.* Garden City, NY: Doubleday.

Pompi, K. F., & Lachman, R. (1967). Surrogate processes in the short-term retention of connected discourse. *Journal of Experimental Psychology, 75,* 143-150.

Pope, A. W., McHale, S. M., & Craighead, W. E. (1988). *Self-esteem enhancement with children and adolescents.* New York: Pergamon Press.

Posner, G. (1989). Field experience: Methods of reflective teaching. New York: Longmans.

Potter, E. (1984). Impact of developmental factors on motivating the school achievement of young adolescents: Theory and implications for practice. *Journal of Early Adolescence, 4,* 1-10.

Premack, D. (1965). Reinforcement theory. In David Levine (Ed.), *Nebraska symposium on motivation: Vol. 13.* Lincoln, NE: University of Nebraska Press.

Pressley, M., & Harris, K. R. (1990, September). What we really know about strategy instruction. *Educational Leadership,* 31-34.

Prewitt, P. W. (1988). Dealing with Ijime (bullying) among Japanese students. *School Psychology International, 9,* 189-195.

Price, R. H., Cowen, E. L., Lorion, R. P. & Ramos-McKay. (1988). *14 ounces of prevention.* Washington, DC: American Psychological Association.

Pugach, M. (1985). The limitations of federal special education policy: The role of classroom teachers in determining who is handicapped. *The Journal of Special Education, 19,* 123-137.

Q

Quackenbush, M., and Villarreal, S. (1988). *Does AIDS hurt?* Santa Cruz: Network Publications.

R

Rahman, R., & Bisanz, G. (1986). Reading ability and use of a story schema in recalling and reconstructing information. *Journal of Educational Psychology, 75,* 323-333.

Ramsey, P. (1987). *Teaching and learning in a diverse world.* New York: Teachers College Press.

Ratliff, J. D. (1988). Motivation and the perceived need deficiencies of secondary teachers. *High School Journal, 72,* 8-16.

Redl, F., & Wattenberg, W. (1959). *Mental hygiene in teaching.* New York: Harcourt, Brace and Jovanovich.

Reigeluth, C. Y. (Ed.). (1983). *Instructional design theories and models.* Hillsdale, NJ: Erlbaum.

Reis, S. (1989). Reflections on policy affecting the education of gifted and talented students. *American Psychologist, 44,* 399-408.

Reith, H., Bahr, C., Okolo, C., & Polsgrove, L. (1988). An analysis of the use of microcomputers on the secondary special education classroom ecology. *Journal of Educational Computing Research, 4,* 425-441.

Renzuli, J. (1985). *The enrichment triad model.* Mansfield Center, CT: Creative Learning Press.

Renzulli, J. (Ed.). (1986). *Systems and models for developing programs for the gifted and talented.* Mansfield Center, CT: Creative Learning Press.

Repp, A. C., & Singh, N. N. (Eds.). (1990). *Perspectives on the use of non-aversive and aversive interventions for persons with developmental disabilities.* Sycamore, IL: Sycamore Publishing Co.

Rescorla, R. A. (1978). Some implications of a cognitive perspective on Pavlovian conditioning. In S. H. Hulse, H. Fowler, and W. K. Honig (Eds.), *Cognitive Processes in Animal Behavior.* Hillsdale, NJ: Erlbaum.

Rescorla, R., & Holland, P. (1976). Some behavioral approaches to the study of learning. In M. Rosenzweig and E. Bennett (Eds.), *Neural mechanisms of learning and memory.* Cambridge, MA: MIT Press.

Resnick, L. (1981). Instructional psychology. In M. Rosenzweig and L. Porter (Eds.), *Annual review of psychology.* Palo Alto, CA: Annual Reviews.

Rest, J. (1983). Morality. In P. Mussen (Ed.), *Handbook of child psychology.* New York: John Wiley.

Reynolds, C. R., & Kaiser, S. M. (1990). Test bias in psychological assessment. In T. B. Gutkin and C. R. Reynolds (Eds.), *The handbook of school psychology* (2nd ed.). (pp. 487-525). New York: John Wiley & Sons.

Reynolds, G. S. (1961). Attention in the pigeon. *Journal of the Experimental Analysis of Behavior, 4,* 203-208.

Rice, F. P. (1990). *The Adolescent.* Boston: Allyn and Bacon.

Rich, D. (1988). *Megaskills: How families can help children succeed in school and beyond.* Boston: Houghton-Mifflin.

Rimm, D., & Masters, J. (1979). *Behavior therapy* (2nd ed.). New York: Academic Press.

Ringness, T. (1976). Whatever happened to the study of classical conditioning? *Phi Delta Kappan, 57,* 447-455.

Rogoff, B. (1981). Schooling and the development of cognitive skills. In H. C. Triadis and W. W. Lambert (Eds.), *Handbook of cross cultural psychology.* Boston: Allyn and Bacon.

Rogoff, B. (1990). *Apprenticeship in thinking.* New York: Oxford.

Rogoff, B., & Morelli, G. (1989). Perspectives on children's development from cultural psychology. *American Psychologist, 44,* 343-349.

Rohrkemper, M., & Brophy, J. (1983). Teachers' thinking about problem students. In J. Levine and M. Wong (Eds.), *Teacher and student perceptions.* Hillsdale, NJ: Erlbaum.

Rohwer, W. D., Ammon, P., & Cramer, P. (1974). *Intellectual Development.* Hinsdale, IL: Dryden Press.

Rohwer, W., Ammon, P., & Cramer, P. (1975). *Understanding intellectual development.* Hinsdale, IL: Dryden Press.

Romberg, T., & Carpenter, T. (1986). Research on teaching and learning mathematics. In M. Wittrock (Ed.), *Handbook of research on teaching.* New York: Macmillan.

Rose, S. (1987). *The conscious brain.* New York: Knopf.

Rose, T. L. (1984). Current uses of corporal punishment in American schools. *Journal of Educational Psychology, 76,* 427-441.

Rosen, L. A., Taylor, S. A., O'Leary, S. G., & Sanderson, W. (1990). A survey of classroom management practices. *Journal of School Psychology, 28,* 257-269.

Rosenfield, S., & Shinn, M. R. (Eds.). Mini-series on curriculum-based assessment. *School Psychology Review, 18 (3),* 297-370.

Rosenshine, B. (1973). Teacher behavior and student attitudes revisited. *Journal of Educational Psychology, 65,* 117-180.

Rosenshine, B., & Stevens, R. Teaching functions. In M. Wittrock (Ed.), *Handbook of research on teaching.* New York: Macmillan.

Rosenthal, R. & Jacobson, L. (1968). *Pygmalion in the classroom.* New York: Holt, Rinehart and Winston.

Rosenthal, T. L. & Zimmerman, B. J. (1978). *Social learning and cognition.* New York: Academic Press.

Rosenzweig, M., & Bennett, E. (Eds.). (1976). *Neural mechanisms of learning and memory.* Cambridge, MA: MIT Press.

Rosenzweig, M., Bennett, E., & Diamond, M. (1972). Brain changes in response to experience. *Scientific American, 10,* 22-29.

Rothkopf, E. Z. (1981). *Macroscopic model of instruction and purposive learning: An overview.* Bell Laboratories, NJ: Elsevier Scientific Pub. Co.

Rotter, J. (1966). Generalized expectancies for internal versus external control of reinforcement. *Psychological Monographs, 80,* no. 609.

Rotter, J. (1975). Some problems and misconceptions related to the construct of internal versus external control of reinforcement. *Journal of Consulting and Clinical Psychology, 43,* 56-67.

Rourke, B., Bakker, D., Fisk, J., & Strang, J. (1983). *Child neuropsychology.* New York: Guilford.

Routman, R. (1988). *Transitions: From literature to literacy.* Portsmouth, NH: Heinemann.

Rubin, K., Fein, G., & Vandenberg, B. (1983). Play. In P. Mussen (Ed.), *Handbook of child psychology.* New York: Wiley.

Rubin, R., Olmsted, P., & Kelly, P. (1981). Comprehensive model for child services. *Children and Youth Services Review, 3.*

Ruch, G. M. (1929). *The objective or new type examination.* Glenview, IL: Scott, Foresman.

Rummelhart, D. (1975). Notes as a schema for stories. In D. Brobow and A. M. Collins (Eds.), *Representation and understanding.* New York: Academic.

Rummelhart, D., & Norman, D. (1981). Analogical processes in learning. In J. R. Anderson (Ed.), *Cognitive skills and their acquisition.* Hillsdale, NJ: Erlbaum.

Russell, E. A. (1981). The pathology and clinical examination of memory. In S. Filskov and T. Boll (Eds.), *Handbook of clinical neuropsychology.* New York: John Wiley.

Russell, T., & Morrow, J. (1986). Reform in teacher education: Perceptions of secondary social studies teachers.

Theory and Research in Social Education, 14, 325-330.

Rust, L. (1977) Interest. In S. Ball (Ed.), *Motivation in Learning.* New York: Academic Press.

Rutter, M. (1975). *Helping troubled children.* New York: Plenum.

Rutter, M. (1979). Maternal deprivation, 1972-1978; new concepts, new approaches. *Child Development, 50,* 283-305.

Rutter, M. (1980). *Changing youth in a changing society.* Cambridge, MA: Harvard University Press.

Rutter, M., & Garmezy, N. (1983). Developmental psychopathology. In P. Mussen (Ed.), *Handbook of child psychology.* New York: Wiley.

S

Sainato, D., Maheady, L., & Shook, G. (1986). The effects of a classroom manager role on the social interaction patterns and social status of withdrawn kindergarten students. *Journal of Applied Behavior Analysis, 19,* 187-195.

Salkind, N. (1981). *Theories of human development.* New York: Van Nostrand.

Salvia, J., & Ysseldyke, J. (1988). *Assessment in special and remedial education.* Boston: Houghton Mifflin.

Sameroff, A. (1975). Early influences on development. *Merrill-Palmer Quarterly.*

Sanders, N. (1966). *Classroom questions: What kinds?* New York: Harper & Row.

Santrock, J. (1992). *Children.* Dubuque, IA: Brown/Benchmark.

Sarason, I. G. (Ed.). (1980). *Anxiety: Theory, research, and applications.* Hillsdale, NJ: Erlbaum.

Scarr, S. (1981). Testing for children. *American Psychologist, 36,* 1159-1166.

Scarr, S., Weinberg, R., & Levine, A. (1986). *Understanding development.* New York: Harcourt, Brace and Jovanovich.

Schiffman, H. (1982). *Sensation and perception* (2nd ed.). New York: John Wiley & Sons.

Schubert, M. A., & Glick, H. M. (1981). Least restrictive environment programs: Why are some so successful? *Education Unlimited, 3,* 11-13.

Schunk, D. (1985). Self-efficacy and classroom learning. *Psychology in the Schools, 22,* 208-223.

Schunk, D. (1989). Self-efficacy and cognitive achievement: Implications for students with learning problems. *Journal of Learning Disabilities, 22,* 14-22.

Schunk, D. (1989). Self-efficacy and cognitive skill learning. In C. Ames and R. Ames (Eds.), *Research on motivation in education: Vol. 3. Goals and cognitions.* San Diego, CA: Academic Press.

Schunk, D. (1990). Introduction to special section on motivation and efficacy. *Journal of Educational Psychology, 82,* 3-6 .

Schunk, D., Hanson, A., & Cox, P. (1987). Peer model attributes and children's achievement behaviors. *Journal of Educational Psychology, 79,* 54-61.

Schwartz, B. (1984). *Psychology of learning and behavior.* New York: Norton.

Scott, J. P. (1968). *Early experiences and the organization of behavior.* Belmont, CA: Brooks-Cole.

Segall, M. (1986). Culture and behavior: Psychology in global perspective. In M. Rosenzweig and L. Porter (Eds.), *Annual review of psychology,* Palo Alto, CA: Annual Reviews.

Seligman, M. E. (1970). On the generality of the laws of learning. *Psychological Review, 77,* 406-418.

Seligman, M. E. (1975). *Helplessness: On depressions, development, and death.* San Francisco: Freeman.

Seligman, M. E., & Maier, S. F. (1967). Failure to escape traumatic shock. *Journal of Experimental Psychology, 74,* 1-9 .

Selinske, J. E., Greer, R. D., & Lodhi, S. (1991). A functional analysis of the comprehensive application of behavior analyses to schooling. *Journal of Applied Behavior Analysis, 24,* 107-117.

Selman, R. (1980). *The growth of interpersonal understanding.* New York: Academic Press.

Serna, L. (1989). Implications of student motivation on study skills instruction. *Elementary School Journal, 24* 503-514.

Shade, B. (1987). Ecological correlates of the educative style of Afro-American children. *Journal of Negro Education, 56,* 88-99.

Shah, B. (1986). Academic reinforcement: Caste and educational development. *Asian Journal of Psychology and Education, 17,* 8-13.

Shannon, C. (1948, July/October). The mathematical theory of communication. *Bell System Technical Journal.*

Shapiro, E. S. (1988). Behavioral assessment. In J. C. Witt, S. N. Elliott, and F. M. Gresham (Eds.), *The handbook of behavior therapy in education.* (pp. 67-98). New York: Plenum.

Shapiro, E. S., & Derr, T. F. (1987). An examination of overlap between reading curricula and standardized achievement tests. *Journal of Special Education, 21,* 59-67.

Shapiro, E. S., & Derr, T. F. (1990). Curriculum-based assessment. In T. B. Gutkin and C. R. Reynolds (Eds.), *The handbook of school psychology* (2nd ed.). (pp. 365-387). New York: John Wiley & Sons.

Shatz, M. (1983). Communication. In P. Mussen (Ed.), *Handbook of child psychology.* New York: John Wiley.

Shaw, R., & Bransford, J. (Eds.). (1977). *Perceiving, acting, and knowing.* Hillsdale, NJ: Erlbaum.

Sheridan, S. W., Kratochwill, T. R., & Elliott, S. N. (1990). Behavioral consultation with parents and teachers: Delivering treatment for socially withdrawn children at home and school. *School Psychology Review, 19,* 33-52.

Sherry, D., & Schachter, D. (1987). The evolution of multiple memory systems. *Psychological Review, 94,* 439-454.

Shinn, M. R. (1989). *Curriculum-based measurement: Assessing special children.* New York: Guilford Press.

Shuell, T. (1986). Cognitive conceptions of learning. *Review of Educational Research, 56,* 411-436.

Shulman, L. (1986). Paradigms and research programs in the study of teaching. In M. Wittrock (Ed.), *The handbook of research on teaching.* New York: Macmillan.

Siegel, M., & Davis, D. (1986). *Understanding computer-based education.* New York: Random House.

Siegler, R. (1983). Information processing approaches to development. In P. Mussen (Ed.), *Handbook of child psychology.* New York: John Wiley.

Sigel, I., & Cocking, R. (1977). *Cognitive development from childhood to adolescence: A constructive perspective.* New York: Holt, Rinehart and Winston.

Silver, A. (1987).*Learning disabilities: A report to the MS Congress.* Washington, DC: U.S. Department of Health and Human Services, Intergroup Committee on Learning.

Simon, H. (1979). *Models of thought.* New Haven: Yale University Press.

Simon, H. A. (1985). Problem solving and education. In D. Tiema and F. Reif (Eds.), *Problem solving and education.* Englewood Cliffs, NJ: Prentice-Hall.

Simon, S., & de Sherbinin, P. (1975). Values clarification: It can start gently and grow deep. *Phi Delta Kappan, 56,* 679-683.

Simon, S., Howe, L., & Kirschenbaum, H. (1972). *Values clarification: A handbook of practical strategies for teachers and students.* New York: Hart Publishing.

Sivan, E. (1986). Motivation in social constructivist theory. *Educational Psychologist, 21,* 209-233.

Sizemore, B. (1990). The Madison elementary school: A turnaround case. In K. Lomotey (Ed.), *Going to school: The African-American experience.* New York: State University of New York Press.

Skeels, H. (1966). Adult status of children with contrasting early life experiences. *Monographs of the Society for Research in Child Development, 31,* No. 3.

Skinner, B. F. (1938). *The behavior of organisms.* New York: Macmillan.

Skinner, B. F. (1953). *Science and human nature.* New York: Macmillan..

Skinner, B. F.(1968). *The technology of teaching.* New York: Appleton-Century-Crofts.

Skinner, B. F. (1971). *Beyond freedom and dignity.* New York: Knopf.

Skinner, B. F. (1974). *About behaviorism.* New York: Knopf.

Skinner, B. F. (1983). *A matter of consequences.* New York: Knopf.

Skinner, B. F. (1984, September). The shame of American education. *American Psychologist,* 947-954.

Skinner, B. F. (1986, March). Some thoughts about the future. *Journal of the Experimental Analysis of Behavior,* 229-235.

Slaughter-Defoe, D., Nakagawa, K., Takanishi, R., & Johnson, D. (1990). Toward cultural/ecological perspectives on schooling and achievement in African-American and Asian-American children. *Child Development, 61,* 361-383.

Slavin, R. (1986). Best-evidence synthesis: An alternative to meta-analytic and traditional reviews. *Educational Researcher, 15,* 5-11.

Slavin, R. (1987a). Cooperative learning: Where behavioristic and humanistic approaches to classroom motivation meet. *Elementary School Journal, 88,* 29-37.

Slavin, R. (1987b, November). Cooperative learning and the cooperative school. *Educational Leadership,* 7-13.

Slavin, R. (1987c). Developmental and motivational perspectives on cooperative learning: A reconciliation. *Child Development, 58,* 1161-1167.

Slavin, R. (1987d). A theory of school and classroom organization. *Educational Psychologist, 22,* 90-99.

Slavin, R. (1988a, September). Synthesis of research on grouping in elementary and secondary schools. *Educational Leadership,* 67-77.

Slavin, R. (1988b, October). Cooperative learning and student achievement. *Educational Leadership,* 31-33.

Slavin, R. E. (1989). Students at risk of school failure: The problem and its dimensions. In R. E. Slavin, N. L. Karweit, and N. A. Madden (Eds.), *Effective programs for students at risk.* Needham Heights, MA: Allyn and Bacon.

Slavin, R. (1991). *Educational psychology.* (3rd ed.). Englewood Cliffs, NJ: Prentice-Hall.

Slavin, R. E., & Madden, N. A. (1989, February). What works for students at risk: A research synthesis. *Educational Leadership,* 4-13.

Slavin, R. E., Madden, N. A., Karweit, N. L., Dolan, L., Wasik, B. A., Shaw, A., Mainzer, K. L., & Haxby, B. (1991). Neverstreaming: Prevention and early intervention as an alternative to special education. *Journal of Learning Disabilities, 24,* 373-378.

Sleeter, C., & Grant, C. (1988). *Making choices for multicultural education.* Columbus, Ohio: Merrill.

Smith, B. M., Schumacher, J., Schaeffer, J., & Sherman, J. (1982). Increasing participation and improving the quality of discussion in seventh-grade social studies classes. *Journal of Applied Behavior Analysis, 15*, 97-110.

Smith, E. C., Shoben, E. J., & Rips, L. J. (1974). Structure and process in semantic memory: A feature model for semantic decisions. *Psychological Review, 81*, 214-241.

Smith, M. (1984). Learning about learning: The contributions of Ausubel's assimilation theory to a teacher education program. *Journal of Learning Skills, 3*, 33-36.

Smith, M. L., & Glass, G. J. (1980). Meta-analysis of psychotherapy outcome studies. *American Psychologist, 32*, 752-760.

Smith, P. K. (1978). A longitudinal study of social participation in preschool children: Solitary and parallel play reexamined. *Developmental Psychology, 14*, 517-523.

Snow, R. (1986). Individual differences and the design of educational programs. *American Psychologist, 41*, 1029-1039.

Snow, R. (1992). Aptitude theory: Yesterday, today, and tomorrow. *Educational Psychologist, 27*, 5-32.

Soldier, L. L. (1989, October). Cooperative learning and the Native American student. *Phi Delta Kappan*, 161-163.

Soulier, J. S. (1988). *The design and development of computer based instruction.* Boston: Allyn and Bacon.

Spencer, M., & Markstrom-Adams, C. (1990). Identity processes among racial and ethnic minority children in America. *Child Development, 61*, 290-310.

Speth, C., & Brown, R. (1988). Study approaches, processes and strategies. Are three perspectives better than one? *British Journal of Educational Psychology, 58*, 247-257.

Spitz, R. (1945). Hospitalism. In O. Fenichel (Ed.), *The psychoanalytic study of the child.* New York: International U. Press.

Spivak, G., & Shure, M. B. (1974). *Social adjustment of young children.* San Francisco: Jossey-Bass.

Sprick, R. S., & Nolet, V. (1991). Prevention and management of secondary-level behavior problems. In G. Stoner, M. R. Shinn, and H. M. Walker (Eds.), *Interventions for Achievement and Behavior Problems* (pp. 519-538). Washington, DC: National Association of School Psychologists.

Springer, S., & Deutsch, G. (1985). *Left brain, right brain.* New York: Freeman.

Sprinthall, N., & Collins, W. A. (1984). *Adolescent psychology.* New York: Random House.

Sroufe, L. A., & Rutter, M. (1984). The domain of developmental psychopathology. *Child Development, 55*, 17-29.

Stallings, J., & Stipek, D. (1986). Research on early childhood and elementary school teaching programs. In M. Wittrock (Ed.), *Handbook of research on teaching.* New York: Macmillan.

Stanley, J. (1976). Identifying and nurturing the intellectually gifted. *Phi Delta Kappan, 58*, 134-237.

Stanley, J., & Davidson, J. E. (Eds.). (1986). *Conceptions of giftedness.* New York: Cambridge U. Press.

Stein, M. I. (1974). *Stimulating creativity.* New York: Academic Press.

Stent, G. (1985). Structuralism and biology. In J. Eccles (Ed.), *Mind and brain.* New York: Paragon.

Stern, D. (1977). *First relationships.* Cambridge, MA: Harvard University Press.

Stern, D. (1985). *The interpersonal world of the infant.* New York: Basic.

Sternberg, R. (1982). Reasoning, problem solving and intelligence. In R. Sternberg (Ed.), *Handbook of human intelligence.* New York: Cambridge University Press.

Sternberg, R. (1985). Critical thinking. In F. Link (Ed.), *Essays on the intellect.* Alexandria, VA: ASCD.

Sternberg, R. (1986). *Intelligence applied.* New York: Harcourt, Brace, Jovanovich.

Sternberg, R. (1987). Teaching intelligence. In J. Baron and R. Sternberg (Eds.), *Teaching thinking skills.* New York: Freeman.

Sternberg, R. (1988). *Mechanics of cognitive development.* Prospect Heights, IL: Waveland Press.

Sternberg, R., & Davidson, J. E. (Eds.). (1986). *Conceptions of giftedness.* New York: Cambridge U. Press.

Sternberg, R., Okagaki, L., & Jackson, L. (1990). Practical intelligence for success in school. *Educational Leadership, 48*, 35-39.

Stevenson, H. (1983). How children learn: The quest for a theory. In P. Mussen (Ed.), *Handbook of child psychology.* New York: Wiley.

Stevenson, H., Lee, S., Chen, C., Lummis, M., Stigler, J., Fan, L., & Ge, F. (1990). Mathematics achievement of children in China and the United States. *Child Development, 61*, 1053-1066.

Stigler, J., Shweder, R., & Herdt, G. (Eds.). (1990). *Cultural psychology.* New York: Cambridge U. Press.

Stinnett, T. A., Oehler-Stinnett, J. & Stout, L. J. (1989). Using the Social Skills Rating System to discriminate behavior of disordered, emotionally disturbed, and handicapped students. *School Psychology Review, 18*, 510-519.

Stipek, D. (1984). The development of achievement motivation. In R. Ames & C. Ames (Eds.), *Research on motivation in education: Vol. 1.* New York: Academic Press.

Stokes, T. F., & Baer, D. M. (1977). An implicit knowledge of generalization. *Journal of Applied Behavior Analysis, 11*, 285-303.

Sue, S., & Okazaki, S. (1990). Asian-American educational achievements: A phenomenon in search of an explanation. *American Psychologist, 45*, 913-920.

Sulzer-Azaroff, B., & Mayer, G. R. (1986). *Achieving educational excellence: Using behavioral strategies.* New York: Holt, Rinehart and Winston.

Sulzer-Azaroff, B., & Mayer, G. R. (1991). *Behavior analysis for lasting change.* Fort Worth: Holt, Rinehart and Winston.

Sulzer-Azaroff, B., & Reese, E. (1982). *Applying behavior analysis.* New York: CBS Publishing.

Suomi, S., & Harlow, H. (1972). Social rehabilitation of isolate-reared monkeys. *Development Psychology, 6*, 487-496.

T

Takaki, R. 1989. *Strangers from a different shore.* Boston: Little, Brown.

Tarpy, R. (1982). *Principles of animal learning and motivation.* Glenview, IL: Scott, Foresman.

Teale, W. (1988). Developmentally appropriate assessment of reading and writing in the early childhood classroom. *Elementary School Journal, 89,* 173-183.

Tennure, J. (1986). Instruction and cognitive development: Coordinating communication and cues. *Exceptional Children, 53,* 109-117.

Terman, L. (1956) In symposium: Intelligence and its measurement. *Journal of Educational Psychology, 12,* 127-133.

Terman, L., & Oden, M. (1959). *Genetic studies of genius: The gifted group at mid-life.* Stanford, CA: Stanford U. Press.

Tharp, R. (1989). Psychocultural variables and constants: Effects on teaching and learning in schools. *American Psychologist, 44,* 349-359.

The National Assessment of Educational Progress. (1988). *The reading report card.* Princeton, NJ: Educational Testing Service.

Thomas, A., & Chess, S. (1977). *Temperament and development.* New York: Brunner/Mazel.

Thomas, A., & Chess, S. (1980). *The dynamics of psychological development.* New York: Brunner/Mazel.

Thomson, P. (1988). The school of hard knocks. A study on the assessment of experiential learning. *The National Center for Research and Development.* Payneham, Australia.

Thorkildsen, T. (1988). Theories of education among academically able adolescents. *Contemporary Educational Psychology, 13,* 323-330.

Thorndike, E. (1913). *Educational psychology: Vol. 1.* New York: Teachers College Press.

Tiedt, P., & Tiedt, I. (1990). *Multicultural teaching.* Boston: Allyn and Bacon.

Tittnich, E., Bloom, L., Schomburg, R., & Szekeres, S. (Eds.). (1990). *Facilitating children's language: Handbook for child-related professionals.* New York: The Haworth Press.

Tobias, S. (1979). Anxiety research in educational psychology. *Journal of Educational Psychology, 71,* 573-582.

Tobias, S. (1986). Anxiety and cognitive processing of instruction. In R. Schwarzer (Ed.), *Self-related cognitions in anxiety and motivation* (p. 35-54). Hillsdale, NJ: Erlbaum.

Tomorrow's teachers: A report of the Holmes group. (1986). East Lansing, MI: Michigan State University.

Torgersen, A. M. (1981). Genetic factors in temperamental individuality. *Journal of the American Academy of Child Psychiatry, 20,* 702-711.

Travers, J. (1982). *The growing child.* Glenview, IL: Scott, Foresman.

Travers, R. (1982). *Essentials of learning.* New York: Macmillan.

Trice, A., & Wood-Shuman, S. (1984). Teacher locus of control and choice between intrinsic or extrinsic motivational techniques. *Educational Research Quarterly, 9,* 11-13.

Triesman, A. (1986). Features and objects in visual processing. *Scientific American, 255,* 1146-1150.

Triesman, A. M. (1960). Verbal cues, language and meaning in selective attention. *Quarterly Journal of Experimental Psychology, 12,* 242-248.

Tulving, E. (1972). Episodic and semantic memory. In E. Tulving and W. Donaldson (Eds.), *Organization and memory.* New York: Academic Press.

Tuma, D. T., & Reif, F. (Eds.). (1980). *Problem solving and education.* Englewood Cliffs, NJ : Prentice-Hall.

Twardosz, S., Cataldo, M. F., & Risley, T. R. (1974). An open environment design for infant and toddler daycare. *Journal of Applied Behavior Analysis, 7,* 529-546.

Tversky, A., & Kahneman, D. (1981). The framing of decisions and the psychology of choice. *Science, 211,* 453-458.

Tyler, R. (1950). *Basic principles of curriculum and instruction.* Chicago: University of Chicago Press.

U

Usher, R. S. (1986). Reflections and prior work experiences: Some problematic issues in relation to adult students in university settings. *Studies in Higher Education, 11,* 245-256.

V

Vazquez-Nuttall, E. (1987). Survey of current practices in the psychological assessment of limited English proficiency handicapped children. *Journal of School Psychology, 25,* 53-61.

Veroff, J., & Veroff, J. (1980). *Social incentives.* New York: Academic Press.

Vidler, D. (1977) Achievement motivation. In S. Ball (Ed.), *Motivation in education.* New York: Academic Press.

Vidler, D. (1977). Curiosity. In S. Ball (Ed.), *Motivation in education.* New York: Academic Press.

Vitz, P. (1990). The use of stories in moral development: New psychological reasons for an old education method. *American Psychologist, 45,* 709-720.

Vygotsky, L. (1962). *Thought and language.* New York: Wiley.

Vygotsky, L. (1978). *Mind in society.* Cambridge, MA: Harvard University Press.

W

Wadsworth, B. (1978). *Piaget for the classroom teacher.* New York: Longman.

Walberg, H. J. (1986). Synthesis of research on teaching. In M. C. Wittrock (Ed.), *Handbook of research on teaching.* New York: Macmillan.

Wallen, N., & Travers, R. (1963). Analysis and investigation of teaching methods. In N. L. Gage (Ed.), *Handbook of research on teaching.* Chicago: Rand McNally.

Walsh, M. E., & Bibace, R. (1990). Developmentally-based AIDS/HIV education. *Journal of School Health, 60,* 256-261.

Walter, J., & Gardner, H. (1985). The development and education of intelligences. In F. Link (Ed.), *Essays on the intellect.* Washington, DC: ASCD.

Wang, M., & Baker, E. (1985/1986). Mainstreaming programs: Design features and effects. *The Journal of Special Education, 19,* 503-521.

Warren, R. M., & Warren, R. P. (1970). Auditory illusions and confusions. *Scientific American, 223,* 30-36.

Watson, J. (1930). *Behaviorism.* New York: Norton.

Wechsler, D. (1958). *The measurement and appraisal of adult intelligence* (4th ed.). Baltimore: Williams and Wilkins.

Weidmann, C. (1933). Written examination procedures. *Phi Delta Kappan,* 78-83.

Weidmann, C. (1941). Review of essay test studies. *Journal of Higher Education, 12,* 41-44.

Weiner, B. (1979). A theory of motivation for some classroom experiences. *Journal of Educational Psychology, 71,* 3-25.

Weiner, B. (1980). *Human motivation.* New York: Holt, Rinehart and Winston.

Weiner, B. (1984). Principles for a theory of student motivation and their application within an attributional framework. In R. Ames & C. Ames (Eds.), *Research on motivation in education: Vol. 1.* New York: Academic Press.

Weiner, B. (1986). A theory of motivation for some classroom experiences. *Journal of Educational Psychology, 71,* 3-25.

Weiner, B. (1990). History of motivational research in education. *Journal of Educational Psychology, 82,* 616-622.

Weiner, B., Russell, D., & Lerman, D. (1978). Affective consequences of causal ascriptions. In J. H. Harvey et al. (Eds.), *New directions in attribution research.* Hillsdale, NJ: Lawrence Erlbaum.

Weinstein, C. E., & Mayer, R. E. (1986). The teaching of learning strategies. In M. C. Wittrock (Ed.), *Handbook of research on teaching* (3rd ed.). New York: Macmillan.

Weinstein, C. E., Ridley, D. S. Dahl, T., & Weber, E. S. (1988/1989, December/January). Helping students develop strategies for effective learning. *Educational Leadership,* 17-19.

Wertheimer, M. (1961). Psycho-motor coordination of auditory-visual space at birth. *Science,* 134.

Wertheimer, M. (1985). A Gestalt perspective on computer simulations of cognitive processes. *Computers in Human Behavior, 1,* 19-33.

Wertsch, J. (1985). *Vygotsky and the growth of mind.* Cambridge, MA: Harvard U. Press.

Whimbey, A., & Lochhead, T. (1985). *Problem solving and comprehension: A short course in analytical reasoning.* Philadelphia: Franklin Institute Press.

White, O. R., &Associates. (1988). Review and analysis of strategies for generalization. In N. G. Haring (Ed.), *Generalization for students with severe handicaps: Strategies and solutions* (pp. 15-51). Seattle: University of Washington Press.

White, R., & Tisher, R. (1986). Research on natural sciences. In M. Wittrock (Ed.), *Handbook of research on teaching.* New York: Macmillan.

Whitehead, A. N. (1949). *The aims of education.* New York: New American Library.

Whiting, B., & Whiting, J. (1975). *Children of six cultures.* Cambridge MA: Harvard University Press.

Whiting, J. (1977). Culture and development. In P. Leiderman, S. Tulkin, and A. Rosenfeld (Eds.), *Culture and infancy.* New York: Academic.

Wickelgren, W. (1974). *How to solve problems.* San Francisco: W. H. Freeman.

Wielkiewicz, R. (1986). *Behavior management in the schools.* New York: Pergamon.

Wigfield, A. (1988). Children's attributions for success and failure: Effects of age and attentional focus. *Journal of Educational Psychology, 80,* 76-81.

Wilcox, R. (1987, October). Rediscovering discovery learning. *The Clearing House,* 53-56.

Williams, J. (1986). Teaching children to identify the main idea of expository text. *Exceptional Children, 53,* 163-168.

Wilson, B. (1987). What is a concept? Concept teaching and cognitive psychology. *Performance and Instruction, 25,* 16-18.

Witt, J. C., Elliott, S. N., Gresham, F. M., & Kramer, J. J. (1988). *Assessment of special children: Tests and the problem solving process.* Glenview, IL: Scott, Foresman and Co.

Wittrock, M. C. (1986). *Handbook of research on teaching.* New York: Macmillan.

Wittrock, M. C., & Lumsdaine, A. (1977). Instructional psychology. In M. Rosenzweig and L. Porter (Eds.), *Annual review of psychology.* Palo Alto, CA: Annual Reviews, Inc.

Wlodkowski, R. (1986). *Motivation and teaching.* Washington, DC: NEA.

Wolfgang, C. H., & Glickman, C. D. (1986). *Solving discipline problems: Strategies for classroom teachers* (2nd ed.). Boston: Allyn and Bacon.

Woodward, J., Cornine, D., & Gersten, R. (1988). Teaching problem solving through a computer simulator. *American Educational Research Journal, 25,* 72-86.

Woodward, J., & Noell, J. (1991). Science instruction at the secondary level: Implications for students with learning disabilities. *Journal of Learning Disabilities, 24,* 277-284.

Workman, E. A. (1982). *Teaching behavioral self-control to students.* Austin, TX: Pro-Ed.

Wynne, E. (1988, February). Balancing character development and academics in the elementary school. *Phi Delta Kappan,* 424-426.

Y

Young, J. Z. (1978). *Programs of the brain.* London: Oxford University Press.

Ysseldyke, J. E., & Algozzine, B. (1990). *Introduction to special education* (2nd ed.). Boston: Houghton Mifflin.

Ysseldyke, J. E., & Christenson, S. L. (1987). *The instructional environment scale: A comprehensive methodology for assessing an individual student's instruction.* Austin, TX: Pro:Ed.

Ysseldyke, J. E., Christenson, S. L., Thurlow, M. L., & Bakewell, D. (1989). Are different kinds of instructional tasks used by different categories of students in different settings? *School Psychology Review, 18,* 98-111.

Z

Zigmond, N., Vallecorsa, A., & Silverman, R. (1983). *Assessment for instructional planning in special education.* Englewood Cliffs, NJ: Prentice-Hall.

Credits

Line Art and Text

Chapter 1

Figure 1.3 From Centra and Potter, *Review of American Educational Research Journal,* 1980. Copyright © 1980 by the American Educational Research Association. Reprinted by permission of the publisher.

Chapter 2

Excerpt, pages 51–52 American Psychological Association. (1990). Ethical principles of psychologists (amended June 2, 1989). *American Psychologist, 45,* 390–395. Copyright 1990 by the American Psychological Association. Reprinted by permission.

Chapter 3

Figure 3.2 From John F. Travers, *The Growing Child.* Copyright © 1982 Scott, Foresman and Company, Glenview, IL. Reprinted by permission of the author. Figure 3.3 From John F. Travers, *The Growing Child.* Copyright © 1982 Scott, Foresman and Company, Glenview, IL. Reprinted by permission of the author. Figure 3.4 From A. P. Kaiser, et al., "Alternative Intervention Strategies for the Treatment of Communication Disorders in Young Children with Developmental Disabilities" in T. R. Kratochwill, S. N. Elliott, and M. Gettinger, (Eds.), *Advances in School Psychology,* Vol. VIII, pp. 7–43, 1992. Copyright © 1992 Lawrence Erlbaum Associates, Hillsdale, NJ. Reprinted by permission of the publisher and the authors.

Chapter 5

Figure 5.1 From Albert Bandura, *American Psychologist.* Copyright © 1978 by the American Psychological Association, Washington, DC. Reprinted by permission.

Chapter 6

Figure 6.1 From Benjamin B. Lahey, *Psychology: An Introduction,* 3d ed. Copyright © 1989 Wm. C. Brown Communications, Inc., Dubuque, Iowa. All Rights Reserved. Reprinted by permission.

Chapter 7

Illustration, page 195 From Köhler, Wolfgang *The Task of Gestalt Psychology,* with Introduction by Carroll C. Pratt. Copyright © 1969 by Princeton University Press. Reproduced by permission of Princeton University Press.

Chapter 8

Figure 8.4 Sternberg, R., et al., (1990). "Practical Intelligence for Success in School." *Educational Leadership* 48, 1:35–39. Reprinted with permission of the Association for Supervision and Curriculum Development. Copyright © 1990 by ASCD. All rights reserved. Figure 8.5 Sternberg, R., et al., (1990). "Practical Intelligence for Success in School." *Educational Leadership* 48, 1:35–39. Reprinted with permission of the Association for Supervision and Curriculum Development. Copyright © 1990 by ASCD. All rights reserved.

Chapter 9

Box Figure 9.1 a and b From Dr. Beau Fly Jones, *Educational Leadership,* 1988, pages 22–23. Reprinted by permission of Dr. Beau Fly Jones, North Central Regional Educational Labortory, 1900 Spring Road, Oak Brook, IL. Table 9.1 From D. Lewis and J. Greene, Thinking Better. Copyright © 1982 Holt, Rinehart and Winston, Orlando, FL. Box Figure 9.2 From M. A. Bash, *Think Aloud Classroom Resource Manual, Grades 1–2.* Copyright © Research Press, Champaign, IL.

Chapter 10

Figure 10.2 From B. Weiner, *Human Motivation.* Copyright © 1980 Holt, Rinehart and Winston, Orlando, FL. Box 10.1 Alderman, M. K. 1990. "Motivation for At-Risk Students." *Educational Leadership* 48, 1. Reprinted with permission of the Association for Supervision and Curriculum Development. Copyright © 1990 by ASCD. All rights reserved. Box 10.2 Alderman, M. K. 1990. "Motivation for At-Risk Students." *Educational Leadership* 48, 1. Reprinted with permission of the Association for Supervision and Curriculum Development. Copyright © 1990 by ASCD. All rights reserved.

Chapter 12

Figure 12.1 From Maribeth Gettinger, *Best Practices.* Copyright 1990 by the National Association of School Psychologists. Reprinted by permission of the publisher. Box Figure 12.1 From J. Ysseldyke and S. Christianson, *The Instructional Environmental Scale.* Copyright © 1987 Pro-Ed, Austin, TX. Reprinted by permission of the publisher and authors. Figure 12.5 From *Homework* by Harris Cooper. Copyright © 1989 by Longman Publishing Group. Figure 12.6 *Homework* by Harris Cooper. Copyright © 1989 by Longman Publishing Group.

Chapter 13

Figure 13.2 From Mary Lou Kelley, *School-Home Notes: Promoting Children's Classroom Success.* Copyright © 1990 The Guilford Press, New York, NY. Reprinted by permission.

Chapter 14

Excerpt, page 430 Ysseldyke, James E. and Bob Algozzine. *Introduction to Special Education,* Second Edition. Copyright © 1990 by Houghton Mifflin Company. Used with permission. Box Figure 14.1 From C. R. Ponti, et al., "Implementing a Consultation-Based Service Delivery System to Decrease Referrals for Special Education: A Case Study of Organizational Considerations" in *School Psychology Review,* 17, 89–100, 1988. Copyright 1988 by the National Association of School Psychologists. Reprinted by permission of the publisher. Figure 14.1 a and b Ysseldyke, James and Robert Algozzine, *Introduction to Special Education,* Second Edition. Copyright © 1990 by Houghton Mifflin Company. Used with permission. Figure 14.2 From H. M. Walker and M. Bullis, "Behavior Disorders and the Social Context of Regular Class Integration: A Conceptual Dilemma?" in John W. Lloyd, et al.,

(Editors), *The Regular Education Initiative: Alternative Perspectives on Concepts, Issues, and Models.* Copyright © 1991 Sycamore Publishing Company, Sycamore, IL. Reprinted by permission.

Chapter 15

Figure 15.2 Reprinted with the permission of Macmillan Publishing Company, Inc. from *Measurement and Evaluation In Teaching,* Sixth Edition by Norman E. Gronlund and Robert L. Linn. Copyright © 1990 by Macmillan Publishing Company. Figure 15.3 Walden III's Rite of Passage Experience (ROPE). *Horace.* (March 1990), p. 10. Reprinted by permission.

Chapter 16

Figure 16.2 From Howard Lyman, *Test Scores and What They Mean.* Copyright © 1986 Prentice Hall, Inc., Englewood Cliffs, NJ.

Illustrations

Precision Graphics

1.1, 1.2, 1.3, 2.1, 2.3, 3.1, p. 64, 3.2, 3.3, 3.4, 5.1, 5.2, Box 5.1, 5.3, 5.4, 6.1, 6.2, 6.3, p. 184, p. 195, p. 203 lower left, p. 203 upper right, p. 203 lower right, p. 204, 7.1, p. 206, p. 207 upper left, p. 207 lower left, p. 207 upper right, p. 207 lower right, p. 208, 7.2, 7.3, p. 213, 7.4, 8.1, 8.2, 8.3, 8.4, 8.5, Box 9.1 a and b, p. 267 lower left, p. 267 upper right, p. 267 lower right, p. 273, Box 9.2, 10.1, 10.2, 10.3, 10.4, Box 10.1, Box 10.2, p. 328, 12.1, Box 12.1, 12.2, 12.3, 12.4, 12.5, 12.6, 13.1, 13.2, Box 14.1, 14.1 a and b, 14.2, 15.1, 15.2, 15.3, 15.4, 16.1, 16.2

Part Openers

Part openers 1, 2, 3, 4, 5: © Superstock, Inc.

Chapter 1

Chapter opener 1: © T. Rosenthal/Superstock, Inc.; **page 4 a and b:** Jim Shaffer; **p. 9:** © Lawrence Migdale/Photo Researchers, Inc.; **p. 12, 14:** Jim Shaffer

Chapter 2

Chapter opener 2: © R. Llewellyn/Superstock, Inc.; **p. 30:** © Michael Siluk; **2.2:** Tom Kratochwill

Chapter 3

Chapter opener 3: © T. Rosenthal/Superstock, Inc.; **p. 59 top left:** John Travers; **b-d:** © Michael Siluk; **p. 62:**

The Bettman Archive; **p. 66 a:** © Michael Siluk; **b:** Jim Shaffer; **c:** © Will & Deni McIntyre/Photo Researchers, Inc.; **p. 66d, p. 70:** Jim Shaffer; **p. 79 top and middle:** © Michael Siluk; **bottom:** Jim Shaffer; **p. 85:** © Will & Deni McIntyre/Photo Researchers, Inc.

Chapter 4

Chapter opener 4: © R. Llewellyn/Superstock, Inc.; **p. 94:** The Bettman Archive; **p. 100 left:** © Lawrence Migdale/Photo Researchers, Inc.; **middle:** © Michael Siluk; **right:** © Y. Arthus Bertrand/Photo Researchers, Inc.; **p. 107:** © Sidney/The Image Works, Inc.

Chapter 5

Chapter opener 5: © Superstock, Inc.; **p. 120 a:** © Will & Deni McIntyre/Photo Researchers, Inc.; **b:** © Blair Seitz/Photo Researchers, Inc.; **c:** © David Frazier PhotoLibrary; **d:** © Michael Sulik; **p. 128:** Jim Shaffer; **p. 139:** Courtesy of Penelope L. Peterson, Michigan State University; **p. 144:** Jim Shaffer

Chapter 6

Chapter opener 6: © Superstock, Inc.; **p. 156:** The Bettman Archive; **p. 160:** Archives of the History of American Psychology; **p. 161:** Journal of Applied Behavior Analysis, Vol. 23, No. 4, Winter 1990, Society for the Experimental Analysis of Behavior; **p. 164:** Photo by G. K. Hare, Fred S. Keller, "Burrhus Frederick Skinner" in *Journal of Applied Behavior Analysis*, Vol. 23, No. 4, Winter 1990, Society for the Experimental Analysis of Behavior; **p. 165:** © Will & Deni McIntyre/Photo Researchers, Inc.; **p. 172:** Jim Shaffer; **p. 174, 175:** A. Bandura, D. Ross & S. Ross, Imitation of Film-Mediated Aggressive Models, *Journal of Abnormal and Social Psych.*, Vol. 66, 1963, fig. 2-2, pg. 3-11; **p. 176:** c Will McIntyre/Photo Researchers, Inc.; **p. 180:** Jim Shaffer

Chapter 7

Chapter opener 7: © Superstock, Inc.; **p. 192:** Michael Siluk; **p. 202:** © Will & Deni McIntyre/Photo Researchers, Inc.; **p. 203:** Jim Shaffer

Chapter 8

Chapter opener 8: © Superstock, Inc.; **p. 232:** Courtesy of Robert Sternberg; **p. 233:** Courtesy of Howard Gardner, Harvard University; **p. 236:** Courtesy of David Perkins, Harvard University; **p.**

246: © Lawrence Migdale/Photo Researchers, Inc.

Chapter 9

Chapter opener 9: © T. Rosenthal/Superstock, Inc.; **p. 255 left:** © Bob Daemmrich/The Image Works, Inc.; **middle and right:** © Michael Sulik; **p. 263:** © Bob Daemmrich/The Image Works, Inc.

Chapter 10

Chapter opener 10: © Superstock, Inc.; **p. 288:** © Blair Seitz/Photo Researchers, Inc.; **p. 293:** Jim Shaffer; **p. 302:** © Lawrence Migdale/Photo Researchers, Inc.

Chapter 11

Chapter opener 11: © Superstock, Inc.; **p. 341:** © Lawrence Migdale/Photo Researchers, Inc.

Chapter 12

Chapter opener 12: © R. Heinzen/Superstock, Inc.; **p. 353 a:** © Michael Siluk; **b:** © Frank Pedrick/The Image Works, Inc.; **c:** © David Frazier Photolibrary; **d:** © Michael Siluk; **p. 365:** Jim Shaffer; **p. 375:** © Richard Hutchins/Photo Researchers, Inc.; **p. 381:** Courtesy of Madeline Hunter

Chapter 13

Chapter opener 13: © R. Llewellyn/Superstock, Inc.; **p. 391, 402:** Jim Shaffer; **p. 416:** © Michael Siluk

Chapter 14

Chapter opener 14: © Superstock, Inc.; **p. 429:** © Bob Daemmrich/The Image Works, Inc.; **p. 431:** Jim Shaffer; **p. 434:** © Wells/The Image Works, Inc.; **p. 446:** Jim Shaffer; **p. 447:** © Beringer/Dratch/The Image Works, Inc.

Chapter 15

Chapter opener 15: © R. Llewellyn/Superstock, Inc.; **p. 481:** © Michael Siluk; **p. 488:** AGS Catalog, 1991, American Guidance Service, Circle Pines, MN; **p. 494:** © Michael Siluk

Chapter 16

Chapter opener 16: © R. Llewellyn/Superstock, Inc.; **p. 501 top:** Jim Shaffer; **bottom:** © David Frazier PhotoLibrary; **p. 520:** © Elizabeth Crews/The Image Works, Inc.

Name Index

Subject Index

A

Ability, in attribution theory, 292
Ability grouping, 399, 429-30
About Behaviorism (Skinner), 160
Academic function, 6
Academic goals, 323
Acceleration, 448-49
Accommodation, 63
Achievement motivation, 291, 292-94. See also Motivation
Achievement tests, 502, 504-5, 506-7, 508, 523
Acronyms, 270
Acrostics, 270-71
Active responding, principle of, 371-72
Active teaching, 354-56
Activities. *See* Classroom activities
Activity reinforcers, 179
Adaptation
    in cognitive development, 63
    macroadaptation, 377-80
    microadaptation, 380-82
    in multicultural classroom, 382-85
    of teaching, 377-85
ADHD (attention-deficit hyperactivity disorder), 456-58
Adolescence
    cognitive development in, 72-74
    developmental tasks of, 394
    egocentric thinking in, 73
    moral development in, 111-12, 117
    peer relationships in, 132
Advance organizers, 198-99
Affect. *See* Emotion
Affective entry characteristics, 368, 369
African-American students
    cognitive development of, 61
    instructional objectives and, 322
    mathematical performance of, 336-37
    multicultural classrooms and, 14-16
    reading levels of, 335
Aggression
    classroom management of, 404-7
    development and, 405
    modeling of, 174-75
    parents and, 405
    sex differences in, 131-32, 404
    of teacher, 405
    understanding, 415
AIDS prevention, 76-78
Alderman's Link Model, 308-9
America 2000, 4-5
American Association on Mental Retardation, 460
American Psychiatric Association, 432, 456
American Psychological Association, 391
Amputation, 455

Analysis

assessment of, 476
behavior, 413-14
meta-analysis, 45, 47
perceptual-conceptual, 212
primary, 44
secondary, 44-45
of self, 183
task, 327-29
of thinking skills, 238-43, 249, 250
Anchoring ideas, 198
Anger, control of, 130-31. See also Aggression
Animism, 69
Anxiety
    motivation and, 297-99
    separation, 96, 101
    test, 298-99
    trait, 297
Appearance, and relationships, 126
Applied behavior analysis, 413-14
Appreciation, 9
Apraxia, 454
Aptitude tests
    learning and, 231
    standardized, 502, 505-8, 523
Aptitude-treatment interaction, 377
Artificialism, 69
Art of Teaching, The (Flinders), 8-9
ASCD Panel on Moral Education, 113
ASCII, 344
Asian-American students
    bilingualism and, 85-86
    cognitive learning and, 201
    mathematical performance of, 336
    special education and, 444
Assertion, 128
Assessment, 467-96
    authentic, 471, 488-90
    comparison of types of, 489
    curriculum-based, 487-88
    defined, 468
    of exceptional students, 430-34
    integrated learning and, 471-72, 495
    of multicultural students, 469-71
    new trends in, 487-94, 496
    performance, 489
    phases of, 432
    portfolio, 490
    preschool, 513-15
    self-assessment, 183, 490
    teacher-constructed tests and, 472-87, 495-96
    uses of, 469
Assimilation, 63
Asthma, 455
At-risk students, 308-9, 428-29
Attachment, 95, 112
Attention deficit, 459

Attention-deficit hyperactivity disorder (ADHD), 456-58
Attention management, 268
Attitude
    change of, 299-300
    about classroom life, 397
    defined, 299
    motivation and, 299-301, 310-11, 314
Attribution theory, 139-40, 291-93
Audience
    in feedback loop, 300
    imaginative, 73
Authentic assessment, 471, 488-90
Authority, 29
Autonomy, 97-98, 102
Aversive control, 413
Aversive stimulus, 162, 166, 167, 169, 171, 413
Avoidance behavior, 167

B

Babbling, 81
Baby and Child Care (Spock), 29
Baby biographies, 32-35
Bandura, A.
    on reciprocal determinism model of human behavior, 125-26
    on social cognitive learning, 172-78, 188, 295-96, 297, 315
Becoming a Nation of Readers, 333
Beginning Teacher Evaluation Studies (BTES), 354
Behavior
    avoidance, 167
    causes of, 413-20
    cognitive entry, 368-69
    escape, 167
    five domains of, 128
    language development and, 87
    misbehavior, 407-8
    of multicultural students, 408
    observable, 156
    problems with, 391-93, 395-96, 406-8
    reciprocal determinism model of, 125-26
    recording, 184
    of teachers, 405, 409-10, 416-17, 420-24
Behavior analysis, applied, 413-14
Behavior disorders, 455-58
Behavior influence, 412
Behaviorism, 155-88
    classical conditioning, 156-58, 159, 188
    cognitive theory vs., 194
    ethics in, 185
    future and, 185-87, 188
    modeling in, 173-77
    neobehaviorism, 156
    operant conditioning, 156, 160-72, 188, 294, 296, 297, 315, 363-65, 370, 412

559

Glossary

A

Ability grouping   The technique of helping students achieve individual goals by placing those of similar ability together, either by groups in the same classroom (homogeneous grouping) or in separate classrooms (tracking). 429

Academic function   One of the four major categories of instructional responsibility. In this case, it is helping students to achieve as much as their potential allows. 6

Acceleration   A change in the regular school program that permits a gifted student to complete a program in less time or at an earlier age than usual. 448

Accommodation   Piaget's term that refers to a change in cognitive structures that produces corresponding behavioral changes. 63

Achievement test   Measures accomplishment in such specific subjects as reading, arithmetic, etc. 502

Achievement tests   Developed by testing specialists; concern today is that these tests may not reflect what is actually taught in the classroom. 487

Activity reinforcers   High-frequency behaviors used to reinforce low-frequency behavior. 179

Adaptation   Piaget's term for one of the two psychological mechanisms used to explain cognitive development (organization is the other). 63

Adolescent egocentric thinking   A characteristic of adolescent thought in which adolescents assume that everyone thinks as they do. 73

Advance organizers   Ausubel's term to describe a type of teaching that explains what is to come. 198

Affective entry characteristics   Bloom's phrase to describe a student's motivation to learn new material. 368

America 2000   A statement of national educational goals. 4

Anchoring ideas   Those ideas that students already possess and that can be related to new, potentially meaningful material. 198

Animism   Piaget's term to describe a child's tendency to attribute life to inert objects. 69

Anxiety   Feelings of apprehension that can affect student performance, either positively or negatively. 297 .

Appreciation   The realization that you have done a good job. 9

Aptitude test   Tests that assess a student's general or specific abilities. 502

Aptitude-treatment interaction   Adapting instruction and materials to students' aptitudes. 377

Artificialism   Piaget's term to describe a preoperational child's tendency to assume that everything is the product of human creation. 69

Assertion   Such behaviors as asking others for information; also behaviors that respond to others' actions. 128

Assessment   The process of gathering information about a student's abilities or using such information to make decisions about the student. 468

Assimilation   Piaget's term to describe how we take information into our minds; one part of adaptation. 63

At risk   A term used to describe those children who have a high probability of becoming handicapped. 428

Attachment   Behavior intended to keep a child (or adult) in close proximity to a significant other. 95

Attention management   A term that refers to the effective use of time. 268

Attitude   A relatively permanent way of thinking, feeling, and behaving toward something or somebody. 299

Attribute–treatment interaction   The manner in which teaching methods interact with student characteristics. 385

Attribution theory   A motivational theory that assumes people want to know the causes of their behavior. 292

Authentic assessment   A means of securing information about a student's success or failure on meaningful and significant (authentic) tasks. 488

Autonomy   Erikson's term for a child's growing sense of independence. 97

Aversive control   A technique to eliminate undesirable student behavior, either by introducing an unpleasant event or removing a pleasurable one. 413

Aversive stimuli   Something unpleasant follows a response (a teacher reprimand). 166

Avoidance behavior   Behavior that allows a student to postpone or prevent contact with something the student finds unpleasant (pretending to be sick to avoid something unpleasant at school). 167

B

Babbling   Sounds that children make that resemble speech. 81

Beginning Teacher Evaluation Studies (BTES)   An effort to evaluate beginning teachers by focusing on student activities. 354

Behavior disorders   Any condition in which environmental conflicts and personal disturbance persist and negatively affect academic performance. 455

Behavior influence   One person exercises some control over another. 412

Behavior modification   A deliberate attempt, using learning principles, to control student behavior. 412

Behavior therapy   An attempt to change behavior in a client-therapist relationship. 412

Bilingual education   Program designed to help those with limited English proficiency (LEP) to acquire English by teaching them partly in English and partly in their own language. 444

Bilingualism   Refers to those with facility in two or more languages. 85

C

Centering   Piaget's term to describe a child's tendency to concentrate on only part of an object or activity. Characteristic of preoperational children. 68

Cerebral lateralization   Refers to hemispheric control of certain functions (if you write with your right hand, you are left lateralized for handedness). 227

Classical conditioning   Pavlov's explanation of conditioning in which a neutral (conditioned) stimulus gradually gains the ability to elicit a response because of its pairing with a natural (unconditioned) stimulus. 156

Classification   Piaget's term that refers to the ability to group objects with some similarities within a larger category. 72

Classroom management   Refers to effective teaching techniques, such as setting and maintaining clear rules and maintaining an orderly learning environment. 20

Classroom organization   Refers to effective teaching methods that result in an organized classroom where students know what to expect and have opportunities to respond to and get feedback. 20

Clinical theory of instruction (CTI)   Refers to M. Hunter's theory that the teacher is a decision-making professional. 380

Cognitive entry behaviors   Bloom's term that refers to the prerequisite learning skills needed before attempting new learning. 368

Cognitive operations Piaget's term that refers to the organization of cognitive structures that enables a student to engage in abstract thinking. 72

Cognitive research trust (CoRT) deBono's program intended to help students acquire thinking skills. 247

Commitment Refers to those situations where one or both parties either accept their relationship or work toward insuring its continuance. 123

Communication Any process that transmits information. 9, 453

Comparative research The investigator searches for direct relations among variables that are compared with each other. 37

Complementarity Refers to those interactions in which the behavior of both participants is different yet blends harmoniously. 123

Computer assisted instruction An instructional aid intended to help achieve previously formulated objectives. 343

Computer literacy Sufficient performance proficiency with computers so that they can be used to help with schoolwork. 342

Computer managed instruction The use of computers to track and document classroom activities. 345

Concrete operations Piaget's third stage of cognitive development, extending approximately from seven to eleven years of age. 65

Conditioned reflex Pavlov's term for the flow of saliva at the sight of food. 156

Conditioned stimulus A previously neutral stimulus that now has attained the power to elicit a response. 157

Conjunctive concepts A concept formed by the joint presence of several attributes. 199

Connectionism Thorndike's explanation of learning (by selecting and connecting). 156

Conservation Piaget's term that refers to the realization that the essence of something remains constant although surface features may change. 71

Construct validity A test has construct validity when it actually measures the knowledge domain or behavior it claims to measure. 475

Content Piaget's term for behavior. 64

Content of interactions What participants in a relationship do together. 122

Content theory of intelligence Perkins' term that refers to intelligence as a rich knowledge base. 236

Content validity A test has content validity if it adequately samples behavior that has been the goal of instruction. 475

Context strategy A term to describe how teachers urge students to search for relationships between new material and material they already know. 268

Contingency contracting A teacher and student decide on a behavioral goal and what the student will receive when the goal is achieved. 413

Control theory A theory suggesting that behavior is always the attempt to satisfy powerful forces at work within. 419

Conventional level Kohlberg's second level of moral development when children desire approval both from others and society, about ten to thirteen years of age. 111

Cooing Sounds resembling vowels and consonants. 81

Cooperation Behaviors, such as helping others, sharing materials, and complying with rules. Teaching that refers to smooth classroom functioning when students and teachers get along well together. 9, 128

Cooperative learning Instructional methods in which students are encouraged or required to work together on academic tasks. 307

Correlational research The researcher attempts to determine if a relation exists between two or more variables. 36

Criterion-referenced tests A type of testing used to determine if a student has achieved predetermined behavioral or learning objectives. A student's performance is interpreted by comparing the performance to a set of objective criteria. 490

Criterion-related validity A test has criterion-related validity if its results parallel some other, external criteria. 475

Critical thinking Mental strategies used to solve problems. 224

Cross-cultural research Research conducted across different cultures to determine which factors are related to a particular culture. 43

Cross-sectional research A research method that entails the selection of different groups of individuals at a variety of age levels for study. 42

Cues Techniques to help us recall; particularly effective if we generate them ourselves. 269

Curriculum-based assessment (CBA) An assessment technique linked to curriculum and instruction whereby a student's success is evaluated by that student's progress in the curriculum and whose purpose is to determine further instructional needs. 487

D

Dangles Leaving some direction unfinished. 409

Decoding Using the sounds and grammar of a language to interpret a message. 454

Dependent variable The variable on which subjects respond to the manipulation of the independent variable. 37

Descriptive research The investigator examines and reports things the way they are. 36

Desists A teacher's actions to stop misbehavior. 408

Didactic teaching Refers to those effective teachers who persistently seek appropriate goals and insist on student responsibility. 20

Discovery learning Bruner's term for learning that involves the rearrangement and transformation of material that leads to insight. 199, 289

Discrimination Refers to the process by which we learn not to respond to similar stimuli in an identical manner. 158

Disjunctive concepts A concept with many attributes, any one of which may be used in classification. 199

Diversity of interactions The participants in a relationship engage in many types of interactions and provide greater understanding of each other. 123

DUPE A problem-solving model intended to mean: don't let yourself be deceived. 254, 259

E

Effective schools Those schools with certain defining characteristics (a respected principal, an orderly environment, etc.). 16

Egocentric speech Piaget's term for that time when children do not care to whom they speak or whether anyone is listening to them (about six years of age). 88

Egocentrism Piaget's term to describe children's tendency to see things as they want them to be. 68

Elaboration Adding information to what you are trying to learn so the material becomes more personally meaningful. 271

Emotional arousal Bandura's term to describe how stressful situations can be a source of personal information. 296

Empathy Behavior that shows concern for the feelings of others. 128

Enactive Bruner's term for knowing the world by acting on it; usually refers to the infancy period.

Encoding A speaker wishes to convey a message to a listener and must fit the message to the language. 453

Enrichment   A method of instruction for gifted students in which they are furnished with additional, challenging experiences. 449

Episodic memory   The recall of personal experiences within a specific context or period of time. 211

Equilibration   Piaget's term to describe the balance between assimilation and accommodation. 63

Escape behavior   A response eliminates something unpleasant (finishing an assignment permits a student to join a group engaged in a pleasant activity). 167

Essay test   A teacher-constructed test that allows students considerable latitude in their answers to questions. 472

Evaluation   Data obtained from tests and measurements are interpreted. 472

Exclusion component   A means of more accurately identifying students with learning disabilities. 458

Exhibitions   A form of authentic assessment in which students are required to demonstrate the integration of the knowledge and skills they have acquired. 490

Expectancy-value   An explanation of motivation based on an individual's expectancy of success, the incentive value of success, and the strength of the motive. 290

Expected learner outcomes (ELO)   A method of expressing learning expectations to students, teachers, and parents. 327

Experimental research   The researcher actively manipulates an independent variable to observe changes in the dependent variable. 37

Extended response   A form of essay question that permits students to make any kind of answer they desire. 477

External representation   A method of problem solving in which a person uses symbols or some other observable type of representation. 263

Externals   Those who attribute the causes of their behavior to something outside themselves. 302

Extinction   Refers to the process by which conditioned responses are lost. 157

Extrinsic motivation   Those rewards and inducements external to students. 286

F

Field sensitive   A tendency to be influenced by personal relationships and praise from authority figures. 76

Fixed interval   A response results in reinforcement after a definite time. 164

Fixed ratio   Reinforcement depends on a definite number of responses. 164

Flip-flops   Changing from one activity to another and then back again; the opposite of transition smoothness. 409

Forgetting   The loss of previously acquired material. 214

Forgiveness   A special application of mercy; focuses on the individual who forgives, not on the one seeking forgiveness. 115

Formal operations   Piaget's term that refers to that period of cognitive development that sees the beginning of logical, abstract thinking (begins at about eleven years of age). 72

Formative evaluation   Intended to aid learning by providing feedback about what has been learned and what remains to be learned. 367

Fragmentation   A form of slowdown in which a teacher has individual students do something it would be better for the entire group to do. 409

Frame   Refers to the manner in which a teacher presents material. 218

Frequency and patterning of interactions   Refers to interactions of different types in a relationship and not merely the number of interactions. 123

Frequency distribution   The frequency with which a score appears in a score category. 516

Functional asymmetry   Refers to differences between the cerebral hemispheres. 228

Functional invariants   Piaget's term for the two cognitive mechanisms: adaptation and organization. 63

G

General instructional objective   Broadly phrased objectives that offer general guidelines for a school. 326

Generalized reinforcers   A form of secondary reinforcers; they acquire their power because they have accompanied several primary reinforcers. 163

General strategies   A set of principles and guidelines that apply to any situation. 257

Generativity   Similar to productivity and creativity. 107

Genetic Studies of Genius   Terman's famous study of the gifted. 449

Gifted   Those with abilities that give evidence of high performance capabilities. 447

Givens   Facts that are presented in a problem. 261

Goals   Clear, precise statements of what is needed to solve a problem. 262

Goodness of fit   The resonance or fit between the properties of the classroom (including the teacher) and student characteristics. 127

Grade equivalent   A student's performance on a test is the same as that of students in a particular grade. If a student's raw score is 32 on a particular test, this may be the grade equivalent score of 5.0. 516

Grading   Assigning a symbol to a student's performance. 468

Group alertness   Instructional methods that maintain interest and contribute to lively classes. 409

Groupers   Those who prefer a global, wholistic approach to a problem. 274

H

Hard of hearing   Those individuals with sufficient hearing potential (with a hearing aid) to process linguistic information through audition. 452

Hearing impairment   Refers to any type of hearing loss, from mild to profound. 452

Heuristics   Using alternative search patterns to solve problems; generating new possible solutions. 272

Historical research   Studying, understanding, and explaining past events. 36

Holophrastic speech   A child uses one word to communicate many meanings and ideas. 81

Homework   School-assigned academic work to be completed outside of school, usually in the home. 8

I

Iconic   Bruner's term (a mode of representation) for our perceptual organization of the world. 362

IDEA   *Individuals with Disabilities Education Act*, designed to provide services for handicapped students in the least restrictive environment. 430

Identical elements   An explanation of the transfer of learning, stating learning can be applied to new situations only if there are similar features in both situations. 160

Identity achievement   Committing oneself to choices about identity and maintaining that commitment. 104

Identity confusion   Those who experience doubt and uncertainty about who they are. 104

Identity crisis   Erikson's term for those situations, usually in adolescence, that cause us to make major decisions about our identity. 104

Identity diffusion   An inability to commit oneself to choices—the lack of a sense of direction. 104

Identity foreclosure   Making a commitment under pressure, not as the result of the resolution of a crisis. 104

Identity moratorium Desiring to make a choice but being unable to do so. 104

Imagery The tendency to visualize objects or events. 271

Imaginative audience The belief of adolescents that everyone is focusing on them. 73

Incidental learning Cognitive growth that results from a changing environment. 244

Independent variable The experimental or treatment condition variable. 37

Individual guided education A detailed plan of individualized instruction; associated with the work of Klausmeier. 379

Individually prescribed instruction (IPI) A form of individualized instruction utilizing precise planning for a student's program. 377

Industry (versus inferiority) Erikson's term to describe a child's sense of being able to do things well; they want to win recognition by doing things well. 100

Inferencing A term that describes how students are taught to question themselves about the implications of material they have learned. 268

Influence techniques Methods intended to maintain classroom control. 417

Initiative (versus guilt) Erikson's term for children's ability to explore the environment and test their world. 99

Inquiry teaching Bruner's belief that teaching should permit students to be active partners in the search for knowledge, thus enhancing the meaning of what they learn. 360

Insensitive classmates Those students unaware of the needs of their classmates with handicaps. 434

Instantiation Furnishing an example. 268

Institutional function Refers to a teacher's responsibility to perform nonacademic duties (eg., collecting lunch money). 6

Instrumental enrichment Feuerstein's program designed to help students acquire thinking skills. 244

Integrity (versus despair) In old age, one looks back and sees meaning in life. 107

Interactions An exchange of behaviors by the partners in a relationship. 122

Interest boosting A classroom management technique designed to prevent discipline problems. 417

Intermittent reinforcers Reinforcers occasionally are implemented. 164

Internal representation A mental model of how to solve a problem. 267

Internals Those who attribute the causes of their behavior to themselves. 302

Interpersonal perception Refers to how each partner in a relationship views the other. 123

Interval reinforcement A schedule of reinforcement in which the reinforcement occurs at definite established time intervals. 164

Interviews A research method in which an investigator asks another individual questions designed to obtain answers relevant to a research problem. 39

Intimacy Hinde's term that refers to the extent to which participants in a relationship are willing to reveal aspects of themselves to each other. 123

Intimacy (versus isolation) Erikson's term for the ability to be involved with another without fearing a loss of self-identity. 106

Intrinsic motivation Students themselves want to learn and do not need external inducements. 286

Irreversibility Piaget's term to describe children's inability to reverse their thinking. 68

K

Knowledge-acquisition components Our ability to acquire and use language, thus helping us solve problems. 232

L

Language Refers to verbal or nonverbal communication between individuals. 453

Language acquisition device (LAD) Chomsky's term for his belief that humans have an innate knowledge of language. 88

Learned helplessness After repeated failure, some individuals become frustrated and simply give up. 303

Learning disabilities Refers to a handicapping condition characterized by a discrepancy between ability and achievement, most commonly manifested in reading, writing, reasoning, and/or mathematics. 458

Least restrictive environment A learning environment or classroom situation that provides necessary support for a handicapped student's continuing educational progress while also minimizing the time the student is removed from a normalized educational environment. In many ways, it is similar to the concept of mainstreaming. 430

Legally blind Refers to those individuals with vision of 20/200 or less in the better eye (after correction). 452

Levels of processing Describes the depth at which we process information. 212

Locus of control Refers to the causes of behavior; some individuals believe it resides within them, while others believe it resides outside themselves. 302

Longitudinal research A research method in which subjects are assessed repeatedly over a lengthy period of time. 42

Long-term store The ability to hold both conscious and unconscious data in memory for long periods of time; related to meaningfulness of material. 211

M

Macroadaptation Long-range decisions, perhaps involving program change. 377

Mainstreaming Integrating physically, mentally, and behaviorally handicapped students into regular classes. 434

Managerial function Refers to a teacher's need to conduct a well-run classroom. 6

Marking Refers to the assessment of a test or an oral or written report. 483

Mastery learning Instructor and student decide on time needed and what is necessary for mastery, usually about 90 percent of possible achievement score. 367

Matching items A test item utilizing two columns, each item in the first column to be matched with an item in the second column. 483

Mean The average of the raw scores. 517

Meaningful learning Ausubel's term to describe the acquisition of new meanings. 198

Measure Assigning a number to a student's performance. 468

Measurements To quantify or place a number on student performance. 472

Median That point in the distribution above which and below which 50 percent of the scores lie. 517

Mediated learning Feuerstein's term that refers to the training given to learners by experienced adults. 245

Mediated learning experience (MLE) Feuerstein's program designed to help students acquire thinking skills. 245

Mental images Cognitive representation of information. 202

Mental representation The coding of external events so they are retrievable in an internal form. 193

Mental retardation Significantly subaverage general intellectual functioning. 460

Meta-analysis A statistical technique used to synthesize and interpret the results of multiple data-based studies. 45

Metacognition The ability to think about thinking. 83, 216, 254

Metacognitive experiences Cognitive or affective experiences that relate to cognitive activities. 216

Metacognitive knowledge Refers to our knowledge and beliefs about cognitive matters gained from experiences we have stored in our long-term memory. 216

Metacomponents Higher order control processes used to evaluate a planned course of action, the executive components of intelligence. 232, 272

Method of Loci Using familiar locations (the chairs in your living room) to help you store things in your memory and to retrieve them more easily. 271

Microadaptation Moment-by-moment changes in classroom activities. 377

Minimum competency tests A means of determining a student's minimal satisfactory performance. 519

Mode The score obtained by the largest number of individuals taking a test. 517

Modes of representation Bruner's designation of the mental stages a child passes through. 362

Monitoring A term that describes how students are taught to monitor their own learning. 268

Moral dilemma A conflict causing subjects to justify the morality of their choices. 113

Morpheme The smallest unit of language to have meaning, may be a whole word or part of a word (old—er). 80

M-space Mental space. 78

Multicultural classrooms Classrooms with students and teachers from different ethnic or cultural groups. 13

Multilevel survey batteries Test batteries that assess separate curricular topics over a wide range of grades. 505

Multiple-choice items Presents students with a question or incomplete statement and several possible responses, one of which is correct. 472

Multiple coding The ability to represent material in more than one way (verbally or visually). 268

Multiple intelligences Refers to Gardner's seven relatively autonomous intelligences. 233

N

Natural incentives Spontaneously occurring motivational elements that appear at certain times in our lives. 314

Need achievement theory An explanation of motivation that is related to competence, judging it, and increasing it. 290

Negative reinforcers Stimuli whose withdrawal strengthens behavior. 165

Neobehaviorists Those behaviorists who believe that behavior results from the interactions between the person and environment. 156

Neverstreaming A term introduced by Slavin which refers to a determined effort to keep students functioning within normal limits by preventing academic problems. 442

Normal anxiety A tendency to be anxious in some situations but not in others. 297

Norms Interpreting test scores by comparing them with many scores derived from an identified sample. 503

Number concept Piaget's term that refers to the ability to understand numbers. 72

O

Objectives Those instructional and learning outcomes deemed worthy of attainment. 320

Observation A research method designed to assess individuals in as natural a setting as possible by trained observers. 41

Operant conditioning Refers to Skinner's explanation of learning that emphasizes the consequences of behavior. 156

Operations Piaget's term to describe actions we perform mentally in order to gain knowledge or the actions that can be performed on the givens in a problem. 68, 261

Organization Piaget's term to describe the connections among cognitive structures. 63

Overcorrection A form of classroom management involving both restitution and positive practice. 167, 413

Overdwelling A form of slowdown in which a teacher spends excessive time on a topic. 409

Overextension Applying a label too widely, e.g., cat for anything with four legs. 82

Overlapping Teachers can handle two or more classroom issues simultaneously. 409

Overregularity Too rigid an interpretation of a language rule, e.g., comed for came. 82

P

Parallel distributed processing Processing information by appearance, meaning, and pronunciation. 335

Pattern matching Refers to the match between our cognitive capacities and the external world. 227

Peer Refers to others of about the same age. 129

Percentile score A score that tells the percentage of individuals taking a test who are at or below a particular score; a percentile rank of 74 means that this student did as well or better than 74 percent of those taking the test. 516

Perception As used to describe teaching, refers to those teachers who are sensitive to the mood of their class; a sensitivity to students. 9, 219

Performance accomplishments The acquisition of personal and effective information from what we do. 295

Performance-based grading benchmarks The use of objective standards by which students' accomplishments are evaluated. 90

Performance components The implementation aspect of intelligence. 232

Performance test A test used to assess a student's ability to translate information into behavior. 472

Personal investment Refers to an individual's persistence, motivation, variation in activity, and goals. 291

Personalized system of instruction (PSI) Keller's technique for individualized instruction. 163

Philosophical viewpoints A view of research that emphasizes the relationship between children's early experiences and future adult life. 32

Philosophy for Children Lipman's program designed to help students acquire thinking skills. 247

Phonemes The distinctive, fundamental sounds of a language. 80

Phonology The use of sounds to form words. 80

Planful ignoring Overlooking an incident if a student regains control; particularly useful with well-behaved students. 417

Plasticity The ability to recover from trauma, both biological and psychological. 227

Portfolio assessment A means of assessing a student's behavior based upon a collection of the student's work that the student believes to be important evidence of learning. 490

Positive reinforcement A procedure wherein the rate of a response increases as a function of the consequences and presentation of a positive reinforcer. 161, 293

Positive reinforcer Those stimuli whose presentation as a consequence of a response strengthens or increases the rate of the response. 165

Postconventional level Kohlberg's third level of moral development when individuals act according to an enlightened conscience. 111

Power theory of intelligence Perkins' term that refers to intelligence as dependent on the neurological efficiency of the brain. 236

Practical intelligence Tactical knowledge necessary for success both inside and outside of school. 243

Pragmatics Refers to the ability to take part in a conversation, using language in a correct social manner. 80

Preconventional level Kohlberg's first level of moral development when children respond mainly to reward and punishment, about four to ten years of age. 108

Premack principle Access to high-frequency behaviors acts as a reinforcer for the performance of low-frequency behaviors. 170

Preoperational Piaget's term to describe a child who has begun to use symbols but is not yet capable of mentally manipulating them. The preoperational period extends from about two to six years of age. 68

Preschool assessment A method of identifying children who need help before entering formal schooling. 512

Pretend play A characteristic of the early childhood youngster in which a child shows an increasing ability to let one thing represent another, a feature that carries over to their play. 99

Primary reinforcers Reinforcers that influence behavior without learning: food, water. 163

Prior knowledge Previously learned material that affects present learning. 193

Proactive classroom management Reactive responding to problems and proactive planning for productive behavior. 391

Professional development function Refers to the rising level of minimal competence necessary to teach. 6

Profiles An authentic assessment procedure using evaluative schemes that permit reliable judgments about a student's proficiency. 490

Programmed instruction Skinner's classroom application of the principles of operant conditioning; a method of instruction. 363

Prototype A type of categorization that utilizes common standard form. 209

Proximity control Moving close to a troublesome student. 417

Psycholinguistics Based on Chomsky's work on language development, a combination of psychology and linguistics. 88

Q

QAIT An instructional model proposed by Slavin that emphasizes the quality of instruction, appropriate levels of instruction, individualized instruction, and time. 399

Quality of an interaction How participants behave in a relationship, e.g., a teacher may discipline either firmly or harshly. 123

Quality of instruction Bloom's term that refers to the needed cues, practice, and reinforcement necessary to make learning meaningful for students. 356

R

Ratio schedule Refers to reinforcement occurring after a certain number of responses. 164

Raw score Uninterpreted data; often the number of correct items. 516

Realism Piaget's term to describe a child's growing ability to distinguish and accept the real world. 69

Recall Retrieving information from memory with a minimum of cues. 213

Reciprocal determinism Bandura's term to describe the interactions among a person's thoughts, behaviors, and environmental factors. 125

Reciprocal interactions We respond to those around us and they change; their changed behavior then causes changes in us; emphasizes a student's active involvement in teacher-student interactions, that is, students are not merely passive recipients in any exchange. 95, 124

Reciprocity Those interactions in relationships in which the participants do the same thing either simultaneously or in turn, e.g., children playing tag. 123

Recognition Comparing an incoming representation with a representation already in memory. 213

Regular Education Initiative (REI) A movement to include more of the mildly handicapped in regular classrooms. 441

Reinforcement Usually refers to an increase in the frequency of a response when certain consequences immediately follow it. 161

Reinforcer A consequential stimulus that occurs contingent on a behavior that increases the behavior. 161

Relational concepts A concept formed by the relationship that exists among defining attributes. 199

Relationship Refers to a continuity among interactions. 122

Reliability A test is reliable if a student's scores are nearly the same in repeated measurements. 474

Reminiscence After rest, memory seems to improve. 215

Reporting Manner in which teachers communicate the results of student evaluation to parents. 483

Representation The manner in which information is recorded or expressed. 201

Response cost The loss of a positive reinforcer (e.g., after misbehavior, a student may no longer be a classroom monitor). 166

Responsibility Behaviors that demonstrate the ability to communicate with adults and that indicate concern with one's property. 128

Restricted response A form of essay question that asks for specific information. 477

Retrieval Recognizing, recalling, and reconstructing what we have previously stored in memory. 212

Retrieving Ability to access stored memory. 269

Reversibility Piaget's term for a child's ability to use cognitive operations ``to take things apart,'' to reverse their thinking. 76

Ripple effect Punishment is not confined to one student; its effects spread to other class members. 408

Role Behavior or expectancies about behavior associated with a particular position. 137

S

Schema (schemata) Mental frameworks that modify incoming data. 196

Schemes Piaget's term for our organized patterns of thought. 64

Secondary reinforcers Reinforcers that acquire the power to influence behavior because they have been associated with primary reinforcers. 163

Selection items A form of objective test in which students must choose from several possible answers. 477

Self-actualization Using our abilities to the fullest extent of our potentialities. 287

Self-assessment Refers to students examining their own behavior to determine whether they have performed some behavior or thought process. 183

Self-control Self-directed behaviors that emerge during social interaction, such as responding appropriately to teasing or to corrections from an adult. 128

Self-efficacy Individuals' beliefs in their abilities to exert control over their lives; feelings of competency. 173, 304

Self-esteem An evaluation of the information contained in the self-concept. 105

Self-fulfilling prophecy   When teachers expect more of children, the students tend to meet the expectations. 383

Self-monitoring   Students record their performance or keep a record of what they are doing. 183

Self-reinforcement   Students give themselves a reward following successful completion of the activity being monitored. 183

Semantic memory   Memory necessary for the use of language. 211

Semantics   Refers to the meaning of words, the relationship between ideas and words. 80

Sensitive responsiveness   The individual manner in which persons respond to particular stimuli; the ability to respond to cues. 96, 126

Sensorimotor   Piaget's term for the first stage of cognitive development, extending from birth to about two years of age. 65

Sensory register   Our ability, which is highly selective, to hold information in memory for a brief period. 211

Seriation   Piaget's term that refers to the ability to arrange objects by increasing or decreasing size. 71

Shaping   A form of classroom management in which teachers determine the successive steps needed to master a task and then teach them separately, reinforcing each step. 413

Short-term store   Our working memory; consciousness is involved. 211

Signal interference   A classroom management technique in which a teacher notices restlessness and uses physical proximity to counter it. 404

Situational anxiety   A tendency to be anxious in some situations and not in others. 297

Slowdowns   Refers to a teacher's behavior slowing down an activity. 409

Social cognitive learning   Bandura's theory that refers to the process whereby the information we glean from observing others influences our behavior. 172

Social discipline   A theory of classroom management based on the conviction that misbehavior can be eliminated by changing a student's goals. 416

Socialized speech   Piaget's term for that time in children's language development when they begin to exchange views with others, ask questions, give answers, etc. (about seven or eight years of age) 88

Social perspective-taking   The manner in which we relate to others cannot be separated from our personal theories concerning the psychological characteristics of individuals. 133

Social reinforcers   Interpersonal activities, such as the attention of others, can be a powerful reinforcer. 179

Sociometrics   A method of summarizing a student's status with peers. 134

Specific instructional objective   A detailed statement of precise outcomes to be attained. 326

Speech   Refers to the use of sound as a vehicle for conveying meaning. 453

Spiral curriculum   Bruner's term for teaching a subject in an ever more abstract manner; tied to his interpretation of readiness. 361

SQ3R   A popular method for improving studying skills. 74

Standard deviation units   Tells how much a score varies from the mean. 517

Standardized tests   Tests that are commercially constructed and sampled under uniform conditions. 472, 502

Standard score   Any of several derived scores (any score other than a raw score) based on number of standard deviations between a specified raw score and the mean of the distribution. 517

Stanford-Binet Intelligence Test (presently called the Stanford-Binet Intelligence Scale)   Binet's famous measure of human intelligence originally revised for American use by Terman and most recently by Thorndike and colleagues. 510

Stanine scores   A standard score that classifies those taking a test into one of nine groups. 517

State anxiety   A tendency to be anxious in some situations and not others. 297

Stimulus generalization   The process by which a conditioned response transfers to other stimuli. 157

Storage   Putting information into memory. 212

Storing   The ability to hold information in memory. 269

Strange situation   Placing youngsters in an unfamiliar situation enables researchers to classify their reactions after reunion with their mothers. 96

Stringers   Those who prefer a systematic, methodical analysis of a problem. 274

Strong strategies   Problem-solving strategies designed for a specific subject. 258

Structures   Piaget's term to describe the psychological units of the mind that enable us to think and know. 63

Structuring strategy   A term that describes how students search for relations in learning materials. 268

Student self-assessment   Students are encouraged to review and analyze their performance. 490

Summative evaluation   Measuring a student's achievement at the completion of a block of work. 367

Supply items   A form of objective test that requires students to give the answer (as opposed to choosing between possible answers). 477

Surveys   A research technique in which the investigator asks subjects questions about a particular issue, usually with structural questionnaires. 38

Symbolic   As used here, Bruner's term (a mode of representation) to indicate the ability to engage in abstract activities. 362

Syntax   Refers to the grammar of a language, putting words together to form sentences. 80

T

Tactical theory of intelligence   Perkins' term that refers to intelligence as knowing different ways of using our minds. 236

Task analysis   Gagne's term for breaking a task into its essential elements. 327

Taxonomy of educational objectives   Bloom's hierarchy of objectives intended to clarify the terminology often used in formulating objectives. 332

Teacher characteristics   Refers to the personal features of the teacher, such as well-organized, task-oriented, etc. 20

Teacher-constructed tests   One method for assessing a student's learning or behavior that is developed by the teacher. 68

Teaching   Those actions designed to help one or more students learn. 4

Teaching machine   Those instructional devices that divide material to be learned into small units and that reinforce successful responses. 170

Telegraphic speech   A child uses two or three words to convey more sophisticated meanings (``milk gone'' means ``my milk is all gone'') 81

Temperament   An individual's characteristic style in interacting with the environment. 126

Terminal behavior   Skinner's term for what students should be able to do after instruction. 364

Test anxiety   Anxiety generated by planning for and taking tests. 298

Tests   One method of student assessment. 472

Test-wiseness   Knowing how to take tests; can be improved by teaching. 492

Theoretical viewpoints   A view of research that focuses on either subjects or methodology. 32

Thinking frames Perkins' term that refers to those representations that guide the thought process. 236

Thinking skills Skills and strategies that enable students to adapt to constant change. 224

Thinning Reinforcement is provided less frequently in an attempt to reduce dependency on reinforcers. 179

Time-on-task Time actively engaged with learning material. 366

Time-out A form of punishment in which a student loses something desirable for a period of time. 166

Time-series research The repeated analysis of a group or individuals over a definite period of time. 44

Token economy A form of classroom management in which students receive tokens for desirable behavior. These may then be exchanged for something pleasurable. 413

Trait anxiety Refers to those individuals in a constant state of anxiety. 297

Transactions Same meaning as reciprocal interactions: our behavior towards others causes them to change; as a result of these changes, we also change. 96

Transductive reasoning Piaget's term to describe a preoperational child's reasoning technique—from particular to particular. 69

Transition smoothness Teachers have no difficulty in handling activities and movement in their classes. 409

Transmission Refers to the way that the speech organs produce sound. 453

Triad model Renzulli's enrichment model for working with the gifted. 450

Triarchic theory of intelligence Sternberg's view of intelligence as consisting of three elements: componential, experiential, and contextual. 231

Tribal dance Refers to those discipline problems in which a student misbehaves, the teacher acts, the student reacts, etc. 404

True-false question Presents subjects with a statement that must be judged true or false. 472

T–score A standard score with a mean of 50 and a standard deviation of 10. 517

V

Validity The extent to which a test measures what it is supposed to measure. 474

Variable interval The time between reinforcements varies. 164

Variable ratio The number of responses needed for reinforcement varies from one reinforcement to the next. 164

Verbal persuasion Leading students, through persuasion, into believing they can overcome any difficulty. 296

Verbal processing Representing information in a different form; language is a good example (the word car to represent an actual car). 202

Vicarious experience Learning from observing others. 295

Visual impairment Any type of reduction in vision. 451

Visually limited Those who have difficulty seeing under ordinary conditions but can adapt with glasses. 451

Vocables Consistent sound patterns to refer to objects and events. 81

W

WAIS-III (the Wechsler Adult Intelligence Scale III) Wechsler's intelligence test designed for adults. 510

Well-defined and ill-defined Refers to problems in which the steps to solution are either clearly or poorly defined. 261

Whole language A technique in which all language processes are studied in a more natural context (as a whole and not as a series of facts). 7, 84

WISC-III (the Wechsler Intelligence Scale for Children III) Wechsler's intelligence test designed for children. 510

Withitness Teachers know and understand what's happening in their classrooms. 409

WPPSI-R (the Wechsler Preschool and Primary Scale of Intelligence–Revised) Wechsler's intelligence test designed for children four to six and one-half years of age. 511

Z

Zone of proximal development The distance between a child's actual developmental level and a higher level of potential development with adult guidance (what children can do independently and what they can do with help). 60

Z scores A score that tells the distance of a student's raw score from the mean in standard deviation units. 517